SOCIAL COGNITION

Key Readings in Social Psychology

General Editor: ARIE W. KRUGLANSKI, University of Maryland at College Park

The aim of this series is to make available to senior undergraduate and graduate students key articles in each area of social psychology in an attractive, user-friendly format. Many professors want to encourage their students to engage directly with research in their fields, yet this can often be daunting for students coming to detailed study of a topic for the first time. Moreover, declining library budgets mean that articles are not always readily available, and course packs can be expensive and time-consuming to produce. **Key Readings in Social Psychology** aims to address this need by providing comprehensive volumes, each one of which will be edited by a senior and active researcher in the field. Articles will be carefully chosen to illustrate the way the field has developed historically as well as current issues and research directions. Each volume will have a similar structure to include:

- an overview chapter, as well as introduction to sections and articles
- questions for class discussion
- annotated bibliographies
- full author and subject indexes

Published Titles

The Self in Social Psychology	Roy F. Baumeister
Stereotypes and Prejudice	Charles Stangor
Motivational Science	E. Tory Higgins and Arie W. Kruglanski
Social Psychology and Human Sexuality	Roy F. Baumeister
Emotions in Social Psychology	W. Gerrod Parrott
Intergroup Relations	Michael A. Hogg and Dominic Abrams
The Social Psychology of Organizational Behavior	Leigh L. Thompson
Social Psychology: A General Reader	Arie W. Kruglanski and E. Tory Higgins
Social Psychology of Health	Peter Salovey and Alexander J. Rothman
The Interface of Social and Clinical Psychology	Robin M. Kowalski and Mark R. Leary
Political Psychology	John T. Jost and James Sidanius
Close Relationships	Harry T. Reis and Caryl Rusbult
Social Neuroscience	John T. Cacioppo and Gary G. Berntson
Social Cognition: Key Readings	David L. Hamilton

Titles in Preparation

Attitudes	Richard E. Petty and Russell Fazio
Group Processes	John Levine and Richard Moreland
Language and Communication	Gün R. Semin
Persuasion	Richard E. Petty and Russell Fazio
Social Comparison	Diederik Stapel and Hart Blanton

For continually updated information about published and forthcoming titles in the Key Readings in Social Psychology series, please visit: **www.keyreadings.com**

SOCIAL COGNITION
Key Readings

Edited by

David L. Hamilton
University of California, Santa Barbara

Psychology Press
New York and Hove

Published in 2005 by
Psychology Press
270 Madison Avenue
New York, New York 10016
www.psypress.com

Published in Great Britain by
Psychology Press
27 Church Road
Hove
East Sussex BN3 2FA U.K.
www.psypress.co.uk

Copyright © 2005 by Taylor & Francis Books, Inc.

Psychology Press is an imprint of the Taylor & Francis Group.
Printed in the United States of America on acid-free paper.
www.socialpsychologyarena.com
www.keyreadings.com

10 9 8 7 6 5 4 3 2 1

Library of Congress Cataloging-in-Publication Data
Social cognition : key readings / edited by David L. Hamilton.
     p. cm. — (Key readings in social psychology)
  Includes bibliographical references and index.
  ISBN 0-86377-590-X (hardcover : alk. paper) — ISBN 0-86377-591-8 (pbk. : alk. paper)
  1. Social perception. I. Hamilton, David L. (David Lewis), 1941- II. Series.

  BF323 . S63S63 2004
  302'.12—dc22

                                                                                          2004009845

Contents

About the Editor

David L. Hamilton received his Ph.D. from the University of Illinois in 1968. He has served on the faculties at Yale University and the University of California, Santa Barbara. A leading scholar in social cognition, he has written extensively on social perception, impression formation, stereotyping, attribution, and intergroup relations. He has edited five books and has published more than 100 scientific research articles, chapters, and commentaries. Dr. Hamilton has been awarded honorary degrees from two European universities (University of Lisbon, Portugal; Eotvos Lorand University, Budapest, Hungary) and in 2000 received the Thomas M. Ostrom Award for Outstanding Contributions to Social Cognition.

Acknowledgments

The editor and publisher are grateful to the following for permission to reproduce the articles in this book:

Reading 1: Heider, F. (1958). Perceiving the other person. In R. Taguiri & L. Petrullo (Eds.), *Person perception and interpersonal behavior.* Stanford: Stanford University Press. Copyright © 1958 by Stanford University Press. Reprinted with permission.

Reading 2: White, J.D., & Carlston, D.E. (1983). Consequences of schemata for attention, impression, and recall in complex social interactions. *Journal of Personality and Social Psychology, 45,* 538–549. Copyright © 1983 by the American Psychological Association. Reprinted with permission.

Reading 3: Dunning, D., & Sherman, D.A. (1997). Stereotypes and tacit inference. *Journal of Personality and Social Psychology, 73,* 459–471. Copyright © 1997 by the American Psychological Association. Reprinted/adapted with permission.

Reading 4: Kim, H.S. (2002). We talk, therefore we think? A cultural analysis of the effect of talking on thinking. *Journal of Personality and Social Psychology, 83,* 828–842. Copyright © 2002 by the American Psychological Association. Reprinted with permission.

Reading 5: Klein, S.B., & Kihlstrom, J.F. (1998). On bridging the gap between social-personality psychology and neuropsychology. *Personality and Social Psychology Review, 2,* 228–242. Copyright © 1998 by Lawrence Erlbaum Associates Inc. Reprinted with permission.

Reading 6: Bruner, J.S. (1957). On perceptual readiness. *Psychological Review, 64,* 123–152. Copyright © 1957 by the American Psychological Association. Reprinted/adapted with permission.

Reading 7: Medin, D. (1989). Concepts and conceptual structure. *American Psychologist, 44,* 1469–1481. Copyright © 1989 by the American Psychological Association. Reprinted with permission.

Reading 8: Wittenbrink, B., Gist, P.L., & Hilton, J.L. (1997). Structural properties of stereotypic knowledge and their influences on the construal of social situations. *Journal of Personality and Social Psychology, 72,* 526–543. Copyright © 1997 by the American Psychological Association. Reprinted/adapted with permission.

Reading 9: Srull, T.K., & Wyer, R.S., Jr. (1979). The role of category accessibility in the interpretation of information about persons: Some determinants and implications. *Journal of Personality and Social Psychology, 37,* 1660–1672. Copyright © 1979 by the American Psychological Association. Reprinted with permission.

Reading 10: Tversky, A., & Kahneman, D. (1974). Judgment under uncertainty: heuristics and biases. *Science, 185,* 1124–1131. Copyright © 1974 AAAS. Reprinted with permission.

Reading 11: Schwarz, N., Bless, H., Strack, F., Klumpp, G., Rittenauer-Schatka., H., & Simons, A. (1991). Ease of retrieval as information: Another look at the availability heuristic. *Journal of Personality and Social Psychology, 61,* 195–202. Copyright © 1991 by the American Psychological Association. Reprinted with permission.

of Personality and Social Psychology, *44*, 20–33. Copyright © 1983 by the American Psychological Association. Reprinted with permission.

Reading 28: Correll, J., Park, B., Judd, C.M., & Wittenbrink, B. (2002). The police officer's dilemma: Using ethnicity to disambiguate potentially threatening individuals. *Journal of Personality and Social Psychology*, *83*, 1314–1329. Copyright © 2002 by the American Psychological Association. Reprinted/ adapted with permission.

Reading 29: Macrae, C.N., Milne, A.B., & Bodenhausen, G.V. (1994). Stereotypes as energy-saving devices: A peek inside the cognitive toolbox. *Journal of Personality and Social Psychology*, *66*, 37–47. Copyright © 1994 by the American Psychological Association. Reprinted with permission.

Reading 30: Hastorf, A.H., & Cantril, H. (1954). They saw a game: A case study. *Journal of Abnormal and Social Psychology*, *49*, 129–134. Copyright © 1954 by the American Psychological Association. Reprinted with permission.

Reading 31: Kunda, Z. (1987). Motivated inference: Self-serving generation and evaluation of causal theories. *Journal of Personality and Social Psychology*, *53*, 636–647. Copyright © 1987 by the American Psychological Association. Reprinted with permission.

Reading 32: Ditto, P.H., & Lopez, D.F. (1992). Motivated skepticism: Use of differential decision criteria for preferred and nonpreferred conclusions. *Journal of Personality and Social Psychology*, *63*, 568–584. Copyright © 1992 by the American Psychological Association. Reprinted with permission.

Reading 33: McFarland, C., Ross, M., & Giltrow, M. (1992). Biased recollections in older adults: The role of implicit theories of aging. *Journal of Personality and Social Psychology*, *62*, 837–850. Copyright © 1992 by the American Psychological Association. Reprinted with permission.

Reading 34: Loftus, E.F. (1997). Memories for a past that never was. *Current Directions in Psychological Science*, *6*, 60–65. Copyright © 1997 by Cambridge University Press. Reprinted with permission.

Reading 35: Markman, K.D., Gavanski, I., Sherman, S.J., & McMullen, M. N. (1993). The mental simulation of better and worse possible worlds. *Journal of Experimental Social Psychology*, *29*, 87–109. Copyright © 1993 Elsevier Science. Reprinted with permission.

Reading 36: Medvec, V.H., Madey, S.F., & Gilovich, T. (1995). When less is more: Counterfactual thinking and satisfaction among Olympic medalists. *Journal of Personality and Social Psychology*, *69*, 603–610. Copyright © 1995 by the American Psychological Association. Reprinted with permission.

Reading 37: Snyder, M., Tanke, E.D., & Berscheid, E. (1977). Social perception and interpersonal behavior: On the self-fulfilling nature of social stereotypes. *Journal of Personality and Social Psychology*, *35*, 656–666. Copyright © 1977 by the American Psychological Association. Reprinted with permission.

Reading 38: Wilson, T.D., Wheatley, T., Meyers, J.M., Gilbert., D.T., & Axsom, D. (2000). Focalism: A source of durability bias in affective forecasting. *Journal of Personality and Social Psychology*, *78*, 821–836. Copyright © 2000 by the American Psychological Association. Reprinted/adapted with permission.

Preface

In our everyday lives we are continually processing and using information we encounter in our world. We often think of the term "processing information" as referring to occasions when we are diligently trying to learn something new, to read a text, or to master some problem that has stymied us. Yet it is equally true that in our social lives we are continually processing information. When we listen to a friend's description of her weekend experiences, when we consider the options of either going skiing or just hanging out at home with friends during an upcoming school vacation, when we get to know someone we've just met during an interaction — in all of these cases we are processing new information and using it for our current purposes (sharing weekend stories, planning a future vacation, forming an impression of a potential new friend). Moreover, we use this information in a variety of ways: as we perceive others, as we make decisions, and as we guide our own behavior and respond to the behaviors of others.

Social cognition is the study of how people process, store, and use the information they process from the social world. During the last two decades it has been an immensely active and important area of research in social psychology. This book attempts to convey some of the knowledge that has been gained through adopting a social cognition approach to understanding social psychological phenomena. The readings reproduced here illustrate the kinds of new questions, new ideas, new theories, and new methodologies that have developed as a result of thinking about social psychology through the lens of social cognition. Most of the articles reproduced in this book were originally published during the last fifteen or so years.

Although social cognition has been most prominent and has had its enormous impact on theory and research within the last 20 years, the roots of this approach to studying social psychology reflect a much longer history. Therefore, in most sections of this book I have tried to include a "classic" reading that laid the groundwork for and anticipated the developments that would evolve at a later time.

As any reader of this volume is well aware, social psychology is a broad subject area that incorporates a variety of topics — attitude change, group processes, person perception, aggression, close relationships, decision making, intergroup relations, and many others. Where does social cognition fit within this framework? Unlike the topic areas I've just listed, social cognition is not a specific substantive focus. Rather, it is an *approach* that can be taken to thinking about and studying any topic area in social psychology. What do I mean by this? It is a way of thinking conceptually, and a way of doing research on any given topic, by investigating the cognitive underpinnings of whatever is being studied. As I said at the outset, in virtually all areas of social psychology people are processing information from the social world. A social cognition approach tries to understand *how* that information is being processed and used as people respond to persuasive messages, decide whether to respond aggressively to another, participate in group decision-making contexts, and any other domain of interest in social psychology. In that sense, social cognition is as broad as the field of social psychology itself.

In developing a book of readings on social cognition, I was faced with a dilemma: how to present a coherent set of readings that illustrate the ways of thinking, the ways of doing research, and the variety of new discoveries that have occurred from adopting a social cognition approach to social psychological topics? In taking on this task, I decided that it would be almost impossible to include examples that cover the entire spectrum of social psychological subject matter. Therefore, although I have tried to be broad in my coverage, this book "tilts" toward social perception (including both person perception and intergroup perception). This focal area seemed appropriate in that much of the early development of the social cognition work had its origins (and continues to be influential) in these domains. Examples of the social cognitive approach in other topic areas are also included in this set of readings, and are also readily available elsewhere (including in other volumes in the series of which this book is a part).

Preparing a book of this nature is a large undertaking, and in the course of my work on it I have benefited from conversations with and comments from many people. I particularly want to thank Leonel Garcia-Marques, Jim Geiwitz, Arie Kruglanski, and Jim Sherman for the very helpful feedback they provided at various stages of the project. I also appreciate the comments of several anonymous reviewers who provided insightful and very useful commentary on an early draft of the materials. The feedback I received from all of these people improved the final product. Finally, I thank Kit Filan for her tolerance, support, and encouragement during this seemingly endless endeavor.

Social Cognition: An Introductory Overview

David L. Hamilton

Imagine the following scene. For lack of something better to do, you go to a party at a friend's place on Friday night. When you arrive you find a number of people already there, talking and laughing in small groups. The music is on, people are drinking beer and munching on snacks, and generally having a good time. As the evening goes on, you enjoy talking with friends and meeting new people. One fellow in particular, named Mark, intrigues you. You hadn't known him prior to this party, and he seems interesting when you talk with him (easy-going style, good taste in music, seems to read a lot, interesting political ideas). As the evening progresses, you notice that he's always on the periphery of the room, never the center of attention. At the same time, he doesn't seem shy as he's always engaged in lively conversation with someone — but only one person at a time. The next day, a friend asks if you had a good time and met anyone interesting. You pause, and then describe Mark and your impression of him: "A nice guy, pretty bright, but reserved."

Now imagine another scene. You are driving to the mall one afternoon along Maple Street, having a lively conversation with your friend Sheila as you drive. You're following a blue Honda, and are approaching an intersection with Victoria Avenue, where there are Stop signs on all four corners. You notice that, although the Honda slows down, it doesn't come to a complete stop but rather cruises through the Stop sign at modest speed. Suddenly you notice a teenager on a bicycle coming quickly into the intersection from the right. The car and the bicycle collide, and you hear the strident sounds of screeching brakes, crunching metal, and broken glass. You pull over to the side of the road and get out of your car to check if everyone is OK. The bicycle is mangled, there has been considerable damage to one fender and headlight of the car, the cyclist fortunately has only a few scrapes, but both the driver and the cyclist are shaken (and more than a little upset). A policeman arrives, talks with the individuals and with several people who witnessed the event, and eventually he asks you to describe what happened. You describe the incident as best you can, retrieving as much detail from memory as possible. You relate your recollection that the Honda hadn't fully stopped at the Stop sign, suggesting that the driver was at fault. On the other hand, you don't say much about the cyclist approaching from the right on Victoria Avenue, as you hadn't seen him until the last moment.

These two scenarios describe incidents that could easily happen to any of us. We certainly form impressions of people we meet in a variety of contexts, and most of us have been in, witnessed, or heard first-hand accounts of traffic accidents. These scenarios are illustrative of many such occasions in everyday life in which we are faced with comprehending and responding to complex aspects of the social world in which we live. This book is about how we perceive and understand the people and events that we encounter all the time.

These everyday occurrences seem quite second nature to us. In fact, you probably don't give any serious thought to, for example, *how* you formed that impression of Mark (Nisbett & Wilson, 1977). After all, we meet people all the time, and getting to know what they're like doesn't seem difficult.

1

We observe things happening all the time and often describe what we've seen with ease. However, there are in fact a variety of complex processes underlying these everyday perceptions, and whereas such things as forming impressions and perceiving events around us may be quite common, what underlies them may not be so simple. For a long time, social psychologists (among others) have been interested in how people perceive and understand the people and events they experience, and a great deal of research has accumulated in their effort to account for how these things are accomplished. This book reports some of the fruits of that research.

Social psychology focuses on the study of the individual in a social context, that is, understanding how the individual's thoughts, feelings, and behaviors are influenced by the presence of others and the social situation in which that behavior occurs. *Social cognition* is a conceptual and empirical approach to understanding social psychological topics by investigating the cognitive underpinnings of whatever social phenomenon is being studied. That is, its focus is on an analysis of how information is processed, stored, represented in memory, and subsequently used in perceiving and interacting with the social world. Social cognition is not a content area within social psychology; rather, it is an approach to studying any topic area in social psychology. Thus, a social cognition perspective can be adopted in studying topics as wide-ranging as person perception, attitudes and attitude change, stereotyping and prejudice, decision-making, the self-concept, social communication and influence, and intergroup discrimination.

In many contexts we can conceive of the individual as participating in social interactions by processing and using information that is available in that situation. Consider some examples that illustrate the variety of social contexts we're talking about: getting acquainted with a new neighbor, weighing the arguments for and against the death penalty, coordinating tasks with a coworker, forming an impression of a stranger, being a jury member and hearing evidence about a defendant, evaluating a political candidate's record and issue positions, debating the strengths of your baseball team vs your friend's favorite team, evaluating the relative merits of two kinds of car you're considering buying. In all of these cases, we form thoughts and opinions about a person, product, or issue from information that we acquire, and we use that information in making judgments and decisions that guide our behaviors. This focus on processing information does not necessarily mean that we are always logical and rational in these efforts. A young man's impression of a new acquaintance may be heavily swayed by her blue eyes and bright smile; our opinion of a Ford Mustang may be influenced by our evaluation of the movie star advocating the product in a commercial; and our liking for a political candidate may be based as much on charisma as on his or her positions on important political issues. Nevertheless, in all cases, one or another kind of information is being processed and used as a basis for judgment.

In all of these cases, the social perceiver is acquiring new information from the social environment, is processing that information in various ways, is integrating it with previously acquired knowledge, and is using it to understand others, to make decisions, and to guide behavior. In other words, the social perceiver is an active processor of social information, and as such, actively contributes to the perception process in a variety of ways.

To illustrate these points, let us return to our earlier examples. At the party Friday night your impression of Mark developed rather quickly. You immediately regarded him as easy-going, and in conversation with him you quickly realized that he's well read and you learned about his musical tastes and political leanings. Your impression formed sufficiently so that the next day you could easily describe him in terms of more general personality attributes (nice, bright, reserved) that extend well beyond the specific encounter you had with him. Similarly, although the accident at the corner of Maple Street and Victoria Avenue happened very quickly, you're able to provide the policeman with information about the Honda driver's lack of attention to the Stop sign.

But these are your perceptions, and even though you might be quite convinced not only about what Mark is like but also about what happened at that intersection, others may dispute your opinions. Someone else at the party might have come away thinking that Mark is a bit of a nerd, one who tends to corner some poor soul and then talks endlessly about his own ideas, and who never mingles with the group as a whole. And someone walking along Victoria Avenue may have seen the cyclist racing recklessly to get across Maple Street before the Honda got there.

What I have described here are differing views of everyday incidents, and as such they seem quite understandable. But we can readily think of other times when the same kinds of things, the same processes, the same differing perceptions of an identical incident, can have more serious consequences. If the two "eyewitness" accounts were not of a minor traffic collision but rather of a murder scene, then the resolution of what actually happened, of people's recollections of who did what and when, becomes of considerably greater import. And if such an incident then ends up in the hands of a jury (who must grapple with the conflicting accounts), then such differing views may have implications for the life or death of a defendant. How are these perceptions formed? Why do different observers of the same event often differ in their conclusions? The conceptual and methodological tools of social cognition can be applied to answer these kinds of questions.

Cognitive Processing

The information we encounter in our social world is not simply recorded, as if by a videocamera, and stored verbatim in a memory file, as if the brain were a computer. There are several ways in which the information that, in actuality, is encountered is only partially recorded, is embellished and expanded, and is transformed as the perceiver actively works on that stimulus information. We can identify several distinct aspects of this process.

Attention and Encoding

At any given moment the stimulus world we perceive is likely to be a complex, constantly changing, and potentially confusing display of people doing things, saying things, expressing feelings, all amidst noises of various kinds impinging on us, and all of it occurring in a specific situation that may or may not give meaning to what is happening. Think back to that party you went to Friday night. The room is filled with people, many of whom you'd not met before, some you seem to remember meeting somewhere once before, and (thank goodness!) a few good friends you know well. There are multiple conversations going on around you, you're trying to simultaneously focus on the person you're looking at while at the same time being cognizant of the others around you. There's lots of noise — people laughing, the stereo playing at what seems like full volume, glasses clinking with ice cubes, and through it all, people trying to maintain at least somewhat reasonable conversations with you. Can you pay attention to all of what's going on in that room? Of course not! The general point is that the stimulus environment typically contains more information than we as perceivers can attend to at any given time. Therefore the perceiver necessarily must selectively attend to certain aspects of this complex stimulus environment, while other aspects of that information are not registered. Suppose during that party you are talking with two friends, Beth and Kevin, when you hear your name being mentioned in another conversation somewhere behind you. Immediately your attention shifts, trying to hear what's being said (especially what's said about you!) in that group, and of course, you also lose focus on what Beth and Kevin are saying . . . which you realize when you become aware that they're waiting for you to answer a question you never heard! Your attention can focus selectively, but not on all things simultaneously (White & Carlston, 1983).

Thus the cognitive processing system performs a "gatekeeping" function in adapting to this rich stimulus environment. This selectivity is not random, however. Our cognitive system is well attuned to direct our attention in certain ways. Hopefully, we will focus on the most important aspects of what's happening around us (e.g., the person you're looking at and what she's saying at the moment) but there are other factors that can command our attention as well (e.g., that person's amazing pink hair and hideous attire).

This selectivity is necessary, for the reasons that these examples illustrate. However, that selectivity can have important consequences. Information that we attend to is encoded, processed, and stored and will be available to influence subsequent perceptions, decisions, and memories. In contrast, information that we selectively ignore and don't pay attention to may not be encoded and consequently may not play a role in subsequent processes and outcomes. So there is some good news and some bad news about this gatekeeping function of selective attention. On the one hand, it is very functional in that it helps us focus on the most relevant aspects of our complex stimulus environment. On the other hand, because it is selective, other aspects of the potentially available information will not be encoded and retained, and hence there can be a loss of information.

Elaboration

Information that we acquire from our social world is not simply registered verbatim and deposited in memory. Rather, the information processing system elaborates on that information in a variety of ways. These operations are all a part of the means by which the perceiver comprehends and understands the information being acquired, and they provide important mechanisms in adapting to the social environment. Let us briefly consider several of these processes.

The information available in the environment has no particular meaning for the perceiver until it is given some *interpretation*. Information about other people — their behaviors, their facial expressions, their motives — is often open to multiple possible interpretations, and the perceiver imposes meaning on that information through this interpretation process. How do you interpret the fact that Mark stays on the social sidelines and avoids being the center of attention? One could interpret his behavior as meaning that he's unfriendly, but instead you concluded that he's reserved — two very different interpretations of the same behavior that leads to quite different impressions of Mark.

Once it has been given some interpretation, the perceiver "goes beyond the information given" (Bruner, 1957) by making *inferences* about the behavior observed, about the actor who performed the behavior, about the group of participants. During your brief conversation with Mark, his comments on music and politics led you to infer that he is "bright." Note that you cannot directly "see" his "brightness" (as if it were apparent on his forehead), and no one comment or incident definitely conveyed that attribute. Instead, it represents an inference you made from the behavior you witnessed. These inferences not only give additional meaning to the events being perceived but also embellish the person, group, or behavior with additional features and attributes.

One particular type of inference is of particular importance and has been of special interest to social psychologists. The perceiver engages in an *attribution* process, determining the reasons for an actor's behavior, thereby inferring the causes for the behavior. For example, when you noticed that the blue Honda hadn't stopped at the intersection, you may have wondered (particularly after it resulted in a collision) why the driver hadn't stopped. A number of possibilities might easily come to mind — the Stop sign was partially hidden by a parked vehicle so he couldn't see it, he was in a hurry, he'd been drinking, etc. These are all possible causes for why he failed to stop, and again, it is you — the perceiver — who decides which is the most appropriate, most compelling explanation. Note, however, that the result of your attribution process can have important consequences. If you attribute his behavior to his hurriedness (or especially to his drinking), then you are locating the cause of this event in the driver himself and hence he would be judged responsible for the accident. On the other hand, if you attribute the event to the partially obstructed Stop sign, then it's the kind of mistake anyone (who similarly would not be able to see the sign) might make, and the driver in that case would be judged less responsible for the accident. The attribution process not only helps us understand why events we observe have happened (by generating an explanation for them) but also helps us anticipate future events of the same type (by determining the causal relations that govern behavior in social contexts). In sum, this process not only enhances the comprehension and meaning of the event but also provides a basis for anticipating future interactions.

Our perceptions of the people and events that we encounter are rarely neutral; they are almost always imbued with *evaluation*. It's difficult to imagine meeting someone and forming an impression that is entirely neutral; we like some groups, but don't care for others; even individual behaviors are evaluated as good or bad, appropriate or inappropriate, admirable or despicable. Even after your brief interaction with Mark at the party, you know whether you'd like to see him again sometime. The social perceiver routinely evaluates the people, behaviors, and events that are encountered in social life. Again, the information conveyed by and about those people, behaviors, and events is evaluatively neutral until the perceiver imposes some evaluation on it, and another person might have quite different evaluations of the same thing. This additional way in which we "go beyond the information given" adds further meaning to our perceptions and can further transform the actual information we have encountered.

Representation in Memory

The information acquired by the perceiver is then represented in memory and stored for later use. There are a number of important questions regarding how information is represented and stored in memory. For example, when we observe a behavioral episode — say, an interaction between a couple of people — what is it that gets stored in memory? Do we simply retain the actual information we've observed, for example, the specific behaviors we have witnessed each participant perform? Or do we extract from that episode some more general characterizations, for example, that the two people were having an argument, and include that characterization in our memory representation of the event? Or do we do both?

Different theories of memory have provided different answers to these questions, some emphasizing discrete representation of individual pieces of information, others emphasizing organized grouping of information according to thematic content. For example, *exemplar theories* posit that each piece of information acquired — each experience we have — is represented as an exemplar, is stored, and is potentially retrievable at a later time. Thus, all of the individual pieces of information you acquired about Mark at the party would be represented individually in memory. Whereas exemplar theories posit that these individual items are stored separately from each other, *network theories* propose that these items may become interconnected with each other, in a network representation, organized in terms of some "node" to which these items of information are attached. From this perspective, all bits of knowledge you learned about Mark would be stored under a "person node" representing Mark. These items would be connected to that node, and some of them may be connected directly with each other as well, forming a network representation. *Abstraction-based theories* propose that, as we acquire those bits of information, we abstract out some meaning, some more general concept, conveyed by that information, and the items of information are stored in terms of those more abstract structures (sometimes called schemas or prototypes). Theorists advocating each of these perspectives have debated which type of representation is most accurate, and it seems safe to assume that each perspective has some merit. Clearly we retain memory records of individual experiences, we somehow extract more abstract meanings from those experiences, and different bits of knowledge become integrated into meaningfully organized representations. The questions of when and how each type of representation is formed are the focus of ongoing research in both cognitive and social psychology.

Whatever one's theoretical view on how information is stored in memory, it is important to recognize that what is retained is not necessarily a verbatim representation of the stimulus information that was actually encountered. Due to the various elaborative processes we have discussed, that information has been encoded, interpreted, evaluated, and used as the launching pad for inferences of various kinds. Your mental representation of the car accident includes the "facts" that the Honda did not adequately stop before crossing the intersection, that the driver appeared to be in quite a hurry, and therefore, in your mind, he is probably responsible for the collision. Note, however, that your understanding of what happened includes not only what you saw but also how you interpreted it and what you inferred from it.

Therefore, the mental representation of information may differ in meaningful ways from the actual stimulus information that was initially perceived and on which that representation is based. However, it is that representation — accurate or inaccurate; complete or partial; valid or biased — that will be the basis for further action by the perceiver.

Retrieval from Memory

The representation that is developed and stored in memory can then be retrieved at a later time for use in making judgments and guiding behavior. This retrieval process itself is flexible and open to influence by various factors. That is, the response at any given time may reflect one or another aspect of the information, as represented. Obviously our immediate goals or purposes in retrieving memories will guide our search of memory, and hence will determine what is brought back to mind. That is, what we "remember" about a person or event often reflects a sampling of our memory, not a thorough search of all that is stored. In addition, some exemplars may be easily retrievable because the information they contain represents experiences that are very important to us, or very unusual stimuli, or very salient aspects of an event, etc. Similarly, retrieval of one item of information or one incident may trigger recall of others with which it is associated in memory storage. Moreover, our current needs and goals can lead us to "reconstruct" the past so that our memory of it fits with our current beliefs and objectives. In later sections we discuss several variables that can influence what and how much is retrieved. The point here is that retrieval from cognitive representations is not a simple, straightforward process. Retrieval can be guided by numerous factors that will influence what it is that we "remember" — at any given moment — about the person or event in question.

Response

All of these processes eventually lead to the perceiver's response, which may include judgments, affective reactions, decisions, and behaviors. Again, however, it is important to recognize that the response is guided by and based on the mental representation of the information acquired, not directly on that information itself. Thus, understanding the various ways that the perceiver operates on the information as it is processed will be important for grasping how and why those responses come about. It therefore becomes clear that these cognitive processes will play a crucial role in guiding the individual's social behavior.

In this regard, it is also important to recognize that these same processes can lead to apparent inconsistencies in a person's responses at different times. They can also lead to differences between persons in their response to the same situation. First, consider the response of the same person at different times. As we have seen, different aspects of the mental representation may be retrieved at different times (as a function of momentary salience, differences in information accessibility, use of different retrieval strategies, etc.). If so, then the perceiver's response may differ accordingly, and hence the individual may appear to be inconsistent across time or in different contexts. Perhaps at one later time you'll refer to Mark's political astuteness, but at another time his social reticence may lead you to emphasize his hesitancy in social situations. Mark is obviously the same person throughout, but your retrieved impressions of him can differ substantially, depending on what aspects of your memory are accessed at any given time. Given that all persons include a mixture of good and bad qualities, one can even experience strong evaluative shifts about a person over time, depending upon which aspects of his or her personality come to mind (i.e., are retrieved). Second, consider two different persons responding to the same person or situation. Different persons may base their responses to the same event on different representations of the same information, or on different retrieved aspects of that information. If so, then these individuals will differ in their response to the same "objective" situation. Thus, for example, you were quite convinced that the driver of the blue Honda had caused the accident. Another witness, who observed the incident from a different perspective, may not have seen the Honda's failure to stop completely, but did see the cyclist racing along Victoria Avenue, completely ignoring the oncoming traffic on Maple Street (which you could not see from your vantage point). This second witness, then, would make a quite different attribution, judging the cyclist to be seriously at fault. So we have two widely differing mental representations of the same event. They are based on somewhat different information (reflecting different points of observation), but importantly, they also include widely differing interpretations, inferences, and attributions for why the accident occurred.

Cognitive Structures

To this point we have discussed the way information in our social world becomes the basis for under-standing the people and events we encounter. We have considered a variety of processes that intersect with the acquisition and use of information, hopefully focusing on relevant aspects of that information but also expanding on it in ways that may or may not further our understanding. This is not, however, the whole story. After all, social information is not processed by naive, unsophisticated perceivers. When interacting with others and observing their behaviors, people are not simply taking in totally unfamiliar material. Rather, all of us have been observing, interacting with, getting to know, and cop-ing with others for a long time. In the process we have learned a lot about what people are like, and we also have come to believe a lot of things about people as well. More generally, perceivers have accu-mulated many years of experience in processing information from the social world, and the benefits of those experiences are stored in cognitive structures in memory.

Cognitive structures represent the accumulated knowledge, beliefs, and expectancies the individual has developed in various domains of life. For example, when I learn that Sarah attends church regularly, says a prayer before meals, and donates generously to church-related organizations, I can easily char-acterize her as being a "religious" person. Similarly, if you learn that Randy has written letters to con-gressmen advocating stronger laws regulating gun possession, and has participated in rallies demonstrating on this issue, then you know his attitude on the gun control issue. Personality traits and attitudes are *concepts* that we can use to summarize a complex range of behaviors manifested by a person, and these concepts usefully summarize a pattern of information in a single attribute. At a more complex level, cognitive structures might also represent the relations among several concepts. For example, I might assume that someone who is witty is also intelligent, that those two attributes "go together" in people, and this belief would then be a part of my own general notions about the nature of people's personali-ties. More generally, *implicit personality theories* (Schneider, 1973) represent our knowledge and beliefs about the nature of people's personalities, and these theories develop as a result of knowing many people and "understanding" their personalities. In a similar manner, *stereotypes* represent our knowledge and beliefs about groups of people — the attributes shared by most members of a religious, ethnic, gender, or national group. Our *self-concepts* represent our knowledge and beliefs about our-selves — our own personalities, our strengths and our weaknesses, etc. The general point is that, through ever-accumulating experiences, perceivers develop cognitive structures that represent and store the knowledge and beliefs that they have acquired through those experiences.

Our knowledge and beliefs, based on past experiences, provide us with *expectancies* for the future. That is, having learned the sequence of steps that happen the first time we go to donate blood, we then know what to expect on subsequent visits to donate at the blood bank. Having met and known a few religious fundamentalists in the past, we have some idea what to expect when we meet a new person who fits this mold. Having seen, on several occasions, what happens when antiabortion and pro-choice groups of demonstrators confront each other in the streets, we have expectancies about what will tran-spire, and who will do what, when this situation reoccurs in the future. In other words, the accumulated knowledge and beliefs from past experiences provide a basis for anticipating future occurrences, and these expectancies are enormously important in directing our information processing, decision-making, and behavior. Both in the remainder of this chapter and in the readings produced in this book, we will see many examples of the impact of expectancies on information processing, on self-understanding, on interactions between individuals, and on intergroup behavior.

These cognitive structures can be an important guide in the processing of new information. In fact, they can influence each of the phases of information processing outlined earlier. For example, when observing an argument between two individuals, one White and one Black, a perceiver who holds a very traditional stereotype of Blacks might *interpret* the Black's behavior as more aggressive, might *infer* that the Black is an aggressive person (personality trait) and that he doesn't like White people (attitude), might *evaluate* the Black person more negatively, and might *attribute* any hostile action to internal, dis-positional causes rather than to provocation from the other person. And those aspects of the interaction that "fit" with those stereotypic expectancies would be more likely to be represented in *memory* and hence would be more available for any later description of what happened. In other words, the perceiver's stereotypic expectancies would have guided all aspects of the way information acquired about the incident was processed and used. Moreover, this example illustrates an important point about the influence of expectancies, namely, that they serve to maintain the status quo. That is, with a few exceptions, expectancies bias information processing in such a way that confirms the *a priori* expectancies that produced those outcomes.

There are several important implications of this influence of cognitive structures on processing social information. First, because they represent the accumulated knowledge of past experience, they can enhance comprehension of the present situation. Hence they are clearly adaptive. Second, they can enhance anticipation of the future. Effective social behavior depends heavily on our ability to anticipate what is likely to happen in various situations, how others are likely to behave and respond, and what behavior would be appropriate in some context. Cognitive structures aid in this aspect of social adaptation as well. That is, the knowledge and beliefs represented in cognitive structures are extracted from multiple experiences in the past, and therefore they reflect the regularities we have experienced in those past situations. As such, they can usefully help us anticipate those regularities in the future. Third, for the very same reasons, there is a "down side" to cognitive structures as well. Because they often represent generalized products of past experience, which then are used as guides to the future, they can lead us astray. That is, assumptions based on past experiences can be inappropriately applied to new, and especially novel, situations. Because of this, the use of cognitive structures can lead to biased outcomes and can therefore be potentially maladaptive.

Activation and Use of Cognitive Structures

The cognitive structures we've discussed are the repositories of our stored knowledge from past experience, as well as the beliefs and expectancies we have formed based on those experiences. Given that we have a multitude of such cognitive structures, pertaining to all the diverse areas of life, you might wonder what determines which structure will be used at any given time. Moreover, you might wonder how we use this information that is stored in these memory structures. There are in fact several answers to that question. Here we highlight a few of the factors that influence the activation and use of cognitive structures.

Priming

With our accumulated knowledge organized and stored in these structures, what will activate one particular cognitive structure, instead of others, for use at a particular moment? In the jargon of the literature, this is called *priming*. When some stimulus brings a particular concept to mind, then that stimulus has "primed" that cognitive structure. Priming is an important process because the cognitive structure that is active at the moment will be used in processing new information, and as we have seen, that processing can include the interpretation and evaluation of that information. Suppose you see a movie in which an African American male is portrayed as very mean and aggressive, the villain in the plot. Afterward, you see a Black male walking toward you on the sidewalk. The portrayal in the movie may have primed the stereotype of Black males as aggressive. The stereotype (a cognitive structure) contains expectancies that may or may not be accurate, either in general or about this particular person, but once that stereotype has been activated (or primed), those expectancies can guide information processing and your perceptions of this individual.

One important determinant of concept activation is the immediate stimulus environment. Suppose you are on a job interview, waiting in an office for the interviewer to arrive. A middle-aged man walks in, wearing a business suit and his manner conveys that he "belongs" there. You will, of course, immediately assume that this is the interviewer; you are unlikely to assume that this is the custodian coming by to empty the wastebasket. Your assumption is based on your "cognitive structures" about what interviewers are like, what happens at an interview, etc. Moreover, your accumulated knowledge and beliefs about such interactions will guide your thinking about the person you meet (he or she will be polite, will ask you questions, etc.) as well as about how you should respond (be polite, put your "best foot forward" in answering questions, etc.). Thus, the nature of the immediate stimulus environment, and the task at hand, will determine what cognitive structures are likely to be called into play at the moment. And this is good, for it is in using those cognitive structures, and the accumulated knowledge from past experiences that they contain, that we adapt to new, unfamiliar, and ever-changing situations. These cognitive structures are the repository of our previous experience, and we would be foolish not to use that benefit.

There are, however, two important points to recognize when we think about the activation and use of cognitive structures. First, just as we have numerous cognitive structures available for use, there are numerous variables that influence concept activation. Some of these structures will be more useful, and more appropriate, in any given situation than will others. Second, whatever structure is activated, it is likely to have an impact on both processing and the results of that processing. One reason for the importance of this process is the intriguing realization that much of social behavior is, to some degree anyway, ambiguous, and therefore it is open to alternative interpretations. Why is this important? It is important because cognitive structures influence the interpretation and use of the information we process. Therefore, the same information (e.g., a behavioral episode involving a few persons) can be "seen," interpreted, evaluated, and hence responded to, in quite different ways by two people who are employing different cognitive structures for comprehending and understanding the available information.

A great deal of research points to the importance of two factors as influencing the likelihood of activation of a given cognitive structure or concept. These factors are the *recency* and the *frequency* of prior activation (Higgins, Rholes, & Jones, 1977; Srull & Wyer, 1979). Consider Hank, who had parked his car on the street overnight, only to discover in the morning that someone had broken into it and stolen the audio equipment from it. When Hank then sees a stranger ambling slowly toward him on the sidewalk, a guy who seems shifty and it's not clear why he's there, then Hank's recent experience is likely to make him suspect that that person has evil intent . . . robbery. In other words, a concept (trait, motive, etc.) that has recently been activated remains easily accessible for a period of time and therefore can influence the interpretation of new, objectively unrelated, and especially ambiguous, stimuli. But that's not the whole story of poor Hank. It turns out that just last week his apartment was burglarized, and all of this reminds him of those other times when someone took some CDs he had left on his desk at work, when his tennis racket was stolen at the club, when his wallet had been picked as he walked through a crowded store. In addition to the recent car incident, the frequency with which Hank has had similar experiences, all of which have activated that same concept, has made it particularly accessible for guiding his interpretation of new events.

Now consider the implications of these findings on a long-term scale. If a particular concept is activated repeatedly, its frequency of activation would be high and, because of its frequency, it probably has been activated recently as well. Thus, both of these factors would work to make the concept readily available for use on a fairly consistent basis. In fact, under such conditions, certain concepts can become *chronically accessible*, and hence would be used with regularity in processing new information about people and events (Higgins, King, & Mavin, 1982). Moreover, because individuals would differ in their specific experiences, they might also differ in the concepts that become chronically accessible. Research evidence has shown that in fact there are individual differences in the constructs that become chronically accessible for use in judgments of both others (Bargh, Bond, Lombardi, & Tota, 1986) and ourselves (Markus, 1977).

Heuristics

When the police officer asks you about the accident at the corner of Victoria and Maple, you probably try to remember everything as thoroughly and as accurately as you can. You search your memory for anything and everything that you saw before, during, and after the incident. There certainly are times when we use such care in retrieving information from memory, but there undoubtedly are many other times when we don't trouble ourselves to be so conscientious. In those cases we use shortcuts, or rules of thumb, to make judgments based on information in memory. The term commonly used by psychologists for such shortcuts is *heuristics*.

Tversky and Kahneman (1974) identified several heuristics that people use in making judgments of probability and frequency, and their work elucidates ways that people bypass the rigorous demands of thoroughly analyzing memory and relevant information in such judgments. Suppose you see a male who looks like he weighs about 260 lb, and you wonder if he is a varsity football player. To answer the question, you might logically want to know how many male students at the university are 6'4" and 260 lb, how many members of the football team are that size, and knowing those things, you can then calculate the probability that this particular individual is a football player. If that's the way you want to answer the question, fine; your answer may be correct. Instead, though, in making this judgment most people will use the *representativeness heuristic*. Instead of carrying out those calculations, they will judge the *similarity* of this person to their conception of what football players are like, and if the "fit" is good, then they will perceive him to be a member of the team. Thus, the representativeness heuristic estimates probabilities based on the similarity between the specific instance and the general category. This strategy is often quite effective, but several factors can lead us astray and cause erroneous inferences. For example, there may be many male students who are big and athletic looking, but are not football players, and hence relying on representativeness would lead to incorrect judgments for all of those cases.

Another heuristic, commonly used in estimating frequencies, is the *availability heuristic*. This heuristic is used in judging how often something has happened, or how many people in a particular group have some characteristic, or any other frequency-related judgment. Rather than thoroughly surveying one's knowledge of the relevant category of events or people, the availability heuristic relies on the *ease of retrieving* instances of that event or members of that category of people. If it is easy to think of group members who have a particular attribute, then there must be a lot of them. If it's difficult to think of times when the event in question has happened, then it must not occur with much frequency. Again, the heuristic is useful because, in fact, in many cases we can easily remember instances of some category simply because there are a lot of them. The problem is that the ease of retrieving examples is a useful, but not a perfectly valid, indicator of actual frequency. In the availability heuristic, it is the ease of retrieving instances that drives the judgment, rather than the actual frequency of membership in the category. As with the representativeness heuristic, other variables can bias these estimates. For example, if we have just recently been interacting with members of the group, then instances of members of the group will come readily to mind. Similarly, if the group is very salient, or unusual, then examples of the category in question will be easily retrieved.

Research stimulated by Tversky and Kahneman's (1974) proposed heuristics has been immensely important in understanding social judgment processes (Nisbett & Ross, 1980). This work has shed new light on the ways in which we use the information and knowledge contained in our cognitive structures.

Deliberative and Automatic Processing of Social Information

Up to this point I have described the observer's processing of social information as if it were a very deliberative, thoughtful process. For example, my description of your evolving impression of Mark at the party referred to the variety of things you noticed about him — his varied interests, his intense conversations with others, his tendency to stay on the sidelines, etc. — and what they meant to you. Similarly, in describing the car accident, I said that you noticed that the Honda driver didn't stop, that the two participants were visibly upset in post-collision conversation, etc. Both of these scenarios portray the social perceiver as seriously engaged, consciously and thoughtfully, in trying to understand his or her social surroundings and the events transpiring in them. It is certainly the case that in many contexts social perceivers are in fact consciously engaged in trying to ascertain what is happening, what others are saying, why they are doing what they're doing, and what it all means. However, that is not the whole story.

One of the most important advances made by the social cognition approach has been the recognition of the extent to which we process social information spontaneously or "automatically." That is, information that we do not consciously or deliberatively attend to and think about may still be processed, stored, and used. Moreover, this automatic processing can in turn produce "automatic" effects on our judgments, feelings, and behaviors.

What do I mean by automatic processing? That is a matter of some debate among researchers (cf. Bargh, 1994), but several properties associated with the automatic processing of information have been identified. First, information can be processed without our conscious awareness, and in fact, without our even having conscious recognition of the stimulus being processed. Second, such processing does not require intentionality. That is, processing of information can occur without our intending to process it, or even focusing our attention on it. Third, being automatic, such processing occurs without requiring extensive cognitive resources being devoted to it. That is, when we consciously weigh the alternatives between two courses of action, our cognitive capacities are consumed by this mental activity, and we cannot attend to other tasks at the same time (and if we do, then the first task is disrupted). In contrast, a process that occurs automatically occurs without demanding conscious attention and therefore does not consume the cognitive resources that deliberative, thoughtful analysis requires. One consequence of this fact is that an automatic process can occur without disrupting other cognitive tasks that might be occurring simultaneously.

Do such automatic or "implicit" processes influence the processing of social information, and if so, do they have effects on subsequent judgments and behaviors? The results of an increasing body of research literature demonstrate that the effects of automatic processes are pervasive. For example, in one of the earliest demonstrations in social psychology, Bargh and Pietromonaco (1982) showed that priming certain trait concepts subliminally, without people's awareness, could influence the impressions formed of a target person. Specifically, in the first part of a two-phase study, participants performed a vigilance-like task in which they were to detect stimuli flashing briefly on a screen. Those stimuli were words, although they appeared so briefly that participants really couldn't detect what they were. In fact, however, either 0%, 20%, or 80% of the words, which participants could not recognize, were related to hostility (words like "insult," "unkind," "rude," "hurt"). Having completed this task, the next phase of the study was an impression formation task in which participants read a paragraph about a person named Donald. At several points Donald was described as having performed behaviors that could be interpreted as being unfriendly or even hostile, but that were open to more benign interpretations as well. Participants then rated their impression of Donald on a series of trait scales. Bargh and Pietromonaco (1982) found that people who had had the hostility construct strongly primed subliminally (80% of word exposures in the vigilance task) rated Donald more negatively than did participants in the other conditions. Thus, a concept that had been automatically activated outside of their awareness influenced participants' interpretation of the material they read about Donald, and consequently formed a less favorable impression of him.

Research has demonstrated comparable effects in a variety of social contexts. For example, people are "automatically vigilant" for negative or undesirable information, and this automatic (unintended) effect can influence performance in other (attended) tasks (Pratto & John, 1991). Other research has demonstrated that attitude objects automatically induce an evaluative reaction (Fazio, Sanbonmatsu, Powell, & Kardes, 1986). And subliminal priming of stereotypes and prejudicial attitudes can influence not only subsequent evaluative impressions and attitude judgments (Devine, 1989; Fazio, Jackson, Dunton, & Williams, 1995) but also overt behavior (Bargh, Chen, & Burrows, 1996; Dovidio, Kawakami, Johnson, Johnson, & Howard, 1997) and interactions toward members of the targeted group (Chen & Bargh, 1997; Dovidio et al., 1997).

In light of findings such as these, some have concluded that our behavior is influenced and controlled by automatic processes to a far greater extent that we have realized (Bargh, 1999). In any event, it is clear that some very important aspects of the way we process social information occurs automatically, outside of our awareness, by processes that we do not fully control, and that can have important influences on outcomes. The interplay between such automatic influences and the more deliberative, thoughtful, and controlled aspects of our processing system is likely to be the focus of continuing research.

Developing Mental Representations: Impressions and Stereotypes

I stated earlier that in the course of our social experiences we acquire information and form mental representations of those persons and events. Given the vast and varied experiences that all of us have, we develop a broad and rich array of mental representations, which we store in memory and use in making judgments and guiding behavior. That is, we develop mental representations pertaining to all aspects of our lives. Two very important kinds of mental representations have been studied extensively by social cognition researchers, and will be highlighted here: impressions of individuals and stereotypes of groups. We are all familiar with these concepts from everyday experience. The question I want to raise in this section is: How are these mental representations formed?

Impression Formation

In an article published more than 50 years ago, Solomon Asch (1946) theorized that our first impression of another person begins to form from the earliest information acquired about the person, and later information is assimilated into the evolving impression. As such, the meaning or connotation of later information can be affected by the impression that has been created from earlier information. In Asch's view there is a "dynamic interaction" among traits such that the impression, as a whole, is more than the sum of its parts. Rather, the various elements become integrated into an organized impression of the person.

Asch developed a simple method and procedure for studying first impression formation: he read a series of trait-descriptive adjectives to his participants, and their task was to form an impression of a person who possessed all of these traits. The participants were then given a list of additional trait-descriptive adjectives and were asked to make a check mark next to those they thought would also characterize the person. Using this procedure, Asch conducted a series of experiments that produced a number of important findings. In one study, for example, he compared the impressions formed by two groups of participants. For one group, the person was described as *intelligent, skillful, industrious, warm, determined, practical*, and *cautious*. For the other group, the list of traits was exactly the same, except that the word *warm* was replaced by the word *cold*. Despite the fact that six of the seven terms were identical, these two groups of participants formed dramatically different impressions. This difference documented what Asch (1946) called *central traits*. His idea was that our impressions are built upon, and organized around, certain central themes that define a person's personality, and in his view, the warm–cold distinction in this study constituted such a central trait.

In another study, Asch presented the exact same list of traits to two groups of participants, but changed the order of their presentation. One group learned that the person is *intelligent, industrious, impulsive, critical, stubborn*, and *envious*. The other group was presented the same traits in the reverse order. As I'm sure you have already detected, the only difference is in whether the traits progress from very favorable to very unfavorable traits or from unfavorable to favorable. If our impressions are simply based on the information we acquire, then the two impressions should be identical, as the descriptive terms were the same in both cases. However, Asch found that people formed much more favorable impressions in the first case than in the second case. This outcome is called a *primacy effect*, and refers to the greater impact of early information on the resulting impression. This result supported Asch's argument that perceivers begin to form an impression of a person from the very earliest information acquired, and then later information is incorporated, or assimilated, into that impression. Another experiment provided evidence for Asch's explanation of how that assimilation occurs. Specifically, any given attribute is open to different interpretations; it can have different meanings or connotations, depending on the context in which it occurs. For example, suppose a person is *kind, wise*, and *clever*.

What is your evaluation of the trait *clever*? It seems a good quality, one that implies that the person has insights, can solve problems, has interesting ideas. Now suppose a person is *cruel, shrewd*, and *clever*. What is your evaluation of the trait *clever* in this case? Here it is a more negative attribute, and has quite different implications: it suggests that the person may be devious, unscrupulous, not to be trusted. Clearly the first two traits in the list establish a context in which the third trait is construed, and therefore the same trait can take on different meanings in different contexts. Asch argued that this *change in meaning* is a function of the context of what else is known about the person. More generally, the impression we already have of a person can guide our interpretation and meaning of new information we learn about her as that new information is assimilated into the existing impression.

Asch was interested in studying the ways that information we learn about a person is assembled and integrated into an impression of that person. At the time he did his research, however, the methodologies were limited and, although his results were consistent with his predictions, it remained for a later era of research to use newer techniques to test his ideas anew. In this more recent era, research on *person memory* has been able to study more directly the way information is acquired and represented in memory (Hastie, Ostrom, Ebbesen, Wyer, Hamilton, & Carlston, 1980).

Person memory researchers took advantage of advances made by cognitive psychologists studying memory, and they adapted both the theoretical models of memory representation and the methodological tools developed to study them. Consider, for example, that you learn a series of behaviors performed by a person and are asked to form an impression of the person. That person is represented as a particular location in memory — a "person node" — and all information associated with that person (e.g., representations of the behaviors) is attached to that node in memory through a series of pathways. In some cases these behaviors themselves may be linked with each other in what emerges as a network of information. In one theory of this type, originating in the work of Hastie (1980) and Srull (1981), the information comprising one's impression of the person is stored in such a network in memory. Later, when asked to retrieve that information (or to use it for other purposes), the perceiver refers to the person node and proceeds across the pathways in the network, recalling items as they are encountered in one's search through the network. This type of model has been very effective in accounting for a variety of empirical findings.

In addition to representing specific instances of behavior performed by the person in memory, we also infer the person's more general qualities on the basis of that information. That is, we infer that the person is friendly, intelligent, outspoken, moody, liberal, etc. Sometimes these inferences are made as we are encoding the specific information that implies such traits. For example, as you were talking with Mark at the party, you couldn't help but notice that he was well read, knew a lot about current events, and could talk knowledgeably about different kinds of music. Therefore you quickly drew the inference that he's smart. When the perceiver makes such an inference as the information is being processed, it is called an *on-line* judgment. On the other hand, suppose that the next day someone asks you if Mark is a good dancer. "Hmmm . . . ," you pause and think, "no one was dancing at the party, but he was somewhat reticent and aloof from others, except when engaged in seemingly serious conversations, so I'd guess he's not the good-dancer type." In contrast to an on-line judgment, in this case you had not formed an evaluation of Mark's dancing abilities as you were conversing with him, but rather, you had to use whatever information you could remember to form a judgment at the time you were asked. This is called a *memory-based* judgment, as it is based on recall of specific facts from memory. This important distinction, introduced by Hastie and Park (1986), refers to the time at which the judgment is made: as the information is being processed (on-line) or later, on the basis of the information retrieved from memory (memory-based). Although we commonly make judgments of both types, there are important differences between them, and they are subject to different kinds of bias.

Stereotypes

In the course of our experiences in the social world we not only acquire information about individual persons but also about groups of people. And in turn, we develop mental representations of those groups. The processes here are similar, but also involve some differences.

In order to develop a conception of a group, it is first necessary to recognize that a group exists. This initial step involves the categorization process, whereby a number of people are perceived as being members of the same class of persons. Categorization is a fundamental cognitive process that is an important tool in adapting to the very complex stimulus environment in which we live. Thus, for example, just as we group various four-legged creatures we encounter — poodles, setters, terriers, pit-bulls — into one category called "dogs," we categorize people into groups on some basis — skin color, gender, nationality, and the like. This act of categorization has certain benefits, for it alleviates the need to attend to each individual member of the category as an individual. In addition, knowing something about the members of the category enables us to assume things about how this "new" member is like the others. Moreover, once members are categorized into one group, it implies that they are different from members of another group. In sum, two important consequences of categorization are, first, that members of the same group are perceived as being similar to each other, and second, that members of different categories are perceived as being very different from each other. Each of these tendencies represents an exaggeration of the actual degree of similarity and differentiation.

It is important to note that categorizing people into groups does not, by itself, mean that stereotypes of those groups have formed. However, after having decided that all people who have a certain attribute constitute a group (Italians, Jews, nerds), we often associate certain characteristics with that group, including characteristics that extend well beyond the basis of categorization ("they're dirty"; "they're intelligent"; "they're aggressive"). Once those associations are formed, then a stereotype has formed, and those beliefs comprise the stereotype. Moreover, like any cognitive structure, stereotypes include expectancies that can bias the processing and use of new information. In the case of stereotypes, the consequences can be particularly insidious.

Stereotypes, then, are mental representations of groups, in a manner paralleling impressions of individuals. Are stereotypes formed in the same way as impressions of individuals? One of the hallmarks of Asch's (1946) view of impression formation was that information describing a person becomes integrated into a coherent whole, an organized impression of the person's personality. Thus, the perceiver is guided by an overarching expectancy that the individual is a unified, coherent being, that his personality is much the same yesterday, today, and tomorrow, that the personality to some degree drives the person's behavior, and therefore one can expect consistency across time and situation in the behaviors the person manifests. Because of this assumption, the perceiver strives to integrate the information learned about a target person, identifying the prominent themes of the person's personality, and striving to explain any apparent inconsistencies in the person's behaviors. Hamilton and Sherman (1996; Hamilton, Sherman, & Lickel, 1998) have argued that perceivers do not make that assumption of unity to the same degree about groups. That is, the group is comprised of many individuals, they may vary among themselves in their behavior patterns, and therefore the group may behave differently at different times, and as a consequence, the perceiver is less likely to assume that the group is an organized and unified entity. Therefore, Hamilton and Sherman argued, perceivers are less likely to engage in the kinds of integrated processing that characterizes the formation of individual impressions. The result is that the mental representation of groups may be less organized and structured than our impressions of individuals, and because of that, judgments made about groups are more likely to be memory-based rather than having been formed on-line. Finally, perceivers are also cognizant of the variety of individuals and groups they encounter in everyday life. Although we assume that individuals are well integrated and coherent beings, we are all aware of the variety of individuals in our world, some of whom would be less aptly characterized in this way. When we lack certainty that an individual possesses a typical degree of personality integration, we are less confident in our impressions of and inferences about him or her. Similarly, although on average we expect less unity and coherence in groups than in individuals, groups obviously vary in the extent to which they are well-organized units. We can form clearer impressions of groups that appear to be well structured and organized than of groups that lack such integration. Thus, the impressions we develop of both individuals and groups — how they are formed, how they guide perceptions and interactions — can be influenced by the extent to which we perceive (or assume) that individual or group to be an integrated, coherent entity (Hamilton, Sherman, & Castelli, 2002; Yzerbyt, Rocher, & Schadron, 1997).

Trait Inferences

We have already encountered several examples of how people elaborate on the information they acquire by making inferences that build on and extend their "knowledge." In considering our opening scenarios, we've seen inferences about personality characteristics (Mark is a nice guy, smart, reticent), about motives (the driver of the blue Honda was in a hurry), and attributional inferences (he caused the accident by not stopping at the intersection). How are these inferences made? When are they made? How much do we have to think about people's behaviors in making these inferences, or (to quote a popular commercial) do we "just do it"? These questions have been the focus of a lot of research.

We know from research on implicit personality theories that people have rich networks of associations representing their beliefs about "what goes with what" in the personalities of people, beliefs that certain pairs of attributes are likely to co-occur ("a person who is witty is also likely to be intelligent"). Therefore, given knowledge that a person possesses one trait, we can use our implicit personality theory to infer that the person probably has certain other, correlated attributes as well. Beyond those associations between trait concepts, however, we often infer dispositional qualities from observation or knowledge of a person's behavior. How and when are these inferences made?

Research has shown that perceivers often make dispositional inferences about an actor in the very process of comprehending behavior. Winter and Uleman (1984) conducted an important study in which they showed that people spontaneously infer a dispositional attribute directly from a person's behavior. Participants in their study read a series of statements, each of which described a behavior performed by a person. For example, one of the statements read, "The plumber left a $20 bill in his wife's purse." The person's behavior is generous; therefore, an inference about the person's corresponding attribute would be that he himself is a generous person. However, Winter and Uleman did not directly ask their participants for such inferences. Instead, they administered a cued recall task in which they provided certain words that were associated with aspects of the stimulus sentence, words that were not, however, actually in those sentences. The rationale is as follows. If the trait inference that the plumber is "generous" was made spontaneously as the stimulus sentence was read and encoded, then that trait is associated in memory with that sentence, and therefore the word "generous" should serve as a useful cue to retrieving the sentence. In fact, that is what Winter and Uleman found. Traits that would be inferred from the actors' behaviors were effective cues to recalling the sentences, and in fact, these inferred disposition words were more effective than other kinds of cues, such as associates of the actor's occupation ("pipes").

Winter and Uleman's (1984) findings were provocative and stimulated a considerable amount of research by other scholars. As you know, no matter how strongly a study's results support the hypotheses and no matter how compelling the findings seem to be, any study leaves certain questions unanswered and is open to alternative interpretation. The most viable alternative interpretation is that the trait words were effective retrieval cues not because a dispositional inference had spontaneously been made while reading the sentence, but instead because it also captured the meaning of the action described. The word "generous" might simply reflect the gist of the behavior, and not have been inferred as a trait of the plumber. That is, perhaps the cue word was effective as an associate of the verb, not as an inferred trait of the actor of the sentence (Bassili & Smith, 1986). The challenge of such interpretive issues then generates new research, seeking alternate means of testing the same hypothesis but avoiding the particular interpretive pitfall of the previous study. (For some of us, that challenge is what makes doing science fun!). In this case, Carlston, Skowronski, and their colleagues (Carlston & Skowronski, 1994; Carlston, Skowronski, & Sparks, 1995) have carried out a series of studies using a different paradigm, and their results also indicate that spontaneous dispositional inferences are commonly made as people encode behavioral information.

The notion that trait inferences are made spontaneously, without thought or intention, raises the specter of a cognitive system that is inflexible and rigid. However, this is not the case, for several reasons. First, some research stimulated by Winter and Uleman's findings (e.g., Bassili & Smith, 1986) showed that making these trait inferences is not automatic (as defined in the previous two paragraphs) but in fact is dependent on the availability of cognitive resources and occurs much more readily under some goal conditions (impression formation) than others (memory). Second, other research (Hilton, Fein, & Miller, 1993) has shown that such inferences are not made when the perceiver is suspicious that the actor's behavior reflects ulterior motives and therefore may not warrant an inference that the actor possesses the corresponding disposition. Hence, making spontaneous correspondent inferences is not inevitable. And third, research has shown that even when a correspondent inference is made, it is tentative, functions as a hypothesis, and is correctable in light of other information (Trope, 1986). For example, Gilbert, Pelham, and Krull (1988) showed that dispositional inferences may be made spontaneously, but they can be "corrected" in light of information about the social context. However, whereas the spontaneous inference occurs quickly and without much thought, the correction process is more demanding and requires cognitive resources.

In sum, perceivers spontaneously make inferences about the dispositional qualities of an actor that would seem to underlie observed behaviors. Perceivers "go beyond the information available" in this way as a part of comprehending the behavioral information they process. However, that process is neither automatic nor inflexible. It can be enhanced or disrupted, depending on the perceiver's processing goal and the situational context, and even after having made such an inference, it can be corrected in light of new information. In all of these cases, however, it is important to recognize this inference process as a useful means by which perceivers elaborate on their understanding of the people and events they encounter.

Attribution

As the preceding discussion indicates, people are quite versatile in making inferences based on the information they have encountered. There is one particular kind of inference, however, that is very important and has captured a lot of research attention.

People process and use the information they acquire about others in order to enhance their adaptation to the social environment. That adaptation is greatly facilitated when one can anticipate, in any given situation, what others are likely to do, how they are likely to react, what they are thinking, planning, intending to do, and how they feel. Understanding and anticipating what is likely to transpire in our social relationships requires that we understand something about the causes of people's behavior. If we understand those causal relations — why people respond in certain ways under certain circumstances — then it helps us anticipate their likely actions and reactions in the future. The study of how perceivers make inferences about the causes for people's behaviors is called the study of *attribution* processes.

The earliest ideas on attribution in the psychological literature were advanced by Fritz Heider (1944, 1958), whose writings were of immense importance and whose ideas guided attribution research for many years. Heider's theory analyzed the perception of causality from the perceiver's perspective, or as he called it, "phenomenal causality." Heider was not concerned with the actual determinants of people's behavior but rather with the perception of causation by the perceiver, and more specifically, with how the perceiver makes that judgment. One of the most important conceptual distinctions he focused on was concerned with the perceived locus of causation. The cause for any given behavior can reside either in the person or in the situational context. Specifically, at any given time a person's behavior might be due to his motives and goals, his personality, his attitudes, his emotions (e.g., "he went to the movie because he likes works by that director"), or it might be in response to some external pressures or constraints imposed by the situation ("he went to the movie because his friends wanted to see it"). This fundamental distinction is highly informative for the perceiver's goal of understanding causality and for anticipating the future. If we judge that the behavior is due to internal (dispositional) causes, then we've learned something about the nature of the actor and can anticipate that those attributes will guide similar behaviors in the future. On the other hand, if the behavior is perceived as having been due to situational constraints — the person felt social pressure, or simply had no choice, so the behavior would have been enacted by virtually anyone under those conditions — then we would have little basis for inferring anything about the attributes of the person. (Heider's theory included several other important ideas that influence attributional inferences, but in our limited space we'll focus on this one, as it had great impact on subsequent theory and research.)

Although Heider's writings were rich in ideas and fascinating in their implications, they were not well formulated as a basis for developing specific experiments testing specific ideas. However, several prominent theories of attribution, guided by Heider's writings, were developed to lend experimental clarity and to make the ideas empirically tractable. Most prominent among these were theories proposed by Jones and Davis (1965) and Kelley (1967), both of which attempted to delineate bases on which the perceiver could infer the locus of causality. The ideas advanced by both theories generated an enormous amount of research on attribution.

Jones and Davis's Correspondent Inference Theory was specifically concerned with the conditions under which the perceiver will infer that a person's behavior reflects an underlying dispositional characteristic, which could then provide a causal account for that behavior. In fact, Jones and Davis's Correspondent Inference Theory was concerned with exactly the issues discussed in the preceding section on Trait Inferences (Hamilton, 1998). A correspondent inference occurs when the perceiver observes a person enact some behavior and infers that the actor has the "corresponding" disposition. For example, if you see someone helping another person carry packages, you might infer that the person is helpful; if you see someone lose his temper and yell at a colleague, you might infer that he is temperamental. A correspondent inference is one in which the actor is perceived as possessing a trait that is directly manifested in behavior. In a correspondent inference, both the behavior and the disposition can be described by the same term (e.g., helpful). In essence, Jones and Davis proposed that, when observing a person's behaviors, a correspondent inference will be made unless certain factors are present that would suggest a situational cause. Factors they discussed include the following: (1) *Choice*. If the actor had no choice in enacting the behavior, but was forced to do so, then one would be less likely to make a correspondent inference. (2) *Commonality*. Typical, normative, desirable behaviors — the kinds of things anyone would do under the circumstances, because they are maintained by social norms — are less likely to lead to correspondent inferences because they are "caused" by adherence to social norms rather than by the internal characteristics of the actor.

Kelley's (1967) theory was focused specifically on the question of how the perceiver might decide whether the locus of causation for a given behavior was internal or external. Consider once again the party you went to Friday evening. Soon after you arrived you briefly met Kevin, who seemed pleasant. Later you saw him across the room talking with Sandy, when suddenly he erupted into an outburst of temper, saying rude things to her in a loud voice. This episode of course captured your (and everyone else's) attention, and you in effect asked yourself the attributional question, "Why did he do that?" Is Kevin a temperamental guy who is prone to losing control? Did Sandy provoke his response by insulting him? Kelley proposed that in answering such questions, three sources of information are relevant and can be used by the perceiver. One is the *consistency* with which the actor has engaged in this behavior toward this person in the past. Is this the first time Kevin has ever lost his temper at Sandy, or has it happened before? The second concerns the *distinctiveness* of this behavior toward others. Was Kevin irritable in his interactions with other people at the party also, or was this response unique to his interaction with Sandy? The third source of information is the *consensus* of this particular behavior in other people. Do other people also get irritated when interacting with Sandy, or is Kevin unusual in doing so? These three types of information, singly and in combination, help clarify the likely locus of causation. For example, if a person consistently performs some behavior toward another person (high consistency), if he does it to many people and not simply to that individual (low distinctiveness), and if few others engage in this behavior (low consensus), then the behavior likely reflects something about the actor's dispositional characteristics (i.e., it is internally caused). On the other hand, if the behavior is infrequently performed by this actor (low consistency), is directed only at this particular target person (high distinctiveness), and many other people also behave that way (high consensus), then the behavior is probably caused by something external to the actor (e.g., it was induced by the person or persons to whom he was responding, or it was constrained by aspects of the situation). Thus, these sources of information can aid in the attribution process.

Both of these theories provided quite plausible accounts of how the perceiver might use relevant information in making an inference about the causal basis for observed behavior. They present quite straightforward ideas that, if followed, would lead to very reasonable judgments. However, research spawned by a social cognition approach to analyzing social perception has revealed that the actual processes engaged in by perceivers often deviate in systematic ways from those prescribed, or at least implied, by these theories.

Strategies and Biases in Using Social Information

We have already seen that the individual, in perceiving and responding to the social world, may actively utilize the information available to her in systematic ways. She may selectively attend to only portions of the relevant information; she may interpret ambiguous information in expectancy-consistent ways; she may infer and elaborate on that information; she may make inferences explaining the causes for what has occurred; and in making judgments later, she may be guided by expectancies in searching and retrieving from memory. In all of these ways, the individual may transform the information that was actually encountered in the social environment. These processing strategies for dealing with complex social information may be highly adaptive, but they may also lead to misrepresentations of that environment and to biases in the use of the information acquired. In other words, in our processing and use of information, not all of our mechanisms would conform to a purely rational handling of that information.

The attribution theories we have just discussed had the flavor of conveying highly rational approaches to dealing with relevant information in trying to understand social causality. That is, if we were to consider all of the factors specified by these theories, then we would probably make sound attributional judgments. But consider what's involved. In Kelley's theory, for example, in order to make an attributional judgment one should consider (1) whether the person has usually behaved this way toward this target person in the past, (2) whether he has behaved this way toward other persons as well, and (3) whether other people also behave this way toward the target person. That's a lot to think about whenever we'd like to know why someone did something. I'm sure there are times — for example, when we're faced with very important situations or decisions — when we do consider and weigh all of these factors, but if we were to do so routinely, we wouldn't get much else done in life! Therefore it's perhaps not surprising to learn that we take shortcuts in our use of information. Social cognition research has documented a variety of strategies that we have developed for dealing with complex social information, strategies that are effective in easing our cognitive burden but that also, being shortcuts, can produce less-than-optimal consequences. In this section I discuss some of the research on these strategies, along with the biases and pitfalls that can emanate from their use.

Sometimes scientific advances are made when we least suspect them. This can happen when the results of a study do not totally conform to our hypotheses, but include some anomaly that lacks easy explanation. Evidence that perceivers may not fully appreciate the implications of the information they acquire was interestingly revealed in a study by Jones and Harris (1967). In their study participants read a speech advocating a certain political argument, presumably prepared for a debate. Some participants were told that the speaker had chosen which side of the issue to argue, whereas others were told he had been assigned that side in the debate. Afterward, they were asked to rate the speaker's true attitude on the issue. When the speaker was free to choose which side to argue, participants of course assumed that that position reflected his own personal opinion. In contrast, as noted in Correspondent Inference Theory, in the "no choice" condition there would be little if any basis for assuming that the views he expressed reflected his privately-held opinions, since the position advocated in his speech was assigned, not chosen. Nevertheless, participants still perceived the speaker as subscribing to those views.

A similar phenomenon emerged in a study by Ross, Amabile, and Steinmetz (1977). Two participants were randomly assigned to the roles of "questioner" and "contestant" in a quiz game in which the questioner tried to ask difficult "general knowledge" questions, to which she knew the answers, in an attempt to stump the contestant. Because the questioner could ask any question she chose, she could draw on trivial facts and remote topic areas about which she happened to have some knowledge, but which the typical person would not. Thus the "rules of the game" strongly favored the questioner, and the poor contestant was destined to have difficulty answering such questions (and in fact did have difficulty). Observers who watched the quiz game then rated both of the participants on their extent of overall general knowledge. Despite the fact that "the cards were stacked" in favor of one participant over the other, observers in fact perceived the questioner as being much more knowledgeable than the contestant. That is, they were oblivious to the fact that the situation was created in such a way that it essentially determined the outcome. Nevertheless, perceivers made dispositional inferences corresponding to the behaviors they witnessed and, equally importantly, they were insensitive to the powerful impact of the situation (i.e., the game rules) in determining the participants' behaviors. This effect, which has been called the *correspondence bias* (Jones, 1990) and the *fundamental attribution error* (Ross, 1977), reflects a perceiver's tendency to view behavior as reflecting underlying dispositions, even when that behavior was performed under situational constraints. This effect has been replicated many times under a variety of conditions (cf. Gilbert & Malone, 1995; Jones, 1979; Ross, 1977).

This tendency to view manifest behavior as reflecting internal properties is particularly true in our judgments of others, and is less prominent in our inferences about ourselves (Jones & Nisbett, 1972). When asked why we ourselves engaged in some behavior, we are less likely to refer to our personality traits and more likely to explain our behavior as being in response to situational demands. That is, we explain the behaviors of others in terms of their dispositional characteristics (personality, motivation, attitudes), whereas we are more likely to view our own behavior as responsive to external constraints.

All of these biases are subject to another important influence, namely, the perceiver's own self-interest. That is, our judgments are subject to motivational factors in which we seek to view ourselves in a favorable light. For example, although perceivers tend to explain their own behavior as being in response to external influences, they are particularly likely to cite such factors in explaining their undesirable behaviors and failings. They are more likely to account for their successes and desirable actions in terms of their internal, stable, redeeming features. Moreover, research has shown that this bias can influence not only our explanations for our behaviors but the very ways in which we perceive and interpret what has happened. Such motivated construal processes are fundamental and pervasive.

Influence of Goals and Motives on Information Processing

The concepts, theories, and research we have discussed to this point might generate an image of a person as information processor who is thoroughly consumed with processing and analyzing information in order to comprehend and understand the people and events that he or she encounters. In fact, the social cognition tradition has sometimes been criticized as focusing too narrowly on the role of cognitive processes, to the exclusion on other important factors. However, the research we consider in this section portrays the information processor as goal driven and motivated toward certain outcomes in preference to others. That is, people usually have goals and motives that drive their perceptions and behavior at the moment. Recent research has shown that these goals and motives can influence not only *what* information people process from the social context but also *how* they process it.

The nature of one's processing goals has a strong effect on information processing. Suppose, for example, you are asked to form an impression of a person by reading a series of statements describing a variety of behaviors, all of which were performed by that person. Later, you are asked to recall as many of those behaviors as you can. Now suppose instead that, instead of forming an impression of someone, you were simply asked to read those same sentences and were then asked to recall them. These two cases reflect different goals or objectives that you might have in processing the same information. Research has shown that the impression formation goal leads to better, and more coherently organized, recall of the same information than does the memory goal (Hamilton, Katz, & Leirer, 1980). Moreover, if you anticipated that you would later be interacting with that person, memory for the relevant information would be even better (Devine, Sedikides, & Fuhrman, 1989). Processing goals have also been shown to influence categorization of another person. Pendry and Macrae (1996) had participants watch a 2-min video of a businesswoman performing a variety of tasks (reading a report, writing some notes, getting things out of her briefcase, etc.). Three groups of participants were given different processing goal instructions. Some were told to judge the visual clarity of the video, some were told to estimate the woman's height, and some were instructed to form an impression of the woman, which they would then have to justify. Participants in all conditions then performed a task assessing the level and detail with which the stimulus woman had been categorized. Participants in the first two conditions simply viewed her as a woman, whereas those in the "accountable impression" condition categorized her at a more detailed level and were more likely to think of her as having the attributes characteristic of businesswomen. Thus, a person's goals or task objectives can guide one's attention to the most task-relevant information, can influence the amount of attention and processing devoted to various items of information, and these processing characteristics can influence our memory for and categorization of social stimuli.

Achieving our goals often involves more than simply focusing on the task at hand or getting a job done. We *want* to achieve our goals. We are motivationally invested in achieving our objectives. Moreover, our goals and motivations often have a self-serving orientation — we want to be right, we want to be liked, we want to do well. Such motivations can dramatically influence the way we interpret and use information, in a number of different ways. For example, Kunda (1987) has shown that people's reasoning processes can be influenced by their motivations. In one study, people read a story about a person, describing a number of characteristics of the person's attributes and background (e.g., introvert or extrovert; religious or nonreligious; mother was employed or unemployed). The person was married a number of years ago, and the subject's task was to indicate which of the person's features (described in the paragraph) would help make for a stable marriage and which ones might make divorce more likely. The results showed that those features rated most favorably (i.e., made a stable marriage more likely) were those that matched the subject's own characteristics. Thus, people see their own attributes (and therefore similar attributes in another person) as contributing to favorable outcomes. Moreover, other research has shown that this bias works in the service of maintaining and/or enhancing self-esteem (Dunning, Leuenberger, & Sherman, 1995).

Consistent with this evidence are other findings showing that people more readily accept conclusions that are consistent with their preferences. In many situations we typically know what outcome we would like to happen. When we learn something that is consistent with our goals, objectives, motives, and self-interest, we not only are pleased but also accept the arguments or evidence without much question (Ditto & Lopez, 1992; Lord, Ross, & Lepper, 1979). On the other hand, if the outcome is counter to our motives and preferences, then we resist the argument or conclusion. If we're honest with ourselves, we can easily find this bias in our own lives. When I first saw the headline of a newspaper article reporting that drinking a glass or two of red wine per day is beneficial to one's health, I didn't need to read much further. Being a wine lover, I immediately accepted the conclusion, and in fact never doubted that the evidence was convincing. If, on the other hand, I had read that two glasses of red wine has detrimental effects on one's health, I immediately would have been motivated to question and challenge that conclusion, generating questions about "direction of causation," reservations about the (in)adequacy of sampling and research design in the reported study, etc. Very often, the mind is not neutral in its evaluation of evidence and outcomes.

How does this bias operate? After all, if some event we didn't want to happen occurs, then we can't simply fantasize it away. As a friend of mine once said, "Reality does happen." The human mind is, however, a clever strategist and it has a variety of tools at its disposal to deal with unwanted outcomes. For example, we often generate hypotheses to understand how the event came about, and we often generate explanatory hypotheses to understand why the event happened. But again we are not neutral in this regard. Research has shown that we analyze information less extensively if the event is consistent with our motives and desires than if it opposes our wishes (Kunda, 1987, 1990; Mayseless & Kruglanski, 1987). We may require more evidence for, and we may generate more opposing arguments against, unwanted outcomes and conclusions (Ditto & Lopez, 1992). Thus, we process information less extensively and less critically when it is consistent with our favored outcome.

In addition to a pervasive motive to view both events and ourselves in a favorable manner, other motives can influence the nature and extent of information processing. Kruglanski and his colleagues (Kruglanski & Webster, 1995) have shown that there are times and circumstances when people feel a "need for cognitive closure," a desire to arrive at an outcome (decision, agreement, etc.) in a short time and with a minimum of ambiguity. Perhaps you are under a lot of pressure to get a lot of things done, or you are facing a deadline, or you've simply been working on some task for so long you just feel a need to have it done. Or perhaps there's a loud, persistent noise in the hallway outside the room where you're working, making you wish you could get finished and out of there. Under such circumstances, you will feel a need for closure, with consequences for the way you process task-relevant information. For example, people experiencing need for closure often process less information before arriving at a judgment or decision, and they generate fewer alternative hypotheses or possibilities once the decision has been made. Thus, heightened need for closure can influence people's openness to new information and hence their response to persuasive communications (Kruglanski, Webster, & Klem, 1993) and, in a group setting, can influence their tolerance for a deviant member who doesn't adhere to group norms (Kruglanski & Webster, 1991). Moreover, once such closure has been achieved, people often feel more confidence in the outcome (Kruglanski & Webster, 1995). In addition to situational factors that can induce this motive, individuals vary in their chronic need for closure (Webster & Kruglanski, 1994).

In sum, our goals and motives can guide our attention to, interpretation of, and use of information in ways that serve those goals and motives.

Understanding the Past, Anticipating the Future

Understanding the Past

We often think of memory as a repository of "facts" gleaned from our experiences that can be retrieved at a later time, as they are needed. A popular image views memory as the verbatim record of those experiences, and therefore our memories are rather accurate recreations of those experiences. We have already seen that memory representations of our experiences may be only partially factual as those experiences are selectively registered, enhanced, and altered through potentially biased interpretation, evaluation, inference, and causal attribution. These processes transform what was observed in the external world into one's own comprehension of that social environment, which then becomes the individual's mental representation of what has transpired. So what is actually stored in memory may differ in important ways from what was actually experienced. But that is only part of the story. It turns out that even those representations may not be recalled accurately, for the cognitive system also works in fascinating ways on our retrieval of that information as well. In fact, memory can be quite malleable. In this section I discuss several ways in which our memory for the past can be biased and massaged by our mental systems.

Let's begin with a simple example by going back to our scenario involving the collision at the intersection of Maple and Victoria. Imagine that a few days later you are being questioned by authorities about exactly what happened. You explain that the Honda driver didn't stop, and you're asked, "How fast was the Honda going when it smashed into the bicycle?" It turns out that your estimate of speed would be greater in that case than if you were asked, "How fast was the Honda going when it bumped into the bicycle?" (Loftus & Palmer, 1974). In other words, what we recall can be guided by such leading questions. This type of effect can occur not only in legal matters but also in many aspects of everyday life. Recent experiences, prior expectancies, current mood states, and the social context can all function in the same way as leading questions — by guiding our search of memory and our interpretation of what we find there.

When we learn that some outcome has happened, we often have the experience of "knowing" that "Of course . . . it was bound to happen, given the circumstances." This sense that "I knew it would turn out that way" is known as the *hindsight bias* (Fischhoff, 1975). It is called a bias because it reflects a distorted view of the past, a biased interpretation and use of our "knowledge" that is represented in memory. Fischhoff (1975) conducted several clever experiments in which he gave people descriptions of events and manipulated the outcome of those events (e.g., the home team won or lost; the British army was or was not victorious in the battle). Participants were then asked how likely they thought it was that that outcome, and possible alternative outcomes, would occur, given the circumstances described. Participants in both conditions (they won, they lost) viewed the outcome as likely, and justified its occurrence in terms of the conditions that had existed at the time (Hawkins & Hastie, 1990). Thus, knowledge of the present can influence our memory of the past. Moreover, knowledge of present outcomes can also bias judgments. For example, Allison, Mackie, and Messick (1996) have found that knowledge of an outcome can influence perceptions of the degree of support for an issue. Suppose that a town votes on an issue that requires a two-third majority to pass. If the vote fails to pass because only 61% of the people voted for it, people may then conclude that "most people" were not in favor of the position advocated.

In addition to seemingly "knowing" (in retrospect) that what happened would happen, sometimes our memory of the past is also biased by what we now know or believe . . . or want to believe. This is most likely to happen when our memories of things that happened some time ago are vague and imprecise. In such cases, we *reconstruct* those past events in our minds (Ross, 1989). That is, we use implicit notions or theories to guide (and perhaps create, or recreate) our memories of the way things were. Ross discusses two different variations on such reconstructive memory. In some cases, we reconstruct the past in such a way that it maintains the apparent *stability* in our lives (Ross, McFarland, & Fletcher, 1981). We want to believe that our attitudes, beliefs, and behavior patterns are the same today as they were in the past. But memories of the past are malleable, and when asked how we felt on an issue, or how often we engaged in some behavior, our recollections may be biased in the direction of our current attitudes, beliefs, and habits. At other times, Ross argues, we reconstruct the past to enhance the appearance of *change*. To demonstrate this effect, Conway and Ross (1984) conducted a study in which participants signed up for a program aimed at improving study skills (covering such topics as reading comprehension, effective note taking, etc.). At the outset, all participants evaluated their study skills on a variety of measures. Half of the participants completed a 3-week program, while the other half were on a waiting list for the program. After completion of the program, both groups of participants again evaluated their study skills, and also predicted whether their grades would improve. The study-skills program produced no measurable effects: grades of students in the program did not improve and were not higher than those in the control (waiting list) group. Nevertheless, students who completed the program thought their study skills had improved and predicted higher grades. One basis for this misperception is their reconstruction of the past. When asked to recall their earlier (preprogram) assessment of their study skills, the group that had the program remembered that they had made worse self-evaluations than they actually had; participants in the control group did not show this bias. Thus, the students were able to hold their belief in change (improvement) by retrospectively altering their memory of their previous self-evaluations.

Another means by which we seek to "understand the past" is by reconsidering what has happened and the events leading up to it. Let's return once more to our accident scenario. Instead of being behind the blue Honda, imagine that you were the driver of the Honda, and it was you that collided with the crossing bicycle rider. Later, after assuring yourself that the biker is OK and assessing your damage, you might replay that event in your mind, and wonder how the accident could have been avoided. You recall being late getting out of work as that last project took longer than expected, and then chatting briefly with a colleague as you were preparing to leave, then driving hurriedly to get home to prepare for your date that evening with someone who (you're hoping) will turn out to be someone pretty special. All of these factors converged to mean that you arrived at the intersection just at the same time as the bicyclist, and because of your lateness and sense of urgency, you only slowed briefly at the Stop sign. You might then think, "If only . . .," and you then consider some of the alternatives. If only I'd finished up that project sooner; if only I hadn't stopped for that chat; if only I'd stopped fully at the Stop sign . . . if only any of these things were true, the accident would not have happened. But of course all of those things did in fact occur, so in thinking this way, you are engaging in *counterfactual thinking* (Kahneman &

Miller, 1986). In doing so, you reconstruct a past incident and think of alternative scenarios that would have resulted in different outcomes (Roese & Olson, 1997).

Counterfactual thinking most often occurs after we have experienced some negative outcome. A bad grade, not getting a job, an interpersonal snub, an accident — such incidents lead us to think about those events analytically, counterfactually. This may seem odd, in that being negative outcomes, thinking about them — and how they might *not* have come about — often induces negative feelings as a consequence (although not always; Medvec, Madey, & Gilovich, 1995). So why would we want to think at length about something that makes us feel bad? Counterfactual thinking can often be very functional in that it helps us understand some of the contingencies in our world and therefore helps us prepare for similar occurrences in the future. The bad grade? If I had studied more (instead of going to that movie) I would have done better on the test. The accident? If I had stopped and looked before beginning to cross Victoria Avenue, I never would have hit the cyclist. Such reconsideration of the past, and creating alternatives to what actually transpired, can be very useful in helping us adapt, and improve outcomes, in similar circumstances when they arise in the future (Mandel & Lehman, 1996; Roese, 1994).

Anticipating the Future

The social mind not only processes current information and uses past information stored in memory, it also looks to, anticipates, and forecasts the future. Earlier we discussed some ways in which people's expectancies can guide their processing of new information and can guide their search of memory in retrieving previously acquired information. People also need to anticipate the future, and their expectancies also play an important role in that process. Being based largely on accumulated knowledge from past experiences, people's expectancies are often well grounded in reality and provide a very useful basis for anticipating future events and interactions. However, as we have already seen in other sections, those same expectancies can be inherently biasing in some ways, and these biases can create difficulties. In this section I discuss two such effects.

Expectancies not only can influence people's perceptions of what they observe, their interpretation and evaluation of information, and their search of memory, but also can serve to guide one's own behavior. If my impression (expectancy) is that you are a cold and aloof person, then in my interactions with you I will probably be somewhat hesitant and perhaps maintain some distance. In your view, my behavior toward you would seem unfriendly and lacking in warmth, which in turn will make you somewhat guarded in your response to me. When I observe that behavior in you, my initial impression will be confirmed — "Yep, I was right — he's not very outgoing and friendly." This effect is known as the *self-fulfilling prophecy*, and is a particularly insidious consequence of prior expectancies. Why do I say it's insidious? For two reasons, both of which are crucially important. First, the expectancy holder is likely to be completely unaware of his or her own role in creating the expectancy confirmation. In this brief interaction, I may be aware of my initial impression of you, and I certainly will recognize that your behavior conforms to that impression. What I probably will *not* be aware of is my own role in generating your behavior. That is, my expectation guided my behavior toward you in such a way that it constrained your response, and importantly, your behavior was constrained in exactly such a way that it would confirm the very expectancy that generated the whole sequence. Thus, my expectancy has created a "behavioral confirmation" (Snyder, 1981) of that expectancy. Second, the self-fulfilling prophecy differs from other expectancy effects in an important (and unnerving) way. In the other effects of expectancies that we have already encountered in previous sections, the expectancy biases some aspect of information processing and use, so that one's perception of reality is somehow distorted. In contrast, the self-fulfilling prophecy does not reflect a biased *perception* of another person's behavior; that person in fact behaves in a way that confirms the expectancy. From the perceiver's perspective, the prior belief has ("yet again . . .") proven to be true. Of course, as I just noted, the perceiver is largely oblivious to the fact that the confirming behavior was induced by the perceiver's own behavior, which in turn was driven by that expectancy.

The self-fulfilling prophecy effect of expectancies has been demonstrated in a variety of contexts. They can be the result of expectancies about a person's trait attributes, one's first impression of another person, a teacher's beliefs about a student's inherent abilities, and a perceiver's stereotype-based expectancies about group members (Olson, Roese, & Zanna, 1996). Self-fulfilling prophecies represent a way that people not only perceive their social environments but also create the social world in which they participate.

We've seen a variety of ways that expectancies can help us predict the future. Our expectancies can guide what we *perceive*, how we perceive it and how we *behave* in response to those perceptions. However, we also anticipate the future in other ways. Sometimes as we look to the future, we foresee how we will *feel*, based on our current (or even anticipated) experiences. And as with expectancies, such *affective forecasting* may be correct or may be biased in systematic ways (Gilbert & Wilson, 2000).

Imagine that, for the last few months, you have been in a relationship that you hope will continue to develop into a long-term commitment. But things don't always work out as we hope, and your partner ends the relationship. You are devastated and are convinced that something very special has just left your life. Understandably, you are in a very unhappy state of mind, really in the dumps. Now consider the following question. How happy will you be two months from now? And how will you actually feel two months from now? Questions such as these have been asked, and analyzed, by Gilbert, Wilson, and their colleagues. Although we know that we are currently very happy or rather depressed about our current situation, when we try to predict our feelings in the future there are several factors that can bias our affective forecasting. In effect, all of these factors lead us to anticipate that our feeling states are more durable and long lasting than they actually are. For example, in anticipating their long-term reactions to an important, emotionally powerful event, people tend to focus on that event and do not consider the affective impacts of other events that will occur during the interim. In focusing on your loss of your beloved partner, you fail to consider the affective uplift that you will get from getting a raise at your job, having a terrific weekend trip with friends, or seeing a hilarious movie. In addition, the mind has a variety of mechanisms for dealing with negative outcomes ("I can see now that that relationship wasn't as good as I thought") — mechanisms that we are not cognizant of when we think about how we'll feel in the future.

In a series of experiments researchers have shown that people overestimate the durability of their affective states for a variety of life outcomes, including the breakup of a romantic relationship, being hired or not hired for a job, learning about a tragic accident, and failing to get tenure. In all of these cases, people expected that their current affective state (positive or negative) would endure into the future longer than was evidenced by people who actually experienced those outcomes (Gilbert, Pinel, Wilson, Blumberg, & Wheatly, 1998; Wilson, Wheatley, Meyers, Gilbert, & Axsom, 2000).

In previous sections we have discussed a variety of ways that the mind processes and works on (through inferences, evaluations, attributions, etc.) the information with which we are confronted in the immediate context. In this section we have seen that the mind also deals in interesting ways with both the past and the future. Consistent with our earlier discussions, it turns out that in both looking back and looking ahead the mind is actively working on the information available and using our expectancies based on past experience to guide our thinking. In most cases these cognitive mechanisms are quite useful, although their processing characteristics also leave us vulnerable to bias and misunderstanding.

Cultural Differences

Social cognition is concerned, in large part, with how people think — how they interpret and understand the information they encounter in the social world, their reasoning as they make decisions and solve problems they encounter. The focus of this approach is on "basic" cognitive processes and the way they underlie and influence the complexities of social perception and social interaction.

For a long time the assumption has been that, although different people may make different inferences or may arrive at different judgments from the same information, the processes involved in making those inferences and judgments are the same. That is, these processes are assumed to be universal among all people. However, the viability of that assumption has been challenged by recent research on cultural differences in behavior and in thought processes. In particular, the increasing research literature comparing people from Western (European, North American) societies with those from Eastern (Asian) cultures has revealed widespread differences in both thought and behavior. For example, people from Western societies are inclined to present themselves in a self-enhancing manner, whereas in Eastern cultures a self-effacing presentation is more common (Heine & Lehman, 1997a). Also, while people in Western countries seek to resolve cognitive inconsistencies, Asians appear less bothered by such contradictions (Heine & Lehman, 1997b).

How do we interpret these differences? One possibility is that different values and traditions have fostered and guided the development of different patterns of overt behavior. Some explanations emphasize a cultural difference between focusing on individualism and independence vs. construing persons as being interdependent within a larger social unit or collective (Markus & Kitayama, 1991; Triandis, 1995). In Western countries there is a strong emphasis on the individual as the focal point in understanding behavior, as the cause of behavior and its outcomes, whereas in Eastern societies there is much heavier emphasis on viewing the individual as part of a larger social entity, that behavior is guided not so much by individual motives and attributes as by expectations of a group. Therefore, in contrast to Western individual agency, in Eastern contexts there is the sense of collective agency. For example, whereas an American might grow up believing that it is acceptable, and even encouraged, to question the views of their parents and teachers, in young Japanese people such overt challenge of authority figures (especially within one's own family or other group) would be viewed as quite inappropriate. In cases like this one, we would observe cultural differences in patterns of behavior, but the same basic processes of learning and socialization would have shaped those different outcomes. That is, the observed differences reflect different valuations on the same underlying processes. Thus, despite cultural differences, the basic processes would be universal.

The more intriguing possibility is that the nature of those fundamental processes may themselves differ between cultures. That is, perhaps the effect of culture extends to developing different psychological processes, different mechanisms for processing and using information. In fact, scholars have proposed that such differences can be summarized by a distinction between holistic thinking and analytic thinking (Nisbett, Peng, Choi, & Norenzayan, 2001). In Western thought, thinking is analytic, rooted in logical analysis of the rules that bind categories and objects together. In contrast, Eastern societies are characterized by modes of thought that are dialectical and holistic (Peng & Nisbett, 1999). In dialectical thinking, opposites (e.g., good and bad) can comfortably coexist – in events, in behaviors, in people — with no compelling need to view matters in one way *or* the other. Holistic thinking emphasizes the interconnectedness of all things to each other, so that any single instance — an event, a behavior, a person — is construed as one element in a larger context. This perspective places greater focus on the social context in which people (and objects) exist and the effects of that context on both psychological processes and behavior.

There is now a growing research literature that documents numerous differences between Eastern and Western cultures in many facets of social behavior. The challenge for future research is to identify and understand the nature of the processes underlying those differences, and therefore, how they can be explained.

Social Neuroscience

Whatever we learn about how the mind functions, it seems safe to assume that those functions have their underpinnings in the brain. Ever since Darwin introduced evolutionary theory well over a century ago, there has been interest in understanding the biological bases of behavior. This interest, of course, was initially and most prominently manifested in the biological sciences, but has always had social psychological implications as well. In fact, one of Darwin's (1872/1998) books — titled *Expression of the Emotions in Man and Animals* — focused on a topic that is of great interest in and relevance to social psychology. After all, emotional expressions are often in response to social stimuli and are communicative to a social audience. During the intervening decades much research has explored numerous aspects of the interface between the psychological and the physical systems, especially in understanding arousal and the nature of emotional experience (Blascovich, 2000; Caccioppo, Berntson, & Crites, 1996). Recent developments in social neuroscience offer important new opportunities for understanding the neural bases of cognitive functioning. As such, this research investigates the brain mechanisms that are central to many topics of interest in social psychology generally and social cognition in particular.

A variety of research strategies and techniques can be used to investigate the neural foundations on which psychological experiences are built (for a sampling, see Harmon-Jones & Devine, 2003). I will illustrate with two examples, one being a method that has been used effectively for many years, the other being a more recent approach resulting from new technology.

One approach involves the careful and systematic testing of patients who have experienced some specific loss of cognitive function due to brain damage, for example, through injury or disease. If the researcher knows what area of the brain has been damaged, then it is possible to study what cognitive processes (as seen, for example, in impaired abilities) rely on that brain location for effective performance. The most famous case of this type is that of Phineas Gage. In 1848, while working on a railway, Gage suffered a devastating injury when an accidental explosion propelled an iron rod through his skull, destroying certain sections of the brain. Although Gage lived for several more years, his personality was markedly different from what it had been prior to the accident. This case provided an early demonstration of specialization of function in the brain (particularly cerebral cortex). More recently, studies of people who have suffered damage due to epilepsy, Alzheimer's disease, amnesia, and other conditions, as well as patients who have suffered injuries to various parts of the brain, have been very useful in localizing parts of the brain that are involved in various cognitive functions associated with thinking, problem solving, and memory, as well as their effects on personality and social interactions (Klein & Kihlstrom, 1998).

A second, and very different, strategy is known as functional brain imaging. Recently developed technological advances have provided several techniques for identifying, in a nonintrusive way, the areas of the brain that are engaged in various forms of mental activity. One of these techniques, functional magnetic resonance imaging (fMRI), provides a means of measuring blood flow in the brain. The assumption underlying this method is that neural activity (e.g., engaged by various forms of thought) increases the need for oxygen (transmitted by blood) in those areas. Thus, if fMRI recordings indicate increased blood flow in an area of the brain, the inference can be drawn that that region is somehow activated by the mental activity engaged at the moment. In this way, researchers can have the potential to identify areas of the brain that have specialized roles in various forms of mental activity.

The use of these techniques (particularly fMRI and other methods using new technologies) has proven very useful in localizing the areas of the brain that are implicated in various mental processes. This research is important because an understanding of those links between brain function and cognition can potentially increase our knowledge of the role of cognition in various social psychological processes, such as person perception, stereotype use, and decision-making. Determining specialization of function and localizing neural mechanisms is difficult, and one cannot — and should not — assume a simple parallel between cognitive process and brain location (see Caccioppo, Bernston, Lorig, Norris, Rickett, & Nusbaum, 2003; Willingham & Dunn, 2003). Nevertheless, these research strategies offer great potential for increasing our knowledge of the interplay between cognitive mechanisms and their underlying neural activities.

PART 1

Processing Information from the Social World

Introduction and Preview

Social perception occurs in social settings. We observe, and in fact participate in, the active flow of social interaction, which is a dynamic process among dynamic people. The people and groups that we perceive and interact with have their own characteristics — their attributes, motives, goals, attitudes, needs, moods, styles of behaving, etc. How they behave, and how we perceive them, have implications for our own needs, goals, and moods, as well as for our ability to satisfy our needs and to feel good about ourselves. In perceiving, interacting with, and responding to these people, we therefore need to understand them as we try to have effective and satisfying interactions with them.

The complexities of this process are well described in Reading 1 in this part, by Fritz Heider (1958). Heider was one of the intellectual leaders in the early development of social psychology during the 1940s and 1950s, and his writings had great impact on later research developments. In this brief reading, Heider discusses a variety of ways in which social perception differs from perceptions of the physical world (what he calls "thing perception"). In contrast to the objects we perceive in our environment (a building, a bike, a ball), the people in our social world are what Heider calls "action centers" that do things, and what they do has implications for us (and what we do has implications for them). Moreover, whereas the properties of any given chair or table are manifestly obvious, the important properties of persons — their traits, intentions, ways of responding — are not so obvious. To understand them we need to "study" them longer and to infer what's "inside" them that makes them tick. As we have continuing experiences with another person, her behaviors can change over time, and hence she can almost seem to be "different persons" on different occasions. However, we know (or at least assume) that there is an underlying continuity to any person, and therefore in "comprehending" what this person is all about, we seek to identify the stable characteristics of the person. Why? Because if we can understand the person's continuity, we can predict and anticipate what she will be like in future interactions. As Heider indicates, all of this can be a complex and challenging task for we simple perceivers. However, as remarkable as it may seem, we do it all the time and with great efficiency and effectiveness. How is this achieved? The readings in this part reveal some of the cognitive mechanisms that are inherent in these social perceptions.

Our perceptions of others are based, in large part, on the information we acquire about them as we observe and interact with them. In virtually any social situation — meeting a person for the first time, participating in a group discussion planning a project, talking with a friend who has just revealed that he's gay, listening to a political candidate who is seeking votes — our comprehension and understanding of what we witness is based on the information we have acquired in those contexts. Social perception, then, involves information processing.

As I try to make my way through social life, it would be convenient, I suppose, if my mind functioned as a videorecorder that "sees" people and events as I experience them, and thereby records into my memory an accurate and verbatim record of my experiences. If that were so, then my perceptions — including my perceptions of the people and groups that play a role in my life — would be quite accurate representations of my experiences. I would simply store those "mental videotapes" on the "mental VCR shelf" in my brain. Later, when I want to remember some incident or retrieve my impression of some person, then I would simply pull out the relevant videotape, play it back, and the resulting "memory" would provide an accurate portrayal of the past. If that's how my mind worked, then I could be confident that my recollections are in fact accurate memories, that things really happened the way I remember them having occurred. Yes, Dad was in fact being unreasonable in not letting me take the car last night; the other members of the committee really didn't pay attention to what I was saying; and yes, Chauncey Thorngood was in fact "coming on" to Tiffany Peckington at the party Saturday night. ("I know I'm right because I saw it myself!") Oh yes, it would be very nice if my "mental representations" of the social world were in fact accurate and trustworthy.

But alas, such an assumption is not warranted. Our minds are neither videorecorders nor computers, and they do not produce verbatim records of our experiences. Our minds are incredible instruments that perform an immense array of functions with impressive efficiency, but they can also introduce some biases and inaccuracies, both in what we perceive and in what we remember of what we have perceived. The important point here is that the social perceiver is an active participant in the perception process. That statement may sound a bit trite, but in fact it opens the door to a number of important questions and issues. The readings in this part (and indeed, throughout this book) illustrate a variety of ways in which the perceiver influences the nature of what is perceived.

As perceivers, we typically are dealing with "information overload": we cannot process all of the information that is available to us at the moment. Consequently, there is an important first step in processing information: we must somehow select what aspects of that information we will attend to. Optimally, as perceivers we direct our *attention* at the most important, the most task relevant, and the most interesting aspects of the stimulus environment. By doing so we increase our effectiveness in adapting to and responding to that stimulus environment, and we thereby increase the likelihood of achieving our goals. However, there are other factors that can draw our attention as well, and these can introduce biases into the way we process social information. Stimuli that are highly salient and vivid capture attention, and when that happens, some other, potentially more important, stimuli can be ignored and subsequent processing can be biased. For example, McArthur and Post (1977) had participants watch a videotape in which several people were having a discussion. Perceptions of these persons and their interaction were unduly influenced by one person who "stood out" due to some inconsequential stimulus cue, such as wearing a brightly colored shirt that differed from what others were wearing, or rocking in a rocking chair while others were seated in straight chairs (and hence not in motion). The person who became visually salient in these ways was perceived as having been more active and more influential in the group discussion.

Stimulus information can capture attention not simply by being vivid or unusual but also because it goes against what we expect to occur. That is, information that disconfirms a prior expectancy — such as an initial impression of a person — can draw attention and, again, would be particularly well encoded and retained in memory. Reading 2 by White and Carlston (1983) documents this

phenomenon in what might be called the "cocktail party effect." Specifically, participants in their study listened, through headphones, to two conversations simultaneously, one presented to each ear. Participants were able to focus their attention on one or the other conversation by flipping a switch. When one of the conversations revealed that a person had behaved in a way that clearly contradicted the impression of that person, attention was quickly directed to that person and what he was saying. Thus, expectancy-inconsistent information captures attention.

Once we attend to some behavior, we encode that information and store it in memory. As I discussed in the introductory overview information is *encoded* and, as a part of that process, the perceiver interprets the meaning of that information. Sometimes this interpretive process is straightforward: when we see a man kiss a woman, we generally assume that it is a sign of affection. In many cases, however, social behavior is ambiguous with regard to its meaning, and hence is open to more than one interpretation. For example, a sarcastic remark may be nothing more than poking fun or it may reflect real underlying bitterness. In such cases — in fact, in many cases — the meaning of the behavior is open to interpretation, and it is the perceiver who makes that interpretation. In fact, behavior has meaning for the perceiver only when that perceiver has imposed some *interpretation* on it. It therefore becomes important to understand the factors that guide the perceiver's interpretation of behaviors whose meaning is ambiguous. One important factor is the perceiver's prior expectancies. These expectancies may be based on an understanding of what kinds of behaviors normally transpire in a particular setting (Jim's loud voice and laughter is "normal" at a party, but not in the library; Abelson, 1981), one's existing impression of the person performing the behavior (Jim is a real extrovert), or one's stereotype of the group to which the person belongs (Italians are endlessly talkative). And it is the behavior *as interpreted* that gets stored in memory and becomes the basis for the perceiver's understanding of the event.

The perceiver, having attended to, encoded, and interpreted some aspect of the social environment, does not stop there. The cognitive system then elaborates on the information, as encoded, through a number of processes that build upon this recently gained knowledge. The perceiver will make *inferences* about the target of that information, assuming that, if the person did behavior B or expressed opinion O, then it's likely that she also has other attributes C, D, and E, or also has attitudes P, Q, and R. The perceiver may also react *evaluatively* to this information, feeling that she likes (or doesn't like) people with such attributes or attitudes. All of these elaborations on the basic information, like the interpretation initially imposed on the acquired information, represent ways that the perceiver uses her own knowledge and beliefs to expand on what she has just observed or learned about the target of that information. It is this view of the person or group, construed through interpretation and expanded through inferential and evaluative elaboration, that then becomes the perceiver's *cognitive representation* of the information acquired. That cognitive representation (e.g., one's impression of another person, or one's stereotype of a group) can then influence the way new information about that person or group is processed in the future.

Reading 3 by Dunning and Sherman (1997) illustrates a number of these processes at work. These authors investigated how stereotypes can guide the interpretation of ambiguous behaviors and how those different interpretations can foster different inferences about a person. Participants were shown a series of sentences describing behaviors performed by a person whose occupation was identified. Two versions of each sentence were presented, using different occupational identifications that had diverging stereotypic implications. Thus the same behavioral act was presented, but the stereotypic expectancy could influence the interpretation, and hence the meaning, of that behavior. Later, participants were shown test sentences and were asked to identify whether or not each one had been presented earlier. Some of these sentences were distortions of the original statement, slanted to be consistent with one or the other stereotype activated during the stimulus presentation. Participants were more likely to indicate that the stereotype-consistent version had been presented earlier, when in fact it had not been. Dunning and Sherman's results show that the same behavior can "mean" quite different things, and can lead to different inferences, depending on the stereotype activated by the group membership of the actor. In similar manner, many of the readings presented in this book demonstrate the functioning of various aspects of the information processing system (encoding, inference, representation, retrieval) and show how cognitive structures (such as stereotypes, for example) can bias those processes.

As I discussed in the Introductory Overview, psychologists in recent years have become increasingly aware of potential cultural differences in the phenomena they study. This work has posed interesting questions about the generality of results that have been obtained in predominantly Western cultures. It may be, for example, that some of the findings, and even some of the processes underlying those findings, are not as universal as researchers had previously assumed. Reading 4 by Kim (2002) illustrates some of the issues raised by these questions. Kim proposed that one difference between Eastern and Western thought has to do with the role of verbalization in thinking. Specifically, due to differential value placed on being talkative, voicing opinions, and the like, versus being quiet and observant, talking is a much more common element in thinking for Westerners than for Asian people. To test this hypothesis, she compared European American and Asian American students on a test of creative reasoning processes that requires analytic thinking. Half of the participants from each cultural group were asked to "think out loud" as they solved the problems. This "talking while thinking" procedure should be much the same as what Westerners typically do as they are thinking about problems, whereas for Asian participants this mental activity would be atypical and hence would disrupt their performance on the task. Kim's (2002) results supported these hypotheses, and they suggest that there may be cultural differences not only in the *content* of, for example, the inferences people make (e.g., that a person's manner reflects his individuality vs the influence of his social group) but also in the nature of the *processes* underlying performance on various tasks.

Reading 5 in this part, by Klein and Kihlstrom (1998), reflects the growing interest in and enthusiasm for social neuroscience as an approach to learning about cognitive functioning. The authors summarize a number of recent findings that have been very informative about the nature of the brain mechanisms that are important for a variety of topics of interest to personality and social psychologists. Patients with various neuropsychological impairments (due, for example, to amnesia, autism, damage to frontal lobe) have been studied and, from examining their performance on various psychological tasks, we have learned a great deal about how those particular impairments can affect one's self knowledge, as well as one's ability to understand the past and anticipate the future, to integrate information about others, to experience and control emotion, and to recognize familiar faces. As

Klein and Kihlstrom argue, studying neuropsychological impairments is not only beneficial for understanding the particular characteristics of these clinical conditions but can also provide useful opportunities for testing psychological theories about the nature of the cognitive and neural mechanisms underlying a broad range of phenomena.

Earlier I said that, despite its impressive features, the mind is not comparable to a videorecorder or a computer because of limitations on what it can do. In this preview section I have discussed several ways in which the perceiver uses the information available to contend with those limits and to adapt to the social environment. These information processing strategies include some biases that can, under some conditions, result in inaccuracies. We cannot attend to all of the information available to us, we cannot retain in memory all that we do process, and at subsequent times we cannot retrieve all that we have retained. Moreover, our judgments may not reflect optimal use of the information on which they are based. The readings in this and subsequent parts provide many demonstrations of ways in which the human perceiver manifests such shortcomings. These biases may create the appearance of the human perceiver as inept, as misusing information in ways that will produce faulty decisions and judgments. Yes, the limitations of our mental resources do make us fallible at times. However, to characterize the perceiver as inept overlooks a very important point, for in other ways the mind is remarkably efficient in finding effective and beneficial means of overcoming those limitations. What is equally important, and impressive, about the way perceivers process and use information is that the cognitive system has devised means of dealing with its limits, ways of going beyond those constraints, and strategies for using the information available to adapt to a rich and varied social environment. The cognitive strategies we develop would not continue to be used if they didn't serve us well. That is, despite these cognitive constraints and the biases they can engender, they are often effective in helping us make correct inferences, useful decisions, and appropriate behaviors. If instead they continually led us into bad decisions and failures, then they wouldn't be useful and we would no longer use them. Despite our cognitive shortcomings, we do pretty well!

Discussion Questions

1. In what ways does social perception differ from perception of the physical environment (e.g., objects)?
2. What variables influence the perceiver's attention to certain aspects of the stimulus environment?
3. What variables influence the way perceivers interpret the meaning of the behaviors they observe?
4. Can you think of some examples of cultural differences in the way people and social interactions are perceived? What might these differences suggest about the way information is processed and used in these cultures?
5. Summarize some examples of what neuroscience research has learned about one's knowledge of oneself and others.

Suggested Readings

Kunda, Z. (1999). *Social cognition: Making sense of people*. Cambridge, MA: MIT Press.

Bless, H., Fiedler, K., & Strack, F. (2004). *Social cognition*. London, UK: Psychology Press.

Devine, P. G., Hamilton, D. L., & Ostrom, T. M. (Eds.) (1994). *Social cognition: Impact on social psychology*. San Diego: Academic Press.

Gilbert, D. T. (1998). Ordinary personology. In D. T. Gilbert, S. T. Fiske, & G. Lindzey (Eds.), *Handbook of social psychology* (4th ed., Vol. 2, pp. 89–50). New York: McGraw-Hill.

Higgins, E. T. (2000). Social cognition: Learning about what matters in the social world. *European Journal of Social Psychology*, *30*, 3–39.

Nisbett, R. E., Peng, K., Choi, I., & Norenzayan, A. (2001). Culture and systems of thought: Holistic versus analytic cognition. *Psychological Review*, *108*, 291–310.

Berntson, G. G., & Cacioppo, J. T. (2000). Psychobiology and social psychology: Past, present, and future. *Personality and Social Psychology Review*, *4*, 3–15.

Perceiving the Other Person[1]

Fritz Heider

In discussing the perception of other persons I want to talk about four points: First, the relevant objects or contents; second, the stimulus patterns; third, the mechanism of attribution; and, finally, the balanced sentiment configurations.

MacLeod has called our attention to the fact that the term "social perception" is used in two senses as referring, on the one hand, to the problem of the social determination of perception and, on the other hand, to the problem of the perception of the social [4, 229]. This paper will deal only with the second problem, and furthermore, we shall disregard the perception of groups or institutions and limit ourselves to the perception of other persons, or, briefly, to person perception.

In thing perception we see objects that have color, that are placed within the surrounding space in a particular position, and that have functional properties which make them fit or not fit into our purposes, properties which define their place in the space of means-end relations, and which also define their possible effects on us. There is a chair on which one can sit, there is an object with which one can cut paper, tie a package, or write a note.

In contrast to things, persons are rarely mere manipulanda; rather, they are action centers, they can do something to us, they can benefit or harm us intentionally, and we can benefit or harm them. Persons are perceived as having abilities, as acting purposefully, as having wishes or sentiments, as perceiving or watching us. They are systems having representations, they can be our friends or our enemies, and each has his characteristic traits. Enumerating the contents of the perception of other persons is equal to listing the concepts of naïve, common-sense psychology.

The second question to be considered deals with the conditions of the impressions we get of other people and their traits, acts, intentions, or sentiments. What are the proximal stimulus patterns, the data or raw materials which are coordinated to the contents of person perception? To begin with, it is probably fair to say that the stimulus patterns basic to person perception are usually more extended in time than those relevant to thing perception. Let us assume that we enter an unfamiliar room for the first time and that in it we find a few people we have never met before. A glance around the room will suffice to get an approximately correct idea of the shape of the room and of the objects in it. We shall be much more insecure about our judgments of people. We may get a global first impression of them but we do not right away perceive the relevant properties of the social situation; we do not know whether A likes or dislikes B, whether C intends to thwart D, and so on. Many more data, a much wider manifold of stimuli are needed to give us this information. We have to get acquainted with these people, we have to interact with them, and we have to observe how they interact with each other. We are familiar with the so-called reduction screen from experiments with color constancy, and we might say that person perception will be like reduction screen vision if we exclude the perception of events and actions. While we believe that we get to know something about a person from the shape of his face, or even the

[1] This paper was read at a symposium on "Theory and Research in Interpersonal Perception" at the meeting of the American Psychological Association in New York in 1954. Parts of this and the following paper are incorporated in a book on *The Psychology of Interpersonal Relations*, which will be published by John Wiley & Sons, Inc.

color of his hair, these physiognomic properties are far outweighed by his actions as clues to his personality. In most cases we cognize a person's traits, and especially his wishes, sentiments, or intentions from what he does and says and we know considerably less when we are limited to what we can see of him as a static object.

However, just to say that in person perception the stimulus patterns are usually extended in time does not tell very much about them. We have to ask whether it is not possible to go further and to specify more exactly the relevant features of these time-extended patterns. It has been shown that a motion picture containing merely movements of a few dots produces in the observer impressions of a great variety of interpersonal events [2]. The subjects perceive a social world in which the persons are dots, and these persons have apparent personalities and sentiments and manifest apparent social behavior. One could talk of ordinal stimulation, in the sense in which Gibson uses the term in space perception, and one could point out features of the space-time manifold which are, to a certain degree, coordinated to impressions of social events. Event patterns showing equifinality seem to be of special importance for the perception of actions. Or, to take another example, the impression of one dot chasing another is based on an event pattern in which two dots move along the same path but with a distance between them. Michotte observed similar phenomena in his studies of phenomenal causality. However, though we often find coordinations between stimulus patterns and impressions, these coordinations are rarely univocal. The same pattern can be seen as *A* chasing *B*, or as *B* leading *A*, which are two events of entirely different social meaning. In order to determine whether the pattern will be seen as chasing or as leading we have to consider the surrounding events, we have to consider the way in which this part event is embedded in the sequence of events. It is probably correct to say that *A* will be seen as chasing *B* if on the basis of previous stimulation *A* is seen as the more powerful person, as the person with greater initiative. If *B* is seen as the more powerful person, or the person with higher status, the event will be seen as one of *B* leading *A*, not as one of *A* chasing *B*. Not only the immediately preceding happenings can influence the interpretation of this pattern; also stereotypes may play this role. If we see two animals running single file we will interpret this event in accordance with our stereotypes. If the one in front is a rabbit and the one behind is a dog, we will see the dog chasing the rabbit. If the first one is a big rabbit and the second a small one we will see the big one leading the small one.

Thus, it is very unlikely that we will be able to coordinate univocally certain characteristics of the stimulus manifolds to impressions of personality traits, social acts, or sentiments in a simple way. In order to understand the connection between the stimulus pattern and the impression, we have to resort to thought models which are more complicated, and this will be especially true when we think of the role of verbal behavior. As an example of these more complicated connections we could mention "attribution," the way in which impression are anchored in the social world.

Hilgard, in talking about thing perception, mentions the tendency of the organism to seek a perceptually stable environment [3]. This feature of the perceptual process can also be described in terms of information theory. Attneave says that "a major function of the perceptual machinery is ... to describe or encode incoming information in a form more economical than that in which it impinges on the receptors" [1, 189]. Hochberg makes use of similar ideas.

In person perception the manifold of incoming messages is encoded in terms of — or referred to, attributed to — the motives, sentiments, or beliefs of other persons. These are the relatively stable features of the environment which are relevant to us and which make possible an economical description of the bewildering mass of data.

This attribution or anchoring of incoming stimuli in a stable environment can go on in a hierarchy of layers.

Let us assume that a person, whom we will designate by the letter *p*, is confronted with a disagreeable experience. This is the raw material which has to be related to some stable reference points, and which is also used as a source of information about these points. The first step in the anchoring of the event will be to connect it with a source; the negative experience will be seen as caused by chance, or as caused by the perceiver himself, or as caused by another person *o*. Which one of these interpretations is realized will depend partly on the way they fit into the subjective environment, partly on the stimulus pattern.

If we assume that another person is accepted as the cause, the question of intention arises. Did *o* do it in order to harm *p*, or was the harm that was done to *p* only an accidental by-product of *o*'s true goal, which had nothing to do with *p*? Or, is it possible that *o* really wanted to benefit *p* and that the harm was only a necessary means to that end? When a parent punishes a child, or when a physician hurts a patient, the harm is usually not the ulterior goal, and it will probably not be seen as such by the recipient.

If *p* perceives the other person as really wanting to harm him, there can be still deeper layers of interpretation. This temporary need to harm may be caused by a momentary bad humor, it may be displaced aggression, or it may come from a more permanent sentiment of dislike.

Finally, this sentiment itself may be traced to further sources: *p* can feel that *o*'s sentiment toward himself is based in *o*'s personality; *o* is an aggressive, snobbish, and rejecting person. Or, the dislike stems from what a third person has told *o* about *p*. Or, at this level too there may be an intropunitive interpretation: *p* feels that *o* dislikes him because of *p*'s own faults; *o* is really justified in not liking *p*.

All that can, of course, go on at different cognitive levels: At the level of perception as well as at a level which one would be more inclined to call "judgment." But the important point is that, just as the schema of a constant object allows us to encode in a simple way all the manifold appearances of an object, so the schemata — or, if it is permitted to use the term, the perceptual construct — of intention, or sentiment, or of a constant person makes possible a simple and unified representation of an otherwise very involved and confused sequence of events. Attribution serves the attainment of a stable and consistent environment, gives a parsimonious and at the same time often an adequate description of what happens, and determines what we expect will occur and what we should do about it.

As a final point, I want to say a few words about still another aspect of this tendency to discover the invariancies of the environment. Not only is there a tendency to find the pivotal constancies which allow us to predict in a detached way what will happen. We also want to attain stable and orderly evaluations; we want to find the good and the bad distributed in a simple and consistent fashion. The codification in terms of positive and negative value is simpler when the positive features are grouped in one unit and the negative ones in another unit. For instance, there is a tendency to see only the positive traits in a person we like. We find again and again that the sentiments and perceptions arrange themselves in such a way that simple harmonious configurations result. If we hear that a person we like has done something we dislike, we are confronted with a disharmonious situation, and there will arise a tendency to change it to a more balanced situation; for instance, we can refuse to believe that the person performed this negative action.

Often, these evaluations are decisive in person perception, and, since we can often determine with a certain degree of exactness which configurations are harmonious and which are not, we have a means of predicting how experiences will be fitted, not only into a world of neutral objects, but also into a world of persons, social acts, or intentions full of significant values.

REFERENCES

1. Attneave, F. Some informational aspects of visual perception. *Psychol. Rev.*, 1954, *61*, 183–193.
2. Heider, F., and Simmel, Marianne. An experimental study of apparent behavior. *Amer. J. Psychol.*, 1944, *57*, 243–259.
3. Hilgard, E. R. The role of learning in perception. In Blake and Ramsay, *Perception.* New York: Ronald, pp. 95–120.
4. MacLeod, R. B. The place of phenomenological analysis in social psychological theory. In J. H. Rohrer and M. Sherif (eds.), *Social psychology at the crossroads.* New York: Harper, 1951, pp. 215–241.

Consequences of Schemata for Attention, Impressions, and Recall in Complex Social Interactions

J. Dennis White and Donal E. Carlston

A study was conducted to assess the effects of personality schemata on attentional allocation, impressions, and memory among observers of a complex social interaction. Subjects were first primed with schematic descriptions of an actor, and then they listened to an audiotape in which that actor and another participated in several separate conversations, with the primed actor either in the foreground or in the background. Other subjects could throw a switch to shift either actors' conversations into the foreground. As predicted, subjects in this last group shifted their attention away from the primed actor after determining that his behavior did not violate the schema they had been given and shifted their attention back when the primed actor acted in a schema-inconsistent manner. Analyses of all three attentional conditions revealed that the less attention subjects were able to pay to the primed actor, the more they relied on their schemata in making impression "false alarm" behaviors, and the less confident they were in the occurrence of schema-inconsistent and schema-irrelevant behaviors. These results are discussed in terms of subject strategies in dealing with information overload when processing complex stimuli.

In recent years, the concept of schema has been widely used in psychological theory and research (Abelson, 1981; Fiske & Linville, 1980; Hastie, 1981; Rumelhart & Ortony, 1977). Although the concept has been applied under a variety of different names in different areas (e.g., scripts, frames, implicational molecules, prototypes, impressions, and expectancies), the generic concept of schema refers to a knowledge structure abstracted from previously encountered stimuli that provides a goal-directed form of information processing (Thorndyke & Hayes-Roth, 1979). In the area of social cognition, research concerning the role of schemata or expectancies in social judgment and memory has demonstrated that schemata have important effects on social inference and on recall for traits and behaviors (Cantor & Mischel, 1977; Cohen & Ebbesen, 1979; Rothbart, Evans, & Fulero, 1979).

The social research on schema effects is generally confined to relatively simple and nondemanding information-processing situations (Hastie, 1981). That is, subjects are asked to deal with only a single stimulus at a time and are allowed to study that stimulus at a leisurely pace. Hence, attention is undivided, and subjects' information-processing capacities are rarely exceeded. However, many real-world social situations require that information be processed about several

This study was conducted as a master's thesis at the University of Iowa by the first author under the direction of the second author. This research was partially supported by Biomedical Research Support Grant SS07 RR07035 awarded by the National Institutes of Health.

Requests for reprints should be sent either to J. Dennis White, who is now at the Department of Marketing, College of Business, Florida State University, Tallahassee, Florida, 32306 or to Donal Carlston, Department of Psychology, University of Iowa, Iowa City, Iowa 52242.

different people or events at once. Because people are limited in their capacities to process information (Broadbent, 1958; Norman & Bobrow, 1975), such situations create conditions of cognitive overload: Attention must be divided and periodically withdrawn entirely from some aspects of the stimulus field.

Under such circumstances, schemata may play an important role both in allocating attention and in compensating for information lost through inattention. Schemata have been hypothesized to "drive" attentional focusing and stimulus encoding in a "top-down" fashion by providing hypotheses that the perceiver attempts to verify from the stimulus (Bobrow & Winograd, 1977; Norman & Bobrow, 1976; Tesser, 1978). In addition, schemata have been hypothesized to provide simplifying heuristics (cf. Nisbett & Ross, 1980) that allow gaps in known information to be filled in with "default options" (Minsky, 1975). Consequently, schemata may help observers compensate for their inability to attend to all important aspects of a complex social interaction.

These considerations lead us to propose several hypotheses concerning the effects of schemata on attention, impressions, and memory in social situations. First, such expectancies should influence the allocation of attention by observers free to focus on different aspects of the social stimulus. And second, such expectancies should have larger effects on impressions and recognition for those aspects of the stimulus interaction that are relatively unattended.

Effects of Schemata on Attention

Because attentional capacity is limited, observers need some method or mechanism for allocating attention among the many elements of a complex social situation. In a non-social domain, Kanarick and Petersen (1969) determined that cognitively overloaded individuals focus their attention on the "highest value" information in a complex stimulus array. Similarly, the observer in a social interaction seems likely to focus attention on those individuals about whom information would be most valuable.

Although a number of factors may determine the potential "value" of social information (cf. McArthur, 1981; Taylor & Fiske, 1978; Zadny & Gerard, 1974), two are important here. First, information that might confirm or disconfirm an existing schema or expectancy should have high value (Bower, Black, & Turner, 1979). A study by Enquist, Newtson, and LaCross (Note 1) indicates that subjects do allocate

more attention to an actor about whom they have expectancies. Second, information that is not already schematically represented should be more valuable, because schematically represented information can be inferred from the schema. These two objectives would seem to operate at cross-purposes in many situations. That is, the first objective would tend to steer attention toward schematically represented material, whereas the second objective would tend to steer attention away from such material. It may nonetheless be possible for observers to satisfy both objectives by first ascertaining that their schema is adequate and applicable and by then relying on that schema while diverting their attention to nonschematic material. It is possible that some periodic monitoring of the schematically represented material may continue even while attention is diverted elsewhere so that the observer can shift back anytime the schema appears inadequate to substitute for actual observation.

Effects of Schemata on Impressions

Carlston (1980a, 1980b) argued that people's impressions of others may be based both on behaviors actually observed and on traits initially abstracted from those behaviors. Similarly, it seems likely that impression judgments made by observers of complex social interactions will reflect both the implications of the observers' prior impressions or expectancies and the implications of behaviors that were actually observed. Indeed, there is considerable research demonstrating that such preexisting schemata can influence impressions formed from behavioral information (Cantor & Mischel, 1977; Markus, 1977). Moreover, it seems probable that the less an individual is attended to, the more schemata will be relied on in forming impressions of that individual. That is, observers whose attention is diverted completely away from an actor must base their impressions solely on their schemata, whereas those who focus directly on the actor are likely to be much more influenced by the actor's actual behavior. Observers who can shift their attention freely to and away from the actor seem likely to form impressions somewhere in between, reflecting the influence of both their schemata for that actor and the actor's actual behavior. Of course, these differing contributions will have the greatest impact and be most evident when some of the actor's actual behavior is inconsistent with the implications of the observer's schemata for the actor.

Effects of Schemata on Behavioral Recognition

One of the most potent consequences of the reliance on schemata under overloaded conditions may be the insertion or substitution of schemata-consistent material into memory. When attention is diverted away from an actor, certain information is necessarily missed, and this missing information may be filled in by the "default values" provided by a schema (Minsky, 1975). This process leads to what Taylor and Crocker (1981) refer to as an "illusory data base," that is, "a set of assumptions, inferences or bits of information that are not actually present in the stimulus configurations encountered by the perceiver, but that rather constitute the contributions the schema makes to the stimulus configuration" (p. 117). The perceiver may actually store schema-generated default values in such a way that at retrieval the perceiver is unable to distinguish between internally and externally generated data (Raye, Johnson, & Taylor, 1980). Similar effects have been reported by several researchers (Bower et al., 1979; Cantor & Mischel, 1977; Picek, Sherman, & Shiffrin, 1975).

In general, research subjects who pay less attention to an actor should tend to indicate higher confidence in the occurrence of schema-consistent "false alarms." These errors should be most pronounced among subjects whose attention is diverted completely away from an actor but should also occur, to a lesser extent, among subjects who must divide their attention among several stimuli.

Method Overview

The present study was designed to examine the effects of person schemata in social situations sufficiently complex to cause informational overload. Subjects in the experiment were first presented with "background information" intended to create a coherent impression of one of two target actors. Then subjects listened to a stereophonic tape of these two actors engaged in separate conversations under "cocktail party" conditions. That is, on each channel, subjects heard one actor converse with three other individuals while the conversations involving the other actor could be heard more faintly in the background. Some subjects listened exclusively to one channel or the other, whereas "free-focus" subjects could throw a switch that moved one or the other of the conversations into the foreground. Timers attached to this switch allowed analysis of the attentional focus to the free-focus subjects at different times during the stimulus interac-

tions. The conversations were structured so that the stimulus character who had been described schematically (the primed actor) behaved in a schema-irrelevant manner during the first two conversations and in a schema-inconsistent manner during the final conversation.

We hypothesized the following: First, free-focus subjects should initially focus on the primed actor, but when they discover nothing at odds with their schema, they should then shift their attention to the unprimed actor. Second, assuming that some monitoring of the primed actor continues during the later conversations, subjects' attention should revert to the primed actor when he begins acting in a schema-inconsistent manner in the final conversation. Third, subjects should report more schema-consistent impressions, as well as more schematic memory intrusions, to the extent that their attention is diverted from the primed actor. Consequently, these effects should be the greatest among subjects made to focus exclusively on the unprimed actor. Subjects in the free-focus conditions were expected to fall between the other two groups, because their attention is divided, and they may observe some behaviors while missing others.

Method

Subjects

Fifty-five male and female students enrolled in the introductory psychology course at the University of Iowa took part in the study as part of a research participation requirement. The experiment was a 3 (free focus, focus on primed actor only, focus on unprimed actor only) × 2 (primed trait:kindness or honesty) × 2 (stimulus version) between-subjects design with actor rated (primed or unprimed) as an additional within-subjects factor in most analyses. The primed trait and the trait-actor factors provided multiple stimulus replications. All subjects were either run individually (free-focus conditions) or in separate cubicles (all other conditions).

Impression Priming Materials

Prior to the presentation of the stimulus tapes, subjects were given background information about the two central characters. Although equal amounts of information were provided about each character, one of the two (the primed actor) was described in a way likely to prompt a clear personality impression or schema of either a kind or an honest individual, depending on condition. The description used in the "kind-prime" condition was as follows:

Friends and acquaintances describe Brian as a very thoughtful, warm person who is seemingly always ready to listen to a problem, lend someone a hand, or help a friend in need. One person summed up his description of Brian by saying, "He's the kind of guy who would give you the shirt off his back."

The description used in the "honest-prime" condition was

Friends and acquaintances describe Brian as a very candid person, who would never tell a lie, and never put someone else at an unfair disadvantage. One person summed up his descriptions of Brian saying, "He'd look you up just to return a borrowed dime."

The other character (the unprimed actor) was described uninformatively:

Paul has played competitive soccer ever since grade school, and admits to being addicted to most types of sports. While he enjoys life in Iowa City and the Midwest, Paul plans to move to New Mexico following his graduation this May.

Paul was the primed character in half of the conditions, whereas Brian was the primed character in the other half. Each description was presented in an audiotape recording concurrent with a videotaped picture of the actor being described.

Stimulus Tapes

The stimulus tapes presented to subjects were made by recording a series of simultaneous conversations between two central characters and some secondary actors. The central characters, Paul and Brian, were seated at opposite ends of a long table, apparently studying in a library. Each engaged in three 2.5-minute conversations with students who "happened" to pass by the table. Each of these secondary actors entered and left within about 5 sec of the student at the other end of the table. Approximately 10 sec intervened between the departure of one pair and the arrival of the next.

The conversations occurring at each end of the table were completely independent. At no time did any of the central or secondary actors at one end of the table acknowledge those at the other end. Furthermore, within any condition, each secondary actor appeared only once and only at one end of the table.

The conversations were tape recorded using a Roberts Four-Track stereo recorder. One microphone (recording a separate stereo channel) was placed at each end of the table so that it would primarily pick up the conversations occurring at that end, although the opposite conversation could be heard in the background. This produced a cocktail party effect in which subjects could most readily make out the conversation on whichever channel they were listening to but could also discern the outlines of the other conversation in the back-channel.

In addition, the conversations were videotaped using a Sony Port-a-Pack system. From these videotapes, a still shot was selected showing each pair of secondary actors engaged in conversations with the central characters. These stills were shown to subjects on a video monitor concurrent with the audiotape of each pair of conversations, which gave subjects a clearer picture of the interactions than they might have received from the sound track alone. The full videotapes were not used because subjects might have visually attended to one channel while aurally attending to the other.

The central and secondary actors were all undergraduate volunteers. Although they were provided with a basic outline of necessary behaviors for each conversations, the actors were allowed to ad-lib the actual dialogue to provide maximum realism. These actors made several tapes, and the most realistic were used in the experiment.

During the first two conversations, each of the central characters behaved in a neutral fashion (exhibiting neither positive nor negative aspects of the relevant trait). However, in the third conversation, one of the central characters acted unkindly (refusing to lend his chemistry notes to his sick friend), whereas the other character acted dishonestly (admitted to having a stolen a textbook from a friend). This procedure allowed us to assess the extent to which subjects shifted their attention to the primed actor when he engaged in schema-inconsistent behavior and to check on the amount of schematic substitution in the impression and memory data. Furthermore, because negative behaviors occurred in both channels, and these behaviors occurred almost simultaneously, negativity biases (Fiske, 1980) by themselves would not cause shifts in attention.

Channel Switch Mechanism

Subjects in the free-focus condition were given a mechanism that allowed them to switch between audio channels and consequently change the conversation they could hear most clearly. When subjects held the switch mechanism to the left, they could hear primarily the left channel to the tape recorder, whereas when they held it to the right, they could hear primarily the right channel. When released, the switch returned to a neutral position, cutting off sound from both channels. Therefore, subjects had to hold the switch in one position or the other to hear the conversations; they could not simply set and forget the channel selector.

Procedure

Research subjects were recruited to participate in an experiment entitled "Evaluations of Conversations." Subjects were told that they would be asked to listen to a tape recording of conversations between two individuals and several of the individuals' friends. To provide some "background information," subjects were then shown pictures of the actors while the subjects listened to the "priming" tapes. Depending on their condition, subjects heard either Paul or Brian (stimulus version) characterized as kind or honest (priming trait) and the other characterized neutrally, as described above.

Subjects then listened to voice samples of Paul and Brian to facilitate their recognition of these characters on the tapes. Finally, in an effort to further reduce confusion, subjects were given a chart showing the names of all the various actors and the order and the locations in which they would appear. Follow-up interviews with subjects found no hint of confusion between voices.

Subjects in the free-focus condition received instructions concerning the use of the channel-switch selector and were told that they could listen to whichever channel they wished during any part of the tape. Subjects in the restricted-focus conditions were not allowed to use the switching mechanism. Their listening channel was set by the experimenter to one channel or the other. Although they were told that they would hear the conversations from a particular vantage point, these subjects were in all other respects instructed exactly as the free-focus subjects had been. Some subjects in the restricted-focus conditions listened to the channel emphasizing the actor for whom they had been primed, whereas other subjects listened to the opposite channel.

All subjects heard a tape in which the primed character ultimately acted in a manner incongruent with the prime. That is, both the subjects who were given the kindness prime for Paul and those who were given the honesty prime for Brian heard the tape in which Paul acted unkindly and Brian acted dishonestly during the third conversation. On the other hand, those subjects who received the honest prime for Paul and those who received the kindness prime for Brian heard the tape in which Paul acted dishonestly and Brian acted unkindly during the third conversation. The experiment thus involved four stimulus replications, which represented all combinations of priming trait (kindness or honesty) with primed character (Paul or Brian).

Counterbalancing Controls

These replications control several possible attentional biases through counterbalancing. For example, each channel of the stimulus tape served as both a primed channel and an unprimed channel, depending on which actor was primed. If any conversation was inherently more attention grabbing than the simultaneous conversation in the opposing channel, the resultant attentional shifts would be toward the primed channel in one condition but away from the primed channel in the counterbalanced condition. Consequently, such stimulus differences could not contribute to any observed differences between the primed and the unprimed conditions. Similarly, depending on the priming manipulation, each central actor served as both the primed and the unprimed actor, controlling for differences in their personalities or interestingness. Likewise, kindness and honesty served equally often as primed and unprimed traits. The complete counterbalanced design thus assures that any systematic attentional shifts towards or away from the primed channel do not simply reflect the relative interestingness of one channel, one actor, or one trait over its opposing member.[1]

The counterbalanced design does have one inherent limitation. The control channels (e.g., the unprimed characters) are always presented in opposition to the experimental channels (e.g., the primed characters). Thus, for example, the control for a primed honest actor would logically be an unprimed honest actor, but when an unprimed honest actor is presented in one channel, a primed kind actor will always be presented in the opposite channel. Consequently, the results in any particular

---

[1] Including a no-schema group in this design would not be beneficial. No-schema subjects merely provide information about the relative salience of individual channels (e.g., the Brian-kind channel) in the absence of any prime. But because each channel contributes both to the primed-channel results and to the unprimed-channel results in the experiment, the salience of individual channels is irrelevant to the results reported. To the extent that the nonschematic salience of a channel contributes to attention when that channel is primed, it must also detract from attention when the opposing channel is primed. Consequently, a no-schema group is uninformative with respect to the priming hypotheses.

condition reflect the dynamics of two different channels; for example, attentional shifts toward a primed character are also shifts away from an unprimed character. The results must thus be interpreted in terms of the two channel alternatives rather than as characteristics of just one channel.

Dependent Measures

In the free-focus conditions, subjects' attention to the different conversations was assessed through two Hunter electric timers connected to the channel-selector mechanism. These timers allowed the experimenter to determine how much time each subject spent listening to each conversation and to determine when switches were made from one channel to the other. The timers were accurate to hundredths of a second.

Subjects in all conditions completed a questionnaire at the end of the experiment that assessed their impressions of the actors and their memories for the conversations. Impressions of both primary actors were measured on 7-point scales that assessed the traits relevant to the primes and to the actors' behaviors: Kindness (kind–unkind, warm–cold) and honesty (honest–dishonest, trustworthy–untrustworthy). Several other scales were also included to assess possible differences between the central actors or the stimulus tapes (likable–dislikable, intelligent–unintelligent, interesting–uninteresting, outgoing–reserved). Although these scales indicated that minor differences existed between actors and stimulus versions, those differences did not interact with the effects of interest, and will not be discussed further.

Subjects were also given a recognition test in which they stated their confidence that various behaviors had or had not occurred in the stimulus conversations. Included among these items were six behaviors that had not actually occurred but that were consistent with a kindness schema and six other nonoccurring behaviors that were consistent with an honesty schema. All behaviors were attributed to one of the primary actors (Paul or Brian) and also named a secondary actor from one of the three conversations. Each set of six false alarms thus consisted of two behaviors ostensibly occurring during each of the three conversations.

Also included in the recognition test were a number of true items, including some that were schema inconsistent and some that were schema irrelevant. Like the false alarms, these behaviors were attributed to one of the primary actors and also named a secondary actor, so that they clearly pertained to a single conversation.

Unfortunately, it was not possible to obtain items of each type from each conversation; the schema-inconsistent items necessarily came from the final conversations, whereas the schema-irrelevant items all pertained to one of the first two conversations. Each subject responded to four different true behaviors, which represented schema-inconsistent and schema-irrelevant behaviors from both the primed and the unprimed channels.[2] A different set of four behaviors was used for each stimulus version, and though all subjects actually responded to all eight items, only the four items pertaining to their own stimulus version could be considered "true," and the other four items simply served as fillers.

Subjects responded to each item on a 4-point scale in which 1 = high confidence that an item was false, 2 = slight confidence that the item was false, 3 = slight confidence that the item was true, and 4 = high confidence that the item was true. The scale intentionally lacked a midpoint so that subjects were forced to choose whether an item was true or false.

Results

Attentional Measures

Free-focus subjects' attention to the primed and the unprimed conversations was assessed through their use of the channel-switching mechanism. For each subject in this condition, the percentage of time spent listening to the primed channel was calculated for nine different intervals. These intervals represented the beginning, middle, and ending third of each of the three conversations. These percentages were then analyzed with conversations (first, second, or third) and segment (beginning, middle, and ending) as within-subjects factors and with the priming trait (kindness or honest) and stimulus version (Paul kind and Brian honest or Paul honest and Brian kind) as between-subjects, replication factors.

This analysis revealed only a significant interaction between conversations and segments: $F(4, 48) = 2.74$,

---

[2] It would have been desirable to have more than one exemplar of each type of true behavior in each cell. However, due to an oversight, as few as one item representing some types pertained to some conditions, whereas more items of some types pertained to other conditions. To insure that all means were based on an equal number of items, one item of each type was randomly selected for each cell of the design from all those items with the appropriate characteristics.

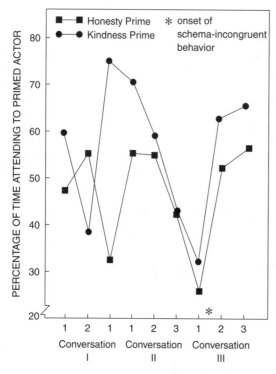

FIGURE 2.1 ■ Percentage of time spent attending to primed actor by priming trait and time period.

$p < .05$. It is noteworthy that the lack of a statistical interaction with any of the replication factors (priming trait or stimulus version) suggests that the primed groups in the kindness and the honesty conditions showed parallel patterns of results, particularly in the latter time periods, which are most critical to the experimental hypotheses. To highlight this, Figure 2.1 presents the channel-time percentages for attention to the primed channel broken down by priming trait. It is evident from this figure that the initial shift in attention toward the primed actor was followed by a general shift in attention toward the unprimed actor throughout the second conversation and the beginning of the final conversation. In the final conversation, there was a radical shift in attention back to the primed actor at about the time he began acting in a schema-inconsistent manner.

A second analysis of these data was undertaken using a slightly different statistic. Instead of analyzing the percentage of time each subject spent focusing on each channel, this analysis examined the percentage of subjects who were tuned to each channel at each of nine

moments (representing the exact midpoints of the nine segments used in the first analysis). This analysis reveals a pattern essentially the same as that shown in Figure 2.1. When collapsed across priming trait, the percentage of subjects attending to the primed channel declined from .69 in the final segment of Conversation 1 to .31 in the final segment of Conversation 2, $X^2(1) = 4.50$, $p < .05$. In addition, the percentage of subjects attending to the primed channel jumped from .31 in the final segment of Conversation 2 to .75 in the second segment of Conversation 3, $X^2(2) = 6.15$, $p < .05$. These results support the hypothesis that attention tends to shift toward characters who are not schematically represented but that enough monitoring of schematically represented characters occurs to allow detection of schema-inconsistent behaviors and the return of attention to a character acting in that manner.

Impression and Recognition Analyses

The basic analyses of the impression and recognition data involved split-plot designs (Kirk, 1968) combining both within-subjects factors (e.g., the trait dimension being rated, and the channel/actor being evaluated) and between-subjects factors (focus condition, stimulus version, and priming trait). However, in this basic design, the two factors of principal interest (focus and actor, channel being rated) are not arranged in the most meaningful way. Hence, these factors were recoded to reflect whether the subjects' ratings pertain to the attended channel (ratings of the primed channel by those focusing on the primed channel and ratings of the unprimed channel by those focusing on the unprimed channel), a partially attended channel (the free-focus conditions), or the unattended channel (ratings of the primed channel by those focusing on the unprimed channel and ratings of the unprimed channel by those focusing on the primed channel). We will refer to this recoded variable as the attention factor to distinguish it from the original focus factor. Although the attention factor is more meaningful and understandable, it does pose a problem in that the attention main effect and the Attention × Channel Rated interaction come to have both within- and between-subjects components, making tests of the overall effects impossible. Therefore these two effects were broken into orthogonal comparisons representing each of their constituent degrees of freedom. These comparisons reflect the linear and quadratic trends comprising each effect (cf. Kirk, 1968; Lindquist, 1953), with the latter trend being equivalent to a test of the "residual" or "nonlinearity" among the three levels of attention. Each of these comparisons has an appropriate within- or between-subjects error term, which allows proper F tests to be conducted.

For simplicity of analysis and presentation, overall split-plot analyses of variance (ANOVAS) were first performed to determine whether the various replication factors (e.g., stimulus version and priming trait) interacted with the focus or the channel effects. Except as noted below, there were no such interactions with the effects of primary interest, and the data were collapsed across the replication factors in computing the reported planned comparisons.

Impression Judgments

At the conclusion of the experiment, subjects in all conditions indicated their impressions of both of the primary actors by completing several trait-rating scales. The two scales intended to assess impressions of honesty (honesty and trustworthiness) were highly correlated (.89 for Brian, .88 for Paul) and were combined into a single honesty composite. Similarly, the two scales intended to assess impressions of kindness (kindness and warmth) were highly correlated (.68 for Brian, .77 for Paul) and were combined into a single kindness composite. These two trait composites were then included as a within-subjects factor (kindness ratings/ honesty ratings) in an overall split-plot ANOVA along with the other experimental factors. Neither the trait dimension rated nor any of the other replication factors interacted with the effects of primary interest.

Planned comparisons were therefore computed to assess the effects of attention on ratings of the primed and the unprimed actors. As shown in Figure 2.2, there was a linear increase in ratings of the primed and the unprimed actor as less attention was devoted to them, $F(1, 28) = 6.68$, $p < .05$. Hence, as subjects paid less attention to an actor, their impression ratings became more consistent with the positive schemata they were given than with the negative behaviors in which the actors actually engaged. The contrast testing the nonlinear residual was nonsignificant, $F(1, 28) < 1$, indicating that the free-focus subjects made ratings between those obtained by subjects who were attending to the actors and those made by subjects who were not attending to the actors.

It is fairly evident from Figure 2.2 that these attentional effects are primarily due to ratings made of the primed actor. However, the comparison that reflected the linear interaction between attention and actor rated did not attain conventionally accepted levels of significance,

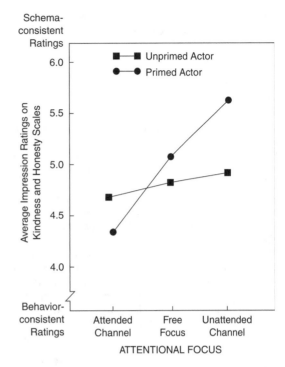

FIGURE 2.2 ■ Effects of attentional focus on impression ratings of primed and unprimed actor.

$F(1, 28) = 2.24$, $p < .16$. The nonlinear contrast for the interaction was also nonsignificant, $F(1, 28) < 1$.

Recognition of False Alarms

The recognition test that subjects completed at the end of the experiment included 12 false alarms, which represented two kindness-related and two honesty-related behaviors alleged to have been enacted by the primary actors in each of the three conversations. Subjects' recognition confidence ratings were averaged across the two primed channel behaviors and across the two nonprimed channel behaviors that pertained to each conversation. Then these averages were subjected to a split-plot ANOVA with conversations as a within-subjects factor along with the various other factors comprising the basic experimental design. In this analysis, the factors of primary interest did interact with one of the replication factors, conversations, $F(4, 56) = 2.80$, $p < .05$. However, this interaction simply indicated that the effects of interest were slightly weaker in the second conversation than in the other two conversations, so the data were again collapsed across all other factors in computing the planned comparisons.

It was hypothesized that the less attention subjects paid to a channel, the more confidence they would have in the occurrence of schematically consistent, but nonoccurring, behaviors pertinent to that channel. As shown in Figure 2.3, confidence in the false alarms in both the primed and the unprimed channel did increase linearly as attention to that channel decreased, $F(1, 28) = 19.88, p < .001$. Furthermore, this increase in confidence with inattention was greater for false alarms in the primed channel than for those in the unprimed channel, producing a significant linear component to the Attention × Channel interaction, $F(1, 28) = 5.98$, $p < .05$. The comparisons reflecting nonlinearity were nonsignificant for both the attention main effect, $F(1, 28) = 1.29, p > .50$, and the Attention × Channel interaction, $F(1, 28) < 1$. It is therefore appropriate to conclude that subjects in the free-focus conditions, whose attention was divided between the two channels, reported confidence in the false alarms that was intermediate between those who attended to the channel to which these behaviors were pertinent and those who did

not. Post hoc Newman–Keuls tests indicate that the free-focus subjects were significantly more confident in the occurrence of schema-consistent false alarms than were subjects attending to the channel to which these items pertained ($p < .05$) but were significantly less confident in the occurrence of these items than were subjects who attended to the other channel ($p < .05$).

The only other effect attaining significance in this set of analyses was a main effect for conversation in the overall split-plot analysis, $F(2, 28) = 15.50, p < .001$. Subjects were less confident in the occurrence of the false alarms (and consequently more correct) during the final conversation ($M = 1.85$) than in the first ($M = 2.29$) or second ($M = 2.22$) conversation. This finding might indicate that subjects were particularly attentive during the final conversation because of the negative behaviors occurring in both channels. However, this finding might also simply reflect a recency effect.

Recognition of True Behaviors

Subjects indicated their confidence in the occurrence of four true behaviors, representing one schema-consistent and one schema-irrelevant behavior in each the primed and the unprimed channels. These confidence ratings were first subjected to a full split-plot ANOVA with item type (schema consistent or irrelevant) as a within-subjects measure, along with all of the other factors involved in the complete design. This overall analysis indicated that only item type interacted significantly with the factors of primary interest (focus and channel), $F(4, 56) = 7.70, p < .001$. Because of this interaction, the planned comparisons involving the attention factor were computed separately for each item type. The results of both analyses are summarized in Figure 2.4.

The planned comparisons on the schema-inconsistent items revealed only a strong linear effect for attention, $F(1, 28) = 35.46, p < .001$. As shown in the top panel of Figure 2.4, the less attention subjects paid to a channel, the less confident they were that schema-inconsistent true behaviors had occurred in that channel. The comparison that tested the nonlinear residual for this data was not significant, $F(1, 28) < 1$, indicating that free-focus subjects made confidence ratings in-between the two fixed attention groups. Although this attentional effect appears to be stronger in the primed channel than in the unprimed channel, the Attention × Channel interaction was not significant at conventional levels, $F(1, 28) = 2.00, p < .15$. However, it should be noted that because the schema presented to subjects pertained

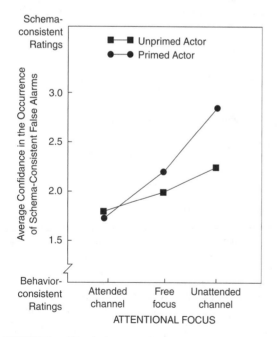

FIGURE 2.3 ■ Effects of attentional focus on confidence in the occurrence of false alarms.

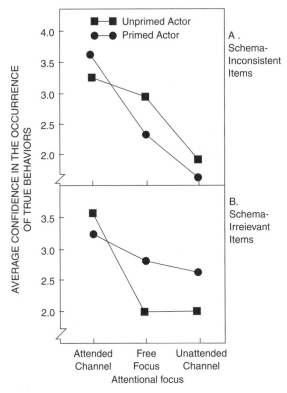

FIGURE 2.4 ■ Effects of attentional focus on confidence in the occurrence of true behaviors.

only to the primed channels, schema-inconsistent behaviors in the unprimed channel were actually schema irrelevant.

Analysis of the schema-irrelevant true items revealed both a significant linear component, $F(1, 28) = 19.59$, $p < .001$, and a significant nonlinear component, $F(1, 28) = 5.41$, $p < .05$, to the attention main effect. The nature of these effects is clear from the bottom panel of Figure 2.4. The linear effect indicates that subjects who paid less attention to a channel were less confident in schema-irrelevant true behaviors that occurred in that channel. The nonlinear component reflects the low confidence in schema-irrelevant behaviors among free-focus subjects, who were essentially as uncertain about these behaviors as subjects whose attention was confined to the opposite channel from the behavior. The linear and the nonlinear components of the Attention × Channel interaction were not significant at conventional levels, $Fs = 2.23$ and 3.08, and $ps < .13$ and $.10$, respectively.

Discussion

The present experiment was intended to examine the effects of schemata on the processing of information in a complex social interaction. It was hypothesized that the informational overload characteristic of such interactions would force subjects to take short-cuts in processing the available information and that previously learned schemata would be instrumental in these simplifying processes. More specifically, it was predicted that schemata would guide the allocation of attention between competing sources of information and would influence impression and recognition judgments made concerning less-attended sources.

Subjects in the free-focus conditions were used to assess the effects of previously learned schemata on attention to schematically represented or nonrepresented individuals. It was predicted that attention would initially be directed to the schematically represented actor to assess the adequacy of the schema and that attention would then shift to the nonrepresented actor, until the schematically represented individual began to act in a manner inconsistent with the schema. The pattern of attention shown in Figure 2.1 corresponds closely to these predictions. This gradual decline in attention to the primed actor supports the argument that schemata substitute for actual observation, allowing perceivers to divert their attention to non-schematically represented material.

When the primed actor began to behave in a manner inconsistent with the schematic description given to subjects, the percentage of subjects attending to the primed channel increased dramatically. We have argued that this shift in attention reflects subjects' periodic sampling of the primed channel after they have directed their attention elsewhere, coupled with the high utility that schema-inconsistent information has for the perceiver. Two other possibilities should be acknowledged. First, it is possible that attention is cyclical and that some shifting back to the primed actor might have occurred irrespective of his behavior. Although additional controls would be necessary to rule out such a possibility, the rather sudden shift that occurred immediately following the onset of the schema-inconsistent behavior seems more consistent with our interpretation. Second, it is possible that attention may have been diverted back to the primed actor because he engaged in schema-relevant behavior for the first time and that such a shift would have occurred regardless of whether the behavior was schema inconsistent or schema consistent. This interpretation, like our own, suggests that subjects continued to monitor the primed channel after they diverted their attention, though it suggests that the attention "rebound" occurred for different reasons than we suggest. Further research might usefully focus on the specific kinds of behaviors that may attract attention back to a schematically represented actor.

It should be evident that these particular patterns of attention reflect the particular nature of the stimuli used and that with other sorts of stimuli, other patterns of attention would be likely. For example, if observed actors initially act in a schema-inconsistent manner, then shifts of attention to other actors seem less likely to occur. Furthermore, in many situations, motivational and stimulus factors that were controlled in this study may have considerable influence on attention. Finally, it must also be acknowledged that the procedures used in the free-focus conditions do not exactly parallel the conditions that would exist in a real-world situation such as a cocktail party. It seems plausible that the present procedures may have encouraged more channel switching than would ordinarily occur in aural attention. A subsidiary analysis of the data indicates that subjects switched channels an average of 3.81 times during the first conversation, declined to 2.81 times during the second conversation, and to 2.69 times during the final conversation, $F(4, 48) = 6.39$, $p < .01$. Most probably, the tendency for subjects to change channels because "the switch was there" simply introduced nuisance variance into the analyses, particularly during the first conversation. Nonetheless, attempts should ultimately be made to replicate these attentional results using less-artificial procedures.

The second major set of hypotheses in this research concerned the effects of inattention on schematic biases and intrusions in social judgments. As predicted, the less attention subjects were able to pay to the primed actor's behavior, the less consistent their impressions were with that behavior and the more consistent they were with the priming schema. A similar, though lesser, effect occurred in ratings of the nonprimed channel, which produced a linear main effect for attention rather than the predicted interaction between attention and channel. It seems likely that people ordinarily have somewhat positive expectancies concerning the behavior of others (cf. Jones & Davis, 1965), so that even in observing the behavior of the unprimed actor, people were slightly affected by a positive schema. Presumably, if negative priming information had been used, the interaction between attention and channel would have been much stronger.

Schematic intrusions in subjects' recognition performance are evident both in the analyses of schematic false alarms and in the analyses of memory for true behaviors. As predicted, subjects who were less able to devote attention to the primed actor indicated higher confidence in the occurrence of schema-consistent false alarm behaviors, which did not actually occur. A similar trend occurred among false items in the nonprimed channel, which indicates that diminished attention also led to greater confidence in the occurrence of positive behaviors irrelevant to the presented schema. However, for these data, the linear component of the Channel × Attention interaction was significant: Inattention led to relatively greater confidence in the occurrence of the false alarms when these items were schematic than when these same items were irrelevant to the schema.

On the true items, inattention led to decreased confidence in the occurrence of schematically inconsistent and schematically irrelevant items from both the primed and the unprimed channels. When these same items occurred in the nonprimed channel, so that both types were essentially schema irrelevant, confidence in the occurrence of both types of items declined with inattention.

Perhaps the most important aspect to these results is that the effects were strictly linear across levels of attention for every variable except confidence in the schema-irrelevant items. This indicates that subjects in the free-focus conditions, who were free to attend to either of the two ongoing conversations, made judgments directly between those made by subjects who focused only on the person being judged and those made by subjects who focused only on the other conversation. The free-focus subjects appear to have dealt with their information overload by dividing their attention between the two conversations and then relying on their schemata partially, but not totally, to make judgments concerning the primed conversation. The result was impression and recognition judgments that were influenced by the behaviors observed and by the schemata held by the subjects.

The only variable in which free-focus subjects did not make judgments intermediate to the attending and nonattending groups involved the irrelevant true behaviors. The free-focus subjects' confidence in the occurrence of these behaviors was as low as the confidence of subjects whose attention was entirely diverted to the other channel. Perhaps this is the cost of the considerable cognitive effort necessary to monitor several individuals at once: Schematically irrelevant behaviors are simply ignored.

This research thus supports several hypotheses concerning the effects of schemata on attention and judgments in complex social interactions. These effects are generally consistent with those that have been found using simpler paradigms, in which subjects' cognitive capacities are not taxed. However, this research suggests that the effects of schemata are likely to be even greater when attention is divided in more complex situations.

REFERENCE NOTE

1. Enquist, G., Newtson, D., & LaCross, K. *Prior expectations and the perceptual segmentation of ongoing behavior.* Unpublished manuscript, University of Virginia, 1978.

REFERENCES

Abelson, R. P. Psychological status of the script concept. *American Psychologist*, 1981, *36*, 715–729.

Bobrow, D. G., & Winograd, T. An overview of KRL, a knowledge representation language. *Cognitive Science*, 1977, *1*, 3–46.

Bower, G. H., Black, J. B., & Turner, T. J. Scripts in memory for text. *Cognitive Psychology*, 1979, *11*, 177–220.

Broadbent, D. E. *Perception and communication.* New York: Pergamon Press, 1958.

Cantor, N., & Mischel, W. Traits as prototypes: Effects on recognition memory. *Journal of Personality and Social Psychology*, 1977, *35*, 38–48.

Carlston, D. E. Events, inferences and impression formation. In R. Hastie, T. M. Ostrom, E. B. Ebbesen, R. S. Wyer, Jr., D. S. Hamilton, & D. E. Carlston (Eds.), *Person memory: The cognitive basis of social perception.* Hillsdale, N. J.: Erlbaum, 1980. (a)

Carlston, D. E. The recall and use of traits and events in social inference processes. *Journal of Experimental Social Psychology*, 1980, *16*, 303–329. (b)

Cohen, C. E., & Ebbesen, E. G. Observational goals and schema activation: A theoretical framework for behavior perception. *Journal of Experimental Social Psychology*, 1979, *15*, 305–329.

Fiske, S. T. Attention and weight in person perception: The impact of negative and extreme behavior. *Journal of Personality and Social Psychology*, 1980, *38*, 889–906.

Fiske, S. T., & Linville, P. W. What does the schema concept buy us? *Personality and Social Psychology Bulletin*, 1980, *6*, 543–557.

Hastie, R. Schematic principles in human memory. In E. T. Higgins, C. P. Herman, & M. P. Zanna (Eds.), *Social cognition: The Ontario symposium* (Vol. 1). Hillsdale, N. J.: Erlbaum, 1981.

Jones, E. E., & Davis, K. From acts to dispositions: The attribution process in person perception. In L. Berkowitz (Ed.), *Advances in experimental social psychology* (Vol. 2). New York: Academic Press, 1965.

Kanarick, A. F., & Petersen, R. C. Effects of value on the monitoring of multi-channel displays. *Human Factors*, 1969, *11*, 313–320.

Kirk, R. E. *Experimental design: Procedures for the behavioral sciences.* Monterey, Calif.: Brooks/Cole, 1968.

Lindquist, E. F. *Design and analysis of experiments in psychology and education.* Boston: Houghton Mifflin, 1953.

Markus, H. Self-schemata and processing information about the self. *Journal of Personality and Social Psychology*, 1977, *35*, 63–78.

McArthur, L. S. What grabs you? The role of attention in impression formation and causal attribution. In E. T. Higgins, C. P. Herman, & M. P. Zanna (Eds.), *Social cognition: The Ontario symposium* (Vol. 1). Hillsdale, N. J.: Erlbaum, 1981.

Minsky, M. A framework for representing knowledge. In P. H. Winston (Ed.), *The psychology of computer vision.* New York: McGraw-Hill, 1975.

Nisbett, R. E., & Ross, L. *Human inference: Strategies and shortcomings of social judgment.* Englewood Cliffs, N.J.: Prentice-Hall, 1980.

Norman, D. A., & Bobrow, D. G. On data-limited processes. *Cognitive Psychology*, 1975, *7*, 44–64.

Norman, D. A., & Bobrow, D. G. On the role of active memory processes in perception and cognition. In C. Cofer (Ed.), *The structure of human memory.* San Francisco: Freeman, 1976.

Picek, J. S., Sherman, S. J., & Shiffrin, R. M. Cognitive organization and coding of social structures. *Journal of Personality and Social Psychology*, 1975, *31*, 758–768.

Raye, C. L., Johnson, M. K., & Taylor, T. H. Is there something special about memory for internally-generated information? *Memory & Cognition*, 1980, *8*, 141–148.

Rothbart, M., Evans, M., & Fulero, S. Recall for confirming events: Memory processes and the maintenance of social stereotypes. *Journal of Experimental Social Psychology*, 1979, *4*, 343–355.

Rumelhart, D. E., & Ortony, A. The representation of knowledge in memory. In R. C. Anderson, R. J. Spiro, & W. E. Montague (Eds.), *Schooling and the acquisition of knowledge.* Hillsdale, N.J.: Erlbaum, 1977.

Taylor, S. E., & Crocker, J. Schematic bases of social information processing. In E. T. Higgins, C. P. Herman, & M. P. Zanna (Eds.), *Social cognition: The Ontario symposium* (Vol. 1). Hillsdale, N.J.: Erlbaum, 1981.

Taylor, S. E., & Fiske, S. T. Salience, attention, and attribution: Top of the head phenomena. In L. Berkowitz (Ed.), *Advances in experimental social psychology* (Vol. 11). New York: Academic Press, 1978.

Tesser, A. Self-generated attitude change. In L. Berkowitz (Ed.), *Advances in experimental social psychology* (Vol. 11). New York: Academic Press, 1978.

Thorndyke, P. W., & Hayes-Roth, B. The use of schemata in the acquisition and transfer of knowledge. *Cognitive Psychology*, 1979, *11*, 82–106.

Zadny, J., & Gerard, H. B. Attributed intentions and informational selectivity. *Journal of Experimental Social Psychology*, 1974, *10*, 34–52.

Received May 11, 1982
Revision received December 30, 1982 ■

Stereotypes and Tacit Inference

David Dunning and David A. Sherman

To judge another person's behavior, one often has to come to an understanding of what that behavior was in its detail. Five studies demonstrated that stereotypes influence the tacit inferences people make about the unspecified details and ambiguities of social behavior (e.g., what the behavior specifically was, what stimulus the individual reacted to, what caused the individual to act) and that these inferences occur when people encode the relevant information. One study found that participants who scored low on a measure of modern sexism were just as likely to make tacit inferences based on gender stereotypes as were those who scored high. Discussion centers on the implications of these findings for identification processes in social judgment, as well as whether stereotypes influence tacit inferences at an implicit level.

To what extent are stereotypes inferential prisons? To what degree do people think they "know" a person once they discover his or her ethnic group, gender, social class, or occupation? Are stereotypes maximum

---

Editor's Note: This article reported five experiments. Experiments 1, 4, and 5 are reproduced here.

David Dunning, Department of Psychology, Cornell University; David A. Sherman, Department of Psychology, Stanford University.

David A. Sherman was supported by a National Science Foundation predoctoral fellowship during the conduct of some of this research. We thank Nenshad Bardoliwalla and Jeannine Delwiche for coding the data from Study 3 and Joy Geng for running the participants of Study 5. We also thank Paul Whitmore as well as the participants of the Social/Personality Proseminar at Cornell University for their comments on a previous version of this article. Finally, we extend our gratitude to Karin Mogg for generously supplying us with stimulus materials from Eysenck, Mogg, May, Richards, and Mathew's (1991) study, which served as an inspiration for many aspects of our own materials.

Correspondence concerning this article should be addressed to David Dunning, Department of Psychology, Uris Hall, Cornell University, Ithaca, New York 14853–7601. Electronic mail may be sent via the Internet to dad6@cornell.edu.

security prisons, with people's inferences and impressions of the person never escaping far from the confines of the stereotype? Or are the prisons not so secure, with people escaping the influence of their stereotypes as they learn more about the individual?

Social psychological research gives conflicting evidence on the persistence of stereotypes in the face of individuating information. On the one hand, people have been shown to abandon their stereotypes just as soon as they garner individuating information about a person (Ashmore, 1981; Glick, Zion, & Nelson, 1988; Heilman, 1984). As an example, Locksley and colleagues discovered that stereotypes about gender had no impact on judgments of aggressiveness once participants received concrete information about an individual (Locksley, Borgida, Brekke, & Hepburn, 1980; Locksley, Hepburn, & Ortiz, 1982). On the other hand, researchers have also shown that people hold onto stereotypes as they judge others. For instance, for any given act of aggressiveness, people see a man performing it as more aggressive than a woman

(Futoran & Wyer, 1986; Krueger & Rothbart, 1988). People take individuating information into account, but simply add it to a baseline of aggressiveness they associate with men and women.

In this article we portray the cognitive prison of stereotypes to be rather secure, for the impact of the stereotype may not be reduced by specific information about the individual. We argue that stereotypes often lead people to make *tacit inferences* about individuating information. These inferences alter the meaning of the information to affirm the stereotype people possess. Indeed, such inferences can alter the behavior or information about which people believe they have been informed. As an example, consider the sentence *Some felt that the politician's statements were untrue.* Although not specified, we propose that the stereotype of politicians would lead people to make tacit inferences about why people have such feelings in that passage. In particular, it would lead people to believe that the politician was lying, although that was not specified in the passage. Such an inference, however, would not be made if the character belonged to another stereotyped group, such as physicists. In this case the stereotype of physicists might lead people to assume that the physicist was only mistaken in his or her assertions.

We propose that social information often leaves room for these types of tacit inferences. People must often specify the exact nature of the action taken, to identify exactly the behavior under consideration or the exact situation confronting the actor. To the extent that the information is ambiguous about the behavior or situation, stereotypes may guide people in their inferences about that information. Indeed, it is easy to see how such tacit inferences may lead people to confirm their stereotypes and apply them in making social judgments. For example, if the information given above leads people to believe that the politician is lying, but that the physicist is only mistaken, then people may conclude that the politician is more dishonest than the physicist, even though people have received ostensibly the same information about both.

In this regard, our logic is consistent with the notions of Trope (1986; Trope, Cohen, & Alfieri, 1991) concerning the specific processes people follow in making social judgments. According to Trope, before people make judgments about another individual, they must complete a preliminary but important step: They must *identify* the behavior that is to be judged. Many stimuli in the social realm are ambiguous, open to many interpretations. As such, people must form an interpretation of the stimulus before making judgments. For example,

suppose one turns the corner in the hallway and sees that a person is weeping. Is that behavior an example of sadness, or one of happiness? It can be either, depending on the context surrounding the act. If the person has just failed an exam, the behavior should properly be identified as sadness. However, if the person has just gotten into her first-choice law school, then the behavior should be identified as unbridled joy. Only after the behavior has been identified can people then proceed to make dispositional judgments about the individual.[1]

In this article we propose that stereotypes alter the tacit inferences people make when comprehending descriptions of social behavior. In Trope's (1986) terms, stereotypes influence identification processes in social judgment, leading people to different conclusions about the exact behavior about which they have been informed. We propose that such inferences are made spontaneously, that is, without prompting from any external agent. Moreover, we propose that these inferences can be so strong that people often mistakenly believe that those inferences were not inferences at all, but rather information presented in the original description.

We assessed these proposals by observing people's memory for passages about individuals in differing stereotyped groups. In five studies, we presented people with passages that invited them to make tacit inferences. In subsequent memory tests, we presented them with altered passages that contained the tacit inferences suggested by the relevant stereotype. We predicted that people would be more likely to falsely remember these altered passages as previously presented when the inferences contained in the sentences were consistent with the stereotype contained in them than when they were inconsistent with the stereotype.

Do People Make Tacit Inferences?

There is a long history of work in cognitive psychology, coming mostly from research on text comprehension, demonstrating that people make tacit inferences about social stimuli with which they are confronted. More than 20 years ago, Johnson, Bransford, and Solomon (1973; see also Bransford. Barclay, & Franks, 1972) demonstrated how tacit inferences appeared in memory

---

[1] A careful reader may have noticed that we specified the gender of the person crying in the hall rather late in the example. If this was noticed, we congratulate the reader for reading carefully. If it was not, it may be evidence that the reader made a tacit inference about the person in the example at the time he or she read the passage.

for text. They presented participants with passages such as *John was trying to fix the bird house. He was pounding the nail when his father came out to watch him and to help him do the work.* Subsequent memory tests revealed that participants had inferred that John was using a hammer, even though no such instrument had been mentioned in the original passage. That is, they misremembered the sentence as *John was using the hammer to fix the bird house when his father came out to watch him and to help him do the work.*

Several years of text comprehension work has confirmed that people readily make tacit inferences about what they read. They have been shown to make inferences regarding the meaning of ambiguous words (Small, Cottrell, & Tanenhaus, 1988; Woll, Weeks, Fraps, Pendergrass, & Vanderplas, 1980; Woll & Yopp, 1978), to specify how different components of the passage refer to one another (O'Brien, Shank, Myers, & Rayner, 1988), to determine the causes and consequences of actions (Singer & Ferreira, 1983; van den Broek, 1990), to specify the emotions felt by the characters in the passage (Gernsbacher, Goldsmith, & Robertson, 1992), and to arrive at the overall theme of the passage (Till, Mross, & Kintsch, 1988). Related work in social psychology has shown that people make inferences regarding the personality traits of the actors in the passage (Winter & Uleman, 1984).

Some researchers have articulated more formal and computational theories about the cognitive processes involved in text comprehension, to show how these processes necessarily involve tacit inference and to demonstrate how such inferences are incorporated into memory of the passage. In one influential model, Kintsch (1988) described text comprehension as a two-step process. First, people decompose the propositions contained in any utterance. For example, in the sentence *The bosses discussed the inadequate work of their summer sales staff, and decided that Scott was the most responsible*, people must break the sentence down into its information units (e.g., work was discussed, the work was inadequate, it was discussed by the bosses, the work was done by the summer sales staff, etc.). Second, people must add propositions to their representation of the sentence to comprehend it. For example, in the sentence above, Scott is portrayed as responsible, but to what does *responsible* refer? Does it refer to a desirable personality trait, or does it refer to the fact that Scott is the one most responsible for the inadequate work? Kintsch suggested that people add such propositions to form a coherent comprehension of the presented message, adding propositions to the memorial

representation of the passage. Thus, when a new sentence containing those inferences is shown to an individual, the new sentences will provide a good match to that individual's memorial representation and will be mistakenly remembered as previously encountered (Kintsch, Welsch, Schmalhofer, & Zimny, 1990).

To be sure, there is much in this work that remains controversial. Researchers differ on the types of inferences people are likely to make when reading a narrative, and they also disagree on whether these inferences are made strategically or automatically (see recent discussions, for example, by Graesser, Singer, & Trabasso, 1994, and McKoon & Ratcliff, 1992). However, there is a consensus among researchers in the field that people do make some types of tacit inferences in narrative passages that describe people's actions.

Would Stereotypes Influence the Tacit Inferences People Make?

Although the work discussed above suggests that people make many tacit inferences while reading narratives about others, it provides no evidence for the specific hypothesis that stereotypes would prompt people to make different tacit inferences about the exact same information about individuals in different stereotypical groups.

More direct evidence of this hypothesis does exist, although it is scant. Kunda and Sherman-Williams (1993) directly asked whether stereotypes would alter the way people construed the features and details of an ambiguous behavior. They presented participants with sentences such as *X hit someone who annoyed him* and asked them explicitly to report the elaborative inferences they made on reading it, that is, what specific, detailed scenarios came to mind as they considered the sentence. Participants reported different acts based on differing stereotypes. When told that a construction worker had hit another person, they described him as punching a coworker. When told that a housewife had hit another person, participants described the action in more benign terms, such as spanking a naughty child. It is important to note that judgments of the target's aggressiveness were dependent on these interpretations. When these inferences about the details of the event were controlled for, either statistically or experimentally, Kunda and Sherman-Williams found no difference in how participants rated the aggressiveness of target individuals.

In a related vein, Slusher and Anderson (1987) discovered that having people imagine the situation surrounding a person's behavior encouraged stereotypical inferences. They presented participants with sentences involving stereotyped occupations (e.g., *Frank, a lawyer, is trying to reach the check-out counter in a crowded department store*) and asked them to spend some time imagining the scene the sentences depicted. In one study, participants tended to imagine details that tended to be stereotypical (e.g., they imagined that the lawyer had acted in an aggressive manner). In another study, Slusher and Anderson found that asking participants to imagine the scene surrounding the sentence tended to prompt them to overestimate the number of stereotype-relevant trait terms (e.g., *aggressive*) that had been explicitly presented in the those sentences.

However, although these two sets of findings support our assertion that stereotypes influence how people interpret the specifics of behavior, they are not conclusive. It is our view that stereotypes influence how people construe the details at the time they read the passage, without any prompting from external forces. Kunda and Sherman-Williams (1993) explicitly asked participants to provide their interpretations of the passages given to them. As such, it is unclear whether the inferences that participants made occurred while they were reading the passage. Indeed, it is unclear whether participants, without prompting, would have made any inferences at all. Instead, they may have taken the passage at face value and made no inferences about the specific behaviors they read about or the circumstances surrounding those behaviors. A similar critique can be applied to Slusher and Anderson (1987). They expressly asked participants to imagine particular situations, and so it is unclear whether participants would have made any stereotypical tacit inferences without the experimenter's prompting.

Goals of the Present Research

In five studies, we tested whether stereotypes influence the tacit inferences people make of individuating information about other people. We tested whether these inferences were made without prompting and whether they occur at the time of comprehension. We also tested whether their strength is reflected in people's memorial representation of the passage — whether these inferences can be held so confidently that they are confused and mistaken for previously presented information.

In all studies, participants were presented with sentences that invited tacit inferences. Each sentence associated an ambiguous action or piece of information with one of two stereotypes, such as *Amy found it hard to*

disguise her feelings toward the Hollywood actor or Amy found it hard to disguise her feelings toward the criminal. People were soon after presented with sentences containing inferences that were either consistent or inconsistent with the one stereotype that had been presented to them (e.g., *Amy found it hard to disguise her attraction toward the Hollywood actor versus Amy found it hard to disguise her repulsion toward the Hollywood actor*). We predicted that people would be more likely to falsely recognize a new sentence when it was consistent with the stereotype contained in it than when it was inconsistent with the stereotype.

In the first study we presented participants with a recognition memory test containing stereotype-consistent and -inconsistent sentences. We predicted that participants would be more likely to false-alarm to the former than to the latter. In the second study we explored whether this effect was due to tacit inferences or to a response bias for plausibility. In the third study we examined whether the effect was influenced by the specific task we asked participants to do while they read the sentences. In the fourth study we examined *when* participants make their stereotype-based inferences: At the time of comprehension (i.e., while reading the passage) or at the time of retrieval (i.e., while completing the recognition memory test). Finally in a fifth study we examined whether this phenomenon would generalize to gender stereotypes, as well as whether even low-sexist individuals would make tacit inferences based on gender.

Study 1: Memory for Stereotype-Consistent and -Inconsistent Inferences

In Study 1 we investigated whether stereotypes influence the tacit inferences made from individuating information and alter memory of that information. Participants were presented with passages about individuals that invited tacit inferences. Different participants had different stereotypes associated with those passages. For example, all participants were given a sentence saying that *Amy found it hard to disguise her feelings toward X*. Half the participants were told that "X" was a Hollywood actor: Half were told that "X" was a criminal. Afterward, participants were given a memory test that contained different sentences containing an inference that could plausibly be made from one of the stereotypes (e.g., *Amy found it hard to disguise her attraction toward the Hollywood actor*). For half the sentences like this in the memory test, the sentence included an inference consistent with the stereotype presented to participants. For the other half, the sentence included an inconsistent inference, that is, an inference consistent with the unpresented stereotype (e.g., *Amy found it hard to disguise her repulsion toward the Hollywood actor*). Our prediction was straightforward: Participants would falsely recognize more sentences containing stereotype-consistent inferences than sentences containing stereotype-inconsistent ones.

Method

Participants
Participants were 10 Cornell University undergraduates enrolled in a senior/graduate student level course on research methods. They participated as a class exercise on data analysis.

Procedure
The experiment was run in one session during class time. Participants were told that they would be reading several sentences about different individuals. After they indicated that they understood the task, they signed consent forms and sat in front of Macintosh LC III computers, which presented them with a few preliminary instructions and told participants that they should simply "try to form immediate impressions of the person or people" in the sentences they saw. The computer then presented participants with 50 sentences that either described the behavior of an individual or provided some descriptive information about him or her. The computer presented each sentence for 6 s, with no delay between sentence presentation.

After the computer presentation was complete, participants were introduced to a distracter task. They were asked to list as many prime numbers as they could, starting with the number 2, for 1 min. They were then given a recognition test for the presented sentences. The experimenter gave participants a list of 48 sentences and told them that some of the sentences had been presented previously and others had not. Participants were told to indicate whether they had seen the *exact same* sentence on the computer screen. Participants responded on a 4-point recognition confidence scale ranging from 1 (*definitely there*) to 4 (*definitely not there*).

Participants then filled out a few follow-up questionnaires that included a probe for suspicion. The goals and design of the study were described. Participants were later given the data gathered at the session to complete as a data analysis exercise for the class.

Materials
The 50 sentences shown on the computer consisted of 34 filler and 16 critical items. There were two versions of each of the 16 critical sentences, differing in the occupation of the actor in the sentence. For example, one sentence read *The X was unhappy about the amount of liquor being served at the party*. In one version of the sentence, the main character was described as a nun. In the other, the main character was described as a rock musician. For each version of the sentence, a stereotype-consistent interpretation was generated. For example, for the nun version of the sentence above, the stereotype-consistent interpretation presented on recognition test was *The nun was unhappy about the large amount of liquor being served at the party*. For the rock musician version, the stereotype-consistent interpretation was *The rock musician was unhappy about the small amount of liquor being served at the party*. Table 3.1 presents the 16 critical sentences with the stereotype-consistent interpretations included in the recognition test. For each sentence, inconsistent interpretations consisted of pairing each interpretation with the alternative stereotype associated with each sentence.

In a preliminary study, we asked 25 people to read the four versions of the stimulus sentences (two were stereotype consistent, and two were stereotype inconsistent) and then to judge the plausibility of each version on a 9-point scale. Stereotype-consistent versions for each critical sentence were rated as more plausible than their stereotype-inconsistent counterparts, mean $t = 5.94$ (ts ranged from 2.30 to 9.91), all ps < .05.

For the experiment proper we randomly selected one occupation for each sentence and placed it into Occupation Set A. The remaining occupation for each sentence was placed into Occupation Set B. Table 3.1 indicates which occupation for each sentence was in Occupation Sets A and B. In the experiment, half of the participants saw sentences containing Occupation Set A, and the other half saw Set B. These critical sentences were randomly interspersed among the filler items, with one proviso: To avoid primacy and recency effects in memory, the first five and the last five sentences in the acquisition set were filler items.

Each critical sentence in the acquisition set had a corresponding sentence in the recognition memory task. Prior to the experiment, the 16 critical sentences in the recognition memory task were divided equally into two groups: Interpretation Sets 1 and 2. Table 3.1 describes which sentences were contained in each set. For some participants, the 8 sentences comprising Interpretation Set 1 were interpretations consistent with the stereotypes that had been shown to participants. For those same participants, the sentences from Interpretation Set 2 were stereotype-inconsistent items. The remaining participants read recognition sentences that contained

TABLE 3.1 Critical Acquisition and Recognition Sentences Used in Study 1

Acquisition Sentence	Stereotype-Consistent Interpretation Used for Occupation Set	
	A	B
1. Some felt that the (physicist's/politician's) statements were untrue.	Some felt that the physicist's statements were mistaken.	Some felt that the politician's statements were lies.
2. The management discussed the poor performance of their summer sales staff and concluded that the (straight-A student/company president's son) was the most responsible.	The management discussed the poor performance of their summer sales staff and concluded that the straight-A student was the most dependable.	The management discussed the poor performance of their summer sales staff and concluded that the company president's son was the most responsible for it.
3. After weighing all the circumstances, the (head of the computer software company/ drug dealer) decided that he would have to terminate a few of his employees.	After weighing all the circumstances, the head of the computer software company decided that he would have to fire a few of his employees.	After weighing all the circumstances, the drug dealer decided he would have to kill a few of his employees.
4. The (accountant's/Marine drill sergeant's) personality was a little hard to take.	The accountant's obsessive personality was a little hard to take.	The Marine drill sergeant's overbearing personality was a little hard to take.
5. The (nurse/bar bouncer) hurriedly rushed through the people to the check-out counter in the crowded department store.	The nurse gingerly dodged her way through the people to the check-out counter in the crowded department store.	The bar bouncer hurriedly pushed his way through the people to the check-out counter in the crowded department store.
6. The punch that the (truck driver/bartender) gave the guy just knocked him out.	The punch that the truck driver threw at the guy just knocked him out.	The drink that the bartender gave the guy just knocked him out.
7. Amy found it hard to disguise her feelings toward the (criminal/Hollywood actor).	Amy found it hard to disguise her repulsion toward the criminal.	Amy found it hard to disguise her attraction toward the Hollywood actor.
8. The (fashion model/triathlete) had to be concerned every day about her physical condition.	The fashion model had to be concerned every day about her physical appearance.	The triathlete had to be concerned every day about her physical fitness.
9. After a few drinks, the two (marriage counselors/lumberjacks) had a fight in the restaurant.	After a few drinks, the two marriage counselors had a quarrel in the restaurant.	After a few drinks, the two lumberjacks had a fist fight in the restaurant.
10. The (nun/rock musician) was unhappy about the amount of liquor being served at the party.	The nun was unhappy about the large amount of liquor being served at the party.	The rock musician was unhappy about the small amount of liquor being served at the party.
11. The two men questioned the (priest/gambling casino operator) about his convictions.	The two men questioned the priest about his beliefs.	The two men questioned the gambling casino operator about his prison record.
12. The student couldn't make sense of the (psychiatric patient's/neurobiology professor's) language.	The student couldn't make sense of the psychiatric patient's incoherent language.	The student couldn't make sense of the neurobiology professor's jargon.
13. The (librarian/investment banker) purchased a brand new car.	The librarian purchased a brand new compact car.	The investment banker purchased a brand new sports car.
14. The (used car salesman/computer hacker) was not known for being the most socially skilled person.	The used car salesman was not known for being the most courteous, socially skilled person.	The computer hacker was not known for being the most outgoing, socially skilled person.
15. The (gangster/police officer) felt he had his reputation to uphold.	The gangster felt he had his tough reputation to uphold.	The police officer felt he had his honest reputation to uphold.
16. Everyone giggled when the (TV talk show host/foreign exchange student) spoke.	Everyone giggled in delight when the TV talk show host spoke.	Everyone giggled in embarrassment when the foreign exchange student spoke.

Note. In the far left column, the first occupation listed in parentheses is the occupation used in Set A, and the second is the one used in Set B. Sentences 1–6 and 13–14 comprise Interpretation Set 1, and Sentences 7–12 and 15–16 comprise Interpretation Set 2. The interpretations listed in Columns 2 and 3 include the occupation that render them stereotype consistent. These sentences were made stereotype inconsistent by replacing the stereotype included with the alternative (e.g., exchanging *politician* and *physicist* in Sentence 1).

stereotype-consistent interpretations from Set 2 and stereotype-inconsistent ones from Set 1.

As such, two factors were counterbalanced across participants. The first was the occupation set shown to participants as they read the acquisition sentences. The second was the specific interpretations shown during the recognition test that were stereotype consistent and inconsistent. There were 2 to 3 participants in each individual cell of the 2×2 factorial that arose from this counterbalancing.

Of the 32 remaining items on the recognition test, 14 were filler items that had been shown in the acquisition set, and 18 were either altered or completely new sentences.

Results and Discussion

The two counterbalancing factors (occupation and interpretation set) had no impact on any results reported below. They are discussed no further.

To assess memory for the presented sentences, we examined the portion of sentences in the recognition test that participants said had been presented (that is, they circled 1 or 2 on the recognition response scale). Analyses indicated that participants had good memory for presented sentences. Participants correctly recognized an average of 78% of the previously presented filter items and mistakenly recognized only 1% of the filter items that had not been presented, $t(9) = 11.98$, $p < .0001$. However, participants made a greater number of mistakes when dealing with critical items. As predicted, participants mistakenly recognized an average of 35% of stereotype-consistent interpretations, but only 15% of stereotype-inconsistent ones, $t(9) = 4.71$, $p < .002$.[2]

In sum, Study 1 provided initial evidence that stereotypes influence interpretations of another person's behavior. Participants in Study 1 mistakenly recognized sentences that contained tacit inferences when those inferences were consistent with stereotypes of the sentence's protagonist. Indeed, they falsely recognized over a third of those sentences, even though none of these sentences had actually been previously presented. In contrast, when the sentence contained inferences that were inconsistent with the stereotype in question, participants were significantly less likely to claim to have seen the sentence before.

---

[2] Analyses in which recognition confidence was the dependent measure produced virtually identical results in all studies reported herein.

Study 4: Do Tacit Inferences Occur at Encoding or Retrieval?

Although Studies 1–3 provide evidence that differing stereotypes can impel people to make divergent tacit inferences about the same piece of information, they still leave one important question unanswered: When do people make these inferences — at the time they read the relevant passage or at the time they confront the recognition test? We contend that people make these inferences at encoding (see von Hippel, Sekaquaptewa, & Vargas, 1995, for arguments that virtually all stereotype processes occur at encoding), when people initially read the passages. However, people may instead remember stimulus sentences veridically, and reinterpret those sentences only at retrieval, when they see similar and plausible sentences on the recognition test.

We designed Study 4 to test whether people make tacit inferences at the time of encoding or at retrieval. We did so by borrowing a procedure used by Winter and Uleman (1984; see also Winter, Uleman, & Cunniff, 1985) to test whether people make inferences about the personality traits of others as they read about their behavior. In these studies, participants were presented with a series of behaviors and then were asked to recall those behaviors using a cued-recall task. The cues used to promote recall were the personality traits people had presumably inferred as they read the original sentence. If people had spontaneously inferred the traits as they read the original sentences, then the traits should have facilitated recall for the original sentences. If the trait had not been inferred, then no facilitation of recall should have occurred. Consistent with their arguments, Winter and Uleman found that people had indeed inferred personality traits concerning the people about whom they had read. When cued with relevant personality traits, they recalled a greater number of sentences than they did when given no cues at all.

In Study 4 we adopted this technique to see if participants made their inferences at the time they read stimulus passages. We presented them with the ambiguous sentences used in the previous studies (e.g., *Amy found it difficult to disguise her feelings toward the Hollywood actor*) and then asked them to recall those sentences a few minutes later. For some of the sentences, participants were given stereotype-consistent cues. That is, they were given short phrases describing the inferences we presumed that participants were making (e.g., *romantically attracted to him*). For other sentences, they were given stereotype-inconsistent cues (e.g., *disgusted and repulsed by him*). For other sentences, they were given no cues at all. If participants made tacit inferences at encoding, then they should recall a greater number of sentences when given stereotype-consistent cues than when given stereotype-inconsistent cues or no cues.

Method

Participants
Participants were 14 Cornell University undergraduates enrolled in an introductory design and environmental analysis class. Participants were given extra credit toward their course grades for taking part.

Procedure
Participants were tested in groups of up to 8. The procedure closely mirrored that of the previous three studies, with all participants given instructions to "form immediate impressions" of the people about whom they read, except that participants viewed only 16 sentences during acquisition. Those sentences consisted of the 12 critical items used in the first two studies, plus 4 filler items. These filler items were included to buffer our results against primacy and recency effects in memory. That is, 2 of the filler items appeared first, and 2 appeared last, in the series of sentences we presented to participants. The 12 critical sentences were shown in random order in the middle of the series.

After viewing the sentences, participants completed a 5-min distracter task in which they wrote down the names of their past jobs and good friends. They then were given a cued-recall task. They were asked to recall as many as they could of the 16 sentences they had seen earlier, but to be as accurate as possible. For 8 of the sentences, they were given cues to aid them in their recall. Participants were asked to write down the sentence associated with each cue. Four of the cues were stereotype consistent, in that they contained the inference we presumed participants would make when exposed to the stereotype mentioned. For example, for the sentence *The nun was unhappy about the amount of liquor being served at the party*, the relevant cue was *didn't like all the alcohol*. The remaining four cues were stereotype inconsistent, in that they presented an inference that contradicted the stereotype in the sentence (and were consistent with the alternative stereotype also connected to the sentence). For example, for the nun sentence above, the stereotype-inconsistent cue was *wanted more alcohol*. A list of all the stereotype-consistent and inconsistent cues is provided in Table 3.2. For the remaining 8 sentences, participants were given eight empty slots to recall as many of the non-cued sentences as they could remember.

As in the previous three studies, participants viewed sentences containing occupations listed in Set A or B. The specific sentences cued by stereotype-consistent or -inconsistent phrases, or by no cue, were counterbalanced across participants. We randomly grouped the 12 critical sentences into three groups of 4. By means of Latin square, one of these groups of sentences was cued by stereotype-consistent phrases, another by stereotype-inconsistent phrases, and the third by no phrase. In this way, each sentence fell into one of the cue conditions approximately one third of the time.

After completing the recall test, participants filled out a few follow-up questionnaires that included a probe for suspicion. They were then debriefed.

To determine which sentences participants had accurately recalled, we gave participant protocols to two coders who were blind to the hypothesis of the study. These coders classified recall of a particular sentence as correct if the participant accurately conveyed the "gist" of the sentence. Interrater reliability was 91%. Disagreements were resolved by means of discussion between the coders.

Results and Discussion

Both counterbalancing factors (occupation and cue set) failed to influence any results reported below. They are discussed no further.

An analysis of participants' recall performance suggested that they made their tacit inferences at the time of encoding. For each participant, we calculated the percentage of sentences accurately recalled when given stereotype-consistent cues, stereotype-inconsistent cues, or no cue. A one-way within-subject ANOVA revealed that there were significant differences depending on the cues that participants received, $F(2, 26) = 18.63$, $p < .0001$. As predicted, participants recalled a higher percentage of sentences cued by stereotype-consistent phrases ($M = 64\%$) than they did sentences cued by inconsistent phrases ($M = 28\%$), $t(13) = 5.04$, $p < .0002$, or by no phrase ($M = 21\%$), $t(13) = 4.64$, $p < .0005$. The difference in recall for stereotype-inconsistent cues and no cues was not significant, $t(13) = 1.44$.

In sum, Study 4 provided evidence that stereotypical tacit inferences are made at encoding and not at retrieval. Stereotype-consistent cues at the time of recall facilitated memory for the original sentences. Such a pattern would occur only if participants made these inferences at encoding, before they confronted the memory test, so that the presence of the cue reminded participants of the sentence associated with it. The data also fail to support an

TABLE 3.2 Acquisition Sentences and Cues Used in Study 3

	Stereotype-Consistent Cue for Occupation Set	
Acquisition Sentence	**A**	**B**
1. Some felt that the (physicist's/politician's) statements were untrue.	Thought comments were mistakenly in error	Thought comments were lies
2. The management discussed the poor performance of their summer sales staff and concluded that the (straight-A student/company president's son) was the most responsible.	The most dependable worker	Caused a business slump
3. After weighing all the circumstances, the (head of the computer software company/drug dealer) decided that he would have to terminate a few of his employees.	Fired a few people	Killed a few people
4. The (accountant's/Marine drill sergeant's) personality was a little hard to take.	Was too obsessive and compulsive	Was too mean and strict
5. The (nurse/bar bouncer) hurriedly rushed through the people to the check-out counter in the crowded department store.	Gingerly weaved through the people	Pushed way through masses
6. The punch that the (truck driver/bartender) gave the guy just knocked him out.	The jab that was thrown floored him	The drink that was served floored him
7. Amy found it hard to disguise her feelings toward the (criminal/Hollywood actor).	Was disgusted and repulsed by him	Was romantically attracted to him
8. The (fashion model/triathlete) had to be concerned every day about her physical condition.	Was worried about looks and appearance	Was worried about fitness and stamina
9. After a few drinks, the two (marriage counselors/lumberjacks) had a fight in the restaurant.	Had a verbal spat	Had a fist fight
10. The (nun/rock musician) was unhappy about the amount of liquor being served at the party.	Didn't like all the alcohol	Wanted more alcohol
11. The two men questioned the (priest/gambling casino operator) about his convictions.	Was queried about beliefs	Was queried about criminal record
12. The student couldn't make sense of the (psychiatric patient's/neurobiology professor's) language.	Incoherent babble was unintelligible	Technical jargon was unintelligible

Note. In the far left column, the first occupation listed in parentheses is the occupation used in Set A, and the second is the one used in Set B. These cues listed in Columns 2 and 3 were made stereotype inconsistent by pairing them with the alternative stereotype (e.g., for Sentence 1, pairing *thought comments were mistakenly in error* with *politician*).

alternative account of how participants approached the memory task. One could argue that participants first recalled sentences and then hunted for the cues associated with those sentences. Such a process could have produced the difference we observed between stereotype-consistent and -inconsistent cues. However, if people recalled sentences first, prior to consulting the cues we provided them, then participants would have recalled just as many no-cue sentences as stereotype-consistent ones.

Study 5: Tacit Inferences Based on Gender

We designed Study 5 with two goals in mind. The first was to generalize our findings to groups that have been of traditional interest to social psychologists. Thus, we

created a number of ambiguous sentences that could potentially be interpreted differently depending on whether the protagonist was a man or a woman. For example, if a person saw the sentence *Elizabeth was not very surprised upon seeing her quantitative SAT score*, would that person be more likely to infer that Elizabeth's score was low than if the protagonist had been named "Bob"?

The second goal was to assess whether participants' attitudes toward gender and gender roles moderated any of our effects. Thus, we selected participants who scored high or low on a scale of modern sexism (Swim, Aikin, Hall, & Hunter, 1995). We wanted to see if participants who scored low would make gender-based tacit inferences at the same rate, or at a lower rate, than their high-scoring counterparts. To the extent that they did, we would have evidence that the prisons that stereotypes create are secure ones, for people who score low on a sexism scale presumably constitute a group that is most likely to be motivated to escape the prison and *not* to make inferences about other people based on their gender.

Method

Participants and selection
Participants were 40 Cornell University undergraduates enrolled in intermediate-level psychology courses. They received extra credit toward their course grade for participating.

Participants were selected according to their scores on the Modern Sexism Scale (Swim et al., 1995). The scale had been administered to several hundred students in intermediate-level psychology courses at the beginning of the semester. Of the participants taking part in Study 5, 18 (16 women) had scored in the bottom 40% of the distribution of the pretest and were termed the *low-sexism group* ($M = 15.2$, $SD = 3.7$). The 22 participants (18 women) who were included in the *high-sexism group* had scored in the top 40% ($M = 26.5$, $SD = 3.0$).[3]

Procedure
The procedure was identical to the one used in Study 1. Presentation of the 12 critical and 38 filler sentences was done on PowerComputing Power Center 132 personal computers.

Materials
The 50 sentences shown on the computer consisted of 38 filler and 12 critical items. There were two versions of each of the 12 critical items, differing in the gender of the actor in the sentence. For each version of the sentence, a stereotype-consistent interpretation was written. Table 3.3 presents the 12 critical sentences with the stereotype-consistent interpretations included in the recognition test. For each sentence, inconsistent interpretations consisted of pairing each interpretation with the other gender associated with each sentence.

In a preliminary study we asked 20 people to read the four versions of the stimulus sentences (two were stereotype-consistent, and two were stereotype-inconsistent) and then to judge the plausibility of each version on a 9-point scale. For each critical sentence, the stereotype-consistent versions were rated as more plausible than their stereotype-inconsistent counterparts,

mean $t = 3.28$ (*ts* ranged from 1.80 to 6.70), all *ps* $< .05$, one-tailed.

For the experiment proper we randomly selected one gender for each sentence and placed it into Gender Set A. The remaining gender for each sentence was placed into Gender Set B. Table 3.3 indicates which gender for each sentence was in Gender Sets A and B. In the experiment, half of the participants saw sentences containing Gender Set A, and the other half saw sentences containing Gender Set B.

Each critical sentence in the acquisition set had a corresponding sentence in the recognition memory task. Prior to the experiment, we divided the 12 critical sentences in the recognition memory task equally into two groups: Interpretation Sets 1 and 2 (see Table 3.3). For some participants, the 6 sentences comprising Interpretation Set 1 were interpretations consistent with the stereotypes shown to participants. For those same participants, the sentences from Interpretation Set 2 were stereotype-inconsistent items. The remaining participants read recognition sentences that contained stereotype-consistent interpretations from Set 2 and stereotype-inconsistent ones from Set 1. Thus, gender set and interpretation set were counterbalanced across participants.

Results and Discussion

The two counterbalancing factors (gender and interpretation set) had no impact on any results reported below. They are discussed no further. Two participants were dropped from the analyses presented below. One (from the high-sexism group) showed no ability to discriminate between old and new filler items on the recognition tests. Indeed, the number of false positives this participant exhibited for new filler items was 13 *SD* higher than the grand mean. The second participant (from the low-sexism group) exceeded the grand mean of false alarms to stereotype-inconsistent items by 3.4 *SD* (1.2 *SD* from the nearest neighbor).

To assess memory for the presented sentences, we again examined the proportion of sentences in the recognition test that participants labeled as "old" (they circled 1 or 2 on the recognition response scale). Analyses indicated that participants had good memory for presented sentences. Participants correctly recognized an average of 77% of the previously presented filler items and mistakenly recognized only 9% of the filler items that had not been presented, $t(37) = 28.5$, $p < .0001$.

Participants again falsely recognized a greater number of stereotype-consistent interpretations (29%) than they did stereotype-inconsistent ones (18%). A 2 (participant had high or low modern sexism score) × 2

---

[3] In contrast to Swim et al. (1995), we scored the Modern Sexism Scale so that high scores indicated more evidence of modern sexism. Swim et al. scored the scale in the opposite direction.

TABLE 3.2 Acquisition and Recognition Sentences Used in Study 5

Acquisition Sentence	Stereotype-Consistent Interpretation Used for Gender Set	
	A	B
1. Jane (Bill) administered the medicine to the patient.	Jane, the nurse, administered the medicine to the patient.	Bill, the doctor, administered the medicine to the patient.
2. Melanie (Don) got into a fight with her boyfriend (his girlfriend) about how much she (he) wanted to have sex.	Melanie got into a fight with her boyfriend about how little she wanted to have sex.	Don got into a fight with his girlfriend because he wanted to have sex more often.
3. Carol (Bob) didn't like Bob's (Carol's) attitude toward sports.	Carol didn't like Bob's enthusiastic attitude toward sports.	Bob didn't like Carol's negative attitude toward sports.
4. Gloria (Mike) argued with Mike (Gloria) about how much he (she) was committed to the relationship.	Gloria argued with Mike about how little he was committed to the relationship.	Mike argued with Gloria about her being committed to the relationship too much.
5. Cindy (Richard) was concerned every day about her (his) physical condition.	Cindy was concerned every day about her physical appearance.	Richard was concerned every day about his physical fitness.
6. Archie's (Edith's) friends were amazed at the shape he (she) kept his (her) room in.	Archie's friends were amazed at how messy he kept his room.	Edith's friends were amazed at how neat she kept her room.
7. The women (men) at the office liked to talk around the water cooler.	The women at the office liked to gossip around the water cooler.	The men at the office liked to talk sports around the water cooler.
8. Dick (Jane) was unhappy about the amount of liquor being served at the party.	Dick was unhappy about the small amount of liquor being served at the party.	Jane was unhappy about the large amount of liquor being served at the party.
9. When Jack (Jill) found out that his (her) friend had been murdered, he (she) became very upset.	When Jack found out that his friend had been murdered, he became very angry.	When Jill found out that her friend had been murdered, she became very sad.
10. Elizabeth (Bob) was not very surprised upon receiving her (his) math SAT scores.	Elizabeth was not very surprised upon receiving her low math SAT scores.	Bob was not very surprised upon receiving his high math SAT scores.
11. Laura (Luke) had a problem with expressing her (his) emotions.	Laura had a problem with expressing her emotions too much.	Luke had a problem with not expressing his emotions.
12. Paul (Linda), the lawyer, made a plea to the jury.	Paul, the lawyer, made a logical plea to the jury.	Linda, the lawyer, made an emotional plea to the jury.

Note. In the far left column, the first gender listed in parentheses is the gender used in Set A, and the second is the one used in Set B. Sentences 1–6 comprise Interpretation Set 1, and Sentences 7–12 comprise Interpretation Set 2. The interpretations listed in Columns 2 and 3 include the gender that render them stereotype consistent. These sentences were made stereotype inconsistent by replacing the stereotype included with the alternative (e.g., exchanging *Bill* and *Jane* in Sentence 1).

(percentage of stereotype-consistent vs.-inconsistent interpretations falsely recognized) mixed model ANOVA indicated that this tendency was significant, $F(1, 36) = 8.48$, $p < .01$, and did not interact with levels of modern sexism, interaction $F(1, 36) = 0.01$, ns. Simple effects tests revealed that participants who scored low on modern sexism were almost as likely to display evidence of stereotype-consistent memory errors ($Ms = 27\%$ and 17% for stereotype-consistent and -inconsistent interpretations, respectively, $t(36) = 1.88$, $p < .08$, two-tailed) as were their peers who scored high on modern sexism ($Ms = 30\%$ and 20% for stereotype-consistent and -inconsistent interpretations, respectively, $t(36) = 2.22$, $p < .05$).

In sum, Study 5 provided evidence of the generality of stereotype-driven tacit inferences. The tacit inferences that participants made about a brief description of a person's behavior were different depending on whether that person was male or female. This tendency was not qualified by level of sexism. Even participants who scored low on modern sexism, and who presumably were the most committed to gender egalitarianism, still made different inferences of protagonists based on their gender. Indeed, the rate at which they made such inferences was statistically equivalent to that of participants who expressed a greater degree of sexist thought on the modern sexism scale.

General Discussion

How do people deal with specific, concrete information about others in stereotyped groups? Do they abandon their stereotypes once they are given such individuating information, taking the data at face value, or do they use their stereotypes to alter their impressions of other individuals? In the five studies we conducted, we found evidence that people use their stereotypes as they encounter individuating information about other people. Indeed, we found that stereotypes, in a sense, may render the information given as not "individuating" at all. For example, with the same description of an altercation in a restaurant, stereotypes can lead people to believe that two lumberjacks had a fist fight but that two marriage counselors had only a verbal spat. When told that a person is worried about her physical condition, stereotypes can lead people to believe that a fashion model is vain but that a triathlete is health conscious. After these tacit inferences, the information that people are given is altered so that it is no longer the "same" information. People extract a specific meaning from the information provided that confirms their stereotype.

Five studies provided convergent support for these assertions. In Study 1, participants read passages about stereotyped individuals and then were given a recognition test. Participants falsely recognized sentences that were consistent with their stereotypes to a greater degree than they recognized sentences that were inconsistent with their stereotypes. Study 2 replicated those effects and found that they were not the byproduct of response biases. Study 3 further demonstrated that these inferences were not a product of asking participants about their impressions of the individuals depicted in the sentences. Study 5 found similar recognition memory effects to sentences containing tacit inferences inspired by the gender of the protagonist, an effect that occurred to an equal degree for individuals who scored high or low on a test of sexist thought. Study 4 provided convergent evidence for stereotypical inference in a cued-recall procedure.

Study 4 also provided evidence that participants made such inferences while encoding the original information at acquisition. Providing participants with stereotype-consistent inferences at the time of recall facilitated their memory for those sentences. They recalled a greater number of sentences with this type of cue than they did with stereotype-inconsistent cues or no cue at all. Because these stereotype-consistent inferences successfully aided recall, it can be assumed that they had been made at the time when people read the original sentence. If such inferences were made later, such as at the time of the recall test, they would have failed to facilitate accurate recall.

Questions for Future Research

The five studies described in this article leave many open questions to be addressed by further research. For example, what specific kinds of inferences do stereotypes commonly and effectively influence? In the present research we did not attempt to ascertain the types of inferences that stereotypes might alter, or the types of inferences that stereotypes leave unaffected. Instead, we created stimulus sentences that contained a number of different kinds of ambiguities. We presented words that carried different lexical meanings (e.g., does *convictions* stand for beliefs or a prison record?), sentences that left the stimulus to which characters were reacting unclear (e.g., was the nun unhappy about too much or too little alcohol?), or phrases that could fit a variety of specifications (e.g., *feelings* can refer to positive as well as negative emotions).

Future research could profit by creating a typology of differing types of tacit inference that may occur when people encounter information about their social world, and then exploring which types of inferences are influenced by stereotypes. In this regard, it may be helpful to monitor the growing work in cognitive psychology on text comprehension (e.g., Graesser, Singer, & Trabasso, 1994; McKoon & Ratcliff, 1992), which is struggling over similar issues. These researchers are striving to enumerate all the various categories of inferences that people might make, and seeing if people make them naturally as they comprehend text. As such, this research is relevant to the present set of studies, as the type of text material participants confront in the text comprehension work bears a strong resemblance to our methodology.

However, we do not propose that the processes we have described here are constrained to text; they can occur for visual stimuli as well. Is Mona Lisa's smile (or is it a smirk?) one of wryness, discomfort, or coquettishness? Facial expressions, voice tone, gestures, and actions are often ambiguous. They require context in order to be interpretable. Part of that context may be the stereotype associated with someone's group (see Biernat & Manis, 1994; Biernat, Manis, & Nelson, 1991, for related arguments). Keltner (1995), for example, found that people more readily identify facial expressions as embarrassment, shame, or anger when they come from demographic groups traditionally of low status (e.g., African Americans) as opposed to those of high status (e.g., Whites). Such differences in perception occur even though the faces from the different groups were chosen to reflect similar levels of movement and intensity. Similarly, people differ in their perceptions of when push comes to shove, perceiving more aggression in behaviors performed by African Americans than by Whites (Sagar & Schofield, 1980).

On Identification Processes

The present research is also relevant to Trope's (1986) model of social judgment. According to his model, social judgment is a two-step process, involving (1) *identification* of the behavior to be judged and (2) *inferences* about the dispositions of the person doing the behavior. In his model, and in the experiments he has conducted to test the model, Trope described the identification task as one of classification. The social perceiver must take a stimulus, such as seeing someone weeping, and classify it as a happy or sad act. The five studies we report here, however, suggest that there are many other tasks to be completed in the identification stage of social judgment. People may have to specify the exact nature of the behavior (e.g., was the fight a fist fight or merely a verbal spat?), the meaning of vague terms (e.g., does *physical condition* refer to one's appearance or health?), and the exact stimulus to which the individual is reacting (e.g., is the person upset because there is too much or too little liquor?). They may infer the emotional state or attitude of others (e.g., are the person's feelings positive or negative toward the Hollywood actor?), their likely personality traits (e.g., what about the Marine drill sergeant's personality makes it hard to take?), or the causal antecedents of their behavior (e.g., why did people think the politician's statements were untrue?).

This is not to suggest that Trope (1986) is inaccurate in his characterization of the identification process. Far from it, for identification processes obviously require people to classify the behaviors to which they are exposed. Rather, our analysis just expands the types of judgments or inferences people must make during the identification process, before they can begin to reach any conclusions about the dispositions possessed by the person they are judging. In short, our experiments heighten the importance of the identification stage and suggest that it should receive more scrutiny in work on social cognition.

Are Tacit Inferences Implicit?

The five studies we conducted suggest that stereotypes prompt tacit inferences that are spontaneous in nature. That is, they occur at the time that participants encounter information about others. Tacit inferences

also occur without prompting by an outside agent. In future work, it would be profitable to address whether tacit inferences inspired by stereotypes are also *implicit*, that is, made without intention or awareness of the perceiver (Greenwald & Banaji, 1995). This consideration is important, for the scope and impact of stereotypes and tacit inferences in social judgment may hinge on whether they are implicit.

For example, consider the work of Devine (1989) on automatic versus controlled components of prejudice. According to Devine, almost all people possess stereotypes that can be automatically activated when the "appropriate" stimulus person appears. What distinguishes high-versus low-prejudiced people is whether they succeed at inhibiting the effects of those stereotypes. Low-prejudiced individuals exert effort to countervail the influence of the unwanted stereotype. However, consider the possibility that tacit inferences occur implicitly, outside of conscious control or awareness. If that is the case, low-prejudiced individuals may never have a chance to counteract the effects of stereotypes on tacit inferences. The "meaning" of the stimulus might be determined before low-prejudiced individuals have a chance to negate it, before they have an opportunity to identify and consider other possible and less stereotypical interpretations. If that is the case, then their judgments and actions may carry a good deal of prejudice even though those individuals have no intention to discriminate. Indeed, with every intention *not* to discriminate, the operation of these inference processes may constrain even those low-prejudiced individuals to consider stimuli that "look" stereotypical, thus influencing their responses. Results from Study 5 suggest that this process may occur for low-prejudiced people. In that study, participants who scored low on a measure of modern sexism made as many stereotypical tacit inferences about men and women, as indexed by recognition memory errors, as did participants who scored higher on the measure.

The presence of tacit inferences also carries implications for any well-intentioned attempt to rid oneself of stereotypes. One plausible way to rid oneself of a stereotype is to garner individuating information about members of a stereotyped group. If one found out how "they" behave in concrete, specific situations, one would discover whether members of a stereotyped group behaved in a stereotypical way. However, consider the impact that tacit inferences, made automatically and outside awareness, may have on such an enterprise. If one's interpretation of individuating information is shaped by tacit inferences, one might be left with information and an impression that confirms the stereotype. As a consequence, even when well intentioned, one may confirm one's stereotype when trying to disprove it by gathering individuating information.

Although we have no specific data on whether the tacit inferences made by our participants were implicit, two findings from the five studies suggest that they may have been. First, we tested for tacit inferences by examining participants' *memory* for stimulus sentences. If tacit inferences were not implicit, that is, if they were made under conscious control, we can presume that participants would have been aware of this fact. As such, they would have had little trouble recognizing that the stereotype-consistent interpretations in the recognition test were alterations of the original sentences, ones that just happened to contain the same inferences they themselves had mindfully made. Second, in Study 3 we observed tacit inferences even in a condition that did not require participants to make any tacit inferences whatsoever. That is, when participants were merely asked to assess the readability of stimulus sentences, their memory of those sentences was still distorted by stereotype-based tacit inferences.

Finally, in Study 5 we found that low-sexist participants made gender-related tacit inferences at virtually the same rate as their high-sexist counterparts. If the production of stereotypical tacit inferences were under the control of the individual, one would assume that this group would have been less likely than their high-sexist counterparts to make such inferences. After all, it is safe to presume that this group would be the most motivated to think about men and women in an egalitarian manner, and not to make inferences that women are gossips, are emotional, score low on math tests, are more committed to relationships than men, are less interested in sex, more likely to be teetotalers, more concerned about their physical appearance, and to assume that a stimulus woman must be a nurse. However, their answers on the recognition memory test suggested that they were just as likely as their high-sexist counterparts to make such inferences.

However, all these observations are only suggestive, not conclusive, evidence of the implicit nature of these tacit inferences. Further, and more rigorous, evidence is necessary before we can conclude that the tacit inferences we observed were made implicitly, outside the control or awareness of the individual making them.

Concluding Remarks

Life is fraught with ambiguities. Although this fact is one all people recognize in the abstract, it is one people may often miss in their day-to-day affairs. When people describe themselves or others, they often fail to recognize that the common and mundane terms they use (e.g., *She is intelligent, I have good leadership skills*) are indeterminate in their meaning. The net result of this lack of recognition is judgmental bias (Dunning, Meyerowitz, & Holzberg, 1989; Gilovich, 1990; Griffin, Dunning, & Ross, 1990) and interpersonal disagreement (Dunning & Cohen, 1992; Dunning & McElwee, 1995; Hayes & Dunning, 1997). The five studies described in this article suggest another way in which ambiguity, unrecognized, may play a role in thought and judgments about others. When information about another person is indeterminate in meaning, people may fill in ambiguities and details based on stereotypical cues about that person.

Thought of in this way, stereotypes may confer both the benefits and the costs that prisons provide for their inmates. On the benefit side, much like prisons guide and constrain the behaviors of prisoners in presumably helpful ways, stereotypes may similarly guide and constrain people in the interpretations they can make about other individuals out of all the infinite number of interpretations that are possible in human life. However, this benefit in interpretation may carry some obvious costs. Real prisons provide a life for their prisoners that hardly resembles life as it looks like in the real world. Similarly, the interpretations of behavior prompted by stereotypes may provide people with impressions of other people's behavior that does not resemble what that behavior looks like in reality.

REFERENCES

Anderson, J. R., & Reder, L. M. (1979). An elaborative processing explanation of depth of processing. In L. S. Cermak & F. I. M. Craik (Eds.), *Levels of processing in human memory* (pp. 385–403). Hillsdale, NJ: Erlbaum.

Ashmore, R. D. (1981). Sex stereotypes and implicit personality theory. In D. Hamilton (Ed.), *Cognitive processes in stereotyping and intergroup behavior* (pp. 37–81). Hillsdale, NJ: Erlbaum.

Bassili, J. N., & Smith, M. C. (1986). On the spontaneity of trait attribution: Converging evidence for the role of cognitive strategy. *Journal of Personality and Social Psychology, 50,* 239–245.

Biernat, M., & Manis, M. (1994). Shifting standards and stereotype-based judgments. *Journal of Personality and Social Psychology, 66,* 5–20.

Biernat, M., Manis, M., & Nelson, T. E. (1991). Stereotypes and standards of judgment. *Journal of Personality and Social Psychology, 60,* 485–499.

Bransford, J. D., Barclay, J. R., & Franks, J. J. (1972). Sentence memory: A constructive versus interpretive approach. *Cognitive Psychology, 3,* 193–209.

Devine, P. G. (1989). Stereotypes and prejudice: Their automatic and controlled components. *Journal of Personality and Social Psychology, 56,* 5–18.

Dunning, D., & Cohen, G. L. (1992). Egocentric definitions of traits and abilities. *Journal of Personality and Social Psychology, 63,* 341–355.

Dunning, D., & McElwee, R. O. (1995). Idiosyncratic trait definitions: Implications for self-description and social judgment. *Journal of Personality and Social Psychology, 68,* 936–946.

Dunning, D., Meyerowitz, J. A., & Holzberg, A. D. (1989). Ambiguity and self-evaluation: The role of idiosyncratic trait definitions in selfserving assessments of ability. *Journal of Personality and Social Psychology, 59,* 1082–1090.

Eysenck, M. W., Mogg, K., May, J., Richards, A., & Mathews, A. (1991). Bias in interpretation of ambiguous sentences related to threat in anxiety. *Journal of Abnormal Psychology, 100,* 144–150.

Futoran, G. C., & Wyer, R. S., Jr. (1986). The effects of traits and gender stereotypes on occupational suitability judgments and the recall of judgment-relevant information. *Journal of Experimental Social Psychology, 22,* 475–503.

Gernsbacher, M. A., Goldsmith, H. H., & Robertson, R. R. (1992). Do readers mentally represent character's emotional states? *Cognition & Emotion, 6,* 89–112.

Gilovich, T. (1990). Differential construal and the false consensus effect. *Journal of Personality and Social Psychology, 59,* 623–634.

Glick, P., Zion, C., & Nelson, C. (1988). What mediates sex discrimination in hiring decision? *Journal of Personality and Social Psychology, 55,* 178–186.

Graesser, A. C., Singer, M., & Trabasso, T. (1994). Constructing inferences during narrative text comprehension. *Psychological Review, 101,* 371–395.

Greenwald, A. G., & Banaji, M. R. (1995). Implicit social cognition: Attitudes, self-esteem, and stereotypes. *Psychological Review, 102,* 4–27.

Griffin, D. W., Dunning, D., & Ross, L. (1990). The role of construal processes in overconfident predictions about the self and others. *Journal of Personality and Social Psychology, 59,* 1128–1139.

Hayes, A. F., & Dunning, D. (1997). Construal processes and trait ambiguity: Implications for self–other agreement in personality judgment. *Journal of Personality and Social Psychology, 72,* 664–678.

Heilman, M. E. (1984). Information as a deterrent against sex discrimination: The effects of applicant sex and information type on preliminary employment decision. *Organizational Behavior and Human Performance, 33,* 174–186.

Johnson, M. K., Bransford, J. D., & Solomon, S. K. (1973). Memory for tacit implications of sentences. *Journal of Experimental Psychology, 98,* 203–205.

Keltner, D. (1995). Signs of appeasement: Evidence for the distinct displays of embarrassment, amusement, and shame. *Journal of Personality and Social Psychology, 68,* 441–454.

Kintsch, W. (1988). The role of knowledge in discourse comprehension: A construction–integration model. *Psychological Review, 95,* 163–182.

Kintsch, W., Welsch, D., Schmalhofer, F., & Zimny, S. (1990). Sentence memory: A theoretical analysis. *Journal of Memory and Language, 29,* 133–159.

Krueger, J., & Rothbart, M. (1988). Use of categorical and individuating information in making inferences about personality. *Journal of Personality and Social Psychology, 55,* 187–195.

Kunda, Z., & Sherman-Williams, B. (1993). Stereotypes and the construal of individuating information. *Personality and Social Psychology Bulletin, 19,* 90–99.

Locksley, A., Borgida, E., Brekke, N., & Hepburn, C. (1980). Sex stereotypes and social judgment. *Journal of Personality and Social Psychology, 39,* 821–831.

Locksley, A., Hepburn, C., & Ortiz, V. (1982). Social stereotypes and judgments of individuals. *Journal of Experimental Social Psychology, 18,* 23–42.

McKoon, G., & Ratcliff, R. (1992). Inference during reading. *Psychological Review, 99,* 440–466.

O'Brien, E. J., Shank, D. M., Myers, J. L., & Rayner, K. (1988). Elaborative inferences during reading: Do they occur on-line? *Journal of Experimental Psychology: Learning, Memory, and Cognition, 14,* 410–420.

Sagar, H., & Schofield, J. W. (1980). Racial and behavioral cues in black and white children's perceptions of ambiguously aggressive acts. *Journal of Personality and Social Psychology, 39,* 590–598.

Singer, M., & Ferreira, F. (1983). Inferring consequences in story comprehension. *Journal of Verbal Learning and Verbal Behavior, 22,* 437–448.

Slusher, M. P., & Anderson, C. A. (1987). When reality monitoring fails: The role of imagination in stereotype maintenance. *Journal of Personality and Social Psychology, 52,* 653–662.

Small, S. I., Cottrell, G. W., & Tanenhaus, M. K. (1988). *Lexical ambiguity resolution.* San Mateo, CA: Morgan Kaufman.

Swim, J. K., Aikin, K. J., Hall, W. S., & Hunter, B. A. (1995). Sexism and racism: Old-fashioned and modern prejudices. *Journal of Personality and Social Psychology, 68,* 199–214.

Till, R. E., Mross, E. F., & Kintsch, W. (1988). Time course of priming for associate and inference words in a discourse context. *Memory & Cognition, 16,* 283–298.

Trope, Y. (1986). Identification and inferential processes in dispositional attribution. *Psychological Review, 93,* 239–257.

Trope, Y., Cohen, O. & Alfieri, T. (1991). Behavior identification as a mediator of dispositional inference. *Journal of Personality and Social Psychology, 61,* 873–883.

Uleman, J. S., & Moskowitz, G. B. (1994). Unintended effects of goals on unintended inferences. *Journal of Personality and Social Psychology, 66,* 490–501.

Broek, P. van den (1990). Causal inferences and the comprehension of narrative text. In A. C. Graesser & G. H. Bower (Eds.), *Inferences and text comprehension* (pp. 175–196). San Diego, CA: Academic Press.

Hippel, W. von, Sekaquaptewa, D., & Vargas, P. (1995). On the role of encoding processes in stereotype maintenance. In M. Zanna (Ed.). *Advances in experimental social psychology* (Vol. 27, pp. 117–254). San Diego, CA: Academic Press.

Winter, L., & Uleman, J. S. (1984). When are social judgments made? Evidence for the spontaneousness of trait inferences. *Journal of Personality and Social Psychology, 47,* 237–252.

Winter, L., Uleman, J. S., & Cunniff, C. (1985). How automatic are social judgments? *Journal of Personality and Social Psychology, 49,* 904–917.

Woll, S., Weeks, D. G., Fraps, C. L., Pendergrass, J., & Vanderplas, M. A. (1980). Role of sentence context in the encoding of trait descriptors. *Journal of Personality and Social Psychology, 39,* 59–68.

Woll, S., & Yopp, H. (1978). The role of context and inference in the comprehension of social action. *Journal of Experimental Social Psychology, 14,* 351–362.

Received March 21, 1996
Revision received December 16, 1996
Accepted December 23, 1996 ■

We Talk, Therefore We Think? A Cultural Analysis of the Effect of Talking on Thinking

Heejung S. Kim

The Western assumption that talking is connected to thinking is not shared in the East. The research examines how the actual psychology of individuals reflects these different cultural assumptions. In Study 1, Asian Americans and European Americans thought aloud while solving reasoning problems. Talking impaired Asian Americans' performance but not that of European Americans. Study 2 showed that participants' beliefs about talking and thinking are correlated with how talking affects performance, and suggested that cultural difference in modes of thinking can explain the difference in the effect of talking. Study 3 showed that talking impaired Asian Americans' performance because they tend to use internal speech less than European Americans. Results illuminate the importance of cultural understanding of psychology for a multicultural society.

A professor ... encourages his Asian students to speak up in class by making it part of the class grade. He makes speaking in front of the class mandatory for some assignments. "Once they understand this is the norm you expect, they'll get used to it," he says. "But you have to make it clear." (Lubman, 1998, p. A12)

This article draws on a dissertation completed by Heejung S. Kim under the guidance of Hazel Rose Markus at Stanford University, which received the 2002 Society of Experimental Social Psychology Dissertation Award. This research was supported by a Social Science Research Council student research grant and a Standard University Graduate Research Opportunity grant.

I thank Yosup Joo, Joan Chiao, and Eddie Kim for their help with data collection, and David K. Sherman, Hazel Rose Markus, R. B. Zajonc, Eric D. Knowles, and Keren Gudeman for commenting on earlier versions of this article.

Correspondence concerning this article should be addressed to Heejung S. Kim, who is now at the Department of Humanities and Social Sciences, Harvey Mudd College, 301 East 12th Street. Claremont, California 91711–5990. E-mail: Heejung_kim@hmc.edu

As reported in the *San Jose Mercury News* (Lubman, 1998), many colleges in the United States with a large population of Asian and Asian American students are concerned about the students' silence in class. The silence of Asian students is a concern for universities who want their students to be "independent thinkers." Motivating this concern is the notion that getting students to talk is a way to make them "better" thinkers. In discussing this issue, the news article details the concern of many educators who are trying to make silent students more vocal, and at the same time, reveals a number of educational assumptions about the relationship between talking and thinking.

One assumption is that talking is a positive act, and there are at least two reasons for this. First, talking is a positive act because it is an expression of the individual (Bellah, Madsen, Sullivan, Swidler, & Tipton, 1985). Talking is a basic means through which individuals express their ideas, points of view, and individuality — the core value of American culture. Therefore, the effort to encourage verbal expression of thoughts is a good and justifiable act. Second, talking is a positive act because it is closely connected with thinking. Language and its verbal expression in talking can create, change, and signify thinking, and hence, one can generally equate talking and thinking. Thus, talking is often taken to mean that the speaker is engaged in thinking, obviously an important act. Underpinning the assumption that talking is a positive act is the assumption of psychic unity (Bruner, 1996; Shweder, 1995), that is, it is assumed that the close relationship between talking and thinking is true for everyone, and the same positive meaning of talking should be shared by everyone.

These assumptions are commonly held in Western cultural contexts. Indeed, the Western assumption about near equivalence of talking and thinking is still very pervasive and fundamental to the study of the mind, despite the abundant research to show that the positive meaning of talking is culturally specific rather than universal (e.g., Azuma, 1986; Gudykunst, Gao, & Franklyn-Stokes, 1996; Kim & Markus, 2002; Marsella, 1993; Minami, 1994; Smith & Bond, 1999; Tobin, Wu, & Davidson, 1989). The potential influence of cultural meanings and practices on the assumption of closeness of talking and thinking is usually overlooked, and the equivalence is thought to be "the nature of human nature" (Bruner, 1996, p. 16). The present research addresses this question of whether the assumption of equivalence of talking and thinking is a product of particular Western sociocultural experiences that may not necessarily generalize to other cultural contexts. More specifically, in three studies participants from different cultural contexts (i.e., East Asia and America) engaged in cognitive problem solving while talking, showing the different effects of talking on performance (i.e., facilitating, interfering, or no effect) and the underlying process that contributes to this difference.

Cultural Differences in the Assumptions About Talking and Thinking

The assumption that talking and language are closely related to human thinking can be easily found in the Western intellectual tradition throughout history from the ancient philosophers (Barnes, 1965) to contemporary linguists and psychologists (e.g., Ericsson & Simon, 1980, 1993; Whorf, 1956; Wierzbicka, 1992). In the Western intellectual tradition, thinking and talking have been thought to be interdependent since ancient Greek civilization. For example, Homer considered one

of the most important skills for a man to have to be that of the debater (Nisbett, Peng, Choi, & Norenzayan, 2001). Sophists commonly emphasized the eristic methods that are skills of disputation (Barnes, 1965). Also, Socrates viewed knowledge as existing within people and needing only to be recovered through verbal reasoning, as reflected in his dialectic method (Barnes, 1965; M. Hunt, 1993), and Plato believed that thought is "the soul's discourse with itself (as shown in Miller, 1981)." In Judeo–Christian and Islamic beliefs, the "Word" is considered sacred because of its divine power to create (Armstrong, 1993). In the Bible, for example, the word is equated with God and with the divine tool of creation (Metzger & Coogan, 1993).

This assumption about the connectedness of thinking and talking persists and has been incorporated into many psychological models of thinking. Language is both a central topic in the study of human cognition as well as an important tool to study how people think. For example, J. B. Watson (1924) viewed thinking as consisting of primarily subvocal speech. Also, the well-known Whorfian hypothesis (Whorf, 1956) asserts that thoughts are molded by the syntax and vocabulary of one's native language. Although the strict Whorfian view that thought is entirely determined by language is no longer accepted, variations of this view are still widely discussed (e.g., E. Hunt & Agnoli, 1991; Markman & Hutchinson, 1984; Slobin, 1996). Certainly, many psychologists have also pointed out that talking can often be at odds with thinking because people do not often have conscious access to their thought processes or because some thought processes are not easily verbalizable (e.g., Fallshore & Schooler, 1995; Nisbett & Wilson, 1977; Schooler & Engstler-Schooler, 1990; Schooler, Ohlsson, & Brooks, 1993; Wilson & Schooler, 1991). Nevertheless, verbal reports of thinking processes (e.g., thinking aloud) continue to be used as valid data for analysis of many cognitive processes (for reviews, see Ericsson & Simon, 1980, 1993). These examples suggest that language occupies an important position in the Western study of the human mind.

The assumptions about language and talking are different in the East Asian cultural tradition (Kim & Markus, 2002). Since ancient Chinese civilization, East Asians did not assume the connectedness between talking and thinking. Not only are philosophical and religious discussions on language and thought and a tradition of debate largely absent, but also, East Asians believe that states of silence and introspection are considered beneficial for high levels of thinking, such as the pursuit of the truth. This assumption is well expressed in Buddhist and Taoist practices, such as meditation (Gard, 1962; Rinpoche, 1987; Robinet, 1993; Stein, 1979). According to Buddhist teaching, one can reach the power of living without getting stained by impurities through the stillness in meditation (Rinpoche, 1987). Moreover, Taoist teaching emphasizes the practices of silence, internal visualization, concentration, and regulation of breathing to reach the "Supreme Truth" (Robinet, 1993).

This overview of how talking has been conceived in these cultural contexts is, of course, a summary of idealized modes of thinking in each cultural tradition, rather than how these ideals are used in everyday life. In everyday situations, both sets of seemingly contradictory assumptions can be found in both cultural contexts. Also, there is an overlap of these assumptions across cultures as well as diversity in the assumptions within a cultural context reflecting the complex nature of human life. Nevertheless, there are differences in the emphasis placed on each set of assumptions and in the prevalence and dominance of the assumptions in different cultural contexts. The cultural difference in the dominance of the assumptions on the relationship between talking and thinking is significant as these dominant assumptions can influence and reflect the modal cultural institutions and practices, and consequently how individuals engage in thinking itself.

Talking as a Cultural Practice

Cultural assumption are often "conventionalized" in cultural ways of doing things in which these assumptions are reflected, and individual psychology may be influenced by these cultural ways of doing things (Bruner, 1996). When there are large differences in practices and interactions in different cultural contexts, there might be different psychological tendencies related to the practices and interactions. Therefore, the examination of cultural differences in how people are engaged in talking practices along with the examination of beliefs should provide valuable information on the contexts in which the psychological phenomenon of the effect of talking on thinking takes place.

Cultural assumptions are often manifested in processes of socialization (Bruner, 1996; Minami, 1994; Segall, Dasen, Berry, & Poortinga, 1999). For example, how people raise and teach their children is influenced by the cultural ideals of how a child should be. Indeed, the cultural differences found in interactions and practices regarding the act of talking are largely

consistent with cultural differences in the assumptions about talking and thinking.

According to Caudill and Weinstein (1969), Japanese middle-class mothers speak much less frequently to their young children than do their American counterparts. Moreover, Chinese preschool teachers see quietness as a means of control, rather than passivity, and appreciate silence more than American teachers (Tobin et al., 1989). Consequently, East Asian children tend to be not as verbal as their European American counterparts. Japanese children produce significantly fewer utterances per turn than North American children (Minami, 1994), and they use verbal expression to communicate emotions less frequently than do American children (Caudill & Schooler, 1973). Also, Chinese infants at 7 months of age and older generally vocalize less than European American infants in response to laboratory events (Kagan, Kearsley, & Zelazo, 1977). This cultural difference in the relative importance of verbal communication demonstrated at a very early age holds for adults as well.

In East Asian cultural contexts, indirect and nonverbal communication of meanings in conversations are more strongly assumed than in European American cultural contexts (Azuma, 1986; Clancy, 1986; Gudykunst et al., 1996; Gudykunst, Ting-Toomey, & Chua, 1988; Hall, 1976; Minami, 1994; Markus, Kitayama & Heiman, 1996; Smith & Bond, 1999). Thus, in a Stroop task in which words are presented in a vocal tone with contradictory emotional meanings (e.g., hearing *enjoy* in an angry tone), Japanese participants' judgment was more influenced by nonverbal cues than was American participants' judgment (Kitayama & Ishii, 2002). These results suggest the relatively greater importance of nonverbal aspects of communications in East Asian cultural contexts than in European American cultural contexts. Cultural practices are often shaped to promote and foster certain psychological tendencies desired by a particular cultural worldview (Bruner, 1996). Thus, psychological tendencies of talking and thinking might differ across cultures as much as cultural practices of talking differ across cultures.

Cultural Modes of Thinking and Their Psychological Effects

Understanding the cultural influence on the relationship between talking and thinking also requires the examination of the modes of thinking that are common and idealized in different cultural contexts because how talking affects thinking should depend on the nature of thinking as well as the nature of talking. Cultural analyses on cognition have suggested that the particular cultural meanings and practices tend to foster particular modes of thinking that are idealized in the given cultural context (Bruner, 1996; Greenfield, 1997). It has been well documented that there are reliable differences in the modes of thinking between people from the East and people from the West (e.g., Fiske, Kitayama, Markus, & Nisbett, 1998; Lin, 1935; Nakamura, 1964; Needham, 1962; Nisbett et al., 2001). People from East Asian cultural contexts tend to adopt a holistic style of reasoning in which many elements are held at the same time in thought in order to grasp the gestalt of the parts. In contrast, people from Western cultural contexts tend to adopt an analytic style of reasoning in which objects are broken up into their component elements (Fiske et al., 1998; Lin, 1935; Nakamura, 1964; Needham, 1962; Nisbett et al., 2001; Peng & Nisbett, 1999).

One of the corollaries of these differences might be the importance of language in cognitive processes. Research has shown that the nature of the effect of verbalization largely depends on the type of task (for reviews, see Ericsson & Simon, 1993; Wilson, 1994). Thinking processes involved with analytical cognitive tasks are found to be easily verbalizable, and hence, performance tends not to be impaired by verbalization (Ericsson & Simon, 1993; Schooler et al., 1993). However, thought processes involved with insight problem solving (Schooler et al., 1993), affective judgment (Wilson & Schooler, 1991), or holistic tasks (Penney, 1975) are not easy to verbalize, and performance tends to be hurt by verbalization because people do not necessarily have conscious access to their thought processes. Putting together these findings on the effect of verbalization on different types of cognitive tasks and cultural difference in the mode of thinking (i.e., holistic vs. analytical), it is reasonable to hypothesize that East Asians who tend to use holistic thinking would be negatively affected by talking, but European Americans who tend to adopt analytical thinking would not be negatively affected by talking. The present research provides a direct examination of the cultural differences in the effect of talking and thinking, and investigates the mechanism through which these differences emerge.

Overview

The purpose of the present research is to examine the effect of talking on thinking (i.e., cognitive problem solving) in relation to the cultural assumptions about talking and thinking in East Asian and European American cultural contexts. Three studies were conducted to show that cultural assumptions about the relationship between talking and thinking are indeed consistent with the psychological realities in respective cultural contexts. In all three studies, thinking was operationalized as performance on a standardized reasoning test, and therefore, better performance means "good thinking."

Study 1 was designed as an initial demonstration of the cultural differences between East Asian Americans and European Americans in the actual effect of talking on thinking and illustrates that the actual effect of talking on thinking is consistent with the cultural assumptions regarding the relationship between talking and thinking. Using the *thinking-aloud* method, the study tested how verbalization of the problem-solving process influences performance on a reasoning test depending on whether participants were from an East Asian American or European American cultural context.

Study 2 was conducted to examine the relationship between the effect of talking on thinking and cultural assumptions that are expressed in the forms of individual beliefs on talking and thinking, and socialization practices regarding talking and thinking. Study 2 replicated the basic findings from Study 1 and also included measures of explicit beliefs on talking and thinking, parental practices, and modes of thinking to better understand the role of cultural beliefs and socialization practices in the shaping of psychological processes.

Study 3 was designed to examine the cross-cultural differences in the underlying cognitive mechanism that might give rise to the phenomenon demonstrated in Study 1 and builds on the findings on the modes of thinking in Study 2. More specifically, Study 3 tested the hypothesis that the diverging effect of talking on thinking across cultures can be explained by a different level of dependency on language in the process of problem solving adopted by people from different cultural contexts.

Study 1

Study 1 tested the idea that the different cultural assumptions on the relationship between talking and thinking would be reflected in a difference in the actual effect of talking on cognitive problem-solving performance of people from different cultural contexts. It was hypothesized that European Americans from a cultural tradition in which talking is thought to be closely related to thinking would not be hindered in their performance on a reasoning test by talking, as previously demonstrated by other researchers (for a review, see Ericsson & Simon, 1980). It was also hypothesized that East Asian Americans from a cultural tradition where talking is thought to interfere with thinking would perform worse when they are talking than when they are silent.

Method

Participants
Thirty-four East Asian American (24 women and 10 men) and 41 European American (28 women and 13 men) undergraduates at Stanford University participated in the study in return for credit in an introductory psychology course. All the participants indicated that their native and dominant language was English. All European American participants were third- or older-generation Americans (i.e., both of their parents were also born and raised in the United States), whereas all East Asian Americans were second-generation Americans (i.e., both of their parents were immigrants from East Asian countries).[1]

Materials
Participants completed Advanced Raven's Progressive Matrices Set II (Raven, 1941). Raven's Progressive Matrices were used in the study because the task has been found to be closely linked to general intelligence (see Snow, Kyllonen, & Marshalek, 1984), and to measure "domain-free reasoning processes" (Carpenter, Just, & Shell, 1990). Moreover, the task is supposed to require analytical thinking, and previous research with participants from Western cultural contexts showed that although the matrices themselves are nonverbal in nature, the participants tend to work on more challenging matrices in a verbal way (Sokolov, 1972).

Advanced Raven's Progressive Matrices Set II consist of a series of items, each including various abstract figures that are arranged in nine cells in a 3×3 matrix. The lower right cell is always blank. The contents of the eight filled cells are determined by various rules that must be figured out by the participant and then applied to generate the correct contents of the empty cell. Eight possible options for the empty cell are given under the

matrix, and the participant is expected to choose one of the eight options that best fit the empty cell.

Raven's Progressive Matrices are devised to begin with a relatively easy item and become progressively more difficult as the item number goes up. Among the total of 36 Advanced Matrices Set II, only items 17–36 — the more difficult items — were used in the study. The order of items in the presentation was randomized to avoid the progressive nature of the test, hence making the test more difficult. Once the items were selected, the test was computerized using PsyScope (Cohen, MacWhinney, Flatt, & Provost, 1993).

Procedure
When the participant arrived at the lab, an experimenter, who was unaware of the hypothesis, explained that the purpose of the study was to examine the cognitive processes of problem solving. The participant was randomly assigned to one of two conditions: *control* condition or *thinking-aloud* condition. In the control condition, the participant did not receive any additional instructions apart from the basic instructions on how to solve the problems. In the thinking-aloud condition, the experimenter instructed the participant to talk aloud his or her thought process while working on the problems. Then, the experimenter set up a tape recorder and informed the participant that his or her vocalization of thinking process would be recorded for future analysis. Once the participant understood the task, the experimenter left the room, and the participant worked on the task alone.

During most thinking-aloud experiments, the experimenter is present in the same room as a participant (Ericsson & Simon, 1993). However, participants in the present studies were kept in a room alone to minimize any evaluation apprehension (Cottrell, Wack, Sekerak, & Rittle, 1968). It is possible that East Asian American participants might feel more self-conscious than European American participants might, because people from the East Asian cultural contexts tend to care more about others' view of themselves (Lim, 1994). Thus, privacy was ensured in the present studies to minimize this potential confound.

The task and instructions were presented on a computer. First, the participant was instructed to solve one practice item. When the answer for the item was typed, the correct answer was given to ensure that the participant understood the instructions for the test. Then, the real test began and 20 matrices were presented on the computer screen. The participant was instructed to type the number of the correct answer using the keyboard. There was no time limit for the test, and the participant

---

[1] These East Asian American participants were preselected because their parental upbringing is more likely to reflect East Asian parenting styles, yet their English proficiency would be as good as their European American counterparts.

was allowed to work on the task at his or her own pace. The session in the thinking-aloud condition was recorded to ensure that participants would follow instructions by thinking aloud. Participants' performance — both accuracy (number correct) and time spent to complete the test — was automatically measured by the computer.

After participants finished the task, they were instructed to fill out a questionnaire that contained a subset of the Positive and Negative Affect Schedule (PANAS; D. Watson, Clark, & Tellegen, 1988) that is relevant to evaluation apprehension, such as *afraid, ashamed, distressed, nervous*, and *scared*. The mood questionnaire was included to measure the level of nervousness experienced by participants to make sure that the manipulation did not induce different levels of evaluation apprehension for the different cultural groups. Finally, once participants completed the experiment, they were debriefed, thanked, and excused.

Results

The results supported the hypothesis that European Americans' performance would not be impaired by talking, whereas East Asian Americans' performance would be impaired by talking. Participants' gender did not have any effect, and thus, will not be mentioned further. The primary dependent variable was the number of

items answered correctly. The numbers of items answered correctly was subjected to a 2 (culture: European American vs. East Asian American) × 2 (condition: Control vs. thinking aloud) analysis of variance (ANOVA). The test revealed that there was no main effects of culture. $F (1, 74) = 2.50$, *ns.* or of condition, $F(1, 74) = 2.39$, *ns*, on how many items were answered correctly. However, there was the predicted interaction between condition and culture. $F(1, 74) = 5.23$, $p < .05$. Planned comparisons with independent samples *t* tests revealed that East Asian American participants' performance was worse when they had to think aloud ($M = 9.24$, $SD = 4.04$, $n = 17$) than when they were not thinking aloud ($M = 12.35$, $SD = 2.62$, $n = 17$), $t(32) = 2.67$, $p < .05$. European American participants' performance, however, did not differ whether they were thinking aloud ($M = 9.76$, $SD = 3.48$, $n = 21$) or not ($M = 9.35$, $SD = 3.01$, $n = 20$), $t(39) = 0.40$, *ns* (see Figure 4.1).

Next, I subjected the length of time (in minutes) taken to complete the task to a 2 (culture: European American vs. East Asian American) × 2 (condition: Control vs. thinking aloud) ANOVA. The length of time was not significantly affected by the condition, $F(1, 74) = 1.66$, *ns*, nor by the culture, $F(1, 74) = 0.59$, *ns*. There was also no significant interaction between culture and condition, $F(1, 74) = 0.04$, *ns*. These results show that the length of time spent to complete the task

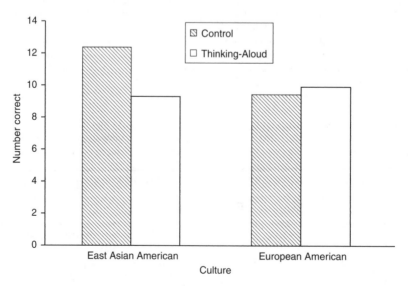

FIGURE 4.1 ■ Mean number correct as a function of talking and culture in Study 1.

was not a confounding factor. In other words, the interaction of culture and condition in performance was not due to the different length of time participants spent on the task in different conditions.

Finally, the mood measured by the PANAS to assess the level of evaluation apprehension due to talking was also subjected to a 2 (culture: European American vs. East Asian American) × 2 (condition: Control vs. thinking-aloud) ANOVA. There was no significant main effect or interaction on any of the mood measures. The analysis revealed that East Asian American participants did not experience any more evaluation apprehension in the thinking-aloud condition.

Discussion

The results support the hypothesis that talking would not interfere with European American participants' cognitive performance whereas talking would interfere with East Asian American participants' performance. When the prevailing cultural assumption is that talking is closely related to thinking, talking can indeed be closely related to thinking. At the same time, when the prevailing cultural assumption is that talking is a disturbance to thinking, talking can interfere with the thinking process.

These results provide initial support for cultural differences in how talking affects thinking, and that this difference would be consistent with the cultural assumptions on the relationship between talking and thinking. However, the study alone does not explain the cultural differences in how talking affects thinking. In Study 2, I address how the psychological differences demonstrated in Study 1 are connected to culture, more specifically to the beliefs and practices shared within a culture.

Study 2

The present research argues that cultural assumptions regarding the relationship between talking and thinking vary across cultures, and these differences in cultural assumptions can lead to the actual psychological phenomenon of how talking affects thinking. Thus, Study 2 was conducted to understand the connectedness between cultural assumptions and the effect of talking on thinking, focusing on the role of cultural beliefs and practices as potential carriers of cultural assumptions through which psychology is shaped.

There were a few specific questions asked in Study 2. The first question was whether East Asian Americans and European Americans would differ in their explicit beliefs about talking and thinking. The second question was whether there are differences in cultural practices between East Asian Americans and European Americans, more specifically parenting style regarding talking, and whether these cultural practices reflect the respective cultural assumptions. The third question was whether East Asian Americans and European Americans differ in their self-perceptions of how much they rely on language in their thinking when solving problems. This question was addressed in the study because cultural differences in how people think might be a potential underlying mechanism for the demonstrated phenomenon. Research suggests that there are cultural differences in modes of thinking (Nisbett et al., 2001) in which East Asians tend to be more holistic whereas Westerners tend to be more analytic in their cognitive processes. These cultural differences in modes of thinking might be related to how much a thinker relies on internal speech that, in turn, might lead to cultural differences in the effect of talking on thinking. Finally, the fourth question was how these explicit and implicit representations of cultural assumptions are related to the actual effect of talking on thinking.

In Study 2, a few procedural changes were made from Study 1. First, the participants in the control condition were explicitly told not to talk in Study 2, thus the condition will be referred to as the *Silence* condition. This change was made to ensure that participants would work on the task in silence because some participants might naturally think aloud in the control condition in which there is no specific instructions to be silent. Second, comparisons between the silence condition and the talking condition were made using a within-subject design in Study 2, unlike the between-subjects design in Study 1. Thus, participants' performance in the silence condition provides a within-subject baseline comparison. Third, the whole session, including the silence condition, was recorded to ensure that participants closely followed the experimental instructions either to talk or not to talk.

The hypothesis was that there would be cultural differences in beliefs, practices, and modes of thinking, and that these beliefs, practices, and modes of thinking would be correlated with the actual effect of talking on thinking.

Method

Participants
Twenty-two East Asian American (8 women and 14 men) and 23 European American (12 women and 11 men) undergraduates at the University of California.

Los Angeles participated in the study in return for credit in an introductory psychology course. As in Study 1, all the participants indicated that their native language is English.

Material

The same items of Advanced Raven's Progressive Matrices Set II as in Study 1 were used in Study 2. The 20 items were divided into two within-subject sections (i.e., silence condition and talking condition) so that each section presented 10 items.[2]

Questionnaires

Three sets of questions were used in the study. The first set of questions was created to measure individuals' explicit beliefs regarding the relationship between talking and thinking. The questions asked participants how much they agree with statements such as "talking clarifies thinking" or "only in silence, can one have clear thoughts and ideas."

The second set of questions was created to measure differences in the cultural practices (i.e., parenting style). The questionnaire asked participants how verbal their interactions with their parents have been, and how much they were encouraged to articulate their point of view throughout the course of their relationships.

The third set of questions examined participants' perception of their own mode of thinking. More specifically, it asked participants to indicate how much they relied on language when they work on Raven's Progressive Matrices. All three questionnaires used 8-point scales and can be found in the Appendix.

Procedure

When a participant arrived at the lab, an experimenter, who was unaware of the hypotheses of the study, explained that the purpose of the study was to examine the cognitive processes of problem solving. At the beginning of the study, participants received the talking-belief questionnaire and the talking-practice questionnaire presented on the computer. Then, the participant was asked to solve a set of 20 problems selected from Raven's Progressive Matrices according to specific instructions shown on the computer screen. The experimenter set up a tape recorder for the participant, pushed the record button, and left the room where the participant worked on the problems alone, and subsequent instructions were given by the computer.

There were two parts in the experiment. In each part, participants were asked to solve 10 problems. In the first part of the experiment, every participant was instructed to solve a set of 10 problems in silence. After participants completed the first part, but before they began the second part, they received the mode-of-thinking questionnaire. The timing of this questionnaire was chosen for participants to reflect on their mode of thinking with the specific task (i.e., Raven's Progressive Matrices) but not to be influenced by their performance in the second part of the experiment. Finally, in the second part of the experiment, every participant was instructed to think aloud. In other words, the study had a 2 (culture: European American vs. East Asian American) $\times$ 2 (talking: silence vs. thinking aloud) design in which talking was a within-subject variable.

Once participants completed the experiment, they were debriefed, thanked, and excused. Participants' responses to the questionnaires and performance in terms of both accuracy (number correct) and time to complete each session was measured by the computer.

Results

The Effect of Talking on Performance

The results replicated the basic pattern of interaction of culture and thinking aloud as only East Asian American participants' performance was impaired by thinking aloud, but not European American participants' performance. The number of items answered correctly was subjected to a 2 (culture: European American vs. East Asian American) $\times$ 2 (talking: Silence vs. thinking aloud) multivariate analysis of variance (MANOVA). Overall, there was no main effect of culture. $F(1, 43) = 3.30$, *ns*, or talking, $F(1, 43) = 0.01$, *ns*. However, there was the expected two-way interaction between culture and talking, $F(1, 43) = 9.99$, $p < .01$.

To examine specifically how thinking aloud affected performance of participants from different cultural contexts, the number correct was subjected to planned comparisons with paired t tests. The analyses showed that East Asian American participants' performance was negatively affected by thinking aloud (silence condition: $M = 5.27$, $SD = 2.07$; thinking-aloud condition: $M = 4.45$, $SD = 2.13$), $t(22) = 2.25$, $p < .05$, whereas European American participants' performance was enhanced by thinking-aloud (silence condition: $M = 3.30$, $SD = 2.32$; thinking-aloud condition: $M = 4.17$, $SD = 2.48$), $t(23) = 2.23$, $p < .05$ (see Figure 4.2).

The effect of talking on the length of time (in minutes) taken to complete the task was also subjected to a

---

[2] The level of difficulty in these two parts was the same according to participants' performance in Study 1.

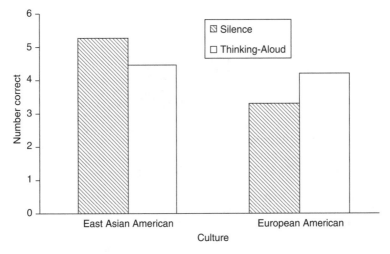

FIGURE 4.2 ■ Mean Number Correct as a Function of Talking and Culture in Study 2.

2 (culture: European American vs. East Asian American) × 2 (talking: Silence vs. thinking aloud) MANOVA. Overall, there was no main effect of culture, $F(1, 43) = 3.01$, ns, or interaction that involves culture, $F(1, 43) = 0.12$, ns. Again, these results show that the interaction effect of culture and talking on performance was not due to the different length of time participants spent on the task in different conditions.

Beliefs, Practices, and Modes of Thinking
Participants' responses to the three questionnaires were examined. First, responses to the three sets of questions (i.e., talking belief, talking practice, mode of thinking) were reverse-coded with necessary items, and averaged for each set of questions so that higher numbers indicate greater importance of talking in thinking, and these numbers were used for further analyses. Talking-practice questions and mode-of-thinking questions were highly intercorrelated (Cronbach's $\alpha = .78$ for practice and .89 for mode of thinking). Talking-beliefs questions were weakly intercorrelated (Cronbach's $\alpha = .24$).[3]

As predicted, significant cultural differences emerged on the measures of beliefs, practices, and modes of

TABLE 4.1 Beliefs, Practices, and Modes of Thinking as a Function of Culture

Talking/thinking Representations	European Americans		East Asian Americans	
	M	SD	M	SD
Talking beliefs	5.14	0.97	4.54	0.90*
Talking practices	5.89	1.01	4.51	1.23***
Modes of thinking	4.02	1.89	2.86	1.68*

* $p < .05$.   *** $p < .001$.

thinking (see Table 4.1). With the talking-belief questionnaire. European American participants ($M = 5.14$, $SD = 0.97$) agreed more with statements in which talking is connected with good thinking than East Asian American participants did ($M = 4.54$, $SD = 0.90$), $t(42) = 2.14$, $p < .05$. This result suggests that cultural assumptions on talking and thinking in East Asian and European American cultures are shared by individuals from their respective cultural contexts in spite of the fact that East Asian American participants in the present study were born and raised in the United States.

Moreover, there was a large cultural difference in participants' responses to the talking-practice questionnaire. European American participants were more likely to report that they have more verbal interaction with their parents ($M = 5.89$, $SD = 1.01$) than were East Asian American participants ($M = 4.51$, $SD = 1.23$),

---

[3] The intercorrelation of talking belief questions was probably low because the questions include multiple factors (i.e., "talking is a sign of intelligence" and "talking clarifies thinking"). Development of a scale with a more extended version of the questionnaire is currently underway. Meanwhile, the combined responses on talking beliefs were used for analysis in the present study.

$t(42) = 4.08$, $p < .001$. This large difference between two cultural groups supports the idea that cultural assumptions are reflected in parental practices.

Also, significant cultural difference was found with the questionnaire on mode of thinking. European American participants reported that they rely on language more in their thinking ($M = 4.02$, $SD = 1.89$) than East Asian American participants did ($M = 2.86$, $SD = 1.68$), $t(42) = 2.15$, $p < .05$. Thus, these results provide initial support for the cultural difference in the modes of thinking as a potential underlying mechanism for the cultural difference in the effect of talking on thinking.

In addition, correlational analyses were also conducted and these analyses suggested that the effect of thinking aloud on performance is related to various measures of representations of cultural assumptions. First, to examine the effect of talking on performance, the talking effect score was calculated by subtracting participants' performance in the silence condition from the thinking-aloud condition. Hence, positive numbers of the talking effect score indicate enhancement due to talking, and negative numbers indicate interference from talking. These talking effect scores were then examined in relation to other measures in which a greater number also indicates greater importance of talking.

Correlational analyses showed that the talking beliefs, $r(44) = .39$, $p < .05$, and the mode of thinking, $r(44) = .31$, $p < .05$, were significantly correlated with the talking effect score (see Table 4.2). In other words, participants who believed that talking and thinking are closely related tend to perform better with talking, and participants who reported that they rely on language in their thinking also tend to perform better with talking.

The analyses showed that the talking practice was not significantly correlated with the talking effect score, $r(44) = .15$, ns. Thus, the nature of parental practices did not seem to be directly related to the way in which talking affected performance. However, further analyses revealed that the talking practice was significantly correlated with the talking beliefs, $r(44) = .39$, $p < .01$, and also with the mode of thinking, $r(44) = .38$, $p < .05$ (see Table 4.2). That is, participants who have more verbal interactions with their parents are more likely to both believe that talking and thinking are closely related and report that they rely on language when they think. Given that both the talking beliefs and the mode of thinking are significantly correlated with performance, parental practices might have an indirect effect on performance.

TABLE 4.2 Correlations Among Beliefs, Practices, Modes of Thinking, and the Effect of Talking on Thinking

Talking/thinking representations	1	2	3	4
1. Practices	—			
2. Beliefs	.39**	—		
3. Modes of thinking	.38*	.17	—	
4. Effect of talking on thinking	.15	.39**	.31*	—

* $p < .05$. ** $p < .01$.

Discussion

Results from Study 2 showed the cultural nature of the effect of talking on thinking. First of all, East Asian American participants differ from European American participants in all representations of cultural assumption. That is, European American participants are more likely to believe that talking is good for thinking, more likely to interact in verbal manners with their parents, and more likely to rely on language in their thinking than East Asian American participants are.

Moreover, correlational analyses support the cultural nature of the effect of talking on thinking. Although the talking practice was not shown to be significantly correlated with the effect of talking, it was related both with the talking belief and the mode of thinking that are, in turn, significantly related with the effect of talking on thinking. Thus, people who were engaged in practices that emphasize talking tend to share the belief that talking and thinking are closely related, and also report that language is important in their thinking. Those who believed that talking is closely related to thinking, and also those who claimed that talking is important in their thinking, tend to indeed think better while talking than those who did not. These results show a link between parental practices and individual beliefs, and the way in which talking affects thinking. These results are correlational and obviously cannot show any causal relationships. However, these clearly provide support for the idea that the effect of talking on thinking is connected to cultural assumptions through various cultural representations, such as practices and beliefs.

In addition, these results suggest a potential underlying mechanism through which the cultural difference in the effect of talking can be explained, and that is the role of the mode of thinking. Results indicated that there is not only a cultural difference in how important language is in thinking, but also a significant relationship between the importance of language in thinking and the effect of talking on thinking. In other words, it is plausible that people from a cultural context where talking is considered to be important and beneficial for thinking might be more likely to process their thoughts through language, whereas people from a cultural context where talking is considered to be less important and harmful to thinking might be less likely to process their thoughts through language. On the basis of the cultural differences in the self-perceptions of how much people rely on language in their thinking. I hypothesized that cultural assumptions on talking and thinking influence the actual effect of talking on thinking through the mode of thinking that reflects the idealized mode of thinking within each cultural context. I conducted Study 3 to examine the idea further.

Study 3

Study 3 tested a possible underlying mechanism that can explain the demonstrated cultural difference in Studies 1 and 2. The hypothesis examined in Study 3 is based on the research findings on the effect of verbalization on different types of tasks. When thinking is more verbal in nature, thinking aloud does not seem to affect thinking much, but when thinking is not verbal, thinking aloud appears to interfere with thinking (Schooler et al., 1993). Because people from different cultural contexts tend to adopt different thinking styles (i.e., analytical vs. holistic), their thinking processes might differ in the degree in which they are verbalizable.

Research suggests that East Asians are relatively weak in verbal compared with nonverbal abilities, as measured by standardized tests (Ho, 1994; Vernon, 1982). Also, in a study on the ability to visualize objects from an unusual visual perspective from the Torrance Tests of Creative Thinking, participants from Eastern cultures demonstrated a significantly greater frequency of internal visualizations than did participants from Western cultures (Ball & Torrance, 1978). Although to date there is only limited and indirect empirical support for this hypothesized cultural difference in verbal thinking, the difference in verbal thinking of people from different cultural contexts may explain the demonstrated cultural difference in how talking affects cognitive performance.

To test this idea, Study 3 modified and adopted the procedure used by Merz (1969). The procedure was devised to examine how participants process problem solving by comparing the effect of thinking aloud and articulatory suppression on their performance.

The rationale for the procedure is as follows: The articulatory suppression task (e.g., saying the alphabet out loud) is designed to interfere with the activation of covert articulation by preoccupying the articulating mechanism with irrelevant overt vocal activity. Thus, if a person is engaged in more verbal thinking, the task of thinking aloud should not affect the performance on problem solving very much, because his or her thoughts are ready to be vocalized as words. However, the articulatory-suppression task should strongly impair the performance of a person who is thinking verbally, because the task directly distracts the verbal problem-solving process.

In contrast, if a person is not engaged in verbal thinking, the thinking-aloud task should impair performance, because the person would need to work on an extra task of converting his or her thoughts into words on top of the main problem-solving task. However, articulatory suppression should not distract the problem solving as much because the task does not directly interfere with the person's nonverbal cognitive process that is required for the main task. In other words, for a nonverbal thinker, only thinking aloud, but not articulatory suppression, should significantly impair performance.

Thus, it was hypothesized that European American participants' problem-solving performance would not be impaired by thinking aloud, but that it would be impaired by articulatory suppression. In contrast, it was hypothesized that East Asian American participants' performance would be impaired by thinking aloud, but that their performance would not be affected by articulatory suppression.

Method

Participants
Forty-four East Asian American (29 women and 15 men) and 42 European American (21 women and 21 men) undergraduates at Stanford University participated in the study in return for credit in an introductory psychology course. As in Study 1, all the participants indicated that their native and dominant language was English. Again, all European American participants were third- or older-generation Americans, whereas all East Asian Americans were second-generation Americans.

Material
The same items of Advanced Raven's Progressive Matrices Set II from Studies 1 and 2 were used in the study. The 20 items were divided into two within-subject sections (i.e., silence condition and talking condition) so that each section presented 10 items, as in Study 2.

Procedure

When a participant arrived at the lab, the experimenter, who was unaware of condition assignment, explained that the purpose of the study was to examine the cognitive processes of problem solving. The participant was then instructed to solve a set of 20 problems selected from Raven's Progressive Matrices as presented on the computer screen according to specific instructions shown on the computer screen. The experimenter informed the participant that in a part of the experiment, the participant would be asked to talk aloud. The experimenter set up a tape recorder for the participant, pushed the record button, and left the room where the participant worked on the problem solving alone, and subsequent instructions were given on the computer.

As in Study 2, there were two parts in the experiment. In each part, the participant was asked to solve 10 problems. In the first part of the experiment, the participant in every condition was instructed to solve a set of 10 problems in silence. In the second part of the experiment, the participant in every condition was instructed to talk aloud, but the participant was randomly assigned to one of two conditions of talking aloud: Thinking-aloud condition and articulatory-suppression condition. In the thinking-aloud condition, the participant was instructed to talk aloud through their thought processes while working on the problems. In the articulatory-suppression condition, the participant was instructed to repeat the alphabet from A to Z aloud while he or she was working on the test. Once participants completed the experiment, they were debriefed, thanked, and excused. Participants' performance — both accuracy (number correct) and time to complete each session — was measured by the computer.

Results

The results supported the hypothesis that the cultural difference in the effect of talking on thinking could be explained by the fact that European Americans tend to process cognitive information more verbally than East Asian Americans. First, the number of items answered correctly in the silence condition (i.e., baseline performance) was examined, and there was no main effect or interaction, showing that the baseline performance was comparable across different conditions (see Table 4.3). The effect of talking on the number of items answered correctly was then calculated by subtracting participants' performance in the talking condition from their performance in the silence condition to yield the talking effect score. Thus, positive talking effect scores

TABLE 4.3 Means of Number Correct and Talking Effect Score in Study 3

Talking Type	Silence		Talking	
	M	SD	M	SD
European American				
Thinking aloud ($n = 20$)	4.85	1.98	5.30	2.11
Articulatory suppression ($n = 22$)	5.05	1.84	3.73	1.61
East Asian American				
Thinking aloud ($n = 22$)	6.18	2.11	4.73	2.10
Articulatory suppression ($n = 22$)	5.50	2.02	5.09	1.90

indicate that the performance was better when the participants were talking than when they were in silence, and negative talking effect scores indicate that the performance was worse when the participants were talking than when they were silent.

The talking effect scores were subjected to a 2 (culture: European American vs. East Asian American) × 2 (talking type: Thinking aloud vs. articulatory suppression) ANOVA. Overall, there was no main effect of culture, $F(1, 85) = 1.20$. ns, or talking type, $F(1, 85) = 0.60$, ns, on the effect of talking on thinking. However, there was the expected two-way interaction between culture and talking type, $F(1, 85) = 11.01, p < .01$.

To examine whether thinking aloud or articulatory suppression significantly changed performance, the talking effect scores were compared with zero. One-sample t test revealed that the results in the thinking-aloud condition replicated the findings from Study 1. East Asian American participants' performance was negatively affected by thinking aloud, as measured by the talking effect score ($M = -1.45$, $SD = 1.95$), $t(21) = 3.51$, $p < .01$, whereas European American participants' performance was not affected by thinking aloud ($M = 0.45$, $SD = 2.48$), $t(19) = 0.81$, ns (see Figure 4.3).

The results in the articulatory-suppression condition showed a different pattern from that in the thinking-aloud condition. As predicted, only European American participants' performance was significantly hindered by articulatory suppression, as measured by the talking effect score ($M = -1.32$, $SD = 1.64$), $t(21) = 3.76$, $p < .01$. In contrast, East Asian American participants' performance was not significantly hindered by articulatory suppression ($M = -0.41, SD = 1.74$), $t(21) = 1.11$, ns (see Figure 4.3).

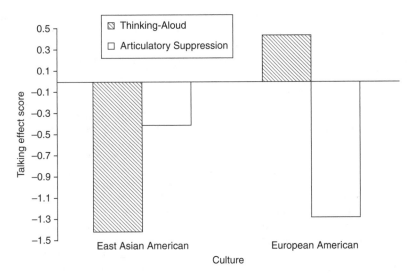

FIGURE 4.3 ■ Mean talking effect score as a function of task type and culture in Study 3.

Additional two-sample *t* tests revealed that East Asian American participants' performance in thinking aloud was, in fact, marginally worse than in articulatory suppression, $t(42) = 1.88$, $p < .07$. It was also shown that European American participants' performance was interfered by articulatory suppression to a somewhat greater degree than East Asian American participants' performance, $t(42) = 1.78$, $p < .09$. These between-group comparisons provided further support that the effect of articulatory suppression was not as debilitating for the performance of East Asian Americans as the thinking-aloud procedure. In addition, articulatory suppression was much more debilitating for the European Americans. In spite of the fact that the articulatory-suppression task is still a distraction for East Asian Americans, even though not a crucial one, it is important to note that East Asian Americans were more negatively affected by thinking aloud than by articulatory suppression.

Finally, the effect of talking on the length of time (in minutes) taken to complete the task was subjected to a 2 (culture: European American vs. East Asian American) × 2 (talking type: Thinking aloud vs. articulatory suppression) ANOVA. Overall, there was no main effect, $F(1, 85) = 2.20$, *ns*, or interaction that involves culture, $F(1,85) = 0.01$, *ns*. Again, these results show that the interaction of culture and talking type with the performance was not due to the different

length of time participants spent on the task in different conditions.

Discussion

The results from Study 3 support the hypothesis. European American problem-solving performance did not differ whether they were thinking aloud or silent. However, it was significantly worse when they were distracted by the articulatory-suppression task than when they were silently working on the task, supporting the hypothesis that their problem-solving process is more verbal. In contrast, East Asian American problem-solving performance was impaired only by thinking aloud but not by articulatory suppression, as predicted by the hypothesis that their problem solving is less verbal.

These results provide support for the idea that European Americans tend to process cognitive information more verbally than East Asian Americans. European Americans only needed to vocalize their thoughts when they were thinking aloud, and it was not necessary to take the extra step of conversion from thoughts to words. In contrast, it seems that East Asian Americans needed to engage in an extra task of transforming their thoughts to words and did not perform as well as in silence. At the same time, when European Americans confronted the articulatory-suppression task while solving problems, the task distracted participants from the problem solving and, consequently, their performance was hurt by the task, whereas East Asian American performance was not hurt by the articulatory-suppression task. The articulatory-suppression task that was designed to suppress internal articulation was distracting for European American participants who are more likely to assume covert articulation. In contrast, the articulatory-suppression task was not as distracting for East Asian participants because they are less likely to use verbal thinking (i.e., internal articulation) and more likely to use nonverbal thinking. The overall pattern of these results suggests that the cultural difference demonstrated in Studies 1 and 2 between European Americans and East Asian Americans in how talking affects thinking can be explained, at least in part, by the fact that European Americans process cognitive information in a more verbal manner than East Asian Americans.

These results emphasize the difference in modes of thinking that people from different cultural contexts use to solve the same set of problems. Although the overall performance of both groups of participants was comparable, the process by which they solved the problems seems to differ, as East Asian American participants tended to use more nonverbal thinking and European American participants tended to use more verbal thinking. This cultural difference in the cognitive process was made salient by the examination of the effect of the manipulations of thinking aloud and articulatory suppression used in the study.

General Discussion

Summary

The present research examined the effect of talking on thinking by focusing on how different cultural assumptions about the relationship between talking and thinking in East Asian and European American cultural contexts are reflected in how talking affects the cognitive processes of East Asians and European Americans. Study 1 examined whether cultural differences in the assumptions about the effect of talking on thinking are reflected in actual individual psychological processes, the problem solving of a standardized reasoning test. Using the thinking-aloud method, the study demonstrated how verbalization of the problem-solving process damaged the performance of East Asian Americans, whereas it did not change the performance of European Americans.

Study 2 tested the relationships between cultural beliefs and practices, and the effect of talking on thinking more directly. The results support the idea that different representations of cultural assumptions are linked to the cultural differences in the effect of talking on thinking demonstrated in Study 1. Also, the results suggested cultural difference in modes of thinking as a potential underlying mechanism for the phenomenon.

On the basis of the finding from Study 2, Study 3 tested the cross-cultural differences in modes of thinking that might give rise to the phenomenon. Study 3 showed that the differential effect of talking on thinking across cultures can be explained by a different degree of dependency on language in the process of problem solving. Indeed, East Asian American's performance was distracted by thinking aloud but not by articulatory suppression, suggesting that they tend not to rely on language in their thinking to the same degree. In contrast, European Americans' performance was not affected by thinking aloud, but strongly impaired by articulatory suppression, showing that they tend to rely on language more in their thinking.

Alternative Explanations for the Findings

The explanation suggested in the present research for the cultural difference in the effect of talking on thinking is the influence of cultural assumptions on the interplay between talking and modes of thinking. Whereas the idea has been supported by the results from the present research, other explanations might be suggested for the phenomenon demonstrated. These explanations include the influence of the language and stereotype threat.

First, the results from the present studies could be explained by the difference in the languages of the participants. Research has shown that language plays an important role in shaping human thoughts. For example, it is argued that speakers with different languages are forced by the structure of their languages to pay attention to certain aspects over other aspects of their experience while they are speaking (Slobin, 1996). Thus, the cultural difference in the effect of talking on thinking might be explained by the fact that the structure of English facilitates analytical thinking whereas the structure of East Asian languages (i.e., Chinese and Japanese) inhibits analytical thinking.

Although accepting the idea that language has a powerful influence on human thoughts and probably plays some role in the cultural differences demonstrated, the findings cannot be explained by the cross-linguistic difference only. It is because the cultural difference was demonstrated in English with European American and East Asian American participants who are native English speakers.

Second, the results might be explained by stereotype threat (Steele, 1997). Stereotype threat is a situational threat that can affect the members of any group about whom a negative stereotype exists, and where negative stereotypes about these groups apply, members of these groups can fear being reduced to that stereotype. Because there is a stereotype about East Asians as being quiet and nonverbal, stereotype threat may have been experienced when East Asian American participants in the experiments were asked to engage in an act of talking that is associated with this stereotype. Stereotype threat suggests another factor that might be related to why East Asian students might have difficulty while talking in class.

One aspect of stereotype threat is that it is a reaction to immediate situational cues as well as a reaction to larger societal level stereotypes. In other words, situational cues such as making one's ethnicity salient or framing the task as a diagnostic test of ability that is relevant to a certain negative stereotype can trigger stereotype threat (Steele & Aronson, 1995). Although stereotype threat might contribute to the negative effect of talking on thinking of East Asian in various social settings, it does not seem to explain the finding from the present research.

In the present studies, the ethnicity of participants was not a salient factor. None of the participants knew that they were recruited to the study because of their ethnicity, and ethnicity was never mentioned or made salient in any way. Moreover, the task was not presented in an evaluative way. Even if working on a reasoning test implied evaluative nature of the task to participants, the evaluative focus of the study was on their performance on the task, not on their ability to articulate. Thus, stereotype threat does not fully explain the results.

Limitations and Future Questions

The purpose of the present research was to demonstrate cultural difference in the effect of talking on thinking and to seek a possible mechanism in how people from different cultural contexts process information. Although the studies were designed to achieve these goals, there are some other important questions that were not yet answered.

First, the present research demonstrated and contextualized the cultural differences in how talking affects thinking and tried to make a connection between culturally shared assumptions and individual psychological tendencies. Whereas the results provide support for the connectedness between culture and the psychological tendencies, the correlational results do not provide a causal explanation about how cultural assumptions and the effect of talking on thinking are related. Thus, it would be beneficial to conduct more direct research that connects cultural practices of talking with the shaping of people's beliefs regarding talking and thinking and also the development of how they think and how they talk. Further examination of the cognitive enculturation process of individuals should provide access to more direct understanding on how culture influences individuals' modes of thinking, and consequently, the effect of talking on thinking.

Second, the present research used a particular type of cognitive task that is supposed to involve more verbal thinking according to previous research, but this task requires neither verbal nor nonverbal thinking by nature, and participants have some flexibility to adopt modes of thinking that they might prefer. Obviously, these are very specific types among many different types of thinking, and whereas the results from the present studies reveal important cultural influence, further research is needed to generalize the findings. A very different pattern of results might emerge with tasks that require more specific styles of thinking, such as entirely verbal tasks or holistic tasks. For example, on the basis of findings on the effect of verbalization on insight problem solving (Penney, 1975; Schooler et al., 1993) where verbalization interfered with problem solving of European Americans, much smaller or no cultural difference might be expected when a task requires holistic thinking. This future research would advance the understanding of the cognitive mechanism for the cultural difference in the effect of talking on thinking.

Third, the present research focused on modes of thinking as an underlying mechanism through which the cultural difference in the effect of talking on thinking is manifested. However, there are probably multiple mechanisms that are likely to contribute to the effect. For example, the act of talking might draw attention to self as one hears his or her voice, and this self-awareness-inducing nature of talking might play a role in how talking affects thinking to the extent that there are cultural differences in the concept of self. Drawing attention to oneself by talking is more likely to be experienced as arousing in East Asian cultural contexts because being singled out is a less common and less positive event (Kim & Markus, 1999; Markus

& Kitayama, 1994), and this arousal might contribute to the impairing effect of talking on thinking. In contrast, it might not lead to the same level of arousal in European American cultural contexts where standing out is a more common and positive event, and hence their thinking is not impaired by talking. Arousal caused by such other social factors might well be contributing to the effect additively along with the difference in cognitive style as shown in the present research, and future research should examine the role of arousal in how talking affects psychology.

Cultural Assumptions, Social Practices, and Psychology

The present research was designed to illustrate an example of the way in which psychological tendencies and processes are interdependent with cultural assumptions (Greenfield, 1997). The results support the hypothesis that the different cultural assumptions about the relationship between talking and thinking are consistent with the respective psychological realities in which talking and thinking relate to each other. The framework of mutual constitution between culture and psychology suggests that this consistency occurs because the cultural assumptions reflect psychological realities and, at the same time, cultural assumptions create reality (Bruner, 1996; Fiske et al., 1998; Markus et al., 1996). The cultural assumptions about talking and thinking become the philosophical and scientific bases of social practices and interactions, and social institutions that become the means by which individual ways of thinking are shaped (Bruner, 1996; Herskovits, 1948; Shweder & Sullivan, 1990). In turn, these actual psychological tendencies reinforce the cultural assumptions represented in the psychological realities.

When there is the assumption that talking is closely related to thinking because good thinking is defined as analytical thinking, people will build their institutions, such as school curricula and teaching philosophy (e.g., Gao, Ting-Toomey, & Gudykunst, 1996; Tobin et al., 1989), and formulate social practices, such as child rearing (e.g., Caudill & Weinstein, 1969; Minami & McCabe, 1995) or interpersonal evaluation (e.g., Henderson & Furnham, 1982; Jones, Briggs, & Smith, 1986), according to the assumptions. Talking will be encouraged and emphasized by parents and teachers to make their children better thinkers, and being articulate becomes a sign of good thinking. Tasks such as talking while thinking are made natural in this cultural context. Thus, these institutions and practices that implicitly

represent cultural assumptions about talking and thinking contribute to the development of an analytical thinking style that can be most aided by talking and foster individual minds in which there is a close connection between talking and thinking.

Undoubtedly, the relationships among cultural assumptions, sociocultural institutions and practices, and individual psychology are not quite as consistent and straightforward as the above example illustrates. Often, coexisting sociocultural practices even in the same cultural context can contradict each other by simultaneously reinforcing inconsistent tendencies from individuals. This inconsistency and complexity in cultural practices and meanings are the nature of culture. However, it is also undeniable that sociocultural institutions and practices are founded on certain sets of assumptions, rather than on random events. Thus, no matter how inconsistent and complex the relationships might be, the sociocultural assumptions, institutions, and practices, and individual psychology are interconnected with each other.

Through these processes of mutual reflection and construction of the culture and psychological reality, there might be as divergent psychological realities as different cultural assumptions. Specific cultural assumptions about psychology are real in the particular cultural contexts because the assumptions reflect and also influence the shaping of psychology in the specific cultural contexts. The assumption that thinking is closely related to talking is true in Western cultural contexts, and at the same time, the assumption that talking and thinking are unrelated to each other is true in East Asian cultural contexts. Psychological reality in one cultural context is not any more real than psychological reality in another cultural context.

Implications for a Multicultural Society

The present research on talking, thinking, and culture suggests a reconsideration of the specific cultural assumptions represented in the growing multicultural America. One implication of the findings is to question the role of culture in the issue of talking and thinking, and more general social and cognitive behaviors. In American education and work settings, talking is strongly emphasized and communicative assertiveness is generally regarded as a sign of a healthy personality (e.g., Cook & St. Lawrence, 1990; Henderson & Furnham, 1982), and anyone who keeps silent tends to be devalued as shy, passive, or lacking independent opinions (e.g., Jones et al., 1986; Zimbardo, 1977). The consequence of the collective silence of East Asians in America is that they are associated with some of these culturally negative traits of people who do not raise their voice.

The present studies suggest that the assumption of talking as a good tool for better thinking may not apply for people who do not share the same set of assumptions. Basic cognitive processes, such as verbal problem solving, are thought of as universally shared "human" tendencies rather than as socioculturally constructed processes (Shweder, 1995). The results from this study support the idea of the social and cultural influence on even "basic" psychological processes.

Another implication of the findings is the importance of recognizing that even very common and basic acts and tasks might imply culturally specific beliefs and assumptions. This idea leads to challenging questions about acculturation and one-way assimilation. Should East Asian students be encouraged to take debate or theatre classes so as to become more comfortable with standing out and expressing oneself, or should mainstream educational principles be encouraged to reflect the fact that there is diversity in styles and conditions of thinking? The findings of this research should lead to a greater appreciation of the value of tolerance for others with different ways of being, and the importance of developing multicultural places in which people from diverse cultural backgrounds can comfortably exist and adjust to different expectations without experiencing a sense of inadequacy.

Problems arise when certain cultural practices are imposed on people who do not share the cultural values behind the practices. The implications of this research should not be limited to East Asian Americans nor to the effects of talking. Often in evaluating people's abilities, people talk about "objective" criteria, such as intelligence or achievement, and desirable personality traits, such as assertiveness or confidence. The present research suggests that before the merit of a person is discussed, the question that needs to be addressed is how culturally "objective" these criteria are, given many of these criteria reflect culturally specific assumptions and realities.

Conclusion

The goal of the present study was to show the consistency between cultural assumptions about thinking and talking and actual psychological tendencies by focusing on basic cognitive process. Whereas future research is left to generalize the findings to different types of think-ing, such as creativity or argumentation, and to different populations, the present research provides an initial demonstration that the relationship between talking and thinking is a lot closer for European Americans than for East Asians. Although one of the goals of the study is certainly to demonstrate the cultural differences in cognition between East Asians and European Americans, the findings from the study illustrate and imply three larger theoretical and practical points.

First, the studies show that cultural assumptions regarding the relationship between talking and thinking can reflect the cultural realities in East Asian cultural contexts and European American contexts. When there is an assumption that talking is closely related to thinking in European American cultural contexts, there is a reality in which talking and thinking are closely related with each other. When there is an assumption that talking interferes with thinking in East Asian cultural contexts, there is an actual reality in which talking interferes with thinking.

Second, how people process information is not free or independent from the social and cultural contexts of the process, and therefore, can have quite divergent behavioral and social consequences. These findings provide a concrete illustration that even very basic psychological realities can be products of cultural beliefs and assumptions that cannot be thought of outside of their cultural contexts.

Third, an implication of the study is that the seemingly same act does not necessarily have the same consequence, if actors are not from cultural contexts where the cultural assumptions behind the act are shared. Because the task of thinking aloud is based on certain cultural assumptions, even with exactly the same task, the consequences of the task for people from cultural contexts where the assumptions are shared is not the same as the consequences of the task for people from cultural contexts where the assumptions are not shared.

To conclude, perhaps making students speak up in class might not be the only way to make them better thinkers for the colleges who are concerned about East Asian students' silence. Another way might be for the colleges to realize that the meaning of students' silence can be the engagement in thoughts, not the absence of ideas. Perhaps instead of trying to change their ways, colleges can learn to listen to their sound of silence.

REFERENCES

Armstrong, K. (1993). *A history of God: The 4000-year quest of Judaism, Christianity and Islam.* New York: Knopf.

Azuma, H. (1986). Why study child development in Japan? In H. Stevenson, H. Azuma, & K. Hakuta (Eds.), *Child development and education in Japan* (pp. 3–12). New York: Freeman.

Bail, O. E., & Torrance, E. P. (1978). Culture and tendencies to draw objects in internal visual perspective. *Perceptual & Motor Skills, 47*, 1071–1075.

Barnes, H. E. (1965). *An intellectual and cultural history of the Western world*. London, England: Dover.

Bellah, R. N., Madsen, R., Sullivan, W. M., Swidler, A., & Tipton, S. M. (1985). *Habits of the heart: Individualism and commitment in American life*. New York: Harper & Row.

Bruner, J. S. (1996). *The culture of education*. Cambridge, MA: Harvard University Press.

Carpenter, P. A., Just, M. A., & Shell, P. (1990). What one intelligence test measures: A theoretical account of the processing in the Raven Progressive Matrices Test. *Psychological Review, 97*, 404–431.

Caudill, W., & Schooler, C. (1973). Child behavior and child rearing in Japan and the United States: An interim report. *Journal of Nervous and Mental Disease, 157*, 323–338.

Caudill, W., & Weinstein, H. (1969). Maternal care and infant behavior in Japan and America. *Psychiatry, 32*, 12–43.

Clancy, P. M. (1986). The acquisition of communicative styles in Japanese. In B. B. Schieffelin & E. Ochs (Eds.), *Language socialization across cultures* (pp. 213–230). Cambridge, England: Cambridge University Press.

Cohen, J. D., MacWhinney, B., Flatt, M., & Provost, J. (1993). PsyScope: A new graphic interactive environment for designing psychology experiments. *Behavioral Research Methods, Instruments, and Computers, 25*, 257–271.

Cook, D. J., & St. Lawrence, J. S. (1990). Variations in presentation format: Effect on interpersonal evaluations of assertive and unassertive behavior. *Behavior Modification, 14*, 21–36.

Cottrell, N. B., Wack, K. L., Sekerak, G. J., & Rittle, R. (1968). Social facilitation in dominant responses by the presence of an audience and the mere presence of others. *Journal of Personality and Social Psychology, 9*, 245–250.

Ericsson, K. A., & Simon, H. A. (1980). Verbal reports as data. *Psychological Review, 87*, 215–251.

Ericsson, K. A., & Simon, H. A. (1993). *Protocol analysis: Verbal reports as data*. Cambridge, MA: MIT Press.

Fallshore, M., & Schooler, J. W. (1995). Verbal vulnerability of perceptual expertise. *Journal of Experimental Psychology: Learning, Memory, and Cognition, 21*, 1608–1623.

Fiske, A. P., Kitayama, S., Markus, H. R., & Nisbett, R. E. (1998). The cultural matrix of social psychology. In D. Gilbert, S. Fiske, & G. Lindzey (Eds.), *Handbook of social psychology* (pp. 915–981). New York: McGraw-Hill.

Gao, G., Ting-Toomey, S., & Gudykunst, W. B. (1996). Chinese communication processes. In M. H. Bond (Ed.), *The handbook of Chinese psychology* (pp. 280–293). Quarry Bay, Hong Kong: Oxford University Press.

Gard, R. A. (Ed.), (1962). *Buddhism*. New York: George Braziller. Inc.

Greenfield, P. M. (1997). You can't take it with you: Why ability assessments don't cross cultures. *American Psychologist, 52*, 1115–1124.

Gudykunst, W. B., Gao, G. & Franklyn-Stokes, A. (1996). Self-monitoring and concern for social appropriateness in China and England. In J. Pandey, D. Sinha, & D. P. S. Bhawuk (Eds.). *Asian contributions to cross-cultural psychology* (pp. 255–267). New Delhi, India: Sage.

Gudykunst, W. B., Ting-Toomey, S., & Chua, E. (1988). *Culture and interpersonal communication*. Newbury Park. CA: Sage.

Hall, E. T. (1976). *Beyond culture*. New York: Doubleday.

Henderson, M., & Furnham, A. (1982). Self-reported and self-attributed scores on personality, social skills and attitudinal measures as compared between high nominated friends and acquaintances. *Psychological Reports, 50*, 88–90.

Herskovits, M. J. (1948). *Man and his works: The science of cultural anthropology*. New York: Knopf.

Ho, D. Y. F. (1994). Cognitive socialization in Confucian heritage cultures. In P. M. Greenfield & R. R. Cocking (Eds.), *Cross-Cultural roots of minority child development* (pp. 285–313). Hillsdale, NJ: Erlbaum.

Hunt, E., & Agnoli, F. (1991). The Whorfian hypothesis: A cognitive psychology perspective. *Psychological Review, 98*, 377–389.

Hunt, M. (1993). *The story of psychology*. New York: Doubleday.

Jones, W. H., Briggs, S. R., & Smith, T. G. (1986). Shyness: Conceptualization and measurement. *Journal of Personality and Social Psychology, 51*, 629–639.

Kagan, J., Kearsley, R. B., & Zelazo, P. R. (1977). The effects of infant day care on psychological development. *Evaluation Quarterly, 1*, 109–142.

Kim, H., & Markus, H. R. (1999). Deviance or uniqueness. harmony or conformity? A cultural analysis. *Journal of Personality and Social Psychology, 77*, 785–800.

Kim, H. S., & Markus, H. R. (2002). Freedom of speech and freedom of silence: An analysis of talking as a cultural practice. In R. Schweder, M. Minow, & H. R. Markus (Eds.), *Engaging cultural differences: The multicultural challenge in liberal democracies* (pp. 432–452). New York: Russell Sage Foundation.

Kitayama, S. & Ishii, K. (2002). Word and voice: Spontaneous attention to emotional speech in two cultures. *Cognition and Emotion, 16*, 29–59.

Lim, T. (1994). Facework and interpersonal relationships. In S. Ting-Toomey (Ed.), *The challenge of facework* (pp. 209–229). Albany, NY: State University of New York Press.

Lin, Y. (1935). *My country, my people*. New York: Halcyon House.

Lubman, S. (1998, February 23). Some students must learn to question. *San Jose Mercury News*, pp. A1, A12.

Markman, E., & Hutchinson, J. (1984). Children's sensitivity to constraints on word meaning: Taxonomic versus thematic relations. *Cognitive Psychology, 16*, 1–27.

Markus, H. R., & Kitayama, S. (1994). A collective fear of the collective: Implications for selves and theories of selves. *Personality and Social Psychology Bulletin, 20*, 568–579.

Markus, H. R., Kitayama, S., & Heiman, R. J. (1996). Culture and "basic" psychological principles. In E. T. Higgins & A. W. Kruglanski (Eds.), *Social psychology: Handbook of basic principles* (pp. 857–913). New York: Guilford Press.

Marsella, A. J. (1993). Counseling and psychotherapy with Japanese Americans: Cross-cultural considerations. *American Journal of Orthopsychiatry, 63*, 200–208.

Merz, F. (1969). The effect of verbalization upon the performance on intelligence tests. *Zeitschrift fuer Experimentelle and Angewandte Psychologie, 16*, 114–137.

Metzger, B. M., & Coogan, M. D. (Eds.). (1993). *The Oxford companion to the Bible*. New York: Oxford University Press.

Miller, G. A. (1981). *Language and speech*. San Francisco: Freeman.

Minami, M. (1994). English and Japanese: A cross-cultural comparison of parental styles of narrative elicitation. *Issues in Applied Linguistics, 5*, 383–407.

Minami, M., & McCabe, A. (1995). Rice balls and bear hunts: Japanese and North American family narrative patterns. *Journal of Child Language, 22,* 423–445.

Nakamura, H. (1964). *Ways of thinking of Eastern peoples: India-China-Tibet-Japan* (4th ed.). Honolulu, HI: East–West Center Press.

Needham, J. (1962). *Science and civilization in China: Physics and physical technology* (Vol. 4). Cambridge, England: Cambridge University Press.

Nisbett, R. E., Peng, K., Choi, I., & Norenzayan. A. (2001). Culture and systems of thought: Holistic versus analytic cognition. *Psychological Review, 108,* 291–310.

Nisbett, R. E., & Wilson, T. D. (1977). Telling more than we can know: Verbal reports on mental processes. *Psychological Review, 84,* 231–259.

Peng, K., & Nisbett, R. E. (1999). Culture, dialectics, and reasoning about contradiction. *American Psychologist, 54,* 741–754.

Penney, C. G. (1975). Modality effects in short-term verbal memory. *Psychological Bulletin, 82,* 68–84.

Raven, J. C. (1941). Standardization of progressive matrices, 1938. *British Journal of Medical Psychology, 19,* 137–150.

Rinpoche, K. (1987). *Foundation of Buddhist meditation.* New Delhi, India: Indraprastha Press.

Robinet, I. (1993). *Taoist meditation.* Albany, NY: State University of New York Press.

Schooler, J. W., & Engstler-Schooler, T. Y. (1990). Verbal overshadowing of visual memories: Some things are better left unsaid. *Cognitive Psychology, 22,* 36–71.

Schooler, J. W., Ohlsson, S., & Brooks, K. (1993). Thoughts beyond words: When language overshadows insight. *Journal of Experimental Psychology: General, 122,* 166–183.

Segall, M. H., Dasen, P. R., Berry, J. W., & Poortinga. Y. H. (1999). *Human behavior in global perspective: An introduction to cross-cultural psychology.* Needham Heights, MA: Allyn & Bacon.

Shweder, R. (1995). Cultural psychology: What is it? In N. R. Goldberger & J. B. Veroff (Eds.), *The cultural and psychology reader* (pp. 41–86). New York: New York University Press.

Schweder, R. A., & Sullivan, M. A. (1990). The semiotic subject of cultural psychology. In L. A. Pervin (Ed.), *Handbook of personality: Theory and research* (pp. 399–416). New York: Guilford Press.

Slobin, D. I. (1996). From "thought and language" to "thinking for speaking." In J. Gumperz & S. Levinson (Eds.), *Rethinking linguistic relativity* (pp. 70–96). Cambridge, MA: Cambridge University Press.

Smith, P. B., & Bond, M. H. (1999). *Social psychology across cultures.* Needham Heights, MA: Allyn and Bacon.

Snow, R. E., Kyllonen, P. C., & Marshalek, B. (1984). The topography of ability and learning correlations. In R. J. Sternberg (Ed.), *Advances in the psychology of human intelligence* (Vol. 2, pp. 47–103). Hillsdale. NJ: Erlbaum.

Sokolov, A. N. (1972). *Inner speech and thought.* New York: Plenum Press.

Steele, C. M. (1997). A threat in the air: How stereotypes shape intellectual identity and performance. *American Psychologist, 52,* 613–629.

Steele, C. M., & Aronson, J. (1995). Stereotype threat and the intellectual test performance of African Americans. *Journal of Personality and Social Psychology, 69,* 797–811.

Stein, R. A. (1979). Religious Taoism and popular religion from the second to seventh centuries. In W. Holmes & A. Seidel (Eds.). *Facets of Taoism* (pp. 53–81). New Haven. CT: Yale University Press.

Tobin, J. J., Wu, D. Y. H., & Davidson, D. H. (1989). *Preschool in three cultures: Japan, China and the United States.* New Haven, CT: Yale University Press.

Vernon, P. E. (1982). *The abilities and achievements of Orientals in North America.* New York: Academic Press.

Watson, D., Clark, L. A., & Tellegen, A. (1988). Development and validation of brief measures of positive and negative affect: The PANAS scales. *Journal of Personality and Social Psychology, 54,* 1063–1070.

Watson, J. B. (1924). The place of kinesthetic, visceral and laryngeal organization in thinking. *Psychological Review, 31,* 339–347.

Whorf, B. L. (1956). *Language, thought, and reality; selected writings.* Cambridge, MA: MIT Press.

Wierzbicka, A. (1992). Talking about emotions: Semantics, culture, and cognition. *Cognition & Emotion, 6,* 285–319.

Wilson, T. D. (1994). The proper protocol: Validity and completeness of verbal reports. *Psychological Science, 5,* 249–252.

Wilson, T. D., & Schooler, J. W. (1991). Thinking too much: Introspection can reduce the quality of preferences and decisions. *Journal of Personality and Social Psychology, 60,* 181–192.

Zimbardo, P. G. (1977). *Shyness.* New York: Jove.

Appendix

Talking Questionnaire Items in Study 2

Talking Belief Questions

1. An articulate person is usually a good thinker.
2. Eloquence does not have very much to do with intelligence.
3. Talking clarifies one's thoughts and ideas.
4. Only in silence, can one have clear thoughts and ideas.

Talking Practice Questions

1. Do your interactions with your mother tend to be more non-verbal or verbal?
2. Do your interactions with your father tend to be more non-verbal or verbal?
3. Which matters more, the verbal or non-verbal interactions with your mother?
4. Which matters more, the verbal or non-verbal interactions with your father?
5. How often do you express your thoughts and opinions to your mother?
6. How often do you express your thoughts and opinions to your father?
7. How often does your mother encourage you to articulate your point of view?
8. How often does your father encourage you to articulate your point of view?

Mode of Thinking Questions

1. How often do you speak aloud your thoughts to YOURSELF when you are trying to clarify your thoughts on how to solve problems such as the problem set you just completed?
2. In general, do you think that you think verbally or nonverbally?
3. How much do you think you rely on language when you think?

Received January 5, 2000
Revision received February 4, 2002
Accepted April 3, 2002 ■

On Bridging the Gap Between Social-Personality Psychology and Neuropsychology

Stanley B. Klein and John F. Kihlstrom

Although cognitive psychology has learned much from the study of patients with neuropsychological impairments, social and personality psychologists have been slow to do the same. In this article we argue that the domain of clinical neuropsychology holds considerable untapped potential for formulating and testing models within social and personality psychology and describe some of the ways in which questions of interest to social and personality psychologists can be addressed with neuropsychological data. Examples are drawn from a variety of neuropsychological syndromes, including amnesia, autism, anosognosia, commissurotomy, frontal lobe damage, and prosopagnosia. We conclude that consideration of the personal and social lives of patients with neuropsychological impairments ultimately will lead to a richer understanding of the person, one that bridges the gap between social and cognitive levels of analysis.

For a very long time psychology thought it could get along without looking at the brain. Skinner and other functional behaviorists treated the organism as a "black box" that connected stimuli with responses but whose

The point of view represented by this article is based in part on research supported by an Academic Senate Research Grant from the University of California, Santa Barbara, and National Institute of Mental Health Grant MH35856.

Preliminary versions of this article were presented at the annual meeting of the Society for Experimental Social Psychology (SESP), Santa Barbara, CA, October 1993 and the 1st Annual SELF preconference at the annual meeting of the SESP, Sturbridge, MA, October 1996.

We thank Jennifer Beer, Lawrence Couture, Elizabeth Glisky, Martha Glisky, Judith Loftus, Shelagh Mulvaney, Michael Polster, Victor Shamas, Michael Valdiserri, and Susan Valdiserri for their comments.

Requests for reprints should be sent to either Stanley B. Klein, Department of Psychology, University of California, Santa Barbara, CA 93106, E-mail: klein@psych.ucsb.edu, or John F. Kihlstrom, Department of Psychology, MC 1650, Tolman Hall #3210, University of California, Berkeley, Berkeley, CA 94720–1650.

internal workings could safely be ignored. Classic cognitive psychology and artificial intelligence also endorsed a version of the doctrine of "empty organism" by focusing on the analogy between mind and software and embracing the notion of a Turing machine that could be made out of neurons, silicon chips, or even old radio parts — thus making the biological substrates of mind irrelevant (for a review, see Gardner, 1985).

All that began to change in the mid-1950s, when theory oriented psychologists began to take notice of patients being seen in the neurological clinic and realized that experimental studies of such cases might provide evidence for theories about how the mind is organized (for comprehensive coverage of the neuropsychological syndromes, see Ellis & Young, 1988; Gazzaniga, Ivry, & Mangun, 1998; Heilman & Valenstein, 1993; Kolb & Whishaw, 1996; McCarthy & Warrington, 1990). The most famous case, of course, is the patient known as H. M., who underwent a bilateral resection of the medial portion of the temporal lobes, including the hippocampus and mammillary bodies, in a desperate attempt to ameliorate intractable epilepsy (e.g., Milner, Corkin, & Teuber, 1968; Scoville & Milner, 1957). H. M. emerged from surgery greatly relieved of his epileptic symptoms; the down side was that he now suffered a profound anterograde amnesia, which prevented him from remembering anything that happened to him from the day of surgery until the present.

Studies of H. M., and patients like him, have provided evidence for a *medial temporal lobe memory system* (e.g., Squire & Zola-Morgan, 1991) that seems to be critical for encoding lasting representations of new experiences. That much is clear, but what exactly do these neural structures do? This, of course, is a question for psychological theory, and over the years various theories about memory structure and processing have been proposed to explain the behavior of H. M. and others like him.

Initially, amnesic patients were thought to lack a capacity for transferring information from short-term to long-term memory (e.g., Baddeley & Warrington, 1970; Cermak, 1972; Milner, 1966; Wickelgren, 1973). This view, however, soon ran into problems. Consider, for example, what happens when amnesic patient K. C.[1] is tutored in the basics of computer operation (e.g., Glisky, Schacter, & Tulving, 1986b). A few minutes following completion of a lesson, K. C. has no conscious recollections of what he was taught or even that he had a lesson. Nonetheless, he shows clear evidence of having acquired complex knowledge about the programming and operation of a computer; he can understand computer related vocabulary (e.g., *software, modem, save, print*), can perform disk storage and retrieval operations, and even can be taught to write simple programs (e.g., Glisky, 1995; Glisky, Schacter, & Tulving, 1986a; Glisky et al., 1986b). Yet, if asked how he knows the procedure for downloading a file or writing a program, K. C. is likely to respond that these are just ordinary facts about the world that everyone knows (cf. Tulving, Hayman, & Macdonald, 1991).

Observations such as these (for related findings, see Brooks & Baddeley, 1976; Graf, Squire, & Mandler, 1984; Warrington & Weiskrantz, 1970) suggest that amnesic patients show a dissociation between two forms of long-term memory: *Episodic memory*, which enables people to become consciously aware of specific past events from their life, is impaired, whereas *semantic*

memory, which enables people to retrieve knowledge abstracted from events but does not entail recollection of the events themselves, is intact (e.g., Cermak, 1984; Evans, Wilson, Wraight, & Hodges, 1993; Kinsbourne & Wood, 1975; Klein, Loftus, & Kihlstrom, 1996; Schacter & Tulving, 1982; Tulving, 1983, 1993; Van der Linden, Bredart, Depoorter, & Coyette, 1996).[2] Characterizing the difference between types or systems of memories is a major growth industry within contemporary cognitive psychology (see, for example, Foster & Jelicic, in press; Schacter & Tulving, 1994), but cognitive psychologists didn't really start asking questions about multiple memory systems until they started contemplating evidence from brain damaged patients (for a review, see Polster, Nadel, & Schacter, 1991). In this way, a great advance in psychological theory began with data from the neurological clinic.

Cognitive psychologists now agree on the value of neurological evidence. For example, psycholinguists are interested in syndromes like Broca's and Wernicke's aphasias for the insights they can provide into the nature of language processing (e.g., Berndt & Caramazza, 1980; Brown, 1972; Goodglass, 1993; Pinker, 1994). Vision scientists are interested in phenomena like blindsight, prosopagnosia, and visual neglect for what they can tell us about perceptual processes (e.g., Coslett, 1997; Prigatano & Schacter, 1991; Weiskrantz, 1997).

The central question addressed in this article is whether the study of patients with neuropsychological impairments should interest personality and social psychologists. We believe the answer to this question is "yes" and hope the arguments we present will challenge our colleagues to join us in considering neuropsychological evidence in theorizing about personality and social processes. Brain damage isn't just for cognitive psychologists anymore; it has a great deal to tell personality and social psychologists about the things

---

[1] Patient K. C. (e.g., Tulving, 1989, 1993) receives more detailed treatment in the next section of this article.

[2] More recently, documentation of spared priming effects, coupled with the observation that amnesic patients can acquire new semantic knowledge and procedural knowledge that does not depend on episodic memory for their performance, has led cognitive scientists to draw a distinction between two expressions of memory: Explicit memory entails conscious recollection of past events, whereas implicit memory reflects the influence of past events on ongoing experience, thought, and action independent of conscious recollection (e.g., Schacter, 1987; see also Squire & Knowlton, 1995). The dissociation between explicit and implicit cognition is now a major research enterprise within cognitive psychology (e.g., Kihlstrom, in press-a), but it is not relevant to the present context.

we're interested in. However, before that happens, we have to ask the appropriate questions. In the following sections we suggest ways in which neuropsychological evidence can provide important new insights into the role of cognition in personality and social interaction.

H. M., Amnesias, and Knowledge of Self

Reading a case like H. M. can be extremely frustrating to personality and social psychologists because there is so much we want to know, yet so few answers. For example, H. M.'s surgery was in 1953, when he was 27 years old. So what happens now, 45 years later, when H. M. goes into the bathroom to shave in the morning: Does he look in the mirror and say: "Who the hell are you?" What can the self-concept of a person who lacks episodic memory for the past 45 years be like? Can a person preserve a sense of identity, including changes in identity over a long period of time, without also preserving an autobiography? More generally, to what extent is our knowledge of what we are like dependent on our ability to remember the behavioral evidence on which that knowledge is based? Unfortunately, with rare exceptions (e.g., Klein, Loftus, et al., 1996; O'Connor, Cermak, & Seidman, 1995; Tulving, 1993), neuropsychological investigations of the amnesic syndrome seldom have considered the impact of catastrophic memory loss on the patient's personal identity.

In the last few years, however, this situation has begun to change as psychologists come to appreciate the ways in which theoretical issues surrounding the self can be addressed with neurological data. Consider, as an example, the case of W. J. (Klein, Loftus, et al., 1996), an 18-year-old undergraduate who suffered a concussive blow to the head shortly after completing her first quarter in college. Brain scans revealed no neurological abnormalities, but she complained of memory and concentration difficulties and testing revealed that she had, in fact, forgotten much of what had happened in her life during the preceding 6 to 7 months — a period of time covering approximately her first quarter at college. Over the next month, W. J.'s amnesia remitted completely.

W. J.'s amnesic deficit in episodic memory was documented by the Galton (1879) memory cueing procedure popularized by J. A. Robinson (1976) and Crovitz (e.g., Crovitz & Quina-Holland, 1976; Crovitz & Schiffman, 1974). In this task, participants are read cue words (representing affects, objects, and activities) one at a time and for each are asked to recall a specific personal event from any time in the past and provide as precise a date as possible for that event. When tested 5 days after her accident, W. J. showed little episodic memory for personal events from recent years. Four weeks later her performance had improved considerably and was indistinguishable from that of three neurologically healthy women who served as controls.

W. J. was also asked both during her amnesia and after its resolution to provide personality ratings describing what she was like during her first term at college. In contrast to the change in her episodic memory performance over the month following her accident, W. J.'s personality ratings of herself at college did not change at all over the same period of time; her trait ratings made during her amnesic period agreed with those she made afterward. Thus, although she was amnesic, W. J. knew what she had been like in college despite the fact that she couldn't recall anything from her time in college.

Of course, it is conceivable that W. J.'s personality didn't change much between high school and college. If so, then she could have achieved reasonably reliable ratings of her personality simply on the basis of her memories from high school, without accessing any information from her college years. To check this possibility, W. J. was asked during her amnesia to rate how she saw herself during high school. Statistical analyses revealed that the correlation between her ratings of herself at high school and ratings of herself at college was reliable ($r = .53$), meaning that some degree of reliability in W. J.'s ratings of her college self could have been achieved by reliance on her memories of her precollege behaviors and experiences. However, this figure was significantly lower than the correlation obtained between W. J.'s two ratings of herself at college, taken during and after her amnesia ($r = .74$; $p < .05$). So, there is reliable variability in her college self which is not accounted for by her high school self. Put another way, although she was amnesic, W. J. knew something about what she was like in college, which was different from what she was like in high school; she knew this despite the fact that she could not recall any personally experienced events from her time in college.

To explain these findings, Klein, Loftus, et al. (1996; see also Kihlstrom & Klein, 1994, 1997; Klein, 1993, in press; Klein, Babey, & Sherman, 1997; Klein & Loftus, 1993; Klein, Sherman, & Loftus, 1996) proposed that knowledge of personality traits and recollections of specific personal events involving those traits reflect the operations of two distinct, neutrally dissociable types of personal memory: Semantic personal memory and episodic personal memory (see also Brewer, 1986; Cermak & O'Connor, 1983; Kihlstrom et al., 1988; Tulving, 1993; Wheeler, Stuss, & Tulving, 1996). *Episodic personal memory* stores the specific details of personally experienced events, whereas *semantic personal memory* stores generalizations about the self abstracted from those experiences. The fact that during her amnesia W. J. had access to trait abstractions about herself, but not the particular episodes on which that knowledge was based, was taken as evidence that these two types of self-knowledge are served by different neural systems, one of which had become dysfunctional as a result of her concussion, whereas the other remained unimpaired (e.g., Kihlstrom & Klein, 1994, 1997; Klein & Loftus, 1993; Klein et al., 1997).[3]

Admittedly, Klein, Loftus, et al.'s (1996) conclusion could be questioned on the basis of W. J.'s continued access to episodic memories that were not covered by her amnesia and the possibility that she drew on those memories, not her semantic personal knowledge, for her ratings of self-at-college. However, there is other evidence indicating that accurate self-description can occur even with total episodic memory loss. Tulving (1993), for example, found that patient K. C., who lost his entire fund of episodic memory (and underwent a marked personality change) following a motorcycle accident, was able to describe his postmorbid personality with considerable accuracy. Tulving asked K. C. to judge a list of trait adjectives for self-descriptiveness. Tulving also asked K. C.'s mother on two separate occasions to rate K. C. on the same traits, the first time rating K. C. as he currently was and the second time rating him as he was before his accident. K. C.'s choices were highly correlated with his mother's judgments of his postmorbid personality. Thus, K. C. was able to acquire accurate knowledge of his new personality (with his mother's ratings serving as the criterion) without being able to retain any episodic knowledge of the specific actions and experiences on which that knowledge was based.

Although theorists differ concerning the precise interpretation of the findings just discussed (e.g., Schneider, Roediger, & Kahn, 1993), this much is clear: Neurally impaired individuals who have lost the ability to recall personal experiences show no obvious impairment in the ability to make accurate personality judgments about themselves, and (in the case of K. C.) even maintain the ability to revise those judgments based on new episodes that they cannot remember. Apparently you do not need to remember how you behaved in the past to know what you are like.

Additional support for this conclusion recently was presented by Craik et al. (in press). Using positron emission tomography (PET), these investigators discovered that requiring participants to judge trait adjectives for self-descriptiveness produced activation of cortical areas associated with semantic memory retrieval (left frontal regions) but not those associated with episodic memory retrieval (right frontal regions).[4]

The dissociations between episodic and semantic self-knowledge have made several things clear. First, contrary to long-held beliefs about the memorial basis of self (e.g., Grice, 1941; James, 1890; Keenan, 1993; Locke, 1690/1731; Quinton, 1962; Tulving, 1984), episodic memory is not the sole repository of self-knowledge. The fact that a loss of episodic memory does not lead to a complete loss of self-knowledge has led theorists to expand the basis of self-knowledge to

---

[3] The finding that one function is impaired and another one is spared reveals the basic methodology of cognitive neuropsychology: The *functional dissociation* (e.g., Shallice, 1988; Teuber, 1955; Weiskrantz, 1989). This term is rather confusing, because to most psychologists the term *dissociation* refers to the isolation of some percepts, memories, thoughts, or actions from conscious awareness (Kihlstrom, 1993). What neuropsychologists mean by dissociation, social psychologists recognize as the *interaction:* An independent variable (reflecting a state, condition, or experimental manipulation) affects one dependent variable but not another.

The dissociations that interest neuropsychologists come in four types (e.g., Dunn & Kirsner, 1988; Kelley & Lindsay, 1996; Neely, 1989). In the case of a *single dissociation*, a single independent variable, A, selectively affects performance on one task, X but not on another, Y. In the *double dissociation*, one independent variable, A, affects dependent variable X but not dependent variable Y, whereas another independent variable, B, affects Y but not X. The double dissociation can be uncrossed or crossed: *Crossed* double interactions are especially interesting to neuropsychologists, because they are especially good evidence that two different processes are involved in the two tasks. Otherwise one would worry about artifacts like differential task difficulty. Even better evidence is provided by the *reversed association*, in which there is a positive correlation between dependent variables X and Y under conditions of independent variable A, but a negative correlation between these same variables under conditions of independent variable B. Reversed associations are particularly difficult to account for in terms of task difficulty (e.g., Dunn & Kirsner, 1988; Klein et al., 1997; Neely, 1989).

---

[4] Craik et al. (in press) also concluded that the cognitive processes involved in self-reference were no different from those involved in referring to other individuals or in performing nonsocial semantic analyses. Thus, the neuroscience method of brain imaging confirmed conclusions that already had been reached on the basis of traditional experimental procedures employing behavioral measures (e.g., Kihlstrom et al., 1988; Klein & Kihlstrom, 1986).

include both episodic and semantic memory (e.g., Cermak & O'Connor, 1983; Conway, 1992; Evans et al., 1993; Klein & Loftus, 1993; Klein, Loftus, et al., 1996; Tulving, 1993; Tulving, Schacter, McLachlan, & Moscovitch, 1988). Second, the finding that individuals can have accurate and detailed knowledge of their personalities despite having no conscious access to behavioral episodes suggests these two types of self-knowledge are represented independently in memory and perhaps mediated by separate cognitive systems.

Over and above these specific issues, the analysis of cases like W. J. and K. C. shows a little of what is possible when neurological disorders are approached with personality and social theories in mind. We hope that these studies stimulate other self-theorists to consider the theoretical promise of patients with neuropsychological impairments, for it would seem there is much such patients can teach us about the representation and function of knowledge about the self.

Autism, Theory of Mind, and Theory of Self

An interesting implication of the proposal that episodic and semantic self-knowledge are served by different cognitive systems is that a person could, in principle, have complete access to his or her episodic self-knowledge yet be unable to know whether a particular trait adjective was descriptive of self. Although this question has not been addressed empirically, some intriguing hints at an answer are found from a rather unusual source — the study of patients with autism (Klein, 1996).

In a series of publications, Baron-Cohen, Leslie, U. Frith, and colleagues (e.g., Baron-Cohen, 1989, 1990, 1991, 1995; Baron-Cohen, Leslie, & Frith, 1985; Baron-Cohen, Tager-Flusberg, & Cohen, 1993; U. Frith, 1989; Leslie, 1987, 1991; Leslie & Frith, 1988; Leslie & Thaiss, 1992) have argued that a defining feature of the autistic syndrome is the failure of autistic individuals to develop what Premack and Woodruff (1978) termed *a theory of mind* — a capacity to attribute mental states (e.g., intentions, desires, thoughts, beliefs) to other persons in order to make sense of their behavior (see also, Flavell, Green, & Flavell, 1995; Gopnik & Metzloff, 1997; Wellman, 1990).

Leslie (1987), in a pioneering paper on the topic, suggested that the failure of autistic individuals to explain behavior in terms of mental states (i.e., to mentalize) stemmed from their inability to form "second order representations." By this account, autistic individuals are able to form "first order representations" of people,

things, and events based directly on perceptual experience (e.g., "Robert smiled when he got the candy bar"). They are, however, deficient in forming second order representations — that is, representations of first order representations (e.g., "Robert smiled because he thought [or knew, or hoped, or believed] he would get the candy bar"). The capacity to represent representations, Leslie argued, is the essence of a theory of mind and is a capacity that fails to fully develop in autistic individuals (a recent review can be found in Baron-Cohen, 1995).

What about the autistic individual's awareness of his or her own mental states? If autism involves a dysfunction of the neural structures necessary for forming a theory of other minds, it is reasonable to wonder whether these individuals might also show an impaired ability to reflect on their own mental states — to know about their own knowing.[5]

Surprisingly, the question of whether the problems autistic patients experience in understanding and recognizing mental states in others extend to their understanding of their own mental states has been largely overlooked (for a recent discussion, see Carruthers, 1996). However, the few empirical findings that are available do suggest that autistic patients have trouble reflecting on their own mental states (e.g., Baron-Cohen, 1989, 1991; Baron-Cohen, Ring, Moriarty, Schmitz, Costa, & Ell, 1994; Jordan, 1989; Tager-Flusberg, 1992). For example, several recent studies reported that compared to normally developing children, autistic children have problems in acquiring a normal grasp of the personal pronouns *I* and *me* (e.g., Fay, 1979; Jordan, 1989; Lee, Hobson, & Chiat, 1994).

---

[5] Nicholas Humphrey's (1984, 1986, 1990) recent writings on the evolution of self-awareness in humans are suggestive of such a possibility. According to Humphrey, self-awareness, having been designed by natural selection, must contribute to our biological success. However, what selective advantage is provided by an ability to reflect on one's own mental states?

Humphrey proposed that the answer is to be found in the social challenges faced by our ancestors. From their initial appearance approximately 150,000 years ago (e.g., Dunbar, 1996), modern humans lived in a highly complex interpersonal milieu; accordingly, their survival depended on their being able to explain, predict, and manipulate the behavior of others. Self-reflective awareness served this function: By showing us how our own mind works, it provided us, by analogy, with a tool for understanding the minds of others like ourselves (for a related view, see Sedikides & Skowronski, 1997). Thus, a necessary precondition for developing a theory of other minds is the possession of a theory of one's own mind. By implication, the absence of a theory of other minds may be diagnostic of a failure to develop a theory of self.

Tager-Flusberg (1992) showed that autistic individuals use significantly less spontaneous speech than matched controls when referring to their own cognitive mental states (e.g., beliefs, desires, traits). Along similar line, Baron-Cohen (1991) found that autistic individuals have as much trouble attributing beliefs to themselves as they do in attributing beliefs to others. Finally, clinical descriptions of autistic individuals often make reference to their inability to self-reflect or to self-monitor (e.g., Baron-Cohen, 1989; Bishop, 1993).

Admittedly, the evidence that autistic individuals may be lacking in awareness of their own mental states is small, indirect, and often anecdotal. Nonetheless, if this hypothesis is correct, it suggests the interesting possibility that an autistic individual, although capable of recalling trait-relevant personal behaviors (e.g., "I remember getting a high score on a math test"), may be unable to make trait-based generalizations about the self on the basis of those behaviors (e.g., "I know [or think, or hope, or believe] that I am an intelligent person"). If such an outcome were obtained, it would provide strong converging evidence in support of the proposed independence between episodic and semantic self-knowledge.

Self-Awareness and the Brain: Locating the Jamesian Self-as-Knower

In light of the previous discussion, it is interesting to wonder whether we know enough about the neural correlates of mentalizing to identify where in the brain such capacity resides. Although a definitive answer is not yet available, some fascinating clues can be found. For example, neuroimaging studies conducted on individuals engaged in theory of mind tasks (e.g., tasks requiring inferences about mental states) report evidence for selective activation of the frontal lobes during task performance, suggesting a role for these structures in the capacity to mentalize (e.g., Baron-Cohen et al., 1994; Fletcher et al., 1995; Goel, Grafman, Sadato, & Hallett, 1995). This possibility receives support from two additional sources. First, there is some evidence that patients with frontal lobe damage show deficits on theory of mind tasks (e.g., Price, Daffner, Stowe, & Mesulam, 1990; Stone, Baron-Cohen, & Knight, 1996). Second, a number of investigators have noted strong parallels between the behavior of autistic individuals and that of patients suffering frontal lobe damage (e.g., Bishop, 1993; Damasio & Maurer, 1987; C. D. Frith & U. Frith, 1991; Ozonoff, Pennington, & Rogers, 1991;

Prior & Hoffman, 1990). Specifically, both groups show (a) limited ability to plan for the future, or to anticipate the long-term consequences of their behavior, (b) deficits in the capacity to self-reflect or self-monitor, and (c) difficulties learning from mistakes, persevering with maladaptive strategies even when repeatedly made aware of their errors (for comprehensive reviews, see Damasio, 1985, and Fuster, 1997).

Interestingly, the psychological processes compromised in patients with frontal lobe dysfunction — the capacity to monitor and reflect on one's mental states — are defining features of James's (1890) *self-as-knower*, the subjective experience of self as a thinking, feeling, wanting, doing being. Although there is much we do not understand about this self-reflective aspect of self (for discussions, see Greenwald & Pratkanis, 1984; Kihlstrom & Klein, 1994; Stuss, 1991), we are perhaps a step closer to knowing where in the brain such a capacity resides. By capitalizing on what we know about frontal lobe function in both normal and brain damaged individuals, we may come to a better understanding of the structure and function of this most elusive of Jamesian concepts.

Anosognosia and Attribution Theory

H. M. is aware of his memory deficit (he describes it as "like waking from a dream"), and he knows that there are things that he can't remember. However, there are other patients suffering from a variety of problems with memory, language, perception, or voluntary movement who appear to have no awareness of their deficits. This lack of awareness of a mental deficit was named *anosagnosia* by Babinski (1914, 1918; for recent reviews, see McGlynn & Schacter, 1989; Prigatano & Schacter, 1991). Anosognosic patients may acknowledge some difficulty in their impaired domains, but they attribute their problems to something besides their own deficits. It should be understood that these patients' behavior is not mere denial of deficit or indifference to it (when a patient acknowledges deficit but seems unconcerned about it, the syndrome is called *anosodiaphoria*).

Most of the classical descriptions of anosognosia are in cases of acute hemiplegia, hemianesthesia, and hemianopia (Bisiach & Geminiani, 1991). In *hemiplegia*, the person is paralyzed on one side of the body, due to damage to the contralateral hemisphere; in *hemianopia*, the person has a loss of sight in one side of the visual field. Interestingly, anosognosia is more likely to occur when the loss is localized on the left side of the body, implying that it is caused by damage to structures in the right cerebral hemisphere. However, the syndrome also occurs in cases of left-hemisphere damage, as for example in aphasia (e.g., Rubens & Garrett, 1991). Many aphasics, both expressive and receptive, attempt to correct their faulty speech production; by virtue of hesitations, pauses, and self-corrections they show clearly that they know that what they have intended to say hasn't come out as planned. However, many do not realize this, a failure that is common in cases of *jargon aphasia*, a special form of receptive aphasia in which the patient's speech is freely littered with meaningless utterances and phonemic and semantic paraphasias (using the wrong sounds or words). Such patients do not seem to realize that they are not communicating with their listeners, and, furthermore, they do not seem to realize that they don't understand what is being said to them. Interestingly, jargon aphasia seems to be more common in cases of bilateral damage; again, this implies that the right hemisphere plays a special role in awareness of deficits.

Anosognosia is a real danger to the patient, of course. People who don't realize that they are paralyzed on one side are headed for disaster if they should try to get up; those who don't realize they are blind on one side are unlikely to take special steps to avoid obstacles and oncoming objects on the affected side. In the dementing disorders, such as Alzheimer's disease and even schizophrenia, anosognosia is particularly insidious because it occurs in the late stages of illness (e.g., McGlynn & Kaszniak, 1991), when the patient is most impaired. Interestingly, however, anosognosics sometimes implicitly acknowledge their difficulties. The hemiplegic may not complain about being confined to a hospital bed or attempt some task that must be performed with both hands, and the hemianopic may actively ignore the affected portion of the environmental field. Neurological patients who are unaware of their deficits are poorly motivated for rehabilitation.

From a social-psychological view one wants to know what these patients make of their own behavior, given that they don't acknowledge their deficits. Some patients attribute their inability to move to arthritis or rheumatism rather than paralysis; others, when asked to move the affected limb, appear distracted or move the unaffected limb or respond that they have moved the affected limb, when in fact they have not (this even happens when patients look at the affected limb during the examination). The explanations can sometimes become bizarre or delusional.

For example, the patient may claim that the affected limb is not his or her own, but rather belongs to someone else — forgotten by a previous patient or belonging to someone else lying at their side (often doing something naughty). One woman studied by Bisiach & Geminiani (1991) was anosognosic for her hemiplegia. She claimed that her left hand did not belong to her, but rather had been forgotten in the ambulance by another patient. She acknowledged that her left shoulder was her own and agreed with the inference that her left arm and elbow were also her own, because they were attached to her shoulder, but this inference did not extend to her left hand (she could not explain why that hand carried her wedding ring). Another hemiplegic patient stated that his own left arm was the examiner's. When the examiner placed the patient's left hand between his own two hands, the patient continued to deny that his arm hand was his own and attributed three arms and three hands to the examiner.

What we're seeing here, of course, are phenomena of attribution; the patients are trying to make sense of their experiences, given their beliefs about themselves and the world at large. These attributions may be convenient laboratory models for other kinds of beliefs, including those that are frankly delusional (for a review of attributional accounts of delusions, see Kihlstrom & Hoyt, 1988). Consider the following scenario: A hemiplegic patient is unaware of the loss of function on his left side and denies that his left arm and hand are his. Then what's he doing in bed? Why is someone else wearing his wedding ring? Where is the rest of that person, anyway? If he's forgotten his left hand, doesn't he miss it? Why doesn't the patient retrieve his wedding ring and put it back on his own left hand? Anomalous perceptual experiences arouse anxiety until they are satisfactorily explained, and in the course of formulating acceptable explanations, the patient must go through the sorts of processes studied by attribution theory. Accordingly, cases of anosognosia can provide an interesting proving ground for testing and refining theories about causal attributions, self-other differences, and other aspects of social judgment and inference.

Split Brains and Self-Perception

Few neuropsychological syndromes have generated greater interest among neuroscientists (e.g., Gazzaniga, 1970; Sperry, 1968, 1974; Springer & Deutsch, 1998) and philosophers (e.g., Marks, 1981; Nagel, 1971; Puccetti, 1973) than that of the commissurotomized (colloquially referred to as *split-brain*) patient. These patients have suffered from severe and uncontrollable epileptic seizures, much like those experienced by H. M., but their treatment is quite different. In an effort to alleviate the effects of otherwise intractable epilepsy, a procedure known as a complete cerebral commissurotomy is performed (e.g., Bogen, Fisher, & Vogel, 1965; Bogen & Vogel, 1962) in which the *corpus callosum*,[6] a large transverse band of approximately 200 million nerve fibers that directly connect the left and right cerebral hemispheres, is surgically cut.[7] Because epileptic seizures, which originate as electrical outbursts at a particular cortical site, tend to spread from one cerebral hemisphere to the other (thereby increasing the magnitude of the disturbance), cutting the corpus callosum is seen as a way of limiting the disturbance to one hemisphere, thereby decreasing its magnitude (e.g., Gazzaniga & LeDoux, 1978; Kolb & Whishaw, 1996; Sperry, 1974).

Medically, complete cerebral commissurotomy proved quite successful; confined to a single hemisphere, patients' epileptic seizures became less frequent or disappeared entirely (e.g., Kolb & Whishaw, 1996; Springer & Deutsch, 1998). Moreover, initial reports revealed no obvious postsurgical changes in their perceptual, cognitive, or everyday behavior (e.g., Akelaitis, 1941a, 1941b, 1944; Bogen, 1985).

However, extensive psychological testing by Roger Sperry and his colleagues (e.g., Franco & Sperry, 1977; Levy-Agresti & Sperry, 1968; Sperry, 1968) eventually uncovered some peculiar psychological consequences of hemispheric disconnection. Sperry's approach to testing split-brain patients depended on two key assumptions. First, that under suitable experimental control, it is possible to confine input presented to a split-brain patient to a single hemisphere (e.g., Sperry, 1968, 1974). Second, that in the vast majority of people, verbal reports issue from the left cerebral hemisphere. By contrast, the right hemisphere, although capable of limited linguistic analyses, lacks access to the speech mechanisms of the left hemisphere and thus is unable to initiate speech (e.g., Corballis, 1991; Kolb & Whishaw, 1996; Springer & Deutsch, 1998).

Using several subtle experimental techniques, Sperry and his colleagues were able to direct input exclusively to a single hemisphere and request a response of it (e.g., Franco & Sperry, 1977; Gordon & Sperry, 1969; Levy, Trevarthen, & Sperry, 1972; Levy-Agresti & Sperry, 1968; Sperry, 1968, 1974; Sperry, Gazzaniga, & Bogen, 1969; Zaidel, 1975). For example, when an object was visually presented to the left hemisphere, split-brain patients reported seeing it and could identify it verbally. However, when the same object was presented to the nonspeaking right hemisphere, patients claimed they saw nothing at all. Nevertheless, the right hemisphere could demonstrate nonverbally what it had seen by pointing at the correct object with the left hand (which is controlled by the right hemisphere). Similar findings were obtained using olfactory stimuli. When a clove of garlic was presented to a split-brain patient's right nostril (which stimulates the right hemisphere), he verbally denied smelling anything. However, when asked to point with his left hand to the object corresponding to the odor he smelled, he correctly selected the clove from among a set of smell related objects, at the same time verbally protesting that he didn't smell anything!

Findings such as these led Sperry to propose that surgery had left split-brain patients with two separate minds, each with its own separate sphere of consciousness (e.g., Sperry, 1966, 1968, 1974). In Sperry's (1968) words:

> Each hemisphere seems to have its own separate and private sensations; its own perceptions; its own concepts; and its own impulses to act, with related volitional, cognitive, and learning experiences. Following surgery, each hemisphere also has thereafter its own separate chain of memories that are rendered inaccessible to the recall processes of the other. (p. 724)

A particularly intriguing case is that of patient P. S. (e.g., Gazzaniga & LeDoux, 1978; LeDoux, 1985; LeDoux, Wilson, & Gazzaniga, 1977). P. S. is unique among split-brain patients in that his right hemisphere, although unable to generate speech, has extensive linguistic abilities, enabling it to respond to a wide variety of verbal commands. For example, when the experimenters asked his right hemisphere to "laugh," it did as told and P. S. laughed aloud. Interestingly, however, when asked why he was laughing, the left hemisphere replied "Oh you guys are really something" (Gazzaniga & LeDoux, 1978, p. 146). In another study the experimenters simultaneously flashed an image of a snow scene to P. S.'s right hemisphere and an image of a chicken claw to his left hemisphere. Each hemisphere

---

[6] In addition to sectioning the corpus callosum, the Bogen and Vogel (1962) procedure also involved complete sectioning of the anterior and hippocampal commissures. It is via these three links that direct interhemispheric communication and integration takes place.

[7] Strictly speaking, the designation *split-brain surgery* is a somewhat of a misnomer — although the corpus callosum and minor commissures are surgically severed, the subcortical regions linking the two hemispheres are left untouched by the surgery.

then was shown a set of pictures and instructed to select the one most closely associated with the image it had seen. The right responded by choosing (with his left hand) a picture of a shovel, and the left selected (with the right hand) a picture of a chicken to match the claw. When asked why he chose these particular pictures, his left hemisphere responded "I saw a claw and I picked a chicken, and you have to clean out the chicken shed with a shovel" (Gazzaniga & LeDoux, 1978, p. 148).

In each of these examples, P. S.'s left hemisphere was faced with a problem — it had observed a response but did not know why the response was performed. When asked "Why are you doing that?", the talking left hemisphere had to come up with a plausible explanation for a behavior performed in response to a command directed to the mute right hemisphere. As Gazzaniga and LeDoux (1978) noted, the left hemisphere proved quite adept at this task, interpreting the actions of the right as though it had insight into the cause of the behavior (when in fact it did not). On the basis of these findings, Gazzaniga and LeDoux concluded that the left hemisphere acts as the interpreter of action, attempting to provide as plausible an account as possible for the individual's behavior (for related views, see Jaynes, 1976; Popper & Eccles, 1977; Sperry, 1974).

Gazzaniga and LeDoux (1978; see also LeDoux, 1985) go on to suggest that the left hemisphere plays a similar role in individuals with intact brains. A considerable body of evidence suggests that we are not consciously aware of the causes of all the behaviors we produce or feelings we experience (for reviews, see Gazzaniga, 1998; Kihlstrom, 1987, in press-a, in press-b; Nisbett & Wilson, 1977; Oakley & Eames, 1985; Velmans, 1996). When an activity is initiated by a neural system whose motives are not consciously accessible, the verbal left hemisphere finds itself confronted with behavior carried out for unknown reasons. Under these circumstances, it attempts to attribute a cause to the action, thereby integrating the action into a coherent personal narrative (e.g., Gazzaniga, 1998; LeDoux, 1985). As Gazzaniga and LeDoux (1978) remarked: "It is as if the verbal self [i.e., left hemisphere] looks out to see what the person is doing, and from that knowledge it interprets reality" (p. 150).[8]

What Gazzaniga and LeDoux have provided us with, of course, is a neuropsychological model of Bem's (1967, 1972) influential theory of self-perception — the idea that people "come to know their own attitudes, emotions, and other internal states partially by inferring them from observations of their own overt behavior and/or the circumstances in which this behavior occurs" (Bem, 1972, p. 5). We believe that such a model can contribute in important ways to our understanding of the process involved in self-perception. The relation between lateralization and hemispheric specialization is becoming increasingly well-mapped experimentally (for a recent review, see Springer & Deutsch, 1998). By drawing on that knowledge, self-perception theorists may gain an understanding of the functional properties of the neural system responsible for drawing inferences about behavior whose origins are outside conscious awareness — an understanding that ultimately may lead to a better appreciation of the ways in which individuals attempt to construct a coherent story of self. And, by learning which of a person's behaviors are likely to be initiated by the nonverbal right hemisphere, theorists may be better able to identify the types of behaviors whose explanation require the inference-making capacities of the left hemisphere. Although the contributions of these particular neuropsychological perspectives on self-perception theory remain to be determined, it seems clear to us that, in the long run, research and theory both will benefit from a greater understanding of the neuropsychological mechanisms that make self-perception possible.

Phineas Gage and the Question of Cognition and Emotion

The relevance of neuropsychology for personality and social psychology is also illustrated by the classic case of Phineas Gage (e.g., Macmillan, 1986). In 1848, this young railway worker was preparing some explosive charges for use in an excavation. In so doing, he accidentally set off a spark that exploded the gunpowder, driving his custom-made tamping iron right through his skull — entering under his left eye socket, traveling behind his eye (severing the optic nerve), and emerging from the top of his head. Gage lived for a dozen more years, which is extraordinary in itself, but he also showed a marked change in personality. Whereas before the accident he had been described as shrewd, smart, energetic, and persistent, he now was described as fitful, irreverent, grossly profane, lacking in deference,

---

[8] Additional support for this idea comes from studies of normal participants showing that the right hemisphere is greatly inferior to the left at drawing inferences and making decisions nonverbally (e.g., Gazzaniga & Smylie, 1984; Phelps & Gazzaniga, 1992; Vallar, Bisiach, Cerizza, & Rusconi, 1988).

impatient, obstinate, capricious and vacillating, child-like in his intellectual capacity, and with strong animal passions — in short, as the physician who attended his wounds put it, he was "no longer Gage" (Harlow, 1868).

The significance of the Gage case was not lost on the phrenologists. Nelson Sizer (1882), an American disciple of Gall and Spurzheim, concluded that the injury had obviously destroyed brain tissue "in the neighborhood of Benevolence and the front part of Veneration" (pp. 193–194). Even after the abandonment of phrenology, the Gage case was used, along with Broca's and Wernicke's cases of expressive and receptive aphasia, as a primary example of specialization of function in the cerebral cortex — in particular, for the localization of faculties relating to personality, social relationships, and emotion in the frontal lobe.[9] Modern neuropsychology has generally confirmed this conclusion, although we now know that the frontal lobes support cognitive as well as emotional and interpersonal functions (for a review of other cases of frontal lobe damage, see Damasio, 1985).

Neuropsychological evidence also can be brought to bear on the vexatious question of the relation between emotion and cognition. Is emotion a cognitive construction or an independent mental faculty? Although cognitive processing undoubtedly plays a role in emotion (e.g., Clark & Fiske, 1982), neuropsychological evidence does seem to show that some brain structures are specialized for emotion and for the processing of emotional as opposed to nonemotional memories. Consider, for example, the Kluver–Bucy syndrome (Kluver & Bucy, 1939), resulting from bilateral destruction of the amygdala and associated inferior portions of the temporal cortex. Humans and nonhuman animals with

such lesions show a loss of fear and other emotional responses and increased and inappropriate sexual activity, among other symptoms. Such outcomes suggest that the amygdala plays a special role in emotion, a hypothesis that has been supported by LeDoux's (1987, 1996) finding that bilateral amygdalectomy impairs classical fear conditioning. Of course, cortical structures also are involved in emotion; patients with lesions in the right hemisphere, and in particular the temporal-parietal regions of the right hemisphere, have special difficulties in judging the mood of others from vocal or facial cues, choosing which uncaptioned cartoons are funny, selecting the correct punchlines to joke set-ups, and matching scenes for emotional valence. Cognition and emotion are certainly related, but the neuropsychological evidence seems to indicate that there are certain brain systems that are specialized for emotional processing, suggesting that cognition and emotion are also different mental faculties.

Prosopagnosia and Face Recognition

Neuropsychological evidence would seem to be especially relevant to understanding a basic social-cognitive process: How one person recognizes the face of another. The face is the fundamental social stimulus. It is the point of contact in the infant's very earliest social interactions; the smiles exchanged between infant and caregiver are the beginnings of life-long social bonds. Perceiving, identifying, and comprehending faces is absolutely basic to social interaction. We have to know who we are dealing with, what they are like, and how we relate to them, before we can interpret their behavior or plan our own. Even when dealing with strangers, the face provides cues to the emotional state of the other person, as well as hints of other things, like deception, that are important in negotiating an interaction. If we want to understand how we come to know another person, we have to understand how we read the face.

As it happens, neuropsychology has been very interested in the face, and, in fact, there is a specific form of visual agnosia involving the face. In general, *visual agnosia* — a term coined by Sigmund Freud (1891/1953) before he turned from neurology to psychoanalysis — refers to the inability to recognize objects (or pictures of objects). A person with visual object agnosia can describe an object, but cannot name it, recognize it as familiar, or demonstrate how it is used. Visual agnosia specific to the face is called *prosopagnosia*, a term coined by Bodamer (1947; for a

---

[9] Incidentally, despite appearances, the Gage case did not lay the foundation for prefrontal lobotomy (originally called *prefrontal leucotomy*) as treatment for mental illness. The inventor of psychosurgery, Egas Moniz (who won the 1949 Nobel prize in Physiology or Medicine for his efforts), was much more influenced by the case of Joe A., reported by Brickner (1936). However, Freeman and Watts (1950), who were chiefly responsible for importing prefrontal lobotomies into the United States, made much of the Gage case (for a critical review of psychosurgery, see Valenstein, 1973). Why they did so is not at all clear, insofar as damage to Gage's frontal lobes seem to have made him very much worse as a person. Perhaps they were reassured by the preliminary reports of Harlow (1849) and Bigelow (1850), which suggested that Gage had suffered no mental impairment. However, by the time of Harlow's final reports (1868, 1869), it was clear that Gage had suffered a serious disorder of the emotions.

recent review, see Damasio, Damasio, & Van Hoesen, 1982), and refers to the inability to recognize faces. Prosopagnosic patients can describe the physical features of faces, but they cannot name the individuals to whom they belong; interestingly, they are able to identify people from such characteristics as their voice, dress, posture, or gait. However, given the face alone, these patients have no idea who the person is or what to expect from them. This deficit is linked to bilateral damage in the occipital lobe, especially those areas adjacent to the temporal lobe. As social animals, we seem to have been built by evolution with brain structures specifically tuned to that most social of stimuli, the face (e.g., Brothers, 1997).

Prosopagnosia has been taken as evidence that there is a particular brain system specialized for the identification of faces (e.g., Farah, 1990; Farah, Wilson, Drain, & Tanaka, 1998). This proposal is not unreasonable, given our status as social animals and the obvious evolutionary advantages of being able to identify faces and discriminate among them, quickly and reliably. However, there is an interesting controversy here. It has been suggested that prosopagnosics have difficulty identifying any particular visual stimulus, not just faces. Unfortunately, the clinical evidence is equivocal. One prosopagnosic farmer was unable to recognize his own cows, as well as members of his own family (Bornstein, Sroka, & Munitz, 1969), whereas another prosopagnosic farmer — What's the chance of that? — lost the ability to recognize both his family members and his cows, but eventually recovered the former but not the latter (Assal, Favre, & Anderes, 1984). However, case studies are always difficult to interpret, and recent experimental and neuroimaging studies of both prosopagnosic patients and intact participants strongly suggests that the "face area" damaged in prosopagnosia is actually specialized for expert recognition of objects at subordinate levels of categorization — objects which include, but are not limited to, faces (Gauthier, 1998).

Although prosopagnosia is dramatic, it turns out that there are many different forms of facial agnosia, each reflecting the selective impairment of some functions and the sparing of others. In general, the finding that two functions are dissociable from each other supports the hypothesis that the functions in question are qualitatively different. For example, some prosopagnosics are able to interpret the emotional meaning of facial expressions without being able to recognize the faces themselves, and others recover the ability to identify familiar faces but not the ability to interpret facial expressions. Interestingly, single-unit analyses of face perception in monkeys finds separate neurons (or, more likely, separate clusters of neurons) that are responsive to identity and expression.

In an attempt to summarize the neuropsychological evidence, Bruce and Young (1986) proposed that facial perception involves several different processes that are carried out in parallel. According to their view, input from a facial stimulus is first processed by a structural encoding system that creates two different descriptions of the face — one which is view-centered (e.g., full-face or profile) and one that is independent of the particular expression on the face. Output from this structural encoding system then passes to other systems specialized for analysis of facial expressions, speech (actually, lip-reading), sameness or difference (as between full-face or profile views), and facial recognition. These functions are performed by separate systems, as indicated by the fact that they are dissociable. For example, prosopagnosic patients can identify facial expressions even though they do not recognize the faces as familiar, and there is at least one patient who has lost the ability to analyze facial expressions of emotion, but who retains the ability to lip-read.

In addition, among brain-damaged patients performance on a test of memory for unfamiliar faces is essentially unrelated to the ability to recognize famous faces. All of these results indicate that remembering unfamiliar faces and recognizing familiar faces are mediated by separate systems. The face recognition system is a sort of visual lexicon containing template representations of familiar faces. Information processed by the face recognition system then contacts associated information pertaining to the identity of the person whose face has been recognized and by this route retrieves the name associated with the familiar face. Thereafter, other information about the person is retrieved through the generic cognitive system. Note that the general cognitive system can influence some facial processing systems (e.g., expression analysis, facial speech analysis, and directed visual processing), but it cannot directly influence facial recognition. That influence must be mediated by cognitive activation of the person-identity nodes.

A model like this makes some interesting predictions about face processing that should interest social psychologists. For example, priming with the name attached to a face should influence face recognition, but not expression analysis; priming with the label of an emotional state should influence expression analysis, but not face recognition. We don't know yet whether this is true. A prediction that has been tested, however, is that familiarity should influence identity matching but not expression analysis. In an experiment performed by Young, Ellis, and their colleagues (e.g., Young, McWeeny, Hay, & Ellis, 1986), intact participants were asked whether two photographs showed the same type of facial expression or whether they showed the same person. Half the photographs were of individuals who were familiar from the news or entertainment media, the other half were mere mortals. In terms of response latencies, familiarity affected identity matching but not expression matching. This is especially interesting, insofar as other research indicates that facial expression analysis and face recognition rely on the same facial features. Although these features may be analyzed by a single structural encoding system, the output from this module appears to be passed to different task-specific systems operating in parallel.

We don't mean to imply that the Bruce-Ellis model has been tested and proven in every respect; it hasn't, and it might be wrong in significant ways. The point is only to show how neuropsychological evidence can contribute to social-psychological theory: First, by providing empirical evidence of a sort that would be difficult or impossible to obtain in laboratory studies of college sophomores or interviews of people in airports and laundromats; second, by providing specific theoretical models of cognitive processes that can be tested in laboratory studies of the sort that we do.

Toward a Social Neuropsychology

One of the most exciting trends in cognitive psychology over the past 20 years has been the increasing application of data and conceptual tools derived from the study of patients with neuropsychological syndromes. To date, however, social and personality psychologists have rarely considered neuropsychological case material when developing theories about social and personality processes. We hope this situation changes, for we believe the domain of clinical neuropsychology holds considerable untapped potential for formulating and testing models within personality and social psychology.

In this article we have described some of the ways in which questions of interest to social and personality psychologists can be addressed with neuropsychological data. For example, we have shown (a) how studying both the preserved and impaired capacities of patients suffering amnesia and autism can provide important new insights into the mental representation of self, (b) how understanding the ways in which anosognosic patients attempt to make sense of their disabilities can

shed new light on the process of causal attribution, and (c) how consideration of the data from frontal lobe patients can help address questions concerning the relation between cognition and emotion. As we hope our review shows, there clearly is much social and personality psychologists can learn from the study of patients with neuropsychological syndromes.

Although our focus in this article has been on ways in which personality and social psychology can benefit from a consideration of neuropsychological case material, we also are convinced that neuropsychological theory and research can benefit from insights derived from personality and social psychology. To date, almost all of the work on patients with neuropsychological impairments has been done within the confines of cognitive psychology and cognitive neuropsychology, with relatively little attention paid to the interpersonal, emotional, and motivational lives of these individuals. Yet, the syndromes described in this article invariably are accompanied by profound changes in the individual's personal, social, and professional life (e.g., Blumer & Benson, 1975; Damasio, 1994; Hilts, 1995; Luria, 1972; O'Connor et al., 1995; M. F. Robinson & Freeman, 1954; Sacks, 1985), changes that have important implications for the way we approach treatment, conduct research, and formulate theory. Thus, it would seem that an important agenda item for the near future would be the adoption by cognitive neuropsychologists of the concepts and principles that have served their social and personality colleagues so well and the systematic extension of research on neuropsychological impairment beyond the purely cognitive to include the personal and social.

The study of the interpersonal and emotional lives of patients with neuropsychological syndromes promises to provide new perspectives on the relation between cognitive neuropsychology and social-personality psychology. However, this will not happen until psychologists interested in social and personality issues start considering neuropsychological case material and psychologists interested in neuropsychology begin to inquire into their patients' personal and social lives. Such an interdisciplinary approach is exciting because it would represent the beginning of a collaboration that ultimately might bridge a gap between social-personality psychology and cognitive neuropsychology.

REFERENCES

Akelaitis, A. J. (1941a). Psychobiological studies following section of the corpus callosum: A preliminary report. *American Journal of Psychiatry, 97,* 1147–1157.

Akelaitis, A. J. (1941b). Studies on the corpus callosum: II. The higher visual functions in each homonymous field following complete section of the corpus callosum. *Archives of Neurology and Psychiatry, 45*, 788–796.

Akelaitis, A. J. (1944). The study of gnosis, praxis and language following section of the corpus callosum and anterior commissure. *Journal of Neurosurgery, 1*, 94–102.

Assal, G., Favre, C., & Anderes, J. P. (1984). Non-reconnaissance d'animaux familiers chez un paysan: Zooagnosie ou prosopagnosie pour les animaux [Nonrecognition of familiar animals by a peasant: Zooagnosia or Prosopagnosia for animals]. *Revue Neurologique, 140*, 580–584.

Babinski, J. (1914). Contribution a l'etude des troubles mentaux dans l'hemiplegie organique cerebrale (anosognosie) [Contribution to the study of mental disturbance in organic cerebral hemiplegia (anosognosia)]. *Revue Neurologie, 1*, 845–848.

Babinski, J. (1918). Anosognosie [Anosognosia]. *Revue Neurologie, 31*, 365–367.

Baddeley, A. D., & Warrington, E. K. (1970). Amnesia and the distinction between long- and short-term memory. *Journal of Verbal Learning and Verbal Behavior, 9*, 176–189.

Baron-Cohen, S. (1989). Are autistic children "behaviorists"? An examination of their mental–physical and appearance–reality distinctions. *Journal of Autism and Developmental Disorders, 19*, 579–600.

Baron-Cohen, S. (1990). Autsim: A specific cognitive disorder of "mind-blindness." *International Review of Psychiatry, 2*, 79–88.

Baron-Cohen, S. (1991). The development of a theory of mind in autism: Deviance or delay? *Psychiatric Clinics of North America, 14*, 33–51.

Baron-Cohen, S. (1995). *Mindblindness: An essay on autism and theory of mind.* Cambridge, MA: MIT Press.

Baron-Cohen, S., Leslie, A. M., & Frith, U. (1985). Does the autistic child have a "theory of mind"? *Cognition, 21*, 37–46.

Baron-Cohen, S., Ring, H., Moriarty, J., Schmitz, B., Costa, D., & Ell, P. (1994). Recognition of mental state terms: Clinical findings in children with autism and a functional neuroimaging study in normal adults. *British Journal of Psychiatry, 165*, 640–649.

Baron-Cohen, S., Tager-Flusberg, H., & Cohen, D. (Eds.). (1993). *Understanding other minds: Perspectives from autism.* Oxford, England: Oxford University Press.

Bem, D. J. (1967). Self-perception: An alternative interpretation of cognitive dissonance phenomena. *Psychological Review, 74*, 183–200.

Bem, D. J. (1972). Self-perception theory. In L. Berkowitz (Ed.), *Advances in experimental social psychology* (Vol. 6, pp. 1–62). New York: Academic.

Berndt, R. S., & Caramazza, A. (1980). A redefinition of the syndrome of Broca's aphasia: Implications for a neuropsychological model of language. *Applied Linguistics, 1*, 225–278.

Bigelow, H. J. (1850). Dr. Harlow's case of recovery from the passage of an iron bar through the head. *American Journal of Medical Sciences, 19*, 13–22.

Bishop, D. V. M. (1993). Annotation: Autism, executive functions and theory of mind: A neuropsychological perspective. *Journal of Child Psychology and Psychiatry, 34*, 279–293.

Bisiach, E., & Geminiani, G. (1991). Anosognosia related to hemiplegia and hemianopia. In G. P. Prigatano & D. L. Schacter (Eds.), *Awareness of deficit after brain injury: Clinical and theoretical issues* (pp. 17–39). New York: Oxford University Press.

Blumer, D., & Benson, D. F. (1975). Personality changes with frontal and temporal lobe lesions. In D. F. Benson & D. Blumer (Eds.), *Psychiatric aspects of neurological disease* (pp. 151–169). New York: Grune & Stratton.

Bodamer, J. (1947). Die prosopagnosia [Prosopagnosia]. *Archiv fur Psychiatrie und Zeitschrift fur Neurologie, 179*, 6–54.

Bogen, J. E. (1985). The callosal syndromes. In K. M. Heilman & E. Valenstein (Eds.), *Clinical neuropsychology* (2nd ed., pp. 295–338). Oxford, England: Oxford University Press.

Bogen, J. E., Fisher, E. D., & Vogel, P. J. (1965). Cerebral commisurotomy: A second case report. *Journal of the American Medical Association, 194*, 1328–1329.

Bogen, J. E., & Vogel, P. J. (1962). Cerebral commissurotomy in man: Preliminary case report. *Bulletin of the Los Angeles Neurological Societies, 27*, 169–172.

Bornstein, B., Sroka, M., & Munitz, H. (1969). Prosopagnosia with animal face agnosia. *Cortex, 5*, 164–169.

Brewer, W. F. (1986). What is autobiographical memory? In D. C. Rubin (Ed.), *Autobiographical memory* (pp. 25–49). Cambridge, England: Cambridge University Press.

Brickner, R. M. (1936). *The intellectual functions of the frontal lobes.* New York: Macmillan.

Brooks, D. N., & Baddeley, A. D. (1976). What can amnesic patients learn? *Neuropsychologia, 14*, 111–122.

Brothers, L. (1997). *Friday's footprint: How society shapes the human mind.* New York: Oxford University Press.

Brown, J. W. (1972). *Aphasia, apraxia, agnosia.* Springfield, IL: Thomas.

Bruce, V., & Young, A. (1986). Understanding face recognition. *British Journal of Psychology, 77*, 305–327.

Carruthers, P. (1996). Autism as mind-blindness: An elaboration and partial defence. In P. Carruthers & P. K. Smith (Eds.), *Theories of theories of mind* (pp. 257–273). Cambridge, England: Cambridge University Press.

Cermak, L. S. (1972). *Human memory: Theory and research.* New York: Ronald Press Company.

Cermak, L. S. (1984). The episodic-semantic distinction in amnesia. In R. L. Squire & N. Butters (Eds.), *Neuropsychology of memory* (pp. 45–54), New York: Guilford.

Cermak, L. S., & O'Connor, M. (1983). The anterograde and retrograde retrieval ability of a patient with amnesia due to encephalitis. *Neuropsychologia, 21*, 213–234.

Clark, M. S., & Fiske, S. T. (1982). *Affect and cognition: The seventeenth annual Carnegie symposium on cognition.* Hillsdale, NJ: Lawrence Erlbaum Associates, Inc.

Conway, M. A. (1992). A structural model of autobiographical memory. In M. A. Conway, D. C. Rubin, H. Spinnler, & W. A. Wagenaar (Eds.), *Theoretical perspectives on autobiographical memory* (pp. 167–194). Amsterdam: Kluwer.

Corballis, M. C. (1991). *The lopsided ape: Evolution of the generative mind.* New York: Oxford University Press.

Coslett, H. B. (1997). Neglect in vision and visual imagery: A double dissociation. *Brain, 120*, 1163–1171.

Craik, F. I. M., Moroz, T. M., Moscovitch, M., Stuss, D. T., Winocur, G., Tulving, E., & Kapur, S. (in press). In search of the self: A PET investigation of self-referential information. *Psychological Science.*

Crovitz, H. F., & Qunia-Holland, K. (1976). Proportion of episodic memories from early childhood by years of age. *Bulletin of the Psychonomic Society, 7*, 61–62.

Crovitz, H. F., & Schiffman, H. (1974). Frequency of episodic memories as a function of their age. *Bulletin of the Psychonomic Society, 4*, 517–518.

Damasio, A. R. (1985). The frontal lobes. In K. M. Heilman & E. Valenstein (Eds.), *Clinical neuropsychology* (pp. 339–375). New York: Oxford University Press.

Damasio, A. R. (1994). *Descartes' error: Emotion, reason, and the human brain*. New York: Grosset/Putnam.

Damasio, A. R., Damasio, H., & Van Hoesen, G. W. (1982). Prosopagnosia: Anatomic basis and behavioral mechanisms. *Neurology, 32*, 331–341.

Damasio, A. R., & Maurer, R. G. (1987). A neurological model for childhood autism. *Archives of Neurology, 35*, 777–786.

Dunbar, R. (1996). *Grooming, gossip, and the evolution of language*. Cambridge, MA: Harvard University Press.

Dunn, J. C., & Kirsner, K. (1988). Discovering functionally independent mental processes: The principle of reversed association. *Psychological Review, 95*, 91–101.

Ellis, A. W., & Young, A. W. (1988). *Human cognitive neuropsychology*. London: Lawrence Erlbaum Associates, Inc.

Evans, J., Wilson, B., Wraight, E. P., & Hodges, J. R. (1993). Neuropsychological and SPECT scan findings during and after transient global amnesia: Evidence for the differential impairment of remote episodic memory. *Journal of Neurology, Neurosurgery, and Psychiatry, 56*, 1227–1230.

Farah, M. (1990). *Visual agnosia: Disorders of object recognition and what they tell us about normal vision*. Cambridge, MA: MIT Press.

Farah, M. J., Wilson, K. D., Drain, M., & Tanaka, J. N. (1998). What is "special" about face perception? *Psychological Review, 105*, 482–498.

Fay, W. H. (1979). Personal pronouns and the autistic child. *Journal of Autism and Developmental Disorders, 9*, 247–260.

Flavell, J. H., Green, F. L., & Flavell, E. R. (1995). Young children's knowledge about thinking. *Monographs of the Society for Research in Child Development, 60* (1, Serial No. 243).

Fletcher, P. C. Happe, F., Frith, U., Baker, S. C., Dolan, R. J., Frackowiak, R. S. J., & Frith, C. D. (1995). Other minds in the brain: A functional imaging study of "theory of mind" in story comprehension. *Cognition, 57*, 109–128.

Foster, J. K., & Jelicic, M. (Eds.). (in press). *Unitary and multiple system accounts of memory*. New York: Oxford University Press.

Franco, L., & Sperry, R. W. (1977). Hemisphere lateralization for cognitive processing of geometry. *Neuropsychologia, 15*, 107–113.

Freeman, W., & Watts, J. W. (1950). *Psychosurgery in the treatment of mental disorders and intractable pain*. Springfield, IL: Charles C. Thomas.

Freud, S. (1953). *On aphasia*. New York: International Universities Press. (Original work published 1891)

Frith, C. D., & Frith, U. (1991). Elective affinities in schizophrenia and childhood autism. In P. Bebbington (Ed.), *Social psychiatry: Theory, methodology and practice* (pp. 66–88). New Brunswick, NJ: Transactions.

Frith, U. (1989). *Autism: Explaining the enigma*. Oxford, England: Blackwell.

Fuster, J. M. (1997). *The prefrontal cortex: Anatomy, physiology, and neuropsychology of the frontal lobe*. Philadelphia: Lippincott-Raven.

Galton, F. (1879). Psychometric experiments. *Brain, 2*, 149–162.

Gardner, H. (1985). *The mind's new science: A history of the cognitive revolution*. New York: Basic Books.

Gauthier, I. (1998). *Dissecting face recognition: The role of categorization level and expertise in visual object recognition*. Unpublished doctoral dissertation, Yale University, New Haven, CT.

Gazzaniga, M. S. (1970). *The bisected brain*. New York: Appleton-Century-Crofts.

Gazzaniga, M. S. (1998). *The mind's past*. Berkeley, CA: University of California Press.

Gazzaniga, M. S., Ivry, R. B., & Mangun, G. R. (1998). *Cognitive neuroscience: The biology of the mind*. New York: Norton.

Gazzaniga, M. S., & LeDoux, J. E. (1978). *The integrated mind*. New York: Plenum.

Gazzaniga, M. S., & Smylie, C. S. (1984). Dissociation of language and cognition: A psychological profile of two disconnected right hemispheres. *Brain, 107*, 145–153.

Glisky, E. L. (1995). Computers in memory rehabilitation. In A. D. Baddeley, R. A. Wilson, & F. N. Watts (Eds.), *Handbook of memory disorders* (pp. 557–575). Chichester, England: Wiley.

Glisky, E. L., Schacter, D. L., & Tulving, E. (1986a). Computer learning by memory-impaired patients: Acquisition and retention of complex knowledge. *Neuropsychologia, 24*, 313–328.

Glisky, E. L., Schacter, D. L., & Tulving, E. (1986b). Learning and retention of computer-related vocabulary in memory-impaired patients: Method of vanishing cues. *Journal of Clinical and Experimental Neuropsychology, 8*, 292–312.

Goel, V., Grafman, J., Sadato, N., & Hallett, M. (1995). Modeling other minds. *Neuroreport, 6*, 1741–1746.

Goodglass, H. (1993). *Understanding aphasia*. San Diego, CA: Academic.

Gopnik, A., & Metzloff, A. N. (1997). *Words, thoughts, and theories*. Cambridge, MA: MIT Press.

Gordon, H. W., & Sperry, R. W. (1969). Lateralization of olfactory perception in the surgically separated hemispheres in man. *Neuropsychologia, 12*, 111–120.

Graf, P., Squire, L., & Mandler, G. (1984). The information that amnesic patients do not forget. *Journal of Experimental Psychology: Learning, Memory and Cognition, 10*, 164–178.

Greenwald, A. G., & Pratkanis, A. R. (1984). The self. In R. S. Wyer & T. K. Srull (Eds.), *Handbook of social cognition* (Vol. 3, pp. 129–178). Hillsdale, NJ: Lawrence Erlbaum Associates, Inc.

Grice, H. P. (1941). Personal identity. *Mind, 50*, 330–350.

Harlow, J. M. (1849). Letter in "Medical miscellany." *Boston Medical and Surgical Journal, 39*, 506–507.

Harlow, J. M. (1868). Recovery form the passage of an iron bar through the head. *Publications of the Massachusetts Medical Society, 2*, 327–347.

Harlow, J. M. (1869). *Recovery from the passage of an iron bar through the head*. Boston: Clapp.

Heilman, K. M., & Valenstein, E. (1993). *Clinical neuropsychology* (3rd ed). New York: Oxford University Press.

Hilts, P. J. (1995). *Memory's ghost: The strange tale of Mr. M. and the nature of memory*. New York: Simon & Schuster.

Humphrey, N. (1984). *Consciousness regained: Chapters in the development of mind*. Oxford, England: Oxford University Press.

Humphrey, N. (1986). *The inner eye*. London: Faber & Faber.

Humphrey, N. (1990). The uses of consciousness. In J. Brockman (Ed.), *Speculations: The reality club* (pp. 67–84). New York: Prentice Hall.

James, W. (1890). *The principles of psychology* (Vol. 1). New York: Holt.

Jaynes, J. (1976). *The origin of consciousness in the breakdown of the bicameral mind*. Boston: Houghton Mifflin.

Jordan, R. R. (1989). An experimental comparison of the understanding and use of speaker–addressee personal pronouns in autistic children. *British Journal of Disorders of Communication, 24*, 169–179.

Keenan, J. M. (1993). An exemplar model can explain Klein and Loftus' results. In T. K. Srull & R. S. Wyer (Eds.), *Advances in social cognition* (Vol. 5, pp. 69–77). Hillsdale, NJ: Lawrence Erlbaum Associates, Inc.

Kelley, C. M., & Lindsay, D. S. (1996). Conscious and unconscious forms of memory. In E. L. Bjork & R. A. Bjork (Eds.), *Memory* (pp. 31–63). New York: Academic.

Kihlstrom, J. F. (1987). The cognitive unconscious. *Science, 237,* 1445–1452.

Kihlstrom, J. F. (1993, October). *Toward a neuropsychology of social cognition.* Paper presented at the Annual Meeting for the Society for Experimental Social Psychology, Santa Barbara, CA.

Kihlstrom, J. F. (in press-a). Conscious and unconscious cognition. In R. J. Sternberg (Ed.), *The concept of cognition* New York: Oxford University Press.

Kihlstrom, J. F. (in press-b). The psychological unconscious. In L. Pervin (Ed.), *Handbook of personality: Theory and research* (2nd ed.). New York: Guilford.

Kihlstrom, J. F., Cantor, N., Albright, J. S., Chew, B. R., Klein, S. B., & Niedenthal, P. M. (1988). Information processing and the study of the self. In L. Berkowitz (Ed.), *Advances in experimental social psychology* (Vol. 21, pp. 145–178). San Diego, CA: Academic.

Kihlstrom, J. F., & Hoyt, E. P. (1988). Hypnosis and the psychology of delusions. In T. F. Oltmanns & B. A. Maher (Eds.), *Delusional beliefs* (pp. 66–109). New York: Wiley-Interscience.

Kihlstrom, J. F., & Klein, S. B. (1994). The self as a knowledge structure. In R. S. Wyer & T. K. Srull (Eds.), *Handbook of social cognition* (Vol. 1, pp. 153–208). Hillsdale, NJ: Lawrence Erlbaum Associates, Inc.

Kihlstrom, J. F., & Klein, S. B. (1997). Self-knowledge and self-awareness. In J. G. Snodgrass & R. L. Thompson (Eds.), *Annals of the New York Academy of Sciences: Vol. 818. The self across psychology: Self-awareness, self-recognition, and the self-concept* (pp. 5–17). New York: New York Academy of Science.

Kinsbourne, M., & Wood, F. (1975). Short-term memory processes and the amnesic syndrome. In D. Deutsch & J. A. Deutsch (Eds.), *Short-term memory* (pp. 257–291). New York: Academic.

Klein, S. B. (1993, October). *The mental representation of self-knowledge: Evidence from clinical amnesia.* Paper presented at the Annual Meeting for the Society for Experimental Social Psychology, Santa Barbara, CA.

Klein, S. B. (1996, October). *The self and cognition.* Paper presented at the 1st Annual SELF Preconference at the Annual Meeting for the Society for Experimental Social Psychology, Sturbridge, MA.

Klein, S. B. (in press). Memory and the self. *McGraw-Hill 1999 yearbook of science and technology.* New York: McGraw-Hill.

Klein, S. B., Babey, S. H., & Sherman, J. W. (1997). The functional independence of trait and behavioral self-knowledge: Methodological considerations and new empirical findings. *Social Cognition, 15,* 183–203.

Klein, S. B., & Kihlstrom, J. F. (1986). Elaboration, organization, and the self-reference effect in memory. *Journal of Experimental Psychology: General, 115,* 26–38.

Klein, S. B., & Loftus, J. (1993). The mental representation of trait and autobiographical knowledge about the self. In T. K. Srull & R. S. Wyer (Eds.), *Advances in social cognition* (Vol. 5, pp. 1–49). Hillsdale, NJ: Lawrence Erlbaum Associates, Inc.

Klein, S. B., Loftus, J., & Kihlstrom, J. F. (1996). Self-knowledge of an amnesic patient: Toward a neuropsychology of personality and social psychology. *Journal of Experimental Psychology: General, 125,* 250–260.

Klein, S. B., Sherman, J. W., & Loftus, J. (1996). The role of episodic and semantic memory in the development of trait self-knowledge. *Social Cognition, 14,* 277–291.

Kluver, H., & Bucy, P. C. (1939). Preliminary analysis of the functions of the temporal lobes in monkeys. *Archives of Neurology and Psychiatry, 42,* 979–1000.

Kolb, B., & Whishaw, I. Q. (1996). *Fundamentals of human neuropsychology* (4th ed.). New York: Freeman.

LeDoux, J. E. (1985). Brain, mind and language. In D. A. Oakley (Ed.), *Brain and mind* (pp. 197–216). London: Methuen.

LeDoux, J. E. (1987). Emotion. In F. Plum (Ed.), *Handbook of physiology: Section 1. The nervous system; Vol. 5. Higher functions of the brain* (pp. 419–460). Bethesda, MD: American Physiological Society.

LeDoux, J. E. (1996). *The emotional brain: The mysterious underpinnings of emotional life.* New York: Simon & Schuster.

LeDoux, J. E., Wilson, D. H., & Gazzaniga, M. S. (1977). A divided mind: Observations on the conscious properties of the separated hemispheres. *Annals of Neurology, 2,* 417–421.

Lee, A., Hobson, R. P., & Chiat, S. (1994). I, you, me, and autism: An experimental study. *Journal of Autism and Developmental Disorders, 24,* 155–176.

Leslie, A. M. (1987). Pretense and representation: The origins of "theory of mind". *Psychological Review, 94,* 412–426.

Leslie, A. M. (1991). The theory of mind impairment in autism: Evidence for a modular mechanism of development. In A. Whiten (Ed.), *Natural theories of mind* (pp. 63–78). Oxford, England: Blackwell.

Leslie, A. M., & Frith, U. (1988). Autistic children's understanding of seeing, knowing and believing. *British Journal of Developmental Psychology, 6,* 315–324.

Leslie, A. M., & Thaiss, L. (1992). Domain specificity in conceptual development: Neuropsychological evidence from autism. *Cognition, 43,* 225–251.

Levy, J., Trevarthen, C., & Sperry, R. W. (1972). Perception of bilateral chimeric figures following hemispheric disconnection. *Brain, 92,* 61–78.

Levy-Agresti, J., & Sperry, R. W. (1968). Differential perceptual capacities in major and minor hemispheres. *Proceedings of the National Academy of Science, 61,* 1151.

Locke, J. (1731). *An essay concerning human understanding.* London: Edmund Parker. (Original work published 1690)

Luria, A. R. (1972). *The man with a shattered world: The history of a brain wound.* Cambridge, MA: Harvard University Press.

Macmillan, M. B. (1986). A wonderful journey through skull and brains: The travels of Mr. Gage's tamping iron. *Brain & Cognition, 5,* 67–107.

Marks, C. E. (1981). *Commissurotomy consciousness and unity of mind.* Cambridge, MA: MIT Press.

McCarthy, R. A., & Warrington, E. K. (1990). *Cognitive neuropsychology: A clinical introduction.* San Diego, CA: Academic.

McGlynn, S. M., & Kasczniak, A. W. (1991). Unawareness of deficits in dementia and schizophrenia. In G. P. Prigatano & D. L. Schacter (Eds.), *Awareness of deficit after brain injury: Clinical and theoretical perspectives* (pp. 84–110). New York: Oxford University Press.

McGlynn, S. M., & Schacter, D. L. (1989). Unawareness of deficits in neuropsychological syndromes. *Journal of Clinical & Experimental Neuropsychology, 11,* 143–205.

Milner, B. (1966). Amnesia following operations on the temporal lobes. In C. W. M. Whitty & O. L. Zangwill (Eds.), *Amnesia.* London: Butterworth.

Milner, B., Corkin, S., & Teuber, H.-L. (1968). Further analysis of the hippocampal amnesic syndrome: 14-year follow up study of H. M. *Neuropsychologia, 6,* 215–234.

Nagel, T. (1971). Brain bisection and the unity of consciousness. *Synthese, 22,* 396–413.

Neely, J. H. (1989). Experimental dissociations and the episodic/semantic memory distinction. In H. L. Roediger & F. I. M. Craik

(Eds.), *Varieties of memory and consciousness: Essays in honor of Endel Tulving* (pp. 229–270). Hillsdale, NJ: Lawrence Erlbaum Associates, Inc.

Nisbett, R. E., & Wilson, T. D. (1977). Telling more than we can know: Verbal reports on mental processes. *Psychological Review, 84*, 231–236.

Oakley, D. A., & Eames, L. C. (1985). The plurality of consciousness. In D. A. Oakley (Ed.), *Brain and mind* (pp. 217–251). London: Methuen.

O'Connor, M. G., Cermak, L. S., & Seidman, L. J. (1995). Social and emotional characteristics of a profoundly amnesic postencephalitic patient. In R. Campbell & M. A. Conway (Eds.), *Broken memories: Case studies in memory impairment* (pp. 45–53). Oxford, England: Blackwell.

Ozonoff, S., Pennington, B. F., & Rogers, S. J. (1991). Executive function deficits in high-functioning autistic individuals: Relationship to theory of mind. *Journal of Child Psychology and Psychiatry, 32*, 1081–1105.

Phelps, E. A., & Gazzaniga, M. S. (1992). Hemispheric differences in mnemonic processing: The effects of left hemisphere interpretation. *Neuropsychologia, 30*, 293–297.

Pinker, S. (1994). *The language instinct: How the mind creates language*. New York: Harper Collins.

Polster, M. R., Nadel, L., & Schacter, D. L. (1991). Cognitive neuroscience analyses of memory: A historical perspective. *Journal of Cognitive Neuroscience, 3*, 95–116.

Popper, K. R., & Eccles, J. C. (1977). *The self and its brain*. Berlin, Germany: Springer-Verlag.

Premack, D., & Woodruff, G. (1978). Does the chimpanzee have a theory of mind? *The Brain and Behavioral Sciences, 4*, 515–526.

Price, B., Daffner, K., Stowe, R., & Mesulam, M. (1990). The compartmental learning disabilities of early frontal lobe damage. *Brain, 113*, 1383–1393.

Prigatano, G. P., & Schacter, D. L. (Eds.). (1991). *Awareness of deficit after brain injury: Clinical and theoretical issues*. New York: Oxford University Press.

Prior, M. R., & Hoffman, W. (1990). Brief report: Neuropsychological testing of autistic children through an exploration with frontal lobe tests. *Journal of Autism and Developmental Disorders, 20*, 581–590.

Puccetti, R. (1973). Brain bisection and personal identity. *British Journal for the Philosophy of Science, 24*, 339–355.

Quinton, A. (1962). The soul. *Journal of Philosophy, 59*, 393–409.

Robinson, J. A. (1976). Sampling autobiographical memory. *Cognitive Psychology, 8*, 578–595.

Robinson, M. F., & Freeman, W. (1954). *Psychosurgery and the self*. New York: Grune & Stratton.

Rubens, A. B., & Garrett, M. F. (1991). Anosognosia of linguistic deficits in patients with neurological deficits. In G. P. Prigatano & D. L. Schacter (Eds.), *Awareness of deficit after brain injury: Clinical and theoretical issues* (pp. 40–52). New York: Oxford University Press.

Sacks, O. (1985). *The man who mistook his wife for a hat*. New York: Doubleday.

Schacter, D. L. (1987). Implicit memory: History and current status. *Journal of Experimental Psychology: Learning, Memory, and Cognition, 13*, 501–518.

Schacter, D. L., & Tulving, E. (1982). Memory, amnesia, and the episodic/semantic memory distinction. In R. L. Isaacson & N. E. Spear (Eds.), *The expression of knowledge* (pp. 33–65). New York: Plenum.

Schacter, D. L., & Tulving, E. (Eds.). (1994). *Memory systems 1994*. Cambridge, MA: MIT Press.

Schneider, D. J., Roediger, H. L., & Khan, M. (1993). Diverse ways of accessing self-knowledge: Comment on Klein and Loftus. In T. K. Srull & R. S. Wyer (Eds.), *Advances in social cognition* (Vol. 5, pp. 123–136). Hillsdale, NJ: Lawrence Erlbaum Associates, Inc.

Scoville, W. B., & Milner, B. (1957). Loss of recent memory after bilateral hippocampal lesions. *Journal of Neurology, Neurosurgery, & Psychiatry, 20*, 11–21.

Sedikides, C., & Skowronski, J. J. (1997). The symbolic self in evolutionary context. *Personality and Social Psychology Review, 1*, 80–102.

Shallice, T. (1988). *From neuropsychology to mental structure*. New York: Cambridge University Press.

Sizer, N. (1882). *Forty years in phrenology: Embracing recollections of history, anecdote, and experience*. New York: Fowler & Wells.

Sperry, R. W. (1966). Brain bisection and the mechanisms of consciousness. In J. C. Eccles (Ed.), *Brain and conscious experience* (pp. 298–313). Heidelberg, Germany: Springer-Verlag.

Sperry, R. W. (1968). Hemisphere deconnection and unity in conscious awareness. *American Psychologist, 23*, 723–733.

Sperry, R. W. (1974). Lateral specialization in the surgically separated hemispheres. In F. O. Schmitt & F. G. Worden (Eds.), *The neurosciences third study program* (pp. 5–19). Cambridge, MA: MIT Press.

Sperry, R. W., Gazzaniga, M. S., & Bogen, J. E. (1969). Interhemispheric relationships: The neocortical commissures: Syndromes of hemisphere disconnection. In P. J. Vinken & G. W. Bruyn (Eds.), *Handbook of clinical neurology* (Vol. 4, pp. 273–290). New York: North Holland.

Springer, S. P., & Deutsch, G. (1998). *Left brain right brain: Perspective from cognitive neuroscience*. New York: Freeman.

Squire, L. R., & Knowlton, B. J. (1995). Memory, hippocampus, and brain systems. In M. S. Gazzaniga (Ed.), *The cognitive neurosciences* (pp. 825–837). Cambridge, MA: MIT Press.

Squire, L. R., & Zola-Morgan, S. (1991). The medial temporal lobe memory system. *Science, 253*, 1380–1386.

Stone, V. E., Baron-Cohen, S., & Knight, R. T. (1996). Frontal lobe contributions to theory of mind. *Journal of Cognitive Neuroscience, 10*, 640–656.

Stuss, D. T. (1991). Self-awareness, and the frontal lobes: A neuropsychological perspective. In J. Strauss & G. R. Goethals (Eds.), *The self: Interdisciplinary approaches* (pp. 255–278). New York: Springer-Verlag.

Tager-Flusberg, H. (1992). Autistic children's talk about psychological states: Deficits in the early acquisition of a theory of mind. *Child Development, 63*, 161–172.

Teuber, H.-L. (1955). Physiological psychology. *Annual Review of Psychology, 9*, 267–296.

Tulving, E. (1983). *Elements of episodic memory*. New York: Oxford University Press.

Tulving, E. (1984). Precis of elements of episodic memory. *The Behavioral and Brain Sciences, 7*, 223–268.

Tulving, E. (1989). Remembering and knowing. *American Scientist, 77*, 361–367.

Tulving, E. (1993). Self-knowledge of an amnesic patient is represented abstractly. In T. K. Srull & R. S. Wyer (Eds.), *Advances in social cognition* (Vol. 5, pp. 147–156). Hillsdale, NJ: Lawrence Erlbaum Associates, Inc.

Tulving, E., Hayman, C. A. G., & Macdonald, C. A. (1991). Long-lasting perceptual priming and semantic learning in amnesia: A case experiment. *Journal of Experimental Psychology: Learning, Memory, and Cognition, 17*, 595–617.

Tulving, E., Schacter, D. L., McLachlan, D. R., & Moscovitch, M. (1988). Priming of semantic autobiographical knowledge: A case study of retrograde amnesia. *Brain and Cognition, 8,* 3–20.

Vallar, G., Bisiach, E., Cerizza, M., & Rusconi, M. L. (1988). The role of the left hemisphere in decision making. *Cortex, 24,* 399–410.

Valenstein, E. S. (1973). *Brain control: A critical examination of brain stimulation and psychosurgery.* New York: Wiley.

Van der Linden, M., Bredart, S., Depoorter, N., & Coyette, F. (1996). Semantic memory and amnesia: A case study. *Cognitive Neuropsychology, 13,* 391–413.

Velmans, M. (1996). *The science of consciousness: Psychological, neuropsychological and clinical reviews.* London: Routledge.

Warrington, E. K., & Weiskrantz, L. (1970). Amnesic syndrome: Consolidation or retrieval? *Nature, 228,* 628–630.

Weiskrantz, L. (1989). Remembering dissociations. In H. L. Roediger & F. I. M. Craik (Eds.), *Varieties of memory and consciousness: Essays in honor of Endel Tulving* (pp. 101–120). Hillsdale, NJ: Lawrence Erlbaum Associates, Inc.

Weiskrantz, L. (1997). *Consciousness lost and found.* New York: Oxford University Press.

Wellman, H. M. (1990). *The child's theory of mind.* Cambridge, MA: MIT Press.

Wheeler, M. A., Stuss, D. T., & Tulving, E. (1996). Toward a theory of episodic memory: The frontal lobes and autonoetic consciousness. *Psychological Bulletin, 121,* 331–354.

Wickelgren, W. A. (1973). The long and the short of memory. *Psychological Bulletin, 80,* 425–438.

Young, A. W., McWeeny, K. H., Hay, D. C., & Ellis, A. W. (1986). Matching familiar and unfamiliar faces on identity and expression. *Psychological Research, 48,* 63–68.

Zaidel, E. (1975). A technique for presenting lateralized visual input with prolonged exposure. *Vision Research, 15,* 283–289.

PART 2

Representation of Social Knowledge

Introduction and Preview

In Part 1, I emphasized a view of the perceiver as an active participant in processing social information. The perceiver selectively attends to certain aspects of the information available, she interprets and endows that information with meaning, she has evaluative reactions, she infers additional "knowledge" about the people and events she encounters, and she stores the result of all of this activity in memory. In Part 2 we examine a bit more closely how that information becomes represented and stored in memory. In doing so, we will learn more about the nature of cognitive structures that can guide information processing.

Categorization

We are so accustomed to "perceiving" things in our world — objects, people, events — that it seems to be a simple and natural process. It is indeed a natural process, but it is far from simple. Consider the object you are now looking at as you read these words — what is it? Obviously, it is a book. Very simple. But suppose some papers by an open window were blowing in the breeze, and you used this object to hold them down. This book would then be a paperweight. If you needed to elevate some other object off the surface of your desk (e.g., to see it better), then this book could become a stand on which something else can rest. If you needed to get something off a high shelf that is just out of reach, then this book (along with a few others) could be stacked to form a "footstool" on which you could step in order to reach it. So the same object can be perceived in different ways. Similarly, when we

101

observe the behaviors of others, what we see can be perceived in different ways. When Rick shows his answers on a take-home exam to Darren, is it an instance of one friend being helpful to another, or is it an act of cheating? Even persons can be seen in quite different ways. Is the Black man wearing the white lab coat and the stethoscope perceived as a doctor or as an African American (Rothbart & John, 1985)? In each case, the same object, behavior, or person has been categorized in one way or another, and in each case the nature of that categorization can make a big difference in how we regard the object, how we evaluate the behavior, and how we think about the person.

The first reading in this part presents excerpts from a classic article by Jerome Bruner (1957), who outlined many ideas about categorization that stimulated thinking and research into the role of stimulus categorization in the perception process. Bruner argued that perception involves an act of categorization in which the stimulus cues of the object that is perceived are used to place it in one category rather than another. Categorization, then, is an inference process that transpires between the cues and the categorical judgment. This process underlies all perception. In making this argument Bruner was among the first to highlight the importance of cognitive, inferential processes that mediate between the stimuli impinging on the organism and the perception that is experienced by the observer. In other words, the objects and events that we "perceive" gain their meaning through this cognitive act of categorization. Bruner explicitly highlighted the distinction between the perceptual world "out there" and the perceptual world as represented in the mind of the perceiver. The relation between external stimuli and internal representations of those stimuli can vary, so that the "meanings" one extracts as a result of this process can vary in their veridicality. Moreover, Bruner notes that much of this cognitive activity is "silent," by which he means that we often are not aware that we are doing it. And

finally, he argues that the results of this categorization process not only are responsive to the stimulus cues of what is "seen" in the external world but also can reflect the *context* in which the object or person is perceived, the prior knowledge and *expectancies* of the perceiver, and the perceiver's *temporary states*, such as needs and motives. All of these factors can increase the accessibility of alternative categorical systems, increasing the perceiver's "readiness" to categorize an object or event in one way vs. another.

At about the same time that Bruner's article was published, Gordon Allport (1954) provided a parallel analysis of the importance of the categorization process in group perception and its implications for stereotyping and prejudice. Allport noted that social perception involves grouping people into categories (based on race, gender, religion, nationality, etc.), an act that has several important consequences. For example, placing people into categories has the effect of exaggerating both the perceived similarities among members of the same group and the perceived differences between different categories.

These theoretical developments regarding the categorization process have also had a fundamental impact on our understanding of intergroup perception, in at least a couple of ways. First, if the perception of *similarities within* a group are exaggerated as a result of categorization ("They're all alike!"), then it becomes easier to make generalizations about the group's members, and such generalizations ("They're dirty, lazy, mean to people.") are the very stuff of which stereotypes are made (see Part 7). Thus, categorization has direct implications for stereotyping. Second, if categorization has the effect of augmenting the perceived *differences between* groups, then such perceptions ("They're really not like us at all!") can become the basis for intergroup differentiation, discrimination, and prejudice. Many factors can influence the dynamics of both stereotyping and intergroup discrimination, including competition for resources, affective reactions, and historical conflict between groups. However, as these examples illustrate, categorization is an inherent process of intergroup perception that often forms the foundation on which stereotyping and prejudice are built. More generally, categorization is an important process by which people incorporate — encode, comprehend, store — new information from their informationally rich environment.

Both Bruner and Allport emphasized that categorization is a fundamental cognitive process that underlies much of social perception. By grouping similar objects, people, or events together in a single category, emphasizing their similarities and diminishing their differences, the process can introduce biases and errors in our perceptions. However, categorization is also a highly adaptive process, one that greatly facilitates our perception and comprehension of a complex stimulus world. In effect, these categories represent the accumulated benefit of our past experiences and they enable us to use that "knowledge" to understand and adapt to new situations.

How does this categorization process work, and how are these categories represented in memory? It is here that this natural, intuitively simple question becomes complex, for the question is nothing less than, "How do we know the meaning of things in our environment?" That is, when we perceive something, we comprehend what it is by understanding it in terms of some concept or category. This applies to our perceptions of objects ("Is that a snake, or merely a branch, on the path?"), behaviors ("Was that remark a joke or was he being sarcastic?"), and people ("Is he gay or straight?"). How we construe (categorize) these perceptions can determine what those objects, behaviors, and people mean for us. We do so by considering the specific instance in relation to some mental representation that helps us make this categorization judgment.

For many years the assumption was that concepts have certain criterial properties and that all members of the category possessed these defining characteristics. A square has four sides of equal length connected, at 90° angles, etc. When I perceive a geometric shape, I can assess whether it has these properties. If it does, fine; if it doesn't, then it isn't a square.

However, it became clear that for many categories it is impossible to specify the defining criteria possessed by all members. Even a "simple" concept like *chair* poses problems of this kind. Whereas we might define a chair as an object with four legs, a seat, and a backrest, the variety of objects we refer to as chairs includes many that violate these criteria (some chairs have three legs instead of four; some have a seat to sit on but no back support; a beanbag chair has neither legs nor back; etc.). These conceptual difficulties led to newer theoretical accounts that posited a probabilistic view in which category members resembled other category members on numerous features, none of which were *necessary* criteria. A given object might be viewed as a member of a category if it shared a "family resemblance" to other objects in the category. In some theoretical accounts a category becomes represented by a *prototype*, a generalized mental representation of the category. This abstract representation is then used when encountering new objects. Specifically, the similarity or resemblance of the object to the prototype is assessed to determine if the object is a member of the category. "This chair doesn't quite look like my prototype of a chair, but it's more similar to this prototype than to prototypes of other categories (tables, cars, etc.) so I'll categorize it as a chair." Other theoretical accounts have argued that people do not form these abstract prototype representations but rather that the category representation consists of mental representations of category members, or *exemplars* of the category. When a new object is encountered, it is compared not to some prototype but rather to the exemplars of the category that are stored in memory. "It looks like other chairs I've seen in the past (as I sample these exemplars from my memory), so this must be a chair." Both the prototype view and the exemplar view have generated a considerable amount of research (as well as a lot of debate) comparing their respective strengths and weaknesses. It seems highly likely that our mental representation of a category includes both an abstract prototype of the category as well as exemplars of category members that we have encountered in past experience (Hamilton & Sherman, 1994; Klein & Loftus, 1990; Medin, 1989).

The conceptual structures we develop in our minds can also be represented in hierarchical relations. We know, for example, that dogs are a subgroup of animals, and that within the category of dogs there are setters, poodles, Dalmatians, and lots of other breeds (as well as mutts!). Each of these categories has associated features, but that knowledge is stored in a hierarchical structure. At any given "level" within the hierarchy, the concepts represented share some features with the superordinate concept under which they are represented (dogs and cats share some attributes that make them both animals; setters and poodles share features of dogs), but they also have unique features that make them meaningfully separate subgroups (dogs and cats, setters and poodles, have differentiating features that allow them to be represented by separate concepts within the overall structure). In the same way, our perceptions of the social world often recognize, and therefore represent, people and groups within a hierarchical system of concepts and categories. For example, Brewer, Dull, and Lui (1981) showed that people make conceptual distinctions — and have different stereotypes — of three subcategories of "old people," which they called the "grandmother type," "elder statesman type," and "senior citizen type." Similarly, Devine and Baker (1991) showed that perceivers have cognitive

representations of different subgroups within the larger category of Blacks (ghetto Blacks, Black athletes, Black businessmen, etc.). Thus, the features associated with the overall category (Blacks) may not apply with consistency to all subgroups of that category, and those subgroups will have different features that distinguish them from each other in one's belief system. In this sense, the cognitive structure we refer to as a "stereotype" may be quite different depending on which subgroup is being thought of at the moment.

In both the prototype view and the exemplar view, a crucial element is the assessment of similarity between an instance and either a prototype or exemplars sampled from memory. Instances that share similar features are classified in the same category. Although similarity plays a crucial role in categorization, Medin (1989) argues that similarity is not enough. A category consists of more than a listing of features shared by members of the category; it also provides some intuitive theory, some rationale, some explanation as to *why* the category members are a part of the same category and how those features are related to each other. Thus, Medin states, the category must have some structure that specifies causal relations among the features, and it is that structure of relations that provides a basis for comprehending why instances become associated with the category. A simple example provided by Medin (1989) makes the point effectively. Consider the three colors white, gray, and black, and think about the similarities among them. Is gray more similar to white or to black? It turns out (Medin & Shoben, 1988) that the particular "theory" that is operative at the moment can influence these judgments of similarity. When thinking about clouds, gray is similar to black — both of them foreboding inclement conditions. On the other hand, when thinking about hair color, gray is more similar to white, both of them reflecting a more advanced age. Thus, the structural organization of a category can both determine perceived similarities and can also — as a "theory" of the category — provide an explanatory basis for understanding the relations among elements of the category. Reading 7 by Medin (1989) reviews these various theoretical accounts of categorization (see also Yzerbyt, Rocher, & Schadron, 1997).

At this point you may be wondering, "What does all of this have to do with *social* cognition?" The simple answer: A lot. When we perceive people's behaviors, we categorize their acts according to traits that those behaviors manifest (religious behaviors, dishonest behaviors, friendly behaviors, etc.). When we perceive others, we often categorize them into social groups according to ways that they are similar and dissimilar to each other (male/female; Black/White/Brown; gay/straight; Catholic/Protestant/Jew; "us"/"them"). These categories provide a structure for organizing our perceptual experiences and also provide a conceptual framework for understanding and explaining those experiences. The categories we use provide our "ways of thinking" about our social world.

These points are well illustrated in Reading 8 by Wittenbrink, Gist, and Hilton (1997). Drawing on Medin's (1989) argument about the explanatory function of categories, these authors showed how the causal relations underlying a particular cognitive structure — specifically, people's stereotypes of African Americans — can influence the processing and interpretation of information in a simulated jury decision context. People differ in the causal assumptions they make about African Americans, for example, about their low social status in American society. Some believe that the low social and economic status of Blacks reflects a lack of motivation and values that foster success, whereas others account for that lower status in terms of the disadvantages in opportunities (education, employment, etc.) that constrain economic advancement by

African Americans. Wittenbrink et al. (1997) argued that these differences in the causal structure underlying stereotypic beliefs can influence the way people construe information, in this case, information presented to them about a criminal case involving an intergroup (Black–White) situation. They showed that the same information was interpreted quite differently as a function of the structural relations underlying the stereotypic beliefs. The results of this study demonstrate that a cognitive structure (stereotype) consists of more than a listing of attributes and that it includes a structural framework that integrates those features in a way that offers explanatory understanding.

Representation Systems

The categories we use when we process information from our social world reflect concepts that we have developed and retained from past experience. An important question for understanding how knowledge is stored in memory concerns the way those concepts are configured in memory. This actually includes several related questions concerning how those concepts are represented and organized, and also how they are used, both in processing new information and in retrieving already-stored information. There are several theories about the nature of these representations, and these theories reflect a variety of assumptions (for a review, see Carlston & Smith, 1996). In this brief introduction I present a view that has been influential in social psychological applications.

As I have just summarized, the concepts we learn are represented in memory in such a way that they form associations with other concepts with which they are related, often being features that characterize and add meaning to the concept. For example, we know that birds have wings, can fly, eat worms, etc. The same thing happens in the social domain. When we meet a person and get to know him, we accumulate a lot of instances of his behavior, and we group (categorize) them into meaningful units as a means of understanding the person. All of this processing lends coherence to what we have learned about him. For example, we might have a concept representing our friend Anthony, and associated with that representation might be prominent features (smart, funny, good looking, Italian) along with other things we know about him (owns a boat and sails, works late and sleeps late, likes jazz, drinks good wine). We also have representations of groups that contain our knowledge and beliefs about those groups ("Italians talk all the time, are emotionally expressive, are disorganized but can be wonderfully romantic"). In each case the concept (Anthony, Italians) is a location or "node" in memory, and the features or attributes are connected to it. In this way, knowledge (e.g., our knowledge or impression of Anthony, our beliefs about Italians) becomes represented in memory through concept nodes and their associated features, all of which is stored in a package that pertains to that concept. By extension, our little network for Anthony can itself be associated with other nodes (e.g., for networks containing knowledge about Italians, about sailors, about wine lovers). These associations tie our impression of Anthony to other concepts that extend our representation of him, such that we come to believe that certain things ("Boats are expensive, so Anthony must be rich." "Italians are romantic, so Anthony . . .") are likely to be true of Anthony, even though we haven't learned them specifically about Anthony ("I really don't know how much money he makes."). As these examples illustrate, our "knowledge" can include not only factually valid information that we have acquired but also inferred beliefs and attributes. Of course, even if erroneous, this inferred knowledge is a part of our cognitive representation of the person, group, or event represented by the concept node.

When we see Anthony, or even when we simply think of him, the concept or node in memory corresponding to Anthony is "activated," with the consequence that the knowledge (features, attributes, etc.) linked to that node becomes accessible. Concepts that are activated in memory can then be used in processing and using new information. Therefore our knowledge and expectancies about Anthony can guide our interpretation of his behavior, the inferences we draw from it, and so forth. Another important element of associative networks is the notion of spreading activation. The idea here is that the activation of a node spreads through associative pathways to the features and attributes associated with it. Hence, hearing someone mention Anthony's name not only stimulates those specific features of Anthony (likes jazz, works late at night, etc.) but can also increase the likelihood of related concepts (beliefs about Italians) coming to mind. Once these associated concepts have been activated, they too can influence the way new information about Anthony is processed (e.g., his behavior might be construed in terms of its compatibility with the stereotype of Italians). Moreover, as we will see in later parts, once activated (for whatever reason), this increased accessibility of associated concepts can influence our processing about and our perceptions of other social stimuli, even of people and events unrelated to Anthony. For example, the activation of the stereotype of Italians, due to an encounter with Anthony, could make that stereotype available to use in perceptions of other persons and events.

In the same way that we can think of concepts being organized into networks of associative relations, we can also think of larger, more complex cognitive structures that emerge as smaller, more focused networks become associated with each other. These more complex cognitive structures — sometimes called schemas — contain one's knowledge, beliefs, and expectancies about a broader range of phenomena. So, for example, whereas one's impression of Anthony represents one's knowledge, beliefs, and expectancies about this individual person, one's stereotype of the group known as Italians (of which Anthony is a member) contains one's knowledge, beliefs, and expectancies about that group. The nature and functioning of cognitive structures is assumed to be much the same, whether it is a limited and very focused set of beliefs (a group of 12 men who followed Jesus and became known as "the disciples") or a very broad, inclusive category of people (those who believe Jesus is the Son of God, that is, "Christians"). In all cases, activation of a cognitive structure and its associated attributes can guide and influence information processing in systematic ways. More specifically, all of the various aspects of cognitive processing that I discussed in Introductory Overview — encoding, interpretation, inference, representation, retrieval — can be influenced and guided by the cognitive structures that are activated at the moment. Later parts in this book provide many illustrations of how activation of a cognitive structure can influence subsequent perceptions and behaviors.

In summary, the human information processor has an array of cognitive structures at his disposal for use in comprehending and adapting to the complexities of the social environment he encounters each day. The people and events he perceives are categorized and interpreted, using concepts that he has developed through past experience. In doing so, the experiences he encounters take on a meaning that did not exist (for him) prior to this cognitive step. These people and events are further understood by representing them in memory and developing associations with them. In this way the individual's knowledge about those people and events becomes organized and coherent, reflecting not only what he has learned directly but also what he has inferred as he has gone beyond the information acquired and expanded through inference and evaluation. These cognitive structures can become complex and abstract, providing a rich knowledge framework for guiding the way that new information is processed.

Discussion Questions

1. What is prototype? What is an exemplar?
2. Medin discusses several theories of conceptual structure. Summarize the main points of the classical view, the similarity-based view, and the theory-based views of categorization.
3. The readings in the chapter argue that categorization is an important cognitive aspect of processing information. What benefits do we gain from this process? What are its liabilities?

Suggested Readings

Carlston, D. E., & Smith, E. R. (1996). Principles of mental representation. In E. T. Higgins & A.W. Kruglanski (Eds.), *Social psychology: Handbook of basic principles* (pp. 184–210). New York: Guilford.

Klein, S. B., & Loftus, J. (1993). The mental representation of trait and autobiographical knowledge about the self. In T. K. Srull & R. S. Wyer, Jr. (Eds.), *Advances in social cognition* (Vol. 5, pp. 1–50). Hillsdale, NJ: Erlbaum.

Yzerbyt, V. Y., Rocher, S., & Schadron, G. (1997). Stereotypes as explanations: A subjective essentialistic view of group perception. In R. Spears, P. J. Oakes, N. Ellemers, & S. A. Haslam (Eds.), *The social psychology of stereotyping and group life* (pp. 20–50). Cambridge, UK: Blackwell.

On Perceptual Readiness[1]

Jerome S. Bruner

On the Nature of Perception

Perception involves an act of categorization. Put in terms of the antecedent and subsequent conditions from which we make our inferences, we stimulate an organism with some appropriate input and he responds by referring the input to some class of things or events. "That is an orange," he states, or he presses a lever that he has been "tuned" to press when the object that he "perceives" is an orange. On the basis of certain defining or criterial attributes in the input, what are usually called cues although they should be called clues [35], there is a selective placing of the input in one category of identity rather than another. The category need not be elaborate: "A sound," "a touch," "a pain," are also examples of categorized inputs. The use of cues in inferring the categorial identity of a perceived object, most recently treated by Bruner, Goodnow, and Austin [9] and by Binder [4], is as much a feature of perception as the sensory stuff from which percepts are made. What is interesting about the nature of the inference from cue to identity in perception is that it is in no sense different from other kinds of categorial inferences based on defining attributes. "That thing is round and nubbly in texture and orange in

Editor's Note: Selected excerpts from the original article are reproduced here.

[1] The present paper was prepared with the invaluable assistance of Mr. Michael Wallach. I also benefitted from the comments of Professors W. C. H. Prentice, Karl Pribram, and M. E. Bitterman, and from various associates at Princeton University, Kansas University, and the University of Michigan, where versions of this paper were presented.

color and of such-and-such size — therefore an orange; let me now test its other properties to be sure." In terms of process, this course of events is no different from the more abstract task of looking at a number, determining that it is divisible only by itself and unity, and thereupon categorizing it in the class of prime numbers. So at the outset, it is evident that one of the principal characteristics of perceiving is a characteristic of cognition generally. There is no reason to assume that the laws governing inferences of this kind are discontinuous as one moves from perceptual to more conceptual activities. In no sense need the process be conscious or deliberate. A theory of perception, we assert, needs a mechanism capable of inference and categorizing as much as one is needed in a theory of cognition.

Let it be plain that no claim is being made for the utter indistinguishability of perceptual and more conceptual inferences. In the first place, the former appear to be notably less docile or reversible than the latter. I may know that the Ames distorted room that looks so rectangular is indeed distorted, but unless conflicting cues are put into the situation, as in experiments to be discussed later, the room still looks rectangular. So too with such compelling illusions as the Miller-Lyer: In spite of knowledge to the contrary, the line with the extended arrowheads looks longer than the equal-length one with those inclined inward. But these differences, interesting in themselves, must not lead us to overlook the common feature of inference underlying so much of cognitive activity.

Is what we have said a denial of the classic doctrine of sense-data? Surely, one may argue (and Hebb [36] has done so effectively) that there must be certain forms of primitive organization within the perceptual field that make possible the differential use of cues in identity categorizing. Both logically and psychologically, the point is evident. Yet it seems to me foolish and unnecessary to assume that the sensory "stuff" on which higher order categorizations are based is, if you will, of a different sensory order than more evolved identities with which our perceptual world is normally peopled. To argue otherwise is to be forced into the contradictions of Locke's distinction between primary and secondary qualities in perception. The rather bold assumption that we shall make at the outset is that all perceptual experience is necessarily the end product of a categorization process.

And this for two reasons. The first is that all perception is generic in the sense that whatever is perceived is placed in and achieves its "meaning" from a class of percepts with which it is grouped. To be sure, in each thing we encounter, there is an aspect of uniqueness, but the uniqueness inheres in deviation from the class to which an object is "assigned." In short, when one specifies something more than that an element or object belongs to a universe, and that it belongs in a subset of the universe, one has categorized the element or object. The categorization can be as intersecting as "this is a quartz crystal goblet fashioned in Denmark," or as simple as "this is a glassy thing." So long as an operation assigns an input to a subset, it is an act of categorization.

If we have implied that categorizing is often a "silent" or unconscious process, that we do not experience a going-from-no-identity to an arrival-at-identity, but that the first hallmark of *any* perception is some form of identity, this does not free us of the responsibility of inquiring into the origin of categories. Certainly, Hebb [36] is correct in asserting like Immanuel Kant, that certain primitive unities or identities within perception must be innate or autochthonous and not learned. The primitive capacity to categorize "things" from "background" is very likely one such, and so too the capacity to distinguish events in one modality from those in others.

A second feature of perception, beyond its seemingly categorial and inferential nature, is that it can be described as varyingly veridical. This is what has classically been called the "representative function" of perception: What is perceived is somehow a representation of the external world. What we generally mean when we speak of representation or veridicality is that perception is predictive in varying degrees. That is to say, the object that we *see* can also be *felt* and *smelled* and there will somehow be a match or a congruity between what we see, feel, and smell. The categorial placement of the object leads to appropriate consequences in terms of later behavior directed toward the perceived object: It appears as an apple, and indeed it keeps the doctor away if consumed once a day.

The meaning of a proposition is the set of hypothetical statements one can make about attributes or consequences related to that proposition. "Let us ask what we mean by calling a thing *hard*. Evidently, that it will not be scratched by many other substances" (White [84]). The meaning of a thing, thus, is the placement of an object in a network of hypothetical inference concerning its other observable properties, its effects, and so on.

All of this suggests, does it not, that veridicality is not so much a matter of representation as it is a matter of what I shall call "model building." In learning to perceive, we are learning the relations that exist between the properties of objects and events that we encounter, learning appropriate categories and category systems, *learning to predict and to check what goes with what.*

The reader will properly ask whether the notion of perceptual representation set forth here is appropriate to anything other than situations where the nature of the percept is not "clear" — perceptual representation under peripheral viewing conditions, in tachistoscopes, under extreme fatigue. If I am given a very good look at an object, under full illumination and with all the viewing time necessary, and end by calling it an orange, is this a different process from one in which the same object is flashed for a millisecond or two on the periphery of my retina with poor illumination? In the first and quite rare case the cues permitting the identification of the object are superabundant and the inferential mechanism operates with high probability relationships between cues and identities. In the latter, it is less so. The difference is of degree. What I am trying to say is that under *any* conditions of perception, what is achieved by the perceiver is the categorization of an object or sensory event in terms of more *or* less abundant and reliable cues. Representation consists of knowing how to utilize cues with reference to a system of categories. It also depends upon the creation of a system of categories-in-relationship that fit the nature of the world in which the person must live. In fine, adequate perceptual representation involves the learning of appropriate categories, the learning of cues useful in placing objects appropriately in such systems of categories, and the learning of what objects are likely to occur in the environment, a matter to which we will turn later.

To summarize, we have proposed that perception is a process of categorization in which organisms move inferentially from cues to categorial identity and that in many cases, as Helmholtz long ago suggested, the process is a silent one. If you will, the inference is often an "unconscious" one. Moreover, the results of such categorizations are representational in nature: They represent with varying degrees of predictive veridicality the nature of the physical world in which the organism operates. By predictive veridicality I mean simply that perceptual categorization of an object or event permits one to "go beyond" the properties of the object or event perceived to a prediction of other properties of the object not yet tested. The more adequate the category systems constructed for coding environmental events in this way, the greater the predictive veridicality that results.

What must now be dealt with are the phenomena having to do with selectivity: Attention, set, and the like.

Cue Utilization and Category Accessibility

A fruitful way of thinking of the nature of perceptual readiness is in terms of the accessibility of categories for use in coding or identifying environmental events. Accessibility is a heuristic concept, and it may be defined in terms of a set of measures. Conceive of a person who is perceptually ready to encounter a certain object, an apple let us say. *How* he happens to be in this state we shall consider later. We measure the accessibility of the category "apples" by the amount of stimulus input of a certain pattern necessary to evoke the perceptual response "there is an apple," or some other standardized response. We can state the "minimum" input required for such categorization by having our observer operate with two response categories, "yes" and "no," with the likelihood of occurrence of apples and non-apples at 50:50, or by using any other definition of "maximum readiness" that one wishes to employ. The greater the accessibility of a category, (*a*) the less the input necessary for categorization to occur in terms of this category, (*b*) the wider the range of input characteristics that will be "accepted" as fitting the category in question, (*c*) the more likely that categories that provide a better or equally good fit for the input will be masked. To put it in more ordinary language: Apples will be more easily and swiftly recognized, a wider range of things will be identified or misidentified as apples, and in consequence the correct or best fitting identity of these other inputs will be masked. This is what is intended by accessibility.

Obviously, categories are not isolated. One has a category "apples," to be sure, but it is imbedded by past learning in a network of categories: "An apple a day keeps the doctor away" is one such category system. So

too, are "apples are fruits" and other placements of an object in a general classification scheme. Predictive systems are of the same order: e.g., "The apple will rot if not refrigerated." We have spoken of these systems before as the "meaning" of an object. We mention them again here to indicate that though we speak analytically of separate or isolated categories as being accessible to inputs, it is quite obvious that category systems vary in accessibility as a whole.

It follows from what has just been said that the most appropriate pattern of readiness at any given moment would be that one which would lead on the average to the most "veridical" guess about the nature of the world around one at the moment — best guess here being construed, of course, as a response in the absence of the necessary stimulus input. And it follows from this that the most ready perceiver would then have the best chances of estimating situations most adequately and planning accordingly. It is in this general sense that the ready perceiver who can proceed with fairly minimal inputs is also in a position to use his cognitive readiness not only for perceiving what is before him but in foreseeing what is likely to be before him. We shall return to this point shortly.

We must turn now to the question of cue utilization, the "strategies" in terms of which inferences are made (by the nervous system, of course) from cue to category and thence to other cues. Given a set of cues, however presented, my nervous system must "decide" whether the thing is an airplane or a sea gull, a red or a green, or what not.

There appears, moreover, to be a sequence of such decisions involved in categorizing an object or event. A common-sense example will make this clear. I look across to the mantelpiece opposite my desk and see a rectangular object lying on it. If I continue this pursuit, subsequent decisions are to be made: Is it the block of plastic I purchased for some apparatus or is it a book? In the dim light it can be either. I remember that the plastic is downstairs in one of the experimental rooms: The object "is" a book now, and I search for further cues on its dark red surface. I see what I think is some gold: It is a McGraw-Hill book, probably G. A. Miller's *Language and Communication* that I had been using late this afternoon. If you will, the process is a "bracketing" one, a gradual narrowing of the category placement of the object.

Let us attempt to analyze the various stages in such a decision sequence.

a. Primitive categorization. Before any more elaborate inferential activity can occur, there must be a first, "silent" process that results in the perceptual isolation of an object or an event with certain characteristic qualities. What is required simply is that an environmental event has been perceptually isolated and that the event is marked by certain spatio-temporal-qualitative characteristics. The event may have no more "meaning" than that it is an "object," a "sound," or a "movement."

b. Cue search. In highly practiced cases or in cases of high cue-category probability linkage, a second process of more precise placement based on additional cues may be equally silent or "unconscious." An object is seen with phenomenal immediacy as a "book" or an "ash tray." In such instances there is usually a good fit between the specifications of a category and the nature of the cues impinging on the organism — although "fit" and "probability of linkage" may stand in a vicarious relation to each other. Where the fit to accessible categories is not precise, or when the linkage between cue and category is low in probability in the past experience of the organism, the conscious experience of cue searching occurs. "What is that thing?" Here, one is scanning the environment for data in order to find cues that permit a more precise placement of the object. Under these circumstances, the organism is "open" to maximum stimulation, in a manner described below.

c. Confirmation check. When a tentative categorization has occurred, following cue search, cue search changes. The "openness" to stimulation decreases sharply in the sense that now, a tentative placement of identity having occurred, the search is narrowed for additional confirmatory cues to check this placement. We shall speak of a selective gating process coming into operation in this stage, having the effect of reducing the effective input of stimulation not relevant to the confirmatory process.

d. Confirmation completion. The last stage in the process of perceptual identification is a completion, marked by termination of cue searching. It is characteristic of this state that openness to additional cues is drastically reduced, and incongruent cues are either normalized or "gated out."

The question of fit between cue and category specification brings us to the key problem of the nature of categories. By a category we mean a rule for classing objects as equivalent. The rule specifies the following about the instances that are to be comprised in the category.

(a) The properties or *criterial attribute values* required of an instance to be coded in a given class.

(b) The manner in which such attribute values are to be combined in making an inference from properties to category membership: Whether conjunctively (e.g., a_i and b_i), relationally (e.g., a_i bears a certain relation to b_i), or disjunctively (e.g., a_i or b_i).

(c) The weight assigned various properties in making an inference from properties to category membership.

(d) The acceptance limits within which properties must fall to be criterial. That is to say, from what range of attribute values may a_i, b_i ... k_i be drawn.

When we speak of rules, again it should be made clear that "conscious rules" are not intended. These are the rules that govern the operation of a categorizing mechanism.

The likelihood that a sensory input will be categorized in terms of a given category is not only a matter of fit between sensory input and category specifications. It depends also on the accessibility of a category. To put the matter in an oversimplified way, given a sensory input with equally good fit to two nonoverlapping categories, the more accessible of the two categories would "capture" the input. It is in this sense that mention was earlier made about the vicarious relationship between fit and accessibility.

We have already noted that the accessibility of categories reflects the learned probabilities of occurrence of events in the person's world. The more frequently in a given context instances of a given category occur, the greater the accessibility of the category. Operationally, this means that less stimulus input will be required for the instance or event to be categorized in terms of a frequently used category. In general, the type of probability we are referring to is not absolute probability of occurrence, where each event that occurs is independent of each other. Such independence is rare in the environment. Rather, the principal form of probability learning affecting category accessibility is the learning of contingent or transitional probabilities — the redundant structure of the environment.

But the organism to operate adequately must not only be ready for likely events in the environment, the better to represent them, and in order to perceive them quickly and without undue cognitive strain: It must also be able to search out unlikely objects and events essential to its maintenance and the pursuit of its enterprises. If I am walking the streets of a strange city and find myself hungry, I must be able to look for restaurants regardless of their likelihood of occurrence in the environment where I now find myself. In short, the accessibility of categories I employ for identifying the objects of the world around me must not only reflect the environmental probabilities of objects that fit these categories, but also reflect the search requirements imposed by my needs, my ongoing activities, my defenses, etc. And for effective search behavior to occur, the pattern of perceptual readiness during search must be realistic: Tempered by what one is likely to find in one's perceptual world at that time and at that place as well as by what one seeks to find.

Let me summarize our considerations about the general properties of perception with a few propositions. The first is that *perception is a decision process.* Whatever the nature of the task set, the perceiver or his nervous system decides that a thing perceived is one thing and not another. A line is longer or shorter than a standard, a particular object is a snake and not a fallen branch, the incomplete word L*VE in the context MEN L*VE WOMEN is the word LOVE and not LIVE.

The second proposition is that *the decision process involves the utilization of discriminatory cues,* as do all decision processes. That is to say, the properties of stimulus inputs make it possible to sort these inputs into categories of best fit.

Thirdly, *the cue utilization process involves the operation of inference.* Going from cue to an inference of identity is probably the most ubiquitous and primitive cognitive activity. The utilization of inference presupposes the learning of environmental probabilities and invariances relating cues to cues, and cues to behavioral consequences. Cue utilization involves various stages: A primitive step of isolating an object or event from the flux of environmental stimulation, stages of cue searching where the task is to find cues that can be fitted to available category specifications, a tentative categorization with more search for confirming cues, and final categorization, when cue searching is severely reduced.

Fourth, *a category may be regarded as a set of specifications* regarding what events will be grouped as equivalent — rules respecting the nature of criterial cues required, the manner of their combining, their inferential weight, and the acceptance limits of their variability.

Fifth, *categories vary in terms of their accessibility*, the readiness with which a stimulus input with given properties will be coded or identified in terms of a category. The relative accessibility of categories and systems of categories seems to depend upon two factors: The expectancies of the person with regard to the likelihood of events to be encountered in the environment; and the search requirements imposed on the organism by his needs and his ongoing enterprises. To use the functionalist's language, perceptual readiness or accessibility serves two functions: *To minimize the surprise value of the environment* by matching category accessibility to the probabilities of events in the world about one, and *to maximize the attainment of sought-after objects and events.*

Veridical perception, so our sixth proposition would run, *consists of the coding of stimulus inputs in appropriate categories* such that one may go from cue to categorial identification, and thence to the correct inference or prediction of other properties of the object so categorized. Thus, veridical perception requires the learning of categories and category systems appropriate to the events and objects with which the person has commerce in the physical world. When we speak of the representative function of perception, we speak of the adequacy of the categorizing system of the individual in permitting him to infer the nature of events and to go beyond them to the correct prediction of other events.

Seventh, *under less than optimal conditions, perception will be veridical in the degree to which the accessibility of categorizing systems reflects the likelihood of occurrence of the events that the person will encounter.* Where accessibility of categories reflects environmental probabilities, the organism is in the position of requiring less stimulus input, less redundancy of cues for the appropriate categorization of objects. In like vein, nonveridical perception will be systematic rather than random in its error insofar as it reflects the inappropriate readiness of the perceiver. The more inappropriate the readiness, the greater the input or redundancy of cues required for appropriate categorization to occur — where "appropriate" means that an input is coded in the category that yields more adequate subsequent predictions.

REFERENCES

1. Allport, F. H. *Theories of perception and the concept of structure.* New York: Wiley, 1955.
2. Asch, S. E. *Social psychology.* New York: Prentice-Hall, 1952.
3. Bartlett, F. C. *Remembering.* Cambridge, England: Cambridge Univer. Press, 1932.
4. Binder, A. A statistical model for the process of visual recognition. *Psychol. Rev.,* 1955, *62,* 119–129.
5. Bitterman, M. E., & Kniffin, C. W. Manifest anxiety and "perceptual defense." *J. abnorm. soc. Psychol.,* 1953, *48,* 248–252.
6. Bricker, P. D., & Chapanis, A. Do incorrectly perceived tachistoscopic stimuli convey some information? *Psychol. Rev.,* 1953, *60,* 181–188.
7. Brown, D. R. Stimulus similarity and the anchoring of subjective scales. *Amer. J. Psychol.,* 1953, *66,* 199–214.
8. Bruner, J. S. Personality dynamics and the process of perceiving. In R. R. Blake & G. V. Ramsey (Eds.), *Perception: An approach to personality.* New York: Ronald, 1951. pp. 121–147.
9. Bruner, J. S., Goodnow, J. J., & Austin, G. A. *A study of thinking.* New York: Wiley, 1956.

10. Bruner, J. S., Miller, G. A., & Zimmerman, C. Discriminative skill and discriminative matching in perceptual recognition. *J. exp. Psychol.*, 1955, *49*, 187–192.

11. Bruner, J. S., & Minturn, A. L. Perceptual identification and perceptual organization. *J. gen. Psychol.*, 1955, *53*, 21–28.

12. Bruner, J. S., & Postman, L. Emotional selectivity in perception and reaction. *J. Pers., 1947, 16*, 69–77.

13. Bruner, J. S., & Postman, L. Perception, cognition, and behavior. *J. Pers.*, 1949, *18*, 14–31.

14. Bruner, J. S., & Postman, L. On the perception of incongruity: A paradigm. *J. Pers.*, 1949, *18*, 206–223.

15. Bruner, J. S., Postman, L., & John, W. Normalization of incongruity. Research memorandum. Cognition Project, Harvard Univer., 1949.

16. Bruner, J. S., Postman, L., & Rodrigues, J. Expectation and the perception of color. *Amer. J. Psychol.*, 1951, *64*, 216–227.

17. Brunswik, E. *Systematic and representative design of psychological experiments.* Berkeley: Univer. of California Press, 1949.

18. Bush, R. R., & Mosteller, C. F. *Stochastic models for learning.* New York: Wiley, 1955.

19. Chapman, D. W. Relative effects of determinate and indeterminate Aufgaben. *Amer. J. Psychol.*, 1932, *44*, 163–174.

20. Cowen, E. L., & Beier, E. G. The influence of "threat expectancy" on perception. *J. Pers.*, 1951, *19*, 85–94.

21. Eccles, J. C. *The neurophysiological basis of mind.* Oxford: Oxford Univer. Press, 1953.

22. Edwards, W. The theory of decision making. *Psychol. Bull.*, 1954, *51*, 380–417.

23. Estes, W. K. Individual behavior in uncertain situations: An interpretation in terms of statistical association theory. In R. M. Thrall, C. H. Coombs, & R. L. Davis (Eds.), *Decision processes.* New York: Wiley, 1954. Pp. 127–137.

24. Fry, D. P., & Denes, P. Mechanical speech recognition. In W. Jackson (Ed.), *Communication theory.* New York: Academic Press, 1953.

25. Galanter, E., & Gerstenhaber, M. On thought: Extrinsic theory of insight. *Amer. Psychologist*, 1955, *10*, 465.

26. Gibson, J. J. *The perception of the visual world.* Boston: Houghton Mifflin, 1950.

27. Gibson, J. J., & Gibson, E. J. Perceptual learning: Differentiation or enrichment? *Psychol. Rev.*, 1955, *62*, 32–41.

28. Golambos, R., Sheatz, G., & Vernier, V. G. Electrophysiological correlates of a conditioned response in cats. *Science*, 1956, *123*, 376–377.

29. Goodnow, J. J. Determinants of choice distribution in two-choice situations. *Amer. J. Psychol.*, 1955, *68*, 106–116.

30. Goodnow, J. J., & Pettigrew, T. E. Some difficulties in learning a simple pattern of events. Paper presented at annual meeting of the East. Psychol. Ass., Atlantic City, March, 1956.

31. Graham, C. H. Perception and behavior. Presidential address to the East. Psychol. Ass., Atlantic City, March, 1956.

32. Granit, R. *Receptors and sensory perception.* New Haven: Yale Univer. Press, 1955.

33. Haire, M., & Grunes, W. F. Perceptual defenses: Processes protecting an organized perception of another personality. *Hum. Relat.*, 1950, *3*, 403–412.

34. Hake, H. W., & Hyman, R. Perception of the statistical structure of a random series of binary symbols. *J. exp. Psychol.*, 1953, *45*, 64–74.

35. Harper, R. S., & Boring, E. G. Cues. *Amer. J. Psychol.*, 1948, *61*, 119–123.

36. Hebb, D. O. *The organization of behavior.* New York: Wiley, 1949.

37. Helson, H. Adaptation-level as a basis for a quantitative theory of frames of reference. *Psychol. Rev.*, 1948, *55*, 297–313.

38. Hernandez-Péon, R., Scherrer, R. H., & Jouvet, M. Modification of electric activity in the cochlear nucleus during "attention" in unanesthetized cats. *Science*, 1956, *123*, 331–332.

39. Hornbostel, E. M. von. Unity of the senses. *Psyche*, 1926, *7*, 83–89.

40. Howes, D. On the interpretation of word frequency as a variable affecting speed of recognition. *J. exp. Psychol.*, 1954, *48*, 106–112.

41. Irwin, F. W. Stated expectations as functions of probability and desirability of outcomes. *J. Pers.*, 1953, *21*, 329–335.

42. Ittleson, W. H. *The Ames demonstrations in perception.* Princeton, N. J.: Princeton Univer. Press, 1952.

43. Jarrett, J. Strategies in risk-taking situations. Unpublished doctor's dissertation, Harvard Univer. Library, 1951.

44. Jarvik, M. E. Probability learning and a negative recency effect in the serial anticipation of alternative symbols. *J. exp. Psychol.*, 1951, *41*, 291–297.

45. Jenkin, N. Two types of perceptual experience. *J. Clin. Psychol.*, 1956, *12*, 44–49.

46. Klein, G. S. The personal world through perception. In R. R. Blake & G. V. Ramsey (Eds.), *Perception: An approach to personality.* New York: Ronald, 1951. Pp. 328–355.

47. Kohler, I. Rehabituation in perception. Published separately in three parts, in German, in *Die Pyramide*, 1953, Heft 5, 6, and 7 (Austria). Translated by Henry Gleitman and edited by J. J. Gibson. Privately circulated by the editor.

48. Köhler, W. *Dynamics in psychology.* New York: Liveright, 1940.

49. Kuffler, S. W., Hunt, C. C., & Quillian, J. P. Function of medullated small-nerve fibers in mammalian ventral roots: Efferent muscle spindle innervation. *J. Neurophysiol.*, 1951, *14*, 29–54.

50. Kuffler, S. W., & Hunt, C. C. The mammalian small nerve fibers: A system for efferent nervous regulation of muscle spindle discharge. *Proc. Assoc. Res. Nerv. Ment. Dis.*, 1952, Vol. 30.

51. Lashley, K. S. Experimental analysis of instinctive behavior. *Psychol. Rev.*, 1938, *45*, 445–471.

52. Lashley, K. S. In search of the engram. *Symp. Soc. Exp. Biol.*, 1950, *4*, 454–482.

53. Lazarus, R. S., Eriksen, C. W., & Fonda, C. P. Personality dynamics and auditory perceptual recognition. *J. Pers.*, 1951, *19*, 471–482.

54. Lazarus, R. S., & McCleary, R. A. Autonomic discrimination without awareness: A study of subception. *Psychol. Rev.*, 1951, *58*, 113–222.

55. Leksell, L. The action potential and excitatory effects of the small ventral root fibers to skeletal muscles. *Acta Physiol. Scand.*, 1945, *10*, Suppl. 31.

56. Lenneberg, E. H. An empirical investigation into the relationship between language and cognition. Unpublished doctoral dissertation, Harvard Univer. Library, 1956.

57. Lorente de No, R. Transmission of impulses through cranial motor nuclei. *J. Neurophysiol.*, 1939, *2*, 402–464.

58. McGinnies, E. Emotionality and perceptual defense. *Psychol. Rev.*, 1949, *56*, 244–251.

59. MacKay, D. M. Toward an information-flow model of human behavior. *Brit. J. Psychol.*, 1956, *47*, 30–43.

60. Marks, R. W. The effect of probability, desirability, and "privilege" on the state of expectations of children. *J. Pers.*, 1951, *19*, 332–351.

61. Miller, G. A., Bruner, J. S., & Postman, L. Familiarity of letter sequences and tachistoscopic identification. *J. gen. Psychol.*, 1954, *50*, 129–139.

62. Miller, G. A., Heise, G. A., & Lichten, W. The intelligibility of speech as a function of the context of the test materials. *J. exp. Psychol.*, 1951, *41*, 329–335.
63. Peirce, C. S. How to make our ideas clear. *Popular Sci. Mon.*, 1878, *12*, 286–302.
64. Penfield, W. Memory mechanisms. *Arch. Neurol. & Psychiat.*, 1952, *67*, 178–191.
65. Piaget, J. *Play, dreams, and imitation in childhood*. New York: Norton, 1951.
66. Pratt, C. C. The role of past experience in visual perception. *J. Psychol.*, 1950, *30*, 85–107.
67. Prentice, W. C. H. Paper read at the Symposium on Conceptual Trends in Psychology, at Amer. Psychol. Ass., New York, September, 1954.
68. Postman, L., & Bruner, J. S. Perception under stress. *Psychol. Rev.*, 1948, *55*, 314–323.
69. Postman, L., Bruner, J. S., & Walk, R. D. The perception of error. *Brit. J. Psychol.*, 1951, *42*, 1–10.
70. Postman, L., & Crutchfield, R. S. The interaction of need, set, and stimulus structure in a cognitive task. *Amer. J. Psychol.*, 1952, *65*, 196–217.
71. Selfridge, O. Pattern recognition and learning. Memorandum of Lincoln Laboratory, Massachusetts Institute of Technology, 1955.
72. Solomon, R. L., & Postman, L. Frequency of usage as a determinant of recognition thresholds for words. *J. exp. Psychol.*, 1952, *43*, 195–201.
73. Smith, J. W., & Klein, G. S. Cognitive control in serial behavior patterns. Dittoed manuscript, available from author, 1951.
74. Stevens, S. S. Chapter I in S. S. Stevens (Ed.), *Handbook of experimental psychology*. New York: Wiley, 1951.
75. Stevens, S. S. The direct estimation of sensory magnitudes — loudness. *Amer. J. Psychol.*, 1956, *69*, 1–25.
76. Tanner, W. P., Jr., & Swets, J. A. A decision-making theory of human detection. *Psychol. Rev.*, 1954, *61*, 401–409.
77. Tinbergen, N. *The study of instinct*. Oxford: Oxford Univer. Press, 1951.
78. Titchener, E. B. *A beginner's psychology*. New York: Macmillan, 1916.
79. Tolman, E. C. Discussion. *J. Pers.*, 1949, *18*, 48–50.
80. Uttley, A. M. *The conditional probability of signals in the nervous system*. Radar Research Establ., British Ministry of Supply, Feb., 1955.
81. Vernon, M. D. *A further study of visual perception*. Cambridge, England: Cambridge Univer. Press, 1952.
82. Volkmann, J. In M. Sherif & J. H. Rohrer (Eds.), *Social psychology at the crossroads*. New York: Harpers, 1951.
83. Wallach, H. Some considerations concerning the relation between perception and cognition. *J. Pers.*, 1949, *18*, 6–13.
84. White, M. *The age of analysis*. New York: New American Library, 1955.
85. Woodworth, R. S. Reenforcement of perception. *Amer. J. Psychol.*, 1947, *60*, 119–124.
86. Wyatt, D. F., & Campbell, D. T. On the liability of stereotype or hypothesis. *J. abnorm. soc. Psychol.*, 1951, *46*, 496–500.
87. Yokoyama, J. Reported in E. G. Boring, *A history of experimental psychology*. (2nd Ed.). New York: Appleton-Century, 1954.
88. Young, J. Z. *Doubt and certainly in science*. Oxford: Oxford Univer. Press, 1951.

Received June 4, 1956 ■

Concepts and Conceptual Structure

Douglas L. Medin

Research and theory on categorization and conceptual structure have recently undergone two major shifts. The first shift is from the assumption that concepts have defining properties (the classical view) to the idea that concept representations may be based on properties that are only characteristic or typical of category examples (the probabilistic view). Both the probabilistic view and the classical view assume that categorization is driven by similarity relations. A major problem with describing category structure in terms of similarity is that the notion of similarity is too unconstrained to give an account of conceptual coherence. The second major shift is from the idea that concepts are organized by similarity to the idea that concepts are organized around theories. In this article, the evidence and rationale associated with these shifts are described, and one means of integrating similarity-based and theory-driven categorization is outlined.

What good are categories? Categorization involves treating two or more distinct entities as in some way equivalent in the service of accessing knowledge and making predictions. Take psychodiagnostic categories as an example. The need to access relevant knowledge explains why clinical psychologists do not (or could not) treat each individual as unique. Although one would expect treatment plans to be tailored to the needs of individuals, absolute uniqueness imposes the prohibitive cost of ignorance. Clinicians need some way to bring their knowledge and experience to bear on the problem under consideration, and that requires the appreciation of some similarity or relationship between the current situation and what has gone before. Although clinical psychologists may or may not use a specific categorization system, they must find points of contact between previous situations and the current context; that is, they must categorize. Diagnostic categories allow clinicians to predict the efficacy of alternative treatments and to share their experiences with other therapists. Yet another reason to categorize is to learn about etiology. People who show a common manifestation of some problem may share common precipitating conditions or causes. Ironically, the only case in which categorization would not be useful is where all individuals are treated alike; thus, categorization allows diversity.

More generally speaking, concepts and categories serve as building blocks for human thought and behavior. Roughly, a *concept* is an idea that includes all that is characteristically associated with it. A *category* is a partitioning or class to which some assertion or set of assertions might apply. It is tempting to think of categories as existing in the world and of concepts as corresponding to mental representations of them, but this analysis is misleading. It is misleading because concepts need not have real-world counterparts (e.g., unicorns) and because people may impose rather than discover structure in the world. I believe that questions about the nature of categories may be psychological questions as much as metaphysical questions. Indeed, for at least the last decade my colleagues and I have been trying to address the question of why we have the categories we have and not others. The world could be partitioned in a limitless variety of ways, yet people find only a miniscule subset of possible classifications to be meaningful. Part of the answer to the categorization question likely does depend on the nature of the world, but part also surely depends on the nature of the organism and its goals. Dolphins have no use for psychodiagnostic categories.

Given the fundamental character of concepts and categories, one might think that people who study concepts would have converged on a stable consensus with respect to conceptual structure. After all, Plato and Aristotle had quite a bit to say about concepts, medieval philosophers were obsessed with questions about universals and the essence of concepts, and concept representation remains as a cornerstone issue in all aspects of cognitive science. However, we have neither consensus nor stability. The relatively recent past has experienced at least one and probably two major shifts in thought about conceptual structure, and stability is the least salient attribute of the current situation. In the remainder of this article, I will briefly describe these shifts and then outline some ways of integrating the strong points of the various views.

The First Shift: Classical Versus Probabilistic Views

It is difficult to discuss concepts without bringing in the notion of similarity at some point. For example, a common idea is that our classification system tends to maximize within-category similarity relative to between-category similarity. That is, we group things into categories because they are similar. It will be suggested that alternative views of conceptual structure are associated with distinct (though sometimes implicit) theories of the nature of similarity.

The Classical View

The idea that all instances or examples of a category have some fundamental characteristics in common that determine their membership is very compelling. The classical view of concepts is organized around this notion. The classical view assumes that mental representations of categories consist of summary lists of features or properties that individually are necessary for category membership and collectively are sufficient to determine category membership. The category *triangle* meets these criteria. All triangles are closed geometric forms with three sides and interior angles that sum to 180 degrees. To see if something is a triangle one has only to check for these three properties, and if any one is missing one does not have a triangle.

What about other concepts? The classical view suggests that all categories have defining features. A particular person may not know what these defining features are but an expert certainly should. In our 1981 book, *Categories and Concepts*, Ed Smith and I reviewed the status of the classical view as a theory of conceptual structure. We concluded that the classical view was in grave trouble for a variety of reasons. Many of the arguments and counterarguments are quite detailed, but the most serious problems can be easily summarized:

1. Failure to specify defining features. One glaring problem is that even experts cannot come up with defining features for most lexical concepts (i.e., those reflected in our language). People may believe that concepts have necessary or sufficient features (McNamara & Sternberg, 1983), but the features given as candidates do not hold up to closer scrutiny. For example, a person may list "made of wood" as a necessary property for violins, but not all violins are made of wood. Linguists, philosophers, biologists, and clinical psychologists alike have been unable to supply a core set of features that all examples of a concept (in their area of expertise) necessarily must share.

2. Goodness of example effects. According to the classical view, all examples of a concept are equally good because they all possess the requisite defining features. Experience and (by now) a considerable body of research undermines this claim. For example, people judge a robin to be a better example of bird than an ostrich is and can answer category membership questions more quickly for good examples than for poor examples (Smith, Shoben, & Rips, 1974). Typicality effects are nearly ubiquitous (for reviews, see Medin & Smith, 1984; Mervis & Rosch, 1981; Oden, 1987); they hold for the artistic style (Hartley & Homa, 1981), chess (Goldin, 1978), emotion terms (Fehr, 1988; Fehr & Russell, 1984), medical diagnosis (Arkes & Harkness, 1980), and person perception (e.g., Cantor & Mischel, 1977).

Typicality effects are not, in principle, fatal for the classical view. One might imagine that some signs or features help to determine the presence of other defining features. Some examples may have more signs or clearer signs pointing the way to the defining properties, and this might account for the difference in goodness of example judgments or response times. This distinction between identification procedures (how one identifies an instance of a concept) and a conceptual core (how the concept relates to other concepts) may prove useful if it can be shown that the core is used in some other aspect of thinking It seems, however, that this distinction serves to insulate the classical view from empirical findings, and Smith, Rips, and Medin (1984) argued that there are no sharp boundaries between core properties and those used for purposes of identification.

3. Unclear cases. The classical view implies a procedure for unambiguously determining category membership that is, check for defining features. Yet there are numerous cases in which it is not clear whether an example belongs to a category. Should a rug be considered furniture? What about a clock or radio? People not only disagree with each other concerning category membership but also contradict themselves when asked about membership on separate occasions (Barsalou, 1989; Bellezza 1984; McCloskey & Glucksberg, 1978).

These and other problems have led to disenchantment with the classical view of concepts. The scholarly consensus has shifted its allegiance to an alternative, the probabilistic view.

The Probabilistic View

The rejection of the classical view of categories has been associated with the ascendance of the probabilistic view of category structure (Wittgenstein, 1953). This view holds that categories are "fuzzy" or ill-defined and that categories are organized around a set of properties or clusters of correlated attributes (Rosch, 1975) that are only characteristic or typical of category membership Thus, the probabilistic view rejects the notion of defining features.

The most recent edition of the *Diagnostic and Statistical Manual of Mental Disorders* (*DSM-IIIR*, American Psychiatric Association, 1987) uses criteria based or lists of characteristic symptoms or features to describe diagnostic categories and thereby endorses the probabilistic view. For example, a diagnosis of depression can be made if a dysphoric mood and any five of a set of nine symptoms are present nearly every day for a period of at least two weeks. Thus, two people may both be categorized as depressed and share only a single one of the nine characteristic symptoms!

The probabilistic view is perfectly at home with the typicality effects that were so awkward for the classical view. Membership in probabilistic categories is naturally graded, rather than all or none, and the better or more typical members have more characteristic properties than the poorer ones. It is also easy to see that the probabilistic view may lead to unclear cases. Any one example may have several typical properties of a category but not so many that it clearly qualifies for category membership.

In some pioneering work aimed at clarifying the structural basis of fuzzy categories, Rosch and Mervis (1975) had subjects list properties of exemplars for a variety of concepts such as *bird, fruit*, and *tool*. They found that the listed properties for some exemplars occurred frequently in other category members, whereas others had properties that occurred less frequently. Most important, the more frequently an exemplar's properties appeared within a category, the higher was its rated typicality for that category. The correlation between number of characteristic properties possessed and typicality rating was very high and positive. For example, robins have characteristic bird properties of flying, singing, eating worms, and building nests in trees, and they are rated to be very typical birds. Penguins have none of these properties, and they are rated as very atypical birds. In short, the Rosch and Mervis work relating typicality to number of characteristic properties put the probabilistic view on fairly firm footing.

1. Mental representations of probabilistic view categories. If categories are not represented in terms of definitions, what form do our mental representations take? The term, probabilistic view, seems to imply that people organize categories via statistical reasoning. Actually, however, there is a more natural interpretation of fuzzy categories. Intuitively, probabilistic view categories are organized according to a *family resemblance* principle. A simple form of summary representation would be an example or ideal that possessed all of the characteristic features of a category. This summary representation is referred to as the *prototype*, and the prototype can be used to decide category membership. If some candidate example is similar enough to the prototype for a category, then it will be classified as a member of that category. The general notion is that, based on experience with examples of a category, people abstract out the central tendency or prototype that becomes the summary mental representation for the category.

A more radical principle of mental representation, which is also consistent with fuzzy categories, is the exemplar view (Smith & Medin, 1981). The exemplar view denies that there is a single summary representation and instead claims that categories are represented by means of examples. In this view, clients may be diagnosed as suicidal, not because they are similar to some prototype of a suicidal person, but because they remind the clinician of a previous client who was suicidal.

A considerable amount of research effort has been aimed at contrasting exemplar and prototype representations (see Allen, Brooks, Norman, & Rosenthal, 1988; Estes, 1986a, 1986b; Medin, 1986; Medin & Smith,

1984; Nosofsky, 1987, 1988a; and Oden, 1987). Genero and Cantor (1987) suggested that prototypes serve untrained diagnosticians well but that trained diagnosticians may find exemplars to be more helpful. For my present purposes, however, I will blur over this distinction to note that both prototype and exemplar theories rely on roughly the same similarity principle. That is, category membership is determined by whether some candidate is sufficiently similar either to the prototype or to a set of encoded examples, where similarity is based on matches and mismatches of independent, equally abstract, features.

2. Probabilistic view and similarity. To give meaning to the claim that categorization is based on similarity, it is important to be specific about what one means by similarity. Although the consensus is not uniform, I believe that the modal model of similarity with respect to conceptual structure can be summarized in terms of the four assumptions as follows: (a) Similarity between two things increases as a function of the number of features or properties they share and decreases as a function of mismatching or distinctive features. (b) These features can be treated as independent and additive. (c) The features determining similarity are all roughly the same level of abstractness (as a special case they may be irreducible primitives). (d) These similarity principles are sufficient to describe conceptual structure, and therefore, a concept is more or less equivalent to a list of its features. This theory of similarity is very compatible with the notion that categories are organized around prototypes. Nonetheless, I will later argue that each of these assumptions is wrong or misleading and that to understand conceptual structure theories of similarity are needed that reject each of these assumptions. Before outlining an alternative set of similarity assumptions, however, I will first describe a set of observations that motivate the second, still more recent, shift in thinking concerning conceptual structure.

Problems for Probabilistic View Theories

Problems for Prototypes

Although the general idea that concepts are organized around prototypes remains popular, at a more specific, empirical level, prototype theories have not fared very well. First of all, prototype theories treat concepts as context-independent. Roth and Shoben (1983), however, have shown that typicality judgments vary as a function of particular contexts. For example, tea is judged to be a more typical beverage than milk in the context of secretaries taking a break, but this ordering reverses for the context of truck drivers taking a break. Similarly, Shoben and I (Medin & Shoben, 1988) noted that the typicality of combined concepts cannot be predicted from the typicality of the constituents. As an illustrative example, consider the concept of *spoon*. People rate small spoons as more typical spoons than large spoons, and metal spoons as more typical spoons than wooden spoons. If the concept *spoon* is represented by a prototypic spoon, then a small metal spoon should be the most typical spoon, followed by small wooden and large metal spoons, and large wooden spoons should be the least typical. Instead, people find large wooden spoons to be more typical spoons than either small wooden spoons or large metal spoons (see also Malt & Smith, 1983). The only way for a prototype model to handle these results is to posit multiple prototypes. But this strategy creates new problems. Obviously one cannot have a separate prototype for every adjective noun combination because there are simply too many possible combinations. One might suggest that there are distinct subtypes for concepts like *spoon*, but one would need a theory describing how and when subtypes are created. Current prototype models do not provide such a theory. A third problem for prototype theories grows out of Barsalou's work (1985, 1987) on goal-derived categories such as "things to take on a camping trip" and "foods to eat while on a diet." Barsalou has found that goal-derived categories show the same typicality effects as other categories. The basis for these effects, however, is not similarity to an average or prototype but rather similarity to an ideal. For example, for the category of things to eat while on a diet, typicality ratings are determined by how closely an example conforms to the ideal of zero calories.

Laboratory studies of categorization using artificially constructed categories also raise problems for prototypes. Normally many variables relevant to human classification are correlated and therefore confounded with one another. The general rationale for laboratory studies with artificially created categories is that one can isolate some variable or set of variables of interest and unconfound some natural correlations. Salient phenomena associated with fuzzy categories are observed with artificially constructed categories, and several of these are consistent with prototype theories. For example, one observes typicality effects in learning and on transfer tests using both correctness and reaction time as the dependent variable (e.g., Rosch & Mervis, 1975). A striking phenomenon, readily obtained, is that the prototype for a category may be classified more accurately during transfer tests than are the previously seen examples that were used during original category learning (e.g., Homa & Vosburgh, 1976; Medin & Schaffer, 1978; Peterson, Meagher, Chait, & Gillie, 1973).

Typicality effects and excellent classification of prototypes are consistent with the idea that people are learning these ill-defined categories by forming prototypes. More detailed analyses, however, are more problematic. Prototype theory implies that the only information abstracted from categories is the central tendency. A prototype representation discards information concerning category size, the variability of the examples, and information concerning correlations of attributes. The evidence suggests that people are sensitive to all three of these types of information (Estes, 1986b; Flannagan, Fried, & Holyoak, 1986; Fried & Holyoak, 1984; Medin, Altom, Edelson, & Freko, 1982; Medin & Schaffer, 1978). An example involving correlated attributes pinpoints part of the problem. Most people have the intuition that small birds are much more likely to sing than large birds. This intuition cannot be obtained from a single summary prototype for birds. The fact that one can generate large numbers of such correlations is a problem for the idea that people reason using prototypes. More generally, prototype representations seem to discard too much information that can be shown to be relevant to human categorizations.

Yet another problem for prototypes is that they make the wrong predictions about which category structures should be easy or difficult to learn. One way to conceptualize the process of classifying examples on the basis of similarity to prototypes is that it involves a summing of evidence against a criterion. For example, if an instance shows a criterial sum of features (appropriately weighted), then it will be classified as a bird, and the more typical a member is of the category, the more quickly the criterion will be exceeded. The key aspect of this prediction is that there must exist some additive combination of properties and their weights that can be used to correctly assign instances as members or nonmembers. The technical term for this constraint is that categories must be linearly separable (Sebestyn, 1962). For a prototype process to work in the sense of accepting all members and rejecting all nonmembers, the categories must be linearly separable.

If linear separability acts as a constraint on human categorization, then with other factors equal, people should find it easier to learn categories that are linearly separable than categories that are not linearly separable. To make a long story short, however, studies employing a variety of stimulus materials, category sizes, subject populations, and instructions have failed to find any evidence that linear separability acts as a constraint on human classification learning (Kemler-Nelson, 1984; Medin & Schwanenflugel, 1981; see also Shepard, Hovland, & Jenkins, 1961).

The cumulative effect of these various chunks of evidence has been to raise serious questions concerning the viability of prototype theories. Prototype theories imply constraints that are not observed in human categorization, predict insensitivity to information that people readily use, and fail to reflect the context sensitivity that is evident in human categorization. Rather than getting at the character of human conceptual representation, prototypes appear to be more of a caricature of it. Exemplar models handle some of these phenomena, but they fail to address some of the most fundamental questions concerning conceptual structure.

Exemplar-Based Theories

The problems just described hold not only for prototype theories in particular but also for any similarity-based categorization model that assumes that the constituent features are independent and additive. To give but one example, one could have an exemplar model of categorization that assumes that, during learning, people store examples but that new examples are classified by "computing" prototypes and determining the similarity of the novel example to the newly constructed prototypes. In short, the central tendency would be abstracted (and other information discarded) at the time of retrieval rather than at the time of storage or initial encoding. Such a model would inherit all the shortcomings of standard prototype theories.

Some exemplar storage theories do not endorse the notion of feature independence (Hintzman, 1986; Medin & Schaffer, 1978), or they assume that classification is based on retrieving only a subset of the stored examples (presumably the most similar ones or, as a special case, the most similar one). The idea that retrieval is limited, similarity-based, and context-sensitive is in accord with much of the memory literature (e.g., Tulving, 1983). In addition, these exemplar models predict sensitivity to category size, instance variability, context, and correlated attributes. It is my impression that in head-to-head competition, exemplar models have been substantially more successful than prototype models (Barsalou & Medin, 1986; Estes, 1986b; Medin & Ross, 1989; Nosofsky, 1988a, 1988b; but see Homa, 1984, for a different opinion).

Why should exemplar models fare better than prototype models? One of the main functions of classification is that it allows one to make inferences and predictions on the basis of partial information (see Anderson, 1988). Here I am using classification loosely to refer to any means by which prior (relevant) knowledge is brought to bear, ranging from a formal classification scheme to an idiosyncratic reminding of a previous case (which, of course, is in the spirit of exemplar models; see also Kolodner, 1984). In psychotherapy, clinicians are constantly making predictions about the likelihood of future behaviors or the efficacy of a particular treatment based on classification. Relative to prototype models, exemplar models tend to be conservative about discarding information that facilitates predictions. For instance, sensitivity to correlations of properties within a category enables finer predictions: From noting that a bird is large, one can predict that it cannot sing. It may seem that exemplar models do not discard any information at all, but they are incomplete without assumptions concerning retrieval or access. In general, however, the pairs of storage and retrieval assumptions associated with exemplar models preserve much more information than prototype models. In a general review of research on categorization and problem-solving, Brian Ross and I concluded that abstraction is both conservative and tied to the details of specific examples in a manner more in the spirit of exemplar models than prototype models (Medin & Ross, 1989).

Unfortunately, context-sensitive, conservative categorization is not enough. The debate between prototype and exemplar models has taken place on a platform constructed in terms of similarity-based categorization. The second shift is that this platform has started to crumble, and the viability of probabilistic view theories of categorization is being seriously questioned. There are two central problems. One is that probabilistic view theories do not say anything about why we have the categories we have. This problem is most glaringly obvious for exemplar models that appear to allow any set of examples to form a category. The second central problem is with the notion of similarity. Do things belong in the same category because they are similar, or do they seem similar because they are in the same category?

Does Similarity Explain Categorization?

1. Flexibility. Similarity is a very intuitive notion. Unfortunately, it is even more elusive than it is intuitive. One problem with using similarity to define categories is that similarity is too flexible. Consider, for example, Tversky's (1977) influential contrast model, which defines similarity as a function of common and distinctive

features weighted for salience or importance. According to this model, similarity relationships will depend heavily on the particular weights given to individual properties or features. For example, a *zebra* and a *barber pole* would be more similar than a *zebra* and a *horse* if the feature "striped" had sufficient weight. This would not necessarily be a problem if the weights were stable. However, Tversky and others have convincingly shown that the relative weighting of a feature (as well as the relative importance of matching and mismatching features) varies with the stimulus context, experimental task (Gati & Tversky, 1984; Tversky, 1977), and probably even the concept under consideration (Ortony, Vondruska, Foss, & Jones, 1985). For example, common properties shared by a pair of entities may become salient only in the context of some third entity that does not share these properties.

Once one concedes that similarity is dynamic and depends on some (not well-understood) processing principles, earlier work on the structural underpinnings of fuzzy categories can be seen in a somewhat different light. Recall that the Rosch and Mervis (1975) studies asked subjects to list attributes or properties of examples and categories. It would be a mistake to assume that people had the ability to read and report their mental representations of concepts in a veridical manner. Indeed Keil (1979, 1981) pointed out that examples like *robin* and *squirrel* shared many important properties that almost never show up in attribute listings (e.g., has a heart, breathes, sleeps, is an organism, is an object with boundaries, is a physical object, is a thing, can be thought about, and so on). In fact, Keil argued that knowledge about just these sorts of predicates, referred to as ontological knowledge (Sommers, 1971), serves to organize children's conceptual and semantic development. For present purposes, the point is that attribute listings provide a biased sample of people's conceptual knowledge. To take things a step further, one could argue that without constraints on what is to count as a feature, any two things may be arbitrarily similar or dissimilar. Thus, as Murphy and I (Murphy & Medin, 1985) suggested, the number of properties that plums and lawn mowers have in common could be infinite: Both weigh less than 1000 Kg, both are found on earth, both are found in our solar system, both cannot hear well, both have an odor, both are not worn by elephants, both are used by people, both can be dropped, and so on (see also Goodman, 1972; Watanabe, 1969). Now consider again the status of attribute listings. They represent a biased subset of stored or readily inferred knowledge. The correlation of attribute listings with typicality judgments is a product of such knowledge and a variety of processes that operate on it. Without a theory of that knowledge and those processes, it simply is not clear what these correlations indicate about mental representations.

The general point is that attempts to describe category structure in terms of similarity will prove useful only to the extent that one specifies which principles determine what is to count as a relevant property and which principles determine the importance of particular properties. It is important to realize that the explanatory work is being done by the principles which specify these constraints rather than the general notion of similarity. In that sense similarity is more like a dependent variable than an independent variable.

2. Attribute matching and categorization. The modal model of similarity summarized in Table 7.1 invites one to view categorization as attribute matching. Although that may be part of the story, there are several ways in which the focus on attribute matching may be misleading. First of all, as Armstrong, Gleitman, and Gleitman (1983) emphasized, most concepts are not a simple sum of independent features. The features that are characteristically associated with the concept *bird* are just a pile of bird features unless they are held together in a "bird structure." Structure requires both attributes and *relations* binding the attributes together. Typical bird features (laying eggs, flying, having wings and feathers, building nests in trees, and singing) have both an internal structure

and an external structure based on interproperty relationships. Building nests is linked to laying eggs, and building nests in trees poses logistical problems whose solution involves other properties such as having wings, flying, and singing. Thus, it makes sense to ask why birds have certain features (e.g., wings and feathers). Although people may not have thought about various interproperty relationships, they can readily reason with them. Thus, one can answer the question of why birds have wings and feathers (i.e., to fly).

In a number of contexts, categorization may be more like problem solving than attribute matching. Inferences and causal attributions may drive the categorization process. Borrowing again from work by Murphy and me (1985), "jumping into a swimming pool with one's clothes on" in all probability is not associated directly with the concept *intoxicated*. However, observing this behavior might lead one to classify the person as drunk. In general, real world knowledge is used to reason about or explain properties, not simply to match them. For example, a teenage boy might show many of the behaviors associated with an eating disorder, but the further knowledge that the teenager is on the wrestling team and trying to make a lower weight class may undermine any diagnosis of a disorder.

3. Summary. It does not appear that similarity, at least in the form it takes in current theories, is going to be at all adequate to explain categorization. Similarity may

TABLE 7.1. Comparison of Two Approaches to Concepts

Aspect of Conceptual Theory	Similarity-Based Approach	Theory-Based Approach
Concept representation	Similarity structure, attribute lists, correlated attributes	Correlated attributes plus underlying principles that determine which correlations are noticed
Category definition	Various similarity metrics, summation of attributes	An explanatory principle common to category members
Units of analysis	Attributes	Attributes plus explicitly represented relations of attributes and concepts
Categorization basis	Attribute matching	Matching plus inferential processes supplied by underlying principles
Weighting of attributes	Cue validity, salience	Determined in part by importance in the underlying principles
Interconceptual structure	Hierarchy based on shared attributes	Network formed by causal and explanatory links, as well as sharing of properties picked out as relevant
Conceptual development	Feature accretion	Changing organization and explanations of concepts as a result of world knowledge

be a byproduct of conceptual coherence rather than a cause. To use a rough analogy, winning basketball teams have in common scoring more points than their opponents, but one must turn to more basic principles to explain why they score more points. One candidate for a set of deeper principles is the idea that concepts are organized around theories, and theories provide conceptual coherence. In the next section, I will briefly summarize some of the current work on the role of knowledge structures and theories in categorization and then turn to a form of rapprochement between similarity and knowledge-based categorization principle.

The Second Shift: Concepts as Organized by Theories

Knowledge-Based Categorization

It is perhaps only a modest exaggeration to say that similarity gets at the shadow rather than the substance of concepts. Something is needed to give concepts life, coherence, and meaning. Although many philosophers of science have argued that observations are necessarily theory-labeled, only recently have researchers begun to stress that the organization of concepts is knowledge-based and driven by theories about the world (e.g., Carey, 1985; S. Gelman, 1988; S. Gelman & Markman, 1986a, 1986b; Keil, 1986, 1987; Keil & Kelly, 1987; Lakoff, 1987; Markman, 1987; Massey & R. Gelman, 1988; Murphy & Medin, 1985; Oden, 1987; Rips, 1989; Schank, Collins, & Hunter, 1986; and others).

The primary differences between the similarity-based and theory-based approaches to categorization are summarized in Table 7.1, taken from Murphy and Medin (1985). Murphy and Medin suggested that the relation between a concept and an example is analogous to the relation between theory and data. That is, classification is not simply based on a direct matching of properties of the concept with those in the example, but rather requires that the example have the right "explanatory relationship" to the theory organizing the concept. In the case of a person diving into a swimming pool with his or her clothes on, one might try to reason back to either causes or predisposing conditions. One might believe that having too much to drink impairs judgment and that going into the pool shows poor judgment. Of course, the presence of other information, such as the fact that another person who cannot swim has fallen into the pool, would radically change the inferences drawn and, as a consequence, the categorization judgment.

One of the more promising aspects of the theory-based approach is that it begins to address the question of why we have the categories we have or why categories are sensible. In fact, coherence may be achieved in the absence of any obvious source of similarity among examples. Consider the category comprised of children, money, photo albums, and pets. Out of context the category seems odd. If one's knowledge base is enriched to include the fact that the category represents "things to take out of one's house in case of a fire," the category becomes sensible (Barsalou, 1983). In addition, one could readily make judgments about whether new examples (e.g., personal papers) belonged to the category, judgments that would not be similarity based.

Similarity effects can be overridden by theory-related strategies even in the judgments of young children. That fact was very nicely demonstrated by Gelman and Markman (1986a) in their studies of induction. Specifically, they pitted category membership against perceptual similarity in an inductive inference task. Young children were taught that different novel properties were true of two examples and then were asked which property was also true of a new example that was similar to one alternative but belonged to a different category, and one that was perceptually different from the other examples but belonged to the same category. For example, children might be taught that a (pictured) flamingo feeds its baby mashed-up food and that a (pictured) bat feeds its baby milk, and then they might be asked how a (pictured) owl feeds its baby. The owl was more perceptually similar to the bat than to the flamingo, but even four-year-olds made inferences on the basis of category membership rather than similarity.

Related work by Susan Carey and Frank Keil shows that children's biological theories guide their conceptual development. For example, Keil has used the ingenious technique of describing transformations or changes such as painting a horse to look like a zebra to examine the extent to which category membership judgments are controlled by superficial perceptual properties. Biological theories determine membership judgments quite early on (Keil, 1987; Keil & Kelly, 1987). Rips (1989) has used the same technique to show that similarity is neither necessary nor sufficient to determine category membership. It even appears to be the case that theories can affect judgments of similarity. For example, Medin and Shoben (1988) found that the terms *white hair* and *grey hair* were judged to be more similar than *grey hair* and *black hair*, but that the terms *white clouds* and *grey clouds* were judged as less similar than *grey clouds* and *black clouds*. Our interpretation is that white and grey hair are linked by a theory (of aging) in a way that white and grey clouds are not.

The above observations are challenging for defenders of the idea that similarity drives conceptual organization. In fact, one might wonder if the notion of similarity is so loose and unconstrained that we might be better off without it. Goodman (1972) epitomized this attitude by calling similarity "a pretender, an imposter, a quack" (p. 437). After reviewing some reasons to continue to take similarity seriously, I outline one possible route for integrating similarity-based and theory-based categorization.

The Need for Similarity

So far I have suggested that similarity relations do not provide conceptual coherence but that theories do. Because a major problem with similarity is that it is so unconstrained, one might ask what constrains theories. If we cannot identify constraints on theories, that is, say something about why we have the theories we have and not others, then we have not solved the problem of coherence: It simply has been shifted to another level. Although I believe we can specify some general properties of theories and develop a psychology of explanation (e.g., Abelson & Lalljee, 1988; Einhorn & Hogarth, 1986; Hilton & Slugoski, 1986; Leddo, Abelson, & Gross, 1984), I equally believe that a constrained form of similarity will play an important role in our understanding of human concepts. This role is not to provide structure so much as it is to guide learners toward structure.

The impact of more direct perceptual similarity on the development of causal explanations is evident in the structure of people's naive theories. Frazer's (1959) cross-cultural analysis of belief systems pointed to the ubiquity of two principles, homeopathy and contagion. The principle of homeopathy is that causes and effects tend to be similar. One manifestation of this principle is homeopathic medicine, in which the cure (and the cause) are seen to resemble the symptoms. In the Azande culture, for example, the cure for ringworm is to apply fowl's excrement because the excrement looks like the ringworm. Schweder (1977) adduced strong support for the claim that resemblance is a fundamental conceptual tool of everyday thinking in all cultures, not just so-called primitive cultures.

Contagion is the principle that a cause must have some form of contact to transmit its effect. In general, the more contiguous (temporally and spatially similar) events are in time and space, the more likely they are to be perceived as causally related (e.g., Dickinson, Shanks, & Evenden, 1984; Michotte, 1963). People also tend to assume that causes and effects should be of similar magnitude. Einhorn and Hogarth (1986) pointed out that the germ theory of disease initially met with great resistance because people could not imagine how such tiny organisms could have such devastating effects.

It is important to recognize that homeopathy and contagion often point us in the right direction. Immunization can be seen as a form of homeopathic medicine that has an underlying theoretical principle to support it. My reading of these observations, however, is not that specific theoretical (causal) principles are constraining similarity but rather that similarity (homeopathy and contagion) acts as a constraint on the search for causal explanations. Even in classical conditioning studies, the similarity of the conditioned stimulus and the unconditioned stimulus can have a major influence on the rate of conditioning (Testa, 1974). Of course, similarity must itself be constrained for terms like homeopathy to have a meaning. Shortly, I will suggest some constraints on similarity as part of an effort to define a role for similarity in conceptual development.

Similarity is likely to have a significant effect on explanations in another way. Given the importance of similarity in retrieval, it is likely that explanations that are applied to a novel event are constrained by similar events and their associated explanations. For example, Read (1983) found that people may rely on single, similar instances in making causal attributions about behaviors. Furthermore, Ross (1984) and Gentner and Landers (1985) have found that superficial similarities and not just similarity with respect to deeper principles or relations play a major role in determining the remindings associated with problem solving and the use of analogy.

In brief, it seems that similarity cannot be banished from the world of theories and conceptual structures. But it seems to me that a theory of similarity is needed that is quite different in character from the one summarized in Table 7.1. I will suggest an alternative view of similarity and then attempt to show its value in integrating and explanation with respect to concepts.

Similarity and Theory in Conceptual Structure

A Contrasting Similarity Model

The following are key tenets of the type of similarity theory needed to link similarity with knowledge-based categorization: (a) Similarity needs to include attributes, relations, and higher-order relations. (b) Properties in general are not independent but rather are linked by a variety of interproperty relations. (c) Properties exist at multiple levels of abstraction. (d) Concepts are more than lists. Properties and relations create depth or structure. Each of the four main ideas directly conflicts with the corresponding assumption of the theory of similarity outlined earlier. In one way or another all of these assumptions are tied to structure. The general idea I am proposing is far from new. In the psychology of visual perception, the need for structural approaches to similarity has been a continuing, if not major, theme (e.g., Biederman, 1985, 1987; Palmer, 1975, 1978; Pomerantz, Sager, & Stoever, 1977). Oden and Lopes (1982) have argued that this view can inform our understanding of concepts: "Although similarity must function at some level in the induction of concepts, the induced categories are not 'held together' subjectively by the undifferentiated 'force' of similarity, but rather by structural principles" (p. 78). Nonindependence of properties and simple and higher-order relations add a dimension of depth to categorization. Depth has clear implications for many of the observations that seem so problematic for probabilistic view theories. I turn now to the question of how these modified similarity notions may link up with theory-based categorization.

Psychological Essentialism

Despite the overwhelming evidence against the classical view, there is something about it that is intuitively compelling. Recently I and my colleagues have begun to take this observation seriously, not for its metaphysical implications but as a piece of psychological data (Medin & Ortony, 1989; Medin & Wattenmaker, 1987; Wattenmaker, Nakamura, & Medin, 1988). One might call this framework "psychological essentialism." The main ideas are as follows: People act as if things (e.g., objects) have essences or underlying natures that make them the thing that they are. Furthermore, the essence constrains or generates properties that may vary in their centrality. One of the things that theories do is to embody or provide causal linkages from deeper properties to more superficial or surface properties. For example, people in our culture believe that the categories *male* and *female* are genetically determined, but to pick someone out as male or female we rely on characteristics such as hair length, height, facial hair, and clothing that represent a mixture of secondary sexual characteristics and cultural conventions. Although these characteristics are more unreliable than genetic evidence, they are far from arbitrary. Not only do they have some validity in

a statistical sense, but also they are tied to our biological and cultural conceptions of *male* and *female*.

It is important to note that psychological essentialism refers not to how the world is but rather to how people approach the world. Wastebaskets probably have no true essence, although we may act as if they do. Both social and psychodiagnostic categories are at least partially culture specific and may have weak if any metaphysical underpinnings (see also Morey & McNamara, 1987).

If psychological essentialism is bad metaphysics, why should people act as if things had essences? The reason is that it may prove to be good epistomology. One could say that people adopt an *essentialist heuristic*, namely, the hypothesis that things that look alike tend to share deeper properties (similarities). Our perceptual and conceptual systems appear to have evolved such that the essentialist heuristic is very often correct (Medin & Wattenmaker, 1987; Shepard, 1984). This is true even for human artifacts such as cars, computers, and camping stoves because structure and function tend to be correlated. Surface characteristics that are perceptually obvious or are readily produced on feature listing tasks may not so much constitute the core of a concept as point toward it. This observation suggests that classifying on the basis of similarity will be relatively effective much of the time, out that similarity will yield to knowledge of deeper principles. Thus, in the work of Gelman and Markman, (1986a) discussed earlier, category membership was more important than perceptual similarity in determining inductive inferences.

Related Evidence

The contrasting similarity principles presented earlier coupled with psychological essentialism provide a framework for integrating knowledge-based and similarity-based categorization. Although it is far short of a formal theory, the framework provides a useful perspective on many of the issues under discussion in this article.

1. Nonindependence of features. Earlier I mentioned that classifying on the basis of similarity to a prototype was functionally equivalent to adding up the evidence favoring a classification and applying some criterion at least X out of Y features). Recall also that the data can strongly against this idea. From the perspective currently under consideration, however, there ought to be two ways to produce data consistent with prototype theory. One would be to provide a theory that suggests the prototype as an ideal or that makes summing of evidence more natural. For example, suppose that the characteristic properties for one category were as follows: It is made of metal, has a regular surface, is of medium size, and is easy to grasp. For a contrasting category the characteristic properties were: It is made of rubber, has an irregular surface, is of small size, and is hard to grasp. The categories may not seem sensible or coherent but suppose one adds the information that the objects in one category could serve as substitutes for a hammer. Given this new information, it becomes easy to add up the properties of examples in terms of their utility in supporting hammering. In a series of studies using the above descriptions and related examples, Wattenmaker, Dewey, Murphy, and I (1986) found data consistent with prototype theory when the additional information was supplied, and data inconsistent with prototype theory when only characteristic properties were supplied. Specifically, they found that linearly separable categories were easier to learn than nonlinearly separable categories only when an organizing theme was provided (see also Nakamura, 1985).

One might think that prototypes become important whenever the categories are meaningful. That is not the case. When themes are provided that are not compatible with a summing of evidence, the data are inconsistent with prototype theories. For instance, suppose that the examples consisted of descriptions of animals and that the organizing theme was that one category consisted of prey and the other of predators. It is a good adaptation for prey to be armored and to live in trees, but an animal that is both armored and lives in trees may not be better adapted than an animal with either characteristic alone. Being armored and living in trees may be somewhat incompatible. Other studies by Wattenmaker et al. using directly analogous materials failed to find any evidence that linear separability (and, presumably, summing of evidence) was important or natural. Only some kinds of interproperty relations are compatible with a summing of evidence, and evidence favoring prototypes may be confined to these cases.

The above studies show that the ease or naturalness of classification tasks cannot be predicted in terms of abstract category structures based on distribution of features, but rather requires an understanding of the knowledge brought to bear on them, for this knowledge determines inter-property relationships. So far only a few types of interproperty relationships have been explored in categorization, and much is to be gained from the careful study of further types of relations (e.g., see Barr & Caplan, 1987; Chaffin & Hermann, 1987; Rips & Conrad, 1989; Winston, Chaffin, & Herman, 1987).

2. Levels of features. Although experimenters can often contrive to have the features or properties comprising stimulus materials at roughly the same level of abstractness, in more typical circumstances levels may vary substantially. This fact has critical implications for descriptions of category structure (see Barsalou & Billman, 1988). This point may be best represented by an example from some ongoing research I am conducting with Glenn Nakamura and Ed Wisniewski. Our stimulus materials consist of children's drawings of people, a sample of which is shown in Figure 7.1. There are two sets of five drawings, one on the left and one on the right. The task of the participants in this experiment is to come up with a rule that could be used to correctly classify both these drawings and new examples that might be presented later.

One of our primary aims in this study was to examine the effects of different types of knowledge structures on rule induction. Consequently, some participants were told that one set was done by farm children and the other by city children; some were told that one set was done by creative children and the other by noncreative children; and still others were told that one set was done by emotionally disturbed children and the other by mentally healthy children. The exact assignment of drawings was counterbalanced with respect to the categories such that half the time the drawings on the left of Figure 7.1 were labeled as done by farm children and half the time the drawings on the right were labeled as having been done by farm children.

Although we were obviously expecting differences in the various conditions, in some respects the most striking result is one that held across conditions. Almost without exception the rules that people gave had properties at two or three different levels of abstractness. For example, one person who was told the drawings on the left were done by city children gave the following rule: "The city drawings use more profiles, and are more elaborate. The clothes are more detailed, showing both pockets and buttons, and the hair is drawn in. The drawings put less emphasis on proportion and the legs and torso are off." Another person who was told the same drawings were done by farm children wrote: "The children draw what they see in their normal life. The people have overalls on and some drawings show body muscles as a result of labor. The drawings are also more detailed. One can see more facial details and one drawing has colored the clothes and another one shows the body under the clothes." As one can see, the rules typically consist of a general assertion or assertions coupled with either an operational definition or examples to illustrate and clarify the assertion. In some cases these definitions or examples extend across several levels of abstractness.

FIGURE 7.1 ■ Children's Drawings of People Used in the Rule Induction Studies by Nakamura, Wisniewski, and Medin.

One might think that our participants used different levels of description because there was nothing else for them to do. That is, there may have been no low-level perceptual features that would separate the groups. In a followup study we presented examples one at a time and asked people to give their rule after each example.

If people are being forced to use multiple levels of description because simple rules will not work, then we should observe a systematic increase in the use of multiple levels across examples. In fact, however, we observed multiple levels of description as the predominant strategy from the first example on. We believe that multiple levels arise when people try to find a link between abstract explanatory principles or ideas (drawings reflect one's experience) and specific details of drawings.

There are several important consequences of multilevel descriptions. First of all, the relation across levels is not necessarily a subset, superset, or a part-whole relation. Most of the time one would say that the lower level property "supports" the higher level property; for example, "jumping into a swimming pool with one's clothes on" supports poor judgment. This underlines the point that categorization often involves more than a simple matching of properties. A related point is that features are ambiguous in the sense that they may support more than one higher level property. When the drawings on the right were associated with the label *mentally healthy*, a common description was "all the faces are smiling." When the label for the same drawing was *noncreative*, a common description was "the faces show little variability in expression." Finally, it should be obvious that whether a category description is disjunctive (e.g., pig's nose or cow's mouth or catlike ears) or conjunctive or defining (e.g., all have animal parts) depends on the level with respect to which the rule is evaluated.

3. Centrality. If properties are at different levels of abstraction and linked by a variety of relations, then one might imagine that some properties are more central than others because of the role they play in conceptual structure. An indication that properties differ in their centrality comes from a provocative study by Asch and Zukier (1984). They presented people with trait terms that appeared to be contradictory (e.g., kind and vindictive) and asked participants if these descriptions could be resolved (e.g., how could a person be both kind and vindictive?). Participants had no difficulty integrating the pairs of terms, and Asch and Zukier identified seven major resolution strategies. For present purposes, what is notable is that many of the resolution strategies involve making one trait term more central than the other one. For example, one way of integrating *kind* and *vindictive* was to say that the person was fundamentally evil and was kind only in the service of vindictive ends.

In related work, Shoben and I (Medin & Shoben, 1988) showed that centrality of a property depends on the concept of which it is a part. We asked participants to judge the typicality of adjective noun pairs when the adjective was a property that other participants judged was not true of the noun representing the concept. For example, our participants judged that all bananas and all boomerangs are curved. Based on this observation, other participants were asked to judge the typicality of a straight banana as a banana or a straight boomerang as a boomerang. Other instances of the 20 pairs used include *soft knife* versus *soft diamond* and *polka dot fire hydrant* versus *polka dot yield sign*. For 19 of the 20 pairs, participants rated one item of a pair as more typical than the other. Straight banana, soft knife, and polka dot fire hydrant were rated as more typical than straight boomerang, soft diamond, and polka dot yield sign. In the case of boomerangs (and probably yield signs), centrality may be driven by structure-function correlations. Soft diamonds are probably rated as very atypical because hardness is linked to many other properties and finding out that diamonds were soft would call a great deal of other knowledge into question.

Most recently, Woo Kyoung Ahn, Joshua Rubenstein, and I have been interviewing clinical psychologists and psychiatrists concerning their understanding of psychodiagnostic categories. Although our project is not far enough along to report any detailed results, it is clear that the *DSM-IIIR* guidebook (American Psychiatric Association, 1987) provides only a skeletal outline that is brought to life by theories and causal scenarios underlying and intertwined with the symptoms that comprise the diagnostic criteria. Symptoms differ in the level of abstractness and the types and number of inter-symptom relations in which they participate, and as a consequence, they differ in their centrality.

Conclusions

The shift to a focus on knowledge-based categorization does not mean that the notion of similarity must be left behind. But we do need an updated approach to, and interpretation of, similarity. The mounting evidence on the role of theories and explanations in organizing categories is much more compatible with features at varying levels linked by a variety of interproperty relations than it is with independent features at a - single level. In addition, similarity may not so much constitute structure as point toward it. There is a dimension of depth to categorization. The conjectures about psychological essentialism may be one way of reconciling classification in terms of perceptual similarity or surface properties with the deeper substance of knowledge-rich, theory-based categorization.

REFERENCES

Abelson, R. P., & Lalljee, M. G. (1988). Knowledge-structures and causal explanation. In D. J. Hilton (Ed.), *Contemporary science and natural explanation: Commonsense conceptions of causality* (pp. 175–202). Brighton, England: Harvester Press.

Allen, S. W., Brooks, L. R., Norman, G. R., & Rosenthal, D. (1988, November). *Effect of prior examples on rule-based diagnostic performance.* Paper presented at the meeting of the Psychonomic Society, Chicago.

American Psychiatric Association. (1987). *Diagnostic and statistical manual of mental disorders* (rev. ed.). Washington, DC: Author.

Anderson, J. R. (1988). The place of cognitive architectures in a rational analyses. In *The Tenth Annual Conference of the Cognitive Science Society* (pp. 1–10). Montreal, Canada: University of Montreal.

Arkes, H. R., & Harkness, A. R. (1980). Effect of making a diagnosis on subsequent recognition of symptoms. *Journal of Experimental Psychology: Human Learning and Memory, 6,* 568–575.

Armstrong, S. L., Gleitman, L. R., & Gleitman, H. (1983). What some concepts might not be. *Cognition, 13,* 263–308.

Asch, S. E., & Zukier, H. (1984). Thinking about persons. *Journal of Personality and Social Psychology, 46,* 1230–1240.

Barr, R. A., & Caplan, L. J. (1987). Category representations and their implications for category structure. *Memory and Cognition, 15,* 397–418.

Barsalou, L. W. (1983). Ad hoc categories. *Memory and Cognition, 11,* 211–227.

Barsalou, L. W. (1985). Ideals, central tendency, and frequency of instantiation as determinants of graded structure in categories. *Journal of Experimental Psychology: Learning, Memory and Cognition, 11,* 629–654.

Barsalou, L. W. (1987). The instability of graded structure: Implications for the nature of concepts. In U. Neisser (Ed.), *Concepts and conceptual development: The ecological and intellectual factors in categorization* (pp. 101–140). Cambridge, England: Cambridge University Press.

Barsalou, L. W. (1989). Intra-concept similarity and its implications for inter-concept similarity. In S. Vosniadou & A. Ortony (Eds.), *Similarity and analogical reasoning* (pp. 76–121). Cambridge, England: Cambridge University Press.

Barsalou, L. W., & Billman, D. (1988, April). *Systematicity and semantic ambiguity.* Paper presented at a workshop on semantic ambiguity, Adelphi University.

Barsalou, L. W., & Medin, D. L. (1986). Concepts: Fixed definitions or dynamic context-dependent representations? *Cahiers de Psychologie Cognitive, 6,* 187–202.

Bellezza, F. S. (1984). Reliability of retrieval from semantic memory: Noun meanings. *Bulletin of the Psychonomic Society, 22,* 377–380.

Biederman, I. (1985). Human image understanding: Recent research and a theory. *Computer Vision, Graphics, and Image Processing, 32,* 29–83.

Biederman, I. (1987). Recognition-by-components: A theory of human image understanding. *Psychological Review, 94,* 115–147.

Cantor, N., & Mischel, W. (1977). Traits as prototypes: Effects on recognition memory. *Journal of Personality and Social Psychology, 35,* 38–48.

Carey, S. (1985). *Conceptual change in childhood.* Cambridge, MA: Massachusetts Institute of Technology Press.

Chaffin, R., & Herrmann, D. J. (1987). Relation element theory: A new account of the representation and processing of semantic relations. In D. Gorfein & R. Hoffman (Eds.), *Learning and memory: The Ebbinghaus centennial conference* (pp. 221–245). Hillsdale, NJ: Erlbaum.

Dickinson, A., Shanks, D., & Evenden, J. (1984). Judgment of act-outcomes contingency: The role of selective attribution. *Quarterly Journal of Experimental Psychology, 36A*(1), 29–50.

Einhorn, J. H., & Hogarth, R. M. (1986). Judging probable cause. *Psychological Bulletin, 99*, 3–19.

Estes, W. K. (1986a). Memory storage and retrieval processes in category learning. *Journal of Experimental Psychology: General, 115*, 155–175.

Estes, W. K. (1986b). Array models for category learning. *Cognitive Psychology, 18*, 500–549.

Fehr, B. (1988). Prototype analysis of the concepts of love and commitment. *Journal of Personality and Social Psychology, 55*, 557–579.

Fehr, B., & Russell, J. A. (1984). Concept of emotion viewed from a prototype perspective. *Journal of Experimental Psychology: General, 113*, 464–486.

Flannagan, M. J., Fried, L. S., & Holyoak, K. J. (1986). Distributional expectations and the induction of category structure. *Journal of Experimental Psychology: Learning, Memory and Cognition, 12*, 241–256.

Frazer, J. G. (1959). *The new golden bough*. New York: Criterion Books.

Fried, L. S., & Holyoak, K. J. (1984). Induction of category distribution: A framework for classification learning. *Journal of Experimental Psychology: Learning, Memory and Cognition, 10*, 234–257.

Gati, I., & Tversky, A. (1984). Weighting common and distinctive features in perceptual and conceptual judgments. *Cognitive Psychology, 16*, 341–370.

Gelman, S. A. (1988). The development of induction within natural kind and artifact categories. *Cognitive Psychology, 20*, 65–95.

Gelman, S. A., & Markman, E. M. (1986a). Categories and induction in young children. *Cognition, 23*, 183–209.

Gelman, S. A., & Markman, E. M. (1986b). Young children's inductions from natural kinds: The role of categories and appearances. *Child Development, 58*, 1532–1541.

Genero, N., & Cantor, N. (1987). Exemplar prototypes and clinical diagnosis: Toward a cognitive economy. *Journal of Social and Clinical Psychology, 5*, 59–78.

Gentner, D., & Landers, R. (1985). *Analogical reminding: A good match is hard to find*. Paper presented at the International Conference of Systems, Man and Cybernetics, Tucson, AZ.

Goldin, S. E. (1978). Memory for the ordinary: Typicality effects in chess memory. *Journal of Experimental Psychology: Human Learning and Memory, 4*, 605–616.

Goodman, N. (1972). Seven strictures on similarity. In N. Goodman (Ed.), *Problems and projects*. New York: Bobbs-Merrill.

Hartley, J., & Homa, D. (1981). Abstraction of stylistic concepts. *Journal of Experimental Psychology: Human Learning and Memory, 7*, 33–46.

Hilton, D. J., & Slugoski, B. R. (1986). Knowledge-based causal attribution: The abnormal conditions focus model. *Psychological Review, 93*, 75–88.

Hintzman, D. L. (1986). "Schema abstraction" in a multiple-trace memory model. *Psychological Review, 93*, 411–428.

Homa, D. (1984). On the nature of categories. In G. Bower (Ed.), *The psychology of learning and motivation* (Vol. 18, pp. 49–94). New York: Academic Press.

Homa, D., & Vosburgh, R. (1976). Category breadth and the abstraction of prototypical information. *JEP: Human Learning and Memory, 2*, 322–330.

Keil, F. C. (1979). *Semantic and conceptual development: An ontological perspective*. Cambridge, MA: Harvard University Press.

Keil, F. C. (1981). Constraints on knowledge and cognitive development. *Psychological Review, 88*, 197–227.

Keil, F. C. (1986). The acquisition of natural kind and artifact terms. In W. Demopoulos & A. Marras (Eds.), *Language learning and concept acquisition* (pp. 133–153). Norwood, NJ: Ablex.

Keil, F. C. (1987). Conceptual development and category structure. In U. Neisser (Ed.), *Concepts and conceptual development: Ecological and intellectual factors in categorization* (pp. 175–200). Cambridge, England: Cambridge University Press.

Keil, F. C., & Kelly, M. H. (1987). Developmental changes in category structure. In S. Harnad (Ed.), *Categorical perception: The groundwork of cognition* (pp. 491–510). Cambridge, England: Cambridge University Press.

Kemler-Nelson, D. G. (1984). The effect of intention on what concepts are acquired. *Journal of Verbal Learning and Verbal Behavior, 23*, 734–759.

Kolodner, J. L. (1984). *Retrieval and organizational structures in conceptual memory: A computer model*. Hillsdale, NJ: Erlbaum.

Lakoff, G. (1987). *Women, fire, and dangerous things: What categories tell us about the nature of thought*. Chicago: University of Chicago Press.

Leddo, J., Abelson, R. P., & Gross, P. H. (1984). Conjunctive explanation: When two explanations are better than one. *Journal of Personality and Social Psychology, 47*, 933–943.

Malt, B. C., & Smith, E. E. (1983). Correlated properties in natural categories. *Journal of Verbal Learning and Verbal Behavior, 23*, 250–269.

Markman, E. M. (1987). How children constrain the possible meanings of words. In U. Neisser (Ed.), *Concepts and conceptual development: The ecological and intellectual factors in categorization* (pp. 256–287). Cambridge, England: Cambridge University Press.

Massey, C. M., & Gelman, R. (1988). Preschoolers' ability to decide whether a photographed unfamiliar object can move itself. *Developmental Psychology, 24*, 307–317.

McCloskey, M., & Glucksberg, S. (1978). Natural categories: Well-defined or fuzzy sets? *Memory and Cognition, 6*, 462–472.

McNamara, T. P., & Sternberg, R. J. (1983). Mental models of word meaning. *Journal of Verbal Learning and Verbal Behavior, 22*, 449–474.

Medin, D. L. (1986). Commentary on "Memory storage and retrieval processes in category learning." *Journal of Experimental Psychology: General, 115*(4), 373–381.

Medin, D. L., Altom, M. W., Edelson, S. M., & Freko, D. (1982). Correlated symptoms and simulated medical classification. *Journal of Experimental Psychology: Learning, Memory and Cognition, 8*, 37–50.

Medin, D. L., & Ortony, A. (1989). *Psychological essentialism*. In S. Vosniadou & A. Ortony (Eds.), *Similarity and analogical reasoning* (pp. 179–195). New York: Cambridge University Press.

Medin, D. L., & Ross, B. H. (1989). The specific character of abstract thought: Categorization, problem-solving, and induction. In R. J. Sternberg (Ed.), *Advances in the psychology of human intelligence* (Vol. 5, pp. 189–223). Hillsdale, NJ: Erlbaum.

Medin, D. L., & Schaffer, M. M. (1978). A context theory of classification learning. *Psychological Review, 85*, 207–238.

Medin, D. L., & Schwanenflugel, P. J. (1981). Linear separability in classification learning. *Journal of Experimental Psychology: Human Learning and Memory, 7*, 355–368.

Medin, D. L., & Shoben, E. J. (1988). Context and structure in conceptual combination. *Cognitive Psychology, 20,* 158–190.

Medin, D. L., & Smith, E. E. (1984). Concepts and concept formation. In M. R. Rosenzweig & L. W. Porter (Eds.), *Annual Review of Psychology, 35,* 113–118.

Medin, D. L., & Wattenmaker, W. D. (1987). Category cohesiveness, theories, and cognitive archeology. In U. Neisser (Ed.), *Concepts and conceptual development: The ecological and intellectual factors in categories* (pp. 25–62). Cambridge, England: Cambridge University Press.

Mervis, C. B., & Rosch, E. (1981). Categorization of natural objects. In M. R. Rosenzweig & L. W. Porter (Eds.), *Annual Review of Psychology, 32,* 89–115.

Michotte, A. (1963). *Perception of causality.* London: Methuen.

Morey, L. C., & McNamara, T. P. (1987). On definitions, diagnosis, and DSM-III. *Journal of Abnormal Psychology, 96,* 283–285.

Murphy, G. L., & Medin, D. L. (1985). The role of theories in conceptual coherence. *Psychological Review, 92,* 289–316.

Nakamura, G. V. (1985). Knowledge-based classification of ill-defined categories. *Memory and Cognition, 13,* 377–384.

Nosofsky, R. M. (1987). Attention and learning processes in the identification and categorization of integral stimuli. *Journal of Experimental Psychology: Learning, Memory, and Cognition, 13,* 87–108.

Nosofsky, R. M. (1988a). Exemplar-based accounts of relations between classification, recognition, and typicality. *Journal of Experimental Psychology: Learning, Memory, and Cognition, 14,* 700–708.

Nosofsky, R. M. (1988b). Similarity, frequency, and category representations. *Journal of Experimental Psychology: Learning, Memory, and Cognition, 14,* 54–65.

Oden G. C. (1987). Concept, knowledge, and thought. In M. R. Rosenzweig & L. W. Porter (Eds.), *Annual Review of Psychology, 38,* 203–227.

Oden G. C., & Lopes, L. (1982). On the internal structure of fuzzy subjective categories. In R. R. Yager (Ed.), *Recent developments in fuzzy set and possibility theory* (pp. 75–89). Elmsford, NY: Pergamon Press.

Ortony, A., Vondruska, R. J., Foss, M. A., & Jones, L. E. (1985). Salience, smiles, and the asymmetry of similarity. *Journal of Memory and Language, 24,* 569–594.

Palmer, S. E. (1975). Visual perception and world knowledge. In D. A. Norman & D. E. Rumelhart (Eds.), *Explorations in cognition* (pp. 279–307). San Francisco: W. H. Freeman.

Palmer, S. E. (1978). Structural aspects of visual similarity. *Memory and Cognition, 6,* 91–97.

Peterson, M. J., Meagher, R. B., Jr., Chait, H., & Gillie, S. (1973). The abstraction and generalization of dot patterns. *Cognitive Psychology, 4,* 378–398.

Pomerantz, J. R., Sager, L. C., & Stoever, R. G. (1977). Perception of wholes and their component parts: Some configural superiority effects. *Journal of Experimental Psychology: Human Perception and Performance, 3,* 422–435.

Read, S. J. (1983). Once is enough: Causal reasoning from a single instance. *Journal of Personality and Social Psychology, 45,* 323–334.

Rips, L. (1989). Similarity, typicality, and categorization. In S. Vosniadou & A. Ortony (Eds.), *Similarity and analogical reasoning* (pp. 21–59). New York: Cambridge University Press.

Rips, L. J., & Conrad, F. G. (1989). The folk psychology of mental activities. *Psychological Review, 96,* 187–207.

Rosch, E. (1975). Cognitive representations of semantic categories. *Journal of Experimental Psychology: General, 104,* 192–233.

Rosch, E., & Mervis, C. B. (1975). Family resemblances: Studies in the internal structure of categories. *Cognitive Psychology, 7,* 573–605.

Ross, B. H. (1984). Remindings and their effects in learning a cognitive skill. *Cognitive Psychology, 16,* 371–416.

Roth E. M., & Shoben, E. J. (1983). The effect of context on the structure of categories. *Cognitive Psychology, 15,* 346–378.

Schank, R. C., Collins, G. C., & Hunter, L. E. (1986). Transcending induction category formation in learning. *The Behavioral and Brain Sciences, 9,* 639–686.

Schweder, R. A. (1977). Likeness and likelihood in everyday thought: Magical thinking in judgments about personality. *Current Anthropology, 18,* 4.

Sebestyn, G. S. (1962). *Decision-making processes in pattern recognition.* New York: Macmillan.

Shepard, R. H. (1984). Ecological constraints on internal representation: Resonant kinematics of perceiving, imagining, thinking, and dreaming. *Psychological Review, 19,* 417–447.

Shepard, R. N., Hovland, C. I., & Jenkins, H. M. (1961). Learning and memorization of classifications. *Psychological Monographs, 75,* (13, Whole No. 517).

Smith, E. E., & Medin, D. L. (1981). *Categories and concepts.* Cambridge, MA: Harvard University Press.

Smith, E. E., Rips, J. J., & Medin, D. W. (1984). A psychological approach to concepts: Comments on Rey's "Concepts and stereotypes." *Cognition,* 17, 265–274.

Smith, E. E., Shoben, E. J., & Rips, J. J. (1974). Structure and processes in semantic memory: A featural model for semantic decisions. *Psychological Review, 81,* 214–241.

Sommers, F. (1971). Structural ontology. *Philosophia, 1,* 21–42.

Testa, T. J. (1974). Causal relationships and the acquisition of avoidance responses. *Psychological Review, 81,* 491–505.

Tulving, E. (1983). *Elements of episodic memory.* New York: Oxford University Press.

Tversky, A. (1977). Features of similarity. *Psychological Review, 84,* 327–352.

Watanabe, S. (1969). *Knowing and guessing: A formal and quantitative study.* New York: Wiley.

Wattenmaker, W. D., Dewey, G. I., Murphy, T. D., & Medin, D. L. (1986). Linear separability and concept learning: Context, relational properties, and concept naturalness. *Cognitive Psychology, 18,* 158–194.

Wattenmaker, W. D., Nakamura, G. V., & Medin, D. L. (1988). Relationships between similarity-based and explanation-based categorization. In D. Hilton (Ed.), *Contemporary science and natural explanation: Commonsense conceptions of causality* (pp. 205–241). Brighton, England: Harvester Press.

Winston, M. E., Chaffin, R., & Herrmann, D. (1987). A taxonomy of part-whole relations. *Cognitive Science, 11,* 417–444.

Wittgenstein, L. (1953). *Philosophical investigations* (G. E. M. Anscombe, trans.). Oxford, England: Blackwell.

Structural Properties of Stereotypic Knowledge and Their Influences on the Construal of Social Situations

Bernd Wittenbrink, Pamela L. Gist, and James L. Hilton

This research focused on the role that higher order structural properties of stereotypic knowledge play in the processing of social information. It is argued that stereotypic assumptions about cause–effect relations provide important constraints for the causal structure underlying the perceiver's subjective representation of social information. Experiment 1 shows how, within the context of a jury decision experiment, the causal structure underlying stereotypic knowledge about African Americans influences the construal of causality in a situation involving a member of that group. Results from 2 additional experiments indicate that this construal effect is based in part on stereotypic knowledge affecting the encoding of the trial evidence instead of on biasing responses at the output stage. The implications of these findings are discussed, and a theoretical framework is offered according to which the application of category knowledge involves not only the matching of stereotypic attributes but also the alignment of structural relations in the environment.

The notion that subjective experience goes beyond the bare sensation of stimuli, that we actively construe reality instead of passively registering our environment, has long guided psychological analysis (Asch, 1952;

Editor's Note: This article reported three experiments. Experiments 1 and 3 are reproduced here.

Bernd Wittenbrink, Department of Psychology, University of Colorado; Pamela L. Gist and James L. Hilton, Department of Psychology, University of Michigan.

Of the many people who have guided this research with their helpful suggestions, we are particularly indebted to Eugene Burnstein, Charles Judd, Bernadette Park, and Norbert Schwarz. Many thanks also go to Robert Bartsch and Gideon Markman for their assistance with the data collection.

Correspondence concerning this article should be addressed to Bernd Wittenbrink, who is now at the Center for Decision Research, Graduate School of Business, University of Chicago, 1101 East 58th Street, Chicago, Illinois 60637. Electronic mail may be sent via the Internet to bernd.wittenbrink@gsb.uchicago.edu.

Bartlett, 1932; Heider, 1944; Lewin, 1936; Neisser, 1967; Ross & Nisbett, 1991; Wertheimer, 1925). Frequently, psychologists have focused on the process of categorization, the grouping of our stimulus environment into classes of similar entities, as one of the important means by which we go "beyond the information given" (Bruner, 1957). In identifying an object as a member of a certain category, we are able to draw on our knowledge and past experiences with similar objects and can thus infer stimulus properties that go beyond those that we directly observe. In the same way that we tend to base judgments and inferences about physical objects not on the individual stimulus but on knowledge about the group of stimuli as a whole, we also often make social judgments and inferences on the basis of our social categorical knowledge (Allport, 1954; Tajfel, 1969; Vinacke, 1957). Stereotypes, the perceiver's generalized assumptions about members of a social group, allow us to employ a wealth of knowledge that helps to enrich our subjective representation of the social environment and thereby place information about a given individual into a context of subjective meaning (cf. Leyens, Yzerbyt, & Schadron, 1992; Oakes & Turner, 1990; Stangor & Lange, 1994).

Indeed, the field has accumulated impressive evidence documenting the effects that perceivers' stereotypes have on the subjective meaning of the social environment (e.g., Darley & Gross, 1983; Duncan, 1976; Sagar & Schofield, 1980; Vallone, Ross, & Lepper, 1985). Stereotypes have been found to direct the perceiver's attention (e.g., Bodenhausen, 1988; Cohen, 1981; Hilton, Klein, & von Hippel, 1991), to affect the information recalled (e.g., Rothbart, Evans, & Fulero, 1979; Hastie & Kumar, 1979; Stangor & Duan, 1991), and to alter the perceiver's interpretation of relevant information (e.g., Banaji, Hardin, & Rothman, 1993; Biernat, Manis, & Nelson, 1991; Darley & Gross, 1983; Duncan, 1976; Kunda & Sherman-Williams, 1993).

Although there has clearly been a long-standing interest in understanding the effects that stereotypes have on the construal of social information, much of this work has focused on the influence of *trait attributes* that are associated with a given stereotype. Banaji and her colleagues, for example, found that after incidental exposure to either stereotypically female or male attributes (i.e., "dependent," "aggressive"), participants perceived a target individual to be relatively more aggressive when the target was a man and relatively more dependent when the target was a woman (Banaji et al., 1993). Of course, stereotypic knowledge often contains assumptions more complex than beliefs about the presence or absence of certain group characteristics. For example, Andersen and Klatzky (1987) demonstrated that stereotype labels evoke substantially richer associations than do trait descriptions. Similarly, Fiske (1993) has described stereotypes as rich "Gestalt-like" entities that aid the perceiver in explaining the social environment. In fact, beyond knowledge about group attributes, stereotypic knowledge frequently includes a causal structure that links these attributes to each other and to the perceiver's external knowledge about the world. In particular, these structural aspects of stereotypic knowledge may specify presumed cause–effect relations among stereotypic attributes. People's knowledge about African Americans, for example, may include assumptions regarding the underlying causes of stereotypic attributes such as *poor, uneducated,* and so on.

So far, the role these higher order structural properties of stereotypic knowledge play in the subjective construal of the social environment has received relatively little attention among stereotyping researchers. To this end, our goal in the present research was to examine more closely the processes by which the relational structure contained in stereotypic knowledge influences the processing of social information.

Structural Properties of Stereotypic Knowledge

Women are "dependent," Germans are "nationalistic," and Blacks are "poor." When thinking of the content of common cultural stereotypes, people usually think of the attributes that members of these groups allegedly share. So it is perhaps not too surprising that social psychological research on the phenomenon of stereotyping has most often been concerned with stereotypic group attributes. This focus characterizes stereotyping research from early on, when Katz and Braly (1933) asked participants to indicate the trait attributes descriptive of a given group in order to assess the content of cultural stereotypes, to more recent investigations of how stereotypes function in the processing of social information. In adopting this approach, the field has, over the years, made significant progress in determining, for example, how people incorporate inconsistent information regarding a certain group attribute into their existing stereotypes (e.g., Gurwitz & Dodge, 1977; Rothbart & John, 1985; Weber & Crocker, 1983), how sensitive people are to variability within the group on a certain attribute dimension (e.g., Linville, Fischer, & Salovey, 1989; Park & Judd, 1990), or how the accessibility of certain stereotypic attributes may influence social judgments (e.g., Banaji et al., 1993; Devine, 1989).

Yet, because stereotypes essentially consist of our knowledge about social categories (Hamilton & Troiler, 1986), they, like categorical knowledge in general, extend beyond assumptions about characteristic category attributes. For instance, Armstrong, Gleitman, and Gleitman (1983) pointed out that a list of bird attributes (e.g., lays eggs, flies, has wings and feathers, and builds nests) will not make a bird, unless those attributes are held together by a structure of attribute relations. After all, a bird is an animal, has wings, lays eggs, and lives in trees. Moreover, nest building is linked to laying eggs, and because of birds' ability to fly, the nests may be located in trees.

Similarly important are the relations that link group attributes into a meaningful entity for the categories with which people partition the social environment. One may, for example, believe that Germans can be described by attributes such as "nationalistic" and at the same time believe that this trait is due to Germans' authoritarian upbringing. Or, to a use more pernicious example, the anti-Semite may believe that Jews are rich because they are greedy and sly, whereas Protestants' affluence is seen as a result of diligence and hard labor. In this latter case, the causal assumptions underlying the stereotype are in fact indispensable in determining the meaning of a given group attribute.

The importance of causal assumptions for people's social-categorical knowledge is further illustrated by Whites' beliefs about African Americans. In trying to identify sets of beliefs that predict various kinds of race-related social judgments and behaviors (i.e., voting behavior, hiring decisions, etc.), researchers have focused increasingly on people's causal explanations for the situation of African Americans in U.S. society (cf. Bobo & Kluegel, 1993; Gilens, 1995; I. Katz & Hass, 1988; Kinder & Sears, 1981; Kluegel & Smith, 1986; Sears, 1988). Although this literature differs widely in its assumptions about the origins of existing belief differences (e.g., realistic group conflict, value differences, or social influence), it consistently has identified two opposing causal models for Whites' beliefs about African Americans. The first model holds that African Americans are individually responsible for economic failure and low social status. African Americans are believed to lack motivation and proper values necessary to function successfully in society, and they are thought to use claims of discrimination to gain unfair advantages and escape their social responsibilities. In contrast, the alternative explanation assumes that the lower social status and economic failure of African Americans is due to structural disadvantages. These structural circumstances, such as lack of job opportunities or an inadequate education system, are thought to result from both discrimination and ignorance on the part of the White majority. At a more general level, these two models may be characterized by whether African Americans are perceived to be the victims or the perpetrators of racial conflict and inequity (Ryan, 1976).

Structural Properties of Stereotypic Knowledge and the Construal of Causality

In the present article, our goal was to demonstrate that causal assumptions such as these play an important role in how stereotypes influence the perceiver's construal of social situations. That is, we believe that structural properties of stereotypic knowledge serve as a kind of causal blueprint when a stereotype is applied to a specific stereotype target. This blueprint aids the perceiver in integrating social information about a given event into a structure of underlying cause–effect relations.

Let us illustrate this argument with an example from research in the area of problem solving, a field in which the use of structural properties of knowledge for the subjective understanding of available information has long been of interest (e.g., Duncker, 1935; Gentner, 1983; Holyoak, 1985; Vosniadou & Ortony, 1989). Within this area, a series of experiments by Gick and Holyoak (1980, 1983) nicely documented the consequences of prior activation of a given relational structure on people's subjective construals of a subsequently encountered stimulus set. Specifically, Gick and Holyoak provided their participants with a classic task from problem-solving research that asks participants to identify a cure for an inoperable stomach tumor (Duncker, 1935). In this task, participants are told that the tumor could be treated with radiation; however the intensity of radiation necessary to destroy the tumor would also destroy the surrounding healthy tissue. Usually, participants have great difficulty finding a solution that would treat the tumor without affecting the healthy tissue. Gick and Holyoak were able to significantly improve performance by first presenting participants with a story that contained a problem analogous to the radiation problem. In this story, a general chooses to divide his troops into smaller units and have them converge on a fort from several directions rather than using a dangerous frontal attack. Similarly, one possible solution to the Duncker task consists of having several radiation sources of low intensity converge on the tumor. Although the various attributes of these two problems are relatively dissimilar ("fortress" vs. "tumor," "troops" vs. "rays," "conquer" vs. "cure," etc.), the ways in which these attributes relate to one another match quite well in both problems. The relational structure of the first task specifying cause–effect relations among the attributes apparently provides participants with a frame that allows for an adequate construal of the radiation problem.

In returning to the premise of this article, we propose that stereotypes serve as explanatory frameworks for the construal of cause–effect relations in social situations in a manner similar to that in which the fortress story in Gick and Holyoak's (1980, 1983) experiments provided participants with a structure for Duncker's radiation problem. That is, stereotypes provide a "theme" around which the perceiver organizes social information (Bodenhausen, 1988). In placing a given piece of information encountered into a specific context of cause–effect relations, stereotypic background knowledge specifies potential links to other information and determines the generation of inferences related to the information available. Stereotypic construal, then, is not only a consequence of the perceiver's stereotypic assumptions regarding additional, potentially unobserved, or so far unnoticed, trait characteristics but also a result of the constraints stereotypic knowledge places on the potential causal connections among the various pieces of information observed.

We emphasize that this characterization focuses on a particular function that stereotypic causal assumptions may serve in the processing of social information. That is, the present argument is concerned with the influences stereotypic causal assumptions have on the encoding of available information when the perceiver attempts to integrate this information into a coherent representation. Of course, stereotypes may also influence the construal of social information in alternative ways, such as by allowing the perceiver to rationalize a biased evaluation (e.g., Allport, 1954; Kunda, 1990; Schaller, 1992). However, our focus at present is on the ways in which stereotypic causal assumptions influence the encoding of stereotype-relevant information.

Overview of the Present Experiments

The three experiments reported in this article were designed to explore this notion that stereotypic knowledge provides constraints for the causal structure of the perceiver's representation of social information. Specifically, the studies were designed to investigate the potential influences of causal assumptions contained in participants' stereotypic beliefs about African Americans on their construals of social information.

Experiment 1 was designed to demonstrate that the differential stereotypic causal assumptions that we referred to earlier as victim or perpetrator models influence participants' perceptions of causality in a social situation involving an African American target. The second and third studies then examined more closely our contention that stereotypic knowledge provides a causal structure into which available information is integrated, thus altering the subjective meaning of available information on its encoding. Specifically, Experiment 2 was designed to contrast this hypothesis with the alternative assumption that differences in construal merely reflect post hoc rationalizations of preferred outcomes by demonstrating that construal effects persist in situations

in which the perceiver is less motivated to maintain a stereotype-consistent construal. Experiment 3, in turn, was designed to show that stereotypic construal of causality takes place during information encoding by demonstrating that construal effects between participants are attenuated when encoding is made more difficult.

In all studies, potential participants were screened for their stereotypic explanations of African Americans' socioeconomic status several weeks prior to the experimental session. Our goal in this prescreening was to identify White participants who subscribed to either of the belief systems that we earlier characterized as the victim model or the perpetrator model of African Americans. To do this, we used a common measure of racial beliefs, the Modern Racism Scale (MRS; McConahay, Hardee, & Batts, 1981).

The MRS is one of a number of different questionnaire measures that have been used in the past to differentiate between alternative explanations for African Americans' socioeconomic status (for alternative measures, see, for example, Bobo & Kluegel, 1993; I. Katz & Hass, 1988; Kinder & Sears, 1981; McConahay & Hough, 1976; Sears & Kinder, 1971). Among the authors of these various instruments there is considerable disagreement about why people subscribe to the belief systems tapped by the scales. McConahay, for example, has been careful to differentiate his own concept of *modern racism* from Kinder and Sears's (1981) notion of *symbolic racism* (McConahay, 1986). Yet, despite theoretical differences about the belief systems' origins, their actual content has been less contested. Indeed, the various measurement instruments used to assess racial beliefs are in fact quite similar. For example, all but one item used by Sears and Kinder (1971) to assess symbolic racism can, with more or less identical wording, also be found on McConahay's MRS. Likewise, data from a series of studies reported in greater detail elsewhere (Wittenbrink, Judd, & Park, 1997; Wittenbrink, Judd, Park, & Stone, 1996), suggest that alternative questionnaire scales such as I. Katz and Hass's (1988) Pro-Black and Anti-Black scales, the MRS, the Subtle Racism Scale of Pettigrew and Meertens (1995), and a scale assessing Gaertner and Dovidio's (1986) *ambivalent racism* are all highly intercorrelated and would seem to be getting at the same underlying construct.

We decided to use the MRS in the current research for two reasons. First, it is a measure of stereotypic beliefs that has been widely used in experimental work on racial stereotyping (e.g., Devine, 1989; Swim, Aikin, Hall, & Hunter, 1995). Second, and more importantly, Wittenbrink et al. (1996) found that scores on the MRS are highly correlated with a set of items containing explicit perpetrator and victim explanations of African Americans' socioeconomic status (e.g., "Blacks have a tendency to blame Whites too much for problems that are of their own doing"; "More and more, Blacks use accusations of racism for their own advantage"). Across three independent studies that included 246 White college students, the MRS yielded correlation coefficients with the average responses to these explicit explanatory belief items of .78, .73, and .72, respectively (Wittenbrink et al., 1996). In other words, individuals who score high on the MRS are more likely to subscribe to beliefs consistent with a Perpetrator model of African Americans, whereas individuals who score low on the MRS are more likely to subscribe to a Victim model.

Experiment 1

Approximately 1,200 students enrolled in an introductory psychology course participated in the prescreening session. White students with either a Victim (low MRS score) or a Perpetrator model (high MRS score) of African Americans were eligible for participation in the experiment.

During the experimental session, participants were provided with information about a trial in which a member of a high school basketball team was accused of having assaulted one of his teammates. The defendant's race was manipulated such that he was either an African American student on a predominantly White team, or a White student on a predominantly African American team. Whereas the defendant always belonged to the minority of the team, the victim was always a member of the team majority. In all conditions, the prosecution argued that the defendant was guilty of the assault, whereas the defense argued that he was provoked by racial slurs made by the victim and by chronic discrimination from his teammates.

The experimental manipulations resulted in a 2 (MRS score: High–low) × 2 (race of defendant: African American–White) between-subjects design. It was predicted that the participants' subjective explanations for the disputed events would match their stereotypic knowledge about African Americans. Specifically, high-MRS participants were expected to construe a representation of the incident that located responsibility for the conflict with the African American protagonists. In contrast, low-MRS participants were expected to be more likely to see the White protagonists as the initiating agents. Moreover, on the basis of previous research on

social judgment, we expected these representations to influence their trial-related judgments (cf. Devine & Ostrom, 1985; Pennington & Hastie, 1988). In other words, participants' stereotypic explanations for the trial-related events were expected to mediate their judgments about the defendant.

Method

Participants
Sixty introductory psychology students participated in the experiment in partial fulfillment of their course requirements. Only White students from the upper and lower 20th percentile of the MRS were included in the study. One participant was eliminated from the study because of reactance to the subject matter.

Procedure
Participants entered the laboratory in groups of 2 to 5, were seated at individual tables, and were randomly assigned to conditions. Participants were told that the study concerned juror decision making and that they would read the summary of a trial and individually come to a verdict. The experimenter, who remained unaware of the participants' MRS scores, then gave them a package containing introductory materials, a summary of the case, jury instructions, and sentencing guidelines. Once participants read the materials, they were each given a questionnaire that asked for a verdict, a sentence, ratings of the defendant on a variety of traits, and the evidence they used to reach their verdict.

Materials
Trial summary. The trial summary consisted of testimony by a series of witnesses. This testimony provided background information that the victim had recently replaced the defendant as a starter on the team and described the more immediate conflict between the two. The defendant was said to have exchanged insults with the victim and an eyewitness who was a friend of the victim. During this exchange, the victim allegedly fell and hit his head. He consequently suffered a temporary coma and permanent hearing loss. The cause of the fall was in dispute. The prosecution argued that the defendant pushed the victim in the course of the argument, whereas the defense argued that the victim simply tripped over a locker-room bench. The testimony included numerous references to the protagonists' race. During the course of the testimony, it became clear that the defendant was not well integrated into the team, that he was friends only with the one other minority member of the team, and that

he was having emotional problems stemming from his parents' divorce. The trial summary was identical in all conditions, with the exception of the race and names of the defendant and his teammates.

Causal agency. To assess participants' explanations for the events described in the trial materials, we asked participants to summarize the evidence they considered to reach their verdicts. The narratives obtained in response to this query were analyzed for their explanatory structure. To this end, the summaries were coded by three independent coders unaware of condition and hypotheses for the extent to which the summaries contained explanations consistent with either a Victim or a Perpetrator model of the African American protagonists. Specifically, the opended responses were coded for explicit references to the defendant's or victim's responsibility, as well as for how participants placed central aspects of the trial evidence within the cause–event sequence of the disputed incident. Six coding categories were used in the analysis of these responses: (a) whether responsibility was directly assigned to the defendant or to the victim; (b) whether the defendant intended the actions that led to the assault; (c) whether the defendant's behavior was seen as a justified response to external threats; (d) whether the defendant's underlying motives were described as racist (hitting the victim as a result of the defendant's prejudice) or paranoid (hitting the victim in defense against perceived, but nonexistent, victim's prejudice); (e) whether the victim's underlying motives were characterized as discriminating against the defendant; and (f) whether the available eyewitness testimony was believed to be veridical or a result of the team majority's conspiracy against the defendant.

Initial coding resulted in an interrater reliability across all six items of .75. Differences in the coding were then reconciled, resulting in 100% final agreement for each of these variables. Because we expected that participants' stereotypic knowledge would lead to differences in perceived causal agency of the trial protagonists, we obtained an overall index of perceived causal agency from these coding results. For this index, the six items were combined by scoring answers locating agency with the defendant as $+1$ and those locating agency with the victim as -1. Thus, responses that yielded more positive than negative scores were categorized as reflecting a causal model in which the defendant was the primary initiating agent, whereas those with more negative than positive scores were categorized as reflective of a causal model with the victim as the initiating agent.

Verdict and sentence. Verdicts were measured on a 6-point Likert-type scale, with points labeled *completely confident, not guilty; moderately confident, not guilty; not confident, but leaning toward not guilty; not confident, but leaning toward guilty; moderately confident, guilty*; and *completely confident, guilty*. Sentencing was indicated in months, with a possible range of 0–24 months. For participants finding the defendant not guilty, sentencing was coded as 0 months.

Target impression. The defendant was rated on a checklist of 25 adjectives (e.g., *violent, cautious, rational, aggressive, impulsive*). The list included 19 evaluative traits and 6 traits without any obvious evaluative dimension that were added as filler items (e.g., *athletic*). Participants were asked to indicate how well each adjective fit the defendant on a scale that ranged from 1 (*not at all*) to 7 (*extremely*). Positive adjectives were reversed and the evaluative adjective ratings averaged to achieve an overall impression rating of the defendant with higher scores reflecting a more negative impression of the defendant.

Results and Discussion

Causal Agency

The central prediction of this initial study was that participants with high and low MRS scores would bring to bear different stereotypic models for the integration of the trial evidence, leading to different causal explanations for the trial-relevant events. To examine the causal structure underlying participants' construals of the incident, the coders' ratings of participants' trial explanations were submitted to a hierarchical log-linear analysis.[1] Consistent with predictions, a three-way MRS Score (high–low) × Defendant's Race (African American–White) × Causal Agency (defendant–victim) interaction emerged, $\chi^2 (1, N = 43) = 10.42, p = .001$. As can be seen in the top half of Table 8.1 high-MRS participants who read about a White defendant and low-MRS participants who read about an African American defendant were more likely to perceive the assault victim as the initiating agent than were high-MRS participants who read about an African American defendant and low-MRS participants who read about a White defendant, $\chi^2 (1, N = 20) = 8.36, p = .004$. Similarly,

---

[1] For 16 of the 59 participants, causal agency could not be determined because either the participant did not provide enough information upon which the coders could base their judgments ($n = 12$) or the participant's comments were coded as attributing blame equally to the victim and the defendant ($n = 4$). These participants were distributed evenly across conditions, with no effect of prejudice level, defendant's race, or interaction between the two on the distribution.

accounts given by high-MRS participants who read about an African American defendant and by low-MRS participants who read about a White defendant tended to include the defendant as the initiating agent more often than did those of high-MRS participants who read about a White defendant and of low-MRS participants who read about an African American defendant, χ^2 (1, $N = 23$) = 2.65, $p = .10$ (see bottom half of Table 8.1).

Verdict, Sentence, and Target Impression
We hypothesized that participants' explanations for the disputed events would, in turn, influence their trial-related judgments. Participants' verdicts, sentences, and impression ratings of the defendant were submitted to separate 2 (MRS score: High–low) × 2 (race of defendant: African American–White) analyses of variance (ANOVAs). No main effects emerged from this analysis. As expected, however, conceptually similar interactions emerged for both verdicts, $F(1, 56) = 4.48$, $p = .04$, and participants' impressions of the defendant, $F(1, 57) = 8.72$, $p = .005$. The means for participants' sentencing recommendations were also in the predicted directions, but they did not achieve significance, $F(1, 56) = 2.48$, $p = .12$. As can be seen in Table 8.2 consistent with their perceptions of causal agency, high-MRS participants tended to rate the African American defendant as more guilty, to form a more negative impression of him, and to recommend harsher sentences for him. In contrast, low-MRS participants tended to rate the White defendant as more guilty, to form a more negative impression of him, and to recommend harsher sentences for him.

Although the results for participants' trial-related judgments show the predicted interactions, the interactions are clearly not symmetrical. The race manipulation consistently showed stronger effects for low- than high-MRS

TABLE 8.1. Causal Agency: Experiment 1

	Participant's MRS score	
Agency	Low	High
Victim as initiating agent		
African American defendant	62%	17%
White defendant	10%	44%
Defendant as initiating agent		
African American defendant	15%	50%
White defendant	60%	33%

Note: Agency × Defendant's Race × Participant's MRS Score interaction, $\chi^2(1, N = 43) = 10.42$, $p = .001$. MRS = Modern Racism Scale.

TABLE 8.2. Average Judgments of Guilt, Target Impression, and Recommended Sentences: Experiment 1

	Participant's MRS score	
Judgment	Low	High
Judgments of guilt[a]		
African American defendant	3.31	4.06
White defendant	4.40	3.76
Target impression[b]		
African American defendant	4.08	4.46
White defendant	4.50	4.36
Recommended sentences[c]		
African American defendant	0.92	2.50
White defendant	4.50	2.33

Note: MRS = Modern Racism Scale.
[a] Responses ranged from 1 (*very confident, not guilty*) to 6 (*very confident, guilty*). Defendant's Race × Participant's MRS Score interaction, $F(1, 56) = 4.48$, $p = .04$.
[b] Responses ranged from 1 (*very positive impression*) to 7 (*very negative impression*). Defendant's Race × Participant's MRS Score interaction, $F(1, 57) = 8.72$, $p = .005$.
[c] Responses ranged from 0 to 24 months. Defendant's Race × Participant's MRS Score interaction, $F(1, 56) = 2.48$, $p = .12$.

participants, resulting in statistically reliable differences for low-MRS participants' verdicts, $F(1, 23) = 5.21$, $p = .03$, and target impressions, $F(1, 23) = 9.92$, $p = .004$, and marginally significant differences for their recommended sentences, $F(1, 23) = 3.14$, $p = .09$. In contrast, the mean differences obtained for high-MRS participants proved to be unreliable (all $Fs < 1$).

At first, this finding that low-MRS participants were more affected by the manipulation than were high-MRS participants may appear somewhat surprising. In interpreting these results, however, it is necessary to keep in mind that we did not expect low-MRS participants to be "color blind." Indeed, we anticipated information about race to provide a crucial part of the causal framework that allowed low-MRS participants to arrive at a subjective understanding of the evidence. The present results indicate that this was the case. Moreover, the fact that low-MRS participants were more affected by the race manipulation than were high-MRS participants might reflect an increased sensitivity on their part to the potential relevance of race in social interaction.[2] At any rate, what remains critical to our broader thesis is that the pattern of judgments for low- and high-MRS participants differed, not that they differed in a particular way.

---

[2] We are grateful to a reviewer who alerted us to this possibility.

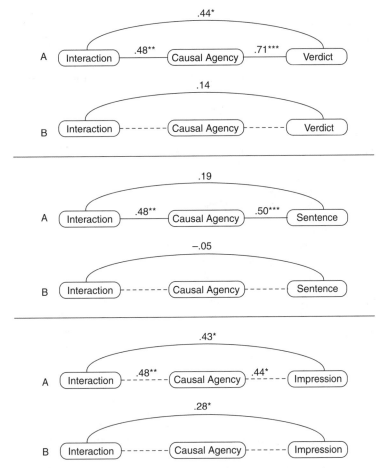

FIGURE 8.1 ■ A: Partial Correlations Controlling for Participant's Level of Prejudice and Defendant's Race. B: Controlling for Causal Agency.
*$p < .05$. **$p < .001$. ***$p < .0001$.

The Mediating Role of Causal Explanations for the Trial Events

As stated earlier, we expected the differences in participants' trial-related judgments to result from their differential construal of the trial events. To examine whether the effects on participants' trial-related judgments were indeed mediated by participants' causal explanations, we performed a series of separate bivariate correlational analyses. According to Baron and Kenny (1986), two conditions must be met to support the hypothesis that a given effect is mediated by another variable. First, the hypothesized mediator needs to be correlated with the effect, and second, the effect has to be no longer reliable when controlling for differences on the mediating variable. The relationships between the hypothesized mediator (causal agency) and the effects obtained for participants' trial-related judgments (i.e., the interactive effects of target race and participants' MRS score on the 3 outcome measures verdict, sentence, and target impression) are presented in Figure 8.1.[3]

---

[3] The independent effects of participants' MRS scores and race of the target were controlled for in these analyses.

For all three outcome variables — verdict, sentence, and target impression — the mediator *causal agency* was significantly correlated with the effect of interest, thus meeting Baron and Kenny's (1986) first condition ($rs = .71$, .50, and .44, respectively; $ps < .0001$, .0001, and .05, respectively; see sections labeled A in Figure 8.1). Moreover, when causal agency was controlled for in the analyses, the effect of the interaction on the outcome variables consistently dropped, thus meeting Baron and Kenny's second condition (see sections labeled B in Figure 8.1). Two complications are worth noting. First, consistent with the ANOVA results for the sentencing dependent measure, although the relationship between the interaction and sentencing dropped substantially when causal agency was controlled for the relationship between these two variables was only marginally significant before entering causal agency ($r = .19$ vs. $r = -.05$). Second, although the relationship between the interaction and the target impression dependent measure dropped substantially when controlling for causal agency, the relationship remained significant ($r = .43$ vs. $r = .28$).

The main goal of this first experiment was to demonstrate that structural aspects of stereotypic beliefs influence the construal of causality in social situations involving a stereotyped target. The present data suggest that participants' assumptions about the underlying causes of the socioeconomic status of African Americans did indeed affect their construal of the trial events. Although slight variations among the analyses emerged, when the hierarchical log-linear analysis, ANOVAs, and mediational analyses are taken together, they indicate that participants with either high or low MRS scores constructed different causal explanations for the incident, and these explanations influenced their judgments of guilt and their perceptions of the defendant.

The question remains, however, what processes underlie these effects of stereotypic knowledge on participants' construal. Earlier, we argued that stereotypic knowledge operates by providing the perceiver with a causal structure for the integration of available information, and we likened this process to the use of analogies in order to successfully structure a problem-solving task. The mediational analyses are consistent with this argument in that they suggest that the trial judgments depended on participants' perceptions of causal agency in the trial episodes. Still, the question of whether participants' explanations for the trial events reflect stereotypic effects on the encoding of the trial evidence, as we suggested earlier, or whether they merely reflect processes that happen after the fact remains unanswered. It is possible, for example, that

participants did not encode the events differently, but that, instead, they simply developed post hoc accounts for the trial events that were consistent with their general attitudes toward the African American protagonists. The remaining two experiments were designed to identify more specifically the processes by which structural aspects of stereotypic knowledge affect the encoding of social situations.

Experiment 3

Previous work on social judgment and story comprehension suggests that presentation order is crucial to the perceiver's representation of information (Baker, 1978; Devine & Ostrom, 1985; Ostrom, Lingle, Pryor, & Geva, 1980; Pennington & Hastie, 1988, 1992). More specific, it has been argued that when evidence is presented in a way that preserves order, the evidence is more easily integrated into subjectively coherent representations (Baker, 1978; Haviland & Clark, 1974; Moeser, 1976; Pennington & Hastie, 1988). For example, Moeser (1976) presented participants with a number of sentences, some of which were relevant to a particular event, such as a picnic under a tree (e.g., "the ants ate the jelly," "the jelly was on the table," "the table was under the tree"). Whereas some participants received the sentences in an order that allowed them to apply the relevant causal framework (i.e., going on a picnic), other participants were provided with the sentences in random order. Participants in the causal framework condition had no difficulty judging related inferences (e.g., "the ants were under the tree") as correct or incorrect, but participants who had been given the sentences in random order had considerable difficulty with the inference task. Presumably, participants in the random order condition, although learning each separate statement, failed to generate inferences about how the various pieces of information related to one another and therefore missed various aspects of the information that were implied, yet not explicitly stated, in the stimulus materials.

In a similar manner, Experiment 3 was designed to manipulate the likelihood with which the trial information used in the previous experiments could be integrated into a coherent representation of the disputed events. Specifically, high- and low-MRS participants were again presented with information from a trial involving a conflict between an African American defendant and his White teammates and were again asked to provide verdicts based on the trial. For half of the participants, the information about the case was presented witness by witness, whereas for the remaining participants, the information was presented in a random order.

The witness order condition, in essence, paralleled the manipulation used in Experiment 1, and we therefore expected to replicate our initial findings that construal of the trial events depends on participants' stereotypic causal assumptions. As noted above, when information is presented in this way, it is relatively easy to integrate it into a coherent causal representation, and this integration process should be influenced in important ways by participants' stereotypic knowledge. That is, for a given witness statement to have implications for participants' understandings of the trial-related events, participants have to construe how this statement relates to other aspects of the evidence. A given statement might, for example, provide information about the protagonists' motives, it might contradict previously encountered testimony, it might call into question the other witnesses' credibility, or it might generate hypotheses about aspects of the evidence that are still missing. Stereotypic background knowledge should influence this process by specifying, among other things, hypotheses and default assumptions regarding the causal structure underlying these linkages.

In contrast, the random order condition limits participants' ability to draw substantive inferences about a given statement. Here, for each individual statement, participants first have to resolve important aspects of the information itself (e.g., Who says this? What event does it refer to? When did this happen? What other statements has this witness made in regard to this particular event?). This presentation order thus effectively increases the difficulty of generating the inferences that are necessary to obtain a coherent understanding of the trial-related events.

In other words, if our contention is correct that the causal structure underlying participants' explanations of the trial episodes is critically dependent on the stereotypic casual structure participants impose on the evidence, the differences between high- and low-MRS participants' construals of the evidence and their trial judgments observed in the previous studies should once again emerge when the application of this causal structure is facilitated (i.e., in the witness order). When application of the stereotypic knowledge is made difficult, however, differences between high- and low-MRS participants should be minimal.

Method

Participants

One hundred thirty-nine introductory psychology students participated in the experiment in partial fulfillment of their course requirements. White participants were again preselected from the upper and lower 20th percentile of the MRS.

Materials

A set of 66 items was constructed from the trial summaries used in Experiment 1 (see Table 8.3). The items were selected to preserve the relevant evidence from the original accounts and to eliminate redundant and irrelevant information. Each item consisted of a source identification (i.e., name of witness), followed by a single-sentence statement.

Procedure

With two exceptions, the experiment proceeded in the same fashion as the jury decision making sections of the previous experiments. First, instead of receiving booklets with witness testimony, participants read the set of

TABLE 8.3. Sample of Evidence Items: Experiment 3

Item	Evidence Item
1	I am Andrew Graham, a teammate of Chris and Odell on the Sibley High School varsity basketball team. Witness for the Prosecution.
2	The entire afternoon had been overshadowed by an argument between 2 players on the team, Odell and Chris, during a practice game.
3	Odell got angry and accused Chris of disrupting other people's play and purposely fouling other players.
4	I think Odell's accusations were pretty far fetched.
5	After the game, I returned to the locker room where Odell and Chris were already arguing again, calling each other names.
6	I walked up to Odell and asked him to cool down.
7	Odell just angrily yelled something like "you would be the one to try to get into this; you are all alike …" and shoved me so that I fell against one of the lockers.
8	Chris tried to intervene and stepped between me and Odell.
9	Chris stumbled and fell backwards onto a bench in the locker room.
10	By this time other teammates were entering the room, and soon a number of people were standing around Chris who was out cold and his head was bleeding.

Note: In both the witness order and the random order conditions, each item was presented together with the name of the witness who allegedly made the statement. All sample items listed here were associated with a single witness.

evidence items on the display of a Macintosh IIci computer. Each item appeared alone on the screen until the participant pressed the computer mouse button to advance to the next statement. The computer program did not allow participants to retrieve and reread previous items. For half the participants, the statements were arranged in an order close to that of the original narrative accounts. That is, the statements associated with each witness were presented together. For the remaining half of the participants, the items appeared in a fixed random order. Second, and consistent with Experiment 2, the race of the defendant was held constant. For all participants, he was portrayed as an African American.

Once all of the evidence was presented, participants received jury instructions and sentencing guidelines, followed by a booklet containing the dependent measures used in the previous experiments. Thus, the experiment used a 2 (MRS score: High–low) $\times$ 2 (witness–random order) between-subjects factorial design.

Dependent Measures

The dependent measures used to assess participants' construal of the trial episodes were conceptually the same as those used in the previous experiments. To address the different hypotheses of this study, however, a few changes in their administration were necessary. Specifically, after participants indicated their verdicts, sentence suggestions, and trait ratings of the defendant, they were asked to list as many items as they could remember from the testimony. Participants were handed a sheet with 20 lines and were asked to limit each item description to one line. Their responses on this sheet were taken as a measure for participants' memories of the information presented. The administration of this recall measure, however, precluded the use of the open-ended response format that was used in Experiment 1 to assess the underlying causal structure of the participants' representations of the trial evidence. Therefore, a procedure from previous research on the role of mental models in social judgment was adopted (Leddo, Abelson, & Gross, 1984; Read & Marcus-Newhall, 1993). Specifically, the recall measure was followed by a set of five items containing different explanations for the information presented (see Table 8.4). For each account, participants were asked to indicate "how good of an explanation each one provides for the trial events" on a scale ranging from 1 (*not at all what happened*) to 7 (*exactly what happened*). Of the five explanations provided, Item A represented an account with the victim as the initiating agent, Items B and D represented two

Table 8.4. Measurement of Causal Agency: Experiment 3

Item	Explanation
A	During an argument, the defendant, Odell Jackson, shoved the victim, Chris Henley, causing Henley to fall and be injured. Jackson assaulted Henley after having been provoked by Henley and his friend Graham. This assault was ultimately the result of Jackson being ostracized by the team and of continuous discrimination against Jackson by Henley as well as by other white team members.
B	During an argument, the defendant, Odell Jackson, shoved the victim, Chris Henley, causing Henley to fall and be injured. Jackson assaulted Henley as a result of his frustration with his own performance on the team, as well as his difficult family and school situation. The defendant's claims of being provoked and a victim of racial discrimination were just excuses to avoid conviction.
C	During an argument, the defendant, Odell Jackson, shoved the victim, Chris Henley, causing Henley to fall and be injured. Jackson assaulted Henley because he thought Henley was responsible for the team's consistently poor performance.
D	During an argument, the defendant, Odell Jackson, shoved the victim, Chris Henley, causing Henley to fall and be injured. Jackson assaulted Henley because he felt ostracized by the team and thought he was continuously discriminated against by Henley as well as by other White team members. But in reality the team was not ostracizing Jackson or discriminating against him.
E	Chris Henley's injuries are due to an accident. During a solely verbal argument, Henley accidentally tripped and fell.

alternative accounts (i.e., "imagined discrimination" and "discrimination used as a pretense") that included the defendant as the initiating agent, and Items C and E provided explanations added as fillers to the task.

Finally, the relatively low ratings obtained on the sentencing measure used in Experiment 1 led us to assess this variable with two separate questions, asking participants for a "minimum sentence" and a "maximum sentence." The responses were measured on 7-point Likert-type scales that ranged from *0 months* to *16–18 months*.

Results and Discussion

Memory for Trial Evidence

The experimental manipulation of participants' ability to integrate the trial information was intended to demonstrate that stereotypic knowledge critically influences the construal of cause–effect relations. To ensure that our manipulation represented a viable test of encoding effects, it was first necessary to make sure that certain recall prerequisites were met. After all, if participants in the random order conditions were less likely to notice the race of the defendant, it would be possible to argue that potential differences between the order conditions emerged simply because high- and low-MRS participants failed to process the race of the defendant in the random order conditions. We thus analyzed the overall amount of information participants listed during the recall task as well as the likelihood of mentioning the defendant's race during this task, as a function of the integration manipulation.

These analyses suggest that the prerequisites were met. First, there was no indication that the order in which participants saw the evidence items affected the overall amount of information recalled. In both conditions, participants listed an equal number of evidence items during the recall task (witness order $M = 15.45$; random order $M = 15.40$; $F < 1$). Second, although the majority of participants (73%) did mention the defendant's race, these references did not differ as a function of the order manipulation. Seventy-four percent and 73% of the participants mentioned the defendant's race in the witness order and random order conditions, respectively, $\chi^2(1, N = 104) = 0.01$, $p = .92$. Thus, there is no indication that the salience of the defendant's race varied as a function of the order manipulation. Although there is a hint that low-MRS participants mentioned the defendant's race more frequently than did high-MRS participants (82% and 63%, respectively), $\chi^2(1, N = 104) = 1.63$, $p = .20$, this was not statistically reliable, nor was it qualified by the order manipulation (64.7% and 79.5%, respectively, for high- and low-MRS participants in the random order conditions, $\chi^2[1, N = 57] = 0.58$, $p = .45$, and 62.1% and 85.3% respectively in the witness order conditions, $\chi^2[1, N = 47] = 1.13$, $p = .29$).

Causal Agency
We predicted that high- and low-MRS participants would again bring to bear different stereotypic causal assumptions for their integration of the trial evidence, resulting in a construal of the trial evidence that was consistent with either a Victim or Perpetrator framework of the African American defendant. However, in the random order conditions, where the application of stereotypic frameworks was made more difficult, these differences were expected to be attenuated.

TABLE 8.5. Causal Agency: Experiment 3

	Participant's MRS score	
Explanation	Low	High
Victim as initiating agent		
Random order	4.22	4.12
Witness order	4.59	3.23
Defendant as initiating agent		
Random order	2.98	2.96
Witness order	2.46	3.17

Note. Responses ranged from 1 (*not at all what happened*) to 7 (*exactly what happened*). Presentation Order × Participant's MRS Score × Explanation interaction, $F (1, 138) = 8.74$, $p = .004$. MRS = Modern Racism Scale.

Table 8.5 summarizes the means obtained for participants' evaluations of the alternative explanations for the trial evidence. Item A from the set of given explanations represented an account with the defendant as the victim of the other trial participants' actions, whereas Items B and D represented two alternative explanations with the defendant as the initiating agent (see Table 8.4). Items B and D were averaged to obtain an overall measure for the acceptance of this latter explanatory scheme.

Consistent with our predictions, participants with high and low MRS scores showed differential preferences for the alternative causal explanations only in the witness order conditions. In these conditions, high-MRS participants were more likely to see the defendant as the initiating agent and less likely to use a causal structure with the trial victim as the initiating agent than were low-MRS participants. In contrast, the two groups of participants show virtually no difference in the random order condition. A 2 (MRS score: High–low) × 2 (random–witness order) × 2 (explanation: Victim–defendant) mixed multivariate analysis of variance with the last factor being a within-subject measure revealed this three-way interaction to be statistically reliable, $F(1, 138) = 8.74$, $p = .004$. It is worth noting that this interaction emerged despite the fact that participants in the random order and the witness order conditions were equally aware of the defendant's race.

Two additional effects emerged from this analysis. First, a highly significant main effect, $F(1, 138) = 47.10$, $p < .0001$, for the explanation factor indicates that, in general, participants tended to be more likely to see the trial victim rather than the defendant as the initiating agent. This result seems to be consistent with the overall level of participants' verdict and sentencing ratings obtained in the previous experiments. Second, a two-way interaction between the explanation factor and MRS score emerged, $F(1, 138) = 10.25$, $p = .002$. Inspection of the mean suggests, however, that this effect is attributable to the differences found in the witness order condition.

Verdict, Sentence, and Target Impression

The observed differences in participants' construals of causality are again reflected in participants' trial-related judgments (see Table 8.6). Specifically, the witness order conditions replicated the findings from the first experiment, with high-MRS participants finding the African American defendant more guilty and forming a more negative impression of the target than low-MRS participants. These differences were virtually eliminated when the evidence was presented in random order. In separate 2 (MRS score: High–low) × 2 (random–witness order) ANOVAs, the predicted two-way interaction emerged for participants' verdicts. $F(1, 138) = 4.78$, $p = .031$, and their impressions of the defendant, $F(1, 138) = 4.28$, $p = .041$. Moreover, simple effect analyses confirm that the mean differences obtained in the witness order condition were reliable, $F(1, 63) = 7.74$, $p = .007$ for

TABLE 8.6. Average Judgments of Guilt, Target Impression, and Recommended Sentences: Experiment 3

Judgment	Participant's MRS score	
	Low	High
Judgments of guilt		
Random order	3.90	3.88
Witness order	3.44	4.63
Target impression		
Random order	4.02	3.90
Witness order	3.86	4.26
Recommended maximum sentences		
Random order	1.51	1.62
Witness order	1.47	1.83

Note: Responses for judgment of guilt ranged from 1 (*not guilty, very confident*) to 8 (*guilty, very confident*). Presentation Order × Participant's MRS Score interaction, $F(1, 138) = 4.78$, $p = 0.31$. Responses for target impression ranged from 1 (*very positive impression*) to 7 (*very negative impression*). Presentation Order × Participant's MRS Score interaction, $F(1, 138) = 4.28$, $p = .041$. Responses for recommended maximum sentence ranged from 1 (*0 months*) to 7 (*16–18 months*). Presentation Order × Participant's MRS Score interaction ($F < 1$). MRS = Modern Racism Scale.

verdict: $F(1, 63) = 4.11$, $p = .047$ for impression, whereas they remained statistically insignificant for the random order condition ($Fs < 1$).

Evidence for an *independent* effect of MRS score failed to emerge on any of the dependent measures. A significant effect for participants' scores on the MRS did emerge in the analysis of participants' verdicts, with high-MRS participants being more likely to find the defendant guilty, $F(1, 138) = 3.81, p = .053$. As with the conceptually equivalent two-way interaction obtained for the causal agency variable, however, this effect was largely confined to the witness order conditions.

The manipulations had virtually no effect on the sentences participants recommended. Although the patterns of results were in the predicted directions, analyses of both maximum and minimum recommended sentences revealed no significant differences ($Fs < 1$).[4]

Taken together, the results from Experiment 3 provide strong support for the assertion that stereotypic knowledge influenced participants' construals of the trial situation by altering the inferences they drew when putting together the various pieces of evidence. These encoding effects were obtained without stereotypic knowledge affecting participants' memory for the trial evidence. We need to emphasize, however, that the absence of any recall effects is most likely attributable to our deliberate attempts to simplify the trial evidence. As in previous research (cf. Devine & Ostrom, 1985; Pennington & Hastie, 1992), the simplified nature of the stimulus materials allowed us to test possible differences in knowledge organization in the absence of additional memory effects. Under more realistic conditions, that is, in a more complex stimulus environment, stereotypic conceptual knowledge should serve not only to organize information, but also to selectively direct the perceiver's attention (cf. Bodenhausen, 1988; Cohen, 1981; Hilton et al., 1991) and to guide information retrieval (cf. Brewer & Dupree, 1983; Hastie, 1981; Lichtenstein & Brewer, 1980).

General Discussion

In the present research, stereotypic knowledge proved to be a powerful tool for participants' construals of social reality. As such, the present results concur with

---

[4] For simplicity, Table 8.6 contains only the results of participants' maximum sentencing. Participants' recommended minimum sentence showed even less variation than this variable.

numerous other studies that have documented the prevalence of stereotypes in shaping human experience and providing subjective meaning through the process of social categorization (cf. Banaji et al., 1993; Darley & Gross, 1983; Duncan, 1976; Kunda & Sherman-Williams, 1993; Sagar & Schofield, 1980; Vallone et al., 1985). These studies have consistently shown how stereotypes may affect participants' interpretations of ambiguous information. The present data demonstrate that such interpretational effects are due, at least in part, to causal assumptions that are contained in stereotypic knowledge.

In the same way that an analogous story may help participants to successfully structure a given thought problem, stereotypic knowledge aids in the structuring of information about the social environment. In Experiment 1, specific causal assumptions about the underlying causes of socioeconomic disadvantage among African Americans influenced participants' construals of causality in a social situation that involved a stereotyped target. In Experiment 3, we found that interfering with participants' ability to integrate the available evidence into a coherent representation on encoding reduced the stereotyping effects substantially. Despite the fact that participants in the random order condition of Experiment 3 were cognizant of the protagonists' race, their construal of causal agency in the trial events remained uninfluenced by the racial stereotypes they held. Taken together, the results suggest that stereotypes shape the construal of causal relations at the time of encoding.

This is not to say, of course, that stereotypic influences on social judgments and behavior are limited solely to the encoding of information. Stereotypes have been found to operate at all stages in social information processing (cf. Hamilton & Sherman, 1994). But what the studies reported here do suggest is that the influence of stereotypic assumptions about causality begin at encoding and involve more than the motivation for consistency.

The fact that stereotypic beliefs may critically influence social judgments has important social implications, of course. In the case of judicial decisions, the context used for the present experiments, the potential of jurors' stereotypic beliefs to influence the outcome of a jury's decisions challenges the basic principle upon which the judicial system is based, the right of every individual to be judged equally independent of race, gender, or class. Indeed, a review of archival records of actual criminal trials suggests that White juries have found African Americans to be the perpetrators of alleged crimes with disproportionate frequency (cf. Gross & Mauro, 1989;

Howard, 1975; Petersilia, 1983). Naturally, these studies lack the rigorous controls available in experimental investigation, which makes them susceptible to methodological criticisms and alternative interpretations (cf. Greenberg & Ruback, 1982). In this respect, the present experimental data nicely complement the findings from these reviews, despite the fact that our experimental procedure diverted in many ways from the proceedings of an actual court trial (e.g., presentation of trial evidence, jury' deliberation, implications of the judgment). The present data confirm that, depending on a juror's racial stereotypes, the same evidence may obtain an entirely different meaning when the defendant happens to be African American rather than White.

Application of Stereotypic Structure

In this research, we focused on a particular set of causal beliefs that tend to be associated with the social stereotype of African Americans, namely participants' assumptions regarding the underlying causes of racial conflict and inequity. Although we consistently observed that participants' stereotypic causal assumptions influenced their construal of causality in the experimental situations that involved a stereotype target, we expect these effects to be limited to situations in which the causal structure is potentially applicable. Rather than resulting in general and broad effects on the denotative meaning of social information, we believe stereotyping effects to be more specific and dependent on the particular content of the stereotype.

Conclusion

At the outset of this article, we emphasized that stereotypes consist of rich sets of knowledge that aid the perceiver in explaining the social environment. This knowledge, of course, is in large part shared in society. That is, although stereotypic knowledge may sometimes be idiosyncratic, because of one's individual experience with members of the group, it is, nevertheless, more likely acquired as a complete package in the process of a person's socialization (cf. Allport, 1954; Gardner, 1994; Pettigrew, 1981; Wittenbrink & Henly, 1996). Indeed, society offers an abundance of stereotypic images about various social groups. Importantly, these images not only contain assumptions about a group's attributes but also include stereotypic explanations for why these attributes presumably exist. In the case of African Americans in U.S. society, these images range from arguments concerning the "culture of poverty," which allegedly perpetuates inadequate values among the largely African American urban poor (M. B. Katz, 1989), to Herrnstein and Murray's (1994) insidious revival of genetic explanations for African Americans' presumed intellectual inferiority.

As stereotyping research of the past decades has documented quite convincingly, abstract group-level knowledge may influence the perceiver's subjective construal of specific social situations. Likewise, our argument in the present article has been that such stereotypic explanations about cause–effect relations at the group level have the potential to affect perceptions of social causation in specific instances. To the same extent that stereotypic attributes are likely to be used in the perceiver's construal of social information, these structural aspects of stereotypic knowledge are likewise used, from the very beginning, providing a blueprint for the construal of cause–effect relations.

REFERENCES

Allport, G. W. (1954). *The nature of prejudice*. Cambridge. MA: Addison-Wesley.

Andersen. S. M., & Klatzky, R. L. (1987). Traits and social stereotypes: Levels of categorization in person perception. *Journal of Personality and Social Psychology, 53*, 235–246.

Armstrong, S. L., Gleitman, L. R., & Gleitman, H. (1983). What some concepts might not be. *Cognition, 13*, 263–308.

Asch, S. E. (1952). *Social psychology*. Englewood Cliffs. NJ: Prentice Hall.

Baker, L. (1978). Processing temporal relationships in simple stories: Effects of input sequence. *Journal of Verbal Learning and Verbal Behavior, 17*, 559–572.

Banaji, M. R., Hardin, C., & Rothman, A. J. (1993). Implicit stereotyping in person judgment. *Journal of Personality and Social Psychology, 65*, 272–281.

Baron, R. M., & Kenny, D. A. (1986). The moderator–mediator variable distinction in social psychological research: Conceptual, strategic, and statistical considerations. *Journal of Personality and Social Psychology, 51*, 1173–1182.

Bartlett, F. C. (1932). *Remembering*. London: Cambridge University Press.

Biernat, M., Manis, M., & Nelson, T. E. (1991). Stereotypes and standards of judgment. *Journal of Personality and Social Psychology, 60*, 485–499.

Bobo, L., & Kluegel, J. R. (1993). Opposition to race-targeting: Self-interest, stratification ideology, or racial attitudes? *American Sociological Review, 58*, 443–464.

Bodenhausen, G. V. (1988). Stereotypic biases in social decision making and memory: Testing process models of stereotype use. *Journal of Personality and Social Psychology, 55*, 726–737.

Brewer, W. F., & Dupree, D. A. (1983). Use of plan schemata in the recall and recognition of goal-directed actions. *Journal of Experimental Psychology: Learning, Memory, and Cognition, 9*, 117–129.

Bruner, J. S. (1957). Going beyond the information given. In J. S. Bruner, et al. (Eds.), *Contemporary approaches to cognition* (pp. 218–238). Cambridge, MA: Harvard University Press.

Cohen, C. E. (1981). Person categories and social perception: Testing some boundaries of the processing effect of prior knowledge. *Journal of Personality and Social Psychology, 40*, 441–452.

Darley, J. M., & Gross, P. H. (1983). A hypothesis-confirming bias in labeling effects. *Journal of Personality and Social Psychology, 44*, 20–33.

Devine, P. G. (1989). Stereotypes and prejudice: Their automatic and controlled components. *Journal of Personality and Social Psychology, 56*, 5–18.

Devine, P. G., & Ostrom. T. M. (1985). Cognitive mediation of inconsistency discounting. *Journal of Personality and Social Psychology, 49*, 5–21.

Duncan, B. L. (1976). Differential social perception and attribution of intergroup violence: Testing the lower limits of stereotyping of Blacks. *Journal of Personality and Social Psychology, 34*, 590–598.

Duncker, K. (1935). *Zur psychologie des produktiven denkens* [On problem solving]. Berlin: Springer-Verlag.

Erdley, C. A., & D'Agostino, P. R. (1988). Cognitive and affective components of automatic priming effects. *Journal of Personality and Social Psychology, 54*, 741–747.

Fazio, R. H., Sanbonmatsu, D. M., Powell, M. C., & Kardes, F. R. (1986). On the automatic activation of attitudes. *Journal of Personality and Social Psychology, 50*, 229–238.

Fiske, S. T. (1993). Social cognition and social perception. *Annual Review of Psychology, 44*, 155–194.

Gaertner, S. L., & Dovidio, J. F. (1986). The aversive form of racism. In J. F. Dovidio & S. L. Gaertner (Eds.), *Prejudice, discrimination, and racism* (pp. 61–89). Orlando, FL: Academic Press.

Gardner, R. C. (1994). Stereotypes as consensual beliefs. In M. P. Zanna & J. M. Olson (Eds.), *The psychology of prejudice: The Ontario Symposium* (Vol. 7, pp. 1–31). Hillsdale, NJ: Erlbaum.

Gentner, D. (1983). Structure-mapping: A theoretical framework for analogy. *Cognitive Science, 7*, 155–170.

Gentner, D., Rattermann, M. J., & Forbus, K. D. (1993). The roles of similarity in transfer: Separating retrievability from inferential soundness. *Cognitive Psychology, 25*, 524–575.

Gick, M. L., & Holyoak, K. J. (1980). Analogical problem solving. *Cognitive Psychology, 12*, 306–355.

Gick, M. L., & Holyoak, K. J. (1983). Schema induction and analogical transfer. *Cognitive Psychology, 15*, 1–38.

Gilens, M. (1995). Racial attitudes and opposition to welfare. *The Journal of Politics, 57*, 994–1014.

Greenberg, M. S., & Ruback, R. B. (1982). *Social psychology of the criminal justice system*. Monterey, CA: Brooks/Cole.

Greenwald, A. G., & Banaji, M. R. (1995). Implicit social cognition: Attitudes, self-esteem, and stereotypes. *Psychological Review, 102*, 4–27.

Gross, S. R., & Mauro, R. (1989). *Death and discrimination: Racial disparities in capital sentencing*. Boston: Northeastern University Press.

Gurwitz, S. B., & Dodge, K. A. (1977). Effects of confirmations and disconfirmations on stereotype-based attributions. *Journal of Personality and Social Psychology, 35*, 495–500.

Hamilton, D. L., & Sherman, J. W. (1994). Stereotypes. In R. S. Wyer & T. K. Srull (Eds.), *Handbook of social cognition* (Vol. 2, 2nd ed., pp. 1–68). Hillsdale, NJ: Erlbaum.

Hamilton, D. L., & Troiler, T. K. (1986). Stereotypes and stereotyping: An overview of the cognitive approach. In J. F. Dovidio, &

S. L. Gaertner (Eds.), *Prejudice, discrimination, and racism* (pp. 127–163). Orlando, FL: Academic Press.

Hastie, R. (1981). Schematic principles in human memory. In E. T. Higgins. C. P. Herman, & M. P. Zanna (Eds.), *Social cognition: The Ontario Symposium* (Vol. 1, pp. 39–88). Hillsdale, NJ: Erlbaum.

Hastie, R., & Kumar, P. (1979). Person memory: Personality traits as organizing principles in memory for behaviors. *Journal of Personality and Social Psychology, 37*, 25–38.

Haviland, S. E., & Clark, H. H. (1974). What's new? Acquiring new information as a process in comprehension. *Journal of Verbal Learning and Verbal Behavior, 13*, 512–521.

Heider, F. (1944). Social perception and phenomenal causality. *Psychological Review, 51*, 358–374.

Heider, F., & Simmel, M. (1944). An experimental study of apparent behavior. *American Journal of Psychology, 57*, 243–249.

Herrnstein, R. J., & Murray, C. (1994). *The bell curve: Intelligence and class structure in American life*. New York: Free Press.

Higgins, E. T., Rholes, W. S., & Jones, C. R. (1977). Category accessibility and impression formation. *Journal of Experimental Social Psychology, 13*, 141–154.

Hilton, J. L., Klein, J. G., & von Hippel, W. (1991). Attention allocation and impression formation. *Personality and Social Psychology Bulletin, 17*, 548–559.

Holyoak, K. J. (1985). The pragmatics of analogical transfer. In G. H. Bower (Ed.), *The psychology of learning and motivation* (Vol. 19, pp. 59–87). New York: Academic Press.

Howard, J. C. (1975). Racial discrimination in sentencing. *Judicature, 59*, 120–125.

Katz, D., & Braly, K. W. (1933). Racial stereotypes of one hundred college students. *Journal of Abnormal and Social Psychology, 28*, 280–290.

Katz, I., & Hass, R. G. (1988). Racial ambivalence and American value conflict: Correlational and priming studies of dual cognitive structures. *Journal of Personality and Social Psychology, 55*, 893–905.

Katz, M. B. (1989). *The undeserving poor: From the war on poverty to the war on welfare*. New York: Random House.

Kinder, D. R., & Sears, D. O. (1981). Prejudice and politics: Symbolic racism versus racial threats to the good life. *Journal of Personality and Social Psychology, 40*, 414–431.

Kluegel, J. R., & Smith, E. R. (1986). *Beliefs about inequality: Americans' views of what is and what ought to be*. Hawthorne, NY: Aldine de Gruyter.

Krueger, J., & Rothbart, M. (1988). Use of categorical and individuating information in making inferences about personality. *Journal of Personality and Social Psychology, 55*, 187–195.

Kunda, Z. (1990). The case for motivated reasoning. *Psychological Bulletin, 108*, 480–498.

Kunda, Z., & Oleson, K. C. (1995). Maintaining stereotypes in the face of disconfirmation: Constructing grounds for subtyping deviants. *Journal of Personality and Social Psychology, 68*, 565–579.

Kunda, Z., & Sherman-Williams, B. (1993). Stereotypes and the construal of individuating information. *Personality and Social Psychology Bulletin, 19*, 90–99.

Leddo, J., Abelson, R. P., & Gross, P. H. (1984). Conjunctive explanations: When two reasons are better than one. *Journal of Personality and Social Psychology, 47*, 933–943.

Lewin, K. (1936). *Principles of topological psychology*. New York: McGraw-Hill.

Leyens, J. P., Yzerbyt, V. Y., & Schadron, G. (1992). The social judgeability approach to stereotypes. In W. Stroebe & M. Hewstone (Eds.), *European review of social psychology* (Vol. 3, pp. 91–120). London: Wiley.

Lichtenstein, E. H., & Brewer, W. F. (1980). Memory for goal-directed events. *Cognitive Psychology, 12*, 412–445.

Linville, P. W., Fischer, G. W., & Salovey, P. (1989). Perceived distributions of the characteristics of in-group and out-group members: Empirical evidence and a computer simulation. *Journal of Personality and Social Psychology, 57*, 165–188.

Macrae, C. N., Stangor, C., & Milne, A. B. (1994). Activating social stereotypes: A functional analysis. *Journal of Experimental Social Psychology, 30*, 370–389.

Martin, L. L. (1986). Set/reset: Use and disuse of concepts in impression formation. *Journal of Personality and Social Psychology, 51*, 493–504.

Martin, L. L., & Achee, J. W. (1992). Beyond accessibility: The role of processing objectives in judgment. In L. L. Martin & A. Tesser (Eds.), *The construction of social judgment* (pp. 195–216). Hillsdale, NJ: Erlbaum.

McConahay, J. B. (1986). Modern racism, ambivalence, and the modern racism scale. In J. F. Dovidio & S. L. Gaertner (Eds.), *Prejudice, discrimination, and racism* (pp. 91–125). Orlando, FL: Academic Press.

McConahay, J. B., Hardee, B. B., & Batts, V. (1981). Has racism declined in America? It depends on who is asking and what is asked. *Journal of Conflict Resolution, 25*, 563–579.

McConahay, J. B., & Hough, J. C. (1976). Symbolic racism. *Journal of Social Issues, 32*, 23–45.

Medin, D. L., Goldstone, R. L., & Gentner, D. (1993). Respects for similarity. *Psychological Review, 100*, 254–278.

Michotte, A. (1963). *The perception of causality*. New York: Basic Books.

Moeser, S. D. (1976). Inferential reasoning in episodic memory. *Journal of Verbal Learning and Verbal Behavior, 15*, 193–212.

Morris, M. W., & Peng, K. (1994). Culture and cause: American and Chinese attributions for social and physical events. *Journal of Personality and Social Psychology, 67*, 949–971.

Neisser, U. (1967). *Cognitive psychology*. Englewood Cliffs, NJ: Prentice Hall.

Oakes, P. J., & Turner, J. C. (1990). Is limited information processing capacity the cause of social stereotyping? In W. Stroebe & M. Hewstone (Eds.), *European review of social psychology* (Vol. 1, pp. 112–135). London: Wiley.

Ostrom, T. M., Lingle, J. H., Pryor, J. B., & Geva, N. (1980). Cognitive organization of person impressions. In R. Hastie, T. M. Ostrom, E. B. Ebbesen, R. S. Wyer, D. L. Hamilton, & D. E. Carlston (Eds.), *Person memory: The cognitive basis of social perception* (pp. 55–88). Hillsdale, NJ: Erlbaum.

Park, B., & Judd, C. M. (1990). Measures and models of perceived group variability. *Journal of Personality and Social Psychology, 59*, 173–191.

Pennington, N., & Hastie, R. (1988). Explanation-based decision making: Effects of memory structure on judgment. *Journal of Experimental Psychology: Learning, Memory, and Cognition, 14*, 521–533.

Pennington, N., & Hastie, R. (1992). Explaining the evidence: Tests of the story model for juror decision making. *Journal of Personality and Social Psychology, 62*, 189–206.

Petersilia, J. (1983). *Racial disparities in the criminal justice system*. Santa Monica, CA: Rand Corporation.

Pettigrew, T. F. (1981). Extending the stereotype concept. In D. L. Hamilton (Ed.), *Cognitive processes in stereotyping and intergroup behavior* (pp. 303–331). Hillsdale, NJ: Erlbaum.

Pettigrew, T. F., & Meertens, R. W. (1995). Subtle and blatant prejudice in Western Europe. *European Journal of Social Psychology, 25*, 57–75.

Read, S. J., & Marcus-Newhall, A. (1993). Explanatory coherence in social explanations: A parallel distributed processing account. *Journal of Personality and Social Psychology, 65*, 429–447.

Ross, L., & Nisbett, R. E. (1991). *The person and the situation. Perspectives of social psychology*. New York: McGraw-Hill.

Rothbart, M., Evans, M., & Fulero, S. (1979). Recall for confirming events: Memory processes and the maintenance of social stereotypes. *Journal of Experimental Social Psychology, 15*, 343–355.

Rothbart, M., & John, O. P. (1985). Social categorization and behavioral episodes: A cognitive analysis of the effects of intergroup contact. *Journal of Social Issues, 41*, 81–104.

Ryan, W. (1976). *Blaming the victim*. New York: Vintage.

Sagar, H. A., & Schofield, J. W. (1980). Racial and behavioral cues in Black and White children's perceptions of ambiguously aggressive acts. *Journal of Personality and Social Psychology, 39*, 590–598.

Schaller, M. (1992). In-group favoritism and statistical reasoning in social inference: Implications for formation and maintenance of group stereotypes. *Journal of Personality and Social Psychology, 63*, 61–74.

Schwarz, N., & Bless, H. (1992). Constructing reality and its alternatives: An inclusion/exclusion model of assimilation and contrast effects in social judgment. In L. L. Martin & A. Tesser (Eds.), *The construction of social judgment* (pp. 217–245). Hillsdale, NJ: Erlbaum.

Sears, D. O. (1988). Symbolic racism. In P. A. Katz & D. A. Taylor (Eds.), *Eliminating racism: Profiles in controversy* (pp. 53–84). New York: Plenum.

Sears, D. O., & Kinder, D. R. (1971). Racial tensions and voting in Los Angeles. In W. Z. Hirsch (Ed.), *Los Angeles: Viability and prospects for metropolitan leadership* (pp. 51–88). New York: Praeger.

Seifert, C. M., McKoon, G., Abelson, R. P., & Ratcliff, R. (1986). Memory connections between thematically similar episodes. *Journal of Experimental Psychology: Learning, Memory, and Cognition, 12*, 220–231.

Skowronski, J. J., Carlston, D. E., & Isham, J. T. (1993). Implicit versus explicit formation: The differing effects of overt labeling and covert priming on memory and impressions. *Journal of Experimental Social Psychology, 29*, 17–41.

Snyder, M., & Swann, W. B. (1978). Hypothesis-testing processes in social interaction. *Journal of Personality and Social Psychology, 36*, 1202–1212.

Srull, T. K., & Wyer, R. S. (1979). The role of category accessibility in the interpretation of information about persons: Some determinants

and implications. *Journal of Personality and Social Psychology, 37*, 1660–1672.

Stangor, C., & Duan, C. (1991). Effects of multiple task demands upon memory for information about social groups. *Journal of Experimental Social Psychology, 27*, 357–378.

Stangor, C., & Lange, J. E. (1994). Mental representations of social groups: Advances in understanding stereotypes and stereotyping. In M. P. Zanna (Ed.), *Advances in experimental social psychology* (Vol. 26, pp. 357–416). San Diego, CA: Academic Press.

Swim, J. K., Aikin, K. J., Hall, W. S., & Hunter, B. A. (1995). Sexism and racism: Old-fashioned and modern prejudices. *Journal of Personality and Social Psychology, 68*, 199–214.

Tajfel, H. (1969). Cognitive aspects of prejudice. *Journal of Social Issues, 25*, 79–97.

Vallone, R. P., Ross, L., & Lepper, M. R. (1985). The hostile media phenomenon: Biased perception and perceptions of media bias in coverage of the Beirut massacre. *Journal of Personality and Social Psychology, 49*, 577–585.

Vinacke, W. E. (1957). Stereotypes as social concepts. *Journal of Social Psychology, 46*, 229–243.

Vosniadou, S., & Ortony, A. (Eds.). (1989). *Similarity and analogical reasoning*. Cambridge, England: Cambridge University Press.

Weber, R., & Crocker, J. (1983). Cognitive processes in the revision of stereotypic beliefs. *Journal of Personality and Social Psychology, 45*, 961–977.

Wegener, D. T., & Petty, R. E. (1995). Flexible correction processes in social judgment: The role of naive theories in corrections for perceived bias. *Journal of Personality and Social Psychology, 68*, 36–51.

Wertheimer, M. (1925). *Drei Abhandlungen zur Gestalttheorie* [Three essays on Gestalt theory]. Erlangen, Germany: Palm-Enke.

Wittenbrink, B., & Henly, J. R. (1996). Creating social reality: Informational social influence and the content of stereotypic beliefs. *Personality and Social Psychology Bulletin, 22*, 598–610.

Wittenbrink, B., Judd, C. M., & Park, B. (1997). Evidence for racial prejudice at the implicit level and its relationship with questionnaire measures. *Journal of Personality and Social Psychology, 72*, 262–274.

Wittenbrink, B., Judd, C. M., Park, B., & Stone, M. H. (1996). *The valenced content of racial stereotypes: Assessing prejudice at implicit and explicit levels*. Manuscript submitted for publication.

Zeigarnik, B. (1927). Das behalten von erledigten und unerledigten handlungen [Remembering finished and unfinished tasks]. *Psychologische Forschung, 9*, 1–85.

Received October 16, 1995
Revision received May 18, 1996
Accepted May 29, 1996 ■

PART 3

Activation and Use of Cognitive Structures

Introduction and Preview

Imagine that you have been out during the evening, at a friend's apartment, and you have been enjoying a lot of fun and laughter with a group of good friends. It's getting late, so the party is finally breaking up. As you're walking the two blocks to where you parked your car, you notice a large man approaching from the other direction. You're still in a good mood from the party, so you smile and say "hello" as you pass him, arrive at your car, and drive home. It's been a good evening.

Now let's change the scenario slightly. You have spent the evening at a friend's apartment, but instead of being at a party you've been watching a movie with your friend — a very scary crime movie in which evil and danger lurk around every corner. It's late when the movie is over, so you leave and, as you walk toward your car, you again notice a large man approaching. In this case, however, instead of smiling as you pass, you are nervous and wondering if this man poses in any danger to you.

All of us have probably had experiences similar to those portrayed in both of these episodes. The difference in our reactions in the two cases reflects the continuing influence of recent experience (a fun party or a scary movie) on our perception and interpretation of subsequent events. Although these different reactions seem sensible, it isn't immediately clear exactly why and how these effects occur. After all, you have left the apartment where the party or movie took place, the man approaching you has no logical relation to either one, yet your perception and reaction to him differs dramatically in the two cases. Why? The articles in Part 3 help us to more fully understand the

147

cognitive processes that play a role in creating these differing reactions. They also inform us about how we use our knowledge in making judgments of this type.

Accessibility Through Priming

In Part 2, I discussed cognitive structures — how our accumulated knowledge is represented in memory and how cognitive structures can guide information processing. I referred to a concept or structure being "activated" when some stimulus (a person, an experience, a conversation, etc.) brings that concept to mind. This is often called *priming*: the stimulus has *primed* the concept. When an event primes a concept and thereby increases the activation of stored knowledge, we refer to that knowledge as being more *accessible*. Once it is accessible, that stored knowledge, or cognitive structure, is more easily retrieved and will be available for use in judgments, in decision-making, and for guiding behavior.

An important question then concerns the conditions that activate cognitive structures and thereby make their contents more accessible. One important variable is the "fit" between the stimulus event and the concept stored in memory. For example, consider the use of concepts to interpret and encode behaviors that one observes. Behaviors can vary considerably in the clarity versus ambiguity of their meaning. For example, if you observe a man who is yelling and cursing at another person, and who then hits that person, you would perceive the man's behavior as an aggressive act. There is a very good "fit" between the stimulus pattern you observe and your concept of aggressive behavior. On the other hand, much behavior carries some level of ambiguity, in the sense that it can be interpreted in more than one way and hence can have quite different meanings for the perceiver. In such cases, the degree of fit between stimulus and concept is not definitive. If I give a large sum of money to a nonprofit organization, you might interpret my behavior as a generous act. However, if that donation qualifies as a tax deduction, you might interpret my "apparent generosity" as motivated by self-interest, in which case my behavior (donating money) has quite a different meaning for your perception of me. In such cases, other factors can influence the concept that will be used to interpret and encode the observed stimulus.

The research reported in Reading 9 by Srull and Wyer (1979) demonstrates the importance to two such variables, namely, the *recency* and the *frequency* of activation of a concept. That is, a concept that has recently been primed is more accessible to influence information processing than is a concept that has not been primed recently. Apparently, then, the activation that results from priming a concept persists for some period of time and is therefore accessible to influence future processing (the period of time such activation endures is a matter of some debate, and is likely a function of several factors). In addition, frequently priming the same concept can increase its activation level, and therefore its accessibility to influence processing persists. Srull and Wyer orthogonally manipulated both of these variables in studying the extent to which priming of trait concepts influences judgments of an ambiguous target person on a subsequent impression formation task. Both recency and frequency of activation of the trait concepts (prior to the impression formation task) had substantial, and persisting, effects on judgments of the person.

If we think about frequency of activation a bit more, it suggests other implications. A concept (e.g., a trait) that is frequently and regularly activated becomes continuously accessible, and if so, then it is likely that it is continuously being used in perceiving the world. The consequence is that use of that trait concept becomes habitual — because it has been frequently activated, it has repeatedly been used in processing information, and that frequent use effectively maintains its accessibility for future use. Hence the concept is always accessible for construing and interpreting people and events. In that case, a trait becomes *chronically accessible* (Higgins, King, & Mavin, 1982). It also seems likely that different people, because of their differing experiences, would develop different chronically accessible concepts. Therefore the frequency of activation of a concept not only can make some traits chronically accessible but also can be reflected in individual differences in how people interpret and perceive experience.

Heuristic Strategies in the Use of Social Knowledge

Individuals use their knowledge of others and of their world in order to facilitate their adaptation to that world. At several points I have referred to the complexity of the information available to the individual. In most social situations the individual encounters a rich array of stimuli, more than he or she can really attend to and make use of, and hence the cognitive processing system exerts some selectivity in both attention and use of that information. In a similar manner, when we think about the amount of information stored in memory — information that might potentially be drawn upon and used in making decisions and guiding behavior — it's obvious that there is an enormity of potential knowledge. Therefore, the individual again must, of necessity, be selective. Hopefully, that selectivity reflects the appropriateness and relevance of information to the task at hand. When deciding whether to go to College A or College B, the choice presumably should be based on educational opportunities, costs, and the like, not on how pretty the buildings are (or even on the success of its football team!). However, other factors can also influence what kinds of knowledge become accessible. As we have

just seen, recent events as well as frequently activated structures can make some kinds of information more accessible.

The activation of knowledge is, however, only part of the story. Once information has become accessible, the individual then uses that information for specific purposes — making judgments, decisions, behavioral choices, etc. In some cases these judgments and choices are the result of careful and deliberative thought, of weighing alternatives, of considering the relevance of information, of comparing options. However, given the extent and the complexity of information available, as well as the busy (even hectic) nature of our daily lives, we often use shortcuts that ease the burden. These shortcuts are called *heuristics* and are commonly used in making judgments.

The landmark work of Amos Tversky and Daniel Kahneman (1974) provided new insights into the use of cognitive structures in making judgments. Heuristics are relatively simple rules of thumb or strategies for using information to make judgments. They often generate valid or reasonably accurate judgments (if they didn't, they wouldn't be useful to us), but because they are shortcut strategies rather than optimal procedures for making decisions and judgments, they can also result in biased or erroneous judgments. Tversky and Kahneman (1974) discussed several important heuristics that are often used in judging likelihood or frequency of events that people encounter in everyday life. The *representativeness heuristic* involves the use of resemblance or "goodness of fit" in judging category membership. That is, given a particular instance — a person, a behavior, an event — one assesses the extent to which this instance is representative of a broader class or category, evaluating the degree to which the instance resembles the prototype or other members of the category. If there is a good match, then the specific exemplar is considered an instance of (a member of) that category. The second judgmental strategy, the *availability heuristic*, assesses the frequency of some class of stimuli (people, objects, events) by relying on the ease with which instances of that class can be retrieved from memory or imagined. If it is easy to think of several instances of the category, then it seems reasonable to infer that there are a lot of them. A third heuristic, *anchoring and adjustment*, is based on the fact that, in many cases when we make judgments, we have a starting value or anchor (e.g., an opening price, a first-guess estimate), and we later adjust our judgment value in the light of new information. However, as Tversky and Kahneman showed, people often do not adjust enough to arrive at the correct value, so their judgments are biased by the initial anchor. Tversky and Kahneman were ingenious in their ability to produce simple yet convincing experimental demonstrations of these heuristics at work. Reading 10 provides several illustrative studies that effectively reveal these heuristic strategies.

The *representativeness heuristic* evaluates category membership through assessing fit or similarity between an instance and a category. If I see a large tree with many branches and full of large, beautiful leaves, I might think it's a maple tree. It certainly resembles most maple trees I've seen. Without taking the time or mental effort to examine the tree closely, to consider the distinguishing features of maple trees vs elm trees, oak tress, etc., the similarity of this tree to my general mental representation of maples means that I can quickly and easily identify this instance as a member of that category (i.e., the probability is high that this exemplar is a member of that category). Representativeness is a heuristic strategy for making this judgment because I did not thoroughly examine this tree for the defining properties of maples. It is a useful strategy in that, in most cases, my judgments of maple vs oak tress will be correct, yet I have made those judgments very quickly. At the same time, the

strategy is potentially problematic in that there will be times when I am wrong, and if those cases prove to be important, the use of a heuristic can lead to erroneous outcomes.

Several factors can lead to inadvertent use of the representativeness heuristic. One problematic factor is people's failure to recognize *base rates* in evaluating probabilities. Some categories are much larger than others are, so they are more likely to occur simply by chance. There are many more physicians than there are diamond cutters in the world, but as one of Tversky and Kahneman's examples reveals, if I told you about someone who was very knowledgeable about precious stones, you might assume that he is more likely to be employed as a diamond cutter than as a physician. In other words, your "guess" would ignore the base-rate frequency of the two occupations and would be biased by the similarity of this particular person to the category prototype.

A particularly interesting example of representativeness is the *conjunction fallacy* (Tversky & Kahneman, 1983). These researchers presented the following scenario to their participants.

> Linda is 31 years old, single, outspoken, and very bright. She majored in philosophy. As a student, she was deeply concerned with issues of discrimination and social justice, and also participated in anti-nuclear demonstrations. Which of the following alternatives is more probable?
>
> a. Linda is a bank teller.
> b. Linda is a bank teller and active in the feminist movement.

Because of the description of Linda, the second alternative seems more likely — it "fits" with our image of her, based on her college experiences. However, notice that this description of Linda actually falls within the broader class of bank tellers in general. Therefore it is impossible that the description in "b" is more probable than the description in "a." Obviously a subset cannot be more probable than the set of which it is a part. In this case, reliance on representativeness has led us astray.

Tversky and Kahneman (1974) also demonstrated that people believe that even short sequences of events (e.g., coin tosses resulting in heads and tails) that presumably are random should produce outcomes that look random. So coin tosses should generate 50% heads and 50% tails, even in the short run. However, "chance" is very inclusive and will reveal actual probabilities only in the long run. Short sequences that deviate from these probabilities are viewed as not due to chance but rather as reflecting the operation of systematic influences. An interesting manifestation of this bias is the belief in the "hot hand" in basketball, that is, that some players are streak shooters (Gilovich, Vallone, & Tversky, 1985). The idea is that, after making a couple of baskets, a player gets "in the groove" so that the likelihood of his making his next shot is higher, at least as long as the "hot hand" is working. In fact, on many basketball teams certain players become known as streak shooters, and when those players have the hot hand, their teammates "feed" the ball to them so they can shoot while they're hot. Gilovich et al. (1985) analyzed the shot-by-shot records, for an entire season, of each member of the Philadelphia 76ers, a professional basketball team, to determine whether certain players produced noticeable (i.e., statistically meaningful) "runs" or sequences of making their shots. In fact, despite the fact that at least one of the players of the team was widely known as a streak shooter, there was no evidence that any of the players scored baskets in streaks that were abnormally long, given their overall likelihood of making a basket.

A second judgmental strategy, the *availability heuristic*, is used to judge frequencies, such as "How many people of Type X are there?" or "How often does Event Y happen?"

In answering such questions, the availability heuristic uses the ease of retrieving instances of the relevant category as an indicator of their frequency. "If I can easily remember some of those cases, there must be a lot of them." This heuristic is useful because in many situations one of the reasons that you would be able to easily recall several instances is that, in fact, there are a lot of them. However, as with representativeness, other factors can influence this process as well. That is, variables other than actual frequency can make some things easily accessible, and when that happens, basing judgments of frequency on availability can lead to erroneous judgments.

Earlier in this section I described research showing that priming a category can make that category more accessible. Therefore, anything that primes a particular concept or category will increase the ease with which those instances come to mind. The result is that the perceiver might judge that there are many such instances, when in fact there are not.

Reading 11 by Schwartz, Bless, Strack, Klumpp, Rittenauer-Schatka, and Simmons (1991) provides a clever demonstration that the crucial variable underlying the availability heuristic is the experienced *ease* with which instances can be recalled. In different experimental conditions they arranged participants' perceptions so that they thought that recalling a particular class of events (e.g., examples of times they had been assertive) was made to seem easy or difficult. Specifically, they were asked to recall either 6 or 12 times when they had acted in an assertive manner. Generating 6 such instances was a relatively easy task for most people, but recalling 12 times was more challenging and difficult. Despite the fact that participants in both conditions actually recalled an equivalent number of such instances, those who experienced this task as easy rated themselves as more assertive than did those who had experienced the task as difficult.

For most of us, the things that we ourselves do are more salient and accessible to us than are things that other people do. Hence, our own thoughts, feelings, and behaviors are more available than are those of others, even people who are close to us. But suppose my partner and I engage in a certain activity equally often. Use of the availability heuristic might lead each of us to think we perform that behavior more often than the other does. Ross and Sicoly (1979) demonstrated the implications of this fact for interpersonal relations. For example, married couples were asked to estimate the percentage of times both they and their spouse performed a variety of household chores. If these participants were accurate, the husband's estimate of how often he takes the garbage out plus the wife's estimate of how often she does that task should add to 100%. In fact, for a variety of such chores, the summed percentages consistently exceeded 100. Similar effects were observed for other social contexts as well. Ross and Sicoly also demonstrated that heightening one's awareness of the partner's contributions could undermine this bias. Thus, the enhanced ease of accessibility of our own actions (even our, compared to others', contributions to joint tasks) can lead us to take greater relative credit for the combined activities of group members.

Tversky and Kahneman described a third heuristic, which they called *anchoring and adjustment*. In many cases when we make judgments, we are uncertain about the correct answer and we begin with some (perhaps tentative) initial estimate. The initial value may be suggested by the way the judgment task is presented ("Do you think the ticket for the Broadway musical will be more or less than $20?") or by prior consideration of a value ("When Fred sold his car he got $8000 for it. I wonder what I could get for mine?"). This initial value, even if quite arbitrarily determined, then serves as an *anchor* for a subsequent judgment. In making this

new judgment, the person *adjusts* the value in the appropriate direction, but insufficiently so ("Well, tickets on Broadway usually cost a lot more than $20 — probably more like $50."). This bias in making judgments can occur in either direction. If the initial question asked whether a Broadway ticket costs more or less than $200, then one's judgment would be adjusted lower, but again, insufficiently so ("Oh, tickets don't cost that much! I'd guess they go for around $125."). Thus, a low anchor keeps a subsequent judgment, even when adjusted, too low; a high anchor keeps a judgment too high.

Many studies have followed this type of procedure in which widely discrepant starting values have been arbitrarily instilled in the participants' minds, and their subsequent judgments have moved in the appropriate direction, but remained quite different. The initial value serves as an anchor, and subsequent adjustments move only modestly from that starting point. Research has shown that this bias in people's judgments is quite pervasive and can occur in a wide variety of domains where initial estimates are subsequently revised (e.g., Strack & Mussweiler, 1997), including real estate agents' judgments of an appropriate selling price of a home (Northcraft & Neale, 1987) and people's judgments of the likelihood of nuclear war (Plous, 1989).

The heuristic processes outlined by Tversky and Kahneman (1974) have been enormously important in helping us understand how people use their knowledge and make everyday judgments. These heuristics are illustrative of the variety of ways that humans engage in shortcuts as they deal with complex judgment and decision tasks. Rather than pursuing a logical and analytic, but cognitively demanding and time-consuming, approach to making judgments, people use these heuristics that often will provide very good approximations of correct judgments.

As the examples from research have shown, these heuristics can sometimes lead to not only biases but also errors in the judgments we make. Yet it is important to realize that these heuristics, while imperfect strategies, draw on principles that are often "accurate enough" to be useful. That is, judging the likelihood that an instance is a member of a category by assessing how typical it is of our mental image of that category seems plausible — members of a category usually are representative (to some extent, at least) of the category as a whole. Likewise, judging frequency by the ease of retrieval of instances is not unreasonable, for the simple reason that in many, many cases, it's easy to think of a few instances of a category for the very reason that there are in fact a lot of them. As cognitive shortcuts, then, these strategies provide extremely useful and highly efficient means of making judgments. The problems occur in those instances where other factors (e.g., insensitivity to base rates, ignoring sample size biases) can mislead our judgments of typicality, or when other factors (e.g., recency, salience, etc.) can influence the ease of retrieval that are independent of actual frequency. Thus, once again, the human information processor has devised strategies to assist in coping with the complex tasks and demands of the social world, strategies that are generally quite adaptive, but that under certain conditions can lead to biased and erroneous outcomes.

Discussion Questions

1. What is priming? What variables influence the accessibility of concepts?
2. Describe the representativeness heuristic and cite three variables that can lead to biased estimates using this heuristic.
3. The readings by Schwarz et al. and by Ross and Sicoly highlight two variables that can influence judgments based on availability. What are they and how were they demonstrated in these studies?
4. In making estimations, we often begin with some initial value and then adjust that estimate in light of other considerations. According to Tversky and Kahneman, how and why can this process result in inaccurate estimates?

Suggested Readings

Macrae, C. N., & Bodenhausen, G. V. (2000). Social cognition: Thinking categorically about others. *Annual Review of Psychology*, 51, 93–120.

Higgins, E. T. (1996). Knowledge activation: Accessibility, applicability, and salience. In E. T. Higgins & A. W. Kruglanski (Eds.), *Social psychology: Handbook of basic principles* (pp. 133–168). New York: Guilford.

Gilovich, T. (1991). *How we know what isn't so: The fallibility of human reason in everyday life.* New York: Free Press.

Nisbett, R., & Ross, L. (1980). *Human inference: Strategies and shortcomings of social judgment.* Englewood Cliffs, NJ: Prentice-Hall.

The Role of Category Accessibility in the Interpretation of Information About Persons: Some Determinants and Implications

Thomas K. Srull and Robert S. Wyer, Jr.

Many personality trait terms can be thought of as summary labels for broad conceptual categories that are used to encode information about an individual's behavior into memory. The likelihood that a behavior is encoded in terms of a particular trait category is postulated to be a function of the relative accessibility of that category in memory. In addition, the trait category used to encode a particular behavior is thought to affect subsequent judgments of the person along dimensions to which it is directly or indirectly related. To test these hypotheses, subjects first performed a sentence construction task that activated concepts associated with either hostility (Experiment 1) or kindness (Experiment 2). As part of an ostensibly unrelated impression formation experiment, subjects later read a description of behaviors that were ambiguous with respect to hostility (kindness) and then rated the target person along a variety of trait dimensions. Ratings of the target along these dimensions increased with the number of times that the test concept had previously been activated in the sentence construction task and decreased with the time interval between these prior activations and presentation of the stimulus information to be encoded. Results suggest that category accessibility is a major determinant of the way in which social information is encoded into memory and subsequently used to make judgments. Implications of this for future research and theory development are discussed.

The present research was supported by U.S. Public Health Service Training Grants MH-14257 and MH-15140 to the first author and National Science Foundation Grant BNS 76-24001 to the second author. We thank Frank Costin for generously providing us with many of his stimulus materials. We would also like to extend our sincere appreciation to two anonymous reviewers, each of whom provided us with trenchant but very constructive criticism of an earlier draft of the manuscript.

Requests for reprints should be sent to Thomas K. Srull or Robert S. Wyer, Department of Psychology, University of Illinois, Champaign, Illinois 61820.

When individuals are asked to judge themselves or another person, they are unlikely to perform an exhaustive search of memory for all cognitions that have implications for this judgment. Rather, they are likely to base their judgment on some subset of these cognitions that is most readily accessible (Tversky & Kahneman, 1973, 1974). Using quite different research methodologies, Carlston (1977) and Lingle and Ostrom (in press) have both shown that once a judgment of a stimulus person has been made on the basis of new information, this judgment is subsequently used as a basis for later inferences about the person independent of the information upon which the judgment was originally based. Similarly, Ross and his colleagues (Ross, Lepper, & Hubbard, 1975; Ross, Lepper, Strack, & Steinmetz, 1977) have found that once a person has constructed an explanation of an event involving himself or another person, this construction, rather than the information that stimulated it, is used to predict the likelihood of future events. Each body of research therefore suggests that the most easily accessible cognitions about an object or event (i.e., those that have been acquired and used most recently) have a major influence on future judgments.

Similar considerations arise when a person is asked to interpret new information about a social stimulus. In many instances, the information one receives is ambiguous; that is, it can be interpreted in more than one way. For example, information that someone told his girl friend that her new hair style is unattractive could be interpreted, or *encoded*, as either "honest" or "unkind." Which encoding is actually made may depend upon which of the two relevant concepts (honest or unkind) is most easily accessible at the time the information is received (cf. Bruner, 1957). Once the behavior is encoded as an instance of one of these trait concepts, the implications of this encoding, rather than those of the original behavioral information, may be used as a basis for subsequent judgments about the person (Carlston, 1977; Higgins, Rholes, & Jones, 1977). If this is true, judgments of a person may often be affected substantially by rather fortuitous events that lead one or another concept to be more accessible to the judge at the time information about the person is initially received.

This paper reports two in a series of studies designed to investigate the possibility raised above and to explore its implications. In so doing, they supplement and extend an earlier study by Higgins, Rholes, and Jones (1977). These authors reasoned that if subjects were required to use trait terms in the course of performing one task, these terms would become more accessible and therefore more likely to be used to encode subsequent behavioral information about a person in an unrelated context. To test this hypothesis, subjects first performed a color-naming task that required them to remember four trait terms. In experimental conditions, the traits were all potentially applicable for encoding a normatively based set of behavioral descriptions (e.g., thinking about crossing the Atlantic in a sailboat), whereas in control conditions they were all inapplica-

ble. Moreover, in some cases the four terms all had positive evaluative implications (e.g., "adventurous"), while in other cases they all had negative evaluative implications (e.g., "reckless"). As part of a second, ostensibly unrelated experiment, subjects read a story about a stimulus person that contained these behavioral descriptions. Subjects then both wrote a description of the target person in their own words and estimated how much they liked this person. Experimental subjects tended to describe the target person with trait terms that were the same as or synonymous with those to which they had been exposed in the color-naming task. In addition, their subsequent ratings of the target person were biased in the direction of the evaluative implications of these terms. In contrast, control subjects who were exposed to trait terms that were inapplicable for encoding the target's behavior did not vary systematically in either the evaluative implications of their free descriptions of the target or their ratings of him.

The findings of Higgins et al. provide intriguing support for the general hypothesis that once a concept is activated or "primed" as a result of its use for one purpose, its relative accessibility is enhanced, and its likelihood of being used to encode subsequent information increases. Moreover, the implications of the encoding, rather than those of the original stimulus material, are used as a basis for later judgments. Several additional questions are raised by these results, however. First, in the Higgins et al. study, subjects were primed with specific trait labels, each of which presumably represented a particular cognitive category or concept. To the extent that trait and behavioral concepts are interrelated in memory, however, the accessibility of trait concepts may also be increased by priming specific behaviors that exemplify these trait concepts. In this regard, it may be useful to conceptualize the representation of person information in memory in terms of schemata, or configurations of interconnected traits and behaviors at different levels of generality (cf. Cantor & Mischel, 1977). Such schemata may be hierarchical, with trait terms centrally located and behavioral instances of the traits more peripheral. Once a schema is activated, it may then be used to interpret and organize subsequent information (Bransford & Johnson, 1972; Lingle & Ostrom, in press). Thus, exposure to behavioral instances of a trait in one context may activate a schema associated with this trait, and the schema may then serve as a basis for interpreting subsequent behavioral information that is received in other contexts (Wyer & Srull, in press).

This reasoning implies that it is not necessary to prime the name of a trait in order to increase the likelihood that the schema associated with it will be used to interpret subsequent information. Rather, one needs only prime behavioral instances of the trait that are represented in the schema. It is conceivable, however, that several such instances must be primed in order to activate the schema itself. One reason for this is that behaviors are often ambiguous; that is, they can be considered instances of several different traits. To this extent, they are less likely to be interpreted as representative of any given trait when considered in isolation. Thus, it is reasonable to expect that the likelihood of activating a trait schema will increase with the number of behavioral instances used to prime it.

Once a trait concept or schema is activated as a result of exposure to representative behaviors, its accessibility, and thus its effect on the interpretation of subsequent information, is likely to decrease over time. This prediction is both intuitively reasonable and formally derived on the basis of several existing theoretical formulations. For example, Wyer and Srull (in press) have developed a model of social information processing in which the accessibility of a primed concept is postulated to decrease as a function of the number of other potentially relevant concepts used during the subsequent time interval. Since the likelihood of using at least one other potentially relevant concept becomes greater as the time interval increases, the likelihood of using the initially primed concept to interpret new information becomes correspondingly less.

Wyer and Carlston (1979) have formulated a model of person memory that also predicts this decrease. According to this formulation, which in many respects is similar to the semantic memory model of Collins and Loftus (1975), the residual "excitation" that remains at the location of a previously activated trait concept decreases over time once the concept is no longer used. As a result, increasingly greater amounts of excitation are required to reactivate the concept as time goes on, and the trait category is less likely to be invoked.[1] The two models therefore differ in that the first attributes the decrease in accessibility to be a function of interference effects (the likelihood of which increases over time), while the second attributes the decrease to

be a function of time per se, independent of any interference produced by other concepts.

To summarize, then, the above reasoning implies that the accessibility of a trait schema, and therefore the likelihood that it will be used to interpret new information, will increase with the number of schema-related behavioral concepts that have been activated prior to the receipt of this information but will decrease with the length of time between the activation of these concepts and acquisition of the new information to be interpreted. The present set of experiments tests these hypotheses.

The experiments reported extend upon the findings of Higgins et al. in one other important way. Specifically, Higgins et al. found that the accessibility of trait terms that were inapplicable for encoding the behavioral information did not affect subsequent evaluations of the target person. This suggests that priming does not have a direct influence on subjects' judgments of the target but affects these judgments only through its mediating influence on the interpretation of the target's behavior. Once the behavior has been encoded in terms of a given trait (e.g., "hostile"), however, and an overall impression of the target has been formed on the basis of this encoding, the target may then be ascribed other, evaluatively similar traits (e.g., "unintelligent") that are related only on the basis of subjects' implicit personality theories (Rosenberg & Sedlak, 1972). This possibility was also explored in the present set of experiments.

Method

Overview

Two experiments were run. The first investigated the effects of priming concepts related to hostility. The second was a conceptual replication in which concepts related to kindness were primed. The procedure used was the same in each experiment. Subjects first performed a "word comprehension" task in which they constructed sentences from sets of words. These sets were constructed so that each sentence completed would describe a behavior either related or unrelated to hostility (kindness). The total number of questionnaire items and the proportion of items related to the concept being primed were both systematically varied. Then, as part of a separate experiment on impression formation, subjects read a paragraph about a hypothetical target person who manifested a series of behaviors that were ambiguous with respect to the trait being primed. Judgments of both the target person and of individual behaviors were then

---

[1] The effects of priming appear to dissipate very rapidly with the semantic tasks that are typically used to test the Collins and Loftus model. Wyer and Carlston's extension of the model does not postulate this rapid a decay of excitation, however. More important, the stimulus domain and judgment tasks to which the Wyer and Carlston model is theoretically applied are quite different from those considered by Collins and Loftus.

analyzed as a function of the length of the priming questionnaire (30 or 60 items), the proportion of hostile (kind) priming items in the questionnaire (20% or 80%), and the time interval between completion of the priming task and the presentation of the target information (no delay, 1 hour, or 24 hours).

Ninety-six introductory psychology students (8 in each experimental condition) participated in Experiment 1 for course credit, and a different group of 96 students participated in Experiment 2.

Selection of Behavioral Descriptions

Experiment 1

To select behavioral descriptions that varied both in terms of the hostility they conveyed and in terms of the ambiguity of their implications, 43 subjects who did not participate in the main experiment were asked to rate a large pool of individual behaviors along a scale from 0 ("not at all hostile") to 10 ("extremely hostile"). From this pool were selected 5 behaviors that were judged to convey high hostility ($M = 8.08$) and 5 that were judged to convey low hostility ($M = .58$). In addition, 10 "ambiguous" behaviors were selected on the basis of two criteria: First, the mean hostility rating of each ambiguous behavior ($M = 3.99$) was lower than the mean rating of any behavior identified as hostile and higher than that of any behavior identified as nonhostile; second, the standard deviation of ratings for each ambiguous item was greater than the largest standard deviation of any item in either of the other two groups ($SD = 2.76$). The 10 ambiguous items were randomly divided into two groups of 5, and each group was then used to construct a vignette describing a hypothetical target person. In addition, all 20 behaviors were used as test items to be rated individually in a manner to be described.

Experiment 2

A procedure similar to that described above was used to select behavioral descriptions related to kindness. In this case, the mean ratings ($n = 40$) of the items selected as kind, ambiguous, and unkind were 8.71, 4.24, and .81, respectively. Again, the standard deviation of each ambiguous item was greater than the largest standard deviation of any item in the other two groups ($SD = 2.92$).

Procedure

Except where noted, the procedures described were identical in both experiments.

Administration of the Priming Task

Subjects, who were run in groups of four to eight, were greeted by a male experimenter. The experimenter introduced himself as a graduate student and stated that subjects had not actually been assigned to him but that the "real" experimenter had agreed to let him pretest a word comprehension test he was trying to develop. The exercise was described as a test of how people perceive word relationships based on their first immediate impressions. The task consisted of a number of items adapted from materials developed by Costin (1969, 1975). Each item consisted of a set of four words, and the subject's task was to underline three of the words that would make a complete sentence. The subject was told to complete each item as quickly as possible. Each item listed the words in random order and was constructed in such a way that the subject could form at least two possible sentences. In Experiment 1, however, each possible sentence formed from the hostile priming items (e.g., "leg break arm his") necessarily conveyed hostility while each item formed from other (filler) items (e.g., "her found knew I") did not. In Experiment 2, the filler items were identical, but each possible sentence formed from the kind priming items (e.g., "the hug boy kiss") conveyed kindness.

Although the effects of priming were expected to increase with the number of times an instance of the trait concept was primed, a more diagnostic test of these effects was constructed by varying both the total number of items in the questionnaire and the proportion of these items that was relevant to the trait concept. Specifically, subjects completed a total of 30 or 60 items, either 20% (6 or 12 items) or 80% (24 or 48 items) of which were related to the concept being primed. (Items of each type were distributed randomly throughout the questionnaire.) The influence of the number of priming items per se would then be indicated by significant effects for both of these manipulations. Moreover, the proportion variable should have a greater effect when the total number of questionnaire items is large than when it is small.

To avoid suspicion, all subjects within any given experimental session received a questionnaire of the same length, but the proportion of priming items was varied. In addition, the particular priming items used in constructing the questionnaire were varied, so that pooled over subjects within each condition, each item occurred the same number of times.

Presentation of Stimulus Materials

After completing the priming task, the graduate student thanked the subjects for helping him. They were then turned over immediately to the "real" experimenter, told to return 1 hour later, or told to return 24 hours later. (In the latter two cases, subjects had previously been notified through the mail that they were scheduled for those times as well. The early dismissal from the first session was attributed to a small mix-up that prevented one of the planned experiments from being ready on time.)

The second experimenter (a female) then led subjects to believe that the scheduled experiment consisted of three separate and unrelated tasks. The first task (the only one relevant to the present article) was described as a task of impression formation. Subjects were asked to read a short vignette about a stimulus person (Donald) that described a series of events occurring during the course of one afternoon. Two vignettes, serving as stimulus replications, were constructed for use in each experiment. Each vignette contained a different set of five behaviors that were ambiguous with respect to their implications for the primed trait. These behaviors were embedded within other information that was irrelevant to the trait. For example, one of the vignettes used in Experiment 1, which described behaviors that were ambiguous with respect to hostility, was the following.

> I ran into my old acquaintance Donald the other day, and I decided to go over and visit him, since by coincidence we took our vacations at the same time. Soon after I arrived, a salesman knocked at the door, but Donald refused to let him enter. He also told me that he was refusing to pay his rent until the landlord repaints his apartment. We talked for a while, had lunch, and then went out for a ride. We used my car, since Donald's car had broken down that morning, and he told the garage mechanic that he would have to go somewhere else if he couldn't fix his car that same day. We went to the park for about an hour and then stopped at a hardware store. I was sort of preoccupied, but Donald bought some small gadget, and then I heard him demand his money back from the sales clerk. I couldn't find what I was looking for, so we left and walked a few blocks to another store. The Red Cross had set up a stand by the door and asked us to donate blood. Donald lied by saying he had diabetes and therefore could not give blood. It's funny that I hadn't noticed it before, but when we got to the store, we found that it had gone out of business. It was getting kind of late, so I took Donald to pick up his car and we agreed to meet again as soon as possible.

Similar vignettes that were ambiguous with respect to kindness, were used in Experiment 2.

In each case, subjects were asked after reading the vignettes to form an impression of the person described and then rate him along a series of trait dimensions, six of which (hostile, unfriendly, dislikable, kind, considerate, and thoughtful) were assumed to imply either a high or a low degree of hostility/kindness, and the others of which (boring, selfish, narrow-minded, dependable, interesting, and intelligent) were expected to be evaluatively loaded but descriptively unrelated to either hostility or kindness. These ratings were made along a scale from 0 ("not at all") to 10 ("extremely") and in each case included reverse scoring on half the items.

Ratings of Individual Behaviors

After rating the target person, subjects rated the hostility (in Experiment 1) or kindness (in Experiment 2) conveyed by each of the 20 individual behaviors selected on the basis of the pretest data described earlier. These ratings were made along a scale from 0 ("not at all hostile/kind") to 10 ("extremely hostile/kind").

Ratings of Trait Co-occurrence

Finally, subjects were asked to estimate the co-occurrence of hostility (in Experiment 1) and kindness (in Experiment 2) with each of the other 11 traits. Items were of the form "If a person is hostile [kind], how likely is it that he is — ?" and were rated along a scale from 0 ("not at all") to 10 ("extremely").

Postexperimental Data

To check on the extent to which subjects might have had insight into the objectives of the experiment despite the several precautions taken to dissociate the priming questionnaire from the impression-formation task, subjects in Experiment 2 were asked to indicate which of the four tasks they performed during the experimental session(s) were most likely to be related to the same hypothesis. Following this question, they were also asked to indicate any other tasks they thought might be related.

Collection of Normative Data

To facilitate the interpretation of the expected priming effects, normative data were collected on the 20 behaviors used in each experiment. To avoid possible context effects associated with the large pool of behaviors originally tested, different groups of subjects rated the amount of hostility conveyed by each behavior used in Experiment 1 ($n = 28$) and the amount of kindness conveyed by each behavior used in Experiment 2 ($n = 34$) on scales ranging from 0 ("not at all hostile/kind") to 10 ("extremely hostile/kind"). These ratings were all made under neutral testing conditions and were later used for comparative purposes.

Results

Experiment 1

Preliminary Analysis

The traits *unfriendly, dislikable, kind, considerate*, and *thoughtful* were assumed to be denotatively related to the trait *hostile*. Ratings of the estimated co-occurrence of these traits with hostility, which ranged (after reverse scoring on the last three) from 8.79 to 8.98, indicate that they were all thought to covary with hostility to a substantial degree. Thus the six traits were summed across to produce a single index of the perceived hostility of the target. Similarly, ratings of the remaining six traits were summed after appropriate reverse scoring to provide a single index of the unfavorableness of the target along dimensions that are evaluatively loaded but not descriptively related to hostility, as evidenced by co-occurrence ratings ranging from 5.52 to 6.45.

Ratings of Target Person

Mean ratings of the target along both hostility-related dimensions and evaluative dimensions not directly related to hostility are shown in Figure 9.1 as a function of the length of the priming questionnaire, the proportion of hostile priming items, and the delay between completion of the priming task and presentation of the stimulus materials. Analyses as a function of these variables and the stimulus replication are relevant to several hypotheses. First, ratings of the target along both sets of dimensions were expected to increase with the number of times hostility-related concepts had previously been activated. Support for this can be seen in Figure 9.1, which shows that ratings of the target increased monotonically with the number of hostility-related items contained in the questionnaire. The hypothesis is supported statistically by significant main effects of both questionnaire length, $F(1, 72) = 123.74, p < .001$, and the proportion of hostile priming items, $F(1, 72) = 590.67, p < .001$. If the effect of priming is a linear function of the number of times hostility was previously primed, the effect of proportion should be greater when the questionnaire is long than when it is short. While the interaction of proportion and questionnaire length was not significant ($F < 1$), the pattern of results is consistent with predictions; specifically, when collapsed over delay conditions, the difference in the mean trait ratings of the target between low and high proportion lists was greater for the long questionnaire (2.70) than for the short questionnaire (2.51).

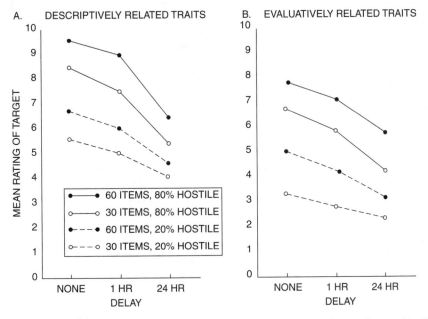

FIGURE 9.1. ■ Mean Ratings of Target Person along (A) Descriptively and (B) Evaluatively Related Traits to Hostility as a Function of Questionnaire Length, Proportion of Hostile Priming Items, and Delay.

Second, the effect of priming was expected to decrease with the time interval between the priming task and presentation of the stimulus information to be encoded. The data shown in Figure 9.1 clearly support this hypothesis, which is tested statistically by the main effect of delay interval, $F(2, 72) = 133.32$, $p < .001$.[2] Figure 9.1 also suggests that the magnitude of the decrease in priming effects over time is a positive function of the number of times the category was initially activated (i.e., the number of relevant priming items in the questionnaire). Only the interaction of delay and proportion of priming items was statistically significant, $F(2, 72) = 8.30$, $p < .001$, indicating that the effect of delay increased with the proportion of priming items in the initial questionnaire. Since the number of relevant items presented differed more as a function of proportion than as a function of overall questionnaire length, the greater contingency of delay on the former variable is not surprising.

Finally, priming effects on judgments of hostility were expected to generalize to ratings along dimensions that are evaluative but related to hostility only indirectly through subjects' implicit personality theories. Data in the right panel of Figure 9.1 clearly support this hypothesis. However, these effects were not as pronounced as they were on judgments along dimensions that were descriptively related to the primed concept (left panel of Figure 9.1). This hypothesis is supported by significant interactions of trait type with both delay, $F(2, 72) = 5.13$, $p < .01$, and the proportion of hostile priming items, $F(1,72) = 5.70$, $p < .05$. Specifically, the effect of delay interval on judgments of the target along descriptively related dimensions was greater ($M = 7.65, 6.94$, and 5.28 in the immediate, 1-hour, and 24-hour conditions, respectively) than its effect on judgments along evaluative but not descriptively related dimensions ($M = 5.77, 5.00$, and 3.90, respectively). However, the proportion of hostile priming items had less effect on hostility-related judgments ($M = 5.41$ and 7.83 under 20% and 80% conditions) than on evaluative judgments along other dimensions ($M = 3.49$ and 6.29, respectively).

Ratings of Individual Behaviors

The mean ratings of hostile, ambiguous, and nonhostile behaviors are plotted in Figure 9.2 as a function of experimental variables. Analyses of these data yielded an obviously significant effect of behavior type, along with the predicted main effects of delay, proportion of hostile priming items, and length of the priming questionnaire (in each case, $p < .001$). By far the greatest effects occurred on ratings of ambiguous behaviors, as evidenced by significant interactions of behavior type with questionnaire length, $F(2, 144) = 65.64$, $p < .001$; proportion of hostile priming items, $F(2, 144) = 352.95$, $p < .001$; and delay, $F(4, 144) = 223.69$, $p < .001$. The 4-way interaction among these variables was also significant, $F(4, 144) = 3.38$, $p < .02$. This reflects the fact that the interaction among delay, number of priming items, and proportion of critical priming items was greater for the ambiguous behaviors than for the other two behavior types, $F(2, 72) = 4.79$, $p < .02$. In fact, this component accounts for 73.8% of the total interaction sums of squares.

The differences in ratings under the 24-hour delay conditions are sufficient to justify the conclusion that the priming task influenced judgments even after a fairly long time interval had elapsed. However, they do not indicate in an absolute sense whether the delayed ratings were positively affected by priming under all conditions. Evidence bearing on this question is provided by a comparison of these ratings with normative ratings of the behaviors made by subjects who were not exposed to the priming task. These normative ratings are also presented in Figure 9.2. Unfortunately, the comparisons are not easy to interpret. Subjects who completed priming questionnaires in which only 20% (6 or 12) of the items were hostility-related made *less hostile* ratings of both the hostile and ambiguous behaviors than subjects who received no priming at all. Taken at face value, this suggests that priming under these conditions had a negative effect after a delay of 24 hours. However, since comparable results did not obtain in Experiment 2 (see below) and such negative effects are difficult to account for theoretically, such a conclusion must be treated very cautiously pending replication. (Indeed, it seems more reasonable to attribute the finding to spuriously high normative ratings of the behaviors than to negative effects of priming.)

Experiment 2

Preliminary Analysis

The traits *considerate, thoughtful, hostile, unfriendly*, and *dislikable* were assumed to be descriptively related to the trait *kind*. Mean estimates of the co-occurrence of these traits with kindness (after reverse scoring on the

---

[2] It should be noted that all of the results reported in this paper are based on analyses of variance that assume homogeneity of treatment–difference variances. The small positive bias that results when this assumption is not completely satisfied (see, e.g., Huynh & Feldt, 1970) would appear insignificant in relation to the general strength of the results.

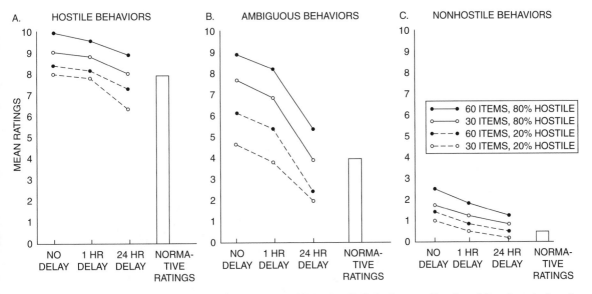

FIGURE 9.2. ■ Mean Ratings of (A) Hostile, (B) Ambiguous, and (C) Nonhostile Behaviors as a Function of Questionnaire Length, Proportion of Hostile Priming Items, and Delay.

last three) ranged from 8.54 to 8.85, indicating that they were all thought to covary with kindness to a substantial degree. Ratings of the six traits were therefore summed across to produce a single index of the perceived kindness of the target. Ratings of the remaining six traits were also summed after appropriate reverse scoring to provide a single index of the perceived favorableness of the target along dimensions that are evaluatively but not descriptively related to kindness. Ratings of the estimated co-occurrence of these traits with kindness ranged from 5.69 to 6.24.

Ratings of Target Person
Mean ratings of the target person along dimensions both descriptively and evaluatively related to kindness are plotted in Figure 9.3 as a function of experimental variables. These effects are similar in most respects to those obtained in Experiment 1. The hypothesis that ratings would increase monotonically with the number of times concepts related to kindness were previously activated is supported by main effects for both questionnaire length, $F(1, 72) = 35.62$, $p < .001$, and the proportion of kind priming items in the questionnaire, $F(1, 72) = 158.67$, $p < .001$. Moreover, the effect of proportion was significantly greater when the questionnaire was long ($M = 4.54$ and 6.05 under 20% and 80%

conditions) than when it was short ($M = 4.24$ and 5.18, respectively), $F(1, 72) = 8.85$, $p < .01$.

The hypothesis that priming effects would decrease over the time interval between the priming task and stimulus presentations was again strongly supported, $F(2, 72) = 47.79$, $p < .001$. Moreover, the magnitude of this decrease was greater when the proportion of kind priming items in the questionnaire was high than when it was low, $F(2, 72) = 19.66$, $p < .01$, and greater when the questionnaire was long than when it was short, $F(2,72) = 5.98$, $p < .01$. These findings indicate that the effect of delay is a positive function of the number of times that kindness was initially primed.

Finally, the priming manipulations had very similar effects on ratings of both dimensions that are descriptively related to kindness and those that were evaluative but descriptively unrelated. This again supports the hypothesis that once the target's behavior is encoded in terms of a trait, it will also be assigned other characteristics that are evaluatively associated with this trait. However, the effect of delay on ratings of descriptively related dimensions ($M = 5.94$, 5.15, and 4.54 in the immediate, 1-hour, and 24-hour conditions, respectively) was greater than for ratings of evaluatively related dimensions ($M = 5.23$, 4.88, and 4.29, respectively), $F(2, 72) = 3.61$, $p < .05$. Moreover, the effect of

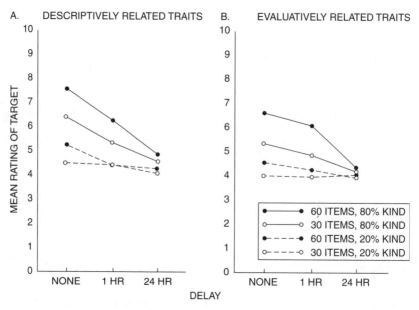

FIGURE 9.3. ■ Mean Ratings of Target Person along (A) Descriptively and (B) Evaluatively Related Traits to Kindness as a Function of Questionnaire Length, Proportion of Kind Priming Items, and Delay.

proportion was greater for descriptively related judgments (M = 4.55 and 5.87 under 20% and 80% conditions) than for evaluative judgments along other dimensions (M = 4.23 and 5.36, respectively). However, this difference was not reliable, $F(1, 72)$ = 1.54, *ns*.

There are two related differences between these data and those obtained in the first experiment. First, the delay interval in Experiment 1 had an appreciable effect at all combinations of questionnaire length and proportion of critical priming items, whereas the effect of delay in the present experiment was negligible when the proportion of priming items was low, $F(2, 72)$ = 1.68, *ns*. Second, the effect of the two priming variables after a 24-hour delay was pronounced in the first experiment, but was much less so in this study. In fact, neither questionnaire length ($F < 1$) nor proportion of kind priming items, $F(1, 72)$ = 3.12, *ns*, had reliable effects after such a delay. In sum, these data suggest that a greater number of priming items was necessary to increase the accessibility of a schema associated with kindness than was required to increase the accessibility of a schema associated with hostility. Moreover, the accessibility of kindness-related concepts appears to decrease more rapidly over time than does the accessibility of concepts related to hostility.

Ratings of Individual Behaviors

Mean ratings of individual behaviors designated as kind, ambiguous, and unkind on the basis of normative data are shown in Figure 9.4 as a function of experimental variables. The effects of these variables are generally similar to their effects on ratings of the target person; that is, the estimated kindness of all three types of behaviors increased with both questionnaire length and the proportion of kind priming items contained in the questionnaire, each $F(1, 72) \geq 43.60$, $p < .001$, while decreasing as a function of the time interval between the priming task and making these estimates, $F(2, 72)$ = 51.73, $p < .001$. Moreover, the effects of the time delay increased with both questionnaire length, $F(2, 72)$ = 6.75, $p < .01$, and the proportion of kind priming items, $F(2, 72)$ = 25.75, $p < .001$. As in the case of target ratings, priming had virtually no effect when only 6 or 12 kindness-related items were involved, and the effect of priming after a 24-hour delay was negligible.

In addition to the above effects, there was an interaction between behavior type and the proportion of kind priming items, $F(2, 144)$ = 10.53, $p < .001$. This interaction reflects the fact that the proportion variable had a greater effect on ratings of ambiguous items than on

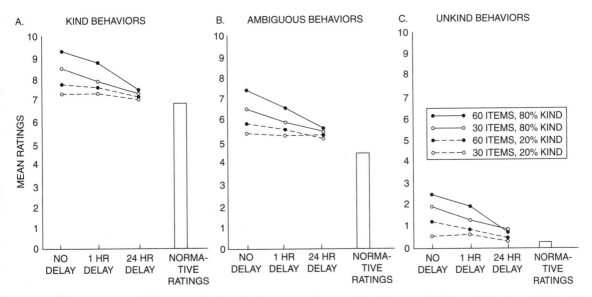

FIGURE 9.4. ■ Mean Ratings of (A) Kind, (B) Ambiguous, and (C) Unkind Behaviors as a Function of Questionnaire Length, Proportion of Kind Priming Items, and Delay.

unambiguous ones, $F(1, 72) = 14.42$, $p < .001$. This component accounts for 74.5% of the total interaction sums of squares. Finally, there was also an interaction among behavior type, proportion of kind priming items, and delay, $F(4, 144) = 2.44$, $p < .05$, which is again attributable to the greater effect of experimental variables on ratings of ambiguous behaviors than on ratings of unambiguously kind or unkind behaviors, $F(2, 72) = 3.31, p < .05$. This component accounts for 73.9% of the total interaction sums of squares.

The mean normative ratings of each type of behavior under neutral conditions are also shown in Figure 9.4 for comparison. These ratings, unlike the corresponding ones in Experiment 1 (see Figure 9.2), are invariably below subjects' ratings in any one of the priming conditions. Thus, each level of priming increased the perceived kindness of all three types of behaviors. However, this effect was much less pronounced after a 24-hour delay than after either of the shorter delays.

Supplementary Analysis

Despite the elaborate precautions taken to separate the priming and experimental tasks, a postexperimental questionnaire was administered to determine whether subjects had insight into their actual relatedness. Two findings suggest that subjects were not complying with

any implicit demand characteristics. First, only 5 of 96 subjects thought the first (priming) task was related to any of the other three tasks performed during the course of the experimental session(s). Moreover, only 1 of these 5 connected the priming task to the subsequent impression-formation experiment. Thus, subjects were just as likely to relate the priming task to an objectively irrelevant experiment as to the ratings of actual concern. Since each of the four tasks was highly dissimilar, subjects appeared to be guessing randomly and to have no insight at all into the relationship of the two tasks.

Discussion

The two experiments reported in this paper are consistent in their implications for the processing of information about persons. Specifically, once a trait concept or schema is made more accessible by previous cognitive activity, the likelihood that the same schema will be used to encode new information is increased. The accessibility of these concepts, and therefore the likelihood that they are subsequently used, increases with the number of times that instances of them have been activated in the past. Moreover, although these effects decrease with the time interval between their activation and the acquisition of information to be interpreted or encoded, they are sometimes detectable even after 24 hours. In addition, the effect of category accessibility on the encoding of behavioral information is much more pronounced when the implications of this information are relatively ambiguous.

Finally, once behavioral information is encoded, these encodings affect judgments of the person who manifested the behavior with respect to both the trait originally primed and other traits that are related to it only indirectly through subjects' implicit personality theories. The fact that these effects were typically less on judgments of the latter than of the former traits suggests that this generalizability is not simply due to a halo effect produced by exposure to "good" or "bad" concepts on the priming task. Moreover, this generalization process is very likely to be contingent upon the original encoding of the information about the person being judged. As Higgins et al. (1977) found, increasing the accessibility of a trait concept has little effect on later evaluations of a target person unless the concept is applicable for encoding the information about this person. Once the encoding takes place and an overall impression of the target is formed, however, it may then be used as a basis for inferring traits of the target that are unrelated to either the original behavioral information or the material in the priming task.

In combination, the present experiments and the earlier study reported by Higgins et al. suggest that category accessibility is an important mediator of social judgment processes. However, direct evidence of encoding was not obtained in the present study. Such evidence is suggested by Higgins et al., who found that only the priming of trait terms that were potentially applicable for describing the target's behavior affected subjects' later characterizations of him. Thus, primed traits that were evaluatively toned but inapplicable for describing the target's behavior had no effect. While similar data were not collected in the present study, the paradigm used is sufficiently similar to suggest tentatively that similar processes were operating.

At least two other approaches could be used to examine directly the mediating role of category accessibility and the conditions under which it affects encoding. First, reaction time procedures may be useful. For example, once a particular trait concept such as *hostile* is primed and is thus theoretically made more accessible, subjects should encode information with hostile implications more quickly, as well as be capable of making judgments based upon it more rapidly. Second, our analysis has assumed that encoding effects occur at the time the stimulus information is received. If this is true, priming trait concepts *after* presenting behavioral information about a target (i.e., after the information has already been encoded) should not have any effect on subsequent judgments of the person. Evidence that priming produces no effect under these conditions would provide clear evidence that priming effects are in fact mediated by the encoding of behavioral information.

The difference between the ultimate duration of priming effects obtained in this type of situation and those typically obtained with semantic and lexical decision-making tasks is striking. For example, the effects of priming a familiar noun category (e.g., "bread") on the time required to respond to other concepts that are closely associated with it (e.g., "butter") appear to dissipate in a matter of milliseconds (for a summary, see Schvaneveldt & Meyer, 1973). This suggests that the processes underlying these phenomena are quite different from those that underlie priming effects obtained in the experiments reported here. It also suggests that an "interference" interpretation of the sort postulated by Wyer and Srull (in press) may be more appropriate for describing the processing of complex social stimulus information than the spreading activation approach that is typically used to account for priming effects (cf. Collins & Loftus, 1975). On the other hand, the fact that the present effects are sometimes still detectable after a period of 24 hours remains intriguing. It is possible that factors such as the experimental laboratory, the presence of the same fellow subjects, and other situational conditions provided a variety of relatively novel contextual cues that were rich enough to "reprime" the trait categories originally made salient. This possibility should also be explored in future research.

The generalizability of the main findings over experiments suggests that these effects are not unique to particular trait concepts or to traits at a given level of favorableness. The amount of priming required to activate different trait concepts appears to differ, however. In the first experiment, as few as six instances of hostile behavior were sufficient to activate the schema related to this trait and thus to affect subsequent judgments. However, many more instances of kindness were apparently required to increase the accessibility of a kindness-related schema. It is possible that this difference is due to unique characteristics of the two traits or the particular set of priming behaviors used. However, to the extent that these materials are representative of favorable and unfavorable traits, it would appear that favorable trait concepts are generally more difficult to activate using the present procedures. Impression formation research (e.g., Birnbaum, 1974; Wyer & Hinkle, 1976) has consistently shown that favorable information has less influence on judgments than unfavorable information does. One reason is that favorable information is typically more ambiguous (for direct evidence of this, see Wyer, 1974). In the present case, since favorable behaviors are socially desirable, instances of these behaviors may be considered less indicative of traits to which they correspond (cf. Jones & Davis, 1965). Therefore, when considered in isolation, these behaviors are less likely to activate a particular trait schema. This possibility may deserve further investigation using a broader sample of trait concepts than those considered in the present studies.

While the effects of manipulations of category accessibility decrease over the interval between the priming task and presentation of the information to be encoded, they appear to increase with the time interval between the presentation of this information and subsequent judgments (Higgins et al., 1977). These two effects should be distinguished. The likelihood that a trait category is accessed and used to interpret information should decrease over the time period since it was most recently activated, for reasons noted earlier. Different considerations arise in explaining the effect of a delay between the encoding of information and judgments. Immediately after exposure to the stimulus information, both the raw information and the encoded representation of it are easily accessible. To the extent that the encoding does not capture all the implications of the original information for the judgment to be made, the judgment may be based on a composite of both. However, the accessibility of the original input material may decrease more rapidly over time than the encoded representation of it, producing the increased effect of encoding reported by Higgins et al. Additional evidence of increased effects of encoding over time has been reported by Carlston (1977), and an investigation of comparable effects within the present paradigm may also be worthwhile.

A final issue to be considered concerns the way in which various target persons will be differentially affected by prior activations of a particular trait schema. The interpretation of information about persons is obviously an overdetermined process, and the accessibility of a particular trait schema is likely to be only one of several determinants. Wyer and Srull (in press) have proposed that schematic representations of specific individuals are built up on the basis of repeated experiences. In this regard, the effects of increased accessibility of a particular trait schema on the encoding of new information may be an inverse function of the amount of information already known about the target person. Thus priming effects may be most pronounced when the target person is previously unknown.

REFERENCES

Birnbaum, M. H. The nonadditivity of personality impressions. *Journal of Experimental Psychology*, 1974, *102*, 543–561.

Bransford, J. D., & Johnson, M. K. Contextual prerequisites for understanding: Some investigations of comprehension and recall. *Journal of Verbal Learning and Verbal Behavior*, 1972, *11*, 717–726.

Bruner, J. S. On perceptual readiness. *Psychological Review*, 1957, *64*, 123–152.

Cantor, N., & Mischel, W. Traits as prototypes: Effects on recognition memory. *Journal of Personality and Social Psychology*, 1977, *35*, 38–48.

Carlston, D. E. *The recall and use of observed behaviors and inferred traits in social inference processes.* Unpublished PhD dissertation, University of Illinois, 1977.

Collins, A. M., & Loftus, E. F. A spreading-activation theory of semantic processing. *Psychological Review*, 1975, *82*, 407–428.

Costin, F. The scrambled sentence test: A group measure of hostility. *Educational and Psychological Measurement*, 1969, *29*, 461–468.

Costin, F. Measuring hostility with the scrambled sentence test. In L. K. Verma & C. Bagley (Eds.), *Race and education across cultures*. London: Heinemann, 1975.

Higgins, E. T., Rholes, W. J., & Jones, C. R. Category accessibility and impression formation. *Journal of Experimental Social Psychology*, 1977, *13*, 141–154.

Huynh, H., & Feldt, L. S. Conditions under which mean square ratios in repeated measurements designs have exact F-distributions. *Journal of the American Statistical Association*, 1970, *65*, 1582–1589.

Jones, E. E., & Davis, K. E. From acts to dispositions: The attribution process in person perception. In L. Berkowitz (Ed.), *Advances in experimental social psychology* (Vol. 2). New York: Academic Press, 1965.

Lingle, J. H., & Ostrom, T. M. Thematic effects of attitudes on the cognitive processing of attitude relevant information. In R. E. Petty, T. M. Ostrom, & T. C. Brock (Eds.) *Cognitive responses in persuasive communications: A text in attitude change.* Hillsdale, N.J.: Erlbaum, in press.

Rosenberg, S., & Sedlak, A. Structural representations of implicit personality theory. In L. Berkowitz (Ed.) *Advances in experimental social psychology* (Vol. 6). New York: Academic Press, 1972.

Ross, L., Lepper, M., & Hubbard, M. Perseverance in self-perception and social perception: Biased attributional processes in the debriefing paradigm. *Journal of Personality and Social Psychology*, 1975, *32*, 880–892.

Ross, L., Lepper, M. R., Strack, F., & Steinmetz, J. Social explanation and social expectation: Effects of real and hypothetical explanations on subjective likelihood. *Journal of Personality and Social Psychology*, 1977, *35*, 817–829.

Schvaneveldt, R. W., & Meyer, D. E. Retrieval and comparison processes in semantic memory. In S. Kornblum (Ed.) *Attention and performance IV*. New York: Academic Press, 1973.

Tversky, A., & Kahneman, D. Availability: A heuristic for judging frequency and probability. *Cognitive Psychology*, 1973, *5*, 207–232.

Tversky, A., & Kahneman, D. Judgment under uncertainty: Heuristics and biases. *Science*, 1974, *185*, 1124–1131.

Wyer, R. S. *Cognitive organization and change: An information-processing approach*. Potomac, Md.: Erlbaum, 1974.

Wyer, R. S., & Carlston, D. E. *Social cognition, inference and attribution*. Hillsdale, N.J.: Erlbaum, 1979.

Wyer, R. S., & Hinkle, R. L. Informational factors underlying inferences about hypothetical persons. *Journal of Personality and Social Psychology*, 1976, *34*, 481–495.

Wyer, R. S., & Srull, T. K. The processing of social stimulus information: A conceptual integration. In R. Hastie, E. B. Ebbesen, T. H. Ostrom, R. S. Wyer, D. L. Hamilton, & D. E. Carlston (Eds.), *Person memory: Cognitive bases of social perception*. Hillsdale, N.J.: Erlbaum, in press.

Received August 25, 1978 ■

Judgment Under Uncertainty: Heuristics and Biases

Amos Tversky and Daniel Kahneman

| Biases in judgments reveal some heuristics of thinking under uncertainty

Many decisions are based on beliefs concerning the likelihood of uncertain events such as the outcome of an election, the guilt of a defendant, or the future value of the dollar. These beliefs are usually expressed in statements such as "I think that ... ." "chances are ... ." "it is unlikely that ... ." and so forth. Occasionally, beliefs concerning uncertain events are expressed in numerical form as odds or subjective probabilities. What determines such beliefs? How do people assess the probability of an uncertain event or the value of an uncertain quantity? This article shows that people rely on a limited number of heuristic principles which reduce the complex tasks of assessing probabilities and predicting values to simpler judgmental operations. In general, these heuristics are quite useful, but sometimes they lead to severe and systematic errors.

The subjective assessment of probability resembles the subjective assessment of physical quantities such as distance or size. These judgments are all based on data of limited validity, which are processed according to heuristic rules. For example, the apparent distance of an object is determined in part by its clarity. The more sharply the object is seen, the closer it appears to be. This rule has some validity, because in any given scene the more distant objects are seen less sharply than nearer objects. However, the reliance on this rule leads to systematic errors in the estimation of distance. Specifically, distances are often overestimated when visibility is poor because the contours of objects are blurred. On the other hand, distances are often underestimated when visibility is good because the objects are seen sharply. Thus, the reliance on clarity as an indication of distance leads to common biases. Such biases are also found in the intuitive judgment of probability. This article describes three heuristics that are employed to assess probabilities and to predict values. Biases to which these heuristics lead are enumerated, and the applied and theoretical implications of these observations are discussed.

Representativeness

Many of the probabilistic questions with which people are concerned belong to one of the following types: What is the probability that object A belongs to class B? What is the probability that event A originates from process B? What is the probability that process B will generate event A? In answering such questions, people typically rely on the representativeness heuristic, in which probabilities are evaluated by the degree to which A is representative of B, that is, by the degree to which A resembles B. For

The authors are members of the department of psychology at the Hebrew University, Jerusalem, Israel.

example, when A is highly representative of B, the probability that A originates from B is judged to be high. On the other hand, if A is not similar to B, the probability that A originates from B is judged to be low.

For an illustration of judgment by representativeness, consider an individual who has been described by a former neighbor as follows: "Steve is very shy and withdrawn, invariably helpful, but with little interest in people, or in the world of reality. A meek and tidy soul, he has a need for order and structure, and a passion for detail." How do people assess the probability that Steve is engaged in a particular occupation from a list of possibilities (for example, farmer, salesman, airline pilot, librarian, or physician)? How do people order these occupations from most to least likely? In the representativeness heuristic, the probability that Steve is a librarian, for example, is assessed by the degree to which he is representative of, or similar to, the stereotype of a librarian. Indeed, research with problems of this type has shown that people order the occupations by probability and by similarity in exactly the same way.(1) This approach to the judgment of probability leads to serious errors, because similarity, or representativeness, is not influenced by several factors that should affect judgments of probability.

Insensitivity to Prior Probability of Outcomes

One of the factors that have no effect on representativeness but should have a major effect on probability is the prior probability, or base-rate frequency, of the outcomes. In the case of Steve, for example, the fact that there are many more farmers than librarians in the population should enter into any reasonable estimate of the probability that Steve is a librarian rather than a farmer. Considerations of base-rate frequency, however, do not affect the similarity of Steve to the stereotypes of librarians and farmers. If people evaluate probability by representativeness, therefore, prior probabilities will be neglected. This hypothesis was tested in an experiment where prior probabilities were manipulated (1). Subjects were shown brief personality descriptions of several individuals, allegedly sampled at random from a group of 100 professionals — engineers and lawyers. The subjects were asked to assess, for each description, the probability that it belonged to an engineer rather than to a lawyer. In one experimental condition, subjects were told that the group from which the descriptions had been drawn consisted of 70 engineers and 30 lawyers. In another condition, subjects were told that the group

consisted of 30 engineers and 70 lawyers. The odds that any particular description belongs to an engineer rather than to a lawyer should be higher in the first condition, where there is a majority of engineers, than in the second condition, where there is a majority of lawyers. Specifically, it can be shown by applying Bayes' rule that the ratio of these odds should be $(.7/.3)^2$, or 5.44, for each description. In a sharp violation of Bayes' rule, the subjects in the two conditions produced essentially the same probability judgments. Apparently, subjects evaluated the likelihood that a particular description belonged to an engineer rather than to a lawyer by the degree to which this description was representative of the two stereotypes, with little or no regard for the prior probabilities of the categories.

The subjects used prior probabilities correctly when they had no other information. In the absence of a personality sketch, they judged the probability that an unknown individual is an engineer to be .7 and .3, respectively, in the two base-rate conditions. However, prior probabilities were effectively ignored when a description was introduced, even when this description was totally uninformative. The responses to the following description illustrate this phenomenon:

> Dick is a 30 year old man. He is married with no children. A man of high ability and high motivation, he promises to be quite successful in his field. He is well liked by his colleagues.

This description was intended to convey no information relevant to the question of whether Dick is an engineer or a lawyer. Consequently, the probability that Dick is an engineer should equal the proportion of engineers in the group, as if no description had been given. The subjects, however, judged the probability of Dick being an engineer to be .5 regardless of whether the stated proportion of engineers in the group was .7 or .3. Evidently, people respond differently when given no evidence and when given worthless evidence. When no specific evidence is given, prior probabilities are properly utilized; when worthless evidence is given, prior probabilities are ignored (1).

Insensitivity to Sample Size

To evaluate the probability of obtaining a particular result in a sample drawn from a specified population, people typically apply the representativeness heuristic. That is, they assess the likelihood of a sample result, for example, that the average height in a random sample of ten men will be 6 feet (180 centimeters), by the similarity of this result to the corresponding parameter (that is, to the average height in the population of men). The similarity of a sample statistic to a population parameter does not depend on the size of the sample. Consequently, if probabilities are assessed by representativeness, then the judged probability of a sample statistic will be essentially independent of sample size. Indeed, when subjects assessed the distributions of average height for samples of various sizes, they produced identical distributions. For example, the probability of obtaining an average height greater than 6 feet was assigned the same value for samples of 1000, 100, and 10 men (2). Moreover, subjects failed to appreciate the role of sample size even when it was emphasized in the formulation of the problem. Consider the following question:

A certain town is served by two hospitals. In the larger hospital about 45 babies are born each day, and in the smaller hospital about 15 babies are born each day. As you know, about 50 percent of all babies are boys. However, the exact percentage varies from day to day. Sometimes it may be higher than 50 percent, sometimes lower.

For a period of 1 year, each hospital recorded the days on which more than 60 percent of the babies born were boys. Which hospital do you think recorded more such days?

- The larger hospital (21)
- The smaller hospital (21)
- About the same (that is, within 5 percent of each other) (53)

The values in parentheses are the number of undergraduate students who chose each answer.

Most subjects judged the probability of obtaining more than 60 percent boys to be the same in the small and in the large hospital, presumably because these events are described by the same statistic and are therefore equally representative of the general population. In contrast, sampling theory entails that the expected number of days on which more than 60 percent of the babies are boys is much greater in the small hospital than in the large one, because a large sample is less likely to stray from 50 percent. This fundamental notion of statistics is evidently not part of people's repertoire of intuitions.

A similar insensitivity to sample size has been reported in judgments of posterior probability, that is, of the probability that a sample has been drawn from one population rather than from another. Consider the following example:

Imagine an urn filled with balls, of which 2/3 are of one color and 1/3 of another. One individual has drawn 5 balls from the urn, and found that 4 were red and 1 was white Another individual has drawn 20 balls and found that 12 were red and 8 were white. Which of the two individuals should feel more confident that the urn contains 2/3 red balls and 1/3 white balls, rather than the opposite? What odds should each individual give?

In this problem, the correct posterior odds are 8 to 1 for the 4 : 1 sample and 16 to 1 for the 12 : 8 sample, assuming equal prior probabilities. However, most people feel that the first sample provides much stronger evidence for the hypothesis that the urn is predominantly red, because the proportion of red balls is larger in the first than in the second sample. Here again, intuitive judgments are dominated by the sample proportion and are essentially unaffected by the size of the sample, which plays a crucial role in the determination of the actual posterior odds (2). In addition, intuitive estimates of posterior odds are far less extreme than the correct values. The underestimation of the impact of evidence has been observed repeatedly in problems of this type (3,4). It has been labeled "conservatism."

Misconceptions of Chance

People expect that a sequence of events generated by a random process will represent the essential characteristics of that process even when the sequence is short. In considering tosses of a coin for heads or tails, for example, people regard the sequence H-T-H-T-T-H to be more likely than the sequence H-H-H-T-T-T, which does not appear random, and also more likely than the sequence H-H-H-H-T-H, which does not represent the fairness of the coin (2). Thus, people expect that the essential characteristics of the process will be represented, not only globally in the entire sequence, but also locally in each of its parts. A locally representative sequence, however, deviates systematically from chance expectation: It contains too many alternations and too few runs. Another consequence of the belief in local representativeness is the well-known gambler's fallacy. After observing a long run of red on the roulette wheel, for example, most people erroneously believe that black is now due, presumably because the occurrence of black will result in a more representative sequence than the occurrence of an additional red. Chance is commonly viewed as a self-correcting process in which a deviation in one direction induces a deviation in the opposite direction to restore the equilibrium. In fact, deviations are not "corrected" as a chance process unfolds, they are merely diluted.

Misconceptions of chance are not limited to naive subjects. A study of the statistical intuitions of experienced research psychologists (5) revealed a lingering belief in what may be called the "law of small numbers," according to which even small samples are highly representative of the populations from which they are drawn. The responses of these investigators reflected the expectation that a valid hypothesis about a population will be represented by a statistically significant result in a sample — with little regard for its size. As a consequence, the researchers put too much faith in the results of small samples and grossly overestimated the replicability of such results. In the actual conduct of research, this bias leads to the selection of samples of inadequate size and to overinterpretation of findings.

Insensitivity to Predictability

People are sometimes called upon to make such numerical predictions as the future value of a stock, the demand for a commodity, or the outcome of a football game. Such predictions are often made by representativeness. For example, suppose one is given a description of a company and is asked to predict its future profit. If the description of the company is very favorable, a very high profit will appear most representative of that description: If the description is mediocre, a mediocre performance will appear most representative. The degree to which the description is favorable is unaffected by the reliability of that description or by the degree to which it permits accurate prediction. Hence, if people predict solely in terms of the favorableness of the description, their predictions will be insensitive to the reliability of the evidence and to the expected accuracy of the prediction.

This mode of judgment violates the normative statistical theory in which the extremeness and the range of predictions are controlled by considerations of predictability. When predictability is nil, the same prediction should be made in all cases. For example, if the descriptions of companies provide no information relevant to profit, then the same value (such as average profit) should be predicted for all companies. If predictability is perfect, of course, the values predicted will match the actual values and the range of predictions will equal the range of outcomes. In general, the higher the predictability, the wider the range of predicted values.

Several studies of numerical prediction have demonstrated that intuitive predictions violate this rule, and that subjects show little or no regard for considerations of predictability (1). In one of these studies, subjects were presented with several paragraphs, each describing the performance of a student teacher during a particular practice lesson. Some subjects were asked to *evaluate* the quality of the lesson described in the paragraph in percentile scores, relative to a specified population. Other subjects were asked to *predict*, also in percentile scores, the standing of each student teacher 5 years after the practice lesson. The judgments made under the two conditions were identical. That is, the prediction of a remote criterion (success of a teacher after 5 years) was identical to the evaluation of the information on which the prediction was based (the quality of the practice lesson). The students who made these predictions were undoubtedly aware of the limited predictability of teaching competence on the basis of a single trial lesson 5 years earlier; nevertheless, their predictions were as extreme as their evaluations.

The Illusion of Validity

As we have seen, people often predict by selecting the outcome (for example, an occupation) that is most representative of the input (for example, the description of a person). The confidence they have in their prediction depends primarily on the degree of representativeness (that is, on the quality of the match between the selected outcome and the input) with little or no regard for the factors that limit predictive accuracy. Thus, people express great confidence in the prediction that a person is a librarian when given a description of his personality which matches the stereotype of librarians, even if the description is scanty, unreliable, or outdated. The unwarranted confidence which is produced by a good fit between the predicted outcome and the input information may be called the illusion of validity. This illusion persists even when the judge is aware of the factors that limit the accuracy of his predictions. It is a common observation that psychologists who conduct selection interviews often experience considerable confidence in their predictions, even when they know of the vast literature that shows selection interviews to be highly fallible. The continued reliance on the clinical interview for selection, despite repeated demonstrations of its inadequacy, amply attests to the strength of this effect.

The internal consistency of a pattern of inputs is a major determinant of one's confidence in predictions based on these inputs. For example, people express more confidence in predicting the final grade-point average of a student whose first-year record consists entirely of B's than in predicting the grade-point average of a student whose first-year record includes many A's and C's. Highly consistent patterns are most often observed when the input variables are highly redundant or correlated. Hence, people tend to have great confidence in predictions based on redundant input variables. However, an elementary result in the statistics of correlation asserts that, given input variables of stated validity, a prediction based on several such inputs can achieve higher accuracy when they are independent of each other than when they are redundant or correlated. Thus, redundancy among inputs decreases accuracy even as it increases confidence, and people are often confident in predictions that are quite likely to be off the mark (1).

Misconceptions of Regression

Suppose a large group of children has been examined on two equivalent versions of an aptitude test. If one selects ten children from among those who did best on one of the two versions, he will usually find their performance on the second version to be somewhat disappointing. Conversely, if one selects ten children from among those who did worst on one version, they will be found, on the average, to do somewhat better on the other version. More generally, consider two variables X and Y which have the same distribution. If one selects individuals whose average X score deviates from the mean of X by k units, then the average of their Y scores will usually deviate from the mean of Y by less than k units. These observations illustrate a general phenomenon known as regression toward the mean, which was first documented by Galton more than 100 years ago.

In the normal course of life, one encounters many instances of regression toward the mean, in the comparison of the height of fathers and sons, of the intelligence of husbands and wives, or of the performance of individuals on consecutive examinations. Nevertheless, people do not develop correct intuitions about this phenomenon. First, they do not expect regression in many contexts where it is bound to occur. Second, when they recognize the occurrence of regression, they often invent spurious causal explanations for it (1). We suggest that the phenomenon of regression remains elusive because it is incompatible with the belief that the predicted outcome should be maximally representative of the input, and, hence, that the value of the outcome variable should be as extreme as the value of the input variable.

The failure to recognize the import of regression can have pernicious consequences, as illustrated by the following observation (1). In a discussion of flight training, experienced instructors noted that praise for an exceptionally smooth landing is typically followed by a poorer landing on the next try, while harsh criticism after a rough landing is usually followed by an improvement on the next try. The instructors concluded that verbal rewards are detrimental to learning, while verbal punishments are beneficial, contrary to accepted psychological doctrine. This conclusion is unwarranted because of the presence of regression toward the mean. As in other cases of repeated examination, an improvement will usually follow a poor performance and a deterioration will usually follow an outstanding performance, even if the instructor does not respond to the trainee's achievement on the first attempt. Because the instructors had praised their trainees after good landings and admonished them after poor ones, they reached the erroneous and potentially harmful conclusion that punishment is more effective than reward.

Thus, the failure to understand the effect of regression leads one to overestimate the effectiveness of punishment and to underestimate the effectiveness of reward. In social interaction, as well as in training, rewards are typically administered when performance is good, and punishments are typically administered when performance is poor. By regression alone, therefore, behavior is most likely to improve after punishment and most likely to deteriorate after reward. Consequently, the human condition is such that, by chance alone, one is most often rewarded for punishing others and most often punished for rewarding them. People are generally not aware of this contingency. In fact, the elusive role of regression in determining the apparent consequences of reward and punishment seems to have escaped the notice of students of this area.

Availability

There are situations in which people assess the frequency of a class or the probability of an event by the ease with which instances or occurrences can be brought to mind. For example, one may assess the risk of heart attack among middle-aged people by recalling such occurrences among one's acquaintances. Similarly, one may evaluate the probability that a given business venture will fail by imagining various difficulties it could encounter. This judgmental heuristic is called availability. Availability is a useful clue for assessing frequency or probability, because instances of large classes are usually recalled better and faster than instances of less frequent classes. However, availability is affected by factors other than frequency and probability. Consequently, the reliance on availability leads to predictable biases, some of which are illustrated below.

Biases Due to the Retrievability of Instances

When the size of a class is judged by the availability of its instances, a class whose instances are easily retrieved will appear more numerous than a class of equal frequency whose instances are less retrievable. In an elementary demonstration of this effect, subjects heard a list of well-known personalities of both sexes and were subsequently asked to judge whether the list contained more names of men than of women. Different lists were presented to different groups of subjects. In some of the lists the men were relatively more famous than the women, and in others the women were relatively more famous than the men. In each of the lists, the subjects erroneously judged that the class (sex) that had the more famous personalities was the more numerous (6).

In addition to familiarity, there are other factors, such as salience, which affect the retrievability of instances. For example, the impact of seeing a house burning on the subjective probability of such accidents is probably greater than the impact of reading about a fire in the local paper. Furthermore, recent occurrences are likely to be relatively more available than earlier occurrences. It is a common experience that the subjective probability of traffic accidents rises temporarily when one sees a car overturned by the side of the road.

Biases Due to the Effectiveness of a Search Set

Suppose one samples a word (of three letters or more) at random from an English text. Is it more likely that the word starts with r or that r is the third letter? People approach this problem by recalling words that begin with r (road) and words that have r in the third position (car) and assess the relative frequency by the ease with which words of the two types come to mind. Because it is much easier to search for words by their first letter than by their third letter, most people judge words that begin with a given consonant to be more numerous than words in which the same consonant appears in the third position. They do so even for consonants, such as

r or k, that are more frequent in the third position than in the first (6).

Different tasks elicit different search sets. For example, suppose you are asked to rate the frequency with which abstract words (thought, love) and concrete words (door, water) appear in written English. A natural way to answer this question is to search for contexts in which the word could appear. It seems easier to think of contexts in which an abstract concept is mentioned (love in love stories) than to think of contexts in which a concrete word (such as door) is mentioned. If the frequency of words is judged by the availability of the contexts in which they appear, abstract words will be judged as relatively more numerous than concrete words. This bias has been observed in a recent study (7) which showed that the judged frequency of occurrence of abstract words was much higher than that of concrete words, equated in objective frequency. Abstract words were also judged to appear in a much greater variety of contexts than concrete words.

Biases of Imaginability

Sometimes one has to assess the frequency of a class whose instances are not stored in memory but can be generated according to a given rule. In such situations, one typically generates several instances and evaluates frequency or probability by the ease with which the relevant instances can be constructed. However, the ease of constructing instances does not always reflect their actual frequency, and this mode of evaluation is prone to biases. To illustrate, consider a group of 10 people who form committees of k members. $2 \leq k \leq 8$. How many different committees of k members can be formed? The correct answer to this problem is given by the binomial coefficient $\binom{10}{k}$ which reaches a maximum of 252 for $k = 5$. Clearly, the number of committees of k members equals the number of committees of $(10 - k)$ members, because any committee of k members defines a unique group of $(10 - k)$ nonmembers.

One way to answer this question without computation is to mentally construct committees of k members and to evaluate their number by the ease with which they come to mind. Committees of few members, say 2, are more available than committees of many members, say 8. The simplest scheme for the construction of committees is a partition of the group into disjoint sets. One readily sees that it is easy to construct five disjoint committees of 2 members, while it is impossible to generate even two disjoint committees of 8 members. Consequently, if frequency is assessed by imaginability, or by availability for construction, the small committees will appear more numerous than larger committees, in contrast to the correct bell-shaped function. Indeed, when naive subjects were asked to estimate the number of distinct committees of various sizes, their estimates were a decreasing monotonic function of committee size (6). For example, the median estimate of the number of committees of 2 members was 70, while the estimate for committees of 8 members was 20 (the correct answer is 45 in both cases).

Imaginability plays an important role in the evaluation of probabilities in real-life situations. The risk involved in an adventurous expedition, for example, is evaluated by imagining contingencies with which the expedition is not equipped to cope. If many such difficulties are vividly portrayed, the expedition can be made to appear exceedingly dangerous, although the ease with which disasters are imagined need not reflect their actual likelihood. Conversely, the risk involved in an undertaking may be grossly underestimated if some possible dangers are either difficult to conceive of, or simply do not come to mind.

Illusory Correlation

Chapman and Chapman (8) have described an interesting bias in the judgment of the frequency with which two events co-occur. They presented naive judges with information concerning several hypothetical mental patients. The data for each patient consisted of a clinical diagnosis and a drawing of a person made by the patient. Later the judges estimated the frequency with which each diagnosis (such as paranoia or suspiciousness) had been accompanied by various features of the drawing (such as peculiar eyes). The subjects markedly overestimated the frequency of co-occurrence of natural associates, such as suspiciousness and peculiar eyes. This effect was labeled illusory correlation. In their erroneous judgments of the data to which they had been exposed, naive subjects "rediscovered" much of the common, but unfounded, clinical lore concerning the interpretation of the draw-a-person test. The illusory correlation effect was extremely resistant to contradictory data. It persisted even when the correlation between symptom and diagnosis was actually negative, and it prevented the judges from detecting relationships that were in fact present.

Availability provides a natural account for the illusory-correlation effect. The judgment of how frequently two events co-occur could be based on the strength of the associative bond between them. When the association is strong, one is likely to conclude that the events have been frequently paired. Consequently, strong associates will be judged to have occurred together frequently. According to this view, the illusory correlation between suspiciousness and peculiar drawing of the eyes, for example, is due to the fact that suspiciousness is more readily associated with the eyes than with any other part of the body.

Lifelong experience has taught us that, in general, instances of large classes are recalled better and faster than instances of less frequent classes; that likely occurrences are easier to imagine than unlikely ones; and that the associative connections between events are strengthened when the events frequently co-occur. As a result, man has at his disposal a procedure (the availability heuristic) for estimating the numerosity of a class, the likelihood of an event, or the frequency of co-occurrences, by the ease with which the relevant mental operations of retrieval, construction, or association can be performed. However, as the preceding examples have demonstrated, this valuable estimation procedure results in systematic errors.

Adjustment and Anchoring

In many situations, people make estimates by starting from an initial value that is adjusted to yield the final answer. The initial value, or starting point, may be suggested by the formulation of the problem, or it may be the result of a partial computation. In either case, adjustments are typically insufficient (4). That is, different starting points yield different estimates, which are biased toward the initial values. We call this phenomenon anchoring.

Insufficient Adjustment

In a demonstration of the anchoring effect, subjects were asked to estimate various quantities, stated in percentages (for example, the percentage of African countries in the United Nations). For each quantity, a number between 0 and 100 was determined by spinning a wheel of fortune in the subjects' presence. The subjects were instructed to indicate first whether that number was higher or lower than the value of the quantity, and then to estimate the value of the quantity by moving upward or downward from the given number. Different groups were given different numbers for each quantity, and these arbitrary numbers had a marked effect on estimates. For example, the median estimates of the percentage of African countries in the United Nations were 25 and 45 for groups that received 10 and 65, respectively, as starting points. Payoffs for accuracy did not reduce the anchoring effect.

Anchoring occurs not only when the starting point is given to the subject, but also when the subject bases his estimate on the result of some incomplete computation. A study of intuitive numerical estimation illustrates this effect. Two groups of high school students estimated, within 5 seconds, a numerical expression that was written on the blackboard. One group estimated the product

$$8 \times 7 \times 6 \times 5 \times 4 \times 3 \times 2 \times 1$$

while another group estimated the product

$$1 \times 2 \times 3 \times 4 \times 5 \times 6 \times 7 \times 8$$

To rapidly answer such questions, people may perform a few steps of computation and estimate the product by extrapolation or adjustment. Because adjustments are typically insufficient, this procedure should lead to underestimation. Furthermore, because the result of the first few steps of multiplication (performed from left to right) is higher in the descending sequence than in the ascending sequence, the former expression should be judged larger than the latter. Both predictions were confirmed. The median estimate for the ascending sequence was 512, while the median estimate for the descending sequence was 2,250. The correct answer is 40,320.

Biases in the Evaluation of Conjunctive and Disjunctive Events

In a recent study by Bar-Hillel (9) subjects were given the opportunity to bet on one of two events. Three types of events were used: (i) simple events, such as drawing a red marble from a bag containing 50 percent red marbles and 50 percent white marbles; (ii) conjunctive events, such as drawing a red marble seven times in succession, with replacement, from a bag containing 90 percent red marbles and 10 percent white marbles; and (iii) disjunctive events, such as drawing a red marble at least once in seven successive tries, with replacement, from a bag containing 10 percent red marbles and 90 percent white marbles. In this problem, a significant majority of subjects preferred to bet on the conjunctive event (the probability of which is .48) rather than on the simple event (the probability of which is .50). Subjects also preferred to bet on the simple event rather than on the disjunctive event, which has a probability of .52. Thus, most subjects bet on the less likely event in both comparisons. This pattern of choices

illustrates a general finding. Studies of choice among gambles and of judgments of probability indicate that people tend to overestimate the probability of conjunctive events (10) and to underestimate the probability of disjunctive events. These biases are readily explained as effects of anchoring. The stated probability of the elementary event (success at any one stage) provides a natural starting point for the estimation of the probabilities of both conjunctive and disjunctive events. Since adjustment from the starting point is typically insufficient, the final estimates remain too close to the probabilities of the elementary events in both cases. Note that the overall probability of a conjunctive event is lower than the probability of each elementary event, whereas the overall probability of a disjunctive event is higher than the probability of each elementary event, whereas the overall probability of a disjunctive event is higher than the probability of each elementary event. As a consequence of anchoring, the overall probability will be overestimated in conjunctive problems and underestimated in disjunctive problems.

Biases in the evaluation of compound events are particularly significant in the context of planning. The successful completion of an undertaking, such as the development of a new product, typically has a conjunctive character: for the undertaking to succeed, each of a series of events must occur. Even when each of these events is very likely, the overall probability of success can be quite low if the number of events is large. The general tendency to overestimate the probability of conjunctive events leads to unwarranted optimism in the evaluation of the likelihood that a plan will succeed or that a project will be completed on time. Conversely, disjunctive structures are typically encountered in the evaluation of risks. A complex system, such as a nuclear reactor or a human body, will malfunction if any of its essential components fails. Even when the likelihood of failure in each component is slight, the probability of an overall failure can be high if many components are involved. Because of anchoring, people will tend to underestimate the probabilities of failure in complex systems. Thus, the direction of the anchoring bias can sometimes be inferred from the structure of the event. The chain-like structure of conjunctions leads to overestimation, the funnel-like structure of disjunctions leads to underestimation.

Anchoring in the Assessment of Subjective Probability Distributions

In decision analysis, experts are often required to express their beliefs about a quantity, such as the value of the Dow-Jones average on a particular day, in the form of a probability distribution. Such a distribution is usually constructed by asking the person to select values of the quantity that correspond to specified percentiles of his subjective probability distribution. For example, the judge may be asked to select a number, X_{90}, such that his subjective probability that this number will be higher than the value of the Dow-Jones average is .90. That is, he should select the value X_{90} so that he is just willing to accept 9 to 1 odds that the Dow-Jones average will not exceed it. A subjective probability distribution for the value of the Dow-Jones average can be constructed from several such judgments corresponding to different percentiles.

By collecting subjective probability distributions for many different quantities, it is possible to test the judge for proper calibration. A judge is properly (or externally) calibrated in a set of problems if exactly π percent of the true values of the assessed quantities falls below his stated values of X_n. For example, the true values should fall below X_{01} for 1 percent of the quantities and above X_{99} for 1 percent of the quantities. Thus, the true values should fall in the confidence interval between X_{01} and X_{99} on 98 percent of the problems.

Several investigators (11) have obtained probability distributions for many quantities from a large number of judges. These distributions indicated large and systematic departures from proper calibration. In most studies, the actual values of the assessed quantities are either smaller than X_{01} or greater than X_{99} for about 30 percent of the problems. That is, the subjects state overly narrow confidence intervals which reflect more certainty than is justified by their knowledge about the assessed quantities. This bias is common to naive and to sophisticated subjects, and it is not eliminated by introducing proper scoring rules, which provide incentives for external calibration. This effect is attributable, in part at least, to anchoring.

To select X_{99} for the value of the Dow-Jones average, for example, it is natural to begin by thinking about one's best estimate of the Dow-Jones and to adjust this value upward. If this adjustment — like most others — is insufficient, then X_{90} will not be sufficiently extreme. A similar anchoring effect will occur in the selection of X_{10}, which is presumably obtained by adjusting one's best estimate downward. Consequently, the confidence interval between X_{10} and X_{90} will be too narrow, and the assessed probability distribution will be too tight. In support of this interpretation it can be shown that subjective probabilities are systematically altered by a procedure in which one's best estimate does not serve as an anchor.

Subjective probability distributions for a given quantity (the Dow-Jones average) can be obtained in two different ways: (i) by asking the subject to select values of the Dow-Jones that correspond to specified percentiles of his probability distribution and (ii) by asking the subject to assess the probabilities that the true value of the Dow-Jones will exceed some specified values. The two procedures are formally equivalent and should yield identical distributions. However, they suggest different modes of adjustment from different anchors. In procedure (i), the natural starting point is one's best estimate of the quantity. In procedure (ii), on the other hand, the subject may be anchored on the value stated in the question. Alternatively, he may be anchored on even odds, or 50–50 chances, which is a natural starting point in the estimation of likelihood. In either case, procedure (ii) should yield less extreme odds than procedure (i).

To contrast the two procedures, a set of 24 quantities (such as the air distance from New Delhi to Peking) was presented to a group of subjects who assessed either X_{10} or X_{90} for each problem. Another group of subjects received the median judgment of the first group for each of the 24 quantities. They were asked to assess the odds that each of the given values exceeded the true value of the relevant quantity. In the absence of any bias, the second group should retrieve the odds specified to the first group, that is, 9 : 1. However, if even odds or the stated value serve as anchors, the odds of the second group should be less extreme, that is, closer to 1 : 1. Indeed, the median odds stated by this group, across all problems, were 3 : 1. When the judgments of the two groups were tested for external calibration, it was found that subjects in the first group were too extreme, in accord with earlier studies. The events that they defined as having a probability of .10 actually obtained in 24 percent of the cases. In contrast, subjects in the second group were too conservative. Events to which they assigned an average probability of .34 actually obtained in 26 percent of the cases. These results illustrate the manner in which the degree of calibration depends on the procedure of elicitation.

Discussion

This article has been concerned with cognitive biases that stem from the reliance on judgmental heuristics. These biases are not attributable to motivational effects such as wishful thinking or the distortion of judgments by payoffs and penalties. Indeed, several of the severe errors of judgment reported earlier occurred despite the fact that subjects were encouraged to be accurate and were rewarded for the correct answers (2, 6).

The reliance on heuristics and the prevalence of biases are not restricted to laymen. Experienced researchers are also prone to the same biases — when they think intuitively. For example, the tendency to predict the outcome that best represents the data, with insufficient regard for prior probability, has been observed in the intuitive judgments of individuals who have had extensive training in statistics (1, 5). Although the statistically sophisticated avoid elementary errors, such as the gambler's fallacy, their intuitive judgments are liable to similar fallacies in more intricate and less transparent problems.

It is not surprising that useful heuristics such as representativeness and availability are retained, even though they occasionally lead to errors in prediction or estimation. What is perhaps surprising is the failure of people to infer from lifelong experience such fundamental statistical rules as regression toward the mean, or the effect of sample size on sampling variability. Although everyone is exposed, in the normal course of life, to numerous examples from which these rules could have been induced, very few people discover the principles of sampling and regression on their own. Statistical principles are not learned from everyday experience because the relevant instances are not coded appropriately. For example, people do not discover that successive lines in a text differ more in average word length than do successive pages, because they simply do not attend to the average word length of individual lines or pages. Thus, people do not learn the relation between sample size and sampling variability, although the data for such learning are abundant.

The lack of an appropriate code also explains why people usually do not detect the biases in their judgments of probability. A person could conceivably learn whether his judgments are externally calibrated by keeping a tally of the proportion of events that actually occur among those to which he assigns the same probability. However, it is not natural to group events by their judged probability. In the absence of such grouping it is impossible for an individual to discover, for example, that only 50 percent of the predictions to which he has assigned a probability of .9 or higher actually came true.

The empirical analysis of cognitive biases has implications for the theoretical and applied role of judged probabilities. Modern decision theory (12, 13) regards subjective probability as the quantified opinion of an idealized person. Specifically, the subjective probability of a given event is defined by the set of bets about this event that such a person is willing to accept. An internally consistent, or coherent, subjective probability measure can be derived for an individual if his choices among bets satisfy certain principles, that is, the axioms of the theory. The derived probability is subjective in the sense that different individuals are allowed to have different probabilities for the same event. The major contribution of this approach is that it provides a rigorous subjective interpretation of probability that is applicable to unique events and is embedded in a general theory of rational decision.

It should perhaps be noted that, while subjective probabilities can sometimes be inferred from preferences among bets, they are normally not formed in this fashion. A person bets on team A rather than on team B because he believes that team A is more likely to win; he does not infer this belief from his betting preferences. Thus, in reality, subjective probabilities determine preferences among bets and are not derived from them, as in the axiomatic theory of rational decision (12).

The inherently subjective nature of probability has led many students to the belief that coherence, or internal consistency, is the only valid criterion by which judged probabilities should be evaluated. From the standpoint of the formal theory of subjective probability, any set of internally consistent probability judgments is as good as any other. This criterion is not entirely satisfactory, because an internally consistent set of subjective probabilities can be incompatible with other beliefs held by the individual. Consider a person whose subjective probabilities for all possible outcomes of a coin-tossing game reflect the gambler's fallacy. That is, his estimate of the probability of tails on a particular toss increases with the number of consecutive heads that preceded that toss. The judgments of such a person could be internally consistent and therefore acceptable as adequate subjective probabilities according to the criterion of the formal theory. These probabilities, however, are incompatible with the generally held belief that a coin has no memory and is therefore incapable of generating sequential dependencies. For judged probabilities to be considered adequate, or rational, internal consistency is not enough. The judgments must be compatible with the entire web of beliefs held by the individual. Unfortunately, there can be no simple formal procedure for assessing the compatibility of a set of probability judgments with the judge's total system of beliefs. The rational judge will nevertheless strive for compatibility, even though internal consistency is more easily achieved and assessed. In particular, he will attempt to make his probability judgments compatible with his knowledge about the subject matter, the laws of probability, and his own judgmental heuristics and biases.

Summary

This article described three heuristics that are employed in making judgments under uncertainty: (i) representativeness, which is usually employed when people are asked to judge the probability that an object or event A belongs to class or process B; (ii) availability of instances or scenarios, which is often employed when people are asked to assess the frequency of a class or the plausibility of a particular development; and (iii) adjustment from an anchor, which is usually employed in numerical prediction when a relevant value is available. These heuristics are highly economical and usually effective, but they lead to systematic and predictable errors. A better understanding of these heuristics and of the biases to which they lead could improve judgments and decisions in situations of uncertainty.

REFERENCES AND NOTES

1. D. Kahneman and A. Tversky, *Psychol. Rev.* **80**, 237 (1973).
2. ——, *Cognitive Psychol.* **3**, 430 (1972).
3. W. Edwards, in *Formal Representation of Human Judgment*, B. Kleinmuntz, Ed. (Wiley, New York, 1968), pp. 17–52.
4. P. Slovic and S. Lichtenstein, *Organ. Behav. Hum. Performance* **6**, 649 (1971).
5. A. Tversky and D. Kahneman, *Psychol. Bull.* 76, 105 (1971).
6. ——, *Cognitive Psychol.* **5**, 207 (1973).
7. R. C. Galbraith and B. J. Underwood, *Mem. Cognition* **1**, 56 (1973).
8. L. J. Chapman and J. P. Chapman, *J. Abnorm. Psychol.* **73**, 193 (1967); *ibid.*, 74, 271 (1969).
9. M. Bar-Hillel, *Organ. Behav. Hum. Performance* **9**, 396 (1973).
10. J. Cohen, E. I. Chesnick, D. Haran, *Br. J. Psychol.* **63**, 41 (1972).
11. M. Alpert and H. Raiffa, unpublished manuscript; C. A. S. von Holstein, *Acta Psychol*, **35**, 478 (1971); R. L. Winkler, *J. Am. Stat. Assoc.* 62, 776 (1967).
12. L. J. Savage, *The Foundations of Statistics* (Wiley, New York, 1954).
13. B. De Finetti, in *International Encyclopedia of the Social Sciences*, D. E. Sills, Ed. (Macmillan, New York, 1968), vol. 12, pp. 496–504.
14. This research was supported by the Advanced Research Projects Agency of the Department of Defense and was monitored by the Office of Naval Research under contract N00014-73-C-0438 to the Oregon Research Institute, Eugene. Additional support for this research was provided by the Research and Development Authority of the Hebrew University, Jerusalem, Israel.

Ease of Retrieval as Information: Another Look at the Availability Heuristic

Norbert Schwarz, Fritz Strack, Herbert Bless, Gisela Klumpp,
Helga Rittenauer-Schatka, and Annette Simons

Experienced ease of recall was found to qualify the implications of recalled content. Ss who had to recall 12 examples of assertive (unassertive) behaviors, which was difficult, rated themselves as less assertive (less unassertive) than subjects who had to recall 6 examples, which was easy. In fact, Ss reported higher assertiveness after recalling 12 unassertive rather than 12 assertive behaviors. Thus, self-assessments only reflected the implications of recalled content if recall was easy. The impact of ease of recall was eliminated when its informational value was discredited by a misattribution manipulation. The informative functions of subjective experiences are discussed.

One of the most widely shared assumptions in decision making as well as in social judgment research holds that people estimate the frequency of an

The reported research is based in part on the diploma theses of Gisela Klumpp, Annette Simons (Experiment 1), and Helga Rittenauer-Schatka (Experiment 2), conducted at the Universität Heidelberg under the direction of Norbert Schwarz, Herbert Bless, and Fritz Strack. The studies were supported by Grants Schw278/2 and Str264/2 from the Deutsche Forschungsgemeinschaft to Norbert Schwarz and Fritz Strack and Grant Schw278/5 to Norbert Schwarz, Herbert Bless, and Gerd Bohner.

We thank Leslie Clark, Tory Higgins, Bob Wyer, and three anonymous reviewers for helpful comments on a draft of the article.

Correspondence concerning this article should be addressed to Norbert Schwarz, Zentrum für Umfragen, Methoden und Analysen, ZUMA, P.O. Box 122155, D-6800 Mannheim, Federal Republic of Germany.

event, or the likelihood of its occurrence, "by the ease with which instances or associations come to mind" (Tversky & Kahneman, 1973, p. 208). Since Tversky and Kahneman introduced this *availability heuristic*, it has stimulated a tremendous amount of research in social cognition (see Sherman & Corty, 1984; Strack, 1985, for reviews). However, the classic studies on the issue are surprisingly ambiguous regarding the underlying process. For example, in the most frequently cited study (Tversky & Kahneman, 1973, Experiment 8), subjects were read two lists of names, one presenting 19 famous men and 20 less famous women and the other presenting 19 famous women and 20 less famous men. When asked, subjects reported that there were more men than women in the first list but more women than men in the second list, even though the opposite was true (by a difference of 1). Presumably, the famous names were easier to recall than the nonfamous ones, resulting in an overestimate. In fact, subjects were able to recall about 50% more of the famous than of the nonfamous names. It remains unclear, however, what drives the overestimate: Were subjects' judgments based on the phenomenal experience of the ease or difficulty with which they could bring the famous and nonfamous names to mind, as Tversky and Kahneman's interpretation suggests? Or were their judgments based on the content of their recall, with famous names being overrepresented in the recalled sample?

In a related study (Tversky & Kahneman, 1973, Experiment 3), subjects were found to overestimate the number of words that began with the letter *r* but to underestimate the number of words that had *r* as the third letter. Similarly, Gabrielcik and Fazio (1984) observed that exposing subjects to subliminally presented words containing the letter *t* increased subjects' estimates of the frequency of *t* words. Again, these findings may reflect either that subjects could generate more words beginning with an *r*, or including a *t* if primed or that they relied on the ease with which relevant exemplars could be called to mind. Similar ambiguities apply to other studies (see Sherman & Corty, 1984; Strack, 1985; Taylor, 1982, for reviews). Typically, the manipulations that are introduced to increase the subjectively experienced ease of recall are also likely to affect the amount of subjects' recall. As a result, it is difficult to evaluate if the obtained estimates of frequency, likelihood, or typicality are based on subjects' subjective experiences or on a biased sample of recalled information. As Taylor (1982) noted, the latter possibility would render the availability heuristic rather trivial — after all, "one's judgments are always based on what comes to mind" (p. 199).

In the present article, we report three studies that were designed to disentangle the impact of content of recall and of the subjective experience of ease or difficulty that may accompany recall. In all studies, we introduced conditions under which the implications of experienced ease of recall were opposite to the implications of the content of recall per se. In addition, we manipulated the perceived diagnosticity of the experienced ease of recall, using misattribution manipulations (Experiment 3). We first introduce the basic logic and the findings of our experiments and subsequently discuss the informational functions of experienced ease of recall in the context of a more general conceptualization of the informational functions of subjective experiences (Schwarz, 1990; Schwarz & Clore, 1988).

Experiment 1: If It Is So Difficult to Recall, It Cannot Be Typical

Suppose that people are asked to report a certain number of examples of particularly assertive, or of particularly unassertive, behaviors that they have recently engaged in. Presumably, reporting these behaviors would increase their cognitive accessibility in memory, making it more likely that these behaviors come to mind when the people are later asked to evaluate their own assertiveness. As a result, one should find that people who had to report assertive behaviors report higher assertiveness than people who had to report unassertive behaviors, reflecting that the previously reported examples resulted in a biased sample of relevant behaviors. As long as people consider only the content of what they recall, the more examples they have to report, the more pronounced this effect should be. Such content-based predictions may be derived from numerous models of self-related judgment (e.g., Bem, 1972; Wyer & Srull, 1989).

Suppose, however, that people not only rely on what comes to mind but also pay attention to the subjective experiences that accompany the recall process. If so, the subjective experience that it is very difficult to recall examples of one's own assertive behaviors may imply that one cannot be that assertive after all, or thinking of examples would not be that difficult. To the extent that the experienced difficulty of recall increases with the number of examples that are to be reported, ease of recall and content of recall would lead to different conclusions: Whereas the content of the recalled examples would suggest that one is very assertive (or very unassertive), the difficulty experienced in recalling these examples would suggest that they cannot be frequent and typical. Hence, one may conclude that one is probably not as assertive (or unassertive) as the recalled behaviors would seem to imply. Accordingly, the experienced difficulty of recall may qualify the implications of recalled content.

In Experiment 1, we tested this prediction by asking subjects to describe either 6 or 12 examples of very assertive or very unassertive behaviors in which they had engaged. Pretests indicated that most subjects could easily generate 8 or 9 behaviors but found it very difficult to generate more than 10. Subsequently, subjects were asked to rate their own assertiveness along several items.

If subjects base assessments of their own assertiveness solely on the relevant behavior that comes to mind, subjects who have to report examples of assertive behavior should rate themselves as more assertive than subjects who have to report examples of unassertive behavior. Moreover, the more examples subjects have to report, the more pronounced the impact of recalled content should be. Thus, a content-based judgment process will predict additive effects of type of example and number of examples requested. If subjects consider the content of their recall in the light of the ease or difficulty with which they can generate the requested examples, however, these additive effects should not be obtained. Rather, the impact of recalled content should be less pronounced, the more examples subjects have to report because the difficulty of doing so should imply that the recalled examples are not very frequent and typical. Hence, subjects should rate themselves as less assertive (or unassertive) after recalling 12 rather than 6 examples, indicating that the implications of recalled content are qualified by the ease or difficulty with which this content could be brought to mind.

Method

Forty female students at a German university participated in a 2 (examples of assertive vs. unassertive behaviors) × 2 (6 vs. 12 examples) factorial between-subjects experiment. Subjects were randomly assigned to conditions and tested in groups of 4.

All subjects were informed that the study was concerned with developing role-playing scenarios that could be used in future relaxation training. To help with the development of these scenarios, they were asked to describe either 6 or 12 examples of situations in which they "behaved very assertively and felt at ease" or of situations in which they "behaved unassertively and felt insecure." Pretests indicated that generating 6 examples was experienced as an easy task, whereas generating 12 examples was difficult. Subjects reported their examples on answer sheets that provided three lines for each example.

After completion of this task, subjects were asked to answer some general questions, purportedly designed to explore students' interest in participating in a relaxation-training program. These questions asked subjects to evaluate their assertiveness, their feelings of insecurity, and their feelings of anxiety along 10-point scales. Given the high internal consistency of these ratings (Cronbach's alpha = .76), the mean of these ratings was used as the major dependent variable; higher values indicated higher assertiveness.

In addition, subjects rated how difficult it was to generate the requested number of examples on a scale ranging from *not at all difficult* (1) to *very difficult* (10), thus providing a direct measure of experienced ease of recall.

TABLE 11.1. Ratings of Assertiveness as a Function of Valence and Number of Recalled Behaviors

	Type of Behavior	
No. Recalled Examples	Assertive	Unassertive
6	6.3	5.2
12	5.2	6.2

Note: n = 9 or 10 per condition. Mean score of three questions is given; possible range is 1 to 10; higher values reflect higher assertiveness.

Results

Manipulation Check

Analyses of subjects' reported ease of retrieval indicated that subjects found it easier to report 6 ($M = 5.1$) rather than 12 ($M = 7.2$) examples, $F(1, 36) = 4.2$, $p < .05$. No other effect emerged ($F < 1$).

Mean Differences

As shown in Table 11.1, subjects who had to describe examples of assertive behaviors rated themselves as more assertive after describing 6 ($M = 6.3$) rather than 12 ($M = 5.2$) examples. Conversely, subjects who had to describe examples of unassertive behaviors rated themselves as less assertive after describing 6 ($M = 5.2$) rather than 12 ($M = 6.2$) examples. This crossover pattern was reflected in a marginally significant Valence × Number of Examples Requested interaction, $F(1, 36) = 3.40$, $p < .07$[1], whereas neither of the main effects reached significance ($F < 1$).[1]

These findings indicate that subjects did consider the experienced ease of recall in evaluating their own assertiveness. In fact, subjects rated themselves as more assertive after describing examples of assertive rather than unassertive behaviors only if the recall task was easy. When the recall task was difficult, their self-rating was opposite to the implications of recalled content, despite the fact that more examples had been recalled. This pattern of findings could not be accounted for on the basis of recalled content per se.[2] Rather, it reflected that the implications of recalled content were qualified by the ease with which the respective content could be brought to mind.

---

[1] The statistical weakness of this interaction is of little concern because this pattern replicates consistently in subsequent experiments.
[2] It was conceivable, however, that the representativeness of the recalled examples decreased with increasing number of examples requested. This issue was addressed in Experiment 2, which ruled out this possibility, as described below.

Correlational Analyses

This conclusion is further supported by correlational analyses. Specifically, the more difficult subjects who had to recall assertive behaviors found the recall task, the lower the assertiveness they reported, $r(20) = -.35$, $p = .12$. In contrast, the more difficult subjects who had to report examples of unassertive behaviors found the task, the higher the assertiveness they reported, $r(20) = .66$, $p < .002$. Both correlations differ reliably from one another ($z = 3.38$, $p < .001$).

Discussion

In summary, the present findings suggest that the content of recall affected self-judgments in the direction of the valence of the recalled behaviors only if the recall process itself was experienced as easy. If the recall process elicited experiences of difficulty, on the other hand, the content of recall affected self-judgments in a direction opposite to the implications of the recalled behaviors. Hence, we may conclude that the phenomenal experience of ease or difficulty of recall may qualify the implications of what comes to mind, even to the extent that the inferences drawn are opposite in valence to the implications of recalled content.

Experiment 2: An Extended Replication

Given the marginal significance of the interaction obtained in Experiment 1, a replication of this finding would be welcome. Experiment 2 was designed to provide this replication and extended the previous study by manipulating the perceived diagnosticity of experienced ease of retrieval. Subjects were again asked to report 6 or 12 examples of assertive or unassertive behavior. However, some subjects were informed that most participants of a previous study had found it easy to complete this task, whereas other subjects were told that most previous participants found the task difficult. We expected that subjects who were told that their subjective experience of ease or difficulty of recall was shared by most other subjects would be likely to attribute their experience to characteristics of the task. If so, they might perceive their subjective experience of ease or difficulty as being less diagnostic and might therefore be less likely to consider it when making a self-judgment (cf. Kelley, 1967). In contrast, subjects who were told that their own experience of ease or difficulty contradicted the typical experience of similar others might be more likely to perceive their apparently unique phenomenal experience as

reflecting the frequency of the respective behaviors in their own repertoire. If so, they would be more likely to rely on their subjective experience of ease or difficulty of retrieval in making self-judgments.

Method

One hundred fifty-eight students (113 women and 45 men) of a West German teachers' college were asked to report either 6 or 12 examples of assertive or unassertive behavior and were informed either that most previous participants had found it easy or that most previous participants had found it difficult to complete this task. The latter manipulation should increase the perceived diagnosticity of ease or difficulty of retrieval under conditions in which subjects' own experience deviates from the alleged experience of previous participants, that is, in which subjects find the task easy (6 examples) but are told others found it difficult or in which subjects find the task difficult (12 examples) but are told others found it easy. Conversely, this information should decrease perceived diagnosticity under conditions in which subjects' experience coincides with the alleged experience of most other participants.

In combination, these manipulations constituted a 2 (examples of assertive vs. unassertive behaviors) × 2 (6 vs. 12 examples) × 2 (low vs. high diagnosticity of ease of recall) factorial between-subjects design. Subjects were randomly assigned to conditions, and all subjects were tested in one session in a lecture hall setting.

The cover story and procedure used closely followed the procedure described in Experiment 1, except that the study was said to be concerned with the development of assertiveness (rather than relaxation) training. After completing the requested number of examples, subjects responded to a short questionnaire that purportedly assessed students' interest in participating in assertiveness training. Specifically, subjects rated their own assertiveness, their desire to be more assertive, and their interest in assertiveness training along 9-point bipolar scales. The mean score of these variables (Cronbach's alpha = .72) was used as the dependent variable; high values indicated high assertiveness.

Results

Manipulation Check

Analysis of variance again indicated that subjects experienced recalling 6 examples as easier ($M = 4.8$) than recalling 12 examples ($M = 7.4$), $F(1, 142) = 5.2$, $p < .02$. No other effect reached significance.

TABLE 11.2. Ratings of Assertiveness as a Function of Valence and Number of Recalled Behaviors and Others' Ease of Recall

No. Recalled Examples	Diagnosticity of Ease of Recall			
	Low		High	
	Assert	Unassert	Assert	Unassert
6	5.1	5.0	5.2	4.5
12	4.7	5.2	4.7	5.4

Note. n = 18 to 20 per condition. Mean score of five questions is given; possible range is 1 to 9; higher values reflect higher assertiveness. Assert = assertive; Unassert = unassertive.

Mean Differences

Analyses of variance including subjects' sex revealed a main effect of sex, $F(1, 142) = 7.15$, $p < .01$, indicating that men reported higher assertiveness than did women. However, sex of subjects did not interact with any of the experimental variables (all $F < 1$) and was therefore ignored in the following analyses.

As shown in Table 11.2, the present study replicated the previous findings. Specifically, subjects who had to describe examples of assertive behaviors rated themselves as more assertive after describing 6 examples $(M = 5.2)$ rather than 12 examples $(M = 4.7)$. Conversely, subjects who had to describe examples of unassertive behavior rated themselves as less assertive after describing 6 examples $(M = 4.7)$ rather than 12 examples $(M = 5.3)$. This crossover pattern was reflected in a significant Valence × Number of Examples Requested interaction, $F(1, 142) = 6.35$, $p < .02$. As in Experiment 1, no main effects of valence or number of examples emerged $(F < 1)$.

Contrary to predictions, however, the manipulation of the perceived diagnosticity of the experienced ease of recall had no significant impact on subjects' self-assessment. Although separate analyses revealed a significant Valence × Number of Examples interaction under high-diagnosticity conditions, $F(1, 76) = 5.98$, $p < .03$, but not under low-diagnosticity conditions $(F < 1)$, the triple interaction failed to reach significance $(F < 1)$. We return to this issue below.

Correlational Analyses

The interpretation that subjects' self-assessments of assertiveness were mediated by the subjective experience of ease of retrieval is again supported by correlational analyses. Specifically, subjects who had to report examples of unassertive behavior reported higher assertiveness the more difficult they found the task $(r = .32$, $p < .002)$. In contrast, subjects who had to report examples of assertive behavior reported lower assertiveness the more difficult they found the task $(r = -.12$, $p = .15)$, and both correlations differ significantly from one another $(z = 2.77, p < .003)$.

Self-perception

A possible alternative account of the obtained findings of this and the previous experiment required additional analyses. To the extent that recalling many examples is difficult, the more examples subjects are to report, the more the representativeness of the recalled examples may decrease. Thus, subjects who have to recall 12 examples may eventually include examples that are less extreme to complete their task. If so, a content-based judgmental process may produce a similar pattern of findings, reflecting that the inclusion of less extreme examples may dilute the impact of more extreme ones (cf. Nisbett, Zukier, & Lemley, 1981).

To test this possibility, the extremity of the last two examples provided by 5 randomly selected subjects from each condition of Experiment 2 was rated by two independent judges on a scale ranging from *very unassertive* (1) to *very assertive* (11). Interrater reliability was high $(r = .92)$, and examples of assertive behaviors $(M = 9.6)$ differed reliably from examples of unassertive behaviors $(M = 2.8)$, $F(1, 32) = 663.0, p < .001$. More important, planned comparisons indicated that the last 2 examples provided by subjects who had to report 12 examples were, if anything, better exemplars of the requested type of behavior than the last 2 examples provided by subjects who had to recall only 6 examples: $(Ms = 9.8$ and $9.4)$, $F < 1$, for 12 and 6 assertive behaviors, respectively; $(Ms = 2.3$ and $3.3)$, $F(1, 32) = 4.26, p < .05$, for 12 and 6 unassertive behaviors, respectively.

Thus, although differences in the quality of the recalled behaviors did emerge in the unassertive examples conditions, these differences were opposite to those found in subjects' judgments, lending no support to the hypothesis that subjects' judgments were mediated by differential content rather than by the subjective experience of ease of recall.

Discussion

In summary, Experiment 2 replicated the previously obtained interaction, indicating that the implications of recalled content were qualified by the ease with which this content could be brought to mind. In contrast to our expectations, however, informing subjects that most previous participants found the task easy or difficult, respectively, did not result in a significant triple interaction, although separate analyses under each diagnosticity condition provided some support for our reasoning. In retrospect, the standard that we introduced might have been less relevant for subjects' self-judgments than we had assumed a priori: Whereas the diagnosticity manipulation referred to others' experience, the requested judgment was not a comparative one. Individuals may use their own feelings and aspirations, rather than the behavior of others, in evaluating how assertive they are. If they can easily recall situations in which they behaved unassertively, for example, this may be bothersome no matter if others can do so just as easily or not. Moreover, informing subjects about others' experienced ease or difficulty of recall may have focused their attention even more on their own phenomenal experience, thus increasing its impact. Accordingly, a different manipulation of the diagnosticity of ease of retrieval is used in Experiment 3.

At the same time, the failure to obtain a pronounced impact of the alleged typical recall performance renders a possible variation of the ease-of-recall account less plausible. Specifically, one might argue that asking subjects to report 12 examples of a given class of behaviors may convey that most people are probably able to do so. If so, the experienced difficulty in meeting this expectation might imply that one has less of the respective trait than many other people. Accordingly, the obtained findings would reflect the experience of ease or difficulty in meeting a certain standard, rather than the experience of ease or difficulty of recall per se. If so, however, one would expect a pronounced impact of explicit information about the ease or difficulty with which others can perform the recall task. That this manipulation showed little effect renders an ease-of-meeting-a-standard account less compelling.

Experiment 3: Misattributing the Ease of Recall

Reflecting the assumption that others' performance may not be germane to the informational value of subjective experiences, as discussed above, a different manipulation of perceived diagnosticity of ease of retrieval was used in Experiment 3. As previous research on the informational functions of another subjective experience — namely mood — indicated, the diagnosticity of subjective states can be manipulated by misattribution manipulations. For example, attributing one's feelings correctly (Schwarz & Clore, 1983, Experiment 1) or incorrectly (Schwarz & Clore, 1983, Experiment 2; Schwarz, Servay, & Kumpf, 1985) to a transient source that is irrelevant to the judgment at hand was found to

eliminate the impact of affective states on subsequent judgments (see Schwarz, 1987, 1990; Schwarz & Clore, 1988, for reviews). Similarly, misattributing one's arousal to an irrelevant source (e.g., Zanna & Cooper, 1974; Zillman & Bryant, 1974) was found to eliminate the effects of arousal states (see Zanna & Cooper, 1976; Zillman, 1978, for reviews).

Following these lines of research, we introduced a misattribution manipulation in Experiment 3. Specifically, we informed subjects that the study was concerned with the impact of different types of music on the recall of autobiographical experiences. All subjects were exposed, by means of headphones, to a piece of meditation music. Some subjects were informed that this music facilitated the recall of situations in which one behaved assertively and felt at ease, whereas others were informed that it facilitated the recall of situations in which one behaved unassertively and felt insecure. After these instructions, subjects had to describe either 6 or 12 examples of assertive or unassertive behaviors, replicating the previous experiments.

Following Kelley's (1972) reasoning about augmentation and discounting effects, we expected the alleged side effects of exposure to meditation music to moderate the impact of subjects' experienced ease of recall on their self-assessment of assertiveness. Most important, subjects whose subjective experience contradicted the alleged side effect of the music would consider this experience particularly diagnostic and would use it in their self-assessment. Accordingly, their self-rating would only reflect the content of recall if recall was easy, and not if it was difficult, replicating the previously obtained findings.

Predictions are somewhat more complex, however, for subjects who can attribute their subjective experience to the music, thus rendering it nondiagnostic. On the one hand, these subjects may turn to the content of their recall to evaluate their assertiveness, given that the informational value of their subjective experience has been discredited. If so, they should report higher assertiveness after recalling 12 rather than 6 examples of assertive behaviors and lower assertiveness after recalling 12 rather than 6 examples of unassertive behaviors, despite the difficulty that they experienced in doing so. Thus, within each valence condition, discrediting the informative value of experienced ease or difficulty of recall should result in a data pattern that is opposite to the pattern observed in the previous experiments.

On the other hand, discrediting the informational value of experienced ease of retrieval may lead to self-assessments that are opposite to the implications of recalled content under some conditions. Much as self-assessments were found to deviate from the content of recall when recall was difficult, they may be expected to deviate from the content of recall if recall is easy, but for the wrong reasons. Specifically, subjects who can easily recall 6 examples of assertive (or unassertive) behavior but attribute the experienced ease to the alleged impact of the music may discount their subjective experience. This may render the typicality and frequency of the recalled behaviors dubious, resulting in lower ratings of assertiveness (or unassertiveness, respectively). If so, subjects who had to report 6 examples of assertive behavior may actually rate themselves as less assertive than subjects who had to recall 6 examples of unassertive behaviors under these conditions. A similar prediction cannot be derived, however, for subjects who have to recall 12 examples under low-diagnosticity conditions. In this case, the misattribution manipulation implies that the impact of the music may render recall difficult, suggesting that the content of recall is informative despite the experienced difficulty. Accordingly, these subjects' self-ratings should reflect content, and no reversal between valence conditions should be obtained.

In summary, discrediting the informative value of experienced ease of recall may result in a data pattern that is opposite to the pattern observed in the previous experiments, either within or between the valence conditions, whereas the previously obtained pattern should replicate when the informational value of subjects' phenomenal experience is not called into question.

Method

Seventy-eight female students of a West German university participated in a 2 (examples of assertive vs. unassertive behaviors) $\times$ 2 (6 vs. 12 examples) $\times$ 2 (high vs. low diagnosticity of experienced ease of recall) factorial between-subjects experiment. Subjects were randomly assigned to conditions and received all instructions from cassette players by means of headphones.

Subjects were told that the study was part of a research program concerned with the impact of music on the recall of autobiographical memories of different emotional valence. The present study was said to investigate the recall of a specific type of situation, namely situations in which one felt insecure or felt assertive and at ease, respectively. Accordingly, subjects were asked to describe either 6 or 12 examples of situations in which they "behaved *assertively* and felt at ease" or of situations in which they "behaved *unassertively* and felt

insecure" while listening to meditation music, presented by means of headphones.

To manipulate the perceived diagnosticity of experienced ease of recall, subjects were told that the music was known to facilitate the recall of autobiographical memories that pertain to experiences characterized by assertiveness or by insecurity, respectively. If the music is said to facilitate the respective recall task, this alleged side effect should result in low diagnosticity of the experienced ease of retrieval associated with recalling 6 examples but high diagnosticity of the difficulty associated with recalling 12 examples. Conversely, if the music is said to facilitate recall of experiences that are opposite in valence to those the person is asked to recall, this should imply high diagnosticity of easy recall but low diagnosticity of difficult recall.

To draw attention to the alleged impact of the music, subjects were exposed to the music for 30 s and were asked to rate the music along several items before they began to work on the recall task. In addition, it was emphasized that the music might only develop its impact after a certain amount of exposure, and subjects were told that the time of exposure was varied in the present study. This information seemed necessary because the subjective experience of difficulty of recall does only emerge after a certain number of examples are reported. To draw attention to this information, subjects received a note that said the following:

> You will be exposed to the music
> ( ) for the first four minutes,
> ( ) for the first eight minutes,
> ( ) for the full duration of the recall task.

For all subjects, the full duration option was checked by the experimenter.

Following this information, subjects provided descriptions of the requested behavioral examples while listening to the music. Subsequently, they rated their own assertiveness, as well their desire to be more assertive, along 9-point scales. The mean score of these ratings was used as the major dependent variable, with higher values indicating higher assertiveness. In addition, a rating of the experienced ease of retrieval was obtained on a scale ranging from *easy* (1) to *difficult* (9).

Results and Discussion

Manipulation Check
As in the previous studies, subjects reported that recalling 6 examples ($M = 5.9$) was easier than recalling 12

examples ($M = 6.7$), although this difference did not reach significance, $F(1, 70) = 1.76$, *ns*. No other effects emerged.

Mean Differences

Subjects' self-ratings of assertiveness are shown in Table 11.3, as a function of the experimental variables. Analysis of variance again indicated a significant Valence × Number of Examples Requested interaction, $F(1, 70) = 4.09$, $p < .04$. However, this interaction was qualified by a significant triple interaction, $F(1, 70) = 9.75$, $p < .001$, involving level of diagnosticity of experienced ease of retrieval.

Diagnoses of this triple interaction revealed that the previously obtained Valence × Number of Examples Requested interaction was restricted to conditions in which the alleged side effects of the music did not discredit the diagnosticity of experienced ease or difficulty of retrieval, $F(1, 70) = 5.97$, $p < .02$, for the simple interaction under high diagnosticity. Specifically, subjects who had to recall assertive behaviors reported higher assertiveness after describing 6 examples ($M = 5.6$) rather than 12 examples ($M = 4.5$), $t(70) = 1.55$, $p < .06$, one-tailed. Conversely, subjects who had to recall unassertive behaviors rated themselves as less assertive after describing 6 examples ($M = 3.1$) rather than 12 examples ($M = 4.4$), $t(70) = 1.91$, $p < .03$, one-tailed. This pattern replicates the key findings of Experiments 1 and 2, further illustrating the robustness of the effect, although no crossover was obtained in the present study.

This was not so, however, under low-diagnosticity conditions, in which the alleged side effects of the music rendered the experienced ease or difficulty of retrieval uninformative. In that case, comparisons within each valence condition suggest that subjects tended to rely on the content of recall, rather than on the ease with which that content came to mind. Specifically, subjects who

had to report examples of assertive behaviors reported higher assertiveness after recalling 12 ($M = 4.8$) rather than 6 ($M = 3.9$) examples, $t(70) = 1.27$, $p < .10$, one-tailed. Similarly, subjects who had to recall examples of unassertive behaviors reported being less assertive after recalling 12 ($M = 4.0$) rather than 6 ($M = 5.11$) examples, $t(70) = 1.52$, $p < .06$, one-tailed. This impact of content of recall is reflected in a simple interaction that is opposite in direction to the one obtained under high diagnosticity conditions, $F(1, 70) = 3.88$, $p < .06$.

At the same time, diagnosis of this simple interaction by comparisons between both valence conditions indicates that subjects who had to recall 6 examples of assertive behaviors rated themselves as less assertive ($M = 3.9$) than subjects who had to recall 6 examples of unassertive behaviors ($M = 5.1$), $t(70) = 1.59$, $p < .06$, one-tailed. This suggests that subjects discounted the experienced ease of retrieval, resulting in a reversal between both valence conditions. Finally, such a reversal was not obtained when subjects had to recall 12 examples ($M = 4.8$ and 4.0 for assertive and unassertive examples, respectively), as suggested by the reasoning outlined in the introduction to this study.

In summary, the previously obtained Valence × Number of Examples interaction only emerged when the informational value of subjects' subjective experience of ease or difficulty of recall was not discredited. When the alleged side effects of the music did discredit the implications of subjects' subjective experience, subjects did not rely on their subjective experience. Rather, subjects who had to recall 6 examples of assertive behaviors reported lower assertiveness than subjects who had to recall 6 examples of unassertive behavior, presumably reflecting that they discounted the experienced ease of retrieval. This latter finding renders comparisons within each valence condition under low diagnosticity somewhat ambiguous, which would otherwise suggest that subjects in the low diagnosticity conditions relied primarily on the content of recall, as reflected in the more pronounced impact of recalling 12 rather than 6 examples.

TABLE 11.3. Ratings of Assertiveness as a Function of Valence, Number of Recalled Behaviors, and Diagnosticity of Ease of Recall

| No. Recalled Examples | Diagnosticity of Ease of Recall | | | |
| | Low | | High | |
	Assert	Unassert	Assert	Unassert
6	3.9	5.1	5.6	3.1
12	4.8	4.0	4.5	4.4

Note. n is 9 or 10 per condition. Mean score of two questions is given; possible range is 1 to 9; higher values reflect higher assertiveness. Assert = assertive; Unassert = unassertive.

Correlational Analyses

As in the previous experiments, subjects who had to recall examples of unassertive behaviors reported higher assertiveness the more difficult they found the recall task ($r = .23$, $p = .15$), provided that the diagnosticity of ease of recall was not called into question. When the diagnosticity of ease of recall was discredited, on the other hand, both variables were uncorrelated ($r = .05$), as would be expected on the basis of the present theorizing, although the difference between correlations did not reach significance ($z = .60$). Finally, no significant correlation of reported ease of recall and assertiveness emerged under either high ($r = .03$) or low ($r = -.02$) diagnosticity conditions for subjects who had to report examples of assertive behavior, in contrast to the previous experiments. Subjects might have taken the induced expectations into account in making their ratings, thus obscuring the correlational relationships obtained in the previous experiments.

General Discussion

Ease of Recall as Information

In combination, the reported findings provide consistent support for the assumption that the implications of recalled content may be qualified by the ease or difficulty with which that content can be brought to mind. Although this assumption has enjoyed great popularity since Tversky and Kahneman's (1973) introduction of the availability heuristic, it had not been adequately tested in previous studies. Most important, these studies were open to the alternative interpretation that manipulations that affected the ease of recall could just as well affect the content of recall. Accordingly, the obtained findings could either be attributed to biased recall, reflecting what has been called the accessibility bias (cf. Iyengar, 1990) or to the accompanying subjective experience of greater ease of retrieval, reflecting the operation of the availability heuristic (Tversky & Kahneman, 1973), as Taylor (1982) noted.

By constructing conditions under which the implications of what was recalled contradicted the implications of the subjectively experienced ease or difficulty with which it came to mind, we could disentangle the impact of both sources of information. In three experiments, subjects attributed themselves higher assertiveness after recalling 6 rather than 12 examples of assertive behavior and lower assertiveness after recalling 6 rather than 12 examples of unassertive behavior. If their judgment was solely based on the content of what they recalled, their self-attributions should have been more extreme the more examples they recalled — in particular because content analyses of the reported examples (presented as part of Experiment 2) provided no evidence that the larger number of examples requested decreased their representativeness. Accordingly, a judgmental process that is based on recalled content as the only

source of information cannot account for the observed results.

Rather, the present findings indicate that people paid attention to the subjective experience of ease or difficulty of recall in drawing inferences from recalled content. Apparently, our subjects concluded that they can't be that assertive (or unassertive) if it is so difficult to recall the requested number of examples. In line with that assumption, their ratings of ease of recall were positively correlated with their self-assessment of assertiveness if they had to report examples of assertive behavior but were negatively correlated if they had to report examples of unassertive behavior. Most important, however, discrediting the experienced ease of recall by misattribution manipulations (Experiment 3) reversed the otherwise obtained pattern of findings. In this case, subjects reported higher assertiveness after recalling 12 rather than 6 examples of assertive behavior and lower assertiveness after recalling 12 rather than 6 examples of unassertive behavior.

In summary, we conclude that people not only consider what they recall in making a judgment but also use the ease or difficulty with which that content comes to mind as an additional source of information. Most notably, they only rely on the content of their recall if its implications are not called into question by the difficulty that they experience in bringing the relevant material to mind. In Experiments 1 and 2, the difficulty of recalling 12 examples qualified the conclusions drawn from the content of recall to such a degree that the obtained judgments were, in fact, opposite to the implications of recalled content. Thus, the present studies extend previous research on the availability heuristic by drawing attention to the other end of the ease-of-recall continuum: Our findings suggest that difficulty in recall may decrease judgments of frequency, probability, or typicality, much as ease of recall has been assumed to increase these judgments.

Informative Functions of Subjective Experiences

In addition to bearing on the operation of the availability heuristic, the present studies extend previous research on the informative functions of subjective experiences. This research has primarily been concerned with the informational value of affective states (see Schwarz, 1987, 1990; Schwarz & Clore, 1988, for reviews) and has demonstrated that people may use their perceived affective state as a source of information, according to a "how do I feel about it" heuristic (e.g., Schwarz & Clore, 1983; Schwarz et al., 1985; Schwarz, Strack, Kommer, & Wagner, 1987). In doing so, people (mis)interpret their pre-existing affective state as a reaction to the object of judgment, resulting in more favorable evaluations under elated than under depressed moods, unless the diagnosticity of their feelings for the judgment at hand is called into question. Accordingly, people were found to rely on their feelings at the time of judgment only under conditions in which they could assume those feelings to reflect their affective reaction to the object of judgment.

As Clore and Parrott (in press) noted, it is informative to apply this logic to the operation of the availability heuristic. In principle, the availability heuristic reflects the correct insight that it is easier to recall frequent rather than rare events. What renders this heuristic error prone is that the experienced ease of retrieval may reflect the impact of variables other than frequency, such as the event's salience or vividness (cf. Nisbett & Ross, 1980). Hence, we may conclude that inappropriate applications of the availability heuristic reflect a process of misattribution: People rely on their subjective experience of ease of retrieval to the extent that they (mis)attribute it to frequency of occurrence, rather than to the impact of other variables.

The same logic may be extended to other subjective experiences, such as feelings of familiarity. For example, Jacoby and Dallas (1981; see also Jacoby & Kelley, 1987; Jacoby, Kelley, Brown, & Jasechko, 1989) observed in a recognition experiment that subjects could accurately identify rare words that had previously been shown to them but provided numerous false alarms in response to common words. As Clore and Parrot (in press) noted, subjects "apparently misattributed to recency of exposure the sense of familiarity that actually came from frequency of exposure."

In fact, the current analysis may be extended to the operation of priming phenomena in general (cf. Clore & Parrott, in press). This research (see Higgins & Bargh, 1987; Martin & Clark, 1990, for reviews) indicates that exposure to a concept increases the likelihood that this, rather than another, concept is subsequently used in interpreting ambiguous information. However, this effect is only obtained if subjects are not aware of the potential impact of the priming episode. Specifically, correlational analyses reported by Lombardi, Higgins, and Bargh (1987) indicated that priming effects were limited to subjects who were not able to consciously recall the primed concepts. In a more direct experimental test, Strack, Schwarz, Bless, Kübler, and Wänke (1990) observed that priming effects were not obtained

when subjects were subtly reminded of the priming episode. These findings suggest that priming effects may only emerge if people misattribute the thoughts that come to mind to the impact of the stimulus information. If they, correctly, attribute the emerging thoughts to the impact of the priming procedure, on the other hand, priming effects seem unlikely to be obtained.

As this discussion indicates, social cognition research may benefit from paying closer attention to phenomenal experiences, a theme that has only recently captured researchers' attention (see Bargh, 1989; Jacoby & Kelley, 1987, for reviews). Although the default option is probably to use the content that comes to mind without further qualification, judgmental processes may also involve the use of subjective experiences as an additional source of data, which may qualify the implications of thought content. In using these data — be they affective states, the ease of retrieval, a sense of familiarity, or an emerging train of thoughts — people may pay attention to their possible causes to determine their informational value. Most important, they will only use these subjective experiences as a basis of judgment if they can (mis)attribute them to the impact of the object of judgment. Whereas much remains to be learned about the informative functions of different subjective experiences, the present discussion suggests that the general logic developed in research on the informative functions of affective states (see Clore & Parrott, in press; Schwarz, 1990; Schwarz & Clore, 1988) may provide a fruitful heuristic framework for their conceptualization.

REFERENCES

Bargh, J. A. (1989). Conditional automaticity: Varieties of automatic influence in social perception and cognition. In J. S. Uleman & J. A. Bargh (Eds.), *Unintended thought* (pp. 3–51). New York: Guilford Press.

Bem, D. J. (1972). Self-perception theory. In L. Berkowitz (Ed.), *Advances in experimental social psychology* (Vol. 6, pp. 1–62). San Diego, CA: Academic Press.

Clore, G. L., & Parrott, W. G. (in press). Moods and their vicissitudes: Thoughts and feelings as information. In J. Forgas (Ed.), *Emotion and social judgment.* Elmsford, NY: Pergamon Press.

Gabrielcik, A., & Fazio, R. H. (1984). Priming and frequency estimation: A strict test of the availability heuristic. *Personality and Social Psychology Bulletin, 10,* 85–89.

Higgins, E. T., & Bargh, J. A. (1987). Social cognition and social perception. *Annual Review of Psychology, 38,* 369–425.

Iyengar, S. (1990). The accessibility bias in politics: Television news and public opinion. *International Journal of Public Opinion Research, 2,* 1–15.

Jacoby, L. L., & Dallas, M. (1981). On the relationship between autobiographical memory and perceptual learning. *Journal of Experimental Psychology: General, 110,* 306–340.

Jacoby, L. L., & Kelley, C. M. (1987). Unconscious influences of memory for a prior event. *Personality and Social Psychology Bulletin, 13*, 314–336.

Jacoby, L. L., Kelley, C. M., Brown, J., & Jasechko, J. (1989). Becoming famous overnight: Limits on the ability to avoid unconscious influences of the past. *Journal of Personality and Social Psychology, 56*, 326–338.

Kelley, H. H. (1967). Attribution theory in social psychology. In D. Levine (Ed.), *Nebraska symposium on motivation* (Vol. 15, pp. 192–238). Lincoln: University of Nebraska Press.

Kelley, H. H. (1972). *Causal schemata and the attribution process.* Morristown, NJ: General Learning Press.

Lombardi, W. J., Higgins, E. T., & Bargh, J. A. (1987). The role of consciousness in priming effects on categorization: Assimilation versus contrast as a function of awareness of the priming task. *Personality and Social Psychology Bulletin, 13*, 411–429.

Martin, L. L., & Clark, L. F. (1990). Social cognition: Exploring the mental processes involved in human social interaction. In M. W. Eysenck (Ed.), *Cognitive psychology: An international review* (pp. 265–310). New York: Wiley.

Nisbett, R. E., & Ross, L. (1980). *Human inference: Strategies and shortcomings of social judgment.* Englewood Cliffs, NJ: Prentice-Hall.

Nisbett, R. E., Zukier, H., & Lemley, R. (1981). The dilution effect: Nondiagnostic information weakens the impact of diagnostic information. *Cognitive Psychology, 13*, 248–277.

Schwarz, N. (1987). *Stimmung als Information: Untersuchungen zum Einfluβ von Stimmungen auf die Bewertung des eigenen Lebens* [Mood as information]. West Berlin, Federal Republic of Germany: Springer-Verlag.

Schwarz, N. (1990). Feelings as information: Informational and motivational functions of affective states. In E. T. Higgins & R. Sorrentino (Eds.), *Handbook of motivation and cognition: Foundations of social behavior* (Vol. 2, pp. 527–561). New York: Guilford Press.

Schwarz, N., & Clore, G. L. (1983). Mood, misattribution, and judgments of well-being: Informative and directive functions of affective states. *Journal of Personality and Social Psychology, 45*, 513–523.

Schwarz, N., & Clore, G. L. (1988). How do I feel about it? Informative functions of affective states. In K. Fiedler & J. Forgas (Eds.), *Affect, cognition, and social behavior* (pp. 25–43). Toronto, Ontario, Canada: Hogrefe International.

Schwarz, N., Servay, W., & Kumpf, M. (1985). Attribution of arousal as a mediator of the effectiveness of fear-arousing communications. *Journal of Applied Social Psychology, 15*, 74–84.

Schwarz, N., Strack, F., Kommer, D., & Wagner, D. (1987). Soccer, rooms, and the quality of your life: Mood effects of judgments of satisfaction with life in general and with specific life-domains. *European Journal of Social Psychology, 17*, 69–79.

Sherman, S. J., & Corty, E. (1984). Cognitive heuristics. In R. S. Wyer & T. K. Srull (Eds.), *Handbook of social cognition* (Vol. 1, pp. 189–286). Hillsdale, NJ: Erlbaum.

Strack, F. (1985). Urteilsheuristiken [Judgmental heuristics]. In D. Frey & M. Irle (Eds.), *Theorien der Sozialpsychologie* (Vol. 3, pp. 239–267). Bern, Switzerland: Huber.

Strack, F., Schwarz, N., Bless, H., Kübler, A., & Wänke, M. (1990). *Remember the priming episode: A test of Jacoby's bifocational model of memory.* Manuscript submitted for publication.

Taylor, S. E. (1982). The availability bias in social perception and interaction. In D. Kahneman, P. Slovic, & A. Tversky (Eds.), *Judgment under uncertainty: Heuristics and biases* (pp. 190–200). Cambridge, England: Cambridge University Press.

Tversky, A., & Kahneman, D. (1973). Availability: A heuristic for judging frequency and probability. *Cognitive Psychology, 5*, 207–232.

Wyer, R. S., & Srull, T. K. (1989). *Memory and cognition in its social context.* Hillsdale, NJ: Erlbaum.

Zanna, M. P., & Cooper, J. (1974). Dissonance and the pill: An attribution approach to studying the arousal properties of dissonance. *Journal of Personality and Social Psychology, 29*, 703–709.

Zanna, M. P., & Cooper, J. (1976). Dissonance and the attribution process. In J. Harvey, W. Ickes, & R. F. Kidd (Eds.), *New directions in attribution research* (Vol. 1, pp. 199–217). Hillsdale, NJ: Erlbaum.

Zillman, D. (1978). Attribution and misattribution of excitatory reactions. In J. H. Harvey, W. I. Ickes, & R. F. Kidd (Eds.), *New directions in attribution research* (Vol. 2, pp. 335–368). Hillsdale, NJ: Erlbaum.

Zillman, D., & Bryant, J. (1974). Effect of residual excitation on the emotional response to provocation and delayed aggressive behavior. *Journal of Personality and Social Psychology, 30*, 782–791.

Received August 8, 1990
Revision received March 6,1991
Accepted March 21, 1991 ■

Egocentric Biases in Availability and Attribution

Michael Ross and Fiore Sicoly

Five experiments were conducted to assess biases in availability of information in memory and attributions of responsibility for the actions and decisions that occurred during a previous group interaction. The subject populations sampled included naturally occurring discussion groups, married couples, basketball teams, and groups assembled in the laboratory. The data provided consistent evidence for egocentric biases in availability and attribution: One's own contributions to a joint product were more readily available, that is, more frequently and easily recalled; individuals accepted more responsibility for a group product than other participants attributed to them. In addition, statements attributed to the self were recalled more accurately and the availability bias was attenuated, though not eliminated, when the group product was negatively evaluated (Experiment 2). Finally, when another participant's contributions were made more available to the individual via a selective retrieval process, the individual allocated correspondingly more responsibility for the group decisions to the coparticipant (Experiment 5). The determinants and pervasiveness of the egocentric biases are considered.

One instance of a phenomenon examined in the present experiments is familiar to almost anyone who has conducted joint research. Consider the following: You have worked on a research project with another person, and the question arises as to who should be "first author" (i.e., who contributed more to the final product?). Often, it seems that both of you feel entirely justified in claiming that honor. Moreover, since you are convinced that your view of reality must be shared by your colleague (there being only one reality), you assume that the other person is attempting to take advantage of you. Sometimes such concerns are settled or prevented by the use of arbitrary decision rules, for example, the rule of "alphabetical priority" — a favorite gambit of those whose surnames begin with letters in the first part of the alphabet.

We suggest, then, that individuals tend to accept more responsibility for a joint product than other contributors attribute to them. It is further proposed that this is a pervasive phenomenon when responsibility for a joint venture is allocated by the participants. In many common endeavors, however, the participants are unaware of their divergent views, since there is no need to assign "authorship"; consequently, the ubiquity of the phenomenon is not readily apparent. The purpose of the current research was to assess whether these egocentric perceptions do occur in a variety of settings and to examine associated psychological processes.

This research was supported by a Canada Council grant to the first author. We are grateful to the following people for their comments on earlier versions of this article: Dick Bootzin, Leslie McArthur, Hildy Ross, Lee Ross, Shelley Taylor, Amos Tversky, and Mark Zanna. We thank Vicky Vetere for collecting the data in Experiment 5.

Requests for reprints should be sent to Michael Ross, Department of Psychology, University of Waterloo, Waterloo, Ontario, Canada N2L 3G1.

In exploring the bases of such differential perceptions, we are not so naive as to suggest that intentional self-aggrandisement never occurs. Nonetheless, it is likely that perceptions can be at variance in the absence of deliberate deceit; it is from this perspective that we approach the issue.

To allocate responsibility for a joint endeavor, well-intentioned participants presumably attempt to recall the contributions each made to the final product. Some aspects of the interaction may be recalled more readily, or be more available, than others, however. In addition, the features that are recalled easily may not be a random subset of the whole. Specifically, a person may recall a greater proportion of his or her own contributions than would other participants.

An egocentric bias in availability of information in memory, in turn, could produce biased attributions of responsibility for a joint product. As Tversky and Kahneman (1973) have demonstrated, people use availability, that is, "the ease with which relevant instances come to mind" (p. 209), as a basis for estimating frequency. Thus, if self-generated inputs were indeed more available, individuals would be likely to claim more responsibility for a joint product than other participants would attribute to them.

There are at least four processes that may be operating to increase the availability of one's own contributions: (a) selective encoding and storage of information, (b) differential retrieval, (c) informational disparities, and (d) motivational influences.

Selective Encoding and Storage

For a number of reasons, the availability of the person's own inputs may be facilitated by differential encoding and storage of self-generated responses. First, individuals' own thoughts (about what they are going to say next, daydreams, etc.) or actions may distract their attention from the contributions of others. Second, individuals may rehearse or repeat their own ideas or actions; for example, they might think out their position before verbalizing and defending it. Consequently, their own inputs may receive more "study time," and degree of retention is strongly related to study time (Carver, 1972). Third, individuals' contributions are likely to fit more readily into their own cognitive schema, that is, their unique conception of the problem based on past experience, values, and so forth. Contributions that fit into such preexisting schemata are more likely to be retained (Bartlett. 1932; Bruner, 1961).

Differential Retrieval

The availability bias could also be produced by the selective retrieval of information from memory. In allocating responsibility for a joint outcome, the essential question from each participant's point of view may be, "How much did *I* contribute?" Participants may, therefore, attempt to recall principally their own contributions and inappropriately use the information so retrieved to estimate their *relative* contributions, a judgment that cannot properly be made without a consideration of the inputs of others as well.

Informational Disparities

There are likely to be differences in the information available to the contributors that could promote egocentric recall. Individuals have greater access to their own internal states, thoughts, and strategies than do observers. Moreover, participants in a common endeavor may differ in their knowledge of the frequency and significance of each other's independent contributions. For example, faculty supervisors may be less aware than their student colleagues of the amount of time, effort, or ingenuity that students invest in running subjects, performing data analyses, and writing preliminary drafts of a paper. On the other hand, supervisors are more cognizant of the amount and of the importance of the thought, reading, and so on that they put into the study before the students' involvement begins.

Motivational Influences

Motivational factors may also mediate an egocentric bias in availability. One's sense of self-esteem may be enhanced by focusing on, or weighting more heavily, one's own inputs. Similarly, a concern for personal efficacy or control (see deCharms, 1968; White, 1959) could lead individuals to dwell on their own contributions to a joint product.

The preceding discussion outlines a number of processes that may be operating to render one's own inputs more available (and more likely to be recalled) than the contributions of others. Consequently, it may be difficult to imagine a disconfirmation of the hypothesis that memories and attributions are egocentric. As Greenwald (Note 1) has observed, however, the egocentric character of memory "is not a necessary truth. It is possible, for example, to conceive of an organization of past experience that is more like that of some reference work, such as a history text, or the index of a thesaurus" (p. 4). In addition, we were unable to find published data directly supportive of the hypothesized bias in availability. Finally, recent developments in the actor–observer literature seem inconsistent with the hypothesis that memories and attributions are egocentric. Jones and Nisbett (1971) speculated that actors are disposed to locate the cause of their behavior in the environment, whereas observers attribute the same behavior to stable traits possessed by the actors. Though a variety of explanations were advanced to account for this effect (Jones & Nisbett, 1971), the recent emphasis has been on perceptual information processing (Storms, 1973; Taylor & Fiske, 1975). The actor's visual receptors are aimed toward the environment; an observer may focus directly on the actor. Thus, divergent aspects of the situation are salient to actors and observers, a disparity that is reflected in their causal attributions. This proposal seems to contradict the thesis that actors in an interaction are largely self-absorbed.

Two studies offer suggestive evidence for the present hypothesis. Rogers, Kuiper, and Kirker (1977) showed that trait adjectives were recalled more readily when subjects had been required to make a judgment about self-relevance (to decide whether each trait was descriptive of them) rather than about a number of other dimensions (e.g., synonymity judgments). These data imply that self-relevance increases availability; however, Rogers et al. did not contrast recall of adjectives relevant to the self with recall of adjectives relevant to other people — a comparison that would be more pertinent to the current discussion. Greenwald and Albert (1968) found that individuals recalled their own arguments on an attitude issue more accurately than the written arguments of other subjects. Since the arguments of self and other were always on opposite sides of the issue, the Greenwald and Albert finding could conceivably reflect increased familiarity with, and memory for, arguments consistent with one's own attitude position rather than enhanced memory for self-generated statements (although the evidence for attitude-biased learning is equivocal, e.g., Greenwald & Sakumura, 1967; Malpass, 1969).

We conducted a pilot study to determine whether we could obtain support for the hypothesized bias in availability. Students in an undergraduate seminar were asked to estimate the number of minutes each member of the seminar had spoken during the immediately preceding class period. An additional 26 subjects were obtained from naturally occurring two-person groups approached in cafeterias and lounges. The participants in these groups

were asked to estimate the percentage of the total time each person had spoken during the current interaction.

It was assumed that subjects would base their time estimates on those portions of the conversation they could recall readily. Thus, if there is a bias in the direction of better recall of one's own statements, individuals' estimates of the amount of time they themselves spoke should exceed the average speaking time attributed to them by the other member (s) of the group.

The results were consistent with this reasoning. For seven of the eight students in the undergraduate seminar, assessments of their own discussion time exceeded the average time estimate attributed to them by the other participants ($p < .05$, sign test). Similarly, in 10 of the 13 dyads, estimates of one's own discussion time exceeded that provided by the other participant ($p < .05$, sign test). The magnitude of the bias was highly significant over the 13 dyads, $F (1, 12) = 14.85$, $p < .005$; on the average, participants estimated that they spoke 59% of the time. These data provide preliminary, albeit indirect, evidence for the hypothesized availability bias in everyday situations.

The principle objectives of the current research were (a) to assess the ocurrence of egocentric biases in availability and attributions of responsibility in different settings; (b) to examine factors that were hypothesized to influence these biases; and (c) to offer preliminary evidence of a relation between a bias in availability and a bias in attributions of responsibility. Experiment 1 assessed the occurrence of egocentric biases in availability and allocations of responsibility in a natural setting and examined the relation between the two biases. Next, a laboratory experiment was conducted to address the issue of whether the quality of the group's performance affects the availability bias: Is the tendency for one's own inputs to be more available reduced substantially when the group's performance is poor, as a *motivational* interpretation would suggest? Experiment 3 further examined the effects of success and failure in a natural setting. The experimental manipulations in Experiments 4 and 5 were designed to influence availability, and changes in attributions of responsibility were assessed. The manipulation in Experiment 4 induced *differential encoding*; the manipulation in Experiment 5 varied the *retrieval* cues provided to the subjects.

Experiment 1

In this experiment, we wished to examine egocentric biases in naturally occurring, continuing relationships.

Married couples appeared to represent an ideal target group. Spouses engage in many joint endeavors of varying importance. This circumstance would appear to be rife with possibilities for egocentric biases.

Accordingly, the first experiment was conducted (a) to determine if egocentric biases in allocations of responsibility occur in marital relationships; (b) to replicate, using a different dependent measure, the egocentric bias in availability obtained in the pretest; and (c) to correlate the bias in availability with the bias in responsibility. If the bias in responsibility is caused by a bias in availability, the two sets of data should be related.

Method

Subjects

The subjects were 37 married couples living in student residences. Twenty of the couples had children. The subjects were recruited by two female research assistants who knocked on doors in the residences and briefly described the experiment. If the couple were willing to participate, an appointment was made. The study was conducted in the couple's apartment; each couple was paid $5 for participating.

Procedure

A questionnaire was developed on the basis of extensive preliminary interviews with six married couples. In the experiment proper, the questionnaire was completed individually by the husband and wife; their anonymity was assured. The first pages of the questionnaire required subjects to estimate the extent of their responsibility for each of 20 activities relevant to married couples by putting a slash through a 150-mm straight line, the endpoints of which were labeled "primarily wife" and "primarily husband."[1] The twenty activities were making breakfast, cleaning dishes, cleaning house, shopping for groceries, caring for your children, planning joint leisure activities, deciding how money should be spent, deciding where to live, choosing friends, making important decisions that affect the two of you, causing arguments that occur between the two of you, resolving conflicts that occur between the two of you,

---

[1] In the preliminary interviews, we used percentage estimates. We found that subjects were able to remember the percentages they recorded and that postquestionnaire comparisons of percentages provided a strong source of conflict between the spouses. The use of the 150-mm scales circumvented these difficulties; subjects were not inclined to convert their slashes into exact percentages that could then be disputed.

making the house messy, washing the clothes, keeping in touch with relatives, demonstrating affection for spouse, taking out the garbage, irritating spouse, waiting for spouse, deciding whether to have children.

Subjects were next asked to record briefly examples of the contributions they or their spouses made to each activity. Their written records were subsequently examined to assess if the person's own inputs were generally more "available." That is, did the examples reported by subjects tend to focus more on their own behaviors than on their spouses'? A rater, blind to the experimental hypothesis, recorded the number of discrete examples subjects provided of their own and of their spouses' contributions. A second rater coded one third of the data; the reliability (Pearson product-moment correlation) was .81.

Results

The responses of both spouses to each of the responsibility questions were summed, so that the total included the amount that the wife viewed as her contribution and the amount that the husband viewed as his contribution. Since the response scale was 150 mm long, there were 150 "units of responsibility" to be allocated. A sum of greater than 150 would indicate an egocentric bias in perceived contribution, in that at least one of the spouses was overestimating his or her responsibility for that activity. To assess the degree of over- or underestimation that spouses revealed for each activity, 150 was subtracted from each couple's total. A composite score was derived for the couple, averaging over the 20 activities (or 19, when the couple had no children).

An analysis of variance, using the couple as the unit of analysis, revealed that the composite scores were significantly greater than zero, $M = 4.67$, $F (1, 35) = 12.89$, $p < .001$, indicating an egocentric bias in perceived contributions. Twenty-seven of the 37 couples showed some degree of overestimation ($p < .025$, sign test). Moreover, on the average, overestimation occurred on 16 of the 20 items on the questionnaire, including negative items — for example, causing arguments that occur between the two of you, $F (1, 32) = 20.38$, $p < .001$. Although the magnitude of the overestimation was relatively small, on the average, note that subjects tended to use a restricted range of the scale. Most responses were slightly above or slightly below the halfway mark on the scale. None of the items showed a significant underestimation effect.

The second set of items on the questionnaire required subjects to record examples of their own and of their spouses' contributions to each activity. A mean difference score was obtained over the 20 activities (averaging over husband and wife), with the number of examples of spouses' contributions subtracted from the number of examples of own contributions. A test of the grand mean was highly significant, $F (1, 35) = 36.0$, $p < .001$; as expected, subjects provided more examples of their own ($M = 10.9$) than of their spouses' ($M = 8.1$) inputs. The correlation between this self-other difference score and the initial measure of perceived responsibility was determined. As hypothesized, the greater the tendency to recall self-relevant behaviors, the greater was the overestimation in perceived responsibility, $r (35) = .50, p < .01$.

The number of words contained in each behavioral example reported by the subjects was also assessed to provide a measure of elaboration or richness of recall. The mean number of words per example did not differ as a function of whether the behavior was reported to be emitted by self ($M = 10.0$) or spouse ($M = 10.1$), $F < 1$. Further, this measure was uncorrelated with the measure of perceived responsibility, $r (35) = -.15, ns$.

In summary, both the measure of responsibility and the measure reflecting the availability of relevant behaviors showed the hypothesized egocentric biases. Moreover, there was a significant correlation between the magnitude of the bias in availability and the magnitude of the bias in responsibility. This finding is consistent with the hypothesis that egocentric biases in attributions of responsibility are mediated by biases in availability. Finally, the amount of behavior recalled seemed to be the important factor, rather than the richness of the recall.

Experiment 2

The data from Experiment 1 indicate that egocentric biases in availability and attributions of responsibility occur in ongoing relationships. The remaining experiments were designed to demonstrate the prevalence of these phenomena, and to investigate some of the factors that were expected to influence their magnitude.

The major purpose of Experiment 2 was to evaluate the self-esteem interpretation of the availability bias. If the availability bias is caused primarily by the motivation to enhance self-esteem, recall of a joint endeavor should facilitate an acceptance of personal responsibility after success and a denial of personal responsibility after failure. Consequently, the self-esteem interpretation implies that self-generated inputs should be more available after success than after failure. The evidence from past research that people accept more responsibility for a success than for a failure is consistent with this reasoning

(e.g., Luginbuhl, Crowe, & Kahan, 1975; Sicoly & Ross, 1977; Wortman, Costanzo, & Witt, 1973).

In Experiment 2, subjects learned several days after participating in a problem-solving task that their group had performed either well or poorly. It was hypothesized that subjects would recall a greater proportion of their own statements when the group product was positively evaluated. Because we moved to the laboratory for this experiment, it was possible to tape record the group's initial interaction. This recording provided a "reality base" against which to compare the subsequent recall of subjects.

Method

Subjects

The subjects were 37 males and 7 females selected from lists of students living at the university. Subjects were paid $5 each. All of the subjects participated in both sessions.

Procedure

The experiment was conducted in two sessions separated by a 3- or 4-day interval. Subjects reported for the first session in groups of two. They were told that the purpose of the study was to determine whether groups exhibit more social awareness than individuals. They were given 10 minutes to read a case study of Paula, a psychologically troubled person (selected from Goldstein & Palmer, 1975). Each subject in the dyad was provided with different portions of the case study. The subjects were next asked questions designed to assess their psychological understanding of Paula's difficulties. They were told to discuss each question and arrive at a joint response, taking into account the different information that each group member brought with him or her to the case. Subjects were told that their discussions were being tape recorded. The experimenter informed them that she would listen to the tapes following the session to evaluate the group's answers.

Subjects returned individually for the second session. In a random one half of the dyads, subjects were led to believe that their group had performed poorly relative to other groups in the experiment (third from the worst). In the remaining dyads, subjects were informed that their group had performed relatively well (third from the best). Subjects were then told, "Write down as much as you can recall of your group's discussion of Paula. You will only have a short time to do this, so it is unlikely that you will be able to report all or even most of what was said. It is, therefore, important that you put things down in the order that they come to you. ... If you remember the idea, but not the exact comment, rephrase it in your own words." Subjects were told not to record who said each statement. They were simply to write what was said.

Subjects were asked to stop writing at the end of 8 minutes and to go back over their responses to indicate who said each statement during the discussion. Finally, they were asked whether, in their opinion, each statement improved or lowered their group's score, or whether they were uncertain. Subjects were debriefed at the end of the second session.

An observer who was blind to the subjects' treatment conditions contrasted subjects' recall with their original comments on the tape to assess accuracy. A statement was judged to be accurate if it represented an idea that the subject expressed during the interaction, even though the actual words used during the discussion might have differed from the words recalled by the subject. A second rater scored a random one third of the tapes, and agreement was 93%.

Results and Discussion

Availability

The proportion of statements that subjects attributed to themselves was calculated for each member of the dyad. The average proportion for each dyad served as the unit of analysis. In 21 of the 22 dyads, the subjects attributed the majority of the statements that they recalled to themselves ($p < .001$, sign test). The average proportion of subjects' own statements was .70 in the success condition and .60 in the failure condition. Each of these proportions was significantly greater than a .50 or chance expectancy, $t(10) = 9.09, p < .001$, and $t(10) = 3.22, p < .01$, respectively. Thus, in both the success and failure conditions, subjects attributed significantly more of the recalled statements to themselves than would be expected by chance. Nevertheless, as hypothesized, subjects attributed a greater proportion of the recalled statements to themselves after a success than after a failure, $F (1, 20) = 7.10, p < .025$. The total number of statements recalled (adding over statements attributed to self and the other person) did not differ significantly as a function of the group's performance ($F = 1.57$).

Accuracy

Subjects' recall was compared with the taped record in a 2 × 2 between-within analysis of variance (Success vs. Failure × Self vs. Partner), with the dyad as the unit of analysis. Subjects recalled a higher percentage of

their own actual statements ($M = 5.6\%$) than of their partner's actual statements ($M = 2.6\%$), $F (1, 19) = 18.37, p < .001.$[2] Although the means seem low, note that subjects were given only an 8-minute recall period. The group's performance level did not affect the percentage of actual statements recalled (main effect and interaction $Fs < 1$).

We also compared the accuracy of the statements subjects attributed to themselves with the accuracy of the statements they attributed to their partners. Sixty-nine percent of the statements that subjects attributed to self were accurate reflections of self-generated comments; 56% of the statements that subjects attributed to their partners were accurate. The difference between these two percentages was significant, $F (1, 19) = 7.06, p < .025$. The group's performance level did not significantly affect the accuracy of the attributed statements (success-fail main effect $F = 1.14$, interaction $F < 1$).

Most of the errors that subjects made were of two types: They recalled material from the case history that had not been mentioned in the discussion; they reported inferences and conclusions that were not contained in the case history or in the discussion. In only a few instances (approximately 2% of the errors) did subjects take credit for statements made by their partners.

Evaluations

Finally, subjects' evaluations of the statements were transcribed onto a 3-point scale: +1 (improved the group's score), 0 (uncertain), and −1 (lowered the group's score). Two scores were obtained for each subject: The average rating of comments attributed to self and the average rating of statements attributed to the other person. An analysis of variance, with the dyad as the unit of analysis, revealed a main effect for success-fail, $F(1, 20) = 14.56, p < .005$, and a Success-Fail × Self-Other interaction, $F (1, 20) = 5.19, p < .05$.

The success-fail main effect indicated that statements were evaluated more positively following success ($M = .75$) than following failure ($M = .41$). The interaction revealed that whereas subjects' evaluations of their own comments were marginally lower in the failure condition than in the success condition (M difference = .18, $t = 1.85, p < .10$), their evaluations of the other person's comments were significantly lower in the failure condition than in the success condition (M difference = .50, $t = 5.14, p < .01$).

---

[2] The tapes from one of the failure groups were lost; this group is omitted from the analysis.

In summary, the present study provided some evidence for the self-esteem maintenance hypothesis. Subjects attributed a higher proportion of the recalled comments to themselves after success than after failure; subjects' evaluations of the recalled statements suggested an attempt to shift the blame for failure onto their partners. On the other hand, contrary to the self-esteem interpretation, recall was egocentric even in the failure condition.

Note that the strong egocentricity obtained on the recall measure and the increased accuracy of self-generated statements may reflect, in part, the fact that subjects initially read different aspects of the case history. Since they subsequently presented this material to the other person in responding to the questions, subjects' own contributions may have received more "study time." Nevertheless, this differential is ecologically valid. A person's inputs are often derived from his or her previous history and experiences.

Experiment 3

In Experiment 3 we examined the effects of success and failure in a more natural setting. We had the players on 12 intercollegiate basketball teams individually complete a questionnaire in which they were asked to recall an important turning point in their last game and to assess why their team had won or lost.

It is a leap to go from the self-other comparisons that we have considered in the previous studies to own team — other team comparisons. There are, however, a number of reasons to expect that the actions of one's own team should be more available to the attributor than the actions of the other team: I know the names of my teammates, and therefore, I have a ready means of organizing the storage and retrieval of data relevant to them; our success in future games against other opponents depends more on our own offensive and defensive abilities than on the abilities of the opposing team. Consequently, I may attend more closely to the actions of my teammates, which would enhance encoding and storage. Also, there are informational disparities: The strategies of my own team are more salient than are the strategies of the opposing team (Tversky & Kahneman, 1973).

If the initiatives of one's own team are differentially available, players should recall a turning point in terms of the actions of their team and attribute responsibility for the game outcome to their team. On the basis of the data from Experiment 2, it may be expected that these tendencies will be stronger after a win than after a loss.

Method

Subjects
Seventy-four female and 84 male intercollegiate basketball players participated in the study. The team managers were contacted by telephone; all agreed, following discussions with their players, to have their teams participate in the study.

Procedure
The questionnaires were administered after six games in which the teams participating in the study played each other. Thus, for the three male games chosen, three of the six male teams in the study were competing against the other three male teams. Similarly, the three female games selected included all six of the female teams. The questionnaires were administered at the first team practice following the target game (1 or 2 days after the game), except in one case where, because of the teams' schedules of play, it was necessary to collect data immediately after the game (two female teams). The questionnaires were completed individually, and the respondents' anonymity was assured. The relevant questions, from the current perspective, were the following:

1. Please describe briefly one important turning point in the last game and indicate in which period it occurred.
2. Our team won/lost our last game because … .

The responses to the first question were examined to determine if the turning point was described as precipitated by one's own team, both teams, or the other team. Responses to the second question were examined to assess the number of reasons for the win or loss that related to the actions of either one's own or the opposing team. The data were coded by a person who was unaware of the experimental hypotheses. A second observer independently coded the responses from 50% of the subjects. There was 100% agreement for both questions.

Results

There were no significant sex differences on the two dependent measures; the results are, therefore, reported collapsed across gender. Since team members' responses cannot be viewed as independent, responses were averaged, and the team served as the unit of analysis.

A preliminary examination of the "turning point" data revealed that even within a team, the players were recalling quite different events. Nevertheless, 119 players recalled a turning point that they described as precipitated by the actions of their own team; 13 players recalled a turning point that they viewed as caused by both teams; 16 players recalled a turning point seen to be initiated by the actions of the opposing team (the remaining 10 players did not answer the question). Subjects described such events as a strong defense during the last 2 minutes of the game, a defensive steal, a shift in offensive strategies, and so on.

The percentage of players who recalled a turning point caused by their teammates was derived for each team. These 12 scores were submitted to an analysis that compared them to a chance expectancy of 50%. The obtained distribution was significantly different from chance, $F(1, 11) = 30.25$, $p < .001$, with a mean of 80.25%. As hypothesized, most reports emphasized the actions of the players' own team.

The percentage of players who recalled a turning point caused by their teammates was examined in relation to the team's performance. The average percentage was higher on the losing team than on the winning team in five of the six games ($p < .11$, sign test). The mean difference between the percentages on losing ($M = 88.5$) and winning ($M = 72.$) teams was nonsignificant ($F < 1$).

The players' explanations for their team's win or loss were also examined. Of the 158 participants, only 14 provided any reasons that involved the actions of the opposing team. On the average, subjects reported 1.79 reasons for the win or loss that involved their own team and .09 reasons that involved the opposing team, $F(1, 11) = 272.91$, $p < .001$. Finally, the tendency to ascribe more reasons to one's own team was nonsignificantly greater after a loss ($M = 1.73$) than after a win ($M = 1.65$), $F < 1$.

Discussion

The responses to the turning point question indicate that the performances of subjects' teammates were more available than those of opposing team members. Further, subjects ascribed responsibility for the game outcome to the actions or inactions of their teammates rather than to those of members of the opposing team. Thus, biases in availability and judgments of responsibility can occur at the group level. Rather and Heskowitz (1977) provide another example of group egocentrism: "CBS (news) became a solid Number One after the Apollo moonshot in 1968. If you are a CBS person, you tend to say our coverage of the lunar landing tipped us over. If you are a NBC person, you tend to cite the break-up of the Huntley-Brinkley team as the key factor" (p. 307).

Contrary to the data from Experiment 2, the availability bias in Experiment 3 was as strong after failure as after success. There are differences between the studies that may contribute to this discrepancy. The "egocentric" availability and attributions in the basketball experiment were team rather than self-oriented; as a result, responsibility for failure was more diffused, and subjects' self-esteem was threatened less directly. Also, unlike the group in the laboratory study, the basketball team had a future: The players could enhance their control over subsequent game outcomes by locating causality within their own team. Finally, and perhaps most important, unlike the laboratory group, the team also had a past. Team members recalled aspects of their behavior that changed and attributed the game outcomes to these variations (e.g., we win because of discipline and hustle; we lose because of a lack of discipline and hustle). What players seemed to ignore, however, was that the opposing teams might contribute to these fluctuations.

It seems likely that a tendency to perceive both teams as responsible for the game outcome might increase with the magnitude of the win or loss (assuming that large wins or losses are atypical). As Kelley (1973) noted, multiple causes are necessary to explain extreme outcomes. Although no such tendency was observed in the current study, there were too few data points (games) to provide an accurate determination.

Experiment 4

In the final two experiments, we examined the hypothesized relation between the bias in availability and the bias in attributions of responsibility more directly by introducing manipulations that should affect availability and measuring changes in attribution. In Experiment 4, subjects were required to record either their own comments (self-focus condition) or those of the other person (partner-focus condition) during a problem-solving session. At a second session, subjects were shown their notes and asked to assess the extent to which either they or their partners had been responsible for various aspects of the decision-making process. It was assumed that the partner-focus condition would enhance encoding and retrieval of the partner's contributions. Thus, the partner's inputs would be more available when assessments of responsibility were made, and subjects should assign their partner more responsibility for group decision-making in the partner-focus condition than in the self-focus condition.

Method

Subjects
The subjects were 40 males recruited from the introductory psychology subject pool.

Procedure
Subjects were scheduled in pairs for the first session. In a few introductory comments, the experimenter described the difficulty of preventing people from smoking. Subjects were then told they were participating in a pilot project to assess the efficacy of "brainstorming techniques" as a means of providing possible solutions to this problem. They were further informed that solutions generated during their discussion would be sent to the Committee for the Prevention of Cigarette Smoking (a government committee). Subjects were told to follow a four-step sequence: Define the problem, generate as many solutions as possible, discuss the pros and cons of each proposed solution, and finally, select a preferred solution and explain the reasons for this choice.

Subjects in the self-focus condition were asked to keep a record of their own contributions to the discussion. Subjects in the partner-focus condition were asked to keep a record of only the other person's inputs: "This will leave you free to think and develop your ideas because your partner will be doing the writing." Subjects were given about 45 minutes for discussion.

Subjects returned individually for a second session 2–3 days later. Each subject was asked to look over the notes he had taken during the previous session, "in order to refresh your recollection of the discussion."

Subjects completed the dependent measures after they had reviewed their notes of Session 1. The principal dependent variable required subjects to indicate who tended to control the course and content of the discussion during the first session. They were asked to assess this overall, and also with respect to the various stages of the discussion, on 150-mm scales with endpoints labeled "the other person" and "me."

Results

A 2×2 analysis of variance was performed on the data. Self- versus partner focus was a between-subjects factor. Since the dyad was treated as an experimental unit, the response made by each member of the pair was considered to be a repeated measure.

The focus manipulation had no reliable impact on attributions of responsibility (all $Fs < .1$). Once again, however, there was strong evidence of an egocentric bias in allocations of responsibility. Subjects reported that they had exerted more control over the course and content of each segment of the discussion than their partners ascribed to them — solutions stage: 85 versus 68, $F(1, 18) = 7.32$, $p < .025$; evaluation stage: 79 versus 70, $F(1, 18) = 4.13$, $p < .07$; final proposal stage: 86 versus 67, $F(1, 18) = 11.31$, $p < .01$; overall discussion: 89 versus 72, $F(1, 18) = 9.21$, $p < .01$. Note that for each item, A's self-attributions were, on the average, beyond the midpoint of the 150-mm scale, indicating a perceived contribution of greater than 50%; on the other hand, the partner viewed A's contributions as being less than 50% in each instance.

Discussion

The results revealed strong egocentric biases in individuals' attributions of responsibility for segments of the problem-solving task. The focus manipulation had surprisingly little effect, however. What we had viewed to be a sledgehammer manipulation turned out to be ineffective.

Why did the attention manipulation have so little impact? One possibility is that subjects may have found the written records to be relatively uninformative and relied more on their memories than on the notes in responding to the questionnaire (hence, the strong egocentric biases). The notes may have appeared inadequate, in part because they were very brief, usually about one page, relative to the length of the interaction (45 minutes). Moreover, much of what subjects wrote may have seemed irrelevant to the final decisions made by the group. In short, we may not have succeeded in focusing subjects' attention on what, from their perspective, were the important aspects of the interaction. To obtain this information they were, perhaps, only too willing to rely on their memories.

Finally, note that recent research on the relation between attention and recall in interpersonal perception settings has yielded inconsistent results (Taylor & Fiske, 1978). This situation stands in marked contrast to the strong relation evident in the cognitive literature (Cofer, 1977; Loftus & Loftus, 1976). Unlike the constrained experimental settings utilized in cognitive research, however, the present study and those reviewed by Taylor and Fiske incorporate rich social environments. Consequently, the manipulation of attention is relatively gross; it is less certain that the individual is attending to those aspects of the situation that are relevant to the dependent measures.

Experiment 5

In Experiment 5, we again attempted to vary the individual's focus of attention so as to affect availability. In this experiment, however, we employed a manipulation designed to promote selective retrieval of information directly relevant to attributions of responsibility.

In our initial analysis, we suggested that egocentric attributions of responsibility could be produced by the selective retrieval of information from memory and that retrieval might be guided by the kinds of questions that individuals ask themselves. Experiment 5 was conducted to test this hypothesis. Subjects were induced to engage in differing retrieval by variations in the form in which questions were posed. Graduate students were stimulated to think about either their own contributions to their BA theses or the contributions of their supervisors. The amount of responsibility for the thesis that subjects allocated to either self or supervisor was then assessed. It was hypothesized that subjects would accept less responsibility for the research effort in the supervisor-focus than in the self-focus condition.

Method

Subjects
The subjects were 17 female and 12 male psychology graduate students. Most had completed either 1 or 2 years of graduate school. All of these students had conducted experiments that served as their BA theses in their final undergraduate year.

Procedure
The subjects were approached individually in their offices and asked to complete a brief questionnaire on supervisor–student relations. None refused to participate. The two forms of the questionnaire were randomly distributed to the subjects; they were assured that their responses would be anonymous and confidential.

One form of the questionnaire asked the subjects to indicate their own contribution to each of a number of activities related to their BA theses. The questions were as follows: (a) "I suggested _____ percent of the methodology that was finally employed in the study." (b) "I provided _____ percent of the interpretation of results." (c) "I initiated _____ percent of the thesis-relevant discussions with my supervisor." (d) "During thesis-related discussions I tended to control the course and content of the discussion _____ percent of the time. (e) "All things considered, I was responsible for _____ percent of the entire research effort." (f) "How would you evaluate your thesis relative to others done in the department?"

The second form of the questionnaire was identical to the above, except that the word *I* (self-focus condition) was replaced with *my supervisor* (supervisor-focus condition) on Questions 1–5. Subjects were asked to fill in the blanks in response to the first five questions and to put a slash through a 150-mm line, with endpoints labeled "inferior" and "superior," in response to Question 6.

Results and Discussion

For purposes of the analyses, it was assumed that the supervisor's and the student's contribution to each item would add up to 100%. Though the experiment was introduced as a study of supervisor–student relations, it is possible that the students may have considered in their estimates the inputs of other individuals (e.g., fellow students). Nevertheless, the current procedure provides a conservative test of the experimental hypothesis. For example, if a subject responded 20% to an item in the "I" version of the questionnaire, it was assumed that his or her supervisor contributed 80%. Yet the supervisor may have contributed only 60%, with an unspecified person providing the remainder. By possibly overestimating the supervisor's contribution, however, we are biasing the data against the experimental hypothesis: The "I" version was expected to reduce the percentage of responsibility allocated to the supervisor.

Subjects' responses to the first five questions on the "I" form of the questionnaire were subtracted from 100, so that higher numbers would reflect greater contributions by the supervisor in both conditions. Question 5 dealt with overall responsibility for the research effort. As anticipated, subjects allocated more responsibility to the supervisor in the supervisor-focus ($M = 33.3\%$) than in the self-focus ($M = 16.5\%$) condition, $F(1, 27) = 9.05$, $p < .01$. The first four questions were concerned with different aspects of the thesis, and the average response revealed a similar result: supervisor-focus $M = 33.34$; self-focus $M = 21.82$; $F(1, 27) = 5.34, p < .05$. Finally, subjects tended to evaluate their thesis more positively in the self-focus condition than in the supervisor-focus condition: 112.6 versus 94.6, $F(1, 27) = 3.59, p < .10$.

The contrasting wording of the questions had the anticipated impact on subjects' allocations of responsibility. The supervisor version of the questionnaire presumably caused subjects to recall a greater proportion of their supervisors' contributions than did the "I" form of the questionnaire. This differential availability was then reflected in the allocations of responsibility. Note, however, that the questions were not entirely successful in controlling subjects' retrieval. The supervisor was allocated only one third of the responsibility for the thesis in the supervisor-focus condition.

In light of the present data, the basketball players' attributions of responsibility for the game outcome in Experiment 3 need to be reexamined. Recall that the players were asked to complete the sentence, "Our team won/lost our last game because ... ." This question yielded a highly significant egocentric bias. With hindsight, it is evident that the form of the question — "Our team ... our last game" — may have prompted subjects to focus on the actions of their own teams, even though the wording does not preclude references to the opposing team. The "turning point" question in Experiment 3 was more neutrally worded and is not susceptible to this alternative interpretation.

The leading questions in these studies emanate from an external source; many of our retrieval queries are self-initiated, however, and our recall may well be biased by the form in which we pose retrieval questions to ourselves. For example, basketball players are probably more likely to think in terms of "Why did we win or lose?" than in terms of a neutrally phrased "Which team was responsible for the game outcome?"

General Discussion

The five studies employed different subject populations, tasks, and dependent measures. As hypothesized, the egocentric biases in availability and attribution appear to be robust and pervasive.

Determinants of the Availability Bias

Several processes were hypothesized to contribute to the increased availability of self-generated inputs. It is possible to consider how well each accounts for the existing data. *Selective encoding* and *storage* cannot have contributed to the effects of success versus failure on availability in Experiment 2 or of supervisor- versus self-focus in Experiment 5 (since these manipulations occurred long after encoding and storage took place).

Informational disparities should not have contributed to the pretest results (subjects' time estimates were based solely on the preceding discussion), to the tendency to attribute a higher proportion of the recalled statements to oneself in the success as compared to the failure condition in Experiment 2, or to the effects of supervisor- versus self-focus in Experiment 5 (since neither performance level, as operationalized here, nor focus could affect the information initially available to the subjects). Two *motivational processes* were posited. Self-esteem maintenance does not seem pertinent to the results obtained from the two-person groups in the pretest. Nor does it account for (a) the over-recall of self-generated inputs in the failure condition of Experiment 2 and (b) the finding that players on losing basketball teams recalled the turning point of the game in terms of the actions of their teammates. The control motivation hypothesis fares somewhat better. Although focusing on one's own inputs in failure situations may lower self-esteem, it does permit one to perceive personal control over the activity. Hence, efficacy motivation could account for these results. Nevertheless, a desire for personal efficacy does not appear to explain all of the data. The two-person groups in the pretest seem to reveal a relatively "pure" information-processing effect: It is unlikely that people would feel a need to report that they dominated casual conversations. Also, the effect of supervisor- versus self-focus in Experiment 5 appears to be mediated by differential retrieval. Efficacy considerations may have induced the subjects to report that they were major contributors to their theses; nonetheless, motivational concerns do not dictate that focusing on the supervisor's contributions will reduce one's need to assume responsibility.

In summary, selective encoding and storage, informational disparities, and motivational influences do not appear to be necessary determinants of the egocentric bias in availability. The one remaining process that was posited, *selective retrieval*, is not precluded by any of the current data; further, it receives direct support from the findings in Experiments 2 and 5.

Nevertheless, it seems premature to eliminate any of the hypothesized processes as sufficient causes of the availability bias. The tendency of spouses to recall their own contributions in Experiment 1 may reflect informational disparities; the desire to maintain self-esteem may have contributed to the effect of performance level in Experiment 2; basketball players' responses to the turning point question in Experiment 3 may well have been influenced by selective encoding and by control motivation.

We suspect that, like many cognitive phenomena (cf. Erdelyi, 1974; Erdelyi & Goldberg, in press; McGuire, 1973), biases in availability are multidetermined in real life. Multidetermination may seem an unsatisfying resolution; however, it is one that social psychologists shall probably confront increasingly as they begin to study cognitive phenomena in situ. Researchers in other sciences face parallel complexities. For example, similar cancers appear to have different etiologies, depending, among other factors, on the environment in which the patient lives (Goodfield, 1976).

The Link Between Availability and Attributions of Responsibility

The focus of the present research has been on demonstrating that the hypothesized biases in availability and attribution exist and are relatively ubiquitous. It was also hypothesized, however, that the egocentric bias in attributions of responsibility would be mediated by the bias in availability. Although the data are suggestive, we have no definitive evidence that the bias in availability *causes* the bias in responsibility. The strongest affirmative evidence is that the two biases were significantly correlated in the marriage study and that a manipulation designed to induce selective retrieval influenced attributions of responsibility (Experiment 5). In opposition, it might be contended that the covariation between the two biases is susceptible to a number of alternative causal interpretations and that there is no direct evidence that the retrieval manipulation in Experiment 5 affected availability. Conceivably, the attributions of responsibility in Experiment 5 were mediated by some other factor not yet identified. Further evidence will be required to establish whether the bias in responsibility is caused by the bias in availability. The present results suggest several additional considerations, however, concerning the determinants and pervasiveness of the biases.

Pervasiveness of the Egocentric Biases

The egocentric biases obtained in the current studies may seem inconsistent with Jones and Nisbett's (1971) proposal that actors locate causality for their actions primarily within their environment. There are a number of differences between the two paradigms that might account for the discrepancy. Most important, Jones and Nisbett were concerned with interpretation, whereas we focused on recall and judgments of responsibility. Actors could presumably overestimate their contributions to a joint product and, at the same time, locate the cause of their behavior within the environment. For example, suppose that a wife who reports that she does 80% of the cleaning is asked *why* she cleans (the central question for Jones and Nisbett). She may respond that the house is dirty, an environmental attribution. Conversely, her husband, who perhaps accepts 30% of the responsibility for cleaning, may answer the same question by pointing out that his wife has a fetish for cleanliness, a trait attribution.

Thus, the current data do not speak directly to the Jones and Nisbett hypothesis. Nevertheless, our data do seem to contradict related evidence that the responses of actors are more salient and available to observers than to actors themselves (Storms, 1973; Taylor & Fiske, 1975). The critical variable may be the extent to which the observer departs from a passive role and interacts with the actor. When, as in the present research, individuals undertake complex social interactions, they alternate between the roles of speaker (actor) and listener (observer), yet much of their attention may be directed at planning and executing their own responses. Although they do not attend to themselves perceptually, they may be cognitively self-focused; therefore, self-generated inputs are likely to be more available in recall. On the other hand, passive observers may concentrate on other persons in their environment. Also, observers may be less self-absorbed when their own responses require little attention, as, for example, when they enact well-practiced behaviors (Langer, 1978, has speculated that a wide range of social behaviors require minimal thought).

These instances notwithstanding, the present research demonstrates the prevalence of self-centered biases in availability and judgments of responsibility. In everyday life, these egocentric tendencies may be overlooked when joint endeavors do not require explicit allocations of responsibility. If allocations are stated distinctly, however, there is a potential for dissension, and individuals are unlikely to realize that their differences in judgment could arise from honest evaluations of information that is differentially available.

REFERENCE NOTE

1. Greenwald, A. G. *The tolitarian ego: Fabrication and revision of personal history*. Unpublished manuscript, 1978.

REFERENCES

Bartlett, F. C. *Remembering*. Cambridge, England: Cambridge University Press, 1932.

Bruner, J. S. The act of discovery. *Harvard Educational Review*, 1961, *31*, 21–32.

Carver, R. P. A critical review of mathagenic behaviors and the effect of questions upon the retention of prose materials. *Journal of Reading Behavior*, 1972, *4*, 93–119.

Cofer, C. N. On the constructive theory of memory. In I. A. Uzgiris & F. Weizmann (Eds.), *The structuring of experience*. New York: Plenum Press, 1977.

deCharms, R. C. *Personal causation: The internal affective determinants of behavior*. New York: Academic Press, 1968.

Erdelyi, M. H. A new look at the new look: Perceptual defense and vigilance. *Psychological Review*, 1974, *81*, 1–25.

Erdelyi, M. H., & Goldberg, B. Let's not sweep repression under the rug: Towards a cognitive psychology of repression. In J. F. Kihlstrom & F. J. Evans (Eds.), *Functional disorders of memory*. Hillsdale, N. J.: Erlbaum, in press.

Goldstein, M. J., & Palmer, J. O. *The experience of anxiety*. New York: Oxford University Press, 1975.

Goodfield, J. *The siege of cancer*. New York: Dell, 1976.

Greenwald, A. G., & Albert, R. D. Acceptance and recall of improvised arguments. *Journal of personality and Social Psychology*, 1968, *8*, 31–34.

Greenwald, A. G., & Sakumura, J. S. Attitude and selective learning: Where are the phenomena of yesteryear? *Journal of Personality and Social Psychology*, 1967, *7*, 387–397.

Jones, E. E., & Nisbett, R. E. *The actor and the observer: Divergent perceptions of the causes of behavior*. Morristown, N. J.: General Learning Press, 1971.

Kelley, H. H. The process of causal attribution. *American Psychologist*, 1973, *28*, 107–128.

Langer, E. J. Rethinking the role of thought in social interaction. In J. H. Harvey, W. J. Ickes, & R. F. Kidd (Eds.), *New directions in attribution research* (Vol. 2). Potomac, Md.: Erlbaum, 1978.

Loftus, G. R., & Loftus, E. F. *Human memory: The processing of information*. Hillsdale, N. J.: Erlbaum, 1976.

Luginbuhl, J. E. R., Crowe, D. H., & Kahan, J. P. Causal attribution for success and failure. *Journal of Personality and Social Psychology*, 1975, *31*, 86–93.

Malpass, R. S. Effects of attitude on learning and memory: The influence of instruction-induced sets. *Journal of Experimental Social Psychology*, 1969, *5*, 441–453.

McGuire, W. J. The yin and yang of progress in social psychology: Seven Koan. *Journal of Personality and Social Psychology*, 1973, 26, 446–456.

Rather, D., & Heskowitz, M. *The camera never blinks*. New York: Ballantine Books, 1977.

Rogers, T. B., Kuiper, N. A., & Kirker, W. S. Self-reference and the encoding of personal information. *Journal of Personality and Social Psychology*, 1977, *35*, 677–688.

Sicoly, F., & Ross, M. The facilitation of egobiased attributions by means of self-serving observer feedback. *Journal of Personality and Social Psychology*, 1977, *35*, 734–741.

Storms, M. D. Videotape and the attribution process: Reversing actors' and observers' points of view. *Journal of Personality and Social Psychology*, 1973, *27*, 165–175.

Taylor, S. E., & Fiske, S. T. Point of view and perceptions of causality. *Journal of Personality and Social Psychology*, 1975, *32*, 439–445.

Taylor, S. E., & Fiske, S. T. Salience, attention, and attribution. Top of the head phenomena. In L. Berkowitz (Ed.), *Advances in experimental social psychology* (Vol. 11). New York: Academic Press, 1978.

Tversky, A., & Kahneman, D. Availability: A heurisitc for judging frequency and probability. *Cognitive Psychology*, 1973, *5*, 207–232.

White, R. W. Motivation reconsidered: The concept of competence. *Psychological Review*, 1959, *66*, 297–333.

Wortman, C. B., Costanzo, P. R., & Witt, T. R. Effect of anticipated performance on the attribution of causality to self and others. *Journal of Personality and Social Psychology*, 1973, *27*, 372–381.

Received February 20, 1978 ■

PART 4

Nonconscious and Automatic Processing

Introduction and Preview

Most of the time, most of us think we know what we're doing, how we're doing it, and why we're doing it. "I'm going to the grocery store to buy some food, I'm doing it because the refrigerator is nearly empty, and I want something more than ice cubes for dinner." Moreover, much of the time, most of us think we know how we do what we do ("I cleverly solved the problem by remembering that . . ."), what makes us act the way we do in various situations ("I was quiet at dinner because I was thinking about getting my term paper done."), and why we feel the way we do ("I was feeling uneasy because Ted can be rude.").

These kinds of statements reflect our "knowledge" not simply of facts, or even of our opinions. Rather, they refer to our sense of *how* we make decisions, *how* we are thinking, and *why* we feel the way we do. More generally, they refer to our knowledge of our own mental processes. Moreover, such knowledge implies that we understand why we have responded in certain ways to certain situations and events.

For many years the implicit assumption underlying much theory and research was that people are quite cognizant of what they're doing when they make judgments and decisions. For example, dissonance theorists portrayed the individual struggling with the discrepancy between some cognitive belief ("Smoking is bad for one's health") and one's behavior ("I smoke") (Festinger, 1957). Research on decision processes considered the way people weigh various factors in arriving at such judgments

(Slovic & Lichtenstein, 1971). The early attribution theories (Jones & Davis, 1965; Kelley, 1967) discussed the various factors one considers in deciding whether some behavior was, for example, the result of internal (e.g., traits, motives) or external (e.g., situational pressures or constraints) causes. In all of these cases, authors would discuss "what people do" in ways that implied that people had some cognizance, some awareness, some conscious recognition of the issues at hand, and how they were resolving them.

Although there certainly are many respects in which we possess such self-understanding, recent social cognition research raises some serious questions about the extent to which we do have access to "knowing" our own mental processes. To what extent do we have access to the cognitive processes that drive our judgments, decisions, and behavior? To what extent do we understand how we know which stimuli in our environment are effectively "making a difference" in how we perceive and respond to that environment?

Reading 13 by Nisbett and Wilson (1977) focused specifically on these questions. These authors argued that a considerable amount of our higher mental activity goes on outside of awareness and, in fact, that people have little or no direct access to their cognitive processes. There are instances, such as when we solve an algebra problem, when we consciously think about the mental steps we go through in trying to arrive at a correct answer ("OK, first I have to multiply these two values, then take the square root of the product, and then . . ."). In many cases, however, and particularly in those cases involving social judgments that are based on less rigorous procedural rules, we have relatively little awareness of *how* we're doing *what* we're doing. I may

be very aware of the end product — for example, my judgment that "I really like that sport coat" — but the mental processes by which that evaluation is made, and the specific factors that determine my reaction to the coat, are not available to me. In a series of studies Nisbett and Wilson (1977) showed that people do a poor job of explaining why they rated some job applicants better than others, what factors cause shifts in their mood states, or why they selected one item of clothing vs another.

Even though people may not have direct access to the mental processes underlying such judgments and behaviors, they do have "intuitive theories" — ideas, inferences, intuitive explanations — about how such judgments are made. And these intuitive theories guide their own understanding of the underlying mental processes. Unfortunately, those intuitive theories may not be correct, and in Nisbett and Wilson's (1977) analysis, they very often are incorrect. They are incorrect because the intuitive theories highlight the importance of factors that in fact are not the determining causal agents. For example, a recent experience, or a salient feature, or a prior belief may guide our thinking about what led us to feel, decide, behave in a particular way, whereas those factors may have in fact been irrelevant to our action.

Can we ever be correct in our notions about our own cognitive processes? Yes, we can. There are times when the important determining stimuli are very salient to us, so that we recognize their importance on our judgments and decisions. As I alluded to earlier, there are some judgment tasks where we make those judgments by consciously probing our thought processes. Those occasions occur, but are not as common as we might think, and in general we rely on our intuitive theories. When will those theories be correct? They will sometimes generate "correct" judgments because our intuitive ideas happen to highlight the important factors that actually determine what we do. Note, however, that in such cases, we have made correct judgments *not* because of our awareness of how we did it (that is, due to our access to our cognitive processes) but instead because of a convenient parallel between our *theories* of how stimuli influence our judgments and the *actual* importance of those stimuli in those cases.

More recent research has extended Nisbett and Wilson's analysis in important ways. Specifically, research has shown that many processes occur entirely outside of awareness, that cognitive functions can be activated and carried out automatically, without intent or conscious awareness. Therefore many everyday experiences — including our perceptions and judgments of others, and even our behavior in social interaction — can be guided by stimuli and processes of which we have no cognizance whatsoever. This kind of phenomenon is called *automatic* or spontaneous processing, and this form of functioning is contrasted with *controlled*, systematic, or deliberative processing.

I began this Introduction and Preview with an example of going to a grocery store to replenish food supplies. In deciding to go to the store, I was doing something that I intended to do, I was aware that I had decided to do so, and while shopping, my mind was consciously focused on completing that chore. On the other hand, if something else had come up, I could change my plans and do something else. All of what I have just described are characteristics of *controlled* or deliberative processes: they are initiated by intention toward achieving some goal, the person is aware of being focused on performing the task,

and because of that, those processes consume the person's mental resources for that period of time. In contrast, *automatic* processes occur without the person's intention or awareness, and are highly efficient in that one's cognitive resources can be applied to other tasks at the same time. A simple example of automatic processing is riding a bicycle. Once you've mastered that skill, you can ride without thinking about it. You don't have to pay attention to how you are pushing the pedals or steering, and you can easily carry on a conversation with another person riding along side of you. The task of riding a bike, then, occurs automatically. If something unusual happens — the pedals don't work, the chain comes off — the conversation is disrupted, one's attention and cognitive resources are immediately drawn to the task, and one has reverted to controlled processing. Hence there is an interplay between the two kinds of processing.

If automatic processes are engaged without the person's intent or awareness, what initiates these processes? In Part 3 I discussed the concept of priming, by which a concept or category in memory can be activated by some salient or recent experience. Once activated the contents of that concept or category can then guide subsequent processing, including perception, judgment, and behavior. In many cases we are perfectly aware of the stimulus that might activate a concept. For example, in any social interaction it is difficult *not* to be aware of the gender of the person one is talking to. However, priming can also occur when the person is unaware of the activating stimulus. In many experiments stimuli have been presented so fast (e.g., on a computer screen) that they literally cannot be detected by the perceiver. This is called *subliminal priming*. Despite not being consciously aware of the stimulus, it is nevertheless detected subconsciously and thereby activates the relevant concept. In either case, priming the concept influences subsequent outcomes by automatic processing.

A great deal of our everyday cognitive processing occurs automatically. The reading by Bargh and Chartrand (1999) summarizes the role of automatic processes in an impressive variety of phenomena — perception of objects and persons, activation of goals, affective reactions, and social behavior. For example, perception occurs automatically, without intentional control: it is not possible to perceive the book on the table to be a grapefruit! Once perceived, other processes can be automatically set in motion. As Bargh and Chartrand (1999) state, "The external environment can direct behavior nonconsciously through a two-stage process: automatic perceptual activity that then automatically creates behavioral tendencies through the perception–behavior link" (p. 466). For example, consider what happens when I, a white person, perceive a person named James, who happens to be a black. Although I might give little conscious thought or attention to the race difference between us, it may have important automatic consequences. That perception would automatically activate the category "black persons" and the stereotypic beliefs associated with it. Once activated, that stereotype could guide the inferences and judgments I make about James, and these effects may even influence my behavior toward him. And these influences can occur automatically, in the absence of my awareness or intention that my perceptions and behavior would be guided and shaped by those beliefs.

Other readings in Part 4 illustrate the nature of automatic effects on social perception and behavior. For example, Pratto and John (1991) suggested that there are certain kinds of information that themselves trigger automatic processing. They proposed that negative stimuli — information that carries, for example, the potential for harm or unpleasantness for the individual — may be more likely to be automatically attended to than positively valued information. To test their hypothesis they used the Stoop task, in which words typed in different colors are presented to the experimental participant, whose task is to name the color of ink in which the word is written. In this task, the meaning of the word can interfere with the naming of the color, and when that happens, the time taken to name the color is somewhat longer. Pratto and John reasoned that if the negativity of information is automatically detected, it would detract from the immediate task of color naming. If so, then this effect would produce longer response times for negatively-valenced words than for positively-valenced words. Their results supported this hypothesis. It appears, then, that perceivers are automatically "vigilant" to detect negative information.

Other research has shown that subliminal priming can influence subsequent processing. In Part 3, Reading 9 by Srull and Wyer (1979) showed that priming a trait concept (hostility), using a scrambled sentence task, influenced participants' interpretations of information about a target person named Donald on a subsequent impression-formation task. Bargh and Pietromonaco (1962) tested the hypothesis that concepts can be activated subliminally, without the participant's awareness, and that such activation would still influence subsequent processing. Instead of completing the scrambled sentence task, their participants initially performed a "vigilance task" in which they watched a screen and every time they saw a flash on the screen they were to push a button. The flashes that they saw were actually words presented at very short exposure times (100 ms) — too fast for participants to be able to consciously recognize the words. For some participants, a high proportion of the words were related to hostility; for others, only a few were related to hostility. This manipulation was designed to produce either strong or weak activation of the trait concept. The question was whether this subliminal activation would automatically influence participants' interpretations of the information they subsequently read about Donald. The results showed that participants in the strong priming condition did in fact rate Donald more negatively than did people in the weak prime condition. Thus, based on these findings, it becomes clear that recent experiences that prime a given concept, even without our awareness of that activation, can guide subsequent information processing and influence inferences and judgments in an unrelated context. These same kinds of effects have been shown in numerous studies of stereotyping. Priming stereotypic attributes, subliminally and without the participants' awareness, can directly and automatically influence perceptions of target persons on subsequent tasks (e.g., Devine, 1989; Fazio, Jackson, Dunton, & Williams, 1995; Fazio, Powell, & Herr, 1983).

The accumulated research provides impressive documentation that automatic processes can influence perceptions, impressions, and other types of cognitive processing. One might wonder, however, if these effects of automatic processing are limited to the mental world of cognitive functioning. In other words, do these effects have anything to do with social behavior? Recent research has provided several compelling demonstrations of subtle, automatic effects on actual interpersonal behavior (e.g., Bargh, Chen, & Burrows, 1996). Reading 16 by Dijksterhuis and van Knippenberg (1998) reports a series of studies showing that such priming can influence complex behavior. In the first phase in their studies, they primed either the concept of intelligence — through priming the stereotype of

"professors" or the trait word "intelligent" — or stupidity — through activating the stereotype of "soccer hooligans" or the trait word "stupid." Then, on a second and presumably unrelated task, participants completed a test of general knowledge, drawn from items in the game Trivial Pursuit. Their results showed that priming significantly influenced performance on this task. Priming "professors" led to higher percentages of correct answers, whereas priming "soccer hooligans" decreased intellectual performance on the test. Thus, priming in the first phase persisted and produced automatic effects on behavior in the second phase.

Although we like to think that we are well aware of the forces driving our judgments and behavior, a considerable amount of evidence now exists showing that automatic processes have pervasive effects on a broad range of our everyday functioning (Bargh & Chartrand, 1999). Our cognitive processes (and consequently numerous outcomes influenced by them) can be governed by automatic processes that are (a) unintended responses to external stimuli, (b) are outside of conscious awareness, and (c) are not under our control. Realization of these facts can be unnerving. Two questions then come to mind that need to be addressed about these processes. First, if they're automatic, can these processes be modified or are their consequences inevitable? Second, does automatic processing produce beneficial or detrimental outcomes? Is it a good thing or a bad thing?

The first question concerns the inevitability of the effects of automatic processing. A process that is unintended and occurs outside of conscious awareness would seem to be something over which the individual can exert very little control. In fact, one commonly-cited characteristic of automatic processes is that, given the occurrence of the activating stimulus, the process is set in motion and cannot be interrupted until it completes its course. When we realize that stereotypic judgments of and responses to outgroup members can be guided by such automaticity, then the negative consequences of such processing become of concern. If stereotypes are automatically activated by group-relevant stimuli, and those stereotypes then influence our perceptions and behavior in unintended ways and for reasons we are unaware of, then the question is reasonably asked: are we destined to stereotype others? Are prejudicial responses unavoidable? These questions have plagued the minds of researchers for several years (Fiske, 1989). Fortunately, there are now several recent studies that show that automatic processes can in fact be modified by a number of circumstances (for a review, see Blair, 2002).

The second question concerns how we view the consequences of automaticity and is a bit more complex. Some of the examples I have discussed might lead us to think that automaticity has undesirable outcomes. For example, Pratto and John's (1991) finding that people are automatically vigilant for negative information suggests that we are inherently attuned to notice the bad things that pose potential threat or harm. Other research indicates that we give differential weight to undesirable qualities in others (Fiske, 1980). Also, evidence indicating that stereotypic judgments and prejudicial evaluations of outgroup members are driven in part by automatic effects are disturbing and highlight the potential for undesirable consequences of automaticity.

It is important to realize, however, that automaticity itself is an evaluatively-neutral process. A process becomes automatic because it has occurred repeatedly over time. To return to our earlier example, learning to ride a bicycle is initially a very attention-demanding and deliberative process. With experience, the various elements of this task become routinized, and eventually automatic, in that they no longer require the focus of our cognitive resources or even awareness. In parallel manner, cognitive and affective responses that occur repeatedly in response to certain stimuli — trait inferences, attitudinal reactions, stereotypic judgments, affective responses — can become routine, and eventually automatic, reactions to those stimuli. Thus, automaticity develops as a result of our experiences, and those experiences and processes can be either positive or negative in evaluative tone.

Moreover, automatic processes arise and are maintained because they prove to be useful and beneficial for the individual. What are those benefits? As I have emphasized before, the individual is continually perceiving and responding to a complex, information-rich stimulus world that imposes many demands on the individual's cognitive resources. Automatic processing, like other cognitive mechanisms we develop (e.g., cognitive structures, judgment heuristics) aid in coping with that complexity. They increase the efficiency with which the individual can process and comprehend social information. Being automatic, they function while using few cognitive resources, thereby freeing those resources for other tasks. In all of these ways, automatic processing facilitates adaptation to a complex social environment.

Discussion Questions

1. According to Nisbett and Wilson (Reading 13), what factors lessen or undermine the accuracy of our verbal descriptions of our cognitive processes? Under what conditions are such verbal reports likely to be accurate, and why?
2. What are the primary characteristics that differentiate automatic and controlled processes?
3. Describe examples of research showing automatic processes influencing (a) perception, and (b) behavior.

Suggested Readings

Fazio, R. H., Sanbonmatsu, D. M., Powell, M. C., & Kardes, F. R. (1986). On the automatic activation of attitudes. *Journal of Personality and Social Psychology*, 50, 229–238.

Greenwald, A.G., & Banaji, M.R. (1995). Implicit social cognition: Attitudes, self-esteem, and stereotypes. *Psychological Review*, 102, 4–27.

Blair, I.V. (2002). The malleability of automatic stereotypes and prejudice. *Personality & Social Psychology Review*, 6, 242–261.

Greenwald, A. G., McGhee, D. E., & Schwartz, J. L. K. (1998). Measuring individual differences in implicit cognition: The implicit association test. *Journal of Personality and Social Psychology*, 74, 1464–1480.

Telling More Than We Can Know: Verbal Reports on Mental Processes

Richard E. Nisbett and Timothy DeCamp Wilson

Evidence is reviewed which suggests that there may be little or no direct introspective access to higher order cognitive processes. Subjects are sometimes (a) unaware of the existence of a stimulus that importantly influenced a response, (b) unaware of the existence of the response, and (c) unaware that the stimulus has affected the response. It is proposed that when people attempt to report on their cognitive processes, that is, on the processes mediating the effects of a stimulus on a response, they do not do so on the basis of any true introspection. Instead, their reports are based on a priori, implicit causal theories, or judgments about the extent to which a particular stimulus is a plausible cause of a given response. This suggests that though people may not be able to observe directly their cognitive processes, they will sometimes be able to report accurately about them. Accurate reports will occur when influential stimuli are salient and are plausible causes of the responses they produce, and will not occur when stimuli are not salient or are not plausible causes.

"**W**hy do you like him?" "How did you solve this problem?" "Why did you take that job?"

In our daily lives we answer many such questions about the cognitive processes underlying our choices,

Editor's Note: Selected excerpts from the original article are reproduced here.

The writing of this paper, and some of the research described, was supported by grants GS-40085 and BNS75-23191 from the National Science Foundation. The authors are greatly indebted to Eugene Borgida, Michael Kruger, Lee Ross, Lydia Temoshok, and Amos Tversky for innumerable ideas and generous and constructive criticism. John W. Atkinson, Nancy Bellows, Dorwin Cartwright, Alvin Goldman, Sharon Gurwitz, Ronald Lemley, Harvey London, Hazel Markus, William R. Wilson, and Robert Zajonc provided valuable critiques of earlier drafts of the paper.

Requests for reprints should be sent to Richard E. Nisbett, Research Center for Group Dynamics, Institute for Social Research, University of Michigan, Ann Arbor, Michigan 48109.

evaluations, judgments, and behavior. Sometimes such questions are asked by social scientists. For example, investigators have asked people why they like particular political candidates (Gaudet, 1955) or detergents (Kornhauser & Lazarsfeld, 1935), why they chose a particular occupation (Lazarsfeld, 1931), to go to graduate school (Davis, 1964) or to become a juvenile delinquent (Burt, 1925), why they got married or divorced (Goode, 1956) or joined a voluntary organization (Sills, 1957) or moved to a new home (Rossi, 1955) or sought out a psychoanalyst (Kadushin, 1958), or failed to use a contraceptive technique (Sills, 1961). Social psychologists routinely ask the subjects in their experiments why they behaved, chose, or evaluated as they did. Indeed, some social psychologists have advocated the abandonment of the social psychology experiment and its deceptive practices and have urged that subjects simply be asked how their cognitive processes *would* work if they were to be confronted with particular stimulus situations (Brown, 1962; Kelman, 1966).

Recently, however, several cognitive psychologists (Mandler, 1975a, 1975b; Miller, 1962; Neisser, 1967) have proposed that we may have no direct access to higher order mental processes such as those involved in evaluation, judgment, problem solving, and the initiation of behavior. The following quotations will serve to indicate the extent to which these investigators doubt people's ability to observe directly the workings of their own minds. "It is the *result* of thinking, not the process of thinking, that appears spontaneously in consciousness" (Miller, 1962, p. 56). "The constructive processes [of encoding perceptual sensations] themselves never appear in consciousness, their products do" (Neisser, 1967, p. 301). And in Neisser's next paragraph: "This general description of the fate of sensory information seems to fit the higher mental processes as well" (p. 301). Mandler's (1975a) suggestions are still more sweeping: "The analysis of situations and appraisal of the environment ... goes on mainly at the nonconscious level" (p. 241). "There are many systems that cannot be brought into consciousness, and probably most systems that analyze the environment in the first place have that characteristic. In most of these cases, only the products of cognitive and mental activities are available to consciousness" (p. 245). And finally: "Unconscious processes ... include those that are not available to conscious experience, be they feature analyzers, deep syntactic structures, affective appraisals, computational processes, language production systems, action systems of many kinds" (p. 230).

It is important to note that none of these writers cites data in support of the view that people have no direct access to higher order mental processes. In fact, when the above quotations are read in context, it is clear that the source of the speculations is not research on higher order processes such as "thinking," "affective appraisal," and "action systems," but rather research on more basic processes of perception and memory. Recent research has made it increasingly clear that there is almost no conscious awareness of perceptual and memorial processes. It would be absurd, for example, to ask a subject about the extent to which he relied on parallel line convergence when making a judgment of depth or whether he stored the meanings of animal names in a hierarchical tree fashion or in some other manner. Miller (1962) has provided an excellent example of our lack of awareness of the operation of memorial processes. If a person is asked, "What is your mother's maiden name?", the answer appears swiftly in consciousness. Then if the person is asked "How did you come up with that?", he is usually reduced to the inarticulate answer, "I don't know, it just came to me."

It is a substantial leap, however, from research and anecdotal examples concerning perception and memory to blanket assertions about higher order processes. In the absence of evidence indicating that people cannot correctly report on the cognitive processes underlying complex behaviors such as judgment, choice, inference, and problem solving, social scientists are not likely to abandon their practice of quizzing their subjects about such processes. The layman is even less likely to abandon his habit of asking and answering such questions.

A second problem with the new anti-introspectivist view is that it fails to account for the fact, obvious to anyone who has ever questioned a subject about the reasons for his behavior or evaluations, that people readily answer such questions. Thus while people usually appear stumped when asked about perceptual or memorial processes, they are quite fluent when asked why they behaved as they did in some social situation or why they like or dislike an object or another person. It would seem to be incumbent on one who takes a position that denies the possibility of introspective access to higher order processes to account for these reports by specifying their source. If it is not direct introspective access to a memory of the processes involved, what is the source of such verbal reports?

Finally, a third problem with the anti-introspectivist view is that it does not allow for the possibility that people are ever correct in their reports about their higher order mental processes. It seems intuitively unlikely that such reports are always inaccurate. But if people are sometimes accurate, several questions arise. (a) What is the basis of these accurate reports? (b) Are accurate reports fundamentally different in kind from inaccurate ones? (c) Is it possible to specify what sorts of reports will be accurate and what sorts will be inaccurate?

The first part of this article is concerned with a review of the evidence bearing on the accuracy of subjective reports about higher mental processes. The second part of the paper presents an account of the basis of such reports. We shall argue for three major conclusions.

1. People often cannot report accurately on the effects of particular stimuli on higher order, inference-based responses. Indeed, sometimes they cannot report on the existence of critical stimuli, sometimes cannot report on the existence of their responses, and sometimes cannot even report that an inferential process of any kind has occurred. The accuracy of subjective

reports is so poor as to suggest that any introspective access that may exist is not sufficient to produce generally correct or reliable reports.

2. When reporting on the effects of stimuli, people may not interrogate a memory of the cognitive processes that operated on the stimuli; instead, they may base their reports on implicit, a priori theories about the causal connection between stimulus and response. If the stimulus psychologically implies the response in some way (Abelson, 1968) or seems "representative" of the sorts of stimuli that influence the response in question (Tversky & Kahneman, 1974), the stimulus is reported to have influenced the response. If the stimulus does not seem to be a plausible cause of the response, it is reported to be noninfluential.

3. Subjective reports about higher mental processes are sometimes correct, but even the instances of correct report are not due to direct introspective awareness. Instead, they are due to the incidentally correct employment of a priori causal theories.

Verbal Reports on Cognitive Processes in Dissonance and Attribution Studies

Much of the evidence that casts doubt on the ability of people to report on their cognitive processes comes from a study of the literature that deals with cognitive dissonance and self-perception attribution processes. Or rather, the evidence comes from a consideration of what was *not* published in that literature. A review of the non-public, sub rosa aspects of these investigations leads to three conclusions: (a) Subjects frequently cannot report on the existence of the chief response that was produced by the manipulations; (b) even when they are able to report the existence of the responses, subjects do not report that a *change process* occurred, that is, that an evaluational or attitudinal response underwent any alterations; and (c) subjects cannot correctly identify the stimuli that produced the response.

Awareness of the Existence of the Response

The central idea of insufficient justification or dissonance research is that behavior that is intrinsically undesirable will, when performed for inadequate extrinsic reasons, be seen as more attractive than when performed for adequate extrinsic reasons. In the view of Festinger (1957)

and other dissonance theorists, attitude change occurs because the cognition "I have done something unpleasant without adequate justification" is dissonant and therefore painful; and the person revises his opinion about the behavior in order to avoid the psychic discomfort.

The central idea of attribution theory is that people strive to discover the causes of attitudinal, emotional, and behavioral responses (their own and others), and that the resulting causal attributions are a chief determinant of a host of additional attitudinal and behavioral effects. Thus, for example, if someone tells us that a particular Western movie is a fine film, our acceptance of that opinion, and possibly our subsequent behavior, will be determined by our causal analysis of the person's reasons for the evaluation: Does he like all movies? All Westerns? All John Wayne movies? Do other people like the movie? Does this person tend to like movies that other people do not like?

Many insufficient-justification studies and many attribution studies where the subject makes inferences about himself have employed behavioral dependent variables. Substantial effects have been shown on behavior of inherent interest and with significant social implications, including pain, hunger and thirst tolerance, psychopathology, task perseverance, and aggressive behavior. Two examples will serve to illustrate research with behavioral consequences.

Zimbardo, Cohen, Weisenberg, Dworkin, and Firestone (1969) asked subjects to accept a series of painful electric shocks while performing a learning task. When the task was completed, subjects were asked to repeat it. Some subjects were given adequate justification for performing the task a second time and accepting another series of shocks (the research was very important, nothing could be learned unless the shocks were given again), while other subjects were given insufficient justification (the experimenter wanted to satisfy his more or less idle curiosity about what would happen). Subjects with insufficient justification for accepting the shocks showed lower GSR responses and better learning performance on the second task than subjects with sufficient justification. The explanation offered for this finding is that insufficient-justification subjects sought to justify taking the shocks, which they did by deciding that the shocks were not all that painful. Thus the evaluation of the painfulness of the shocks was lowered, and physiological and behavioral indicators reflected this evaluation.

A study by Valins and Ray (1967) will illustrate the attribution paradigm. These investigators asked snake-phobic subjects to watch slides while receiving occasional electric shocks. Subjects were wired for what they believed were recordings of heart rate. They were allowed to hear a rhythmic pattern of sounds which, they were told, was the amplified sound of their own heart beats. Subjects were shown a series of slides of snakes interspersed with slides of the word "SHOCK." Following each presentation of the shock slide, subjects were given an electric shock. After a few such pairings, the appearance of the shock slide was accompanied by an increased rate of "heartbeats." Snake slides were never accompanied by any change in apparent heart rate. Following this procedure, subjects were requested to approach, and if possible, to touch, a 30-inch (76.2-cm) boa constrictor. Such subjects approached the snake more closely than subjects who had gone through the identical procedure but who believed that the "heart-beats" were simply "extraneous sounds" (which, of course, they actually were). The finding is explained as follows. Subjects in the heart rate condition learned that their "heart rate" indicated they were appropriately frightened when they saw the shock slide, because of the electric shock it portended, but that they were not frightened by the snake slides. If they were not frightened by the snake slides, perhaps they were not as afraid of live snakes as they had thought. Armed with this new self-attribution of snake fearlessness, they were more willing to approach the boa.

The two experiments just described share a common formal model. Verbal stimuli in the form of instructions from the experimenter, together with the subject's appraisal of the stimulus situation, are the inputs into a fairly complicated cognitive process which results in a changed evaluation of the relevant stimuli and an altered motivational state. These motivational changes are reflected in subsequent physiological and behavioral events. Thus: Stimuli → cognitive process→ evaluative and motivational state change → behavior change. Following traditional assumptions about higher mental processes, it has been tacitly assumed by investigators that the cognitive processes in question are for the most part verbal, conscious ones. Thus the subject consciously decides how he feels about an object, and this evaluation determines his behavior toward it. As several writers (Bem, 1972; Nisbett & Valins, 1972; Storms & Nisbett, 1970; Weick, 1966) have pointed out, there is a serious problem with this implicit assumption: Typically, behavioral and physiological differences are obtained in the absence of *verbally reported* differences in evaluations or motive states. For example, in the study by Zimbardo, Cohen, Weisenberg, Dworkin, and Firestone (1969), experimental subjects

given inadequate justification for taking shock learned much more quickly and showed much less GSR reactivity to the shock than did control, adequate-justification subjects, but the former did not report the shock to be significantly less painful than did the latter. And subjects in the Valins and Ray (1967) experiment who had "inferred" that they were not very frightened of snakes, as indicated by their willingness to approach the boa constrictor, showed no evidence of any such inference when asked a direct question about how frightened they were of snakes.

We have reviewed all the insufficient-justification and attribution studies we have been able to find that meet the following criteria: (a) behavioral or physiological effects were examined, and (b) at approximately the same time, verbal reports of evaluations and motivational states were obtained. Studies that did not permit a clear, uncontroversial comparison of the strength of behavioral and self-report indicators were not included (e.g., Brehm, Back, & Bogdonoff, 1969; Schachter & Singer, 1962), nor were studies that employed controversial, poorly understood techniques such as hypnosis (e.g., Brock & Grant, 1969).

Three striking generalizations can be made about these studies:

1. In the majority of studies, no significant verbal report differences were found at all. This applies to studies by Cohen and Zimbardo (1969), Cottrell and Wack (1967), Davison and Valins (1969), Ferdinand (1964), Freedman (1965), Grinker (1969), Pallak (1970), five experiments by Pallak, Brock, and Kiesler (1967), Experiment 1 in Pallak and Pittman (1972), Schachter and Wheeler (1962), Snyder, Schultz, and Jones (1974), Storms and Nisbett (1970), Valins and Ray (1967), Waterman (1969), Weick and Penner (1969), Weick and Prestholdt (1968), and Zimbardo, Cohen, Weisenberg, Dworkin, and Firestone (1969).

2. In the remainder of studies, the behavioral effects were in most cases stronger (i.e., more statistically reliable) than the verbal report effects (Berkowitz & Turner, 1974; Kruglanski, Friedman, & Zeevi, 1971; Schlachet, 1969; Nisbett & Schachter, 1966; Experiment 2 of Pallak and Pittman, 1972; and Weick, 1964). Exceptions to this are reports by Brehm (1969), Freedman (1963), Mansson (1969), and Zimbardo, Weisenberg, Firestone, and Levy (1969).

3. In two studies where it was reported, the correlation between verbal report about motive state and behavioral measures of motive state was found to be nil

(Storms & Nisbett, 1970; Zimbardo, Cohen, Weisenberg, Dworkin, & Firestone, 1969). The rest of the literature in this area is strangely silent concerning the correlations between verbal report and behavior. Since positive correlations would have constituted support for investigators' hypotheses, while zero or negative correlations would have been difficult to understand or interpret in terms of prevailing assumptions about the nature of the cognitive processes involved, the failure to report the correlations constitutes presumptive evidence that they were not positive. In order to check on this possibility, we wrote to the principal investigators of the studies described above, asking for the correlations between verbal report and behavior. Only three investigators replied by saying that they still had the data and could provide the correlations. In all three instances, the correlations were in fact nonsignificant and close to zero (Davison & Valins, 1969; Freedman, 1965; Snyder, Schultz, & Jones, 1974).

The overall results thus confound any assumption that conscious, verbal cognitive processes result in conscious, verbalizable changes in evaluations or motive states which then mediate changed behavior. In studies where the data are available, no association is found between degree of verbal report change and degree of behavior change in experimental groups. And in most studies no evidence is found that experimental subjects differ from control subjects in their verbal reports on evaluations and motivational states.

What of the studies that do find differences in the verbal reports of experimental and control subjects? (It should be noted that this includes many studies not reviewed here where the *only* dependent measure was a verbal one and where differences between experimental and control groups were obtained.) Should these studies be taken as evidence that the traditional model sometimes works, that subjects are sometimes aware of the cognitive processes that occur in these experiments? Evidence to be discussed below casts doubt on such a conclusion.

Awareness of the Existence of a Change Process

There is an important difference between awareness of the *existence* of an evaluation or motive state and awareness of a *changed* evaluation or motive state. The former sort of awareness does not imply true recognition of the process induced by insufficient justification

and attribution manipulations — which in fact always involves a change in evaluations. Thus if it could be shown that subjects cannot report on the fact that a change has taken place as a consequence of such manipulations, this would suggest that they are not aware of the occurrence of a process.

Bem and McConnell (1970) contrived an experiment to demonstrate that in fact, subjects do not experience a subjective change in their evaluations in response to insufficient-justification manipulations. A stock-in-trade of the dissonance tradition is the counterattitudinal advocacy experiment. In this type of experiment, subjects are asked to write an essay opposing their own views on some topic and are then asked what their attitudes are toward the topic. Subjects who are coerced (or heavily bribed) into writing the essays show no change in evaluation of the topic. Subjects who are given insufficient justification for writing the essay, or who are manipulated into believing that they had free choice in the matter, typically shift their evaluations in the direction of the position advocated in the essay. On the face of it, this would seem to indicate that subjects are aware of the existence of a change process since the means employed for assessing the response is a verbal report, and this report changes from premanipulation measures to postmanipulation measures.

Bem and McConnell contested this assumption by the simple expedient of asking the subjects, at the time of the postmanipulation measure, what their attitude *had been* 1 week earlier, at the time of the premanipulation measure. Control subjects had no difficulty reporting accurately on their previous opinions. In contrast, though the postmanipulation attitudes of experimental subjects were substantially different from their premanipulation attitudes, they reported that their current attitudes were the same as their premanipulation attitudes. Thus subjects apparently changed their attitudes in the absence of any subjective experience of change. This suggests that though subjects can sometimes report on the existence of the new evaluation, they may still be unaware of the fact that the evaluation has changed. If so, then they cannot be aware of the nature of the cognitive process that has occurred, because they are not even aware of the fact that a process has occurred at all.

Such a conclusion gains credence in view of a truly stunning demonstration of the same phenomenon by Goethals and Reckman (1973). These investigators assessed the opinions of high school students on 30 social issues, including attitudes toward busing of school children to achieve racial integration. One to two weeks later, students were called and asked to partici-pate in a group discussion of the busing issue. Each group was composed of three subjects whose pretest opinions indicated that they were all pro-busing or all anti-busing, plus one high school student confederate who was armed with a number of persuasive opinions and whose job it was to argue persistently against the opinion held by all other group members. He was highly successful in this task. Following the discussion, sub-jects indicated their opinions on the busing issue — on a scale different in form from the original measure. The original anti-busing subjects had their opinions sharply moderated in a pro-direction. Most of the pro-busing subjects were actually converted to an anti-busing posi-tion. Then Goethals and Reckman asked their subjects to recall, as best they could, what their original opinions on the busing question had been. Subjects were reminded that the experimenters were in possession of the original opinion scale and would check the accuracy of the sub-jects' recall. Control subjects were able to recall their original opinions with high accuracy. In contrast, among experimental subjects, the original anti-busing subjects "recalled" their opinions as having been much more pro-busing than they actually were, while the original pro-busing subjects actually recalled their original opinions as having been, on the average, anti-busing! In fact, the original pro-busing subjects recalled that they had been more anti-busing than the original anti-busing subjects recalled that they had been.

It would appear that subjects in the Goethals and Reckman (1973) study did not actually experience these enormous shifts as opinion change:

> Some subjects listened carefully to the course of the dis-cussion and began to nod their heads in agreement with the confederate's arguments. They seemed to come to agree with him without any awareness of their earlier attitude. In the debriefing they gave every indication that the position they adopted after the discussion was the position they had basically always held.... Most com-mented that the discussion had served to broaden their awareness of the issues involved or had provided sup-port for their original position. No subject reported that the discussion had had any effect in changing or modi-fying his position. (p. 499)

Thus research in the insufficient-justification and attribution traditions seems to indicate that (a) subjects sometimes do not report the evaluational and motiva-tional states produced in these experiments; and (b) even when they can report on such states, they may not report that a change has taken place in these states.

It may have occurred to the reader that the most direct approach to the question of accuracy of subjects' reports in these experiments would be simply to ask subjects why they behaved as they did and listen to what they have to say about their own cognitive processes. This would indeed be a fruitful approach, and it is dis-cussed below.

Reports About Cognitive Processes

A literal reading of the literature would give the impres-sion that researchers working in the areas of insuffi-cient-justification and attribution have not bothered to ask their subjects about their thought processes. We have been able to find only a single report of the results of such questioning. This is the terse and intriguing report by Ross, Rodin, and Zimbardo (1969) in their experiment on reattribution of arousal symptoms that the subjects "never explicitly mentioned any conflict about, or searching for, the 'explanation' for their arousal. This suggests that attribution may never have been consciously debated by these subjects" (p. 287). Fortunately, additional unpublished data, collected from subjects following their participation in attribution exper-iments by Nisbett and Schachter (1966) and Storms and Nisbett (1970), are available. These data are consistent with the description supplied by Ross et al.

In the experiment by Nisbett and Schachter (1966), subjects were requested to take a series of electric shocks of steadily increasing intensity. Prior to exposure to the shock, some of the subjects were given a placebo pill which, they were told, would produce heart palpita-tions, breathing irregularities, hand tremor, and butter-flies in the stomach. These are the physical symptoms most often reported by subjects as accompanying the experience of electric shock. It was anticipated that when subjects with these instructions were exposed to the shock, they would attribute their arousal symptoms to the pill, and would therefore be willing to tolerate more shock than subjects who could only attribute these aversive symptoms to the shock. And, in fact, the pill attribution subjects took four times as much amperage as shock attribution subjects.

Following his participation in the experiment, each subject in the pill attribution group was interviewed following a Spielberger-type (1962) graded debriefing procedure. (a) Question: "I notice that you took more shock than average. Why do you suppose you did?" Typical answer: "Gee, I don't really know .... Well, I used to build radios and stuff when I was 13 or 14, and maybe I got used to electric shock." (b) Question: "While you were taking the shock, did you think about the pill at all?" Typical answer: "No, I was too worried about the shock." (c) Question: "Did it occur to you at all that the pill was causing some physical effects?" Typical answer: "No, like I said, I was too busy worrying about the shock." In all, only 3 of 12 subjects reported having made the postulated attribution of arousal to the pill. (d) Finally, the experimenter described the hypothesis of the study in detail, including the postulated process of attribution of symptoms to the pill. He concluded by asking the subject if he might have had any thoughts like those described. Subjects typically said that the hypothesis was very interesting and that many people probably would go through the process that the experimenter described, but so far as they could tell, they themselves had not.

A similar blank wall was discovered by Storms and Nisbett (1970) in their experiment on the reattribution of insomnia symptoms. In that experiment, insomniac subjects were asked to report, for 2 consecutive nights, on the time they had gone to bed and the time they had finally gotten to sleep. Arousal condition subjects were then given a placebo pill to take 15 minutes before going to bed for the next 2 nights. These subjects were told that the pill would produce rapid heart rate, breathing irregularities, bodily warmth, and alertness — the physical and emotional symptoms, in other words, of insomnia. Relaxation subjects were told that their pills would produce the opposite symptoms — lowered heart rate, breathing rate, body temperature, and a reduction in alertness. It was anticipated that subjects in the arousal condition would get to sleep more quickly on the nights they took the pills because they would attribute their arousal symptoms to the pills rather than to emotionally laden cognitions concerning work or social life. Relaxation subjects were expected to take longer to get to sleep since they would infer that their emotional cognitions must be particularly intense because they were as fully aroused as usual even though they had taken a pill intended to lower arousal. These were in fact the results. Arousal subjects reported getting to sleep 28% quicker on the nights with the pills, and relaxation subjects reported taking 42% longer to get to sleep. Sleep onset was unaffected for control subjects.

In the interview following completion of the experiment, it was pointed out to subjects in experimental conditions that they had reported getting to sleep more quickly (or more slowly) on experimental nights than on the previous nights, and they were asked why. Arousal subjects typically replied that they usually found it easier to get to sleep later in the week, or that they had taken an exam that had worried them but had done well on it and could now relax, or that problems with a roommate or girlfriend seemed on their way to a resolution. Relaxation subjects were able to find similar sorts of reasons to explain their increased sleeplessness. When subjects were asked if they had thought about the pills at all before getting to sleep, they almost uniformly insisted that after taking the pills they had completely forgotten about them. When asked if it had occurred to them that the pill might be producing (or counteracting) their arousal symptoms, they reiterated their insistence that they had not thought about the pills at all after taking them. Finally, the experimental hypothesis and the postulated attribution processes were described in detail. Subjects showed no recognition of the hypothesized processes and (unlike subjects in the Nisbett and Schachter study) made little pretense of believing that *any* subjects could have gone through such processes.

Thus the explanations that subjects offer for their behavior in insufficient-justification and attribution experiments are so removed from the processes that investigators presume to have occurred as to give grounds for considerable doubt that there is direct access to these processes. Whatever the inferential process, the experimental method makes it clear that something about the manipulated stimuli produces the differential results. Yet subjects do not refer to these critical stimuli in any way in their reports on their cognitive processes.

Demonstrations of Subject Inability to Report Accurately on the Effects of Stimuli on Responses

In order to fill in the gaps in the literature, we have performed a series of small studies investigating people's ability to report accurately on the effects of stimuli on their responses. They were designed with several criteria in mind:

1. The cognitive processes studied were of a routine sort that occur frequently in daily life. Deception was used minimally, and in only a few of the studies.
2. Studies were designed to sample a wide range of behavioral domains, including evaluations, judgments, choices, and predictions.
3. Care was taken to establish that subjects were thoroughly cognizant of the existence of both the critical stimulus and their own responses.

4. With two exceptions, the critical stimuli were verbal in nature, thus reducing the possibility that subjects could be cognizant of the role of the critical stimulus but simply unable to describe it verbally.

5. Most of the stimulus situations were designed to be as little ego-involving as possible so that subjects would not be motivated on grounds of social desirability or self-esteem maintenance to assert or deny the role of particular stimuli in influencing their responses.

In all of the studies, some component of a complex stimulus situation was manipulated and the impact of this stimulus component on responses could thus be assessed. Subjects, as it turned out, were virtually never accurate in their reports. If the stimulus component had a significant effect on responses, subjects typically reported that it was noninfluential; if the stimulus component had no significant effect, subjects typically reported that it had been influential.

Failure to Report the Influence of Effective Stimulus Factors

Erroneous Reports about Position Effects on Appraisal and Choice

We conducted two studies that serendipitously showed a position effect on evaluation of an array of consumer goods. In both studies, conducted in commercial establishments under the guise of a consumer survey, passersby were invited to evaluate articles of clothing — four different nightgowns in one study (378 subjects) and four identical pairs of nylon stockings in the other (52 subjects). Subjects were asked to say which article of clothing was the best quality and, when they announced a choice, were asked why they had chosen the article they had. There was a pronounced left-to-right position effect, such that the right-most object in the array was heavily over-chosen. For the stockings, the effect was quite large, with the right-most stockings being preferred over the left-most by a factor of almost four to one. When asked about the reasons for their choices, no subject ever mentioned spontaneously the position of the article in the array. And, when asked directly about a possible effect of the position of the article, virtually all subjects denied it, usually with a worried glance at the interviewer suggesting that they felt either that they had misunderstood the question or were dealing with a madman.

Precisely why the position effect occurs is not obvious. It is possible that subjects carried into the judgment task the consumer's habit of "shopping around," holding off on choice of early-seen garments on the left in favor of later-seen garments on the right.

Erroneous Reports about the Influence of an Individual's Personality on Reactions to his Physical Characteristics

Perhaps the most remarkable of the demonstrations is one we have described in detail elsewhere (Nisbett & Wilson, in press). This study, an experimental demonstration of the halo effect, showed that the manipulated warmth or coldness of an individual's personality had a large effect on ratings of the attractiveness of his appearance, speech, and mannerisms, yet many subjects actually insisted that cause and effect ran in the opposite direction. They asserted that their feelings about the individual's appearance, speech, and mannerisms had influenced their liking of him.

Subjects were shown an interview with a college teacher who spoke English with a European accent. The interview dealt with teaching practices and philosophy of education. Half the subjects saw the teacher answering the questions in a pleasant, agreeable, and enthusiastic way (warm condition). The other half saw an autocratic martinet, rigid, intolerant, and distrustful of his students (cold condition). Subjects then rated the teacher's likability and rated also three attributes that were by their nature essentially invariant across the two experimental conditions: His physical appearance, his mannerisms, and his accent. Subjects who saw the warm version of the interview liked the teacher much better than subjects who saw the cold version of the interview, and there was a very marked halo effect. Most of the subjects who saw the warm version rated the teacher's appearance, mannerisms, and accent as attractive, while a majority of subjects who saw the cold version rated these qualities as irritating. Each of these differences was significant at the .001 level.

Some subjects in each condition were asked if their liking for the teacher had influenced their ratings of the three attributes, and some were asked if their liking for each of the three attributes had influenced their liking of the teacher. Subjects in both warm and cold conditions strongly denied any effect of their overall liking for the teacher on ratings of his attributes. Subjects who saw the warm version also denied that their liking of his attributes had influenced their overall liking. But subjects who saw the cold version asserted that their disliking of each of the three attributes had lowered their overall liking for him. Thus it would appear that these subjects precisely inverted the true causal relationship. Their disliking of the teacher lowered their evaluation of his appearance, his mannerisms, and accent, but subjects denied such an influence and asserted instead that their dislike of these attributes had decreased their liking of him!

Reporting the Influence of Ineffective Stimulus Factors

Three of our demonstrations involved the manipulation of stimulus factors that turned out to have no effect on subjects' judgments. In each of these studies, subjects reported that at least some of these actually ineffective factors had been highly influential in their judgments.

Erroneous Reports about the Emotional Impact of Literary Passages

In the first of these studies, 152 subjects (introductory psychology students) read a selection from the novel *Rabbit, Run* by John Updike. The selection described an alcoholic housewife who has just been left by her husband and who is cleaning up her filthy home in preparation for a visit by her mother. While drunkenly washing her infant girl, she accidentally allows the child to drown. The selection is well written and has a substantial emotional impact even when read out of the context of the rest of the novel. There were four conditions of the experiment. In one condition, subjects read the selection as it was written. In a second condition, a passage graphically describing the messiness of the baby's crib was deleted. In a third condition, subjects read the selection minus a passage physically describing the baby girl. In the fourth condition, both passages were deleted.

After reading the selection, all subjects were asked what emotional impact it had had. Then the manipulated passages were presented, and subjects were asked how the presence of the passage had affected (or would have affected, for subjects for whom the passage was deleted), the emotional impact of the selection. As it turned out, there was no detectable effect on reported emotional impact due to inclusion versus deletion of either passage. (Both pairs of means differed by less than .10 on a 7-point scale.) Subjects reported, however, that the passages had increased the impact

of the selection. Subjects exposed to the passage describing the messiness of the baby's crib were virtually unanimous in their opinion that the passage had increased the impact of the selection: 86% said the passage had increased the impact. Two thirds of the subjects exposed to the physical description of the baby reported that the passage had had an effect, and of those who reported it had an effect, two and a half times as many subjects said it had increased the impact of the selection as said it decreased the impact. The subjects who were not exposed to the passages on the initial reading predicted that both passages would have increased the impact of the selection had they been included. Predicted effects by these subjects were in fact extremely close to the pattern of (erroneous) reported effects by subjects who were exposed to the passages.

Erroneous Reports about the Effects of Distractions on Reactions to a Film

In another study, 90 subjects (introductory psychology students) were asked to view a brief documentary on the plight of the Jewish poor in large cities. Some subjects viewed the film while a distracting noise (produced by a power saw) occurred in the hall outside. Other subjects viewed the film while the focus was poorly adjusted on the projector. Control subjects viewed the film under conditions of no distraction. After viewing the film, subjects rated it on three dimensions — how interesting they thought it was, how much they thought other people would be affected by it, and how sympathetic they found the main character to be. Then, for experimental conditions, the experimenter apologized for the poor viewing conditions and asked subjects to indicate next to each rating whether he had been influenced by the noise or poor focus. Neither the noise nor the poor focus actually had any detectable effect on any of the three ratings. (Ratings were in general trivially *higher* for distraction subjects.) In the first and only demonstration of reasonably good accuracy in subject report of stimulus effects we found, most of the subjects in the poor focus condition actually reported that the focus had not affected their ratings (although 27% of the subjects reported that the focus had lowered at least one rating, a proportion significantly different from zero). A majority of subjects in the noise condition, however, erroneously reported that the noise had affected their ratings. Fifty-five per cent of these subjects reported that the noise had lowered at least one of their ratings.

Erroneous Reports about the Effects of Reassurance on Willingness to Take Electric Shocks

In a third study, 75 subjects (male introductory psychology students) were asked to predict how much shock they would take in an experiment on the effects of intense electric shocks. One version of the procedural protocol for the experiment included a "reassurance" that the shocks would do "no permanent damage." The other version did not include this "reassurance." Subjects receiving the first version were asked if the phrase about permanent damage had affected their predictions about the amount of shock they would take, and subjects receiving the second version were asked if the phrase would have affected their predictions, had it been included. Inclusion of the phrase in fact had no effect on predicted shock taking, but a majority of subjects reported that it did. Of those reporting an effect, more than 80% reported it had increased their predictions. Subjects who had not received the phrase were similarly, and erroneously, inclined to say that it would have increased their willingness to take shock had it been included.

Taken together, these studies indicate that the accuracy of subject reports about higher order mental processes may be very low. We wish to acknowledge that there are methodological and interpretive problems with some of the individual studies, however. Although the magnitude of effects induced by effective critical stimuli ranged from a ratio of 2:1 over control values to a ratio of 4:1, the critical stimuli may often have been merely necessary and not sufficient causes of the responses in question. Therefore subjects may often have been correct in asserting that some other stimulus was a more important determinant of their responses. In studies where the manipulated stimuli were ineffective (e.g., the literary passage and distraction studies), it is conceivable that perceived experimenter demands could have contributed to the results. And finally, in some of the studies it could be argued that the subjects denied the role of the influential stimulus in order to avoid looking silly or foolish (e.g., the position effect study), and not because they were unaware of its causal role.

We also wish to acknowledge that the studies do not suffice to show that people *could never* be accurate about the processes involved. To do so would require ecologically meaningless but theoretically interesting procedures such as interrupting a process at the very moment it was occurring, alerting subjects to pay careful attention to their cognitive processes, coaching them in introspective procedures, and so on. What the studies do indicate is that such introspective access as may exist is not sufficient to produce accurate reports about the role of critical stimuli in response to questions asked a few minutes or seconds after the stimuli have been processed and a response produced.

The Origin of Verbal Reports about Cognitive Processes

The Fount That Never was

In summary, it would appear that people may have little ability to report accurately on their cognitive processes:

1. Sometimes people are unable to report correctly even about the existence of the evaluative and motivational responses produced by the manipulations.
2. Sometimes people appear to be unable to report that a cognitive process has occurred.
3. Sometimes, people may not be able to identify the existence of the critical stimulus.
4. Even when people are completely cognizant of the existence of both stimulus and response they appear to be unable to report correctly about the effect of the stimulus on the response.

Polanyi (1964) and others (e.g., Gross, 1974) have argued persuasively that "we can know more than we can tell," by which it is meant that people can perform skilled activities without being able to describe what they are doing and can make fine discriminations without being able to articulate their basis. The research described above suggests that the converse is also true — that we sometimes tell more than we can know. More formally, people sometimes make assertions about mental events to which they may have no access and these assertions may bear little resemblance to the actual events.

The evidence reviewed is then consistent with the most pessimistic view concerning people's ability to report accurately about their cognitive processes. Though methodological implications are not our chief concern, we should note that the evidence indicates it may be quite misleading for social scientists to ask their subjects about the influences on their evaluations, choices, or behavior. The relevant research indicates that such reports, as well as predictions, may have little value except for whatever utility they may have in the study of verbal explanations per se.

More importantly, the evidence suggests that people's erroneous reports about their cognitive processes are not capricious or haphazard, but instead are regular and systematic. Evidence for this comes from the fact that "observer" subjects, who did not participate in experiments but who simply read verbal descriptions of them, made predictions about the stimuli which were remarkably similar to the reports about the stimuli by subjects who had actually been exposed to them. In experiments by Latané and Darley (1970), and in several of our own studies, subjects were asked to predict how they themselves, or how other people, would react to the stimulus situations that had actually been presented to other subjects. The observer subjects made predictions that in every case were similar to the erroneous reports given by the actual subjects. Thus Latané and Darley's original subjects denied that the presence of other people had affected their behavior, and observer subjects also denied that the presence of others would affect either their own or other people's behavior. In two of our studies, subjects were asked to predict how they would have responded to stimuli that were actually presented to subjects in another condition. In both cases, predictions about behavior were very similar to the inaccurate reports of subjects who had actually been exposed to the conditions. Thus, whatever capacity for introspection exists, it does not produce accurate reports about stimulus effects, nor does it even produce reports that differ from predictions of observers operating only with a verbal description of the stimulus situation. As Bem (1967) put it in a similar context, if the reports of subjects do not differ from the reports of observers, then it is unneccessary to assume that the former are drawing on "a fount of privileged knowledge" (p. 186). It seems equally clear that subjects and observers are drawing on a similar source for their verbal reports about stimulus effects. What might this be?

A Priori Causal Theories

We propose that when people are asked to report how a particular stimulus influenced a particular response, they do so not by consulting a memory of the mediating process, but by applying or generating causal theories about the effects of that type of stimulus on that type of response. They simply make judgments, in other words, about how plausible it is that the stimulus would have influenced the response. These plausibility judgments exist prior to, or at least independently of, any actual contact with the particular stimulus embedded in a particular complex stimulus configuration. Causal theories may have any of several origins.

1. The culture or a subculture may have explicit rules stating the relationship between a particular stimulus and a particular response ("I came to a stop because the light started to change." "I played a trump because I had no cards in the suit that was led").

2. The culture or a subculture may supply implicit theories about causal relations. In Abelson's (1968) terms, the presence of a particular stimulus may "psychologically imply" a particular response ("Jim gave flowers to Amy [me]; that's why she's [I'm] acting pleased as punch today"). In Kelley's (1972) terms, people growing up in a given culture learn certain "causal schemata," psychological rules governing likely stimulus-response relations ("The ballplayer [I] was paid to endorse Aqua-Velva, that's the only reason he [I] endorsed it").

3. An individual may hold a particular causal theory on the basis of empirical observation of covariation between stimuli of the general type and responses of the general type. ("I'm grouchy today. I'm always grouchy when I don't break 100 in golf.") There is reason to suspect, however, that actual covariation may play less of a role in perceived or reported covariation than do theories about covariation. The Chapmans (Chapman, 1967; Chapman & Chapman, 1967, 1969) have shown that powerful covariations may go undetected when the individual lacks a theory leading him to suspect covariation and, conversely, that the individual may perceive covariation where there is none if he has a theory leading him to expect it. The present position, of course, leads to the expectation that people would be as subject to theory-induced errors in self-perception as in the perception of convariation among purely external events.

4. In the absence of a culturally supplied rule, implicit causal theory, or assumption about covariation, people may be able to generate causal hypotheses linking even novel stimuli and novel responses. They may do so by searching their networks of connotative relations surrounding the stimulus description and the response description. If the stimulus is connotatively similar to the response, then it may be reported as having influenced the response. To the extent that people share similar connotative networks they would be expected to arrive at similar judgments about the likelihood of a causal link between stimulus and response.

We do not wish to imply that all or even most a priori causal theories are wrong. Verbal reports relying on such theories will typically be wrong not because the theories are in error in every case but merely because they are incorrectly applied in the particular instance.

The tools that people employ when asked to make judgments about causality are analogous to the "representativeness heuristic" described by Tversky and Kahneman (1973, 1974; Kahneman & Tversky, 1973). These writers have proposed that when making judgments about the probability that an individual is, say, a librarian, one does so by comparing his information about the individual with the contents of his stereotype concerning librarians. If the information is representative of the contents of the stereotype concerning librarians, then it is deemed "probable" that the individual is a librarian. Information that is more pertinent to a true probability judgment, such as the proportion of librarians in the population, is ignored. We are proposing that a similar sort of representativeness heuristic is employed in assessing cause and effect relations in self-perception. Thus a particular stimulus will be deemed a representative cause if the stimulus and response are linked via a rule, an implicit theory, a presumed empirical covariation, or overlapping connotative networks.

In the experiments reviewed above, then, subjects may have been making simple representativeness judgments when asked to introspect about their cognitive processes. Worry and concern seem to be representative, plausible reasons for insomnia while thoughts about the physiological effects of pills do not. The knit, sheerness, and weave of nylon stockings seem representative of reasons for liking them, while their position on a table does not. And a reassurance that electric shock will cause no permanent damage seems representative of reasons for accepting shock; a passage graphically describing the physical characteristics of a child seems representative of reasons for being emotionally affected by a literary selection ending with the death of a child, and a distracting noise seems representative of reasons for not liking a film.

When subjects were asked about their cognitive processes, therefore, they did something that may have felt like introspection but which in fact may have been only a simple judgment of the extent to which input was a representative or plausible cause of output. It seems likely, in fact, that the subjects in the present studies, and ordinary people in their daily lives, do not even attempt to interrogate their memories about their cognitive processes when they are asked questions about them. Rather, they may resort in the first instance to a pool of culturally supplied explanations for behavior of the sort in question or, failing in that, begin a search through a network of connotative relations until they find an explanation that may be adduced as psychologically

implying the behavior. Thus if we ask another person why he enjoyed a particular party and he responds with "I liked the people at the party," we may be extremely dubious as to whether he has reached this conclusion as a result of anything that might be called introspection. We are justified in suspecting that he has instead asked himself Why People Enjoy Parties and has come up with the altogether plausible hypothesis that in general people will like parties if they like the people at the parties. Then, his only excursion into his storehouse of private information would be to make a quick check to verify that his six worst enemies were not at the party. If not, he confidently asserts that the people-liking was the basis of his party-liking. He is informationally superior to observers, in this account, only by virtue of being able to make this last-minute check of his enemies list, and not by virtue of any ability to examine directly the effects of the stimuli (the people) on his response (enjoyment).

The present view carries two important implications that go beyond a merely anti-introspectivist position: (a) People's reports will sometimes be correct, and it should be possible to predict when they will be likely to be correct. (b) People's reports about their higher mental processes should be neither more nor less accurate, in general, then the predictions about such processes made by observers. An experiment by Nisbett and Bellows (Note 3), reported below, tested both these implications.

Accuracy of Subject Reports and Observer Predictions

The above analysis implies that it should be possible to demonstrate accuracy and inaccuracy in verbal reports in the same experiment by simply asking subjects to make two sorts of judgments — those for which the influential factors are plausible and are included in a priori causal theories, and others which are influenced by implausible factors not included in such theories. In the former case, both subjects and observers should be accurate; in the latter, neither should be accurate.

Nisbett and Bellows (Note 3) asked female subjects to read a lengthy description of a woman who was applying for a job as a counselor in a crisis intervention center. Subjects read what they believed was the application portfolio, a lengthy document including a letter of recommendation and a detailed report of an interview with the center's director. Five stimulus factors were manipulated. (a) The woman's appearance was either described in such a way as to make it clear that she was quite physically attractive, or nothing was said about her appearance. (b) The woman was either described as having superb academic credentials, or nothing was said about her academic credentials. (c) The woman was described as having spilled a cup of coffee over the interviewer's desk, or nothing was said about any such incident. (d) The woman was described as having been in a serious auto accident, or nothing was said about an accident. (e) Subjects were either told that they would meet the woman whose folder they were reading, or they were told that they would meet some other applicant. These stimuli were manipulated factorially.

After reading the portfolio, subjects were asked to make four judgments about the woman: (a) how much they liked her, (b) how sympathetic they thought she would be toward clients' problems, (c) how intelligent they thought she was, and (d) how flexible they thought she would be in dealing with clients' problems. Then subjects were asked how each of the factors (ranging from 0 for some subjects up to 5 for others) had influenced each of the four judgments.

In addition, "observer" subjects were asked to state how each of the five factors would influence each of the four judgments. These subjects did not read any portfolio and, indeed, the factors were described only in summary form (e.g., "Suppose you knew that someone was quite physically attractive. How would that influence how much you would like the person?"). Both observers and subjects answered these questions on 7-point scales ranging from "increase(d) my liking a great deal" to "decrease(d) my liking a great deal."

Two predictions about the results of the study follow from the present analysis.

1. Subjects should be much more accurate in their reports about the effects of the stimulus factors on the intelligence judgment than in their reports about the effects of the factors on their other judgments. This is because the culture specifies more clearly what sorts of factors ought to influence a judgment of intelligence, and in what way they should do so, than it does for judgments such as liking, sympathy toward others, or flexibility. In fact, the other factor-judgment combinations were chosen with malice aforethought. Recent work by social psychologists has shown that several of the factors have implausible effects on several of the judgments, for example, people tend to give more favorable ratings on a number of dimensions to people whom they believe they are about to meet than to people whom they do not expect to meet (Darley & Berscheid, 1967).
2. Whether subjects are generally accurate in reports about the effects of the factors on a given judgment

or generally inaccurate, their accuracy will be equalled by observers working from impoverished descriptions of the factors.

The results gave the strongest possible support to both predictions. Mean subject reports about the effects of the factors, mean observer reports, and mean actual effects (experimental minus control means) were compared for each of the judgments. The most remarkable result was that subject and observer reports of factor utilization were so strongly correlated for each of the judgments that it seems highly unlikely that subjects and observers could possibly have arrived at these reports by different means. Mean subject and observer reports of factor utilization were correlated .89 for the liking judgment, .84 for the sympathy judgment, .99 for the intelligence judgment, and .77 for the flexibility judgment. Such strong correspondence between subject and observer reports suggests that both groups produced these reports via the same route, namely by applying or generating similar causal theories.

As anticipated, subject accuracy was extremely high for the intelligence judgment. Subject reports about the effects of the factors were correlated .94 with true effects of the factors. Also as anticipated, however, observer predictions were fully as accurate as subject reports: Observer predictions were correlated .98 with true effects of the factors on the intelligence judgment.

For the other judgments, the accuracy of subject reports was literally nil. Subject reports were correlated — .31 with true effects on the liking judgment, .14 with true effects on the sympathy judgment, and .11 with true effects on the flexibility judgment. Once again, observers were neither more nor less accurate than subjects. Correlations of their predictions with true effects were highly similar to the correlations of subject reports with true effects.

It should be noted that the experiment provides good justification for requiring a change in the traditional empirical definition of awareness. "Awareness" has been equated with "correct verbal report." The Nisbett and Bellows experiment and the present analysis strongly suggest that this definition is misleading and overgenerous. The criterion for "awareness" should be instead "verbal report which exceeds in accuracy that obtained from observers provided with a general description of the stimulus and response in question." Even highly accurate reports, therefore, provide no evidence of introspective awareness of the effects of the stimuli on responses if observers can equal that level of accuracy.

Accuracy and Inaccuracy in Verbal Explanations

When Will We Be Wrong In Our Verbal Reports?

It is possible to speculate further about the circumstances that should promote accuracy in reports about higher mental processes and those that should impair accuracy. We will need to call on another Tversky and Kahneman (1973) concept to help describe these circumstances. These writers proposed that a chief determinant of judgments about the frequency and probability of events is the *availability* in memory of the events at the time of judgment. Events are judged as frequent in proportion to their availability, and their availability is determined by such factors as the salience of the events at the time they were encountered, the strength of the network of verbal associations that spontaneously call the events to mind, and instructional manipulations designed to make the events more salient at the time of judgment.

The representativeness and availability heuristics are undoubtedly intertwined in the appraisal of cause and effect relations. If a particular stimulus is not available, then it will not be adduced in explanation of a given effect, even though it might be highly representative or plausible once called to mind. Similarly, the representativeness heuristic may be a chief determinant of availability in cause–effect analysis: A particular stimulus may be available chiefly because it is a highly representative cause of the effect to be explained.

It is possible to describe many circumstances that would serve to reduce the availability of a given causal candidate that is in fact influential, or to enhance the availability of a causal candidate that is in fact noninfluential. Similarly, influential causes will sometimes be nonrepresentative of the effects they produce, and noninfluential factors nevertheless will be highly representative causes. Any of these circumstances should promote error in verbal reports.

Removal in Time
Perhaps chief among the circumstances that should decrease accuracy in self-report is a separation in time between the report and the actual occurrence of the process. In almost all the research described above, subjects were asked about a cognitive process immediately after its occurrence, often within seconds of its occurrence. While the present viewpoint holds that there may be no direct access to process even under these circumstances, it is at least the case that subjects are often cognizant of the existence of the effective stimuli at this point. Thus subjects have some chance of accurately reporting that a particular stimulus was influential if it happens to seem to be a plausible cause of the outcome. At some later point, the existence of the stimulus may be forgotten, or become less available, and thus there would be little chance that it could be correctly identified as influential. Similarly, the vagaries of memory may allow the invention of factors presumed to be present at the time the process occurred. It is likely that such invented factors would be generated by use of causal theories. Thus it would be expected that the more removed in time the report is from the process, the more stereotypical should be the reported explanation.

Mechanics of Judgment[1]
There is a class of influential factors to which we should be particularly blind. That class may be described as the mechanics of judgment factors — for example, serial order effects, position effects, contrast effects, and many types of anchoring effects. Such factors should seem particularly implausible as reasons for liking or disliking an object, or for estimating its magnitude on some dimension as high or low. Indeed, it seems outrageous that such a judgment as one concerning the quality of a nightgown might be affected by its position in a series, or that the estimation of the size of an object should be affected by the size of a similar object examined just previously.

Context
Generally, it should be the case that we will be blind to contextual factors, or at any rate be particularly poor at disentangling the effects of the stimulus from the context in which it was encountered. Contextual cues are not likely to be spontaneously salient when we are asked, or ask ourselves, why we evaluated an object as we did. Any question about an object is likely to focus our attention on the properties of the object itself and to cause us to ignore contextual cues. When a question about context is asked directly, on the other hand, as when we questioned our subjects about the effects of noise on their reactions to a film, contextual factors might well be reported as influential even when they are not. Unlike mechanics of judgment factors, many context factors, once they are made available, should seem highly plausible causes.

---

[1] We are indebted to Amos Tversky for this idea.

Nonevents

Ross (in press) has pointed out that many judgments and evaluations probably are based at least in part on the nonoccurrence of certain events. Thus one person may correctly perceive that another person does not like him, and this perception may be based largely on the nonoccurrence of friendly behaviors rather than on the outright manifestation of hostility. There is good reason to suspect that nonbehavior will be generally less available and salient than behavior, and therefore should rarely be reported as influential. But the effect will still require explanation, and thus noninfluential events will often be invoked in preference to influential nonevents.

Nonverbal Behavior

In evaluating other people, we probably rely heavily on nonverbal cues such as posture, distance, gaze, and the volume and tone of voice (Argyle, Solter, Nicholson, Williams, & Burgess, 1970). Yet it seems likely that such nonverbal cues would be less available than verbal behavior, if only because verbal labels for nonverbal behavior are few and impoverished. To the extent that we rely on verbal memory to explain our evaluations of other people there will be proportionately more verbal behaviors to serve as causal candidates than nonverbal behaviors. To the extent that nonverbal behaviors are important to evaluations, relative to verbal behaviors, they will be wrongly overlooked.

Discrepancy Between the Magnitudes of Cause and Effect

In general, we would expect that factors will be perceived as causal to the degree that their magnitudes resemble the magnitude of the effects they are adduced to explain. In the development of causal schemata, both the notion that large causes can produce large effects and the notion that small causes can produce small effects probably precede the development of the notion that large causes can produce small effects. The notion that small causes can produce large effects probably develops very late and never attains very great stability. It is likely that conspiracy theories often feed on the discrepancy between officially provided causal explanations and the large effects they are invoked to explain. It is outrageous that a single, pathetic, weak figure like Lee Harvey Oswald should alter world history. When confronted with large effects, it is to comparably large causes that we turn for explanations. Thus when Storms and Nisbett (1970) interviewed insomniacs and asked them why they slept so little, both on particular occasions and in general, they were inclined to explain their insomnia in terms of the stress of their current life situation or even in terms of neurosis or chronic anxiety. Smaller causes, such as an overheated room, a tendency to work or exercise or smoke just before going to bed, or a tendency to keep irregular hours, were overlooked. Many judgments of the plausibility of cause and effect relations are probably based at least in part on the fittingness of cause and effect magnitudes. Thus both mechanics of judgment factors and nonevents should often be perceived as implausible causes simply because of their smallness and seeming inconsequentiality.

When Will We Be Correct In Our Verbal Reports?

The present analysis corresponds to common sense in that it allows that we will often be right about the causes of our judgments and behavior. If a stranger walks up to a person, strikes him, and walks away, and the person is later asked if he likes the stranger, he will reply that he does not and will accurately report the reason. The interaction he has had with the stranger will be highly salient and a highly plausible reason for disliking someone. And, in general, the conditions that promote accuracy in verbal report will be the opposite of those described previously. These conditions may be summarized briefly by saying that reports will be accurate when influential stimuli are (a) available and (b) plausible causes of the response, and when (c) few or no plausible but noninfluential factors are available.

There is, in fact, some evidence in the literature that people can sometimes accurately report on the stimuli that influenced particular cognitive processes.

The Correspondence Between Actual and Subjective Weights in Judgment Tasks

Slovic and Lichtenstein (1971) have reviewed the literature concerning the ability of subjects to report accurately on the weights they assign to various stimulus factors in making evaluations. Most of the investigations of this question have employed either clinical psychologists or stockbrokers as subjects, and the judgmental domain has been largely limited to clinical diagnoses and assessments of the financial soundness of stocks. Subjects are asked to diagnose patients using Minnesota Multiphasic Personality Inventory (MMPI) scores or to assess stocks using such indicators as growth potential and earnings ratio. Then subjects are asked to state the degree of their reliance on various factors. These subjective weights are then compared to the objective weights derived from regression of the subject's judgments on the various factors. Slovic and Lichtenstein (1971) concluded that self-insight was poor and that of the studies which allowed for a comparison of perceived and actual cue utilization, "all found serious discrepancies between subjective and objective relative weights" (p. 684). While this is a fair assessment of this literature, what strikes one as impressive from the present vantage point is that almost all the studies reviewed by Slovic and Lichtenstein (1971) found evidence of at least some correspondence between subjective and objective weights. This is almost the sole evidence we have been able to uncover that people can be at all accurate in reporting about the effects of stimuli on their responses.

The present framework is useful in understanding this lonely outcropping of accuracy. Clinical psychologists and stockbrokers undertake a formal study of the decision processes they should employ. They are taught explicitly how various factors should be weighed in their evaluations. Thus, for example, elevation of the schizophrenia scale will seem to be a highly plausible reason for a judgment of severe pathology because this is an association that clinicians are formally taught. It seems likely, in fact, that clinicians and stockbrokers could assign accurate weights *prior* to making the series of judgments in these experiments simply by calling on the stored rules about what such judgments should reflect. If so, one would scarcely want to say they were engaging in prospective introspection, but merely that they remember well the formal rules of diagnosis or financial counseling they were taught.

And in general, we may say that people will be accurate in reports about the causes of their behavior and evaluations wherever the culture, or a subculture, specifies clearly what stimuli should produce which responses, and especially where there is continuing feedback from the culture or subculture concerning the extent to which the individual is following the prescribed rules for input and output. Thus university admissions officials will be reasonably accurate about the weights they assign to various types of information in admissions folders, and auto mechanics will be reasonably accurate about the weights they assign to various factors in deciding whether a car has ignition or carburetor troubles. But such accuracy cannot be regarded as evidence of direct access to processes of evaluation. It is evidence for nothing more than the ability to describe the formal rules of evaluation.

The implication of this analysis is that the judgment studies lack what might be called "causal theory controls."

Subjects' reported weights should not be compared directly to their actual weights. Instead, investigators should examine the *increment* in prediction of actual weights that is obtained by asking subjects about their subjective weights over the prediction that is obtained by (a) asking subjects about their subjective weights *prior* to their examination of the data set in question; or (b) asking subjects about their beliefs concerning the weights employed by the average, or ideal, or some particular, clinician or stockbroker; or even (c) by simply asking subjects about the weights they were *taught* to employ in such judgments.

In the present view, little or no "awareness" might be found in studies employing such controls. That is, the subject's actual weights might be as well predicted by his subjective weights for his neighboring stockbroker as by the subject's reports about the weights he himself used.

Why are We Unaware of Our Unawareness?

There is of course a problem with any characterization of "introspection" as nothing more than judgments of plausibility. It does not feel like that at all. While we may sometimes admit to confusion about how we solved a particular problem or why we evaluated a person in a given way, it is often the case that we feel as though we have direct access to cognitive processes. We could retreat behind our data and assert that there is by now enough evidence discrediting introspective reports to allow us to ignore any argument based on introspection. But there is more that can be said than this.

It seems likely that there are regularities concerning the conditions that give rise to introspective certainty about cognitive processes. Confidence should be high when the causal candidates are (a) few in number, (b) perceptually or memorially salient, (c) highly plausible causes of the given outcome (especially where the basis of plausibility is an explicit cultural rule), and (d) where the causes have been observed to be associated with the outcome in the past. In fact, we appeal to introspection to support this view. Does the reader feel there is anything beyond factors such as these that need be adduced to account for occasions of subjective certainty?

The above view, it should be noted, is eminently testable. It should be possible to show that subjective certainty is great when causal candidates are salient and highly plausible, but are in reality noninfluential. Subjective certainty should be lower when the causal candidates are actually influential, but are not salient, not plausible, or compete with more salient or plausible but noninfluential causal candidates.

REFERENCE NOTES

1. Aronson, E. Personal communication, 1975.
2. Zimbardo, P. Personal communication, 1975.
3. Nisbett, R. E., & Bellows, N. *Accuracy and inaccuracy in verbal reports about influences on evaluations.* Unpublished manuscript, University of Michigan, 1976.

REFERENCES

Abelson, R. P. Psychological implication. In R. P. Abelson et al. (Eds.), *Theories of cognitive consistency: A sourcebook.* Chicago: Rand McNally, 1968.

Argyle, M., Salter, U., Nicholson, H., Williams, M., & Burgess, P. The communication of inferior and superior attitudes by verbal and nonverbal signals. *British Journal of Social and Clinical Psychology,* 1970, *9,* 222–231.

Aronson, E., & Mills, J. the effect of severity of initiation on liking for a group. *Journal of Abnormal and Social Psychology,* 1959, *59,* 177–181.

Bem, D. J. Self-perception: An alternative interpretation of cognitive dissonance phenomena. *Psychological Review,* 1967, *74,* 183–200.

Bem, D. J. Self-perception theory. In L. Berkowitz (Ed.), *Advances in experimental social psychology* (Vol. 6). New York: Academic Press, 1972.

Bem, D. J., & McConnell, H. K. Testing the self-perception explanation of dissonance phenomena: On the salience of premanipulation attitudes. *Journal of Personality and Social Psychology,* 1970, *14,* 23–31.

Berkowitz, L., & Turner, C. Perceived anger level, instigating agent, and aggression. In H. London & R. E. Nisbett (Eds.), *Thought and feeling: Cognitive alteration of feeling states.* Chicago: Aldine-Atherton, 1974.

Brehm, J. W. Modification of hunger by cognitive dissonance. In P. G. Zimbardo, *The cognitive control of motivation.* Glenview, Ill.: Scott, Foresman, 1969.

Brehm, M. L., Back, K. W., & Bogdonoff, M. D. A physiological effect of cognitive dissonance under food deprivation and stress. In P. G. Zimbardo, *The cognitive control of motivation.* Glenview, Ill.: Scott, Foresman, 1969.

Broadbent, D. E. *Perception and communication.* London, Pergamon Press, 1958.

Brock, T. C., & Grant, L. D. Dissonance, awareness, and thirst motivation. In P. G. Zimbardo, *The cognitive control of motivation.* Glenview, Ill.: Scott, Foresman, 1969.

Brown, R. Models of attitude change. In R. Brown, E. Galanter, E. H. Hess, & G. Mandler (Eds.), *New directions in psychology* (Vol. 1). New York: Holt, Rinehart & Winston, 1962.

Burt, C. L. *The young delinquent* (4th ed.). London: University of Toronto Press, 1925.

Chapman, L. J. Illusory correlation in observational report. *Journal of Verbal Learning and Verbal Behavior,* 1967, *6,* 151–155.

Chapman, L. J., & Chapman, J. P. Genesis of popular but erroneous diagnostic observations. *Journal of Abnormal Psychology,* 1967, *72,* 193–204.

Chapman, L. J., & Chapman, J. P. Illusory correlation as an obstacle to the use of valid psychodiagnostic signs. *Journal of Abnormal Psychology,* 1969, *74,* 271–280.

Cohen, A. R., & Zimbardo, P. G. Dissonance and the need to avoid failure. In P. G. Zimbardo, *The cognitive control of motivation.* Glenview, Ill.: Scott, Foresman, 1969.

Cottrell, N. B., & Wack, D. L. The energizing effect of cognitive dissonance on dominant and subordinate responses. *Journal of Personality and Social Psychology,* 1967, *6,* 132–138.

Darley, J. M., & Berscheid, E. Increased liking as a result of the anticipation of personal contact. *Human Relations,* 1967, *20,* 29–40.

Davis, J. A. *Great aspirations: The graduate school plans of America's college students.* Chicago: Aldine, 1964.

Davison, G. C., & Valins, S. Maintenance of self-attributed and drug-attributed behavior change. *Journal of Personality and Social Psychology,* 1969, *11,* 25–33.

Dixon, N. F. *Subliminal perception: The nature of a controversy.* London: McGraw-Hill, 1971.

Dulany, D. C. The place of hypotheses and intention: An analysis of verbal control in verbal conditioning. In C. W. Eriksen (Ed.), *Behavior and awareness.* Durham, N. C.: Duke University Press, 1962.

Erdelyi, M. H. A new look at the new look: Perceptual defense and vigilance. *Psychological Review,* 1974, *81,* 1–25.

Eriksen, C. W. Figments, fantasies, and foibles: A search for the unconscious mind. In C. W. Eriksen (Ed.), *Behavior and awareness.* Durham, N. C.: Duke University Press, 1962.

Ferdinand, P. R. *The effect of forced compliance on recognition.* Unpublished master's thesis, Purdue University, 1964.

Festinger, L. *Cognitive dissonance.* Stanford, Calif.: Stanford University Press, 1957.

Freedman, J. L. Attitudinal effects of inadequate justification. *Journal of Personality,* 1963, *31,* 371–385.

Freedman, J. L. Long-term behavioral effects of cognitive dissonance. *Journal of Experimental Social Psychology,* 1965, *1,* 145–155.

Gaudet, H. A model for assessing changes in voting intention. In P. F. Lazarsfeld & M. Rosenberg (Eds.), *The language of social research.* New York: Free Press of Glencoe, 1955.

Ghiselin, B. *The creative process.* New York: Mentor, 1952.

Goethals, G. R., & Reckman, R. F. The perception of consistency in attitudes. *Journal of Experimental Social Psychology,* 1973, *9,* 491–501.

Goode, W. J. *After divorce.* New York: Free Press of Glencoe, 1956.

Greenspoon, J. The reinforcing effect of two spoken sounds on the frequency of two responses. *American Journal of Psychology,* 1955, *68,* 409–416.

Grinker, J. Cognitive control of classical eyelid conditioning. In P. G. Zimbardo, *The cognitive control of motivation.* Glenview, Ill.: Scott, Foresman, 1969.

Gross, L. Modes of communication and the acquisition of symbolic competence. *Seventy-third Yearbook of the National Society for the Study of Education.* Chicago: University of Chicago Press, 1974.

Jones, E. E., & Nisbett, R. E. The actor and the observer: Divergent perceptions of the causes of behavior. In E. E. Jones et al. (Eds.), *Attribution: Perceiving the causes of behavior.* Morristown, N. J.: General Learning Press, 1972.

Kadushin, C. Individual decisions to undertake psychotherapy. *Administrative Science Quarterly,* 1958, *3,* 379–411.

Kahneman, D., & Tversky, A. On the psychology of prediction. *Psychological Review,* 1973, *80,* 237–251.

Kelley, H. H. Attribution theory in social psychology. In D. Levine (Ed.), *Nebraska Symposium on Motivation* (Vol. 15). Lincoln: University of Nebraska Press, 1967.

Kelley, H. H. Attribution in social interaction. In E. E. Jones et al. (Eds.), *Attribution: Perceiving the causes of behavior.* Morristown, N. J.: General Learning Press, 1972.

Kelman, H. Deception in social research. *Transaction,* 1966, *3,* 20–24.

Kornhauser, A., & Lazarsfeld, P. F. The analysis of consumer actions. In P. F. Lazarsfeld & M. Rosenberg (Eds.), *The language of social research.* Glencoe, Ill.: Free Press, 1955.

Kruglanski, A. W., Friedman, I., & Zeevi, G. The effects of extrinsic incentive on some qualitative aspects of task performance. *Journal of Personality,* 1971, *39,* 606–617.

Latané, B., & Darley, J. M. *The unresponsive bystander: Why doesn't he help?* New York: Appleton-Century-Crofts, 1970.

Lazarsfeld, P. F. (Ed.), *Jugend und Beruf.* Jena, Germany: Fischer, 1931.

Maier, N. R. F. Reasoning in humans: II. The solution of a problem and its appearance in consciousness. *Journal of Comparative Psychology,* 1931, *12,* 181–194.

Mandler, G. Consciousness: Respectable, useful and probably necessary. In R. Solso (Ed.), *Information processing and cognition: The Loyola Symposium.* Hillsdale, N. J.: Erlbaum, 1975. (a)

Mandler, G. *Mind and emotion.* New York: Wiley, 1975. (b)

Mansson, H. H. The relation of dissonance reduction to cognitive, perceptual, consummatory, and learning measures of thirst. In P. G. Zimbardo, *The cognitive control of motivation.* Glenview, Ill.: Scott, Foresman 1969.

Miller, G. A. *Psychology: The science of mental life.* New York: Harper & Row, 1962.

Moray, N. *Attention: Selective processes in vision and hearing.* London: Hutchinson Educational, 1969.

Neisser, U. *Cognitive psychology.* New York: Appleton Century-Crofts, 1967.

Nisbett, R. E., & Schachter, S. Cognitive manipulation of pain. *Journal of Experimental Social Psychology* 1966, *2,* 227–236.

Nisbett, R. E., & Valins, S. Perceiving the causes of one's own behavior. New York: General Learning Press, 1972.

Nisbett, R. E., & Wilson, T. D. The halo effect: Evidence for unconscious alteration of judgments. *Journal of Personality and Social Psychology,* in press.

Pallak, M. S. The effects of unexpected shock and relevant or irrelevant dissonance on incidental retention. *Journal of Personality and Social Psychology,* 1970, *14,* 271.

Pallak, M. S., Brock, T. C., & Kiesler, C. A. Dissonance arousal and task performance in an incidental verbal learning paradigm. *Journal of Personality and Social Psychology,* 1967, *7,* 11–21.

Pallak, M. S., & Pittman, T. S. General motivational effects of dissonance arousal. *Journal of Personality and Social Psychology,* 1972, *21,* 349–358.

Polanyi, M. *Personal knowledge: Toward a post-critical philosophy.* New York: Harper, 1964.

Rosenfeld, H. M., & Baer, D. M. Unnoticed verbal conditioning of an aware experimenter by a more aware subject: The double-agent effect. *Psychological Review,* 1969, *76,* 425–432.

Ross, L. D. The intuitive psychologist and his short-comings: Distortions in the attribution process. In L. Berkowitz (Ed.), *Advances in experimental social psychology.* New York: Academic Press, in press.

Ross, L., Rodin, J., & Zimbardo, P. G. Toward an attribution therapy: The reduction of fear through induced cognitive-emotional misattribution. *Journal of Personality and Social Psychology,* 1969, *12,* 279–288.

Rossi, P. H. *Why families move: A study in the social psychology of urban residential mobility.* New York: Free Press of Glencoe, 1955.

Schachter, S., & Singer, J. E. Cognitive, social, and physiological determinants of emotional state. *Psychological Review,* 1962, *69,* 379–399.

Schachter, S., & Wheeler, L. Epinephrine, chlorpromazine, and amusement. *Journal of Abnormal and Social Psychology,* 1962, *65,* 121–128.

Schlachet, P. J. The motivation to succeed and the memory for failure. In P. G. Zimbardo, *The cognitive control of motivation.* Glenview, Ill.: Scott, Foresman, 1969.

Sills, D. L. *The volunteers: Means and ends in a national organization.* Glencoe, Ill.: Free Press, 1957.

Sills, D. L. On the art of asking "Why not?" Some problems and procedures in studying acceptance of family planning. In All India Conference on Family Planning (Fourth, 1961) *Report of the Proceedings: 29th January-3rd February 1961, Hyderabad.* Bombay: Family Planning Association of India, 1961.

Slovic, P., & Lichtenstein, S. Comparison of Bayesian and regression approaches to the study of information processing in judgment, *Organizational Behavior and Human Performance,* 1971, *6,* 649–744.

Snyder, M., Schulz, R., & Jones, E. E. Expectancy and apparent duration as determinants of fatigue. *Journal of Personality and Social Psychology,* 1974, *29,* 426–434.

Spielberger, C. D. The role of awareness in verbal conditioning. In C. W. Eriksen (Ed.), *Behavior and awareness* Durham, N.C.: Duke University Press, 1962.

Storms, M. D., & Nisbett, R. E. Insomnia and the attribution process. *Journal of Personality and Social Psychology,* 1970, *2,* 319–328.

Treisman, A. M. Strategies and models of selective attention. *Psychological Review,* 1969, *76,* 282–299.

Tversky, A., & Kahneman, D. Availability: A heuristic for judging frequency and probability. *Cognitive Psychology,* 1973, *5,* 207–232.

Tversky, A., & Kahneman, D. Judgment under uncertainty: Heuristics and biases. *Science,* 1974, *184,* 1124–1131.

Valins, S., & Ray, A. A. Effects of cognitive desensitization on avoidance behavior. *Journal of Personality and Social Psychology,* 1967, *1,* 345–350.

Waterman, C. K. The facilitating and interfering effects of cognitive dissonance on simple and complex paired-associate learning tasks. *Journal of Experimental Social Psychology,* 1969, *5,* 31–42.

Weick, K. E. Reduction of cognitive dissonance through task enhancement and effort expenditure. *Journal of Abnormal and Social Psychology,* 1964, *68,* 533–539.

Weick, K. E. Task acceptance dilemmas: A site for research on cognition. In S. Feldman (Ed.), *Cognitive consistencey.* New York: Academic Press, 1966.

Weick, K. E., & Penner, D. D. Discrepant membership as an occasion for effective cooperation. *Sociometry,* 1969, *32,* 413–424.

Weick, K. E., & Prestholdt, P. Realignment of discrepant reinforcement value. *Journal of Personality and Social Psychology,* 1968, *8,* 180–187.

Wilson, W. R. *Unobtrusive induction of positive attitudes.* Unpublished doctoral dissertation, University of Michigan, 1975.

Zajonc, R. B. The attitudinal effects of mere exposure. *Journal of Personality and Social Psychology,* 1968, *8* (2, Pt. 2).

Zimbardo, P. G., Cohen, A., Weisenberg, M., Dworkin, L., & Firestone, I. The control of experimental pain. In P. G. Zimbardo, *The cognitive control of motivation.* Glenview, Ill.: Scott, Foresman, 1969.

Zimbardo, P. G., Weisenberg, M., Firestone, I., & Levy, B. Changing appetites for eating fried grasshoppers with cognitive dissonance. In P. G. Zimbardo, *The cognitive control of motivation.* Glenview, Ill.: Scott, Foresman, 1969.

Received December 6, 1976 ■

The Unbearable Automaticity of Being

John A. Bargh and Tanya L. Chartrand

What was noted by E. J. Langer (1978) remains true today: That much of contemporary psychological research is based on the assumption that people are consciously and systematically processing incoming information in order to construe and interpret their world and to plan and engage in courses of action. As did E. J. Langer, the authors question this assumption. First, they review evidence that the ability to exercise such conscious, intentional control is actually quite limited, so that most of moment-to-moment psychological life must occur through nonconscious means if it is to occur at all. The authors then describe the different possible mechanisms that produce automatic, environmental control over these various phenomena and review evidence establishing both the existence of these mechanisms as well as their consequences for judgments, emotions, and behavior. Three major forms of automatic self-regulation are identified: An automatic effect of perception on action, automatic goal pursuit, and a continual automatic evaluation of one's experience. From the accumulating evidence, the authors conclude that these various nonconscious mental systems perform the lion's share of the self-regulatory burden, beneficently keeping the individual grounded in his or her current environment.

The strongest knowledge — that of the total unfreedom of the human will — is nonetheless the poorest in successes, for it always has the strongest opponent: Human vanity.

— Nietzsche, Human, All Too Human

Imagine for a moment that you are a psychology professor who does experiments on conscious awareness. You keep finding that your subtle manipulations of people's judgments and even behavior are successful —

Preparation of this article was supported in part by Grant SBR-9809000 from the National Science Foundation. We thank Ap Dijksterhuis, Wendi Gardner, Ran Hassin, Larry Jacoby, and Dan Wegner for helpful comments on a draft of the article.

Correspondence concerning this article should be addressed to John A. Bargh, Department of Psychology, New York University, 6 Washington Place, Seventh Floor, New York, NY 10003. Electronic mail may be sent to bargh@psych.nyu.edu.

causing your experimental participants to like someone or to dislike that same person, to feel happy or sad, to behave rudely or with infinite patience. However, none of your participants have a clue as to what caused them to feel or behave in these ways. In fact, they don't believe you, and sometimes even argue with you, when you try to explain your experiment to them and how they were caused to feel or behave.

Now, let's say you are home with your family for the holidays or on vacation. Your aunt or brother-in-law asks politely what your job is like. You attempt to explain your research and even some of your more interesting findings. Once again you are met with incredulity. "This can't be so," says your brother-in-law. "I can't remember this ever happening to me, even once."

Our thesis here — that most of a person's everyday life is determined not by their conscious intentions and deliberate choices but by mental processes that are put into motion by features of the environment and that operate outside of conscious awareness and guidance — is a difficult one for people to accept. One cannot have any experiences or memories of being nonconsciously influenced, of course, almost by definition. But let us move from the layperson to the experts (namely, psychological researchers) and see what they have to say about the relative roles played by conscious versus nonconscious causes of daily experience.

The major historical perspectives of 20th-century psychology can be distinguished from one another based on their positions on this question: Do people consciously and actively choose and control (by acts of will) these various experiences and behaviors, or are those experiences and behaviors instead determined directly by other factors, such as external stimuli or internal, unconscious forces?

Freud (e.g., 1901/1965), for example, considered human behavior to be determined mainly by biological impulses and the unconscious interplay of the psychic forces those impulses put into motion. The individual was described as usually unaware of these intrapsychic struggles and of their causal effect on his or her behavior, although it was possible to become aware of them (usually on Freud's couch) and then change one's patterns of behavior.

Early behaviorist theory (e.g., Skinner, 1938: Watson, 1913) similarly proposed that behavior was outside of conscious control, but placed the source of the control not in the psyche but in external stimulus conditions and events. Environmental events directed all behavior in combination with the person's reinforcement history.

A third major perspective emerged in midcentury with Rogers's (1951) self theory and the humanist movement (Kelly, 1955; Rotter, 1954). In what was a reaction to the then-dominant Freudian and behavioristic perspectives, in which "people were thought to be either pushed by their inner drives or pulled by external events" (Seligman, 1991, pp. 8–9), the "causal self" was placed as a mediator between the environment and one's responses to it. In these self-theories, behavior was adapted to the current environment, but it was determined by an act of conscious choice. Fifty years later, this perspective remains dominant among theories of motivation and self-regulation (e.g., Bandura, 1986, 1990; Cantor & Kihlstrom, 1987; Deci & Ryan, 1985; Dweck, 1996; Locke & Latham, 1990; Mischel, Cantor, & Feldman, 1996).

Finally, the contemporary cognitive perspective, in spirit as well as in practice, seeks to account for psychological phenomena in terms of deterministic mechanisms. Although there exist models that acknowledge the role played by higher-order choice or "executive" processes, the authors of these models generally acknowledge that the lack of specification of how these choices are made is an inadequacy of the model. Neisser's (1967) seminal book *Cognitive Psychology*, for example, describes the "problem of the executive," in which the flexible choice and selection processes are described as a homunculus or "little person in the head" that does not constitute a scientific explanation. This position is echoed in Barsalou's (1993) text, in which he too calls free will a homunculus, noting that "most cognitive psychologists believe that the fundamental laws of the physical world determine human behavior completely" (p. 91).[1]

Fortunately, contemporary psychology for the most part has moved away from doctrinaire either–or positions concerning the locus of control of psychological phenomena, to an acknowledgment that they are determined jointly by processes set into motion directly by one's environment and by processes instigated by acts of conscious choice and will. Such dual-process models (see Chaiken & Trope, 1999), in which the phenomenon in question is said to be influenced simultaneously by conscious (control) and non-conscious (automatic) processes, are now the norm in the study of attention and encoding (e.g., Logan & Cowan, 1984; Neely, 1977, 1991; Posner & Snyder, 1975; Shiffrin, 1988), memory (e.g., Jacoby, 1991; Schachter, 1987; Squire, 1987), emotional appraisal (e.g., Lazarus, 1991), emotional disorders (e.g., Beck, 1976), attitudes and persuasion (Chaiken, Liberman, & Eagly, 1989; Fazio, 1990; Petty & Cacioppo, 1986), and social perception and judgment (e.g., Bargh, 1994; Devine, 1989; Fiske & Neuberg, 1990; Gilbert, 1991; Trope, 1986). Thus, the mainstream of psychology accepts both the fact of conscious or willed causation of mental and behavioral processes and the fact of automatic or environmentally triggered processes. The debate has shifted from the existence (or not) of these different causal forces to the circumstances under which one versus the other controls the mind. Is everyday life mainly comprised of

---

[1] The existence of dominant, overarching perspectives concerning free will and self-determination does not mean, of course, that everyone working within a given perspective adheres to its dominant assumption. A notable exception within cognitive psychology is the approach of Varela, Thompson, and Rosch (1991), who argue that higher-order phenomena such as free will and the self are the result of a complex interaction between the mind and the world, and hence cannot be satisfactorily explained through mechanism alone.

consciously or of nonconsciously caused evaluations, judgments, emotions, motivations, and behavior?

As Posner and Snyder (1975, p. 55) noted a quarter century ago, this question of how much conscious control we have over our judgments, decisions, and behavior is one of the most basic and important questions of human existence. The title of the present article makes our position on this question a matter of little suspense, but to make the reasons for that position clear and hopefully compelling, we must start by defining what we mean by a conscious mental process and an automatic mental process. The defining features of what we are referring to as a *conscious* process have remained consistent and stable for over 100 years (see Bargh & Chartrand, in press): These are mental acts of which we are aware, that we intend (i.e., that we start by an act of will), that require effort, and that we can control (i.e., we can stop them and go on to something else if we choose; Logan & Cowan, 1984). In contrast, there has been no consensus on the features of a single form of *automatic* process (Bargh, 1994); instead two major strains have been identified and studied over the past century, similar only in that they do not possess all of the defining features of a conscious process (see Bargh, 1996; Bargh & Chartrand, in press; Wegner & Bargh, 1998).

First, research on skill acquisition focused on intentional, goal-directed processes that became more efficient over time and practice until they could operate without conscious guidance (see J. R. Anderson, 1983; Jastrow, 1906; Shiffrin & Schneider, 1977; Smith & Lerner, 1986). These were intentional but effortless mental processes. Second, research on the initial perceptual analysis or encoding of environmental events (called "preattentive" or "preconscious" processing) showed that much of this analysis takes place not only effortlessly, but without any intention or often awareness that it was taking place (e.g., Neisser, 1967; Posner & Snyder, 1975; Treisman, 1960). The "new look" in perception of the 1940s and 1950s, in which threatening or emotion-laden words or symbols were purportedly shown to be "defended against" through having higher perceptual thresholds than more neutral stimuli (see Allport, 1955; Erdelyi, 1974), is a prototypic example of this line of research. These are the two classic forms of "not-conscious" mental processes; both forms operate effortlessly and without need for conscious guidance, but one (mental skills) requires an act of will to start operation, and the other (preconscious) does not.

So much for how the field of psychology has historically thought about automatic processes; let's return to our aunts and in-laws. What does the concept mean to them? The popular meaning of "automatic" is something that happens, no matter what, as long as certain conditions are met. An automatic answering machine clicks into operation after a specified number of phone rings and then records whatever the caller wants to say. No one has to be at home to turn it on to record whenever the phone happens to ring. Automatic piloting systems on airplanes now perform many sophisticated and complex functions to keep the plane on course and to land it under poor visibility and weather conditions, actually making air travel safer than when such functions were handled entirely by the human pilots.

In modern technological societies one encounters many such automatic devices and systems in the course of daily life. They are all devised and intended to free us from tasks that don't really require our vigilance and intervention, so that our time and energy can be directed toward those that do. And these systems also perform their tasks with a greater degree of reliability, as they are not prone to sources of human error, such as fatigue, distraction, and boredom.

Just as automatic mechanical devices free us from having to attend to and intervene in order for the desired effect to occur, automatic mental processes free one's limited conscious attentional capacity (e.g., Kahneman, 1973; Miller, 1956; Posner & Snyder, 1975) from tasks in which they are no longer needed. Many writers have pointed out how impossible it would be to function effectively if conscious, controlled, and aware mental processing had to deal with every aspect of life, from perceptual comprehension of the environment (both physical and social) to choosing and guiding every action and response to the environment (e.g., Bateson, 1972; Miller, Galanter, & Pribram, 1960; Nørretranders, 1998). But none put it so vividly as the philosopher A. N. Whitehead:

> It is a profoundly erroneous truism, repeated by all copy-books and by eminent people making speeches, that we should cultivate the habit of thinking of what we are doing. The precise opposite is the case. Civilization advances by extending the number of operations which we can perform without thinking about them. Operations of thought are like cavalry charges in a battle — they are strictly limited in number, they require fresh horses, and must only be made at decisive moments. (Whitehead, 1911)

Whitehead (1911) presaged what psychological research would discover 86 years later. Baumeister,

Tice, and their colleagues recently demonstrated just how limited conscious self-regulatory capacities are in a series of studies on what they called "ego depletion" (Baumeister, Bratslavsky, Muraven, & Tice, 1998; Muraven, Tice, & Baumeister, 1998). In their experiments, an act of self-control in one domain (being told not to eat any of the chocolate chip cookies sitting in front of you) seriously depletes a person's ability to engage in self-control in a subsequent, entirely unrelated domain (persistence on a verbal task), which was presented to participants as being a separate experiment. Table 14.1 presents the variety of simple ways in which participants' conscious self-regulatory capacity was depleted to cause performance decrements on the unrelated task that followed.

Tice and Baumeister concluded after their series of eight such experiments that because even minor acts of self-control, such as making a simple choice, use up this limited self-regulatory resource, such conscious acts of self-regulation can occur only rarely in the course of one's day. Even as they were defending the importance of the conscious self for guiding behavior, Baumeister et al. (1998, p. 1252; also Baumeister & Sommer, 1997) concluded it plays a causal role only 5% or so of the time.

TABLE 14.1. Consequences of Various Acts of Choice and Self-Control

Setting this first ...	... makes it difficult to do this
Eating radishes instead of available chocolates	Persist in attempting to solve unsolvable puzzles
Making a choice between two options	Persist in attempting to solve unsolvable puzzles
Suppressing emotional reactions to a movie	Solve (solvable) anagrams
Proofreading	Take action (stop watching a boring movie)
Suppressing emotional responses to a movie	Squeeze a handgrip exerciser for a short time
Suppressing thoughts (about white bears)	Persist in attempting to solve unsolvable puzzles
Suppressing thoughts (about white bears)	Suppress signs of amusement while watching comedy tape

From "Ego Depletion: Is the Active Self a Limited Resource?" by R. F. Baumeister, E. Bratslavsky, M. Muraven, and D. M. Tice, 1998, *Journal of Personality and Social Psychology, 74*. Copyright 1998 by the American Psychological Association. Adapted with permission of the author. Also from "Self-Control as Limited Resource: Regulatory Depletion Patterns," by M. Muraven, D. M. Tice, and R. F. Baumeister, 1998, *Journal of Personality and Social Psychology, 74*. Copyright 1998 by the American Psychological Association. Adapted with permission of the author.

Given one's understandable desire to believe in free will and self-determination, it may be hard to bear that most of daily life is driven by automatic, nonconscious mental processes — but it appears impossible, from these findings, that conscious control could be up to the job. As Sherlock Holmes was fond of telling Dr. Watson, when one eliminates the impossible, whatever remains — however improbable — must be the truth.

It follows, as Lord Whitehead (1911) argued, that most of our day-to-day actions, motivations, judgments, and emotions are not the products of conscious choice and guidance, but must be driven instead by mental processes put into operation directly by environmental features and events. Is this the case? The logical and empirical limits on conscious self-regulation tell us where to look for automatic phenomena — not only in perceptual activity and crude, simple processes (to which cognitive psychologists originally believed they were limited; e.g., Neisser, 1967, ch. 4), but everywhere. We and other researchers have been looking, and here is what we have found.

Perceiving Is for Doing

Humans and other primates have an innate capacity for imitative behavior and vicarious learning (e.g., Bandura, 1977b; Byrne & Russon, 1998). This has led many theorists over many years to argue that there must be a strong associative connection between representations used in perceiving the behavior of others and those used to behave in the same way oneself (Berkowitz, 1984; Koffka, 1925; Lashley, 1951; Piaget, 1946). Some have even argued that the same representation is used both in perceiving others' behavior and to behave that way oneself (Carver, Ganellen, Froming, & Chambers, 1983; Prinz, 1987, 1990). William James (1890), following the ideas of the physiologist William Carpenter (1874), popularized the principle of "ideomotor action" to account for how merely thinking about an action increases its likelihood of occurring. For Carpenter as well as James, the important feature of ideomotor action was that mere ideation about the behavior was sufficient to cause one to act — no separate act of volition was necessary. Although James argued that "thinking is for doing," we sought to extend the source of ideation from inside the head to out in the world — specifically, by considering whether merely perceiving an action increases the person's likelihood of performing the same act.

Automatic Perception Induces the Ideas

Of course, one's own thinking is more or less under one's own conscious control, so the principle of ideo-motor action by itself does not mean the resultant behavior is caused by nonconscious, external environmental events. But because perceptual activity is largely automatic and not under conscious or intentional control (the orange on the desk cannot be perceived as purple through an act of will), perception is the route by which the environment directly causes mental activity — specifically, the activation of internal representations of the outside world. The activated contents of the mind are not only those in the stream of consciousness but also include representations of currently present objects, events, behavior of others, and so on. In short, the "ideo" in ideomotor effects could just as well come from outside the head as within it.

When one considers that this automatic perception of another person's behavior introduces the idea of action — but from the outside environment instead of from internal, intentionally directed thought — a direct and automatic route is provided from the external environment to action tendencies, via perception (see Figure 14.1).[2] The idea that social perception is a largely automated psychological phenomenon is now widely accepted. Many years of research have demonstrated the variety of ways in which behaviors are encoded spontaneously and without intention in terms of relevant trait concepts (e.g., Bargh & Thein, 1985; Winter & Uleman, 1984; Carlston & Skowronski, 1994; Uleman, Newman, & Moskowitz, 1996), how contextual priming of trait concepts changes the perceiver's interpretation of an identical behavior (through temporarily increasing their accessibility or readiness to be used; see Bargh, 1989; Higgins, 1989, 1996; Wyer & Srull, 1989, for reviews), and how stereotypes of social groups become activated automatically on the mere perception of the distinguishing features of a group member (e.g., Bargh, 1994, 1999; Brewer, 1988; Devine, 1989). Perceptual interpretations of behavior, as well as assumptions about an individual's behavior based on identified group membership, become automated like any other representation if they are frequently and consistently made in the presence of the behavioral or group membership features.

---

[2] Consistent with this, Wegner and Wheatley (1999) have shown that the introduction of behavior-relevant ideation through an external means (headphones) produces the same "feeling of will" as when the thought occurs internally and intentionally.

The Perception–Behavior Link

Thus, the external environment can direct behavior non-consciously through a two-stage process: Automatic perceptual activity that then automatically creates behavioral tendencies through the perception–behavior link. That is, the entire environment-perception-behavior sequence is automatic, with no role played by conscious choice in producing the behavior. Berkowitz (1984, 1997) posited that such a mechanism underlies media effects on behavior and modeling effects more generally. In his account, perceiving the aggressiveness (for example) of an actor in a movie or television show activated, in an unintentional and nonconscious manner, the perceiver's own behavioral representation of aggressiveness, thereby increasing the likelihood of aggressive behavior. Carver et al. (1983) experimentally tested this hypothesis by first exposing some participants (and not others) to hostility-related words in a first "language experiment," and then — in what was believed to be a separate experiment — putting the participants in the role of a "teacher" who was to give shocks to a "learner" participant. Those who had been "primed" with hostile-related stimuli subsequently gave longer shocks to the learner than did control participants.

Carver et al. (1983) had explicitly told their participants to give the shocks, however, and so the question remained whether external events could induce the idea of the behavior itself. Bargh, Chen, and Burrows (1996) found that it indeed could. When trait constructs or stereotypes were nonconsciously activated during an unrelated task (i.e., "primed"), participants were subsequently more likely to act in line with the content of the primed trait construct or stereotype. In one experiment, participants were first exposed to words related to either rudeness (e.g., rude, impolite, obnoxious), politeness (e.g., respect, considerate, polite) or neither (in the control condition) in an initial "language experiment." They were then given a chance to interrupt an ongoing conversation (in order to ask for the promised next experimental task). Significantly more participants in the "rude" priming condition interrupted (67%) than did those in the control condition (38%), whereas only 16% of those primed with "polite" interrupted the conversation.

Experiment 2 extended these findings to the case of stereotype activation. In a first task, participants were primed (in the course of an ostensible language test) either with words related to the stereotype of the elderly (e.g., Florida, sentimental, wrinkle) or with words unrelated to the stereotype. As predicted, participants

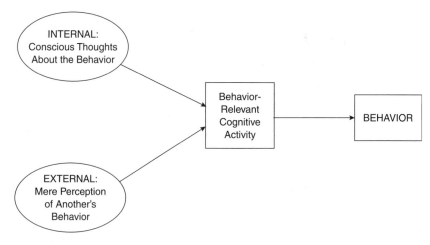

FIGURE 14.1 ■ Internal (intentional) and External (automatic) Sources of Behavior-relevant Cognitions that Automatically Create a Tendency to Engage in that Behavior.

primed with the elderly-related material subsequently behaved in line with the stereotype — specifically, they walked more slowly down the hallway after leaving the experiment. Dijksterhuis, Bargh, and Miedema (in press) have shown that these effects also hold for another central feature of the elderly stereotype — forgetfulness. Those participants whose stereotype for the elderly had been unobtrusively activated in the "first experiment" subsequently could not remember as many features of the room in which that experiment was conducted as could control participants. (For similar findings of behavioral consequences of automatic stereotype activation with different stereotypes, including those for professors and for soccer hooligans, see Dijksterhuis & van Knippenberg [1998]).

Consequences for Social Interaction

In real life, stereotypes aren't triggered by lists of words but by skin color, gender characteristics, and other easily detected features of group members (Brewer, 1988) — in other words, by the actual presence of the person being stereotyped. The effect of stereotypes on behavior could therefore create — entirely nonconsciously — a "self-fulfilling prophecy" (e.g., Rosenthal & Jacobson, 1968; Snyder, Tanke, & Berscheid, 1977) by causing the perceiver to behave in line with stereotypic expectations, to which the stereotyped person might well respond in kind. This possibility was examined in two experiments.

In the first (Bargh, Chen, & Burrows, 1996, Experiment 3), participants who were subliminally presented with faces of young male African Americans subsequently reacted with greater hostility (a component of the African American stereotype [e.g., Devine, 1989]) to a mild provocation, compared with the control condition. Thus the automatic activation of the African American stereotype caused the participants to behave themselves with greater hostility. In the second experiment (Chen & Bargh, 1997), the same subliminal priming manipulation was used but participants then interacted with each other, playing a potentially frustrating game of "Password," in which the object was to get their partner to correctly guess a specific word by giving clues. We recorded both sides of the game, conducted using microphones and headsets, and later had judges rate the degree of hostility of the interaction partners.

As predicted, the partners of participants who had earlier been subliminally primed with African American faces manifested greater hostility than the partners of those who had not been primed. Most important, the primed participants themselves rated their partners as being more hostile than did nonprimed participants. For the primed participants, their own hostile behavior, nonconsciously driven by the content of their stereotype of African Americans, caused their partners to respond in kind, but the primed participants had no clue as to their own role in producing that hostility.

Mental categories are absolutely essential in simplifying and understanding the information-rich environment (e.g., Bruner, 1957; E. E. Smith & Medin, 1981), but stereotypes are maladaptive forms of categories because their content does not correspond to what is actually present or going on in the environment. We reasoned therefore that even though automatic stereotype effects on behavior could cause problems in social interaction as demonstrated by Chen and Bargh (1997), the more natural effect of perception on behavior — when perceptual activity is based on what is actually going on at the moment — would be more positive. In other words, the express link between perception and action likely exists for a good, adaptive reason, such as creating appropriate behavioral readinesses in the absence of conscious guidance and monitoring. Within a social group setting, one is more likely to get along harmoniously with others in the group if one is behaving similarly to them, compared with being "out of sync" and behaving differently. Thus, it makes sense for the default behavioral tendency in an interaction to be based on one's perception of what the other person is doing.

There is a long history of research that suggests that perceptions of the behavior of one's interaction partner leads directly to tendencies to behave that way oneself. This research on mimicry (or "behavioral coordination"; Bernieri & Rosenthal, 1991) includes research on body movements ("movement synchrony"; e.g., Bernieri, 1988; Condon & Ogston, 1966), the imitation of facial expressions of adult models by infants (Meltzoff & Moore, 1977, 1983), and "behavior matching," in which people mimic behavior patterns by adopting similar postures or showing similar body configurations (LaFrance, 1979, 1982; LaFrance & Broadbent, 1976). A major purpose of this latter program of research has been to link similarities in body language to increased feelings of rapport or togetherness between the two people. However, all of these theories hold that the mimicry is for the purpose of establishing a relationship with the other person (i.e., ingratiate him or her). We predicted instead that perceptual effects on bodily movements and postures within social interaction would occur naturally and without the need of a purpose or goal to drive them.

To test this prediction, we (Chartrand & Bargh, 1999a) had participants work on a task along with two different confederates (whom they believed to be fellow participants), one after the other. In each session, the participant and confederate sat at right angles to each other and worked on a task ostensibly to help develop a new projective test based on photographs. We devised this task so as to minimize the chance that the participant would have a goal to form a relationship or make friends with the confederate — the task required the participant to look mostly down at the photographs being discussed, and this helped minimize eye contact. The confederate in session 1 either rubbed his or her face or shook his or her foot, and the confederate in session 2 did whichever mannerism the first confederate did not do. We videorecorded both sessions so that coders could later judge the extent to which participants mimicked the mannerisms of the two confederates. As predicted, participants rubbed their face more times in the presence of the face-rubbing confederate than with the foot-shaking confederate and shook their foot more times with the foot-shaking confederate than with the face-rubbing confederate. No one had any awareness of engaging in these behaviors when asked at the end of the experiment. In a chameleon-like way, the participants' behavior automatically changed as a function of their social environment; as the behavior of their interaction partner changed, so did their own behavior.

Why have humans developed the capacity (and tendency) to behave in line with activated perceptual representations? Is there an adaptive function served by such automatic effects of perception on behavior, by the nonconscious tendency to behave with others as those others are behaving? Our Experiment 2 (Chartrand & Bargh, 1999a) tested the hypothesis that nonconscious mimicry serves a distinct purpose: It increases liking and creates a sense of smooth interactions. As before, each participant worked with another participant — again actually a confederate — on the photograph-projective-test task. But this time it was the confederate who deliberately mimicked the behavioral mannerisms and body posture of the participants, trying as much as possible to be, in a nonobvious way, the "mirror image" of the participant. When the task was over, participants were asked how much they liked the confederate and how smoothly they thought the interaction had gone. Relative to those in the control condition, participants whose mannerisms and posture had been mimicked found the confederate to be more likable and reported that their interaction had gone more smoothly. The natural tendency (because of the automatic effect of perception on behavior) to take on the posture and behaviors of people with whom one interacts, even when that person is a complete stranger, has the positive function of facilitating social interactions and increasing liking between people.

Tinker to Evers to Chance

Much of social behavior occurs without conscious choice or involvement. One major route between the environment and behavior exists because of the simultaneous operation of two different, automatic connections: One is between environmental events and objects (such as people and their behavior) and the individual's perceptual representations of those objects and events, and the other is between those perceptual representations and behavioral impulses. Each of these components of the sequence — automated perception and the perception–behavior link — are old stories in psychology with long research and theoretical histories. What the recent research has demonstrated, therefore, is that "environment to perception to behavior" operates as efficiently and smoothly in producing social behavior as the legendary Chicago Cubs infielders did in producing double plays.

Goals and Motivations

Although the effect of perception on behavior occurs passively, without the need for a conscious choice or intention to behave in the suggested manner, this does not mean that people do not have goals and purposes and are merely passive experiencers of events. People are active participants in the world with purposes and goals they want to attain. Much, if not most, of our responses to the environment in the form of judgments, decisions, and behavior are determined not solely by the information available in that environment but rather by how it relates to whatever goal we are currently pursuing (Bargh, 1989; Gollwitzer & Moskowitz, 1996; Kruglanski, 1996b; Kunda, 1990; Wicklund & Steins, 1996).

For example, when we are trying to get a new acquaintance to like us and perhaps be our friend, the things about that person to which we pay attention and later best remember are quite different than if we meet the same person in a different context, such as if they are a person to whom we are considering subletting our apartment or someone sitting across from us late at night on the subway. And as for behavioral responses to one's environment, the idea that behavior is largely purposive and determined by one's current goals has long had broad support within psychology — not only among those with a humanistic orientation but among cognitive psychologists (e.g., Miller et al., 1960; Wilensky, 1983) and neobehaviorists (e.g., Amsel, 1989; Hull, 1931; Tolman, 1932) as well.

But if the currently-held goal largely determines whether judgments are made (and the quality of those judgments) and how one behaves, this would seem to rule out much of a role for automatic, environmentally driven influences. How can the environment directly control much of anything if goals play such a mediational role?

The answer is as follows: If (and perhaps only if) the environment itself activates and puts the goal into motion (Bargh, 1990, 1997). To entertain this possibility, one must assume that goals are represented mentally (see Bargh, 1990; Kruglanski, 1996a) and like any other mental representation are capable of becoming automatically activated by environmental features. There is no reason, a priori, to assume that goal representations cannot become automated in the same way that stereotypes and other perceptual structures do, as long as the same conditions for development of automatic activation occur.

The Acquisition of Automaticity

What are those conditions? As discussed above, the development of most acquired forms of automaticity (i.e., skill acquisition) depends on the frequent and consistent pairing of internal responses with external events (Jastrow, 1906; Shiffrin & Dumais, 1981; Shiffrin & Schneider, 1977). Initially, conscious choice and guidance are needed to perform the desired behavior or to generate what one hopes are accurate and useful expectations about what is going to happen next in the situation. But to the extent the same expectations are generated, or the same behavior is enacted, or the same goal and plan are chosen in that situation, conscious choice drops out as it is not needed — it has become a superfluous step in the process (see Figure 14.2). According to James (1890),

> It is a general principle in Psychology that consciousness deserts all processes where it can no longer be of use ... We grow unconscious of every feeling which is useless as a sign to lead us to our ends, and where one sign will suffice others drop out, and that one remains, to work alone. (p. 496)

Intentional Acquisition of Automaticity

At some level, people are aware of this phenomenon by which conscious choice-points drop out of mental sequences to the extent they are no longer needed (because the same choice is made frequently and consistently at a given point). This is shown by the fact that

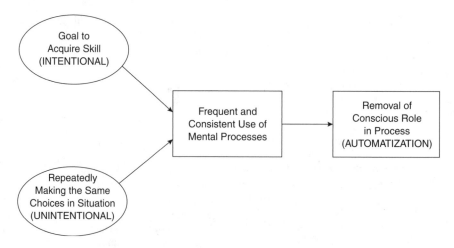

FIGURE 14.2 ■ Intentional and Unintentional Routes to the Automatization of a Psychological Process.

we often use it in a strategic fashion in order to develop a desired skill, such as driving a car or playing the violin. We purposefully engage in the considerable practice (frequent and consistent performances) required to sublimate many of the components of the skill. In this way, the conscious capacity that is freed up from not having to direct and coordinate the lower level components of the skill can be used instead to plot and direct higher-level strategy during the game or performance. And so, one sees the teenager go from being an overwhelmed tangle of nerves at the first attempts to drive a car to soon being able to do so while conversing, tuning the radio, and getting nervous instead over that evening's date.

Unintentional Acquisition of Automaticity
But what we find most intriguing, in considering how mental processes recede from consciousness over time with repeated use, is that the process of automation itself is automatic. The necessary and sufficient ingredients for automation are frequency and consistency of use of the same set of component mental processes under the same circumstances — regardless of whether the frequency and consistency occur because of a desire to attain a skill, or whether they occur just because we have tended in the past to make the same choices or to do the same thing or to react emotionally or evaluatively in the same way each time. These processes also become automated, but because we did not start out intending to make them that way, we are not aware that

they have been and so, when that process operates automatically in that situation, we aren't aware of it (see Figure 14.3).

This is how goals and motives can eventually become automatically activated by situations. For a given individual, his or her motivations (e.g., to gain the love and respect of one's parents) are represented in memory at the most abstract level of an organized hierarchy, followed by the various goals one can pursue to satisfy those motivations (e.g., to be a success, to become a lawyer, to have a family). Each of these motivations is associated with goals that will fulfill it, and these goals in turn have associated with them the various plans and strategies that can be used to attain the goals (e.g., study hard). These plans are in turn linked to specific behaviors by which the plan is carried out (see Carver & Scheier, 1998; Koestler, 1967; Martin & Tesser, 1989, 1996; Vallacher & Wegner, 1987; Wilensky, 1983). However, an individual's motivations are chronic and enduring over time (e.g., Gollwitzer, 1993; Gollwitzer & Moskowitz, 1996; Ryan, Sheldon, Kasser, & Deci, 1996). And thus, because of the stability over time of one's motivations, in many situations a given individual will frequently and consistently pursue the same goal. If the same goal is pursued within the same situation, then conscious choice eventually drops out of the selection of what goal to pursue — the situational features themselves directly put the goal into operation.

According to the above analysis, people should be able to put goals into gear through external means and thereby

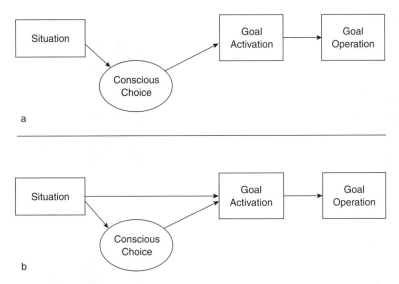

FIGURE 14.3 ■ (a) Conscious, Intentional Mediation of Goal Pursuit within a Situation and (b) Automatic Activation and Operation of Goals by Situational Features following Repeated Choice of the Same Goal.

"bypass the will" entirely. The goal, once activated, should operate to produce the same effects as if it had been consciously chosen. At the same time, the individual should have no awareness of having pursued that goal. We tested this prediction in several different studies.

Automatic Activation of Cognitive Goals

Two experiments by Chartrand and Bargh (1996) demonstrated that information-processing goals (i.e., the goal to remember information and the goal to form an impression of someone) can be activated nonconsciously and then guide subsequent cognition. In the first experiment, we replicated a classic study on person memory by Hamilton, Katz, and Leirer (1980). In the original study, participants read a series of behaviors with instructions either to form an impression of the actor or to memorize the information. Hamilton et al. found that participants who had been given an impression-formation goal recalled more behaviors and showed greater organization of the material in memory around the several trait categories relevant to the target's behaviors (e.g., sociable, intelligent) than those given a memorization goal.

In our replication, however, participants were given no explicit conscious instructions as to what to do with the behavioral information. Instead, prior to being presented

with the various behaviors, either the memorization or the impression-formation goal was unobtrusively primed by means of an ostensible "language test," in which some of the items contained synonyms of memorization (e.g., retain, hold) or evaluation (e.g., judge, evaluate), respectively. Nonetheless, the identical effects on free recall and on memory organization of the material were obtained as in the earlier study (see Figure 14.4).

In a second experiment, all participants were given an initial "reaction-time" task, in the course of which some of them were exposed, subliminally, to words related to evaluation and impression formation, whereas the remaining participants were not. We intended this task to prime the goal of impression formation (or not) for participants. Next, in an ostensibly unrelated study, all participants were presented with a series of behaviors purportedly engaged in by a target person; however, as before, participants were not given any explicit instructions as to what to do with the behavioral information (except that they "would be asked questions about it later"). Those participants whose impression-formation goal had been nonconsciously activated were found to have formed an impression of the target during information acquisition, whereas control participants had not. When questioned extensively, no participant showed any awareness of having a particular goal in mind while encountering the information.

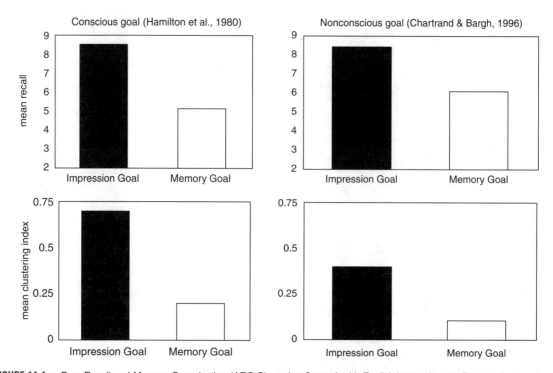

FIGURE 14.4 ■ Free Recall and Memory Organization (ARC Clustering Scores) with Explicit Instructions to Form an Impression or to Memorize the Behavioral Information and With Primed Impression or Memorization Goal and no Explicit Instructions.
Note. The data in the lefthand graphs are from "Organizational Processes in Impression Formation," by D. L. Hamilton, L. B. Katz, and V. O. Leirer in *Person Memory: The Cognitive Basis of Social Perception*, by R. Hastie, T. M. Ostrom, E. B. Ebbesen, R. S. Wyer, D. L. Hamilton, and D. E. Carlston (Eds.), 1980, Hillsdale, NJ: Erlbaum. Copyright 1980 by Erlbaum. Adapted with permission. The data in the righthand graphs are from "Automatic Activation of Impression Formation and Memorization Goals: Nonconscious Goal Priming Reproduces Effects of Explicit Task Instructions," by T. L. Chartrand and J. A. Bargh, 1996, *Journal of Personality and Social Psychology, 71.* Copyright 1996 by the American Psychological Association.

Stereotype Activation and Use

A provocative set of studies by Spencer, Fein, Wolfe, Fong, and Dunn (1998) also provided support for the automatic activation of information-processing goals. These researchers tested the hypothesis that threats to one's self-image automatically trigger the goal of restoring the threatened self-image. One tactic that people often use to restore self-esteem is to denigrate others, especially groups of low power and status within society. Spencer et al. (Experiment 1) replicated procedures of an earlier study that had been successful in eliminating the use of stereotypes (through an attention-demanding secondary task). However, Spencer et al. showed that participants who had just received a blow to their self-esteem, in the form of negative feedback concerning their abilities, still showed evidence of having stereotyped the group member even under these conditions in which stereotyping normally does not occur.

In other words, the threat to self-esteem put into motion a goal to denigrate others that was so automatic and efficient in its working that it produced stereotyping of a minority group member under attention-overload conditions, in which manifestations of stereotyping are normally not obtained. Here is a case in which a situational feature — a failure experience or some other blow to self-esteem — automatically triggers a well-rehearsed goal and plan to restore the sense of self-worth. Unfortunately, it comes at the expense of others.

Corroborating Evidence from Brain Activation Patterns

If information-processing goals operate in the same way regardless of how they were instigated (conscious intention vs. directly by the environment), their consequences should be observable not only in the outcome of the process but also in its known mediational brain processes. We have thus far observed the effects of automatic goal operation on dependent measures such as amount of free recall and judgments made about people. Automatically activated goals produce the same outcomes as do goals set in motion by an act of will, but do they do so in the same way, following the same process? The strong form of our argument asserts that they do: Once activated, a goal operates in the same way whether activated by will or by the environment.

To provide a strict test of this assumption, Gardner, Bargh, Shellman, and Bessenoff (1999) made use of the recent demonstrations of a "right-shift" in lateralized brain activation patterns (occurring about 650 ms after stimulus presentation) when participants are consciously evaluating a series of stimuli (Cacioppo, Crites, & Gardner, 1996). Participants were first primed with stimuli related to evaluation as part of a "verbal task" (i.e., the scrambled-sentence manipulation of Srull & Wyer, 1979). Next they were presented with a series of stimuli but with no explicit conscious instructions except to "listen" to them. Finally, they were presented with a different set of stimuli and were explicitly told to evaluate each one. After a 10-minute videogame distraction task, the same procedure was repeated but with a primed and then an explicit goal to form mental images of each stimulus. (Some participants did the imagery tasks before the evaluation tasks.) During all of these tasks, brain potentials evoked by the stimulus were measured. We could thus compare, on a within-subjects basis, the patterns of brain response under a nonconsciously chosen versus a consciously pursued evaluation goal.

Results confirmed that both the evaluation-priming and the conscious evaluation condition replicated the Cacioppo et al. (1996) findings by showing a significant activation increase in the basal right hemisphere on each trial at about 650 ms postexposure. Neither of the primed-imagery or conscious-imagery conditions produced this pattern. Thus, even though the participants during the operation of the primed evaluation goal did not know they were evaluating and did not intend to evaluate the stimuli (they believed only that they were listening to the names of the stimuli), the same area of the brain unique to the evaluative response reacted to the stimuli as when the participant was consciously evaluating stimuli.

Automatic Activation of Behavioral Goals

Information-processing goals can be put into motion by external events, bypassing the conscious will to become active and produce their effects. Do such automatic goal effects extend to behavioral responses to situations?

Bargh, Gollwitzer, and Lee-Chai (1999; see also Bargh & Gollwitzer, 1994) conducted a series of experiments in which the achievement motive was primed, as part of an allegedly unrelated first "word search" task in which synonyms of achievement (e.g., strive, succeed) were presented (or not, in the control condition). In several experiments, priming the achievement goal in this way caused participants to significantly outperform the control (nonprimed) condition on verbal tasks. As per usual, extensive questioning of the participants revealed no awareness of a possible effect of the priming task on their later performance.

Subsequent experiments provided further evidence that a motivational state had been activated and was guiding participants' performance on the tasks. Goal pursuits have unique properties as pointed to by different theories (e.g., Atkinson & Birch, 1970; Bandura, 1986; Gollwitzer, 1990; Lewin, 1951). One hallmark of an active goal is that the individual will persist on the task, striving to reach the desired goal, in spite of obstacles and interruptions. Therefore, in another experiment, Bargh et al. (1999) primed the achievement goal (or not) and then gave participants three minutes to write down as many words as they could find in a set of seven "Scrabble" letter tiles. They were told over an intercom to stop at the end of the period (the experimenter had left the room) — but hidden videocameras recorded that 55% of those in the achievement condition, compared with only 21% in the control condition, continued to write down words after the stop signal, overcoming the "stop" instructions in order to attain a still higher score. In another study, participants worked on a relatively uninteresting word search task but were then interrupted by a power failure. After power was resumed, those whose achievement goal had been primed (and the goal interrupted) were more likely to opt for returning to the word search task than control participants, who preferred instead the intrinsically more enjoyable "cartoon-humor rating" task option. These and other studies confirmed that nonconsciously activated and operating achievement goals not only produce higher performance but manifest the same classic qualities of motivational states as has been documented for conscious, intentional goal pursuit in years of research.

The process of goal pursuit does not stop with the behavioral attempt to attain the goal, however. Inevitably, the individual either achieves or does not achieve (in varying degrees) the pursued goal and tends to evaluate his or her performance following the attempt. Many researchers have demonstrated the consequences of success or failure at conscious goal pursuit for one's mood and beliefs of self-efficacy (see Bandura, 1997; Gollwitzer, 1990; Heckhausen, 1991). Are there similar consequences of success or failure at nonconscious goals for self-esteem and mood? Our approach suggests that there are such consequences of succeeding or failing, even at goals of which one was not aware of pursuing. Chartrand (1999) has looked beyond the automatic activation and pursuit of a goal to explore what happens once the nonconsciously-held goal is attained or not attained.

In Experiment 1, an achievement goal was primed in half the participants using a scrambled sentence task procedure. Next, participants were led to succeed or fail at this goal through an anagram task, which was downplayed as a "fun" time-filler: The anagrams were either very easy or very difficult to complete in what participants were told was the "average" amount of time. Participants were then administered mood scales as part of an ostensibly separate experiment. As predicted, achievement-primed participants were in a worse mood following the difficult anagram task than following the simple one, but control condition participants' mood was unaffected by the difficulty level of the task. When questioned at the end of the experimental session, no participant reported having a goal to achieve on the anagram task.

This finding was extended in another experiment (Chartrand, 1999, Experiment 3) by replicating the achievement priming and difficult versus easy verbal task procedures. However, instead of completing mood scales at the conclusion of the study, participants worked on a portion of the verbal section of the Graduate Record Examination (GRE), which tested their performance on a task in the same domain as they had just "succeeded" or "failed." If their self-efficacy beliefs were in fact affected by success or failure at the nonconscious achievement goal pursuit (i.e., on the anagram task), then according to Bandura's (e.g., 1977a, 1986, 1990) self-efficacy theory, their subsequent GRE task performance should be affected. That is, they should do better on the GRE if they had previously "succeeded" and worse if they had previously "failed," despite the fact that at a conscious level, they did not know they were pursuing the achievement goal. This is exactly what was found.

Automatic Goal Activation by Situational Features

The studies thus far have demonstrated that goals can become activated by means other than an act of will, and once activated, such goals operate in the same way, and produce the same effects, as when they are put into motion intentionally. However, in these studies the goal was activated by a priming procedure in which the stimuli were semantically related to the goal itself (e.g., achievement, impression formation). Our model, however, posits an automatic link between situational features and the goals that the individual has chronically selected in those situations. A direct test of this hypothesis therefore requires the priming or goal-activating stimuli to be semantically related to the situation, not to the goal itself; otherwise the environment–goal path is assumed but bypassed by the priming manipulation.

To provide this kind of test, we made use of the fact that one situational feature likely to be associated with a person's chronic goal pursuits is that of having (relative) power in that situation. By definition, power is the ability to attain one's desired goals, and so when one is in a position of power those goals are likely to be selected and pursued. In this study (Bargh, Raymond, Pryor, & Strack, 1995), a group already known to have a strong association between power and sex was selected — men who are likely to sexually aggress, as identified by Malamuth's (1989) Attractiveness of Sexual Aggression scale.

In the first experiment, participants were exposed on each trial subliminally to a prime word related either to power, sex, or neither, and then pronounced out loud a target word that immediately followed (also related either to power, sex, or neither) as quickly as possible. Only for men who were likely to sexually aggress (and so for whom we expected that a strong association between power and sex existed) did presentation of the subliminal power-related prime words facilitate (speed up) their times to respond to the sexual target words. This could only happen if there was an automatic connection between the concepts of power and sex for these men (e.g., Neely, 1977). It is important that the reverse connection — between sex and power — was not found to be present. Thus power as a situational feature automatically activated ideas of sex in these men.

In the second study, participants worked on a task in the presence of an attractive woman posing as another participant. Some of the participants were unobtrusively primed (using the scrambled sentence procedure) with power-related words, and the others were not. For men likely to sexually aggress, priming the idea of power caused them to rate the confederate as being more attractive compared with ratings in the no-priming condition; for men not likely to sexually aggress (who do not possess the automatic power–sex connection) the power priming made no difference in their opinion of the woman's attractiveness. The analogy here is the boss who finds his secretary attractive and believes this to be entirely due to her appearance and personality, completely unaware of the role played in his attraction by his relative power over her. What is the moral? This boss would not at all be attracted to the same woman if she were not his secretary, and he had encountered her instead in the corner coffee shop.

Summary

Goals do not require an act of will to operate and guide information processing and behavior. They can be activated instead by external, environmental information and events. Once they are put into motion they operate just as if they had been consciously intended, even to the point of producing changes in mood and in self-efficacy beliefs depending on one's degree of success or failure at reaching the goal. The goal does not know the source of its activation and behaves the same way regardless of where the command to do its thing came from (see Higgins & King, 1981, for a similar argument regarding the various sources of activation of social–perceptual representations).

Note that this argument applies to complex self-regulatory goals — such as those that serve achievement motives — as well as to simpler behavioral goals. Goals vary in their complexity and in how long they need to operate in order to attain the desired state of affairs. But as the achievement-priming studies have shown, one obtains the same qualities of complex and difficult goal pursuit with situationally (nonconsciously) activated goals, such as persistence and resumption of a task in the face of more intrinsically attractive alternatives, as with consciously selected goals.

Given the severe limitations of conscious self-regulation capacity (e.g., Baumeister et al., 1998; Muraven et al., 1998), it makes sense that even complex self-regulatory goals can operate automatically and efficiently, without needing to be instigated and then guided by expensive acts of will and choice. This limited conscious self-regulation is better spared for those occasions when there are real options and choices of which path to take — that is, for situations in which the same conscious choice is not typically made each time.

Subjective Experience

Emotions and Moods

That one's emotional responses to events occur without one intentionally choosing to have that emotion is hardly a controversial statement. Nearly all would agree that the intentional expression of particular emotions is difficult and that the experience of emotion is largely not a matter of conscious choice (e.g., Damasio, 1994; Wegner & Bargh, 1998; Zajonc, 1998; but see Clore, 1994). Consistent with this point is the fact that research on the role played by conscious processes in emotion focuses nearly exclusively on the intentional control of emotional reactions to events after they have occurred. Recently, LeDoux (1996) has put forth a still more radical view of emotions — that, over time, they become direct responses to the presence of the provoking object or event in the environment, with the emotional process bypassing the stage of conscious (cortical) appraisal of the event.

Because the idea of emotions produced without conscious choice is not novel, we turn to a second form of affective experience. *Moods* have been differentiated from emotions as being of lesser intensity but longer duration (e.g., Clark & Fiske, 1982). Moods also tend to develop more gradually than emotions and so typically are not immediate responses to environmental events. Therefore, there is more of a role to be played by conscious, intentional thought in producing moods than in producing emotions. Here again, however, it is not really a matter of intending to be in a good mood or a bad mood. Rather, effortful and strategic mental processes (e.g., thinking about an upcoming vacation in a time of pressure and stress at work) are used in an attempt to change or control the mood once it has settled in. Generally speaking, then, moods are a second form of affective experience that occur, for the most part, without conscious choice.

Evaluations and Judgments

Alternatively, evaluations, such as global judgments as to whether an event or object is good or bad (see Eagly & Chaiken, 1993), are commonly assumed to be made consciously and intentionally. Many theories of attitude formation and of the evaluative process hold that one weighs the pros and cons, or positive and negative features of the object or event, and with intention and deliberation makes a decision about how one feels about it (e.g., N. H. Anderson, 1971; Birnbaum, 1973; see Eagly & Chaiken, 1993, ch. 5). However, prodded by Zajonc's (1980) famous challenge to this position — that "preferences need no inferences" — a substantial body of evidence has now accumulated that one's evaluations often (if not usually) become activated directly, without one needing to think about them, or even be aware that one has just classified the person or event as good or bad. Instead, just the mere presence of the attitude object is sufficient to cause the corresponding evaluation.

The Perception–Evaluation Link

Zajonc (1980) posited the existence of a separate affective information-processing system to account for the fact (among others) that one often knows one's preference among several items before one can explain the reasons for that preference. In response, Fiske (1982) made a counter-proposal that a separate mental system was not necessary — one could consider an evaluation as a node in an associational representation of the environmental object. Moreover, this evaluative "tag" (good vs. bad) to the object representation could become activated immediately on perception of the object, following the principle that all elements of integrated schematic representations become active in an all-or-none fashion (see Hayes-Roth, 1977). Fiske (1982) termed this approach to immediate evaluative experience "category-based affect": Evaluations of objects or events come to be components of their perceptual representations and so become activated immediately in the course of perception of the object or event, without one consciously considering or intending to evaluate it.

In many different areas of research (e.g., social judgment, attitudes) it has been found that people classify their experience as either good or bad and do so immediately, unintentionally, and without awareness that they are doing it. These experiments have, for the most part, used the paradigm developed by Neely (1977) to test for unintended, automatic associative connections between different mental concepts. In this paradigm, a prime word is presented for a short time (e.g., 250 milliseconds), followed by a target word to which the participant responds in some way. To the extent that the prime affects responding to the target, this can only be because of an automatic connection between those two concepts, because the 250-ms time delay between their presentations is too short for an intended, conscious expectancy about the target to have developed (Posner & Snyder, 1975). In the case of "automatic evaluation" research, the prime concept on a given trial is the name of a social group (e.g., White, Asian, male) or other attitude object (e.g., Clinton, tuna, baseball), and the target concept is a positive or negative adjective (e.g., beautiful, phony). If the attitude object (prime) is automatically evaluated by participants as "good," it should speed up responses to positive adjectives and slow down responses to negative adjectives and do the reverse for "bad" attitude objects. If the attitude object has no effect on target responses, this means that it was not evaluated automatically.

Many studies have shown this immediate evaluation effect, with the only contentious issue being just how pervasive the effect is. Some studies (e.g., Fazio, Sanbonmatsu, Powell, & Kardes, 1986) have found it limited to a person's strongest, most important attitudes, whereas others (e.g., Bargh, Chaiken, Govender, & Pratto, 1992; Bargh, Chaiken, Raymond, & Hymes, 1996) have shown the effect for all attitude objects studied, varying widely in the "strength" or importance of the attitude. One clue from this research about the nonconscious nature of evaluation is that those studies that have had fewer conscious, intentionally evaluative aspects to them have found the evaluation effect more pervasive and strong. For instance, Bargh, Chaiken, et al. (1996) had participants pronounce the names of the target words instead of evaluate the targets as good or bad and obtained strong evidence of automatic evaluation of weak as well as strong attitude objects. This study also showed, crucially, that automatic evaluation occurs even when the person has no conscious goal to evaluate.

Automatic Effects on Mood Via Automatic Evaluation

Given this ubiquitous automatic evaluation effect, the question arises as to what functions it serves. It is unlikely that such an immediate and basic mental response would exist in isolation, having no "downstream" consequences for thought, behavior, and phenomenal experience. One possible consequence is an effect on mood state. We've all been in certain moods with no good idea why and in a "funk" or just in a good mood, seemingly at random. We usually don't question our good moods — happy to have them whatever the reason — but when we are in a sad or angry mood, we often try to understand why. The problem is that we are often not very good at figuring out the real reason for our mood (e.g., S. Schachter & Singer, 1962; Schwarz & Clore, 1983) and are thus liable to make bad decisions about what to do about it (e.g., not continuing a relationship because the first date happened to be in a bad neighborhood). It is possible, then, that one reason we can be in moods without knowing why is because of the kind of automatic evaluations being made in our current environment. We recently conducted some studies to test this possibility (Chartrand & Bargh, 1999b).

In both studies, we first subliminally presented participants with nouns associated with either strongly positive (e.g., music, friends), strongly negative (e.g., cancer, cockroach), mildly positive (e.g., parade, clown), or mildly negative (e.g., Monday, worm) attitudes for most people. Following this alleged reaction-time task, participants moved on to what they thought was an unrelated experiment, in which they were given two self-report mood measures: The depression subscale of the Multiple Affect Adjective Check List (MAACL; Zuckerman & Lubin, 1965), and an "affect–arousal" (see Salovey & Birnbaum, 1989) mood measure. On both measures, mood was found to be a direct, increasing function of the evaluative nature of the subliminally presented stimuli — strongly negative attitude objects produced the saddest mood, and strongly positive objects the happiest mood. As predicted, whether a person is making (without knowing it) mainly positive or mainly negative evaluations within the current environment plays out in changes in his or her mood. Because moods last longer than fleeting individual evaluations, they would seem to be a more stable, "rolling average" of the general favorability of one's environment. This is a second way in which automatic, unintended evaluations serve a kind of natural signaling function about the overall safety or danger one is in at the moment.

Behavioral Consequences of Automatic Evaluation

Another possible consequence of automatic evaluative processes is to predispose the individual's behavior toward positive objects and away from negative ones when the conscious mind is elsewhere, thinking about tonight's dinner perhaps or worrying about tomorrow's job interview. And so, Chen and Bargh (1999) tested whether nonconscious evaluations were linked to behavioral dispositions to either approach or to avoid the particular stimulus being evaluated. Recent research has suggested that there is a connection between evaluations and muscular readinesses: Cacioppo, Priester, and Berntson (1993), for example, showed that a participant liked novel stimuli more when his or her arm was currently in a state associated with approach reactions (flexing the arm, as if pulling something toward them) than if it was in a state associated with avoidance reactions (extending the arm, as if pushing something away). Participants were unaware of any relation between the position of their arm and their evaluations of the stimuli. In our experiments, we reversed the causal direction of this effect.

Half of the participants were instructed to push a lever away from them if the stimulus word presented was positive in evaluation and to pull the lever toward them if the stimulus word was negative (the other participants received the opposite instructions). As predicted, people were faster to respond to positive words when they were pulling the lever than pushing the lever, and faster to respond to negative words when they were pushing rather than pulling the lever. In a second experiment, we removed the conscious goal to evaluate the stimuli and just had half the participants push and half pull the lever as quickly as possible when the word appeared, in a straight reaction-time task. Again, those pushing the lever were faster for negative than positive stimuli, and those pulling the lever were faster for positive than negative stimuli, even though nothing in the experiment was explicitly about evaluating anything. Immediately and unintentionally, then, a perceived object or event is classified as either good or as bad, and this results, in a matter of milliseconds, in a behavioral predisposition toward that stimulus. When the conscious mind is elsewhere, automatic evaluative processes prepare the individual to make the appropriate response.

The Relation Between Automatic Evaluations and Conscious Judgments

How do immediate, automatic evaluations impact on deliberate, conscious judgments about the same person, object, or event? The former will occur temporally prior to the latter. Does the automatic influence the conscious? Does it determine it entirely? Ambady and Rosenthal (1992) conducted a meta-analysis of 38 studies of the accuracy of predictions of various behaviors, emotional states, and skills of a target person, made after observations of varying length. Across the studies, the length of time the predictor observed the individual in question ranged from 3 to 300 s. Predictions were made about a variety of outcome variables, such as the effectiveness of a teacher, the quality of a therapist, whether the individual was lying or telling the truth, how he or she was going to vote, how depressed or anxious he or she was, and so forth. Ambady and Rosenthal found that "thin slices" of behavioral and expressive evidence of under 30 s enabled predictions no different in accuracy than those based on observations of 4 or 5 minutes in length. They concluded that a great deal of information about a person is conveyed through unintended and unmanaged expressive behavior, and "these cues are so subtle that they are neither encoded nor decoded at an intentional, conscious level of awareness" (p. 256). More than this, the pick-up of this information occurs almost immediately, and longer, more leisurely conscious observation and deliberation about the judgment to be made leads to judgments no different than those based on only a "thin slice" of evidence.

This conclusion is consistent with other evidence (a) that strangers' personality trait ratings of an individual based on very little and even no interaction with that person are strikingly similar to that person's self-ratings on those traits and (b) that a group of observers rating another person at "zero acquaintance" (they can see the person but have not yet interacted with him or her) have remarkably high consensus about that person's personality (Albright, Kenny, & Malloy, 1988). Certainly, we can quickly pick up information and make judgments about others with little, if any, conscious deliberation. Indeed, other studies have shown that the longer one consciously deliberates about one's preferences and judgments, the less accurate and predictive they become (Wilson & Schooler, 1991).

So it may be, especially for evaluations and judgments of novel people and objects, that what we think we are doing while consciously deliberating in actuality has no effect on the outcome of the judgment, as it has already been made through relatively immediate, automatic means. We know that these evaluations are made constantly without any intention to make them (Bargh, Chaiken, et al., 1996), and so, as Zajonc (1980) first argued, our preferences and many other judgments may be made literally before we know it.

In summary, automatic evaluation of the environment is a pervasive and continuous activity that individuals do not intend to engage in and of which they are largely unaware. It appears to have real and functional consequences, creating behavioral readinesses within fractions of a second to approach positive and avoid negative objects, and, through its effect on mood, serving as a signaling system for the overall safety versus danger of one's current environment. All of these effects tend to keep us in touch with the realities of our world in a way that bypasses the limitations of conscious self-regulation capabilities.

Conclusions

The heavier the burden, the closer our lives come to the earth, the more real and truthful they become. Conversely, the absolute absence of a burden causes man to be lighter than air, to soar into the heights, take leave of the earth and his earthly being, and become only half real, his movements free as they are insignificant. What then shall we choose? Weight or lightness? (Milan Kundera, *The Unbearable Lightness of Being*, 1984, p. 5)

For many years now, researchers have studied two main types of mental processes, both in isolation and in interaction with each other. The two types are known by a variety of names — conscious–nonconscious, controlled–automatic, explicit–implicit, systematic–heuristic — but it is clear which one is "heavy" and which one is "light." To consciously and willfully regulate one's own behavior, evaluations, decisions, and emotional states requires considerable effort and is relatively slow. Moreover, it appears to require a limited resource that is quickly used up, so conscious self-regulatory acts can only occur sparingly and for a short time. On the other hand, the nonconscious or automatic processes we've described here are unintended, effortless, very fast, and many of them can operate at any given time. Most important, they are effortless, continually in gear guiding the individual safely through the day. Automatic self-regulation is, if you will, thought lite — "one third less effort than regular thinking" (Gilbert, 1989, p. 193). The individual is free, in Kundera's (1984) sense, of the burden of their operation.

Some of the automatic guidance systems we've outlined are "natural" and don't require experience to develop. These are the fraternization of perceptual and behavioral representations and the connection between automatic evaluation processes on the one hand and mood and behavior on the other. Other forms of automatic self-regulation develop out of repeated and consistent experience; they map onto the regularities of one's experience and take tasks over from conscious choice and guidance when that choice is not really being exercised. This is how goals and motives can come to operate nonconsciously in given situations, how stereotypes can become chronically associated with the perceptual features of social groups, and how evaluations can become integrated with the perceptual representation of the person, object, or event so that they become active immediately and unintentionally in the course of perception.

To produce the empirical evidence on which these claims rest, we and others have conducted a variety of experiments in which goals, evaluations, and perceptual constructs (traits, stereotypes) were primed in an unobtrusive manner. Through use of these priming manipulations, the mental representations were made active to later exert their influence without an act of will and without the participants' awareness of the influence. Yet in all of these studies, the effect was the same as when people are aware of and intend to engage in that process. Thus it is no coincidence that Figures 14.1, 14.2, and 14.3 have the same essential structure, because the underlying principle is the same in all three: Mental representations designed to perform a certain function will perform that function once activated, regardless of where the activation comes from. The representation does not "care" about the source of the activation; it is blind to it and has no "memory" about it that might cause it to behave differently depending on the particular source. The activated mental representation is like a button being pushed; it can be pushed by one's finger intentionally (e.g., turning on the electric coffeemaker) or accidentally (e.g., by the cat on the countertop) or by a decision made in the past (e.g., by setting the automatic turn-on mechanism the night before). In whatever way the start button is pushed, the mechanism subsequently behaves in the same way.

And so, the evaluations we've made in the past are now made for us and predispose us to behave in consistent ways; the goals we have pursued in the past now become active and guide our behavior in pursuit of the goal in relevant situations; and our perceptions of the emotional and behavioral reactions of others makes us tend to respond in the same way, establishing bonds of rapport and liking in a natural and effortless way. Thus "the automaticity of being" is far from the negative and maladaptive caricature drawn by humanistically oriented writers (e.g., Bandura, 1986; Langer, 1997: Mischel et al., 1996); rather, these processes are in our service and best interests — and in an intimate, knowing way at that. They are, if anything, "mental butlers" who know our tendencies and preferences so well that they anticipate and take care of them for us, without having to be asked.

REFERENCES

Albright, L., Kenny, D. A., & Malloy, T. E. (1988). Consensus in personality judgments at zero acquaintance. *Journal of Personality and Social Psychology, 55*, 387–395.

Allport, F. H. (1955). *Theories of perception and the concept of structure.* New York: Wiley.

Ambady, N., & Rosenthal, R. (1992). Thin slices of expressive behavior as predictors of interpersonal consequences: A meta-analysis. *Psychological Bulletin, 111*, 256–274.

Amsel, A. (1989). *Behaviorism, neobehaviorism, and cognitivism in learning theory: Historical and contemporary perspectives.* Hillsdale, NJ: Erlbaum.

Anderson, J. R. (1983). *The architecture of cognition.* Cambridge, MA: Harvard University Press.

Anderson, N. H. (1971). Integration theory and attitude change. *Psychological Review, 78*, 171–206.

Atkinson, J. W., & Birch. D. (1970). *A dynamic theory of action.* New York: Wiley.

Bandura, A. (1977a). Self-efficacy: Toward a unifying theory of behavioral change. *Psychological Review, 84*, 191–215.

Bandura, A. (1977b). *Social learning theory.* Englewood Cliffs, NJ: Prentice-Hall.

Bandura, A. (1986). *Social foundations of thought and action: A social cognitive theory.* Englewood Cliffs, NJ: Prentice-Hall.

Bandura, A. (1990). Self-regulation of motivation through anticipatory and self-reactive mechanisms. In R. A. Dienstbier (Ed.), *Perspectives on motivation: Nebraska symposium on motivation* (Vol. 38, pp. 69–164). Lincoln: University of Nebraska Press.

Bandura, A. (1997). *Self-efficacy.* New York: Freeman.

Bargh, J. A. (1989). Conditional automaticity: Varieties of automatic influence in social perception and cognition. In J. S. Uleman & J. A. Bargh (Eds.), *Unintended thought* (pp. 3–51). New York: Guilford Press.

Bargh, J. A. (1990). Auto-motives: Preconscious determinants of social interaction. In E. T. Higgins & R. M. Sorrentino (Eds.), *Handbook of motivation and cognition* (Vol. 2, pp. 93–130). New York: Guilford Press.

Bargh, J. A. (1994). The Four Horsemen of automaticity: Awareness, efficiency, intention, and control in social cognition. In R. S. Wyer, Jr., & T. K. Srull (Eds.), *Handbook of social cognition* (2nd ed., pp. 1–40). Hillsdale, NJ: Erlbaum.

Bargh, J. A. (1996). Principles of automaticity. In E. T. Higgins & A. Kruglanski (Eds.), *Social psychology: Handbook of basic principles* (pp. 169–183). New York: Guilford.

Bargh, J. A. (1997). The automaticity of everyday life. In R. S. Wyer, Jr. (Ed.), *The automaticity of everyday life: Advances in social cognition* (Vol. 10. pp. 1–61). Mahwah. NJ: Erlbaum.

Bargh, J. A. (1999). The cognitive monster. In S. Chaiken & Y. Trope (Eds.), *Dual process theories in social psychology* (pp. 361–382). New York: Guilford Press.

Bargh, J. A., Chaiken, S., Govender, R., & Pratto, F. (1992). The generality of the automatic attitude activation effect. *Journal of Personality and Social Psychology, 62*, 893–912.

Bargh, J. A., Chaiken, S., Raymond, P., & Hymes, C. (1996). The automatic evaluation effect: Unconditionally automatic attitude activation with a pronunciation task. *Journal of Experimental Social Psychology, 32*, 185–210.

Bargh, J. A., & Chartrand, T. L. (in press). Studying the mind in the middle: A practical guide to priming and automaticity research. In H. Reis & C. Judd (Eds.), *Research methods in social psychology.* New York: Cambridge University Press.

Bargh, J. A., Chen, M., & Burrows, L. (1996). Automaticity of social behavior: Direct effects of trait construct and stereotype activation on action. *Journal of Personality and Social Psychology, 71*, 230–244.

Bargh, J. A., & Gollwitzer, P. M. (1994). Environmental control of goal-directed action: Automatic and strategic contingencies between situations and behavior. *Nebraska Symposium on Motivation, 41*, 71–124.

Bargh, J. A., Gollwitzer, P. M., & Lee-Chai, A. (1999). *Bypassing the will: Automatic and controlled self-regulation.* Manuscript under review.

Bargh, J. A., Raymond, P., Pryor, J., & Strack, F. (1995). Attractiveness of the underlying: An automatic power-sex association and its consequences for sexual harassment and aggression. *Journal of Personality and Social Psychology, 68*, 768–781.

Bargh, J. A., & Thein, R. D. (1985). Individual construct accessibility, person memory, and the recall–judgment link: The case of information overload. *Journal of Personality and Social Psychology, 46,* 1129–1146.

Barsalou, L. W. (1993). *Cognitive psychology: An overview for cognitive scientists.* Hillsdale, NJ: Erlbaum.

Bateson, G. (1972). *Steps to an ecology of mind.* New York: Ballantine.

Baumeister, R. F., Bratslavsky, E., Muraven, M., & Tice, D. M. (1998). Ego depletion: Is the active self a limited resource? *Journal of Personality and Social Psychology, 74,* 1252–1265.

Baumeister, R. F., & Sommer, K. L. (1997). Consciousness, free choice, and automaticity. In R. S. Wyer, Jr. (Ed.), *Advances in social cognition* (Vol. X, pp. 75–81). Mahwah, NJ: Erlbaum.

Beck, A. T. (1976). *Cognitive therapy and the emotional disorders.* New York: International Universities Press.

Berkowitz, L. (1984). Some effects of thoughts on anti- and prosocial influences of media events: A cognitive-neoassociation analysis. *Psychological Bulletin, 95,* 410–427.

Berkowitz, L. (1997). Some thoughts extending Bargh's argument. In R. S. Wyer (Ed.), *Advances in social cognition* (Vol. 10, pp. 83–94). Mahwah, NJ: Erlbaum.

Bernieri, F. J. (1988). Coordinated movement and rapport in teacher-student interactions. *Journal of Nonverbal Behavior, 12,* 120–138.

Bernieri, F. J., & Rosenthal, R. (1991). Interpersonal coordination: Behavior matching and interactional synchrony. In R. S. Feldman & B. Rimé (Eds.), *Fundamentals of nonverbal behavior* (pp. 401–432). Cambridge, England: Cambridge University Press.

Birnbaum, M. H. (1973). Morality judgment: Test of an averaging model with differential weights. *Journal of Experimental Psychology, 99,* 395–399.

Brewer, M. B. (1988). A dual process model of impression formation. In T. K. Srull & R. S. Wyer, Jr. (Eds.), *Advances in social cognition* (Vol. 1, pp. 1–36). Hillsdale, NJ: Erlbaum.

Bruner, J. S. (1957). On perceptual readiness. *Psychological Review, 64,* 123–152.

Byrne, R. W., & Russon, A. E. (1998). Learning by imitation: A hierarchical approach. *Brian and Behavioral Sciences, 21,* 667–684.

Cacioppo, J. T., Crites, S. L., Jr., & Gardner, W. L. (1996). Attitudes to the right: Evaluative processing is associated with lateralized late positive event-related brain potentials. *Personality and Social Psychology Bulletin, 22,* 1205–1219.

Cacioppo, J. T., Priester, J. R., & Berntson, G. G. (1993). Rudimentary determinants of attitudes: II. Arm flexion and extension have differential effects on attitudes. *Journal of Personality and Social Psychology, 65,* 5–17.

Cantor, N., & Kihlstrom. J. F. (1987). *Personality and social intelligence.* Englewood Cliffs. NJ: Prentice-Hall.

Carlston, D. E., & Skowronski, J. J. (1994). Savings in the relearning of trait information as evidence for spontaneous inference generation. *Journal of Personality and Social Psychology, 66,* 840–856.

Carpenter, W. B. (1874). *Principles of mental physiology.* New York: Appleton.

Carver, C. S., Ganellen, R. J., Froming, W. J., & Chambers, W. (1983). Modeling: An analysis in terms of category accessibility. *Journal of Experimental Social Psychology, 19,* 403–421.

Carver, C. S., & Scheier, M. F. (1998). *On the self-regulation of behavior,* New York: Cambridge University Press.

Chaiken, S., Liberman, A., & Eagly, A. H. (1989). Heuristic and systematic information processing within and beyond the persuasion context. In J. S. Uleman & J. A. Bargh (Eds.), *Unintended thought* (pp. 212–252). New York: Guilford Press.

Chaiken, S., & Trope, Y. (Eds.). (1999). *Dual-process theories in social psychology.* New York: Guilford Press.

Chartrand, T. L. (1999). *Consequences of automatic motivation for mood, self-efficacy, and subsequent performance.* Unpublished doctoral dissertation, New York University.

Chartrand, T. L., & Bargh, J. A. (1996). Automatic activation of impression formation and memorization goals: Nonconscious goal priming reproduces effects of explicit task instructions. *Journal of Personality and Social Psychology, 71,* 464–478.

Chartrand, T. L., & Bargh, J. A. (1999a). The chameleon effect: The perception–behavior link and social interaction. *Journal of Personality and Social Psychology, 76,* 893–910.

Chartrand, T. L., & Bargh, J. A. (1999b). *Consequences of automatic evaluation for current mood.* Manuscript in preparation, New York University.

Chen, M., & Bargh, J. A. (1997). Nonconscious behavioral confirmation processes: The self-fulfilling consequences of automatic stereotype activation. *Journal of Experimental Social Psychology, 33,* 541–560.

Chen, M., & Bargh, J. A. (1999). Nonconscious approach and avoidance behavioral consequences of the automatic evaluation effect. *Personality and Social Psychology Bulletin, 25,* 215–224.

Clark, M. S., & Fiske, S. T. (Eds.), (1982). *Affect and cognition: The 17th Annual Carnegie Symposium on Cognition.* Hillsdale, NJ: Erlbaum.

Clore, G. L. (1994). Why emotions are never unconscious. In P. Ekman & R. J. Davidson (Eds.), *The nature of emotions: Fundamental questions* (pp. 285–290). New York: Oxford University Press.

Condon, W. S., & Ogston, W. D. (1966). Sound film analysis of normal and pathological behavior patterns. *Journal of Nervous and Mental Disease, 143,* 338–347.

Damasio, A. R. (1994). *Descartes' error: Emotion, reason, and the human brain.* New York: Grosset/Putnam.

Deci, E. L., & Ryan, R. M. (1985). *Intrinsic motivation and self-determination in human behavior.* New York: Plenum.

Devine, P. G. (1989). Stereotypes and prejudice: Their automatic and controlled components. *Journal of Personality and Social Psychology, 56,* 680–690.

Dijksterhuis, A., Bargh, J. A., & Miedema, J. (in press). Of men and mackerels: Attention and automatic behavior. In H. Bless & J. P. Forgas (Eds.), *Subjective experience in social cognition and behavior.* Philadelphia: Psychology Press.

Dijksterhuis, A., & van Knippenberg, A. (1998). The relation between perception and behavior or how to win a game of Trivial Pursuit. *Journal of Personality and Social Psychology, 74,* 865–877.

Dweck, C. S. (1996). Implicit theories and organizers of goals and behaviors. In P. M. Gollwitzer & J. A. Bargh (Eds.), *The psychology of action* (pp. 69–90). New York: Guilford Press.

Eagly, A. H., & Chaiken, S. (1993). *The psychology of attitudes.* New York: Harcourt Brace Jovanovich.

Erdelyi, M. H. (1974). A new look at the new look: Perceptual defense and vigilance. *Psychological Review, 81,* 1–25.

Fazio, R. H. (1990). Multiple processes by which attitudes guide behavior: The MODE model as an integrative framework. In M. P. Zanna (Ed.), *Advances in experimental social psychology* (Vol. 23, pp. 75–109). San Diego, CA: Academic Press.

Fazio, R. H., Sanbonmatsu, D. M., Powell, M. C., & Kardes, F. R. (1986). On the automatic activation of attitudes. *Journal of Personality and Social Psychology, 50,* 229–238.

Fiske, S. T. (1982). Schema-triggered affect. In M. S. Clark & S. T. Fiske (Eds.), *Affect and cognition: The 17th Annual Carnegie Symposium on Cognition*. Hillsdale, NJ: Erlbaum.

Fiske, S. T., & Neuberg, S. E. (1990). A continuum of impression formation, from category-based to individuating processes: Influences of information and motivation on attention and interpretation. In M. P. Zanna (Ed.), *Advances in experimental social psychology* (Vol. 23, pp. 1–74). San Diego, CA: Academic Press.

Freud, S. (1965). *The psychopathology of everyday life* (J. Strachey, Ed. & Trans.). New York: Norton. (Original work published 1901)

Gardner, W., Bargh, J. A., Shellman, A., & Bessenoff, G. (1999). *This is your brain on primes: Lateralized brain activity is the same for nonconscious and conscious evaluative processing*. Manuscript under review.

Gilbert, D. T. (1989). Thinking lightly about others: Automatic components of the social inference process. In J. S. Uleman & J. A. Bargh (Eds.), *Unintended thought* (pp. 189–211). New York: Guilford Press.

Gilbert, D. T. (1991). How mental systems believe. *American Psychologist, 46*, 107–119.

Gollwitzer, P. M. (1990). Action phases and mind-sets. In E. T. Higgins & R. M. Sorrentino (Eds.), *Handbook of motivation and cognition* (Vol. 2. pp. 53–92). New York: Guilford Press.

Gollwitzer, P. M. (1993). Goal achievement: The role of intentions. In W. Stroebe & M. Hewstone (Eds.), *European review of social psychology* (Vol. 4, pp. 141–185). London: Wiley.

Gollwitzer, P. M., & Moskowitz, G. (1996). Goal effects on thought and behavior. In E. T. Higgins & A. Kruglanski (Eds.), *Social psychology: Handbook of basic principles* (pp. 361–399). New York: Guilford Press.

Hamilton, D. L., Katz, L. B., & Leirer, V. O. (1980). Organizational processes in impression formation. In R. Hastie, T. M. Ostrom, E. B. Ebbesen, R. S. Wyer, D. L. Hamilton, & D. E. Carlston (Eds.), *Person memory: The cognitive basis of social perception* (pp. 121–153). Hillsdale, NJ: Erlbaum.

Hayes-Roth, B. (1977). Evolution of cognitive structure and process. *Psychological Review, 84*, 260–278.

Heckhausen, H. (1991). *Motivation and action*. New York: Springer-Verlag.

Higgins, E. T. (1989). Knowledge accessibility and activation: Subjectivity and suffering from unconscious sources. In J. S. Uleman & J. A. Bargh (Eds.), *Unintended thought* (pp. 75–123). New York: Guilford Press.

Higgins, E. T. (1996). Knowledge activation: Accessibility, applicability, and salience. In E. T. Higgins & A. W. Kruglanski (Eds.), *Social psychology: Handbook of basic principles* (pp. 133–168). New York: Guilford Press.

Higgins, E. T., & King, G. A. (1981). Accessibility of social construction. Information-processing consequences of individual and contextual ability. In N. Cantor & J. F. Kihlstrom (Eds.), *Personality, cognition and social interaction* (pp. 69–122). Hillsdale, NJ: Erlbaum.

Hull, C. L. (1931). Goal attraction and directing ideas conceived as phenomena. *Psychological Review, 38*, 487–506.

Jacoby, L. L. (1991). A process dissociation framework: Separating as tomatic from intentional uses of memory. *Journal of Memory Language, 30*, 513–541.

James, W. (1890). *The principles of psychology* (Vol. 2). New York:

Jastrow, J. (1906). *The subconscious*. Boston: Houghton-Mifflin.

Kahneman, D. (1973). *Attention and effort*. Englewood Cliffs, NJ: Prentice-Hall.

Kelly, G. A. (1955). *The psychology of personal constructs*. New York Norton.

Koestler, A. (1967). *The ghost in the machine*. London: Hutchinson & Co.

Koffka, K. (1925). *Die grundlagen der psychischen entwicklung* [Foundations of psychological development]. Osterwieck, Germany: Feldt.

Kruglanski, A. W. (1996a). Goals as knowledge structures. In P. M. Gollwitzer & J. A. Bargh (Eds.), *The psychology of action*. (pp. 599–618). New York: Guilford Press.

Kruglanski, A. W. (1996b). Motivated social cognition: Principles of the interface. In E. T. Higgins & A. W. Kruglanski (Eds.), *Social psychology: Handbook of basic principles* (pp. 493–520). New York: Guilford Press.

Kunda, Z. (1990). The case for motivated reasoning. *Psychological Bulletin, 108*, 480–498.

Kundera, M. (1984). *The unbearable lightness of being*. New York: Harper & Row.

LaFrance, M. (1979). Nonverbal synchrony and rapport: Analysis by the cross-lag panel technique. *Social Psychology Quarterly, 42*, 66–70.

LaFrance, M. (1982). Posture mirroring and rapport. In M. Davis (Ed.), *Interaction rhythms: Periodicity in communicative behavior* (pp. 279–298). New York: Human Sciences Press.

LaFrance, M., & Broadbent, M. (1976). Group rapport: Posture sharing as a nonverbal indicator. *Group and Organization Studies, 1*, 328–333.

Langer, E. J. (1978). Rethinking the role of thought in social interaction. In J. H. Harvey, W. Ickes, & R. F. Kidd (Eds.), *New directions attribution research* (Vol. 2, pp. 35–58). Hillsdale, NJ: Erlbaum.

Langer, E. J. (1997). *The power of mindful learning*. Reading, MA: Addison-Wesley.

Lashley, K. S. (1951). The problem of serial order in behavior. In L. A. Jeffress (Ed.), *Cerebral mechanisms in behavior: The Hixon symposium* (pp. 112–136). New York: Wiley.

Lazarus, R. S. (1991). *Emotion and adaption*. New York: Oxford University Press.

LeDoux, J. (1996). *The emotional brain*. New York: Simon & Schuster.

Lewin, K. (1951). *Field theory in social science*. Chicago: University of Chicago Press.

Locke, E. A., & Latham, G. P. (1990). *A theory of goal setting and task performance*. Englewood Cliffs, NJ: Prentice-Hall.

Logan, G. D., & Cowan, W. B. (1984). On the ability to inhibit thought and action: A theory of an act of control. *Psychological Review, 91*, 295–327.

Malamuth, N. (1989). The attraction to sexual aggression scale: Part One *Journal of Sex Research, 26*, 26–49.

Martin, L. L., & Tesser, A. (1989). Toward a motivational and structural theory of ruminative thought. In J. S. Uleman & J. A. Bargh (Eds.), *Unintended thought* (pp. 306–326). New York: Guilford Press.

Martin, L. L., & Tesser, A. (1996). Some ruminative thoughts. In R. S. Wyer (Ed.), *Advances in social cognition* (Vol. 9, pp. 1–47). Hillsdale NJ: Erlbaum.

Meltzoff, A. N., & Moore, M. K. (1977). Imitation of facial and gestures by human neonates. *Science, 198*, 75–78.

Meltzoff, A. N., & Moore, M. K. (1983). Newborn infants imitate facial gestures. *Child Development, 54*, 702–709.

Miller, G. A. (1956). The magical number seven, plus or minus two: Some limits on our capacity for processing information. *Psychological 63*, 81–97.

Miller, G. A., Galanter, E., & Pribram, K. H. (1960). *Plans and the structure of behavior.* New York: Holt.

Mischel, W., Cantor, N., & Feldman, S. (1996). Goal-directed self-regulation. In E. T. Higgins & A. W. Kruglanski (Eds.). *Social psychology: Handbook of basic principles* (pp. 329–360). New York: Guilford Press.

Muraven, M., Tice, D. M., & Baumeister, R. F. (1998). Self-control as limited resource: Regulatory depletion patterns. *Journal of Personality and Social Psychology, 74,* 774–789.

Neely, J. H. (1977). Semantic priming and retrieval from lexical memory: Roles of inhibitionless spreading activation and limited-capacity attention. *Journal of Experimental Psychology: General, 106,* 226–254.

Neely, J. H. (1991). Semantic priming effects in visual word recognition: A selective review of current findings and theories. In D. Besner & G. Humphreys (Eds.), *Basic processes in reading: Visual word recognition* (pp. 264–336). Hillsdale, NJ: Erlbaum.

Neisser, V. (1967). *Cognitive psychology.* New York: Appleton-Century-Crofts.

Nørretranders, T. (1998). *The user illusion.* New York: Viking.

Petty, R. E., & Cacioppo, J. T. (1986). *Communications and persuasion: Central and peripheral routes to attitude change.* New York: Springer-Verlag.

Piaget, J. (1946). *La formation du symbole chez l'enfant* [The development of symbolic thought]. Paris: Delachaux & Niestlé.

Posner, M. I., & Snyder, C. R. R. (1975). Attention and cognitive control. In R. L. Solso (Ed.), *Information processing and cognition: The Loyola symposium* (pp. 55–85). Hillsdale, NJ: Erlbaum.

Prinz, W. (1987). Ideo-motor action. In H. Heuer & A. F. Sanders (Eds.), *Perspectives on perception and action* (pp. 47–76). Hillsdale, NJ: Erlbaum.

Prinz, W. (1990). A common coding approach to perception and action. In O. Neumann & W. Prinz (Eds.), *Relationships between perception and action* (pp. 167–201). Berlin, Germany: Springer-Verlag.

Rogers, C. (1951). *Client-centered therapy: Its current practice, implications, and theory.* Boston: Houghton-Mifflin.

Rosenthal, R., & Jacobson, L. (1968). *Pygmalion in the classroom.* New York: Holt, Rinehart, & Winston.

Rotter, J. B. (1954). *Social learning and clinical psychology.* Englewood Cliffs, NJ: Prentice-Hall.

Ryan, R. M., Sheldon, K. M., Kasser, T., & Deci, E. L. (1996). All goals are not created equal: An organismic perspective on the nature of goals and their regulation. In P. M. Gollwitzer & J. A. Bargh (Eds.), *The psychology of action* (pp. 7–26). New York: Guilford Press.

Salovey, P., & Birnbaum, D. (1989). Influence of mood on health-relevant cognitions. *Journal of Personality and Social Psychology, 57,* 539–551.

Schacter, D. L. (1987). Implicit memory: History and current status. *Journal of Experimental Psychology: Learning, Memory, and Cognition, 13,* 501–518.

Schachter, S., & Singer, J. E. (1962). Cognitive, social, and physiological determinants of emotional state. *Psychological Review, 69,* 379–399.

Schwarz, N., & Clore, G. L. (1983). Mood, misattribution, and judgments of well-being: Informative and directive functions of affective states. *Journal of Personality and Social Psychology, 45,* 513–523.

Seligman, M. E. P. (1991). *Learned optimism.* New York: Knopf.

Shiffrin, R. M. (1988). Attention. In R. C. Atkinson, R. J. Hernstein, G. Lindzey, & R. Duncan Luce (Eds.), *Stevens' handbook of experimental psychology.* (2nd ed., Vol. 2, pp. 739–811). New York: Wiley Inter-science.

Shiffrin, R. M., & Dumais, S. T. (1981). The development of automatism. In J. R. Anderson (Ed.), *Cognitive skills and their acquisition* (pp. 111–140). Hillsdale, NJ: Erlbaum.

Shiffrin, R. M., & Schneider, W. (1977). Controlled and automatic human information processing: II. Perceptual learning, automatic attending, and a general theory. *Psychological Review, 84,* 127–190.

Skinner, B. F. (1938). *The behavior of organisms.* New York: Appleton-Century-Crofts.

Smith, E. E., & Medin, D. L. (1981). *Categories and concepts.* Cambridge, MA: Harvard University Press.

Smith, E. R., & Lerner, M. (1986). Development of automatism of social judgments. *Journal of Personality and Social Psychology, 37,* 2240–2252.

Snyder, M., Tanke, E. D., & Berscheid, E. (1977). Social perception and interpersonal behavior: On the self-fulfilling nature of social stereotypes. *Journal of Personality and Social Psychology, 35,* 656–666.

Spencer, S. J., Fein, S., Wolfe, C. T., Fong, C., & Dunn, M. A. (1998). Automatic activation of stereotypes: The role of self-image threat. *Personality and Social Psychology Bulletin, 24,* 1139–1152.

Squire, L. R. (1987). *Memory and brain.* New York: Oxford University Press.

Srull, T. K., & Wyer, R. S., Jr. (1979). The role of category accessibility in the interpretation of information about persons: Some determinants and implications. *Journal of Personality and Social Psychology, 37,* 1660–1672.

Tolman, E. C. (1932). *Purposive behavior in animals and men.* New York: Appleton-Century-Crofts.

Treisman, A. M. (1960). Contextual cues in selective listening. *Quarterly Journal of Experimental Psychology, 12,* 242–248.

Trope, Y. (1986). Identification and inferential processes in dispositional attribution. *Psychological Review, 93,* 239–257.

Uleman, J. S., Newman, L. S., & Moskowitz, G. B. (1996). People as flexible interpreters: Evidence and issues from spontaneous trait inference. In M. P. Zanna (Ed.), *Advances in experimental social psychology* (Vol. 28, pp. 211–279). New York: Academic Press.

Vallacher, R. R., & Wegner, D. M. (1987). What do people think they're doing? Action identification and human behavior. *Psychological Review, 94,* 3–15.

Varela, F. J., Thompson, E., & Rosch, E. (1991). *The embodied mind: Cognitive science and human experience.* Cambridge. MA: MIT Press.

Watson, J. B. (1913). Psychology as a behaviorist sees it. *Psychological Review, 20,* 158–167.

Wegner, D. M., & Bargh, J. A. (1998). Control and automaticity in social life. In D. Gilbert, S. Fiske, & G. Lindzey (Eds.), *Handbook of social psychology* (4th ed., pp. 446–496). Boston: McGraw-Hill.

Wegner, D. M., & Wheatley, T. P. (1999). Why it feels as if we're doing things: Sources of the experience of will. *American Psychologist, 54,* 480–492.

Whitehead, A. N. (1911). *An introduction to mathematics.* New York: Holt.

Wicklund, R. A., & Steins, G. (1996). Person perception under pressure: When motivation brings about egocentrism. In P. M. Gollwitzer & J. A. Bargh (Eds.), *The psychology of action* (pp. 511–528). New York: Guilford Press.

Wilensky, R. (1983). *Planning and understanding.* Reading, MA: Addison-Wesley.

Wilson, T. D., & Schooler, J. W. (1991). Thinking too much: Introspection can reduce the quality of preferences and decisions. *Journal of Personality and Social Psychology, 60*, 181–192.

Winter, L., & Uleman, J. S. (1984). When are social judgments made? Evidence for the spontaneousness of trait inferences. *Journal of Personality and Social Psychology, 47*, 237–252.

Wyer, R. S., Jr., & Srull, T. K. (1989). *Memory and cognition in its social context*. Hillsdale, NJ: Erlbaum.

Zajonc, R. B. (1980). Feeling and thinking: Preferences need no inferences. *American Psychologist, 35*, 151–175.

Zajonc, R. B. (1998). Emotions. In D. Gilbert, S. Fiske, & G. Lindzey (Eds.), *Handbook of social psychology* (4th ed., pp. 591–632). Boston: McGraw-Hill.

Zuckerman, M., & Lubin, B. (1965). *Manual for the Multiple Affect Adjective Check List*. San Diego, CA: Educational and Industrial Testing Service.

Automatic Vigilance: The Attention-Grabbing Power of Negative Social Information

Felicia Pratto and Oliver P. John

One of the functions of automatic stimulus evaluation is to direct attention toward events that may have undesirable consequences for the perceiver's well-being. To test whether attentional resources are automatically directed away from an attended task to undesirable stimuli, Ss named the colors in which desirable and undesirable traits (e.g., honest, sadistic) appeared. Across 3 experiments, color-naming latencies were consistently longer for undesirable traits but did not differ within the desirable and undesirable categories. In Experiment 2, Ss also showed more incidental learning for undesirable traits, as predicted by the automatic vigilance (but not a perceptual defense) hypothesis. In Experiment 3, a diagnosticity (or base-rate) explanation of the vigilance effect was ruled out. The implications for deliberate processing in person perception and stereotyping are discussed.

There is a fundamental asymmetry in people's evaluations of gains and losses, of joy and pain, and of positive and negative events. A considerable body of research, in fields as diverse as decision making,

This research was supported, in part, by National Institute of Health Grant MH39077 and by Biomedical Research Grants 87-20 and 88-24 (University of California) to Oliver P. John.

We are indebted to Celeste Schneider and Kristina Whitney Robins for assisting as experimenters, to Bud Viera for his help in decoding the MEL programming language, and to John Bargh, Asher Cohen, Lewis R. Goldberg, Shinobu Kitayama, Richard Lazarus, Delroy Paulhus, Steven J. Sherman, Arthur Shimamura, and Shelley E. Taylor for their comments on a draft. The support and resources of the Institute of Personality Assessment and Research, where Felicia Pratto spent 2 postdoctoral years, are also gratefully acknowledged.

Correspondence concerning this article should be addressed to Felicia Pratto, who is now at the Department of Psychology, Jordan Hall, Building 420, Stanford University, Stanford. California 94305-2130, or to Oliver P. John, Department of Psychology, University of California, Berkeley, California 94720.

impression formation, and emotional communication, has shown that people exhibit loss aversion (Kahneman & Tversky, 1984): They assign relatively more value, importance, and weight to events that have negative, rather than positive, implications for them. In decision making, potential costs are more influential than potential gains (e.g., Kahneman & Tversky, 1979). In impression formation, negative information is weighted more heavily than positive information (e.g., Anderson, 1974; Fiske, 1980; Hamilton & Zanna, 1972). In nonverbal communication, perceivers are more responsive to negatively toned messages than to positive ones (Frodi, Lamb, Leavitt, & Donovan, 1978). Quite generally, then, "losses loom larger than gains" (Kahneman & Tversky, 1984, p. 348).

There are good evolutionary reasons for this widespread and pronounced asymmetry in people's evaluative reactions. Events that may negatively affect the individual are typically of greater time urgency than are events that lead to desirable consequences. Averting danger to one's well-being, such as preventing loss of life or limb, often requires an immediate response. In comparison, positively valenced activities, such as feeding and procreation, are less pressing; although they are of crucial importance in the long term, pleasure is simply less urgent than pain. Negative affect carries an important signal value because it signifies to the organism the need to change or adjust its current state or activity.

Given the adaptive significance of fast responses to undesirable stimuli (e.g., Fiske, 1980), an adaptive advantage would accrue for organisms that have the capacity to attend to them quickly and with little effort. In humans, quick and effortless cognitive processes have been termed *automatic:* That is, they can occur without the perceiver's intention or control (for a review, see Shiffrin, 1988). In this article, we postulate and provide evidence for *automatic vigilance*, a mechanism that serves to direct attentional capacity to undesirable stimuli. Previous research suggests that people automatically process the subjective evaluation of social stimuli, such as liked and disliked attitude objects (Fazio, Sanbonmatsu, Powell, & Kardes, 1986), and this research is reviewed below. The present studies of automatic vigilance build on these earlier demonstrations of automatic evaluation effects and are designed to show that undesirable social stimuli are more likely to attract attention than are desirable social stimuli.

Automatic-Evaluative Processing

Evaluation of stimuli as good or bad, liked or disliked, and desirable or undesirable is a basic and ubiquitous aspect of the way people respond to their environment in both its social and nonsocial aspects. A variety of psychological theories view evaluation as a central and even primary response. For example, in factor analyses of semantic differential ratings, Osgood, Suci, and Tannenbaum (1957) found that evaluation was the first and largest factor of connotative meaning, a finding replicated across numerous cultures and languages. Lazarus (e.g., 1966, 1982) has suggested that emotions depend on the person's appraisal of an event and that one aspect of primary appraisal is the simple, immediate ascertainment of whether a stimulus is "good for me" or "bad for me."

Consistent with this view of evaluation as primary appraisal, a number of recent studies suggest that people can and do evaluate stimuli easily, readily, and quickly and that sometimes they do so without intention or much conscious thought. For example, when subjects who had no particular processing goal were exposed very briefly (1–3 ms) to physical shapes, their liking judgments of previously presented shapes differed from those of new shapes (Kunst-Wilson & Zajonc, 1980; Seamon, Brody, & Kauff, 1983; Seamon, Marsh, & Brody, 1984). The accuracy of affective choices was found to exceed recognition accuracy at short exposures (Seamon et al., 1983, 1984), although subjects became accurate at recognition judgments at only slightly longer exposures (Seamon et al., 1984).

Accurate evaluative judgments can also be made for semantically meaningful material at exposure speeds at which accurate recognition does not occur. For example, Bargh, Litt, Pratto, and Spielman (1988) presented trait adjectives at speeds below each subject's threshold of stimulus recognition (i.e., subjects could not accurately recognize whether a stimulus word or a blank card had been presented). Subjects were able to make correct evaluative judgments although they were unable to make correct synonymy judgments. Thus, subjects were able to ascertain the evaluative information in symbolic representations (words) before recognition.

In research on attitudes, Fazio (e.g., 1986; Fazio et al., 1986) found that the evaluation associated with a person's attitude toward an object becomes accessible automatically on exposure to relevant stimuli and that attitude-behavior consistency can be explained in terms of this accessibility. The role of evaluation in intergroup perception has been addressed by Fiske (e.g., 1982), who argued that evaluation becomes immediately accessible when stereotypes are activated.

In all, this research suggests that the evaluation of a stimulus can be detected before conscious recognition occurs and that evaluation is one of the first aspects of semantic meaning to be ascertained. Although it appears to be widely assumed that the evaluative aspects of many different types of stimuli are processed quickly and without much effort, differences between the desirable and undesirable poles of the evaluative continuum have not been examined systematically. The present studies were designed to demonstrate experimentally that automatic attention to desirable and undesirable stimuli is asymmetrical.

Testing the Automatic Vigilance Hypothesis

One way to demonstrate that an automatic mechanism directs attention to undesirable stimuli is to use a task in which the evaluative component of the stimulus is irrelevant to task performance but may interfere with it. Interference with the performance of an attended task is usually taken as an indicator of automaticity: "If a process produces interference with attentive processes despite the subject's attempts to eliminate the interference, then the process in question is surely automatic" (Shiffrin, 1988, p. 765). The key feature of an automatic process is thus its inescapability.

In the present studies, we used a task modeled after Stroop's (1935) color-interference paradigm. In the standard Stroop task, subjects name the colors in which a set of words is presented; attending to the meanings of the words leads to interference, particularly when the letters spell a color name different from the color in which the word is printed. To test whether attention is directed to negatively evaluated stimuli even when subjects try not to attend to that aspect of the stimuli, we presented a series of personality-trait adjectives, such as *sadistic, honest*, and *outgoing*, and subjects named the color in which the adjectives were presented. We predicted that although they had no intention or reason to do so, subjects would attend more to undesirable than to desirable traits and that this additional attention would lead to relatively longer color-naming latencies for undesirable traits. In our stimulus sets, we included traits covering a wide range of evaluation, ranging from extremely undesirable (e.g., sadistic, wicked, mean) to extremely desirable (e.g., kind, friendly, honest). This allowed us to examine the relation between the desirability values of the traits and subjects' latencies in naming their colors.

When rating the desirability of a set of traits, subjects can make fine-grained distinctions among traits on the evaluative continuum. One might therefore assume that gradations in trait desirability would affect color-naming latencies. In that case, trait desirability would be linearly related to color-naming latency, as shown in the middle panel of Figure 15.1. Across the whole range of desirability values, the more negative the trait, the more it should attract the perceiver's attention and distract from the color-naming task. In correlational terms, one would expect a negative association between desirability and latency even within the two valence categories.

However, we have argued that one function of automatic evaluation is to monitor the environment for undesirable stimuli. If this hypothesis is correct, it may be of little importance exactly how undesirable the stimulus is. It would be sufficient for the initial screening to tag any potentially undesirable event; the specific meaning of the tagged stimulus, including its severity, can be ascertained by subsequent, more controlled,

processing. Moreover, automatic evaluations seem to occur very rapidly and early in processing, so that the evaluative distinctions afforded by this process may be relatively crude, possibly no more complex than a simple categorical distinction between desirable and undesirable (see also Bargh et al., 1988). The relation between trait desirability and color-naming latencies might then take the categorical form depicted in the top panel of Figure 15.1. According to that hypothesis, desirable and undesirable traits differ from each other in their color-naming latencies; within the two valence categories, however, desirability and latency should not be related.

We also examined whether evaluative extremity might influence color-naming latencies. If that were the case, more extremely undesirable and desirable traits should elicit the longest latencies, with latencies decreasing from the extremes towards the more neutral traits, as shown in the bottom panel of Figure 15.1. In summary, we examined three different types of relations between desirability and response latency: Categorical, linear, and quadratic.

Experiment 1

Method

Subjects
Sixteen undergraduates at the University of California at Berkeley participated in exchange for partial course credit: Data from 5 subjects who indicated that they did not learn English before 5 years of age were excluded from all analyses.[1] No color-blind subjects were included in any of the experiments.

Design and Stimuli
In the color-naming task, each subject named the colors in which 40 desirable and 40 undesirable personality-trait adjectives were presented; trait valence was thus a within-subjects factor. To achieve a broad and fairly representative coverage of the domain of commonly used English trait adjectives, traits were drawn from each of the Big Five domains of personality description (Norman, 1963; see John, 1990, for a review). We assessed the social desirability of the traits using Hampson, Goldberg, and John's (1987) instructions;

---

[1] Subjects who did not learn English as their first language (e.g., foreign students, immigrants) tend to be slower at color naming; thus, we did not include them in any data analyses.

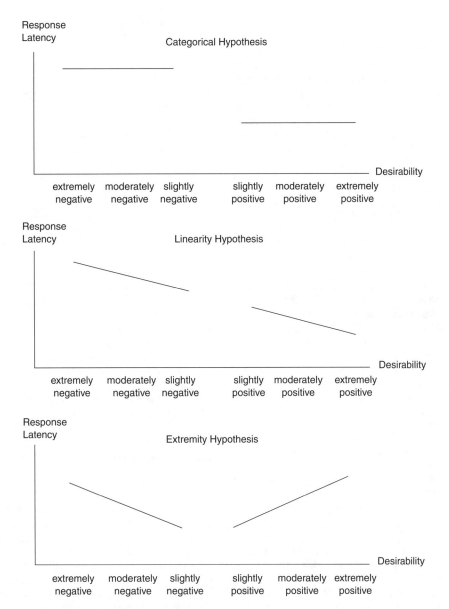

FIGURE 15.1 ■ Categorical, Linear, and Curvilinear Relations Between Color-naming Latencies (reaction time in ms) and Desirability Scale Values.

10 judges rated the 80 adjectives on a scale ranging from *extremely undesirable*(1) through *neutral* (5) to *extremely desirable* (9). The mean ratings were highly reliable (Cronbach's coefficient alpha = .98); the mean of the pairwise correlations among the judges was .85, indicating that gradations in trait desirability were highly reliable and that the mean ratings would closely approximate the personal evaluations of most subjects. Indeed, the mean ratings were indistinguishable from those obtained earlier by Hampson et al. (1987); across

the 67 adjectives included in both studies, the two sets of mean ratings correlated .96.

Across the mean ratings of the 80 adjectives, the mean was exactly at the scale midpoint of 5.0 ($SD = 2.5$). The mean values spanned almost the entire range of the scale (i.e., from 1.1 to 8.6); *sadistic, mean*, and *hostile* were the most undesirable, and *kind, sincere*, and *talented* were among the most desirable traits. The distribution, however, was bimodal, reflecting the distribution in a comprehensive set of English trait adjectives (Goldberg, 1982); that is, the vast majority of traits are either positively or negatively evaluated. The mean desirability ratings were 7.3 for the 40 desirable traits and 2.7 for the 40 undesirable traits. There was no difference in extremity (i.e., the absolute value of the distance from the scale midpoint of 5.0) between the undesirable traits ($M = 2.30$) and the desirable traits ($M = 2.28$), $t(78) < 1$, and extremity and desirability were uncorrelated ($r = -.08$). Thus, valence and extremity were independent. Word length was counterbalanced between desirable and undesirable trait adjectives; the average number of letters was 7.4 for undesirable adjectives and 7.6 for desirable adjectives.

To permit tests of the linearity and extremity hypotheses in trend analyses, we divided the traits into six categories of desirability values (scale values in parentheses): *Extremely undesirable* (range from 1 to 2. $M = 1.5$, $n = 11$ traits), *moderately undesirable* (range from 2 to 3, $M = 2.5$, $n = 16$), *slightly undesirable* (range from 3 to 4, $M = 3.5$, $n = 8$), *slightly desirable* (range from 6 to 7, $M = 6.4$, $n = 12$), *moderately desirable* (range from 7 to 8, $M = 7.4$, $n = 13$) and *extremely desirable* (range from 8 to 9, $M = 8.3$, $n = 12$).[2] These six categories differed significantly from each other in their desirability values (all pairwise $ps < .01$) but did not differ in word length or word frequency.

Apparatus

The experimenter presented instructions and stimuli to subjects on an IBM-PC computer with an EGA color board and monitor running a program in Micro-Experimental Lab. A voice key triggered by microphone input communicated with the software clock through the computer's printer port. Subjects were seated at

such a distance that all stimulus words would fall within the foveal area (e.g., Rayner, 1978).

Procedure

The experimenter told the subjects that they would be participating in a color-naming experiment: On each trial a word would appear in the center of the screen, and their task was to name the color in which the word appeared as quickly and as accurately as possible. Subjects completed 15 practice trials, the first 5 of which illustrated the color names. The first 4 experimental trials served as warm-up trials and were not part of the design. The adjective stayed on the screen until the subject triggered the voice key. The experimenter recorded whether the subject named the correct color and whether there was any reason to disregard the response-latency datum (e.g., the voice key was triggered by a cough). After that, 1 s elapsed before the next adjective appeared.

The 80 adjectives were presented in random order; their colors were chosen randomly from the set of blue, green, gold, pink, and red — with the constraint that the same color was never repeated on two consecutive trials, to avoid bias because of accessibility of the color name. After the first 40 trials, subjects were told to take a short break; the first 4 trials after the break did not include experimental stimuli. After the color-naming task, the subjects were probed for suspicion about the purpose of the experiment, were asked at what age they had learned English, and then were debriefed.

Results and Discussion

In this and the other two experiments, subjects made very few color-naming errors ($M = 0.5$), and these errors always occurred with equal frequency for undesirable and desirable traits. Error trials and trials on which a noise other than the color name triggered the voice key were omitted from the analyses. In addition, response times that noticeably deviated from the distribution (under 300 ms or over 1,500 ms) were omitted. In all, less than 1% of the trials were omitted in Experiment 1, and less than 2% in each of the other two experiments.

Effect of Valence

To test whether undesirable traits interfered more with the color-naming task than did desirable traits, we tested the effect of trait valence (desirable vs. undesirable) on response latency in a within-subjects analysis of variance (ANOVA), using subjects' response means

---

[2] Because of the bimodal distribution of desirability values in English, the neutral range of desirability, from 4 to 6 on the 1 to 9 rating scale, was represented by only eight traits. These traits also elicited lower agreement among the desirability rates than the more extremely valenced traits, so we omitted them from the present analyses.

aggregated across all valid trials as the dependent variable. The effect of valence was significant and in the expected direction, $F(1, 10) = 19.3$, $p = .001$.[3] Subjects took about 29 ms longer to name the color of undesirable traits ($M = 679$ ms) than that of desirable traits ($M = 650$ ms). The mean latency for undesirable traits was greater than the mean latency for desirable traits for 9 (82%) of the 11 subjects.

Although undesirable traits produced significantly more interference than desirable traits for almost all subjects, none of them indicated during debriefing that undesirable traits were more distracting than desirable ones. In fact, subjects reported that they ignored the words and concentrated on recognizing the colors, as they had been instructed. The valence effect occurred although the subjects did not intend to process the trait terms and although they were not aware of their differential attention to desirable and undesirable traits.

Correlations Across the Traits

In a second set of analyses, we tested whether valence was the only stimulus characteristic related to color-naming latency. Word length had been controlled experimentally. Moreover, word frequency did not affect response latency; the correlation between the mean color-naming latency for each adjective and its frequency in written American English (Francis & Kucera, 1982) was close to 0 ($r = .09$, ns). Thus, neither word length nor word frequency could have caused the valence effect.[4]

Additional correlational analyses examined the linearity and extremity hypotheses. If the valence effect simply reflects a linear association, the Pearson product–moment correlation of latency with the continuous desirability values should exceed the point-biserial correlation with valence, and the correlation should be negative within each of the two valence categories. The extremity effect predicts a negative correlation for undesirable traits (i.e., the more extremely undesirable, the longer the latencies) and a positive correlation for desirable traits (i.e., the more extremely desirable, the longer the latencies).

Congruent with the within-subject ANOVA, valence was related to the mean response latencies (point-biserial $r = -.23$, $p < .05$); the Pearson correlation between the desirability ratings and mean latency was also $-.23$ ($p < .05$). That is, the use of continuous desirability values (as opposed to the two valence categories) did not increase the association between latency and negativity. More important, both the linearity and the extremity predictions were contradicted by the two desirability–latency correlations within each valence category: Neither correlation was significantly different from 0, and among the undesirable traits the correlation was positive.

Trend Analyses

Linear and curvilinear effects were also tested in a series of trend analyses, with desirability as a within-subjects factor. The mean desirability values of the six desirability categories were used as coefficients in the trend analyses (see Keppel & Zedeck, 1989). The mean color-naming latencies are given for each desirability category in the bottom panel of Figure 15.2. Neither the linear trend nor the quadratic trend (representing the extremity

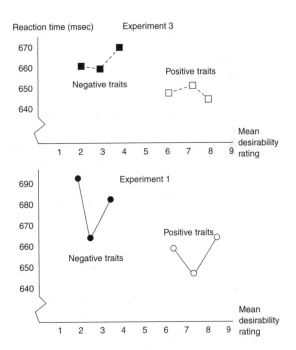

FIGURE 15.2 ■ Relation Between Color-naming Latencies (reaction time) and Desirability Scale Values in Experiment 1 (bottom panel) and Experiment 3 (top panel).

---

[3] All effects significant in the within-subjects analyses reported in this article were also significant when the error term was computed across trials.

[4] Independent of valence, longer words interfered less with color naming than shorter words, $r(78) = -.36$, $p < .01$. The findings for word length and word frequency were the same in all three experiments: These two parameters are therefore not discussed further.

hypothesis) was significant (both $Fs < 1$). The valence contrast effect, however, was significant, $F(11, 54) = 31.3$, $p < .001$, and its regression coefficient was significantly different from 0, $t(1) = 3.8$, $p < .001$.

In conclusion, the results of Experiment 1 show that undesirable traits interfered more with the color-naming task than did desirable traits. Both in trend analyses (across subjects) and in correlational analyses (across traits), we found no support for either a linear or an extremity effect of desirability on latencies, suggesting that the effect is categorical. Moreover, this effect cannot be explained by word length or word frequency. Our findings thus confirm previous findings that the evaluation of social stimuli is processed automatically. More important, they support our hypothesis of an asymmetry in the automatic processing of evaluation: The unattended occurrence of an undesirable stimulus interfered more with a primary task requiring attentional resources than did the occurrence of a desirable stimulus.

Experiment 2: Vigilance and Defense in Incidental Learning

In principle, the longer time subjects needed to respond to the undesirable traits could be due to two quite different mechanisms. Our account postulates perceptual vigilance: Undesirable traits require more time in the color-naming task because negatively valenced stimuli are automatically attended. In general, the material that subjects attend to during presentation will be recalled better (e.g., Fisk & Schneider, 1984). If attention is indeed diverted away from the color-naming task to undesirable traits, as the vigilance account suggests, some incidental learning of these traits should occur, and recall should be greater for undesirable than for desirable traits.

Finding superior incidental recall for undesirable traits would not only strengthen the directed-attention mechanism proposed here, but it would also rule out an alternative, perceptual defense explanation: The color responses to the undesirable traits may have been slower because cognitive effort was required to keep their undesirable content out of consciousness. The notion of defensiveness implies a process motivated by the need to avoid the disturbing affect associated with particular stimuli or memories (see Holmes, 1974, for a review). One type of repression, called *primal repression or perceptual defense*, implies that threatening material is kept from entering consciousness (Holmes, 1974, p. 633). A second type, repression proper, suggests that after the material has been consciously

recognized, it is relegated to the unconscious. As the stimuli in our color-naming task are not presented subliminally, either type of defense could be involved. Nonetheless, both types lead to the same prediction: The more threatening (undesirable) material should be particularly difficult to retrieve from memory. This line of reasoning is based on the assumption that at least some of the undesirable traits are disturbing or "ego threatening." Therefore, Experiment 2 does not provide a test of whether repression can occur but whether it is responsible for the longer latencies of undesirable traits.

In Experiment 2, then, we tested the vigilance and defensiveness accounts of the negativity effect by comparing the incidental learning of undesirable and desirable traits. Incidental learning was measured by free recall directly following the presentation of desirable and undesirable traits in the color-naming task. However, memory for stimulus aspects unrelated to an attended task tends to be minimal (e.g., Fisk & Schneider, 1984). For example, Bargh and Pratto's (1986) subjects, who named the colors of 50 common noun and trait words, recalled less than 10% of the stimulus words. We therefore modified the design of Experiment 1 in ways that would increase incidental learning. In particular, we presented each adjective twice, used only 40 of the 80 adjectives from Experiment 1, and to compensate for the resulting loss in power, we doubled the number of subjects. Thus, Experiment 2 provides a replication of the color-interference effect with a less extensive set of traits, and the repeated presentation of the traits allows us to examine whether this effect is influenced by habituation and practice.

Method

Subjects

Subjects were 32 undergraduates from the University of California, Berkeley, who volunteered to participate and received partial course credit. Data from 3 subjects who had learned English after age 5 and from 4 additional subjects who indicated during debriefing that they had expected the incidental-recall task were omitted from the analyses, leaving a total of 25 subjects.

Trait Stimuli

To ensure that the 40 traits included a similar range and diversity of content as the initial set, the 80 traits were grouped into 40 pairs of quasi synonyms (e.g., *sadistic* and *mean*), and only one of the synonyms was included in the abbreviated set. As in Experiment 1, word length was controlled, and the 20 desirable and 20 undesirable traits differed significantly in desirability but not in extremity. The 40 traits were presented in two different random orders: To control for primacy and recency effects on recall, one order began with two desirable traits and ended with two undesirable ones, whereas the other had the opposite pattern. Subjects received both orders, in either Block 1 or Block 2, and the assignment of orders to blocks was counterbalanced across subjects. The five colors were counterbalanced across desirable and undesirable traits, and the same color was never presented in consecutive trials. Within these constraints, colors were assigned randomly to the traits.

Procedure
The color-naming part of the experiment followed the same procedure as in Experiment 1, except that the color name *yellow* was used instead of *gold*. All 80 trials were presented consecutively without a break. Immediately after the last color-naming trial, instructions appeared on the computer screen asking the subjects to write down all of the words they could remember on a blank sheet of paper. When subjects could not recall any more words, they were interviewed about the task and then were debriefed.

Results

Color-naming Latencies
Because the same 40 traits had been presented twice in two different orders in the two blocks, we were able to test the joint effects of valence and block on the response latencies in a 2 × 2 within-subjects ANOVA, using as the dependent variable each subject's mean response time for undesirable and for desirable traits in each of the two blocks. As in Experiment 1, there was a significant main effect for valence, $F(1, 24) = 9.1$, $p = .006$. Again, the mean response latencies were longer for undesirable traits ($M = 612$ ms) than for desirable ones ($M = 601$ ms), and this effect held for 19 (76%) of the 25 subjects. As shown in Figure 15.3, subjects were slightly faster in the second block, but neither the main effect of block, $F(1, 24) = 1.6$, $p = .22$, nor the interaction ($F < 1$) was significant. Neither the two orders in which the traits had been presented nor their assignment to Block 1 or 2 had any effect on the color-naming latencies. Regardless of block and order, then, the present findings replicated those of Experiment 1.

Correlations Across the Traits
The power of correlational (and trend) analyses is limited by the small number of traits presented. Nonetheless,

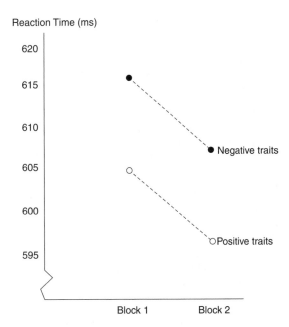

FIGURE 15.3 ■ Color-naming Latencies (reaction times) by Valence and Block in Experiment 2.

the pattern of correlations closely mirrored the categorical pattern found in Experiment 1. We again found the negative point-biserial correlation between response latency and valence ($r = -.24$, $p < .05$, one-tailed), and that correlation was larger than the Pearson correlation between latency and the graded desirability values ($r = -.18$, *ns*). Within the two valence categories, the correlations between latency and desirability were almost exactly 0.

Free Recall
Subjects recalled, on the average, only 3.9 traits, with a range from 0 to 7; subjects expressed surprise at being asked to recall the words, and most apologized for being able to recall so few. They did, however, recall twice as many undesirable ($M = 2.6$, range = 0 to 5) as desirable ($M = 1.3$, range = 0 to 3) traits. The difference in the number of undesirable and desirable words recalled by each subject was significantly different from 0, $t(24) = 3.4$, $p < .01$.

Individual-differences analyses showed a substantial floor effect associated with a low level of recall; subjects recalling more traits overall were likely to show a more pronounced difference between undesirable and desirable traits, $r(23) = .50$, $p < .01$. Nonetheless, the superior recall of undesirable traits held for almost two thirds of the subjects; 16 recalled more undesirable than desirable traits, 8 recalled equal numbers of undesirable and desirable traits (including the 1 subject who recalled none), and 1 recalled more desirable than undesirable traits.[5]

Analyses across the 40 traits showed that all 20 of the undesirable traits had been recalled by at least 1 subject, whereas only 15 of the desirable traits had been recalled by at least 1 subject. That is, the valence effect on recall was not due to the superior recall of a small set of undesirable traits. Across the 40 traits, the correlation between valence and the number of subjects who recalled the trait was $-.31$ ($p < .05$). The correlation between social desirability and the number of subjects who recalled the trait was $-.39$ ($p < .05$), which did not reliably differ from the point-biserial correlation ($p = .29$).

Response Latency, Recency of Exposure, and Recall
We have argued that longer color-naming latencies indicate greater attention to a stimulus and that the stimuli to which subjects pay more attention should be better recalled. If this is true, the mean color-naming latency for a word should be positively related to its frequency of recall. Indeed, across the 40 traits, the correlation between the mean response latency and the number of subjects recalling the trait was positive. This positive association was more pronounced for response latencies measured immediately before recall, that is, in the second block ($r = .31$, $p < .05$), than for latencies measured in the first block ($r = .16$, *ns*), suggesting a recency effect; the most recent presentation of a word is the more potent determinant of recall. However, this recency effect was not particularly strong; when frequency of recall was computed separately for subjects receiving Order A and for those receiving Order B, in the second (more recent) block, the correlation between the resulting two measures of recall was .45 ($p < .01$) across the 40 words, indicating that the valence of the trait stimulus determined its recall, rather than the order and recency of its presentation.

Discussion

The results of Experiments 1 and 2 showed that undesirable traits are more likely than desirable traits to attract attention even when attention is deliberately focused elsewhere. The latency difference established in

Experiment 1 was replicated in Experiment 2 in both the first and second stimulus presentations. Moreover, the correlations between desirability and latency followed the same categorical pattern as in the first study.

The free-recall data suggest two major conclusions. First, unintentional processing of the meaning of the trait stimuli produced very little memory. The "best" subject recalled only 7 words, and the average subject recalled less than 10% of the 40 stimuli, each of which had been presented twice. The low rate of recall is consistent with the short response latencies in the color-naming task, both suggesting that subjects focused their attention on the colors of the terms, not on their meanings. In fact, some subjects did not even realize that the stimuli had been adjectives.

Second, we found that the longer color-naming latencies for undesirable traits were associated with greater accessibility in memory. Across subjects, undesirable traits were recalled twice as often as desirable traits; across traits, there were twice as many subjects showing superior recall for undesirable traits as there were subjects showing no differential recall. These findings rule out the defensiveness hypothesis and, more important, provide overwhelming support for the vigilance interpretation. Undesirable traits require longer response times in the color-naming paradigm not because cognitive work is required to shut out the perception of such negative stimuli or to relegate them to the unconscious once recognized. Rather, our findings are most consistent with the hypothesis that undesirable traits automatically attract more attention and are therefore better remembered than desirable traits. The positive correlation between mean response latency and frequency of recall is consistent with the assumption that differential attention influences recall.

Experiment 3: Automatic Processing of Base Rate and Valence

The findings of Experiment 2 strengthen the automatic vigilance hypothesis. However, in studies of impression formation and person perception (e.g., Anderson, 1974; Fiske, 1980; see Skowronski & Carlston, 1989; Taylor & Fiske, 1978, for reviews), the stronger weighing of negative than of positive information has been explained in informational terms by the higher informativeness (or diagnosticity) of negative information. Negative information tends to be perceived as more diagnostic than positive information because people's expectations about events and outcomes in the world are generally positive. For example, people expect others to behave in socially

---

[5] Of the 7 excluded subjects who had learned English after the age of 5 or expected the incidental recall task, 4 showed the valence effect and 3 did not. When their data are included, the difference is still significant, $t(31) = 2.5, p < .02$.

desirable or at least socially appropriate ways (Kanouse & Hanson, 1972). According to the widely demonstrated positivity effect in person perception (e.g., Sears, 1983), people assume that most individuals have desirable characteristics. The Pollyanna principle (Matlin & Stang, 1978) suggests that people expect positive outcomes even when faced with information to the contrary. In other words, desirable events tend to be viewed as common, frequently occurring, and typical, whereas undesirable events tend to be seen as uncommon, infrequent, and atypical. The informational value of undesirable traits should be higher than that of desirable traits, as uncommon and atypical events are seen as more informative (see Fiske, 1980) and diagnostic (Skowronski & Carlston, 1989; see also Lay, Burron, & Jackson, 1973).

Rating studies have shown a positive and substantial relation between the desirability of personality traits and their perceived base rate (or frequency in the population): The more desirable the trait, the more frequent is it perceived to be (e.g., Fulero, 1979; Funder & Dobroth, 1987; Rothbart & Park, 1986). If this relation holds in the present studies, the lower base rate of undesirable information might account for the negativity effect. To test this possibility, we obtained estimates of desirability and perceived base rate from additional groups of subjects and conducted a third color-naming experiment to test whether our earlier findings are best interpreted in terms of valence, base rate, or both.

An experimental comparison of the valence and the infrequency hypotheses requires trait stimuli for which one hypothesis predicts interference but the other does not: Desirable traits considered infrequent and undesirable traits considered frequent. The 80 traits used in Experiment 1 had been selected without prior consideration of their perceived base rates. To this initial set, we added another 51 traits to represent the two conditions needed to unconfound valence from base rate. We obtained both desirability and base-rate ratings and constructed a set of trait stimuli to manipulate valence and base rate independently. All 131 traits were then used as stimuli in the color-naming task, thus permitting us to replicate earlier analyses with the original set of 80 traits, to test the joint effects of valence and base rate in an unconfounded set of 88 traits, and to replicate the linear and quadratic trend analyses in a large set of stimuli, consisting of all 131 traits.

Method

Base-rate and Desirability Ratings for 131 Traits
The 51 additional traits were selected from previous rating studies by Fulero (1979), Funder and Dobroth

(1987), Hampson et al. (1987), Norman (1967), and Rothbart and Park (1986) or were newly generated on the basis of these studies.[6] Roughly one half of the additional traits were expected to be undesirable but common (low valence, high base rate) and the other half desirable but uncommon (high valence, low base rate).

We drew two samples from the same population as the experimental subjects. One sample ($n = 12$) rated all 131 traits on the nine-step social desirability scale used in Experiment 1, and the other ($n = 16$) estimated the base rate of each of the traits. The base-rate judges were asked to round their estimates to the nearest 5%. Part of their instructions read as follows:

> What percentage of people can be characterized by a particular personality trait? In this study, we are trying to discover the "base rate" — that is, the relative frequency — of each of a number of personality characteristics in the general population .... Consider only those persons who are of the same sex as you are and of your approximate age. Of such persons, please indicate the *percentage* that are characterized by each of the following traits.

Both types of ratings proved highly reliable across judges (both Cronbach coefficient alphas = .98). The mean desirability values ranged from 1.3 (*bigoted*) to 8.5 (*honest*), with a mean of 5.2 (*SD* = 2.3) and correlated .96 with our earlier ratings across the common set of 80 traits. The mean base-rate values ranged from 7% (*saintly*) to 78% (*curious*), with a mean of 42% (*SD* = 15%); in contrast to the desirability ratings, they had a unimodal distribution.

Across the 80 traits studied previously, the base rates correlated .43 with the original desirability ratings, .34 with the new desirability ratings, and .30 with valence (all *ps* < .01). In contrast, across all 131 traits, the correlations were not significant, with correlations of −.12 for desirability and −.14 for valence and with correlations of zero within the subsets of desirable and undesirable traits. That is, valence and base rate were confounded in the initial set of traits but not in the new set.

Manipulation of Valence and Base Rate
From the 131 traits, 88 were selected to form a 2×2 Valence × Base Rate design with 22 traits per condition. These 88 traits in the 4 Valence × Base Rate cells, as well as the mean ratings of the traits in the 4 cells, are listed in the Appendix. The traits classified as common ranged from 44% to 78%; those classified as uncommon

[6] We are indebted to David Funder and Myron Rothbart for providing us with base-rate ratings and to Eileen Donahue and Delroy Paulhus for their imaginativeness in helping us generate additional traits.

ranged from 7% to 42%. For the mean desirability ratings, undesirable traits ranged from 1.3 to 4.0, and
desirable traits ranged from 6.3 to 8.5. An ANOVA on
the mean base-rate ratings yielded a significant effect for
base-rate condition, $F(1, 84) = 247$, but not for valence
($F < 1$) or their interaction ($F = 1.2$). Conversely, an
ANOVA on the mean desirability ratings yielded a
significant effect for valence, $F(1, 84) = 1,333$, but not
for base-rate condition or their interaction (both $Fs < 1$).
Thus, base rate and valence were completely unconfounded in this design.

Subjects and Procedure in the Color-naming Task
Subjects were 17 Berkeley undergraduates, who volunteered to participate in exchange for partial course
credit. The 131 traits were presented in one random
order; otherwise, the procedures were the same as in
Experiment 1, except that the color name *yellow* was
used instead of *gold*.

Results and Discussion

Joint Effects of Base Rate and Valence
The mean of the 22 traits in each condition served as the
dependent variable in a 2 (valence) × 2 (base rate)
within-subjects ANOVA. As shown in Figure 15.4, the
main effect of valence was significant, $F(1, 16) = 52.5$,
$p < .001$; once again, subjects took longer to name the
color of undesirable traits ($M = 676$ ms) than of desirable traits ($M = 647$ ms), and all 17 subjects showed
this effect. In contrast, both the main effect of base rate
and its interaction with valence were not significant,
$Fs(1, 16) = 3.2$ and 1.6, respectively. More important,
the direction of the base-rate effect was opposite to
expectations; as shown in Figure 15.4, common traits
elicited slightly longer latencies ($M = 667$ ms) than
uncommon traits ($M = 656$ ms). This insignificant difference was due to the common undesirable traits,
which elicited the longest response latencies.

In a second ANOVA, the 2 (valence) × 2 (base rate)
design was analyzed across the 88 traits, using the mean
response latency across subjects as the dependent variable and each trait as an observation. This ANOVA also
showed a significant valence effect, $F(1, 84) = 11.2$,
$p = .001$, and neither a main effect of base rate ($p = .21$)
nor a Base Rate × Valence interaction ($p = .27$).

*Base-rate Effects in the Traits Used in Experiments
1 and 2*
To examine the generalizability of these findings, we
used median splits to divide the 80 traits studied in

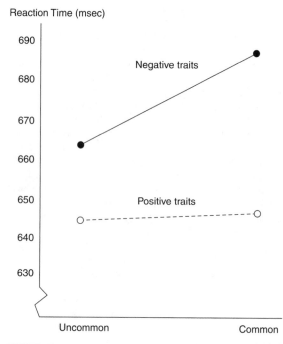

FIGURE 15.4 ■ Color-naming Latencies (reaction times) by
Valence and Base-rate Condition in Experiment 3.

Experiment 1 into a 2 (valence) × 2 (base-rate conditions) design and subjected the mean response latencies
to each trait to an unbalanced ANOVA across traits.
As in Experiment 3, the valence effect was significant,
$F(1, 76) = 4.2, p < .05$, and there was neither a main
effect of base rate nor an interaction (both $Fs < 1$),
despite the fact that valence and base rate were positively correlated.

The same picture emerged in a series of correlational
analyses. In particular, the correlations between the
mean response latencies and base rate were not significant in all three studies: For the 80 traits in Experiment 1
($r = -.14$), the 40 traits in Experiment 2 ($r = .02$), and
the 131 traits in Experiment 3 ($r = -.03$). These findings provide no support for a base-rate interpretation of
the negativity effect; in fact, in the 88 traits in
Experiment 3 for which base rate and valence were
independent, the size of the valence effect was just as
strong (29 ms) as in Experiment 1.

*Categorical versus Linear and Quadratic Effects on
Latency*
In another test of the linear and extremity hypotheses,
we performed trend analyses analogous to those in

Experiment 1, using the combined set of traits to create desirability categories. Again, we used six categories, which differed pairwise in their mean desirability ratings (all $ps < .01$). As in Experiment 1, the linear and quadratic trends were all insignificant (all $Fs < 1$). Only the valence contrast was significant; the overall contrast effect was $F(17, 84) = 71.3$, $p = .001$, and for the regression weight of the valence variable, $t(1) = 3.0$, $p < .005$. Across the 131 traits in this analysis, 15 of the 17 subjects (88%) showed the negativity effect. When the data from Experiments 1 (bottom panel of Figure 15.2) and Experiment 3 (top panel of Figure 15.3) are considered together, there is little evidence for any consistent trends in the data except the categorical effect of valence.[7]

These conclusions are borne out by the correlational analyses, regardless of the experiment or the subset of words analyzed. In the set of 88 traits for which we selected only clearly desirable and clearly undesirable traits, the correlation of response latency and valence was .34 ($p < .01$), as contrasted with .11 among the desirable traits and $-.14$ among the undesirable traits. For all 131 traits, the correlation with valence was still $-.17$ ($p < .05$), as contrasted with $-.03$ and .02 for the desirable and undesirable subsets, respectively. These correlations are very similar to those in the other two experiments and show a significant effect of valence but no evidence for any linear or curvilinear effects of the graded desirability values.

General Discussion

One purpose of automatic evaluation, we have argued, is to direct attention to negatively evaluated stimuli, and this shift in attention occurs without the perceiver's intent. In each of three experiments, we found that undesirable traits attracted more attention (as reflected in response latencies) than desirable traits; combined across studies, 85% of all subjects showed the valence effect. The difference between undesirable and desirable traits was 29 ms in Experiments 1 and 3; in Experiment 2, which used fewer stimuli, the size of the effect was somewhat smaller. Neither word length nor word frequency mediated the effect in any of the experiments.

Moreover, we ruled out two of the most plausible alternative explanations. The incidental-learning findings

in Experiment 2 are inconsistent with a perceptual-defense interpretation of the valence effect and instead strengthen the vigilance hypothesis: The interference in the color-naming task was associated with better recall, supporting the hypothesis that more attentional resources were devoted to undesirable stimuli.

In Experiment 3, we manipulated both the valence and the perceived base rate of the traits. Whereas the valence effect was exactly replicated, the effect of base rate was not significant and not consistent with the hypothesis that infrequent traits attract more attention. Our reanalysis of the data from Experiment 1 and the correlational analyses relating base rate to mean latencies in all three experiments led to the same conclusion: The valence effect cannot be explained by base-rate differences among the traits, and base rate does not seem to play an important role in the color-naming paradigm. Taken together, the results of the three experiments provide converging evidence for the hypothesis that people's attention is drawn to negative information without their intention and that the cause of this effect lies in the valence of the traits, not their informational value or diagnosticity.

The Categorical Nature of the Valence Effect

In all three studies, we examined the data for possible linear and quadratic trends, using both correlational analyses (across stimuli) and within-subjects trend analyses. In all of these analyses, we found no support for any effect but the categorical one. The absence of linear and quadratic effects cannot be explained by the reliability of the desirability scale values because these effects failed to emerge even in the within-subjects trend analyses involving highly reliable contrasts, such as those between Desirability Categories 1 and 3 among the undesirable traits and between Categories 4 and 6 among the desirable traits. This finding is particularly surprising because the power of linear models, even improper ones, has been well demonstrated (Dawes, 1979). Linear models approximate categorical effects, which are therefore more difficult to establish than linear ones; it is extremely rare for a Pearson correlation, which is based on a continuous variable (e.g., desirability) to be eclipsed by the point-biserial correlation, which is based on a dichotomized measure of the same variable (e.g., valence).

Nonetheless, the finding that undesirable traits, regardless of their extremity, are more likely to attract attention than desirable traits requires further comment. In particular, the evolutionary argument (that it is adaptive

---

[7] Because different sets of traits were used in the two experiments, the mean desirability values of the six desirability categories differed slightly across experiments.

to attend to stimuli associated with negative conse-quences) might be misunderstood to mean that only specific subclasses of undesirable traits should show attention-grabbing effects, namely, only those traits of others that directly endanger our personal well-being, such as *sadistic or violent*. However, this interpretation confuses distal (evolutionary) with proximal (psycho-logical) mechanisms and automatic processing with controlled processing.

In particular, we postulated that an adaptive behavior (i.e., monitoring the environment for potential danger) is accomplished through a psychological mechanism, which we have called *automatic vigilance*. This mecha-nism is not contingent on the physical presence of another person posing a threat; after all, our effects were obtained with colored words presented on a com-puter screen. Moreover, given its speed, we did not expect the attention-grabbing effect to be very differen-tiated. Automatic vigilance functions as a signal, rather than by providing a detailed analysis of the stimulus. Indeed, as we argue below, linear and extremity effects are more likely to result from controlled processing in deliberate evaluative judgments, such as desirability ratings and impression formation.

Automatic Evaluation and Automatic Vigilance

Given the consistency of our results across studies, one may wonder why this effect was not discovered in previous studies on automatic evaluation. Fazio et al. (1986), for example, did not find significant differences between positively and negatively valenced attitude objects. However, being interested in demonstrating the automatic evaluation effect, not a negative-positive asym-metry, they used only a few stimuli, which were selected idiographically for each subject. Our findings suggest that relatively large and systematic selections of stimuli may be necessary to demonstrate the automatic vigilance effect. In Experiment 2, which used fewer stimuli, we found that the effect was smaller than in the two other experiments.

A second difference between the present and past studies is the nature of the task. An interference task, such as the color-naming task, is the ideal paradigm to study automatic vigilance. This paradigm mimics in the laboratory a real-life setting in which the subject is con-cerned with other activities (i.e., the attended task) while automatically monitoring the perceptual field for undesirable events or stimuli. In this kind of situation, automatic vigilance is important because it can redirect attention to information about potentially undesirable events. In settings in which redirection of attention is not possible or not necessary, however, automatic vigi-lance is irrelevant. For example, when subjects are already attending to the evaluation of the stimulus, or when the response mode makes the evaluation of the stimuli salient, automatic vigilance effects may not be observed. The automatic vigilance mechanism does not imply that undesirable stimuli are necessarily recog-nized faster or more accurately than desirable ones; rather, when attentional resources are directed else-where, undesirable stimuli are more likely to attract such resources.

What happens once an undesirable stimulus has attracted attention? How does that attention influence subsequent processing? The answer to these questions depends on the particular task the perceiver is trying to accomplish. In the color-naming task, vigilance was unwarranted and interfered with subjects' goals. Note that although undesirable traits elicited longer response latencies, they did not cause more color-naming errors, nor did the subjects necessarily become conscious of the attentional shift to the evaluative aspects of the stim-ulus. Thus, just as subjects can inhibit the word meaning in the Stroop (1935) interference paradigm, they were here able to control the automatically grabbed attentional resources, so that the intrusive effects of automatic vigilance were not noticed.

Unintended Effects of Automatic Processing on Intentional Processing

However, the color-naming task is unusual in that auto-matic vigilance is rendered inappropriate, even dysfunc-tional. In more typical contexts, the attention shifted to an undesirable stimulus permits more deliberate and controlled processing of that stimulus. In general, atten-tional focus has been shown to influence social judg-ment (see Taylor & Fiske, 1978), and automatic vigilance can thus lead to negative bias in judgment.

A second link between automatic vigilance and social judgment is suggested by our second experiment. Even in the color-naming paradigm, the greater atten-tional resources allocated to undesirable traits increased subsequent memory for these traits. Automatic vigilance made these undesirable stimuli relatively more accessible in memory. Judgment can be heavily influenced by the information accessible in memory; therefore negatively biased memory may contribute to negatively biased judgments. This link, relating auto-matic vigilance to biased memory and, in turn, biased memory to biased judgment, may provide an important theoretical connection between the present research and earlier research on the differential weighing of desirable and undesirable information about others.

In particular, the link between vigilance, memory, and judgment would predict greater weighing of undesirable stimuli in impression formation tasks. For example, if the traits whose colors the subjects named were a description of an individual or a social group, our finding that subjects remembered twice as many undesirable than desirable traits (although an equal number was presented) would predict that subjects' impressions of that individual or group would be negatively biased. More generally, automatic vigilance is a mechanism that could explain why unfavorable information about individuals and stereotyped groups is often noticed and remembered better than favorable information, even when the social perceiver is not intentionally processing this information.

In summary, our findings and the close associations between attention, memory, and judgment suggest that automatic vigilance alone could lead to the differential weighing of undesirable information that is typically observed in impression formation studies. However, additional processes must be involved because the differential weighing effects seem considerably more complex than the automatic effects demonstrated in the present research. In particular, in her study of looking time and weighing of desirable and undesirable behaviors, Fiske (1980) found that very undesirable behaviors differed from somewhat undesirable behaviors, whereas we found no such linear effect. Moreover, very desirable behaviors elicited longer looking times and greater weights than did somewhat desirable traits, an extremity effect we did not obtain. Finally, Fiske (1980) explained her findings in terms of informativeness, assuming that regardless of their valence, extreme behaviors are more informative than less extreme behaviors, whereas we ruled out infrequency as an explanation of the automatic vigilance effect.[8]

The difference, we suppose, lies in the deliberate and controlled processing that occurred in Fiske's (1980) impression formation task: Subjects were instructed to examine the information presented as long as they wished and to form an impression of the target person. Such intentional processing was prevented in the color-naming task. The linear and extremity effects, observed in impression formation but not in the color-naming task, thus seem to depend on intentional processing. Once attention has been directed at negative information, the subsequent use and weighing of this information during deliberate processing may depend on a number of factors, including informativeness or diagnosticity (see Skowronski & Carlston, 1989).

In conclusion, we view automatic vigilance as a "default" response: It monitors potentially undesirable information when specific impression formation goals are not active, and it serves as an input to deliberate processing when such goals are (or have become) active. In principle, the effects of automatic vigilance can be overridden by other goals (as in the color-naming task), although the presence of negativity bias in our incidental-learning study and in the numerous impression formation studies suggests that these conditions are unlikely to completely eliminate its effect. However, when perceivers can determine what information is made available to them (as in interviews), the goal to be accurate can lead them to be less biased in seeking negative information and to form less negatively biased impressions, even when they have negative expectancies about the target (Neuberg, 1989). Thus, bias toward undesirable information and the influence of such information on judgment seem most pronounced when people do not realize that such influences are occurring or when they are not motivated to prevent them from occurring (see Bargh, 1989). These two conditions probably hold for most situations in which intergroup contact occurs and beliefs about out-groups are formed and confirmed. In these situations, automatic vigilance might foster the formation and maintenance of unfavorable impressions and stereotypes. Thus, people's greater attention to negative information may protect them from immediate harm but it may also contribute to prejudice and conflict in social interaction.

---

[8] Fiske (1980) manipulated the desirability of the behaviors presented on the slides but did not measure their perceived frequency (or base rate).

REFERENCES

Anderson, N. H. (1974). Cognitive algebra: Integration theory applied to social attribution. In L. Berkowitz (Ed.), *Advances in experimental social psychology*, (Vol. 7, pp. 2–102). San Diego, CA: Academic Press.

Bargh, J. A. (1989). Conditional automaticity: Varieties of automatic influence in social perception and cognition. In J. S. Uleman & J. A. Bargh (Eds.), *Unintended thought: Causes and consequences for judgment, emotion, and behavior* (pp. 3–51). New York: Guilford Press.

Bargh, J. A., Litt, J. E., Pratto, F., & Spielman, L. A. (1988). On the preconscious evaluation of social stimuli. In K. McConkey & A. Bennet (Eds.), *Proceedings of the XXIV International Congress of Psychology* (Vol. 3, pp. 1–57). Amsterdam: Elsevier/North-Holland.

Bargh, J. A., & Pratto, F. (1986). Individual construct accessibility and perceptual selection. *Journal of Experimental Social Psychology, 22,* 293–311.

Dawes, R. M. (1979). The robust beauty of improper linear models in decision making. *American Psychologist, 34,* 571–582.

Fazio, R. H. (1986). How do attitudes guide behavior? In R. M. Sorrentino & E. T. Higgins (Eds.), *The handbook of motivation and cognition: Foundations of social behavior* (pp. 204–243). New York: Guilford Press.

Fazio, R. H., Sanbonmatsu, D. M., Powell, M. C., & Kardes, F. R. (1986). On the automatic activation of attitudes. *Journal of Personality and Social Psychology, 50,* 229–238.

Fisk, A. D., & Schneider, W. (1984). Memory as a function of attention, level of processing, and automatization. *Journal of Experimental Psychology: Learning, Memory and Cognition, 10,* 181–197.

Fiske, S. T. (1980). Attention and weight in person perception: The impact of negative and extreme behavior. *Journal of Personality and Social Psychology, 38,* 889–906.

Fiske, S. T. (1982). Schema-triggered affect: Applications to person perception. In M. S. Clark & S. T. Fiske (Eds.), *Affect and cognition* (pp. 55–78). Hillsdale, NJ: Erlbaum.

Francis, W. N., & Kucera, H. (1982). *Frequency analysis of English usage.* Boston: Houghton Mifflin.

Frodi, L. M., Lamb, M. E., Leavitt, L. A., & Donovan, W. L. (1978). Fathers' and mothers' responses to infants' smiles and cries. *Infant Behavior and Development, 1,* 187–198.

Fulero, S. (1979). *Recall of confirming events as a function of favorability and frequency.* Unpublished doctoral dissertation, Department of Psychology, University of Oregon, Eugene.

Funder, D. C., & Dobroth, K. M. (1987). Differences between traits: Properties associated with interjudge agreement. *Journal of Personality and Social Psychology, 52,* 409–418.

Goldberg, L. R. (1982). From Ace to Zombie: Some explorations in the language of personality. In C. D. Spielberger & J. N. Butcher (Eds.), *Advances in personality assessment* (Vol. 1, pp. 203–234). Hillsdale, NJ: Erlbaum.

Hamilton, D. L., & Zanna, M. (1972). Differential weighing of favorable and unfavorable attributes in impressions of personality. *Journal of Experimental Research in Personality, 6,* 204–212.

Hampson, S. E., Goldberg, L. R., & John, O. P. (1987). Category-breadth and social desirability values for 573 personality terms. *European Journal of Personality, 1,* 241–258.

Holmes, D. S. (1974). Investigations of repression: Differential recall of material experimentally or naturally associated with ego threat. *Psychological Bulletin, 81,* 632–653.

John, O. P. (1990). The "Big Five" factor taxonomy: Dimensions of personality in the natural language and in questionnaires. In L. A. Pervin (Ed.), *Handbook of personality: Theory and research* (pp. 66–100). New York: Guilford Press.

Kahneman, D., & Tversky, A. (1979). Prospect theory: An analysis of decision under risk. *Econometrica, 47,* 263–291.

Kahneman, D., & Tversky, A. (1984). Choices, values, and frames. *American Psychologist, 39,* 341–350.

Kanouse, D. E., & Hanson, L. R. (1972). Negativity in evaluations. In E. E. Jones, D. Kanouse, H. H. Kelley, R. E. Nisbett, S. Valins, &

B. Weiner (Eds.), *Attribution: Perceiving the causes of behavior* (pp. 47–62). Morristown, NJ: General Learning Press.

Keppel, G., & Zedeck, S. (1989). *Data analysis for research designs.* New York: Freeman.

Kunst-Wilson, W. R., & Zajonc, R. B. (1980). Affective discrimination of stimuli that cannot be recognized. *Science, 207,* 557–558.

Lay, C. H., Burron, B. F., & Jackson, D. N. (1973). Base rate and informational value in impression formation. *Journal of Personality and Social Psychology, 28,* 390–395.

Lazarus, R. S. (1966). *Psychological stress and the coping process.* New York: McGraw-Hill.

Lazarus, R. S. (1982). Thoughts on the relations between emotion and cognition. *American Psychologist, 37,* 1019–1024.

Matlin, M., & Stang, D. (1978). *The Pollyanna principle.* Cambridge, MA: Schenkman.

Neuberg, S. L. (1989). The goal of forming accurate impressions during social interactions: Attenuating the impact of negative expectancies. *Journal of Personality and Social Psychology, 56,* 374–386.

Norman, W. T. (1963). Toward an adequate taxonomy of personality attributes: Replicated factor structure in nomination of personality ratings. *Journal of Abnormal and Social Psychology, 66,* 574–583.

Norman, W. T. (1967, April). *2,800 personality trait descriptors: Normative operating characteristics for a university population* (Tech. Rep.). Ann Arbor, MI: University of Michigan. Department of Psychology.

Osgood, C. E., Suci, G. J., & Tannenbaum, P. H. (1957). *The measurement of meaning.* Urbana: University of Illinois Press.

Rayner, K. (1978). Foveal and parafoveal cues in reading. In J. Requin (Ed.), *Attention and performance VIII* (pp. 149–161). Hillsdale, NJ: Erlbaum.

Rothbart, M., & Park, B. (1986). On the confirmability and disconfirmability of trait concepts. *Journal of Personality and Social Psychology, 50,* 131–142.

Seamon, J. G., Brody, N., & Kauff, D. M. (1983). Affective discrimination of stimuli that are not recognized: Effects of shadowing, masking, and cerebral laterality. *Journal of Experimental Psychology: Learning, Memory, and Cognition, 9,* 544–555.

Seamon, J. G., Marsh, R. L., & Brody, N. (1984). Critical importance of exposure duration for affective discrimination of stimuli that are not recognized. *Journal of Experimental Psychology: Learning, Memory, and Cognition, 10,* 465–469.

Sears, D. O. (1983). The person-positivity bias. *Journal of Personality and Social Psychology, 44,* 233–250.

Shiffrin, R. M. (1988). Attention. In R. C. Atkinson, R. J. Herrnstein, G. Lindzey, & R. D. Luce (Eds.), *Stevens handbook of experimental psychology: Vol 2. Learning and cognition* (pp. 739–811). New York: Wiley.

Skowronski, J. J., & Carlston, D. E. (1989). Negativity and extremity biases in impression formation: A review of explanations. *Psychological Bulletin, 105,* 131–142.

Stroop, J. R. (1935). Studies of interference in serial verbal reactions. *Journal of Experimental Psychology, 18,* 643–662.

Taylor, S. E., & Fiske, S. T. (1978). Salience, attention, and attribution: Top of the head phenomena. In L. Berkowitz (Ed.), *Advances in experimental social psychology* (Vol. 11, pp. 249–288). San Diego, CA: Academic Press.

APPENDIX

The 88 Trait Terms Used in the Base-Rate Study (Experiment 3)

Undesirable		Desirable		Undesirable		Desirable	
Uncommon	Common	Uncommon	Common	Uncommon	Common	Uncommon	Common
rude	bigoted	exact	tolerant	sassy	messy	charming	kind
wicked	selfish	polished	curious	forgetful	gossipy	ingenious	talented
sadistic	irritable	refined	extroverted	glum	stubborn	scholarly	smart
mean	immature	humble	vigorous	curt	contradictory	musical	happy
hostile	tactless	worldly	stable	finicky	fickle	artistic	caring
intolerant	jealous	concise	inquisitive	sad	gullible	inventive	creative
annoying	cranky	saintly	active	passive	insecure	wise	loving
bossy	shallow	dignified	organized	naive	sarcastic	brilliant	honest
stingy	nosy	gracious	confident				
sluggish	biased	cultured	polite			Mean desirability	
lazy	moody	original	reliable	2.6	2.7	7.5	7.5
pesty	boastful	elegant	perceptive				
stupid	wasteful	heroic	helpful			Mean base rate	
domineering	impatient	witty	sincere	30%	56%	27%	57%

Note. Within each of the four conditions, the traits are ordered by their desirability values, from more undesirable to more desirable.

Received December 17, 1990
Accepted March 22, 1991 ■

The Relation Between Perception and Behavior, or How to Win a Game of Trivial Pursuit

Ap Dijksterhuis and Ad van Knippenberg

The authors tested and confirmed the hypothesis that priming a stereotype or trait leads to complex overt behavior in line with this activated stereotype or trait. Specifically, 4 experiments established that priming the stereotype of professors or the trait *intelligent* enhanced participants' performance on a scale measuring general knowledge. Also, priming the stereotype of soccer hooligans or the trait *stupid* reduced participants' performance on a general knowledge scale. Results of the experiments revealed (a) that prolonged priming leads to more pronounced behavioral effects and (b) that there is no sign of decay of the effects for at least 15 min. The authors explain their results by claiming that perception has a direct and pervasive impact on overt behavior (cf. J. A. Bargh, M. Chen, & L. Burrows, 1996). Implications for human social behavior are discussed.

I am a camera with its shutter open, quite passive, recording, not thinking.

— Christopher Isherwood

Some time ago, a few members of the Department of Social Psychology of the University of Nijmegen visited a soccer match. After they had parked their car, they walked the remaining mile to the stadium. The psychologists, behaving calmly and orderly as ever, were surrounded by hundreds of soccer fans and hooligans, many of whom were yelling and shouting. After some time, one of the members of the department engaged in somewhat unusual behavior. He saw an empty beer can, and, in what seemed to be an impulsive act, he kicked it as far away as possible. During the next few minutes, he and a slightly embarrassed colleague pondered on possible explanations.

One explanation is that, upon seeing soccer hooligans, one may — without being aware of it — start to act like them. That is, the activation of the representation of soccer hooligans leads to the tendency to behave similarly. Recent research showed that this is indeed possible. The mere perception of a person or a group of persons triggers a mechanism producing the tendency to behave correspondingly. In a series of studies, Bargh, Chen, and Burrows (1996) demonstrated such unconscious and unintentional effects of perception on social behavior. It was established that priming someone with a trait

Ap Dijksterhuis and Ad van Knippenberg, Department of Social Psychology, University of Nijmegen, Nijmegen, the Netherlands.

This research was facilitated by a Royal Netherlands Academy of Sciences Fellowship awarded to Ap Dijksterhuis. We thank the many colleagues who gave us valuable advice during conferences at which we presented these findings.

Correspondence concerning this article should be addressed to Ap Dijksterhuis, Department of Social Psychology, University of Nijmegen, P.O. Box 9104, 6500 HE Nijmegen, the Netherlands. Electronic mail may be sent to dijksterhuis@psych.kun.nl.

(e.g., rudeness) or a stereotype (e.g., elderly, African American) indeed leads to behavior in line with the activated constructs (see also Carver, Ganellen, Froming, & Chambers, 1983; Neuberg, 1988). For example, priming participants with the stereotype of the elderly made participants walk more slowly than participants who were not primed (Bargh, Chen, & Burrows, 1996, Experiment 2).

In our view, the notion that behavior is under direct perceptual control is of central importance for the understanding of human behavior. After all, upon meeting someone, one usually makes several categorizations instantly. One infers personality traits from the behavior of others spontaneously (Winter & Uleman, 1984). One activates stereotypes automatically (Devine, 1989). Hence, it is not immoderate to conclude that social interaction usually involves the activation of trait constructs and stereotypes. In this light, the findings of Bargh, Chen, and Burrows (1996), establishing that people's actions are unintentionally affected by these activated traits and stereotypes, do warrant further exploration.

With the present research, we want to make two contributions. First, we address the question of whether the effects of perception on behavior are confined to relatively simple actions or whether one can also evoke more complex behavioral patterns this way. Second, we explore the parameters of the perception–behavior link. Specifically, we study the relation between the strength of the prime and the strength of the resulting behavioral effect. Furthermore, we investigate the decay function of the effects of perception on behavior.

In should be noted in advance that throughout this article, we use the term *perception* rather loosely. The object of investigation is perception, or the activation of perceptual representations. In our research, as well as in most of the research we discuss and in most social cognition research in general, the researcher does not activate representations (e.g., a stereotype) by presenting participants with the real object of perception (e.g., a group member). Instead, the researcher uses priming manipulations to activate these perceptual representations. Hence, for the sake of simplicity, receiving priming (including the somewhat unorthodox priming manipulations we use) is treated as functionally equivalent to perception. We realize, however, that our priming procedures do not literally reflect social perception processes.

Perception and Overt Behavior

The notion that perception (or the activation of a perceptual representation) may lead to corresponding overt behavior has been recognized since long ago by some of our most influential thinkers (see, e.g., Arnold, 1946; Charcot, 1886; James, 1890; Koffka, 1925; Piaget, 1946). Underlying this idea is the assumption that apart from perceptual or cognitive representations (e.g., traits, stereotypes), behaviors are mentally represented as well and that these perceptual and behavioral representations are somehow intimately linked. Indeed, many theorists (e.g., Bargh, in press; Berkowitz, 1984; Carver & Scheier, 1981; Mischel, 1973; Schank & Abelson, 1977; Vallacher, 1993) have discussed this possibility. Prinz (1990), in a review of the research on the "common coding" hypothesis, explained why mere perception can affect overt behavior relatively easily:

> Acts are completely commensurate and continuous with percepts. Percepts and acts both refer to events with comparable attributes. Both are characterized by location (in space and time) and contents (in terms of physical and non-physical properties), the only difference being that percepts refer to ongoing, actor-independent events and acts to to-be-generated, actor-dependent events. (pp. 171–172).

Research by Rosch and Mervis (1975; see also Carver & Scheier, 1981) supports the notion of common coding of percepts and acts. Participants in their study were asked to generate attributes of a target word. Participants listed not only perceptual attributes but also behavioral responses. Carver and Scheier (1981), in discussing the research by Rosch and Mervis (1975), provided a nice example. The target *apple* elicited "red," "round," and "grows on trees" but also "you can eat it." Hence, it seems that, in line with the common coding hypothesis, actions are encoded in much the same way as other (perceptual) attributes of a given stimulus (see Carver & Scheier, 1981, p. 121). This suggests that perception and action have shared representational systems, again, an idea that has been postulated by several other researchers (e.g., Bandura, 1977; Koffka, 1925; Piaget, 1946).

Toward Priming Complex Behavior

The available evidence for effects of the activation of mental representations on overt behavior is largely confined to areas of behavior of a relatively elementary nature, such as arm movements (Eidelberg, 1929; Smeets & Brenner, 1995). The early research of Eidelberg (1929) can be taken as an example. Eidelberg (1929; see also Prinz, 1990) instructed participants to point at their nose at the verbal instruction "nose" and to point to a lamp upon hearing the word "lamp." During this task, the experimenter also pointed to his nose or to the lamp. As soon as the experimenter started to make mistakes (pointing at his nose after the instruction "lamp"), participants made mistakes too, although they were explicitly instructed to follow the verbal instructions and not the experimenter's movements. Thus, it seems that the activation of a mental representation of a specific movement (here, the perception of a movement) resulted in the tendency to actually make this movement. Another domain in which perception has been shown to affect action is speech production. It was shown that people unconsciously take over accents of others (Dell, 1986). Moreover, people that are primed with a certain syntax tend to use this syntax when producing a sentence (e.g., Bock, 1986, 1989), even when the syntax is grammatically incorrect (Levelt & Kelter, 1982). Speech production, thus, is also partly under perceptual control.

Recently, Bargh and colleagues went a step further. Bargh, Chen, and Burrows (1996) reported an experiment in which participants were subliminally primed with the stereotype of African Americans. Participants thus primed behaved more hostile toward a confederate (see also Carver et al., 1983). In comparison with participants in a control condition, primed participants showed more aggressive facial expressions, and, more pertinent to our present argument, they expressed more verbal hostility. Hence, the influence of perception on behavior goes beyond relatively simple, motoric responses (e.g., arm movements).

We want to take another step by establishing the generalizability of the perception–behavior link to behavior of an even greater complexity. The question is, can very complex behavior be evoked by mere perception? The relation between perception and behavior in, for instance, the studies by Eidelberg (1929) was assumed to be very direct. The mental representation that is activated refers directly to behavior (cf. the "common coding hypothesis" formulated by Prinz). For more complex behaviors, this relation is, of necessity, more complicated. If, for instance, we activate the mental representation of intelligence, this should, according to the same principle, result in the onset of "intelligent behavior." However, unlike arm movements, intelligence is not a behavior. If one assumes, though, that more abstract constructs such as intelligence refer to classes of behavior, or behavioral patterns (such as harder thinking or better concentration) on a more concrete level, and if one further assumes that behavioral representations are hierarchically structured so that abstract behavioral constructs can activate more

concrete behaviors, it is conceivable that the activation of a more abstract mental representation also leads to overt behavior in line with the primed construct. Below, we attempt to explicate the assumed underlying process in some detail.

Theoretically, one can understand the unconscious instigation of complex behavior on stereotype activation as the unrollment of a partly hierarchically structured chain of events. As stereotypes are associated with traits (e.g., Hamilton & Sherman, 1994; Stangor & Lange, 1994), the priming of a stereotype would activate the related trait constructs (Blair & Banaji, 1996; Devine, 1989; Dijksterhuis & van Knippenberg, 1996; Dovidio, Evans, & Tyler, 1986; Macrae, Stangor, & Milne, 1994). In our view, the activation of a trait (e.g., aggressive) may, in turn, activate a number of behavioral representations characteristic of the trait involved (e.g., looking angrily, speaking in an offensive tone of voice, and maybe even wanting to hit someone or something). In fact, in recent research on emotions, such action components have been shown to be evoked by emotion concepts (Frijda, Kuipers, & ter Schure, 1989). We assume that traits are also associated with behavioral representations that constitute instantiations of the trait in question. Suggestive evidence to that effect may be found in early spontaneous trait inference research in which, although the claim of spontaneous linkage is in the reverse direction, trait cues facilitate recall of behavioral episodes (Winter & Uleman, 1984; Winter, Uleman, & Cunnif, 1985). As a result of the existence of the trait–behavioral representation links, the priming of a stereotype may elicit the unconscious tendency to perform more or less complex behaviors typical of the traits associated with this stereotype. Thus, for instance, the activation of the trait *intelligent* (either by directly priming the trait or by priming a stereotype that contains this trait) may lead to the activation of a set of concrete behavioral representations stored under it (e.g., to concentrate on a problem, to adopt an analytical approach, to think systematically about possible solutions).

The presumed hierarchical linkage of mental representations with concrete behaviors has already been argued to exist. There are existing theories that conceive of the mental representation of goals and behavior as hierarchical structures with associations between more abstract classes of behaviors (e.g., eating and drinking) by means of intermediate levels (e.g., going out for a meal) to very specific actions (e.g., moving my arm to grab the raw herring with onions). Several theorists assume that behavior on all (or at least many different) levels of abstractness is mentally represented (e.g., Carver & Scheier, 1981; Martin & Tesser, 1989; Powers, 1973; Vallacher & Wegner, 1985, 1987; Wegner & Vallacher, 1987; see also Schank & Abelson, 1977). As Carver and Scheier (1981) noted, "in any set of perceptions the level of analysis to which one is attending dictates the level of behavioral standard that becomes salient. And what standard becomes salient dictates what action (if any) is subsequently taken" (p. 128). Thus, we assume that the activation of a stereotype leads to a broad set of behavioral tendencies in line with this stereotype. In concrete terms, just as the representation of "I'm hungry" leads to eating and later to moving one's arm to grab the food, it is conceivable that the representation of intelligence leads to a quite differentiated set of more concrete behavioral representations at a lower level.

The Present Research

As was mentioned at the outset, we hope to make two contributions with our research. First, we tested the effects of perception on action for behavior that is clearly more complex than earlier demonstrations. Second, we explored some parameters of the effects of perception on behavior.

Complex Behavior: Priming Ability-Related Performances

To demonstrate the effect that stereotype activation can lead to complex behavior or a behavioral pattern in line with this stereotype, we attempted to affect people's performance on an ability-related task. With regard to performance on an ability-related task such as, for instance, a general knowledge task, it may be argued that the mental activation of the concept of intelligence (or knowledgeability) might enhance one's performance (cf. Bargh, Gollwitzer, & Barndollar, 1996), whereas the mental activation of stupidity might reduce it, compared with one's average performance under normal circumstances. In our experiments, we aimed to increase or decrease performance on a general knowledge test by priming participants with the stereotype of either professors or soccer hooligans. The prime of professor, then, may lead to a set of more specific behavioral changes, such as higher concentration, more analytical and systematic thinking, and more confidence in one's own knowledgeability, whereas the hooligan prime may lead to reduced concentration and sloppier thinking.

It should be noted in advance that effects on performance, specifically improvements, are obviously constrained by objective limitations (e.g., it seems unlikely that one could all of a sudden play the violin merely upon hearing Beethoven's Violin Concerto in E), but given natural within-person variations in task performance over time, theoretically, perceptions or mental representations of superior or inferior performance may have corresponding effects on the person's performance. Thus, if one is a reasonably skilled violin player, one may indeed play better after hearing Beethoven's violin concertos.

We hypothesized that priming a stereotype (professor, hooligan) would affect task performance in line with traits (intelligence, stupidity) associated with the stereotype; specifically, we predicted that these stereotype primes would lead to increased or decreased performance on a general knowledge task. As with the Beethoven example, this general prediction presumes that individual task performance, including performance on ability-related tasks, may vary over time. Specifically, it is assumed that although there obviously exist circumstances that hamper task performance, there may also exist (social and mental) conditions that temporarily enhance one's level of performance. The occurrence of both task performance facilitation and debilitation is documented in the social facilitation and inhibition literature (e.g., Zajonc, 1965). Mostly, social facilitation and inhibition effects are theorized to be mediated by capacity and motivational mechanisms (e.g., Manstead & Semin, 1980; Sanders, 1981), but for the present purpose, it suffices to realize that base-rate performance levels tend to be suboptimal, allowing not only for further deterioration but also for enhancement (see also Bargh, Gollwitzer, & Barndollar, 1996). Hence, in general terms, it is conceivable that priming mechanisms may improve as well as impair human task performance.

Parameters

For exploratory reasons, we include tests of some of the parameters of the relation between perception and behavior in the experiments. First, we investigate the relation between the magnitude of the prime and the magnitude of the behavioral effect. Furthermore, we try to shed light on the decay function of behavior evoked by perception. For both parameters, we briefly present the tentative hypotheses formulated on the basis of earlier findings.

As for the relation between strength of prime and strength of effect, the relevant earlier findings come from studies investigating the relation between priming and social judgment. On the basis of the literature on the effects of priming on judgments, one may hypothesize that the more intense or more prolonged the instigating perception, the more intense the resulting behavior (see Higgins, Bargh, & Lombardi, 1985; Srull & Wyer, 1979, 1980, for such results in the domain of social judgments). In concrete terms, considering that these predictions hold for the effects of priming on behavior, it may be argued that one may walk slowly after being primed with the stereotype of the elderly (cf. Bargh, Chen, & Burrows, 1996), a bit faster when one is primed with the stereotype of psychologists, again faster when one is primed with Carl Lewis for 1 min, and, more important, still faster when one is primed with Carl Lewis for 15 min. We test this hypothesis pertaining to the relation between magnitude of perceptual input and magnitude of behavioral output in the context of ability-related performance.

Furthermore, we try to shed light on the decay function of behavior evoked by perception. Like Bargh, Chen, and Burrows (1996), we assume that in this respect the effects of perception on behavior represents a different mechanism than the effects of automatic goal priming on behavior. In a test of their automotive model, Bargh, Gollwitzer, and Barndollar (1996) primed participants with either achievement or affiliation goals. They obtained evidence that participants behaved accordingly but only on the earlier trials of the dependent variables. Later, no trace of the primed goal was found. However, unlike goal-directed action, the behavior we are considering is not instigated to lead to a desired outcome. Therefore, there is no reason to assume that it ends when a specific state is reached. It does not contain a "stop mechanism," so to speak. Once instigated, it is "left to operate by default" (Bargh, Gollwitzer, & Barndollar, 1996, p. 4). It follows from this reasoning that once instigated, the termination of perception-induced action (e.g., walking very slowly, in the Bargh, Chen, & Burrows, 1996, study) is left to other mechanisms (e.g., a conscious decision to walk faster upon being told that the bus leaves in a minute), or it may be overruled by competing behavioral effects set off by other perceptual cues (e.g., bumping into Carl Lewis). In sum, in the absence of external intervention, there is, theoretically, no reason to expect decay over time. We tested this hypothesis in our experiments.

The Experiments

In the experiments, we investigated the impact of stereotype priming on overt behavior. In Experiments 1 and 2, participants were primed with the stereotype of professors, of which intelligence and knowledgeability are central features. We hypothesized that on a subsequent, ostensibly unrelated, general knowledge task, the participants' performance would be enhanced when compared with performance in no-prime and intelligence-irrelevant control conditions. In Experiment 3 participants were primed with the stereotype of soccer hooligans. As soccer hooligans are perceived as stupid (see, e.g., Dijksterhuis & van Knippenberg, 1996), the primed participants' performance on the general knowledge scale was expected to decrease when compared with the no-prime control condition. In Experiment 4, we investigated whether priming participants directly with traits (intelligent and stupid) led to the same effects as priming participants with stereotypes associated with these traits (professor and hooligan).

In Experiments 1, 2, and 3, we also studied stability of the prime effect over time; that is, we looked at potential (absence of) decay over time. Another manipulation was added to Experiments 2 and 3: Whether the magnitude of the effects varies depending on the length of the prime. In these experiments, participants who were primed for a long period of time (9 min) were compared with participants who were primed for a short period (2 min).

Experiment 1

In the first experiment, participants were primed with the stereotype of professors. We expected these primed participants to perform better on a general knowledge task, in line with the attributes of the stereotype of professors, such as intelligence and knowledgeability. We compared these results with two conditions, one in which participants were not primed and one in which participants were primed with secretaries, a stereotype supposedly unrelated to knowledgeability and intelligence. Both were treated as control conditions.

The priming procedure consisted of a task seemingly unrelated to the rest of the experiment (cf. Bargh & Pietromonaco, 1982; Dijksterhuis & van Knippenberg, 1996, 1997; Higgins, Rholes, & Jones, 1977; Macrae et al., 1994). One may note that our priming manipulation differs from the one used by Bargh, Chen, and Burrows (1996) in that our participants were aware of the content of the prime. However, of critical importance for our test of unconscious effects of stereotype activation on behavior is the fact that participants should be unaware of the link between the priming manipulation and the task on which the resulting effect is measured. In our experiments, participants should not have been aware of the fact that the prime may have influenced their performance. Whether participants were aware of the specific content of the prime itself (e.g., a professor) is irrelevant for our purposes (see, e.g., Bargh, 1994; Bargh & Pietromonaco, 1982; Dijksterhuis & van Knippenberg, 1996; Higgins & King, 1981; Higgins et al., 1977; Macrae et al., 1994; Niedenthal & Cantor, 1986; Srull & Wyer, 1979, 1980, for a similar argument).

The general knowledge task consisted of a questionnaire with 42 difficult multiple-choice questions borrowed from the game Trivial Pursuit (1984/1987).

Method

Participants and design. Sixty undergraduate students of the University of Nijmegen were randomly assigned to one of three experimental conditions: A professor prime condition, a secretary prime (control) condition, or a no-prime control condition. Participants received 5 Dutch guilders (Dfl) (approximately U.S. $3) for participating.

Participants and materials. Participants were told that they would participate in a number of unrelated pilot studies. The pilot studies were allegedly for the purpose of gathering stimulus materials for forthcoming experiments. Upon entering the laboratory, participants were placed in cubicles containing an Apple Macintosh (LCIII) computer. Participants were told that all instructions would be provided by the computer. Subsequently, the experimenter started the computer program and left the cubicle. After some general instructions were provided, the computer randomly assigned participants to one of three experimental conditions: Participants either were primed with the stereotype of professors or the stereotype of secretaries or were not primed at all. The latter participants started with the questionnaire containing the dependent variable immediately.

The priming procedure we used was the same procedure used earlier by Macrae et al. (1994) and by Dijksterhuis and van Knippenberg (1996). Participants were asked, by the computer, to imagine a typical professor (or secretary) for 5 min and to list the behaviors, lifestyle, and appearance attributes of this typical professor (or secretary). Participants were requested to list their thoughts on a blank sheet of paper that had been provided by the experimenter when participants entered their cubicles. Participants were told that this information would be used for forthcoming experiments of the Department of Social Psychology. The choice for stereotypes of professors and secretaries was based on a

pilot study in which 40 participants rated these (and other) groups on 56 traits. In this pilot study, 9-point scales were used, with poles labeled *professors [secretaries] are not at all* — (1) and *professors [secretaries] are very* — (9). Professors were perceived as intelligent ($M = 7.78$) and as knowledgeable ($M = 7.56$). Secretaries were chosen as an additional control condition. They were rated near the midpoint of the scale (i.e., as neutral) with respect to the traits intelligent ($M = 5.05$) and knowledgeable ($M = 4.83$).

After they had completed the priming procedure, participants were asked to start with a second, purportedly unrelated task. The computer program asked the participants to open an envelope that was on the table next to the computer. This envelope contained a booklet with 42 multiple-choice questions, each with four choice options. The booklet consisted of six pages. On each page, seven questions were listed. Participants were told that the Personality Department was currently developing a "general knowledge" scale. This scale consisted of five subscales, each containing 42 questions. The subscales ranged from *very easy* (1) to *very difficult* (5). At that time, we told participants, we were testing the differences in difficulty between the five subscales. For ethical purposes we told all participants that they would receive the most difficult subscale (prestudies indicated that students answered about 50% correctly, indicating that the questions were fairly difficult, considering that a score of 25% would be obtained by mere guessing). Participants were asked to answer the questions by choosing one out of four options. They were told that there were no time constraints. They were asked to push a button before they started and after they finished. This was done to measure the time participants spent on the task.

The 42 questions were all taken from the game Trivial Pursuit. For each question, in addition to the correct answer, three incorrect choice options were also provided. Examples of questions and choice options are "Who painted *La Guernica?*" (a. Dali, b. Miro, c. Picasso, d. Velasquez), "What is the capital of Bangladesh?" (a. Dhaka, b. Hanoi, c. Yangon, d. Bangkok) and "Which country hosted the 1990 World Cup soccer?" (a. the United States, b. Mexico, c. Spain, d. Italy). The right answer was option a on 11 questions, option b on 11 questions, option c on 10 questions, and option d on 10 questions. To control for possible order effects, we constructed six different booklets. In different versions, each page appeared as the first page, as the second page and so on, to the last page. Ten copies were made of all six versions. The booklets were randomly distributed among the participants.

After completing the questionnaire, participants were debriefed carefully. First, participants who were primed were asked which departments were conducting the experiments. With just three exceptions, participants correctly recalled that the first experiment was conducted by the Department of Social Psychology, whereas the second experiment was conducted by the Department of Personality. Subsequently, participants were asked whether the first task might have influenced performance on the second task. None of the participants believed the first task to have affected the second. In sum, none of the participants indicated suspicion as to the actual relation between the tasks. In fact, upon being told about the hypothesis, many participants found it very hard to believe that the priming procedure might have influenced their performance on the general knowledge task. After the debriefing, participants were thanked, paid, and dismissed.

Results and Discussion

Number of Correct Answers

We expected that priming would influence performance on the general knowledge task. Specifically, we hypothesized that participants who had been primed with the professor stereotype would outperform the other participants, who either had been primed with the stereotype of a secretary or had not been primed at all.

We counted the number of correct answers for each participant. The percentages were subjected to a 3 (prime: No prime vs. secretary prime vs. professor prime) between-subjects analysis of variance (ANOVA). The predicted main effect was highly significant, $F(2, 57) = 5.64$, $p < .007$. The percentages of correctly answered questions are listed in Table 16.1. As can be seen, participants primed with the stereotype of professors ($M = 59.5$) outperformed those who were primed with the stereotype of secretaries ($M = 46.6$), $F(1, 57) = 10.45$, $p < .003$, and the no-prime control participants ($M = 49.9$), $F(1, 57) = 5.84$, $p < .02$. There were no differences between participants primed with the stereotype of secretaries and no-prime control participants, $F(1, 57) = .46$, $p < .50$.

To examine possible decay over time, we divided the overall score in three scores. The first score represented the proportion of correct answers on the first two pages of the booklet, the second score represented the proportion on pages 3 and 4, and the third score represented the proportion on the last two pages. These proportions are listed in Table 16.1.

Table 16.1 shows that there might be some reason to assume decay of the priming effects during the

TABLE 16.1. Experiment 1: Number of Correct Answers (Percentages)

Prime	All Questions	Score 1	Score 2	Score 3
No prime	49.9	51.3	46.1	52.3
Professors	59.5	60.0	62.1	56.4
Secretaries	46.4	44.4	46.4	48.4

completion of the questionnaire. The differences between experimental conditions with respect to the proportions of correct answers are more pronounced for the first four pages (Score 1 and Score 2) than for the last two pages (Score 3). To test the significance of the decay, we compared linear and quadratic trends of the professor prime condition with the control conditions. A downward linear trend may be seen as an indication of immediate decay (i.e., decay that starts immediately after the priming procedure ends). A quadratic trend might be indicative of delayed onset of decay (e.g., after a few minutes). We subjected the scores to a 3 (prime: No prime vs. secretary prime vs. professor prime) × 3 (time phase: Score 1 vs. Score 2 vs. Score 3) within-participants ANOVA. The within-subject score was analyzed in terms of linear and quadratic trends. First, there were no interaction effects of prime with time phase, neither with the linear trend, $F(2, 57) = .80$, $p < .46$, nor with the quadratic trend, $F(2, 57) = 1.70$, $p < .20$. Also, comparisons between the professor prime condition and the two other conditions revealed no significant interactions, so there is no apparent relative decay of enhanced performance of the professor prime condition compared with the other two conditions.

Speed

For exploratory purposes, we measured the time participants spent on the questionnaire. Unfortunately, the time of the first 11 participants was not recorded because of a technical problem. Therefore, only 49 participants were included in the analyses. The time participants spent on the task was subjected to a 3 (Prime: No prime vs. secretary prime vs. professor prime) between-subjects ANOVA. We obtained a main effect, $F(2, 46) = 3.62$, $p < .04$. Participants primed with the stereotype of secretaries were considerably faster ($M = 6$ min, 16 s) than both participants primed with the professor stereotype ($M = 8$ min, 3 s) and no-prime control participants ($M = 7$ min, 54 s). These differences were reliable: For secretaries versus professors, $F(1, 46) = 5.73$, $p < .03$; for secretaries versus no-prime controls, $F(1, 46) = 4.91$, $p < .04$. There were no differences between participants primed with professors and no-prime control participants, $F(1, 46) = 0.11$, ns. It may be conjectured that the specific content of the stereotype of secretaries was responsible for this speed of processing effect. Obviously, secretaries deal with a lot of paper work. It is not unlikely that secretaries are perceived as efficient workers who manage to handle a lot of problems in a short period of time. If this is the case, priming this stereotype would lead participants to complete forms and questionnaires with greater speed. However, because we did not test these possible attributes of the stereotype of secretaries in our pilot study, the validity of this post hoc explanation can not be verified with the current data.

The results of Experiment 1 lend support to our prediction. Participants who were primed with the professor stereotype, of which intelligence and knowledgeability are central features, showed enhanced general knowledge in comparison with participants who were not primed and with participants who were primed with a stereotype supposedly unrelated to intelligence and knowledgeability. The results on the speed of completion of the booklets provided tentative additional support for the idea that priming a social category leads one to behave as a (stereotypical) member of this social category (cf. Bargh, Chen, & Burrows, 1996). In other words, the activation of a perceptual representation leads one to behave accordingly.

Although the data on decay were not even close to statistical significance, the conclusion that there was no decay of the effects may be premature. It is possible that the somewhat weaker professor priming effect on the final pages was just the first sign of decay. The mean time that participants primed with the stereotype of professors spent on the task was about 8 min. It is conceivable that the onset of decay was at, say, 6 min and that it would have become plainly visible if only the task has lasted longer. In sum, the picture is not clear. Therefore, we attempted to give decay a better chance in Experiment 2.

Apart from the decay function of the observed effects of stereotype activation on behavior, we also studied the relation between the duration of the prime and the magnitude of the resulting behavioral effect.

Experiment 2

Experiment 2 served three goals. First, we tried to replicate the findings of Experiment 1. Second, we made a more serious attempt to show (lack of) decay of priming effects. To do this, we asked participants to answer more questions (60) while at the same time we fixed the processing pace. Participants were requested to answer questions by pushing a button on the keyboard. Every

question appeared on the screen for 15 s. After 15 s, the next question appeared, regardless of whether participants had answered the previous question. This way, all participants answered questions for exactly 15 min. Third, we examined the relation between strength of the prime (or, more precisely, the length of the prime) and the duration and magnitude of the effect. Therefore, apart from a no-prime control condition, we used a condition in which participants were primed for 2 min and one condition in which participants were primed for 9 min. The priming procedure was (apart from its length) the same as in Experiment 1. We used only the stereotype of professors in Experiment 2.

Method
Participants and design. Fifty-eight undergraduate students of the University of Nijmegen were randomly assigned to one of three experimental conditions: A 2-min prime condition, a 9-min prime condition, or a no-prime control condition. Participants received Dfl. 5 (approximately U.S. $3) for participating.

Procedure and materials. The procedure was largely the same as in Experiment 1. Participants were again told that they would participate in two unrelated pilot studies, one conducted by the Department of Social Psychology and the other by the Department of Personality. Participants were placed in individual cubicles containing an Apple Macintosh (LCIII) computer. A computer program provided the instructions. Participants in the two priming conditions were asked to imagine a typical professor and to list the behaviors, lifestyle, and appearance attributes of this typical professor on a blank sheet provided by the experimenter at the beginning of the experiment. Participants were either given 2 min or 9 min to complete this task. One third of the participants were not primed and started to answer the questions of the general knowledge scale immediately.

After the priming procedure ended, participants were asked, by the computer, to complete the general knowledge scale. We used the 42 questions of the scale of Experiment 1 and added 18 new questions to the list. These 60 questions were presented on a computer screen in random order. This time, the choice options were labeled 1, 2, 3, and 4. Participants had to answer by pushing the corresponding button. All questions appeared on the screen for 15 s, whether an answer was given or not. The screen indicated how many seconds a participant had left to answer the question.

Funneled debriefing again indicated that participants were not suspicious. We first asked participants which departments were involved in these experiments. This time, all participants recalled the right departments. Subsequently, we asked participants whether the first task could have influenced the second. As in Experiment 1, no participants suspected the first stage to have influenced the second. In sum, the tasks were perceived as unrelated. After debriefing, participants were thanked, paid, and dismissed.

Results and Discussion

Number of Correct Answers
The computer recorded the number of correct answers. No answer (2.7%) was, of course, treated as a wrong answer. The percentages of correct answers are listed in Table 16.2. It can be seen that, as in Experiment 1, priming improved performance. Furthermore, the length of the prime influenced the magnitude of the effect.

The percentages of correct answers were subjected to a 3 (prime: No-prime vs. 2-min prime vs. 9-min prime) between-subjects ANOVA. This analysis yielded a significant main effect, $F(2, 55) = 8.18, p < .002$. Simple contrasts revealed that participants primed for 9 min ($M = 58.9$) outperformed those who were primed for 2 min ($M = 51.8$), $F(1, 55) = 4.09, p < .05$, and those who were not primed ($M = 45.2$), $F(1, 55) = 16.36$, $p < .001$. In addition, participants primed for 2 min answered more questions correctly than no-prime control participants, $F(1, 55) = 4.83, p < .04$.

Decay
In an attempt to detect possible decay, we partitioned the overall score into three different blocks, each representing the percentage of correct answers to 20 consecutive questions (i.e., questions answered correctly in a 5-min interval). These scores are listed in Table 16.2. These scores were subjected to a 3 (prime: No-prime vs. 2-min prime vs. 9-min prime) $\times$ 3 (score for the first 5 min, score for the second 5 min, score for the last 5 min) within-participants ANOVA. The within-subject variable was analyzed in terms of linear and quadratic trends. Again, no reliable Prime $\times$ Linear Trend interaction, $F(2, 55) = 1.97, p < .15$, and no reliable

Prime $\times$ Quadratic Trend interaction, $F(2, 55) = .10$, $p < .91$, were obtained. We compared the condition in which participants were primed for 2 min with the no-prime control condition. The Prime $\times$ Linear Trend interaction was marginally significant, $F(1, 55) = 2.98$, $p < .10$. However, as can be seen in Table 16.2, this interaction is caused by the fact that participants who were primed improved their performance over the course of time. Hence, this statistically weak effect may be interpreted as evidence against decay. The Prime $\times$ Quadratic Trend interaction was not reliable, $F(1, 55) = .09, ns$. The comparison between scores for no-prime control participants and participants primed for 9 min revealed no significant Prime $\times$ Linear Trend interaction, $F(1, 55) = .03, p < .85$, and no significant Prime $\times$ Quadratic Trend interaction, $F(1, 55) = .15$, $p < .71$. In sum, this examination of the scores indeed revealed that performance was stable over time under all experimental conditions.

In Experiment 2, then, the results of Experiment 1 were replicated. Participants primed with the stereotype of a professor performed better on a general knowledge task than no-prime control participants. Furthermore, the length of the prime influenced the strength of the effect. Participants primed for 9 min outperformed participants primed for 2 min. As expected, it seems that prolonged perceptual input leads to stronger behavioral effects (cf. Srull & Wyer, 1979, 1980, who found such effects in the judgmental domain).

We did not find any evidence for decay of the priming effects during the 15 min participants were occupied with the general knowledge task. There is, however, one important difference between the procedures of Experiment 1 and Experiment 2. In Experiment 1, participants were allowed to think about the questions for as long (or as short a time) as they wanted to, whereas in Experiment 2, the pace was controlled by the experimenter. It is possible that the fixed pace in Experiment 2 somehow interfered with the occurence of decay. Therefore, we let the participants control their own pace in Experiment 3 (as in Experiment 1).

Experiment 3

In Experiment 3, we tried to obtain additional evidence for the idea that the length of the prime influences the strength of the effect. Therefore, we again primed participants for 2 min, for 9 min, or not at all.

Again, as in Experiment 2, we use the 60-question version of the general knowledge scale. However, we had the participants process the task in their own pace,

TABLE 16.2. Experiment 2: Number of Correct Answers (Percentages)

Prime	All Questions	Score 1	Score 2	Score 3
No prime	45.2	45.2	45.9	44.6
2 min	51.8	49.1	51.2	55.0
9 min	58.9	59.2	58.9	58.6

as in Experiment 1. This way, we hoped to be able to assess the impact of the somewhat rigid form of presentation used in Experiment 2 on the absence of decay of the behavioral effects.

An important modification in Experiment 3 was the stereotype under consideration. In Experiments 1 and 2, we used positive stereotypes (professors and secretaries). Corresponding behavioral consequences, such as enhanced performance on a general knowledge task, are positive or desirable as well. As we argued, the behavioral effects are assumed to be unconscious and unintentional and, therefore, not confined to only positive effects. This argument is in line with Bargh, Chen, and Burrows (1996), who primed both positive and negative behavior in their experiment. In their view and in ours, evidence for behavioral effects that are negative or undesirable may even constitute a stronger case for the unintentional nature of the effects, simply because usually, people will not engage in undesirable or negative behavior on purpose. Or, in terms of performance on our general knowledge task, nobody really wants to perform poorly on such a task and run the risk of coming across as stupid or dumb. Therefore, in Experiment 3, we use the stereotype of soccer hooligans. Soccer hooligans are associated with stupidity, and hence, activation of this stereotype should have impaired the performance of the participants.

Method

Participants and Design
Ninety-five undergraduate students of the University of Nijmegen were randomly assigned to one of three experimental conditions: A 2-min prime condition, a 9-min prime condition, and a no-prime control condition. Participants received Dfl. 5 (approximately U.S. $3) for participating.

Procedure and Materials
Apart from the stereotype used, the priming procedure used in Experiment 3 was the same as in Experiment 2. All instructions were again provided by a computer program. Here, we primed participants with the stereotype of soccer hooligans. This choice was based on a pilot study in which 40 participants rated social groups on traits. Nine-point scales were used, with poles labeled *soccer hooligans are not at all* — (1) and *soccer hooligans are very* — (9). Soccer hooligans were rated low on intelligence ($M = 2.12$) and low on knowledgeability ($M = 1.98$). As in Experiment 2, participants were primed for 2 min, for 9 min, or not at all.

We used the same 60 questions as in Experiment 2. However, as in Experiment 1, the questions were listed in a booklet, and participants were allowed to work on the task at their own pace. On each page, 6 questions were listed. We made 10 different versions so that all pages were 10 times page 1, 10 times page 2, and so on, to the last page. Again, we measured the time participants spent on the booklet.

The debriefing procedure was the same as in Experiments 1 and 2. Answers on the questions again indicated that participants perceived the priming task and the general knowledge task as unrelated, distinct tasks. After debriefing, participants were thanked, paid, and dismissed.

Results and Discussion

Number of Correct Answers
The number of correct answers was counted for each participant. As can be seen in Table 16.3, where percentages are given, priming again influenced performance. As expected, performance was worse after priming. The number of correct answers was subjected to a 3 (prime: No-prime vs. 2-min prime vs. 9-min prime) between-subjects ANOVA. The main effect was significant, $F(2, 92) = 5.50, p < .007$. Simple contrasts showed that participants that were primed with the stereotype of soccer hooligans for 9 min performed worse ($M = 43.1$) than participants who were primed for 2 min ($M = 48.6$), $F(1, 92) = 4.22, p < .05$, and worse than no-prime control participants ($M = 51.3$), $F(1, 92) = 10.58, p < .003$. The difference between the scores for no-prime control participants and participants primed for 2 min failed to reach significance, $F(1, 92) = 1.35, p < .24$.

For every participant, we calculated three different scores, one for the first 20 questions, one for Questions 21 to 40, and one for the last 20 questions. A 3 (prime: No-prime vs. 2-min prime vs. 9-min prime) × 3 (score for the first 20 questions vs. score for Questions 21 to 40 vs. score for the last 20 questions) within participants ANOVA on these scores revealed no sign of decay. Neither the Prime × Linear Trend interaction,

TABLE 16.3. Experiment 3: Number of Correct Answers (Percentages)

Prime	All Questions	Score 1	Score 2	Score 3
No prime	51.3	49.6	53.6	50.6
2 min	48.6	48.1	48.5	49.1
9 min	43.1	45.7	42.9	40.8

$F(2, 92) = .88$, $p < .42$, nor the Prime $\times$ Quadratic Trend interaction, $F(2, 92) = .57$, $p < .57$, approached significance. Moreover, the comparison between no-prime control participants and participants primed for 2 min revealed no Prime $\times$ Linear Trend interaction, $F(1, 92) = .00$, ns, and no No-prime $\times$ Quadratic Trend interaction, $F(1, 92) = .82$, $p < .37$. The comparison between no-prime control participants and participants primed for 9 min showed a nonsignificant Prime $\times$ Linear Trend interaction, $F(1, 92) = 1.28$, $p < .27$, and a nonsignificant Prime $\times$ Quadratic Trend interaction, $F(1, 92) = .92$, $p < .35$. Again, one may conclude that performance was stable over time under all experimental conditions.

Speed
The average time participants spent on the booklet was 10 min, 11 s. Although the duration differed between conditions (10 min, 41 s for no-prime control participants; 9 min, 10 s for participants primed for 2 min; and 10 min, 47 s for participants who were primed for 9 min), these differences were not statistically significant, $F(2, 92) = .69$, $p < .50$.

In Experiment 3, we again obtained evidence that activating a stereotype leads to corresponding behavior. By using the stereotype of soccer hooligans instead of the stereotype of professors, we were able to show undesirable behavioral effects (cf. Bargh, Chen, & Burrows, 1996). After being primed with soccer hooligans, participants' performance on a general knowledge task deteriorated. Furthermore, we also obtained additional evidence for the relation between the length of the prime and the strength of the behavioral effect. Participants that were primed for 9 min performed worse than participants that were primed for only 2 min. Again, no sign of decay of the effects was found during the 10 min the participants were occupied with the task.

Experiment 4

Experiment 4 was conducted to investigate whether the activation of traits (e.g., intelligent) would have the same effect as stereotypes associated with these traits (e.g., professor). At the beginning of this article, we argued that stereotypes affect behavior by means of the activation of traits. In concrete terms, activation of the professor stereotype is expected to result in intelligent behavior because activation of the professor stereotype leads to activation of intelligence. It follows from this reasoning that the direct activation of traits should also evoke corresponding behavior.

In Experiment 4 we tested this assumption. Participants were primed either with a stereotype or with a trait and also were primed either with a construct designating intelligence or with a construct designating stupidity. Participants, thus, were primed with the stereotype of professors or with the stereotype of soccer hooligans, or directly with the trait intelligent or with the trait stupid.

Method
Participants and design. Forty-three undergraduate students were randomly assigned to the cells of 2 (direction of prime: Intelligent vs. stupid) $\times$ 2 (target: Stereotype vs. trait) between-subjects design. All participants received Dfl. 5 (approximately U.S. $3) for their participation.

Procedure and stimulus materials. Upon entering the laboratory, participants were placed in cubicles containing an Apple Macintosh (LCIII) computer. They were told that a number of unrelated pilot studies were being conducted for the purpose of gathering stimulus materials for forthcoming experiments. Participants were told that the computer would provide all the experimental instructions. Subsequently, the experimenter started the computer program and left the cubicle.

The computer randomly assigned participants to cells of a 2 (direction of prime: Intelligent vs. stupid) $\times$ 2 (target: Stereotype vs. trait) between-subjects design. For the stereotype-prime conditions, the priming procedure was the same as in the earlier experiments. In this experiment, participants were primed for 5 min. Participants who were primed with a trait (i.e., intelligent or stupid) were asked to think about the concept of intelligence (or stupidity) for 5 min and to list synonyms and behaviors characteristic of this trait. Participants were asked to list their thoughts on a blank sheet of paper that had been provided by the experimenter when they entered their cubicles.

After completing the priming procedure, the second, purportedly unrelated task was administered. The procedure was the same as in Experiments 1 and 3. The only difference was that participants in Experiment 4 were presented with a short questionnaire containing only 20 multiple-choice questions.

After completing the questionnaire, participants were probed for suspicion very carefully. First, participants were asked which departments were conducting the experiments. With one exception, everyone correctly recalled that the first experiment was conducted by the Department of Social Psychology and the second experiment was conducted by the Department of Personality.

TABLE 16.4. Experiment 4: Number of Correct Answers (Percentages)

Target	Direction of Prime	
	Intelligent	Stupid
Stereotype	55.6	42.5
Trait	46.0	37.9

Participants were then asked whether the first task might have influenced performance on the second task. None of the participants believed the first task to have affected the second. In sum, none of the participants indicated suspicion as to the actual relation between the tasks. After the debriefing, participants were thanked, paid, and dismissed.

Results and Discussion

The number of questions answered correctly was counted for each participant. These scores were subjected to a 2 (direction of prime: Intelligent vs. stupid) × 2 (target: Stereotype vs. trait) between-subjects ANOVA. The only reliable effect was the expected main effect of direction of prime, $F(1, 39) = 7.12$, $p < .02$. (see Table 16.4 for means). Participants primed with intelligence (either by priming professor or by priming intelligent) outperformed participants primed with stupidity (either by priming soccer hooligan or by priming stupid). As in the earlier experiments, priming affected behavior. Participants behaved in line with the activated construct.

On the basis of these results, one may indeed draw the conclusion that the activation of traits, like the activation of stereotypes, evokes corresponding behavior. This finding corroborates the idea of a perception–behavior link discussed at the beginning of this article.

General Discussion

The activation of a mental representation of a social group (e.g., professors) leads to behavior corresponding with specific attributes of the stereotype (e.g., intelligence). In Experiment 1, we primed participants either with the stereotype of professors or with the stereotype of secretaries or not at all. Later, in the second, ostensibly unrelated task, participants completed a list containing 42 general knowledge questions. As predicted, participants primed with the stereotype of professors answered more questions correctly than both participants who had

been primed with the stereotype of secretaries and no-prime control participants. Furthermore, participants primed with the stereotype of secretaries completed the questionnaire considerably faster than the other participants. This might be attributed to the specific content of the secretary stereotype. With these results, the findings of Bargh, Chen, and Burrows (1996) were replicated using a different priming procedure, different stereotypes, and a different dependent measure.

With our findings, we also contribute to knowledge about the nature of the relation between perception and behavior. In two experiments, we demonstrated that the magnitude of the behavioral effects simply mirrored the magnitude of the perceptual input. In Experiments 2 and 3, participants who were primed for 9 min showed stronger behavioral effects than participants who were primed for 2 min. In other words, longer priming led to greater behavioral changes. These results underscore the fact that the process under consideration can be characterized as rather passive (cf. Bargh, Chen, & Burrows, 1996). Also, these results parallel findings from experiments in which the relation between perception and judgment is investigated (e.g., Higgins et al., 1985; Srull & Wyer, 1979, 1980).

The present research also showed an absence of decay of the effects of perception on behavior at least for a short period of time. The effects were stable over time at least until participants finished the dependent measure (which took, on average, 8 min in Experiment 1, 15 min in Experiment 2, and 10 min in Experiment 3). At first sight, this finding seems to be at odds with findings from the social judgment domain. An interesting assumption that may resolve this discrepancy is that semantic priming effects decay rather fast unless one is in the process of applying the primed construct one way or another. That is, it is very well possible that if we prime participants with the stereotype of professors, the semantic activation starts to decay immediately under conditions in which the stereotype is not somehow applied (e.g., for making judgments), but conversely, we may find no signs of decay as long as the primed stereotype is being applied in some way.

By changing ability-related performances, we demonstrated the effects of perception on behavior in a new domain. The behavior we studied is considerably more complex than the actions that were investigated in earlier research. It must be granted that the model explaining these results is still a rather crude one, and it needs to be refined in further research. Also, there may be alternative explanations that cannot be rejected on the basis of the current data.

In the next sections, we first discuss possible explanations for the findings as well as suggestions for refinements. Second, we discuss possible mediators of the effects of the intelligence and professor primes on performance on the general knowledge task. Later, we try to reject some alternative explanations. Finally, we ponder on some implications of our findings.

From Perception to Action in Two Steps

In order to explain why priming a trait or a stereotype leads to behavioral changes, it may be fruitful to explicate the route from the activation of a trait (e.g., aggressive) to the behavior (e.g., hitting somebody) in terms of two distinctive steps. First, one must explain why a semantic construct can lead to action — in concrete terms, how aggressive results in aggressive behavior. Second, one has to explain how some abstract behavioral class of actions results in all kinds of more specific behaviors. In other words, how can an abstract term that does not refer to concrete behaviors ("aggressive behavior") result in specific acts?

The first step to be taken is the one from activation of some semantic construct to overt behavior. For example, how does activation of a construct implying "slow" lead to a slower walking speed (see Bargh, Chen, & Burrows, 1996)? It is known that people do not necessarily need an intention in order to act. Actually, action can be instigated by the intention not to act (see Ansfield & Wegner, 1996). It is known that people do not have to be aware of our actions in order for them to occur. Despite this knowledge, more direct routes from perception or cognition to action, although demonstrated empirically, are not well understood.

One way of dealing with the relation among perception, cognition, and action is offered by Vallacher (1993). Vallacher assumes that (complex) behavior must be represented verbally in order to be executed successfully. If one wants to do something (e.g., eat an orange) that requires a specific order of subactions, one engages in action queuing (e.g., first peel it and only then bite). This requires a sophisticated coordination process for which verbal representation seems to be much more appropriate than visual representation. If one assumes that action is verbally represented and combines this with the notion that all sorts of actions are, in evolutionary terms, much older than language, one may even posit that language developed because of the need to execute more complex behaviors. According to this — admittedly very speculative — view, an explanation would be required if priming the semantic concept slow

would *not* result in a slower walking speed (see also James, 1890), because after all, evoking action may have been the original function of this concept.

From an evolutionary point of view, it may be argued that the existence of a direct perception–behavior link allows for imitation (cf. Bargh, Chen, & Burrows, 1996). A mechanism that fosters imitation of others is, in terms of evolution, beneficial because it may have survival value, not only for fish and gnus but also for human beings. Unlike fish and gnus, however, humans seem to be capable not only of imitating visually represented, simple actions (e.g., moving as fast as possible in a certain direction). In addition, humans can "imitate" much more complex behavioral patterns because they use abstract concepts such as traits and stereotypes. These concepts permit predictions regarding complex behavior of others and can both improve and speed up imitation processes. In other words, the participants in our experiments may have fallen prey to the same mechanism a gnu uses to escape from a lion, except that human beings can apply this mechanism for much more complex actions.

Obviously, these perspectives are based on very speculative assumptions, and there are alternative approaches to the issue at hand. Whichever perspective one favors, it is clear that a lot of further thinking and research in various areas is needed before the relation between perception (and cognition) and action can be properly understood.

The second step needed to explain our findings is the one from complex and abstract behavior (such as intelligent behavior) to simple actions. This step rests on the notion that behavior is organized and represented hierarchically. This step is relatively well understood, and many theorists have posited the idea (Broadbent, 1977; Carver & Scheier, 1981; Lashley, 1951; Martin & Tesser, 1989; Powers, 1973; Vallacher & Wegner, 1985).[1] Nevertheless, the perceptual representations investigated in this article (traits and stereotypes) are abstract and refer to actions only rather indirectly. To corroborate our assumed route from traits to specific behaviors, it may be worthwhile to assess which behaviors are associated most strongly with a certain trait and

---

[1] As the example about deciding to eat an orange implies, actions must be represented hierarchically to enable their intended execution. It would be silly to assume that one intentionally decides to peel the orange completely independently of the next step: The first bite. Instead, one intentionally decides to eat an orange, which in turn elicits the subactions needed.

to determine whether trait activation would indeed primarily evoke these behaviors.

From Priming Professor to Winning a Game of Trivial Pursuit

To explain the observed priming effects on complex behaviors, we assume that mental representations of traits are associated with behavioral instantiations characteristic of the trait involved. Thus, as we outlined at the beginning of this article, priming a stereotype activates the traits associated with it. The trait activation is assumed to bring about (or maybe even "imply") the activation of a set of behavioral representations. The latter may actually constitute the core of the participants' understanding of what it is like to have that trait.

How can one, on a more concrete level, interpret the obtained priming effects on behavior? Specifically, how can one explain the observed phenomenon that participants primed with the professor stereotype showed significantly better performance on a general knowledge task than participants not so primed?

Obviously, one explanation can be rejected immediately: Participants do not become more knowledgeable as a result of the prime; that is, they do not know things they did not know before merely because they were primed with the word *professor*. The effect must have come about because the prime triggered behaviors beneficial to performance on a general knowledge task that already were part of the participants' behavioral repertoire.

What, then, are the more specific behavioral changes one can expect to occur on the basis of the prime? That is, which more specific actions can be elicited by activating the stereotype of professors, a stereotype of which traits such as intelligence and knowledgeability are central features?[2]

Several behaviors may be evoked that may improve performance on multiple-choice general knowledge questions. First, participants may allocate their effort differently. Assuming that base-rate performances on our general knowledge questions are suboptimal, the prime may automatically and subconsciously induce participants to concentrate on the task and to think harder about possible answers.

Second, the professor prime may induce participants to use smarter and more varied strategies for problem solving. If one is asked "Who painted *La Guernica?*" and the choices are Dali, Miro, Picasso, and Velasquez, one can, for instance, begin with dismissing incorrect options (e.g., "It can't be Velasquez who painted *La Guernica* because I know he was not a modern painter") or thinking of additional cues (such as differences in painting styles between Miro, Dali, and Picasso). Thus, priming participants with the stereotype of professors may lead them to use more of these strategies and also to use them more often.

Third, it is very well possible that participants have an altered "feeling of knowing," which may result in a different use of their own knowledge. An example is that participants might be more confident regarding their own knowledge. It is possible that primed participants rely, because of enhanced confidence, more on the first answer that comes to mind. In general, people have been shown to benefit from awareness of idiosyncratic aspects of their knowledge (see, e.g., Jameson, 1990; Lovelace, 1984; Nelson, Leonesio, Landwehr, & Narens, 1986; Underwood, 1966).

These and other possible effects of the professor prime may, separately or in unison, have enhanced participants' ability to perform well on a general knowledge task. This short list of potentially invoked behaviors is a tentative one; their causal role might be examined in further study in combination with a search for other potentially intervening behavioral mechanisms.

Rejecting Alternatives

During several encounters, colleagues have wondered whether the empirical results under consideration can be explained by a process of spreading activation. Although the idea of spreading activation may play a role in our perception–behavior explanation, we do not endorse a purely semantic spreading activation account of our results. Yet one might try to explain the present findings in terms of priming of semantic constructs. It is possible that our priming manipulation, by means of spreading activation (cf. Collins & Loftus, 1975) increased (in the case of the professor prime) or decreased (in the case of the soccer hooligan prime) the accessibility of general knowledge. Although it is possible that enhanced access to relevant knowledge plays a role in our experiment, we feel it is implausible that it can on its own account for our data.

First, the idea of spreading activation is based on the logic of what may be called "semantic space." Activation of a construct (e.g., mother) leads to activation of a

---

[2] Unfortunately, the protocols containing what the participants listed during the priming stage were not very helpful. Because of our instructions, participants wrote down about everything that could possibly be associated with college professors (and even some things that one would never associate with college professors). These protocols are not suitable for a reasonably elegant quantitative analysis.

semantically related construct (e.g., caring). This logic implies that the effects of spreading activation diminish when the semantic resemblance of constructs is low or almost absent. The longer the "semantic route" from one construct to the other, the less plausible the possibility that activation of one construct will result in the activation of the other construct. For this reason it is hard to believe that activation of professor would lead to activation of Dali or Hanoi or World Cup soccer (see the examples of the questions used in the *Method* section of Experiment 1). In brief, it seems implausible that the professor concept is semantically related to the right answers on the questions in our general knowledge task.

Quite another way in which the term *professor* may be argued to have activated relevant knowledge is by assuming that a lot of knowledge is acquired through lectures given by professors. Considering that our participants were mostly psychology students, this explanation could have been plausible if our questions had pertained to psychology, because most of this knowledge would indeed be acquired through lectures given by professors. However, the questionnaire did not contain such questions. If knowledge relevant to our questions had been acquired through lectures (instead of by reading books or watching TV, for instance), such lectures probably would have been given by high school teachers, that is, teachers who are not members of the social category of professors.[3] Thus, in sum, it is unlikely that the effects reported are the result of a process of spreading activation.

The second consideration that speaks against knowledge accessibility as an explanation for our results is that this explanation would entail the idea of knowledge inhibition in case of Experiments 3 and 4. In Experiments 3 and 4, participants performed worse on a general knowledge task after being primed with soccer hooligans (or with stupidity). Although there is a some evidence for the existence of spreading inhibition (see, e.g., Anderson & Spellman, 1995; Blair & Banaji, 1996; Dijksterhuis & van Knippenberg, 1996; Neumann & DeSchepper, 1992), this evidence is largely confined to constructs that are clearly inconsistent with each other. For instance, activation of the stereotype of soccer hooligans leads to inhibition of the trait friendly (Dijksterhuis & van Knippenberg, 1996). In other words, inhibition seems to be restricted to constructs that are, in terms of

their meaning, almost mutually exclusive. On the basis of this evidence, there is no reason to expect soccer hooligan to inhibit Dali or Hanoi. These terms are no more than merely unrelated to the stereotype. Hence, the assumption of spreading inhibition to account for our data is even more problematic than the assumption of spreading activation. In sum, there is little to say for a purely knowledge activation explanation for our results.

Implications for Human Interaction

As Bargh, Chen, and Burrows (1996) noted, the perception–behavior link may be of crucial importance to our understanding of a large number of social psychological phenomena: Compliance and conformity, emotional and behavioral contagion, empathic reactions, imitating and modeling, mass media effects on behavior, and behavioral confirmation of stereotypes are, according to Bargh, Chen, and Burrows (1996), expected to be at least partly under the influence of the perception–behavior link. In view of the findings that (a) the influence of perception on behavior does not seem to be restricted to desirable behavior, (b) decay seems to be absent — for at least a couple of minutes — all else being equal, and (c) the magnitude (i.e., duration) of the perceptual input is positively related to the magnitude of the resulting behavioral effects, the implications of this mechanism for social behavior may be very important indeed.

It is not feasible, within the confines of the present article, to give an exhaustive account, but let us briefly consider some of the ways in which the perception–behavior link may play a role in human interaction. First, imitating somebody may well trigger automatic empathic reactions (Bargh, Gollwitzer, & Barndollar, 1996). In general, people seem to like other people who are similar to themselves (e.g., Byrne, 1971; Newcomb, 1961). The perception–behavior link, then, may unwittingly help us to get other people to like us. There is some evidence suggesting that this might be the case. It is established that people are attracted to other people who have similar attitudes (e.g., Newcomb, 1961). As Baldwin and Holmes (1987) showed, people change their attitudes in the direction of the attitude of others upon thinking about these others. In sum, unconscious imitation may serve an important function in everyday interactions: It may enhance cohesion between people in interaction. Specific features of the perception–behavior link, such as that it is not restricted to a limited behavioral domain, that it does not decay over time, and that prolonged perception leads to stronger effects, may all contribute to its success in supporting interaction.

---

[3] This may not be true for other countries. In the Netherlands, however, high school teachers are never referred to as professors. They are always simply referred to as teachers.

The same mechanisms underlying its success may also cause problems. Because people unconsciously imitate each other, perceptual cues may also trigger undesirable behaviors. Just as friendly behavior evokes friendly behavior in return, hostile behavior will result in hostile behavior in others. As Chen and Bargh (1997) recently established, perception-induced behavior can lead to self-fulfilling prophecies (Darley & Fazio, 1980; Snyder, Tanke, & Berscheid, 1977) and to stereotype confirmation. Encountering people that one perceives as aggressive may inadvertently elicit facial expressions, a tone of voice, or acts evoking aggressive reactions in return. It is quite conceivable that such snowball effects (Gilbert, 1995; Miller & Turnbull, 1986) lead to escalated hostility in a variety of social situations.

These examples show that the perception–behavior link can have both desirable and undesirable consequences in everyday human interaction. Of course, questions remain. For one thing, it is important to gain insight into the range and frequency of these perception-induced behaviors, as well as the prevalence of perceptual action instigators, in order to be able to assess their impact on human behavior. For the time being it seems to us that because of its inconspicuous nature, the pervasiveness of the impact of percepts on human behavior may easily be underestimated. The literature to date, including the present study, has only begun to unravel the first rough features of this intriguing phenomenon.

REFERENCES

Anderson, M. C., & Spellman, B. A. (1995). On the status of inhibitory mechanisms in cognition: Memory retrieval as a model case. *Psychological Review, 102,* 68–100.

Ansfield, M. E., & Wegner, D. M. (1996). The feeling of doing. In P. M. Gollwitzer & J. A. Bargh (Eds.), *The psychology of action*, pp. 482–506. New York: Guilford Press.

Arnold, M. B. (1946). On the mechanism of suggestion and hypnosis. *Journal of Abnormal and Social Psychology, 41,* 107–128.

Baldwin, M. W., & Holmes, J. G. (1987). Salient private audiences and awareness of self. *Journal of Personality and Social Psychology, 52,* 1087–1098.

Bandura, A. (1977). *Social learning theory.* Englewood Cliffs, NJ: Prentice Hall.

Bargh, J. A. (1994). The four horsemen of automaticity: Awareness, intention, efficiency and control in social cognition. In R. S. Wyer, Jr. & T. K. Srull (Eds.), *The handbook of social cognition: Vol. 2. Basic processes* (pp. 1–40). Hillsdale, NJ: Erlbaum.

Bargh, J. A. (in press). The automaticity of everyday life. In R. S. Wyer, Jr. (Ed.), *Advances in social cognition.* Hillsdale, NJ: Erlbaum.

Bargh, J. A., Chen, M., & Burrows, L. (1996). The automaticity of social behavior: Direct effects of trait concept and stereotype activation on action. *Journal of Personality and Social Psychology, 71,* 230–244.

Bargh, J. A., Gollwitzer, P. M., & Barndollar, K. (1996). *Social ignition: The automatic activation of motivational states.* Unpublished manuscript, New York University.

Bargh, J. A., & Pietromonaco, P. (1982). Automatic information processing and social perception: The influence of trait information presented outside of conscious awareness on impression formation. *Journal of Personality and Social Psychology, 43,* 437–449.

Berkowitz, L. (1984). Some effects of thoughts on anti- and prosocial influences of media events: A cognitive-neoassociation analysis. *Psychological Bulletin, 95,* 410–427.

Blair, I. V., & Banaji, M. R. (1996). Automatic and controlled processes in stereotype priming. *Journal of Personality and Social Psychology, 70,* 1142–1163.

Bock, J. K. (1986). Syntactic persistence in language production. *Cognitive Psychology, 18,* 355–387.

Bock, J. K. (1989). Closed-class immanence in sentence production. *Cognition, 31,* 163–186.

Broadbent, D. E. (1977). Levels, hierarchies, and the locus of control. *Quarterly Journal of Experimental Psychology, 29,* 181–201.

Byrne, D. (1971). *The attraction paradigm.* New York: Academic Press.

Carver, C. S., Ganellen, R. J., Froming, W. J., & Chambers, W. (1983). Modeling: An analysis in terms of category accessibility. *Journal of Experimental Social Psychology, 19,* 403–421.

Carver, C. S., & Scheier, M. F. (1981). *Attention and self-regulation: A control-theory approach to human behavior.* New York: Springer-Verlag.

Charcot, J. M. (1886). *Neue Vorlesungen über die Krankheiten des Nervensystems (Autorisierte Deutsche Ausgabe von S. Freud).* Leipzig, Germany: Toeplitz & Deuticke.

Chen, M., & Bargh, J. A. (1997). Nonconscious behavioral confirmation processes: The self-fulfilling nature of automatically activated stereotypes. *Journal of Experimental Social Psychology, 33,* 541–560.

Collins, A. M., & Loftus, E. F. (1975). A spreading activation theory of semantic processing. *Psychological Review, 82,* 407–428.

Darley, J. M., & Fazio, R. H. (1980). Expectancy confirmation processes arising in the social interaction sequence. *American Psychologist, 35,* 867–881.

Dell, G. S. (1986). A spreading activation theory of retrieval in sentence production. *Psychological Review, 93,* 283–321.

Devine, P. G. (1989). Stereotypes and prejudice: Their automatic and controlled components. *Journal of Personality and Social Psychology, 56,* 5–18.

Dijksterhuis, A., & van Knippenberg, A. (1996). The knife that cuts both ways: Facilitated and inhibited access to traits as a result of stereotype-activation. *Journal of Experimental Social Psychology, 32,* 271–288.

Dijksterhuis, A., & van Knippenberg, A. (1997). *Unconscious control of unintentional and unconscious behavior.* Manuscript in preparation.

Dovidio, J. F., Evans, N., & Tyler, R. B. (1986). Racial stereotypes: The contents of their cognitive representations. *Journal of Experimental Social Psychology, 22,* 22–37.

Eidelberg, L. (1929). Experimenteller Beitrag zum Mechanismus der Imitationsbewegung. *Jahrbücher für Psychiatrie und Neurologie, 46,* 170–173.

Frijda, N. H., Kuipers, P., & ter Schure, E. (1989). Relations among emotions, appraisal, and emotional action readiness. *Journal of Personality and Social Psychology, 57,* 212–228.

Gilbert, D. T. (1995). Attribution and interpersonal perception. In A. Tesser (Ed.), *Advanced social psychology* (pp. 98–147). New York: McGraw-Hill.

Hamilton, D. L., & Sherman, J. W. (1994). Stereotypes. In R. S. Wyer & T. K. Srull (Eds.), *Handbook of social cognition: Vol. 2. Applications* (p. 1–68). Hillsdale, NJ: Erlbaum.

Higgins, E. T., Bargh, J. A., & Lombardi, W. (1985). Nature of priming effects on categorization. *Journal of Experimental Psychology: Learning, Memory, and Cognition, 11*, 59–69.

Higgins, E. T., & King, G. A. (1981). Accessibility of social constructs: Information-processing consequences of individual and contextual variability. In N. Cantor & J. F. Kihlstrom (Eds.), *Personality, cognition, and social interaction* (pp. 69–122). Hillsdale, NJ: Erlbaum.

Higgins, E. T., Rholes, W. S., & Jones, C. R. (1977). Category accessibility and impression formation. *Journal of Experimental Social Psychology, 13*, 141–154.

James, W. (1890). *Principles of psychology*. New York: Holt.

Jameson, A. (1990). *Knowing what others know: Studies in intuitive psychometrics*. Unpublished doctoral dissertation, University of Amsterdam, Amsterdam, the Netherlands.

Koffka, K. (1925). *Die Grundlagen der psychischen Entwicklung*. Osterwieck, Germany: Zickfeldt.

Lashley, K. (1951). The problem of serial order of behavior. In L. A. Jeffres (Ed.), *Cerebral mechanisms in behavior: The Hixon symposium* (pp. 112–136). New York: Wiley.

Levelt, W. J. M., & Kelter, S. (1982). Surface form and memory in question answering. *Cognitive Psychology, 14*, 78–106.

Lovelace, E. A. (1984). Metamemory: Monitoring future recallability during study. *Journal of Experimental Psychology: Learning, Memory, and Cognition, 10*, 756–766.

Macrae, C. N., Stangor, C., & Milne, A. B. (1994). Activating social stereotypes: A functional analysis. *Journal of Experimental Social Psychology, 30*, 370–389.

Manstead, A. S. R., & Semin, G. R. (1980). Social facilitation effects: More enhancement of dominant responses? *British Journal of Social and Clinical Psychology, 19*, 119–136.

Martin, L., & Tesser, A. (1989). Toward a model of ruminative thought. In J. S. Uleman & J. A. Bargh (Eds.), *Unintended thought* (pp. 306–326). New York: Guilford Press.

Miller, D. T., & Turnbull, W. (1986). Expectancies and interpersonal processes. *Annual Review of Psychology, 37*, 233–256.

Mischel, W. (1973). Toward a cognitive social learning reconceptualization of personality. *Psychological Review, 80*, 252–283.

Nelson, T. O., Leonesio, R. J., Landwehr, R. S., & Narens, L. (1986). A comparison of three predictors of an individual's memory performance: The individual's feeling of knowing vs. the normative feeling of knowing vs. base-rate item difficulty. *Journal of Experimental Psychology: Learning, Memory, and Cognition, 12*, 279–287.

Neuberg, S. L. (1988). Behavioral implications of information presented outside of conscious awareness: The effect of subliminal presentation of trait information on behavior in the prisoner's dilemma game. *Social Cognition, 6*, 207–230.

Neumann, E., & DeSchepper, B. G. (1992). An inhibition-based fan effect: Evidence for an active suppression mechanism in selective attention. *Canadian Journal of Psychology, 46*, 1–40.

Newcomb, T. M. (1961). *The acquaintance process*. New York: Holt, Rinehart and Winston.

Niedenthal, P. M., & Cantor, N. (1986). Affective responses as guides to category-based influences. *Motivation and Emotion, 10*, 505–527.

Piaget, J. (1946). *La information du symbole chez l'enfant*. Paris: Delachaux & Niestlé.

Powers, W. T. (1973). *Behavior: The control of perception*. Chicago: Aldine.

Prinz, W. (1990). A common coding approach to perception and action. In O. Neumann & W. Prinz (Eds.), *Relationships between perception and action* (pp. 167–201). Berlin, Germany: Springer-Verlag.

Rosch, E., & Mervis, C. (1975). Family resemblances: Studies in the internal structure of categories. *Cognitive Psychology, 7*, 573–605.

Sanders, G. S. (1981). Driven by distraction: An integrative review of social facilitation theory and research. *Journal of Experimental Social Psychology, 13*, 303–314.

Schank, R. C., & Abelson, R. P. (1977). *Scripts, plans, goals, and understanding*. Hillsdale, NJ: Erlbaum.

Smeets, J. B. J., & Brenner, E. (1995). Perception and action are based on the same visual information: Distinction between position and velocity. *Journal of Experimental psychology: Human Perception and Performance, 21*, 19–31.

Snyder, M., Tanke, E. D., & Berscheid, E. (1977). Social perception and interpersonal behavior: On the self-fulfilling nature of social stereotypes. *Journal of Personality and Social Psychology, 35*, 656–666.

Srull, T. K., & Wyer, R. S., Jr. (1979). The role of category accessibility in the interpretation of information about persons: Some determinants and implications. *Journal of Personality and Social Psychology, 37*, 1660–1672.

Srull, T. K., & Wyer, R. S., Jr. (1980). Category accessibility and social perception: Some implications for the study of person memory and interpersonal judgments. *Journal of Personality and Social Psychology, 38*, 841–856.

Stangor, C., & Lange, J. E. (1994). Mental representations of social groups: Advances in understanding stereotypes and stereotyping. *Advances in Experimental Social Psychology, 26*, 357–416.

Trivial Pursuit (Triviant). (1984/1987). *Tweede Genus editie* (2nd ed.). Hastings, England: Horn Abbott International.

Underwood, B. J. (1966). Individual and group predictions of item difficulty for free learning. *Journal of Experimental Psychology, 71*, 673–679.

Vallacher, R. R. (1993). Mental calibration: Forging a working relationship between mind and action. In D. M. Wegner & J. W. Pennebaker (Eds.), *Handbook of mental control* (pp. 443–472). Englewood Cliffs, NJ: Prentice Hall.

Vallacher, R. R., & Wegner, D. M. (1985). *A theory of action identification*. Hillsdale, NJ: Erlbaum.

Vallacher, R. R., & Wegner, D. M. (1987). What do people think they're doing? Action identification and human behavior. *Psychological Review, 94*, 3–15.

Wegner, D. M., & Vallacher, R. R. (1987). The trouble with action. *Social Cognition, 5*, 179–190.

Winter, L., & Uleman, J. S. (1984). When are social judgments made? Evidence for the spontaneousness of trait inferences. *Journal of Personality and Social Psychology, 47*, 237–252.

Winter, L., Uleman, J. S., & Cunnif, C. (1985). How automatic are social judgments? *Journal of Personality and Social Psychology, 49*, 904–917.

Zajonc, R. B. (1965). Social facilitation. *Science, 149*, 269–278.

Received March 22, 1996
Revision received May 15, 1997
Accepted June 9, 1997 ■

PART 5

Dispositional and Attributional Inferences

Introduction and Preview

At several points in this book we have seen examples whereby perceivers go beyond the information available to them in meaningful ways, thereby guiding and shaping the nature of the ultimate perception. Perceivers use the available information in order to elaborate on their comprehension of what they have observed in their social environment, they impose some interpretation on the information, and they form evaluative reactions to it. These processes can result in biases in the way perceivers come to understand the world around them, but at the same time these processes facilitate comprehension, understanding, and adaptation.

In Part 5 we look more closely at some additional processes by which perceivers expand on the information they are processing. Specifically, they take some piece of information — someone's behavior, or spoken word, or facial expression — and from that observation they make *inferences* about the person. That is, we are not content to simply record in our minds the events that transpire around us and in which we participate. We are inclined to understand those events by making inferences about the persons who engage in those behaviors.

Why would we engage in this process? Why do we want to understand events in terms of the dispositional qualities of the people involved? Wouldn't this process lead us (at least sometimes) to make inferential errors, and hence to be wrong in our perceptions? If so, when does that happen, and why? These questions have intrigued social psychologists for many years and have generated some fascinating and very informative research. The readings in Part 5 are concerned with the nature and functioning of those inference processes.

The first reading in Part 5 is taken from an important book by Fritz Heider (1958), whose ideas stimulated a great deal of research on these topics for many years. Heider was interested in the "naïve psychology" of the everyday person. He viewed people as "intuitive theorists" (Ross, 1977) who try to understand the regularities in the behaviors of others and of themselves. The perceiver is motivated to understand these regularities in order to increase his or her ability to predict the future, to anticipate the behavior of others with whom he interacts. Why would the perceiver be so motivated? Why would she spend her time and mental energy trying to understand such things? The answer is compellingly simple. If she can accurately predict how others will act, then she can increase the effectiveness of her future interactions by guiding her own behavior accordingly. Hence, Heider analyzed the ways people would seek and identify stabilities in people's behaviors (as well as stabilities in the environment). He noted that perceivers make inferences about people's abilities ("can") and about their motives ("want"), and in doing so, they seek to identify the bases of stability and regularity that govern people's behaviors. The readings in Part 5 illustrate two kinds of inference processes that occur frequently and normally in social perception: dispositional inferences and attributional inferences.

Dispositional inferences occur when the perceiver uses what she sees and knows about a person to infer something about the person's underlying characteristics, such as personality traits, motives, attitudes, or intentions (Gilbert & Malone, 1995; Jones, 1990). In the words of Jones and Davis (1965), the perceiver moves "from acts to dispositions." Sometimes this step might be a conscious

activity, as when friends compare their impressions of the attributes of someone they know. At other times, these dispositional inferences are made spontaneously, without conscious thought or intention. The research reported in Reading 18 by Winter and Uleman (1984) showed that such inferences can be made in tasks where people are not purposefully forming impressions or thinking about other people. Their participants thought they were taking part in a study on memory for verbal descriptions of behavior, so nothing in the instructions mentioned anything about traits, impressions, or the like. In the study participants read a series of sentences, each of which described a behavior performed by a person. Later their memory for the information they read was assessed using a cued recall procedure, in which cue words were presented as aids to recall. Winter and Uleman (1984) found that if the cue word was a trait that was implied by the actor's behavior, then it increased the likelihood of recalling the sentence. The interpretation is that participants, when they first read the behavior-descriptive sentences, spontaneously inferred a disposition that characterized the actor. Having inferred that disposition while encoding the behavioral information, that trait word became associated with the stimulus sentence as it was stored in memory. As a consequence, that trait word could later serve as a useful retrieval cue to aid recalling the sentence. So, for example, upon learning that Tom made a large donation to charity, you might spontaneously infer that Tom is generous person, and his inferred quality of being "generous" is then stored in memory with your representation of his charitable act. Later, the word "generous" then cues recall of the behavior itself.

The Winter and Uleman reading stimulated a lot of research investigating the extent to which, and when, people make spontaneous dispositional inferences in course of comprehending social behavior (Carlston &

Skowronski, 1994; Uleman, Newman, & Moskowitz, 1996). One implication of this work is that people seem to be "locked in" to making such inferences. If so, then their perceptions of others would be heavily guided by the dispositional characteristics they infer. Moreover, if this process often happens without prior intention, without giving it much thought, then perceptions of others might be biased by such inferences. Reading 19 by Gilbert, Pelham, and Krull (1988) addresses this question. Their participants watched a videotape, with sound turned off, of a woman conversing with another person about several topics, which were identified by subtitles at the bottom of the screen. The woman appeared to be very anxious, moving in a fidgety manner. For some participants, the topic subtitles indicated that she was discussing very personal and private matters, the kinds of things most people would be nervous talking about; for other participants the topics were innocuous and presumably would not generate anxiety. In addition, half of the participants in each of these conditions were given a second task to perform at the same time, namely, to remember the list of topics being discussed, as shown in the subtitles. After viewing the tape, participants were asked to rate the extent to which they thought the woman is a nervous sort of person who is often uncomfortable in social situations. Their results showed that dispositional inferences were made quickly and easily, but that they could be "corrected" by information considered after the inference has been made. However, whereas the initial inference occurs spontaneously, that correction process requires cognitive resources. When those resources are consumed by another task (i.e., those participants who also had to remember the list of topics discussed), the correction process did not occur and the woman was seen as being a very anxious type of person. Thus, dispositional inferences are made spontaneously, without conscious thought or intention, as part of the process of comprehending social

behavior. However, those initial inferences can be corrected or adjusted in light of relevant information — if the perceiver is not distracted or consumed by other simultaneous tasks or activities. The problem, of course, is that in everyday life we often are busy and distracted by other demands on our time and cognitive resources, so the correction will not always occur, even when it should.

Heider's writings drew particular attention to a specific kind of inference, namely, *attributional inferences*. Whereas a dispositional inference about an actor might be spontaneously drawn from that person's behavior, sometimes we make inferences specifically aimed at explaining *why* the person engaged in that behavior. An important part of Header's naïve psychology concerned how the everyday person comes to understand the causes that govern the behaviors he observes. He made an important distinction concerning the perceived *locus of causation*. Specifically, Heider pointed out that some causes are inside the person — *internal* causes, such as personality traits, motives, attitudes, intentions — and some causes are outside the person — *external* causes, such as social pressure, situational constraints and demands, social obligations. As I discussed in the Introductory Overview, several prominent theories were developed in an effort to elucidate, in more detail, the cognitive mechanisms by which perceivers arrive at internal vs external attributions. Those attribution theories have generated an enormous amount of research (for reviews, see Fiske & Taylor, 1991; Jones, 1990; Ross, 1977; Smith, 1994).

One common finding in that research literature was that people are biased towards making internal attributions for people's behavior. That is, perceivers tend to "see" other's behaviors as being caused by their personality or other dispositional characteristics, and they seem remarkably immune from recognizing the power of situational factors that might influence, if not determine, what one does in a particular situation. This tendency has been so pervasively observed in many studies that Ross (1977) referred to it as the *fundamental attribution error*. Reading 20 by Ross, Amabile, and Steinmetz (1977) illustrates this bias well. Participants played a quiz game in which one participant was to ask difficult and challenging questions to the other participant, who had to try to answer these questions. The goal was to stump the respondent if one could. And of course, one easily could do so. Why were the questioners so successful? One simple reason: the questioner was at a considerable advantage. He could ask any question he wanted, he of course tried to generate questions from areas of knowledge where he knew a lot but would suspect that most others knew less, etc. And of course, the respondent had considerable difficulty in answering those questions. Subsequently, both the participants and observers of the game rated the questioner as being much more knowledgeable than the respondent is. What these raters — both the participants and the observers alike — failed to recognize was the extent to which the structure of the game essentially determined the outcome (external causation). Instead, they made differing dispositional attributions (internal causation) about the two participants (the questioner performed well because he is very smart; the answerer performed poorly because he is less knowledgeable). They *explained* the outcome by attributing it to internal qualities of the participants, but were oblivious to the external constraints (rules of the game) that essentially determined that outcome.

But how pervasive is this bias? Although it has been called the "fundamental" attribution error, and although some have viewed it as nearly universal, it may be that this bias is culture-bound and is pervasive primarily in Western societies. In earlier parts of this book we have developed the view that Eastern and Western cultures differ in the way they construe the social world, and they do so in ways that have clear implications for perceptions of causality. In Western societies the individual person is seen to be the unit of analysis, the locus of causation, the origin of one's behavior. It naturally follows that perceivers would "explain" the person's behavior in terms of his or her internal attributes — traits, motives, goals, attitudes. In contrast, in Eastern societies the individual is seen to be a part of a larger social unit (family, friends, co-workers, nation), and the individual's behavior is perceived to be much more responsive to the influence of those groups than as emanating from the person's unique personal attributes.

Reading 21 by Menon, Morris, Chiu, and Hong (1999) develops and tests this possibility in interesting ways. In three studies they showed a consistent tendency on the part of American students to attribute the cause of behavior to the individual agent involved in the setting. In contrast, students in Hong Kong showed a different pattern, manifested in two different but related ways. In the first two studies the individual's actions, rather than being attributed to that person's own agency, were attributed to the influence of the group of which that person is a part. These results are consistent with the collectivist tendency to construe the individual as part of a larger entity that holds some responsibility for his or her behavior. The third study extended this pattern and showed that Hong Kong students attributed the individual's actions to external, situational causes to a much greater extent than did American students, who again referred to individual dispositional causes. In sum, Menon et al.'s (1999) findings show that some of our basic tendencies to infer the causes for behavior may take different form in cultures that subscribe to different underlying views of human nature and different conceptions of causality.

Discussion Questions

1. In what ways are dispositional inferences and attributional inferences similar and in what ways do they differ?
2. Describe two examples of studies that demonstrated that perceivers tend to perceive actors' behaviors as reflecting their inner dispositions (even when that inference is not warranted).
3. How does the characterization-correction model presented in the article by Gilbert, Pelham, and Krull (Reading 19) relate to the anchoring-and-adjustment heuristic described by Tversky and Kahneman (Reading 10)?
4. Summarize the cultural differences in the perception of causal agency were found in studies by Menon, Morris, Chiu, and Hong.

Suggested Readings

Beike, D. R., & Sherman, S. J. (1994). Social inference: Inductions, deductions, and analogies. In R. S. Wyer, Jr & T. K. Srull (Eds.), *Handbook of social cognition* (2nd ed., Vol. 1, pp. 209–285). Hillsdale, NJ: Erlbaum.

Jones, E. E. (1990). *Interpersonal perception*. New York: McMillan.

Gilbert, D. T., & Malone, P. S. (1995). The correspondence bias. *Psychological Bulletin*, 117, 21–38.

Hamilton, D. L. (1998). Dispositional and attributional inferences in person perception. In J. M. Darley & J. Cooper (Eds.), *Attribution and social interaction: The legacy of Edward E. Jones* (pp. 99–114).Washington, D.C.: American Psychological Association

Sherman, S. J., Crawford, M., Hamilton, D. L., & Garcia-Marques, L. (2003). Social inference and social memory: The interplay between systems. In M. A. Hogg & J. Cooper (Eds.), *Sage handbook of social psychology* (pp. 65–86). London: Sage.

Malle, B. F. (2004). *How the mind explains behavior: Folk explanations, meaning, and social interaction*. Cambridge, MA: MIT Press.

The Naïve Analysis of Action

Fritz Heider

In this chapter we shall be concerned with the actions of another person, in particular with the basic constituents of an action sequence which lead us to know that another person is trying to do something, intends to do something, has the ability to do something, etc. The concepts also apply to one's own actions, but our main emphasis will be on actions in interpersonal relations. We shall also explore the consequences of such cognition — how we utilize knowledge of the basic constituents of action in interpreting action and in predicting and controlling it. The concepts involved in the naive analysis of action stand, as we shall see, in systematic relations to each other just as do the terms of a good scientific system of concepts. Our task will be to formulate this system more explicitly.

This task requires a description of the causal nexus of an environment which contains not only the directly observable facts about the behavior of another person, but also their connection with the more stable structures and processes underlying that behavior. It is an important principle of common-sense psychology, as it is of scientific theory in general, that man grasps reality, and can predict and control it, by referring transient and variable behavior and events to relatively unchanging underlying conditions, the so-called dispositional properties of his world. This principle, already discussed in this book, will become increasingly familiar as we continue the investigation of common-sense psychology. It is time that we examined it more fully.

Editor's Note: Selected excerpts from the original article are reproduced here.

Dispositional Properties

The Nature of and Search for Dispositional Properties

The term dispositional properties is applied to those properties that "dispose" objects and events to manifest themselves in certain ways under certain conditions. Dispositional properties are the invariances that make possible a more or less stable, predictable, and controllable world. They refer to the relatively unchanging structures and processes that characterize or underlie phenomena.

Instances of relatively unchanging structures are such object properties as color and size, such person properties as character and ability. We feel, for example, that John's good grades make sense when we refer his achievement, a relatively momentary event, to his high intelligence, a more or less permanent property, and we then believe we are safe in predicting a successful college career. But static structures are not the only ones that can serve as reference points for understanding. Processes may also provide a basis for understanding as long as they show relatively constant coordination to changes in underlying structures or to other processes. For example, "practice makes perfect" is satisfying as an explanatory principle insofar as the process of repetition is felt to be highly coordinated to skill.

The causal structure of the environment, both as the scientist describes it and as the naive person apprehends it, is such that we are usually in contact only with what may be called the offshoots or manifestations of underlying core-processes or core-structures. For example, if

I find sand on my desk, I shall want to find out the underlying reason for this circumstance. I make this inquiry not because of idle curiosity, but because only if I refer this relatively insignificant offshoot event to an underlying core event will I attain a stable environment and have the possibility of controlling it. Should I find that the sand comes from a crack in the ceiling and that this crack appeared because of the weakness in one of the walls, then I have reached the layer of underlying conditions which is of vital importance for me. The sand on my desk is merely a symptom, a manifestation that remains ambiguous until it becomes anchored to dispositional properties — cracks and stresses in this case.

The Depth Dimension of the Invariances

The search for relatively enduring aspects of our world, the dispositional properties in nature, may carry us quite far from the immediate facts or they may end hardly a step from them. That is, there exists a hierarchy of cognitive awarenesses which begin with the more stimulus-bound recognition of "facts," and gradually go deeper into the underlying causes of these facts. What is called "fact" here is similar to what Ichheiser (1949) calls the "raw material" of social perception: "Let us call those data which are interpreted and misinterpreted by mechanisms of social perception the 'raw material' of social perception" (p. 12). The raw material is the stuff, so to speak, of which the organism forms a conclusion. Thus, in the hierarchy of cognitive awareness, each previous layer stands to the succeeding one in the relation of raw material to interpretation.

For a concrete illustration, let us assume that a person, p, is confronted with an agreeable, happy experience, x. This is the raw material at a level close to the peripheral stimulus. The next step of interpretation may be: What is the immediate source of x? Is it chance? Am I the cause of it? Or is another person, o, the cause? If o is accepted as cause, the question of motive or intention may well arise. Did he do it in order to please me, or was the event only an accidental by-product of a different goal? Perhaps he was ordered to help me, perhaps he did it to put me under an obligation to him, or to relieve his conscience, or to please someone else. But if p perceives o as really wanting to please him, there are still deeper layers of interpretation possible. The need "o wants to please p" may be caused by temporary goodwill in o; it may be "displaced love"; or it may come from a more permanent sentiment that o feels toward p. Finally, the underlying attitude itself may be

traced to further sources. For example, p may feel that o's attitude toward him is a function of o's personality, that o is a kind person. Or, p may feel that the sentiment stems from the compatibility in their natures, etc.

Underscoring the main points of this illustration, we note first, that man is usually not content simply to register the observables that surround him; he needs to refer them as far as possible to the invariances of his environment. Second, the underlying causes of events, especially the motives of other persons, are the invariances of the environment that are relevant to him; they give meaning to what he experiences and it is these meanings that are recorded in his life space, and are precipitated as the reality of the environment to which he then reacts.

As applied to the actions of another person, the depth dimension of relevant invariances is often of the following order: There is first the raw material which provides the information that change x occurs or has occurred and that o causes or has caused x (though this can already be a further level of interpretation). Then, further meaning is given to these facts when, relating them to certain dispositional properties of the person and of the environment, we conclude that o can do x, o wants to do x, o is trying to do x, o likes to do x, etc. These conclusions become the recorded reality for us, so much so that most typically they are not experienced as interpretations at all. We shall now investigate certain features surrounding the actions of another person which lead us to penetrate the depth dimension of the invariances and precipitate into reality the meaning of actions.

Effective Forces of the Person and Environment in the Action Outcome

In common-sense psychology (as in scientific psychology) the result of an action is felt to depend on two sets of conditions, namely factors within the person and factors within the environment. Naive psychology also has different terms to express the contributions of these factors. Consider the example of a person rowing a boat across a lake. The following is but a sample of expressions used to refer to factors that are significant to the action outcome. We say, "He is *trying* to row the boat across the lake," "He has the *ability* to row the boat across the lake," "He *can* row the boat across the lake," "He *wants* to row the boat across the lake," "It is *difficult* to row the boat across the lake," "Today there is a good *opportunity* for him to row the boat across the lake," "It is sheer *luck* that he succeeded in rowing the boat across the lake." These varying descriptive statements have reference to personal factors on the one hand and to environmental factors on the other. One may speak of the effective force (*ff*) of the person or of the environment when one means the totality of forces emanating from one or the other source.

The action outcome, *x*, may then be said to be dependent upon a combination of effective personal force and effective environmental force, thus:

$$x = f\,(\mathit{ff}\,\text{person},\,\mathit{ff}\,\text{environment})$$

One is tempted to formulate the underlying relation between the two independent variables as an additive one, for if the effective environmental force is zero (which would mean that the combination of environmental factors neither hinders nor furthers the result *x*), then *x* will depend only on the effective personal force. One would also have to assume that *x* would occur without any personal intervention if the effective environmental force were greater than zero (that is if those environmental factors favorable to *x* were greater than those unfavorable to *x*). This would be the case if the wind carried the boat safely to shore while the rower was asleep.

The effective personal force is also analyzed into two contributing factors: A power factor and a motivational factor. We shall have more to say about these components in the course of our discussion, but here let it suffice to point out that the power factor is often represented by ability; there are other characteristics of a person that affect his power, temperament for example, but ability is commonly felt to head the list. The motivational factor refers to what a person is trying to do (his intention) and how hard he is trying to do it (exertion). The contribution of the rower to the outcome *x*, therefore, depends on his ability to maneuver the boat and on how hard he tries to accomplish the goal.

Thus, the schema that is used is the following:

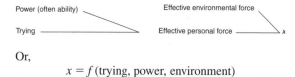

Or,

$$x = f\,(\text{trying, power, environment})$$

The personal constituents, namely power and trying, are related as a multiplicative combination, since the effective personal force is zero if either of them is zero. For instance, if a person has the ability but does not try at all he will make no progress toward the goal.

The personal and environmental contributions to action do not have the same status. The effective personal force shows the traits of personal causality (see

later, pp. 100 ff.); it is truly directed toward the goal in the sense that this direction is an invariant characteristic of the force, invariant to the changing circumstances. When we talk of direction toward or away from the goal in regard to impersonal environmental forces, we are using the term in a different sense. Notice that in the above schema, "trying" was not given as a constituent of the effective environmental force. The wind has the direction of furthering or hindering the progress of the boat only accidentally. It is not "trying" or "exerting itself" to produce a certain state of affairs. Only when we think of the wind in an anthropomorphic way would we say: "It could hold up the boat if it only tried hard enough."

Whether a person tries to do something and whether he has the requisite abilities to accomplish it are so significantly different in the affairs of everyday life that naive psychology has demarcated those factors still further by regrouping the constituents of action in such a way that the power factor and the effective environmental force are combined into the concept "can," leaving the motivational factor clearly separate and distinct. The conceptual groupings may be indicated as follows:

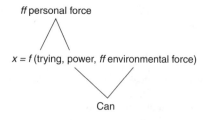

Our plan is first to examine the concept of can, to discuss the properties and conditions underlying its power and environmental components and end with an analysis of the concept of "try" in action.

The Concept of Can

Dispositional Character of Can

Can generally, though not exclusively, is a dispositional concept, which means that it refers to a relatively stable relationship between the person and the environment. As a dispositional concept it allows the person to ask and answer such questions as, "Will I be able to do the task again?" "Will other people be able to do it as well?" Temporary factors that affect an action outcome are generally ascribed to luck or to transitory personal states such as fatigue rather than to the "can." Thus, if I accidentally hit the bull's eye, I will not feel that I can hit it in the sense of being able to hit it again should I try. I was just lucky.

Sometimes, however, can is used to represent temporary relations between person and environment. We say, "I can't do it now because I am too tired." Or we say, "He can swim the channel when the weather conditions are just right." Notice, however, that the temporary factors, fatigue in the first case and opportunity in the second, are explicitly indicated as disrupting the usual state of affairs obtaining between the powers of the person and the environmental situation.

Can and Try as Conditions of the Outcome

It will be helpful to restate the basic constituents of can and the position of can in the action outcome:

Thus, all the relatively permanent factors that influence the effect but are not ascribed to the motivational factor — that is, the "trying" of the person — are lumped together and become the factor of "can." If a person can do something and he tries to do it, then he will do it (barring temporary circumstances). Common expressions are: "He could do it if he only tried," "He tries very hard but he just cannot do it," or "I will do it as soon as I can."

Ichheiser (1933) says that the experience of "I can" is a knowledge that one is able to reach a goal or to produce an effect if one only wills it. This hypothetical clause, "if one only wills it," i.e., if one only really tries, if one exerts all one's powers, is important. If one tries one's best to produce an effect, and one can produce it, then the effect will come about (excluding, of course, cases of "bad luck"). Both "p tries to cause x" and "p can cause x" are conceived of as conditions of "p causes x." Both are necessary but neither is sufficient.

Relating the roles of "can" and "try" in the action outcome to the effective forces of the person and of the environment, we can state the following: When we say: "He can do it, but fails only because he does not try sufficiently" then we mean that the effective personal force is smaller than the restraining environmental force only because the exertion is not great enough; with greater exertion he would succeed. The concept "can" means that if a person tries to do x, no environmental force away from

x is likely to arise that would be greater in its resultant effects than the effective personal force of p toward x.

Constituents of Can

As already noted, can refers to the relation between the power or ability of the person and the strength of the environmental forces. The relationship might be further specified as:

$$\text{can} = f\,(\text{power, ability} - \text{difficulty of environmental factors})$$

If the task is easy, then even a person with little ability can do it; if it is difficult, the person cannot do it unless he has greater ability. Or, we may say, if a person succeeds, then his ability must be greater than the environmental difficulty; if he fails (and has maximally exerted himself), his ability must be less than the environmental difficulty. We see, therefore, that though "can" is a function of ability or power, it is not identical with it.

To avoid possible confusion, we wish to make explicit that the term power is used not only to express a meaning different from can. In ordinary conversation, the sentence "p has the power to do x" is often used as identical in meaning to the sentence "p can do x." In our formulation, however, "can" refers to a relation between the person and the environment; the nonmotivational factors contributed by the person are encompassed by the generic term, power. Yet, in some places in the discussion that follows, it will be seen that we have used power and can more or less interchangeably. This occurs when, to all intents and purposes, the environmental factors can be disregarded. Furthermore, our use of power differs from the topological one in which power is restricted to social power, that is to the case "p can cause o to do something."

The Cognition of Can Through Action

The most direct recognition that p can do something is given by his actual behavior. If he causes a change in the environment, we conclude that he can cause this change. Ichheiser (1933) has also pointed out that we get to know what we can do through realization, i.e., by transforming the potential can into real action. In reality testing or testing the limits, a person may attempt a task in order to learn just what he can and cannot do, or what he may do without suffering negative consequences. On the other hand, if a person only talks about effecting a change in the environment, that is if he only expresses his intention of doing something, then we may attribute the absence of the action effect to the absence of the can, one of the necessary conditions of action. A person who only threatens harm but does not execute his threat is judged feeble; the one who carries out the threat, strong. In the first case it is concluded that the person cannot harm me, in the second case that he can. "Actions speak louder than words" is an expression not only applying to intentions, but also applying to abilities.

However, action outcome as the criterion for the determination of can is sometimes misleading. A person's failure is often seen as proving that the task is too difficult or that he lacks the requisite ability, i.e., can factors, when actually motivational factors are mainly responsible. Or a particular success, when a matter of luck, may sometimes be erroneously ascribed to can. The boy who accidentally hits the bull's eye may feel that he is a good marksman.

As we shall see later, in addition to the perceptual data given by the outcome of an action, there are other bases for believing that a person can or cannot do something. Not all of these are equally reliable. For example, a strong need may lead to an unjustified belief that one is able to do something. Factors that indirectly influence beliefs about can will be considered in the following sections which deal with the personal and environmental properties significant in can.

As with most psychological phenomena, what a person can do is not always apprehended in consciousness. As Stern (1935) has suggested, much of the time "can" exists as a background, like a mental set (pp. 570 ff.). We walk, recount events and digest food without at the same time having a conscious experience that we can do these things. However, when what one can do becomes problematic, then we tend to think about it and become aware of it. The question of what can and cannot be accomplished with an arm prosthesis is in the foreground when a person is being fitted with it for the first time. The insecure swimmer will wonder whether he can swim the lake when he is put to the test. The confident student is sure that he can solve the equation when challenged by another. Questioning, wondering about, and knowing the can are all conscious experiences of can. But the can that does not penetrate into our consciousness also belongs to the explication of the concept of can.

In the events of everyday life, we are interested not only in what people can do. We want to know whether what a person can do is primarily due to his own characteristics, his abilities for example, or primarily due to favorable environmental conditions. Such knowledge enables the person to profit from experience as well as

to influence the outcome of actions involving other people. Let us suppose that the speeches of a certain politician were poorly received. He might ascribe the failure to the shortcomings of the speeches, that is, to his own creations and therefore to himself: They were too rough, too highbrow, too emotional, too general, or too factual. He might ascribe the failure to his appearance or to the fact that he was not enough of a regular guy, or that he got stage fright. On the other hand, the source of the failure might be placed outside himself, on the audience, for example. He might feel that it was too primitive, that it fell only for slogans, or was too prejudiced. He might attribute the failure to the physical setting: The acoustics were poor, it was too cold, the seats were uncomfortable. In any case, he would then try to avoid that to which he attributes his failure and strengthen that to which he attributes success. The learning, of course, may be based on the experience of others. If the politician sees another man succeed or fail, he will try to imitate that to which he attributes the success and avoid that to which he attributes the failure.

Attribution, the linking of an event with its underlying conditions, involves a kind of unit formation. In the case of "can" a unit is formed between the possibility of success or failure and person or environment. If the success "belongs" to the person, then the person is felt to be responsible for it; if it belongs to the environment, then the environment is held accountable. Therefore, though "can" is a resultant of two contributing sources, it is sometimes ascribed more to the person and sometimes more to the environment. We shall now inquire into the conditions of attribution to one or the other source and also examine further the properties of the person and of the environment that are important in can.*

Difficulty — an Important Dispositional Property of the Environment

Often, as we have just seen, the success or failure of an action provides the raw material for the perception of "can." If a person successfully completes an action, we say, "He can do it" but the implications are very different if we conclude "He can do it because it is so easy" or

---

* In the sectional headings below, sometimes "power", sometimes "environment," and sometimes "can" appears. Where the factors under consideration apply more or less clearly to one of the components of can, namely power or environment, the corresponding term designates the section. Where, however, ambiguity as to attribution exists, or where "can" as such is being emphasized, then "can" is used.

"He can do it because he has such great ability." In both instances the personal force is permanently greater than the environmental force but in one case the reason is that the environmental force is small and in the other case that the personal force is great. That is, the superiority of the personal force is attributed either to the person or to the environment.

An important basis for such attribution is the following. If we know that only one person succeeded or only one person failed out of a large number in a certain endeavor, then we shall ascribe success or failure to this person — to his great ability or to his lack of ability. On the other hand, if we know that practically everyone who tries succeeds, we shall attribute the success to the task. The task is then described as being easy. If hardly anyone succeeds it is felt to be difficult.

Sometimes the knowledge concerning group performance and the appraisal of task difficulty is inferred from the performance of a single individual. If a child, for example, successfully bakes a cake or reads a book, we conclude that the recipe or book was easy. In effect we have made use of the postulates linking can with power and environmental difficulty: (1) Since success has occurred, the task difficulty must be smaller than the ability. (2) Since a child has effected the success, we presume that the ability is low. (3) Therefore, we conclude that the task is easy and that most adults would be able to accomplish it.

Exertion, often, is the dominant clue for inferring task difficulty. When we see a person performing a skilled act, like dancing or diving or playing a musical instrument with elegance and ease, we may well feel that the task is probably not so hard after all. Only our rational knowledge about "what it takes" checks us from this tempting conclusion; we modify our interpretation and say, "It looks so easy." The high pressure salesman effortlessly demonstrates a new gadget in order to convince a gullible public of the simplicity of the operation, when in reality considerable skill may be required. As for self-exertion, if I find that I can do something with little effort, I am likely to judge that the task is easy unless I think I have special ability. If it takes considerable application, then I judge it to be difficult. But unless I place my ability in the framework of others' I will not be able legitimately to predict how another will fare with the same task.

The unit forming character of attribution is clearly seen in judgments concerning task difficulty. If p is the only person who can do a certain act, or if there are only a few other people who can do it, then the task is difficult and the action belongs in a peculiar way to p. A strong unit

between the possibility of success in this action and p is formed. If, however, the task is felt to be so easy that anyone could do it, then the possibility of the action lies in the environment. Difficulty is one of the important properties assigned to the environmental side of the can complex; it is invariably connected with an object or situation. Even so, there is an implied relation to a person acting. When we say "this is an impossible task," we do not merely mean "it is impossible that this happens." The meaning most important for us is that "If any person tries to do this he is bound to fail," or "No matter how hard I try, I cannot succeed."

Finally, difficulty has a dispositional quality (cf. pp. 80–82). Referring to a permanent characteristic of the task helps us predict the action outcome on future occasions.

Opportunity and Luck — The More Variable Environmental Factors

As stated before, man is interested in the invariances of the environment and of the person so he can establish himself in a stable world in which the future can be anticipated and controlled. It is therefore important that a person "diagnose" the temporary conditions that disturb the more permanent coordination between outcome and the dispositional properties of the task and person.

On the environmental side two terms are commonly used to designate the more temporary states. One of these is opportunity. Another is luck. If the strength and direction of the environmental factors fluctuate, the person may wait until they are optional for reaching his goal; i.e., he waits for a good opportunity to do x. Likewise, a person is felt to succeed because he is lucky when the resultant environmental force in the direction of the goal is at a maximum, or when the force away from it is at a minimum. Thus, when the success is attributed to luck or opportunity, two things are implied: First, that environmental conditions, rather than the person, are primarily responsible for the outcome, and second, that these environmental conditions are the product of chance; at least this is true for "luck."

As with difficulty, there is a diversity of conditions that lead to the cognition of luck. One of these is consistency, or conversely, variability, of performance. If a person succeeds only once in a great number of trials we will attribute the success to luck, especially if it is followed by a number of failures so it cannot be interpreted as "He has learned it at last." If he fails only once and succeeds at other times, the failure is attributed to bad luck (sometimes temporary personal factors are held accountable). In line with the dispositional character of can, the unusual is attributed to luck and not to the permanent "can" constituents. Whyte (1943) reports that the members of the Norton Street gang judged a bowler not by his strikes — knocking down all the pins with the first ball — but by his ability to get spares, that is, to knock down the pins remaining after the first ball; the strike, a highly inconsistent occurrence, was considered merely a matter of chance (p. 17).

Drawing upon the more lasting properties of the person and environment for judgments concerning "can" serves in effect to make such judgments more realistic. If a person has failed consistently in 50 trials and then suddenly shows a success, it would be very unrealistic to change one's opinion about his ability or about the environmental difficulty: It is more realistic to attribute the success to chance.

Whether or not the outcome of an action is attributed to luck also depends upon our ideas concerning the person's abilities (again a dispositional property). For instance, if we have a very low opinion of a person's ability then any success will be attributed to luck.

The important point is that correct attribution, whether to the stable or to the vacillating conditions underlying an event, always serves to build up and support the constancy of our picture of the world. Naive psychology has therefore found it necessary to isolate those wavering, more fortuitous conditions that interfere with this constancy. Sometimes these conditions are designated luck; events that deviate from constancy are then relegated to good or bad luck depending upon whether or not they favor the person's fortunes. If action outcome is correctly made accountable, then future performance becomes more predictable.

Ability — a Main Power Factor

Thus far in the discussion, "power" as the personal contribution to "can," was represented by ability, and for good reason. First of all, ability is clearly a property of the person. Though environmental factors may augment or deplete ability, it describes the person and not the environment. Also, ability is a dispositional concept. It characterizes a person over time and therefore its use is in line with the general tendency to analyze experience in terms of underlying invariances. At the same time it is to be noted that certain facets of ability, for example, knowledge (knowledge is power), are less permanently an integral part of the person than others, as for example, intelligence or strength. We may become shockingly aware of how easily knowledge has been kept from us or with what facility we forget what we have learned. Last

but certainly not least, ability, both mental and physical, plays a frequent and significant role in determining a person's power. A person with strength and skill can row the boat farther than one less favorably equipped. A clever man can do more things than a stupid one.

Degree of ability, as has already been pointed out, is sometimes determined by relative standing in the group as measured by success and failure on particular tasks. If p is among the few people who can do a task, his ability is high; if he is among the few who fail, his ability is low.

The Contribution of Personality Traits and Attitudes to Power

Personality traits and attitudes are also personal factors that have an important bearing on what a person can do. Power is not merely a matter of physical and mental ability skills. It is also highly affected by attitudes of self-confidence, attitudes that assert, "I can do something worth while here. Thinking new thoughts and carrying out new activities belong to my space of free movement."

The feeling of one's power or lack of power on a particular task may be connected with a pervasive mood of competence in which one feels that one can do anything, or with a despondent mood in which one despairs of one's powers and abilities. Sometimes the feeling of personal power may encompass a philosophical view of the course of world events as a whole in which, at one extreme, one feels that the world can always be changed in such a way that it fits one better; or, at the other extreme, one may feel that one can do nothing, that one must remain at the mercy of imposed forces. Literature abounds with plots whose dramatic effect pivots around the world outlook of the superman and of the fatalist.

Many psychologists have stated that one can do more when one is confident, less if one mistrusts one's own power. The impact of personality traits is pointed up when a person with high ability is made powerless in a group because of his diffidence. Moreover, there is ample clinical evidence that even so stable a characteristic as a person's abilities may be grossly and permanently affected by attitudes of self-confidence. When a person's self-confidence is destroyed, his abilities may also be. He becomes the person he thinks he is.

Certainly a person's apparent self-confidence often influences our judgment of his abilities. The candidate who is sure of himself casts the most favorable light on his abilities. This may decide for which presidential aspirant we vote, which job applicant we hire. Naive psychology is so clear about these connections that the person himself, aware that manifest self-confidence often speaks for underlying abilities, may consciously feign this attitude as the core of his strategy.

Some Variable Personal Factors Affecting Power

Just as on the environmental side of the can matrix, vacillating, unpredictable chance events were set apart from the more consistent characteristics, so the less persistent power factors are recognized on the personal side. Fatigue and mood, for instance, represent for the most part temporary states, and unless they should persist, their effect on the power component of can is likely to be temporary also.

Since can tends to be used as a dispositional concept, when failure is attributed to fatigue, the conclusion is usually not drawn that the person cannot do the task. On the other hand, success, even when understood as due to a transitory positive state in the person, often leads to the conclusion that the person can do the task. As an illustration we may draw upon the performance of an alcoholic or psychotic who is able to hammer a nail, read a book, and so on only on a rare day of lucidity. We are led to feel that he can do these things even though there are few occasions when he can actually do them. It is as though we perceive the "real person" through his chronic alcoholic or psychotic state and coordinate the ability to this.

We have thus far attempted to make explicit the constituents of "can" as grasped by naive psychology and to point out some important factors that bear on them. The second essential component of action remains to be discussed, namely the motivational factor that becomes manifest in trying, the factor that propels and guides the action and gives it its purposive character. This is the feature par excellence that distinguishes instigation by a person from other "causes" of events. It is so central to the interpretation of actions that we shall introduce the analysis of trying by a rather full consideration of the difference between personal and impersonal causality.

Personal and Impersonal Causality

Intention, the Central Factor In Personal Causality

What we have designated as personal causality refers to instances in which p causes x intentionally. That is to say, the action is purposive. This has to be distinguished from other cases in which p is a part of the sequence of events. For example, p may cause x unintentionally merely because his physical or social being exerts some influence on the environment. He may cause a board on which he stands to break or he may act as a social stimulus for others. Sometimes the statement, "He did it" is really a short cut for "It was the weight of his body that caused the board to break." But unless intention ties together the cause–effect relations we do not have a case of true personal causality.

A more complicated case which is also excluded from personal causality occurs when p causes x because x is an unintended consequence of a change y which is intended; p may or may not be aware that y leads to x. For instance, p may acquire an object that o also desires. If the true goal of p is only to obtain the object, then the fact that this has negative consequences for o is not part of p's intention. Of course, the fact that the aftereffects of the action were not intended by the person does not mean that we can neglect them in the analysis of action, or that they are irrelevant for psychological processes. The person himself and other persons will react to these effects in a specific way which will derive precisely from the fact that they are not intended. A case in point is an outcome that is very injurious to the person and is the aftereffect of an action from which the person hoped to gain great benefits. This often produces the impression of tragic fate; that the person causes his own destruction is an element in many tragedies (Reardon, 1953).

True personal causality is restricted to instances where p tries to cause x, where x is his goal. This, by the way, does not exclude unconscious action; often, it is precisely because such action displays the features of personal causality as delineated below that inferences are drawn concerning unconscious motivations and unconscious goals. But cases of personal causality must be distinguished from effects involving persons but not intentions. The latter are more appropriately represented as cases of impersonal causality. They not only are different phenomenally from cases of purposive action, that is, in the way in which we experience them, but the causal nexus that links the person to the effect is also different. Consequently, to influence the outcome of an action in these cases one would have to change a different set of conditions.

The Causal Network in Personal and Impersonal Causality

When I am threatened by a danger from a nonpersonal source, all I usually need to do is change the conditions in order to escape the danger. If I am threatened by falling stones on a mountain, I can get out of the danger area and seek shelter. The stones will not change their paths in order to find me behind the shelter. If, however, a person wants to hit me with a stone and he can run faster than I can, I am exposed to the danger of being hit to a much greater degree and I have to use very different means in order not to be hit: I can hit him back and disable him before he has hit me, I can ask for mercy, or I can try to move in such a way that he will not know where I have gone.

In other words, if I meet a person who has certain intentions in regard to myself — for instance, who wants to get me into a certain state — that means that my environment contains conditions that are convergently directed towards this state, and if the person has enough power, this state will sooner or later be brought about whatever I do. In short, personal causality is characterized by equifinality, that is, the invariance of the end and variability of the means. Vicarious mediation with respect to an end point is an essential feature of the operational definition of purpose (Tolman, 1932; Brunswik, 1952).

Yet this is not the only characteristic of personal causality, for we must distinguish the equifinality in this case from that which sometimes occurs in physical systems, for instance, a system like a pendulum or a marble in a bowl which, in the end, will always come to rest at the lowest point regardless of where it started. In the inorganic world where a particular end state may be enforced, the forces leading to that unitary effect are not controlled by any part of the system. There is no power hierarchy, no leader-led distinction between the parts, and the process is understood in terms of the whole system. On the other hand, in the case of personal causality, the invariant end is due to the person. Because the person controls the causal lines emanating from himself, he not only is the initial source of the produced change, but he remains the persistent cause. Here, if anywhere, one can speak of a local cause, the second characteristic of the causal network in personal causality. Actually, within a wide range of environmental conditions, the person may be thought of as the one necessary and sufficient condition for the effect to occur, for within that wide range the person changes the means to achieve the end, the end itself remaining unaltered. However, equifinality is characteristic of personal causality only within certain limits, and these limits define what the person "can" do if he tries.

The Concept of Trying

Early in this chapter we noted that the outcome of an action, x, is commonly acknowledged to be a function of factors that reside in the environment and in the person. The effective personal force was dissected yet further and the constituents of action realigned in such a way that "p tries to cause x" and "p can cause x" became the two conditions of x. These conditions are almost always taken into account in considering the actions of other people. Both are necessary but neither of them is sufficient.

In the condition "p tries to do x" the factor of personal causality may be recognized. The local cause of the event x is the person. His trying is the central factor that controls the forces exerted on the environment to produce the equifinality. The condition "p can do x" points to the possibility of an action. The distinction between can and try is related to the distinction between learning and motivation in scientific psychology.

Intention and Exertion: The Constituents of Trying

"Trying" has a directional aspect and a quantitative aspect. In describing it we have to define first what p is trying to do, and second how hard he is trying to do it. The first aspect is usually called intention, the second exertion (Allport, 1947). In psychology they are often thought of as the direction and strength of motivation. As expressed in "trying" they make up the vectorial component of action.

The Conditions of Action and Personal Responsibility

It has already been stressed that intention is the central factor in personal causality, that it is the intention of a person that brings order into the wide variety of possible action sequences by coordinating them to final outcome. Therefore, if we are convinced that o did x intentionally we generally link the x more intimately with the person than if we think that o did x unintentionally. By the same token, if we account for an act by a person's stupidity or clumsiness, that is by ability factors we tend to hold him less responsible than if we take the act as an indication of his motives. Thus it is that the question of premeditation is important in the decisions regarding guilt.

Ability is also attributed to the person, but not in the same way as motivation. If a person tries to help but cannot, then it may not be considered his fault if he does not help. People are held responsible for their intentions and exertions but not so strictly for their abilities.

Moreover, as we have seen in the naive analysis of action, the change x is not always attributed to the person. Sometimes it is attributed luck, for example, or at least partly to such environmental factors as task difficulty. Personal responsibility then varies with the relative contribution of environmental factors to the action outcome; in general, the more they are felt to influence the action, the less the person is held responsible. One may consider the different forms in which the concept of responsibility has been used as successive stages in which attribution to the person decreases and attribution to the environment increases.

At the most primitive level the concept is a global one according to which the person is held responsible for each effect that is in any way connected with him or that seems in any way to belong to him. For example, a person may be accused of the presumed wrong doings of his church or his country for centuries back. Similarly, a person may be congratulated upon the victory of his school's football team.

At the next level anything that is caused by p is ascribed to him. Causation is understood in the sense that p was a necessary condition for the happening, even though he could not have foreseen the outcome however cautiously he had proceeded. Impersonal causality rather than personal causality as we have defined it, characterizes the judgment of responsibility at this level. In an "achievement ethics" the person is judged not according to his intention but according to the actual results of what he does.

Then comes the stage at which p is considered responsible, directly or indirectly, for any aftereffect that he might have foreseen even though it was not a part of his own goal and therefore still not a part of the framework of personal causality. For instance, p may be perceived as having done it because he was stupid, negligent, or morally that a wider field would exert were lacking. Thus, p may be accused of bringing harm to o, though this was not p's intention. That he was not deterred from pursuing his goal by the thought of harm to o is taken as a sign that he is ruthless, though not necessarily malicious. A nicer person would not have carried out the action. The moral restraining forces were lacking in p.

Next, only what p intended is perceived as having its source in him. This corresponds to what Piaget has called subjective responsibility and pertains to actions whose structure may be described by personal causality.

Finally there is the stage at which even p's own motives are not entirely ascribed to him but are seen as having their source in the environment. We may say about an action of p's, "It is not his fault that he behaves like that. He has been provoked." We mean by this that anybody would have felt and acted as he did under the circumstances. The causal lines leading to the final outcome are still guided by p, and therefore the act fits into the structure of personal causality, but since the source of the motive is felt to be the coercion of the environment and not p himself, responsibility for the act is at least shared by the environment. The criminal may blame the environment for his ill-fated career and thereby excuse himself. We view traitorous acts committed under duress differently from those that are premeditated. In extreme cases in which the act coerced by the environment does not fit the individual's personality organization, the behavior appears alien and the person is described by himself and others as "not being himself."

It will be recognized that the issue of responsibility includes the problem of attribution of action. That is, it is important which of the several conditions of action — the intentions of the person, personal power factors, or environmental forces — is to be given primary weight for the action outcome. Once such attribution has been decided upon the evaluation of responsibility is possible.

Cognition of Trying

The cognition of both intention and exertion has important bearing on our interpretation of action. We have seen, for instance, how the diagnosis of intention may affect the judgment of responsibility and the appraisal of ability. Above all, it is the goal of an action, its source in the intention of the person, that often determines what the person really is doing, or what really is happening. The situation is quite different, and carries different implications for the future, if something is done to me intentionally or accidentally. It is the difference between a stone accidentally hitting me and a stone aimed at me. The particular path the stone travels might be the same in both cases; still the events are very different because the movement of the stone is only a part of the whole event to which we react and which is of vital importance for us. The position of intention in the expectation and control of action has been elaborated in the main discussion of personal causality.

Less obvious, perhaps, is the fact that the cognition of exertion also may have important repercussions on the meaning of an act. For one thing, exertion circumscribes the degree of motivation or intention, that is, how much a person wants something. The cognition of exertion even helps differentiate genuine intention from the more superficial or less sincere variety. For instance, if a person gives up easily, we might conclude that he was not really interested. Or, if a benefit does not presuppose some self-sacrifice on the part of the benefactor, that is, if the necessary exertion was minimal, then the recipient may discount the benefit and feel little obligation to reciprocate. Exertion also, as has already been pointed out, may be taken as an indicator of both ability and intelligence. As a matter of fact, the most convincing raw material for the perception that "*o* cannot do it" is to see someone trying very hard and not succeeding.

Egocentric Cognition and Attribution in the Case of Can and Try

Sometimes the data make it very clear in the absence or failure of action, whether it is the "can" or the "try" that is the missing condition. But sometimes the data are sufficiently ambiguous so that the person's own needs or wishes determine the attribution.

An example of such egocentric attribution is the sour grapes fable. The fox pretends, or perhaps is even convinced, that he does not want the grapes rather than that he cannot get them. He attributes the failure to the "not want" (and the "not intend" and "not try") instead of the "not can," since in this case the former is neutral as far as his self-esteem is concerned, and the latter is damaging. Another example is the thief who, having no opportunity to steal, considers himself an honest man. In reality he does not steal because the condition "can" is lacking: He has had no opportunity. However, he attributes the not stealing to the fact that he has no intention to steal and is thereby able to claim credit for being law abiding. Examples of egocentric attribution to "cannot" are not hard to find. The child affirms that he cannot do the chore when in fact he does not wish to.

Finally, when a person wants to absolve himself of responsibility for the action outcome, he may find a good ally in fate. If neither of the personal contributions to action — namely, the ability factor in "can" and the intention in "try" — is manifestly suspect, he may blame the tricks or commands of fate for what he has done: He could not do otherwise.

Summary

We have attempted to show the complexities, the wisdom, and the failings of the naive psychology of action by making explicit what is not always phenomenally explicit. In the analysis, "can" and "trying" were shown to be the two necessary and sufficient conditions of purposive action. Each is analyzable into constituent elements: Can into personal power and environmental factors; trying into intention and exertion. The nature of dispositional properties as well as the meaning of

personal causality were singled out as being of special significance in the understanding of these concepts. Factors that influence the conditions of action and their constituents were also discussed.

The naive factor analysis of action permits man to give meaning to action, to influence the actions of others as well as of himself, and to predict future actions. The framework of the many examples in the chapter rests on the fact implicit in naive psychology that can and try are the conditions of action. Thus, our reactions will be different according to whether we think a person failed primarily because he lacked adequate ability or primarily because he did not want to carry out the action. In the first case, we will expect him to succeed as soon as the condition "can" is fulfilled. Moreover, we may bring this condition about by making the task easier, by removing obstacles, by teaching the person requisite skills, and so on. In the second case, however, we will not expect the person to perform the action even when such changes are realized.

Only by affecting the want is there a possibility of establishing the necessary condition, try. Consequently, the direction of our efforts will be quite different. We may attempt to convince the person that this is something he wants to do, we may highlight the positive features of the goal, or appeal to ethical considerations. In this case, the conditions of motivation become the focus. In addition to differences of expectation and control in the two cases, our value judgments may be quite different also. The person may be held far more responsible for the action outcome in the one case than in the other.

The above example seems obvious. But after all, our intention was to show the connections given by naive psychology that permit action and the interpretation of behavior in everyday interpersonal relations. At the same time, in delineating the "logic" of the naive analysis of action, we do not imply that the conclusions based thereon always fit objective reality. Sometimes, as we have seen, erroneous inferences are made when the conditions of action are only partially given or when egocentric influences distort cognition.

It is quite remarkable that the naive psychology of action works as well as it does and applies to such a wide range of cases involving action. It permits statements about the attribution of action, the cognition of its components, and the prediction and control of behavior. Similar functions were seen to emerge from the naive analysis of perception and in this area as well as that of action, man's meaningful association with his environment and control over it is thereby widened.

When Are Social Judgments Made? Evidence for the Spontaneousness of Trait Inferences

Laraine Winter and James S. Uleman

Do people make trait inferences, even without intentions or instructions, at the encoding stage of processing behavioral information? Tulving's encoding specificity paradigm (Tulving & Thomson, 1973) was adapted for two recall experiments. Under memory instructions only, subjects read sentences describing people performing actions that implied traits. Later, subjects recalled each sentence under one of three cuing conditions: (a) a dispositional cue (e.g., generous), (b) a strong, nondispositional semantic associate to an important sentence word; or (c) no cue. Recall was best when cued by the disposition words. Subjects were unaware of having made trait inferences. Interpreted in terms of encoding specificity, these results indicate that subjects unintentionally made trait inferences at encoding. This suggests that attributions may be made spontaneously, as part of the routine comprehension of social events.

Although research on social inferences has dominated social psychology for well over a decade, the lion's share of scientific attention has centered on inferences made in response to explicit instructions. But as several researchers have recently pointed out (Berscheid, Fraziano, Monson, & Dermer, 1976; Pyszczynski & Greenberg, 1981; Wong & Weiner, 1981), there is little research on whether and when such inferences occur spontaneously. This issue of whether and when social

inferences are initiated in the absence of investigators' instructions is important in its own right and has serious import for research in social cognition. The spontaneousness of these inferences largely determines their frequency outside the laboratory and is therefore crucial to any claim regarding their psychological importance.

Early researchers in person perception and impression formation (e.g., Asch, 1946; Tagiuri, 1958) expressed complete confidence that the phenomena they studied were not only spontaneous but pervasive and central to everyday psychological functioning. For example, Asch wrote in 1946,

> We look at a person and immediately a certain impression of his character forms itself in us. A glance, a few spoken words are sufficient to tell us a story about a highly complex matter. We know that such impressions form with remarkable rapidity and great ease. Subsequent observations may enrich or upset our first

We wish to thank John J. Winters, John Bargh, and two anonymous reviewers for their helpful criticisms of an earlier draft of this article, Bert Holland for his assistance with data analysis, and Frederick D. Miller for contributing to this work's earlier stages. This research was supported in part by National Institute of Mental Health Grant MH08573 to the first author.

Requests for reprints should be sent to James S. Uleman, Department of Psychology, New York University, 6 Washington Place, 7th Floor, New York, New York 10003.

view, but we can no more prevent its rapid growth than we can avoid perceiving a given visual object or hearing a melody. (Asch, 1946, p. 258).

In a marked contrast, more recent person perception research has at least implicitly characterized social judgments as deliberate, even laborious mental operations, performed under particular and unusual conditions. These conditions include having a mental set induced by experimental instruction (e.g., Enzle & Schopflocher, 1978) or a need to feel in control (e.g., Berscheid et al., 1976). Underlying this research is the assumption that making attributions is always a discrete mental operation, easily separable from other stages in the information-processing sequence, and that it is an optional stage that is engaged only under special circumstances (e.g., Pryor & Kriss, 1977, with regard to causal attributions). Indeed, authors who discuss person perception in terms of an explicit processing sequence (e.g., Schneider, Hastorf, & Ellsworth, 1979, chap. 1) commonly identify trait attributions as a relatively late stage, dependent on the outcome of several earlier operations performed on the behavioral information.

This characterization may have unwittingly arisen from the kinds of paradigms that attribution researchers have used most heavily. In these paradigms, subjects are presented with all the information necessary to make judgments and are instructed to carry out the specified mental operation. Clearly, an inference or trait attribution may occur deliberately, at the instigation of experimental instructions or with some other particular purpose in mind, or be based on previously encoded information that has been retrieved from memory. We wish to point out, however, that many researchers seem to have assumed that social judgments outside the laboratory share the cognitive characteristics of these laboratory judgments, that is, they require intention and effort and represent a later, optional processing step.

A few recent researchers, working in the conceptual framework of information processing, have discussed the possibility that attributions are as spontaneous as early theorists like Asch posited. The notion that attributional phenomena are an integral part of the process of encoding information, rather than a separate mental operation occurring at retrieval, was raised by Smith and Miller (1979), who proposed that attributional processing is "intrinsically involved in the initial comprehension of sentences and therefore that it goes on all the time, not just when a subject is asked an attributional question" (1979, p. 2247). Similarly, Carlston (1980) considered the effects of spontaneous inference making on subsequent memories for behavior and impressions.

The present research was a direct test of the possibility that inferences about personality can be part and parcel of the encoding of behavioral information, carried out without instructions or other unusual motivating conditions (i.e., spontaneously). Although this does not imply that trait inferences must always be spontaneous, or that they must always occur at encoding, a demonstration that trait inferences may also occur spontaneously at encoding would strongly suggest that they are ordinarily an integral part of the process of observing behavior and not essentially discrete operations motivated by particular purposes and dependent on information retrieval. Our basic proposal is that people sometimes make spontaneous social inferences as part of their initial comprehension of social information. Even without explicit questions or goals, they do not simply store some representation of the information as it is presented. Instead, they make inferences and store both the information and their inferences in memory.

To test the notion that trait inferences ordinarily are made at encoding, we adapted the encoding specificity paradigm developed by Tulving and his associates (Thomson & Tulving, 1970; Tulving & Osler, 1968; Tulving & Pearlstone, 1966; Tulving & Thomson, 1973). The encoding specificity principle holds that "specific encoding operations performed on what is perceived determine what is stored, and what is stored determines what retrieval cues are effective in providing access to what is stored" (Tulving & Thomson, 1973, p. 369). The principle stresses "the importance of encoding events at the time of input as the primary determinant of the storage format and retrievability of information in the episodic memory system..." (Tulving, 1972, p. 392). Thus, an effective retrieval cue for any input will be another piece of information that was encoded at the same time. Cue effectiveness is defined as "the probability of recall of the target item in the presence of a discrete retrieval cue" (Tulving & Thomson, 1973, p. 354) and is determined by comparison with the free-recall rate (i.e., noncued recall).

In encoding specificity experiments, target words like *chair* are paired with weak semantic associates, such as *glue*. Subjects study lists of such pairs with the expectation that their memory for the target words will be tested. They are then asked to recall the target words in the presence of either the input cue (*glue*), a strong semantic associate of the target (e.g., *table*), or no cue. Tulving's results (e.g., Thomson & Tulving, 1970) showed that recall was best when the input cue was present, whereas recall cued by the strong semantic associate was in fact no better than noncued recall.

If people make trait inferences when they observe behavior and encode the information, those inferred traits should be stored in memory along with the information on which they were based. Therefore, as part of the encoding context of the behavioral information, the attributed trait itself should serve as a self-generated covert input cue and thus as an effective retrieval cue for the behavioral information. It should be possible, then, to show that people make trait inferences at encoding by demonstrating the retrieval effectiveness for the behavioral information of subjects' most likely trait inference. For instance, if reading "The librarian carries the old woman's groceries across the street," subjects infer that the librarian is helpful, then the word *helpful* ought to be a good retrieval cue for the sentence.

Disposition cues were selected that were related to the sentences primarily by the subjects' inferences. This was done so that the disposition words would be unlikely to cue the sentences because of some association in semantic memory. Tulving's (1972) distinction between episodic and semantic memory is heuristic here. Tulving defined episodic memory as the memory organization "concerned with storage and retrieval of temporally dated episodes or events, and temporal-spatial relations among these events" (1972, p. 385), events such as stimuli presented in a memory experiment. This was contrasted with semantic memory, the organized knowledge of symbols and concepts. Tulving's distinction has generated considerable controversy, chiefly surrounding the issue of separate memory stores for the two kinds of information (e.g., Anderson & Ross, 1980). The present use of the distinction as a conceptual heuristic is designed primarily as a fruitful new way of viewing person-perception issues. It does not provide a test of the notion of separate episodic and semantic memory stores. In the present research, the inferred disposition *helpful* and the librarian sentence would be associated episodically, because the subject has made the inference (*helpful*) at the time she or he encoded the sentence. *Helpful* would thus become the de facto input cue, even though not physically present at encoding and not a strong semantic associate.

The retrieval effectiveness of the disposition cues was defined by comparison with noncued recall and was also compared with the effectiveness of strong semantic associates to important sentence parts (e.g., books, a strong associate to librarian, and bags, a strong associate to carries the groceries). The retrieval effectiveness of such semantic associations has been established in verbal-learning research. This "extralist cuing effect" has been explained from a variety of conceptual frameworks (e.g., Bilodeau & Blick, 1965; Bahrick, 1969,

1970; Tulving & Thomson, 1973). These semantic associates were included as a control for the possibility that the retrieval effectiveness of the disposition words might be due to a priori semantic associations to sentence words rather than to dispositional inferences. Sets of strong associates to actors or predicates were derived in free-association tests. Our purpose was to pit the disposition cues against another set of cues that empirically had strong semantic associations with the sentences. If the disposition cues facilitate sentence recall merely because of associative contiguity with sentences, one would expect the semantic cues to produce stronger recall, because those a priori relations are empirically very strong, whereas the a priori associations between disposition words and sentences are extremely weak. But if the disposition cues were as effective as, or more effective than, the strong semantic associates, this strength must be due to the episodic link between sentence and cue, that is, to their temporal cooccurrence and consequent proximity in episodic memory organization.

We can thus posit that the strongest link between the sentences and the disposition words is provided by an inference made by the subject at encoding, rather than by a priori semantic associations between the dispositions and sentences. The association between the sentence words and the disposition words is provided by episodic memory. Whatever link exists in semantic memory between disposition cues and sentences must be weaker than that between the sentences and semantic cues, because the disposition cues do not show up in the free-association pretests, whereas the semantic cues do.

Hence, the semantic and disposition cues are hypothesized to facilitate recall for different reasons. The semantic cues are closely associated with the semantic representations of the words that constitute the sentences. Presenting subjects with the semantic associate during the recall phase should facilitate retrieval of the target sentence parts on the basis of the extralist cuing effect (cf. Tulving & Thomson, 1973). The encoding-specific cue (the inferred disposition), by contrast, is hypothesized to facilitate retrieval primarily because of the inferred trait's close episodic relation to the target information. Therefore, presenting subjects with the encoding-specific cue should provide access to the whole target sentence even though there is little or no semantic association between cues and sentence parts. The sentences and their corresponding semantic and disposition cues are presented in Table 18.1.

This research comprised two phases, construction of the stimuli and the recall experiments. Each experiment presented subjects with behavior descriptions that were to

TABLE 18.1. Sentence Stimuli, Their Cues, and Characteristics

Sentences[a]	Semantic Cues[b]		Disposition Cues[b]	Attribution Rating[c]	Vividness Rating[d]
	Actor	Verb			
The plumber slips an extra $50 into his wife's purse.	pipes (28)		generous (25)	2.23	3.55
The receptionist steps in front of the old man in line.	telephone (21)		rude (18)	1.81	3.45
The electrician *gets a promotion* and a raise.	wires (37)	work (17)	good worker (18)	1.59	2.77
The librarian *carries the* old woman's *groceries* across the street.	books (49)	bag (17)	helpful (10)	1.78	3.18
The tailor picks his teeth during dinner at the fancy restaurant.	clothes (16)		ill-mannered (25)	1.59	3.78
The elevator-operator *saves* enough *money* to buy a new house.	floors (13)	bank (17)	thrifty (13)	1.71	2.84
Mother *gets her poem into the* NewYorker.	father (20)	writes (14)	talented (13)	1.30	4.17
The farmer *paints* a swastika on the synagogue wall.	crops (10)	colors (19)	bigot (05)	1.62	4.61
The professor *has* his new *neighbors over* for dinner.	teacher (14)	party (32)	friendly (60)	1.25	2.19
The butcher writes a letter to the editor about air pollution.	meat (44)		concerned citizen (55)	1.69	2.94
The pianist leaves her purse on the subway seat.	music (13)		absent-minded (38)	1.76	3.13
The accountant *takes* the orphans *to the circus.*	numbers (16)	fun (16)	kindhearted (25)	1.71	3.66
The successful film-maker gives his ailing mother $10 a month.	movie (21)		cheap (43)	2.08	1.91
The secretary *solves the mystery* half-way through the book.	typewriter (19)	detective (22)	clever (23)	1.27	3.24
The sailor *leaves* his wife *with 20* pounds of *laundry*	sea (20)	wash (13)	inconsiderate (28)	1.79	2.69

TABLE 18.1. (*Continued*)

Sentences[a]	Semantic Cues[b]		Disposition Cues[b]	Attribution Rating[c]	Vividness Rating[d]
	Actor	Verb			
The barber *loses 20 lbs.* in 6 weeks on a new diet.	hair (45)	fat (21)	willpower (25)	2.14	3.5
The carpenter *stops his car* and motions the pedestrians to cross.	wood (24)	brakes (15)	considerate (23)	1.79	2.62
The reporter *steps on* his girlfriend's *feet* as they foxtrot.	newspaper (21)	ouch (15)	clumsy (43)	1.71	1.68

[a] The italicized portion served as stimuli in the pretest for Experiment 2, obtaining semantic associations to verbs.
[b] Semantic cues, actor, came from Pretest 1; semantic cues, verb, came from the pretest for Experiment 2; and disposition cues came from Pretest 3. Numbers in parentheses indicate the percentage of subjects who gave the response.
[c] Attribution ratings, Pretest 2; 1 = dispositional, 4 = situational.
[d] Vividness ratings, Pretest 6.

be recalled later in the presence either of (a) a personality attribute of the actor implied by the described action, (b) a semantic associate to one of the words of the sentence, or (c) no cue. Stimuli with the appropriate specifications were established through six pretests. Short declarative sentences were written that described simple actions in behavioral, non-evaluative terms, avoiding implications about actors' intentions, traits, attitudes, or feelings. Accordingly, verbs like *helps* were avoided in favor of phrases that described only the behavior (e.g., ". . . carried the groceries across the street"). No inferences were provided explicitly for the subject (see Table 18.1).

Development of Sentence Stimuli

Pretest 1: Semantic associates to actors. The first pretest was conducted to gather semantic word association norms to a large number of common nouns that could represent the actors in sentences. One-hundred eight undergraduates enrolled in social psychology and personality courses at New York University (NYU) were given pamphlets containing a list of 80 occupations and roles (e.g., architect, brother), preceded by instructions to look at each and write the first word it made them think of, avoiding the words *man* and *woman*. To determine the strongest associate to each, the responses were tallied and the most frequently given response was selected as the semantic associate. Fifteen nouns that

generated more than 25% dispositional attributions as associates (e.g., nurse: Kind) were excluded. Of the remaining 65 nouns, the 39 with the strongest consensus on their semantic associates were selected for use as actors in the sentence stimuli. Sentences were constructed by pairing the 39 nouns with sentence stems describing actions, half positive, half negative. Actors and sentence stems were matched in such a way that subjects and predicates were neither bizarre or striking in combination, nor redundant in terms of the information they contained. For example, pairing businessman with the stem "doubles his investment in a *business venture*" was avoided as redundant, because a cue like thrifty is an associate of each.

Pretest 2: Sentences evoking dispositional attributions. This pretest was designed to identify those sentences that most reliably generated dispositional attributions to the actors, rather than situational attributions. Forty-four female undergraduates taking the introductory psychology course at NYU were asked to read the sentences and make causal attributions for each. Their instructions were to ". . . make a judgment about what probably caused the event — why it probably occurred, given the minimal information you have. A phrase or short sentence should be sufficient."

A subject's response received a score of 1 if it was judged to be totally dispositional (e.g., "she is a helpful person"), 2 if it evoked a person-centered cause (e.g., "she felt sorry for the old woman"), 3 if it evoked situational considerations ("the old woman dropped her groceries"), or 4 if it was totally situational. We calculated an average rating for each sentence, ranging from 1 to 4 with a 1 indicating *unanimous dispositional attributions* and 4 indicating *unanimous situational attributions*. Two independent judges made attribution ratings for a set of 20 responses selected at random. The interjudge reliability was found to be .89, and the first judge's scoring was followed. We chose the 18 sentences that scored closest to the dispositional end of the scale. The mean attribution rating was 1.71, and they ranged from 1.25 to 2.23 (see Table 18.1).

Pretest 3: Dispositions inferred from whole sentences. The personality traits most frequently attributed to actors, in subjects' own words, were obtained in this pretest. For each of the 18 sentences, 40 additional female undergraduates in the introductory psychology course answered the question, "What kind of person is this?" They were asked to write as many as three words, if that many came to mind. We tallied each response and then selected the most frequently given word as the dispositional cue for that sentence, in the same way that the most frequently given semantic associate in Pretest 1 had been selected as the semantic cue for each sentence.

Pretest 4: Dispositional associates of other noun phrases. We conducted this pretest to ensure that sentence nouns that had not already been pretested (e.g., in prepositional phrases) were not associated with dispositional concepts. The purpose of detecting such a priori relations was to rule out the possibility that the disposition words might accidentally cue sentences on the basis of semantic relations, rather than the hypothesized episodic memory connection provided by the personality inference. Sentence actors with dispositional associates had already been eliminated in Pretest 1.

Twenty-five NYU undergraduates received booklets containing 37 items (direct and indirect objects, and prepositional phrases), listed in random order, with instructions to write the first word(s) that came to mind on the line following each item. The responses for each item were recorded and tallied. No item generated more than 10% disposition concepts, and so no sentences were eliminated.

Pretest 5: Behavioral associates of dispositions. This was a further attempt to detect a priori associations between the dispositions identified in Pretest 3 and the sentence stimuli. It was done to rule out the possibility that the disposition words might accidentally cue the sentences themselves, or parts of the sentences, through semantic relations rather than through the link in episodic memory established by inferring the disposition at encoding.

Twenty-seven NYU undergraduates were asked "what kinds of behaviors or actions do you associate with" each of 11 dispositions. The dispositions were listed in alphabetical order and were the strongest associates from Pretest 3, where they had been given by at least 25% of the subjects. Subjects listed up to five behavioral associates of each disposition.

The dispositions elicited between 2.8 and 3.4 behavioral associates per subject. None of these were identical to or paraphrases of the sentences that had elicited the dispositions. More lenient scoring criteria showed that an average of only 5.5% (and a maximum less than 17%) of the behavior associates produced to each disposition were in the same general class of behaviors as the sentence behaviors (e.g., "looses something" for sentence 11, Table 18.1). Therefore, none of the sentences were eliminated on the basis of this pretest.

As a further check that disposition cues were not facilitating recall through semantic associations to behaviors, the frequencies of the leniently scored behavioral associates for each cue were subsequently correlated with the sentence recall scores for each of these 11 dispositional cues from Experiment 1. These behavior-associate frequencies were unrelated to disposition-cued recall ($r = -.06$, $n = 11$, $p > .25$).

Pretest 6: Vividness. The purpose of this pretest was to rule out the possibility that the vividness or strikingness of some sentences could affect their memorability, because this would confound the effect of dispositional judgment on recall for sentences. Each sentence was read by 40 additional undergraduates in the introductory psychology course, who were asked to rate each sentence on how unusual or striking each event seemed on a 5-point scale, with a 1 indicating *an ordinary event* and a 5 indicating *a highly striking or extraordinary event*. We calculated the average vividness rating for each sentence. Each block of sentences in Experiment 1 was then composed of sentences whose average vividness ratings were approximately equal to each other. The sentences' ratings ranged from 1.68 to 3.78, but the blocks' average ratings fell between 1.98 and 2.46 (see Table 18.1).

Experiment 1

Method

Subjects

Ninety male and female undergraduates enrolled in the introductory psychology course at NYU participated in the experiment in partial fulfillment of a course requirement. They were tested in groups of 2 to 12, and sessions lasted about 30 min.

Materials
The 18 sentences were presented one at a time by a Kodak Carousel Slide Projector. In addition, there were three slides containing a distractor task, with instructions on one slide and three anagrams on each of the other two slides. After the slide presentation, each subject received a recall sheet containing the recall cues, on which responses were to be written. There were three kinds of cues on each sheet, counterbalanced across sentence blocks. Thus, one-third of the subjects had a particular six-sentence block cued by semantic cues, another block cued by disposition cues, and the last by no cue. There were three groups of subjects that differed only in the type of cue they received for each block of sentences. A postrecall questionnaire followed the recall sheets, for the last 60 subjects tested.

Procedure
Following Tulving's procedure (e.g., Tulving & Thomson, 1973), written instructions informed subjects that they were participating in a memory experiment. They were asked to study the sentences carefully because they would be tested on them later. Subjects viewed each of the 18 sentence slides for 5 s. We randomly determined the order of the slides for each group of subjects.

The distractor task (included to allow short-term memory to dissipate) followed the presentation of the sentences. Immediately after the last sentence was presented, a slide with instructions to unscramble the six anagrams that followed was shown for 5 s. The anagrams were shown on two slides, three anagrams on each. Subjects were allowed 1 min for each slide. The recall sheets were then distributed. Subjects were allowed 10 min to recall as many sentences and as much of each as they could.

After the recall sheets were collected, the first 30 subjects were informally questioned about their recollection of the mental operations they had used (a) as they read the sentences and (b) later as they tried to recall them. Their responses helped to clarify which questions could profitably be asked and the best wording to use. On the basis of this, a postrecall questionnaire was constructed, and these questionnaires were given to the last 60 subjects tested. The first question was open-ended, asking whether they had used any method or strategy to remember the sentences and if so to describe it briefly. The second question presented

them with four plausible strategies for committing the sentences to memory (visual imagery, judgments about causality, judgments about personality, and word-meaning associations) and asked them to estimate the percentage of the time they had used each. The third question explained the three cuing conditions and asked them to rate how heavily they had relied on each type of cue (word-meaning or personality trait) or had applied cues of their own, by using 11-point scales to indicate their answers.

Results and Discussion

Each sentence had a similar four-part structure, generally consisting of actor (A), verb (V), direct or indirect object (O) and a prepositional phrase or second object (P). One point was given for recall of each of the four parts. Thus the maximum score for one sentence was four points. Because there were 18 sentences, the highest possible score a subject could receive was 72. We used lenient scoring. No consideration was given for verbatim recall or spelling. Credit was given for appropriate recall of consistent sentence parts: That is, when subjects responded to the cue bag with "The farmer carries the old woman's groceries," they received credit for recall of verb and object but not for actor recall (because the appropriate actor was the librarian). We also used this scoring practice for noncued recall when occasional words were erroneously recalled as parts of the wrong sentence. The first five recall protocols in each condition were scored by two independent coders. The interrater agreement was 96.4%.

We assessed the hypothesis that recall cued by dispositions would be at least as strong as semantic-cued recall and superior to noncued recall by using a split-plot factorial analysis of variance (ANOVA). On the recall sheets, three blocks of sentences had been rotated through the three cuing conditions in a Latin square. Hence, block-cue pairing was a 3-level between-subjects factor. Type of cue was a 3-level within-subjects factor, as all subjects received all three types of cues. The other within-subjects factor was the sentence part recalled, a 4-level factor (A, V, O, and P). This yielded a $3 \times 3 \times 4$ (Pairing $\times$ Cue Type $\times$ Sentence Part) ANOVA.

The analysis revealed significant main effects for cue type, $F(2, 168) = 23.00$, $p < .001$) and for sentence part, $F(3, 252) = 12.40$, $p < .001$. The interaction between cue type and sentence part was also significant, $F(6, 504 = 67.65, p < .001)$.

The mean recall rates of the three types of cues were ordered as predicted. Mean recall with the disposition cue was strongest (2.42), followed by recall with the semantic cue (2.14) and by noncued recall (1.36). The significance of these differences was assessed by using Newman-Keuls multiple comparison tests (Kirk, 1968), which use a stairstep approach to the error rate, according to which the critical value for differences between means varies with the number of means in a set. This test showed that recall cued with disposition words was significantly stronger than noncued recall, $W(.01) = .97$, and nonsignificantly stronger than recall with the semantic cues. Semanticcued recall was also significantly stronger than noncued recall, $W(.01) = .644$.

The main effect for sentence part was revealed by a Newman-Keuls test to be due to the superiority of actor recall (2.12) to that of preposition (1.88) and Verb (1.90) recall, $W(.01) = .23$ and .21.

The significant Cue × Sentence Part interaction is depicted in Figure 18.1. Analyses of simple main effects within each cue type showed that sentence parts were differentially recalled for the semantic cue, $F(3, 258) = 74.05, p < .001$, and for the disposition cue, $F(3, 258) = 22.91, p < .001$, but not for noncued recall. For semantic-cued recall, protected t tests (Cohen & Cohen, 1975) showed actors to be more often recalled than verbs, objects, and prepositions, $ts(86) > 8.55, ps < .001$, and prepositions to be recalled less often than verbs and objects, $ts(86) > 2.78, ps < .001$. For disposition-cued recall, protected t tests showed actors were recalled less often than verbs, objects, and prepositions, $ts(86) > 4.23, ps < .001$, and objects were recalled more often than verbs or prepositions, $ts(86) > 2.39, ps < .02$.

We computed another set of simple main effects and protected t tests in order to compare recall of each sentence part in the three cuing conditions. Actors were recalled differentially by cue type, $F(2, 172) = 41.52, p < .001$. Semantic cues were more effective for actors than disposition cues, $t(86) = 4.90, p < .001$, which were in turn more effective than no cues, $t(86) = 4.92, p < .001$. As Figure 18.1 suggests, this is a different ordering than that for the other three sentence parts across cue conditions. The simple main effects for verbs, objects and prepositions were also significant, $Fs(2, 172) > 20.35, ps < .001$; and for each sentence part, disposition-cued recall was greater than semantic-cued recall, $ts(86) > 3.46, ps < .001$, which was in turn greater than noncued recall, $ts(86) > 1.99, ps < .05$.

In summary, as Figure 18.1 suggests, both disposition- and semantic-cued recall were superior to noncued recall but not different from each other overall. The disposition cues' effectiveness was greatest for sentence verbs,

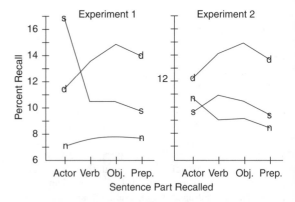

FIGURE 18.1 ■ Percentage Recall of Sentence Parts, for Disposition Cues (d), Semantic Cues (s) and No Cue (n). Percentage Recall = Mean Recall Divided by .18 for Experiment 1, and .12 for Experiment 2.

objects, and prepositions, whereas the semantic cues' effectiveness was greatest for sentence actors.

We also tallied the combination of sentence parts that were recalled primarily to examine differences in the kinds of sentence information each type of cue had retrieved best. We tabulated the recall for each of the 15 possible combinations of parts (e.g. actor, actor + verb). These sums are presented in Table 18.2. Inspection of this table reveals, first, that sentence recall overall was primarily due to recall of total sentences rather than sentence parts, and secondarily to recall of predicates. These observations were confirmed by the results of a 3 × 3 × 15 (Block-Cue Pairing × Cue Type × Combination of Parts) split-plot ANOVA. It showed significant main effects for cue type, $F(2, 168) = 22.92, p < .001$; for combination, $F(14, 1176) = 188.17, p < .001$; and for the interaction between these two within-subject factors, $F(28, 2352) = 13.34, p < .001$. Newman-Keuls tests were computed between all pairs of means involved in the main effect for combination of parts. They showed that this main effect occurred because the recall of the total sentence (AVOP) was stronger than that of any other sentence-part combination, $W(.01)$ from .389 to .583; and the recall of the VOP combination (i.e., the predicate) was stronger than any other combination except AVOP, $W(.01)$ from .40 to .60.

Another theoretically interesting comparison lies in the difference in actor recall among the three cuing conditions. Inspection of Table 18.2 suggests that semantic cues retrieved actors best. This was supported

TABLE 18.2. Recall Frequency of Combinations of Sentence Parts As a Function of Cue Type

Recalled Combination	Study 1 (N = 87)			Study 2 (N = 63)		
	Actor Association	Disposition	No Cue	Verb Association	Disposition	No Cue
Actor (A)	101	3	17	12	2	24
Verb (V)	0	1	0	2	1	2
Object (O)	2	2	1	1	1	1
Preposition (P)	0	2	2	0	1	0
A + V	1	0	0	1	0	
A + O	2	4	2	1	1	
A + P	0	0	1	1	2	
V + O	1	5	1	9	1	
V + P	0	2	1	1	1	
O + P	0	8	2	1	2	
A + V + O	13	9	4	4	12	4
A + V + P	5	2	1	4	2	
A + O + P	3	12	0	2	6	
V + O + P	6	43	27	14	22	11
A + V + O + P	138	149	86	48	68	47

Note. To obtain cell means referred to in the text, compute $(F \times P)/N$, where $F =$ is the frequency above; $P =$ the number of sentence parts in the combination (1 to 4); and $N =$ the sample size.

by a test for simple main effects and found to be significant, $F(2, 172) = 63.54$, $p < .001$. Protected t tests on the differences between pairs of means showed semantic-cued recall to be higher than either disposition-cued, $t(86) = 8.98$, $p < .001$, or noncued recall, $t(86) = 7.36$, $p < .001$, and noncued recall to be superior to disposition-cued recall, $t(86) = 3.51$, $p < .001$. We conducted another test for simple main effects on recall of the VOP combination (the predicate) among the three cuing conditions. This was found to be significant, $F(2, 172) = 15.92$, $p < .001$. Protected t tests revealed the disposition cue to be more effective than either the semantic cue, $t(86) = 5.35$, $p < .001$, or no cue, $t(86) = 2.27$, $p = .026$. Noncued recall was also superior to semantic-cued recall, $t(86) = 3.69$, p $< .001$.

We conducted a final test of simple main effects on the three means for recall of the total sentence (AVOP). This was also significant, $F(2, 172) = 12.12$, $p < .001$, and was shown by a protected t test to be due to the inferiority of noncued recall to semantic-cued, $t(86) = 3.53$, $p < .001$ and disposition-cued recall, $t(86) = 4.70$, $p < .001$.

In summary, as Table 18.2 suggests, the most frequently recalled combination of sentence parts was the whole sentence, for which both the disposition and the semantic cues were more effective than no cue. The entire predicate (VOP) was also frequently recalled, most often with disposition cues. And actors alone were most frequently cued by semantic cues.

The question of subjects' awareness of making social judgments was assessed in several ways. The first 30 subjects were questioned informally about their recollections of having made personality-related or cause-related inferences as they read the sentences. Although demand characteristics would predict that subjects in such situations would strive to be agreeable and confirm the experimenter's suggestions, most subjects regretfully reported having made no such judgments at all. Even after the debriefing, some did not believe they had made trait inferences and were greatly surprised by evidence supplied by their own recall sheets that trait cues had actually been effective in promoting their recall.

For the remaining 60 subjects, the formal postrecall questionnaire was employed to assess introspective awareness. Alternative memory and recall strategies were described equally plausibly, since Nisbett and Wilson (1977) have pointed out that the a priori causal theories people use to explain events are preeminently those that seem plausible. The four strategies were (a) visual imagery, (b) association to word meanings, (c) judgments about causality, and (d) judgments about personality. Subjects were asked to estimate the percentage of time they had used each.

TABLE 18.3. Pearson Product-Moment Correlations Between Introspective Reports of Dispositional Inferences and Actual Disposition-cued Recall Measures

Measures	Experiment 1		Experiment 2	
	Score	Ratio	Score	Ratio
Mention of persons on open-ended question	.16 ($p = .21$)	.13 ($p = .32$)	.10 ($p = .43$)	− .01 ($p = .93$)
Reported thoughts about causality during encoding	.20 ($p = .13$)	.24 ($p = .06$)	.15 ($p = .23$)	− .03 ($p = .82$)
Reported thoughts about personality during encoding	.13 ($p = .31$)	.10 ($p = .46$)	− .12 ($p = .34$)	.12 ($p = .36$)
Reported usefulness of disposition cues during recall	.13 ($p = .31$)	.12 ($p = .34$)	− .10 ($p = .45$)	− .07 ($p = .60$)

To the open-ended question, virtually no subjects reported having made causal- or personality-related judgments, and only 10 mentioned anything at all about the persons in the sentences. The mean percentage of time subjects reported using each strategy were as follows: 36.5% for visual imagery, 18.3% for causality-related thoughts, 36.6% for personality-related thoughts, and 45.5% for word-meaning associations.

To assess the question of introspective awareness more precisely, Pearson product-moment correlations were computed between self-reports and actual recall scores. In addition to the scores, we calculated for each subject the ratio of the disposition-cued recall score to the total recall score. This was taken as an additional index of the retrieval effectiveness of the disposition cues. For example, if a subject had a total recall score of 20 and had recalled 10 items (i.e., parts of sentences) that were cued with the disposition cues, his or her ratio would be .5. Both the disposition-cued scores and the ratios were correlated with the self-reports.

Table 18.3 presents the Pearson product-moment correlations between the two indices of disposition-cued recall and the four self-reports of having made dispositional or causal inferences during encoding (i.e., while reading the sentences) or during recall. Only one coefficient approaches significance ($r = -.24$, $p = .06$), and this is in the opposite direction from that predicted by introspective awareness. So there is no evidence that subjects were aware of having made personality inferences while encoding the behavioral information or aware of the effectiveness of disposition cues during retrieval.

Experiment 2

One criticism that may be leveled at Experiment 1 is that semantic-cued recall may have been unfairly matched against disposition-cued recall because the semantic cue was an associate of only the actor, and actors had been chosen specifically for their semantic independence from the rest of the sentence. Dispositions, although not strong semantic associates of any of the sentence parts, might still be preferentially relevant to the other major syntactic division of the sentence, the predicate. Because the predicates comprised three parts and the actors only one, disposition cues may have been superior in recall only because they were relevant to a larger portion of each sentence. Indeed, there is evidence that semantic and disposition cues retrieved sentence parts differentially, as Table 18.2 shows. Of the sentences recalled through semantic cues, 37% consisted of the actor alone, and 3% the predicate only. Disposition cues retrieved actors alone only 1% of the time, and predicate parts alone 26% of the time. Free recall fell between these two, with 12% actors alone and 24% predicates alone.

We conducted Experiment 2 to meet this criticism by pitting disposition-cued recall against recall cued by strong associates to the sentence verbs.

Method

Pretest: Semantic Associates to Verbs.
The verbs or verb phrases of the 18 sentences used in Experiment 1 were shown to 40 subjects enrolled in the introductory psychology course at NYU. (These words are italicized in Table 18.1). Instructions were to read each word or phrase and write the first word that came to mind. Verb phrases were used in most cases because the verb alone was often too general or ambiguous (e.g., gets in "*gets* a promotion"). Thus most of these prompts were short phrases.

The strongest associates to six of the verb phrases turned out to be dispositions (e.g., "slips money into purse" yielded the associate *generous*). These six sentences were dropped from the set, and Experiment 2 therefore employed 12 sentences. The verb associates were used as the semantic cues for the second recall experiment.

Recall Experiment.
Sixty-three students enrolled in the introductory psychology course at NYU served as subjects. They were given general memory instructions and then shown the 12 sentences on slides, presented in one of three previously fixed random orders, for 5 s each. The original 2-min distractor task followed the sentence presentation. Subjects then received the recall sheets, which provided the disposition cues (from Experiment 1) for four sentence, the new semantic associates to another four, and no cue for the third block of four. These cues were counterbalanced, as in Experiment 1. Subjects were allowed 10 min to recall the sentences.

Results and Discussion

We scored recall, as in Experiment 1, for a maximum of four points per sentence, one for each of the four parts (i.e., actor, verb, object, and preposition or second object). Because there were 12 sentences, the highest possible score was 48. As in Experiment 1, we computed a split-plot factorial ANOVA on the recall scores, with block cue pairing a three-level between-subjects factor, cue type a three-level within-subjects factor, and sentence part a four-level within-subjects factor. Both cue type, $F(2, 120) = 5.35$, $p = .006$, and sentence part, $F(2, 180) = 2.86$, $p = .038$, produced significant main effects, and the interaction between these factors was also significant, $F(6, 360) = 4.41$, $p < .001$.

As in Experiment 1, mean disposition-cued recall was highest (1.66), followed by semantic-cued recall (1.22) and noncued recall (1.13). A Newman-Keuls test showed that disposition-cued recall was significantly stronger than either semantic-cued recall, $W(.01) = .25$, or noncued recall, $W(.01) = .22$. Semantic-cued recall was nonsignificantly higher than noncued recall.

A Newman-Keuls tests on the Sentence-Part factor showed none of the sentence parts to be significantly superior to any other.

The interaction between cue type and sentence part is depicted in Figure 18.1. Analyses of simple main effects within each cue type revealed that sentence parts were differentially recalled for disposition-cued recall, $F(3,186) = 5.26$, $p = .002$, and noncued recall, $F(3,186) = 4.33$, $p = .006$. For disposition-cued recall, protected t tests

showed that actors were recalled less often than either verb, $t(62) = 2.23$, $p = .03$, or object, $t(62) = 3.32$, $p = .001$, and object recall was better than preposition recall, $t(62) = 2.41$, $p = .019$. For noncued recall, protected t tests showed only a significant superiority of actor recall over preposition recall, $t(62) = 2.88$, $p = .005$.

We computed another set of simple main effects within sentence part, comparing the three cue types. Differences in actor recall for the three cuing conditions were not significant. Recall of the verbs was affected by cue type, $F(2, 124) = 5.45$, $p = .005$, with disposition cues superior to both semantic cues, $t(62) = 2.09$, $p = .04$, and no cue, $t(62) = 3.06$, $p = .003$. Recall of objects and prepositions showed the same pattern, $Fs(2, 124) > 7.09$, $ps < .001$, with disposition cues stronger than both semantic cues and no cue, $ts(62) > 2.94$, $ps < .005$.

Hence disposition cues were more effective than other cues overall, and they were also more effective for each part of the predicate, despite the semantic cues being strong associates to words in the predicates.

As in Experiment 1, we also examined the pattern of sentence recall by computing recall for each combination of sentence parts. The sums in each category are presented on the right in Table 18.2. A split-plot factorial ANOVA on these data revealed significant main effects for cue type, $F(2, 120) = 4.34$, $p < .05$, and combination of parts, $F(14, 840) = 88.32$, $p < .001$, as well as a Cue Type $\times$ Combination interaction, $F(28, 1680) = 2.05$, $p < .01$. A Newman-Keuls test revealed that disposition-cued recall (M = .44) was superior to both semantic-cued (M = .34), $W(.05) = .09$, and noncued recall (M = .31), $W(.05) = .11$.

We also evaluated the main effect for combination of parts by using a Newman-Keuls test. This revealed that recall of the total sentence (AVOP) was superior to that of any other combination of sentence parts, $W(.01)$ from .36 to .54 and that recall of the VOP combination (the predicate) was also stronger than recall of any other combination except AVOP, $W(.01)$ from .27 to .46. Hence the whole sentence was most frequently recalled, followed by the predicate alone.

These recall-pattern data afford an opportunity to examine more closely the central issue of whether the disposition cues are linked to sentences via an inference made at encoding or are merely another kind of semantic association to action descriptions. If their retrieval superiority is due to an encoding mechanism, they should be more associated to actors than the verb associates, as well as to predicates, and thus be more effective in eliciting whole sentences and combinations of sentences that include the actor. If on the other hand, they are really just semantic associations, they should produce a pattern of sentence-part retrieval, which resembles that of the verb associates. Specifically, their superiority should reside primarily in their ability to elicit predicates.

One line of reasoning, then, involves the extent to which total sentences (AVOP) were recalled by the three cue types. Evaluated by a test of simple main effects, the effect of cue type on AVOP recall was found to be marginally significant, $F(2, 124) = 2.72$, $p = .07$, and protected t tests revealed that disposition-cued recall was superior to semantic-cued, $t(62) = 2.00$, $p = .05$, and marginally superior to noncued recall, $t(62) = 1.95$, $p = .056$.

We pursued this question further by grouping together the sentence-part combinations that included the actor (i.e., actor, AV, AO, AP, AVO, AVP, AOP, AVOP) and comparing the three cuing conditions in their ability to retrieve these. Again, if trait inferences were made at encoding, the ascribed trait should become associated with the actor as well as with the predicate. So the disposition cues should be stronger than the verb associates in retrieving these actor-included combinations. Assessed by a test of simple main effects, this prediction was confirmed, $F(2, 124) = 3.77$, $p = .026$. The disposition words (M = 5.40) were stronger retrieval cues for these combinations than either the verb-associated semantic cues (M = 3.83), $t(62) = 2.45$, $p = .017$, or noncued recall (M = 3.81), $t(62) = 2.45$, $p = 224$, $p = .029$. These findings support the notion that the disposition cues, more than the verb associates, were associated with actors.

A second implication of the encoding-inference notion is that the overall recall effectiveness of disposition cues should not be due to their superiority in retrieving predicates. Accordingly, predicate recall (VOP) was assessed by a test of simple main effects, which showed that VOP recall did not differ across cuing conditions. We also grouped together the sentence-part combinations that best represented recall of the predicates, those combinations that excluded the actor (i.e., V, O, P, VO, VP, OP, VOP). A test of simple main effects revealed no differences among the three cuing conditions in the extent to which they retrieved these predicate combinations, $F(2, 124) = 2.02$, $p = .137$. Furthermore, disposition-cued recall of these predicate combinations was not significantly better than verb-associate-cued recall, $t(62) = .55$, $p = .587$. Hence, the superiority of the disposition cues does not seem to reside in their ability to retrieve predicates. This indicates that they were not

just more effective semantic associates to descriptions of actions.[1]

We again assessed the question of introspective awareness by using the postrecall questionnaire from Experiment 1. On the open-ended question, virtually no one mentioned having had personality-related thoughts, and only four subjects reported any thoughts about the actors at all. As in the previous experiment, most self-reports dealt with the use of visual imagery. The same correlations were computed between responses to the four self-report questions and the two indices of actual disposition-cued recall, (i.e., subjects' scores and the ratios of disposition-cued to total recall score). The results are shown in Table 18.3. None of the correlations in this experiment even approached significance.

General Discussion

In both experiments, recall of sentences was at least as good with dispositional cues as with either type of strong semantic cue and clearly superior to noncued recall. Yet subjects had not been instructed to make dispositional inferences and seemed unaware of having done so. Thus, the results of the experiments provide evidence that personality inferences may occur in the absence of any particular purpose such as a prediction or a requirement to follow an experimenter's instructions.

How well do these results support the notion that personality inferences are made spontaneously from behavioral information as it is encoded? This question may be rephrased in terms of how well we have ruled out the possibility that a disposition cue like *helpful* may be effective in retrieval if it was not present at

---

[1] A third line of reasoning concerns the total-sentence recall (AVOP) and addresses the possibility that AVOP recall may be an artifact of predicate recall. If the disposition cue is truly working on episodic rather than semantic relations among sentence parts, the frequency with which actor and predicate were recalled, versus predicate alone (VOP), should be greatest in the disposition cue condition. We accordingly examined the difference between the number of instances of AVOP recall and of VOP recall in the three cuing conditions (AVOP-VOP) and found it to be 46 in the disposition condition, 36 in the noncued condition, and 34 in the verb-associate semantic condition. In other words, taking the frequency of predicate recall as a baseline figure, the greatest increase in instances of actor-recall (i.e., AVOP) occurred in the disposition cue condition. The increase in instances of recalled AVOP above VOP recall was in fact slightly worse in the semantic cue condition than in the noncued recall condition. These results are consistent with the prediction that a trait ascription to the actor was made at encoding and is associated episodically with the stored sentence.

encoding. Two major alternatives to the encoding specificity hypothesis present themselves as explanations for the retrieval effectiveness of the disposition words. One is that the disposition cues were actually functioning as semantic associates to sentences, rather than representing outcomes of an encoding-specific inference. The second concerns the locus of the hypothesized inference in the information-processing sequence: Might an inference have occurred at some later stage?

First, are there undetected a priori semantic associations between the disposition cues and the sentences that are strong enough to retrieve the sentences better than the intended semantic associates did? We designed the extensive pretesting to reduce this possibility. Even though pretesting did not identify these disposition words as semantic associates, it is still possible that such associations existed and operated to help subjects retrieve sentences. But if the disposition words were operating as semantic associates, then their effectiveness should have been specific to sentence parts. For instance, had the entire recall advantage of the disposition words resided in the recall of predicates, then it could be argued that the disposition words were merely associated with kinds of behavior in subjects' implicit personality theories (e.g., motioning pedestrians to cross the street is an instance of considerateness). The superiority of the disposition-cued recall might then be accounted for by rival theories of retrieval. For example, according to the generation-recognition theory (e.g., Bahrick, 1969), presentation of a disposition cue might allow subjects to generate a set of behaviors that exemplify the disposition and then to recognize the correct one. (We designed Pretest 5 to minimize this possibility). But in fact the disposition words had an advantage over other retrieval cues in the recall of the entire sentence and combinations of sentence parts that included the semantically unrelated actor. Most telling is the difference between disposition-cued and semantic-cued recall of these combinations in Experiment 2. In that study, both cues related in different ways to sentence verbs; the semantic cues were related by virtue of a priori associations, and the disposition words were related by virtue of inferences that subjects made on reading the sentences. Disposition cues retrieved the entire sentence 65 times as compared with 51 times for the verb associate, a significant superiority, as our a posteriori test revealed. In addition, the disposition words retrieved combinations that included the actor significantly more often than did the semantic-verb associates. These patterns of recall are more consistent with the encoding-specificity notion, which holds that

the sentence is linked in the episodic memory system with the disposition word, which is a de facto input cue because it was inferred at encoding. Although the disposition cues may arguably have a semantic association with some of the sentence predicates (as the pretest for Experiment 2 showed clearly), the actors, which were randomly paired with predicates, certainly had no a priori associations with the disposition words (e.g., carpenter: Considerate). Hence the superior recall of entire sentences, including the semantically unrelated actors, through disposition cuing suggests that those cues were operating on episodic memory of the sentences' representations more than on their semantic representations.

A second issue concerns the most likely locus of the inference in information processing, short-term or long-term store. Even if important a priori associations between disposition words and sentences were ruled out, the possibility would remain that a personality inference is made, not at encoding, but at a later processing stage, during retrieval perhaps (Postman, 1972). Even though this interesting possibility has not been absolutely eliminated in the present experiments, several circumstances make it less plausible than the encoding hypothesis. If inferences were made when the sentences were retrieved, one would expect noncued recall to be as strong as disposition-cued recall, or at any rate much higher than it was, because the sentences must have been retrieved from long-term store before inferences could be made on them. Because noncued recall is much lower than disposition-cued recall, a nonencoding hypothesis must hold that subjects made inferences from the sentences while they were available but not accessible (cf. Tulving & Pearlstone, 1966). In other words, sentences that had not been retrieved from long-term store would be the basis of personality inferences, in this scenario. This possibility seems much less parsimonious than the hypothesis that the inferences are made from the sentences while they are held in short-term store during encoding. Thus, the data suggest that such inferences may be an intrinsic part of the process of encoding information and do not always require a separate mental operation subsequent to information retrieval.

The fact that subjects made covert trait inferences without intentions to do so brings up the intriguing possibility that trait inferences may qualify as automatic processes. This issue has important implications for the question of how spontaneous such social inferences are, because automatic processes possess characteristics that would strongly argue for their spontaneousness (e.g., being difficult to suppress or change). In addition to the absence-of-intentionality characteristic, however, automatic processes may occur without awareness and without interference from other ongoing mental activity (Bargh, 1984; Hasher & Zacks, 1979; Kahneman, 1973; Posner & Snyder, 1975; Schneider & Shiffrin, 1977; Shiffrin & Schneider, 1977). The present evidence for absence of awareness is problematic because the 10-min interval between encoding and reporting leaves open the possibility that subjects may have been momentarily aware of their mental processes but forgot them by the time they were asked to introspect. The criterion of absence-of-interference from simultaneous mental activity has not been addressed in the present experiments. This issue, as well as other criteria for automaticity, is being investigated in current research.

One limit to the generality of these findings must be pointed out. The sentences used in the experiments described actions that, in Jones and Davis' terminology, are correspondent to personality traits. Correspondence, in their theory, means the extent to which "the act and the underlying characteristic or attribute are similarly described by the inference" (Jones & Davis, 1965, p. 223). Our sentences were not only written to represent correspondent acts but were also selected from a set of 39, partly on the basis of pretest subjects' ability to make reliable and consensual correspondent inferences. Thus there were no sentences like, "The man walks down the street." We are not suggesting that people make personality inferences about every piece of behavior they observe. But it should also be remembered that sentences were pretested for vividness or extremeness. Thus it cannot be said that only extreme behaviors instigate trait inferences. Some commonplace behaviors do too.

What are the implications of the possibility that inferred dispositions are often stored in memory with behavioral information? There is a body of research that has explored the relation between the memory status of social information and consequent judgments (e.g., Carlston, 1980; Higgins & King, 1981; Taylor & Fiske, 1978; Reyes, Thompson, & Bower, 1980; Srull & Wyer, 1979). The import of this research is that the accessibility of information has an impact on the outcome of social judgments, such as decisions of guilt or innocence. Our results suggest that dispositional judgments may be made unintentionally at encoding and stored with the information on which they are based. That should increase their subsequent accessibility, and this may influence subsequent judgments. When the original unintended dispositional judgment is evaluative, it may prejudice subsequent judgments, perhaps without the judge's awareness.

A second implication is that the relative effectiveness of dispositional cues in recall of behavioral information may be one basis for the overestimation of behavioral consistency across situations or time. People frequently make this error in perceiving others (Mischel, 1968). There is recent evidence (Lenauer, Sameth, & Shaver, 1976; Moore, Sherrod, Liu, & Underwood, 1979) that people increasingly make this same error in self-perception as time passes.

A third implication is that if dispositions are stored in memory with supportive behavioral information, then memory searches using these dispositions as retrieval cues may be one basis for the occurrence of confirmatory hypothesis testing (Snyder, 1981) and perseverence effects (Ross & Anderson, 1982).

Perhaps the most basic issue concerns the early assumptions expressed by seminal person-perception researchers regarding the facile nature of these processes. The possibility that trait inferences are encoding specific and spontaneous would tend to support these notions and to suggest that such processes occur when behavior is being casually observed, in ordinary situations entirely lacking the character of laboratory experiments. The supposition that they are not occurring when not instructed is therefore gratuitous, and researchers who present subjects with descriptions of behavior, for any experimental purpose, should be mindful of this possibility.

REFERENCES

Anderson, J. R., & Ross, B. H. (1980). Evidence against a semantic-episodic distinction. *Journal of Experimental Psychology: Human Learning and Memory, 6*, 441–465.

Asch, S. E. (1946). Forming impressions of personality. *Journal of Abnormal and Social Psychology, 41*, 258–290.

Bahrick, H. P. (1969). Measurement of memory by prompted recall. *Journal of Experimental Psychology, 79*, 213–219.

Bahrick, H. P. (1970). Two-phase model for prompted recall. *Psychological Review, 77*, 215–222.

Bargh, J. A. (1984). Automatic and conscious processing of social information. In R. S. Wyer, Jr., & T. K. Srull (Eds.), *The handbook of social cognition* (Vol. 3, pp. 1–43). Hillsdale, NJ: Erlbaum.

Berscheid, E., Fraziano, W., Monson, T., & Dermer, M. (1976). Outcome dependency: Attention, attribution, and attraction. *Journal of Personality and Social Psychology, 34*, 978–989.

Bilodeau, E. A., & Blick, K. A. (1965). Courses of misrecall over long-term retention intervals as related to strength of pre-experimental habits of word association. *Psychological Reports, 16*, 1173–1192.

Carlston, D. E. (1980). Events, inferences and impression formation. In R. Hastie, T. M. Ostrom, E. B. Ebbesen, R. S. Wyer, Jr., D. L. Hamilton, & D. E. Carlston (Eds.), *Person memory: The cognitive basis of social perception* (pp. 89–119). Hillsdale, NJ: Erlbaum.

Cohen, J., & Cohen, P. (1975). *Applied multiple regression correlational analysis for the behavioral sciences*. Hillsdale, NJ: Erlbaum.

Enzle, M. E., & Schopflocher, D. (1978). Instigation of attribution processes by attributional questions. *Personality and Social Psychology Bulletin, 4*, 595–599.

Hasher, L., & Zacks, R. T. (1979). Automatic and effortful processes in memory. *Journal of Experimental Psychology: General, 108*, 356–388.

Higgins, E. T., & King, G. (1981). Accessibility of social constructs: Information-processing consequences of individual and contextual variability. In N. Cantor & J. F. Kihlstrom (Eds.), *Personality, cognition, and social interaction*. Hillsdale, NJ: Erlbaum.

Jones, E. E., & Davis, K. E. (1965). From acts to dispositions: The attribution process in person perception. In L. Berkowitz (Ed.), *Advances in experimental social psychology* (Vol. 2, pp. 220–266). New York: Academic Press.

Kirk, R. E. (1968). *Experimental design: Procedures for the behavioral sciences*. Monterey, CA: Brooks/Cole.

Kahneman, D. (1973). *Attention and effort*. Englewood Cliffs, NJ: Prentice-Hall.

Lenauer, M., Sameth, L., & Shaver, P. (1976). Looking back at oneself in time: Another approach to the actor-observer phenomenon. *Perceptual and Motor Skills, 43*, 1283–1287.

Mischel, W. (1968). *Personality and assessment*. New York: Wiley.

Moore, B. S., Sherrod, D. R., Liu, T. J., & Underwood, B. (1979). The dispositional shift in attribution over time. *Journal of Experimental Social Psychology, 15*, 553–569.

Nisbett, R. E., & Wilson, T. D. (1977). Telling more than we can know: Verbal reports on mental processes. *Psychological Review, 84*, 229–259.

Posner, M. I., & Snyder, C. R. R. (1975). Attention and cognitive control. In R. L. Solso (Ed.), *Information processing and cognition: The Loyola Symposium* (pp. 55–85). Hillsdale, NJ: Erlbaum.

Postman, L. (1972). A pragmatic view of organization theory. In E. Tulving & W. Donaldson (Eds.), *Organization of Memory* (pp. 3–48). New York: Academic Press.

Pryor, J. B., & Kriss, M. (1977). The cognitive dynamics of salience in the attribution process. *Journal of Personality and Social Psychology, 33*, 49–55.

Pyszczynski, T. A., & Greenberg, J. (1981). Role of disconfirmed expectancies in the instigation of attributional processing. *Journal of Personality and Social Psychology, 40*, 31–38.

Reyes, R. M., Thompson, W. C., & Bower, G. H. (1980). Judgmental biases resulting from differing availabilities of arguments. *Journal of Personality and Social Psychology, 39*, 2–12.

Ross, L., & Anderson, C. A. (1982). Shortcomings in the attribution process: On the origins and maintenance of erroneous social assessments. In D. Kahneman, P. Slovic, & A. Tversky (Eds.), *Judgment under uncertainty: Heuristics and biases* (pp. 129–152). Cambridge, England: Cambridge University Press.

Schneider, D. J., Hastorf, A. H., & Ellsworth, P. C. (1979). *Person perception*. Reading, MA: Addison-Wesley.

Schneider, W., & Shiffrin, R. M. (1977). Controlled and automatic human information processing: I. Detection, search, and attention. *Psychological Review, 84*, 1–61.

Shiffrin, R. M., & Schneider, W. (1977). Controlled and automatic human information processing: II. Perceptual learning, automatic attending, and a general theory. *Psychological Review, 84*, 127–190.

Smith, E. R., & Miller, F. D. (1979). Salience and the cognitive mediation of attribution. *Journal of Personality and Social Psychology, 37*, 2240–2252.

Snyder, M. (1981). Seek and ye shall find: Testing hypotheses about other people. In E. T. Higgins, C. P. Herman, & M. P. Zanna (Eds.), *Social cognition: The Ontario Symposium* (Vol. I, pp. 277–303). Hillsdale, NJ: Erlbaum.

Srull, T. K., & Wyer, R. S. (1979). The role of category accessibility in the interpretation of information about persons: Some determinants and implications. *Journal of Personality and Social Psychology, 37*, 1660–1672.

Tagiuri, R. (1958). Introduction. In R. Tagiuri & L. Petrullo (Eds.), *Person perception and interpersonal behavior*. Stanford, CA: Stanford University Press.

Taylor, S. E., & Fiske, S. (1978). Salience, attention, and attribution: Top-of-the-head phenomena. In L. Berkowitz (Ed.), *Advances in experimental social psychology* (Vol. 11, pp. 249–288), New York: Academic Press.

Thomson, D., & Tulving, E. (1970). Associative encoding and retrieval: Weak and strong cues. *Journal of Experimental Psychology, 86*, 255–262.

Tulving, E. (1972). Episodic and semantic memory. In E. Tulving & W. Donaldson (Eds.), *Organization of Memory* (pp. 381–403). New York: Academic Press.

Tulving, E., & Osler, S. (1968). Effectiveness of retrieval cues in memory for words. *Journal of Experimental Psychology, 77*, 593–601.

Tulving, E., & Pearlstone, Z. (1966). Availability versus accessibility of information in memory for words, *Journal of Verbal Learning and Verbal Behavior, 5*, 381–391.

Tulving, E., & Thomson, D. M. (1973). Encoding specificity and retrieval processes in episodic memory. *Psychological Review, 80*, 352–373.

Wong, P. T. P., & Weiner, B. (1981). When people ask "why" questions, and the heuristics of attributional search. *Journal of Personality and Social Psychology, 40*, 650–663.

On Cognitive Busyness: When Person Perceivers Meet Persons Perceived

Daniel T. Gilbert, Brett W. Pelham, and Douglas S. Krull

Person perception includes three sequential processes: Categorization (what is the actor doing?), characterization (what trait does the action imply?), and correction (what situational constraints may have caused the action?). We argue that correction is less automatic (i.e., more easily disrupted) than either categorization or characterization. In Experiment 1, subjects observed a target behave anxiously in an anxiety-provoking situation. In Experiment 2, subjects listened to a target read a political speech that he had been constrained to write. In both experiments, control subjects used information about situational constraints when drawing inferences about the target, but cognitively busy subjects (who performed an additional cognitive task during encoding) did not. The results (a) suggest that person perception is a combination of lower and higher order processes that differ in their susceptibility to disruption and (b) highlight the fundamental differences between active and passive perceivers.

Many of us can recall a time when, as students, we encountered a professor at a party and were surprised to find that he or she seemed a very different sort of person than our classroom experience had led us to expect. In part, such discrepant impressions reflect real discrepancies in behavior: Professors may display greater warmth or less wit at a party than they do in the classroom. However, just as the object of perception changes across situations, so too does the perceiver. As *passive perceivers* in a classroom, we are able to observe

This research was supported by National Science Foundation Grant BNS-8605443 to Daniel T. Gilbert.

We thank Bill Swann and several anonymous reviewers for their thoughtful comments on an earlier version of this article, Karen Enquist and Alan Swinkles for serving as target persons, and Mark Fishbein for his help with Experiment 2.

Correspondence concerning this article should be addressed to Daniel Gilbert, Department of Psychology, University of Texas, Mezes Hall 330, Austin, Texas 78712.

a professor without concerning ourselves with the mechanics of social interaction. At a party, however, we are *active perceivers*, busy managing our impressions, predicting our partner's behavior, and evaluating alternative courses of action. Of all the many differences between active and passive perceivers, one seems fundamental: Active perceivers, unlike passive perceivers, are almost always doing several things at once (Gilbert, Jones, & Pelham, 1987; Gilbert & Krull, 1988; Jones & Thibaut, 1958).

How do the complexities of engaging in social interaction affect the process of social perception? This question is tractable only if one recognizes that there is no single process of social perception; rather, there are several different processes that together constitute the act of knowing others. Trope (1986) has argued that person perception has two major components: Behavioral identification (what is the actor doing?) and attributional inference (why is the actor doing it?). The first of these processes involves categorizing an action, whereas the second involves causal reasoning about the categorized act. In addition, Quattrone (1982) has suggested that this second attributional stage may itself be comprised of two minor components: Perceivers first draw a dispositional inference about the actor and then adjust this inference by taking into account the various external forces that may have facilitated or inhibited the actor's behavior. In short, these perspectives suggest that person perception consists of (a) categorization (i.e., identifying actions), (b) characterization (i.e., drawing dispositional inferences about the actor), and finally, (c) correction (i.e., adjusting those inferences with information about situational constraints).

In what ways are these processes qualitatively distinct? Categorization is considered a relatively automatic process[1] that happens immediately and without conscious attention: We see Henry playing poker rather than simply moving his fingers, Herbert cheating rather than simply taking a card from his sleeve, and we are usually unaware of the inferential processes by which such categorizations are achieved (e.g., Bruner, 1957; Fodor, 1983; Nisbett & Wilson, 1977; cf. Gibson, 1979). Characterization and correction, on the other hand, are often considered more deliberate and conscious processes whereby perceivers apply inferential rules (e.g., the law of noncommon effects, the discounting and augmenting principles, etc.) to their observations and calculate the causes of behavior. We may conclude that Herbert is not truly malicious if a cocaine habit or bad luck on Wall Street forced him to raise extra cash with an extra ace, and we can easily articulate the logic by which such a conclusion is derived (Jones & Davis, 1965; Kelley, 1971).

We believe that this view of attributional processes is not entirely correct. In fact, we will suggest that in some senses characterization (the first attributional subprocess) is much more like categorization (the preattributional process) than it is like correction (the second attributional subprocess). Specifically, we will argue that characterization is generally an overlearned, relatively automatic process that requires little effort or conscious attention, whereas correction is a more deliberate, relatively controlled process that uses a significant portion of the perceiver's processing resources.

---

[1] We use the word *automatic* here with some trepidation because this term has a very specific meaning on which few theorists agree. For our purposes, it is enough to say that a process is relatively automatic if it is generally impervious to disruption by concurrent cognitive operations and generally resistant to conscious control.

These contentions have an important consequence for the active perceiver. If they are true, then the peripheral cognitive activities in which active person-perceivers engage (e.g., impression management, social influence, etc.) may disrupt correction without similarly disrupting characterization. Thus, active perceivers may draw dispositional inferences from the behavior of others but be less likely than their passive counterparts to use situational constraint information to correct these inferences, simply because the demands of social interaction leave them unable to do so.

We stress the word *use* in this regard. It is clear that perceivers often fail to notice the situational constraints that impinge upon an actor: We may not realize, for example, the extent to which a husband's domineering manner forces his wife to behave submissively. If active perceivers do not identify situational constraints, then the fact that they do not use such information is unremarkable (Gilbert & Jones, 1986). We wish to suggest that even when active perceivers do identify the situational forces that shape another's behavior, they are often unable to use this information because doing so requires cognitive resources that the complexities of interaction have already usurped.

Experiment 1

We contend that cognitive busyness disables the ability to use situational constraint information (i.e., to augment and discount). It is tempting to test this hypothesis simply by engaging some subjects in social interaction with a target and allowing others to remain passive observers of such an interaction. However, this sort of operationalization would create serious confounds. Although the interactive subject would be cognitively busier than the observer subject, the subjects would also differ in other ways. Active perceivers may be more outcome dependent, may feel more involved and accountable, and may consider the target's actions more personally relevant than do passive perceivers. Thus, a clear test of the hypothesis requires that perceivers differ only in the number of cognitive tasks they perform.

There is, however, a second problem. If cognitively busy perceivers are given some extra task to perform, then they may not use situational constraint information simply because the extra task may leave them unable to gather it. If, for example, cognitively busy perceivers are asked to observe an actor behaving under situational constraint and are also asked to count the pulses of a nearby flashing light, then their failure to use situational constraint information may reflect only the misdirection of attention rather than the consumption of attentional resources.

In Experiment 1 we solved this problem by asking busy perceivers simultaneously to observe a target and to memorize information about the situational constraints on the target's behavior. Memorization requires rehearsal and rehearsal requires resources; thus, we predicted that these busy perceivers would remember the constraint information particularly well but would be unable to use the information they were rehearsing.

Method

Overview

Subjects watched seven silent clips from a videotape of a female target having a discussion with a stranger. In five of the seven clips, the target appeared extremely anxious. Half the subjects learned that in these five clips the target had been discussing anxiety-inducing topics (e.g., her sexual fantasies). The remaining subjects learned that in all seven clips the target had been discussing relaxation-inducing topics (e.g., world travel). Half of the subjects in each of these conditions were required to perform a cognitive rehearsal task (i.e., remembering the discussion topics in their proper sequence) while viewing the tape, and the remaining subjects were not. After viewing the tape, subjects rated the target's trait anxiety, predicted the target's future state anxiety, and attempted to recall the - discussion topics.

Subjects

The subjects were 47 female students at the University of Texas at Austin who participated to fulfill a requirement of their introductory psychology course.

Instructions

On arrival at the laboratory subjects were greeted by a male experimenter who gave them a brief oral introduction to the experiment, provided them with complete written instructions, and then escorted each subject to a cubicle (equipped with video monitor) where she remained for the duration of the experiment.

The written instructions explained that subjects would watch seven short clips from a videotape of a getting-acquainted conversation that had ostensibly taken place earlier in the year. This conversation was alleged to have been part of a project on the role of discussion topics in friendship formation. Subjects were told that two female students (who had never previously met) had been asked to discuss each of seven topics for about 5 min and that

subjects would be seeing a short (approximately 20 s) clip from each of these seven discussions. The instructions explained that during the getting-acquainted conversation the camera had been positioned behind one of the discussants, and thus only one of the discussants (the target) would be visible in the tape.

Situational Constraint Information

Subjects were told that to protect the privacy of the discussants the videotape would be shown without any sound. However, subjects were told that they would be able to tell which of the seven topics was being discussed in any given clip because the topic would appear in subtitles at the bottom of the screen.

Half the subjects were randomly assigned to the anxious topics condition. In this condition five of the seven subtitles indicated that the target was discussing anxiety-inducing topics (e.g., her sexual fantasies). In each of these five instances, the target appeared clearly anxious and uneasy. In the two remaining instances, the subtitles indicated that the target was discussing rather mundane topics (e.g., world travel); in these instances the target appeared relaxed and at ease. The remaining subjects were assigned to the relaxing topics condition. In this condition subjects saw the same behaviors seen by subjects in the anxious topics condition. However, all seven of the subtitles in this condition indicated that the target was discussing mundane and ordinary topics.

In the anxious topics condition, then, the target's apparent anxiety could logically be attributed to the nature of the topics she was discussing and thus was not indicative of dispositional anxiety. In the relaxing topics condition, however, the same behavior could not logically have been caused by the nature of the discussion topics, which should, in fact, have induced precisely the opposite sort of reaction. In this case the target's behavior was an excellent index of dispositional anxiety. The topics and the target's behavior in each of these conditions are shown in Table 19.1.

Cognitive Busyness Manipulation

Half the subjects were randomly assigned to the one-task condition. Subjects in this condition were told that at the end of the experiment they would be asked to make several judgments about the target's personality. The remaining subjects were assigned to the two-task condition. Subjects in this condition were told that in addition to making personality judgments, they should also be prepared to recall each of the seven discussion topics at the end of the experiment. (Subjects were told that this task would enable the experimenter to compare the subject's

TABLE 19.1. Discussion Topics and Target's Behavior

Relaxing topics Condition	Anxious Topics Condition	Target's Behavior
Fashion trends	Public humiliation	Anxious
World travel	Hidden secrets	Anxious
Great books	Sexual fantasies	Anxious
Favorite hobbies	Favorite hobbies	Relaxed
Foreign films	Embarrassing moments	Anxious
Ideal vacations	Ideal vacations	Relaxed
Best restaurants	Personal failures	Anxious

memory for the topics with the discussants' memories for the same topics.) We assumed that this additional memory task would encourage two-task subjects to rehearse the topics while they viewed the videotape.

Dependent Measures
Perceived trait anxiety. Before the experiment began, subjects were allowed to familiarize themselves with the trait anxiety measures. These measures required subjects to rate the target's dispositional anxiety on three 13-point bipolar scales that were anchored with the phrases (a) *is probably comfortable (uncomfortable) in social situations*, (b) *is a calm (nervous) sort of person*, and (c) *is generally relaxed (anxious) with people*. It was stressed that by marking the scales subjects should indicate "what kind of person the target is in her day to day life" and not just "how she was acting."
Recall of discussion topics. After seeing the videotape, subjects completed the trait anxiety measures described. Next, subjects were given 10 min to recall each of the seven discussion topics in their proper order.
Predicted state anxiety. Finally, subjects were asked to predict the target's state anxiety (i.e., how she would feel) in each of three hypothetical situations: (a) when being asked to give an impromptu presentation in a seminar, (b) when noticing that a male acquaintance had seen her lose her bikini at a local pool, and (c) when noticing a run in her stockings during a corporate job interview. Subjects predicted the target's state anxiety in each of these situations on three 13-point bipolar scales anchored with the phrases *extremely anxious* and *not at all anxious*. After completing these measures, subjects were probed for suspicion, debriefed, and dismissed.

Results and Discussion

Recall of Discussion Topics
At the end of the experiment, subjects were asked to recall the discussion topics. Subjects' recall attempts

were coded as follows: No points if the subject failed to recall the topic, 1 point if the subject recalled the topic's meaning but not its precise wording (e.g., global travel rather than world travel), and 2 points if the subject recalled the topic verbatim. Thus, subjects could receive from 0 to 14 points on the recall index.

A 2 (cognitive tasks: one or two) $\times$ 2 (discussion topics: relaxing or anxious) analysis of variance (ANOVA) performed on this recall index revealed only a main effect of cognitive tasks, $F(1, 43) = 6.38$, $p < .02$, $MS_e = 3.98$. Two-task subjects recalled more topics ($M = 11.79$) than did one-task subjects ($M = 10.30$). This seems to indicate that two-task subjects did indeed devote some extra cognitive resources to the rehearsal and memorization of the discussion topics.

Perceived Trait Anxiety
We averaged the three measures of perceived trait anxiety (comfortable-uncomfortable, calm-nervous, and relaxed-anxious) to create a perceived trait anxiety index (coefficient $\alpha = .78$). A 2 $\times$ 2 ANOVA performed on this index revealed a main effect of discussion topic, $F(1, 43) = 7.55$, $p < .01$, $MS_e = 28.92$. This effect, however, was qualified by the predicted Cognitive Task $\times$ Discussion Topic interaction, $F(1, 43) = 4.07$, $p = .05$. As Table 19.2 shows, one-task subjects used the situational constraint information (i.e., the discussion topics) both to discount and to augment. In the anxious topics condition, one-task subjects discounted by rating the target as less dispositionally anxious than she appeared to be, whereas in the relaxing topics condition, one-task subjects augmented by rating the target as more dispositionally anxious than she appeared to be. Thus, the target was seen as more trait-anxious when she displayed anxiety during a discussion of relaxing rather than anxious topics, $F(1, 21) = 7.78$, $p < .01$.

Two-task subjects, however, did not use the situational constraint information (i.e., they neither discounted nor augmented). These subjects concluded that the target was equally trait anxious regardless of which topics she had been asked to discuss, $F(1, 22) < 1$. It is worth nothing that two-task subjects drew this conclusion despite the fact that they were more likely than one-task subjects to recall the discussion topics.

Predicted State Anxiety
Subjects' predictions of the target's state anxiety in three hypothetical situations were averaged to create a predicted state anxiety index (coefficient $\alpha = .76$). A 2 $\times$ 2 ANOVA performed on this index revealed only

TABLE 19.2. Subjects' Perceptions of Target's Trait Anxiety

	One task		Two tasks	
Discussion Topic	M	n	M	n
Relaxing	10.31	12	9.28	13
Anxious	7.79	11	8.88	11
Difference	2.52		0.40	

Note. Higher values indicate greater perceived trait anxiety.

TABLE 19.3. Subjects' Predictions of Target's State Anxiety in Hypothetical Situations

	Cognitive tasks	
Discussion Topic	One Task	Two Tasks
Relaxing	11.58	10.13
Anxious	9.67	10.45
Difference	1.91	−0.32

Note. Higher values indicate greater predicted state anxiety.

the predicted Cognitive Tasks × Discussion Topic interaction, $F(1, 43) = 4.56$, $p < .05$, $MS_e = 29.02$. As Table 19.3 shows, one-task subjects predicted that the apparently anxious target who discussed relaxation-inducing topics would experience more state anxiety in new situations than would the apparently anxious target who discussed anxiety-inducing topics, $F(1, 21) = 4.05$, $p < .06$. Two-task subjects, however, predicted the same amount of state anxiety in both conditions, regardless of which topics the target had been asked to discuss, $F(1, 22) < 1$. This pattern of results is similar to the pattern seen earlier on the perceived trait anxiety index and suggests that those earlier ratings do indeed reflect true dispositional attributions (rather than some potential confusion about the meaning of the scales).

Evidence of Mediating Processes
Memory for the discussion topics may be considered an index of how much of their cognitive resources two-task subjects devoted to the peripheral task. We have claimed that the use of situational constraint information is disabled by peripheral tasks: Thus, those subjects who spent the greatest amount of their cognitive resources on the peripheral task (i.e., who showed the best recall of the topics) should have been the least likely to use the situational constraint information. This means that the two-task subjects in the anxious topics condition who recalled the greatest number of topics (i.e., those

who presumably devoted the most resources to the peripheral task) should have perceived the greatest amount of trait anxiety, whereas those who recalled the fewest number of topics should (like the one-task subjects) have perceived the least amount of trait anxiety. This is precisely what happened. For two-task subjects in the anxious topics condition there was a positive correlation between recall and perceived trait anxiety, $r(9) = .56$, $p < .05$.

Similar logic predicts precisely the opposite pattern of correlation for two-task subjects in the relaxing topics condition. In this condition, subjects who recalled the greatest number of topics should have perceived the least amount of trait anxiety, whereas those who recalled the fewest number of topics should (like the one-task subjects) have perceived the greatest amount of trait anxiety. Again, this was the case. In this condition there was a negative correlation between recall and perceived trait anxiety, $r(11) = -.61$, $p < .05$. These correlations provide strong internal support for our claim that cognitive busyness mediates the tendency to use situational constraint information.

Experiment 2

The results of Experiment 1 are clear: Those subjects who performed an extra task during person perception were particularly unlikely to use information about the situational constraints that were affecting the target. This was true despite the fact that these subjects were particularly likely to recall the situational constraint information. This finding is consistent with our suggestion that initial characterizations require fewer resources than do subsequent corrections.

Two important questions arise. First, does the rehearsal task that subjects performed have any real world analog? We believe it does. For example, active perceivers (unlike passive perceivers) must constantly be prepared to execute behavior. Often this means that one must prepare one's actions at the same time that one's partner is acting. Most of us can remember a conversation in which we wanted to say something but had to wait until our partner finished talking. During this time we probably rehearsed our contribution, thus depleting the cognitive resources available for drawing inferences about our loquacious partner's ongoing behavior. In Experiment 2 we attempted to demonstrate that the rehearsal engendered by behavioral preparation would have the same effects as the rehearsal task used in Experiment 1.

Second, it is important to ask whether these findings apply to verbal behavior as well as to nonverbal behavior. It seems possible that the characterization of nonverbal behavior is (as we have argued) relatively more automatic than subsequent correction, but that the characterization of verbal behavior is not. If this is so, then the effect we have demonstrated (i.e., that peripheral tasks impair correction but not characterization) has a somewhat more limited range of application. Therefore, it seemed important to investigate the effects of cognitive busyness on inferences drawn from verbal behavior.

Method

Overview
Subjects listened to a male target read either a pro- or antiabortion speech that he had been assigned to write. Subjects in the one-task condition merely listened to the speech, whereas subjects in the two-task condition listened to the speech knowing that they would themselves be asked to write and read a speech later in the session. Finally, all subjects attempted to diagnose the target's true attitude toward abortion.

Subjects
The subjects were 37 male and 26 female students at the University of Texas at Austin who participated to fulfill a requirement of their introductory psychology course.

Instructions
On arrival at the laboratory subjects were greeted by a male experimenter who gave them a brief oral introduction to the experiment, provided them with complete written instructions, and then escorted each subject to a cubicle (equipped with an audio speaker) where the subject remained for the duration of the experiment.

The written instruction explained that the study concerned extemporaneous public speaking. Subjects were told that another subject (the target) had arrived 15 min earlier and had been assigned to write either a pro- or antiabortion speech. The target had ostensibly been given two newspaper editorials to help him generate arguments for the speech. Subjects were informed that in a few minutes they would hear (over the audio speaker) the target read his speech from the next room. The subject's job was to listen to this speech and diagnose the target's true attitude toward abortion. It was stressed that the task was difficult because the target had had no choice about which side of the issue he would defend; rather, the experimenter had randomly

assigned the target to defend a pro- or antiabortion position. Thus, subjects were told, "You will have to use all of your skills and intuitions as a person perceiver to figure out what he really believes."

Cognitive Busyness Manipulation
Subjects in the one-task condition were given the preceding instructions and were then allowed to hear the target read either a pro- or antiabortion speech. In fact, the speeches had been previously recorded, and it was this recording that subjects heard.

Subjects in the two-task condition were given further instructions. These subjects were told that after diagnosing the target's true attitude toward abortion

> we will ask you and the other volunteer (the target) to switch booths, so that you are in the booth with the microphone and he is in the booth with the speaker. You will then be given 20 minutes to write a speech on an assigned topic, just like the other volunteer was.

Subjects were assured that they would also be given editorials to help them generate arguments for their speeches and were told "We will give you further instructions when the time comes for you to write and read your speech. For now, just concentrate on your duties as the listener." We suspected that despite these assurances, subjects who expected to give a speech would be preoccupied with thoughts about that upcoming event and would therefore have fewer cognitive resources to devote to the attitude attribution task.

Dependent Measures
After listening to the target read his anti- or proabortion speech, subjects attempted to diagnose the target's true attitude on a 13-point bipolar scale anchored with the phrases *essayist is opposed to (in favor of) legalized abortion*. Subjects then used similar bipolar scales to indicate (a) their certainty about the foregoing judgment, (b) their own attitudes toward abortion, (c) their estimates of the average student's attitude toward abortion, and (d) their memories of the position that the target had been assigned to defend. Finally, subjects were probed for suspicion, debriefed, and dismissed.

Results and Discussion

Perceived Attitude
Subjects' ratings of the target's true attitude toward abortion were subjected to a 2 (essay: proabortion or antiabortion) × 2 (cognitive tasks: one or two) ANOVA

TABLE 19.4. Subjects' Perceptions of Target's Attitude Toward Abortion

Target's Essay	One Task		Two Tasks	
	M	n	M	n
Proabortion	8.7	11	10.6	13
Antiabortion	5.4	13	4.2	10
Difference	3.3		6.4	

Note. Higher values indicate more proabortion attitudes.

that revealed a main effect of essay,[2] $F(1, 43) = 50.77$, $p < .001$, $MS_e = 5.44$. This effect was qualified, however, by the predicted Essay × Cognitive Tasks interaction, $F(1, 43) = 5.03$, $p < .03$. As Table 19.4 shows, all subjects attributed a correspondent attitude to the target; however, those subjects who expected to write a speech themselves were especially likely to do so (i.e., were especially unlikely to use the situational constraint information).

This is worthy of remark. Two-task subjects knew that they would be asked to endorse political positions with which they did not necessarily agree; thus, one might predict that these subjects would be particularly sensitive to the fact that identical constraints had been imposed on the target, and would therefore be likely to discount the target's behavior (cf. Miller, Jones, & Hinkle, 1981). As our hypothesis predicted, however, these subjects were less likely than one-task subjects to discount the target's behavior. As in Experiment 1, those subjects who would seem to have been in the best position to use situational constraint information were in fact the least likely to do so.

Other Measures

In the interest of brevity, the remaining measures may be summarized succinctly: Two-task and one-task subjects were equally certain about the inferences they drew and showed equally good memory for the position

[2] Unfortunately, an experiment using a similar deception was being run concurrently with ours; thus, some of our subjects (all of whom participated in several experiments over the course of the semester) did not believe that the target was actually in an adjacent room. After the experiment was over the experimenter conducted an exhaustive probe for suspicion. In addition, all subjects completed a confidential questionnaire that assessed their suspicion, their knowledge of the hypothesis, and so on. Two raters (who had not been experimenters and who were blind to the subject's condition) separately coded each subject's comments and the experimenter's written notes. As a result, 8 suspicious subjects in the two-task condition and 8 suspicious subjects in the one-task condition were removed from the data set prior to analysis.

(pro- or antiabortion) of the essay they had heard (all Fs < 1). There was an irrelevant tendency for two-task subjects to report more antiabortion attitudes for both themselves ($p < .07$) and the average student ($p < .04$), but this tendency occurred regardless of the speech (pro- or antiabortion) that subjects heard (for all Essay × Cognitive Tasks interactions, $F < 1.3$).

General Discussion

These experiments tell a simple story. When people are cognitively busy, one component of the person-perception process (correction) suffers more than another (characterization). In particular, cognitive rehearsal seems to impair the ability to use information about the situational constraints that may have influenced an actor's behavior; thus, perceivers who are busy performing rehearsal tasks may draw dispositional inferences that are not warranted and fail to draw dispositional inferences that are. It is not that cognitively busy perceivers simply fail to gather situational constraint information; in these studies, busy perceivers were more likely to have this information than were their less busy counterparts. Rather, busy perceivers seem unable to use the information they gather and remember so well.

One interpretation of these findings (and the one that we favor) is that correction requires a significant expenditure of resources and therefore cannot proceed on a limited cognitive budget. Of course, the interpretation of interference effects in general is currently the subject of much controversy (see Hirst & Kalmar, 1987, for a review). The resource metaphor is only one way to describe such effects and, unfortunately, no critical experiment seems capable of distinguishing between resource and other viable interpretations (e.g., structure or skill). Thus, although our data are entirely consistent with the notion of limited processing resources, they do not demand such an account. However, regardless of which metaphor one prefers, these data have several practical implications for our understanding of the person-perception process.

The Mystery of the Correspondence Bias

Person-perceivers often draw dispositional inferences from situationally induced behavior, and this tendency is so common as to warrant the label *fundamental attribution error* (Ross, 1977) or *correspondence bias* (Gilbert & Jones, 1986). Attempts to explain the pervasive bias toward dispositional inference have consistently fallen short, and none seem to provide a complete account of this tendency. The problem is that (with few exceptions) theorists have generally considered dispositional and situational attributions to be alternative consequences of a hypothetical process known as causal attribution.

But consider two different kinds of inferential processes. Perception is a lower order inferential process that occurs automatically and nonconsciously; perceptual inferences have a *given* quality about them because one is usually unaware of the processes by which the percept was produced (M. K. Johnson & Raye, 1981). Reasoning, however, is a higher order inferential process; reasoned inferences have a deliberate and conscious quality about them, and the steps by which they are achieved are easily articulated. Ordinary language captures this phenomenal distinction between higher and lower order inferences: One passively *has* a perception, whereas one actively *draws* an inference.

Our studies, and other recent evidence, suggest that correction is a species of reasoning (a higher order process), whereas characterization is a species of perception (a lower order process; Kassin & Baron, 1985; Lowe & Kassin, 1980; McArthur & Baron, 1983; Newtson, 1980; Winter & Uleman, 1984; Winter, Uleman, & Cunniff, 1985). If this is so, then correspondence bias can be seen as the failure to apply an inferential correction to the initial dispositional perceptions that perceivers cannot help but have (cf. J. T. Johnson, Jemmott, & Pettigrew, 1984; Quattrone, 1982). But why should the second step in this two-step process sometimes fail to occur? Our studies suggest a simple answer: The first step is a snap, but the second one's a doozy. When we recognize that characterizations occur more automatically than, and prior to, inferential corrections, the once mysterious correspondence bias becomes entirely explicable.

The Slow Death of the Person-Perception Process

Having argued that characterization is a lower order perceptual process rather than a higher order inferential process, we are prepared to offer some refinements to a general model of person perception. First, we concur with Quattrone's (1982) contention that attributions are a product of dispositional inferences that are followed by situational adjustments. However, the differences between the characterization and correction processes are of paramount importance. The present experiments argue that characterization is, in general, more automatic than correction. Elsewhere (Gilbert & Krull,

1988) we have argued that drawing dispositional inferences from nonverbal behavior (nonverbal characterization) is, in turn, more automatic than drawing dispositional inferences from verbal behavior (verbal characterization). By arranging these three processes in decreasing order of automaticity (i.e., nonverbal characterization, verbal characterization, and correction), we are in a position to make some predictions about their relative rates of degeneration and thereby to begin painting a portrait of the person perceiver.

Passive Perceivers

Passive perceivers who devote their entire attention to a person-perception task should, according to our model, successfully complete all three operations and thus should draw accurate inferences about others. Why, then, do the passive subjects of attributional research apparently defy this prediction by showing correspondence bias?

First, one of the rarely noted findings in Jones and Harris's (1967, p. 6) original demonstration of the correspondence bias is that there was 10 times more variance among the judgments of perceivers who observed constrained behavior than among the judgments of perceivers who observed unconstrained behavior. In other words, many of the passive perceivers who observed constrained behavior did not draw dispositional inferences about the target (i.e., the bias appeared as a difference between the aggregate scores of the high-variance conditions). This suggests that some passive perceivers do in fact complete all three of the operations in our model and are therefore able to draw accurate inferences from the situationally induced behavior of others.

But what about those who do show the bias? We suspect it is unusual for a person to devote his or her entire attention to any one task. During the dramatic climax of a film or the last movement of a great symphony, we are, for a moment, wholly absorbed by a single perceptual event. These experiences are, however, exceptional. More often we find ourselves attending primarily to one thing, but secondarily and simultaneously to a host of others (e.g., intrusive thoughts, uncomfortable chairs, full bladders, or the anchovy aficionado in the next seat). It is unlikely that the passive perceiver in the psychologist's laboratory ever becomes completely enraptured by a low-budget videotape or a typewritten page; rather, he or she attends to these mundane stimuli while also thinking about the unfamiliar surroundings, the lateness of the hour, or tomorrow's chemistry exam. Our second point, then, is that even so-called passive perceivers are often cognitively busy.

Can this minimal busyness account for a phenomenon as robust as the correspondence bias? To answer this question we must be clear about what the bias is, and moreover, what it is not. Some theorists have interpreted the bias to mean that passive perceivers do not use situational constraint information; this is simply wrong. As we noted earlier, some subjects do not show the bias at all. Furthermore, virtually all passive perceivers do use situational constraint information; what research shows is that some passive perceivers do not make sufficient use of this information, and this distinction is important. The correspondence bias is a very meaningful, very reliable, but inevitably very small effect. We suspect that the diminutive size of this bias reflects a slight impairment of the correction process that is caused by the low levels of cognitive busyness that even passive perceivers must normally endure.

Active Perceivers

In his acerbic critique of the field, Neisser (1980) chastised social psychologists for being "too quick to take detached perceivers and knowers as models of human nature" (p. 604). There are, of course, many instances in which people are merely passive perceivers of others: Almost everyone has an opinion about the president of the United States, although very few have met him. Nonetheless, Neisser's point is well-taken; much of what we know about others is in fact learned during social interaction. In what ways, then, do the judgments of active and passive perceivers differ?

As our research suggests, when perceivers begin to interact with others their cognitive resources may become depleted. The added complexities of interaction may begin to usurp increasing amounts of cognitive energy, impairing the relatively controlled correction process while leaving both the verbal and nonverbal characterization processes unimpaired. Thus, active perceivers often finish the person-perception task with their initial characterizations insufficiently corrected. The present experiments are examples of this effect.

As cognitive busyness increases further (either because of increasing interactional complexity or emerging peripheral demands), the next most fragile process — verbal characterization — may itself be impaired. Interestingly, this can have several different effects on the active perceiver's ultimate construal of the target. If the target's verbal and nonverbal behavior carry the same message, then the inability to draw dispositional inferences from verbal behavior should have little consequence. Such redundancy usually occurs when people

are telling the truth. When people lie, however, their verbal and nonverbal behaviors are often at odds, and under these circumstances nonverbal expressions (both vocal and gestural) may reflect their inner characteristics more accurately than do their words (Depaulo, Stone, & Lassiter, 1985; Ekman & Friesen, 1969). In such cases, active perceivers may actually benefit from impairment of the verbal characterization process because they may be unable to use the deceptive information that is carried on the verbal channel. Consequently, the active perceiver's characterizations may be based largely on the target's highly diagnostic nonverbal behavior. Gilbert and Krull (1988) have shown precisely this effect.

Hyperactive Perceivers

Finally, one can imagine perceivers for whom the mechanics of interaction are so complex that all three operations are impaired. Such perceivers may, in essence, draw no inferences at all. People who are painfully shy, desperately bereft, socially inept, or otherwise preoccupied with their thoughts and actions may have virtually no resources to devote to the act of person-perception and thus may fail to draw dispositional inferences from both the verbal and nonverbal behavior of others. Unfortunately, little is known about the effects of severe cognitive busyness on the person-perception process, and we must not be too quick to extrapolate our findings. It may be, for example, that the characterization of nonverbal behavior is so thoroughly automatized that it cannot be impaired by other concurrent activities (cf. Kassin & Baron, 1985; McArthur & Baron, 1983).

Coda and Reprise

The foregoing discussion may seem to suggest that active perceivers are doomed to make errors because their perceptions are often faulty and their ability to correct these perceptions through reasoning is easily impaired. This conclusion is incorrect for several reasons. First, we have argued that when verbal and nonverbal behaviors are at odds, cognitive busyness can, strangely enough, lead active perceivers to make more normative inferences than do passive perceivers (Gilbert & Krull, 1988). In other words, there are occasional benefits to perceptual ignorance.

Second, and more important, it behooves us to remember that things are often what they appear to be: Tables often look flat because they are flat, and people often act aggressively because they are aggressive sorts.

One reason why people can afford to make dispositional inferences at the perceptual level is that such inferences are at least pragmatically correct (see Gilbert, in press; Swann, 1984). Like any other heuristic assumption, the perceptual assumption of dispositional causation probably could not have evolved if it led to inappropriate conclusions on many occasions (Nisbett & Ross, 1980; Tversky & Kahneman, 1974). Third, when functioning in familiar environments, active perceivers may learn to make inferential corrections automatically. To the extent that the correction process can itself become automatized, active perceivers may become relatively immune to the impairments engendered by cognitive busyness.

The present experiments should remind us that understanding others is a rather complex business: Some of what we come to believe about others is perceptually given and some is deliberately reasoned. Although these processes differ primarily in the speed with which they happen, in our awareness of their operation, and in their susceptibility to conscious control and disruption, these small differences may have profound implications for our ultimate construal of others. The more we learn about the ways in which social perceptions and social inferences form an admixture, the closer we shall move to a true understanding of social understanding itself.

REFERENCES

Bruner, J. (1957). On perceptual readiness. *Psychological Review, 64*, 123–152.

Depaulo, B. M., Stone, J. L., & Lassiter, G. D. (1985). Deceiving and detecting deceit. In B. R. Schlenker (Ed.), *The self in social life* (pp. 323–370). New York: McGraw-Hill.

Ekman, O., & Friesen, W. V. (1969). Nonverbal leakage and clues to deception. *Psychiatry, 32*, 88–106.

Fodor, J. A. (1983). *The modularity of mind.* Cambridge: MIT Press.

Gibson, J. J. (1979). *The ecological approach to visual perception.* Boston: Houghton Miffin.

Gilbert, D. T. (in press). Thinking lightly about others: Automatic components of the social inference process. In J. S. Uleman & J. A. Bargh (Eds.), *Unintended thought: Limits of awareness, intention, and control.* New York: Guilford Press.

Gilbert, D. T., & Jones, E. E. (1986). Perceiver-induced constraint: Interpretations of self-generated reality. *Journal of Personality and Social Psychology, 50*, 269–280.

Gilbert, D. T., Jones, E. E., & Pelham, B. W. (1987). Influence and inference: What the active perceiver overlooks. *Journal of Personality and Social Psychology, 52*, 861–870.

Gilbert, D. T., & Krull, D. S. (1988). Seeing less and knowing more: The benefits of perceptual ignorance. *Journal of Personality and Social Psychology, 54*, 193–201.

Hirst, W., & Kalmar, D. (1987). Characterizing attentional resources. *Journal of Experimental Psychology: General, 116*, 68–81.

Johnson, J. T., Jemmott, J. B., & Pettigrew, T. F. (1984). Causal attribution and dispositional inference: Evidence of inconsistent judgments. *Journal of Experimental Social Psychology, 20*, 567–585.

Johnson, M. K., & Raye, C. L. (1981). Reality monitoring. *Psychological Review, 88*, 67–85.

Jones, E. E., & Davis, K. E. (1965). From acts to dispositions: The attribution process in person perception. In L. Berkowitz (Ed.), *Advances in experimental social psychology* (Vol. 2, pp. 219–266). New York: Academic Press.

Jones, E. E., & Harris, V. A. (1967). The attribution of attitudes. *Journal of Experimental Social Psychology, 3*, 1–24.

Jones, E. E., & Thibaut, J. W. (1958). Interaction goals as bases of inference in interpersonal perception. In R. Tagiuri & L. Petrillo (Eds.), *Person perception and interpersonal behavior* (pp. 151–178). Stanford, CA: Stanford University Press.

Kassin, S. M., & Baron, R. M. (1985). Basic determinants of attribution and social perception. In J. Harvey & G. Weary (Eds.), *Attribution: Basic issues and applications* (pp. 37–64). New York: Academic Press.

Kelley, H. H. (1971). Attribution in social interaction. In E. E. Jones, D. E. Kanouse, H. H. Kelley, R. E. Nisbett, S. Valins, & B. Weiner (Eds.), *Attribution: Perceiving the causes of behavior* (pp. 1–26). Morristown, NJ: General Learning Press.

Lowe, C. A., & Kassin, S. M. (1980). A perceptual view of attribution: Theoretical and methodological implications. *Personality and Social Psychology Bulletin, 6*, 532–542.

McArthur, L. Z., & Baron, R. M. (1983). Toward an ecological theory of social perception. *Psychological Review, 90*, 215–238.

Miller, A. G., Jones, E. E., & Hinkle, S. (1981). A robust attribution error in the personality domain. *Journal of Experimental Social Psychology, 17*, 587–600.

Neisser, U. (1980). On "social knowing." *Personality and Social Psychology Bulletin, 6*, 601–605.

Newtson, D. (1980). An interactionist perspective on social knowing. *Personality and Social Psychology Bulletin, 6*, 520–531.

Nisbett, R. E., & Ross, L. (1980). *Human inference: Strategies and shortcomings of social judgment.* Englewood Cliffs, NJ: Prentice-Hall.

Nisbett, R. E., & Wilson, T. D. (1977). Telling more than we can know: Verbal reports on mental processes. *Psychological Review, 84*, 231–259.

Quattrone, G. A. (1982). Overattribution and unit formation: When behavior engulfs the person. *Journal of Personality and Social Psychology, 42*, 593–607.

Ross, L. (1977). The intuitive psychologist and his shortcomings. In L. Berkowitz (Ed.), *Advances in experimental social psychology* (Vol. 10, pp. 173–220). New York: Academic Press.

Swann, W. B., Jr. (1984). Quest for accuracy in person perception: A matter of pragmatics. *Psychological Review, 91*, 457–477.

Trope, Y. (1986). Identification and inferential processes in dispositional attribution. *Psychological Review, 93*, 239–257.

Tversky, A., & Kahneman, D. (1974). Judgments under uncertainty: Heuristics and biases. *Science, 185*, 1124–1131.

Winter, L., & Uleman, J. S. (1984). When are social judgments made? Evidence for the spontaneousness of trait inferences. *Journal of Personality and Social Psychology, 47*, 237–252.

Winter, L., Uleman, J. S., & Cunniff, C. (1985). How automatic are social judgments? *Journal of Personality and Social Psychology, 49*, 904–917.

Received April 13, 1987
Revision received September 14, 1987
Accepted September 15, 1987 ■

Social Roles, Social Control, and Biases in Social-Perception Processes

Lee D. Ross, Teresa M. Amabile, and Julia L. Steinmetz

To make accurate social judgments, an individual must both recognize and adequately correct for the self-presentation advantages or disadvantages conferred upon actors by their social roles. Two experiments examined social perceptions formed during an encounter in which one participant composed difficult general knowledge questions and another participant attempted to answer those questions. It was found, as predicted, that perceivers fail to make adequate allowance for the biasing effects of these "questioner" and "answerer" roles in judging the participants' general knowledge. Questioners, allowed to display their personal store of esoteric knowledge in composing questions, were consistently rated superior to their partners, who attempted to answer the questions. This bias was stronger for the answerers and the uninvolved observers than for the questioners. Some implications of these results for our understanding of the biased perceptions of the powerful and the powerless in society are noted. More general implications for an understanding of the shortcomings of the "intuitive psychologist" are also discussed.

Interpersonal encounters provide an important informational basis for self-evaluation and social judgment. Often, however, our performances in such encounters are shaped and constrained by the social roles we must play. Typically, roles confer unequal control over the style, content, and duration of an encounter; such social control, in turn, generally facilitates displays of

This research was supported, in part, by Research Grant MH-26736 from the National Institute of Mental Health to the first author. We wish to acknowledge Gary Dexter and Barbara Marshment for their valuable assistance in running this study. We also wish to express our appreciation to William DeJong, Mark Lepper, and Richard Nisbett for their helpful comments on earlier drafts of this paper.

Portions of this study were reported at the 56th Annual Convention of the Western Psychological Association, Los Angeles, April 1976.

Request for reprints should be sent to Lee D. Ross, Department of Psychology, Stanford University, Stanford, California 94305.

knowledge, skill, insight, wit, or sensitivity, while permitting the concealment of deficiencies. Accurate social judgment, accordingly, depends upon the perceiver's ability to make adequate allowance for such role-conferred advantages and disadvantages in self-presentation.

The thesis of the present paper, and of the research it reports, is a simple one: In drawing inferences about actors, perceivers consistently fail to make adequate allowance for the biasing effects of social roles upon performance. The specific empirical demonstration reported here dealt with the particular roles of "questioner" and "answerer" and with the biased perceptions of general knowledge that result from the arbitrary assignment and fulfillment of these roles. Subjects participated in a general knowledge "quiz game," in which one person was assigned the role of questioner and the other the role of answerer, or "contestant." The questioner first composed a set of challenging general knowledge questions and then posed them to the contestant; both participants (and, in a subsequent reenactment, a pair of observers) were then required to rate the questioner's and contestant's general knowledge.

It should be emphasized that the role-conferred advantages and disadvantages in self-presentation of general knowledge in the quiz game were neither subtle nor disguised. Questioners were allowed and encouraged to display their own wealth of general knowledge by asking difficult and esoteric questions, and their role, of course, guaranteed that they would know the answers to the questions asked during the quiz game. The contestant's role, by contrast, prevented any such selective, self-serving displays and made displays of ignorance virtually inevitable. In a sense, the arbitrary assignment and fulfillment of roles forced participants to deal with non-representative and highly biased samples of the questioners' and contestants' general knowledge.

The encounter between questioner and contestant was designed to capture the essential feature of many real-world encounters: One participant defines the domain and controls the style of the interaction and the other must respond within those limits. The quiz game, however, provides a particularly stringent test of our thesis, because the participants seemingly enjoyed an ideal perspective to overcome the proposed bias: In contrast to many real-world encounters, the random nature of the role assignment was salient and unambiguous; furthermore, both participants were fully aware of the obligations and prerogatives associated with each role.

The primary experimental prediction was that the perceivers of the quiz game — the participants themselves and observers as well — would form relatively positive impressions of the questioners' general knowledge and relatively negative impressions of the contestants' knowledge. This prediction, it should be reemphasized, follows from the expectation that perceivers would consistently underestimate, and/or make inadequate allowance for, the biasing effects of the questioners' and contestants' roles upon their ability to display general knowledge advantageously. It was further anticipated, therefore, that impressions would be biased to the extent (and only to the extent) that the relevant perceivers were forced to rely upon biased samples of "evidence." A detailed analysis of the various perceivers' access to and reliance upon biased or unbiased samples, however, will be deferred until our experimental results have been presented.

Experiment 1: Contestants' and Questioners' Perceptions

In Experiment 1, subjects performed the arbitrarily assigned roles of questioner or contestant in an oral quiz of general knowledge. In the experimental condition, questioners asked questions that they had composed themselves; in a yoked control condition they posed questions formulated by a previous questioner. All of the subjects rated their own general knowledge and that of their partners after the quiz session was completed and then again after taking a written general knowledge quiz prepared by the experimenter.[1]

Method

Subjects and Role Assignment
Eighteen male pairs and 18 female pairs of subjects were recruited from an introductory psychology class at Stanford University for a "quiz game" experiment. Upon their arrival at the laboratory, subjects were met by a same-sex experimenter, who explained that the study dealt with the processes by which "people form impressions about general knowledge." The experimenter then introduced the quiz format and explained that one subject would be given the "job of contestant" and the other the "job of questioner." The random and arbitrary nature of the role assignment was then made obvious to the subjects by having them each choose one of the two cards ("Questioner" or "Contestant") that had been shuffled and placed face down before them.

Questioner and Contestant Roles
The questioner and contestant in each session were seated at separate tables in the same room. Each received oral instructions and each heard the instructions given to his or her partner. These oral instructions were supplemented with more detailed written descriptions of their tasks and roles.

---

[1] Half of the 12 experimental condition pairs of each sex completed *only* these ratings and it was these pairs to whom the 6 control pairs of each sex were yoked (i.e., the questions prepared and posed by these questioners were subsequently used by the control-condition questioners). The remaining half of the experimental group pairs also completed a self-rating of general knowledge *before* the initial quiz session but after assignment of roles. There were no significant differences between questioners and contestants on this premeasure and its introduction produced no apparent impact upon subsequent dependent measures.

Twelve pairs of subjects of each sex participated in the *experimental* condition. In this condition, the questioners were instructed to compose 10 "challenging but not impossible" questions for the contestant. They were cautioned to avoid both easy questions (e.g., the number of days in the month of April) and unfair questions (e.g., the name of the questioner's brother) and to draw from any area in which they had interest or expertise ("for example, movies, books, sports, music, literature, psychology, history, science, etc."). The questioner was instructed to complete, in 10 or 15 minutes, 10 questions that could be answered in a word or two and to ask the experimenter for help if he or she had any problems. To aid the questioner in this task the experimenter offered a few sample questions (e.g., "What is the capital of New Mexico?") and suggested some possible areas or question formats (e.g., "You can ask about something you read in the news, or ask about the geography of a particular state, or ask what is the largest ... or the highest ... etc.").

During the period in which the questioner composed difficult quiz items, the contestant also engaged in a question-preparation task. However, the contestant's task involved composing easy questions that would be irrevelant to subsequent advantages and disadvantages in self-presentation.[2] The experimenter's instructions to the contestant emphasized the difference in tasks:

> Your job, as "contestant," will be to answer the questions that the questioner is now composing. Right now,

however, we would like you to "warm up" for the quiz game by composing some questions of your own. These questions won't be used during this experiment; they're just for you to get into the spirit of our study. The questioner's instructions tell him or her to compose 10 challenging questions of the type that are used in TV game shows. However, we want you to compose 10 questions that are relatively *easy*, questions that could be answered by 90% of high school freshmen.

Six pairs of subjects of each sex participated in the *control* condition. In this condition, both questioners and contestants were informed that for the quiz session, the questioner would ask questions prepared beforehand by another individual. Here, both the participants spent 15 minutes before the quiz preparing "easy general knowledge questions"; that is, their preparation task was identical to that of the contestants (but not that of the questioners) in the experimental condition. Again, both participants were fully aware of the details of each other's preparation and quiz game tasks.

The preparation period was followed by the quiz game: As described earlier, questioners in the experimental condition posed their own questions to the contestants; in the control condition, each questioner posed items prepared by a same-sex questioner from the previous experimental condition (see Footnote 1). It should be emphasized that the contestants were always aware of whether or not the questions were prepared by their own questioner or by someone else. During the quiz the questioner faced the contestant and waited about 30 seconds for the contestant's response to each question, acknowledging correct responses and supplying them when the contestant failed to answer or answered incorrectly. To minimize extraneous self-presentation evidence concerning general knowledge, all participants were instructed to say nothing beyond the questioning and answering demanded by their assigned roles.

Throughout the quiz session, the experimenter recorded all responses given by the contestant, and made certain that the two participants properly fulfilled their roles. At the conclusion of the session, the experimenter noted aloud the number of correct responses made by the contestant.

Dependent Measures and Concluding Procedures

Immediately following the quiz game, the participants rated themselves and their partners on several 100-point Likert scales, anchored at "much better than average" and "much worse than average," with midpoints and two additional scale points appropriately labeled. The two most relevant measures required participants to rate themselves and their partners on general knowledge

---

[2] The contestant's task, prior to the quiz game, was designed to resemble superficially the task of the questioner without sacrificing any part of the latter's self-presentation advantage. Nevertheless, it is important to recognize that the present independent-variable manipulation was a compound one, involving a manipulation of the preliminary question-preparation task in addition to that of the contestant-versus-questioner role in the quiz session. It is impossible, therefore, to determine from the present results alone what part, if any, the difference in preparation tasks might have played in producing the experimental effects to be reported. It is worth noting, however, that any procedure requiring contestants to prepare *difficult* questions would have introduced other confounding factors and problems of interpretation. First, the contestants might have felt slighted or frustrated at the lack of opportunity to pose their questions to their coparticipant. More important, such a task might have forced the contestants to recognize their own capacity to pose extremely esoteric and difficult questions. This recognition, in turn, could have attenuated both the questioner's role advantage and the relevant experimental effect. (The encouragement of this insight through such role playing, it should be emphasized, is hardly a typical feature of the contestant role or of other disadvantaged roles in everyday encounters.) Obviously a factorial design, one comparing the effects of "no question preparation task," "easy question preparation," and "difficult question preparation," would be required to isolate any possible influence of the factors described above.

"compared to the average Stanford student"; these were, respectively, the first and seventh items on the questionnaire. Other items provided various manipulation checks and less direct or less relevant estimates of general knowledge.[3]

After completion of this initial set of general knowledge ratings, the experimenter administered to all participants a written general knowledge quiz consisting of 15 moderately difficult items selected from "Jeopardy," a popular general knowledge game (Milton-Bradley, 8th ed.). Typical items on this quiz asked participants to identify "the great lake closest to the Gulf of St. Lawrence" or "the radio show on which the only character who aged was the reporter Jimmy Olsen." This quiz served two purposes: First, it provided a potential "objective" assessment of the subjects' general knowledge that could have been used as a covariate in testing the statistical significance of differences in subjective ratings. (The differences that emerged, however, were sufficiently clear to obviate the need for such covariate analysis.) Second, it gave both contestants and questioners the opportunity to reassess their own general knowledge in light of their performance on items prepared by an unknown outsider. Upon completion of this written quiz, therefore, subjects were given a second questionnaire identical (except for the addition of a few items specifically relevant to the written quiz) to the one they had completed earlier. They were told, "Feel free to revise your ratings or not revise them as you see fit." It should be noted that subjects, on completing these ratings, were aware of their own performances on the written quiz, but unaware of the performances of their partners.

The experimental session concluded with a detailed account by the experimenter of research hypotheses and postulated biases, along with a request that subjects not discuss the study's procedures and purposes with potential subjects.

Results

Contestants' Performances
The quiz sessions of Experiment 1 were designed to confer a self-presentation advantage upon questioners relative

to contestants. Thus it was intended and anticipated that contestants would be unable to answer most of the questions posed by the questioners. This precondition for testing our primary hypothesis was reasonably well met; overall, contestants correctly answered a mean of only 4.0 out of 10 questions posed by questioners. This low performance rate was consistent with the level of difficulty of many of the questions asked (e.g., "What do the initials W. H. in W. H. Auden's name stand for?" and "What is the longest glacier in the world?"). Further analysis, however, revealed a rather striking and unanticipated sex difference. Male contestants answered a mean of 5.2 questions correctly, while females answered only 2.9, $t(34) = 3.15, p < .01$.

This unanticipated difference permits a further test of the study's basic hypothesis. It is apparent that female questioners more fully exercised the prerogative of their role — to ask difficult questions displaying their own esoteric knowledge while revealing deficiencies in the contestants' knowledge.[4] Accordingly, one might expect and predict that female pairs would provide a stronger confirmation of the experimental hypothesis than male pairs.

General Knowledge Ratings
The principal dependent measures were Likert-type ratings of general knowledge completed immediately following the quiz game. The results for experimental and yoked-control subjects in Experiment 1 are reported in Table 20.1.

Several comparisons reveal the extent to which the main experimental hypothesis was confirmed. In 18 of the 24 experimental-condition pairs, the contestant's self-rating was less positive than the questioner's self-rating, and in only 4 cases was the reverse true. The mean difference of 12.2 (see Table 20.1) was clearly significant, $t(23) = 3.00, p < .01$. Similarly, in 18 of 24 cases (with only 5 reverses) the contestants rated their questioners more positively than questioners rated their contestants. Again, the mean difference of 16.2 was statistically significant, $t(23) = 3.93, p < .01$.

An examination of the differences between subjects' self-ratings and their ratings of their partners clarify these results (and, in addition, eliminate the error variance introduced by idiosyncratic differences in scale usage). These scores reveal that the contestants rated

---

[3] These additional items asked subjects to rate their (a) general knowledge relative to other people in general, (b) test-taking ability, (c) memory for isolated facts, (d) ability to formulate general knowledge questions, and (e) ability to answer general knowledge questions made up by others. The data provided by these additional items do not challenge any implications drawn from the results to be discussed, nor do they extend or clarify these results. In the interest of brevity, these items receive no further attention in the present report.

---

[4] In a follow-up procedure, a new population of subjects took written quizzes consisting of questions originally composed by male and female questioners. Analyses revealed that the females' questions were, in fact, more difficult, $F(1, 98) = 11.42, p < .01$.

TABLE 20.1. Mean Ratings of General Knowledge of Questioners and Contestants on Questionnaire Immediately Following Quiz Game

Condition	Measure		
	Subject's Rating of Self[a]	Subject's Rating of Partner[a]	Self-partner Difference
Experimental (n = 24)			
Questioner	53.5	50.6	2.9
Contestant	41.3	66.8	−25.5
Difference	12.2	−16.2	
Control (n = 12)			
Questioner	54.1	52.5	1.6
Contestant	47.0	50.3	−3.3
Difference	7.1	2.2	

[a] All ratings were made on 100-point scales. A higher number indicates more general knowledge relative to other Stanford students.

themselves far inferior to their questioners, $t(23) = 4.66$, $p < .001$, while the questioners rated themselves slightly superior to their contestants, $t < 1$. Furthermore, 20 contestants rated themselves inferior to their questioners, and only a single contestant rated himself superior to his questioner; on the other hand, 12 questioners rated themselves superior and 9 questioners rated themselves inferior to their contestants. These data leave little doubt that it was the contestants and not the questioners whose social perceptions were distorted by the fulfillment of the assigned roles.

Results from the control condition further illustrate the nature and degree of these distortions. The control-group questioners, it will be recalled, were denied the opportunity to display their own stores of esoteric knowledge to their contestants. Instead, they were limited to asking questions prepared by an anonymous previous participant. Control-condition contestants, accordingly, were less prone than experimental-condition contestants to rate themselves negatively in relation to their partners. Control-condition questioners, by contrast, produced ratings of self and partner that were virtually indistinguishable from those of experimental-condition questioners.

Analyses of variance performed on self-ratings, partner ratings, and the crucial self-minus-partner differences largely confirm the experimental hypotheses. The interaction between condition and role was statistically significant for ratings of partner, $F(1, 68) = 6.38$, $p < .05$, but not significant for self-ratings, $F(1, 68) < 1$. For the self-minus-partner difference, the relevant Role × Condition interaction was marginally significant,

$F(1, 68) = 3.83$, $p < .06$. Furthermore, for contestants alone, the main effect of condition on the self-minus-partner difference measure was clearly significant, $F(1, 34) = 6.05$, $p < .05$,[5] while for questioners alone there was no such effect, $F(1, 34) < 1$. Again it is obvious that the primary distortion in social perception in the experimental condition was the contestants' overly positive assessment of their questioners.

Sex differences. As noted earlier, female questioners asked more difficult questions and received fewer correct answers from their partners than male questioners. Female questioners, in other words, more fully exploited the opportunity for advantageous self-presentation (or, perhaps, more carefully obeyed the experimenter's instructions) than did male questioners. Comparisons of general knowledge ratings indicate that it was indeed the female pairs who most strikingly confirmed the experimental predictions. Again, it is the contestants' perceptions of their partners relative to themselves that are most revealing: Female contestants in the experimental condition, on the average, rated themselves 36.4 points less positively than their partners, while male contestants rated themselves only 14.6 points less positively. This difference was statistically significant, $t(22) = 2.14$, $p < .05$.

General Knowledge Ratings After Written Quiz

Performance on the written quiz administered by the experimenter served to emphasize that there was absolutely no basis in fact for the subjects' conviction that questioners were superior in general knowledge to contestants. On the 15-item quiz, questioners in the experimental condition scored a mean of 7.75 correct, while contestants scored 7.71 correct, $t < 1$.

A more important issue concerning the experimenter's quiz was its effect upon the participants' previously biased perceptions of their partners' general knowledge relative to their own. An inspection of the relevant self-minus-partner ratings reveals once more the differing experiences, and the resulting differences in perceptions, of male and female pairs. Among female pairs in the experimental condition, the contestants continued to rate

---

[5] These analyses of variance treated experimental and control conditions as independent. The reader will recall, however, that the 12 control questioners were yoked to 12 of the 24 experimental questioners (i.e., the control questioners posed questions previously prepared and posed by experimental condition questioners). If only the 12 yoked pairs are considered, the effect of condition on the contestant's rating for self minus partner remains significant: For correlated samples, $t(11) = 2.59$, $p < .05$.

themselves far inferior to their questioners, $t(11) = 4.45$, $p < .01$; among male pairs the originally smaller difference disappeared completely, $t(11) < 1$.

Summary of Results

It is clear that contestants in the quiz games failed in their interpersonal assessments to make adequate allowance for the self-presentation advantage enjoyed by their questioners. Thus, they strikingly overestimated the general knowledge of the questioners relative to their own knowledge. It happened that female questioners exploited, more fully than male questioners, the opportunity to display their own idiosyncratic knowledge and to reveal gaps in the knowledge of their contestants. Consistent with our underlying hypothesis, it was thus the female contestants who showed the most positive, and hence the most distorted, perceptions of their questioners.

Experiment 2: Observers' Perceptions

A second demonstration experiment exposed observers to close simulations of the interactions that had occurred between questioners and contestants in Experiment 1. Experiment 2 thus permitted comparison of the observers' relatively impersonal and objective assessments with those of the two personally involved actors in Experiment 1. The experimental prediction paralleled that of Experiment 1. It was predicted that observers, like the actors themselves, would make inadequate allowance for role-conferred advantages and disadvantages in personal presentation and, in so doing, would judge the contestants to be inferior in general knowledge to the questioners.

Female pairs had provided a clearer test — and ultimately a stronger confirmation — of the research hypothesis in Experiment 1. Accordingly, it was the female pairs' sessions from Experiment 1 that were selected for simulation in Experiment 2.

Method

Personnel and Procedures
Two female confederates were recruited to simulate the 12 sessions from Experiment 1 involving the female pairs in the experimental group. Each simulation was observed by one male and one female undergraduate and each of the original sessions was simulated twice (thereby allowing the two confederates to alternate questioner and

answerer roles). A total of 48 subjects, 24 males and 24 females, were recruited from the introductory psychology class to serve as observers in Experiment 2.

The subjects were led to believe that the simulation was authentic — that they personally just happened to be the ones randomly assigned to the role of observers, that the two confederates just happened to receive the two participant roles, and that the quiz game was genuine rather than contrived. The assignment of roles was accomplished through a procedure similar, at least from the subjects' viewpoint, to that followed in Experiment 1. That is, all four participants picked a card at random from among those four shuffled and placed face down before them. All of the cards, in fact, read "Observer": The confederates simply claimed that their cards had read "Questioner" and "Contestant" as dictated by the experimental design.

The simulation unfolded just as the experimental sessions had in Experiment 1. Upon oral instructions from the experimenter (heard by the observers), the confederate playing the role of questioner pretended to compose 10 items for the quiz session, while the contestant pretended to prepare a set of easy questions. During this question-preparation period, the observer subjects also composed easy questions in the manner previously described for Experiment 1 contestants. The questioner's quiz questions and the contestant's responses were identical to those that had been recorded in Experiment 1 for the original pair of subjects. As in the original experimental sessions, the participants refrained from extraneous talking and were generally unexpressive. During the quiz session, the subjects watched the participants closely, without speaking, as instructed by the experimenter.

After the quiz simulation, the observers rated the contestant's and questioner's general knowledge. In virtually all respects the experimenter's instructions and descriptions of purpose were unchanged from Experiment 1. The scales used by the observer subjects to rate the participants' general knowledge were identical in format to those employed in the previous study, except that the items referred to "contestant" and "questioner," rather than "self" and "partner."

Results

Observers' impressions of the participants in the quiz game showed the same bias that was evident in the participants' own perceptions. Overall, the questioner is seen as tremendously knowledgeable ($M = 82.08$); the contestant is seen as only slightly less knowledgeable than the average Stanford student ($M = 48.92$), $F(1, 44) = 65.9$, $p < .001$.

These results further support and clarify the findings for Experiment 1: In a sense, the observers necessarily shared the perspective of the contestants. Like the contestants, the observers almost certainly found that they were unable to answer the difficult questions posed by the questioners. What the observers, like the contestants, failed to recognize was that the questioners did not possess any superiority in general knowledge — they merely had exploited the opportunity to choose the particular topics and specific items that most favorably displayed their general knowledge.

An analysis of variance reveals that there were no significant differences between the perceptions of male and female observers ($F < 1$). This result also illuminates the findings of Experiment 1. When male observers saw the same encounters as female observers, they were no better able to make adequate allowance for the questioner's role-conferred self-presentation advantage. It seems very likely, therefore, that the sex differences in ratings obtained in Experiment 1 occurred because of differences in the quiz sessions, not differences in the perceptual strategies or capacities of the raters.

General Discussion

Attribution Error and Sampling Bias

The two experiments reported here clearly demonstrate that social perceivers may fail to make adequate allowance for the role-conferred advantage in self-presentation enjoyed by questioners relative to contestants. This failure was demonstrated by contestants and by observers but not by questioners. When the relevant advantage was most fully exploited (i.e., among female pairs in the experimental group), the relevant distortion in interpersonal judgment was maximized. Conversely, when the questioner's role retained its title but lost its self-presentation advantage (i.e., in the control condition), the distortion in judgment disappeared.

The reader may recognize that the phenomenon we have described represents a special case of a more fundamental attribution error. This fundamental error (cf. Ross, 1977) is the tendency to underestimate the role of situational determinants and overestimate the degree to which social actions and outcomes reflect the dispositions of relevant actors. That is, man as an intuitive psychologist is too often a "nativist," a proponent of stable individual differences, and too seldom a Watsonian

"behaviorist." He readily infers broad personal dispositions and anticipates more cross-situational consistency in behavior than actually occurs (Mischel, 1968; 1973; 1974). He jumps to conclusions about others too readily and underestimates the potential impact of relevant environmental forces and constraints.

Beyond anecdotes and appeals to subjective experience, the evidence most frequently cited (e.g., Jones & Nisbett, 1972; Kelley, 1972) for this fundamental bias involves the apparent willingness of observers to draw "correspondent" personal inferences (Jones & Davis, 1965) about actors who have yielded to very obvious situational pressures. For instance, Jones and Harris (1967) found that listeners assumed some correspondence between a communicator's pro-Castro remarks and his private opinions despite their knowledge that the communicator was obeying the experimenter's explicit instructions under "no-choice" conditions. A second line of evidence that observers may ignore or underestimate situational forces has been provided by Bierbrauer (1973). This investigator showed that even after personally participating in a verbatim reenactment of the classic Milgram (1963) demonstration, raters consistently and dramatically underestimated the extent to which Milgram's subjects would administer dangerous levels of electric shock in accord with the situational forces compelling "obedience." In so doing, Bierbrauer's subjects erroneously assumed that a particular individual's obedience in the Milgram paradigm reflected distinguishing personal dispositions rather than the potency of situational pressures and constraints.

Social roles thus may be regarded as a special case of situational forces that bias performance and the inferences about actors that are made on the basis of such performances. Accordingly, the present demonstrations may be regarded as a special case, and a particularly powerful demonstration, of the susceptibility of subjects to the fundamental attribution error noted by theorists since Heider (1958).

A conception of the social perceiver as an "intuitive psychologist" who must draw inferences from the social data he samples, stores, retrieves, and analyzes (cf. Ross, 1977) suggests another more general interpretation of the demonstration experiments reported in the present paper. Ratings of general knowledge were made on the basis of data furnished during the quiz game. In fact, it is apparent that distorted judgments about the participants in the game were based on highly unrepresentative data samples, systematically *biased* to favor the questioner. Consider the quiz items prepared by the questioners. These surely were the most biased samples imaginable of their general knowledge; indeed, an item was presented to a contestant (and to observers) only if the questioner both knew the answer *and* anticipated that the contestant would be unlikely to know it. The present findings suggest that this tremendously biased sample of the questioner's knowledge was nevertheless treated by the contestant and by subsequent observers as reasonably representative. These raters apparently failed to make adequate allowance for the fact that, had the role assignments been reversed, the contestants could have just as easily prepared questions that would have stumped their questioners and revealed their own knowledge to best advantage. In fact, a brief review of the pattern of obtained results suggests that distortions in perceptions and judgments occurred precisely to the extent that the perceiver was forced to rely upon an unrepresentative but highly available (cf. Tversky & Kahneman, 1973) data sample.

Judgments About the Questioner

The contestants and observers alike had access to only one sample of the questioner's general knowledge, that flattering sample of 10 difficult questions prepared for the quiz game. The contestants and observers knew, of course, that the relevant sample was not random; indeed, they knew precisely how it was drawn and why it was biased. Nevertheless, they consistently rated the questioners as highly knowledgeable.

The questioners, by contrast, were not forced to rely uniquely upon the 10-item sample available to contestants and observers. The questioners had a lifetime of experience and social comparison to draw upon in assessing their own knowledge; moreover, they were aware of the vast areas of ignorance they had passed over in searching for optimal topics and specific items. It is consistent with our analysis, therefore, that questioners did not rate themselves as superior to the average of their peers.

Judgments About the Contestant

The sample of the contestant's knowledge provided by the quiz game was not really biased or unrepresentative. It was a reasonably random sample of his or her ability to answer relatively difficult and obscure general knowledge questions. As our analysis would dictate, the questioners and observers rated the contestant, overall, as "average" in general knowledge. It is interesting to note that the contestant did downgrade his or her own knowledge somewhat as a result of the quiz game

experience. This probably resulted not from any distortion in self-perception but rather from the basis of comparison (i.e., the "average Stanford undergraduate") used in the rating. The contestant might have been led to overestimate the knowledge of the population from whom his partner was sampled on the basis of this one vivid and concrete experience (cf. Nisbett & Borgida, 1975).

It is also interesting to contrast the observer's perspective with that of the contestant. Each observer knew that *two* individuals (i.e., the observer and the contestant alike) were baffled by the questioner's quiz items. Contestants, of course, enjoyed no such reassuring "consensus" information (Kelley, 1967). Thus the observers were confident that the contestants, like themselves, were simply average, but that the questioners were vastly superior; the contestants, by contrast, seemed to entertain the hypothesis that they themselves were somewhat inferior to the "average Stanford undergraduate," and the questioners were somewhat superior.

In summary, it appears that the various raters' judgments were distorted precisely to the extent that they depended upon biased data samples. The intuitive psychologist's apparent willingness to make social inferences on the basis of highly biased data samples seems worthy of more systematic investigation in future research.

Social Roles and Social Perceptions

The phenomenon demonstrated in the two present experiments has clear implications for role-constrained encounters outside the laboratory. In fact, the specific relationship between advantaged questioners and disadvantaged contestants has obvious parallels within academic settings. Teachers consistently enjoy the prerogatives of questioners and students typically suffer the handicaps of answers (although some students leap at opportunities to reverse these roles). Consider, as a particularly dramatic instance, the role-constrained encounters that characterize the typical dissertation "orals." The candidate is required to field questions from the idiosyncratic and occasionally esoteric areas of each examiner's interest and expertise. In contrast to the examiners, the candidate has relatively little time for reflections and relatively little power to define or limit the domains of inquiry. In light of the present demonstrations, it might be anticipated (correctly so, in the investigators' experience) that the typical candidate leaves the ordeal feeling more relief than pride, while his or her examiners depart with increased respect for each others' insight and scholarship.[6] Such evaluations, of course, may often be warranted; however, they may also reflect in whole or in part the inadequate allowance made for advantages and disadvantages in personal presentation. Perhaps an alternative procedure for the oral examination, one in which the candidate first posed questions for his examiners and then corrected their errors and omissions, might yield more elated candidates. Such a procedure might also produce examiners more impressed with the candidate and less impressed with each other.

The present demonstrations dealt with encounters between questioners and answerers, but there are countless other contexts in which social roles bias interpersonal encounters and, consequently, interpersonal judgments. The basis for role-differentiated behavior in an encounter may be formal, as in the interactions between employers and employees, or it may be informal, as in the encounters between a domineering individual and a reticent one. Regardless of its basis, however, this role differentiation creates unequal control and unequal opportunity for advantaged self-presentation. Thus the employer can discuss his personal triumphs, avocations, and areas of expertise without risk of interruption while the employee enjoys no such opportunity. Similarly, the domineering partner in a friendship can determine whether poetry or poker will furnish the arena for personal presentation, and the choice is apt to be self-serving. Again, we do not contend that the participants or relevant observers are oblivious to the inequality of the participants' opportunities for advantageous self-presentation. Rather, we contend that the social judgments of the disadvantaged and of relevant observers will reveal inadequate *allowance* or *correction for* such inequalities.

It is important to resist premature generalizations and conclusions based on the present specific demonstrations. Nevertheless, if subsequent research demonstrates a more general tendency for disadvantaged social participants and observers to make inadequate allowance for the self-presentation advantages of role and rank, the implications may be all too clear. Individuals who, by accident of birth, favorable political treatment, or even their own efforts, enjoy positions of power, also enjoy advantages in self-presentation. Observers of such social interactions and the disadvantaged participants (although not the advantaged ones, if the present results are representative) are apt to underestimate the extent to which the seemingly positive attributes of the powerful simply reflect the advantages of social control. Indeed, this distortion in social judgment could provide a particularly insidious brake upon social mobility, whereby the disadvantaged and powerless overestimate the capabilities of the powerful who, in turn, inappropriately deem members of their own caste well-suited to their particular leadership tasks.

REFERENCES

Bierbrauer, G. *Effect of set, perspective, and temporal factors in attribution.* Unpublished doctoral dissertation, Stanford University, 1973.

Heider, F. *The psychology of interpersonal relations.* New York: Wiley, 1958.

Jones, E. E., & Davis, K. E. From acts to dispositions: The attribution process in person perceptions. In L. Berkowitz (Ed.), *Advances in experimental social psychology* (Vol. 2). New York: Academic Press, 1965.

Jones, E. E., & Harris, V. A. The attribution of attitudes. *Journal of Experimental Social Psychology*, 1967, 3, 1–24.

Jones, E. E., & Nisbett, R. E. The actor and observer: Divergent perceptions of the causes of behavior. In E. E. Jones et al. (Eds.), *Attribution: Perceiving the causes of behavior.* Morristown, N.J.: General Learning Press, 1972.

Kelley, H. H. Attribution theory in social psychology. In D. Levine (Ed.), *Nebraska Symposium on Motivation* (Vol. 15). Lincoln: University of Nebraska Press, 1967.

Kelley, H. H. Attribution in social interaction. In E. E. Jones et al. (Eds.), *Attribution: Perceiving the causes of behavior.* Morristown, N. J.: General Learning Press, 1972.

Milgram, S. Behavioral study of obedience. *Journal of Abnormal and Social Psychology*, 1963, 67, 371–378.

Mischel, W. *Personality and assessment.* New York: Wiley, 1968.

Mischel, W. Towards a cognitive social learning re-conceptualization of personality. *Psychological Review*, 1973, 80, 252–283.

Mischel, W. Processes in delay of gratification. In L. Berkowitz (Ed.), *Advances in experimental social psychology* (Vol. 7). New York: Academic Press, 1974.

Nisbett, R. E., & Borgida, E. Attribution and the psychology of prediction. *Journal of Personality and Social Psychology*, 1975, 32, 932–943.

Ross, L. The intuitive psychologist and his shortcomings: Distortions in the attribution process. In L. Berkowitz (Ed.), *Advances in Experimental Social Psychology* (Vol. 10). New York: Academic Press, 1977.

Tversky, A., & Kahneman, D. Availability: A heuristic for judging frequency and probability. *Cognitive Psychology*, 1973, 5, 207–232.

Received August 16, 1976 ■

---

[6] This example, and the more general speculations that follow concerning the social relevance of our demonstration, suggest an important question: Do the advantaged and the powerful overestimate the merits of their equally advantaged and powerful peers or does the fulfillment of one's advantageous role lead one to make adequate allowance for similar advantages enjoyed by others? The impact of the observer's own role experiences and perspectives upon their perceptions of others furnishes an interesting and significant avenue for subsequent research.

Culture and the Construal of Agency: Attribution to Individual Versus Group Dispositions

Tanya Menon, Michael W. Morris, Chi-yue Chiu and Ying-yi Hong

The authors argue that cultures differ in implicit theories of individuals and groups. North Americans conceive of individual persons as free agents, whereas East Asians conceptualize them as constrained and as less agentic than social collectives. Hence, East Asian perceivers were expected to be more likely than North Americans to focus on and attribute causality to dispositions of collectives. In Study 1 newspaper articles about "rogue trader" scandals were analyzed, and it was found that U.S. papers made more mention of the individual trader involved, whereas Japanese papers referred more to the organization. Study 2 replicated this pattern among U.S. and Hong Kong participants who responded to a vignette about a maladjusted team member. Study 3 revealed the same pattern with respect to individual and group dispositionism using a different design that compared attributions for an act performed by an individual in one condition and by a group in the other condition.

Tanya Menon and Michael W. Morris, Graduate School of Business, Stanford University; Chi-yue Chiu, Department of Psychology, University of Hong Kong; Ying-yi Hong, Department of Psychology, Hong Kong University of Science and Technology, Hong Kong.

This article has benefited from the comments of Sheena Iyengar, Rod Kramer, Kwok Leung, Richard Nisbett, Jeffrey Pfeffer, and Steve Su. Also beneficial have been the points raised at research presentations at the University of California, Berkeley, Culture and Cognition Group, the Asian Association of Social Psychology Meetings, and the Organizational Behavior Groups at Harvard and Michigan Business Schools. The authors also acknowledge the capable assistance of Chaddus Bruce and the financial support of the Organizational Behavior Group at the Stanford Graduate School of Business.

Correspondence concerning this article should be addressed to Michael W. Morris, Stanford Graduate School of Business, 518 Memorial Way, Stanford University, Stanford, California 94305-5015. Electronic mail may be sent to fmorris@crown.stanford.edu.

Do people everywhere tend to attribute observed actions to properties of the actor? Social psychologists have traditionally assumed that they do, on the basis of Heider's (1958) premise that causal attribution functions to help the perceiver navigate the social environment. Empirical evidence for the tendency to attribute behavior to personal dispositions is so pervasive in the social psychological literature that this bias has been labeled the *fundamental attribution error* (Ross, 1977) and described as a universal human tendency (Gilbert & Malone, 1995). However, cross-cultural studies have raised doubts about whether social perceivers everywhere strive to trace actions to internal, stable properties of the actor. Although the bias toward attributing an observed person's behavior to personal dispositions is robust in Western individualistic settings (Jones & Harris, 1967), it is markedly reduced in more collectivist Asian settings (Miller, 1984). This is not simply because perceivers in different cultures encounter different behaviors. Studies presenting the same social stimuli to participants in different cultures have found that Americans exhibit the familiar bias toward personal dispositions, whereas Chinese participants emphasize social situations (Morris & Peng, 1994).

A lively debate has arisen about the source of cultural differences in dispositional attribution. One interpretation challenges Heider's premise that social perceivers strive to trace actions to actor dispositions and suggests that attributors in Western and East Asian cultures have different *orientations* to social perception. This account posits that the agentic orientation of North Americans contrasts with the situational orientation of Chinese perceivers. Whereas the analytic, mechanistic orientation of Western culture supports attribution to properties of the individual agent, many non-Western cultures interpret behavior in a "non-generalizing, occasion-bound, context-specific" manner (Shweder & Bourne, 1982, p. 105). A more moderate version of this position is the suggestion that social perceivers in collectivist cultural settings attribute an actor's behavior to stable properties of the situation rather than to stable properties of the actor (Krull, 1993). This position is more moderate because it retains Heider's idea that all social perceivers seek inferences to stable properties, although it suggests that Chinese perceivers map the social environment in terms of situations rather than agents.

We defend an alternative interpretation that cultural differences in attribution arise from contrasting *implicit theories* of agency. Perceivers from different cultures may differ in their perceptions of which social actors are agents possessing dispositions and which are controlled by situational forces. As argued by Heider (1958) and many followers, perceivers rely on implicit theories or causal schemata to guide their inferences about persons (Dweck, Chiu, & Hong, 1995; Jones, 1979; Kelley, 1972; Reeder & Brewer, 1979; Schank & Abelson, 1977). Many recent studies have documented that these implicit theories of persons differ across cultures (Choi, Nisbett, & Norenzayan, 1999; Kashima, Siegal, Tanaka, & Kashima, 1992; Morris & Peng, 1994). Although there has been little empirical research on the topic, researchers have recently suggested that social perceivers also possess implicit theories of groups (Su et al., 1999). In this article, we argue that both person and group theories vary across cultures. Whereas prevailing North American theories hold that persons have stable properties that cause social outcomes and groups do not, the theories prevailing in Confucius-influenced East Asian cultures emphasize that groups have stable properties that cause social outcomes. Hence, our implicit theory account yields predictions concerning attributions about collective-level agents, such as groups or organizations, as well as about individual-level agents.

Studying attributions to individual- and collective-level agents cross-culturally tests whether cultures differ in their orientations to agents versus situations or, rather, in their conceptions of which actors in society have agency. If East Asians differ from North Americans primarily with respect to their tendency to attribute causes to an agent's dispositions, then, as with their attributions about individuals, East Asians should be less likely than North Americans to draw dispositional inferences about collective-level actors, such as groups or organizations. However, if the cultures differ primarily in their theories or conceptions of particular social actors, then, in contrast to their attributions about individuals, East Asians should be more likely to attribute to dispositional properties of collectivities.

Our reasoning rests on two assumptions: First, that the group disposition is in fact a meaningful construct to lay perceivers, and second, that cultures differ in their beliefs about the autonomy of individuals and collectives. We address these issues by first reviewing what is known about the perception of individual persons as opposed to collective-level actors and then reviewing the evidence that cultures differ in their implicit theories.

Perceiving Persons and Groups

The construct of dispositionism to individuals is firmly entrenched in social psychology. Research has long focused on perceiving individual persons rather than groups, organizations, and other collective-level agents. The emphasis on person perception begins with the work of Heider (1944), Asch (1946), and other émigrés to social psychology from the Gestalt tradition. Seminal studies documented that perceptions are organized in terms of personality impression. These studies found that perceivers spontaneously organize even minimal displays of behavior into unified personality impressions (Heider & Simmel, 1944) and sustain these impressions by interpreting new data in light of initial trait impressions (Asch, 1946). The key assumption of this research — that an implicit theory of unified, stable personalities supports dispositional inference — has formed a basis from which much attribution research has proceeded (Jones, 1990).

Group perception received some consideration in early Gestalt studies of social perception (Asch, 1946, 1952). Researchers addressed the question of how one comes to perceive a social aggregate as a group — an entity with its own dispositions — rather than merely a collection of individuals. One early article argued that Gestalt principles such as similarity, proximity, and common fate cause individual members of a group to be aggregated into a single perceptual unit (Campbell, 1958). Although the subsequent literature on perceiving groups has been sparse in comparison with the literature on perceiving persons, recently research on perceiving groups has increased. D. L. Hamilton and Sherman (1996) reviewed an impressive convergence of evidence supporting the thesis that perceivers do not expect the same degree of coherence in the actions of a group as in those of an individual person and, accordingly, do not draw inferences about group dispositions as spontaneously as they draw inferences about personal dispositions. Some evidence for this comes from comparing inferences about individual and group behavior. For example, when a series of behaviors was presented as the actions of the same person or as the actions of members of the same group, trait inferences were drawn with greater speed and extremity in the person condition than in the group condition (Susskind & Hamilton, 1994). Other evidence for different patterns of inference about individuals and groups comes through methods traditionally used to study stereotypes (Sanbonmatsu, Sherman, & Hamilton, 1987).

However, several caveats can be raised about the evidence on group perception. First, even research nominally about group perception (e.g., research on stereotypes) tends to emphasize how perceivers draw inferences about individual group members rather than how they perceive group-level properties.

Second, before one delves into research on group-level properties, one should determine whether group dispositions merit distinct consideration apart from other forms of situational attribution. As with nonsocial situational forces, groups occupy the physical space surrounding individual actors. If group dispositions are equivalent to other situational attributions in the minds of social perceivers, then the creation of an additional theoretical construct is unwarranted. On the other hand, groups may be perceived as more than just situations. In contrast to nonagentic, environmental aspects of the situation, the group is a social entity that can direct action. Therefore, it is simultaneously both a situation affecting individual actors and an agent in its own right. Thus, as with persons, groups may be perceived as possessing dispositions (Higgins & Bryant, 1982). Although the perception of collective targets has been studied far less than the perception of individual targets, there is a rich history of research on group dispositions (Cattell, 1973), emotions (Allport, 1962; Cartwright & Zander, 1968), and other group-level properties (Durkheim, 1915; LeBon, 1896; McDougall, 1923; Sandelands & St. Clair, 1993).

Third, as D. L. Hamilton and Sherman (1996) explicitly acknowledge, "virtually all of the research on which our analysis is based was conducted in Western countries, primarily the United States," and cultural traditions of thinking about individuals and groups may contribute to the pattern. They acknowledge recent findings of cultural differences in person perception and go on to say that "cross-cultural evidence relevant to … [our thesis] is not extensive, and more research directed at these issues would be extremely useful" (p. 339). The current research answers this call for cross-cultural study of person and group perception. We propose that the pattern described by these authors reflects the influence of culturally bound theories of individual and group actors, particularly about their degree of autonomy. We next review the history and current evidence that cultures differ in conceptions of individual versus collective autonomy.

Culture and Conceptions of Individual and Collective Autonomy

We propose that cultures differ in their conceptions of individual versus collective autonomy. Autonomy, the power of an agent to exert the law set forth by its internal will rather than that of an external constraint (Kant, 1786/1949), can be possessed by an individual or by a collective. Mainstream North American social thinking rests on conceptions of individual autonomy, with the person characterized as "an independent, self-contained, autonomous entity who comprises a unique configuration of internal attributes such as traits, abilities, motives, and values, and behaves primarily as a consequence of these internal attributes" (Markus & Kitayama, 1991, p. 224). The intellectual history of this folk theory can be traced to the Judeo-Christian belief in the individual soul, the English legal and philosophical tradition of individual rights, Adam Smith's economics of individual self-interest, and the exaltation of individual freedom in social thinkers such as Nietzsche and Freud (see Bellah, Madsen, Sullivan, Swidler, & Tipton, 1985; Lukes, 1973).

Social thinking that is based on group autonomy, developed from the Confucian tradition, predominates in East Asian societies such as China, Korea, and Japan. Central to this tradition is the Confucian ideal of the community man (*qunti de fenzi*) or social being (*shehui de renge*), the individual who derives both role and awareness from the social collective to which he or she belongs (Kubin, 1991). Individuals in East Asian societies are enmeshed in powerful collectivities such as family, school, and work groups that both support and constrain through the lifetime (Hu, 1991). Furthermore, social norms oblige conformity to these groups and institutions (Hsu, 1948; Su et al., 1999). Groups in collectivist societies are "able and entitled to know, even regulate, what individuals do and think in private" (Ho & Chiu, 1994, p. 139). Confucian conceptions of society take relations to family as a core metaphor for relations to other groups. Furthermore, obligations to family must be followed even when they lead to wrongdoing. An example of how the collective and its role structure produce wrongdoing is found in *The Analects*, in which Confucius states that there is integrity when "a father covers up [wrongdoing] for his son, [and] a son covers up [wrongdoing] for his father" (trans. 1997, p. 63). The causal role of groups was recognized in traditional Chinese laws that held groups such as the family responsible for wrongdoing by individual members. The punishment for the attempted murder of an emperor was death not solely for the individual assailant but also for the assailant's entire family (Chiu & Hong, 1992; Nishida, 1985; Zhang, 1984). In contemporary Japan, the power of groups is visible in corporate life, in which the *ringi* system gives decision- making power to groups rather than individuals (Erez, 1992).

Consistent with the historical and institutional differences in the way groups are treated in North American and East Asian cultures, there is also psychological evidence for differences in the lay theories guiding everyday inference. Studies of first-person beliefs about the self suggest that North Americans have an inflated sense of individual control, whereas East Asians perceive that they cannot control their destinies independent of groups (for a review, see Fiske, Kitayama, Markus, & Nisbett, 1998). For example, a study of managerial students found that North Americans have stronger expectations of individual control in a performance task, whereas Chinese have stronger expectations of group control (Earley, 1994). Also, whereas motivation depends on individual control over choice of task for Anglo American children, control by the in-group suffices for Asian American children (Iyengar & Lepper, 1999).

Similar findings have been reported for third-person beliefs about other persons among North Americans and East Asians. Americans assume that individual moral character is fixed and the social world is fluid, whereas Chinese assume individual moral character is fluid and

the social world is fixed (Chiu, Dweck, Tong, & Fu, 1997). These different perceptions of stability are associated with different beliefs about the causal power of individuals and collectives. Australians are more likely than Japanese to believe that an individual's attitudes cause behavior (Kashima et al., 1992), whereas Koreans are more likely than Americans to cite the situational influences on an individual's behavior (Choi et al., 1999). In their reactions to violent crimes, Chinese are more likely than Americans to attribute blame and responsibility to the social groups associated with the criminals (Morris, 1993). In sum, cross-cultural studies point to differences in the perceived stability and causal potency of individual and group attributes. Despite the strong evidence, research that more directly examines cultural differences in these beliefs is called for.

Pilot Study: Testing Assumptions

This pilot study checked two presuppositions of our hypothesis. First, to check that autonomy is ascribed to individuals by North Americans and to collective-level agents by East Asians, we conducted a pilot survey of beliefs about control among demographically comparable college student samples in the United States ($N = 41$) and Singapore ($N = 99$). Second, to distinguish attributions to group dispositions from other attributions to an individual's environment, we presented participants with a vignette that concerned an ambiguous outcome and had them rate the plausibility of causes involving a focal individual, focal group, or nonsocial environmental factors. We expected that these three types of attributions would be distinct for both North American and East Asian social perceivers.

Check of Country Differences in Beliefs

Unlike general values or attitudes, a specific belief can be measured with a few highly similar items (see Dweck, Chiu, & Hong, 1995). We measured agreement with the following three statements, first with *individuals* as the subject and then with *organizations* as the subject:

In my society, individuals [organizations] take control of the situations around them and exercise free will.

The rules and laws in my society say that individuals [organizations] should take control of the situations around them and exercise free will.

Individuals [organizations] set a course for themselves independent of the influences surrounding them.

As expected, there was an association between items for individual autonomy ($r = .31$, $p < .05$) and collective autonomy ($r = .28$, $p < .05$), and hence two summary scores were calculated.[1] As may be seen in the means by country in Table 21.1, Americans endorsed the beliefs related to individual autonomy more than they endorsed those related to collective autonomy, paired sample $t(40) = 3.64$, $p < .01$, whereas Singaporeans endorsed beliefs related to collective autonomy more than they endorsed beliefs related to individual autonomy, paired sample $t(98) = -4.80$, $p < .01$. In support of the predicted divergence in autonomy beliefs, there was a significant interaction of Country (United States vs. Singapore) × Level of Actor (individual vs. collective) in the mixed-model analysis of variance (ANOVA), $F(1, 138) = 24.61$, $p < .01$.

Distinguishing Group Attributions From Nonsocial Attributions

To explore how lay attributers think about collective-level agency in relation to other kinds of causes, we examined the structure of attributions for an outcome that could be explained (by a scientific observer) in three distinct ways: As reflecting the agency of an individual, as reflecting the agency of a group, or as reflecting nonsocial situational factors. The outcome involved social animals rather than humans to make the purpose of the study less transparent. Participants were placed in the role of an assistant to a naturalist observing how penguin colonies manage to feed on fish while avoiding being eaten by killer whales. When an individual penguin enters the water, it may reflect individual recklessness and hunger, it may be the result of pressure from the group to test the waters, or it may simply be an accident caused by wind and ice:

> You are an inexperienced assistant that is observing penguins at the field site for the first time. It is a cold day and the ice is very slick, so you carefully find a place from which to watch them. Soon after you are settled there, you notice a penguin that the other researchers have nicknamed Peter. Through your binoculars, you see Peter standing for several minutes at the water's edge. Peter looks excited and is flapping his wings energetically. The rest of the flock stands close behind him making extremely loud squawking noises. They all crowd behind him, each hoping to be the second penguin in the water

---

[1] We report average interim correlation. The significance indicated is that of the least significant pair of items.

TABLE 21.1. Beliefs About Individuals and Organizations in the United States and Singapore

Actor	United States ($N = 41$)	Singapore ($N = 99$)
Individuals	4.10**	3.50**
Organizations	3.74	3.98

Note. The scores represent answers on a 7-point scale, with higher answers indicating greater belief in the autonomy of that actor. Asterisks indicate significant simple effects within country.
** $p < .01$.

after the first one tests the waters. With a squawk, Peter goes suddenly into the water. As soon as it is clear Peter is safe, several other penguins enter the water. After a few minutes, the rest of the flock dives into the water, eating as much fish as they possibly can.

Table 21.2 reveals that this vignette was not as ambiguous as planned: Both cultures preferred group attributions. However, we can still assess whether these attributions were distinct from nonsocial, environmental attributions. This vignette contains salient cues that the individual is the primary agent ("Peter looks excited and is flapping his wings energetically"), yet also contains other salient cues that the group is the primary agent ("The rest of the flock stands close behind him making extremely loud squawking noises") and plausible nonsocial factors. Participants rated the importance of a series of specific causes falling into these categories, which may be seen in Table 21.2

We performed an ALSCAL (alternating least squares scaling analysis) multidimensional scaling procedure on the 16 ratings of individual, group, and nonsocial factors. The items formed meaningful clusters for both Singapore and the United States, so we pooled the two countries together. A two-dimensional solution fit, with the R^2 (goodness of fit) = .98 and the poorness of fit (stress) = .07. The corresponding statistics for the three-dimensional model were $R^2 = .99$ and poorness of fit = .05, indicating that the three-dimensional model does not provide significant improvement over the two-dimensional model. The one-dimensional model, on the other hand, resulted in a substantial decline in fit, with $R^2 = .95$ and poorness of fit = .13.

Figure 21.1, which displays the two-dimensional solution, reveals three distinct clusters of individual, group, and nonsocial factors. As is also visible in Table 21.2, attribution items corresponding to group and nonsocial factors fall on opposite ends of Dimension 1, suggesting that not only are group and nonsocial attributions distinct, they are negatively associated in the

338 ■ Social Cognition: Key Readings

TABLE 21.2. Individual, Group, and Nonsocial Dimensions of Attribution in the Penguin Case

Items	Dimension 1	Dimension 2
Individual attributions[a]		
Peter was tempted by fish.	0.68	0.89
Peter was carefree and happy.	−0.55	0.65
Peter wanted to enter.	0.01	0.37
Peter wanted more fish.	0.26	0.21
Peter had a lot of energy.	−0.59	0.21
Group attributions[b]		
The flock decided Peter should enter.	2.91	0.49
The dominant birds wanted Peter to enter.	1.90	−0.79
The flock set an example for Peter.	1.73	−0.01
The flock pressured Peter.	0.90	−0.98
The flock was pushy.	0.62	−0.66
Nonsocial attributions[c]		
The wind pushed Peter in.	−1.74	−0.19
The flock slipped on the ice.	−1.47	−0.01
The wind pushed the flock in.	−1.39	−0.13
Peter slipped on the ice.	−1.21	−0.21
The chaos confused Peter.	−1.04	0.09
The cold weather made the water tempting.	−1.04	0.07

[a] α = .80, U.S. M = .17, Hong Kong M = .06.
[b] α = .49, U.S. M = .73, Hong Kong M = .77.
[c] α = .82, U.S. M = −.62, Hong Kong M = −.57.

minds of the participants responding to this vignette. The individual items cluster along Dimension 2, which is orthogonal to the nonsocial group dimension. Despite the fact that this scenario produced no significant cultural differences in attribution to any of the three dimensions, the results establish that North American and East Asian social perceivers both detected consequential differences between group and nonsocial situational attributions.

Cultural Theories in the Resolution of Ambiguity

Given preliminary support for our assumptions, we proposed the hypothesis that differing conceptions of agency in North American and East Asian societies determine how social perceivers in the two cultures make sense of ambiguous social events. Figure 21.2 illustrates our expectations about how the same objective event would be subjectively construed by perceivers relying on the individual agent theory and the collective

agent theory. The stimulus is an outcome (X) that follows activity by a number of individuals (A, B, C, D, E, F, and G). Perceivers relying on the individual agent theory would focus on one plausible individual (e.g., C), construe that individual as the agent, and causally attribute the outcome to properties of that individual. By contrast, perceivers relying on the group agent theory would focus on a plausible collective (e.g., the group of individuals A–G), construe this group as the agent, and attribute the outcome to properties of this group.

Several standard methods were used to test the hypothesis about cultural differences in attribution. We compared the frequency of individual- and organization-level references in American and Japanese newspaper reports about a number of incidents. Also, we measured the perceived weight of dispositional and situational forces in producing several types of outcomes. A common feature of the studies is a focus on deviance, action that departs from social norms. A first reason to focus on deviance is simply that unusual negative outcomes evoke attributions more than other kinds of outcomes (Wong & Weiner, 1981). A second reason is that deviance is particularly likely to illuminate the cultural difference because it involves conflict between an agent and a surrounding collective. Instances of deviance can be read as impingements of autonomous individuals on collectives (as when a parasite invades the body), or they can be read as failures of the collective to reign in and support a member (as when the body rejects a transplanted organ). Hence, instances of deviance or transgression are particularly good stimuli for a test of cultural differences to attribution to individual versus group agents.

Study 1: Focus on Individual and Collective Actors in Newspaper Explanations

Newspaper analyses of real-life events provide a natural context through which cultural differences in causal explanations may be examined (Lee, Hallahan, & Herzog, 1996; Morris & Peng, 1994). We compared newspaper explanations for "rogue trader" scandals in leading papers from a Confucian-influenced East Asian society (Japan) and an individualistic North American society (the United States) to test the hypothesized difference in focus on individual and collective actors.[2]

[2] Confucian classics were especially popular in Japan during the Edo period, but other influences, such as Shinto and Buddhist thought, have also shaped Japanese society extensively.

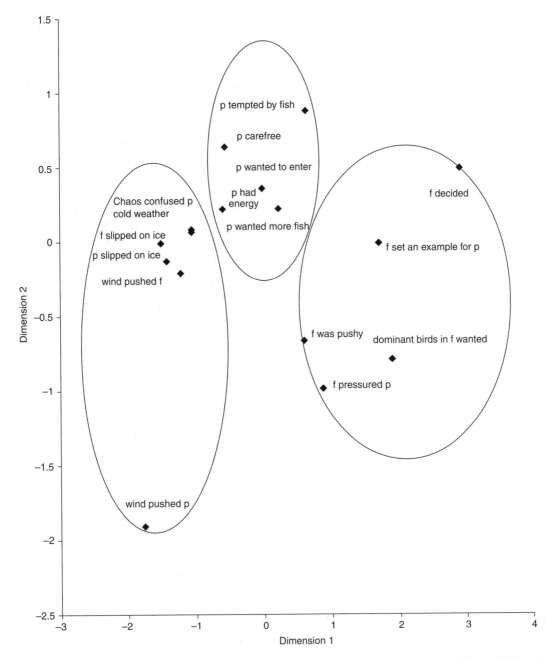

FIGURE 21.1 ■ Multidimensional Scaling Analysis Revealing Three Clusters of Attribution Items, Corresponding to Individual Agent, Collective Agent, and Nonsocial Environment Categories. f = flock, p = Peter. For Complete Attribution Items, See Table 21.2.

Objective Social Stimulus

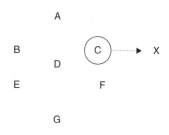

Subjective Construals of Social Stimulus

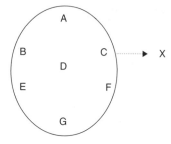

FIGURE 21.2 ■ Hypotheses About How the Same Social Event is Construed Differently on the Basis of Different Implicit Theories of Agency. X = Outcome Following Activity of Individuals; A, B, C, D, E, F, and G = Individuals.

Method

Materials

Event selection. We selected business scandals in which a particular individual and an organization were mutually implicated in a negative outcome. To select several comparable scandals, we searched the ABI/Inform database (1972) of business articles for scandals in

Japan and the United States that had evoked appreciable news coverage. We selected Japan (rather than Hong Kong or China) because of widely noted similarities between recent scandals in Japanese and Western organizations. The Japanese scandals we selected were Daiwa Bank's 1995 discovery of Toshihide Iguchi's loss in derivative trading and Yasuo Hamanaka's 1996 unauthorized copper trading at Sumitomo Bank. The American scandal was Paul Mozer's unauthorized bid in a Treasury auction in 1991, which his firm, Salomon Brothers, had been aware of but had failed to report to the government. The final scandal involved the trades of Nick Leeson that contributed to the 1995 collapse of Britain's oldest bank, Barings. Although Leeson was not an American, his British background made him a character with whom Americans could readily identify.

In addition to the superficial similarities (all scandals were multimillion dollar losses that occurred in banks in the same 5-year period, 1991–1996), these events also had structural parallels. In each, the central individual was a mid-level manager, not a leader of the organization yet not a low-level employee. Further, because neither the individual nor the organizational actor fully controlled the other, causality was not definitively lodged with either. Hence, from an individual responsibility perspective, each case was the consequence of an individual employee's transgression. Yet, from a collective responsibility perspective, each could be viewed as evoked by organization-level factors such as inadequate management. It is in the economic self-interest of traders to make double-or-nothing bets if they have already accumulated career-ending losses. If a firm lacks adequate controls against this happening, this property of the firm could be seen as the cause of the loss.

Newspaper selection. We selected newspapers that were comparable in their quality of news reporting and analysis. In Japan and the United States, two newspapers with superior reputations are respectively the *Asahi Shimbun* (*AS*) and *The New York Times* (*NYT*). A bilingual research assistant collected the relevant articles from the original Japanese-language *AS* and the *NYT*.

Article sampling. We sampled every article in each paper about the scandal during the first 2 weeks in which the story broke. Table 21.3 shows that the frequency of articles about each scandal was very similar across papers.

Procedure

Our first step was to extract the relevant statements from each newspaper article (Schulman, Castellon, & Seligman. 1989). A hypothesis-blind bilingual extractor

TABLE 21.3. Number of Articles About Each Scandal in the Sample Period (Study 1)

Scandal	United States, The New York Times	Japan, Asahi Shimbun
Iguchi at Daiwa	12	12
Hamanaka at Sumitomo	15	13
Mozer at Salomon Brothers	10	7
Leeson at Barings	39	31

identified each of the distinct attributions to an individual or organization. Because of the structure of these scandals, the attribution was to either the primary actors, that is, the individual who was involved with the event (Iguchi, Hamanaka, Mozer, or Leeson), or the firm (Daiwa, Sumitomo, Salomon, or Barings). The extractor segmented each unit referring to an actor, transcribed it, and indicated the source (either the reporter or a cited person). This process yielded 919 units referring to the focal individual or collective. Articles in the *NYT* were longer than those in the *AS* and consequently yielded more units.[3]

Following the extraction process, two hypothesis-blind judges coded whether each unit in question concerned the focal individual or the focal organization. The first judge coded each of the 919 units and the second judge coded all of the units for the Daiwa, Sumitomo, and Salomon cases and the first 50% of the units of each article for the longer Barings case. The percentage of agreement between these two coders was 85.5%.

Results

Table 21.4 shows the frequency of explanatory references to individual and organizational actors, respectively, in the North American (*NYT*) and East Asian (*AS*) newspapers. For Japanese scandals, the *NYT* referred

---

[3] The source of attributions was taken into account in two ways. We selected those ideas in Japanese newspapers expressed by a Japanese speaker and those ideas in American papers expressed by American or Western speakers. By using only speakers from within the culture, we eliminated the complications that could result, for instance, from the *NYT* quoting Japanese sources about Japanese scandals. Further, to maintain the separation in the literature between attributions about the self and other, we excluded explanations in self-defense. Thus, statements by actors themselves, by their lawyers, or by presidents of the affected organizations were not included because they involved some degree of self-attribution. This winnowing did not alter the pattern of results.

more to properties of the individual than the organization, whereas the reverse ordering held in the *AS*; for Daiwa, $\chi^2_2(1, N = 166) = 7.58$, $p < .01$, and for Sumitomo, $\chi^2_2(1, N = 143) = 21.28$, $p < .01$. Likewise, the *NYT* emphasized the individual more and the group less than did the *AS* for American scandals. Most dramatically, in the Salomon case the *AS* did not make a single explanatory reference to the individual actor and exclusively discussed organization-level factors, $\chi^2(1, N = 84) = 7.03$, $p < .01$. In the Barings case, whereas the *NYT* referred more frequently to the individual than to the organization, the *AS* referred more frequently to the organization, $\chi^2(1, N = 526) = 14.79$, $p < .01$. Importantly, as Figure 21.3 illustrates, the cultural difference in locus of attribution holds regardless of the culture in which the scandal took place.

In interpreting the quantitative results, it is instructive to consider the qualitative content of the explanations emphasized by the American and Japanese papers. One *NYT* article described Mozer as "Salomon's errant cowboy" who "attacked his work as aggressively as he hit tennis balls." Another implied Hamanaka's lack of shrewdness in stating that he "was known more for the volume of his trades than his aptness." Whereas the lack of organizational controls was a minor theme of Americans in the *NYT*, it was a major theme of Japanese reporters in the *AS*. Japanese reporters commented that "somebody in Sumitomo should have recognized the fictitious trading since documents are checked every day," and that Daiwa "is embarrassed that its internal controls and procedures were not sufficient to prevent the case."

Discussion

This study showed that cultures differed in their focus on individual- as opposed to collective-level factors when explaining a scandal to which both individual and group actors contributed. Despite the naturalism and validity of newspaper reports, the study did not establish whether these attribution patterns exist more broadly outside the newspaper context and among ordinary social perceivers rather than reporters.

Study 2: Focus on Individual and Collective Actors in a Student Survey

Study 2 replicated Study 1 with a survey of college student attributions for an event within an organization. We presented American and Hong Kong Chinese

TABLE 21.4. Number of References to Individuals and Organizations in American and Japanese Papers (Study 1)

Individuals and organizations	United States, *The New York Times*		Japan, *Asahi Shimbun*		χ^2	df	N
	No. of References	% of Total	No. of References	% of Total			
Iguchi	69	62	21	39	7.58**	1	166
Daiwa	43	38	33	61			
Hamanka	62	61	8	19	21.28**	1	143
Sumitomo	39	39	34	81			
Mozer	30	41	0	0	7.03**	1	84
Salomon	43	59	11	100			
Leeson	229	54	34	33	14.79**	1	526
Barings	194	46	69	67			

**$p < .01$.

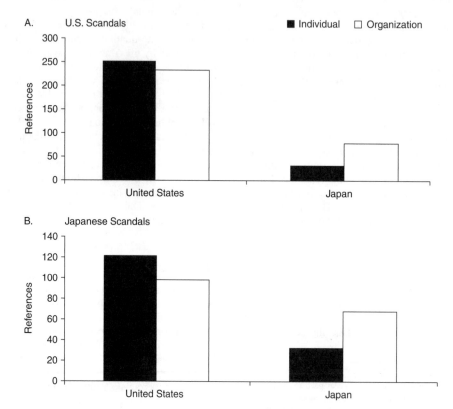

FIGURE 21.3 ■ Frequency of References to Individuals and Groups in U.S. and Japanese Articles About Rogue Trader Scandals (Study 1).

(Chinese) undergraduates with a vignette in which both individual and collective factors contributed to a negative organizational outcome. Instead of a complex financial scandal, the outcome in Study 2 was a decline in teamwork and performance in a work group that included a maladjusted employee. Participants were asked to rate several properties of the individual and the group that were plausible causes of the decline.

Method

Overview of Design
The study used a 2 × 2 design in which country (United States vs. Hong Kong) varied quasi-experimentally and level of actor (individual vs. group) varied within participants.

Participants
We surveyed 41 American students from Stanford University. The ethnic composition of the sample was as follows: 54% European American, 13% Hispanic, 13% Asian American, and 4% African American; 16% did not report this information. Of the sample, 39% were men, 46% were women, and the rest did not report their gender. American participants were 18.9 years old on average. Fifty-two students at the University of Hong Kong were also surveyed, all of whom described themselves as Chinese. Of these students, 31% were men, 69% were women, and they were 19.7 years old on average.

Stimulus Materials
We presented participants with a vignette (translated into Chinese for Hong Kong participants) that could be explained by two plausible stories involving either the individual or the group as the autonomous agent. Participants could construe the individual as a "free rider" who shirked obligations toward the group. Alternatively, they could construe the group as the problematic actor that failed to integrate a member:

> In a particular company, a group of coworkers was responsible for completing a very important project. The project itself involved few complications, but one problem constantly plagued the group. One coworker, who we will call "Z," consistently showed up late for meetings and, worse, missed deadlines. Z had reasonable excuses for every incident. For example, in one case Z was tied up with an emergency personal situation, and in another Z came down with a bad flu. In the final analysis, Z's work did not get done to the group's satisfaction, and the group was often charged with the responsibilities that should have been Z's. Group relations suffered, and the members of the group often lost their patience with Z and became sidetracked from the project. As a result of these issues, the final product did not meet expectations of quality.

We asked participants to evaluate "reasons as to why this project was not as successful as it could have been." We presented a list of possibly relevant factors, including individual and group dispositions and many extraneous filler items. The participants rated items on a 7-point scale with 1 = *not a cause at all* and 7 = *most important cause*.

Results

As reported in Figure 21.4, American students were more likely to endorse individual dispositions, whereas Chinese students were more likely to endorse group dispositions. Ratings were standardized across items before analysis to control for any cultural differences in scale response biases (van de Vijver & Leung, 1996). Table 21.5 reports individual disposition ($\alpha = .85$) and group disposition ($\alpha = .74$) items. The individual dispositions that differed across cultures were "Z was in charge of his own actions and behaviors,"

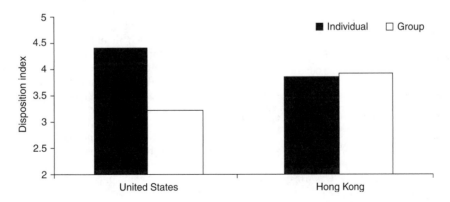

FIGURE 21.4 ■ Dispositional Attributions About the Individual and Group in Student Responses to a Story About a Maladjusted Team Member (Study 2).

TABLE 21.5. Mean Attribution Scores for a Vignette With Individual and Group Causes (Study 2)

Items	United States (N = 38)	Hong Kong (N = 51)
Individual dispositions (α = .85)		
Z was in charge of his own actions and behaviors.		
Raw scores	4.71**	3.21
Standardized scores	.43**	−.60
Z was irresponsible in not completing the work.		
Raw scores	4.92†	4.25
Standardized scores	.59*	.23
Z was inconsiderate to the group.		
Raw scores	4.84†	4.33
Standardized scores	.56	.35
Z was a poor worker.		
Raw scores	4.05	3.61
Standardized scores	−.01	−.26
Z's behavior is rooted in a permanent part of his personality.		
Raw scores	3.74	3.25
Standardized scores	−.21	−.49
Group dispositions (α = .74)		
The group was unfriendly to communication.		
Raw scores	3.11**	4.53
Standardized scores	−.56**	−.48
The group could have resolved Z's problems.		
Raw scores	2.84**	3.80
Standardized scores	−.76**	−.06
The group was unsupportive, unable to handle internal problems.		
Raw scores	4.05**	4.86
Standardized scores	.05**	.73
The group was irresponsible.		
Raw scores	3.05	3.35
Standardized scores	−.63	−.42
The group was selfish, unaccommodating.		
Raw scores	3.00	3.04
Standardized scores	−.63	.62

Note. The raw scores represent answers on a 7-point scale with higher answers indicating greater agreement with the statement. Standardized scores are standardized across items. There were several other individual disposition items not shown.
† $p < .10$ (marginally significant). * $p < .05$. ** $p < .01$.

$F(1, 88) = 36.75$, $p < .01$, and "Z was irresponsible in not completing the work," $F(1, 88) = 4.63$, $p < .05$. Group items that differed included "The group was unfriendly to communication," $F(1, 88) = 27.06$, $p < .01$; "The group could have resolved Z's problems," $F(1, 88) = 12.29$, $p < .01$; and "The group was unsupportive, unable to handle internal problems," $F(1, 88) = 12.19$, $p < .01$. The summary scores for individual and group dispositions produced a significant interaction between country and level of actor, $F(1, 89) = 16.52$, $p < .01$.

Discussion

Our hypothesis that North Americans place relatively more focus on individual persons whereas East Asians place relatively more focus on collective-level actors was clearly supported by the pattern of results in Study 2. However, as in Study 1, Study 2 concerned outcomes that resulted from an interaction of an individual and a surrounding group. Because the group formed part of the situation around a focal individual actor, attributions to dispositions were not fully distinguished from nonsocial, situational attributions. Extending our demonstration in the pilot study that lay attributors distinguish group agents from nonsocial factors in the environment, we designed our final study to demonstrate that East Asian attribution to groups does not derive from a general orientation to situations or context.

Study 3: Attribution to Dispositions and Situations for Individual and Group Acts

Study 3 involved two departures from the previous studies. First, whereas in Study 1 and Study 2 we analyzed attributions about individual and group actors only, in Study 3 we introduced the situation. Our concept of the situation was more specific here than in prior research, given that we separated the social situation (which involves group actors) from the nonsocial situation (which includes chance and task difficult). Second, in the previous studies, the group was simultaneously a situation affecting a focal individual and an actor in its own right. In the group condition of Study 3, the group was unambiguously an actor affected by its own set of situational constraints. This provided a clear test of whether East Asians attribute causality to groups when they are not simply a situation around individuals but agents instead. We expected an interaction whereby American dispositionism to individuals would be accompanied by greater situationalism to groups, and East Asian situationalism about individuals would be accompanied by greater dispositionism to groups.

Method

Overview

Study 3 used a 2 × 2 design in which country (United States vs. Hong Kong) varied quasi-experimentally, and level of actor (person vs. group) was between participants.

Participants

In this study, we collected data at Stanford University and the Hong Kong University of Science and Technology. The 89 American students had an average age of 19.0. The ethnic composition was 49% European American, 19% Asian American, 14% African American, 10% Hispanic, and 8% of other ethnicities. The 100 students from HKUST were 21.2 years old on average, and all reported Chinese ethnicity.

Materials

Hong Kong and American participants were presented (in Chinese and English, respectively) three cases of wrongdoing — the transgression of a duty or norm. Half the participants saw vignettes in which the actor was an individual, and the other half saw an identical vignette in which the actor was a group. The first two cases, "inequitable employees" and "ineffective firemen," described transgressions of duty at the workplace. The third, "rogue cattle," described a transgression by animals. The animal case was included to test whether cultural differences in attribution reflect theories rather than concrete, detailed knowledge of the dynamics of managers, firemen, or other particular social contexts (see Morris & Peng, 1994).

> In a small nonprofit organization, the Society to Cure Cancer in Children, a mid-level employee [group of employees] who had been working there for a long time was charged with making an important decision. His [Their] task was to determine pay scales for the rest of the organization and to determine the value of both his [their] own and other people's work in the organization. Unfortunately, in the first year of implementing his [their] plan, gross inequities were discovered. It was determined that the benefits and wage plans favored this employee [group of employees] overwhelmingly. As a result of this unfair plan, morale in the organization suffered and much time had to be spent in order to reorganize the company.

> Recently a community had what was its most destructive fire in ten years. A disturbing event occurred during the fire. From one window of a building that appeared ready to collapse, a little girl was crying for help because she had no means of escape. A fireman [team of

firemen] with several years of experience was in full uniform and prepared with the necessary equipment. He [They] heard the child's screams but did not enter the building. In the end, the child died in the fire.

> A farmer was grazing a small herd of cattle. One day, things unexpectedly went wrong. At first, a bull [the herd] seemed agitated by something near the farmer. Moments later, the bull [herd] charged directly at the farmer, who fell to the ground as he was hit by its [their] impact. The bull [herd] managed to break free from the enclosed area. It [They] escaped and ran free.

Participants then rated several potential causes generated from a typology of achievement attributions in which internality and externality are crossed with stability and instability (Weiner et al., 1971). They rated three items that referred to internal, stable properties of the actor (i.e., dispositions). They also rated one item each of the other types: Internal, unstable factors (e.g., effort); external, stable factors (e.g., task difficulty); and external, unstable factors (e.g., chance). One benefit of using Weiner's typology was that each of the external items was clearly a nonsocial aspect of the situation. We list each of the specific items that formed the dependent measures in Table 21.6.

Following these cases, they rated their agreement with a list of general social beliefs. We assessed their ratings of statements related to the autonomy of individuals and of social collectives as an indirect check that Hong Kong students, despite diverse cultural influences, differ from American students in conceptions of autonomy. The items covered a broad range of specific topics and were taken from a list of social beliefs designed to be interpretable across cultures (Leung, 1997).

Results

Check of Country Differences in Beliefs

To check our assumption that Hong Kong differs from the United States in implicit theories of individual versus collective autonomy, we assessed the pattern of country differences on proverbial beliefs about tensions between individuals and collectives. These belief items were assessed individually because they tapped beliefs about different kinds of social collectives, rather than one specific belief. As expected, Americans were significantly more likely to endorse beliefs in individual autonomy, such as "Non-conformity is valuable for society," $F(1, 189) = 8.41$, $p < .01$, and "Society is most healthy and moral if each individual follows his or her internal will," $F(1, 189) = 19.75$, $p < .01$. Conversely, Americans were more likely to reject statements about

TABLE 21.6. Summary Measures for Dispositional and Situational Attribution (Study 3)

Scale	Inequitable managers	Ineffective firemen	Rogue cattle
Dispositional attribution	Irresponsible	Lacked courage	Aggressive and dominant
	Greedy	More concerned about own safety	Stubborn
	Lacked a sense of fairness	Not committed to job	Crazy
Interitem r	.47**	.50**	.28*
Situational attribution	Difficult task	Difficult task	Provocation
	Unpredictable complications	Chance made the fire difficult to fight	Accidental escape
Interitem r	.41**	.15*	.21**

Note. For average intercorrelation, asterisks indicate the significance of the least significant pair of items in the group.
* $p < .05$. ** $p < .01$.

the limits of individual autonomy, such as "The company one keeps influence what one becomes," $F(1, 189) = 6.81$, $p = .01$, and "Children should be taught that following duty is more important than following preferences," $F(1, 189) = 76.91$, $p < .01$.

As expected, the reverse pattern held for beliefs about the autonomy of social collectives. Compared with Americans, Chinese were more likely to endorse statements such as "A coherent group has a will that is stronger than any individual person," $F(1, 189) = 9.29$, $p < .01$; "Strong organizations chart a direction for themselves and do not let themselves be affected by the pressures surrounding them," $F(1, 189) = 35.96$, $p < .01$; and "Each nation follows its own internally directed path through history," $F(1, 189) = 59.40$, $p < .01$. Because this pattern held across several types of collective actors, it follows that these beliefs result from a general conception of collectives having stable properties that cause outcomes.[4]

Attribution Patterns
For each scenario, we averaged the standardized scores for the three internal, stable items to form a summary score for dispositional attribution. The external, unstable item and external, stable item were averaged to form a summary score for situational attribution.[5] We used the dispositional and situational attribution summary

scores from each of the three scenarios as dependent variables in a 2 (country) × 2 (level of actor) × 3 (scenario) repeated measures ANOVA. There was no three-way effect for Country × Level of Actor × Scenario for either dispositional or situational attributions, so we averaged across the three scenarios.

Graphs of dispositional attributions (Figure 21.5A) reveal that Americans were more dispositional about acts by individuals than by groups, whereas Chinese were more dispositional about acts by groups than by individuals. As reported in Table 21.7, this Country × Level of Actor interaction was highly significant, $F(1, 184) = 18.73$, $p < .01$. We conducted a priori tests to determine whether the interaction followed the predicted form. We assigned contrast coefficients of $+1$ for conditions involving acts by the agent predicted to be privileged in a culture (the individual in the United States and the group in Hong Kong) and -1 for conditions concerning the agent predicted to be less favored (the group in the United States and the individual in Hong Kong). The test resulted in a highly significant contrast, $t(185) = 4.28$, $p < .01$. Americans were significantly more dispositional about individuals than groups, $t(87) = 4.22$, $p < .01$, whereas Chinese exhibited a marginally significant preference for dispositional attribution to groups over individuals, $t(98) = -1.74$, $p < .10$.

A mirror-image pattern can be seen in graphs of situational attributions (Figure 21.5B). Whereas Chinese

---

[4] Our view is that such beliefs about the world are constructed from implicit theories but are not equivalent with these theories. Theories may exist in the form of attentional schemata or automatized procedures (Duff & Newman, 1997; Gilbert, 1989) rather than as explicit propositional beliefs. In sum, beliefs are just a different way of measuring the theories of interest, not necessarily a more proximal measure.

5 Given that the internal, unstable items are not dispositional properties of the actor, we, of course, did not include them as part of the disposition summary score. Ratings of the internal, unstable items did not differ significantly across cultures in any of the three cases.

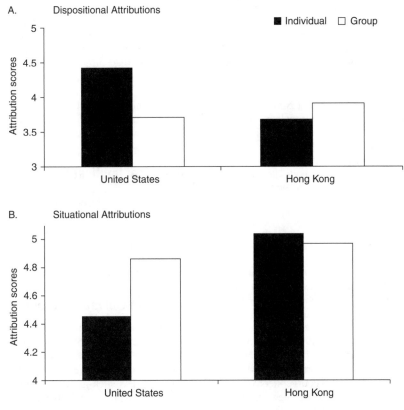

FIGURE 21.5 ■ Attributions to Dispositions and Situations Around Individuals and Groups (Study 3).

TABLE 21.7. Dispositional and Situational Attributions in the Individual and Group Conditions (Study 3)

Attributional Loci	United States (individual, $N = 48$; group, $N = 40$)	Hong Kong (individual, $N = 48$; group, $N = 52$)
Dispositional		
Individual	.20**	−.19†
Group	−.05	−.10
Situational		
Individual	.23**	.64
Group	.55	.56

Note. Scores are standardized across items. Asterisks indicate a significant within–country simple effect of level of actor.
† $p < .10$ (marginally significant). ** $p < .01$.

were much more likely than Americans to make situational attributions about individuals, there was no difference between Chinese and American situational attributions about groups, $F(1, 184) = 10.37$, $p < .01$.

We again performed a priori tests to specify the form of this interaction. As compared with dispositional attributions, we reversed the coefficients we assigned to the conditions for situational attributions. Conditions referring to the actor predicted to be privileged in a culture were assigned contrast coefficients of −1, and the conditions with the other actor were assigned +1. Again, these contrasts were highly significant, $t(185) = 3.11$, $p < .01$. For the within-country simple effects, Americans were significantly more likely to be situational about groups than individuals, $t(87) = −3.17$, $p < .01$, whereas there was no significant difference between Chinese situational attributions to groups and individuals.

Discussion

Study 3 results support our hypothesis that North American and East Asian perceivers differ in their readiness to infer dispositional causes depending on whether the actor is an individual or a group. As Figure 21.5 illustrates, Americans were more confident in inferring internal, stable causes of acts by an individual than acts by a group, whereas the opposite was true for Chinese perceivers. Further, Chinese were more situational than Americans with respect to individual but not group actors. Given our findings that North American dispositionism and East Asian situationalism are specific to the individual level of analysis, we conclude that the source of cultural differences does not lie in contrasting cognitive styles (dispositionism vs. situationalism) but in the application of those styles to the actor privileged by autonomy beliefs in the society (individual vs. group).

General Discussion

We have argued that social perception and attribution is channeled by culturally bound theories about the relative autonomy of individuals and collectivities. Through several methods, we replicated previous findings that North American social perceivers are more likely than East Asians to attribute causality to individuals and their dispositions. The novel findings are the East Asians are relatively more likely than North Americans to focus on, and attribute causality to dispositions of, collective-level agents. In Study 1 we found that American news reporters, compared with their Japanese counterparts, focused more on the central individuals in financial scandals, whereas Japanese reporters focused more on the properties of organizations. In Study 2 we found that American students explained an ambiguous outcome by emphasizing properties of the individual, whereas Chinese students placed relatively more emphasis on properties of the group. Study 3 established that the emphasis on the group was different from a general emphasis on situation or context. Further, in Study 3 we found that cultures differed in readiness to make dispositional and situational attributions about persons and groups. Across several cases, we found that Americans more readily attributed causes to the dispositions of persons than groups, as compared with Chinese.

Our hypothesis is drawn from the premise that cultures differ in implicit theories about the autonomy of individual and collective actors. At two points, we tested this premise directly. An initial pilot study assessed beliefs of American and Singaporean students about the extent to which individuals and organizations control their own destinies. The study revealed a strong interaction

effect whereby Americans were more likely to endorse statements consistent with individual autonomy and Singaporeans were more likely to endorse statements consistent with organizational autonomy. Similarly, in Study 3 we assessed a diffuse set of beliefs relevant to autonomy of individuals versus collectives such as groups, organizations, and nations. Again, Americans endorsed individual autonomy items whereas Chinese were more likely to endorse items concerning the autonomy of the various collective actors.

Theoretical Implications

The current research contributes to the literature in three ways. First, it introduces a more precise specification of cultural differences in attribution patterns. Second, it tests between competing accounts of the sources of these cultural differences. Third, it draws attention to the perceiver's interpretations of group actors.

Patterns of Cultural Divergence

The current findings further the effort toward a fine-grained understanding of patterns of cultural differences in cognition. Hypotheses about cultural differences in cognitive tendencies were advanced by early 20th-century anthropologists such as Levy-Bruhl (1910/1926), who contrasted a "prelogical" mentality in traditional cultures with a logical mentality more predominant in Western cultures. These sweeping claims about broad differences fell from favor because they were both pejorative and underdetermined by ethnographic data (which afford only indirect evidence about cognition). Since then, most anthropologists and psychologists have upheld the doctrine of psychic universality, the position that although tendencies in public behavior differ across cultures, patterns of private cognition such as attributional biases do not differ (for a review, see Shore, 1996).

However, proposals that cognitive tendencies differ across cultures have reemerged in the past 2 decades, on the basis of evidence from cross-cultural psychological studies (for a review, see Morris, Nisbett, & Peng, 1995). Initial proposals about the patterns of difference were less pejorative but no less broad than those of Levy-Bruhl (1910/1926). For instance, Shweder and Bourne (1982) drew a contrast between the holistic, contextual style of inference in non-Western cultures and the analytical, generalizing style in the West. Yet, as more empirical data has accumulated, researchers have identified more specific patterns. For example, Morris and Peng (1994) presented American and Chinese participants with animated displays of different kinds of events, some involving mechanical causality (i.e., one object influences another's movement) and some involving social causality (i.e., one actor influences another's action). Cultural differences in dispositional attribution emerged only in attributions of social causality, not of physical causality, suggesting they reflect differences in domain-specific social theories rather than domain-general cognitive styles. The current research continues this progress toward a more fine-grained understanding by contrasting individual actors with group actors. We find that perceivers in different cultures are equally likely to make dispositional attributions for action, but their proclivity to make dispositional attributions depends on the type of actor. Hence, patterns of cultural divergence are not general across domains or even within the social domain, but they are specific to the type of actor in question.

Culture and the Process of Attribution

The current findings also help disentangle competing accounts of where cultural differences originate in the attribution process. Our account is that cultural socialization and experience determines which implicit social theories are cognitively accessible to a perceiver as a basis for tracing an outcome to an agent's disposition. North American and European cultures confer a highly accessible theory of persons as autonomous agents, whereas East Asian cultures confer a theory of groups as agents. In particular, two predictions follow from this interpretation: (a) that relative to North Americans, East Asian perceivers are more likely to focus on collective-level agents when explaining an outcome for which the agent is ambiguous, and (b) that the relative reluctance among East Asian perceivers to make dispositional attributions for acts by individuals does not extend to acts by groups. In sum, the current findings support the interpretation that attribution biases reflect knowledge structures; that is, North Americans work with the assumption that individual agents are autonomous vis-à-vis social collectives, and East Asians work with the assumption that collective-level agents have some autonomy vis-à-vis individuals.

An alternative account of where cultural differences originate turns on goals. It has been suggested that cultures differ in the degree to which they inculcate the aim of dispositional inference in the first place (Krull, 1993; Shweder & Bourne, 1982). The current findings

disconfirm this interpretation, which predicts that East Asian participants should be as unlikely to attribute causality to the disposition of a group actor as they are with respect to an individual actor.

Concurrent with our work, Choi et al. (1999) have proposed that cultural influences in attribution can be elucidated in terms of the distinction between dispositional inference and situational adjustment. In stage models of the attribution process, dispositional inference is an automatic, heuristic process, whereas situational adjustment is a more deliberate correction of that initial dispositional inference (for a review, see Gilbert, 1989). Integrating findings from person perception studies, Choi et al. (1999) argued that the source of cultural differences lies in the situational adjustment stage. That is, North Americans and East Asians possess identical tendencies toward initial dispositional judgments, yet East Asians respond more dramatically to salient situations by adjusting their initial judgments. Although this account serves well to integrate findings from person perception studies, it does not fare as well with respect to the current studies. It does not account for why East Asians are more likely to focus on the group rather than the individual in responding to an action by an embedded individual, such as an employee in an organization (Study 1 and Study 2). Moreover, it does not account for why the individual-level contrast between North American dispositionism and East Asian situationalism disappears at the group level of analysis (Study 3).

Ongoing research further supports our interpretation of the source of cultural differences in the attribution process. On the basis of findings that the epistemic motive of *need for closure* accentuates reliance on highly accessible knowledge structures (e.g., Kruglanski & Webster, 1996; Jost, Kruglanski, & Simon, 1998), we tested the prediction that individuals exhibit cultural biases to the degree that they have a high need for closure (Chiu, Morris, Hong, Cheng, & Menon, 1998). As predicted, individuals in North American with a chronically high need for closure showed accentuated dispositionism for individual but not group actors, whereas those in Hong Kong with chronically high need for closure showed accentuated dispositionism for group but not individual actors (Chiu et al., 1998). In an experiment that manipulated need for closure situationally by putting participants under time pressure, we obtained the same pattern of results (Chiu et al., 1998). Further support for the implicit theory account comes from evidence that manipulations of cognitive load (which increase reliance on accessible theories) have culturally divergent influences (Knowles, Morris, Chiu, &

Hong, 1998). A final source of evidence that culture has its impact through the accessibility of implicit theories comes from a series of priming experiments (Hong, Morris, Chiu, & Benet-Martinez, 1998). Bicultural participants were randomly assigned to conditions under which they were exposed to images of North American culture, of Chinese culture, or of neutral landscapes. Results showed that American versus Chinese cultural priming skewed subsequent attributions in the direction predicted on the basis of the predominant social theories in these cultures. That is, the increased accessibility of Western social theories led perceivers to attribute causality to individual dispositions, and the increased accessibility of Chinese social theories led perceivers to attribute causality to group dispositions.

Attributions to Group Agents

A third theoretical contribution of the current research lies in drawing research attention to attributions for group action and to the construct of group dispositions. Although a considerable amount of social cognition is devoted to the understanding of groups, organizations, and institutions, this aspect of social perception has received very little research attention as compared with person perception. Perhaps because of the methodological individualism in psychological research, researchers have assumed that lay perceivers construe their social worlds in terms of atomistic individuals (Fiske et al., 1998). Individual- and group-level dispositions are on the same epistemic footing (both are abstract constructs ascribed on the basis of behavioral regularities). Yet, whereas Western psychologists have treated individual dispositions as natural and obvious, they have introduced group dispositions only tentatively, if at all.

We suggest that two types of group dispositions deserve attention: Those that involve aggregated traits of individuals within the group (see Yzerbyt, Rogier, & Fiske, 1998) and those that concern group-level properties (see Allison, Beggan, Midgley, & Wallace, 1995). Our studies found interactions with respect to both of these types of group dispositionism. For example, Study 2 concerned group-level processes, such as "The group had poor communication." Study 3 concerned individual-level traits applied to the group, such as "The managers were greedy." We suggest conducting a more systematic study of both types of group dispositions to further examine their prevalence within East Asian causal reasoning.

The current findings also suggest that several areas of social cognition research may benefit from considering

cultural theories about groups. Impression formation processes involving expectations of stability and coherence in group and individual actors (D. L. Hamilton & Sherman, 1996) may differ depending on cultural theories that emphasize individual or collective autonomy. Similarly, research on attributions of responsibility and blameworthiness in East Asian and North American cultures has proceeded by presenting vignettes about acts of individual wrongdoing to perceivers in both cultures (V. L. Hamilton & Sanders, 1992). Our current findings suggest that a fuller understanding of cultural differences might arise from studies of cases in which a group is the actor. Finally, our research supports prior findings about shared responsibility and blame in Chinese societies (Chiu & Hong, 1992; Morris, 1993).

Issues for Future Research

Although the current studies test the predictions from an implicit theory interpretation of cultural differences against a competing interpretation in terms of differing orientations, they raise and leave unanswered numerous related questions that suggest directions for future research. We review these directions in terms of how the pattern of results may be sensitive to changes in particular variables, although the interest, of course, lies not merely in specifying the pattern of attributions across variables but also in understanding relevant underlying cognitive processes and structures.

Type of Act

The current studies follow in a tradition of research on culture in attributions for wrongdoing or deviance (Miller, 1984; Morris & Peng, 1994). Although acts of deviance are particularly likely to evoke spontaneous attributions, given that they are unusual and negatively valenced outcomes (Wong & Weiner, 1981), they are by no means the only kind of act to evoke attributional processing nor the only kind for which cultures differ. To name just one example, attributions for achievement have also received cross-cultural study, with some findings pointing to a pattern in which internal, stable factors are accorded more weight by North Americans than by East Asians (Hess, Chang, & McDevitt, 1987). Although patterns of cultural differences in the achievement domain resemble those in the deviance domain, they are not exactly the same; for example, internal, unstable factors such as effort seem to be particularly important to East Asians in the achievement domain. Most likely the implicit theories involved are distinct from but related to the ones applied to deviance. In cross-cultural studies of attribution for achievements by groups, it would be interesting to assess whether East Asians accord more weight to internal, stable factors at the group level, or whether their emphasis on internal, unstable factors carries across to their inferences about group achievements.

Type of Actor

Questions concerning the type of individual or group actor would be worth addressing in future studies. First, the current results suggest an answer to a puzzle concerning cultural variation in a pattern of attribution taken to reflect ethnocentrism. The typical finding in studies with Western participants is that negatively valenced acts by out-group individuals are more likely to be attributed to negative dispositions than those by in-group individuals (Pettigrew, 1979). However, attempts to replicate this finding in Chinese cultural settings have not been successful (Morris & Peng, 1994), a surprising finding given the importance of the boundary between the in-group and out-group in Chinese culture and other manifestations of ethnocentrism. The current findings suggest that the problem may be that researchers have looked in the wrong place for the negative dispositional attributions that support Chinese ethnocentrism — they have looked at attributions to individuals rather than attributions to groups.

Another direction for future research is how cultural patterns of attribution for acts by groups depends on the type of group. For instance, a recent investigation (Lickel et al., 1998) distinguished the following four group types: Intimacy groups (family, friends), task groups (committees, work groups), categories of individuals with a common characteristic (religion, nationality,

gender), and temporary loose associations (people at a bus stop, the audience of a movie). These clusters were formed from a larger set of groups varying on dimensions such as interaction frequency and similarity of group members. The first two types — intimacy and task groups — are perceived to be more entity-like (higher in entitativity) than the second two types — categories and associations. Our expectation is that the cultural theory of collective autonomy in East Asian cultures applies to the first two types but not the second. Hence, we expect that the cultural difference in the tendency to attribute group outcomes to group dispositions holds for groups that are high in entitativity.[6]

REFERENCES

ABI/Inform [Electronic database]. (1972). Ann Arbor, MI: University Microfilm [Producer].

Allison, S. T., Beggan, J. K., Midgley, E. H., & Wallace, K. A. (1995). Dispositional and behavioral inferences about inherently democratic and unanimous groups. *Social Cognition, 13*, 105–125.

Allport, F. H. (1962). A structuronomic conception of behavior: Individual and collective. *Journal of Abnormal and Social Psychology, 64*, 3–30.

Asch, S. E. (1946). Forming impressions of personality. *Journal of Abnormal and Social Psychology, 41*, 258–290.

Asch, S. E. (1952). *Social psychology.* Englewood Cliffs, NJ: Prentice Hall.

Bellah, R. N., Madsen, R., Sullivan, W. M., Swidler, A., & Tipton, S. M. (1985). *Habits of the heart: Individualism and commitment in American life.* Berkeley, CA: University of California Press.

Campbell, D. T. (1958). Common fate, similarity, and other indices of the status of aggregates of persons as social entities. *Behavioral Science, 3*, 14–25.

Cartwright, D., & Zander, A. (Eds.). (1968). *Group dynamics: Research and theory* (3rd ed.). New York: Harper & Row.

Cattell, R. B. (1973). *Personality and mood by questionnaire.* San Francisco: Jossey-Bass.

Chiu, C., Dweck, C. S., Tong, J. Y., & Fu, J. H. (1997). Implicit theories and conceptions of morality. *Journal of Personality and Social Psychology, 73*, 923–940.

Chiu, C., & Hong, Y. (1992). The effects of intentionality and validation on individual and collective responsibility attribution among Hong Kong Chinese. *Journal of Psychology, 126*, 291–300.

Chiu, C., Morris, M. W., Hong, Y., Cheng, T.-K., & Menon, T. (1998). *The closing of the American mind and the closing of the Chinese mind: Differential effects of need for closure on the construal of social outcomes.* Unpublished manuscript, Stanford University, Graduate School of Business, Stanford, CA.

Choi, I., Nisbett, R. E., & Norenzayan, A. (1999). Causal attribution across cultures: Variation and universality. *Psychological Bulletin, 125*, 47–63.

Confucius. (1997). *The analects of Confucius* (S. Leys, Trans.). New York: Norton.

Duff, K., & Newman, L. S. (1997). Individual differences in the spontaneous construal of behavior: Idiocentrism and the automatization of the trait inference process. *Social Cognition, 15*, 217–241.

Durkheim, E. (1915). *The elementary forms of religious life: A study in religious sociology* (J. W. Swain, Trans.). New York: Macmillan.

---

[6] Because this paper concerns the contrast between implicit theories about individuals in North America and collectives in East Asia, it generalizes across different types of collective actors and the diverse countries within those regions. However, as a reviewer of this article has noted, one variation obscured in the broad strokes of this generalization is that East Asian countries may differ in their primary group orientation. Scholars have argued that in China the primary collective unit may be the family, whereas in Japan it is the larger social unit, such as the village, company, or nation (Nakane, 1973; Tobin, Wu, & Davidson, 1989). In addition to the broad contrast between North Americans and East Asians, the variation in implicit theory within East Asia may produce different attributional patterns within those cultures.

Dweck, C. S., Chiu, C., & Hong, Y. (1995). Implicit theories and their role in judgments and reactions: A world from two perspectives. *Psychological Inquiry, 6,* 267–285.

Earley, P. C. (1994). *Self or group? Cultural effects of training on self-efficacy and performance* (Working Paper No. OB94004). Irvine, CA: University of California, Graduate School of Management.

Erez, M. (1992). Interpersonal communication systems in organizations and their relationships to cultural values, productivity, and innovation: The case of Japanese corporations. *Applied Psychology: An International Review, 41,* 43–64.

Fiske, A. P., Kitayama, S., Markus, H. R., & Nisbett, R. E. (1998). The cultural matrix of social psychology. In D. T. Gilbert, S. T. Fiske, & G. Lindzey (Eds.), *Handbook of social psychology* (4th ed., pp. 915–981). Boston: McGraw-Hill.

Gilbert, D. T. (1989). Thinking lightly about others: Automatic components of the social inference process. In J. S. Uleman & J. A. Bargh (Eds.), *Unintended thought* (pp. 189–211). New York: Guilford Press.

Gilbert, D. T., & Malone, P. S. (1995). The correspondence bias. *Psychological Bulletin, 117,* 21–38.

Hamilton, D. L., & Sherman, S. J. (1996). Perceiving persons and groups. *Psychological Review, 103,* 336–355.

Hamilton, V. L., & Sanders, J. A. (1992). *Everyday justice: Responsibility and the individual in Japan and the United States.* New Haven, CT: Yale University Press.

Heider, F. (1944). Social perception and phenomenal causality. *Psychological Review, 51,* 358–374.

Heider, F. (1958). *The psychology of interpersonal relations.* New York: Wiley.

Heider, F., & Simmel, M. (1944). An experimental study of apparent behavior. *American Journal of psychology, 57,* 243–259.

Hess, R. D., Chang, C.-M., & McDevitt, T. M. (1987). Cultural variations in family beliefs about children's performance in mathematics: Comparisons among People's Republic of China, Chinese-American, and Caucasian-American families. *Journal of Educational Psychology, 79,* 179–188.

Higgins, E. T., & Bryant, S. L. (1982). Consensus information and the fundamental attribution error: The role of development and in-group versus out-group knowledge. *Journal of Personality and Social Psychology, 43,* 889–900.

Ho, D. Y., & Chiu, C. (1994). Component ideas of individualism, collectivism, and social organization: An application in the study of Chinese culture. In M. Kim, H. C. Triandis, C. Kagitcibasi, S. C. Choi, & G. Yoon (Eds.). *Individualism and collectivism: Theory, method, and application: Cross-cultural research and methodology* (Vol. 18, pp. 137–156). Thousand Oaks, CA: Sage.

Hong, Y.-Y., Morris, M. W., Chiu, C.-Y., & Benet-Martinez, V. (1998). *How cultures move through minds: A dynamic constructivist approach to culture and cognition* (Research Paper No. 1536), Stanford. CA: Stanford University, Graduate School of Business.

Hsu, F. L.-K. (1948). *Under the ancestors' shadow: Chinese culture and personality.* New York: Columbia University Press.

Hu, W. C. (1991). *Encountering the Chinese.* Yarmouth, ME: Intercultural Press.

Iyengar, S., & Lepper, M. (1999). Rethinking the value of choice: A cultural perspective on intrinsic motivation. *Journal of Personality and Social Psychology, 76,* 349–366.

Jones, E. E. (1979). The rocky road from acts to dispositions. *American Psychologist, 34,* 107–117.

Jones, E. E. (1990). *Interpersonal perception.* New York: Freeman.

Jones, E. E., & Harris, V. A. (1967). The attribution of attitudes. *Journal of Experimental and Social Psychology, 3,* 1–24.

Jost, J. T., Kruglanski, A. W., & Simon, L. (1998). *Effects of epistemic motivation on conservatism, intolerance, and other system-justifying attitudes.* Unpublished manuscript, Stanford University, Graduate School of Business, Stanford, CA.

Kant, I. (1949). *The fundamental principles of the metaphysic of morals (T. K. Abbott, Trans.).* New York: Liberal Arts Press. (Original work published 1786)

Kashima, Y., Siegal, M., Tanaka, K., & Kashima, E. (1992). Do people believe behaviours are consistent with attitudes? Towards a cultural psychology of attribution processes. *British Journal of Social Psychology, 31,* 111–124.

Kelley, H. H. (1972). Causal schemata and the attribution process. In D. E. Kanouse, E. E. Jones, H. H. Kelley, R. E. Nisbett, S. Valins, & B. Weiner (Eds.), *Attribution: Perceiving the causes of behavior* (pp. 151–174). Morristown, NJ: General Learning Press.

Knowles, E., Morris, M. W., Chiu, C.-Y., & Hong, Y.-Y. (1998). *People reveal their cultural assumptions when loaded: Culturally varying responses to cognitive load.* Unpublished manuscript, Stanford University, Graduate School of Business, Stanford, California.

Kruglanski, A. W., & Webster, D. M. (1996). Motivated closing of the mind: "Seizing" and "freezing." *Psychological Review, 103,* 263–283.

Krull, D. S. (1993). Does the grist change the mill? The effect of the perceiver's inferential goal on the process of social inference. *Personality and Social Psychology Bulletin, 19,* 340–348.

Kubin, W. (1991). On the problem of the self in Confucianism. In S. Krieger & R. Trauzettel (Eds.), *Confucianism and the modernization of China* (pp. 63–95). Mainz, Germany: V. Hase & Koehler Verlag Mainz.

LeBon, G. (1896). *The crowd: A study of the popular mind.* London: Ernest Bem.

Lee, F., Hallahan, M., & Herzog, T. (1996). Explaining real-life events: How culture and domain shape attributions. *Personality and Social Psychology Bulletin, 22,* 732–741.

Leung, K. (1997, August). *Social axioms.* Paper presented at the meeting of the Asian Association of Social Psychology, Kyoto, Japan.

Levy-Bruhl, L. (1926). *How natives think.* (L. A. Clare, Trans.) London: Allen & Unwin. (Original work published 1910)

Lickel, B., Hamilton, D. L., Wiecaorkowska, G., Lewis, A., Sherman, S. J., & Uhles, A. N. (1998). *Varieties of groups and the perception of group entitativity.* Manuscript submitted for publication.

Lukes, S. (1973). *Individualism.* Oxford, England: Basil Blackwell.

Markus, H. R., & Kitayama, S. (1991). Culture and the self: Implications for cognition, emotion, and motivation. *Psychological Review, 98,* 224–253.

McDougall, W. (1923). *Outline of psychology.* New York: Scribner.

Miller, J. G. (1984). Culture and the development of everyday social explanation. *Journal of Personality and Social Psychology, 46,* 961–978.

Morris, M. W. (1993). *Culture and cause: American and Chinese understanding of physical and social causality.* Unpublished doctoral dissertation, University of Michigan, Ann Arbor.

Morris, M. W., Nisbett, R. E., & Peng, K. (1995). Causal attribution across domains and cultures. In D. Sperber, D. Premack, & A. J. Premack (Eds.), *Causal cognition: A multidisciplinary debate* (pp. 577–612). Oxford, England: Clarendon Press.

Morris, M. W., & Peng, K. (1994). Culture and cause: American and Chinese attributions for social and physical events. *Journal of Personality and Social Psychology, 67,* 949–971.

Nakane, C. (1973). *Japanese society.* Harmonsworth, Middlesex, England: Penguin.

Nishida, T. (1985). *A study of the history of Chinese criminal laws.* Beijing, China: Peking University Press.

Pettigrew, T. F. (1979). The ultimate attribution error: Extending Allport's cognitive analysis of prejudice. *Personality and Social Psychology Bulletin, 5,* 461–476.

Reeder, G. D., & Brewer, M. B. (1979). A schematic model of dispositional attribution in interpersonal perception. *Psychological Review, 86,* 61–79.

Ross, L. D. (1977). The intuitive psychologist and his shortcomings. In L. Berkowitz (Ed.), *Advances in experimental social psychology* (Vol. 10, pp. 174–220). New York: Academic Press.

Sanbonmatsu, D. M., Sherman, S. J., & Hamilton, D. L. (1987). Illusory correlation in the perception of individuals and groups. *Social Cognition, 5,* 1–25.

Sandelands, L., & St. Clair, L. (1993). Toward an empirical concept of a group. *Journal for the Theory of Social Behaviour, 23,* 423–458.

Schank, R. C., & Abelson, R. P. (1977). *Scripts, plans, goals, and understanding: An inquiry into human knowledge structures.* Hillsdale, NJ: Erlbaum.

Schulman, P., Castellon, C., & Seligman, M. (1989). Assessing explanatory style: The content analysis of verbatim explanations and the attributional style questionnaire. *Behavioral Research Therapy, 27,* 505–512.

Shore, B. (1996). *Culture in mind: Cognition, culture, and the problem of meaning.* New York: Oxford University Press.

Shweder, R. A., & Bourne, E. J. (1982). Does the concept of the person vary cross-culturally? In A. J. Marsella & G. M. White (Eds.), *Cultural conceptions of mental health and therapy* (pp. 97–137). Boston: Reidel.

Su, S. K., Chiu, C., Hong, Y., Leung, K., Peng, K., & Morris, M. W. (1999). Self-organization and social organization: American and Chinese constructions. In T. R. Tyler, R. M. Kramer, & O. P. John (Eds.), *The psychology of the social self* (pp. 193–222). Mahwah, NJ: Erlbaum.

Susskind, J., & Hamilton, D. L. (1994, June). *The effects of perceived target unity on trait judgments.* Paper presented at the meeting of the American Psychological Society, Washington, DC.

Tobin, J. J., Wu, D. Y. H., & Davidson, D. H. (1989). *Preschool in three cultures: Japan, China, and the United States.* New Haven, CT: Yale University Press.

van de Vijver, F., & Leung, K. (1996). Methods and data analysis of comparative research. In J. W. Berry, Y. H. Poortinga, & J. Pandey (Eds.), *Handbook of cross-cultural psychology: Vol. 1. Theory and method* (pp. 257–301). Needham Heights, MA: Allyn & Bacon.

Weiner, B., Frieze, I. H., Kukla, A., Reed, L., Rest, S., & Rosenbaum, R. M. (1971). *Perceiving the causes of success and failure.* Morristown, NJ: General Learning Press.

Wong, P. T., & Weiner, B. (1981). When people ask "why" questions, and the heuristics of attributional search. *Journal of Personality and Social Psychology, 40,* 650–663.

Yzerbyt, V. Y., Rogier, A., & Fiske, S. T. (1998). Group entitativity and social attribution: On translating situational constraints into stereotypes. *Personality and Social Psychology Bulletin, 24,* 1090–1104.

Zhang, J. (1984). Exploratory investigations on the characteristics of the judicial system in feudal China. *Theses of Law of China, 1,* 245–266.

Received August 3, 1998
Revision received December 4, 1998
Accepted December 29, 1998 ■

PART 6

Impression Formation and Judgment

Introduction and Preview

Social psychologists often face an interesting problem when teaching classes to bright undergraduate students. Specifically, many of the topics studied by social psychologists are phenomena that occur in everyday life, which people have been not only doing but also talking about for a long time. Therefore, students often have the sense that they "know" about these topics already, without needing to hear what some social psychology professor has to say about them in his or her seemingly endless lectures. While I have no intention of demeaning the value or usefulness of our everyday knowledge, I do want to suggest that "things are not always as they seem," and in fact, seemingly simple phenomena can be a good bit more complex than we might otherwise think. In fact, many of the readings reproduced in this book (in virtually every part of the book) provide examples to support that statement.

The topic of Part 6 is one such case: forming impressions of others. It is something we have all been doing all of our lives. We form first impressions quickly and easily, almost without exception, when we first meet people. Moreover, we spend a lot of time talking with our friends about our impressions of others. Consider some typical conversations between friends:

> *Person A*: "I really like Steve. He's such a nice guy — he's interesting, witty, lots of fun."
> *Person B*: "Are you kidding? Steve is a snob — he talks about himself all the time, and his humor is always putting someone down."

355

Person J: "You know, Chuck is so stable ... he always seems to have it together."

Person K: "Yea, I know what you mean, but I'll never forget that one time when he really lost it . . . blew his stack over nothing. It was so out of character for him."

Person P: "You know, I sometimes can't figure Sandy out. She's warm and outgoing, which I like, but she's sometimes moody and distant, which makes her difficult to be close to. What do you think?"

Person Q: "I agree — she's a real mix. I like her good qualities, but overall, I can't stand it when she's in one of her bad moods, so I've given up on her as a good friend."

Person X: "Jason is 'so California.' I knew it from the moment I met him."

Person Y: "Well, at first I thought so, too. When I first met him, after he had moved here from LA, he sure seemed to reflect the California type. But as I've gotten to know him, he really doesn't fit the stereotype as much as I thought."

Conversations such as these are familiar to all of us. They are instructive because they provide some hints about the nature of our impressions of others. First, as revealed in the comments of Persons A and B, different people can have remarkably different impressions of the same person. Second, even when there is overall agreement (Persons J and K), certain facts can stand out and be highly memorable. Third, these brief interchanges suggest the richness of our impressions, and therefore of the complexity of the processes underlying them. Persons P and Q, for example, agree that Sandy (like all of us) is a blend of good and bad qualities. And for Person Q, anyway,

the bad outweighs the good in the overall impression. Fourth, the conversation between Persons X and Y illustrates two important points about impressions: first, that impressions can change, and second, that impressions can be based, at least in part, on the person's membership in a group (in this case, Jason's being a Californian).

So what at first intuitively seemed to be a fairly straightforward phenomenon, one that we all experience routinely, turns out to be not quite so simple. How are first impressions formed? What determines how they take shape? How can we make sense of this process? Research on impression formation has been very informative in providing answers to these questions.

The study of impression formation began with a now-classic paper published in 1946 by Solomon Asch. Although Asch wrote this paper more than a half century ago, his ideas remain cogent and many of his findings have survived the dual tests of time and replication. Portions of his article, including the two most famous of his experiments, are reproduced in Reading 22. Asch was struck by some simple facts about the way we form impressions. The first was the amount and diversity of information we learn about someone, even in a first meeting. The second was the ease with which that diverse information is integrated into coherent, yet often complex, impressions. How can we understand this process?

Asch argued that we form an impression of the whole person — an impression does not consist merely of an accumulation of bits of facts that we acquire, but rather those facts become integrated into a coherent impression of what the person is like. The goal of impression formation is to understand what the target person is like, and therefore the perceiver's task is to discover the "themes" that define and characterize this person as an individual. The process of forming an impression begins with the first information we learn about a person, and it continually evolves as new information is acquired. Moreover, that new information is assimilated to and incorporated in the emerging impression. In fact, the existing impression can guide the meaning of — that is, our interpretation of — that new information as we try to make it "fit" with what we already "know" (or have come to believe) about the person. Impression formation, then, is a dynamic process in which the impression is continually being modified by new knowledge.

To test his ideas, Asch (1946) presented participants with a series of trait descriptions of a target person, and he asked participants to form an impression of the person. To measure their impressions, Asch had his participants write a paragraph describing their impression of the target person. These paragraphs, some of which are included in his article, provide compelling evidence of the extent to which people grapple with and elaborate on the literal information they have received. To assess these impressions in a quantifiable manner, Asch had participants indicate, on a trait checklist, which other attributes they thought would also be characteristic of the person. In other words, Asch had his participants infer what else might be true of the person. In making these trait inferences, the perceiver embellishes the information acquired, trying to develop an understanding of what the person is like. As Asch's studies showed, these inferences were not random. Rather, they followed certain systematic patterns.

Asch's work was groundbreaking in the sense that it took a complex process — forming an impression of another person — and made it empirically tractable. Although it provided some important clues to this process, it was incomplete. My impression of Sarah is something that I carry around in my head; it is with me all the time, and I can use it in recalling facts about her, in making judgments of her, in guiding my behavior toward her. In that sense, an impression is not simply a set of inferences I've made about her — it is what in previous sections I've called a cognitive structure, in this case, a cognitive structure that contains my knowledge, beliefs, and expectancies about Sarah. A number of lines of research since Asch's initial work have explored these other aspects of impressions.

If an impression is a representation of a person that is stored in memory, then the next question becomes: How is it represented? Research on person memory has been devoted to answering that question. Consistent with Asch's original viewpoint, this work has shown what happens as people integrate items of information into an emerging structure. For example, information we learn about a person is not simply deposited in memory but rather is organized according to the themes that seem to represent the person's personality (Hamilton, Katz, & Léirer, 1980). Other research has developed more specifically the way items of information are represented in memory. The article by Srull (1981) illustrates this approach to learning more about impression formation. Adopting the associative network approach I discussed earlier (see Introduction to Part 2), the impression of a person is stored in a location known as a "person node" for that person, and each item of information learned about the person is represented in memory attached to that node. Of particular interest to Srull was how perceivers encode, store, and retrieve information that is either congruent or incongruent with the existing impression of the person. An item of information that doesn't "fit" with an impression, or somehow violates our expectancies about a person, not only becomes attached to the person node (as do all items) but in addition it triggers additional processes, trying to understand why the person behaved in a way that deviates from our impression. In trying to understand this behavior, the perceiver might think about previously acquired items, trying to incorporate this unexpected outcome into the impression and perhaps to explain why it happened (Hamilton, 1998; Hastie, 1984). This process of retrieving past knowledge leads to the formation of associations directly between certain pairs of behaviors, and once established, these associations influence the retrieval of information from memory. A number of studies using this paradigm (Hastie & Kumar, 1979; Srull, 1981; for a review, see Srull & Wyer, 1989) have found that this process can result in the better recall of items of information that are incongruent, compared to congruent, with an initial impression. (There are, however, constraints on this finding; see Garcia-Marques, Hamilton & Maddox, 2002, Hamilton & Garcia-Marques, 2003.) Also, a number of studies find that, under various conditions, people have better memory for information that is congruent with impression-based expectations; see Stangor & McMillan, 1992.)

The representation in memory includes the stored factual material that is retained, along with inferences that have been made based on that information and integrated into the impression, as Asch studied. The resulting impression is then used as a basis for making judgments about the target of that impression. How are these judgments made? What processes can influence the nature of our judgment processes? These questions have generated an enormous amount of research.

Hastie and Park (1986) differentiated between two fundamentally different and important processes by which judgments might be made. Suppose you meet someone named Jan, and as you're talking with her you find yourself thinking, "Gee, she's pretty bright and has a lot of personality, but she's really full of herself and thinks she's pretty hot stuff." These are inferences or judgments that are being made from the "raw data" you experience — Jan's behavior, her mannerisms, her ways of talking, etc. — and these judgments are made at the time you are processing this information. Hastie and Park called these *on-line judgments* — they are made at the time the information on which they are based is being processed. Suppose, however, that later on someone asks you if Jan is religious. Well, gee, you and Jan never really talked about religion so you didn't form any on-line assessment of her religiosity. Therefore, you think back to what you can remember of your interaction and infer from some bits that yes, probably, she's at least somewhat religious. Hastie and Park called this a *memory-based judgment* because it is based on the retrieval of specific information from memory. The crucial distinction between on-line and memory-based judgments is the time at which they are made — either as the information is being processed (on-line) or later, based on information retrieved from memory (memory-based). As they discuss in their article, different conditions will induce on-line judgments and different factors can be more or less influential, depending on which type of judgment is made.

When we make judgments of other people, however, we often know more about them than a simple listing of traits (as in Asch, 1946) or a sample of the person's behaviors (as in Srull, 1981). We often know the person's membership in various groups, and we may have stereotypic knowledge and beliefs about those groups. Our judgments can obviously be influenced by those category-based beliefs, and they can be based on specific knowledge we've acquired about this individual. How do perceivers incorporate both kinds of information in making judgments, and which kind of information is more important? Fiske and Neuberg's (1990)

"Continuum Model" was developed to address these questions, and specifically to deal with how perceivers use both of these kinds of information in making judgments of target persons. When we encounter a person it is very difficult *not* to notice their membership in certain social groups; at minimum, it is nearly impossible not to be aware of a person's gender, race, and age group. Because of the salience of these (and potentially other) group memberships, Fiske and Neuberg argue that categorization into such groups is an initial step in impression formation. Because this categorization takes priority, the beliefs associated with that category will become the initial basis of one's impression of the person. This category-based impression is nearly an automatic effect. Therefore, one's initial impression is largely category-based, and any judgments of the person at this stage would reflect one's beliefs about that social group. If the perceiver is motivated to learn more about the person, to develop a fuller impression of that person, then the perceiver can attend to information he or she has learned about this individual person. How is that individuating information incorporated into this evolving impression? What will determine the nature of one's judgments? Fiske and Neuberg propose that initially the perceiver attempts to "fit" the specific information about this person with the category that has already been activated. If the fit is good, then the person will still be perceived as a "good" member of the category, and judgments will still be based largely on categorical beliefs. What happens if the new information learned about the person doesn't confirm the initial categorization? There are then a few options. One possibility is that the person will be recategorized as a member of some alternate grouping, such as a subtype of the initial category. Another possibility is to abandon the initial categorization and to view the person in terms of some completely different category. For example,

I might no longer view the person as old (thinking of the person perhaps as inactive and dependent) but instead to think of him/her as a physician (vigorous, a contributing member of society) or some alternate classification that better reflects the information acquired about the person. Both of these alternatives retain the preference of viewing persons in terms of category memberships, and therefore emphasizing the role of category-based beliefs on judgments of the person. Finally, if the individuating information doesn't allow any easy categorization (or recategorization), the perceiver's impression — and resulting judgments — of the person will be based primarily on the information learned specifically about this individual. Judgments will then be based on this information, and in this case those judgments will not reflect any category-based beliefs. Thus, Fiske and Neuberg (1990) have offered a useful model for thinking about the use of both category-based and individuating information in impression judgments, a model that recognizes an important role of categorization in impression formation.

The category-based (stereotypic) judgments emphasized in the Continuum Model (Fiske & Neuberg, 1990) can influence judgments in other ways as well. Specifically, as research by Biernat and her colleagues (see Biernat, 1995) has shown, our knowledge that a person is a member of some category (e.g., women) can create a *standard* by which the person is judged. Moreover, that standard may be different than the standard used to judge members of other categories (men). Thus, a woman who stands up at a public meeting and strongly disagrees with the speaker might be viewed in one way ("Wow, she is one forceful, aggressive woman!"), whereas a man engaging in the same behavior might not be viewed as equally aggressive ("Men are always spouting off, aren't they?"). In fact, to invoke the label "aggressive," a man would have to commit a more extreme form of behavior (e.g., hitting someone). Thus, two people performing the same act might be viewed differently. This difference in judgment is due to the fact that the target persons are judged in comparison to standards expected of their respective groups. In Biernat's terms, the standard "shifts" from one group to another (the woman's outburst is "aggressive" compared to what we expect for women, but not for men). The use of different standards of comparison for construing the behaviors of members of different groups can influence not only our interpretations of these behaviors but also our judgments and evaluations of the person.

Thus far we have been considering processes involved in forming impressions of individual persons. We also develop conceptions of what groups are like. Do the same processes we have been discussing for impressions of individuals apply to the way we form impressions of groups?

This question and its ramifications are discussed in the article by Hamilton, Sherman, and Lickel (1998). They began by stating a "fundamental postulate" and several corollaries, basically a set of principles based on the accumulated findings from research on how perceivers form impressions of individual target persons. The core assertion is that "The perceiver assumes unity in the personalities of others. Persons are seen as coherent entities." Given this assumption, certain consequences follow, all of which have been supported by research on impression formation. These include the fact that (a) perceivers make on-line inferences about target persons as they process information; (b) they assume stability in the person's personality and therefore expect consistency in the person's behaviors across time and situations; (c) they integrate the information they acquire about a target person into a coherent, organized impression; and (d) they strive to resolve any inconsistencies in the information as they incorporate it into the evolving impression. Given these

findings from research on impressions of individual target persons, Hamilton et al. (1998) then considered whether those same principles hold for impressions of groups. They assumed that perceivers do not subscribe to the fundamental postulate in forming impressions of groups. That is, they don't expect the same degree of unity and coherence among members of a group as they do in the personality of an individual. Therefore, when they learn information about a group and form an impression of it, based on information about its members, they are less likely to engage in the processes that are so characteristic of individual impression formation. That is, they are less likely to make on-line inferences, they assume less stability and consistency across group members, their impressions of groups are less organized, and they are less likely to engage in resolving inconsistencies between what is learned about various group members (see Hamilton & Sherman, 1996).

Based on this analysis, then, there are important differences in the way perceivers form impressions of individuals and groups. Hamilton et al. (1998) then go on to consider in greater detail the nature of perceptions of groups, and in particular, how a collection of individuals comes to be perceived as a meaningful entity, as having entitativity. All of us encounter a vast and diverse array of groups in our everyday experiences, and we routinely are able to perceive meaningful differences among them. How do we do that? A group is made up of individuals, but not all collections of individuals are perceived as groups. How does the perceiver recognize some, but not all, collections of persons as having the quality of being a group? Hamilton et al.'s analysis illustrates the complexity of this question, yet it also reveals the complexities of what the human perceiver is able to accomplish in perceiving and adapting to both individual persons and social groups in the social environment.

Discussion Questions

1. The introduction to Part 6 began with four vignettes, each one presenting a conversation between two persons. Each vignette portrays an important principle about impression formation. What are those principles? Can you cite a study demonstrating each one?
2. What is the incongruency effect as demonstrated by Srull (1981)? How is it explained?
3. What is the difference between on-line and memory-based judgments? Describe the process underlying each type.
4. Summarize differences in the ways we form impressions of individuals and of groups. What processes generate these differences?

Suggested Readings

Leyens, J-P., & Fiske, S. T. (1994). Impression formation: From recitals to symphonic fantasique. In P. G. Devine, D. L. Hamilton, & T. M. Ostrom (Eds.), *Social cognition: Impact on social psychology*. San Diego: Academic Press.

Hastie, R., Ostrom, T. M., Ebbesen, E. B., Wyer, R. S. Jr., Hamilton, D. L., & Carlston, D. E. (Eds.) (1980). *Person memory: The cognitive basis of social perception*. Hillsdale, NJ: Erlbaum.

Fiske, S. T., & Neuberg, S. L. (1990). A continuum of impression formation, from category-based to individuating processes: Influences of information and motivation on attention and interpretation. In M. P. Zanna (Ed.), *Advances in experimental social psychology* (Vol. 23, pp. 1–74). New York: Academic Press.

Hamilton, D. L., & Sherman, S. J. (1996). Perceiving persons and groups. *Psychological Review, 103*, 336–355.

Forming Impressions of Personality[*]

Solomon E. Asch

We look at a person and immediately a certain impression of his character forms itself in us. A glance, a few spoken words are sufficient to tell us a story about a highly complex matter. We know that such impressions form with remarkable rapidity and with great ease. Subsequent observation may enrich or upset our first view, but we can no more prevent its rapid growth than we can avoid perceiving a given visual object or hearing a melody. We also know that this process, though often imperfect, is also at times extraordinarily sensitive.

This remarkable capacity we possess to understand something of the character of another person, to form a conception of him as a human being, as a center of life and striving, with particular characteristics forming a distinct individuality, is a precondition of social life. In what manner are these impressions established? Are there lawful principles regulating their formation?

One particular problem commands our attention. Each person confronts us with a large number of diverse characteristics. This man is courageous, intelligent, with a ready sense of humor, quick in his movements, but he is also serious, energetic, patient under stress, not to mention his politeness and punctuality. These characteristics and many others enter into the formation of our view. Yet our impression is from the start unified; it is the impression of *one* person. We ask: How do the

Editor's Note: This article reported twelve experiments. Experiments 1, 5, and 6 are reproduced here.

* The present investigation was begun in 1943 when the writer was a Fellow of the John Simon Guggenheim Memorial Foundation.

several characteristics function together to produce an impression of one person? What principles regulate this process?

We have mentioned earlier that the impression of a person grows quickly and easily. Yet our minds falter when we face the far simpler task of mastering a series of disconnected numbers or words. We have apparently no need to commit to memory by repeated drill the various characteristics we observe in a person, nor do some of his traits exert an observable retroactive inhibition upon our grasp of the others. Indeed, they seem to support each other. And it is quite hard to forget our view of a person once it has formed. Similarly, we do not easily confuse the half of one person with the half of another. It should be of interest to the psychologist that the far more complex task of grasping the nature of a person is so much less difficult.

There are a number of theoretical possibilities for describing the process of forming an impression, of which the major ones are the following:

1. A trait is realized in its particular quality. The next trait is similarly realized, etc. Each trait produces its particular impression. The total impression of the person is the sum of the several independent impressions. If a person possesses traits *a, b, c, d, e*, then the impression of him may be expressed as:

$$\text{I. Impression} = a + b + c + d + e$$

Few if any psychologists would at the present time apply this formulation strictly. It would, however, be an error to deny its importance for the present problem. That it controls in considerable degree many of the procedures for arriving at a scientific, objective view of a person (*e.g.*, by means of questionnaires, rating scales) is evident. But more pertinent to our present discussion is the modified form in which Proposition I is applied to the actual forming of an impression. Some psychologists assume, in addition to the factors of Proposition I, the operation of a "general impression." The latter is conceived as an affective force possessing a plus or minus direction which shifts the evaluation of the several traits in its direction. We may represent this process as follows:

I*a*. Impression =

To the sum of the traits there is now added another factor, the general impression.

2. The second view asserts that we form an impression of the entire person. We see a person as consisting not of these and those independent traits (or of the sum of mutually modified traits), but we try to get at the root of the personality. This would involve that the traits are perceived in relation to each other, in their proper place within the given personality. We may express the final impression as

II. Impression =

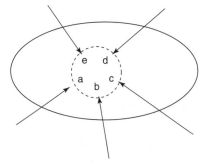

It may appear that psychologists generally hold to some form of the latter formulation. The frequent reference to the unity of the person, or to his "integration," implying that these qualities are also present in the

impression, point in this direction. The generality of these expressions is, however, not suitable to exact treatment. Terms such as unity of the person, while pointing to a problem, do not solve it. If we wish to become clear about the unity in persons, or in the impression of persons, we must ask in what sense there is such unity, and in what manner we come to observe it. Secondly, these terms are often applied interchangeably to Propositions II and I*a*. It is therefore important to state at this point a distinction between them.

For Proposition II, the general impression is not a factor added to the particular traits, but rather the perception of a particular form of relation between the traits, a conception which is wholly missing in I*a*. Further, Proposition I*a* conceives the process in terms of an imposed affective shift in the evaluation of separate traits, whereas Proposition II deals in the first instance with processes between the traits each of which has a cognitive content.

Perhaps the central difference between the two propositions becomes clearest when the accuracy of the impression becomes an issue. It is implicit in Proposition II that the process it describes is for the subject a necessary one if he is to focus on a person with maximum clarity. On the other hand, Proposition I*a* permits a radically different interpretation. It has been asserted that the general impression "colors" the particular characteristics, the effect being to *blur* the clarity with which the latter are perceived. In consequence the conclusion is drawn that the general impression is a source of error which should be supplanted by the attitude of judging each trait in isolation, as described in Proposition I. This is the doctrine of the "halo effect" [9].

Forming a Unified Impression: Procedure

The plan followed in the experiments to be reported was to read to the subject a number of discrete characteristics, said to belong to a person, with the instruction to describe the impression he formed. The subjects were all college students, most of whom were women.[1] They were mostly beginners in psychology. Though they expressed genuine interest in the tasks, the subjects

―――――――――――

[1] The writer wishes to express his gratitude to the following colleagues for their help in the performance of these experiments in their classes: Drs. B. F. Riess, L. Welch, V. J. McGill, and A. Goldenson of Hunter College; Drs. M. Blum and A. Mintz of the College of the City of New York; Dr. Lois Adams, Mr. Michael Newman, and Mr. Herbert Newman of Brooklyn College.

were not aware of the nature of the problem until is was explained to them. We illustrate our procedure with one concrete instance. The following list of terms was read: *Energetic — assured — talkative — cold — ironical — inquisitive — persuasive*. The reading of the list was preceded by the following instructions:

> I shall read to you a number of characteristics that belong to a particular person. Please listen to them carefully and try to form an impression of the kind of person described. You will later be asked to give a brief characterization of the person in just a few sentences. I will read the list slowly and will repeat it once.

The list was read with an interval of approximately five seconds between the terms. When the first reading was completed, the experimenter said, "I will now read the list again," and proceeded to do so. We reproduce below a few typical sketches written by subjects after they heard read the list of terms:

> He seems to be the kind of person who would make a great impression upon others at a first meeting. However as time went by, his acquaintances would easily come to see through the mask. Underneath would be revealed his arrogance and selfishness.
>
> He is the type of person you meet all too often: Sure of himself, talks too much, always trying to bring you around to his way of thinking, and with not much feeling for the other fellow.
>
> He impresses people as being more capable than he really is. He is popular and never ill at ease. Easily becomes the center of attraction at any gathering. He is likely to be a jack-of-all-trades. Although his interests are varied, he is not necessarily well-versed in any of them. He possesses a sense of humor. His presence stimulates enthusiasm and very often he does arrive at a position of importance.
>
> Possibly he does not have any deep feeling. He would tend to be an opportunist. Likely to succeed in things he intends to do. He has perhaps married a wife who would help him in his purpose. He tends to be skeptical.

The following preliminary points are to be noted:

1. When a task of this kind is given, a normal adult is capable of responding to the instruction by forming a unified impression. Though he hears a sequence of discrete terms, his resulting impression is not discrete. In some manner he shapes the separate qualities into a single, consistent view. All subjects in the following experiments, of whom there were over 1,000, fulfilled the task in the manner described.

No one proceeded by reproducing the given list of terms, as one would in a rote memory experiment; nor did any of the subjects reply merely with synonyms of the given terms.

2. The characteristics seem to reach out beyond the merely given terms of the description. Starting from the bare terms, the final account is completed and rounded. Reference is made to characters and situations which are apparently not directly mentioned in the list, but which are inferred from it.

3. The accounts of the subjects diverge from each other in important respects. This will not be surprising in view of the variable content of the terms employed, which permits a considerable freedom in interpretation and weighting.

In the experiments to be reported the subjects were given a group of traits on the basis of which they formed an impression. In view of the fact that we possess no principles in this region to help in their systematic construction, it was necessary to invent groupings of traits. In this we were guided by an informal sense of what traits were consistent with each other.

The procedure here employed is clearly different from the everyday situation in which we follow the concrete actions of an actual person. We have chosen to work with weak, incipient impressions, based on abbreviated descriptions of personal qualities. Nevertheless, this procedure has some merit for purposes of investigation, especially in observing the change of impressions, and is, we hope to show, relevant to more natural judgment.

More detailed features of the procedure will be described subsequently in connection with the actual experiments. We shall now inquire into some of the factors that determine the content and alteration of such impressions.

I. Central and Peripheral Characteristics

A. Variation of a Central Quality

Observation suggests that not all qualities have the same weight in establishing the view of a person. Some are felt to be basic, others secondary. In the following experiments we sought for a demonstration of this process in the course of the formation of an impression.

Experiment I

Two groups, A and B, heard read a list of character-qualities, identical save for one term. The list follows:

A. intelligent — skillful — industrious — *warm* — determined — practical — cautious

B. intelligent — skillful — industrious — *cold* — determined — practical — cautious

Group A heard the person described as "warm"; Group B, as "cold."

Technique. The instructions were as described above. Following the reading, each subject wrote a brief sketch.

The sketches furnish concrete evidence of the impressions formed. Their exact analysis involves, however, serious technical difficulties. It seemed, therefore, desirable to add a somewhat simpler procedure for the determination of the content of the impression and for the purpose of group comparisons. To this end we constructed a check list consisting of pairs of traits, mostly opposites. From each pair of terms in this list, which the reader will find reproduced in Table 22.1, the subject was instructed to select the one that was most in accordance with the view he had formed. Terms were included which were quite different from those appearing in the basic list, but which could be related to them. Of necessity we were guided in the selection of terms for the check list (as well as for the experimental lists) by an informal sense of what was fitting or relevant. Some of the terms were taken from written sketches of subjects in preliminary experiments. In the examination of results we shall rely upon the written sketches for evidence of the actual character of the impressions, and we shall supplement these with the quantitative results from the check list.

There were 90 subjects in Group A (comprising four separate classroom groups), 76 subjects in Group B (comprising four separate classroom groups).

Results. Are the impressions of Groups A and B identical, with the exception that one has the added quality of "warm," the other of "cold"? This is one possible outcome. Another possibility is that the differentiating quality imparts a general plus or minus direction to the resulting impression. We shall see that neither of these formulations accurately describes the results.

We note first that the characteristic "warm-cold" produces striking and consistent differences of impression. In general, the A-impressions are far more positive than the B-impressions. We cite a few representative examples:

Series A ("warm")

> A person who believes certain things to be right, wants others to see his point, would be sincere in an argument and would like to see his point won.

> A scientist performing experiments and persevering after many setbacks. He is driven by the desire to accomplish something that would be of benefit.

Series B ("cold")

> A very ambitious and talented person who would not let anyone or anything stand in the way of achieving his goal. Wants his own way, he is determined not to give in, no matter what happens.

> A rather snobbish person who feels that his success and intelligence set him apart from the run-of-the-mill individual. Calculating and unsympathetic.

This trend is fully confirmed in the check-list choices. In Table 22.2 we report the frequency (in terms of percentages) with which each term in the check list was selected. For the sake of brevity of presentation we state the results for the positive term in each pair; the reader may determine the percentage of choices for the other term in each pair by subtracting the given figure from 100. To illustrate, under Condition A of the present experiment, 91 per cent of the subjects chose the designation "generous"; the remaining 9 per cent selected the designation "ungenerous." Occasionally, a subject would

TABLE 22.1. Check List I

1. generous — ungenerous	7. popular — unpopular	13. frivolous — serious
2. shrewd — wise	8. unreliable — reliable	14. restrained — talkative
3. unhappy — happy	9. important — insignificant	15. self-centered — altruistic
4. irritable — good-natured	10. ruthless — humane	16. imaginative — hard-headed
5. humorous — humorless	11. good-looking — unattractive	17. strong — weak
6. sociable — unsociable	12. persistent — unstable	18. dishonest — honest

TABLE 22.2. Choice of Fitting Qualities (Percentages)

	Experiment I	
	"Warm" *N* = 90	"Cold" *N* = 76
1. generous	91	8
2. wise	65	25
3. happy	90	34
4. good-natured	94	17
5. humorous	77	13
6. sociable	91	38
7. popular	84	28
8. reliable	94	99
9. important	88	99
10. humane	86	31
11. good-looking	77	69
12. persistent	100	97
13. serious	100	99
14. restrained	77	89
15. altruistic	69	18
16. imaginative	51	19
17. strong	98	95
18. honest	98	94

not state a choice for a particular pair. Therefore, the number of cases on which the figures are based is not always identical; however, the fluctuations were minor, with the exception of the category "good-looking — unattractive," which a larger proportion of subjects failed to answer.

We find:

1. There are extreme reversals between Groups A and B in the choice of fitting characteristics. Certain qualities are preponderantly assigned to the "warm" person, while the opposing qualities are equally prominent in the "cold" person. This holds for the qualities of (1) generosity, (2) shrewdness, (3) happiness, (4) irritability, (5) humor, (6) sociability, (7) popularity, (10) ruthlessness, (15) self-centeredness, (16) imaginativeness.
2. There is another group of qualities which is *not* affected by the transition from "warm" to "cold," or only slightly affected. These are: (8) reliability, (9) importance, (11) physical attractiveness, (12) persistence, (13) seriousness, (14) restraint, (17) strength, (18) honesty.

These results show that a change in one character-quality has produced a widespread change in the entire impression. Further, the written sketches show that the terms "warm-cold" did not simply add a new quality, but to some extent transformed the other characteristics.

With this point we shall deal more explicitly in the experiments to follow.

That such transformations take place is also a matter of everyday experience. If a man is intelligent, this has an effect on the way in which we perceive his playfulness, happiness, friendliness. At the same time, this extensive change does not function indiscriminately. The "warm" person is not seen more favorably in all respects. There is a range of qualities, among them a number that are basic, which are not touched by the distinction between "warm" and "cold." Both remain equally honest, strong, serious, reliable, etc.

The latter result is of interest with reference to one possible interpretation of the findings. It might be supposed that the category "warm-cold" aroused a "mental set" or established a halo tending toward a consistently plus or minus evaluation. We observe here that this trend did not work in an indiscriminate manner, but was decisively limited at certain points. If we assume that the process of mutual influence took place in terms of the actual character of the qualities in question, it is not surprising that some will, by virtue of their content, remain unchanged.[2]

The following will show that the subjects generally felt the qualities "warm-cold" to be of primary importance. We asked the subjects in certain of the groups to rank the terms of Lists A and B in order of their importance for determining their impression. Table 22.3, containing the distribution of rankings of "warm-cold," shows that these qualities ranked comparatively high. At the same time a considerable number of subjects relegated "cold" to the lowest position. That the rankings are not higher is due to the fact that the lists contained other central traits.

These data, as well as the ranking of the other traits not here reproduced, point to the following conclusions:

1. The given characteristics do not all have the same weight for the subject. He assigns to some a higher importance than to others.
2. The weight of a given characteristic varies — within limits — from subject to subject.

Certain limitations of the check-list procedure need to be considered: (1) The subject's reactions are forced into an appearance of discreteness which they do not actually possess, as the written sketches show; (2) the check list requires the subject to choose between

---

[2] This by no means excludes the possibility that the nuances of strength, honesty, etc., do change in relation to "warm-cold."

TABLE 22.3. Rankings of "Warm" and "Cold": Experiment 1

	"Warm"		"Cold"	
Rank	N	Percentage	N	Percentage
1	6	14	12	27
2	15	35	8	21
3	4	10	1	2
4	4	10	2	5
5	4	10	3	7
6	3	7	2	5
7	6	14	13	33
	42	100	41	100

extreme characteristics, which he might prefer to avoid; (3) the quantitative data describe group trends; they do not represent adequately the form of the individual impression. Generally the individual responses exhibit much stronger trends in a consistently positive or negative direction. For these reasons we employ the checklist results primarily for the purpose of comparing group trends under different conditions. For this purpose the procedure is quite adequate.

Experiment V
The preceding experiments have shown that the characteristics forming the basis of an impression do not contribute each a fixed, independent meaning, but that their content is itself partly a function of the environment of the other characteristics, of their mutual relations. We propose now to investigate more directly the manner in which the content of a given characteristic may undergo change.

Lists A and B were read to two separate groups (including 38 and 41 subjects respectively). The first three terms of the two lists are opposites; the final two terms are identical.

A. kind — wise — honest — *calm — strong*
B. cruel — shrewd — unscrupulous — *calm — strong*

The instructions were to write down synonyms for the given terms. The instructions read: "Suppose you had to describe this person in the same manner, but without using the terms you heard, what other terms would you use?" We are concerned with the synonyms given to the two final terms.

In Table 22.4 we list those synonyms of "calm" which occurred with different frequencies in the two groups. It will be seen that terms appear in one group

which are not at all to be found in the other; further, some terms appear with considerably different frequencies under the two conditions. These do not, however, include the total group of synonyms; many scattered terms occurred equally in both groups.

We may conclude that the quality "calm" did not, at least in some cases, function as an independent, fixed trait, but that its content was determined by its relation to the other terms. As a consequence, the quality "calm" was not the same under the two experimental conditions. In Series A it possessed an aspect of gentleness, while a grimmer side became prominent in Series B.[3]

Essentially the same may be said of the final term, "strong." Again, some synonyms appear exclusively in one or the other groups, and in the expected directions. Among these are:

Series A: Fearless — helpful — just — forceful — courageous — reliable

Series B: Ruthless — overbearing — overpowering — hard — inflexible — unbending — dominant

The data of Table 22.4 provide evidence of a tendency in the described direction, but its strength is probably underestimated. We have already mentioned that certain synonyms appeared frequently in both series. But it is not to be concluded that they therefore carried the same meaning. Doubtless the same terms were at times applied in the two groups with different meanings, precisely because the subjects were under the control of the factor being investigated. To mention one example: The term "quiet" often occurred as a synonym of "calm" in both groups, but the subjects may have intended a different meaning in the two cases. For this reason Table 22.4 may not reveal the full extent of the change introduced by the factor of embedding.

The preceding experiments permit the following conclusions:

1. There is a process of discrimination between central and peripheral traits. All traits do not have the same

[3] In an earlier investigation the writer [2] has dealt with basically the same question though in a very different context. It was there shown that certain phenomena of judgment, which appeared to be due to changes of evaluation, were produced by a shift in the frame of reference.

TABLE 22.4. Synonyms of "Calm": Experiment V

	"Kind" Series	"Cruel" Series
serene	18	3
cold, frigid, icy, cool, calculating, shrewd, nervy, scheming, conscienceless	0	20
soothing, peaceful, gentle, tolerant, good-natured,	11	0
mild-mannered	11	0
poised, reserved, restful, unexcitable, unshakable	18	7
deliberate, silent, unperturbed, masterful, impassive,collected, confident, relaxed, emotionless, steady, impassive, composed	11	26

rank and value in the final impression. The change of a central trait may completely alter the impression, while the change of a peripheral trait has a far weaker effect (Experiments I, II, and III).

2. Both the cognitive content of a trait and its functional value are determined in relation to its surroundings (Experiment IV).

3. Some traits determine both the content and the function of other traits. The former we call central, the latter peripheral (Experiment IV).

II. The Factor of Direction

If impressions of the kind here investigated are a summation of the effects of the separate characteristics, then an identical set of characteristics should produce a constant result. Is it possible to alter the impression without changing the particular characteristic? We investigate this question below.

Experiment VI
The following series are read, each to a different group:

A. intelligent — industrious — impulsive — critical — stubborn — envious
B. envious — stubborn — critical — impulsive — industrious — intelligent

There were 34 subjects in Group A, 24 in Group B.
The two series are identical with regard to their members, differing only in the order of succession of the latter. More particularly, Series A opens with qualities

of high merit (intelligent — industrious), proceeds to qualities that permit of a better or poorer evaluation (impulsive — critical — stubborn), and closes with a dubious quality (envious). This order is reversed in Series B.

A considerable difference develops between the two groups taken as a whole. The impression produced by A is predominantly that of an able person who possesses certain shortcomings which do not, however, overshadow his merits. On the other hand, B impresses the majority as a "problem," whose abilities are hampered by his serious difficulties. Further, some of the qualities (e.g., impulsiveness, criticalness) are interpreted in a positive way under Condition A, while they take on, under Condition B, a negative color. This trend is not observed in all subjects, but it is found in the majority. A few illustrative extracts follow:

Series A

A person who knows what he wants and goes after it. He is impatient at people who are less gifted, and ambitious with those who stand in his way.

Is a forceful person, has his own convictions and is usually right about things. Is self-centered and desires his own way.

The person is intelligent and fortunately he puts his intelligence to work. That he is stubborn and impulsive may be due to the fact that he knows what he is saying and what he means and will not therefore give in easily to someone else's idea which he disagrees with.

Series B

This person's good qualities such as industry and intelligence are bound to be restricted by jealousy and stubbornness. The person is emotional. He is unsuccessful because he is weak and allows his bad points to cover up his good ones.

This individual is probably maladjusted because he is envious and impulsive.

In order to observe more directly the transition in question, the writer proceeded as follows. A new group (N = 24) heard Series B, wrote the free sketch, and immediately thereafter wrote the sketch in response to Series A. They were also asked to comment on the relation between the two impressions. Under these conditions, with the transition occurring in the same subjects, 14 out of 24 claimed that their impression suffered a change, while the remaining 10 subjects reported no change. Some of the latter asserted that they had waited until the entire series was read before deciding upon their impression. The following are a few comments of the changing group:

> You read the list in a different order and thereby caused a different type of person to come to mind. This one is smarter, more likeable, a go-getter, lively, headstrong, and with a will of his own; he goes after what he wants.
>
> The first individual seems to show his envy and criticism more than the second one.
>
> The first individual seems to show his envy and criticism more than the second one.
>
> This man does not seem so bad as the first one. Somehow, he seems more intelligent, with his critical attitude helping that characteristic of intelligence, and he seems to be industrious, perhaps because he is envious and wants to get ahead.

The check-list data appearing in Table 22.5 furnish quantitative support for the conclusions drawn from the written sketches.

Under the given conditions the terms, the elements of the description, are identical, but the resulting impressions frequently are not the same. Further, the relations of the terms to one another have not been disturbed, as they may have been in Experiments I and II, with the addition and omission of parts. How can we understand the resulting difference?

TABLE 22.5. Choice of Fitting Qualities (Percentages)

	Experiment VI	
	Intelligent→Envious (N = 34)	Envious→Intelligent (N = 24)
1. generous	24	10
2. wise	18	17
3. happy	32	5
4. good-natured	18	0
5. humorous	52	21
6. sociable	56	27
7. popular	35	14
8. reliable	84	91
9. important	85	90
10. humane	36	21
11. good-looking	74	35
12. persistent	82	87
13. serious	97	100
14. restrained	64	9
15. altruistic	6	5
16. imaginative	26	14
17. strong	94	73
18. honest	80	79

The accounts of the subjects suggest that the first terms set up in most subjects a *direction* which then exerts a continuous effect on the latter terms. When the subject hears the first term, a broad, uncrystallized but directed impression is born. The next characteristic comes not as a separate item, but is related to the established direction. Quickly the view formed acquires a certain stability, so that later characteristics are fitted — if conditions permit[4] — to the given direction.

Here we observe a factor of primacy guiding the development of an impression. This factor is not, however, to be understood in the sense of Ebbinghaus, but rather in a structural sense. It is not the sheer temporal position of the item which is important as much as the functional relation of its content to the content of the items following it.[5]

Discussion I

The investigations here reported have their starting-point in one problem and converge on one basic conclusion. In different ways the observations have demonstrated that forming an impression is an organized process; that characteristics are perceived in their dynamic relations; that central qualities are discovered, leading to the distinction between them and peripheral qualities; that relations of harmony and contradiction are observed. To know a person is to have a grasp of a particular structure.

Before proceeding it may be helpful to note two preliminary points. First: For the sake of convenience of expression we speak in this discussion of forming an impression of a person, though our observations are restricted entirely to impressions based on descriptive materials. We do not intend to imply that observations of actual persons would not involve other processes which we have failed to find under the present conditions; we are certain that they would (see p. 288 ff.). But we see no reason to doubt that the basic features we

---

[4] For an instance in which the given conditions may destroy the established direction, see page 273.

[5] In accordance with this interpretation the effect of primacy should be abolished — or reversed — if it does not stand in a fitting relation to the succeeding qualities, or if a certain quality stands out as central despite its position. The latter was clearly the case for the quality "warm-cold" in Experiment I (see Table 22.1) which, though occupying a middle position, ranked comparatively high.

The distinction between the two senses of primacy could be studied experimentally by comparing the recall of an identical series of character-qualities in two groups, one of which reads them as a discrete list of terms, the other as a set of characteristics describing a person.

were able to observe are also present in the judgment of actual persons. Secondly: We have not dealt in this investigation with the role of individual differences, of which the most obvious would be the effect of the subject's own personal qualities on the nature of his impression. Though the issue of individual differences is unquestionably important, it seemed desirable to turn first to those processes which hold generally, despite individual differences. A proper study of individual differences can best be pursued when a minimum theoretical clarification has been reached.

Let us briefly reformulate the main points in the procedure of our subjects:

1. There is an attempt to form an impression of the *entire* person. The subject can see the person only as a unit;[6] he cannot form an impression of one-half or of one-quarter of the person. This is the case even when the factual basis is meager; the impression then strives to become complete, reaching out toward other compatible qualities. The subject seeks to reach the core of the person *through* the trait or traits.
2. As soon as two or more traits are understood to belong to one person, they cease to exist as isolated traits, and come into immediate dynamic interaction.[7] The subject perceives not this *and* that quality, but the two entering into a particular relation. There takes place a process of organization in the course of which the traits order themselves into a structure. It may be said that the traits lead an intensely social life, striving to join each other in a closely organized system. The representation in us of the character of another person possesses in a striking sense certain of the qualities of a system.
3. In the course of this process some characteristics are discovered to be central. The whole system of relations determines which will become central. These set the direction for the further view of the person and for the concretization of the dependent traits. As

a rule the several traits do not have equal weight. And it is not until we have found the center that we experience the assurance of having come near to an understanding of the person.
4. The single trait possesses the property of a part in a whole. A change in a single trait may alter not that aspect alone, but many others — at times all. As soon as we isolate a trait we not only lose the distinctive organization of the person; the trait itself becomes abstract. The trait develops its full content and weight only when it finds its place within the whole impression.
5. Each trait is a trait of the entire person. It refers to a characteristic form of action or attitude which belongs to the person as a whole. In this sense we may speak of traits as possessing the properties of Ehrenfels-qualities. Traits are not to be considered as referring to different regions of the personality, on the analogy of geographical regions which border on another.
6. Each trait functions as a *representative* of the person. We do not experience anonymous traits the particular organization of which constitutes the identity of the person. Rather the entire person speaks through each of his qualities, though not with the same clearness.
7. In the process of mutual interaction the concrete character of each trait is developed in accordance with the dynamic requirements set for it by its environment. There is involved an understanding of necessary consequences following from certain given characteristics for others. The envy of a proud man is, for example, seen to have a different basis from the envy of a modest man.
8. On this basis consistencies and contradictions are discovered. Certain qualities are seen to cooperate; others to negate each other. But we are not content simply to note inconsistencies or to let them sit where they are. The contradiction is puzzling, and prompts us to look more deeply. Disturbing factors arouse a trend to maintain the unity of the impression, to search for the most sensible way in which the characteristics could exist together,[8] or to decide that we have not found the key to the person. We feel that proper understanding would eliminate, not the presence of inner tensions and inconsistencies, but of sheer contradiction. (It may be relevant to point

---

[6] To be sure, we do often react to people in a more narrow manner, as when we have dealings with the ticket-collector or bank teller. It cannot however be said that in such instances we are primarily oriented to the other as a person. The moment our special attitude would give way to a genuine interest in the other, the point stated above would fully apply.

[7] We cannot say on the basis of our observations whether exceptions to this statement occur, *e.g.*, whether some traits may be seen as accidental, having no relation to the rest of the person. It seems more likely that even insignificant traits are seen as part of the person.

---

[8] Indeed, the perception of such contradiction, or of the failure of a trait to fit to the others, may be of fundamental importance for gaining a proper view. It may point to a critical region in the person, in which things are not as they should be.

out that the very sense of one trait being in contradiction to others would not arise if we were not oriented to the entire person. Without the assumption of a unitary person there would be just different traits.)

9. It follows that the content and functional value of a trait changes with the given context. This statement expresses for our problem a principle formulated in gestalt theory with regard to the identity of parts in different structures [8, 10]. A trait central in one person may be seen as secondary in another. Or a quality which is now referred to the person may in another case be referred to outer conditions. (In the extreme case a quality may be neglected, because it does not touch what is important in the person.)

We conclude that the formation and change of impressions consist of specific processes of organization. Further, it seems probable that these processes are not specific to impressions of persons alone. It is a task for future investigation to determine whether processes of this order are at work in other important regions of psychology, such as in forming the view of a group, or of the relations between one person and another.

REFERENCES

1. Allport, G. W. *Personality: A psychological interpretation.* New York: Holt, 1937.
2. Asch, S. E. Studies in the principles of judgments and attitudes: II. Determination of judgments by group and by ego standards. *J. soc. Psychol.*, 1940, *12*, 433–465.
3. Hartshorne, H., & May, M. A. Vol. I, *Studies in deceit*, 1928; Vol. II, *Studies in service and self-control*, 1939; Vol. III (with F. K. Shuttleworth), *Studies in the organization of character*, 1930.
4. Hull, C. L. *Principles of behavior.* New York: Appleton-Century, 1943.
5. Hull, C. L. The discrimination of stimulus configurations and the hypothesis of afferent neural interaction. *Psychol. Rev.*, 1945, *52*, 133–142.
6. Köhler, W. *Gestalt psychology.* New York: Liveright, 1929.
7. Mackinnon, D. W. The structure of personality. *In* Hunt, J. McV. (Ed.), *Personality and the behavior disorders*, Vol. I. New York: Ronald Press, 1944.
8. Ternus, J. Experimentelle Untersuchungen über phänomenale Identität. *Psych. Forsch.*, 1926, *7*, 81–136.
9. Thorndike, E. L. A constant error in psychological rating. *J. appl. Psychol.*, 1920, *4*, 25–29.
10. Wertheimer, M. *Productive thinking.* New York: Harper, 1946.

Person Memory: Some Tests of Associative Storage and Retrieval Models

Thomas K. Srull

An associative model of person memory that emphasizes the processing of behavioral information that is either congruent or incongruent with a prior expectancy was examined in four experiments. According to the model, the encoding of an incongruent item will result in the formation of a large number of associative paths between items, facilitating subsequent recall. The results of Experiment 1 indicate that, as predicted, subjects are much better at recalling items that are incongruent with a prior expectancy than those that are congruent. This was true when the set size for incongruent items was less than, equal to, or greater than that for congruent items, and the difference was as pronounced after a delay of 48 hours as it was after a delay of only a few minutes. Experiments 2 and 3 demonstrated that, holding the number of congruent items constant, adding incongruent items to the list increases the proportion of these congruent items that are subsequently recalled. However, adding congruent items to the list has no effect on the recall of incongruent items. These findings are also predicted by the model. It is suggested that unexpected or incongruent behaviors are difficult to comprehend and are considered in relation to behaviors already known about the target person during the process of encoding. Theoretically, this comparison process results in the formation of associative linkages between items. Experiment 4 demonstrated that requiring subjects to allocate a portion of their processing capacity to an irrelevant task interferes with their ability to form such linkages and therefore reduces the advantage of incongruent over congruent items in a free-recall task. Although the results reported are consistent with a variety of associative models that allow for the formation of linkages between items, it is suggested that the data place important constraints on the way such models may be formulated.

Research and theory in social cognition have recently turned to an explicit consideration of the way in which information about persons is organized in memory. It can generally be assumed that those cognitive processes involved in remembering information about persons are similar to those involved in remembering other types of

Editor's Note: This article reported four experiments. Experiments 1 and 4 are reproduced here.

Part of the present research was reported in a doctoral dissertation submitted to the University of Illinois at Urbana-Champaign. Committee members Jerry Clore, Mike Coles, Steve Golding, and Ed Shoben each offered constructive criticism and committee chairperson Bob Wyer was a constant sounding board for the ideas discussed. Appreciation is also extended to Reid Hastie for making available numerous unpublished papers on which the present report heavily depends. Ray Burke, Reid Haastie, and Leah Light each provided trenchant criticisms of an earlier draft of the paper. The present research was supported by United States Public Health Service Training Grant MH-15140 and a Biomedical Research Grant from the National Institutes of Health.

Requests for reprints should be sent to Thomas K. Srull, Department of Psychology, 603 East Daniel, University of Illinois, Champaign, Illinois, 61820.

information. Thus, established memory models should provide good starting points for developing specific theories of person memory. It is equally important, however, to consider the characteristics of social information that distinguish it from most other types of information. In particular, social information processing is often very "top-down" in nature. One usually has some generalized expectancy of the type of behavior a person will exhibit. These expectancies can be formed in a myriad of ways, based, for example, on descriptions of the target from other people, familiarity with their past accomplishments, knowledge of occupation or social roles, or even manner of dress (see, e.g., Schneider, Hastorf, & Ellsworth, 1979). Moreover, the process of acquiring behavioral information about a target often involves an active attempt to integrate the new information with what one already knows about the person.

Hastie (1980; Hastie & Kumar, 1979) recently reported an impressive set of experiments in which he investigated issues such as these. In a typical experiment, the subject is presented with a short ensemble of personality trait adjectives describing the target person to create an initial expectancy of the types of behaviors that would normally be expected from this person. The subject is then presented with a sequence of behaviors, of which some are congruent, some are incongruent, and some are irrelevant to the initial expectancy. Hastie found several results of interest. Most important, free recall of items incongruent with the expectancy is consistently superior to recall of items congruent with the expectancy, and these in turn are better recalled than irrelevant items. Although this difference exists when there is an equal number of congruent and incongruent behaviors in the presentation list, it increases in magnitude as the set size for incongruent behaviors decreases relative to the set size for congruent behaviors. That is, as the total number of incongruent behaviors presented in the acquisition list is reduced, subjects tend to recall a greater proportion of these behaviors (cf. Murdock, 1962; Roberts, 1972). These basic results have been obtained with a variety of trait expectancies, with written and visual materials, and under short and long delay conditions, and they correspond to a wide array of results previously reported in the experimental literature (for an excellent review, see Hastie, 1981).

Hastie (1980) also reported several more refined experiments related to the study of person memory. Perhaps the most parsimonious interpretation of the results of these studies can be made in terms of an associative storage and retrieval model. Of course many variations are possible. However, it would appear that any viable model would require that specific behavioral items be stored in relation to the superordinate cues that compose the initial expectancy, as well as any additional cues that are provided by other items in the list. Such a model would also allow for associative linkages to be formed between items in the presentation list (cf. Ross & Bower, 1981). Although it is possible that such linkages might be formed on the basis of factors such as contiguity of presentation, it is suggested that the relation of any particular item to the generalized expectancy is the primary determinant of when the linkages are formed (or, alternatively, of the strength of any individual associative link). This reflects the emphasis on top-down processes noted earlier. Finally, such a model would require that the search process traverse the associative pathways that are established during encoding. That is, the probability of retrieving a particular item should be a function of the number (or strength) of associative paths that have been formed during encoding.

Specific Associative Models

Although there are several associative storage and retrieval models that could be used to account for the phenomena described above (see, e.g., the Search of Associative Memory model proposed by Raaijmakers & Shiffrin, 1980, 1981), the present article examines several of the empirical implications of one proposed by Hastie (1980). This is a network model originally based on the human associative memory (HAM) theory of Anderson and Bower (1973).

The experiments reported are specifically concerned with the case in which a subject is given trait information about a target to create an initial expectancy and then exposed to behavioral information that is either congruent or incongruent with the expectancy. As each behavioral item is presented, the subject presumably attempts to comprehend its meaning by relating it to information stored in long-term memory. The comprehension process is assumed to involve the simultaneous use of conceptually driven and data driven processes (see Bobrow & Norman, 1975; Norman & Bobrow, 1976). The conceptually driven component is regulated by the prior expectancy, and confirmation or disconfirmation of the expectancy is noted very early during the stage of comprehension.

The HAM model as originally proposed by Anderson and Bower cannot account for several findings within the present experimental paradigm (for a complete discussion, see Hastie & Kumar, 1979). Most important, Anderson and Bower treat each proposition as an independent fact that does not in any way need to be integrated with other known facts. Thus, there is no meaningful difference between the way in which congruent (expected) and incongruent (unexpected) behaviors are processed, and both would be expected to be recalled with equal likelihood. However, Hastie (1980) proposed that the model can be extended by assuming that behavioral episodes pertaining to the same target will themselves sometimes be directly connected by associative paths. Specifically, this will occur whenever two episodes are considered in relation to one another in working memory. That is, whenever a new behavioral episode is compared to one retrieved from long-term memory (i.e., one already present in the network), an associative linkage will develop between the two.

Hastie (1980) hypothesized that an episode incongruent with a prior expectancy is difficult to comprehend and will be retained in working memory for a relatively long period of time. During this time, the subject is assumed to retrieve additional information (i.e., old behaviors) from long-term memory in an effort to more fully comprehend such an unexpected or incongruent behavior. In addition, the subject may retain such an incongruent behavior in working memory until subsequent behaviors are received as well. In either case, the incongruent episode will make contact with other behaviors (either previously learned or subsequently acquired). Whenever this occurs, an interepisode associative linkage between the two will be established.[1]

Figure 23.1 presents a simplified hypothetical associative network of the type postulated by Hastie that might result from a condition in which four congruent and two incongruent episodes were presented. The structure is a simplified version of that described by Anderson and Bower (1973), with propositions represented only in terms of subjects and predicates (see Hastie, 1980, for a complete discussion). Note, however, that the average number of associative paths emanating from incongruent behaviors is substantially greater than the number emanating from congruent behaviors.

As Hastie (1980) pointed out, this process of establishing interepisode associative paths is conceptually similar to the levels of processing framework (Craik & Lockhart, 1972). As more and more previously stored information is retrieved and makes contact with new information in working memory, more and more interepisode linkages will develop.

In order to see how the Hastie model can account for the fact that a greater proportion of incongruent than congruent episodes are typically recalled, it is necessary to trace the various retrieval processes postulated. When a subject attempts to remember the behavioral information presented, the retrieval process underlying free recall is assumed to be the same as that postulated by Anderson (1972; Anderson & Bower, 1973). The search process originates at the subject node at the highest level of the network and follows the associative paths until an episode node (i.e., a particular predicate) is activated. After the subject recalls an episode, the search continues from that node to traverse the associative paths until another episode is activated. When a number of paths emanate from a single node, the search is assumed to be random and sequential (cf. Anderson, 1976). That is, only one of the several possible paths is followed and it is chosen randomly.

Since the model predicts that incongruent events will generally have more associative paths attached to them than congruent events, a greater proportion of incongruent than congruent episodes should be recalled. However, a number of variables should affect when additional interepisode associative paths will be established and how they will be affected over time. The experiments reported examined several of these.

Specific Theoretical Predictions

Learning conditions. In the experiments reported by Hastie, "impression formation" and "memory" instructions have always been used simultaneously. Thus, subjects are instructed to form a general impression of what the target would be like *and* to remember the behavioral information as well as possible. However, separating the effects due to intentional and incidental learning conditions is important for several interrelated reasons. First, contemporary theories of both social (Wyer & Srull, 1980) and nonsocial (see, e.g., Underwood, 1978) memory have increasingly emphasized the role of subject processing strategies in the way in which information is ultimately represented. Second, the effects obtained in this paradigm are very similar to those found in the "isolation" studies

---

[1] Smith, Adams, and Schorr (1978) recently pointed out that a more abstract integration of various sentences will often occur in nonsocial domains as well and, similar to Hastie, suggested that this integration process can be conceptualized in terms of the formation of interepisode associative linkages. They also noted that this is most likely to occur when the subject has some prior expectancy, and discussed in depth how the basic HAM model begins to break down under these conditions (cf. Reder & Anderson, 1980). The conceptual arguments of Smith et al. are very similar to those presented here. However, since they are tested using reaction time rather than recall procedures, they will not be discussed further.

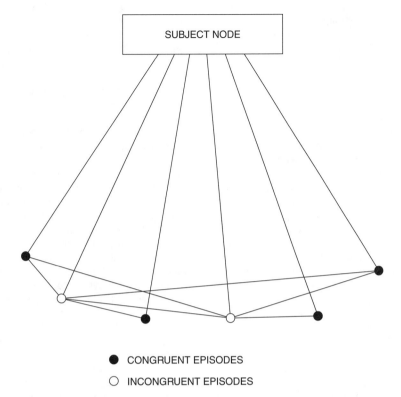

SUBJECT NODE

● CONGRUENT EPISODES

○ INCONGRUENT EPISODES

FIGURE 23.1 ■ Hypothetical Associative Network Representing Information About a Single Individual (after Hastie, 1980).

originally reported by von Restorff (1933). Although von Restorff effects have been found in a variety of contexts (see Wallace, 1965), a long line of failures to find such effects in incidental learning situations has been reported (Gleitman & Gillett, 1957; Koyanagi, 1957a, 1957b; Postman & Phillips, 1954; Saltzman & Carterette, 1959). Finally, it also should be recognized that most social interactions actually occur under conditions that are similar to a general "impression" set.

There is a great deal of evidence in the social cognition literature to suggest that subjects are much more active in integrating discrepant pieces of information under impression formation than memory set instructions (see, e.g., Hamilton, Katz, & Leirer, 1980). Ironically, the theoretical framework guiding the present research predicts that recall for incongruent information will be greatest precisely when such integration occurs. Thus, in contrast to the typical isolation study, the advantage of incongruent information is expected to be

greater under incidental than intentional learning conditions.[2] Indeed, an ideal subject who did not attempt to integrate the various pieces of information into a coherent impression of the target person would not be expected to show any superior recall for incongruent information.

Retention. It is also interesting to note that early interpretations of the von Restorff effect were made in terms of Gestalt theory. Specifically, the Gestalt theorists suggested that isolated or incongruent items would be not

---

[2] It is recognized that not all "incidental" learning conditions are the same, and the "impression set" discussed is only one of an infinite number of orienting tasks that could be investigated. An explicit focus on the impression set seems reasonable, however, because it comes close to representing those conditions to which investigators in the area of social cognition most often wish to generalize. A concern with ecological representativeness is probably also responsible for this set appearing in most of the existing literature.

only more easily learned but also more slowly forgotten. While several studies have supported this prediction (e.g., Bellezza & Cheney, 1973; Newman, 1939; Postman & Phillips, 1954), others have not (e.g., Green, 1956; Saul & Osgood, 1950).

The Hastie model can only account for forgetting in terms of the associative pathways becoming less accessible over time. It is assumed that this decrease in accessibility is constant for all paths (Anderson & Bower, 1973). Thus, the retention curves for congruent and incongruent items would be predicted to be the same, and they would not be expected to interact with intentional or incidental learning conditions. Although this specific hypothesis has never been examined, it is consistent with findings reported by Hastie (1980) under conditions in which memory set and impression formation instructions were used simultaneously.

Note that these predictions are different from the predictions of several schema-based models of person memory. These models predict that although incongruent items may be very well recalled under short delay conditions, only behavioral information that is adequately integrated into the schema will be recalled after a long delay (see Wyer & Srull, 1980, for a complete discussion). These models would therefore predict that incongruent items would be forgotten at a faster rate than congruent items, and the retention curves for the two types of items would not be parallel across various delay conditions. The "forgetting" in these models is typically attributed to some type of cue-dependent retrieval failure.

Types of incongruity. It is important to distinguish between items that are incongruent with a prior expectancy and items that are descriptively inconsistent with the other items in the list. The present research examines situations in which items incongruent with a prior expectancy have a set size that is less than, equal to, or greater than that for congruent items. Of particular interest is the condition in which the number of incongruent items is actually greater than the number of congruent items. This is a very interesting situation because the Hastie model predicts that, contrary to the typical set size effect reported in the verbal learning literature (see e.g., Murdock, 1962; Roberts, 1972), subjects should still recall a greater proportion of incongruent than congruent items.

Potential modifications. of the expectancy One important assumption of the Hastie model is that the initial expectancy will continue to influence how subsequent information is encoded even after more and more information is learned about the target person. It also seems reasonable, however, that the nature of the expectancy may change as additional behavioral information about the target person is acquired. This is particularly likely to be the case when more information incongruent than congruent with the expectancy is acquired. This will be examined in the present investigation by examining whether recall of various types of information changes over successive blocks of presentation.

Potential differences between recall and recognition. One of the most conceptually satisfying aspects of the Hastie model is that it explicitly takes into account the nature of both encoding and retrieval processes. By integrating concerns typically discussed under levels of processing, the model makes quite specific statements about how behavioral episodes are encoded into memory. However, it is only by considering the final structural representation *and* the nature of the retrieval process that one can predict better recall of episodes that are incongruent with an initial expectancy than episodes that are congruent with it. That is, the predicted advantage for incongruent items is based on the assumption that the retrieval process underlying free recall traverses the associative paths that are established during encoding.

However, it is well known that a number of variables have pronounced effects on recall but virtually none on recognition (see, e.g., Brown, 1976). These variables are generally thought to affect a subject's ability to retrieve particular items, and the results are generally interpreted in terms of some "generation–recognition" theory of free recall (for minor variations of this approach, see Anderson & Bower, 1972, 1974; Bahrick, 1969, 1970; Kintsch, 1970; Müller, 1913). Any variable that affects a subject's ability to independently retrieve a given item should, according to the theory, have a pronounced effect on recall but none on recognition accuracy. Since the model being examined postulates that the greater recall of incongruent items is due to their having a greater number of interepisode associative paths attached to them (and thus having a greater probability of being retrieved), it is possible that there will be no differential ability to recognize incongruent and congruent episodes. The reason for this is that the retrieval process is thought to be bypassed with a recognition task. According to the generation–recognition theory, a reliable effect on recall but *not* on recognition would suggest that the superior recall of incongruent over other types of items is localized in the retrieval stage. This possibility will also be examined.

Interindividual and intraindividual variability. A final issue that has been discussed in the social cognition literature concerns the nature of the target. Specifically,

Rothbart, Evans, and Fulero (1979) hypothesized that subjects may be more willing to tolerate information that indicates interindividual inconsistency within a group (e.g., three friendly and three unfriendly behaviors manifested by six different persons in a group) than they are to tolerate intraindividual inconsistency from a single person (e.g., three friendly and three unfriendly behaviors manifested by a single individual). According to the associative memory model being considered, this suggests that subjects would form fewer (or weaker) interepisode associative linkages when given information about members of a group than they would when given information about a single individual. However, the tendency to form fewer (or weaker) interepisode linkages when given information about a group rather than about a single individual may only occur when there is no important psychological bond linking the various members of the group. Under conditions in which there is such a bond linking the various members (e.g., a fraternity), the "group" will become an appropriate unit of analysis, and subjects' reactions to interindividual behavioral inconsistency may be similar to their reactions to intraindividual inconsistency.

It is predicted that subjects will process interindividual variability about members of a group the same as they do intraindividual variability about a single individual whenever they are concerned with forming an impression of the group *as a whole*. When there is no important psychological bond linking the various members of a group, and thus no reason to integrate the information into a unitary impression of the group as a whole, subjects may process the behavioral information about each individual separately (for a more detailed analysis of these issues, see Srull, 1980).

Experiment 1

The first experiment was an initial test of whether the experimental variables discussed above would have the hypothesized effects. Theoretically, these variables should affect the number of interepisode associative paths that are formed and, ultimately, the number and type of items recalled.

Subjects were presented with a brief description of a particular individual or group to create an initial expectancy of the target(s) as being either friendly and sociable or unfriendly and nonsociable. They were then presented with behaviors that were said to have been performed by that person or group. The individual behavior items were either congruent or incongruent

with the initial expectancy. In order to prevent all of the items from falling into one of two discrete categories, a number of irrelevant items (i.e., items unrelated to the initial expectancy) were also included. In various conditions, the congruent items had a set size that was either less than, equal to, or greater than that of the incongruent items. Half of the subjects in each condition received the information under general "impression set" instructions and the remaining subjects received the information under the standard "memory set" instructions. A free-recall test was administered in all cases, and this was completed either immediately or 48 hr. after the behavioral information was presented. The proportion of congruent and incongruent items recalled was then examined across conditions.

Method

Selection of Stimulus Materials
A total of 37 undergraduate students not tested in the actual experiment rated a large pool of behavior statements on a scale ranging from -10 (extremely unfriendly) to $+10$ (extremely friendly) with the scale midpoint indicating that the behavior was irrelevant to the trait dimension. On the basis of these normative ratings, 12 friendly, 12 unfriendly, and 12 irrelevant behaviors were selected for use in the actual experiment. The unfriendly behaviors (e.g., "publically criticized his wife at a party") had a mean rating of -8.92, the irrelevant behaviors (e.g., "ordered a new magazine for a special subscription rate") had a mean rating of .11, and the friendly behaviors (e.g., "pulled off the highway to assist a driver whose car had stalled") had a mean rating of 8.78.

Experimental Design
The design was a $3 \times 3 \times 2 \times 2$ completely balanced factorial with the following factors: Type of target (individual vs. "meaningful group" vs. "nonmeaningful group"), set size (equal numbers of congruent and incongruent items vs. more congruent than incongruent items vs. fewer congruent than incongruent items), learning conditions (memory set vs. impression set), and length of delay before recall (immediate vs. 48 hr.). Eight subjects were randomly assigned to each of the resulting 36 data cells. However, four of the subjects in each cell were told that the target was "friendly and sociable" and four were told that the target was "unfriendly and nonsociable" (although they received identical items). Construction of the presentation lists allowed these groups to be collapsed for purposes of

analysis. Since only the initial expectancy was varied, specific item content was held constant, and the proportions of congruent and incongruent items recalled were based on exactly the same set of items.

Subjects

Two hundred and eighty-eight male and female introductory psychology students participated in the actual experiment. Participation partially fulfilled a course requirement.

Procedure

Subjects were tested in small groups. Although all of the subjects in any given session were in the same delay condition, there was random assignment to all other conditions.

Subjects were given a short booklet containing all experimental instructions and materials. In all cases, the first page of the booklet explained that the experiment was concerned with the way in which people typically process social information and that they would be presented with a list of behaviors that had been manifested by a particular individual (or group of individuals). Half of the subjects, run under memory set conditions, were told that they were to remember the behavioral information as well as possible and that they would later be asked to recall its basic content. The other half, run under impression set conditions, were told that they were to form an impression of what the person (or group) would be like and that they would later be asked to make some simple judgments about the person (or group).

Subjects in the individual target condition were told that each of the behaviors had been manifested by a particular individual named Peter Lacy. Half were told that Peter "tends to be much more friendly and sociable than average. He tends to enjoy making new friends, meeting with old friends, and generally tends to value social activities." The other half were told he "tends to be

much more unfriendly and nonsociable than average. He tends not to enjoy making new friends, nor meeting with old friends, and he generally does not value social activities." Each behavior in the presentation list began with the name Peter.

Subjects in the nonmeaningful group target condition received instructions analogous to those provided by Rothbart et al. (1979). Specifically, they were told that they would receive information about a group of people who tend to be more friendly and sociable (or unfriendly and nonsociable) than average, and that each behavior presented had been manifested by a different member of the group. Each behavior presented was associated with a different male name.

Subjects in the meaningful group target condition were also told that the group tends to be more friendly and sociable (or unfriendly and nonsociable) than average and that each behavior had been manifested by a different member of the group. However, these subjects were also told that "this group of men is a real one, composed of a political caucus of a midwestern state who are meeting regularly in order to select delegates to the upcoming national political convention." Again, each behavior presented was associated with a different male name.

All subjects received a list of 30 behavior statements. The composition of the lists for the various set size conditions is summarized in Table 23.1. In those conditions in which only 6 of a particular behavior type (e.g., friendly) were presented, two separate lists of 6 (exhausting the total pool of 12) were made and administered to half of the subjects in each cell. When collapsed across subjects, this procedure controls for item content.

The 30 behavior statements were also divided into six blocks of five items each. Each block contained the same proportion of congruent, incongruent, and irrelevant items. For example, in the equal set size condition,

TABLE 23.1. The Number of Friendly, Unfriendly, and Irrelevant Items Appearing in the Presentation Lists for Each of the Three Set Size Conditions

Item Type	Expectancy					
	Equal Set Sizes		Smaller Set Size for Congruent Items		Larger Set Size for Congruent Items	
	Friendly	Unfriendly	Friendly	Unfriendly	Friendly	Unfriendly
Friendly	12	12	6	12	12	6
Unfriendly	12	12	12	6	6	12
Irrelevant	6	6	12	12	12	12

each block contained two congruent, two incongruent, and one irrelevant item. The items were then randomly arranged within a block, and the order of the blocks in the final presentation list was also randomized. This procedure permitted an examination of whether the proportion of various types of items recalled changes as a function of the subject learning more about the target.

Each behavior statement was typed on a separate piece of paper, and subjects were paced through the booklet by the experimenter at the rate of 6 sec per item. After reading through the complete list of behavior items, subjects were asked either immediately or 48 hr. later to recall as many of the individual behaviors as possible. They were told that they need not produce verbatim recall, nor associate any behavior with a particular name.

After completing the recall protocols, all subjects were given a 12-min. interpolated task in which they were asked to list as many of the 50 states as possible. This was followed by a final 60-item recognition rating task. The items were composed of the original 30 items and 30 lures with normative ratings that matched those of the old items as closely as possible. That is, subjects in the equal set size condition, who were given 12 congruent, 12 incongruent, and 6 irrelevant items originally, were given a recognition test that contained these same 30 items plus 12 congruent, 12 incongruent, and 6 irrelevant lures. Similarly, subjects who originally received a greater proportion of congruent than incongruent items were given a recognition test containing the original items plus 12 congruent, 6 incongruent, and 12 irrelevant lures. Finally, subjects originally given a greater proportion of incongruent than congruent items received the original items plus 6 congruent, 12 incongruent, and 12 irrelevant lures. Overall, mean normative ratings for the lures were −8.89, .09, and 8.81 for "unfriendly," "irrelevant," and "friendly" items, respectively.

Results

Recall
The free-recall data were scored according to a lenient "general meaning" criterion by a judge blind to the experimental condition. A random selection of 60 protocols was selected and independently scored by a second blind judge; reliability was close to perfect, with the two judges agreeing on 861 of 869 items commonly scored. From a grand total of 3,289 items recalled, only 22, or less than 1%, could be classified as intrusions. Such a low intrusion rate with behavioral items has also been found by Hastie and Kumar (1979) and Rothbart et al. (1979).

The proportion of items recalled was analyzed as a function of four between-subject and two within-subject factors. The between-subject factors were learning conditions (memory set vs. impression set), length of delay (immediate vs. 48-hr.), target type (individual vs. meaningful group vs. nonmeaningful group), and set size (the number of incongruent items being either less than, equal to, or greater than the number of congruent items). The within-subject factors were type of item (incongruent, congruent, or irrelevant with respect to the prior expectancy) and blocks (Positions 1–6 in the presentation list). Theoretically, the most important comparisons involved the proportion of items recalled that are congruent or incongruent to the expectancy.

The main effect of presentation blocks was not significant ($F < 1$), nor did this variable enter into any interactions. Not surprisingly, subjects were able to recall a much higher proportion of items immediately ($M = .538$) than they were after a delay of 48 hr. ($M = .218$), $F(1, 252) = 722.02$, $MS_e = .18$, $p < .001$. The effect of type of item recalled was also highly significant, $F(2, 504) = 144.05$, $MS_e = .08$, $p < .001$. Consistent with predictions from the associative model and previous results reported by Hastie and Kumar (1979), the mean proportions of incongruent, congruent, and irrelevant items recalled were .444, .400, and .289, respectively. Post hoc comparisons indicate that all three means are significantly different from one another (all at $p < .01$).[3]

It was also predicted that subjects would be more likely to integrate discrepant pieces of information, and ultimately recall them better, if the pieces of information pertained to a psychologically meaningful target rather than if they did not. Consistent with this analysis, there was a strong main effect of target type, $F(2, 252) = 24.11$, $MS_e = .18$, $p < .001$. Whereas an equal proportion of items pertaining to a single individual ($M = .401$) or a meaningful group ($M = .412$) were recalled, these levels were each significantly greater ($p < .01$) than the proportion of items recalled about a group whose members shared no important psychological bond ($M = .320$). This suggests that subjects can process information about individuals or groups equally well *if* there is a psychologically meaningful reason to consider the group as a single unit. However, if members of a "group" have nothing psychological in common, subjects may process the behavioral information

---

[3] All post hoc comparisons reported in the present paper were calculated using Newman-Keuls procedures (see, e.g., Keppel, 1973).

separately and make no attempt at integrating inconsistent or discrepant pieces of information. The fact that subjects receiving items about a meaningful group were able to remember as much of the information as those receiving information about a single individual indicates that the decrement in recall associated with the nonmeaningful group is not simply due to a greater number of names being presented. It is also interesting that the interaction between target type and learning conditions was not significant ($F < 1$) and that this effect appears to generalize over both memory set and impression set conditions.

A number of important results were related to learning conditions, however. It was predicted that subjects would generally be more likely to integrate various pieces of information, and thus develop interepisode associative linkages between items, when they were attempting to form a coherent impression of the target than when they were simply trying to learn the material. In general, however, this integration process should be more difficult for items incongruent with a prior expectancy. Thus, these items would be expected to be kept in working memory for a longer period of time and form a greater number of associative links than other items. A number of findings are related to these hypotheses. First, more items were recalled under incidental (impression set) than intentional (memory set) learning conditions, $F(1, 252) = 4.65$, $MS_e = .18$, $p < .05$, replicating earlier indications of such a possibility in both the cognitive (Hyde & Jenkins, 1969, 1973; Mandler, 1967; Postman, 1964) and social (Hamilton et al., 1980) literature. However, there was also an interaction between learning conditions and item type, $F(2, 504) = 4.00$, $MS_e = .08$, $p < .02$. The means associated with this interaction are presented in Table 23.2. While there was no difference between the proportion of congruent or irrelevant items recalled under memory set and impression set conditions, a significantly greater proportion of incongruent items was recalled under the impression set ($M = .470$) than under the memory set ($M = .417$) conditions ($p < .01$). In terms of the underlying theoretical model, this suggests that items incongruent with a prior expectancy undergo additional processing when subjects are attempting to form an integrated impression of what the target would be like. It also suggests that the locus of the effects reported by Hastie and Kumar (1979), who confounded the two types of processing objectives, lies largely in the impression formation component of their instructions.

It is also important to note that there was a crossover interaction between learning conditions and length of

TABLE 23.2. Proportion of Congruent, Incongruent, and Irrelevant Behaviors Recalled as a Function of Learning Conditions

	Learning Condition	
Item Type	Memory Set	Impression Set
Congruent	.401	.400
Incongruent	.417	.470
Irrelevant	.300	.278

delay, $F(1, 252) = 15.27$, $MS_e = .18$, $p < .001$. Although instructions to form an integrated impression of the target person led to significantly ($p < .01$) greater recall than memory set instructions under immediate delay conditions (.574 vs. .502), there was a slight (and nonsignificant) advantage for memory set over impression set subjects in the long delay condition (.228 vs. .208). Since memory set subjects left the first session knowing they would have to recall the material 2 days later, however, they may have intentionally engaged in some additional rehearsal of the items. This would provide them with a spurious "advantage" over impression set subjects who presumably did not anticipate a future recall test and would be unlikely to engage in such additional processing.

Finally, there was a complicated three-way interaction involving target type, item type, and length of delay, $F(4, 504) = 4.12$, $MS_e = .08$, $p < .01$. This interaction, which is displayed in Figure 23.2, is due primarily to the fact that the retention curve for irrelevant items about nonmeaningful group members is much flatter than that for any other type of item or in any other condition. This finding is also responsible for three lower order interactions between length of delay and target type, $F(2, 252) = 8.15$, $MS_e = .18$, $p < .001$; target type and item type, $F(4, 504) = 5.13$, $MS_e = .08$, $p < .001$; and length of delay and item type, $F(2, 504) = 10.65$, $MS_e = .08$, $p < .001$.

In spite of the one exception, Figure 23.2 is noteworthy for the basic symmetry of the retention curves. Not only are the curves essentially the same for different target types but they are also equivalent for all types of items. In fact, the differences between recall of incongruent items under short and long delay conditions (.616 and .271, respectively) and between congruent items under short and long delay conditions (.572 and .229, respectively) are nearly identical, a finding that Hastie (1980) has also found with both visual and written materials.

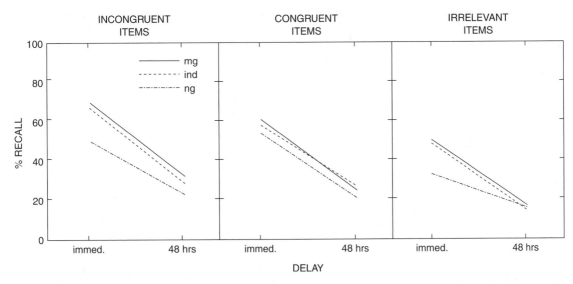

FIGURE 23.2 ■ Proportion of Incongruent, Congruent, and Irrelevant Items Recalled as a Function of Target Type and Length of Delay. (mg = meaningful group; ind = individual; ng = nonmeaningful group.)

Additional Tests of the Model

Output sequence of items recalled. Hastie (1980) and Hastie and Kumar (1979) have reported repeated failures to find any evidence of clustering as assessed by conventional measures (e.g., Bousfield & Bousfield, 1966) in a paradigm very similar to the one used here. An analysis of the present recall data using both the Bousfield and Bousfield (1966) index and the adjusted-ratio-of-clustering (ARC) index (Roenker, Thompson, & Brown, 1971) indicates no significant degree of clustering in the present study as well.

However, several predictions concerning order of output can be made by considering the representational structure of the Hastie model in conjunction with the nature of the retrieval processes hypothesized to underlie recall. Specifically, when an item congruent with a prior expectancy is received, it is simply encoded into memory by associating it with the abstract person node. However, when an incongruent item is received, it is assumed to be retained in working memory until it can make contact with other items; these items may be congruent ones, irrelevant ones, or other incongruent ones. Following the successive presentation of items, interepisode associative paths will have been formed between incongruent items and all other types of items. It follows, therefore, that associative paths emanating from incongruent items will be attached to either other

incongruent items, congruent items, or irrelevant items. In contrast, the overwhelming number of paths emanating from congruent items should be attached only to incongruent items. Assuming that the retrieval process underlying free recall follows these paths, this implies several things. First, the probability of recalling an incongruent item given that one has just recalled a congruent item ($P_{I/C}$) should be greater than the probability of recalling a congruent item given that one has just recalled an incongruent item ($P_{C/I}$). In fact, there is a large difference between these two conditional probabilities, with $P_{I/C}$ equal to .789 and $P_{C/I}$ equal to .319.

All possible conditional probabilities for the recall of incongruent (I), congruent (C), and irrelevant (i) items, calculated across subjects and conditions, are presented in Table 23.3. There are several additional things to note about these data. First, the values for $P_{I/I}$, $P_{C/C}$, and $P_{i/i}$ are extremely low, largely explaining the failure to find any degree of clustering with conventional measures. Second, given that an incongruent item has been recalled, it is almost equally likely that any other type of item will follow. However, given that a congruent item has been recalled, it is extremely likely that the next item recalled will be an incongruent item.

The conditional probabilities concerning irrelevant items are also interesting. In particular, although the absolute proportion of irrelevant items recalled is very

TABLE 23.3. Probability that an Incongruent, Congruent, or Irrelevant Item was Recalled, Conditional On the Type of Item Previously Recalled

Probability of Recall	Type of Item Previously Recalled		
	Con-gruent	Incon-gruent	Irrele-vant
Congruent	.089	.319	.675
Incongruent	.789	.208	.162
Irrelevant	.122	.473	.163

TABLE 23.4. Recognition Confidence Ratings for Old and New Items as a Function of Item Type and Length of Delay

Item Type	Old Items		New Items	
	Short delay	Long delay	Short delay	Long delay
Incongruent	5.117	4.233	1.885	2.069
Congruent	5.141	4.254	1.941	2.084
Irrelevant	5.100	4.207	1.894	2.054

low, when one is recalled it is quite likely to be followed by a congruent item. This might suggest that certain irrelevant items are examined in relation to congruent items to "make sure" they could not, in fact, be considered consistent with the prior expectancy. The problem with this explanation is that it assumes that the irrelevant items are held in working memory for a relatively long period of time, and thus the overall level of recall should be quite high; in fact, it is very low. A more provocative explanation is that irrelevant items are not richly integrated into the network, and they develop few if any interitem associations. Thus, after an irrelevant item is activated, it may be impossible to traverse any of the associative pathways. Subjects might then adopt a retrieval strategy of retreating to the general person node at the highest level of the hierarchy. It is quite possible that entering the network at this point leads to a high probability of then recalling a congruent episode. However, if this is true, there should be a high probability of congruent items being recalled on the very first attempt. That is, if subjects begin their recall attempts by entering at this point in the hierarchy, a high proportion of the first items recalled should be congruent ones. In fact, the data support this; of the 288 recall protocols, 159 began with a congruent item, 71 began with an incongruent item, and 58 began with an irrelevant item. These differences are highly significant, $\chi^2(2) = 62.89$, $p < .001$. This explanation can also account for the fact that fewer irrelevant than congruent or incongruent items were recalled.[4]

These data are taken as very strong support for the assumptions concerning the retrieval processes underlying free recall. They also support the hypothesized formation of interepisode associative paths between items and lead to several additional hypotheses that were examined in subsequent experiments.

Recognition memory. Subjects made recognition confidence ratings for each of the 30 behaviors originally presented and 30 lures that were chosen on the basis of normative ratings. Each item was rated along the following scale: (1) positive the behavior was not presented, (2) fairly certain the behavior was not presented, (3) undecided, but think the behavior was not presented, (4) undecided, but think the behavior was presented, (5) fairly certain the behavior was presented, and (6) positive the behavior was presented.

The recognition confidence ratings for incongruent, congruent, and irrelevant items under short and long delay conditions are presented in Table 23.4. Subjects were able to distinguish quite well between old and new items even after a 48-hr. delay. Most important, however, there was no advantage whatsoever for incongruent items with a recognition task. Concerning only those items previously presented, there was no effect for item type, $F(2, 504) = 2.46$, *ns*, and in fact subjects made slightly higher confidence ratings for congruent than incongruent items. It is also important to note that item type did not interact with any of the other variables previously found to have a strong impact on recall. That is, the interaction of item type with learning conditions, $F(2, 504) = 2.46$; target type ($F < 1$); and set size, $F(4, 504) = 1.08$, were all nonsignificant.

Recognition confidence ratings given to items not previously presented are also shown in Table 23.4. The pattern of ratings given to old and new items is almost identical. Again, the effect of item type was not significant, $F(2, 504) = 2.09$, *ns*, nor did it interact with any other variables. This indicates that the relatively high levels of recognition for congruent and incongruent items are not simply due to a guessing bias. Rather, it appears that the use of a recognition task, which theoretically bypasses (or certainly minimizes the influence of) the retrieval stage, eliminates any advantage for incongruent over other types of items. An analysis of variance of d' scores (see, e.g., McNicol, 1972) also

---

[4] Appreciation is extended to Richard Shiffrin for suggesting this analysis.

indicates no difference in memory discrimination for the various types of items. This is consistent with the above interpretation.

Experiment 4

One of the most novel aspects of the Hastie model is the postulated formation of interepisode linkages between incongruent and other types of items. It is important to note, however, that such paths are hypothesized to be formed only when the subject compares two or more behavioral episodes in working memory. One implication of this is that any procedure that requires the subject to devote part or all of his/her processing capacity to an irrelevant task will effectively prevent the formation of such linkages. Experiment 4 tested this hypothesis by presenting items sequentially and requiring subjects to rehearse aloud the item then being presented. This procedure has been shown to reduce the opportunity of subjects to form associative linkages among items (Schwartz & Humphreys, 1974). Four conditions were run: (1) no irrelevant task was required, (2) the subject was required to rehearse aloud the item then being presented one time, (3) the subject was required to rehearse the item two times, or (4) the subject was required to rehearse the item three times. Theoretically, Conditions 1–4 require more and more of the subject's processing capacity to be devoted to an irrelevant task and thus should prevent the formation of interepisode associative links. As a consequence, it was predicted that the proportion of incongruent items recalled would consistently decline over Conditions 1–4.

Method

Stimulus Materials
The behavior statements used were the same as those in the earlier experiments.

Subjects
A total of 48 male and female introductory psychology students (12 per experimental condition) participated in the experiment in partial fulfillment of a course requirement.

Procedure
The procedure was very similar to that used in the earlier studies. All subjects were tested in individual sessions, given the standard impression formation instructions and received information about a single target person. Each subject received a list with 12 congruent, 12 incongruent, and 6 irrelevant items presented in random order. Subjects were paced through the booklet at the rate of 10 sec. per item and then immediately given the surprise recall test.

Design
The design was a split-plot factorial with one between-subject and one within-subject factor. In various conditions, subjects were (a) simply given the impression formation instructions, (b) given the instructions and told to rehearse aloud each item one time loud enough for the experimenter to hear it, (c) given the instructions and told to rehearse each item aloud two times, or (d) given the instructions and told to rehearse each item aloud three times. (Pilot testing indicated that subjects manifest wide variability in talking speed and some subjects could not rehearse every item three times during the 10-sec. interval. Subjects in the last condition were alerted to this possibility and told to simply go onto the next item if they were still talking when the signal for the next item was given.)

Results

The proportions of congruent, incongruent, and irrelevant items recalled are plotted in Figure 23.3 as a function of the number of overt repetitions required. An analysis of

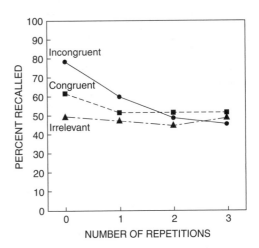

FIGURE 23.3 ■ Proportion of Incongruent, Congruent, and Irrelevant Items Recalled as a Function of the Number of Overt Rehearsals Required.

variance of these data indicates that total recall consistently declined as more repetitions were required, $F(3, 44) = 3.63$, $MS_e = .05$, $p < .02$. There was also a main effect of item type, $F(2, 88) = 13.35$, $MS_e = .01$, $p < .001$, with incongruent items being the best recalled and irrelevant items being the least well recalled. Most important, there was also a significant interaction between item type and number of repetitions, $F(6, 88) = 5.19$, $MS_e = .01$, $p < .001$. As predicted, the proportion of incongruent items recalled consistently declined as the number of overt repetitions increased, $F(3, 44) = 12.95$, $MS_e = .02$, $p < .001$. On the other hand, the number of repetitions had no effect on the proportion of congruent, $F(3, 44) = 1.65$, ns, or the proportion of irrelevant ($F < 1$) items recalled.

General Discussion

As with any new field, current research activity in the area of person memory is very diffuse in nature. One of the reasons for this is that only very crude theoretical structures are currently available to guide empirical work. In fact, the associative model proposed by Hastie (1980) is one of the few formalized theoretical models of person memory that currently exists. As such, it needs to be examined very carefully.

The research reported in the present paper had two complimentary objectives and can be discussed on two different levels. At the descriptive level, it was concerned with identifying some of the factors that influence one's tendency to selectively recall social information that is congruent or incongruent with a prior belief or expectancy. At the theoretical level, the research was designed to test several specific implications of the Hastie model and generate data that place constraints on any associative model of person memory. Each of these will be addressed in turn.

Recall of Information Congruent or Incongruent With a Prior Expectancy

A number of researchers in both person perception and group stereotyping have recently considered whether mental representations of persons or groups are maintained in the face of contradictory evidence by a tendency to selectively remember behavioral information that is congruent with a prior belief or expectancy. Cohen (1981, Note 1), Cantor and Mischel (1977), Rothbart et al. (1979), and Snyder and Uranowitz (1978) have all recently reported evidence in support of

such a position. Moreover, all of these researchers have interpreted their findings in terms of some general schema theory of person memory, usually one that has strong reconstructive properties associated with it. However, the results of Hastie (1980), Hastie and Kumar (1979), and the experiments reported here suggest that there will often be better memory for *incongruent* than congruent information, and these results appear to pose serious difficulties for most of the schema theories that have been proposed (however, see Thorndyke & Hayes-Roth, 1979, for a well-developed exception to this rule). As Hastie and Kumar (1979) note, one of the most immediate problems is to identify those factors that control whether congruent or incongruent information will be better remembered.

A careful examination of the social cognition literature indicates that virtually all of the previous studies finding better memory for congruent than incongruent information have used some form of recognition procedure (Cantor & Mischel, 1977; Cohen, 1981, Note 1; Snyder & Uranowitz, 1978). In fact, the lone exception to this is a study by Rothbart et al. (1979), who used presentation lists in which the number of incongruent behaviors was always substantially smaller than the number of congruent or irrelevant behaviors. However, even in the data of Rothbart et al., it is only when one examines the total number of behaviors recalled that one finds "better" recall for congruent than incongruent behaviors; that is, their data also show that a greater *proportion* of incongruent than congruent behaviors is typically recalled. Experiment 1 extends this finding to conditions in which there is an equal set size for congruent and incongruent items and conditions in which the set size for incongruent items is actually greater than that for congruent items.

A consistent pattern of results therefore emerges, with subjects tending to recall (but not necessarily recognize) a reliably greater proportion of behaviors that are incongruent than congruent with a prior expectancy. The results of Experiment 1 are also consistent in demonstrating that this difference is accentuated by any factor that induces the subject to integrate discrepant pieces of information into a coherent impression.

It is also interesting to note that the proportion of various types of items recalled did not change over successive blocks of presentation, even when the set size of incongruent items was greater than that of congruent items. Future research will need to be directed toward identifying those conditions under which the effect of such an expectancy begins to break down.

Theoretical Implications

The four experiments reported in the present paper all examined associative storage and retrieval models of person memory. Although the Hastie model has been widely investigated in the person memory literature and it was used to generate many of the predictions examined in the present paper, it should be noted that alternative models are available. For example, while Hastie emphasized the importance of encoding operations, the findings are not obviously inconsistent with Raaijmakers and Shiffrin's (1980, 1981) Search of Associative Memory (SAM) model, which places much more conceptual weight on cue-dependent search and retrieval processes. However, it would appear that any associative model that attempts to account for the present results will need to incorporate several key characteristics. For example, behavioral information would need to be stored in relation to superordinate cues that are included in the initial expectancy. Any alternative account would also need to allow for the formation of interepisode associative links. Further, it would appear that the number or strength of these associations would in some way need to be influenced by the initial orienting task of the subject. Finally, some mechanism would need to be included to account for the fact that the accessibility of congruent and incongruent items over time appears to decrease at a constant rate. This could be accomplished by postulating a constant decrease in strength of all of the associative links, a change in the strength of specific links as a function of successive retrieval attempts, a sampling procedure that makes it more difficult to activate appropriate items over time (perhaps due to the cues that are generated), or a variety of other mechanisms that can affect retrieval probabilities. Raaijmakers and Shiffrin (1980, 1981) demonstrated how powerful a model can be that simultaneously incorporates several of these mechanisms.

The most important contribution of Hastie's analysis has been to integrate concerns typically associated with levels of processing into the formal structural network model of HAM. Unlike Anderson and Bower's model, which treats each piece of propositional knowledge independently, Hastie assumed that behavioral episodes that are incongruent with a prior expectancy are difficult to encode and remain in working memory for relatively long periods of time. During this time, they are likely to be considered in relation to other behavioral information known about the target. Any time this occurs, an interepisode associative path will be established between the two items. In conjunction with the retrieval process assumed to underlie free recall, this model easily accounts for the fact that a greater proportion of incongruent than congruent information is recalled. While this modification of HAM is post hoc, it has also led to several additional predictions that are very provocative theoretically. Particularly noteworthy are the data concerning the conditional probabilities of recall in Experiment 1, because they discount any simple rehearsal explanation for why incongruent items might be better recalled than congruent items.

Hastie assumed that incongruent items are held in working memory much longer than congruent items. This suggests that whereas incongruent items can form associative paths with any other type of item, the only paths emanating from congruent items will be associated with incongruent ones. Consistent with this assumption is the finding that nearly 80% of the congruent items recalled were directly followed by the recall of an incongruent item. In contrast, the probability of a congruent item being recalled given that an incongruent item was just previously recalled was only 32%.

Another interesting finding in the present set of data is the fact that the probability of consecutively recalling two items of the same type is only about what one would expect on the basis of chance. This largely explains why no significant degrees of category (type of item) clustering have been found with the present paradigm. It is clear, however, that there is a systematic nature to the order in which items are recalled. The Hastie model seems capable of accounting for the order of output data far better than any competing theoretical framework.

The dramatic difference between recall and recognition is also very important conceptually. The generation–recognition theory continues to be a parsimonious and highly regarded approach to the problem (see, e.g., recent reviews by Brown, 1976; Eysenck, 1977; Watkins & Gardiner, 1979), and it presents a very heuristic framework for interpreting the results of Experiment 1. Since the retrieval process underlying free recall is assumed to traverse the associative paths laid down in the network, any variable that affects the nature of these associations should have an effect on recall. It was hypothesized that the encoding of an incongruent item would form more interepisode associative paths than the encoding of a congruent item, and the establishment of such paths would occur more often when subjects were attempting to form a coherent impression of the target and when the target was a psychologically meaningful unit. All three of these variables had a significant effect on recall. However, when the retrieval stage was bypassed with a recognition task, none of them had a significant influence.

Each of the three variables noted above theoretically affects the subject's tendency to organize and integrate the various pieces of information. Schwartz and Humphreys (1974) recently conducted a study in the area of verbal learning that is conceptually and procedurally similar to the fourth experiment presented here. A list of items was presented sequentially. Subjects were either given standard memory set instructions or required to rehearse aloud only the item then being presented, thus reducing the opportunity to organize the material by forming associative links. The latter condition had no effect on recognition performance but led to substantially reduced levels of recall.

Experiments 2, 3, and 4 provided strong support for other predictions of the associative model as well. Experiment 2 demonstrated that, holding the number of congruent behaviors constant, as more *incongruent* pieces of information are learned about a target, a greater proportion of these congruent behaviors will be recalled. That is, although there is still a greater proportion of incongruent than congruent behaviors recalled, the proportion of congruent behaviors recalled increases as the number of incongruent behaviors in the list increases. Moreover, there is a significant linear relationship between the two. Theoretically, more incongruent behaviors will lead to a greater number of interepisode associative linkages in the network. Since many of these will be attached to congruent episodes, the proportion of congruent behaviors recalled will increase as more and more incongruent behaviors are received. Note, however, that congruent behaviors do not typically establish interepisode paths during encoding. Thus, one would not expect that, all else being equal, adding a number of congruent behaviors to the list would increase the proportion of incongruent behaviors recalled; this is exactly what was found in Experiment 3. Finally, Experiment 4 demonstrated that when subjects are forced to engage in an irrelevant task, subsequent recall of incongruent items systematically decreases as the processing demands of the irrelevant task increase. Theoretically, this decrement is due to the subject's inability to form interepisode associative linkages while simultaneously performing the irrelevant task. It should be noted that the results of Experiments 2, 3 and 4 are all inconsistent with a simple rehearsal explanation for why recall of incongruent items tends to be greater than that of congruent items.

Finally, although the present paradigm bears a strong resemblance to that used in traditional list-learning experiments, Experiment 1 and others in the general area of person memory (see Hamilton et al., 1980) have demonstrated that incidental learning conditions often lead to greater organizational activity on the part of subjects than intentional learning conditions. In particular, impression formation instructions appear to induce high levels of organization in subjects. Not only do they consistently lead to greater levels of recall than memory set instructions, but they lead to particularly high levels of recall for items incongruent with an initial expectancy. Virtually all of the available evidence suggests that the reason for this is that these items are much more difficult to integrate into a coherent impression of the person or group involved (for a fuller discussion of this point, see Wyer & Srull, 1980).

The experiments reported in the present article have important implications for a number of theoretical issues in memory and cognition. In particular, they raise a number of issues related to Anderson and Bower's (1973) HAM model and Craik and Lockhart's (1972) conception of levels of processing as alternative approaches to the study of person memory.

The most serious deficiency in extending the original HAM model into the area of person memory is that it proposes that each item is encoded independently of the rest. The experiments reported demonstrate a number of ways in which such a model fails (see also Smith et al., 1978). First, the original HAM model would predict that the proportion of incongruent and congruent items recalled would be about the same at any given delay interval. The results of the present experiments, along with those reported by Hastie (1980; Hastie & Kumar, 1979), demonstrate that this simply is not the case. Second, the original HAM model also postulates a random sequential search process. However, since it does not postulate the formation of any interepisode associative paths, the probability of any given type of item being recalled should be independent of the type of item previously recalled. However, the results of Experiment 1 demonstrate that the probability of a given type of item being recalled is strongly related to the type of item previously recalled. Finally, the original HAM model cannot explain why increasing the number of incongruent items in a list will lead to greater levels of recall for congruent items or why having the subject engage in an irrelevant task will have a *differential* effect on the types of items subsequently recalled. As discussed previously, Hastie's (1980) integration of certain levels of processing considerations into a general associative storage and retrieval model is quite successful in accounting for all of these empirical findings.

It is also the case, however, that the levels of processing framework by itself cannot account for the results of the present experiments. For example, Eysenck (1978a, 1978b) cogently criticized this approach for paying far too little attention to retrieval processes, and it has been argued (see Lockhart, Craik, & Jacoby, 1976) that the "depth" to which an item is encoded should affect both recall and recognition. This is clearly inconsistent with the results obtained in the present experiments. Nevertheless, the active consideration given to encoding processes seems particularly important to the study of person memory, and several authors have recently alluded to how these processes will be affected by a prior expectancy. For example, Lockhart et al. (1976) wrote, "Thus, paradoxically, when expectancy facilitates initial encoding, it reduces the richness and later effectiveness of the resulting memory trace" (p. 96). This summary statement is an excellent description of the results of all four experiments reported here. Lockhart et al. went on to say, "Expectancy or prior experience in a situation may also reduce the number of cognitive operations required to arrive at an encoding … . If an item is to be remembered, it must be placed in relationship with other events so that a structure involving the item is constructed" (p. 97). The shortcoming of this approach is that it says very little about what such a structure would look like or how the postulation of various retrieval processes might differentially affect recall and recognition. The complex array of data already reported in the person memory literature suggests that a richly interconnected associative network may be the best immediate approach to this problem.

At least for an initial account of person memory, Hastie (1980) has done an impressive job of integrating concerns typically addressed under levels of processing into a basic associative storage and retrieval model. Although alternative models are certainly available, by integrating these two approaches into a unitary theoretical framework, Hastie has presented at least one relatively formal model of person memory that should continue to generate provocative questions in the years ahead. Several of the most fundamental questions that need to be addressed are outlined in the following section.

Several Remaining Issues

The associative model discussed in the present paper accounts for a wide range of results that have thus far been reported. However, several critical issues need to be addressed as the model is further developed.

One conceptual ambiguity in the present model concerns the role of irrelevant items. Most of the studies reported thus far have used irrelevant items to control for overall list length effect. The major comparisons are therefore between items that are congruent and items that are incongruent with a prior expectancy. This was true in the studies reported here, as well as well as those reported by Hastie (1980; Hastie & Kumar, 1979). At the conceptual level, however, these items have been given very little attention. It is not clear how such items should be represented in the network, and it is not clear how the Hastie model *at present* can account for the systematic tendency of subjects to recall fewer irrelevant than congruent items. That is, the encoding operations associated with irrelevant items have not been articulated to any great extent. On the other hand, it may be possible to account for such effects in terms of variables that affect search and retrieval operations. Many of these have been discussed by Raaijmakers and Shiffrin (1980, 1981), but no experiments designed to help discriminate between these approaches have thus far been reported.

Perhaps an even more basic issue concerns exactly what should be considered an "irrelevant" item. Virtually all of the existing studies (including those reported here) have used personality trait information to create the initial expectancy. Conceptually, it would seem that there are at least two distinct types of irrelevant items within this framework. First, some behavioral items will simply be irrelevant to the trait dimension under consideration. For example, "stopping to buy a doughnut on his way to the office" is probably irrelevant to the personality trait of "friendliness." On the other hand, "said goodbye to his secretary as he left the office" may be considered a behavior that is relevant to the trait dimension of "friendliness" but so common that it is irrelevant to discriminating between those who are friendly and those who are not. Thus, it could not be considered consistent *or* inconsistent with the initial expectancy. Although some consideration has been given to such distinctions (see Hastie, 1981), it will be difficult to determine the importance of such variables until the same types of scaling procedures that have been used with individual words are also conducted on the type of sentences typically used in person memory experiments. Again, initial attempts at this have been reported (Rothbart, Note 2) but much more needs to be done.

A detailed examination of these questions is also necessary for the present body of research to make contact with related investigations in cognitive psychology. For example, Graesser and his colleagues (Graesser, Gordon, & Sawyer, 1979; Graesser, Woll, Kowalski, & Smith, 1980; Woll & Graesser, Note 3) conducted a series of investigations on recognition memory for scripted activities. They consistently found that memory discrimination, as measured by d', is greater for atypical than typical behaviors. As Woll and Graesser (Note 3) pointed out, however, their "atypical" actions were simply irrelevant to (as opposed to inconsistent with) the particular script being investigated. Since both of these lines of research are concerned with memory for behaviors that violate a prior expectancy, it is important to keep these distinctions in mind.

It is also interesting to note that Bower, Black, and Turner (1979) investigated recall of scripted activities and found results perfectly analogous to those reported here. In their Experiment 7, they specifically constructed stories that contained events congruent with, irrelevant to, or incongruent with the generalized expectancy or script. Congruent events were routine actions that would be expected in the normal enactment of a script (e.g., examining the menu in a restaurant). Incongruent events were what Schank and Abelson (1977) call "obstacles" or actions that would be unexpected in the normal enactment of a script (e.g., the waiter bringing the wrong food to the table). Finally, irrelevant events were actions "unrelated" to the general script. These actions are not specifically expected but are also not unexpected in the normal enactment of a script (e.g., a woman being seated at another table). Thus, all three types of critical information were represented in the stories. Bower et al. found that recall was reliably greater for incongruent than congruent actions, and both of these were greater than recall for irrelevant actions. Thus very similar results have been found in quite different paradigms.

A final issue that deserves careful consideration in future research concerns whether the types of associations described in the Hastie model, or similar associative storage and retrieval models, are symmetrical or asymmetrical in strength. This includes associations between individual items and associations between single items and the superordinate cues. This question has also been raised with respect to other accounts of person memory (Wyer & Carlston, 1979). Although it may appear parsimonious to assume symmetric relations, and the issues involved in addressing this type of question can become very complicated (Asch & Ebenholtz, 1962), results indicating that asymmetric associations can be formed (at least in a paired-associate task) have been reported (Wollen, 1968). Presumably the Hastie model will need to be developed to the point where quantitative predictions can be made before this issue can be satisfactorily addressed.

In any case, it is clear that future investigators of person memory can (and should) borrow heavily from the techniques and theories developed in general cognitive psychology. It is equally clear, however, that work in experimental psychology can benefit substantially by considering some of the issues that have thus far been raised in social cognition. There is certainly nothing inherently different about the cognitive processes examined in the study of person memory and those examined in verbal learning of general cognitive psychology. For this reason, it is hoped that future theoretical work in these complementary areas will become more closely aligned. Such a closer association should be propaedeutic to gaining further insights into the full complexities of the human cognitive system and its operation in everyday social life.

REFERENCE NOTES

1. Cohen, C. E. Cognitive basis of stereotyping. Paper presented at the American Psychological Association Meeting, San Francisco, September 1977.
2. Rothbart, M. Desirability and frequency ratings of 208 behavior statements. Unpublished manuscript, University of Oregon, 1975.
3. Woll, S. B., & Graesser, A. C. Memory discrimination for information typical or atypical of person schemata. Unpublished manuscript, California State University at Fullerton, 1981.

REFERENCES

Anderson, J. R. FRAN: A simulation model of free recall. In G. H. Bower (Ed.), The psychology of learning and motivation (Vol. 5). New York: Academic Press, 1972.

Anderson, J. R. Language, memory, and thought. Hillsdale, N.J.: Erlbaum, 1976.

Anderson, J. R., & Bower, G. H. Recognition and retrieval processes in free recall. Psychological Review, 1972, 79, 97–123.

Anderson, J. R., & Bower, G. H. Human associative memory. Washington, D.C.: Winston, 1973.

Anderson, J. R., & Bower, G. H. A propositional theory of recognition memory. Memory & Cognition, 1974, 2, 406–412.

Asch, S., & Ebenholtz, S. M. The principle of associative symmetry. Proceedings of the American Philosophical Society, 1962, 106, 135–163.

Bahrick, H. P. Measurement of memory by prompted recall. Journal of Experimental Psychology, 1969, 97, 213–219.

Bahrick, H. P. Two-phase model for prompted recall. Psychological Review, 1970, 77, 215–222.

Belleza, P. S., & Cheney, T. L. Isolation effect in immediate and delayed recall. Journal of Experimental Psychology, 1973, 99, 55–60.

Bobrow, D. G., & Norman, D. A. Some principles of memory schemata. In D. G. Bobrow & A. Collins (Eds.), Representation and understanding: Studies in cognitive science. New York: Academic Press, 1975.

Bousfield, A. K., & Bousfield, W. A. Measurement of clustering and of sequential constancies in repeated free recall. Psychological Reports, 1966, 19, 935–942.

Bower, G. H., Black, J. B., & Turner, T. J. Scripts in memory for text. Cognitive Psychology, 1979, 11, 177–220.

Brown, J. An analysis of recognition and recall and problems in their comparison. In J. Brown (Ed.), Recall and recognition. London: Wiley, 1976.

Cantor, N., & Mischel, W. Traits as prototypes: Effects on recognition memory. *Journal of Personality and Social Psychology*, 1977, *35*, 38–48.

Cohen, C. E. Person categories and social perception: Testing some boundaries of the processing effects of prior knowledge. *Journal of Personality and Social Psychology*, 1981, *40*, 441–452.

Craik, F. I. M., & Lockhart, R. S. Levels of processing: A framework for memory research. *Journal of Verbal Learning and Verbal Behavior*, 1972, *11*, 671–684.

Eysenck, M. W. *Human memory: Theory, research, and individual differences*. Oxford, England: Pergamon Press, 1977.

Eysenck, M. W. Levels of processing: A critique. *British Journal of Psychology*, 1978, *68*, 157–169. (a)

Eysenck, M. W. Levels of processing: A reply to Lockhart and Craik. *British Journal of Psychology*, 1978, *69*, 177–178. (b)

Gleitman, H., & Gillett, E. The effect of intention upon learning. *Journal of General Psychology*, 1957, *57*, 137–149.

Graesser, A. C., Gordon, S. E., & Sawyer, J. D. Recognition memory for typical and atypical actions in scripted activities: Tests of a script pointer + tag hypothesis. *Journal of Verbal Learning and Verbal Behavior*, 1979, *18*, 319–332.

Graesser, A. C., Woll, S. B., Kowalski, D. J., & Smith, D. A. Memory for typical and atypical actions in scripted activities. *Journal of Experimental Psychology: Human Learning and Memory*, 1980, *6*, 503–515.

Green, R. T. Surprise as a factor in the von Restorff effect. *Journal of Experimental Psychology*, 1956, *52*, 340–344.

Hamilton, D. L., Katz, L. B., & Leirer, V. O. Organizational processes in impression formation. In R. Hastie et al. (Eds.), *Person memory: The cognitive basis of social perception*. Hillsdale, N.J.: Erlbaum, 1980.

Hastie, R. Memory for information which confirms or contradicts a general impression. In R. Hastie et al. (Eds.), *Person memory: The cognitive basis of social perception*. Hillsdale, N.J.: Erlbaum, 1980.

Hastie, R. Schematic principles in human memory. In E. T. Higgins, C. P. Herman, & M. P. Zanna (Eds.), *Social cognition: The Ontario symposium on personality and social psychology*. Hillsdale, N.J.: Erlbaum, 1981.

Hastie, R., & Kumar, P. A. Person memory: Personality traits as organizing principles in memory for behaviors. *Journal of Personality and Social Psychology*, 1979, *37*, 25–38.

Hyde, T. S., & Jenkins, J. J. Differential effects of incidental tasks on the organization of a list of highly associated words. *Journal of Experimental Psychology*, 1969, *82*, 472–482.

Hyde, T. S., & Jenkins, J. J. Recall of words as a function of semantic, graphic, and syntactic orienting tasks. *Journal of Verbal Learning and Verbal Behavior*, 1973, *12*, 471–480.

Keppel, G. *Design and analysis: A researcher's handbook*. Englewood Cliffs, N.J.: Prentice-Hall, 1973.

Kintsch, W. Models for free recall and recognition. In D. A. Norman (Ed.), *Models of human memory*. New York: Academic Press, 1970.

Koyanagi, K. Studies in incidental learning: I. Intention of learning and the isolation effect. *Japanese Journal of Psychology*, 1957, *27*, 270–278. (a)

Koyanagi, K. Studies in incidental learning: II. Intraserial interference. *Psychologica Folia*, 1957, *15*, 1–12. (b)

Lockhart, R. S., Craik, F. I. M., & Jacoby, L. Depth of processing, recognition, and recall, In J. Brown (Ed.), *Recall and recognition*. London: Wiley, 1976.

Mandler, G. Organization and memory. In K. W. Spence & J. A. Spence (Eds.), *The psychology of learning and motivation* (Vol. 1). New York: Academic Press, 1967.

McNicol, D. *A primer of signal detection theory*. London: Allen & Unwin, 1972.

Müller, G. E. Zur analyse der gedachtnistatigkeit und des vorstellungsuerlaufe. III. Teil. *Zeitschriftfuer Psychologie*, 1913, *8* (Supplement).

Murdock, B. B. The serial position effect of free recall. *Journal of Experimental Psychology*, 1962, *64*, 482–488.

Newman, E. B. Effect of crowding material on curves of forgetting. *American Journal of Psychology*, 1939, *52*, 601–609.

Norman, D. A., & Bobrow, D. G. On the role of active memory processes in perception and cognition. In C. N. Cofer (Ed.), *The structure of human memory*. San Francisco: Freeman, 1976.

Postman, L. Short-term memory and incidental learning. In A. W. Melton (Ed.), *Categories of human learning*. New York: Academic Press, 1964.

Postman, L., & Phillips, L. W. Studies in incidental learning: I. The effect of crowding and isolation. *Journal of Experimental Psychology*, 1954, *48*, 48–56.

Raaijmakers, J. G. W., & Shiffrin, R. M. SAM: A theory of probabilistic search of associative memory. In G. H. Bower (Ed.), *The psychology of learning and motivation* (Vol. 14). Academic Press, 1980.

Raaijmakers, J. G. W., & Shiffrin, R. M. Search of associative memory. *Psychological Review*, 1981, *88*, 93–134.

Reder, L. M., & Anderson, J. R. A partial resolution of the paradox of interference: The role of integrating knowledge. *Cognitive Psychology*, 1980, *12*, 447–472.

Roberts, W. A. Free recall of word lists varying in length and rate of presentation: A test of total-time hypotheses. *Journal of Experimental Psychology*, 1972, *92*, 365–372.

Roenker, D. L., Thompson, C. P., & Brown, S. C. Comparison of measures for the estimation of clustering in free recall. *Psychological Bulletin*, 1971, *76*, 45–48.

Ross, B. H., & Bower, G. H. Comparisons of models of associative recall. *Memory & Cognition*, 1981, *9*, 1–16.

Rothbart, M., Evans, M., & Fulero, S. Recall for confirming events: Memory processes and the maintenance of social stereotypes. *Journal of Experimental Social Psychology*, 1979, *15*, 343–355.

Saltzman, I. J., & Carterette, T. Incidental and intentional learning of isolated and crowded items. *American Journal of Psychology*, 1959, *72*, 230–235.

Saul, E. U., & Osgood, C. E. Perceptual organization of materials as a factor influencing ease of learning and degree of retention. *Journal of Experimental Psychology*, 1950, *40*, 372–379.

Schank, R. C., & Abelson, R. P. *Scripts, plans, goals, and understanding: An inquiry into human knowledge structures*. Hillsdale, N.J.: Erlbaum, 1977.

Schneider, D. J., Hastorf, A. H., & Ellsworth, P. C. *Person perception* (2nd ed.). Reading, Mass.: Addison-Wesley, 1979.

Schwartz, R. M., & Humphreys, M. S. Recognition and recall as a function of instructional manipulations of organization. *Journal of Experimental Psychology*, 1974, *102*, 517–519.

Smith, E. E., Adams, N., & Schorr, D. Fact retrieval and the paradox of interference. *Cognitive Psychology*, 1978, *10*, 438–464.

Snyder, M., & Uranowitz, S. W. Reconstructing the past: Some cognitive consequences of person perception. *Journal of Personality and Social Psychology*, 1978, *36*, 941–950.

Srull, T. K. *Person memory: The role of processing strategy, expectancy, and level of incongruity in the processing of interindividual and intraindividual behavioral variability*. Unpublished doctoral dissertation, University of Illinois, 1980.

Thorndyke, P. W., & Hayes-Roth, B. The use of schemata in the acquisition and transfer of knowledge. *Cognitive Psychology*, 1979, *11*, 82–106.

Underwood, G. (Ed.). *Strategies of information processing*. London: Academic Press, 1978.

von Restorff, H. Über die Wirkung von Bereichsbildungen in Spürenfeld. *Psychologisch Forschung*, 1933, *18*, 299–342.

Wallace, W. P. Review of the historical, empirical, and theoretical status of the von Restorff phenomenon. *Psychological Bulletin*, 1965, *63*, 410–424.

Watkins, M. J., & Gardiner, J. M. An appreciation of generate-recognize theory of recall. *Journal of Verbal Learning and Verbal Behavior*, 1979, *18*, 687–704.

Wollen, K. A. Effects of maximizing availability and minimizing rehearsal upon associative symmetry in two modalities. *Journal of Experimental Psychology*, 1968, *77*, 626–630.

Wyer, R. S., & Carlston, D. E. *Social cognition, inference, and attribution*. Hillsdale, N.J.: Erlbaum, 1979.

Wyer, R. S., & Srull, T. K. The processing of social stimulus information: A conceptual integration. In R. Hastie et al. (Eds.), *Person memory: The cognitive basis of social perception*. Hillsdale, N.J.: Erlbaum, 1980.

Received March 2, 1981 ■

The Relationship Between Memory and Judgment Depends on Whether the Judgment Task is Memory-Based or On-Line

Reid Hastie and Bernadette Park

Five alternative information processing models that relate memory for evidence to judgments based on the evidence are identified in the current social cognition literature: independent processing, availability, biased retrieval, biased encoding, and incongruity-biased encoding. A distinction between two types of judgment tasks, memory-based versus on-line, is introduced and is related to the five process models. In memory-based tasks where the availability model describes subjects' thinking, direct correlations between memory and judgment measures are obtained. In on-line tasks where any of the remaining four process models may apply, prediction of the memory–judgment relationship is equivocal but usually follows the independence model prediction of zero correlation.

There ought to be a relationship between memory and judgment. Our intuition tells us that we should be able to generate more arguments and information in support of a favored position than against it, that evaluations of people should be related to the amounts of good and bad information we have about them. When a person is able to remember many arguments against a belief, or to cite many good characteristics of an acquaintance, we

This research was supported by funds from the Trout Foundation. Nancy Pennington provided extensive and valuable advice at all stages of this research. Ebbe B. Ebbesen, David L. Hamilton, G. Daniel Lassiter, and Thomas M. Ostrom made helpful comments on the research plan and on the manuscript.

Correspondence concerning this article should be addressed to Reid Hastie, Psychology Department, Northwestern University, Evanston, Illinois 60201, or to Bernadette Park, Psychology Department, University of Colorado, Boulder, Colorado 80309.

are surprised if they endorse the belief or dislike the person. In support of intuitions like these, names have been given to the idea that memory and judgment have a simple direct relationship, including "availability," "dominance of the given," "salience effect," and so forth.

However, empirical studies of the relationship between memory and judgment with subject matter as diverse as social impressions, personal attitudes, attributions of causes for behavior, evaluations of legal culpability, and a variety of probability and frequency estimates have not revealed simple relations between memory and judgment. Some relationships have been found, but strong empirical relations are rare and results are often contradictory.

Some examples seem to support the expectation of a direct relationship between memory and judgment. Tversky and Kahneman (1973) demonstrated that many judgments of numerosity were directly correlated with the "ease with which instances or associations could be brought to mind" (p. 208). In an illustrative series of experiments, they showed that judgments of the frequency of words in English text were correlated with the ease of remembering the words. Beyth-Marom and Fischhoff (1977) provided more definite evidence on the strength of the memory–judgment relationship, and Gabrielcik and Fazio (1984) demonstrated that ease of retrieval exerts a causal (not just correlational) influence on the frequency estimates.

Similar demonstrations have been provided in research studying memory–judgment relationships for more complex naturally occurring events. Lichtenstein, Slovic, Fischhoff, Layman, and Combs (1978; Combs & Slovic, 1979) obtained large correlations between judged frequencies of deaths and the frequencies of reports of causes of death in newspaper articles. For these events, reporting rates were not correlated with actuarial frequencies, supporting the conclusion that newspaper reporting rates biased memory availability, which in turn influenced the frequency estimates. Another neat everyday example is provided by Ross and Sicoly (1979) in their research on the attribution of responsibility. They found simple, direct relationships in joint tasks such as home improvement projects, writing scientific papers, and competing in team sports between subjects' judgments of responsibility for themselves and others and the subjects' ability to remember relevant evidence. These examples imply a direct relationship between memory and judgment: the more a subject can remember and the more easily it comes to mind, the higher the estimates of frequency, probability, or responsibility.

However, there is another side to the literature on memory–judgment relationships. Although researchers almost invariably expect to find the direct relationships illustrated by the first set of examples, this has not always been the case. In a classic experiment by Anderson and Hubert (1963), subjects made likableness ratings of a hypothetical character on the basis of ensembles of trait adjectives. In some conditions of the experiment, subjects were also asked to recall the adjectives. Anderson and Hubert noted that when the recall data were summarized as serial position curves, a recency effect was obtained; however, the likableness rating data showed that early adjectives in the sequence had the greatest impact on subjects' final impressions, a primacy effect. Anderson and Hubert concluded that "the impression memory is distinct from the verbal memory for the adjectives" (p. 391).

Another frequently cited study of memory–judgment relationships is an experiment by Reyes, Thompson, and Bower (1980) in which subjects were asked to make judgments of the apparent guilt of a defendant briefly described in a drunken driving case. These experimenters manipulated information about the defendant's character and the memorability of items of evidence favoring defense or prosecution sides of the case. The authors did not find a relationship between memory and judgment at short delays; however, after a 48-hour delay a significant but low correlation (+.31) was obtained. The authors concluded that "such a low correlation suggests that judgments of apparent guilt were not made simply on the basis of the differential availability of the arguments" (p. 7).

Finally, there is a third relationship between memory and judgment that appears in some person impression formation tasks. Hastie and Kumar (1979; replicated by many others, most notably Srull, 1981) found that when subjects studied sentences describing the behavior of a hypothetical character while making judgments of the character's personality, behaviors that were incongruent with the final trait ratings were the best recalled on a subsequent memory test. This reversal of the commonly expected direct memory–judgment relationship has been explained as resulting from "special processing" accorded to the incongruent acts when they were attributed to a single character in the context of an impression formation task (Hastie, 1984). Empirical results suggest that this special processing involves the subject's effort to explain why the surprising, incongruent actions were performed by the character, a plausible subtask within the larger impression formation task.

The scope of the literature from which these examples were culled is large. We have identified more than 50 published experiments that report correlational or treatment effect findings relevant to the memory–judgment relationship in judgment tasks. The variety of judgment task domains included in these studies is remarkably diverse even within the social judgment area: impression formation involving traits, behaviors, likability, and ability judgments; occupation suitability judgments; attitude formation and change; judgments of historical events' antecedents and consequences; predictions of sports events; psychodiagnosis of clinical cases; causal attribution for individual behavior; statistical decision making; and deductive reasoning.

Theoretical Analysis

The contrast between our expectations that memory–judgment relationships should be direct and pervasive and the mixed results of research on the relationship is puzzling. We believe that a careful analysis of the cognitive processes that could produce or obscure a memory–judgment relationship can explain why the relationship appears or does not appear across experimental tasks. Several specific models for the perception, memory, and judgment processes that could produce correlations between memory and judgment measures have been presented by researchers studying social judgment. To resolve the enigma concerning when memory and judgment will be directly related, we need to clarify the alternate process models and identify the empirical conditions under which each model will apply.

Our theoretical analysis is nested in the context of an information processing approach to social cognition (Hastie & Carlston, 1980; Smith, 1984; Wyer & Srull, 1980). Briefly, we assume that when a person is presented with a judgment task, either in an experimental or natural situation, evidence information is processed by a judgment operator that performs its function to generate a conclusion on which a response is based. Traditionally, judgment researchers have described these operators as algebraic combination rules (e.g., Anderson, 1981; Edwards, 1968; Hammond, Stewart, Brehmer, & Steinmann, 1975), stochastic processes (e.g., Thomas & Hogue, 1976), or cognitive heuristics (e.g., Kelley, 1973; Tversky & Kahneman, 1974).

The judgment operator is limited by working-memory capacities constraining the complexity of elementary information processes that can be executed at any point in time. The same limits apply to the activation of memory representations and constrain the amount of evidence that can be input into the operator at any moment. Information processing researchers have identified many information formats and structures that might characterize the evidence that is input into the operator. They have also described many potential judgment operators that have been learned over a person's lifespan and are stored in long-term memory along with other cognitive skill procedures.

Five Information Processing Models

The current social cognition literature provides several examples of memory–judgment models. They can be separated into three classes according to the causal priority of memory or judgment processes: no priority-independence, memory causes judgment, and judgment causes memory. The most populated class comprises judgment-causes-memory models (biased retrieval, biased encoding, and incongruity-biased encoding), with one example each of an independence model (two-memory hypothesis) and a memory-causes-judgment model (availability-biased judgment). Note that the establishment of a direct or indirect correlation between memory

and judgment measures will not answer the question of whether memory has causal priority and causes judgment or the reverse, judgment causes memory. Furthermore, most research has not attempted to go beyond correlational analysis to resolve the ambiguity and establish causal relationships (Dellarosa & Bourne, 1984; and Gabrielcik & Fazio, 1984, are possibly the only exceptions). However, we will review the alternate theoretical models before we turn to the tough questions of empirical prediction and identifiability.

Independence

First, there is a basic model that postulates independence between judgment and memory processes, with no relationship expected between measures of memory and judgments. Norman Anderson (1981; Anderson & Hubert, 1963) has probably stated this position most clearly in his articles on the two-memory hypothesis in trait-adjective-based impression formation tasks:

> The judgment was based on a memory system different from the recall. ... As each adjective was received, the valuation operation extracted its implications for the task at hand. Further processing, especially the integration, was performed on these implications. The verbal material itself, no longer necessary, was transferred to a verbal memory or forgotten. (Anderson, 1981, pp. 95–96)

Thus, the valuation and integration operations involved in the execution of the judgment operator (usually summarized as an algebraic weighted averaging calculation) and the encoding of evidence information into long-term memory traces occur simultaneously and independently.

Availability

Second is the currently popular family of availability models which assume that memory availability causes judgment. The model has many precedents, but a seminal article by Tversky and Kahneman (1973) on the "availability heuristic" is its most common source. This model can be stated as follows: (a) During the time when evidence information is available in the external environment, the subject encodes that information in working memory. The judgment is not made at this time; usually the subject is unaware that the information is relevant to a future judgment. (b) At this time only one process operates that is relevant to the later memory–judgment relationship, namely, the further encoding of the evidence information by transforming it from working-memory codes into long-term memory traces. (c) At some later point in time when a judgment is called for (by the experimenter or "spontaneously"), the subject initiates the judgment process and retrieves information from long-term memory to use as input into a judgment operator. (d) A judgment is generated and reported to the experimenter at this point on the basis of evidence retrieved from long-term memory. (e) When the experimenter tests memory, the memory retrieval process is repeated (in essentially the same fashion as it occurred to generate input for the judgment operator) and the subject responds on the memory test. A relationship is produced between judgment and memory because any tendency that the subject may have to selectively remember information will be reflected both in biased input to the judgment operator and in the biased sample of information reported on the memory test.

The availability process model we have described is slightly more limited than the original Tversky and Kahneman (1973) heuristic. We exclude cases of perceptual availability and restrict the model to memory availability. We also exclude consideration of the availability of previously made inferences and judgments to focus on memory availability of relatively raw evidence information (see Lingle & Ostrom, 1979, for a different opinion). These more complex cases involving judgments based on the retrieval of other judgments and principles of perceptual salience are treated as derived from our five elementary models (see discussion below).

In the introduction to this article we gave examples of experiments by Tversky and Kahneman, Ross and Sicoly, Lichtenstein et al., and others who reported correlational results consistent with the availability heuristic memory-causes-judgment hypothesis. The memory-causes-judgment process model that we sketched above is surely correct in many applications. However, one point of the present article is that the availability heuristic model has been generalized to many tasks to which it does not apply. The evidence for overgeneralization appears in many articles in which a strong correlation between memory and judgment is not obtained, although the authors often persist with the availability heuristic interpretation in their discussion sections (e.g., Fiske, Kenny, & Taylor, 1982; Reyes et al., 1980).

Biased Retrieval
A second set of causal models assumes that judgment causes memory. The most common process model assumes that the judgment and memory-encoding processes go on at about the same time, independently, but the judgment, once completed, has the potential to bias retrieval. (a) Evidence information occurs in the environment and is encoded into a representation in working memory. (b) During its stay in working memory, the information serves as input for two independent processes; information is transformed and written into long-term memory traces and information is operated on to produce a unitary judgment conclusion. (c) When the experimenter asks the subject to report his or her judgment, the subject responds by considering the judgment conclusion that is stored in working memory or, if time has passed, in long-term memory. (d) When the experimenter tests the subject's memory for the evidence, the subject searches long-term memory to find trace information to respond on the memory test. At this point the subject's judgment plays a special role in that it biases access to traces stored in long-term memory or serves to edit the traces as they are output in the form of responses on the memory test. Thus, the judgment serves a selective function such that traces that "fit" the judgment are likelier to be found in the memory search or to be reported at the memory decision stage. Common names for this class of biases include "selective recall," "confirmatory memory," and "access-biased memory" (Leamer, 1974, 1975; Snyder & Uranowitz, 1978). The selective influence of the judgment during the retrieval phase of a memory task biases recall in a fashion that produces a correlation between the judgment (c) and the memory (d) responses.

There is some controversy in the literature about exactly what mechanism at retrieval produces the bias. Snyder and Uranowitz (1978) suggested that the search phase of retrieval was the locus of the bias, but subsequent studies by Bellezza and Bower (1981) and Clark and Woll (1981) favored an editing or response threshold mechanism to explain the relevant findings. For present purposes it will suffice to cite the Snyder and Uranowitz results as illustrating the basic retrieval bias phenomenon because either biased search or biased responses would fit the slightly more general model we are describing.

Biased Encoding
The fourth model assumes that judgment causes memory by biasing the encoding of evidence information. (a) Evidence information enters working memory and is used as input to the judgment operator in the formation of an initial judgment. (b) The initial judgment filters subsequent evidence information by guiding information search, encoding, and comprehension in such a way that information that fits the initial judgment (or that can be interpreted to fit) has an advantage in subsequent transfer to long-term memory. (c) When the experimenter asks the subject to report his or her

judgment, the subject responds by considering the judgment conclusion that is stored in working memory or, if time has passed, in long-term memory. (d) When the experimenter tests the subject's memory for the evidence, the subject searches long-term memory to find trace information to respond on the memory test. Because the evidence stored in long-term memory was filtered through the lens of the initial judgment, memory search will locate a biased sample of information reflecting the encoding bias.

Oddly enough, although this is the most frequently mentioned judgment–memory model, there is the least support for its applicability to social judgment phenomena (Alba & Hasher, 1983; Hastie, 1981). In our view, the social psychological finding that have been cited as examples of the model are more plausibly interpreted as biased-retrieval phenomena (see Taylor & Crocker, 1981, for a typical review). We must admit, however, that some examples are ambiguous and could represent either biased-encoding or biased-retrieval processes (e.g., Berman, Read, & Kenny, 1983).

Incongruity-biased Encoding
Finally, there is a model which assumes that judgment causes memory during the encoding stage, but the hypothesized memory–judgment relationship is the reverse of the common filtered encoding bias: we call this the incongruity-biased-encoding model. Hastie (1980, 1984) and Srull (1981) have given this model its clearest statement in interpreting the results of a series of studies of impression formation and recall tasks in which judgment-incongruent evidence was better recalled than judgment-congruent evidence (see also Woll & Graesser, 1982, for an interpretation that emphasizes incongruity-biased-encoding processes). (a) Evidence information is encoded in working memory and is input to a judgment operator where an initial judgment is formed. (b) Later incoming information is reviewed in the context of the initial judgment, and information that is incongruent (contradictory) is given special processing that enhances its memorability (e.g., it receives more associative links to other information in working memory, or it receives "special tags" that strongly attach it to a knowledge structure that organizes current events in long-term memory). (c) When the experimenter asks the subject to report a final judgment, the subject responds by considering the judgment that is stored in working memory or in long-term memory. (d) When the experimenter tests the subject's memory for the evidence, the subject searches long-term memory and is especially likely to find incongruent information.

The incongruent information advantage accrues from the rich network of associative links or the special tags that were attached to incongruent evidence during encoding. The most frequently cited examples of this model are found in the Hastie and Kumar (1979) and Srull (1981) person memory experiments cited above.

Given that information processing can plausibly follow one of several alternate models, the derivation of unequivocal predictions concerning the direction and strength of memory–judgment relationships, even at the gross correlational level, will not be a simple matter. Furthermore, it is likely that in many laboratory and naturally occurring judgment tasks more than one of the theoretical process models may apply to a single subject's performance (e.g., both encoding and retrieval biases may operate or both judgment-causes-memory and memory-causes-judgment processes may apply; Hastie, 1981). We should not be surprised that empirical results are mixed, given theoretical hypotheses to account for either direct or indirect relationships. We believe that careful thought about the task conditions that elicit each model can resolve some of the theoretical and empirical confusions.

On-Line Versus Memory-Based Judgment Tasks

The key distinction we would like to make concerns the source of inputs to the judgment operators. In essence our hypothesis is that in some tasks the judgment is necessarily memory based and the subject must perforce rely on the retrieval of relatively concrete evidence from long-term memory in order to render a judgment. Under these memory-based conditions, direct relationships between memory for the evidence and the judgment will be obtained. The direct relationships would be predicted from either of the availability process models that would apply to memory-based tasks. However, these conditions are rare, both in natural and laboratory environments, and ingenuity must be exercised to design tasks that will produce simple, direct memory-judgment relationships. The alternative, more common, class of on-line judgment tasks is associated with several process models that do not all yield predictions of a direct memory–judgment relationship.

In many judgment tasks, information for the operator follows a path from the stimulus environment external to the subject into working memory and directly to the judgment operator. We call tasks of this type on-line judgment tasks because the subject is forming the judgment "on-line" as evidence information is encountered.

For example, in most research on impression formation (Anderson & Hubert, 1963; Asch, 1946), adjectives are presented to subjects as the basis for an impression and they are used by the judgment operator to update the impression almost immediately after they are perceived by the subject.

A second example of an on-line, perception-based task is the abbreviated legal judgment task employed by Reyes et al. (1980), which was also described in the introduction to this article. Another well-known on-line judgment task was introduced by Ward Edwards (1968) and has been used to study judgments that can be characterized as dynamic probability revision judgments. One version of this judgment task involved subjects' inductive inferences concerning which of two bookbags was the source of a sample of poker chips. The bags differed in the composition of chips, of distinctive colors, that they contained, and a random sample of chips from the bag would be informative about which bag had been selected by the experimenter. Lopes (1982; see also Einhorn & Hogarth, 1985) proposed what we believe is the most plausible judgment operator for performance in this task. Her "anchoring and adjustment" model for opinion revision is a prototype of an on-line judgment procedure. In all of these cases, our assumption is that subjects making the judgment revise, on-line, as items of evidence are encountered. Furthermore, the evidence items are used directly, with few intervening inferences, as inputs into the judgment operator.

Our review of the five theoretical processing models implies that it will not be possible to unequivocally predict the relationship that will be obtained between memory and judgment measures when the judgment is made on-line. It should be clear that four of the five models could apply; thus, direct, indirect, or no relationship might be observed. Because previous research has not been sensitive to the possible variety of process models and relationships that might apply in on-line judgment tasks, it is difficult to definitely identify the appropriate process model in most experiments.

The judgment procedure can take a different, memory-based course, with the input to the operator coming from long-term memory into working memory rather than directly from the external environment. The clearest examples of this condition in the judgment literature appear in the Tversky and Kahneman (1973) demonstrations of availability effects. For example, when subjects were asked to estimate the frequency of occurrence of words with certain characteristics (e.g., k as the first letter), they had to rely on information that had been stored in long-term memory to make estimates of frequencies. In addition, in the introduction to the present article we described research on risk judgments by Lichtenstein et al. (1978) and responsibility judgments by Ross and Sicoly (1979) in which subjects appeared to rely on their ability to retrieve instances that were directly relevant to a judgment from long-term memory.

If our theoretical review is valid, prediction of the memory–judgment relationship is possible in memory-based tasks. Only the availability processing model is applicable, and it predicts that there will be a direct relationship between memory and judgment measures.

The on-line versus memory-based distinction has many precedents in the social cognition literature. Two series of experiments, one directed by Lingle (Lingle, Dukerich, & Ostrom, 1983; Lingle, Geva, Ostrom, Lieppe, & Baumgardner, 1979; Lingle & Ostrom, 1979) and one by Carlston (1980) simultaneously introduced the notion of memory-based judgments to the social literature. These authors studied the case in which a subject made an initial judgment and then retrieved the first judgment from memory to serve as the basis for a second judgment. Perhaps McArthur (1980) most clearly distinguished between direct, perception-based judgment and indirect, recall-mediated judgment in the same terms as our distinction between perception and memory sources of input (see also Taylor & Thompson, 1982). Finally, Sherman and his colleagues (Sherman, Zehner, Johnson, & Hirt, 1983) and Lichtenstein and Srull (1985) have also reached the conclusion that direct memory–judgment relationships are likeliest to be found in memory-based tasks.

Why is the on-line versus memory-based task difference the key to understanding the mixed results from empirical research on the memory–judgment relationship? If we can arrange conditions to insure that a subject makes a memory-based judgment, the memory–judgment relationship should fit the availability process model, which predicts a direct relationship between evidence memorability and the judgment conclusion. However, if the judgment task is on-line, four of the five models may apply. Therefore the memory–judgment relationship can be either direct, indirect, or null, and unequivocal prediction is not possible.

Because so many conditions are likely to instigate perception-based, on-line judgments, the difficult question for experimenters on the memory–judgment relationship is how to produce memory-based judgments. Memory-based judgments are usually more effortful than on-line judgments, and people realize that memory processes are less reliable than the perceptual processes involved in on-line judgments. Hence, subjects make on-line judgments when they believe that a judgment is likely to be required at a later point in time.

What are the conditions that will produce memory-based judgments? Probably the most reliable method to produce memory-based judgments is to surprise subjects with a novel judgment that is unlikely to be preceded by a relevant on-line judgment. Everyday examples of memory-based "surprise judgments" abound. A university professor returns from a professional meeting and learns that her department has a position open. Relatively effortful memory-based judgments are made of prospective candidates who had been encountered at the meeting. Similarly, a student might discover that he is looking for a roommate and then review acquaintances on the basis of memory to make preliminary judgments of compatibility. In these examples it is obvious that if the judgments had been anticipated before the evidence was encountered, the judgments would have been on-line.

On-Line Spontaneous Judgments

Normally people make many judgments spontaneously, without waiting for an instruction from one of life's experimenters. We often make spontaneous inferences about other people, particularly in the first encounter situations so frequently simulated in laboratory and field research on impression formation, stereotyping, attribution, moral evaluation, and persuasion. Essentially we assume that most judgments studied by social psychologists are perception-based, on-line processes. Even the reader who believes that people are mindless drones in most natural social interactions (Langer, Blank, & Chanowitz, 1978) will admit that psychology experiments on social judgment are an exception to the norm of mental inactivity. In these experiments judgments of interest to the experimenter are almost always being made on-line by subjects because of the nature of the situation (e.g., "This is a hypothetical acquaintance situation"; "We are interested in your first impressions"; "Suppose that you are a personnel officer"); the task (e.g., "You will make judgments of the likability of 12 individuals"); or specific instructions (e.g., "Attempt to evaluate the relative degrees of responsibility … ").

Recently social psychologists have conducted research that identifies some of the major types of social judgments that will tend to be made spontaneously, on-line, "in the absence of an investigator's instructions" (Winter & Uleman, 1984, p. 237). In accord with our above assumption, trait (Winter & Uleman, 1984) and causal (Weiner, 1985) inferences are likely to be made

spontaneously. Furthermore, several additional classes of factors have been found to elicit spontaneous social judgments.

First are a set of individual difference factors that are frequently referred to as "schematicism" or "chronicity" in the social psychology literature. For example, Markus (1977) demonstrated that people exhibit differential tendencies to make judgments of other people along certain dimensions or with reference to certain attributes. Some people appear to be constantly concerned with the masculinity–femininity of others, some people with the dependence–independence of others, some people with the intelligence of others, and so forth. These individual differences lead subjects to spontaneously make inferences about almost everybody they meet, although the specific dimensions will differ across subjects (see also Bargh, 1982; Higgins, King, & Mavin, 1982).

Second, Hastie (1980, 1984) has speculated that unexpected events will tend to elicit certain types of social judgments, particularly causal attribution judgments. Third, it seems that other stimulus conditions can also invoke spontaneous judgments: stimulus properties that are strikingly and distinctively associated with certain social categories or activities. For example, it is difficult to look at Arnold Schwarzenegger without making a judgment of his athletic prowess. Fourth, there is considerable speculation about the relationships between social goals (e.g., to form a clear impression of another person, to induce another to like oneself, to persuade another to comply with one's desires, to inform another about one's [self-conceived] identity, etc.) and judgment. Weiner (1985) concluded that a goal of "mastery" is the primary instigating condition for causal attribution judgments. Similarly, Jones and Pittman (1982) hypothesized that many types of judgments would be made to facilitate "strategic self presentation" in the service of a motive to exert power over others. More specific social goals have been identified by other theorists (e.g., Hamilton, Katz, & Leirer, 1980; Hoffman, Mischel, & Mazze, 1981; Swann, 1984), but little empirical research on the goal–judgment link has been conducted.

In fact, there is a further complication: even when subjects have not spontaneously made the judgment requested by an experimenter, they seem reluctant to consult long-term memory for evidence on which to base a novel judgment. Rather, they appear to prefer to make a new judgment on the basis of earlier judgments and inferences without retrieving specific evidence from memory (Lingle, Dukerich, & Ostrom, 1983; Lingle & Ostrom, 1979). Thus, true memory-based judgments may be rare because so many judgments are made on-line (spontaneously) and because when a new judgment must be made in the absence of perceptually available evidence, subjects rely on previous judgments rather than remembered evidence.

To summarize, we started with the empirical enigma of the rarity of direct memory–judgment relationships in the results of experiments designed to obtain them. Five models for the information processes that might underlie memory–judgment relationships were abstracted from the social cognition literature: the two-memory independence hypothesis, availability, retrieval bias, encoding bias, and incongruity-biased encoding. The independence model predicts no correlation between memory and judgment measures, the incongruity-biased-encoding model predicts a negative correlation, and the remaining models predict a positive correlation. A distinction was introduced between on-line and memory-based judgment tasks, and we hypothesized that the availability model was the only candidate to apply in memory-based tasks. However, most laboratory and real-world judgments probably occur under on-line task conditions where there is uncertainty about which of the remaining four process models apply, and thus the memory–judgment relationship is equivocal.

The bottom line of our analysis is that to guarantee a direct relationship between memory and judgment measures, we must study memory-based judgment tasks that occur (a) when no previous relevant judgment has been made and (b) when the subject is motivated to use evidence retrieved from memory as input at the time of judgment. In the next section we will summarize the results of four experiments that vary task conditions to produce the predicted direct relationship between memory and judgment.

Empirical Research

The most convincing argument we can make in support of our conceptual analysis is to conduct research showing that empirical phenomena fit our predictions. Results from four experiments that investigated the memory–judgment relationship are summarized in Table 24.1.[1] In each experiment, task conditions were arranged to force subjects to adopt a memory-based judgment strategy, where we would predict substantial

correlations between memory and judgment measures. In the last three experiments we added task conditions that would either encourage on-line judgment strategies or would allow subjects to make the final judgment based on a previous spontaneous judgment retrieved from memory. In these conditions we did not predict correlations between memory and judgment. We will briefly sketch the methods and results from each experiment.

In Experiment 1 subjects were asked to make a judgment of a man's suitability for a job as a computer programmer after hearing a 5-min conversation between two men. Half of the subjects were told of the judgment before hearing the conversation (on-line task condition), and half learned of the judgment only after the conversation (memory-based task condition). Pretesting assured us that the job suitability judgment would not be made spontaneously by subjects in the memory-based task. After the tape-recorded conversation, all subjects made the job suitability judgment (on a 10-point rating scale) and recalled as much information from the conversation as they could. Order of the rating and recall tasks was varied, but it did not affect the results. Experimental instructions, identical except for timing in on-line and memory-based conditions, stressed accuracy in judgment and completeness of recall to counter any tendencies that subjects might have to follow an unspoken experimental demand for agreement between recall and judgment.

Several indices of the strength of recall of items favoring or opposing the job candidate were calculated, and all supported the same conclusions. The measure we will report is a ratio (calculated for each subject) of the number of items recalled favoring suitability divided by the number of items recalled favoring and opposing suitability. A ratio of .50 corresponds to recall of an equal number of items favoring and opposing, greater than .50 indicates more favoring items recalled, and less than .50 indicates more opposing items recalled. A similar ratio was calculated on the basis of only the first five items recalled, on the assumption that in a memory-based judgment process, primacy in retrieval would determine item impact on the judgment (i.e., the subject would probably not recall more than five items before rendering one of our experimental judgments, and the earliest items retrieved would have the greatest impact on the judgment).

The measures of the relationship between memory and judgment reported in Table 24.1 are simple correlation coefficients calculated across subjects in each judgment condition (on-line vs. memory-based) between the subjects' recall ratios and judgments of job suitability.

---

[1] A detailed report, which has been submitted for publications, is available from the authors.

TABLE 24.1. Correlations Between Memory and Judgment Measures From Four Experiments

	Task							
	Total Recall				First Five Recall			
	On-line		Memory		On-line		Memory	
Judgment	*r*	*n*	*r*	*n*	*r*	*n*	*r*	*n*
Experiment 1								
Job suitability	−.14	35	.46	33	.14	35	.42	33
Experiment 2								
Job suitability (nonspontaneous)	.24	20	.39	23	.21	20	.44	23
Gender (spontaneous)	.37	20	.20	22	.26	20	.47	22
Experiment 3								
Exercise (nonspontaneous)	.09	64	.56	65				
Sociability (spontaneous)	.11	65	−.09	64				
Experiment 4								
Intelligence	.15	53	.67	39				
Friendliness	.29	53	.73	41				
Likability	.10	53	.56	43				

In all cases where a relationship was discernible, the function relating judgment and recall measures appeared to be linear, based on an inspection of the residuals from a fitted line. Our prediction was confirmed: the correlations between memory and judgment measures are substantial in the memory-based task (+.46 and +.42, $ps < .05$) but not in the on-line task (−.14 and +.14, *ns*).

Experiment 2 provides a replication of these results for the same job suitability judgment but with new evidence items presented in a written format. A second judgment task was included in the Experiment 2 design, with subjects judging the gender of a respondent interviewed in a national survey of leisure time activities. Subjects in the gender judgment condition were either told before reading the written interview that their task would be to infer the gender of the respondent (on-line), or they were given a general "form an impression" instruction before and the gender judgment instruction only after reading the interview (memory). A single written interview containing items relevant to the job judgment (favoring or opposing) and items relevant to the gender judgment (implying the respondent was male or female) was read by all subjects. Our hypothesis was that the on-line versus memory-based task differences obtained in Experiment 1 would be replicated in the job judgments of Experiment 2. However, the gender judgment would be made spontaneously by all

subjects whether or not they received the experimenter's instruction before reading the interview. Thus, we would not predict a substantial correlation between recall ratio and judgment measures in either on-line or memory-based tasks for the gender judgment.

The results from Experiment 1 are replicated in the job judgment condition of Experiment 2 (*r*s of .39 and .44, $ps < .05$, for memory-based judgments; *r*s of .24 and .21, *ns*, for on-line judgments). Results for the gender judgment are not exactly in line with our predictions, although they do not strictly contradict our hypothesis. Essentially there is no clear difference between on-line and memory-based tasks in the strength of the memory–judgment correlations. The total recall ratio analysis suggests that the relationship in the on-line condition is stronger (.37 vs. .20), whereas the first five recall ratio yields the reverse order (.26 vs. .47). However, although our theoretical analysis left us uncertain about what, if any, relationship to expect in spontaneous conditions, we were surprised to obtain substantial recall ratio–judgment correlations.

Experiment 3 shifts to a new content domain and to judgments of numerosity rather than suitability or category membership. Subjects listened to a tape-recorded monologue attributed to another undergraduate describing his activities during the past week. Two judgment conditions were used: (a) one selected to be spontaneous, a judgment of the frequency with which the speaker interacted with women (sociability and gender were the judgments most commonly cited as spontaneous by pretest subjects) and (b) one selected to be nonspontaneous, a judgment of the frequency with which the speaker engaged in cardiovascular exercise (none of the pretest subjects cited this type of judgment as occurring spontaneously). As before, half of the subjects were given instructions for the judgment task before the tape (on-line) and half only after the tape (memory). In this experiment every subject received one judgment before the tape and both after, so that each subject provided data for one on-line task (sociability or exercise) and one memory-based task (exercise or sociability). Note that because we have identified the sociability judgment as spontaneous, we do not expect to obtain differences between on-line and memory-based subjects for this judgment.

The results from Experiment 3 confirm our predictions for the exercise judgment; a relationship between memory and judgment measures was observed in the memory-based but not in the on-line task conditions (rs of .56, $p < .05$, and .09, ns). The results for the sociability judgment were also in line with our prediction; no relationship between memory and judgment measures in either memory-based or on-line tasks (rs of +.11 and −.09, both ns).

Experiment 4 provides new materials, judgment tasks, and a new operationalization of the on-line versus memory-based task distinction. Subjects listened to a tape-recorded list of 30 sentences describing a person engaged in everyday actions that had implications for the person's intelligence and friendliness (see Hastie & Kumar, 1979, for a description of the materials). Previous research (Winter & Uleman, 1984) and our pretest ratings suggested that personality and ability judgments would usually be made spontaneously by our undergraduate subjects. Thus, the problem of operationalizing the on-line versus memory-based difference becomes the problem of turning a spontaneously made (on-line) judgment into a memory-based judgment. Note that in the previous experiments our problem was to turn a rarely made nonspontaneous judgment into an on-line judgment. In those studies, we used experimenter instructions before presenting evidence to make the nonspontaneous judgment on-line. In Experiment 4 we attempted to interfere with the subjects' tendency to make personality and ability judgments spontaneously by presenting a novel judgment task that we expected would divert the subjects' mental processes from their normal spontaneous judgments. The task we used required

subjects to make a judgment of the grammaticality of each sentence as it was presented on the tape recorder. We believed that making the grammaticality judgment would prevent the subjects from spontaneously integrating information from the sentences into impressions of the person's personality, abilities, or likability. Thus, the interfering grammaticality judgments would make impression judgments, after the tape recording, memory based. The on-line task was established by instructing subjects that they would make personality judgments at the end of the list of sentences and by requiring a likability judgment of the person after each sentence was presented.

Ratings of intelligence, friendliness, and likability from Experiment 4 subjects revealed the predicted pattern: substantial recall ratio–judgment correlations in the memory-based task (rs of .67, .63, and .56, all $ps < .05$) but not in the on-line (grammaticality) task (rs of .15, .29, and .10, ns). We should note that differences in the variances associated with the variables entered into any of these correlational analyses do not account for differences in the magnitudes of the coefficients. For example, there was no tendency for variances to be lower in the on-line task conditions in comparison with memory-based conditions for either recall ratio or judgment measures.

Results from some secondary analyses also fit the theoretical account we have advanced to explain the on-line versus memory-based task differences. Evidence items in Experiments 1 and 2 were separated into judgment-relevant and judgment-irrelevant sets to explore the effects of task (on-line versus memory-based) on the relative recall of these two types of items. One prediction from our initial theoretical account is that relevant and irrelevant items will receive differential attention and encoding in on-line tasks, where relevant items should be well remembered in comparison with irrelevant items. However, under memory-based task conditions there would be no reason to expect differential treatment of the two sets of items until after the judgment task is presented. Thus, there should be little or no difference in the recall of relevant and irrelevant items in memory-based tasks. The pattern of means of proportion recalled measures predicted by this hypothesis was observed in the results from Experiments 1 and 2: distinctively high recall of judgment-relevant items in the on-line task and no advantage in recall of relevant items in the memory-based task (all Task × Item Type interactions significant at the .05 level, means in Table 24.2).

Table 24.2. Proportion Recalled Measures of Memory for Evidence From Experiments 1 and 2

	Task			
	On-line		Memory-based	
Judgment	Relevant	Irrelevant	Relevant	Irrelevant
Experiment 1				
Job suitability judgment	.36	.26	.26	.28
Experiment 2				
Job suitability judgment	.40	.34	.18	.33
Gender judgment	.25	.12	.17	.15

One series of analyses, concerned with subjects' tendency to interpret evidence in a manner biased to fit their final judgments, did not find support for biased interpretation effects. In several of the experiments, subjects were asked, after making their judgments and recalling the evidence, to review each evidence item and to rate its implication for the judgment. We had thought that these ratings might be correlated with the final judgments (e.g., a subject who judged the job candidate as unsuited would also rate the evidence items as more strongly implying unsuited than a subject who judged the candidate to be suited). We also speculated that the biased interpretation effect would be more pronounced in on-line tasks in comparison with memory-based tasks. However, our results did not show significant or consistent correlations between final judgments and postjudgment item ratings under any of our experimental conditions. (Of course, these results may merely indicate that our materials were relatively unambiguous and did not permit much variance in individual interpretations.)

A Recipe for Memory–Judgment Correlations?

At times our research program has seemed like a quest for conditions sufficient to produce a significant correlation between recall ratio and judgment measures. Our theoretical clue was to seek task conditions in which subjects would be forced to rely on evidence previously stored in long-term memory and where no previously made judgment (also stored in memory) was available on which to base the judgment. In fact, our quest has been mostly successful; we did find several experimental

tasks in which sizable memory–judgment relationships were reliably obtained.

The goal of our analysis is to find useful fundamental categories that classify the subject's cognitive processing strategies (five models) and to find judgment tasks (two tasks) that can serve as the building blocks to describe behavior in more complex tasks. Predictive power in the system comes from the links we have hypothesized between process models and tasks. However, we should attach a warning that several of our attempts to obtain memory–judgment correlations were not successful. Most of these failures occurred early in our research program, before we realized the importance of preventing subjects from making spontaneous on-line judgments relevant to the final judgment (in memory-based tasks). The best advice we can give researchers who extend our methods to new domains is to carefully study the types of judgments that subjects make spontaneously in their experimental tasks and then to insure that these judgments are not related to the final judgment of interest to the experimenter.

This warning is not simply a methodological note. The implication is that most judgments, laboratory and real world, do not take the simple forms of the availability and independence models we identified at the start of our analysis. Rather, conditions that invoke the biased-retrieval, biased-encoding, and incongruity-biased-encoding models associated with on-line tasks are quite common, making predictions of memory–judgment relationships difficult or impossible. We would go a step further and warn that most important judgments occur in an extended time frame and do not depend on the application of a simple operator like those identified in the algebraic, stochastic, and heuristic traditions that dominate the psychological literature. For example, even in the present experiments (2 and 3), talk-aloud reports suggest that our spontaneous judgment conditions (gender and sociability) are treated as both on-line and memory-based tasks by the subjects. They both induce an initial impression on-line, spontaneously, and rejudge in a memory-based fashion when the experimenter explicitly requests a judgment at the end of the experiment. Of course, even this complication seems trivial when compared to the duration and complexity of real-world legal (Pennington & Hastie, 1981); medical (Elstein, Shulman, & Sprafka, 1978); or diplomatic (Axelrod, 1976; Jervis, 1976) judgments. Nonetheless, simple models such as the five we begin with here constitute the proper starting point for a reduction of the complex cases to their tractable theoretical components.

Conclusion

In this article we have made the case for a distinction between two types of judgment tasks: on-line and memory-based. In support of the distinction we outlined a theoretical, information processing framework for memory–judgment relationships and identified five alternate models for processing that differed in the causal relations among memory and judgment events. The alternate models were linked to the on-line versus memory-based task distinction. The most persuasive argument for the distinction was the predicted pattern of memory–judgment relationships that we found in the results of four experiments in which on-line and memory-based tasks were presented to subjects in several social judgment domains.

Traditional theories of human judgment do not provide useful concepts to describe memory–judgment relationships. For example, cognitive algebra approaches to judgment have yielded considerable progress in our understanding of process but have not illuminated memory–judgment relationships (Anderson, 1981). Linear statistical models of judgment policies are also mute on the memory–judgment relationship (Hammond & Summers, 1965). Similarly, approaches based on normative mathematical models would not distinguish between the memory-based and on-line task conditions that affected our subjects' behavior (Edwards, 1968).

The judgment heuristics approach was one inspiration for our information processing analysis (Tversky & Kahneman, 1974). We believe that the general form of the judgment heuristics approach provides the best current characterization of the judgment information processing system. However, the description of judgment operators, memory processes, and memory structures is extremely abstract, and specific hypotheses about the task conditions under which availability heuristics will be activated are not included in recent statements of the heuristics and biases approach (Kahneman, Slovic, & Tversky, 1982). This makes the formulation too abstract to yield a priori, testable predictions or even to describe many phenomena in the judgment literature.

The on-line versus memory-based distinction is based on differences in the sources of the information that is entered as input to the hypothetical judgment operator. Research in our laboratory suggests that the two types of tasks may affect performance in ways that are not obvious from the memory–judgment results reported here. In our experiments, talk-aloud protocols suggest that our subjects are using judgment operators that can best be described (within the larger information processing system) as algebraic combination rules similar to the weighted average or weighted sum principles identified by Anderson (1981), Hammond (1955; Hammond & Summers, 1965), and their colleagues. We believe that our subjects' operators are closest to the anchor and adjust procedures proposed by Lopes (1982) and Einhorn and Hogarth (1985) in recent extensions of the algebraic modeling approach. However, subjects do not adopt the anchor and adjust operator as frequently in memory-based tasks as in on-line tasks. Thus, there is a suggestion that the heart of the judgment process, the operator, is affected by on-line versus memory-based task conditions. A second, suggestive observation is that when evidence information is unbalanced to favor one side of the judgment, the final judgment will be both more polarized and held with more confidence in on-line as compared to memory-based tasks.

For the moment, the on-line versus memory-based distinction has made one important contribution to our understanding of human judgment. It is a mistake to look for simple memory–judgment relationships in on-line judgment tasks. Memory and judgment will be directly related, though, when the judgment is based directly on the retrieval of evidence information in memory-based judgment tasks.

REFERENCES

Alba, J. W., & Hasher, L. (1983). Is memory schematic? *Psychological Bulletin, 93*, 203–231.

Anderson, N. H. (1981). *Foundations of information integration theory.* New York: Academic Press.

Anderson, N. H., & Hubert, S. (1963). Effects of concomitant verbal recall on order effects in personality impression formation. *Journal of Verbal Learning and Verbal Behavior, 2*, 379–391.

Asch, S. (1946). Forming impressions of personality. *Journal of Abnormal and Social Psychology, 41*, 258–290.

Axelrod, R. (1976). *Structure of decision.* Princeton, NJ: Princeton University Press.

Bargh, J. A. (1982). Attention and automaticity in the processing of self-relevant information. *Journal of Personality and Social Psychology, 43*, 425–436.

Bellezza, F. S., & Bower, G.H. (1981). Person stereotypes and memory for people. *Journal of Personality and Social Psychology, 41*, 856–865.

Berman, J. S., Read, S. J., & Kenny, D. A. (1983). Processing inconsistent social information. *Journal of Personality and Social Psychology, 45*, 1211–1224.

Beyth-Marom, R., & Fischhoff, B. (1977). Direct measures of availability and judgments of category frequency. *Bulletin of the Psychonomic Society, 9*, 236–238.

Carlston, D. E. (1980). The recall and use of traits and events in social inference processes. *Journal of Experimental Social Psychology, 16*, 303–328.

Clark, L. F., & Woll, S. B. (1981). Stereotype biases: A reconstructive analysis of their role in reconstructive memory. *Journal of Personality and Social Psychology, 41*, 1064–1072.

Combs, B., & Slovic, P. (1979). Newspaper coverage of causes of death. *Journalism Quarterly, 56*, 837–849.

Dellarosa, D., & Bourne, L. E., Jr. (1984). Decisions and memory: Differential retrievability of consistent and contradictory evidence. *Journal of Verbal Learning and Verbal Behavior, 23*, 669–682.

Edwards, W. (1968). Conservativism in human information processing. In B. Kleinmuntz (Ed.), *Formal representation of human judgment* (pp. 17–52). New York: Wiley.

Einhorn, H. J., & Hogarth, R. M. (1985). Ambiguity and uncertainty in probabilistic inference. *Psychological Review, 92*, 433–461.

Elstein, A. S., Shulman, L. S., & Sprafka, S. A. (1978). *Medical problem solving.* Cambridge, MA: Harvard University Press.

Fiske, S. T., Kenny, D. A., & Taylor, S. E. (1982). Structural models for the mediation of salience effects on attribution. *Journal of Experimental Social Psychology, 18*, 105–127.

Gabrielcik, A., & Fazio, R. H. (1984). Priming and frequency estimation: A strict test of the availability heuristic. *Personality and Social Psychology Bulletin, 10*, 85–89.

Hamilton, D. L., Katz, L. B., & Leirer, V. O. (1980). Cognitive representation of personality impressions: Organizational processes in first impression formation. *Journal of Personality and Social Psychology, 39*, 1050–1063.

Hammond, K. R. (1955). Probabilistic functioning and the clinical method. *Psychological Review, 62*, 255–262.

Hammond, K. R., Stewart, T. R., Brehmer, B., & Steinmann, D. (1975). Social judgment theory. In M. Kaplan & S. Schwartz (Eds.), *Human judgment and decision processes* (pp. 2–27). New York: Academic Press.

Hammond, K. R., & Summers, D. A. (1965). Cognitive dependence on linear and nonlinear cues. *Psychological Review, 72*, 215–224.

Hastie, R. (1980). Memory for behavioral information that confirms or contradicts a personality impression. In R. Hastie, T. M. Ostrom, R. S. Wyer, Jr., D. L. Hamilton, & D. E. Carlston (Eds.), *Person memory: The cognitive basis of social perception* (pp. 155–178). Hillsdale, NJ: Erlbaum.

Hastie, R. (1981). Schematic principles in human memory. In E. T. Higgins, C. P. Herman, & M. P. Zanna (Eds.), *Social cognition: The Ontario Symposium* (Vol. 1, pp. 39–88). Hillsdale, NJ: Erlbaum.

Hastie, R. (1984). Causes and effects of causal attribution. *Journal of Personality and Social Psychology, 46*, 44–56.

Hastie, R., & Carlston, D.E. (1980). Theoretical issues in person memory. In R. Hastie, T. M. Ostrom, E. B. Ebbesen, R. S. Wyer, Jr., D. L. Hamilton, & D. E. Carlston (Eds.), *Person memory: The cognitive basis of social perception* (pp. 1–54). Hillsdale, NJ: Erlbaum.

Hastie, R., & Kumar, A. P. (1979). Person memory: Personality traits as organizing principles in memory for behavior. *Journal of Personality and Social Psychology, 37*, 25–38.

Higgins, E. T., King, G. A., & Mavin, G. H. (1982). Individual construct accessibility and subjective impressions and recall. *Journal of Personality and Social Psychology, 43*, 35–47.

Hoffman, C., Mischel, W., & Mazze, K. (1981). The role of purpose in the organization of information about behavior. Trait-based versus goal-based categories in person cognition. *Journal of Personality and Social Psychology, 40*, 211–225.

Jervis, R. (1976). *Perception and misperception in international politics.* Princeton: Princeton University Press.

Jones, E. E., & Pittman, T. S. (1982). Towards a general theory of strategic self-presentation. In J. Suls (Ed.), *Psychological perspectives on the self* (pp. 141–184). Hillsdale, NJ: Erlbaum.

Kahneman, D., Slovic, P., & Tversky, A. (1982). *Judgment under uncertainty: Heuristics and biases.* New York: Cambridge University Press.

Kelley, H. H. (1973). The processes of causal attribution. *American Psychologist, 28*, 107–128.

Langer, E. J., Blank, A., & Chanowitz, B. (1978). The mindlessness of ostensibly thoughtful action: The role of "placebic" information in interpersonal interaction. *Journal of Personality and Social Psychology, 36*, 635–642.

Leamer, E. E. (1974). False models and post-data model construction. *Journal of the American Statistical Association, 69*, 122–131.

Leamer, E. E. (1975). "Explaining your results" as access-biased memory. *Journal of the American Statistical Association, 70*, 88–93.

Lichtenstein, S., Slovic, P., Fischhoff, B., Layman, M., & Combs, B. (1978). Judged frequency of lethal events. *Journal of Experimental Psychology: Human Learning and Memory, 4*, 551–578.

Lichtenstein, M., & Srull, T. K. (1985). Conceptual and methodological issues in examining the relationship between consumer memory and judgment. In L. F. Alwitt & A. A. Mitchell (Eds.), *Psychological processes and advertising effects: Theory, research, and application.* Hillsdale, NJ: Erlbaum.

Lingle, J. H., Dukerich, J. M., & Ostrom, T. M. (1983). Accessing information in memory-based impression judgments: Incongruity versus negativity in retrieval selectivity. *Journal of Personality and Social Psychology, 44*, 262–272.

Lingle, J. H., Geva, N., Ostrom, T. M., Lieppe, M. R., & Baumgardner, M. H. (1979). Thematic effects of person judgments on impression formation. *Journal of Personality and Social Psychology, 37*, 674–687.

Lingle, J. H., & Ostrom, T. M. (1979). Retrieval selectivity in memory-based impression judgments. *Journal of Personality and Social Psychology, 37*, 180–194.

Lopes, L. L. (1982). Toward a procedural theory of judgment. Wisconsin Human Information *Processing Program, Technical Report, 17*, 1–49.

Markus, H. (1977). Self-schemata and the processing of information about the self. *Journal of Personality and Social Psychology, 35*, 63–78.

McArthur, L. Z. (1980). Illusory causation and illusory correlation: Two epistemological accounts. *Personality and Social Psychology Bulletin, 6*, 507–519.

Pennington, N., & Hastie, R. (1981). Juror decision-making: The generalization gap. *Psychological Bulletin, 89*, 246–287.

Reyes, R. M., Thompson, W. C., & Bower, G. H. (1980). Judgmental biases resulting from differing availabilities of arguments. *Journal of Personality and Social Psychology, 39*, 2–12.

Ross, M., & Sicoly, F. (1979). Egocentric biases in availability and attribution. *Journal of Personality and Social Psychology, 37*, 322–336.

Sherman, S. J., Zehner, K. S., Johnson, J., & Hirt, E. R. (1983). Social explanation: The role of timing, set, and recall on subjective likelihood estimates. *Journal of Personality and Social Psychology, 44*, 1127–1143.

Smith, E. R. (1984). Model of social inference processes. *Psychological Review, 91*, 392–413.

Snyder, M., & Uranowitz, W. (1978). Reconstructing the past: Some cognitive consequences of person perception. *Journal of Personality and Social Psychology, 36*, 941–950.

Srull, T. K. (1981). Person memory: Some tests of associative storage and retrieval models. *Journal of Experimental Psychology: Human Learning and Memory, 7*, 440–463.

Swann, W. B., Jr. (1984). Quest for accuracy in person perception: A matter of pragmatics. *Psychological Review, 91,* 457–477.

Taylor, S. E., & Crocker, J. (1981). Schematic bases of social information processing. In E. T. Higgins, C. P. Herman, & M. P. Zanna (Eds.), *Social cognition: The Ontario Symposium* (Vol. 1, pp. 89–134). Hillsdale, NJ: Erlbaum.

Taylor, S. E., & Thompson, S. C. (1982). Stalking the elusive "vividness" effect. *Psychological Review, 89,* 155–181.

Thomas, E. A. C., & Hogue, A. (1976). Apparent weight of evidence, decision criteria, and confidence ratings in juror decision making. *Psychological Review, 83,* 442–465.

Tversky, A., & Kahneman, D. (1973). Availability: A heuristic for judging frequency and probability. *Cognitive Psychology, 5,* 207–232.

Tversky, A., & Kahneman, D. (1974). Judgment under uncertainty: Heuristics and biases. Science, *185,* 1124–1131.

Weiner, B. (1985). "Spontaneous" causal thinking. *Psychological Bulletin, 97,* 74–84.

Winter, L., & Uleman, J. S. (1984). When are social judgments made? Evidence for the spontaneousness of trait inferences. *Journal of Personality and Social Psychology, 47,* 237–252.

Woll, S. B., & Graesser, A. C. (1982). Memory discrimination for information typical or atypical of person schemas. *Social Cognition, 1,* 287–310.

Wyer, R. S., Jr., & Srull, T. K. (1980). The processing of social stimulus information: A conceptual integration. In R. Hastie, T. M. Ostrom, R. S. Wyer, Jr., D. L. Hamilton, & D. E. Carlston (Eds.), *Person memory: The cognitive basis of social perception* (pp. 227–300). Hillsdale, NJ: Erlbaum.

Received July 12, 1985
Revision received October 18, 1985 ■

Perceiving Social Groups: The Importance of the Entitativity Continuum

David L. Hamilton, Steven J. Sherman, and Brian Lickel

In our everyday lives, we encounter people all the time and in all kinds of situations. We are continuously perceiving and interacting with others. Even when we are alone, we spend much of our time thinking about others. We also regularly encounter groups of people in all kinds of social settings. We talk about, worry about, joke about, and anticipate being with these groups. We sometimes value them, we sometimes hate them. Sometimes we see individuals as individuals, sometimes we see them as group members. What leads us to perceive "groupness" in a collection of individuals? Certainly we do not see every aggregate of individuals as a meaningful group; we rarely think of the collection of persons waiting to board an airplane as possessing the quality of "groupness." Yet we do think of people as belonging to a group under a remarkable variety of circumstances.

This chapter is concerned with these issues. It begins by presenting a theoretical analysis of the similarities and differences in the way perceivers form impressions of individuals and of groups, and it briefly summarizes the evidence pertinent to the issues raised in that analysis. The discussion then focuses specifically on the perception of groups, examining some implications of our analysis for questions of when and how we perceive collections of persons to be groups. In doing so, this chapter also considers the relationship between the *perception* of groupness by observers and the definition of groupness by social scientists.

Impressions of Individuals and Groups: A Process Comparison

Theoretical Analysis

Perceiving, understanding, and knowing others involves the perceiver in processing and use of information. When we meet an individual, we immediately begin the process of forming an impression of that person (Asch, 1946). Similarly, perhaps, when we see a gathering of people, and we immediately begin to evolve a conception of what that group is like. Or do we?

Although at first glance these may seem to be fairly commonplace observations, a little thought on these matters quickly leads to a number of puzzling questions, the answers to which are not immediately obvious. Do we always develop conceptions of the individuals and groups of people that we encounter? Are we just as likely to develop a conception of a group as are to form an impression of an individual? When we do, are the same psychological processes involved in forming those individual and group impressions?

In a recent article (Hamilton & Sherman, 1996), we examined how perceivers process information about group members and how conceptions of groups are formed from that information. In doing so, we analyzed the similarities and differences in the way perceivers develop conceptions of groups and impressions of individuals. We developed a set of principles that summarize the way impressions of individuals are formed, and we then evaluated the evidence regarding the development of conceptions of groups in light of those principles. Because the present chapter grows out of this analysis, we begin by briefly summarizing our development of these points.

Our analysis of the impression formation process was organized around "fundamental postulate" that we proposed as underlying this entire process: "The perceiver assumes unity in the personalities of others. Persons are seen as coherent entities." Given this assumption, the perceiver's task in forming an impression of a person becomes that of comprehending and understanding the basic themes that comprise the person's individuality.

From that fundamental postulate, we derived several important principles specifying processes that characterize the impression formation process. These include the following: (a) From the information acquired, the perceiver spontaneously makes inferences about the dispositions that characterize the person's personality, (b) the perceiver assumes that the person will manifest consistency across time and situations, (c) the information acquired about the person is used to develop an organized impression of the person, and (d) the perceiver strives to resolve any inconsistencies in the information acquired about the person. Despite being presented as sweeping generalizations, these principles provide a viable overview of what is known about the impression formation process. In fact, there is at least some evidence in the impression formation literature to support each of these principles (cf. Hamilton & Sherman, 1996).

Having presented this postulate and set of principles, we then analyzed whether the same principles apply when perceivers develop conceptions of groups from information they acquire about group members. Our analysis was based on a "fundamental assumption" that perceivers do not expect the same degree of unity and coherence in a group that they do in an individual person. If this assumption is correct, and if all of the processes summarized in the four principles presented earlier derive from that expectation of unity and coherence, then it follows that the process of developing group conceptions should be characterized by those processes to a lesser degree than is evidenced in forming impressions of individuals.

Between-target Differences

The heart of our analysis, then, was to examine the evidence relevant to this comparison of how individual and group impressions are formed. This section briefly highlights some of this evidence (for a more thorough review, see Hamilton & Sherman, 1996).

Principle 1: Spontaneous Inferences/On-line Processing

When perceiving an individual, the perceiver attempts to understand the dispositions of the person. Inferences about a person's characteristics are made spontaneously and judgments are made on-line as information about the person is processed (Carlston & Skowronski, 1994; Hastie & Park, 1986; Uleman, 1987). In contrast, because perceivers do not expect the same degree of coherence in groups, they are less likely to form impressions on-line. Instead, judgments about the characteristics of groups are more likely to be memory-based, made only when directly called for and based on whatever events the perceiver can access from memory. Evidence from our research supports this difference in processing for individuals and groups (McConnell, Sherman, & Hamilton, 1994, 1997; Sanbonmatsu, Sherman, & Hamilton, 1987; Susskind, Maurer, Thakkar, Sherman, & Hamilton, 1994). Compared with individual targets, strong impressions of groups are less likely to form spontaneously as the information is processed.

Principle 2: Expectations of Consistency

Perceivers expect consistency in target persons. They expect the personality of an individual to remain consistent across time and situation. However, if perceivers expect less unity and coherence in group targets, then they should be less inclined to expect consistency in the behaviors of group members. Although few studies have examined this issue, recent results support this proposition (Park, DeKay, & Kraus, 1994; Weisz & Jones, 1993).

Principle 3: Organization of Impressions

The assumption that perceivers spontaneously organize information about the target person was at the core of Asch's (1946) view of impression formation. Research on person memory has shown that perceivers organize person information according to trait themes, evaluative implications, or perceived goals (Hamilton, Driscoll, & Worth, 1989; Hamilton, Katz, & Leirer, 1980; Hoffman, Mischel, & Mazze, 1981; Srull & Wyer, 1989). Consistent with our analysis of between-target differences, Wyer, Bodenhausen, and Srull (1984) found that perceivers integrate items of information into an organized representation to a greater extent for an individual target than for a group target (particularly for behaviors that were evaluatively relevant to subjects' prior impression-based expectancies about the target).

Principle 4: Processing Inconsistent Information
Our proposal that perceivers assume more coherence in the behavior and dispositions of individuals than of groups has important implications for how people deal with behavior that does not fit easily into an impression of an individual or group target. Research on person memory has shown that, when confronted with an inconsistency in a person's behavior, perceivers (a) spend more time processing the incongruent behavior compared with expectancy-congruent behavior, (b) generate causal explanations for the incongruent behavior, and (c) exhibit better memory for incongruent than congruent behaviors. Consistent with our analysis, research has shown that each of these effects is less likely to occur for a group target than for an individual target. First, Stern, Marrs, Millar, and Cole (1984) found that when the target was an individual, participants spent longer reading incongruent than congruent behaviors. However, when each statement referred to a different member of an unidentified group, this difference in processing time for congruent and incongruent behaviors disappeared. Second, Hastie (1984) showed that when the target was an individual, perceivers spontaneously generated causal explanations for incongruent behaviors to a greater degree than they did for congruent behaviors. Susskind et al. (1997) replicated this finding when the target was an individual, but found that when the behaviors referred to members of a group, the tendency to generate causal explanations for incongruent behavior was no longer evident. Thus, expectancy-incongruent information triggers attributional thinking for individual targets, but not for group targets. Finally, a number of studies have found that perceivers show heightened recall of expectancy-incongruent behavior when it pertains to an individual target, whereas this effect is strongly attenuated when the target is a group (Srull, 1981; Srull, Lichtenstein, & Rothbart, 1985; Stern et al., 1984).

In summary, the research summarized by Hamilton and Sherman (1996) provides considerable evidence for the contention that the same information is processed differently as a function of whether it describes an individual or members of a group. These differences follow from and support our fundamental assumption that perceivers hold differing expectancies about the degree of unity and coherence that typically characterize individual and group targets.

Within-target Variations

Beyond these between-target differences, we can also consider variation within a type of target (individual or group) in the extent to which these processes are engaged. In our theoretical perspective, this variation derives from the same foundation on which those between-target differences were based: expectations of unity and coherence in the target. Thus, in addition to the difference in "default" expectancies about individual and group targets noted earlier, perceivers may also differentiate among (individual or group) targets about whom they hold differing expectations of unity, organization, and consistency. Thus, for example, we expect more internal structure and behavioral consistency from the leader of an important organization than we do from a person diagnosed as borderline manic-depressive. Similarly, a well-trained military unit is a more tightly organized, cohesive group than is a once-a-month book club.

Campbell (1958) introduced the term *entitativity* to refer to the degree to which a group is perceived as having this property of "groupness," of being an entity, and he specifically noted that groups vary in the extent to which they are seen as possessing entitativity. Thus, this concept becomes of central importance for our analysis, in that variation in perceived entitativity will thereby determine the extent to which impression formation processes become significantly engaged as information about group members is acquired and used.

We have investigated whether perceptions of the entitativity of a group of people influence the way in which information about group members is processed, organized, and used in forming impressions of that group (McConnell et al., 1997). In these experiments, entitativity of group targets was manipulated through instructions that generated differing expectations about the degree of consistency and similarity that existed among the various group members. When perceivers expected high entitativity, they engaged in on-line impression formation, attempting to arrive at an integrated impression of the group as the information about its members was being presented (as reflected in several dependent measures, including both memory and judgment data). However, when the group target was presented in a way that suggested low entitativity, perceivers did not form integrated impressions and produced results more typical for group targets, described in the preceding section. Similarly, McConnell et al. (1997) manipulated expectancies about the consistency of an individual target's behaviors. When expectancies of consistency were strong, subjects formed clear and integrated impressions, typical of the findings described for individual targets in the preceding section. However, when expectancies for an individual's consistency were low, a different pattern of results was obtained. In fact, by undermining perceivers' default expectancies of consistency in an individual target, we produced results that more strongly resembled findings typically obtained for group targets (as described previously).

In summary, the concept of entitativity can apply to both individual and group targets; for each type of target, perceived entitativity can influence the way in which impressions of that target are formed (see also McConnell et al., 1994). As documented in our between-target analysis, perceivers expect greater unity or entitativity in individual compared with group targets, and this creates general processing differences for the two types of targets. As these within-target variations indicate, differences in perceivers' expectations about individuals or groups can produce parallel differences in information processing and impression formation.

Hamilton and Sherman's (1996) analysis compared the processing of information in forming impressions of individual and group targets. The remainder of this chapter focuses on groups as targets of social perception. It considers in more detail the variation among groups in the extent to which they are perceived as having entitativity, as possessing "groupness," and examines the variables that contribute to the perception of entitativity. The chapter then discusses the ways that theorists and researchers studying groups have defined what a *group* is, and what elements contribute to a group being a group. Finally, the chapter considers the extent to which social perceivers rely on those same cues and information about groups in their perceptions of group entitativity.

Complexities in Understanding Perceived Entitativity

The concept of entitativity and the variation among groups in the extent to which they are perceived as possessing this attribute are at the core of our analysis. Therefore, we introduce the concept of an *Entitativity Continuum* along which groups are perceived as varying. The Entitativity Continuum is of central importance because the perception of a group's position along that continuum will determine the nature of the information processing that transpires as the observer acquires, processes, and uses information about the group and its members.

A useful way to appreciate the variation of groups along the Entitativity Continuum is by introducing several well-chosen examples of collections of people. Consider the extent to which each one qualifies as a group, and why (or why not):

1. An urban street gang is a relatively small and tightly knit group. The members of the group share a number of features (age, locale, socioeconomic status [SES], ethnic background, etc.), they all know each other well, and they have extensive interaction with each other. Continued membership in the group assumes a high degree of commitment, and leaving the group is difficult and can be dangerous.

2. The thousands of members of the Democratic Party are bound together by certain ill-defined ideological principles that are of varying significance to its members. They are heterogeneous on virtually every imaginable attribute, and most have never met each other. Degree of commitment and length of group membership vary considerably among the members, and leaving the group is a matter of personal choice with little consequence. Still, some members devote most of their lives to the welfare of the group.

3. The Philadelphia Phillies baseball team consists of a limited number of group members who share a variety of attributes (gender, approximate age, athletic ability, etc.) and spend at least part of the year in intense collaborative effort. Most members have had a brief history of association with the group. Although momentary involvement in the group may be quite strong, one's allegiance can easily be shifted to another team (a current outgroup) with virtually no consequence, and this can occur as result of either personal choice (free agency) or action by the group power structure (trade).

4. Americans of Polish descent have in common one defining characteristic of national ancestry. Many members of this group also share cultural similarities that derive from that heritage, although many others do not. Some identify quite strongly with that heritage, feeling strong bonds with relatives in "the old country," including some whom they have never met (and never will); others do not. Although such identification may vary considerably among group members, changing this group membership is not possible.

5. Consider a task force of engineers working together to develop a new computer system for improved airplane guidance and tracking — a project that is of considerable financial importance to the contract

research company by whom they are employed. There is an appointed leader of the task force, and different individual members (or subsets of members) are responsible for developing different aspects of the overall plan. The members of the task force have been working together on this project for several months. They therefore know each other very well, and they respect each other's unique contributions to the combined effort. Each of them also realizes that failure to win the contract for this project may ultimately lead to layoffs for some (perhaps even most) members of the group.

6. Imagine the following scene. It's a hot summer day in a city in the American South in 1955. In the lobby of the city hall, there are two lines of persons waiting their turn for a drink at water fountains. One line is longer than the other. The lines move relatively quickly, so no one is in line for very long. Within either line, no one knows more than 1–2 other persons. Having quenched their thirst, people go their respective ways. A sign over one water fountain says "Colored" and a sign over the other fountain says "Whites Only."

All of these scenarios portray collectives of persons that, to most observers, would be considered to be groups. They obviously vary in a number of properties, a point to which we return later. First, however, consider two other scenarios that have many elements in common with the features portrayed in the preceding examples, but that describe aggregates of persons that, to most observers, would not qualify as meaningful groups.

7. A man enters his local bank and notices that two lines of people have formed, each waiting to be served. One line, the longer one, consists of people waiting to make deposits or withdrawals. The second, shorter line consists of people waiting to gain access to their safe deposit boxes. Fortunately for the customers, both lines move fairly quickly, so no one has to stand in line for very long. Within each line, few if any people know each other. Having completed their business, the people go their respective ways.

8. In a nearly full movie theater, someone notices smoke coming from behind the screen. Suddenly it is very important for everyone to leave the theater. Quickly but calmly, this large gathering of strangers moves toward the exits in an orderly, almost coordinated fashion, everyone having the same goal in mind. A few individuals spontaneously take charge, guiding people toward the appropriate exits. Fortunately, everyone manages to get outside without panic or personal injury.

These examples describe very different types of social settings involving collectives of people. With the exception of the last two examples, these collectives would be considered by most observers to be *groups* in some sense of that term. Yet these capsules describe groups that are characterized and held together by very different properties. As the last two example illustrate, not all collections of persons are perceived to be meaningful groups. We shall see, however, that it can be difficult to specify the properties that differentiate these collectivities from others in whom we more readily perceive an element of groupness.

Bases of Perceived Entitativity

Although the question of what constitutes "groupness" seems fundamental to understanding intergroup perceptions, we know relatively little about the conditions that foster perceptions of groupness. A number of candidates have, however, been proposed. In discussing them, we refer to the scenarios we created earlier in considering the extent to which each property is useful in identifying conditions that contribute to the perception of entitativity.

Perceived Entitativity Based on Group Features

Campbell (1958) sought to address the question of when an aggregate of individuals is perceived as a group. His approach was to apply principles of perceptual organization, derived from research on object perception, to understanding how group entitativity is perceived. That is, Campbell argued, several cues are used by the visual system to identify when several stimulus elements are part of the same physical entity; he suggested that social perceivers may use the same types of cues in their perceptions of human "elements" that sometimes, but not always, are members of a social entity. The three primary cues he suggested follow.

Proximity
In perceptions of the physical world, elements that exist in close proximity to each other are likely to be seen as parts of the same object or organization. Similarly, a collection of individuals may be more likely to be seen as a

group when those persons are physically proximal to each other. For example, proximity may contribute to perceiving entitativity in the urban street gang, the Phillies, the project task force, and the racial groups in line at water fountains. However, to the extent that members of the Democratic Party or Polish Americans are perceived as a group, such perceptions would not be based on proximity, indicating that proximity is not a necessary precondition. Moreover, the examples of the lines at the bank and the people exiting the movie theater, both of which include physical proximity, indicate that proximity is not a sufficient condition for perceiving groupness either.

Similarity

Physical stimuli that are similar to each other are more likely to be perceived as part of the same entity. In the same vein, it seems plausible that perceived similarity may enhance the likelihood that persons will be perceived as comprising a group. In fact, virtually all of the groups described in our scenarios are characterized by some form of similarity among members. However, the bases of similarity vary widely in these examples, including race (water fountain lines), age (street gang, Phillies), national heritage (Polish Americans), education (engineers), abilities (Phillies), and beliefs (Democrats, at least in theory). Other appearance cues — the Phillies' uniforms, identifying dress codes of gang members — may also enhance the perception of similarity, and thereby contribute to perceived entitativity. However, similarity does not guarantee perceived groupness. If everyone in line at the bank happened to be male, would they then be perceived as a group? It seems unlikely.

Common Fate

Physical elements that are seen as moving together in the same direction are perceived as members of the same physical entity. Similarly, it may be that persons whose activities are oriented toward the same end, and who therefore share a common fate, will be more likely to be perceived as a group. This feature is most apparent in the example of the task force of engineers whose plan may or may not be approved; but it is also relevant to sports teams (Phillies), and gang members, and is starkly revealed in discriminatory practices (different water fountains for African Americans and Whites). However, the people who had to quickly exit the movie theater because of fire shared, at least temporarily, a common fate as well. Again, common fate is neither sufficient to nor necessary for the perception of entitativity.

In addition to proximity, similarity, and common fate, Campbell (1958) suggested other possible cues to group entitativity, again drawing on principles of perceptual organization. These included goodness of form and "resistance to intrusion," which may have counterparts in social perception as organization among members and permeability of group boundaries. In our illustrative scenarios, some of the groups are highly organized (the project task force, the Phillies), whereas others clearly are not (Polish Americans, Democrats). Similarly, some groups can be joined or left with relative ease (Democrats), some only with difficulty or risk (street gangs, task force members), and in some cases such changes are virtually impossible (groups based on racial or national descent).

Campbell's analysis is highly original and intriguing. It suggests a number of possible perceptual cues that the social perceiver may use in inferring that an aggregate of individual persons possesses the quality of entitativity — that they comprise a social group. Nevertheless, none of these features is perfectly correlated with entitativity.

Perceived Entitativity Based on Natural Kind Status

Labels for social groups often have important effects on impressions of, reaction to, and behavior toward those groups. Rothbart and Taylor (1992) wondered why our labels for social categories possess such power, and they noted that group labels vary greatly in the strength of these effects. They accounted for these differences in terms of the distinction between natural kinds and artifacts. The concepts of "natural kinds" and "artifacts" were introduced as a way of making an important distinction among category types (Gelman, 1988; Keil, 1989). Natural kinds are objects that exist in the world independently of the behavior and beliefs of humans (e.g., giraffes, calcium). Artifacts are categories of things that reflect the operation of human needs, wishes, and constructions (e.g., chairs, umbrellas). Natural kinds are perceived as possessing underlying essences that serve to make the category unique and distinctive. In contrast, artifacts are seen as sharing only superficial and function-related properties.

Although the distinction between natural kinds and artifacts was developed to apply to nonsocial categories, Rothbart and Taylor (1992) applied this distinction to social categories, arguing that different social groups are viewed as natural kinds to a greater or lesser extent. Just as we argued that social groups differ in the degree to which they are seen as possessing entitativity, Rothbart and Taylor proposed that there is a continuum of "natural kindness" along which social groups are seen to vary. Just as the perception of the degree of entitativity of a group is important for processing information about and developing impressions of that group (Hamilton & Sherman, 1996), so too is the extent to which a group is perceived as a natural kind important in terms of the way we think about and represent that group and its members.

Rothbart and Taylor (1992) identified two dimensions that are most relevant to the perception of groups as natural kinds: inductive potential and unalterability. *Inductive potential* refers to the fact that membership in a natural kind category allows for inferences about a wide variety of attributes and qualities. Some social categories (e.g., race, occupation) are perceived as high in inductive potential, and thus allow for the prediction of diverse and important knowledge about group members. Other social categories (e.g., literature preferences, first name) have little inductive potential. *Unalterability* refers to the ease or difficulty of changing one's category status. Gender and race are highly unalterable, whereas one's political affiliation or hobby is easily changeable. Unalterability is similar to Campbell's (1958) conception of the impenetrability of group boundaries, which he cited as a possible indicator of entitativity.

Which social categories are most likely to be perceived as having natural kind status? According to Rothbart and Taylor, the answer is categories that are judged as high in both inductive potential and unalterability. They proposed that similarity in surface characteristics (e.g., physical appearance) is the most important element for perceptions of both high inductive potential and high unalterability. Physical similarity is used as an indication that group membership has rich inductive potential, and that the group has some essence or core quality. In addition, groups bound together by physical similarity give the suggestion that group membership is highly unalterable. Rothbart and Taylor (1992) suggested that race and gender are the social groupings that have the highest degree of natural kind status, and therefore are the groups most strongly perceived as having core properties or essences — the properties that give these groups meaning and identity. The importance of race and gender in the stereotyping and prejudice literature attests to the perception of these social categories as natural kinds.

In some respects, the concept of natural kindness is similar to our concept of entitativity. The perceiver's belief in a fundamental essence for a social group and a belief in an underlying coherence, consistency, and unity for the attributes of the group members resemble our conception of entitativity. Just as inductive potential is one of the important dimensions of a social category that is relevant to its perception as a natural kind, inductive potential would seem to be a key aspect of entitativity. When group membership is indicative of many traits, abilities, beliefs, and goals, it seems likely that perceived entitativity is high. However, which of these is cause and which is effect is not so clear. Rothbart and Taylor maintained that it is the perception of high inductive potential that leads to the judgment of natural kind status. We too would see the perception of inductive potential as a factor leading to the perceived entitativity of a group. However, we would also maintain that the perception of high entitativity for a group (however that perception is arrived at) will increase the degree of inductive potential regarding inferences about group members.

Rothbart and Taylor's second dimension for the judgment of natural kind status is unalterability. However, we do not regard perceived unalterability as a crucial precursor to the perception of entitativity in a social group. Membership in a fraternity or the Philadelphia Phillies is easily alterable, yet these two groups are quite high in entitativity; they are perhaps higher than social groupings such as gender or nationality, which are characterized by unalterability, but where perceptions of unity and coherence are limited by the size and diversity of the membership.

Finally, Rothbart and Taylor (1992) have argued that groups that are seen as natural kinds will be perceived as relatively homogeneous. However, we (Hamilton & Sherman, 1996) have argued that entitativity and perceived homogeneity are not necessarily related. Outgroups are generally perceived as more homogeneous than are ingroups (the outgroup homogeneity effect), and yet the groups to which we belong and with which we identify (our ingroups) are more likely to be seen as possessing a high degree of entitativity — as having an identity and cohesiveness. As we noted in the preceding subsection, perceptions of similarity or homogeneity are but one element that can contribute to the perception of group entitativity. The group's history, the shared goals of its members, and their interdependence seem likely to play much stronger roles in perceived entitativity than is the extent to which a group is perceived as a natural kind.

Perceived Entitativity Based on Group Size

Mullen (1991) has argued that the relative size of a group can fundamentally influence the way the group is perceived. Is it possible that group size is a key variable that influences the perception of entitativity? Mullen summarized evidence showing that, as the size of a group increases, (a) conformity and social loafing of group members increase, (b) perceived consensus of group members decreases, (c) ingroup bias decreases, and (d) perceived variability of the group decreases. Based on these findings, he concluded that group size is an important determinant of a wide array of effects.

Mullen (1991) explained these effects by proposing that the relative size of a group influences the group's salience to perceivers: as group size decreases, the group's salience increases. He argued that the differential salience of majority and minority groups influences the nature of representations that perceivers develop of these groups. Specifically, he proposed that perceivers develop prototype-based representations of minority groups and exemplar-based representations of majority groups. These representational differences then lead perceivers to process information about majority and minority groups in fundamentally different ways, adopting a simpler, more heuristic processing style when processing information about minority group members.

Although intrigued by Mullen's analyses, we have reservations about his conceptual framework as a means of understanding entitativity. First, although small groups may sometimes be more salient than large groups, this is not always the case. Even when it is, the salience due to differences in group size will not invariably influence perceptions of entitativity. For example, two of our scenarios described two lines of people of differing size. In the bank example, although one line of customers was larger than the other, this difference by itself would not lead observers to view either line as a group or to perceive them as differing in entitativity. Moreover, although the lines at the "Colored" and "White" drinking fountains are perceived as groups having entitativity, it seems unlikely that this perception is based on the fact that one group happens to be smaller than the other. It also seems possible that some effects that Mullen ascribes to salience based on group size instead reflect general expectancies about the nature of minority and majority groups. Brewer, Weber, and Carini (1995) held constant the number of majority and minority persons viewed by experimental participants, yet they found that knowledge of majority/minority status affected perceived entitativity. Thus, information pertaining to minority group members was processed differently, even when they were not themselves a salient minority.

Second, in contrast to the view that perceivers engage in simpler, more heuristic processing for minority group targets than for majority group targets, and that this difference relates to perceived entitativity, the evidence we have reviewed (Hamilton & Sherman, 1996) suggests that perceivers do *not* process information about highly entitative targets (persons or groups) in a simple and heuristic fashion. Rather, perceivers seem to process information more extensively and attend to inconsistencies in behavior to a greater extent for such targets. Therefore, if minority groups did have higher entitativity than majority groups, we would argue that perceivers process information regarding minority groups in a less, not more, heuristic fashion.

Given these considerations, we question the degree to which group size, in and of itself, drives perceivers' perceptions of entitativity. Group size may be correlated with entitativity, but it is undoubtedly correlated with other important variables as well. For example, members of small groups probably have more interpersonal interaction with each other and are more interdependent than are members of large groups. It is variables such as these, not group size per se, that are likely to influence the perception of entitativity.

Functional Bases of Perceived Entitativity

In each of the preceding discussions of bases of perceived entitativity, the analysis has focused on properties of the group being perceived — whether they be perceptual cues, structural properties, or the identification of a group as reflecting a "natural kind" category. In all of these cases, the perception of entitativity is driven by properties of the group — by stimulus features that are "out there" (or at least believed to be out there). As such, perceptions of entitativity should be stable across both time and perceivers. That is, the perceived entitativity of a group should not fluctuate dramatically, and there should be some reasonable level of consensus among observers about a group's entitativity. In a word, from these perspectives, perceived entitativity is driven by group-based properties.

In contrast to these approaches, Brewer and Harasty (1996) highlighted the role of perceiver variables in group perception, including individual differences as well as transitory motivational and contextual determinants. Perceiving a group as a group can, then, be influenced by the perceiver's currently activated expectancies and affective states, and may be beneficial to meeting the perceiver's needs and goals. Because of this emphasis, we refer to this approach as a *functional* perspective on the bases of perceived entitativity.

Brewer and Harasty (1996) discussed a variety of factors that might influence the perception of groupness. For example, the ease or difficulty of the information-processing task faced by perceivers can influence the way information about group members is organized and stored in memory, and can thereby influence perceptions of the group as a whole (Rothbart, Fulero, Jensen, Howard, & Birrell, 1978). Similarly, the perceiver's processing goals can influence the way information about group members is encoded and represented in memory, including the extent to which group members are represented as a unit and the extent of consistency perceived among group members (Park, DeKay, & Kraus, 1994; Seta & Hayes, 1994). Information about ingroup and outgroup members may be represented in memory differently, not only as a function of properties of the information acquired about group members (Park & Rothbart, 1982; Park, Ryan, & Judd, 1992), but also as a function of the relationship between the groups (Brewer, Weber, & Carini, 1995) and the perceiver's motives and goals (Simon, 1993). Finally, there may be individual differences among perceivers in their proclivity to see coherence and structure in groups.

It seems to us that Brewer and Harasty's (1996) approach to the perceived entitativity of groups represents a nice parallel to Brewer's (1991) optimal distinctiveness theory. That theory emphasized the importance of conflicting needs for inclusion and differentiation in determining ingroup identification, and argued that social identity represents a reconciliation of these two needs. The relative importance of these two needs can enhance or diminish an individual's need to feel part of a meaningful ingroup. Parallel concerns may influence the perception of groupness in others. Just as an individual might focus on a need for belonging or a need for distinctiveness at different times, so too might one, at different times, focus on the coherence, structure, and unity of a group versus the lack of similarity and consistency among its members. In fact, to the extent that one's functional focus is more on the need for inclusion, one is more likely to perceive an ingroup as high in entitativity. However, at different times, when one's focus is on the need for uniqueness, that same ingroup might be perceived as rather low in entitativity. Thus, both of these approaches to the perception of groups emphasize the motivations that increase or decrease the amount of groupness that is perceived in a collection of people.

Perceived Entitativity: A Theoretical Perspective

Earlier we presented descriptions of several social collectivities that most people would consider *groups*, at least in some sense of that word: few would doubt that street gangs, political parties, baseball teams, work groups, and people sharing racial, national, religious, and other forms of ethnic heritage are commonly perceived as meaningful groups. Equally obvious is the fact that there are many circumstances when perceivers see aggregates of persons without thinking of them as a group. What is it that binds certain of these collectives together such that we endow them with the quality of being a group? Given that we perceive an aggregate of persons to constitute a group, *how much* entitativity do we see the group as having, and why? How do we determine where any given group falls along the Entitativity Continuum?

In reviewing possible conceptual frameworks for thinking about these questions, we were struck by the variety of properties and concepts that seem relevant to an analysis of possible bases of perceived entitativity: the size of the group; its history and longevity; the permeability of its boundaries; its potential as a "natural kind" category; the similarity, proximity, interdependence, familiarity, and common fate of the group's members; and so on. All of them seem to be factors that plausibly would influence the perception of entitativity in groups, and indeed we submit that all of them contribute to that perception. But which among them are more important, and which are less influential?

Answering these questions is difficult for (at least) two reasons. First, the necessary empirical work has not yet been done, so any answer at this point must be largely speculative. Second, although all of these variables may influence perceived entitativity, many of them undoubtedly are intercorrelated to a substantial degree across a range of actual groups. Members of small groups are more likely to be familiar with each other, have face-to-face interactions, and share physical proximity than are members of large groups. Ethnic groups often have rather impermeable boundaries, and their members are likely to have physical similarities, share history and heritage, and perhaps be subject to common fate. Given these relationships, efforts to tease apart the unique contribution of any given feature or property will be difficult. Moreover, as indicated in our earlier discussion, although these properties may contribute to the perception of entitativity, for most of them it is clear that they are neither necessary nor sufficient conditions for perceiving entitativity.

Nevertheless, we venture the opinion that there is one variable on which groups differ that is a primary clue to any given group's degree of entitativity. We propose that the most useful indicator of a group's position along the Entitativity Continuum is the extent to which it possesses organization and structure among its members. In particular, the presence of organization in a group clearly implies entitativity. Such organization may be reflected in several ways: a hierarchical structure within the group, a differentiation of roles and functions among its members, purposive integration of activity, and/or clear differentials in leadership, power, status, and responsibility. These properties may be manifested in different ways in different groups. For example, a military unit possesses these features explicitly, with relatively little tolerance for variation in or violation of the defined structure; in a family, these properties may be more implicit, with greater tolerance for improvisation, but they are typically present nevertheless (in fact, when they are not present, we often refer to a "dysfunctional" family — and perceive it as less entitative as a consequence). Our main point is that groups that manifest cues reflecting organization and structure will be perceived as entitative units.

Interestingly, Asch (1952) advanced a similar position some 45 years ago:

We do not see a group of men merely according to proximity, distribution, or similarity of its members. A marching platoon is more than a visually perceived unit; it is an organization with psychological properties. ... We grasp the coordination of [its members'] movements as a demonstration of group discipline, an ordering of their separate wills in subordination to a common purpose. We see the platoon as a strong or a threatening formation. The quality of power it reveals is a consequence of the knowledge of its purpose and of the manner in which it is held together. (p. 224)

In another example, Asch observed, "A picket line in front of a plant has a quality of unity that is a product of its organization" (p. 225). We can do no better than Asch's descriptions in conveying the important role of organization in the perception of entitativity.

The groups portrayed in the scenarios presented earlier reflect varying degrees of organization and, we submit, reflect comparable variation in perceived entitativity. At the high end of the Entitativity Continuum, the task force working on the computer system is a well-structured group, and the street gang has leaders and followers, established norms, and other characteristics of group structure and organization. Similarly, the Phillies have clear differentiation of roles among its members, and their success depends on their effectiveness in performing in an organized, coordinated fashion. All of these groups convey a clear sense of groupness, and hence lead to the perception of entitativity. The Democratic Party has a formal organizational structure that implies an entitative character, although it often functions in a manner that suggests an

intermediate degree of organization (at best). Other groups convey this characteristic to lesser degrees. Despite their similarities in national heritage or race, neither the Polish Americans nor the racial groups in the water fountain lines have an organized nature, and hence do not possess entitativity to the same extent as the preceding examples. Finally, at the low end of the Entitativity Continuum are the aggregates of persons described in the bank lines and in the movie theater. These collectives possess an organized nature to a minimal (at best) extent, and hence are not seen as having entitativity — as being "real" groups. In summary, the extent to which groups possess organization and structure seems to define their positions on the Entitativity Continuum.

In characterizing the social perceiver, it may seem odd to suggest that racial, gender, or ethnic groups, about whom stereotypes are so widespread, are not perceived as highly entitative groups. Certainly they would be considered meaningful groups (in some sense) by most observers. Moreover, the history of intergroup relations is replete with examples wherein such groups have been identified and treated as singular groups — in which "they" all look alike and "they" are all treated (i.e., discriminated against) in the same way. In this light, it is important to emphasize that we are discussing groups that vary considerably along the Entitativity Continuum; our analysis suggests that large categories based on race, gender, national origin, and so on probably have an intermediate place along this continuum.

Although categories such as race and gender may not be extremely high in entitativity, these social categories have been identified as being high in "natural kindness," as discussed earlier (Rothbart & Taylor, 1992). That is, gender and race groups are perceived as having a core or essence, and these groups are high in inductive potential. Thus, members of one of these groups can be perceived as "all alike," and it is not surprising that stereotyping and prejudice are widespread with regard to racial, ethnic, and gender groups. However, just because all members of a grouping are perceived as sharing essential qualities and as similar in many important respects does not mean that a collection of these individuals will be highly entitative. The individuals comprising a group may be quite similar with regard to physical characteristics, personalities, and abilities, and yet a group of such individuals need not be cohesive, organized, structured, or interdependent. It is these qualities that, in our analysis, define and determine entitativity. Moreover, it is not clear that knowledge about race or gender groups becomes represented in memory in such an organized fashion, or that violations of expectancies typically lead to efforts to explain such inconsistencies among group members. Thus, we must distinguish between the perception of entitativity in groups and other seemingly related but distinct concepts, such as the perception of a group as a natural kind and the perception of homogeneity within a group (Hamilton & Sherman, 1996).

Does this focus on a group's organization mean that the other determinants of perceived entitativity that we discussed earlier are unimportant? Certainly not. All of these bases of perceived entitativity (i.e., similarity, appearance of a natural kind, salience due to minority status, etc.) contribute to the perception of unity and coherence among group members. Any group that possesses one of these features will be perceived as entitative to some degree, but in our view it will be perceived as more so if it also appears to be (or is expected to be) an organized group. However, a group that clearly has an organized and purposive manner need not have highly similar, proximal, or salient members to be perceived as having high entitativity. It is in this sense that we view perceived organization as having a differentially impactful role in evaluating a group's position along the Entitativity Continuum.

Groups and the Perception of Groups

Groups and Categories

The preceding analysis of the perception of entitativity leads to another important observation. Our emphasis on the importance of a group's apparent organization and structure in the perception of its entitativity is consistent with theorizing by scholars concerned with understanding the nature of groups. In particular, the social psychological literature on groups has always had a somewhat narrower definition of *groups* than has the literature on perceptions of groups. Although a broad range of definitions of the term *group* has been offered (see Cartwright & Zander, 1968, pp. 46–48 for a sampling and discussion of such definitions), most authors include some mention of interdependence, organization, and/or role differentiation among the group's members.

The importance of these features of the definition of a group pertains to a distinction between groups, defined in this way, and the kinds of groups of interest to researchers who study intergroup perceptions, stereotyping, and the like. This distinction was clearly articulated in one of the early, and highly influential, textbooks on social psychology, Krech and Crutchfield's (1948) *Theory and Problems of Social Psychology*, where the authors stated that "A group does not merely mean individuals characterized by some similar property. Thus, for example, a collection of Republicans or farmers or Negroes or blind men is not a *group*. These collections may be called *classes* of people. The term *group*, on the other hand, refers to two or more people who bear an *explicit psychological relationship to one another*" (p. 18; italics in original). The same point was nicely illustrated by Lewin (1948) in the following passage:

> Similarity between persons merely permits their classification, their subsumption under the same abstract concept, whereas belonging to the same social group means concrete, dynamic interrelations among persons. A husband, a wife, and a baby are less similar to each other, in spite of their being a strong natural group, than the baby is to other babies, or the husband to other men, or the wife to other women. Strong and well-organized groups, far from being fully homogeneous, are bound to contain a variety of different sub-groups and individuals. It is not similarity or dissimilarity that decides whether two individuals belong to the same or different groups, but social interaction or other types of interdependence. A group is best defined as a dynamic whole based on interdependence rather than similarity. (p. 184)

This emphasis on the importance of organization, differentiation of roles, and pursuit of a common purpose as defining properties of a group continues in more contemporary definitions of groups among researchers in the group dynamics tradition (e.g., McGrath, 1984). Collections of persons that lack these properties, including people of the same gender or ethnicity, are viewed as classes or, in more contemporary terms, social categories.

In contrast to these perspectives on what constitutes a group is virtually any book, chapter, or article on the perception of groups, intergroup perception, or stereotyping. In this literature, those social categories — membership in which may be defined by nothing more than sharing a single feature, such as skin color, gender, or national heritage — are considered meaningful groups simply because they are so commonly perceived in everyday social life as meaningful groups. Perceivers have richly developed beliefs about such groups, and our language and everyday conversation are filled with references to them. In this view, then, women, Hungarians, African Americans, and gays all qualify as meaningful groups, despite the fact that many members of these groups will never even encounter each other.

Thus, the term *group* has two distinct meanings: one meaning that is preferred by scholars, who seek to understand the properties and functioning of small, inter-active groups; and another, much broader meaning that is used by social perception researchers and that seems commonplace in everyday parlance. At one level, the distinction seems to be a mere semantic difference that social psychologists have lived with for decades. Aside from occasional alcohol-induced, late-night ideological arguments at conferences, it is not a distinction that arouses much passion. Everyone understands that when one researcher talks about group decision making and another talks about a stereotype of a group, the term *group* is referring to quite different entities in the two cases.

However, by considering the placement of these social entities along the Entitativity Continuum, the present analysis offers a potentially unifying framework for understanding these distinctions. Consistent with emphases prevalent in the groups dynamics tradition, we view groups characterized by organization, interdependence, and purposiveness as being distinctly high in entitativity, and we believe that perceivers see them as such. From our perspective, the perception that a group possesses this degree of entitativity typically induces information-processing mechanisms that we earlier identified as being characteristic of forming impressions of individuals: on-line inferences and evaluations, organized representation of information, surprise and attributional processing when a member's behavior clearly violates expectations about the group, and so on (Hamilton & Sherman, 1996: McConnell et al., 1994, 1997). These groups are perceived to be the well-integrated (as well as differentiated) units that group dynamics researchers have always said they are.

What, then, about the large "social categories" that are the life-blood of the intergroup perception researcher? We would argue that these "categories" of people are indeed groups, if for no other reason than they are uniformly perceived as such by virtually everyone (the group dynamics researcher being the lone possible exception). If they were not perceived as meaningful entities, everything from wars between countries to debates about affirmative action would be far less prevalent in our world and our society. Thus, we view these groups as possessing moderate to high entitativity, although not as high as the organized, interdependent groups described earlier.

An Emerging Unification?

Our analysis based on the Entitativity Continuum has grown out of our attempt to understand how perceivers

detect "groupness" in their perceptions of social aggregates. Our proposed Entitativity Continuum stands in contrast to the distinction between groups and nongroups, which has been the focus of much discussion in the group dynamics literature. However, it happens that ideas paralleling our proposals can be found in the more recent writings of some group theorists in their analyses of the nature of and differences among social groups. Consider, for example, the following comments from Moreland (1987):

> An analysis of group formation raises several complex issues. One such issue involves the meaning of the term "group." In order to determine whether a group has formed, someone must be able to specify what a group is. Unfortunately, there is little agreement among social psychologists about the "essential" characteristics of small groups .... And it seems unlikely that anyone will produce a definitive listing of those characteristics anytime soon. Perhaps we should abandon these efforts to distinguish groups from nongroups and consider instead a hypothetical dimension of "groupness" that is relevant to every set of persons. Group formation could then be regarded as a *continuous* phenomenon involving the movement of a set of persons along that dimension, rather than as a *discontinuous* phenomenon involving the transformation of a nongroup into a group. (p. 81; italics in original)

Moreland's conception of a continuous dimension along which groups vary directly parallels our conception of an Entitativity Continuum along which groups are perceived. We believe that the correspondence between these two conceptualizations offers a hope for an emerging unification between research on the analysis of groups and research on the perception of groups. The benefits and limitations of such a unification cannot be fully anticipated at this point, but the prospect of such integration between research on group perception and group behavior justifies, in our view, efforts in this direction.

Earlier we discussed a variety of cues that the perceiver might use to infer the extent of a group's "groupness" or entitativity. We might think of the perceiver's task in terms of a Brunswikian lens model, as shown in Fig. 25.1 In the Figure, $X_1 - X_5$ represent variables that contribute to the groupness or entitativity of a group, and that also might serve as cues for inferring entitativity. P represents the observer's perception of entitativity based on those cues, and G represents the group's actual level of entitativity. The lines connecting the cues (X_1) with P represent the extent to which the perceiver uses these cues in inferring

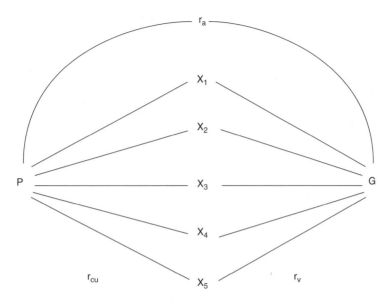

FIGURE 25.1 ■ The lens model.

entitativity, and are called *cue utilization coefficients* (r_{cu}). The extent to which those variables are actually associated with groupness are *validity coefficients* (r_v). To the extent that perceivers' *use* of the available cues (cue utilization coefficients) matches their *usefulness* as valid indicators of groupness (validity coefficients), the perceivers' judgments of entitativity will be accurate (r_a).

As Moreland (1987) noted, there is no "definitive listing" of "essential characteristics" of groups. Nevertheless, various authors have provided lists of candidates. For example, in his textbook on group dynamics, Forsyth (1990) identified several characteristics that define groups, including inter-dependence among members, shared goals, interaction among members, relatively small size of group, cohesiveness, shared goals, and (of particular relevance to our analysis) group structure. It is interesting that these characteristics correspond quite closely to several of the features of social aggregates discussed earlier as possible cues to entitativity. The degree of correspondence between the characteristics perceivers use as cues to entitativity and the characteristics that actually define groupness is, at this juncture, unknown.

Such an analysis, of course, assumes that we have a suitable criterion measure of the extent to which any

group is indeed a group. Unfortunately, group researchers have had difficulty agreeing on such a criterion. Consequently, research assessing the accuracy of perceivers' judgments of group formation has been scarce. In one of the few research programs attempting to investigate this question, Freeman (1992; Freeman & Webster, 1994) studied the interaction patterns of a number of individuals in particular settings over an extended time. These participants were then asked to make judgments about the extent of interaction among pairs of individuals and to sort individuals into groups. The findings of these studies suggest that (a) subjects' reports of interaction patterns (group formation) correspond at a reasonable level to the actual patterns of interaction that occurred among these persons, but that (b) subjects' judgment data reflect some degree of simplification and exaggeration of the observed interaction patterns. Freeman's research is quite useful as a first step toward developing the bridge between group behavior and group perception. Moreover, his findings are fascinating in their suggestion that observers are reasonably accurate while simultaneously manifesting some degree of bias in their mental representations of the groups they observe. Thus, there can be discrepancies between what a group is and how it is perceived.

Conclusion: Organization, the Entitativity Continuum, and the Perception of Individuals and Groups

Our theoretical analysis has generated two central propositions. First, building on previous conceptualizations (Campbell, 1958; Hamilton & Sherman, 1996), we postulated that groups are perceived as existing along an Entitativity Continuum. Second, we postulated that the most important element in the social perceiver's inference about the degree of a group's entitativity is the extent to which the group is an organized entity. A group is more "groupy" when the structural relations among its parts are clearly evident — when it has identifiable leaders, differentiation of roles and functions, established norms, and the like. As was developed earlier in this chapter (and more extensively in Hamilton & Sherman, 1996), the extent to which a group is perceived as being entitative has direct implications for a number of important principles of information processing that will guide the way information about the group and its members will be processed and utilized. Specifically, the perception of entitativity leads to spontaneous, on-line inferences and evaluations, organized representation of acquired information in memory, efforts toward resolution of inconsistencies, and expectations for consistency in the group's performance and the behaviors of its members. Thus, the perception of a group's entitativity has substantial ramifications for a number of aspects of group perception.

Our analysis goes beyond previous efforts to address these issues in postulating the central role of perceived group organization in determining perceptions of entitativity. In our view, the perception of a group as an organized unit is a primary basis for perceivers inferring that the group is indeed a meaningful group. In concluding this chapter, we draw attention to two benefits of this emphasis on perceived organization.

One benefit of the emphasis on the importance of perceiving a group as an organized entity brings us back to our original goal in examining the processes underlying perceptions of groups. As we discussed earlier, the purpose of Hamilton and Sherman's (1996) analysis was to compare the processes mediating perceptions of individuals and of groups — or more specifically, to examine the similarities and differences in how impressions of individuals and conceptions of groups are formed. Based on the extensive literature on forming impressions of individuals, we postulated that perceivers expect an individual to be an organized, coherent unit, and therefore seek to form an impression of the person that identifies and represents his or her primary characteristics in a coherent manner. We then hypothesized that social perceivers expect such coherence in groups to a lesser degree, and found in the literature numerous empirical findings consistent with this view. These observations led us to emphasize the importance of the Entitativity Continuum, which underlies perceptions of both individuals and groups. To the extent that groups are perceived as possessing, or are expected to possess, coherence and organization, they will be perceived as being high in entitativity, and the commonly observed differences in processing information about individual and group targets, based on a priori assumptions about target entitativity, will be diminished. In identifying perceived organization of the target as the primary element underlying this continuum, we have brought the analysis of group perception once again into line with the perception of individual targets, which rests heavily on the assumption that individuals' personalities are unified and organized.

The second benefit of our approach, developed in this chapter, extends this perspective to the interface between group perception and group behavior. In highlighting the importance of a group's organization and structure for the perception of that group, our analysis establishes ties to previous analyses in the group literature regarding the definition of *groupness*. In essence, we view the social perceiver as intuitively engaging in analyses that parallel those of the social scientist, who tries to understand what groups are and what their properties are. Social aggregates are viewed as varying along the Entitativity Continuum, and both the perceiver and the social scientist use information about their properties to understand their placement along that continuum. Given that the literatures on group perception and group process have remained somewhat distinct from each other, this potential bridge may offer some benefits for future analyses and rapprochement.

Acknowledgment

Preparation of this chapter was supported, in part, by NIMH Grant MH-40058. Brian Lickel was supported by a NSF Graduate Fellowship.

REFERENCES

Asch, S. E. (1946). Forming impressions of personality. *Journal of Abnormal and Social Psychology, 41*, 258–290.
Asch, S. E. (1952). *Social psychology*. New York: Oxford University Press.

Brewer, M. B. (1991). The social self: On being the same and different at the same time. *Personality and Social Psychology Bulletin, 17,* 475–482.

Brewer, M. B., & Harasty, A. S. (1996). Seeing groups as entities: The role of perceiver motivation. In R. Sorrentino & E. T. Higgins (Eds.), *Handbook of motivation and cognition Vol. 3: The interpersonal context* (pp. 347–370). New York: Guilford.

Brewer, M. B., Weber, J. G., & Carini, B. (1995). Person memory in intergroup contexts: Categorization versus individuation. *Journal of Personality and Social Psychology, 69,* 29–40.

Campbell, D. T. (1958). Common fate, similarity, and other indices of the status of aggregates of persons as social entities. *Behavioral Science, 3,* 14–25.

Carlston, D. E., & Skowronski, J. J. (1994). Savings in the relearning of trait information as evidence for spontaneous inference generation. *Journal of Personality and Social Psychology, 66,* 840–856.

Cartwright, D., & Zander, A. (1968). Groups and group membership: Introduction. In D. Cartwright & A. Zander (Eds.), *Group dynamics: Research and theory* (3rd ed., pp. 45–62). New York: Harper & Row.

Forsyth, D. R. (1990). *An introduction to group dynamics.* Pacific Grove, CA : Brooks/Cole.

Freeman, L. C. (1992). Filling in the blanks: A theory of cognitive categories and the structure of social affiliation. *Social Psychology Quarterly, 55,* 118–127.

Freeman, L. C., & Webster, C. M. (1994). Interpersonal proximity in social and cognitive space. *Social Cognition, 12,* 223–247.

Freeman, S. A. (1988). The development of induction within natural kind and artifact categories. *Cognitive Psychology, 20,* 65–95.

Hamilton, D. L., Driscoll, D. M., & Worth, L. T. (1989). Cognitive organization of impressions: Effects of incongruency in complex representations. *Journal of Personality and Social Psychology, 57,* 925–939.

Hamilton, D. L., Katz, L. B., & Léirer, V. O. (1980). Organizational processes in impression formation. In R. Hastie, T. M. Ostrom, E. B. Ebbesen, R. S. Wyer, Jr., D. L. Hamilton, & D. E. Carlston (Eds.), *Person memory: The cognitive basis of social perception* (pp. 121–153). Hillsdale, NJ: Lawrence Erlbaum Associates.

Hamilton, D. L., & Sherman, S. J. (1996). Perceiving persons and groups. *Psychological Review, 103,* 336–355.

Hastie, R. (1984). Causes and effects of causal attribution. *Journal of Personality and Social Psychology, 46,* 44–56.

Hastie, R., & Park, B. (1986). The relationship between memory and judgment depends on whether the judgment task is memory-based or on-line. *Psychological Review, 93,* 258–268.

Hoffman, C., Mischel, W., & Mazze, K. (1981). The role of purpose in the organization of information about behavior: Trait-based versus goal-based categories in person cognition. *Journal of Personality and Social Psychology, 40,* 211–225.

Keil, F. C. (1989). *Concepts, kinds, and cognitive development.* Cambridge, MA: MIT Press.

Krech, D., & Crutchfield, R. C. (1948). *Theory and problems of social psychology.* New York: McGraw-Hill.

Lewin, K. (1948). Resolving social conflicts. New York: Harper.

McConnell, A. R., Sherman, S. J., & Hamilton, D. L. (1994). The online and memory-based aspects of individual and group target judgments. *Journal of Personality and Social Psychology, 67,* 173–185.

McConnell, A. R., Sherman, S. J., & Hamilton, D. L. (1997). Target entitativity: Implications for information processing about individual and group targets. *Journal of Personality and Social Psychology, 72,* 750–762.

McGrath, J. E. (1984). *Groups: Interaction and performance.* Englewood Cliffs, NJ: Prentice-Hall.

Moreland, R. L. (1987). The formation of small groups. In C. Hendrick (Ed.), *Group processes: Review of personality and social psychology* (Vol. 8., pp. 80–110). Newbury Park, CA: Sage.

Mullen, B. (1991). Group composition, salience, and cognitive representations: The phenomenology of being in a group. *Journal of Experimental Social Psychology, 27,* 297–323.

Park, B., DeKay, M. L., & Kraus, S. (1994). Aggregating social behavior into person models: Perceiver-induced consistency. *Journal of Personality and Social Psychology, 66,* 437–459.

Park, B., & Rothbart, M. (1982). Perception of out-group homogeneity and levels of social categorization: Memory for the subordinate attributes of in-group and out-group members. *Journal of Personality and Social Psychology, 42,* 1051–1068.

Park, B., Ryan, C. S., & Judd, C. M. (1992). Role of meaningful subgroups in explaining differences in perceived variability for ingroups and out-groups. *Journal of Personality and Social Psychology, 63,* 553–567.

Rothbart, M., Fulero, S., Jensen, C., Howard, J., & Birrell, P. (1978). From individual to group impressions: Availability heuristics in stereotype formation. *Journal of Experimental Social Psychology, 14,* 237–255.

Rothbart, M., & Taylor, M. (1992). Social categories and social reality: Do we view social categories as natural kinds? In G. R., Semin & K. Fiedler (Eds.), *Language, interaction and social cognition* (pp. 11–36). Newbury Park, CA: Sage.

Sanbonmatsu, D. M., Sherman, S. J., & Hamilton, D. L. (1987). Illusory correlation in the perception of individuals and groups. *Social Cognition, 5,* 1–25.

Seta, C. E., & Hayes, N. (1994). The influence of impression formation goals on the accuracy of social memory. *Personality and Social Psychology Bulletin, 20,* 93–101.

Simon, B. (1993). On the asymmetry in the cognitive construal of ingroup and outgroup: A model of egocentric social categorization. *European Journal of Social Psychology, 23,* 131–147.

Srull, T. K. (1981). Person memory: Some tests of associative storage and retrieval models. *Journal of Experimental Psychology: Human Learning and Memory, 7,* 440–462.

Srull, T. K., Lichtenstein, M., & Rothbart, M. (1985). Associative storage and retrieval processes in person memory. *Journal of Experimental Psychology: Learning, Memory, and Cognition, 11,* 316–345.

Srull, T. K., & Wyer, R. S., Jr. (1989). Person memory and judgment. *Psychological Review, 96,* 58–83.

Stern, L. D., Marrs, S., Millar, M. G., & Cole, E. (1984). Processing time and the recall of inconsistent and consistent behaviors of individuals and groups. *Journal of Personality and Social Psychology, 47,* 253–262.

Susskind, J., Maurer, K. L., Thakkar, V., Sherman, J. W., & Hamilton, D. L. (1997). *Perceiving individuals and groups: Expectancies, inferences, and causal attributions.* Unpublished manuscript, University of California, Santa Barbara.

Uleman, J. S. (1987). Consciousness and control: The case of spontaneous trait inferences. *Personality and Social Psychology Bulletin, 13,* 337–354.

Weisz, C., & Jones, E. E. (1993). Expectancy disconfirmation and dispositional inference: Latent strength of target-based and category-based expectancies. *Personality and Social Psychology Bulletin, 19,* 563–573.

Wyer, R. S., Bodenhausen, G. V., & Srull, T. K. (1984). The cognitive representation of persons and groups and its effect on recall and recognition memory. *Journal of Experimental Social Psychology, 20,* 445–469.

PART 7

Stereotypes

Introduction and Preview

Heaven is where . . .
> *the police are British,*
> *the cooks are French,*
> *the mechanics are German,*
> *the lovers are Italian,*
> *and it's all organized by the Swiss.*

Hell is where . . .
> *the police are German,*
> *the cooks are British,*
> *the mechanics are French,*
> *the lovers are Swiss,*
> *and it's all organized by the Italians.*

We can understand and enjoy jokes such as this one because we are familiar with the prevalent beliefs about the characteristics of various national groups and how they differ. Stereotypes about groups are widespread in any society and are routinely used in people's judgments of those groups and their members (Fiske, 1998; Hamilton & Sherman, 1994). Stereotypes also can be harmful to the targets of those beliefs as they paint all members of a large and diverse group with one broad stroke. What exactly are stereotypes? How do they form and why do we use them? How can we understand the ways that stereotypes influence perceptions and behavior? These questions are addressed in Part 7.

421

From the social cognition perspective, stereotypes are cognitive structures and therefore, like any cognitive structure, they can influence information processing, perception, and behavior in a variety of ways. Earlier we defined a cognitive structure as the perceiver's "knowledge, beliefs, and expectancies about some domain." When that domain pertains to some human group (women, Asians, gays), then those cognitive structures are stereotypes.

Why do we form and use these stereotypes? There are several answers to these questions (for a fuller treatment, see Mackie, Hamilton, Susskind, & Rosselli, 1996). Certainly from a very young age we are "taught" — by parents, teachers, friends and peer groups, the media — what our society believes to be the prominent characteristics of many groups (gender, race, nationality, occupations, etc.). Research has also documented that cognitive processes can play important roles in both the formation and use of stereotypes. These processes are fundamentally important in stereotyping, but are perhaps less obvious and therefore warrant some brief discussion.

What cognitive mechanisms are involved in the formation and use of stereotypes, and why? Again, there are several answers. First, stereotypes, as cognitive structures, can greatly reduce the demands on information processing. By categorizing people — lumping them together in a group and assuming that they all have the same characteristics — we bypass the need to attend to each individual that we encounter. In stereotyping, we overlook the individual and the attributes that distinguish that person as a unique person, and instead we assume that all members of the group share a common set of attributes (yes, all those French are great cooks). Such an assumption can be cognitively useful. If indeed most

French are good cooks, then perhaps I can assume that Pierre, whom I've never met, would be quite adept at preparing a good meal. In this way, I have "knowledge gain" through the application of my preconceived beliefs to Pierre. On the other hand, by assuming that Pierre is just like all French, the consequence is "information loss" in that I do not bother to learn about those characteristics that make Pierre a unique and fascinating individual. So the use of stereotypes can produce information gain, but also can result in information loss.

A second reason we form and use stereotypes is that we may obtain some psychological benefit from doing so. That is, if we distinguish "us" from "them," and if we want to feel good about our own group, then it benefits us if we can perceive "those folks" as bad, as undesirable, as unworthy. In comparing our own group to some other group in this way, we can feel pride in belonging to our group and therefore each of us can feel good about ourselves. Of course, you might be wondering, "How do we know that our group is better than those other folks?" Good question. The answer lies in the fact that this social comparison process can itself be biased and selective. After all, what are the relevant criteria for comparing our group to the other group? Well, as long as this process is occurring in our own minds, that choice is ours. This means that we can choose to compare the groups on those very criteria that will favor our group in the comparison process. Not a terribly objective process, to be sure, and one that clearly is motivated by a desire for self-enhancement, but nevertheless, with that goal in mind, it works. These ideas are at the heart of the Social Identity Theory (Tajfel & Turner, 1986), which has stimulated an enormous amount of important research on intergroup categorization and its effects.

Categorization of people into groups is an important foundation of stereotyping (Allport, 1954; Tajfel, 1969). The mere cognitive act of categorizing others has important consequences that provide the building blocks for stereotype formation. For example, categorizing others into distinct groups leads to (a) enhanced perception of the differences between groups, (b) enhanced perception of the similarity among members within a group, and (c) diminished ability to differentiate among the members of a group (Taylor, 1981; Wilder, 1981). These consequences of categorization make it "easy" to believe that the groups are "really" different from each other (and studies have shown that this occurs even in groups defined by arbitrary criteria). Moreover, due to these effects of categorization, the members of each group are seen as being similar to each other. If they are seen as homogeneous, then it becomes easy to generalize across group members, to "see" them all as having the same attributes. This kind of generalizing across all group members is one of the hallmarks of stereotyping (Allport, 1954), and is even reflected in some common sayings in everyday parlance ("they're all alike"; "if you've seen one, you've seen them all"). Thus, the mere act of categorization — a very common and often highly adaptive cognitive process — can lay the foundation for the development of group stereotypes.

In addition, we have already seen that stimuli in our environment can be salient and attention-grabbing for a variety of reasons — for example, because they are bright and colorful, because they are in motion rather than stationary, because they pose a threat to our well-being. The article by Hamilton and Gifford (1976) shows the impact of distinctive stimuli in a different context. Stimulus events can be distinctive not only by being very bright, very loud, or otherwise vivid, but also because they

are unusual. That is, something that is out of the ordinary because it doesn't happen very often can be distinctive and therefore can capture attention. Once that happens, the information is likely to be well represented in memory and therefore to be available to influence later judgments. Hamilton and Gifford suggested that members of small groups are "distinctive" in the social world, simply because perceivers are exposed to them less frequently than they encounter members of larger groups. Similarly, some kinds of behaviors (e.g., undesirable behaviors) occur less frequently than other (e.g., desirable) behaviors, making them distinctive by their statistical infrequency. Hamilton and Gifford proposed that when those two kinds of stimuli co-occur — a member of a small group performs an undesirable behavior — that event will be particularly distinctive, will be noticed and processed, stored in memory, and therefore will have a disproportionate impact on later judgments. In fact, Hamilton and Gifford's research showed that this effect can lead to evaluatively differing perceptions of two groups, even when the information describing the groups was evaluatively equivalent. Thus, different group impressions (stereotypes) were formed, solely due to a bias in the way perceivers process distinctive information (other possible explanations for this effect are reviewed by Stroessner & Plaks, 2001).

Once formed, how do stereotypes function? That is, how do they influence our perceptions of groups and our judgments of individual members of those groups? In the Introductory Overview chapter, I highlighted several aspects of social information processing — attention and encoding, elaboration, representation in memory, retrieval from memory — that characterize the way perceivers comprehend and make use of the information they encounter. And I noted that cognitive structures can influence each of these processes. If stereotypes are cognitive structures, then it seems plausible that the same processes would be involved in the ways we process and use information about groups. The readings in this section (and a great deal of additional research; see Fiske, 1998; Hamilton & Sherman, 1994) document that stereotypes do in fact function in this manner.

Much of the information we encounter in the social world is ambiguous, in the sense that it is open to alternative interpretations. Was her smile genuine or was she merely being polite? Was his temperamental outburst a reflection of an unstable personality or a consequence of the stress he's been under? As I have stated several times in earlier sections, the "meaning" of behavior often is not clear until the perceiver imposes some interpretation on that information. Cognitive structures can aid the perceiver in making sense of this complex and ambiguous information by guiding that interpretive process. Knowing that a person is religious helps me understand why a person pauses briefly, with eyes closed and head bowed, prior to eating a meal. Believing (stereotypically) that African Americans are hostile and aggressive can guide one's interpretation of a black person's behavior (Duncan, 1976; Sagar & Schofield, 1980).

Sometimes the stereotype provides only a tentative "hunch" as to how to interpret others' behaviors, and those hunches can serve as hypotheses that are then evaluated as we learn more about a person. Darley and Gross (1983) demonstrated that stereotypes can serve as a source of such "hypotheses" that can guide a perceiver's interpretation of another's behavior. Their study occurred in two parts. Participants initially learned about a young girl by viewing pictures of her home, neighborhood, and school while they heard an experimenter read about what they were seeing. Two conditions were established at this

phase. In one, the girl was portrayed as coming from an upper-middle-class background, whereas in the other condition they learned that she came from a lower-class urban neighborhood. Participants at that point were asked to rate how well they thought the girl would do academically in school. The manipulation of SES background did not significantly influence these ratings. However, Darley and Gross argued, the stereotypic expectancy that high-SES kids would do better academically than low-SES kids was a hypothesis that would guide interpretation of new information about the girl. All participants then were shown a videotape in which the girl was orally tested on a variety of math problems, some easy, some difficult. She did moderately well, both missing some easy questions but also answering some of the difficult ones correctly. Importantly, in this phase of the study all participants were shown exactly the same videotape. When they were then asked to rate the girl's performance and overall ability, participants in the high-SES condition rated her as having performed better, answered more items correctly, and having performed at a higher grade level, compared to ratings made by participants in the low-SES condition. How do these differences "fit" with the results of the first phase of the study? Darley and Gross propose that stereotypes can serve as intuitive (tentatively held) hypotheses, so that activation of the stereotype by itself may not influence judgments of a group member (as in the first phase of the study). However, once activated, those stereotypes can guide the interpretation of new information. Thus, participants in the high-SES condition "saw" the girl as performing better, as having correctly answered more of the difficult questions and having fewer incorrect answers than did participants who had the stereotype of low-SES students activated by the initial background information.

The findings from this study illustrate the insidious nature of cognitive structures and their influence on social perception. Initially, participants essentially said (in their Phase 1 ratings) "No, knowing a child's SES is not a valid basis for predicting her academic performance." Yet later, after all participants had viewed exactly the same performance, the two conditions diverged in their assessments not only of what they had just seen (the girl's performance) but also in their overall evaluations of her ability.

Stereotypes not only can influence the way we interpret behavior and perceive others, they also can influence our actions. Research by Correll, Park, Judd, and Wittenbrink (2002) simulated the situation faced by police officers when they encounter the potentially dangerous incident in which another person may or may not be armed and attempting to shoot them. In such instances the officer must make a quick decision, on the basis of partial information, as to whether the person is a threat or is harmless. That quick decision will then influence whether he himself should shoot or not. Correll et al. used a videogame format to simulate this situation. Participants saw a person appear on a computer screen, and the person either was or was not holding a gun. The participants' instruction was that if the person had a gun, then they should shoot (by pressing a particular response key); if not holding a gun, do not shoot (indicated by pressing a different key). The computer recorded both the participant's decision (shoot or not shoot) and the time it took to make that decision. Importantly, on some trials the target person was African American, whereas on other trials he was Euro-American. The effect of race of stimulus person on participants' decisions was dramatic. Participants made the decision to shoot an armed target more quickly if that person was African American than if

white, and they were quicker in responding "not shoot" if the target person was white than if African American. Moreover, in one of their studies this same pattern occurred for both white and African American participants, suggesting that the effect is not due to outgroup prejudice but more likely reflects commonly shared stereotypes of African Americans (for similar research, see Payne, 2001).

When we consider the variety of contexts in which our judgments can be biased by stereotypic beliefs (as illustrated by Darley and Gross) and in which stereotype-based expectancies can influence our behavior toward outgroup members (as shown by Correll et al.), we begin to understand how stereotypes can have profound and troubling consequences. Moreover, when we realize that the participants in both of these studies probably were not even aware of these stereotype-based influences on their perceptions and actions, the ramifications of these cognitive processes become even more evident and problematic. This research helps us begin to understand some of the important mechanisms that underlie stereotyping and its detrimental consequences for the targets of those judgments and behaviors.

It is important to realize, however, that cognitive structures do not form *in order to* bias information processing and to victimize targets of perception and behavior. On the contrary, those detrimental effects *are consequences of* an information processing system that in most contexts is highly adaptive and useful in dealing with the cognitive burdens of a complex social world.

Several of the readings in this book provide examples of how perceivers achieve this adaptation. One illustrative case is provided by Reading 28 in this part (Macrae, Milne, & Bodenhausen, 1994). We have seen that the perceiver's expectancies can guide (and sometimes bias) the processing of social information. However, expectancies can also facilitate information processing, particularly information that is consistent with those expectancies. If that is so, then the effect of such expectancies is to reduce the demands on the cognitive processing system and thereby to "free up" cognitive resources for other tasks.

This effect is demonstrated in the research reported by Macrae et al. (1994). Stereotypes are cognitive structures that incorporate our expectancies about social groups, and as we all know, they can slant our views of group members. However, what Macrae et al. show is that the use of a stereotype in processing information about group members can facilitate performance *on another task being performed simultaneously*. Specifically, participants in one of Macrae et al.'s studies had to perform two tasks at the same time. One task involved forming impressions of four men who were described by a variety of traits. Some of the participants were told the occupation of each person, and in each case some of the traits were stereotypic of their group membership. The other participants were shown the same traits describing the same persons, but without the group membership information, so no stereotype was available for their use. While they were doing this task, participants also had to listen to a tape recording describing the geography and economy of Indonesia. Afterward, two measures were taken: (1) participants were asked to recall the traits that described the target persons and (2) they were given a quiz about the information about Indonesia provided in the audiotape. The results showed that participants who had knowledge of the target persons' group memberships, and therefore could use stereotypes in processing information about them, differed on both measures from those who did not have stereotypic knowledge. First, they could recall more of the stereotypic traits that had described the target persons, evidence of the expectancy-confirming bias in processing that I mentioned earlier. Second, and more importantly for my point here, participants who knew the group memberships of the target persons also performed better on the quiz about Indonesia. This result indicates that having stereotypes available made processing information about the target persons easier and less demanding. This in turn freed up cognitive resources for the second, simultaneous task of listening to the descriptive information about Indonesia. As a consequence the information was processed better and better retained, resulting in better performance on the quiz administered to the participants. Thus, the use of prior expectancies eased processing of expectancy-relevant materials and facilitated performance on a second, simultaneously performed task.

Discussion Questions

1. Stereotypes can form through several different means. List several different processes that could lead to the formation of stereotypes.
2. The articles by Darley and Gross and by Cottrell et al. demonstrate that stereotypes can influence perceptions, judgments, and behaviors, but these studies demonstrate quite different processes that can generate these effects. What mechanisms are revealed in each paper, and how do they differ?
3. It has been said that the biases in stereotyping generally serve to maintain the stereotype. Explain what that statement means, and cite research findings that support it.

Suggested Readings

Hamilton, D. L., & Sherman, J. W. (1994). Stereotypes. In R. S. Wyer, Jr., & T. K. Srull (Eds.), *Handbook of social cognition* (2nd Ed., Vol. 2, pp. 1–68). Hillsdale, NJ: Erlbaum.

Fiske, S. T. (1998). Stereotyping, prejudice, and discrimination. In D. T. Gilbert, S. T. Fiske, & G. Lindzey (Eds.), *Handbook of social psychology* (4th Ed., Vol. 2, pp. 357–411). New York: McGraw-Hill.

Schneider, D. J. (2004). *The psychology of stereotyping*. New York: Guilford.

Devine, P. G. (1989). Stereotypes and prejudice: Their automatic and controlled components. *Journal of Personality and Social Psychology, 56*, 5–18.

Jost, J. T., & Banaji, M. R. (1994). The role of stereotyping in system-justification and the production of false consciousness. *British Journal of Social Psychology, 33*, 1–27.

Illusory Correlation in Interpersonal Perception: A Cognitive Basis of Stereotypic Judgments

David L. Hamilton and Robert K. Gifford

Illusory correlation refers to an erroneous inference about the relationship between two categories of events. One postulated basis for illusory correlation is the co-occurrence of events which are statistically infrequent; i.e., observers overestimate the frequency of co-occurrence of distinctive events. If one group of persons "occurs" less frequently than another and one type of behavior occurs infrequently, then the above hypothesis predicts that observers would overestimate the frequency that that type of behavior was performed by members of that group. This suggested that the differential perception of majority and minority groups could result solely from the cognitive mechanisms involved in processing information about stimulus events that differ in their frequencies of co-occurrence. Results of two experiments testing this line of reasoning provided strong support for the hypothesis. Implications of the experiments for the acquisition of stereotypes are discussed.

Chapman (1967) has introduced the concept of illusory correlation to refer to "the report by observers of a correlation between two classes of events which, in reality, (a) are not correlated, or (b) are correlated to a lesser extent than reported" (p. 151). Most research on this topic has been concerned with illusory correlation as a basis for erroneous reports of relationships between symptoms of patients and performance on psychodiagnostic tests (Chapman & Chapman, 1967, 1969; Golding & Rorer, 1971; Starr & Katkin, 1969). The interest of the present research was in studying illusory correlation in the way persons make judgments about other people. Specifically,

This research was supported by NSF Grant GS-3189 and NIMH Grant MH 26049 to the first author. The authors appreciate the assistance of Sally Eisenman and William Trochim in the collection and analysis of the data. R.K.G. is now at Uniformed Services University of the Health Sciences, Bethesda, M.D. Requests for reprints should be sent to David L. Hamilton, Department of Psychology, University of California at Santa Barbara, Santa Barbara, CA 93106.

the two experiments reported here were designed to explore the possibility that stereotypic judgments can be acquired on the basis of purely cognitive, information-processing mechanisms.

In Chapman's (1967) original demonstration of illusory correlation, a series of 12 word pairs — constructed by pairing each of four words from one list with each of three words from a second list — was presented to subjects a number of times. Each word pair was shown the same number of times. When subjects were asked to estimate, for each word on the first list, the percentage of occurrences of that word in which it was paired with each word in the second list, certain systematic biases were observed. When there was a strong associative connection between the words (e.g., *lion–tiger, bacon–eggs*), subjects overestimated the frequency of co-occurrence. In addition, one word in each list was longer than the other words, and subjects consistently overestimated the frequency with which those two words have been paired. Chapman hypothesized that this latter finding was due to the distinctiveness of the long words within their respective lists, and that the co-occurrence of distinctive stimuli can result in an overestimation of the frequency with which the two events occurred together. The long words were distinctive only because the other words were short. Thus, distinctiveness is considered here as due to statistical infrequency. The present research explores the implications of the latter finding — illusory correlation based on the co-occurrence of distinctive stimuli — for social perception.

Why would the co-occurrence of distinctive events result in an illusory correlation? It is well established that observers are more attentive to distinctive than to nondistinctive stimuli, and the heightened attention to a distinctive stimulus should result in a greater encoding of that information. Extending this line of reasoning, the co-occurrence of two distinctive events should be particularly salient to an observer, resulting in increased attention to and more effective encoding of the fact that the two events occurred together, thereby increasing the subjective belief that a relationship exists between them.

Experiment 1

Tajfel (1969) has defined stereotyping as "the attribution of general psychological characteristics to large human groups" (pp. 81–82). Thus stereotyping begins with the differential perception of social groups. When a perceiver differentially evaluates two groups, then the particular content associated with those evaluations constitutes the basis for stereotypic perceptions. Traditional conceptions of the development of stereotypes have emphasized the role of learning and motivational processes (cf. Brigham, 1971; Hamilton, 1976). Recently, however, several lines of research indicate that such differential perceptions of groups can develop simply as a consequence of our normal cognitive processes (see Hamilton, 1976, for a discussion of this research). The present research is consistent with this line of investigation.

The first experiment reported here examined whether the differential perception of groups can be based on the way perceivers process information about co-occurring events, and more specifically, on the co-occurrence of distinctive events. The following conceptual parallel will make the rationale underlying the present research more understandable. In the everyday experience of the typical white suburbanite, interaction with blacks, and even observation of them, is a relatively infrequent occurrence. That is, it is a statistically infrequent event

and hence is "distinctive" in the sense that that term was used above. Also, since for most varieties of behavior the norm is positive in value, undesirable (non-normative) behavior is statistically less frequent than desirable behavior and can also be considered distinctive. Given this framework, the implication of Chapman's (1967) finding is that, even if the distribution of desirable and undesirable behavior is the same for both blacks and whites, the pairing of "blackness" with "undesirable behavior" would lead the typical white observer to infer that those two events co-occur more frequently than they actually do. Such an inference would provide the basis for the differential perception of the majority and minority groups, and hence for stereotypic judgments, based solely on characteristics of how persons process information about other people. The first experiment was designed to subject this line of reasoning to experimental test.

Method

Development of Stimulus Materials

A list of 95 behavior descriptions was developed. The behaviors portrayed in these items for the most part were common, everyday behaviors, such us the following: "Is rarely late for work," "always talks about himself and his problems," "converses easily with people he does not know well." This list of behavior descriptions was given to 36 undergraduate college students who rated each item in terms of how desirable they considered the behavior to be. The mean rating of each item was considered to be the desirability scale value of the behavior. From this list, 27 moderately desirable and 12 moderately undesirable items were selected for use in the stimulus materials.

In this study we were interested in examining "paired distinctiveness" as a possible basis for stereotypic judgment. Consequently, members of any actual minority group could not be used as stimulus persons, since judgments of such persons would in all likelihood already be biased by previously formed associations. Therefore, a minority group was "manufactured." Of the 39 stimulus persons used in the study, 26 were identified as members of Group A and 13 as members of Group B.

The stimulus materials used in the study consisted of a series of statements, each statement describing a behavior performed by one male person who was either a member of Group A or Group B, e.g., "John, a member of Group A, visited a sick friend in the hospital." The distribution of the 39 sentences according to desirability of the behavior and the group membership was as follows: Group A, desirable: 18; Group A, undesirable: 8; Group B, desirable: 9; Group B, undesirable: 4. It can be seen that two-thirds of the statements described behaviors performed by members of Group A; this was true of sentences describing both desirable and undesirable behaviors. Also, desirable behaviors were more frequent than undesirable behaviors; for both Groups A and B, there was a 9:4 ratio of desirable to undesirable behaviors. Thus, Group B is distinctive by its occurring less frequently than A, as is undesirable behavior also distinctive by its statistical infrequency. The four sentences which describe a member of Group B performing an undesirable act therefore represent instances of the co-occurrence of distinctive events.

In assigning behavior descriptions to the two groups, care was taken to ensure that the mean and variability of the desirability values of the two groups of sentences were essentially equal. In addition, in view of the rating scales to be used (see below), an attempt was made to equate the two groups on the proportion of sentences describing interpersonal as opposed to task-related behaviors.

Instructions and Procedures

Subjects were run in small groups of four to six per session. The experiment was described as being concerned with how people process and retain information that is presented to them visually, and after some expansion on this theme, the instructions indicated that subjects would see a series of slides, each slide showing a single sentence describing a behavior performed by a particular person. A few examples of the kinds of sentences they would see were then shown. The sample sentences presented descriptions of a person performing some behavior but did not include identification of the actor's membership in Group A or Group B (e.g., "Alex tried not to take sides when two of his friends had an argument"). These sample slides were included in order to expose subjects to the kinds of behavior that they would see in the experimental set of slides. The instructions then continued as follows.

> In the sentences you will see in the actual experiment, the persons described in the statements will be identified by their membership in a certain group. Each person described in the slides is a member of one of two groups which, to keep things simple, will be referred to as Group A or Group B. In collecting behavior descriptions of people for this experiment we tried to draw a random sample from the population. In the real-world population, Group B is a smaller group than is Group A, Consequently statements describing members of Group B occur less frequently in the slides you will see....

> You will be shown a rather large number of statements like the ones you saw a few minutes ago.... As the slides are presented, simply read each statement carefully.

Following these instructions the sequence of 39 slides was presented to the subjects, Each slide was presented for a period of 8 seconds.

When the series of slides was completed, subjects were given a booklet containing materials for the three dependent measures.

Trait Ratings

This experiment was primarily interested in illusory correlation as a basis of differential perceptions of groups. One section of the booklet therefore asked subjects to rate the members of Groups A and B on a series of characteristics. The questionnaire consisted of a list of 20 attributes, each attribute accompanied by two 10 point inference scales, one for Group A and one for Group B. In order to guarantee some degree of heterogeneity in the inference scales used, the 20 attributes were selected on the basis of Rosenberg, Nelson, and Vivekananthan's (1968) analysis of the dimensions underlying first impressions. These authors found two dimensions to be both empirically satisfactory and conceptually useful, a Social or interpersonal dimension (e.g., *popular, sociable*, vs. *irritable, unhappy*) and an Intellectual or task-related dimension (e.g., *industrious, intelligent*, vs. *lazy, foolish*). Six words representing the positive pole and four words representing the negative pole of each of these two dimensions were used in the trait inference task. If "paired distinctiveness" is a basis for stereotypic judgments, then subjects should give less desirable ratings to members of Group B.

Attributions of Group Membership

Another section of the booklet asked the subject to indicate the group membership of the person who had performed each behavior. The 39 behavior descriptions were listed, each statement beginning with the following phase, "A member of Group ——." For each item, the subjects were asked to write letter A or B in the blank space. If the co-occurrence of distinctive events can result in an overestimate of the frequency of those events, there should be a tendency for negative behaviors to be overattributed to members of Group B.

Frequency Estimates

The last page of the questionnaire booklet told the subjects how many of the statements had described members of Group A and Group B, and asked them to estimate in each case how many of these statements had described *undesirable* behavior. If subjects overestimate the frequency of co-occurrence of the distinctive events, then they should overestimate the number of undesirable behaviors for Group B.

For half of the subjects, the dependent measures occurred in the order described above. The other half of the subjects completed the trait inferences after filling out the group membership attributions. This manipulation provided a check on the effect of completing one dependent measure on the responses to subsequent measures. In all cases the frequency estimates were completed last. (Since the instructions for the frequency estimates measure specifically focused the subjects' attention on the desirability–undesirability variable, it was decided that this should be the last measure completed by all subjects.)

When the subjects had completed the dependent measures, the purpose of the study and the rationale underlying the procedure used were explained.

Subjects

Subjects in the experiment were 20 male and 20 female undergraduate students at a state university in New Haven. Half of the subjects of each sex received the dependent measures in each of the orders described above.

In a task in which stimulus person's name (John, Bill, etc.), group membership (A, B), and the behavior described were all varying, it is possible that some subjects did not attend to the group membership information while viewing the sequence of slides. However, the basic conditions for testing the present hypotheses require that

membership in Group B be recognized as having occurred less frequently than membership in Group A in the series of stimulus sentences. On the attributions of group membership task, if a subject attributed a majority of the behaviors to Group B (which actually occurred one-third of the time), then that subject could not have perceived information about Group B as distinctive due to its infrequency of occurrence, and hence that subject's data do not provide an adequate basis for testing the hypotheses. It was therefore decided to eliminate from the sample any subject who attributed less than half of the behaviors to Group A (the actual majority group). Seven subjects were thereby eliminated from the sample, and the results reported below are based on the remaining 33 subjects. (Analyses based on the total sample yielded very similar results.)

Results

Attributions of Group Membership

On one dependent measure, subjects attributed each behavior description to a member of Group A or a member of Group B. In classifying these data, a 2 × 2 table was constructed in which the rows referred to the evaluation of the behavior (desirable or undesirable) and the columns were defined by the group membership (A or B) assigned by the subject to each behavior description. Each subject's responses to the 39 items were classified according to such a table, and a phi coefficient was calculated from the data for each subject. In the stimulus sentences there was no relationship between behavior desirability and group membership (cf. Table 26.1a).

TABLE 26.1. Results of Experiment 1 for Attributions of Group Membership and Frequency Estimates Measures

(a) Distribution of stimulus sentences

Behaviors	Group		
	A	B	
Desirable	18	9	27
Undesirable	8	4	12
	26	13	39

(b) Attributions of group membership means (conditional probabilities in parentheses)

Behaviors	Group assigned by subject		
	A	B	
Desirable	17.52 (.65)	9.48 (.35)	27.00 (1.00)
Undesirable	5.79 (.30)	6.21 (.52)	12.00 (1.00)
	23.31	15.09	39.00

(c) Proportion of each sentence type recalled accurately (values expected by chance in parentheses)

Behaviors	Group	
	A	B
Desirable	.74 (.60)	.54 (.40)
Undesirable	.55 (.60)	.65 (.40)

(d) Frequency estimates means (conditional proportions in parentheses)

Behaviors	Group		
	A	B	
Desirable	17.09 (.66)	7.27 (.56)	24.36
Undesirable	8.91 (.34)	5.73 (.44)	14.64
	26.00 (1.00)	13.00 (1.00)	39.00

It was hypothesized, however, that subjects would over-attribute undesirable behaviors to members of Group B, a tendency that would result in a nonzero correlation. To test this hypothesis, each subject's phi coefficient was converted to a Fisher's Z-score, and a t-test was conducted to determine whether the mean of this distribution was significantly greater than zero. The results of this test supported the hypothesis, $t(32) = 2.57, p < .02$. A 2 × 2 (Sex of Subject × Order of Dependent Measure) analysis of these Z-scores indicated that there were no significant effects associated with these variables.

To examine the basis for this illusory correlation, the mean number of desirable and undesirable statements attributed to members of Group A and Group B on this task was determined. These data, shown in Table 26.1b, indicate that subjects tended to overattribute the undesirable behaviors to Group B. This effect is reflected in the conditional probabilities (shown in parentheses) for the assignment of behaviors to Groups A and B, given the desirability value of the behavior. In the stimulus slides, the probability that a statement described a member of Group A was .67, regardless of desirability value (18 of 27 desirable and eight of 12 undesirable behaviors described members of that group). While the probability that a desirable behavior would be attributed to Group A was .65 (slightly less than the correct probability), the comparable probability given an undesirable behavior was only .48. In other words, although only one-third of the undesirable statements described members of Group B, over half of them were attributed to Group B on the group membership attribution task. Thus, the bias was associated with the undesirable statements, and the data support the interpretation that the illusory correlation was based on the overattribution of undesirable behaviors to the smaller group.

Responses on the attributions of group membership task were further examined to determine the accuracy with which subjects recalled the group membership for each sentence type. If, as argued earlier, subjects differentially attend to and encode information contained in infrequently co-occurring stimulus events, then they should be better able to recall accurately group membership in the case of undesirable behaviors performed by members of Group B. Table 26.1c shows the proportion of correct responses for each sentence type. The proportions expected by chance are shown in parentheses. In their attributions of group membership subjects assigned "A" to 60% of the sentences and attributed 40% to Group B. Thus for those behaviors actually performed by Group A stimulus persons (left column of the table) chance responding would yield correct answers in 60% of the cases. Similarly, 40% accuracy would be expected for those behaviors performed by members of Group B. The data in this table illustrate three points: (a) Subjects performed above chance level in three of the four cases, (b) the overattribution of undesirable behaviors to Group B, as described above, resulted in below-chance accuracy for undesirable behaviors associated with Group A, and (c) most important, subjects' performance exceeded the chance level by the greatest amount in the case of the infrequently co-occurring stimuli.

Frequency Estimates

Whereas the preceding analyses demonstrated a bias in subjects' attributions of specific behavior instances, the frequency estimates measure was included to determine whether or not an illusory correlation would manifest itself in a subject's overall estimates of the frequency of desirable and undesirable statements characterizing each group. The subject was told that there were 26 statements describing members of Group A, and he was asked how many of those he thought were undesirable. Subtracting the subject's estimate from 26 yielded his estimate of the number of desirable-behavior statements there had been about Group A. A comparable procedure for Group B yielded the subject's estimate for that group. The resulting means are presented in Table 26.1d. The proportions of desirable and undesirable behaviors estimated for each group, based on these means, are shown in parentheses. It can be seen that subjects estimated that a larger proportion of the behaviors describing Group B had been undesirable.

Two statistical analyses were performed on these frequency estimates. Subjects estimated the number of undesirable behaviors for Group A and Group B, and the correct values were 8 and 4, respectively. For each subject, two deviation scores were determined by subtracting these correct values from his corresponding estimates. The resulting means were 0.91 and 1.73, indicating that subjects did tend to overestimate the number of undesirable behaviors for Group B. This difference, however, was not statistically significant. The second analysis consisted of determining a phi coefficient for each subject, based on the 2 × 2 table constructed from his estimates. A t test of the hypothesis that the mean correlation was greater than zero approached significance, $t(32) = 1.92, p < .10$. A 2 × 2 analysis of variance showed that neither sex of subject nor order of dependent measures had a significant effect on these data.

Trait Ratings

The findings reported thus far demonstrate that an illusory correlation was established such that subjects perceived a relationship between group membership and behavior desirability. The question of primary interest to the present research is whether this bias would have an effect upon the subjects' perceptions of the two groups.

Subjects rated Group A and Group B on 20 trait scales. Four kinds of inference scales were used: Good Social, Bad Social, Good Intellectual, and Bad Intellectual. Each subject's average rating for Group A and Group B were determined for each scale category, and these data were analyzed in a 2 (Subject Sex) × 2 (Order of Dependent Measure) × 2 (Social/Intellectual Scales) × 2 (Good/Bad Scales) × 2 (Groups A and B) analysis of variance with repeated measures on the last three factors. Of primary interest is the interaction of Good/Bad Scales with Groups, which was highly significant, $F(1, 29) = 9.36$, $p < .01$. The mean ratings of the two groups for each scale category, presented in Table 26.2, indicate that members of Group A were rated as more likely to have desirable properties and less likely to have undesirable characteristics. These findings provide strong support for the primary hypothesis of this experiment, that the differential perception of groups can be based solely on the cognitive mechanisms involved in processing information about pairs of events that differ in their frequencies of co-occurrence.[1]

Discussion

The results of Experiment 1 clearly supported the hypotheses, and are consistent with the interpretation that subjects developed an illusory correlation based on the co-occurrence of distinctive stimulus events and that this bias resulted in the differential perception of the two groups. However, since desirability and frequency of occurrence were confounded in the stimulus materials, other explanations remain plausible.

One possibility is that the present results were due to "mere exposure" effects (Zajonc, 1968); the greater frequency of occurrence of members of Group A might have resulted in the subjects' developing more positive attitudes toward members of that group. The general enhancement in evaluation of members of Group A evidenced in the trait inferences (Table 26.2) clearly would

TABLE 26.2. Mean Trait Ratings for Groups A and B: Experiment 1

Rating Scales	Group A	Group B
Good Social	6.66	6.03
Bad Social	4.43	5.63
Good Intellectual	7.16	6.26
Bad Intellectual	4.35	4.98

Note: Ratings were made on 10-point scales.

follow from this interpretation. A mere exposure explanation would posit that subjects overresponded to the most frequently occurring class of stimulus items (i.e., members of Group A performing desirable behaviors) and that a bias to do so resulted in a more favorable evaluation of the members of the larger group. Analyses of the Attribution of Group Membership responses, however, indicated that subjects in fact overestimated the frequency with which the distinctive events co-occurred (cf. Table 26.1b), i.e., the bias was associated with the undesirable, not the desirable, statements. Thus the mere exposure hypothesis would seemingly have difficulty accounting for this result. Nevertheless, the extent to which mere exposure contributed to (at least some of) the findings of this study remain undetermined.

Another possibility is that the statement in the instructions that "Group B is a smaller group than Group A" could have led subjects to infer that Group B was a minority group, and if they believe most minority groups are "less good" than the majority, such a bias could have contributed to the results. However, Jones, Stoll, Solernou, Noble, Fiala, and Miller (Note 1) have replicated this study omitting that statement, and report similar findings. Thus it is unlikely that the present results were due to that instructional statement. Nevertheless, any conception the subjects may have had that "smaller groups are less desirable than larger groups" could still have influenced the findings.

Experiment 2

Because of these interpretive problems, a second experiment was undertaken. Since the alternative explanations are tied to evaluation in a manner that the present interpretation is not, a comparative test is straightforward. That is, if the co-occurrence of distinctive events is particularly salient to the observer, then it should be possible to produce a *positive* stereotype of Group B by making desirable behaviors less frequent than undesirable behaviors in the stimulus sequence. The co-occurring

---

[1] While there were some significant effects associated with the other factors, they were few in number, do not qualify the primary findings presented here, and hence will not discussed further.

distinctiveness explanation would then predict that subjects would have a more *favorable* impression of Group B than of Group A, as well as that they would overestimate the frequency with which those desirable behaviors were performed by members of Group B. The alternative hypotheses, on the other hand, would still predict a more favorable impression of Group A.

Method

The methodology and procedures used in this experiment were essentially the same as those employed in Experiment 1. The major difference was in the distribution of desirable and undesirable behaviors included in the stimulus set, which in this case consisted of 36 statements. Of those 36, 24 described undesirable behaviors, while 12 described desirable behaviors. Also, 24 of the 36 statements characterized members of Group A, with 12 sentences describing members of Group B. However, the distribution of desirable and undesirable behaviors was the same for both groups, one-third of the statements for each group describing desirable behaviors. Thus, a sentence describing a member of Group B performing a *desirable* behavior represented an instance of the co-occurrence of events which were infrequent, and therefore distinctive, within the two information categories.

Two replication sets were used. Due to the limited number of behavior descriptions available within the scale intervals used, two independent sets of statements could not be developed. Instead, the same 36 sentences were used for both sets, with the 12 Group B sentences in Set 1 applied to Group A in Set 2 and the Group B descriptions for Set 2 coming from Group A sentences in Set 1. Thus, two-thirds of the sentences were associated with different group memberships in the two sets. Although not providing independent replications, this strategy did afford some basis for examining the generalizability of results.

The sentences in both stimulus sets were assigned to groups so that the mean desirability values of the behaviors describing the two groups were equal and so that approximately the same proportions of interpersonal and task-related behaviors were contained in each group. As in Experiment 1, each statement presented a man's name, his group membership, and a behavior description. Again, the sentences were presented on slides, and each slide was shown for 8 sec. To avoid the possibility of tapping preexisting conceptions of minority groups, no mention was made in the instructions of the relative sizes of Groups A and B. Other than this omission, the instructions and procedures were the same as those used in Experiment 1.

The same dependent measures were obtained in this experiment, i.e., trait inferences, attributions of group membership, and frequency estimates. Trait inference scales were selected from the same two dimensions (Rosenberg *et al.*, 1968), in this case three attributes from each pole of each dimension being included in the questionnaire. As in Experiment 1, the order of the first two dependent measures was counterbalanced. Finally, a series of postexperimental questions asked subjects what aspects of the stimulus information they focused on during the slide presentation and what strategies they developed for remembering those aspects.

Subjects were 70 female students at a state university in New Haven. Each of the two stimulus sets was presented to 35 subjects, and within those groups approximately half completed the dependent measures in each of the two orders used. As in Experiment 1, subjects who, on the attributions of group membership task, assigned more than half of the sentences to Group B were eliminated from the sample. Seventeen subjects were thereby discarded. Examination of their responses to the postexperimental questions confirmed that most were focusing their attention on other aspects of the stimulus information (e.g., the relationship between types of names and types of behaviors) and *not* on group memberships. The results reported below are based on the reduced sample of 53 subjects. Due to failures to complete one or another of the dependent measures, the number of subjects included in the analyses was 52 for the Group Attribution and Frequency Estimates data and 50 for the Trait Rating data. (Results based on the total sample were generally in the predicted direction but did not achieve statistical significance.)

Results

Attributions of Group Memberships
The distribution of stimulus sentences by group and behavior desirability is shown in Table 26.3a. Each subject's responses on the group attribution task were tallied to determine the frequency with which desirable and undesirable behaviors were assigned to the two groups, and a phi coefficient was calculated from each subject's frequency table. These coefficients were converted to Fisher's Z-scores and the mean value was determined. In this case it was predicted that this value would be negative, indicating a perceived relationship of Group B with desirable and Group A with undesirable behaviors. The mean was in fact negative and

TABLE 26.3. Results of Experiment 2 for Attributions of Group Membership and Frequency Estimates Measures

(a) Distribution of stimulus sentences

Behaviors	Group A	B	
Desirable	8	4	12
Undesirable	16	8	24
	24	12	36

(b) Attributions of group membership means (conditional probabilities in parentheses)

Behaviors	Group assigned by Subject A	B	
Desirable	5.87 (.49)	6.13 (.51)	12.00 (1.00)
Undesirable	15.71 (.65)	8.29 (.35)	24.00 (1.00)
	21.58	14.42	36.00

(c) Proportion of each sentence type recalled accurately (values expected by

Behaviors	Group A	B
Desirable	.53 (.60)	.59 (.40)
Undesirable	.73 (.60)	.49 (.40)

(d) Frequency estimates means (conditional proportions in parentheses)

Behaviors	Group A	B	
Desirable	8.23 (.34)	6.62 (.55)	14.85
Undesirable	15.77 (.66)	5.38 (.45)	21.15
	24.00 (1.00)	12.00 (1.00)	36.00

significantly different from zero. $t(51) = -3.04, p < .01$. A 2×2 (Replication Sets × Order of Dependent Measure) analysis of variance conducted on these Z-scores yielded no significant effects.

The mean number of desirable and undesirable statements attributed to the two groups is shown in Table 26.3b. The conditional probabilities for the assignment of behaviors to groups again reveal that the bias was associated with the co-occurrence of infrequent events. As in the first experiment, the probability that a statement (desirable or undesirable) described a member of Group A was .67. In the subjects' responses, the probability that an undesirable behavior would be assigned to this group was .65, rather close to the correct value. On the other hand, the probability of a desirable behavior being attributed to Group A was only .49, i.e., over half of these statements were attributed to Group B, despite the fact that only one-third of them was actually associated with that group. Thus the illusory correlation was due to the subject's tendency to overattribute the desirable behaviors to members of Group B.

Data relevant to the accuracy with which group memberships were recalled are presented in Table 26.3c. In their responses on this task subjects again attributed 60% of the behaviors to Group A and 40% to Group B, so that chance performance would yield a 60% accuracy rate in those cells referring to Group A statements and 40% accuracy for those behaviors performed by members of Group B. The findings show that (a) subjects' performance exceeded chance expectations for three of the four categories of statements, (b) the only

case in which below-chance performance occurred was for desirable behaviors performed by Group A persons, i.e., behaviors which had been overattributed to Group B, and (c) accuracy most exceeded the chance level for desirable behaviors attributed to Group B. Thus, Tables 26.3b and 26.3c show a pattern of results for desirable behaviors remarkably similar to that shown in Table 26.1 for undesirable behaviors, as would be predicted by the present interpretation.

Frequency Estimates
Subjects were told that there had been 24 statements describing members of Group A and 12 describing Group B, and were asked how many statements for each group were highly desirable. For each subject, the correct values (eight and four, respectively) were subtracted from her estimates. The means for these deviation scores were 0.23 and 2.62, and the difference between them was highly significant, $F(1.51) = 8.10$, $p < .01$. Thus, subjects significantly overestimated the number of desirable behaviors performed by members of Group B. These estimates were also used to construct 2×2 frequency tables from which a phi coefficient was calculated for each subject, as in Experiment 1. The mean of these coefficients (converted to Z-scores) was negative and approached being significantly different from zero, $t(51) = -1.75, p < .10$. A 2×2 analysis of variance yielded no significant effects due to either Replication Sets or Order of Dependent Measures.

The means for the frequency estimate data are shown in Table 26.3d. It can be seen that, although only one-third of the statements described desirable behaviors (for each group), subjects on the average estimated that over half of the behaviors associated with Group B were desirable. In contrast the average estimate for Group A was quite accurate.

Trait Ratings

The mean rating on each of the four scale categories (Good Social, Bad Social, Good Intellectual, Bad Intellectual) was determined for each subject. These data were then analyzed by a 2 (Replication Sets) × 2 (Order of Dependent Measures) × 2 (Social/ Intellectual Scales) × 2 (Good/Bad Scales) × 2 (Groups A and B) analysis of variance with repeated measures on the last three factors. The crucial interaction of Good/Bad Scales with Groups was again highly significant, $F(1, 46) = 7.61$, $p < .01$. The mean ratings of Groups A and B for each scale category are shown in Table 26.4. In marked contrast to Experiment 1, members of Group B were rated more favorably in each case.[2]

Discussion

The findings of Experiment 2 provide strong support for the hypotheses. Subjects again developed an illusory correlation between behavior desirability and group membership, but in this case the bias was reflected in the overattribution of *desirable* behaviors to the minority group. Moreover, the illusory correlation had an influence on the subjects' trait ratings, with Group B receiving significantly more favorable ratings than Group A. These results are quite supportive of the interpretation that the co-occurrence of distinctive stimuli results in an overestimation of the frequency with which that event pair occurred, with consequent effects on the subjects' perceptions of the two groups.

TABLE 26.4. **Mean Trait Ratings for Groups A and B: Experiment 2**

Rating Scales	Group A	Group B
Good Social	4.87	6.25
Bad Social	5.98	5.04
Good Intellectual	5.24	5.59
Bad Intellectual	6.12	4.87

Note: Ratings were made on 10-point scales.

[2] There were a few other significant effects due to other factors, but in no case did these results suggest a qualification of the primary findings reported here. Hence a complete description of these results is not necessary.

The results of this experiment are most useful in eliminating from plausibility certain competing explanations for the results of Experiment 1. In particular, while the results of the first study could be viewed as due to mere exposure effects, these results directly contradict the predictions of that explanation for Experiment 2. Whereas the mere exposure hypothesis would predict findings similar to Experiment 1, this study yielded results significantly in the opposite direction. Similarly, any other interpretation which links evaluation with group size (e.g., a tendency to view any smaller or "minority" group as likely to be "less good" than the majority group) now appears implausible as an explanation for the results of Experiment 1.

General Discussion

Illusory correlation refers to an erroneous inference a person makes about the relationship between two categories of events. The present findings demonstrate that distortions in judgment can result from the cognitive mechanisms involved in processing information about co-occurring events, at least when the various events co-occur with differential frequencies. The consequence in these studies was that two groups of stimulus persons were systematically perceived as being different from each other when no informational basis for such differences was available.

Little is known about the means by which observers develop concepts of relationships between variables, or "subjective correlations," and how biases can enter into that process. The concern here is specifically with the case in which events co-occur with differing frequencies, and the present interpretation emphasizes the salience of distinctive stimuli for the observer. While unusual or infrequent events are themselves distinctive, the *co-occurrence* of two distinctive events presumably would be particularly noticeable, differentially drawing the observer's attention to the fact that these events co-occurred. As the observer's attention is differentially directed to several instances of two "unusual" events "going together," the perception of a relationship between them can develop, providing the basis for the illusory correlation. In the experiments reported here, the increased accuracy in recall of this class of stimuli, as well as the overestimation of its frequency of occurrence, lends support to this interpretation of the processes which produced the observed effects. However, further research will be needed to more definitively determine the cognitive processes underlying these biased judgments.

The present study was conceptualized as an investigation of cognitive bases of stereotype formation, and the results indicate that perceptions of group differences can be based on certain characteristics of the way people process information about others. Obviously, this is not to deny, or even question, the importance of socially learned or culturally transmitted bases of stereotypes, and we are *not* suggesting that present-day stereotypes are due as much to information processing biases as to these learning mechanisms. The findings do indicate, however, that not all stereotyping necessarily originates in the learning and motivational processes emphasized in the stereotype literature; cognitive factors alone can be sufficient to produce differential perceptions of social groups (cf. Hamilton, 1976).

It is also possible that the two processes reinforce each other. If, for example, in our society whites learn through acculturation that blacks have a variety of undesirable characteristics, then they would be less likely to want to have much interaction with blacks. This infrequency of interaction, combined with the salience of the negative information received when some form of undesirable behavior *is* observed, would provide the basis for a cognitively based illusory correlation that would reinforce the learned stereotypic judgments. The reverse process may also occur. Some subgroups of the population become distinctive in the experience of others due to such arbitrary factors as geographic location (e.g., "Southerners" for those who live outside the South) or population distribution (e.g., one finds relatively few Catholics in small Midwestern towns). Such accidentally-gained distinctiveness, when combined with the distinctiveness of certain categories of behavior, can provide the basis for an illusory correlation such as that reported here. The erroneous inferences and assumptions acquired by this process can then be transmitted to other members of the predominant group, as well as to the next generation, so that what originally had a purely cognitive basis is now learned by others. It wouldn't seem unreasonable that some of our current stereotypes originated in this way. Thus, the two processes underlying illusory correlations are not only complementary but may, in everyday experience, be confounded and mutually reinforcing.

The present findings also have implications for one long-standing issue in the stereotype literature, the "kernel of truth" controversy (cf. Brigham, 1971). This hypothesis asserts that although stereotypes may be gross overgeneralizations, and may even be maintained by defensive processes that serve individual needs, nevertheless there is some "kernel of truth" underlying the elements comprising the stereotypes of any given group. The results of this experiment suggest that while this may be true of some stereotypes, it may not be a *necessary* condition underlying the formation of all stereotypes. There was no actual informational basis for the perceived differences between Groups A and B that were reported by subjects in the present experiment.

REFERENCES

Brigham, J. C. Ethnic stereotypes. *Psychological Bulletin*. 1971, **76**, 15–38.

Chapman, L. J. Illusory correlation in observational report. *Journal of Verbal Learning and Verbal Behavior*, 1967, **6**, 151–155.

Chapman, L. J., & Chapman, J. P. Genesis of popular but erroneous psychodiagnostic observations. *Journal of Abnormal Psychology*, 1967, **72**, 193–204.

Chapman, L. J., & Chapman, J. P. Illusory correlation as an obstacle to the use of valid psychodiagnostic signs. *Journal of Abnormal Psychology*, 1969, **74**, 271–280.

Golding, S. L., & Rorer, L. G. Illusory correlation and subjective judgment. *Journal of Abnormal Psychology*, 1972, **80**, 249–260.

Hamilton, D. L. Cognitive biases in the perception of social groups. *In* J. S. Carroll & J. W. Payne (Eds.), *Cognition and social behavior*. Hillsdale, N.J.: Lawrence Erlbaum Associates, 1976.

Jones, E. E., & Davis, K. E. From acts to dispositions: The attribution process in person perception. *In* L. Berkowitz (Ed.), *Advances in experimental social psychology*. New York: Academic Press, 1965, Vol. 2.

Rosenberg, S., Nelson, C., & Vivekananthan, P. S. A multidimensional approach to the structure of personality impressions. *Journal of Personality and Social Psychology*, 1968, **9**, 283–294.

Starr, B. J., & Katkin, E. S. The clinician as an aberrant actuary: Illusory correlation and the Incomplete Sentence Blank. *Journal of Abnormal Psychology*, 1969, **74**, 670–675.

Tajfel, H. Cognitive aspects of prejudice. *Journal of Social Issues*, 1969, **25**, 79–97.

Zajonc, R. B. Attitudinal effect of mere exposure. *Journal of Personality and Social Psychology*, 1968, **9**(2, Pt. 2).

REFERENCE NOTE

1. Jones, R. A., Stoll, J., Solernou, J., Noble, A., Fiala, J., & Miller, K: *Availability and stereotype formation*. Unpublished manuscript. University of Kentucky, 1974.

Received November 3, 1975 ■

A Hypothesis-Confirming Bias in Labeling Effects

John M. Darley and Paget H. Gross

The present study examines the process leading to the confirmation of a perceiver's expectancies about another when the social label that created the expectancy provides poor or tentative evidence about another's true dispositions or capabilities. One group of subjects was led to believe that a child came from a high socioeconomic background; the other group, that the child came from a low socioeconomic background. Nothing in the socioeconomic data conveyed information directly relevant to the child's ability level, and when asked, both groups of subjects reluctantly rated the child's ability level to be approximately at her grade level. Two other groups received the social-class information and then witnessed a videotape of the child taking an academic test. Although the videotaped performance series was identical for all subjects, those who had information that the child came from a high socioeconomic background rated her abilities well above grade level, whereas those for whom the child was identified as coming from a lower class background rated her abilites as below grade level. Both groups cited evidence from the ability test to support their conflicting conclusions. We interpret these findings as suggesting that some "stereotype" information (e.g., socioeconomic class information) creates not certainties but hypotheses about the stereotyped individual. However, these hypotheses are often tested in a biased fashion that leads to their false confirmation.

The expectancy-confirmation process is an important link in the chain leading from social perception to social action (Darley & Fazio, 1980; Rosenthal & Jacobson, 1968; Snyder & Swann, 1978a). As research has demonstrated, two processes leading to the confirmation of a perceiver's beliefs about another can be

The authors are grateful for the insightful comments of Nancy Cantor, Ron Comer, Joel Cooper, E. E. Jones, Charles Lord, Mark Zanna, and the members of the Princeton Social Psychology Research Seminar. Robin Akert, Kristin Boggiano, Paul Bree, Kay Ferdinandsen, Hannah McChesney, and Frederick Rhodewalt ably assisted in creating the stimulus materials.

Requests for reprints should be sent to John M. Darley, Department of Psychology, Princeton University, Princeton, New Jersey 08544.

identified. The first, called a "behavioral confirmation effect" (Snyder & Swann, 1978b), is consistent with Merton's (1948) description of the "self-fulfilling prophecy." In this process, perceiver's behaviors toward the individual for whom they hold an expectancy channel the course of the interaction such that expectancy-confirming behaviors are elicited from the other individual (Rosenthal, 1974; Snyder, Tanke, & Berscheid, 1977). The second process leads to what we may call a "cognitive confirmation effect." We use this term to refer to expectancy-confirmation effects that occur in the absence of any interaction between the perceiver and the target person. In these cases, perceivers simply selectively interpret, attribute, or recall aspects of the target person's actions in ways that are consistent with their expectations (Duncan, 1976; Kelley, 1950; Langer & Abelson, 1974). Thus, perceivers with different expectancies about another may witness an identical action sequence and still emerge with their divergent expectancies "confirmed."

The focus of the present article is on the mediation of cognitive confirmation effects. We suggest that there are at least two different processes that bring about the cognitive confirmation of expectancies. The key to separating these processes lies in recognizing that people distinguish between the kinds of information that create conceptions of other people. Perceivers may define a continuum, one end of which involves information that is seen as a valid and sufficient basis for judgments about another; at the other end is evidence that is seen as a weak or invalid basis for those judgments.

As an example of valid information, consider a teacher who receives the results of a standardized test indicating that a particular pupil has high ability. The expectancies this information creates about the child are assumed to reflect the child's actual capabilities and are probably quite automatically applied. At the other end of the continuum, and of primary interest to this article, is expectancy-creating information that most perceivers would regard as incomplete with respect to an individual's abilities or dispositions. Many of our social stereotypes fall into this category. For example, racial or social-class categories are regarded by most of us as an insufficient evidential basis for conclusive judgments of another's dispositions or capabilities. In this case, we suspect that perceivers are highly resistant to automatically applying their expectancies to a target person. A teacher, for example, would be extremely hesitant to conclude that a black child had low ability unless that child supplied direct behavioral evidence validating the application of the label.

The end of the continuum defining information that is seen as insufficient evidence for social judgments is of interest because we find what appears to be a paradox in the literature dealing with social stereotypes. Some recent investigations of the influence of stereotypes on social judgments have demonstrated a "fading" of stereotypic attributions (e.g., Karlins, Coffman, & Walters, 1969; Locksley, Borgida, Brekke, & Hepburn, 1980). For example, investigators have noted participants' increasing unwillingness to make stereotypic trait ascriptions (Brigham, 1971). Moreover, Quattrone and Jones (1980) demonstrate that although people may make stereotype-based judgments about a social group, they are unwilling to use category-based information to predict the behavior of any one member of that group.

Given this resistance to the utilization of expectancies when the social labels establishing them are not seen as valid guides for judgments, one might expect an elimination of the expectancy-confirmation bias. That is, perceivers would not unjustly assume the truth of a stereotype; they would instead require that evidence substantiating the accuracy of that stereotype be provided. This leads to the prediction that, ultimately, judgments about the target person will reflect the actual evidence produced by his or her behavior, unbiased by the perceivers' initial expectancies. Unfortunately, this conclusion stands in contradiction to the bulk of the self-fulfilling prophecy literature in which one finds that confirmation effects are often produced when racial, ethnic, or other negative social labels are implicated — exactly those cases in which one expects perceivers to refrain from using category-based information (e.g., Foster, Schmidt, & Sabatino, 1976; Rist, 1970; Rosenhan, 1973; Word, Zanna, & Cooper, 1974). We suggest that this apparent contradiction can be resolved if the following two-stage expectancy-confirmation process is assumed: Initially, when perceivers have reason to suspect that the information that establishes an expectancy is not diagnostically valid for determining certain of the target person's dispositions or capabilities, they will refrain from using that information to come to diagnostic conclusions. The expectancies function not as truths about the target person but rather as hypotheses about the likely dispositions of that person. If perceivers were asked for judgments at this point in the process, without any behavioral evidence to confirm their predictions, they would not report evaluations based on their expectancies. They would instead report that either they did not have sufficient information or they would make judgments consistent with normative expectations about the general population.

The second stage occurs when perceivers are given the opportunity to observe the actions of the labeled other. They then can test their hypotheses against relevant behavioral evidence. The initiation of a hypothesis-testing process would seem to be an unbiased approach for deriving a valid basis for judgments about another. If, however, individuals test their hypothesis using a "confirming strategy" — as has often been demonstrated — a tendency to find evidence supporting the hypothesis being tested would be expected (Snyder & Cantor, 1979; Snyder & Swann, 1978b). A number of mechanisms operating in the service of a hypothesis-confirming strategy may contribute to this result. First, the search for evidence may involve selective attention to information that is consistent with expectations and a consequent tendency to recall expectancy-consistent information when making final evaluations (Zadny & Gerard, 1974). Second, a hypothesis-confirming strategy may affect how information attended to during a performance will be weighted. Typically, expectancy-consistent information has inferential impact, whereas inconsistent information has insufficient influence in social-decision tasks (Nisbett & Ross, 1980). In fact, a recent study by Lord, Ross, and Lepper (1979) indicates that even when expectancy-inconsistent information is brought to the attention of the perceiver, it may be regarded as flawed evidence and therefore given minimal weight in the evaluation process. Third, it is also possible for inconsistent actions to be attributed to situational factors and thereby be attributionally discounted (Regan, Strauss, & Fazio, 1974). Finally, apparently inconsistent behavior may be reinterpreted as a manifestation of dispositions that are consistent with the initial expectancy (Hayden & Mischel, 1976).

Given the operation of all of these biasing mechanisms, an expectancy-confirmation effect could arise even when the target person's behavior does not objectively confirm the perceiver's expectancies. Nonetheless, the opportunity to observe the diagnostically relevant information is critical to the process because it provides what perceivers consider to be valid evidence, and thus, they can feel that they have made an "unbiased" judgment.

In the present study, we attempted to find evidence of this two-stage expectancy-confirmation process. To do this, perceivers were given information that would induce them to categorize an elementary school child as belonging to a high- or low-socioeconomic-status (SES) class (cf. Cooper, Baron, & Lowe, 1975). Consistent with the two-stage model, we predicted that perceivers given only this demographic information about the child would be reluctant to provide label-consistent ability evaluations. Another group of evaluators were given the identical demographic information about the child (high or low SES) and were then shown a performance sequence that provided ability-relevant information about the child. Owing to the hypothesis-confirming bias, it was predicted that these individuals would find evidence in the identical performance sequence to support their opposing hypotheses and would thus report widely different judgments of the child's ability. Moreover, we expected these perceivers to mislocate the source of their evidence from their own expectancies to the "objective" evidence provided by the performance sequence.

Method

As part of a study on "teacher evaluation methods," students viewed a videotape of a fourth-grade female child and were asked to evaluate her academic capabilities. Variation in the videotape determined the four experimental conditions. The first segment provided demographic information about the child and was used to establish either positive or negative expectations for the child's academic potential. Half of the participants viewed a sequence that depicted the child in an urban, low-income area (negative expectancy); the other half were shown the same child in a middle-class, suburban setting (positive expectancy).

Orthogonal to this manipulation was the performance variable. Half of the participants from each expectancy condition were shown a second tape segment in which the child responded to achievement-test problems (performance). The tape was constructed to be inconsistent and relatively uninformative about the child's abilities. The remaining participants were not shown this segment (no performance).

The design was thus a 2 × 2 factorial one, with two levels of expectancy (positive and negative) and two levels of performance (performance and no performance). In addition, a fifth group of participants viewed the performance tape but were not given prior information about the child's background (performance only). Their evaluations were used to determine if the performance tape was, as intended, an ambiguous display of the child's academic capabilities.

All viewers then completed an evaluation form on which they rated the child's overall achievement and academic skill level. Additional questions about the child's performance and manipulation checks were included. After completing their evaluation form, participants were given a questionnaire designed to probe their suspiciousness about the experiment. Finally, participants were debriefed, thanked, and paid.

Subjects

Seventy (30 male and 40 female) Princeton University undergraduates volunteered for a study on "teacher evaluation and referral" for which they were paid $2.50 for a 1-hour session. Participants were randomly assigned to one of five (four experimental and one control) conditions, with an attempt made to have an equal number of men and women in each condition. None of the students in the study reported having any formal teacher training; two students had informal teaching experience, both at the high school level. Only three of the original subjects were eliminated from the study because of suspiciousness about the experimental procedures.

Instructions

The experimenter introduced herself as a research assistant for a federal agency interested in testing new educational procedures. Students were told that their participation would be useful for determining the reliability of a new evaluation form teachers would use when referring pupils to special programs (these included remedial classes and programs for gifted students). To test the completeness and scorability of the evaluation form, subjects, acting as teachers, were asked to provide an academic evaluation of a selected child on this specially designed form. The experimenter emphasized that all evaluations would be anonymous and confidential and asked participants not to place their names anywhere on the form. She also requested that they replace the form in its envelope and seal it when they were finished. Each participant was further admonished to be as accurate and objective as possible when evaluating their selected pupil.

The research assistant then went on to explain that a videotape file of elementary school children had been prepared for a previous study (numerous videotape reels were on shelves in front of the subject). Participants would be selecting one child from this sample to observe and evaluate. It was made clear that this "randomly selected sample of children includes some who perform well above their grade level, some who would benefit from remedial programs, and some at all levels between these extremes." To select a child from this file, participants drew a number corresponding to a videotape reel. The experimenter, who had been blind to condition until this point, placed the tape on a television monitor and gave the participant a fact sheet appropriate to the child they selected.

The participant actually selected one of five prepared tapes (corresponding to the four experimental and one control conditions). In all conditions, the child observed was a nine-year-old female Caucasian named Hannah, who was a fourth grader attending a public elementary school. The information about the child's name, grade, and so forth appeared on the fact sheet and was reiterated in the narration of the tape.

Demographic Expectancy Manipulation

To establish either positive or negative expectancies about Hannah's ability, participants viewed a tape of Hannah that contained environmental cues indicating either a high or low socioeconomic background. Each tape included 4 minutes devoted to scenes of Hannah playing in a playground (filmed at a distance to prevent clear perception of her physical attractiveness) and 2 minutes devoted to scenes of her neighborhood and school. The tapes were filmed at two different locations.

In the negative-expectancy condition, subjects viewed Hannah playing in a stark fenced-in school yard. The scences from her neighborhood showed an urban setting of run-down two-family homes. The school she attended was depicted as a three-story brick structure set close to the street, with an adjacent asphalt school yard. The fact sheet given to participants included the following information about Hannah's parents: Both parents had only a high school education; her father was employed as a meat packer; her mother was a seamstress who worked at home.

In the positive-expectancy condition, Hannah was seen playing in a tree-lined park. The scenes from her neighborhood showed a suburban setting of five- and six-bedroom homes set on landscaped grounds. Her school was depicted as a sprawling modern structure, with adjacent playing fields and a shaded playground. Further, Hannah's fact sheet indicated that both her parents were college graduates. Her father's occupation was listed as an attorney, her mother's as a free-lance writer.

The Performance Manipulation

Two groups were asked to evaluate Hannah's academic ability immediately after viewing one or the other expectancy tape (no performance); two other groups were given the opportunity to observe Hannah in a test situation (performance).

Subjects in the performance conditions observed a second 12-minute tape sequence in which Hannah responded to 25 achievement-test problems. This portion of the tape was identical for both performance groups. The problems were modified versions of items selected from an achievement-test battery and included problems from the mathematics computation, mathematics concepts, reading, science, and social studies subtests. The grade level for the problems ranged from the second to the sixth grade. Participants were told that the test included "easy, moderate, and difficult problems." The problems were given orally to Hannah by a male tester who held up the possible solutions on cards. The sequence was filmed from behind the child so the viewer was able to see the cards held by the tester but not Hannah's face.

Hannah's performance was prearranged to present an inconsistent picture of her abilities. She answered both easy and difficult questions correctly as well as incorrectly. She appeared to be fairly verbal, motivated, and attentive on some portions of the tape and unresponsive and distracted on other portions of the tape. The tester provided little feedback about Hannah's performance. After each problem, he recorded Hannah's response and went on to the next problem.

To determine what information the tape provided about Hannah's ability in the absence of a priori expectancies, a group of participants, given the same cover story as subjects in the other conditions, were shown only the performance tape. These subjects were given no information about the child other than her name, age, grade, address, and the school she attended.

Dependent Measures

After reviewing the tape, participants were given an evaluation form to complete. The form contained the following sections:

Ability Measures
Nine curriculum areas forming three broad categories were listed. Included in this section were reading (reading comprehension, reading ability, writing, language ability), mathematics (mathematical concepts, mathematical computation), and liberal arts (science, general knowledge, social studies). Each curriculum area was followed by a scale extending from kindergarten to the sixth-grade, ninth-month grade level, with points labeled at 3-month intervals. Subjects were instructed to indicate the grade level that represented the child's ability in each of these areas. For subsequent analyses, mean ratings of items within these three categories were used, and grade levels were converted to a scale with months represented as fractions of a year (i.e., third grade, sixth month would equal 3.5).

Performance Measures
Participants in the performance conditions were asked to estimate the number of easy, moderate, and difficult problems the child answered correctly and to report the overall grade level of the test administered to the child. In an open-ended question, participants were asked to report the "information they found most useful in determining the child's capabilities."

Supplementary Academic Measures
Twenty traits or skills, followed by exemplars of classroom behaviors characterizing both the positive and negative ends of each of these traits, were listed. Subjects were asked to check the point on a 9-point scale that would best characterize the child on the dimension. Next to each scale, a box labeled "insufficient information" was also provided. Subjects were instructed to check this box rather than a scale value if they felt they had not been given sufficient information to rate the child on a given dimension.

These 20 items were selected to form five clusters: Work habits (organization, task orientation, dependability, attention, thoroughness), motivation (involvement, motivation, achievement orientation), sociability (popularity, verbal behavior, cooperation), emotional maturity (confidence, maturity, mood, disposition), and cognitive skill (articulation, creativity, learning capability, logical reasoning). Mean ratings of items within these five categories were used in subsequent analysis.

Manipulation Checks
In the last part of the booklet, subjects were asked to rate the child's "attractiveness" and the "usefulness of socioeconomic information as an indicator of a child's academic ability." The final open-ended question asked subjects to report the child's socioeconomic level.

Suspiciousness Probe
Finally, participants filled out a questionnaire assessing, for the agency, "how they had been treated during the experimental session." This was designed to probe their suspiciousness about the experimental procedures and purpose of the study. Following this, participants were thoroughly debriefed and paid.

Results

Ability-Level Ratings

Our primary hypothesis was that expectancy-confirmation effects occur only when perceivers feel they have definitive evidence relevant to their expectations. Specifically, we predicted that subjects who viewed only the positive- or negative-expectancy tape segment (no performance) would show little, if any, signs of expectancy confirmation in their ratings of the child's ability level, whereas subjects who viewed both the expectancy segment and the test segment (performance) would show considerable signs of expectancy confirmation. As a test of this hypothesis, a 2 (positive vs. negative) $\times$ 2 (performance vs. no performance) analysis of variance (ANOVA) was performed on ability-level ratings.

As shown in Figure 27.1, the results support our predictions. The ANOVA interaction term was significant for each index: Liberal arts, $F(1, 56) = 6.67, p < .02$; reading $F(1, 56) = 5.73$, $p < .03$; and mathematics $F(1, 56) = 9.87$, $p < .01$. Although a main effect for expectancy emerged for each of the three indexes — liberal arts, $F(1, 56) = 19.24$, $p < .01$; reading, $F(1, 56) = 32.98$, $p < .001$; and mathematics, $F(1, 56) = 19.78$, $p < .001$ — Newman-Keuls tests revealed that the subjects in the no-performance conditions did not rate the child's ability level as differing much in either direction from her known school grade. On only one of the indexes (liberal arts) did the no-performance–positive-expectancy subjects

rate the child significantly higher than the negative-expectancy subjects made reliably higher ratings on all three indexes ($p < .05$ in all cases). The fanshaped interaction of Figure 27.1 is consistent with the hypothesized two-stage confirmation process in which subjects first reserve judgment — if that judgment is based on only demographic indicators — but then allow their judgment about an ability to be biased in the direction of hypothesis confirmation.[1]

Manipulation Checks

The manipulation checks indicate that the above results were not artifactually produced. First, the expectancy manipulation was as successful for subjects who viewed the child's test performance as for those who did not. Without exception, positive-expectancy subjects reported the child's socioeconomic status as upper middle or upper class, and negative-expectancy subjects reported the child's socioeconomic status as lower middle or lower class. Second, analyses of ratings of the child's attractiveness and the usefulness of socioeconomic information for predicting ability yielded no differences across groups. The latter result is especially important in indicating that those who had seen the child's test performance did not regard the demographic information as any more diagnostic than those who had not seen it. Thus, the greater impact of induced expectancies in the performance conditions was not attributable to greater confidence in an implicit theory of the social-class–ability relation. Moreover, mean ratings of the usefulness of socioeconomic information (for all groups) were just below the midpoint toward the "not useful" end of the scale.

Finally, as can be seen in Table 27.1, ability ratings of the performance-only group indicate that the performance

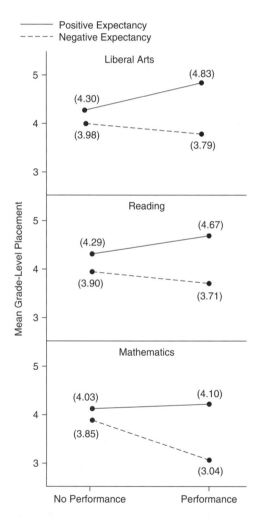

FIGURE 27.1 ■ Mean Grade-level Placements on the Liberal Arts, Reading, and Mathematics Indexes for Experimental Conditions.

TABLE 27.1. Mean Grade-level Placements on Curriculum Areas by the Performance Control Group

Index	M	Grade Level	SD
Liberal arts	4.0	3rd grade, 9th month	.505
Reading	3.8	4th grade	.581
Mathematics	3.5	3rd grade, 6th month	.238

Note: $n = 10$.

---

[1] We also analyzed this data by pooling across the three ability measures. As one would expect, because this increases the number of observations, the significance levels are improved, although the basic interactional pattern ($p = .002$) remains the same. Again, post hoc comparisons reveal that the two performance conditions are reliably different ($p < .01$), whereas the two no-performance groups do not differ reliably.

segment was, as intended, an ambiguous display of Hannah's capabilities.

We hoped that evaluations of the child's ability would tend to be variable, reflecting the inconsistencies in the child's performance; however, mean estimates would be expected to fall close to the child's given grade level. As the data in Table 27.1 indicate, ratings on the three curriculum indexes do show considerable variability, and the perceivers do use the child's grade level as an anchor for their judgments. The mathematics ratings were somewhat lower and less variable than the others, indicating that her performance in this area may have been poorer and more consistent.[2] (This will be discussed at a later point.)

Judgments of the Performance

If performance subjects were no less aware of, or impressed by, the relevance of the expectancy information, it follows that they found support for their divergent hypotheses in the child's performance. Measures from the academic evaluation form indicate several ways in which perceivers obtained support for their diverse hypotheses. (All of these were measures of the subjects' perceptions of the performance and therefore were taken only from the groups that witnessed the test sequence. Recall that all of these subjects witnessed the identical performance tape.)

Test Difficulty
Performance on a test is a joint function of the test taker's ability (and other personal factors) and the difficulty of the test. Therefore, one way of justifying a high-ability inference from an inconsistent test performance is to perceive the test as being very difficult. Conversely, one way of rationalizing a low-ability inference from the same performance would be to perceive the test as easy. This happened: Subjects in the positive-expectancy condition rated the test as significantly more difficult (M grade = 4.8) than did those in the negative-expectancy condition (M grade = 3.9), $t(28) = 2.69$, $p < .02$.

Problems Correct
Subjects also estimated the number of problems the child answered correctly within each of the problem categories: Very difficult, moderately difficult, and easy.

A repeated measures analysis of variance revealed a marginally reliable tendency for subjects with positive expectancies to estimate that the child correctly answered a higher percentage of problems, $F(1, 28) = 3.94$, $p < .06$. Follow-up analyses revealed that subjects with positive expectancies estimated that the child correctly answered more of the easy ($M = 94\%$ vs. 79%) and moderately difficult ($M = 69\%$ vs. 53%) problems than did subjects with negative expectancies, $t(28) = 2.55$ and 2.21, respectively, $ps < .05$. Expectancy did not affect estimates of answers to difficult problems ($M = 37\%$ vs. 36%). The overall pattern suggests a bias to report more instances of expectancy-consistent than expectancy-inconsistent test responses.

Reporting Relevant behaviors
Subjects had been asked to report, in an open-ended format, the performance information "most relevant for determining the child's capabilities." We expected that subjects anticipating a good performance would report more instances of positive behaviors than those expecting a poor performance. For each subject, we computed a positivity index by subtracting the number of negative instances from the number of positive instances. Consistent with predictions, positive-expectancy subjects reported a significantly greater number of positive behaviors relative to negative ones as being relevant in their judgments than did negative-expectancy subjects, $t(28) = 34.65$, $p < .001$.

To summarize the performance judgments, positive- and negative-expectancy subjects, although agreeing that the performance provided information that was sufficient to estimate the child's capabilities, disagreed on how difficult the test was, how many problems the child answered correctly, and how many of her test behaviors reflected either positively or negatively on her achievement level. On every measure, positive-expectancy subjects made interpretations more favorable to the child than did negative-expectancy subjects.

Supplementary Academic Measures

Information Sufficiency
Recall that subjects reporting on these measures were allowed to check a scale value or a box labeled insufficient information. We believed that the no-performance subjects who had only demographic-based expectancies to rely on would display a greater reluctance to evaluate the child and that this reluctance would lead to more frequent use of the insufficient information answer. A 2 × 2 analysis of variance on these data yielded only a

---

[2] An F_{max} test of the difference between several variances indicates no difference between the variances of the liberal arts and reading indexes. The variance of the mathematics index is, however, significantly different from that of the liberal arts index, $F_{max}(9, 9) = 5.92$, $p < .05$, and shows a marginally significant difference from that of the reading index.

TABLE 27.2. Mean Ratings on Trait Measures for Experimental Groups

	Dependent Measure				
Condition	Work Habits	Motivation	Sociability	Maturity	Cognitive Skills
Positive, performance	5.21_a	5.16_a	5.25_a	$5.33_{a,b}$	4.73_a
Positive, no-performance	$4.92_{a,b}$	5.31_a	$4.82_{a,b}$	5.65_b	5.55_b
Negative, no-performance	5.13_a	$4.80_{a,b}$	4.38_b	4.67_a	4.83_a
Negative, performance	4.36_b	4.11_b	$4.58_{a,b}$	$4.77_{a,b}$	4.12_a

Note: $n = 15$ per condition. The higher the number, the more positive the evaluation. Letter subscripts indicate vertical comparisons of cell means by Duncan's multiple-range test. Means that do not share a common subscript are significantly different from each other at the .05 level.

main effect for performance, $F(1, 56) = 12.86, p < .001$, such that no-performance subjects chose this option more often ($M = 43\%$ of the items) than subjects who viewed the test sequence ($M = 22\%$ of the items). A one-way analysis of variance, comparing the no-performance, performance, and performance-only conditions yielded a reliable effect, $F(2, 67) = 12.41, p < .001$. Moreover, comparing these means (via Duncan's test), we find that the performance-witnessing groups were not significantly different from each other, whereas both were significantly different from the no-performance groups ($p < .01$). Thus, the difference found between performance and no-performance groups on the use of the insufficient information option did not seem to depend on the fact that the mere quantity of evidence provided to performance subjects was greater (two tape segments) than that given to no-performance subjects (one tape segment). The performance-only subjects, who also saw only one tape segment, did not differ from performance subjects on this measure. The difference is better attributed to the greater perceived diagnostic utility of the performance segment. Performance subjects apparently felt that the child's test performance provided sufficient diagnostic information on which to base their evaluations.

Trait Measures

A 2 (expectancy) × 2 (performance) analysis of variance was performed on ratings for each of the five trait dimensions. Because participants were given the option of not checking a scale value on these measures, missing values were given a score of 5, which, on a 9-point scale, represents the neutral point.[3] These data are presented in Table 27.2.

Consistent with our findings for the curriculum indexes, a significant interaction emerged for the work habits index such that individuals expecting the child to perform well rated her more positively after viewing the performance tape whereas those expecting her to perform poorly rated her more negatively after viewing the performance tape, $F(1, 56) = 5.15, p < .03$. The predicted interaction effect was not obtained for the motivation, sociability, emotional maturity, or cognitive skill measures. For each of these measures, we found a main effect for expectancy, with the positive-expectancy groups rating the child significantly higher than the negative-expectancy groups, $F(1, 56) = 6.99, 4.57, 5.76$, and 5.84, respectively, $ps < .05$. In addition, there was a significant effect for performance on the cognitive skill index, with the performance groups showing lower ratings than the no-performance groups, $F(1, 56) = 7.73$, $p < .05$. These data indicate that certain expectancy-consistent judgments may not require a two-stage process. Although it may be necessary to provide performance information to obtain judgments of a child's ability level, judgments about other dispositional characteristics may be made without this information.

Discussion

Unlike many previous studies demonstrating expectancy-confirmation effects, the expectancies in the present study were not created by information that most people would regard as definitively establishing their validity. They were not created by objective test results, expert judgments, or other authoritative information. Instead, the expectancies were conveyed by

---

[3] Analyses of these data require a decision about how to treat the responses of subjects who checked the "not enough information to rate" alternative. The means presented in Table 2 are calculated by assigning a score of 5 to missing scale values. This assumes that the

nonresponding subjects would have checked the scale midpoint if forced to respond. Another way of dealing with the same issue is to insert the cell-mean score for each such subject. Using this procedure, the pattern of results is essentially unchanged. The same effects emerged as significant.

such cues as the child's clothes, the bleakness of the playground on which she played, or the high- or low-status character of her parents' occupations.

We suggested that perceivers would realize that expectancies created by this information do not form a completely valid basis for some of the evaluations they were asked to make. The results indicate that this is so: Perceivers who were given only demographic information about the child demonstrated a resistance to making expectancy-consistent attributions on the ability indexes. Their estimations of the child's ability level tended to cluster closely around the one concrete fact they had at their disposal: The child's grade in school. When given the opportunity to avoid making dispositional attributions altogether, nearly half of the time these perceivers chose that option.

In contrast, a marked expectancy-confirmation effect was evident for those perceivers who evaluated the child after witnessing an ability-relevant performance. Those who believed the child came from a high socioeconomic class reported that her performance indicated a high ability level, whereas those who believed the child came from a low socioeconomic class reported that the identical performance indicated a substantially lower level of ability.

This pattern of results suggests that when the diagnostic validity of a perceiver's expectations is suspect, expectancies function as hypotheses, and the task of evaluating an individual for whom one has an expectancy is a hypothesis-testing process. Expectancy confirmation, then, does not always result from an automatic inference process. Instead, it occurs as the end product of an active process in which perceivers examine the labeled individual's behavior for evidence relevant to their hypothesis.[4]

As is apparent from our data, the hypothesis-testing strategy that perceivers use has a bias (as Snyder & Cantor, 1979, have suggested) toward confirmation of the hypothesis being tested. The literature suggests a

number of related mechanisms that can contribute to this effect (see Nisbett & Ross, 1980, for a review). We do have evidence to suggest what some of these mechanisms may have been in our study. First, there seems to be a selective recall of evidence: Perceivers who expected the child to do well reported the child as having answered more easy and more moderately difficult problems correctly than those expecting the child to do poorly. Second, there seems to be a selective weighting of the evidence such that hypothesis-consistent behaviors are regarded as more "typical" of the child's true capabilities. When people were asked to report what evidence they found most useful in determining their evaluations, they reported only those test items on which the child's performance was consistent with their initial expectations. Third, perceivers appeared to develop auxilliary hypotheses that would render apparently inconsistent behavior consistent with their hypotheses. These auxilliary hypotheses did not seem to be revised assessments of the actor but rather assessments of situational factors that could account for discrepancies in the actor's behavior. For instance, we found that persons who expected a good performance decided that the test given to the child was very difficult, a conclusion that would account for instances of otherwise inconsistent poor performance; whereas persons who expected a poor performance reported that the test was easy, which would account for inconsistent good performance. Finally, we found evidence in the open-ended reports of some participants to suggest that the meaning given to the child's behaviors was often consistent with the perceivers' initial hypotheses. For example, a low-SES Hannah was reported to have "difficulty accepting new information," whereas a high-SES Hannah was reported to have the "ability to apply what she knows to unfamiliar problems."

Implicit in this data is the conclusion that perceivers seem to be aware that witnessing a particular test performance does not give them automatic access to an individual's underlying ability. Many other factors, such as luck, task difficulty, or lack of motivation, may intervene (Darley & Goethals, 1980; Weiner et al., 1971). Therefore, the meaning of a person's performance is susceptible to multiple interpretations that can be consistent with, and even supportive of, opposing hypotheses about that person's ability.

Thus far, we have treated information as creating expectancies that are either valid and automatically applied to others or weak and only hypothesis generating. It is more likely that any item of information about a person generates some certainties and some hypotheses,

---

[4] In the experimental paradigm in which expectancy effects are typically demonstrated, perceivers are always provided with the opportunity to observe or interact with the labeled target person. By using this research design, one cannot conclusively determine whether the resulting expectancy effect was due to differential perceptions of the target person, as most researchers suggest, or if subjects had simply based their evaluations on the information provided by the label and had ignored the performance. By including conditions in the present study in which some perceivers are not provided with performance information, it becomes possible to distinguish between expectancy effects arising from a nonobservationally based inference process and those arising from expectancy-guided search processes.

depending on the domain to which it is applied. In the present study, the demographic information seems to have this character of creating both certainties and hypotheses. On the supplemental measures related to school achievement — specifically, on measures of motivation, sociability, and emotional maturity — a simple main effect was obtained such that people who saw the child as coming from a high socioeconomic background judged her more positively, and those who did not see the performance had as extreme ratings as those who did. (But keep in mind that individuals had the opportunity not to rate the child on these measures and that, overall, many more people from the no-performance conditions chose not to rate.) Apparently, some individuals felt that demographic data alone was sufficient evidence on which to base an evaluation of, for example, a child's likely achievement orientation. Thus, the addition of performance information was not necessary for a conclusive judgment in this area. In general, our social categories do trigger expectancies for a constellation of dispositions and behaviors, and for some of these, it may not be necessary to rely on performance evidence to feel certain that one's expectations are accurate.

The Validity of Demographic Evidence

From another perspective, one could ask whether demographic information does not warrant correspondent inferences of ability. Certainly, numerous studies show correlations between social class and school performance (Dreger & Miller, 1960; Kennedy, VanDeReit, & White, 1963; Lesser, Fifer, & Clark, 1965). From this perspective, the differential judgments of people who witnessed the same test with different demographically produced expectancies was less evidence of bias than it was of an understanding of the true workings of the world. Two things can be said about this: First, part of the general argument of those concerned with self-fulfilling prophecies is that the present process is exactly how the link between social class and academic performance comes about. Second, the data from our no-performance perceivers indicate that people regard the question of what exists in the world as a separate question from that addressed in the present study. Base-rate information (i.e., estimates of the frequencies with which an attribute or capability level occurs in a social group) represents probabilistic statements about a class of individuals, which may not be applicable to every member of the class. Thus, regardless of what an individual perceives the actual base rates to be, rating any one member of the class requires a higher standard of

evidence. When one child's ability is being considered, demographic information does not appear to meet the perceiver's criteria for a valid predictor; performance information, on the other hand, clearly does.

There is yet another way to pose the validity question, and that is to consider the use of demographic evidence when perceivers formulate a working hypothesis. From an information-processing perspective, hypothesis formulation serves a useful function: It allows one to make better use of subsequent evidence. The rub, of course, is that once a hypothesis is formulated, regardless of our judgments of the validity of the evidence on which it is based, our cognitive mechanisms are biased toward its eventual confirmation. Thus, when asking whether the final judgments of the perceiver accurately reflect what exists in the world, we should not obscure an important point: How those judgments come about. To clarify further, the "judgmental bias" in the present study does not refer to the indiscriminate use of category-based information, or to the (in)accuracy of final judgments, but to the processes that determine what those judgments will be.

An Alternative Explanation

An alternative explanation for the general pattern of results reported here is possible. The individuals who witnessed only the demographic information may have actually made ability inferences but chose not to report them. Their failure to report their evaluations may have been due to fears that the experimenter would regard the inferences as unjustified. However, in the experiment we minimized the possible cause for this concern by demonstrating to the participants that their responses would be anonymous. The experimenter was not present while the participant filled out the dependent-measures form and did not return until he or she deposited the questionnaire in an anonymity-guaranteeing location. Furthermore, on the final questionnaire, participants were asked if they were sufficiently assured of the anonymity of their responses, and all of them replied affirmatively.

It is, of course, still possible to make a generalized version of the same point: The perceiver's resistance to using the demographic information could, at least in part, be motivated by the awareness that their behavior was under scrutiny by others. This does not necessarily diminish the interest in the phenomenon. In the real world, people who make judgments frequently know their judgments may be public. Teachers classifying students, clinicians diagnosing clients, and employers selecting new personnel are all aware that their actions may be scrutinized by others. Thus, whether this awareness is based on personal knowledge, social pressures, or internalized social desirability concerns, both the processes that bring about those judgments and the consequences in terms of judgmental bias are likely to be the same.

The present study finds results that at first glance seem contradictory to results of some other studies. One thinks particularly of the work of Locksley et al. (1980) and that of Kahneman and Tversky (1973). In the Locksley et al. study, the direction of the interaction appears to be the reverse of that obtained here. A strong stereotype effect in trait ratings is found with category-membership information (gender labels) or when nondiagnostic information accompanies the category label. This stereotype effect disappears with diagnostic information. However, consider the differences in the type of information given to perceivers in the present study and that given to perceivers in the correspondent conditions of the Locksley et al. study. The perceivers in the present study who were reluctant to apply stereotypes (the no-performance conditions) received nondiagnostic case information, as do some in the Locksley et al. study. However, perceivers in the present study observe the child they will rate and are given a fair amount of family data — information that would certainly distinguish the child from others in her social group. The diagnostic information used by Locksley et al. consists of information that could be applied to almost any person and may not have created an individuated impression of the person to be rated. The two conditions, then, are not identical, and comparing them leads us to the following possibility: Stereotype effects persist with information that does not distinguish the target from the target's social category, whereas dilution effects (nonstereotypic judgments) appear when case information successfully creates an individuated impression of the target. Recent studies by Quattrone and Jones (1980) and Locksley, Hepburn, and Oritz (in press) support this conclusion.

In comparing other conditions of the Locksley et al. (1980) and the present study, differences in the type of information given to perceivers produces discrepant results. The diagnostic information given to perceivers in the Locksley et al. study consists of a single behavioral exemplar that confirms or disconfirms a gender-based trait expectancy. A dilution effect is found only with a disconfirming behavior sample. In contrast, the diagnostic test sequence in the present study contains both confirming and disconfirming behavioral evidence. Furthermore, we know from supplementary measures that perceivers found the expectancy-consistent portions

more diagnostically informative than the inconsistent portions. Therefore, with a source of multiple information — with many information elements that serve to confirm expectancies — a confirmation effect is not surprising. Had the performance tape in the present study provided only compelling disconfirming evidence, we suspect a dilution effect might have been found here as well.

Discrepancies between this work and that of Kahneman and Tversky (1973) can be addressed as well. In Kahneman and Tversky's studies, individuals are asked to predict a target person's occupational-category membership from a brief personality description. Predictions are overwhelmingly based on the degree to which the personality information "fits" with an occupational stereotype (i.e., a representativeness effect). This appears inconsistent with the stereotype-resisting judgments of the perceivers in our study who received no performance information. However, the demographic information given to our no-performance perceivers, although it does allow for a judgment of fit to a social category, does not provide information for a judgment on an ability dimension. The condition, then, is similar to Kahneman and Tversky's Experiment 3 in which the personality description is uninformative with regard to the target person's profession (i.e., it contains no occupation-relevant personality traits). In their study, occupational-category predictions were essentially random. That is, they were based neither on prior probabilities nor on similarity. This is essentially the same effect we find for no-performance perceivers in the present study. Apparently, the representativeness effect (or an expectancy effect) depends on the provision of information that allows for a similarity match to the categories perceivers are asked to judge.

Further, the no-performance conditions in the present study are not identical to Kahneman and Tversky's (1973) null-description condition. In that condition, subjects are given no information whatsoever about the target — neither individuating information nor category-relevant information. Here a strong base-rate effect emerges. Although this might cause one to predict a strong stereotype effect in the present no-performance conditions, our earlier point about individuating information may explain why it is not obtained. No-performance perceivers may lack relevant case information, but they do have a significant amount of individuating target information; apparently, this significantly alters the framework for prediction.

We might summarize as follows: Representativeness and expectancy effects are found when relevant case data are provided so that individuals can determine the target person's fit to a category. Base-rate effects (and nonobservationally based stereotypic judgments) are found when neither case data nor individuating information is given. Finally, assume that three conditions are met: Individuating information is given, information about base rates is withheld, and a priori expectancies are not relied on because they may not be applicable to a particular target. Then, without relevant case data, a judgment of fit is precluded, attenuating a representativeness or a biased confirmation effect. In these circumstances, judgments are made at the scale midpoint or the chance level. We find this latter effect in both Kahneman and Tversky's (1973) uninformed condition and in the no-performance conditions of the present study.

A final point is relevant to both of the studies reviewed above. Predicting ability from social-class information may not be equivalent to predicting personality traits from gender labels or occupational membership. The nature of the prediction required (ability rather than personality characteristics) may cause individuals to regard social-class information as at the invalid end of the continuum we have defined. But an individual's gender or occupation, on the other hand, may be regarded as valid information on which to base an inference about personality. Related to this point is that the standards of evidence required for different stereotype-confirming judgments may be different. Automatic assumptions about personality may be made from occupation or gender label, and thus, stereotype effects are obtained with this information alone, or with minimal additional information. To make judgments of a low-SES child's ability, perceivers require more information and, specifically, criterion-relevant information. Thus, stereotypic judgments are not found with only category or nondiagnostic information but are found only when a sufficient amount of apparently confirming diagnostic information is provided.

Limits to the Confirmation Process

The present study finds results consistent with those of many other studies. For instance, Swann and Snyder (1980) found that target individuals labeled as dull witted were still seen as dull witted even after the perceivers had witnessed a sequence in which these target individuals outperformed those labeled as bright, a situation in which a cognitive confirmation effect triumphed over apparently strongly disconfirming evidence. Nonetheless, we suspect that there are limits to the cognitive confirmation process.

We can suggest several variables, some of which we have mentioned, that may determine whether a confirmation or a disconfirmation effect is found. First, there is the clarity of the disconfirming evidence. In the domain of abilities, in spite of the above example, a sustained high-level performance is compelling evidence for high ability. I may perceive another as a slow runner, but if I see him or her do several successive 4-minute miles, my expectancy must change. When this occurs, it is possible that a contrast effect will take place in which the significance of the disconfirming behavior will be exaggerated and the initial expectancy reversed. Intuitively, no such unambiguous evidence exists in the personality realm, where even compelling positive behavior can be attributed to negative underlying motives or dispositions. Second, the strength with which the initial expectancy or hypothesis is held may produce conflicting effects. "Strength of expectancy" is an ambiguous phrase. It may refer to one's degree of commitment to an expectancy of a fixed level, or it may refer to the extremity of the expectancy. In the first instance, the stronger the commitment to the expectancy, the more resistant it would be to disconfirmation. However, the more extreme the expectancy, the more evidence there is that potentially disconfirms it. Finally, the perceiver's motivation may play a role. Under certain circumstances, an individual may prefer to see his or her expectancy confirmed; in other situations he or she may have a preference for the disconfirmation of the same expectancy. All of these suggestions, of course, require empirical testing.

A Final Comment

The self-fulfilling prophecy and the expectancy-confirmation effect have been of interest to psychologists partially because of the social policy implications of the research. However, in many of the research studies that document the effect, the specific and limited character of the material that creates the expectancies is lost, and we talk as if any material that creates expectancies is automatically accepted as valid by the perceiver. The image of the perceiver that emerges is one of an individual who takes his or her stereotypes and prejudices for granted and indiscriminantly applies them to members of the class he or she has stereotyped without any consideration of the unjustness of such a proceeding. The present study suggests that this is an oversimplification that in turn does some injustice to the perceiver. There are times when perceivers resist regarding their expectancies as truths and instead treat them as hypotheses to be confirmed or disconfirmed by relevant evidence. Perceivers in the present study did not make the error of reporting stereotypic judgments without sufficient evidence to warrant their conclusions. They engaged in an extremely rational strategy of evaluating the behavioral evidence when it was available and refraining from judgment when it was not. It was the strategy perceivers employed to analyze the evidence that led them to regard their hypotheses as confirmed even when the objective evidence did not warrant that conclusion. The error the perceivers make, then, is in assuming that the behavioral evidence they have derived is valid and unbiased. Future research could profitably address the question of the conditions under which this general confirmation strategy can be reversed or eliminated. In the meantime, however, the image of the perceiver as a hypothesis tester is certainly more appealing than that of a stereotype-applying bigot, even though the end result of both processes, sadly enough, may be quite similar.

REFERENCES

Brigham, J. C. Ethnic stereotypes. *Psychological Bulletin*, 1971, *76*, 15–38.

Cooper, H. M., Baron, R. M., & Lowe, C. A. The importance of race and social class information in the formation of expectancies about academic performance. *Journal of Educational Psychology*, 1975, *67*, 312–319.

Darley, J. M., & Fazio, R. H. Expectancy confirmation processes arising in the social interaction sequence. *American Psychologist*, 1980, *35*, 867–881.

Darley, J. M., & Goethals, G. R. People's analyses of the causes of ability-linked performances. In L. Berkowitz (Ed.), *Advances in experimental social psychology* (Vol. 13). New York: Academic Press, 1980.

Dreger, R. M., & Miller, S. K. Comparative psychological studies of Negroes and whites in the United States. *Psychological Bulletin*, 1960, *57*, 361–402.

Duncan, B. L. Differential social perception and attribution of intergroup violence: Testing the lower limits of stereotyping of blacks. *Journal of Personality and Social Psychology*, 1976, *34*, 590–598.

Foster, G., Schmidt, C., & Sabatino, D. Teacher expectancies and the label "learning disabilities." *Journal of Learning Disabilities*, 1976, *9*, 111–114.

Hayden, T., & Mischel, W. Maintaining trait consistency in the resolution of behavioral inconsistency: The wolf in sheep's clothing? *Journal of Personality*, 1976, *44*, 109–132.

Kahneman, D., & Tversky, A. On the psychology of prediction. *Psychological Review*, 1973, *80*, 237–251.

Karlins, M., Coffman, T. L., & Walters, G. On the fading of social stereotypes: Studies in three generations of college students. *Journal of Personality and Social Psychology*, 1969, *13*, 1–16.

Kelley, H. H. The warm-cold variable in first impressions of persons. *Journal of Personality*, 1950, *18*, 431–439.

Kennedy, W. A., VanDeReit, V., & White, J. C. A normative sample of intelligence and achievement of Negro elementary school children in the southeastern United States. *Monographs of the Society for Research in Child Development*, 1963, *28*, 13–112.

Langer, E. J., & Abelson, R. P. A patient by any other name … : Clinician group differences in labeling bias. *Journal of Consulting and Clinical Psychology*, 1974, *42*, 4–9.

Lesser, G. S., Fifer, G., & Clark, D. H. Mental abilities of children from different social class and cultural groups. *Monographs of the Society for Research in Child Development*, 1965, *30*, 1–115.

Locksley, A., Borgida, E., Brekke, N., & Hepburn, C. Sex stereotypes and social judgment. *Journal of Personality and Social Psychology*, 1980, *39*, 821–831.

Locksley, A., Hepburn, C., & Ortiz, V. Social stereotypes and judgments of individuals: An instance of the baserate fallacy. *Journal of Experimental Social Psychology*, in press.

Lord, C., Ross, L., & Lepper, M. E. Biased assimilation and attitude polarization: The effects of prior theories on subsequently considered evidence. *Journal of Personality and Social Psychology*, 1979, *37*, 2098–2109.

Merton, R. K. The self-fulfilling prophecy. *Antioch Review*, 1948, *8*, 193–210.

Nisbett, R., & Ross, L. *Human inference: Strategies and shortcomings of social judgment*. Englewood Cliffs, N. J.: Prentice-Hall, 1980.

Quattrone, G. A., & Jones, E. E. The perception of variability within in-groups and out-groups: Implications for the law of small numbers. *Journal of Personality and Social Psychology*, 1980, *38*, 141–152.

Regan, D. T., Strauss, E., & Fazio, R. Liking and the attribution process. *Journal of Experimental Social Psychology*, 1974, *10*, 385–397.

Rist, R. C. Student social class and teacher expectations: The self-fulfilling prophecy in ghetto education. *Harvard Educational Review*, 1970, *40*, 411–451.

Rosenhan, D. L. On being sane in insane places. *Science*, 1973, *179*, 250–258.

Rosenthal, R. *On the social psychology of self-fulfilling prophecy: Further evidence for Pygmalion effects and their mediating mechanisms.* New York: MSS Modular Publications, Module 53, 1974.

Rosenthal, R., & Jacobson, L. *Pygmalion in the classroom.* New York: Holt, Rinehart & Winston, 1968.

Snyder, M., & Cantor, N. Testing hypotheses about other people: The use of historical knowledge. *Journal of Experimental Social Psychology*, 1979, *15*, 330–342.

Snyder, M., & Swann, W. B. Behavioral confirmation in social interaction: From social perception to social reality. *Journal of Experimental Social Psychology*, 1978, *14*, 148–162. (a)

Snyder, M., & Swann, W. B. Hypothesis-testing processes in social interaction. *Journal of Personality and Social Psychology*, 1978, *36*, 1202–1212. (b)

Snyder, M., Tanke, E. D., & Berscheid, E. Social perception and interpersonal behavior: On the self-fulfilling nature of social stereotypes. *Journal of Personality and Social Psychology*, 1977, *35*, 656–666.

Swann, W. B., & Snyder, M. On translating beliefs into action: Theories of ability and their application in an instructional setting. *Journal of Personality and Social Psychology*, 1980, *6*, 879–888.

Weiner, B., et al. *Perceiving the causes of success and failure.* Morristown, N.J.: General Learning Press, 1971.

Word, C. O., Zanna, M. P., & Cooper, J. The nonverbal mediation of self-fulfilling prophecies in interracial interaction. *Journal of Experimental Social Psychology*, 1974, *10*, 109–120.

Zadny, J., & Gerard, H. B. Attributed intentions and informational selectivity. *Journal of Experimental Social Psychology*, 1974, *10*, 34–52.

Received August 31, 1981
Revision received April 2, 1982 ■

The Police Officer's Dilemma: Using Ethnicity to Disambiguate Potentially Threatening Individuals

Joshua Correll, Bernadette Park, Charles M. Judd, and Bernd Wittenbrink

Using a simple videogame, the effect of ethnicity on shoot/don't shoot decisions was examined. African American or White targets, holding guns or other objects, appeared in complex backgrounds. Participants were told to "shoot" armed targets and to "not shoot" unarmed targets. In Study 1. White participants made the correct decision to shoot an armed target more quickly if the target was African American than if he was White, but decided to "not shoot" an unarmed target more quickly if he was White. Study 2 used a shorter time window, forcing this effect into error rates. Study 3 replicated Study 1's effects and showed that the magnitude of bias varied with perceptions of the cultural stereotype and with levels of contact, but not with personal racial prejudice. Study 4 revealed equivalent levels of bias among both African American and White participants in a community sample. Implications and potential underlying mechanisms are discussed.

In February 1999, around midnight, four plain-clothes police officers were searching a Bronx, New York, neighborhood for a rape suspect. They saw Amadou

Editor's Note: Only portions of the results of Study 3 are reproduced here.

Joshua Correll, Bernadette Park, and Charles M. Judd. Department of Psychology, University of Colorado at Boulder; Bernd Wittenbrink, Graduate School of Business, University of Chicago.

This material is based on work supported by a National Science Foundation graduate research fellowship awarded to Joshua Correll. Support for this work also came from National Institute of Mental Health Grant R01-45049 awarded to Bernadette Park and Charles M. Judd and from a sabbatical award from the James McKeen Cattell Fund awarded to Bernadette Park. We thank Paul G. Davies for his invaluable contributions to the conceptual development of this project, and Joshua Ingram and David M. Deffenbacher for their assistance in its implementation.

Correspondence concerning this article should be addressed to Joshua Correll. Department of Psychology, University of Colorado, Boulder, Colorado 80309–0345. E-mail: jcorrell@psych.colorado.edu

Diallo, a 22-year-old West African immigrant, standing in the doorway of his apartment building. According to the police, Diallo resembled the suspect they were tracking. When they ordered him not to move. Diallo reached into his pants pocket. Believing he was reaching for a gun, the police fired a total of 41 shots, 19 of which hit and killed Diallo. Diallo was in fact unarmed. All four officers were later acquitted of any wrongdoing in the case.

The police could not have known for certain that Diallo was harmless. In the dark, they had ordered a potentially dangerous man to freeze, and that man reached for something. If Diallo had been armed, their decision to open fire would never have been questioned. But the decision to shoot a man who later proved to be unarmed did raise questions, one fundamental question in particular: Would the police have responded differently if Diallo had been White? Perhaps Diallo would have been given the benefit of the doubt, perhaps the

451

order to freeze would have been repeated, perhaps a slight delay in the decision to fire would have given the officers time to recognize that this suspect was not reaching for a gun. Though it is impossible to reach a definitive answer with respect to Diallo's case, the dilemma faced by these officers has important consequences for cities nationwide and warrants a systematic investigation. It seems crucial to understand whether or not the decision to shoot is influenced by the target's ethnicity, and if so, what this bias represents.

Social psychology has long held an interest in the way that schemata, including expectancies about social categories like ethnicity, guide the interpretation of ambiguous information (Duncan, 1976; Hilton & von Hippel, 1990; Jacobs & Eccles, 1992; Rothbart & Birrell, 1977; Sagar & Schofield, 1980). The quick and almost effortless classification of a unique individual into a broad social category (Brewer, 1988; Fiske, Lin, & Neuberg, 1999; Fiske & Neuberg, 1990) may lead people to assume that traits generally associated with the category also apply to this particular member. Either in the absence of individuating information (Darley & Gross, 1983; Locksley, Borgida, Brekke, & Hepburn, 1980; see Hamilton & Sherman, 1994, for a review) or in spite of it (Beckett & Park, 1995; Krueger & Rothbart, 1988), stereotypic associations can influence an observer's perceptions in a top-down fashion. A stereotype, in essence, can function as a schema to help clarify or disambiguate an otherwise confusing situation.

Of particular interest to the question of Diallo's death is the possibility that the officers' decision to fire was influenced by the stereotypic association between African Americans and violence. The ambiguity of Diallo's behavior (what was he reaching for?), which ironically provides a justification for the officers' decision, may have set the stage for bias, prompting the officers to draw on other sources of information, including stereotypes, in an effort to understand what was happening. Duncan (1976) showed that the same mildly aggressive behavior is perceived as more threatening when it is performed by an African American than when it is performed by a White person. A White person's light push seems like a violent shove when performed by an African American. Sagar and Schofield (1980), following Duncan, presented 6th-grade boys with line drawings and verbal accounts of ambiguous dyadic interactions, for example, two boys bumping into one another in the hallway, or one boy borrowing a pencil from a classmate without asking. To manipulate the ethnicity of the people interacting, the researchers simply shaded in the drawings. Like Duncan, they found

that when an actor was depicted as African American, rather than White, his behavior seemed more mean and threatening to the participants. Sagar and Schofield further found that this bias in perception was similar for both White and African American participants. That is, the tendency to see an African American's behavior as more mean and threatening than a White person's did not depend on the observer's ethnicity. On the basis of this result, Sagar and Schofield argued that the bias reflects not the internalization of anti-African American attitudes, but rather the application of a widely known and cognitively derived stereotype about the group to the particular target individual.

Devine (1989) went on to demonstrate that the impact of ethnicity on interpretation could occur even without participants' awareness. She asked participants to rate a target's ambiguously hostile behavior after subliminally priming them with words related to both the social category and the stereotype of African Americans (but excluding words directly related to violence). Participants who were primed with a greater number of these words were more likely to interpret the behavior as hostile, even though the target's ethnicity was never mentioned. Lepore and Brown (1997) primed only the social category of African Americans (not the stereotype) and found that the effect of the primes on interpretation of behavior was only evident among the more prejudiced participants. In all of these studies, the association between the social category, African American, and the concept of violence seems to lead participants to interpret an ambiguous target as more dangerous.

Most recently, Payne (2001) demonstrated that participants were faster and more accurate in distinguishing guns from hand tools when they were primed with an African American face, as opposed to a White face. Using Jacoby's (1991; Jacoby, Toth, & Yonelinas, 1993) Process Dissociation Procedure, Payne then separated participants' errors into automatic and controlled components. The magnitude of the automatic estimate represents the degree to which the ethnicity of the prime influences participants' decisions when their ability to control that decision fails. Among participants who were low in motivation to control prejudiced responding, Payne found that greater prejudice was associated with a greater automatic effect.

The primary goal of the current research was to carry this line of inquiry one step further, investigating the effect of a target's ethnicity on participants' decision to "shoot" that target. We present data from a simplified videogame, which roughly simulates the situation of a police officer who is confronted with an ambiguous, but potentially hostile, target, and who must decide whether or not to shoot. In the game, images of people who are either armed or unarmed, and either African American or White, appear unexpectedly in a variety of contexts. Unlike previous research, this game requires participants to make a behavioral shoot/don't shoot decision similar to that of a police officer. And unlike a sequential priming study (such as Payne, 2001), this game simultaneously presents a target person's ethnicity and the object he is holding. A participant need not process ethnicity to determine whether the target is armed. In spite of these differences, the research reviewed above strongly suggests that interpretation of the target as dangerous, and the associated decision to shoot, will vary as a function of the target's ethnicity. In Studies 1 and 2, we test this basic prediction. In Studies 3 and 4, we make an initial effort to understand the processes underlying this bias in the decision to shoot.

Study 1

Method

Participants and Design

Forty undergraduates (24 female, 16 male) at the University of Colorado at Boulder participated in this experiment in return for either $8 or partial credit toward a class requirement.[1] One of the male participants was Latino. All other participants were White. The study used a 2×2 within-subject design, with Target Ethnicity (African American vs. White) and Object Type (gun vs. no gun) as repeated factors.

Materials

Using the PsyScope software package (Cohen, MacWhinney, Flatt, & Provost, 1993), we developed a simplistic videogame that presented a series of background and target images. The videogame used a total of 20 backgrounds and 80 target images. Twenty young men, 10 African American and 10 White, were recruited on college campuses to pose as models for the targets. Each of these models appeared in the game four times, twice as a target in the gun condition and twice as a target in the no-gun condition, with a different object and in

a different pose each time (five basic poses were used in the game). There were four non-gun objects (a silver-colored aluminum can, a silver camera, a black cell phone, and a black wallet) and two guns (a silver snub-nosed revolver and a black 9-mm pistol). Each of the objects, within condition, appeared equally often in each of the five poses. The four target images for each model were superimposed on randomly determined backgrounds, constrained so that each background was used once in each of the four conditions and no target appeared on the same background more than once. Background images included an intentionally diverse assortment of photographs, such as train station terminals, parks, hotel entrances, restaurant facades, and city sidewalks. No people appeared in any of the original background scenes. Examples of the stimuli appear in Figure 28.1.

In total, there were 80 trials in the videogame, with 20 trials in each cell of the 2×2 design created by crossing the ethnicity of the target with whether the target held a gun or a non-gun. Each of the 80 trials began with the presentation of a fixation point, followed by a series of empty backgrounds, presented in slide-show fashion. The number of backgrounds on a given trial was randomly determined, ranging from 1 to 4. The duration of each was also random, ranging from 500 to 1,000 ms. The final background in the series was replaced by the target image, created by superimposing the target on the final background. From the perspective of the participant, a man seemed to simply appear on the background. The design of the game was intended to ensure that the participant never knew when or where the target would appear in the background or when a response would be required.

To play the game, the participant needed to decide as quickly as possible whether the object the man was holding was a gun or not. If it was a gun, the man posed an imminent danger, and the participant needed to shoot him as quickly as possible by pushing the right button, labeled *shoot*, on a button box. If he was holding some object other than a gun, he posed no danger, and the participant needed to press the left button, labeled *don't shoot*, as quickly as possible. Participants were instructed to use separate hands for each button and to rest their fingers on the buttons between trials. The game awarded and deducted points on the basis of performance. A hit (correctly shooting a target holding a gun) earned 10 points, and a correct rejection (not shooting a target holding some non-gun object) earned 5 points. A false alarm (shooting a target holding a non-gun) was punished by taking away 20 points, and a miss (not shooting a target holding a gun) resulted in our harshest penalty: A loss of

---

[1] Gender did not moderate any of the effects we report in this or subsequent studies. In Study 3, there was a main effect of gender, such that men had faster reaction times for all targets than did women, $t(43) = 2.31$, $p = .03$, but this effect did not replicate in the other studies.

FIGURE 28.1 ▪ Target and Background Example Scenes from Videogame. Color Originals are Available at psych.colorado.edu/-jcorrellapod.html

40 points.[2] This payoff matrix represented an effort to partially, if weakly, recreate the payoff matrix experienced by police officers on the street, where shooting an innocent suspect is a terrible mistake (as in the case of Amadou Diallo), but where the stronger motivation is presumably to avoid misidentifying an armed and hostile target, which could result in an officer's death. To minimize nonresponse, the game assessed a timeout penalty of 10 points if participants failed to respond to a target within 850 ms. This time window was selected to force participants to respond relatively quickly, while still allowing enough time such that errors in the game would be minimized. Participants' decisions ("shoot" or "don't shoot") and their reaction times were recorded for each trial. Each trial ended by giving participants feedback on whether they had made the correct decision on that trial and by showing them their cumulative point total.

Procedure

Participants, in groups of 1 to 4, were met by a male experimenter who outlined the study as an investigation of perceptual vigilance, or the ability to monitor and quickly respond to a variety of stimuli. A detailed set of instructions for the videogame task followed, including the point values for each of the outcomes. Participants were also informed that the people with the first, second, and third highest scores in the study would receive a prize ($30, $15, and $10, respectively) and that 5 others, randomly selected from participants with scores in the top 30%, would each receive $10. These prizes were intended to make the payoff matrix personally meaningful. Finally, participants were asked to pay attention to the faces of the targets, because they would be tested on their ability to recognize the targets at the end of the game. Participants then moved to individual rooms to play the game.

At the conclusion of the game, participants were presented with a series of 16 recognition trials in a paper-and-pencil task to determine whether facial characteristics of the targets had been attended to. For each of the 16 faces, participants had to indicate whether they believed it was the face of one of the targets that had been seen during the game or not. Half of the presented targets had in fact been seen previously; half had not. Additionally, half of the targets were African American and half were White.

Following the recognition task, participants were given a short questionnaire, which asked whether they

valued the monetary incentives, whether they remembered the point values for hits, misses, false alarms, and correct rejections. Participants were then fully debriefed, with the experimenter paying particular attention to alleviate any negative feelings aroused by the game.

Results and Discussion

To analyze the resulting reaction times, we excluded all trials on which the participant had either timed-out (i.e., failed to make a decision in the allotted 850-ms window) or made an incorrect response (e.g., shooting a target holding a non-gun). This resulted in the exclusion of data from 7% of the trials across participants, with a maximum of 20% of the trials for any one participant. Response latencies on the remaining trials were log-transformed and then averaged within subject across trials occurring in the same cell of the 2×2 within-subject research design. An analysis of variance (ANOVA) of the resulting mean latencies was then conducted, treating Target Ethnicity (White vs. African American) and Object Type (gun versus no gun) as within-subject factors.

This analysis revealed a significant main effect for Object. $F(1, 39) = 244.16, p < .0001$, and a significant Object × Ethnicity interaction, $F(1, 39) = 21.86, p < .0001$. The resulting cell means (converted back to the millisecond metric) appear in Table 28.1. As these means

TABLE 28.1. Means (and Standard Deviations) for Reaction Times and Error Rates as a Function of Target Ethnicity and Object Type (Studies 1, 2, and 3)

	Reaction Times		Errors per 20 Trials	
Study	White Targets	Afr. Am. Targets	White Targets	Afr. Am. Targets
Study 1				
Armed targets	554 (46)	544 (39)	0.70 (1.07)	0.40 (0.78)
Unarmed targets	623 (38)	634 (39)	1.23 (1.29)	1.45 (1.04)
Study 2				
Armed targets	449 (23)	451 (28)	2.46 (1.83)	1.48 (1.38)
Unarmed targets	513 (32)	523 (38)	2.40 (2.76)	3.29 (2.87)
Study 3				
Armed targets	550 (40)	539 (45)	0.76 (0.86)	0.49 (0.80)
Unarmed targets	607 (38)	620 (38)	0.33 (0.90)	0.65 (1.24)

Note. Afr. Am. = African American.

[2] These point values should, objectively, create a bias to shoot: The two "don't shoot" options yield an average reward of −17.5 points, whereas the "shoot" options yield a less aversive average of −5 points.

reveal, participants were significantly faster at making the correct decision to shoot, when the target held a gun, than the correct decision to not shoot, when the target did not hold a gun. More central to our predictions, the interaction suggests that the speed of responding on gun versus no-gun trials depended on target ethnicity. We decomposed this interaction by examining the simple effects of ethnicity separately for the gun and no-gun trials. Both were significant: Participants fired at an armed target more quickly if he was African American than if he was White, $F(1, 39) = 10.89, p < .005$, and they decided not to shoot an unarmed White target more quickly than an unarmed African American target, $F(1, 39) = 9.77, p < .005$.

We intentionally gave participants a long enough response window (850 ms) in this study to maximize correct responses to examine effects on response latencies. And, as we suspected, the proportions of errors were quite low, averaging 4% of the trials across participants. Nonetheless, it is possible to examine the error rates to see if they depended on Target Ethnicity, Object Type, or their interaction (see mean error rates in Table 28.1). This analysis revealed a main effect for Object, $F(1, 39) = 32.31, p < .0001$, such that errors in the no-gun condition (i.e., false alarms) were more frequent than errors in the gun condition (i.e., misses). The interaction between Ethnicity and Object was also significant, suggesting that the tendency to make more false alarms than misses was more pronounced for African American targets than for White targets, $F(1, 39) = 7.68, p < .01$. That is, whereas participants tended to shoot unarmed targets more frequently than they decided not to shoot armed targets, in general, this tendency was stronger when the target was African American than when the target was White. The simple effects were in the correct direction, but not statistically significant. Participants were marginally more likely to miss an armed target when he was White than when he was African American, $F(1, 39) = 3.66, p = .06$, but errors in response to unarmed targets did not seem to depend on ethnicity, $F(1, 39) = 1.68, p = .20$.

Both the latency and error results attest to the role of target ethnicity in disambiguating potentially threatening stimuli. Clearly, the responses of participants to these stimuli depended at some level on the ethnic category of the target, with potentially hostile targets identified as such more quickly if they were African American rather than White and benign targets identified as such more quickly if they were White rather than African American. Although these results are certainly consistent with our expectations, they are also somewhat surprising

given the fact that the target ethnicity appeared at exactly the same time as the object that had to be identified as a gun or not. Certainly participants could have performed perfectly on the task by attending only to the object held in the target's hand and by completely ignoring the target's ethnicity or any other individuating information.

To examine whether a target's features, other than the object he held, were attended to by participants, we examined their ability to recognize the faces of the targets they had seen during the game. A signal detection analysis revealed that sensitivity to old versus new faces was not above chance level in these recognition data (mean $d' = 0.15$), $t(39) = 1.15, p = .26$. Separate analyses within target ethnicity revealed that participants were unable to recognize African American targets at a better than chance level (mean $d' = -0.08$), $t(39) = -0.48$, $p = .63$, although recognition sensitivity for the White targets did exceed chance levels (mean $d' = 0.33$), $t(39) = 2.26, p < .05$. Our data suggest, then, that target ethnicity affected participants' judgments even while participants remained largely incapable of recognizing the faces of the targets they had seen.

Study 2

Our first study allowed participants a sufficient response window so that they made correct decisions in the case of nearly all targets. That is, error rates were very low. As a result, the strongest results from the first study were found with decision latencies on correct responses, with faster decisions to armed African American targets than to armed Whites, and faster decision to unarmed White targets than to unarmed African Americans. Although significant, the interactive effects of Target Ethnicity and Object Type on response errors were substantially weaker (and the relevant simple comparisons were not significant).

In the second study, we sought to replicate the basic pattern of results from the first study, but this time to make the task substantially harder by shortening the amount of time during which participants had to respond. Clearly, if the effects that we are exploring are to be relevant to more real-life scenarios, such as those encountered by police officers, then we would like to show our effects on actual responses (and errors in responses) rather than simply on the speed with which correct responses are made. Additionally, to increase the importance of performance in the task, we recruited participants exclusively for pay in this study and we offered them incentives directly tied to the quality of their performance, paying up to $20 for a study taking well less than an hour.

Method

Participants and Design

Forty-four undergraduates (33 female, 11 male) participated in this experiment in return for a minimum payment of $10, with the opportunity to earn additional money (up to a total of $20) by scoring points in the game. This incentive was intended to increase the personal significance of the rewards and penalties. One male participant was Latino, and 1 female was Asian. All other participants were White. We used the same 2×2 design, with Target Ethnicity (African American vs. White) and Object Type (gun vs. no gun) as within-subject factors.

Materials and Procedure

The materials and procedure were identical to those of Study 1, with the exception of the following modifications. First, we made clear to participants that they would be paid as a function of their performance. They were told that they started with an initial sum of $14 to their credit. Each point earned or lost (according to the same payoff matrix used in Study 1) was worth 1 cent. It was made clear that if they performed perfectly across all 80 trials, they would earn $20. If they lost points, they could lose up to $4, but they were guaranteed a base pay of $10. Second, we adjusted the game's response window from 850 ms to 630 ms to force participants to make decisions more quickly, with the goal of increasing error rates. Although a 630-ms response window may provide ample time to process simple stimuli such as faces or isolated objects, our images were fairly complex, and the shortened window proved a challenge for our participants. A pretest indicated that the shortened response window had the desired effect, increasing errors, but also dramatically increasing the proportion of trials on which participants failed to respond in time. Because the meaning of a timeout is ambiguous, a third change we made was to discourage timeouts by increasing their associated penalty from 10 to 50 points (i.e., 50 cents) and stressing the importance of responding quickly in the instructions. As participants' point totals directly affected the amount they were paid, this provided a considerable incentive. We also set an a priori limit, such that any participant with more than 10 timeouts would be excluded from the analysis. A final change we made was to the program used to record participants' data. In Study 1, for each trial, the program only recorded the response, response latency, target ethnicity, and target object (gun vs. no-gun), but the exact target and background for the trial were not recorded. We modified this in Study 2 so that we could identify particular stimuli that were associated with a greater number of errors.

Results and Discussion

Before conducting the primary analysis of error rates, we eliminated 5 participants (all female) who exceeded our a priori threshold of 10 timeouts (one eighth of all trials). Additionally, we examined error rates for particular targets to determine if correct responses were particularly difficult for some. In fact, there were a number of targets that were outliers in the overall distribution, inducing many more errors than the other targets. For instance, one unarmed African American target was shot by more than 90% of our participants. Additionally, one armed African American target and four unarmed White targets resulted in errors for more than one third of the participants. In each of these target images, some detail seemed potentially misleading. For example, one target had a stripe in his shorts that could be mistaken for a gun given the position of his arm. We suspect the substantially shorter time-out window was responsible for producing the unusually high error rates for these six targets. To deal with these outliers, we conducted all analyses twice, once with the full dataset and once deleting the six outlying targets. The analyses that we report are based on the partial dataset. However, with only one exception, as noted below, the results were unaffected by their inclusion/exclusion.

Participants' error rates (number of errors divided by the total number of valid trials) were subjected to a 2×2 ANOVA, with Target Ethnicity (White vs. African American) and Object Type (gun vs. no gun) as the independent variables. The relevant cell means are given in Table 28.1. The analysis revealed a significant effect for Object, such that the proportion of errors when a gun was present (i.e., misses) was lower than the proportion of errors when a gun was absent (i.e., false alarms), $F(1, 38) = 6.42$, $p < .02$. We also found the predicted interaction between Ethnicity and Object, $F(1, 38) = 17.83$, $p < .0001$. A test of the simple effects revealed that, when the target was unarmed, participants mistakenly shot him more often if he was African American than if he was White. $F(1, 38) = 6.53$, $p < .02$, though this effect was not significant when all targets were analyzed. When the target was armed, however, participants mistakenly decided not to shoot more often if he was White than if he was African American. $F(1, 38) = 13.31, p < .001$.

In addition to the analyses of the error rates, we also analyzed the decision latencies for correct responses, as in Study 1. Not surprisingly, given the considerably shorter response window in this study, there were no effects in the latencies. It seems that Study 1's interaction in response speed was, in this study, pushed over into error rates, due to the tightened response window.

As in Study 1, participants were unable to recognize presented targets above chance level. An analysis of the mean sensitivity to old versus new faces revealed a nonsignificant overall $d' = -0.02$, $t(38) = -0.15$, $p = .88$. Sensitivity was not above chance for either the White targets (mean $d' = 0.12$), $t(38) = 0.74$, $p = .46$, or for the African American targets (mean $d' = -0.16$), $t(38) = -0.97, p = .34$.

To understand the error rate results in greater detail, further analyses were conducted using the signal detection model (Green & Swets, 1966/1974; MacMillan & Creelman, 1991). Applied to the present context, the signal detection analysis assumes that targets encountered, both those with a gun and those without a gun, vary on a judgment-relevant dimension. For example, in the present studies, the extent to which the targets appeared to be threatening might have served as a critical dimension. On average, targets with guns are more threatening than targets who possess other objects (to the extent that they are discriminated at all), but nevertheless, there is a distribution of targets within each set, and these vary in how threatening they subjectively appear to be. Thus, we have two distributions of targets, one of targets with guns and one of targets without guns, and the signal detection model assumes that these are both normal distributions with equal variances. To some extent, of course, these two distributions overlap and the question of sensitivity is the question of the extent to which this is true. That is, if participants are relatively sensitive or accurate, shooting those targets who have guns and not shooting those targets who don't have guns, then the two distributions are largely separated from each other.

Additionally, because participants make a choice between shooting and not shooting a target on the basis of the subjective sense of how threatening the target appears to be, they set a decision threshold somewhere along the continuum that underlies the two distributions. Above that threshold, they shoot the target; below threshold they do not. Where that threshold is set is commonly referred to as the *decision criterion*.

From the two kinds of errors (false alarms: shooting an unarmed target: misses: not shooting an armed target),

one can derive estimates of both sensitivity, commonly defined as d', and decision criterion, in this case defined as c. We estimated both of these parameters for our participants, once for the White targets and once for the African American targets. Unsurprisingly, given the relatively low percentages of errors, participants showed considerable accuracy (i.e., high levels of d') for both the White and African American targets (White $M = 2.47$ [$SD = 0.87$]; African American $M = 2.48$ [$SD = 0.85$]). A test of differential sensitivity between the two kinds of targets failed to reject the null hypothesis, $F(1, 38) = 0.01$, $p = .93$. There were differences, however, between the two kinds of targets in the response criterion (White $M = 0.03$ [$SD = 0.30$]; African American $M = -0.24$ [$SD = 0.31$]), such that a significantly lower decision criterion to shoot the target was found for African American targets, $F(1, 38) = 22.21$, $p < .0001$. These results are depicted graphically in Figure 28.2. In sum, from the perspective of the signal detection model, the differences between responses to the African American and White targets arose not from differences in the underlying accuracy with which the two kinds of targets, those with a gun and those without a gun, can be discriminated. Rather, in the case of the African American targets, participants simply set a lower threshold for the decision to shoot, being willing to shoot targets who seemed less threatening.[3]

Study 3

Studies 1 and 2 provide evidence that the decision to shoot an armed target is made more quickly and more accurately if that target is African American than if he is White, whereas the decision not to shoot is made more quickly and more accurately if the target is White. This pattern of results is fundamentally consistent with research suggesting that participants may use ethnicity to interpret an ambiguously threatening target. When ambiguous behavior is performed by an African American, it seems more hostile, more mean, and more threatening than when it is performed by a White person (Duncan, 1976; Sagar &

---

[3] The same pattern of signal detection results emerges both for Study 1 and for Study 3. For Study 1, sensitivity did not differ: African American $d' = 3.30$, White $d' = 3.28$, $F(1, 39) = 0.10$, $p = .75$; but the decision criterion did: African American $c = -0.17$, White $c = -0.09$, $F(1, 39) = 10.07, p = .003$. In Study 3, sensitivity did not differ: African American $d' = 3.54$, White $d' = 3.56$, $F(1, 44) = 0.12$, $p = .73$; but the decision criterion did: African American $c = -0.02$, White $c = 0.07$, $F(1, 44) = 6.96, p = .02$.

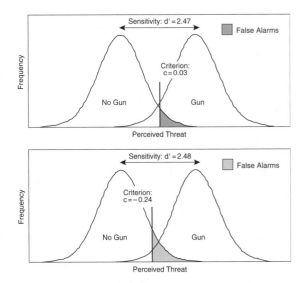

FIGURE 28.2 ■ Hypothetical Normal Distributions Representing Unarmed and Armed Targets for Signal Detection Analyses: White (top panel) and African Americans (bottom panel) targets.

Schofield, 1980). Participants also recognize a weapon more quickly and more accurately after seeing an African American face, rather than a White face (Payne, 2001). Here, we have shown that ethnicity can also influence a behavioral judgment with serious consequences for both target and shooter.

Simply documenting the existence of this bias does not clarify the mechanism by which ethnicity influences the decision to shoot. We suggested earlier that participants may use the stereotypic association between the social category, African American, and concepts like violence or danger as a schema to help interpret ambiguous behavior on the part of any given African American target. Through deductive inference, traits associated with the category may be applied to the individual category member. It is important to recognize that the proposed process does not require a participant to dislike African Americans, or to hold any explicit prejudice against them, nor does it require that the participant endorse the stereotype; it simply requires that, at some level, the participant associates the two concepts "African American" and "violent." Previous research is equivocal in its support of this possibility, suggesting that bias in the interpretation of an ambiguous stimulus may depend on both stereotypic associations and on prejudice. Sagar and Schofield

(1980), for example, provide evidence for a stereotype-driven effect. Recall that these researchers found that both White and African American participants interpreted behavior as more threatening if it had been performed by an African American target. Reasoning that bias among the African American participants is not likely to reflect prejudice against African Americans, they concluded that it reflects instead a common belief, or stereotype, that African Americans are more violent than Whites. A culturally communicated stereotypic association may influence interpretations even if the observer does not personally endorse the stereotype or hold a prejudiced attitude (Devine, 1989). Data presented by both Lepore and Brown (1997) and Payne (2001), however, have shown that more prejudiced participants show greater bias in their interpretations of ambiguous stimuli (for Payne, 2001, this relationship was moderated by motivation to control prejudice). Of course, the effect of prejudice on perceptions may be indirect, operating chiefly through the stronger negative stereotypic associations that accompany prejudiced attitudes. The question is whether stereotypic associations predict bias over and above prejudice. To be clear, we hypothesize that although the magnitude of the bias evident in our videogame may covary with participants' prejudice against African Americans, it is not a function of that prejudice, per se, but rather reflects the deductive application of stereotypic associations (often associated with prejudice) between African Americans and violence. Because participants can use traits associated with the group to disambiguate a particular African American target, they may inappropriately perceive that target as threatening or hostile.

Study 3 represents a first attempt to test these predictions. After playing the videogame, participants completed a questionnaire designed to measure prejudice and two forms of the association between African Americans and violence. The first measure of this association assessed stereotypes that the participant personally endorses or believes. We refer to this as the *personal stereotype*. The second measure, called the *cultural stereotype*, is designed to assess the participant's awareness that a stereotype of African Americans as violent is present in U.S. culture, generally. Though we use the terms *personal stereotype* and *cultural stereotype*, this distinction maps cleanly on to the endorsement/knowledge distinction suggested by Devine (Devine, 1989; Devine & Elliot, 1995), who has shown that, although people often personally disavow negative stereotypes about African Americans, they are well aware that those stereotypes exist. Because this knowledge represents a psychological link between the social category and the trait, activating the concept of the group may predispose a participant to make use of the stereotypic trait in interpretations of an ambiguous target—even if he or she does not personally endorse the stereotype. Both personal and cultural forms of the stereotypic association, then, may influence interpretation of an ambiguous target.

Method

Participants and Design

Forty-eight undergraduates (26 female, 22 male) participated in this experiment in return for either $10 or partial credit toward a class requirement. Two male participants were Latino, and 1 female was Asian. Another female was African American and was excluded from our analyses. All other participants were White. Two White females were also removed from the dataset, one because the game's *shoot* and *don't shoot* labels were reversed, and one because she was working as a research assistant on a different study of African American stereotypes. The final sample included 45 students. This study used the same 2 × 2 within-subject design, with Target Ethnicity (African American vs. White) and Object Type (gun vs. no gun) as repeated factors.

Materials

Videogame. In this study, we used the videogame parameters we had used in Study 1. The response window was set at 850 ms, and we expected effects primarily in the latency of correct responses, rather than in error rates.

Questionnaire. Study 3 added a battery of individual difference measures. First, participants completed the Modern Racism Scale (MRS; McConahay, Hardee, & Batts, 1981), the Discrimination (DIS) and Diversity Scales (DIV) (both from Wittenbrink, Judd, & Park, 1997), all of which are designed to measure prejudice against African Americans, as well as the Motivation to Control Prejudiced Responding Scale (MCP; Dunton & Fazio, 1997; Fazio, Jackson, Dunton, & Williams, 1995), which assesses participants willingness to express any prejudice they may feel. Items from these scales were intermixed (presented in a single, randomly determined order) and responses were given on 5-point scales, ranging from *strongly disagree* to *strongly agree*. The items were intermingled with filler items from the Right-Wing Authoritarianism Scale (RWA, Altemeyer, 1988) and the Personal Need for Structure Scale (PNS; Thompson, Naccarato, Parker, & Moskowitz, 2001), which are

addressed below. Second, to examine the degree to which participants endorsed a negative stereotype of African Americans as aggressive and dangerous, we asked them to estimate, on the basis of their personal beliefs, the percentage of both African Americans and Whites who are dangerous, violent, and aggressive (separate estimates were made for each trait by filling in a value from 0% to 100%). Third, we included a measure of participants' perceptions of the cultural stereotype that African Americans are aggressive and dangerous. Participants were asked to again consider the three attributes (dangerous, violent, and aggressive), giving prevalence estimates, not on the basis of their own personal beliefs, but rather on the basis of their perceptions of what most White Americans would estimate. These estimates were made by marking a 130-mm line anchored with the adjective (e.g., *dangerous*) on the right, and its negation (e.g., *not dangerous*) on the left.

Responses to the contact items were made on 7-point scales. The first contact question asked participants to rate how many African Americans they know, using a scale anchored with *don't know any African Americans* and *know a lot of African Americans*. The second item asked for a rating of how well they know their African American acquaintances on a scale from *don't know well* to *know very well*. The third item asked about the degree of contact with African Americans in their neighborhood, when growing up. The fourth item asked about the number of African American friends they had while growing up. And the fifth item asked about the number of African Americans who had attended their high school. The last three items used a scale ranging from *none* to *many*.

Procedure

As before, a male experimenter greeted participants, in groups of 1 to 4, and introduced the study as an investigation of perceptual vigilance. He went on to note that, because the vigilance task did not require the entire time period, participants would work on a separate questionnaire study afterward. After learning about the rules of the game, participants moved to computer terminals in private rooms and played the videogame. As each participant completed the game, the experimenter moved him or her to a table (still in the private room) and administered the short questionnaire, from Studies 1 and 2, assessing basic reactions to the game. The experimenter subsequently announced that the videogame study was over and provided another consent form, ostensibly for the separate questionnaire study. After collecting the consent form, he handed the participant an envelope containing the questionnaire. We made every effort to stress the confidentiality of the responses on the questionnaire. The experimenter told participants not to put any identifying information on the forms, not even a code number, and to seal the packet in the envelope when they had finished. He then left them alone to complete the questions. As in Studies 1 and 2, participants were fully debriefed. During this process, the experimenter probed for suspicion about the relationship between the game and the subsequent questionnaire.

Results and Discussion

In the debriefing, 6 participants reported that they had noticed that both the game and the questionnaire involved ethnicity, and that this awareness had prompted them to wonder if the two were related. Two of the 6 reported strong suspicion. The following results are based on the complete dataset, but exclusion of the 6 participants does not affect the analyses in either direction or significance. To analyze the videogame data, we submitted the log-transformed reaction times from correct trials to a 2×2 ANOVA, with Target Ethnicity and Object Type as the independent variables (see Table 28.1 for means converted back to milliseconds). The targets that had proved problematic in Study 2 were excluded from this analysis, though their inclusion does not substantially affect the results. Replicating the results from the first study, we found both a pronounced effect for Object, such that armed targets were responded to more quickly than unarmed targets, $F(1, 44) = 171.33$, $p < .0001$, and an Ethnicity $\times$ Object interaction, $F(1, 44) = 22.44$, $p < .0001$. Simple effects tests revealed that, when the target was armed, participants, on average, fired more quickly if he was African American than if he was White, $F(1, 44) = 4.15$, $p < .05$. When presented with an unarmed target, participants chose the "don't shoot" alternative more quickly if he was White than if he was African American, $F(1, 44) = 22.72$, $p < .0001$.

Mean scores on the error rates were largely consistent with those from Study 1. The Ethnicity $\times$ Object interaction was significant. $F(1, 44) = 7.20$, $p = .01$. Simple effects tests showed an ethnicity effect only among targets without guns, $F(1, 44) = 5.76$, $p = .02$. such that these were incorrectly shot more often if they were African American. The simple effect for armed targets was not significant, $F(1, 44) = 2.31$, $p = .14$. A test of the mean recognition sensitivity for the presented targets was significant in this study (mean

$d' = 0.25$), $t(44) = 2.51$, $p = .016$. As in Study 1, however, sensitivity was above chance only for the White targets (mean $d' = 0.62$), $t(44) = 4.71$, $p < .0001$, and not for the African American targets (mean $d' = -0.15$), $t(44) = -1.14$, $p = .26$.

Having replicated the Ethnicity $\times$ Object interaction in the response latency scores, we wanted to examine its correlates. Accordingly, for each participant we computed a within-subject contrast score, assessing the magnitude of the Ethnicity $\times$ Object interaction for that particular participant. Higher scores on this variable, which we refer to as *Shooter Bias*, indicate faster responses to unarmed White than to unarmed African American targets, and to armed African American than armed White targets.

None of the explicit prejudice scales — MRS, DIS, and DIV — show significant correlations with the Shooter Bias from the videogame. That is, those who reported higher levels of prejudice on these scales did not show a stronger ethnicity bias in the videogame. Because these three measures are highly intercorrelated, we also combined them, averaging all items together. This composite scale was similarly uncorrelated with Shooter Bias.

To compute the personal stereotype measure of African Americans as aggressive, we calculated the degree to which participants rated African Americans as more violent than Whites, more dangerous than Whites, and more aggressive than Whites. These three difference scores were averaged together to form the personal stereotype index. The measure reflects perceptions of the prevalence of the negative stereotypic attributes among African Americans relative to Whites. The same process was followed in computing the extent to which participants believed there is a negative cultural stereotype of African Americans as dangerous and aggressive. The measure of personal endorsement of the negative stereotype of African Americans as aggressive and violent did not correlate with the Shooter Bias. However, the perception of a parallel negative cultural stereotype did correlate with the magnitude of the Shooter Bias in the videogame.

Contact scores were calculated by averaging participants' responses to the five 7-point contact items. This measure showed a significant and somewhat surprising correlation with the bias: Participants who reported more contact with African Americans exhibited a more pronounced Shooter Bias in the videogame. We discuss this intriguing effect in the General Discussion when we consider potential mechanisms that may give rise to Shooter Bias.

We suggested that the Shooter Bias evident in this videogame might be a consequence of participants using stereotypic associations about African Americans to help interpret ambiguous African American targets. The data from Study 3 suggest that the magnitude of the bias was related to participants' perceptions of the cultural stereotype about African Americans. The bias was not, however, related to either personally endorsed stereotypes or to prejudice. This is somewhat surprising, because, to the extent that people personally endorse the violent stereotype or hold prejudices against African Americans, we might suppose the negative associations to be stronger and more likely to influence their interpretations of, and behavior toward, an ambiguous target.

There are well-documented social desirability concerns associated with expressing prejudice or negative stereotypic beliefs about African Americans (Dunton & Fazio, 1997; McConahay et al., 1981; Plant & Devine, 1998), so it may be that participants simply refused to express their personal views.

Unlike prejudice and personal stereotypes, our measure of cultural stereotype should be generally free from social desirability concerns. It involves participants' estimates of the stereotype held by American society. The fact that cultural stereotype correlates with Shooter Bias suggests that awareness of the stereotype, itself, even though a person may not believe that stereotype, can be sufficient to produce bias. One might argue, however, that our cultural stereotype measure was just another way of measuring personal prejudice, in a manner that allowed participants to express their own prejudices relatively free from normative constraints. That is, by attributing prejudicial beliefs to others, participants were now able to express more freely the prejudice that they themselves felt.

We were interested in whether cultural stereotype would continue to predict Shooter Bias once we removed the extent to which the cultural stereotype variable is a measure of personal prejudice, particularly among those low in motivation to control prejudice. Accordingly, we estimated a model with Shooter Bias as the criterion, regressing it on the cultural stereotype measure while controlling for our personal prejudice composite, MCP, and the interaction between personal prejudice and MCP. In this model, again, only the cultural stereotype measure related significantly to bias in the videogame, $F(1, 40) = 5.24$, $p < .03$. Thus, even removing personal prejudice levels from the cultural stereotype, and controlling for the fact that personal prejudice levels were more strongly related to the cultural stereotype among those low in MCP, the cultural

stereotype measure continued to predict bias in our videogame.[4] This suggests that it is truly knowledge of the cultural stereotype that is at work here, rather than simply an indirect measure of personal prejudice. We consider this a sobering prospect because it suggests that the bias may be endemic in American society.

A number of studies have shown that cultural stereotypes can be automatically activated even when a perceiver does not endorse them (Banaji & Greenwald, 1995; Devine, 1989; Gilbert & Hixon, 1991: Macrae, Milne, & Bodenhausen, 1994). Cultural influences, including television, movies, music, and newspapers provide a constant barrage of information that often depicts African Americans as violent (Cosby, 1994; Gray, 1989), and those depictions may shape our understanding of the world (Gerbner, Gross, Morgan, & Signorielli, 1986). Popular culture, including Gangsta Rap songs like the Notorious B.I.G.'s "Somebody's Gotta Die," Snoop Dogg's "Serial Killa," or Dr. Dre's "Murder Ink," and movies like *Colors* or *Training Day* may foster bias by enhancing detrimental stereotypic associations, in spite of the fact that the audience knows the characters and events are fictitious.

If cultural stereotypes associating African Americans with violence do, in fact, lead to Shooter Bias, any person exposed to American culture should be liable to demonstrate the bias, regardless of his or her personal views about African Americans. Research suggests that the very people who are targeted by cultural stereotypes are influenced by the media representations they see (Berry & Mitchell-Kernan, 1982; Stroman, 1986; SuberviVelez & Necochea, 1990), know full well that the stereotypes exist (Steele & Aronson, 1995), and even activate those stereotypes automatically (Banaji & Greenwald, 1995). Sagar and Schofield (1980), as noted above, found similar levels of bias among their African American and White participants using their interpretation task. To examine further the possibility that knowledge of the cultural stereotype may, in and of itself, lead to Shooter Bias, we sought to test for bias in a more diverse sample that included African American participants.

---

[4] The attempt to control for the prejudice composite measure, MCP, and their interaction only removes variance based on personal prejudice to the extent that these scales reliably measure that variance. There is reason to assume that these measures only partially assess prejudice, particularly for participants high in MCP. Thus, although the analysis represents our best attempt to examine the effects of cultural stereotypes over and above prejudice in the current dataset, it is nonetheless imperfect. Our thanks to Keith Payne for this insight.

Study 4

Method

Participants and Design
Fifty-two adults from bus stations, malls, and food courts in Denver, Colorado, were recruited to participate in this study in return for $5. The study followed the same 2 × 2 within-subject design used in Studies 1–3, with Target Ethnicity (African American vs. White) and Object Type (gun vs. no gun) as repeated factors, but in Study 4 we added a between-subject factor, namely Participant Ethnicity (African American vs. White). The final sample included 25 African Americans (6 females, 19 males) and 21 Whites (8 females, 13 males). One Asian and 4 Hispanic or Latino participants, and 1 participant who did not indicate his ethnicity, were excluded from the analyses, though the results do not differ if they are included in the White sample.

Materials
In this study, we used the videogame parameters from Studies 1 and 3. The response window was set at 850 ms and, again, we expected effects in the latency of correct responses, rather than in error rates. Before beginning this study, the targets identified as problematic in Study 2 were edited in Photoshop to clarify the object in the picture.

Procedure
At each location, two male experimenters set up 2–3 laptop computers equipped with the videogame program and earphones, to minimize distractions inherent in the nonlaboratory environment. Without a button box, participants pressed the *k* key on the laptop keyboard to indicate *shoot*, and the *d* key to indicate *don't shoot*. While one experimenter circulated and recruited participants, the other oversaw the experiment, giving instructions to each participant individually. After completing the videogame, participants were paid and debriefed. In this study, we did not include instructions to attend to target faces, nor did we test for recognition after the game.

Results and Discussion

Before analyzing the videogame data, we reexamined the targets that were problematic in Study 2. The targets no longer induced unusually high numbers of errors, and they were therefore included in the analyses

reported below. The results reported do not change in direction or magnitude if the targets are excluded. We submitted the log-transformed reaction times from correct trials to a 2 × 2 × 2 mixed-model ANOVA, with Participant Ethnicity as a between-subject factor, and Target Ethnicity and Object Type as within-subject factors (see Table 28.2 for means converted back to milliseconds). Across all participants, we again found a pronounced effect for Object, such that armed targets evoked responses more quickly than unarmed targets, $F(1, 45) = 347.82, p < .0001$. The Target Ethnicity × Object interaction, or Shooter Bias, was also significant, $F(1, 45) = 14.75, p < .001$. Crucially, though, the magnitude of the bias did not depend on Participant Ethnicity, $F(1, 44) = 0.10, p = .75$. Examining the African American and White samples separately, we found that the Target Ethnicity × Object interaction was significant for both, $F(1, 24) = 6.55, p = .017$ and $F(1, 20) = 8.01, p = .01$, respectively.

Simple effects tests again showed that, when the target was armed, participants decided to shoot more quickly if he was African American than if he was White, $F(1, 45) = 7.62, p = .008$. When the target was unarmed, participants pressed the *don't shoot* button more quickly if he was White than if he was African American, resulting in an identical test statistic, $F(1, 45) = 7.62, p = .008$. Neither simple effect depended on Participant Ethnicity,

TABLE 28.2. Means (and Standard Deviations) for Reaction Times and Error Rates as a Function of Target Ethnicity, Object Type, and Participant Ethnicity (Study 4)

Study	Reaction Times		Errors per 20 Trials	
	White Targets	Afr. Am. Targets	White Targets	Afr. Am. Targets
White participants				
Armed targets	590 (43)	578 (36)	1.38 (1.36)	0.76 (0.77)
Unarmed targets	652 (40)	665 (41)	1.19 (0.93)	1.29 (1.49)
Afr. Am. participants				
Armed targets	578 (42)	567 (47)	2.00 (1.53)	1.52 (1.58)
Unarmed targets	645 (47)	659 (41)	1.64 (1.80)	1.44 (1.47)

Note. Afr. Am. = African American.

$F(1, 44) = 0.07$, $p = .79$, for the unarmed targets, and $F(1, 44) = 0.42$, $p = .52$, for the unarmed targets.

An analysis of the error rates revealed that the Target Ethnicity × Object interaction was only marginal, $F(1, 45) = 3.24$, $p = .08$, and its magnitude did not depend on Participant Ethnicity, $F(1, 44) = 0.66$, $p = .42$.

General Discussion

In four studies, we attempted to recreate the experience of a police officer who, confronted with a potentially dangerous suspect, must decide whether or not to shoot. Our goal was to examine the influence of the suspect's ethnicity on that decision. We used a simplified videogame to present African American and White male targets, each holding either a gun or a nonthreatening object. Participants were instructed to shoot only armed targets. We reasoned that participants might use the stereotype, or schema, that African Americans are violent to help disambiguate the target stimuli, and would therefore respond with greater speed and accuracy to stereotype-consistent targets (armed African Americans and unarmed Whites) than to stereotype-inconsistent targets (armed Whites and unarmed African Americans).

In Study 1, participants fired on an armed target more quickly when he was African American than when he was White, and decided not to shoot an unarmed target more quickly when he was White than when he was African American. In Study 2, we attempted to increase error rates by forcing participants to make decisions very quickly. Participants in this study failed to shoot an armed target more often when that target was White than when he was African American. If the target was unarmed, participants mistakenly shot him more often when he was African American than when he was White. A signal detection analysis of these data revealed that, although participants' ability to distinguish between armed and unarmed targets did not depend on target ethnicity, participants set a lower decision criterion to shoot for African American targets than for Whites. That is, if a target was African American, participants generally required less certainty that he was, in fact, holding a gun before they decided to shoot him. In Study 3, we returned to an analysis of reaction times, replicating the Ethnicity × Object Type interaction (Shooter Bias) obtained in Study 1, and examining individual difference measures associated with the magnitude of that effect. Shooter Bias was more pronounced among participants who believed that there is a strong stereotype in American culture characterizing African Americans as

aggressive, violent and dangerous: and among participants who reported more contact with African Americans. Prejudice and personal endorsement of the stereotype that African Americans are violent failed to predict Shooter Bias in the simple correlations, and their predictive power was no stronger among participants low in motivation to control prejudice. The fact that Shooter Bias in Study 3 was related to perceptions of the cultural stereotype, rather than prejudice or personally endorsed stereotypes, suggests that mere knowledge of the stereotype is enough to induce this bias. In Study 4, we obtained additional support for this prediction. Testing both White and African American participants, we found that the two groups display equivalent levels of bias.

The results of these studies consistently support the hypothesized effect of ethnicity on shoot/don't shoot decisions. Both in speed and accuracy, the decision to fire on an armed target was facilitated when that target was African American, whereas the decision not to shoot an unarmed target was facilitated when that target was White. This Shooter Bias effect is consistent with the results reported by Payne (2001). Payne primed participants with African American and White faces, and asked them to identify subsequent target objects as either hand tools or weapons. His results suggest that responses to hand tools were faster (and, in a second study, more accurate) when preceded by White, relative to African American, primes, whereas responses to weapons were faster (but no more accurate) when preceded by African American primes. This priming effect maps nicely onto our results. The consistency between our results and those obtained by Payne is particularly striking given methodological differences between the two paradigms. Four primary differences stand out. Payne used small, decontextualized and relatively simple images of faces (the center portion of the face) and objects, whereas our stimuli were very complex, with target individuals appearing against realistic backgrounds. Payne used a sequential priming task, whereas we used simultaneous presentation of ethnicity and object. A consequence of Payne's priming task, which used a constant 200-ms stimulus onset asynchrony, is that the appearance of a prime in his task should have clearly indicated to participants that a target was imminent. Our task, however, presented targets at random intervals, with no prime, so that participants were never certain about when they would appear. Finally, whereas Payne asked his participants to identify a target object as a tool or a weapon, we asked our participants to decide whether or not to shoot a target person. Although both decisions depend on the presence of a weapon, the psychological implications of the two tasks are quite different. Payne's task was framed as a categorization judgment, whereas our task was characterized as a behavioral response. In spite of these distinctions, both paradigms reveal a pronounced effect of target ethnicity on reactions to weapons.

In line with Sagar and Schofield (1980), we have argued that ethnicity influences the shoot/don't shoot decision primarily because traits associated with African Americans, namely "violent" or "dangerous," can act as a schema to influence perceptions of an ambiguously threatening target. The relationship between cultural stereotype and Shooter Bias obtained in Study 3 provides support for this hypothesis. The subsequent finding that African Americans and Whites, alike, display this bias further buttresses the argument. It is unlikely that participants in our African American sample held strong prejudice against their own ethnic group (Judd, Park, Ryan, Brauer, & Kraus, 1995), but as members of U.S. society, they are, presumably, aware of the cultural stereotype that African Americans are violent (Devine & Elliot, 1995; Steele & Aronson, 1995). These associations, we suggest, may influence reactions to the targets in our videogame. Though ambient cultural associations may impact most members of U.S. society, it is certainly plausible that personal endorsement of stereotypes, and perhaps prejudice, will lead to even stronger negative associations with African Americans, potentially magnifying bias. (Though the data in Study 3, specifically the lack of a relationship between Shooter Bias and personal stereotype, offer little support for this argument, at present.)

It seems appropriate at this juncture to speculate on mechanisms that may underlie Shooter Bias. Our basic findings indicate that a target's ethnicity, though technically irrelevant to the decision task at hand, somehow interferes with participants' ability to react appropriately to the object in the target's hand. This interference seems roughly analogous to a Stroop effect, and research on this extensively studied phenomenon may provide a useful perspective from which to consider our results. The common Stroop experiment presents participants with a word, and requires them to identify the color of the ink in which that word is written (e.g., green ink). Performance on this simple task can be disrupted when the word, itself, refers to a different color than the ink (e.g., RED printed in green ink), relative to performance when the color of the ink and the referent of the word are the same (e.g., GREEN printed in green ink) or when the word does not refer to a color at all (e.g., EGGS printed in green ink). The Stroop paradigm, like our videogame, simultaneously presents participants with information that is relevant to the judgment at hand (ink color and object, respectively) as well as information that is irrelevant (word name and ethnicity, respectively). Participants need not process the irrelevant information to perform the task, but in both cases, the presence of incongruent information on the irrelevant dimension interferes with participants' ability to process the relevant information. Researchers have suggested that, because we so frequently read the words that we see, reading occurs quickly. Ink naming, though, is an unusual and relatively cumbersome task. If these two processes occur in parallel, the quicker word reading may produce interference by winning a kind of horse race, getting to the finish line and influencing responses ahead of the slower ink-naming process, which eventually provides the definitive answer (Cohen, Dunbar, & McClelland, 1990; Posner & Snyder, 1975). Similarly, the speedy categorization of people into ethnic categories, described by Brewer (1988) and Fiske and Neuberg (1990), should quickly activate stereotypes and interfere with the unfamiliar and less automatic gun/no-gun judgment (see Figure 28.3). This analogy is not perfect, of course. Although it may be natural to read the word RED when it appears, the typical day-to-day response to an African American does not involve gunfire. However, to the extent that a person spontaneously associates an African American target with violence, the ethnicity of the target should conflict with the judgment that he is unarmed, and it may therefore inhibit the "don't shoot" response.

Cohen et al. (1990) characterized Stroop interference as an interaction between two variables: Attention to the irrelevant dimension and the strength of the association between the incongruent information and the incorrect response. Both of these variables can moderate Stroop effects independently (see Walley, McLeod, & Khan, 1997; Walley, McLeod, & Weiden, 1994, for research on attention; see Lu & Proctor, 2001, for research on the strength of association). Though it is only speculation at present, we suggest that the two significant predictors of Shooter Bias in Study 3, cultural stereotype and contact, are important because they capture these two components of Stroop interference. We have already presented the argument that a cultural stereotype represents an associative link between African Americans and traits related to violence and danger. We further suggest that the role of contact in predicting Shooter Bias may reflect, at least in part, the other component of Stroop interference: Attention to irrelevant ethnic cues. People who have had extensive contact with African Americans may have, over the course of that experience, learned to naturally parse the world in terms of ethnic categories.

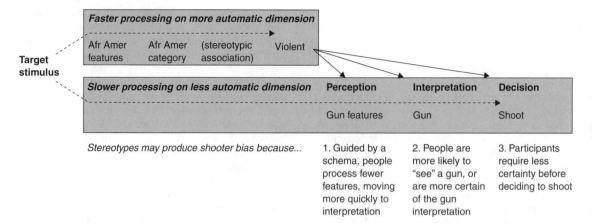

FIGURE 28.3 ■ Faster, more automatic processing on the irrelevant ethnic dimension may bias participants' (a) perception of targets, (b) interpretation of targets, or (c) the criterion of certainty required for the "shoot" response. Afr Amer = African American.

They may be essentially schematic for ethnicity. Greater attention to ethnicity combined with an association between African Americans and violence should, from the Stroop perspective, magnify Shooter Bias. In line with this prediction, Payne (Payne, Lambert, & Jacoby, in press) has shown that asking participants to use ethnic cues in their judgments (like a person engaged in racial profiling) increases the magnitude of the automatic component in error responses in his task, relative to control participants who receive no special instructions. Of greater interest, asking participants to avoid using ethnicity in their judgments also increases the magnitude of the automatic component. This suggests that attention to the irrelevant ethnic cue may produce interference.

The Stroop conceptualization offers another, perhaps more hopeful, prediction. If Shooter Bias is, in part, a function of the automaticity with which ethnic cues are processed relative to the automaticity of the object cues (i.e., ethnicity's ability to win the horse race against the relevant dimension), the bias should be minimized by interventions that speed up the gun/no-gun decision. As the relevant decision becomes more automatic, the effect of the irrelevant dimension should weaken. Experimental research (MacLeod, 1998; MacLeod & Dunbar, 1988) as well as computer simulations (Cohen et al., 1990) have demonstrated that repeated training on ink-naming tasks, which should render that process more automatic, reduces Stroop interference. Similarly, training participants to quickly and effortlessly distinguish guns from cell phones may reduce Shooter Bias.

Though we have characterized Shooter Bias as a result of distorted interpretations of an ambiguous target, there are several stages at which this bias may actually be functioning. Before shooting, a participant must (a) *perceive* the object, (b) *interpret* the object as a gun with some degree of certainty, and (c) *decide* to press the "shoot" button once a criterion of certainty has been reached. Stereotypic schemata may theoretically affect any or all of these processes, and it is difficult to disentangle them theoretically, let alone empirically. Figure 28.3 depicts the three processing stages and how faster, more automatic processing along the irrelevant dimension (as suggested by the Stroop research) might bias each stage of relevant processing (the solid arrows). Throughout this article, we have argued that bias impacts the second stage of this process, changing the interpretation of an ambiguous object. A participant who catches a glimpse of some elongated shape in the target's hand may draw on stereotypic associations, interpreting the shape as a gun if the target is African American but as a cell phone if he is White. Participants may almost "see" different objects.

One problem with this perspective is that we took pains to ensure that the objects presented in our target images were clearly identifiable. Even under time pressure, is it fair to characterize these objects as ambiguous? Certainly, very few of our participants actually misperceived the objects: Our primary effects were in reaction times, not errors, and errors were consistently quite low. It is possible that the bias in reaction time represents the effects of stereotypes on actual perception of the object, not on its interpretation. von Hippel and his associates (von Hippel, Jonides, Hilton & Narayan, 1993) showed that when a participant has a relevant schema, he or she can infer the gist of a stimulus with very few perceptual details. Without a schema, though, more detailed perceptual encoding may be necessary. In the context of the current research, the stereotype of African Americans may influence the number features a participant must process to make the correct object identification. An African American target provides a schema relevant to guns, so participants who see just a few features of a gun quickly identify it and decide to shoot. A White target, perhaps, provides no useful schema, and participants must attend to more features of the gun in his hand before they recognize it, causing them to respond more slowly. von Hippel's research provides an elegant rationale for the differential speed required to shoot an armed target, but we are less confident that perceptual differences underlie reactions to the unarmed targets. Perceptual processes can only account for the simple effect of ethnicity among unarmed targets if we assume that White people stereotypically carry cell phones, wallets, coke cans, and cameras, and that this stereotype reduces the number of perceptual cues necessary to identify these objects relative to African Americans, where no cell phone stereotype exists. Empirically, it should be possible to test the viability of a perceptual encoding account of Shooter Bias. If perceptual differences drive ethnic bias, then memory for trivial details, such as the kind of gun or the color of the cell phone, which should reflect the extent of perceptual encoding, should differ as a function of target ethnicity.

Another, more macroscopic, alternative to our interpretation-based account is that Shooter Bias may reflect changes in the decision criterion that participants use. Bias would clearly emerge if participants require one level of certainty that the object is a gun when deciding to shoot African American targets, but have another, more stringent, criterion for Whites. Even if the perception and interpretation of an object do not differ as a function of target ethnicity (e.g., the participant is 75% certain that the object is a gun for both African American and White targets), a participant who requires 60% certainty for African American targets, but 80% certainty for Whites, will show Shooter Bias. Unfortunately, the current studies do not allow us to discern between the interpretation and decision criterion explanations. Though the signal detection terms, *sensitivity* and *criterion*, might foster an expectation that Study 2 should be able to resolve this question, that is not the case. Study 2 suggested that sensitivity was equal for African American and White targets, and that only the criterion differed. The criterion may differ, though, either because the certainty needed to make the shoot/don't shoot decision differs with target ethnicity (bias in the decision

stage), or because a given object in the hand of an African American target is *simultaneously* more likely to be perceived as a gun and less likely to be perceived as a non-gun, than the same object in a White target's hand (bias in the interpretation stage). The signal detection theory figure from Study 2 assumes that the average armed White target and the average armed African American target seem equally threatening, that the two gun distributions fall at the same point on the *x*-axis. As we have graphed it, the figure suggests that the criterion to shoot shifts down for African American targets. However, it is also possible that participants use the same criterion for White and African American targets, but generally perceive African Americans as more threatening. If this were the case, the criterion line in the chart for African American targets would have the same *x*-coordinate as the White criterion line, but the mean of the two African American distributions (both armed and unarmed) would seem to shift up on the dimension of perceived threat. Even using signal detection theory, we have no way to statistically disentangle these two possibilities in the current data.

Bias in the decision-making stage may be seen as consistent with ideomotor effects. Bargh, Chen, and Burrows (1996, Study 3), for example, found that participants primed with African American faces exhibited more aggressive behavior in response to a rude request from an experimenter. It is possible that the participants' behavior was still driven by bias in their interpretation, that those primed with African American actually perceived the experimenter as more hostile (along the lines of Devine, 1989). But Bargh and others (e.g., Chartrand & Bargh, 1996; Dijksterhuis, Aarts, Bargh, & van Knippenberg, 2000; Stapel & Koomen, 2001) have demonstrated direct behavioral priming effects in a number of situations designed to preclude interpretation-based bias. It is not unreasonable to suppose that participants in our studies were cued by a target's ethnicity to behave aggressively toward African American targets, shooting them more often and more quickly than Whites. Payne (2001), though, did not require a behavioral response. Because his task required that participants classify objects as guns or hand tools, rather than react violently, ideomotor effects cannot account for his findings. In the absence of more definitive evidence, and given the consistency between Payne's results and ours, parsimony argues for an interpretation-based explanation of Shooter Bias, rather than a criterion-based or ideomotor explanation.

These studies have demonstrated that the decision to shoot may be influenced by a target person's ethnicity. In four studies, participants showed a bias to shoot

African American targets more rapidly and/or more frequently than White targets. The implications of this bias are clear and disturbing. Even more worrisome is the suggestion that mere knowledge of the cultural stereotype, which depicts African Americans as violent, may produce Shooter Bias, and that even African Americans demonstrate the bias. We understand that the demonstration of bias in an African American sample is politically controversial given the nature of this task, and we offer two considerations. First, the results of a single study are not definitive. Our findings should be replicated by researchers in other labs with different materials before generalizations are made. Second, our goals as psychologists include understanding, predicting, and controlling behavior. Ultimately, efforts to control (i.e., reduce or eliminate) any ethnic bias in the decision to shoot must be based on an accurate understanding of how target ethnicity influences that decision, even if that understanding is politically or personally distasteful.

Though these studies suggest that bias in the decision to shoot may be widespread, it is not yet clear that Shooter Bias actually exists among police officers. The studies we report use exclusively lay samples, and there is no reason to assume that this effect will generalize beyond this population. There is even a possibility, suggested by literature on the Stroop effect, that police training may actually reduce Shooter Bias by rendering the gun/no-gun decision more automatic for officers. If this is the case, police might show less bias than the average college sophomore. Examining these sorts of effects in a sample of police officers is of the utmost importance.

The studies reported here suggest that Shooter Bias is present among White college students (Studies 1–3) and among a community sample that consists of both Whites and African Americans (Study 4). The effect is robust and clearly a cause for concern, no matter the underlying cause. On the basis of our data, though, bias does not seem to simply reflect prejudice toward African Americans, and there is reason to believe the effect is present simply as a function of stereotypic associations that exist in our culture. That these associations can have such potentially profound consequences for members of stigmatized groups is a finding worthy of great concern. Since the death of Amadou Diallo. New York has witnessed a number of similar, though less publicized, cases, and Cincinnati, Ohio, has added Timothy Thomas's name to the list of unarmed African American men killed by police officers. Social psychological theory and research may prove invaluable in the effort to identify, understand and eventually control processes that bias decisions to shoot (and possibly kill) a person, as a function of his or her ethnicity.

REFERENCES

Altemeyer, B. (1988). *Enemies of freedom: Understanding right-wing authoritarianism.* San Francisco: Jossey-Bass.

Banaji, M. R., & Greenwald, A. G. (1995). Implicit gender stereotyping in judgments of fame. *Journal of Personality and Social Psychology, 68,* 181–198.

Bargh, J. A., Chen. M., & Burrows, L. (1996). Automaticity of social behavior: Direct effects of trait construct and stereotype activation on action. *Journal of Personality and Social Psychology, 71,* 230–244.

Beckett, N. E., & Park, B. (1995). Use of category versus individuating information: Making base-rates salient. *Personality and Social Psychology Bulletin, 21,* 21–31.

Berry, G. L., & Mitchell-Kernan, C. (1982) Introduction. In G. L. Berry & C. Mitchell-Kernan (Eds.), *Television and the socialization of the minority child* (pp. 1–11). New York: Academic Press.

Brewer, M. B. (1988). A dual process model of impression formation. In T. K. Srull & R. S. Wyer (Eds.), *Advances in social cognition* (Vol. 1, pp. 1–36). Hillsdale, NJ: Erlbaum.

Chartrand, T. L., & Bargh, J. A. (1996). Automatic activation of impression formation and memorization goals: Nonconscious goal priming reproduces effects of explicit task instructions. *Journal of Personality and Social Psychology, 71,* 464–478.

Cohen, J. D., Dunbar, K., & McClelland, J. L. (1990). On the control of automatic processes: A parallel distributed processing account of the Stroop effect. *Psychological Review, 97,* 332–361.

Cohen, J. D., MacWhinney, B., Flatt, M., & Provost, J. (1993). PsyScope: An interactive graphic system for designing and controlling experiments in the psychology laboratory using Macintosh computers. *Behavior Research Methods, Instruments & Computers, 25,* 257–271.

Cosby, C. O. (1994). *Television's imageable influences: The self-perceptions of young African-Americans.* Lanham, MD: University Press of America.

Darley, J. M., & Gross, P. G. (1983). A hypothesis-confirming bias in labeling effects. *Journal of Personality and Social Psychology, 44,* 20–33.

Devine, P. G. (1989). Stereotypess and prejudice: Their automatic and controlled components. *Journal of Personality and Social Psychology, 56,* 5–18.

Devine, P. G., & Elliot, A. J. (1995). Are racial stereotypes really fading? The Princeton trilogy revisited. *Personality and Social Psychology Bulletin, 21,* 1139–1150.

Dijksterhuis, A., Aarts, H., Bargh, J. A., & van Knippenberg, A. (2000). On the relation between associative strength and automatic behavior. *Journal of Experimental Social Psychology, 36,* 531–544.

Duncan, B. L. (1976). Differential social perception and attribution of intergroup violence: Testing the lower limits of stereotyping of blacks. *Journal of Personality and Social Psychology 34,* 590–598.

Dunton, B. C., & Fazio, R. H. (1997). An individual difference measure of motivation to control prejudiced reactions. *Personality and Social Psychology Bulletin, 23,* 316–326.

Fazio, R. H., Jackson, J. R., Dunton, B. C., & Williams. C. J. (1995). Variability in automatic activation as an unobtrusive measure of racial attitudes: A bona fide pipeline? *Journal of Personality and Social Psychology, 69,* 1013–1027.

Fiske, S. T., Lin. M., & Neuberg, S. L. (1999). The continuum model: Ten years later. In S. Chaiken & Y. Trope (Eds.). *Dual-process theories in social psychology* (pp. 231–254). New York: Guilford Press.

Fiske, S. T., & Neuberg, S. L. (1990). A continuum of impression formation, from category-based to individuating processes: Influences of information and motivation on attention and interpretation. In M. P. Zanna (Ed.), *Advances in experimental social psychology* (Vol. 23, pp. 1–74). New York: Academic Press.

Gerbner, G., Gross, L., Morgan, M., & Signorielli, N. (1986). Living with television: The dynamics of the cultivation process. In J. Bryant & D. Zillman (Eds.), *Perspectives of media effects* (pp. 14–40). Hillsdale, NJ: Erlbaum.

Gilbert, D. T., & Hixon, J. G. (1991). The trouble of thinking: Activation and application of stereotypic beliefs. *Journal of Personality and Social Psychology, 60*, 509–517.

Gray, H. (1989) Television, Black Americans, and the American dream. *Critical Studies in Mass Communication, 6*, 376–386.

Green, D. M., & Swets, J. A. (1966). *Signal detection theory and psychophysics*. New York: Wiley. (Reprinted 1974, Huntington, NY: Krieger).

Hamilton, D. L., & Sherman, J. W. (1994). Stereotypes. In R. S. Wyer & T. K. Srull (Eds.), *Handbook of social cognition* (pp. 1–68). Hillsdale, NJ: Erlbaum.

Hilton, J. L., & von Hippel, W. (1990). The role of consistency in the judgment of stereotype-relevant behaviors. *Personality and Social Psychology Bulletin 16*, 430–448.

Jacobs, J. E., & Eccles, J. S. (1992). The impact of mothers' gender-role stereotypic beliefs on mothers' and children's ability perceptions. *Journal of Personality and Social Psychology 63*, 932–944.

Jacoby, L. L. (1991). A process dissociation framework: Separating automatic from intentional uses of memory. *Journal of Memory and Language, 30*, 513–541.

Jacoby, L. L., Toth, J. P., & Yonelinas, A. P. (1993). Separating conscious and unconscious influences of memory: Measuring recollection. *Journal of Experimental Psychology: General, 122*, 139–154.

Judd, C. M., Park, B., Ryan, C. S., Brauer, M., & Kraus, S. (1995). Stereotypes and ethnocentrism: Diverging interethnic perceptions of African American and White American youth. *Journal of Personality and Social Psychology, 69*, 460–481.

Krueger, J., & Rothbart, M. (1988). The use of categorical and individuating information in making inferences about personality. *Journal of Personality and Social Psychology, 55*, 187–195.

Lepore, L., & Brown, R. (1997). Category and stereotype activation: Is prejudice inevitable? *Journal of Personality and Social Psychology, 72*, 275–287.

Locksley, A., Borgida, E., Brekke, N., & Hepburn, C. (1980). Sex stereotypes and social judgment. *Journal of Personality and Social Psychology, 39*, 821–831.

Lu, C.-H., & Proctor, R. W. (2001). Influence of irrelevant information on human performance: Effects of S–R association strength and relative timing. *Quarterly Journal of Experimental Psychology: Human Experimental Psychology, 54*(A), 95–136.

MacLeod, C. M. (1998). Training on integrated versus separated Stroop tasks: The progression of interference and facilitation. *Memory & Cognition, 26*, 201–211.

MacLeod, C. M., & Dunbar, K. (1988). Training and Stroop-like interference: Evidence for a continuum of automaticity. *Journal of Experimental Psychology: Learning, Memory, and Cognition, 14*, 126–135.

MacMillan, N. A., & Creelman, C. D. (1991). *Detection theory: A users guide*. Cambridge, England: Cambridge University Press.

Macrae, C. N., Milne, A. B., & Bodenhausen, G. V. (1994). Stereotypes as energy-saving devices: A peek inside the cognitive toolbox, *Journal of Personality and Social Psychology, 66*, 37–47.

McConahay, J. B., Hardee, B. B., & Batts, V. (1981). Has racism declined in America? It depends on who is asking and what is asked. *Journal of Conflict Resolution, 25*, 563–579.

Neuberg, S. L., & Newson, J. T. (1993). Personal need for structure: Individual differences in the desire for simpler structure. *Journal of Personality and Social Psychology, 65*, 113–131.

Payne, B. K. (2001). Prejudice and perception: The role of automatic and controlled processes in misperceiving a weapon. *Journal of Personality and Social Psychology, 81*, 181–192.

Payne, B. K., Lambert, A. J., & Jacoby, L. L. (in press). Best laid plans: Effects of goals on accessibility bias and cognitive control in race-based misperceptions of weapons. *Journal of Experimental Social Psychology*.

Pettigrew, T. F., & Tropp. L. R. (2000). Does intergroup contact reduce prejudice: Recent meta-analytic findings. In S. Oskamp (Ed.), *Reducing prejudice and discrimination* (pp. 93–114). Mahwah, NJ: Erlbaum.

Plant, E. A., & Devine, P. G. (1998). Internal and external motivation to respond without prejudice. *Journal of Personality and Social Psychology, 75*, 811–832.

Posner, M. I., & Snyder, C. R. R. (1975). Attention and cognitive control. In R. L. Solo (Ed.), *Information processing and cognition: The Loyola symposium* (pp. 55–85). Hillsdale, NJ: Erlbaum.

Pratto, F., Sidanius, J., Stallworth, L. M., & Malle, B. F. (1994). Social dominance orientation: A personality variable predicting social and political attitudes. *Journal of Personality and Social Psychology, 67*, 741–763.

Rothbart, M., & Birrell, P. (1977). Attitude and perception of faces. *Journal of Research in Personality 11*, 209–215.

Sagar, H. A., & Schofield, J. W. (1980). Racial and behavioral cues in black and white children's perceptions of ambiguously aggressive acts. *Journal of Personality and Social Psychology 39*, 590–598.

Stapel, D. A., & Koomen, W. (2001). The impact of interpretation versus comparison mindsets on knowledge accessibility effects. *Journal of Experimental Social Psychology, 37*, 134–149.

Steele, C. M., & Aronson, J. (1995). Stereotype threat and the intellectual test performance of African Americans. *Journal of Personality and Social Psychology, 69*, 797–811.

Stroman, C. A. (1986). Television viewing and self-concept among Black children. *Journal of Broadcasting and Electronic Media, 30*, 87–93.

SuberviVelez, F. A., & Necochea, J. (1990). Television viewing and self-concept among Hispanic American children—A pilot study. *Howard Journal of Communications, 2*, 315–329.

Thompson, M. M., Naccarato, M. E., Parker, K. C. H., & Moskowitz, G. B. (2001). The personal need for structure and personal fear of invalidity measures: Historical perspectives, current applications, and future directions. In G. B. Moskowitz (Ed.). *Cognitive social psychology: The Princeton symposium on the legacy and future of social cognition* (pp. 19–39). Mahwah, NJ: Erlbaum.

von Hippel, W., Jonides, J., Hilton, J. L., & Narayan, S. (1993). Inhibitory effect of schematic processing on perceptual encoding. *Journal of Personality and Social Psychology, 64*, 921–935.

Walley, R. E., McLeod, B. E., & Khan, M. (1997). Tests of a translational model of Stroop interference: Translation or attention? *Canadian Journal of Experimental Psychology, 51*, 10–19.

Walley, R. E., McLeod, B. E. & Weiden, T. D. (1994). Increased attention to the irrelevant dimension increases interference in a spatial Stroop task. *Canadian Journal of Experimental Psychology, 48*, 467–492.

Wittenbrink, B., Judd, C. M., & Park, B. (1997). Evidence for racial prejudice at the implicit level and its relationship with questionnaire measures. *Journal of Personality and Social Psychology, 72*, 262–274.

Received February 11, 2002
Revision received July 5, 2002
Accepted July 5, 2002 ■

Stereotypes as Energy-Saving Devices: A Peek Inside the Cognitive Toolbox

C. Neil Macrae, Alan B. Milne, and Galen V. Bodenhausen

By use of a dual-task paradigm, 3 studies investigated the contention that stereotypes function as resource-preserving devices in mental life. In Study 1, Ss formed impressions of targets while simultaneously monitoring a prose passage. The results demonstrated a significant enhancement in Ss' prose-monitoring performance when stereotype labels were present on the impression-formation task. To investigate the intentionality of this effect, in Study 2, the procedures used in Study 1 were repeated using a subliminal priming procedure to activate stereotypes. Subliminal activation of stereotypes produced the same resource-preserving effects as supraliminal activation did. This effect, moreover, was replicated in Study 3 when a probe reaction task was used to measure resource preservation. These findings, which generalized across a range of social stereotypes, are discussed in terms of their implications for contemporary models of stereotyping and social inference.

Human adaptation to the challenging and complex environment has often taken the form of developing tools that facilitate the execution of mundane but necessary tasks, leaving more time and energy available for other, perhaps more interesting or rewarding activities. It is reasonable to suppose, as some contemporary psychologists have, that the development of physical tools, such as plows or printing presses, has been paralleled by the development of cognitive "tools," or routine strategies of inference and evaluation (cf. Tooby & Cosmides, 1990) that permit a sufficiently effective analysis of the social environment to be accomplished in an efficient fashion. The benefit of such mental tools presumably lies in the fact that they free up limited cognitive resources for the performance of other necessary or desirable mental activities.

Social psychologists have frequently characterized stereotypes as energy-saving devices that serve the important cognitive function of simplifying information processing and response generation (e.g., Allport, 1954; Andersen, Klatzky, & Murray, 1990; Bodenhausen & Lichtenstein, 1987; Brewer, 1988; Fiske & Neuberg, 1990; Tajfel, 1969). Building on this tradition, Gilbert and Hixon (1991) aptly characterized stereotypes as "tools that jump out" of a metaphorical cognitive

C. Neil Macrae and Alan B. Milne, 37 School of Psychology, University of Wales College of Cardiff, Cardiff, Wales; Galen V. Bodenhausen, Department of Psychology, Michigan State University.

We thank John Bargh, Dan Gilbert, Chick Judd, Herbert Bless, Chuck Stangor, and an anonymous reviewer for their insightful comments on earlier versions of this article. Thanks are also extended to Riana Griffiths for collecting the data in Studies 2 and 3.

Correspondence concerning this article should be addressed to C. Neil Macrae, School of Psychology, University of Wales College of Cardiff, Cardiff, CF1 3YG, United Kingdom. Electronic mail may be addressed to macrae@taff.cardiff.ac.uk.

toolbox "when there is a job to be done" (p. 510). Anyone who has ever succumbed to the temptation to evaluate others in terms of their social group membership would doubtlessly recognize the power of this contention. Individuation, in its many guises, is a rather time consuming and effortful affair (Brewer, 1988; Fiske & Neuberg, 1990; Fiske & Pavelchak, 1986). Stereotyping, in contrast, relies only on the execution of some rather rudimentary skills: Most notably, the ability to assign people to meaningful social categories (see Hamilton, 1979; Hamilton & Sherman, in press; Hamilton, Sherman, & Ruvolo, 1990; Hamilton & Trolier, 1986). Once achieved, this categorization provides perceivers with a veritable wealth of stereotypic information.

The metaphorical view of humans as cognitive misers has attained a zenith of popularity among contemporary social cognition researchers (see Fiske & Taylor, 1991; Higgins & Bargh, 1987; Sherman, Judd, & Park, 1989), but the notion of stereotypes as simplifying mental devices has its origins in much earlier times. Lippman (1922), for example, argued that reality is too complex for any person to represent accurately. Stereotypes, accordingly, serve to simplify perception, judgment, and action. As energy-saving devices, they spare perceivers the ordeal of responding to an almost incomprehensibly complex social world. Seventy years later, these sentiments are characteristic features of cognitive writings on the topic. As Fiske and Neuberg (1990, p. 14) remarked, "we are exposed to so much information that we must in some manner simplify our social environment ... for reasons of cognitive economy, we categorize others as members of particular groups — groups about which we often have a great deal of generalized, or stereotypic, knowledge."

Stereotypes and Resource Preservation

The view of the social perceiver evident in the writings of Lippman as well as the contemporary social cognition researchers is that of an information processor confronted by limitations that necessitate compromises and shortcuts. The evidence to support this basic contention comes primarily from research demonstrating an increased reliance on stereotypes when social perception occurs under taxing or resource-depleting conditions. The idea that people will fall back on their stereotypic preconceptions whenever they lack the ability or motivation to think more deeply about members of stereotyped groups has been emphasized in a

number of studies (e.g., Bodenhausen, 1990, 1993; Bodenhausen & Lichtenstein, 1987; Bodenhausen, Sheppard, & Kramer, in press; Kim & Baron, 1988; Kruglanski & Freund, 1983; Macrae, Hewstone, & Griffiths, 1993; Pratto & Bargh, 1991; Rothbart, Fulero, Jensen, Howard, & Birrell, 1978; Stangor & Duan, 1991). The message emerging from this research is a fairly consistent one: When the processing environment reaches a sufficient level of difficulty, and perceivers' resources are correspondingly depleted, stereotypes are likely to be activated and applied in judgmental tasks (but see Gilbert & Hixon, 1991).

Although compelling and providing impressive evidence for the heuristic utility of stereotype application, these studies tell only part of the story. In particular, through their emphasis on, and assessment of, perceivers' judgmental and memorial outcomes in demanding task environments, they potentially obscure some of the more covert benefits the information-processing system may accrue as a consequence of stereotype application. The basic assertion driving research in this domain is, after all, that stereotypes function as energy-saving or resource-preserving mental devices (Allport, 1954; Lippman, 1922; Tajfel, 1969). As such, one might reasonably expect to find a range of studies directly demonstrating this effect. For instance, information processing should be easier, and cognitive resources preserved, when stereotypes are present, rather than absent, in judgmental tasks.

On closer inspection, however, this effect remains a largely untested theoretical premise in much of the work in this domain. It seems clear that people do use stereotypes to a greater extent when they are operating under taxing conditions, but it is difficult to draw any definitive conclusions from existing research about why this might be so. It may be that people are often simply lazy and are unwilling to think very deeply about the world around them, especially when there is any cognitive challenge in effect in the concurrent environment. On this view, the cognitive miser is essentially a lazy slob who is prone to stereotype whenever the going gets tough, cognitively speaking. The more charitable view that we have been outlining characterizes the cognitive miser instead as someone who stereotypes not as a way of simply avoiding cognitive work, but rather as a means to free up resources for use in other tasks. Which characterization is most accurate? It is hard to say on the basis of the available evidence. Clearly, existing studies fail to provide direct evidence of the possible information-processing advantages resulting from stereotype application. In an attempt to provide insight into this issue, in the reported research we investigate the widely held belief that stereotypes operate as resource-preserving devices in mental life (Allport, 1954; Lippman, 1922).

Assuming that stereotype application does in fact promote resource preservation, the puzzle remains as to exactly how this benefit arises. A potential answer, however, can be found in the schematic principles that seemingly govern the encoding and representation of stereotype-based information in memory (Cantor & Mischel, 1977; Hastie, 1981; Stangor & McMillan, 1992; Taylor & Crocker, 1981). Schema theories typically assert that expectancy-congruent information should be preferentially encoded into memory because it is easier to assimilate or integrate within existing knowledge structures than expectancy-incongruent information (Neisser, 1976; Taylor & Crocker, 1981). Empirical support for this contention comes primarily from research demonstrating that stereotypes, as guiding themes or organizing structures, favor the encoding and representation of congruent rather than incongruent information in long-term memory (Bodenhausen, 1988; Bodenhausen & Wyer, 1985). This congruency bias, moreover, is exacerbated when perceivers encounter the stereotype-relevant information in cognitively demanding settings (Bodenhausen & Lichtenstein, 1987; Hastie, 1980; Macrae et al., 1993; Srull & Wyer, 1989; Stangor & Duan, 1991). Taken together, these findings suggest that stereotypes simplify processing (hence, they promote resource preservation) through the provision of a mental framework on which perceivers can readily deposit or organize information. In the absence of such a framework, the encoding and representation of information in memory involves a more effortful, resource-dependent process (Srull & Wyer, 1989).

With only finite cognitive resources available, perceivers (or their inferential systems) need to derive economical strategies for the allocation of these resources to the tasks encountered in everyday interaction (see Gilbert, 1989). This executive function, in addition, probably plays a prominent part in the resolution of life's daily puzzles. Allocate too many resources to a single task and one will likely be able to perform little else. Expend too few, and one's chances of task success will rapidly diminish. In this vein, stereotype application is, arguably, one tactic an inferential system can successfully use to expedite the allocation of resources to competing tasks or activities and the intricacies of mental life.

To assess the relative distribution of resources between competing mental activities, researchers have traditionally relied on measures derived from dual-task experimental paradigms (see Kahneman, 1973; Navon & Gopher, 1979; Wickens, 1980). In these studies, subjects are typically required to perform two concurrent tasks under different performance instructions. For example, they may be asked to track the movement of an object on a computer screen, while simultaneously responding to information presented in the auditory domain (Wickens, 1976). Through systematic patterns of interference in performance, researchers are able to estimate both the difficulty and the resource dependence of the competing tasks. According to their specific characteristics (e.g., difficulty), tasks impose differential demands on perceivers' processing resources. For their successful execution and completion, some tasks demand more resources than others. By introducing a secondary task, researchers are able to estimate the residual resources or capacity not used in the primary task (e.g., Ogden, Levine, & Eisner, 1979; Rolfe, 1973). In other words, the secondary task mops up perceivers' spare capacity or free cognitive resources. So, when concurrent tasks are deemed to interfere with each other (i.e., they call on common cognitive resources), secondary-task performance is routinely used as an index of processing capacity not expended in the execution of the primary task (Wickens, 1984).

Dual-task techniques have already been used with some success in the investigation of the resource-preserving properties of schema application. Bargh (1982), for example, demonstrated subjects' enhanced performance on a secondary task (i.e., probe reaction task) when self-relevant, rather than neutral, information was shadowed on a primary, dichotic listening task. The automaticity involved in the processing of self-relevant information freed subjects' attentional resources, thereby enhancing their secondary-task performance. In the present research, we expected stereotype application to produce similar effects. If, as suggested, stereotypes simplify processing and save valuable cognitive resources, then this should be reflected in perceivers' performance on a concurrent mental task. That is, the presence, rather than absence, of stereotypical information on a primary task should result in a simplification of this task. This simplification should save processing resources, which in turn, should enhance perceivers' secondary-task performance. In this article, we report the results of a series of studies investigating the general question of whether using stereotypes really does produce any efficiency-related gains on other cognitive tasks.

Study 1

Method

Overview

Subjects performed two tasks concurrently. While forming impressions of targets using the computer-based presentation of trait descriptors (i.e., Task 1), subjects simultaneously monitored information from a tape-recorded source (i.e., Task 2). To manipulate the difficulty of the impression-formation task, stereotype-based information, describing each of the targets, was either present or absent. It was anticipated that, when present, this information would simplify the impression-formation task, thereby saving processing resources and enhancing performance on the prose-monitoring task. A cued recall task and a multiple-choice questionnaire were utilized respectively to measure performance on the two tasks.

Subjects and Design

Twenty-four female undergraduate students at the University of Wales College of Cardiff were paid £2 for their participation in the experiment. The study had a single-factor (stereotype: present or absent) between-subjects design.

Procedure and Stimulus Materials

Subjects arrived at the laboratory individually, were randomly assigned to one of the experimental conditions, and were seated facing the screen of an Apple Macintosh microcomputer (Mac IIvi). The experimenter then explained that the study involved an investigation of people's ability to perform tasks simultaneously. In particular, in the course of the study, subjects would be required to form impressions of a number of targets while simultaneously monitoring information from an auditory source elsewhere in the laboratory. The impression-formation task (i.e., Task 1) was undertaken on the computer. Subjects observed on the computer screen a target's name (e.g., John) and a number of descriptive personality traits (e.g., *aggressive*). The target's name appeared above, and the trait descriptors below, the fixation point in the center of the screen. Each trait appeared, in turn, beneath the target's name until all the relevant information had been presented (i.e., only one trait was on the screen at any given time). When all the traits for a particular target had been presented, the screen cleared, a new name appeared, and the process was repeated. In addition to the target's name, half of the subjects were also given a stereotype

label (e.g., John — *skinhead*). This was located in the center of the screen on the fixation point (i.e., between the name and the trait). It was anticipated that, for these subjects, this information would simplify the impression-formation task by providing them with a theme to guide or organize their impressions of each target (Bodenhausen, 1988; Hamilton, Katz, & Leirer, 1980). This stereotypical information, together with the target's name, remained on the screen until all the traits had been presented. In total, subjects were given 10 traits for each of four targets (see Table 29.1). In the stereotype-present condition, 5 of the traits describing each target had previously been established to be stereotype-consistent with respect to the label provided. It was expected that these traits would be the focus of stimulus simplification in this condition. The other 5 traits attributed to each target were neutral with respect to the category label provided. All the stimulus materials were selected from an earlier pilot study in which subjects were required to rate the extent to which a large number of traits were characteristic of a range of social categories. Presentation of the targets and the order of traits attributed to each target were randomized for each subject by the computer.

While forming impressions of the targets, subjects were simultaneously required to monitor information played on a tape recorder (i.e., Task 2). Before performing the tasks, subjects were informed that, on their completion, they would be probed about the impressions they had formed and the information they had heard. Thus, each task was given equal priority in the experimental instructions. To eradicate the effects

TABLE 29.1. Stereotype Labels and Personality Traits for Impression-Formation Task

Nigel: doctor	Julian: artist	John: skinhead	Graham: estate agent
Caring	*Creative*	*Rebellious*	*Pushy*
Honest	*Temperamental*	*Aggressive*	*Talkative*
Reliable	*Unconventional*	*Dishonest*	*Arrogant*
Upstanding	*Sensitive*	*Untrustworthy*	*Confident*
Responsible	*Individualistic*	*Dangerous*	*Unscrupulous*
Unlucky	Fearless	Lucky	Musical
Forgetful	Active	Observant	Pessimistic
Passive	Cordial	Modest	Humorless
Clumsy	Progressive	Optimistic	Alert
Enthusiastic	Generous	Curious	Spirited

Note. Stereotypic words are italicized.

of prior knowledge on the prose-monitoring task, a passage describing the basic geography and economy of Indonesia was constructed. Earlier pilot testing had established that undergraduate students have little knowledge of this topic. The passage lasted for 2 min and contained a number of facts woven into a meaningful narrative. To synchronize both tasks, the stimulus presentation rate on the impression-formation task was manipulated to occupy 2 min. This resulted in each personality trait remaining on the computer screen for approximately 3 s. For each subject, then, both experimental tasks ran contemporaneously.

Dependent Measures

Performance on the impression-formation task was assessed by measuring subjects' memory for the presented trait information. A cued recall task was used whereby subjects were given a sheet of paper with each target's name written at the top of the sheet. Their task was simply to recall as many of the traits as possible and correctly attribute them to the appropriate target. To measure prose-monitoring performance, a multiple-choice questionnaire was constructed. This consisted of 20 questions, with four optional responses per question, to tap subjects' knowledge of the passage (e.g., "What is the country's official religion?" "Jakarta is found on which coast of Java?"). After they completed the dependent measures, subjects were debriefed, paid, and dismissed.

Results and Discussion

Cued Recall

It was expected that having an applicable stereotypic label available would facilitate learning of the personality descriptor information, as reflected in cued recall performance. Mean cued recall of both the stereotype-consistent and the neutral trait descriptors are shown in Table 29.2, as a function of whether a stereotypic label was provided. In line with our predictions, subjects for whom a stereotypic label had been made available were in fact able to recall more than twice as many personality descriptors than those for whom no label had been provided. The number of stereotype-consistent and neutral traits recalled and attributed to the correct target were submitted to a 2 (stereotype: present or absent) × 2(trait type: consistent or neutral) mixed-model analysis of variance (ANOVA) with repeated measures on the second factor. This revealed main effects of both stereotype, $F(1, 22) = 5.85$, $p < .03$, and trait type, $F(1, 22) = 17.64$, $p < .004$, on subjects' memory for

TABLE 29.2. Subjects' Mean Task Performance:Study 1

Task	Stereotype	
	Present	Absent
Trait recall		
Consistent	4.42	2.08
Neutral	1.83	1.33
Multiple-choice questionnaire	8.75	6.66

the presented information. These effects were qualified, however, by a Stereotype × Trait Type interaction, $F(1, 22) = 5.33$, $p < .03$. Simple effects analysis revealed an effect of stereotype activation for the consistent, $F(1, 39) = 10.87$, $p < .002$, but not the neutral traits recalled, $F(1, 39) < 1$, ns (see Table 29.2).

Multiple Choice

If stereotypes represent a useful means for economizing cognition, then those subjects for whom a stereotype had been activated should have more resources available for the prose-monitoring task. It was therefore hypothesized that subjects who had been given a stereotypic label would show superior learning of the material in the prose passage, as demonstrated in a multiple choice test on the passage. The relevant means (see Table 29.2) clearly fall in the predicted pattern. A *t* test confirmed that subjects in the stereotypic label condition correctly answered a significantly greater number of test questions, $t(22) = 2.32, p < .04$.

As predicted, the provision of stereotype labels during the impression-formation task reduced the demands imposed on subjects' processing resources, resulting in enhanced performance on the prose-monitoring task. Evidence for simplification of the impression-formation task (hence, preservation of attentional capacity) can be gleaned from subjects' memorial performance. The provision of stereotype labels increased the memorability of the presented information, with this effect most pronounced for the consistent traits. This largely confirms the view that stereotypes, in demanding processing contexts, function as simplifying themes in long-term memory, facilitating the representation of schema-consistent information (e.g., Bodenhausen, 1988; Macrae et al., 1993; Stangor & Duan, 1991).

Stereotypes, then, do appear to function as resource-preserving devices in mental life. Notwithstanding the demonstration of this effect, however, an important theoretical question emerges from Study 1. Whereas the results document resource savings accruing to those perceivers who are able to use a stereotype as an organizing theme in the impression-formation task, it is unclear whether this efficiency-producing strategy is intentionally deployed by the social perceiver. Are stereotypes tools that must be consciously applied in the process of building an impression, or do they spring from the toolbox of their own accord, streamlining social information processing without conscious consent? The present results fail to distinguish between these two possibilities. In Study 2, accordingly, we set out to address this issue. The question motivating our inquiry was as follows: Are processing resources liberated in a task context in which perceivers have no knowledge or awareness of stereotype activation? If indeed they are, this would confirm the intuition that stereotypes economize cognition without perceivers' awareness or conscious consent.

Study 2

To investigate the automaticity of stereotype activation, researchers have typically used modified semantic priming techniques. Central to the successful execution of this approach is the presentation of a priming stimulus outside of subjects' conscious awareness (i.e., subjects have no conscious knowledge of the presentation of the prime). This effect is typically achieved by presenting the prime for a very brief duration and then obscuring it with either another word or a masking stimulus. The surprising finding to emerge from research of this kind is that despite subjects' inability to consciously report the nature or identity of the prime, it is consistently shown to facilitate their responses to semantically related material presented immediately afterward. That is, priming effects prevail even when the primes are presented below perceivers' threshold of stimulus identification.

Several researchers have successfully applied this technique to issues in stereotyping and person perception (Bargh, 1982; Bargh, Bond, Lombardi, & Tota, 1986; Bargh & Pietromonaco, 1982; Devine, 1989; Erdley & D'Agostino, 1988; Perdue, Dovidio, Gurtman, & Tyler, 1990; Perdue & Gurtman, 1990; Smith, Spence, & Klein, 1958; see Bargh, 1989, 1992, for reviews). Perdue and Gurtman (1990), for instance, demonstrated that subjects respond faster to negative traits when subliminally primed with the word *old* rather than *young* and faster to positive traits when primed with the word *young* rather than *old*. There are, of course, compelling advantages inherent in the use of subliminal priming

techniques in the investigation of stereotyping (Perdue et al., 1990; Perdue & Gurtman, 1990). First, the technique minimizes reactivity, particularly the impact of demand characteristics and social desirability biases. Second, it provides a tool for researchers to decompose perceivers' cognitive processes and identify the automatic and controlled components of the phenomenon (e.g., Devine, 1989). If the effects observed in Study 1 can be replicated in a situation in which subjects are unaware of the presence of the stereotype labels in the impression-formation task, this will support the contention that stereotype application simplifies processing and promotes resource preservation without perceivers' awareness or conscious consent.

Method

Overview

Study 1 was replicated, but with one important difference. While performing the impression-formation task, half of the subjects were provided with stereotype labels presented outside their conscious awareness. It was anticipated that if stereotypes simplify processing and preserve valuable mental energy without perceivers' conscious intent, then the present effects should replicate those obtained in Study 1. That is, the provision (albeit subliminal) of stereotype labels should simplify the impression-formation task, thereby saving processing resources and enhancing performance on the prose-monitoring task.

Subjects and Design

Thirty-two female undergraduate students at the University of Wales College of Cardiff were paid £2 for their participation in the experiment. The study had a single-factor (stereotype: present-but-subliminal or absent) between-subjects design.

Procedure and Stimulus Materials

This experiment was identical to Study 1, but with a subliminal presentation of the stereotype labels on the impression-formation task. The experimental stimuli were black and presented on a white background with stimulus timings controlled by the Apple Macintosh's Vertical Blank Manager. Words were drawn in 14-point Geneva type, a proportionally spaced typeface with a maximum cell size of 0.5 cm × 0.5 cm. The target's name was positioned such that its baseline was 1 cm above the fixation point in the center of the screen. The priming words (i.e., category labels) were located with their baseline on the center of the screen, and the trait words were positioned such that the maximum distance between the top pixel of the priming stimulus and the bottom pixel of the trait words was 2 cm. The standard viewing distance (i.e., eye to center of screen) was 55 cm. Thus, the prime and trait words subtended a maximum visual angle of 0.5 ° and were separated by 1 °. These settings ensured that the stimulus materials fell within each subject's foveal visual field. In the center of the computer screen, immediately below each target's name and above the location where the trait descriptives appear, a row of Xs (i.e., XXXXXXXX) was displayed (i.e., masking stimulus). For subjects in the priming condition, immediately before the presentation of each trait descriptive, the mask disappeared and the relevant stereotype label was presented in its place for 30 ms before being overwritten by the mask. Consequently, for each target in the impression-formation task, the priming stimulus appeared on 10 separate occasions. The procedure was identical for subjects in the nonpriming (i.e., no-stereotype) condition; however, rather than a stereotype label appearing behind the mask, subjects simply observed, for each target, ten 30-ms segments of blank computer screen. The brevity of the exposure was intended to prevent subjects' conscious recognition of the priming stimuli, thereby satisfying the critical criterion for the establishment of automatic effects in information processing (Bargh, 1984; Hasher & Zacks, 1979; Marcel, 1983). While subliminal priming effects have been demonstrated with longer exposure durations (e.g., 100 ms), these studies have typically relied on the parafoveal presentation of the priming stimuli (e.g., Bargh & Pietromonaco, 1982; Devine, 1989). The experiment was controlled by a program running on the Apple Macintosh microcomputer. Stimuli were presented on a Apple 13-in. (33-cm) color monitor, which has a refresh rate of 66.67 Hz, giving a frame duration of 15 ms. Person names and traits were drawn on-screen using standard Macintosh library routines. Prime words were drawn into a small off-screen buffer during the inter-stimulus interval using the same graphics routines. On each trial, the program waited until it received a vertical blank signal (indicating that the raster scan was about to return to the top of the screen) and copied the buffer directly into the appropriate screen memory location before the raster scan reached that location. A similar procedure was used to erase the prime after exposure. Thus, the prime display was always synchronized with and preceded screen updating. This procedure ensured that the presentation duration of each priming stimulus was exactly 30 ms.

A number of steps were taken to verify that subjects did indeed process the primes in an unconscious manner (see Cheesman & Merikle, 1986; Greenwald, Klinger, & Liu, 1989; Perdue et al., 1990). These were primarily instigated during each subject's debriefing session. First, on completion of the study, subjects were asked to write down the experimental procedure and list as many of the words that appeared on the computer screen as they could remember. Importantly, none of the subjects listed any of the priming stimuli when performing this task. Second, subjects were then informed that during the study certain words had appeared very quickly in the area of the screen occupied by the row of Xs; their task was simply to guess what these words might have been. Again, none of the subjects correctly guessed any of the primes. This corroborates the results of earlier pilot research, which we undertook to establish an optimal exposure duration for inclusion in the experiment proper. In a variant of the present study, 12 subjects were presented with a number of words (i.e., a total of 40), which were then masked by a row of Xs. Each word remained on the screen for 30 ms. Before the presentation phase, subjects were instructed that a number of words would appear, albeit very quickly, in the center of the computer screen. Their task was simply to identify and report each word. If they were unable to identify the word, subjects were forced by the experimenter to make a guess, even a blind guess if necessary (Bargh & Pietromonaco, 1982; Devine, 1989). Of the 480 responses, subjects correctly identified the words on 16 occasions, a hit rate of only 3.33%. It would seem, then, that the present paradigm satisfies the preconditions necessary for the establishment of automatic effects on social information processing. As in Study 1, the two experimental tasks (impression formation and prose monitoring) ran contemporaneously.

Dependent Measures

Performance on the tasks was again assessed with a cued recall task and multiple-choice questionnaire. After they completed the experiment, subjects were debriefed, paid, and dismissed.

Results and Discussion

Cued Recall

If stereotypes are automatically used to organize person representations, then effects similar to those of Study 1 might occur even when the stereotype is activated outside the bounds of conscious awareness. To evaluate this possibility, the number of stereotype-consistent and neutral traits recalled and attributed to the correct target (see Table 29.3) were submitted to a 2 (stereotype: present-but-subliminal or absent) $\times$ 2 (trait type: consistent or neutral) mixed-model ANOVA with repeated measures on the second factor. This analysis revealed main effects of both stereotype, $F(1, 30) = 6.66$, $p < .02$, and trait type, $F(1, 30) = 17.04$, $p < .0003$, on subjects' memory for the presented information. A greater number of traits was recalled when stereotypes were present rather than absent (respective $Ms = 2.50$ vs. 1.50), and subjects displayed enhanced recall for consistent rather than neutral traits (respective $Ms = 2.63$ vs. 1.37). Unlike in Study 1, the Stereotype $\times$ Trait Type interaction failed to reach statistical significance, $F(1, 30) < 1$, ns.

Multiple Choice
Automatic activation of stereotypes should also produce cognitive savings in the impression-formation task, allowing for better performance on the prose-monitoring task. The means relevant to this prediction are displayed in Table 29.3. Consistent with the view that stereotypes are tools that automatically and effortlessly economize information processing, prose-monitoring performance was clearly enhanced by the subliminal activation of a stereotype, $t(30) = 2.04$, $p < .05$.

As in Study 1, then, the provision of stereotype labels on the impression-formation task reduced the demands imposed on subjects' processing resources, resulting in an enhancement in their performance on the prose-monitoring task. As before, recall performance was facilitated when stereotype labels were present rather than absent in the impression-formation task. In each of the reported experiments, therefore, we observed a general resource-preserving effect, with stereotype application enhancing the memorability of both confirmatory and neutral traits. In Study 1, however, this facilitatory effect was somewhat stronger for the consistent traits; in Study 2 it was equivalent for both trait types.

Notwithstanding the demonstration of these effects across Studies 1 and 2, some limitations of the present

TABLE 29.3. Subjects' Mean Task Performance: Study 2

Task	Subliminal Stereotype	
	Present	Absent
Trait recall		
Consistent	3.26	2.00
Neutral	1.75	1.00
Multiple-choice questionnaire	8.19	6.62

research should be noted. In particular, two main areas of concern can be identified: (a) The experimental manipulation of subliminality in Study 2 and (b) the use of a prose-monitoring task to estimate subjects' residual attentional capacity in Studies 1 and 2. With regard to the subliminal presentation of stereotype labels, two weaknesses limit our earlier study. First, 30-ms stimulus presentations to the fovea are certainly long enough for at least some subjects to identify consciously the priming stimulus. When piloting our experimental manipulation, after all, subjects ($N = 12$) correctly identifed the target word on 16 occasions (i.e., a hit rate of more than one correct identification per subject). Given that it may only take one overt identification per subject to consciously rather than nonconsciously activate the stereotype, we could reasonably question whether subliminal priming was successfully accomplished in Study 2. This difficulty was compounded by the use of a suboptimal masking stimulus (i.e., XXXXXXXX) in the experiment. In retrospect, a central pattern mask would have been the more appropriate choice (Turvey, 1973). This type of mask, which consists of a series of letter patterns (e.g., ZBKWPLSR), is structurally similar to the preceding word stimulus (i.e., masked stimulus). Central pattern masking is appropriate because although it interferes with a prime's path to consciousness, it does not affect its automatic registration by perceivers (Marcel, 1983).

Second, potential difficulties also arise in the interpretation of the data from our prose-monitoring task. In each of the reported studies, we used a technique in which subjects were presented with two concurrent tasks (i.e., impression formation and prose monitoring) and each was given equal priority in the experimental instructions. Unfortunately, these instructions may actively encourage subjects to switch attention between the tasks. Secondary-task performance can provide an indication of capacity usage in the primary task only if subjects devote their attention first and foremost to the primary task (i.e., maximize primary-task performance). If attention switches between the tasks, which is conceivable when they are given equal priority in the experimental instructions, it is difficult to draw any firm conclusions about how much attentional capacity each task requires (Kantowitz, 1974).

In our third experiment, we introduced a number of methodological and procedural refinements in an attempt to address these limitations. To strengthen our manipulation of subliminality, we used a shorter stimulus presentation duration (i.e., 15 ms) and an improved pattern mask. In addition, we also carried out extensive pilot testing of our subliminal manipulation before the experiment proper. Finally, we used a probe reaction task to investigate the resource-preserving properties of stereotype application (Bargh, 1982; Brown, 1964; Gollwitzer, 1993; Johnston, 1978; Johnston & Heinz, 1978; Posner & Boies, 1971). With this technique, subjects are instructed to optimize performance on a primary task and to use their remaining attentional capacity to respond to a subsidiary probe stimulus, such as turning off a randomly illuminated light bulb. The reasoning behind this technique is straightforward. As the attentional requirement of the primary task increases, performance on the secondary, probe task decreases (i.e., subjects offer slower responses to the probe — see Bargh, 1982; Kahneman, 1973; Logan, 1979).

Study 3

Method

Overview
While forming impressions of targets using the computer-based presentation of trait descriptors (i.e., primary task), subjects simultaneously performed a probe reaction task whereby they were required to switch off, by means of a key press, a randomly presented auditory stimulus (i.e., secondary task). To manipulate the difficulty of the impression-formation task, stereotypic information, describing each of the targets, was either available or unavailable. When available, this information was presented either supra-or subliminally. Primary-task performance was assessed, as before, with a cued recall task. Probe reaction times served as our measure of secondary-task performance.

Subjects and Design
Thirty-six female undergraduate students at the University of Wales College of Cardiff were paid £2 for their participation in the experiment. The study had a single-factor (stereotype: present or present-but-subliminal or absent) between-subjects design.

Procedure and Stimulus Materials.
This experiment, in essence, was a combination of the previous two studies. That is, supra-and subliminal priming conditions were included, with a no-prime condition, in a single experiment. Subjects arrived at the laboratory individually, were randomly assigned to one of the treatment conditions, and were seated facing the screen of an Apple Macintosh microcomputer (Mac IIvi).

The experimenter then explained, as before, that the study involved an investigation of people's ability to perform tasks simultaneously (i.e., impression-formation and probe-reaction tasks). In the impression-formation task, subjects in all conditions were presented with the four targets and the relevant trait descriptors. As before, these appeared, respectively, above and below the fixation point in the center of the screen. In all conditions, the target's name remained on the screen continuously and each trait word appeared for 2,400 ms. The inter-stimulus interval between successive trait presentations was 500 ms. In the supraliminal priming condition, each prime (i.e., stereotype label) appeared continuously, in the center of the screen, until all the target's trait descriptors had been presented. The presentation sequence was then repeated for the next target. For subjects in the subliminal condition, immediately before the presentation of each trait descriptive, the prime appeared in the center of the screen for 15 ms and was then masked by a string of randomly selected consonants (e.g., SFPRMWLJ) for a further 135 ms. Consequently, for each target in the impression-formation task, the priming stimulus appeared on 10 separate occasions. The procedure was identical for subjects in the nonpriming (i.e., no-stereotype) condition; however, rather than having a stereotype label appearing behind the mask, subjects simply observed, for each target, ten 15-ms segments of blank computer screen. The experimental setup (i.e., size, composition, and location of stimuli) was identical to that in Study 2, thereby ensuring that the stimulus materials again fell within each subject's foveal visual field.

In a modification of Study 2, the stereotype labels in the subliminal priming condition were presented for only 15 ms. This brevity of exposure duration was intended to strengthen our manipulation of subliminality. Before the experiment proper, we also carried out a pilot study to help achieve this end. In a computer-based word-identification task, 14 subjects were presented with a number of words (i.e., 20 in total), which were then masked by a random string of consonants. Each word was presented for 15 ms before it was overwritten by the mask. Before the presentation phase, subjects were instructed that a number of words would appear in the center of the computer screen. Their task was simply to identify and report each word to the experimenter. If unable to identify the word, subjects were forced by the experimenter to make a guess. Of the 280 responses, subjects correctly identified the words on 6 occasions, for a hit rate of only 2.14%. Before leaving the laboratory, each subject performed an ostensibly unrelated lexical decision task. On the presentation of a letter string on the computer screen, subjects had to respond, by means of a key press, whether it was a "word" or "nonword." Included in the list of to-be-identified letter strings were the 20 words presented earlier plus 20 matched distractors. A single-factor (word: old or distractor) repeated measures ANOVA confirmed that, despite subjects' earlier inability to identify the words, they classified them more quickly than matched distractors in the lexical decision task, $F(1, 13) = 5.79$, $p < .04$ (respective $Ms = 546$ ms vs. 571 ms). This lexical priming effect then clearly reflects word activation without awareness and suggests that an exposure duration of 15 ms satisfies the preconditions necessary for the establishment of automatic effects on information processing. As in Study 2, during each subject's debriefing session, additional measures were taken to confirm that the primes had indeed been processed in an automatic, unconscious manner. As before, subjects demonstrated no awareness of the priming stimuli on any of these measures.

While forming impressions of the targets, subjects simultaneously performed a secondary, probe-reaction task (e.g., Bargh, 1982). Before the subjects performed the tasks, however, the experimenter stressed that the impression-formation task was the more important of the two. During the presentation of the target-related information (i.e., impression-formation task), the computer periodically emitted a bleeping sound. The subjects' task was simply to turn off the sound, when it occurred, by pressing the space bar on the keyboard. Unknown to the subjects, the computer had been programmed to emit the sound four times in the course of the experiment. Presentation of the probe stimuli was randomized for each subject by the computer. Probe reaction times (ms) were recorded by the computer and measured using the Macintosh's Extended Time Manager.

Before the experiment proper, steps were taken to ensure that the probe reaction task was a true measure of subjects' residual attentional capacity. To serve this function, it must be established that the probe task does not itself divert processing resources from the primary, impression-formation task. To confirm this necessary precondition, 24 independent subjects performed a variant of the present experiment. Twelve of these subjects performed both the impression-formation (i.e., no prime condition) and probe-reaction tasks. The others, in contrast, performed only the impression-formation task. We reasoned that if the probe task diverted resources away from the impression-formation task, this would be reflected in differences in trait recall performance between the probe and no-probe conditions. A single-factor (probe task: present or absent) between-subjects ANOVA revealed no effect of the probe-reaction task on subjects' memorial performance, $F(1, 22) < 1$, ns. This, then, validates the use of the probe task as a measure of subjects' residual attentional capacity.

Dependent Measures
Memory for the presented trait information (i.e., cued recall) and probe reaction times (RTs) were taken as respective indicators of subjects' primary-and secondary-task performance. On completion of the experiment subjects were debriefed, paid, and dismissed.

Results and Discussion

Cued Recall
To investigate the effects of stereotype activation on the memorability of person descriptors, we submitted the number of stereotype-consistent and neutral traits recalled and attributed to the correct target to a 3 (stereotype: present or present-but-subliminal or absent) × 2 (trait type: consistent or neutral) mixed-model ANOVA with repeated measures on the second factor. As anticipated, the presence of stereotype labels in the impression-formation task facilitated the memorability of the personality descriptor information, $F(2, 33) = 5.14$, $p < .02$. Post hoc Tukey tests showed that subjects in each of the stereotype-present conditions (i.e., supraliminal and subliminal) recalled significantly more traits than subjects for whom stereotypes had been absent during the impression-formation task (respective $Ms = 5.04, 5.12$, and 3.54; significant $ps < .05$). Also, subjects recalled more consistent than neutral traits, $F(1, 33) = 14.03$, $p < .001$ (respective $Ms = 5.30$ vs. 3.83). These main effects were qualified by a Stereotype × Trait Type interaction, $F(2, 33) = 3.40$, $p < .05$ (see Table 29.4). Simple effects analysis confirmed an effect of stereotype for the consistent, $F(2, 66) = 6.47$, $p < .003$, but not the neutral traits recalled, $F(2, 66) = 1.79$, ns. Post hoc Tukey tests showed that subjects recalled more consistent traits when the stereotype was presented supraliminally than when it was absent (respective $Ms = 6.66$ vs. 4.00). Simple effects analysis also revealed an effect of trait type for the supraliminal priming condition, $F(1, 33) = 18.39$, $p < .0001$. This effect was not apparent, however, in either the subliminal priming, $F(1, 33) < 1$, ns, or stereotype-absent condition, $F(1,33) = 1.36$, ns.

Probe Latencies

After Studies 1 and 2, it was anticipated that when stereotypes were activated in the impression-formation task, subjects would have more attentional resources available for the execution of the probe-reaction task. Accordingly, they should offer faster responses to the probe stimulus than subjects for whom stereotypes had not previously been activated. A single-factor (stereotype: present or present-but-subliminal or absent) between-subjects ANOVA on subjects' mean probe reaction times confirmed this prediction, $F(2, 33) = 3.177$, $p < .05$ (see Table 29.4). Subjects in the no-prime condition exhibited significantly slower responses to the probe stimulus than subjects in either of the priming conditions ($ps < .05$).

With an improved dual-task methodology, the present results replicated the effects observed in Studies 1 and 2. The provision of stereotype labels during the impression-formation task reduced the demands imposed on subjects' attentional resources, resulting in enhanced performance on the probe-reaction task. This effect, moreover, was apparent whether the priming stimulus was presented supraliminally or subliminally. This suggests, then, that awareness of the priming categorical stimulus is not a necessary precondition for the resource-preserving properties of stereotype application. The effect occurs in the absence of perceivers' awareness or conscious consent (see Bargh, 1989). Whereas the provision of stereotype labels facilitated the memorability of both consistent and neutral traits, as in Study 1 the effect was greatest for the consistent items.

Additional Analyses

Whereas stereotypes clearly economize information processing, an important theoretical question emerges from the present research. Specifically, does stereotype application economize cognition in a general (i.e., stereotype-consistent as well as neutral traits) or more specific (i.e., stereotype-consistent traits only) manner?

TABLE 29.4. Subjects' Mean Task Performance: Study 3

Task	Stereotype		
	Supraliminal	Subliminal	Absent
Trait recall			
Consistent	6.66$_a$	5.24	4.00$_a$
Neutral	3.42	5.00	3.08
Probe reaction times (ms)	582$_a$	571$_b$	812$_{ab}$

Note. Means with a common subscript differ significantly: trait recall, $p < .005$; probe reaction times, $p < .05$.

Across the three studies, the recall data are suggestive of a general resource-preserving effect — although it does appear that this effect may be stronger for the consistent traits. To investigate this possibility, we conducted additional statistical tests to determine whether stereotype presence (vs. absence) facilitated the recall of both consistent and neutral traits across the three studies. In this pursuit, we used meta-analytic procedures that enabled us to combine results across studies and to compare the resultant effect sizes (Rosenthal, 1978; Rosenthal & Rubin, 1979). This analysis demonstrated that across the three studies, a reliable effect of stereotype presence was apparent for both consistent traits (weighted average $Z = 3.61$, $p < .0001$, average effect size $= .66$) and neutral traits (weighted average $Z = 2.39$, $p < .008$, average effect size $= .42$). The facilitatory effect of stereotype presence, moreover, was not reliably greater for the consistent than the neutral traits, $X^2(1, N = 92) = .741$, $p < .40$.

Taken together, then, the results of the three experiments suggest that stereotypes economize cognition through the provision of a mental framework on which both confirmatory and neutral information can be located (Bodenhausen, 1988; Bodenhausen & Lichtenstein, 1987; Bodenhausen & Wyer, 1985; Macrae et al., 1993; Stangor & Duan, 1991; Srull & Wyer, 1989). Perhaps only when perceivers are confronted with disconfirmatory information may stereotypes lose their power to preserve mental capacity. Charged with the task of reconciling discrepant information with preexisting stereotypic beliefs, perceivers must engage in effortful processes of inconsistency resolution (Macrae et al., 1993; Srull & Wyer, 1989; Stangor & Duan, 1991). Under these conditions, as such, stereotype application is unlikely to liberate attentional resources for the execution of other mental activities.

General Discussion

Stereotypes and Judgment Processes

The essence of the cognitive approach is that stereotyping is a functional, adaptive process that plays a central role in human social cognition. As Fiske (1989, p. 253) described, "stereotypers categorize because it requires too much mental effort to individuate." It was unclear from previous research whether this tendency simply reflects the mental sloth of social perceivers or their adaptive deployment of a sufficiently effective shortcut strategy. As Sherman and Corty (1984) emphasized, the many heuristic strategies of the social perceiver are likely to persist only insofar as they permit greater efficiency at acceptable levels of incurred costs. Most writings on the subject of stereotyping have understandably been focused on the costs incurred by the targets of social stereotyping, rather than the costs accruing to the stereotyping perceiver. It is likely that such costs are minimal under common, everyday conditions. Although there are clearly cases in which those who stereotype do pay a penalty (e.g., failing to hire the best job applicant because of gender stereotypes), the act of stereotyping may typically produce errors that are more costly to others than to the perceiver him- or herself. The present research has documented the benefits that perceivers may gain by the process of stereotyping — benefits that may often outweigh perceivers' own costs.

Within the spirit of the stereotypes-as-mental-tools metaphor (Gilbert & Hixon, 1991), we anticipated that stereotype application would promote the preservation of processing resources. This prediction follows from related research by Bargh (1982) demonstrating the efficiency of schematic thinking. In all three studies, our speculations were supported. Moreover, the preservation of attentional capacity was not contingent on perceivers' strategic deployment of stereotypical thinking. Resources were liberated in a task context in which perceivers were completely unaware of prior stereotype activation. This effect, as such, satisfies two of the criteria commonly associated with an automatic mental process: (a) It is unintentional and (b) it occurs without perceivers' awareness (see Bargh, 1989).

This demonstration has obvious implications for contemporary treatments of social stereotyping. A characteristic feature of cognitive models of impression formation is the priority they accord to category-based processes in person perception (Brewer, 1988; Fiske & Neuberg, 1990). Perceivers seem at best reluctant, and at worst incapable, of individuating others unless a series of critical cognitive and motivational criteria (e.g., spare attentional resources, self-involvement, outcome dependency, and accountability) have been satisfied (Erber & Fiske, 1984; Neuberg & Fiske, 1987; Tetlock, 1983; Tetlock & Kim, 1987). The primacy of these category-based effects is typically attributed to the utility or adaptability of social stereotyping. The present findings provide direct empirical support for this contention. Through stereotype application, perceivers can economize cognition by managing the demands imposed on their processing capacity. This executive function, moreover, is not simply a reflection of deliberative, strategic processing. It occurs in the absence of

perceivers' explicit intention to instigate stereotype-based modes of thought. In a dauntingly complex social world, this is clearly an efficient way for a mental system to operate (Bargh, 1989; Gilbert, 1989). The attentional resources that are liberated through the operation of covert mental processes (e.g., stereotype application) can be redirected to assist in the execution of perceivers' conscious reasoning strategies. The operation of stereotypes as economizing mental devices does not imply, however, that social interactions must invariably unfold in a stereotype-based manner. As Fiske and Taylor (1991) have recently argued, under certain circumstances, cognitive misers can change personae and become instead motivated tacticians. This switch is characterized by a preference for systematic information-processing strategies and an awareness of the impact of goals, needs, and desires on judgmental outcomes (Showers & Cantor, 1985). The motivated tactician, as such, surrenders the benefits of cognitive expedience (i.e., resource preservation) for a more individuated, but effortful, evaluation of others. These individuated impressions are most likely driven by a host of affective or motivational factors and the demands imposed on perceivers by specific task environments (see Brewer, 1988; Fiske & Neuberg, 1990; Fiske & Pavelchak, 1986).

Evolution of Stereotypical Thinking

Assuming, if we may, that stereotypical thinking is a fundamental property of human inferential systems, then some challenging theoretical questions can be raised. The most basic of these concerns the origins and maintenance of an inferential system that actively sustains stereotype-based modes of thought. If stereotypic judgments are predominantly inaccurate and irrational, why do we continue to make them? The present results, together with related theorizing, provide insight into this puzzle.

In a recent article, Gilbert (1989) outlined the development and evolution of an inferential system that actively favors dispositional, thereby potentially inaccurate, modes of thought. In a two-stage process, this system first draws dispositional inferences from human action; it then corrects or adjusts these inferences when necessary (see Gilbert & Krull, 1988; Gilbert, Krull, & Pelham, 1988; Gilbert, Pelham, & Krull, 1988; Trope, 1986). On encountering the new departmental secretary, for instance, we may conclude that he or she is rather sullen. This inference may subsequently be tempered, however, when we learn of his or her recent broken relationship. The crux of Gilbert's (1989) argument is that the inferential system draws the initial characterological inference with rapidity and consummate ease. Correction of this inference, in contrast, is a more resource-consuming, effortful affair. Here, then, we have an explicit dissociation between the automatic and controlled components of person perception (Bargh, 1989; Devine, 1989). Through automatic, unconscious processes, the inferential system furnishes perceivers with a dispositional explanation for human action. Through more effortful, controlled processing modes, it then adjusts or corrects these inferences in the light of additional information. The evolutionary value of such a system, according to Gilbert (1989), lies in its rapid, automatic, and effortless provision of dispositional inferences. Viable organisms, after all, "produce the best inferences they can for the least investment" (Gilbert, 1989, p. 207). More often than not, our default dispositional characterizations of others are likely to be perfectly adequate for the tasks we routinely face. They can, of course, always be adjusted (albeit effortfully) when the need arises.

The impetus for the evolution of the aforementioned inferential system is perceivers' need to invest cognitive resources in life's daily chores as expeditiously as possible. The present findings, as such, fit rather nicely within Gilbert's (1989) conception of what characterizes an adaptive and viable inferential system. Through stereotype application, perceivers possess an efficient means of simplifying social interaction and preserving valuable processing resources. Such a facility, moreover, makes sound evolutionary sense. Expending resources as cheaply as possible, on social interactions of minimal relevance, enables perceivers to redirect their energy to more pressing environmental contingencies. Given the trivial nature of most of our interactions with others, it is easy to see why stereotypical thinking tends to be the rule rather than the exception (see Fiske & Neuberg, 1990). In most social settings, complex impressions of others are quite unnecessary. Through stereotype application, perceivers are able to derive viable, although potentially erroneous, target-based impressions at very little cognitive cost. Although more accurate, individuated evaluations of others can be computed, they may be generally unattractive to the inferential system under many circumstances because of the cognitive resources they consume. Accordingly, individuated impressions are only likely to prevail when a series of affective or motivational preconditions, such as high self-involvement or interdependence, have been satisfied (Brewer, 1988; Fiske & Neuberg, 1990).

Stereotypical thinking is a ubiquitous feature of everyday life. In the present work, we attempted to discern why this may be so and investigated the popular belief that stereotypes function as energy-saving devices in social cognition. Across three studies, this contention was confirmed. Through their application, stereotypes were shown to simplify judgmental tasks and preserve valuable processing resources. In a sense, then, Gilbert and Hixon's (1991) characterization of stereotypes as tools residing in a metaphorical mental toolbox is an appropriate one. Through the deployment of social stereotypes, perceivers are able to free up limited cognitive resources for the execution of other necessary or desirable activities. This suggests then that researchers should not be content in simply cataloging the negative consequences of social stereotyping. Instead, a more functional perspective should be adopted (cf. Fox, 1992; Jackson, 1992). In our long journey from the primordial soup to intellectual hegemony, we seem to have evolved an inferential system that actively sustains stereotype-based modes of thought. A complete understanding of social stereotyping will certainly require a sobering appraisal of the many possible costs of stereotypic thinking, but it will also require a fuller appreciation of the benefits inherent in such thinking.

REFERENCES

Allport, G. W. (1954). *The nature of prejudice*. Reading, MA: Addison-Wesley.

Andersen, S. M., Klatzky, R. L., & Murray, J. (1990). Traits and social stereotypes: Efficiency differences in social information processing. *Journal of Personality and Social Psychology, 59*, 192–201.

Bargh, J. A. (1982). Attention and automaticity in the processing of self-relevant information. *Journal of Personality and Social Psychology, 43*, 425–436.

Bargh, J. A. (1984). Automatic and conscious processing of social information. In R. S. Wyer, Jr., & T. K. Srull (Eds.), *Handbook of social cognition* (Vol. 3, pp. 1–44). Hillsdale, NJ: Erlbaum.

Bargh, J. A. (1989). Conditional automaticity: Varieties of automatic influence in social perception and cognition. In J. S. Uleman & J. A. Bargh (Eds.), *Unintended thought* (pp. 3–51). New York: Guilford Press.

Bargh, J. A. (1992). Does subliminality matter to social psychology? Awareness of the stimulus versus awareness of its influence. In R. Bornstein & T. Pittman (Eds.), *Perception without awareness: Cognitive, clinical, and social perspectives* (pp. 236–255). New York: Guilford Press.

Bargh, J. A., Bond, R. N., Lombardi, W. J., & Tota, M. E. (1986). The additive nature of chronic and temporary sources of construct accessibility. *Journal of Personality and Social Psychology, 50*, 869–878.

Bargh, J. A., & Pietromonaco, P. (1982). Automatic information processing and social perception: The influence of trait information presented outside of conscious awareness on impression formation. *Journal of Personality and Social Psychology, 43*, 437–449.

Bodenhausen, G. V. (1988). Stereotypic biases in social decision making and memory: Testing process models of stereotype use. *Journal of Personality and Social Psychology, 55*, 726–737.

Bodenhausen, G. V. (1990). Stereotypes as judgmental heuristics: Evidence of circadian variations in discrimination. *Psychological Science, 1*, 319–322.

Bodenhausen, G. V. (1993). Emotion, arousal, and stereotypic judgments: A heuristic model of affect and stereotyping. In D. Mackie & D. Hamilton (Eds.), *Affect, cognition, and stereotyping: Interactive processes in group perception* (pp. 13–37). San Diego, CA: Academic Press.

Bodenhausen, G. V., & Lichtenstein, M. (1987). Social stereotypes and information processing strategies: The impact of task complexity. *Journal of Personality and Social Psychology, 52*, 871–880.

Bodenhausen, G. V., Sheppard, L. A., & Kramer, G. P. (in press). Negative affect and social judgment: The differential impact of anger and sadness. *European Journal of Social Psychology.*

Bodenhausen, G. V., & Wyer, R. S., Jr. (1985). Effects of stereotypes on decision making and information processing strategies. *Journal of Personality and Social Psychology, 48*, 267–282.

Brewer, M. B. (1988). A dual process model of impression formation. In R. S. Wyer, Jr., & T. K. Srull (Eds.), *Advances in social cognition* (Vol. 1, pp. 1–36). Hillsdale, NJ: Erlbaum.

Brown, I. D. (1964). The measurement of perceptual load and reserve capacity. *Transactions of the Association of Industrial Medical Officers, 14*, 44–49.

Cantor, N., & Mischel, W. (1977). Traits as prototypes: Effects on recognition memory. *Journal of Personality and Social Psychology, 35*, 38–48.

Cheesman, J., & Merikle, P. M. (1986). Distinguishing conscious from unconscious perceptual processes. *Canadian Journal of Psychology, 40*, 343–367.

Devine, P. G. (1989). Stereotypes and prejudice: Their automatic and controlled components. *Journal of Personality and Social Psychology, 56*, 5–18.

Erber, R., & Fiske, S. T. (1984). Outcome dependency and attention to inconsistent information. *Journal of Personality and Social Psychology, 47*, 709–726.

Erdley, C. A., & D'Agostino, P. R. (1988). Cognitive and affective components of automatic priming effects. *Journal of Personality and Social Psychology, 54*, 741–747.

Fiske, S. T. (1989). Examining the role of intent: Toward understanding its role in stereotyping and prejudice. In J. S. Uleman & J. A. Bargh (Eds.), *Unintended thought* (pp. 253–286). New York: Guilford Press.

Fiske, S. T., & Neuberg, S. L. (1990). A continuum model of impression formation from category-based to individuating processes: Influences of information and motivation on attention and interpretation. In M. P. Zanna (Ed.), *Advances in experimental social psychology* (Vol. 3, pp. 1–74). San Diego, CA: Academic Press.

Fiske, S. T., & Pavelchak, M. (1986). Category-based versus piecemeal-based affective responses. In R. M. Sorrentino & E. T. Higgins (Eds.), *Handbook of motivation and cognition* (pp. 167–203). New York: Guilford Press.

Fiske, S. T., & Taylor, S. E. (1991). *Social cognition* (2nd ed.). New York: McGraw-Hill.

Fox, R. (1992). Prejudice and the unfinished mind: A new look at an old failing. *Psychological Inquiry, 3*, 137–152.

Gilbert, D. T. (1989). Thinking lightly about others: Automatic components of the social inference process. In J. S. Uleman & J. A. Bargh (Eds.), *Unintended thought* (pp. 189–211). New York: Guilford Press.

Gilbert, D. T., & Hixon, J. G. (1991). The trouble of thinking: Activation and application of stereotypic beliefs. *Journal of Personality and Social Psychology, 60*, 509–517.

Gilbert, D. T., & Krull, D. S. (1988). Seeing less and knowing more: The benefits of perceptual ignorance. *Journal of Personality and Social Psychology, 54*, 193–202.

Gilbert, D. T., Krull, D. S., & Pelham, B. W. (1988). Of thoughts unspoken: Social inference and the self-regulation of behavior. *Journal of Personality and Social Psychology, 55*, 685–694.

Gilbert, D. T., Pelham, B. W., & Krull, D. S. (1988). On cognitive busyness: When person perceivers meet persons perceived. *Journal of Personality and Social Psychology, 54*, 733–740.

Gollwitzer, P. M. (1993). Goal achievement: The role of intentions. In W. Stroebe & M. Hewstone (Eds.), *European review of social psychology* (Vol. 4, pp. 141–185). Chichester, England: Wiley.

Greenwald, A. G., Klinger, M. R., & Liu, T. J. (1989). Unconscious processing of dichoptically masked words. *Memory and Cognition, 17*, 35–47.

Hamilton, D. L. (1979). A cognitive-attributional analysis of stereotyping. In L. Berkowitz (Ed.), *Advances in experimental social psychology* (Vol. 12, pp. 53–84). San Diego, CA: Academic Press.

Hamilton, D. L., Katz, L. B., & Leirer, V. O. (1980). Cognitive representation of personality impressions: Organizational processes in first impression formation. *Journal of Personality and Social Psychology, 39*, 1050–1063.

Hamilton, D. L., & Sherman, J. W. (in press). Stereotypes. In R. S. Wyer, Jr., & T. K. Srull (Eds.), *Handbook of social cognition* (2nd ed.). Hillsdale, NJ: Erlbaum.

Hamilton, D. L., Sherman, S. J., & Ruvolo, C. M. (1990). Stereotype-based expectancies: Effects on information processing and social behavior. *Journal of Social Issues, 46*, 35–60.

Hamilton, D. L., & Trolier, T. K. (1986). Stereotypes and stereotyping: An overview of the cognitive approach. In J. Dovidio & S. Gaertner (Eds.), *Prejudice, discrimination, and racism* (pp. 127–163). San Diego, CA: Academic Press.

Hasher, L., & Zacks, R. T. (1979). Automatic and effortful processes in memory. *Journal of Experimental Psychology: General, 108*, 356–388.

Hastie, R. (1980). Memory for behavioral information that confirms or contradicts a personality impression. In R. Hastie, T. M. Ostrom, E. B. Ebbeson, R. S. Wyer, Jr., D. L. Hamilton, & D. E. Carlston (Eds.), *Person memory: The cognitive basis of social perception* (pp. 141–172). Hillsdale, NJ: Erlbaum.

Hastie, R. (1981). Schematic principles in human memory. In E. T. Higgins, C. P. Herman, & M. P. Zanna (Eds.), *Social cognition: The Ontario Symposium* (Vol. 1, pp. 39–88). Hillsdale, NJ: Erlbaum.

Higgins, E. T., & Bargh, J. A. (1987). Social cognition and perception. *Annual Review of Psychology, 38*, 369–425.

Jackson, L. A. (1992). In what way is the unfinished mind unfinished? *Psychological Inquiry, 3*, 163–165.

Johnston, W. A. (1978). The intrusiveness of familiar nontarget information. *Memory and Cognition, 6*, 38–42.

Johnston, W. A., & Heinz, S. P. (1978). Flexibility and capacity demands of attention. *Journal of Experimental Psychology: General, 107*, 420–435.

Kahneman, D. (1973). *Attention and effort.* Englewood Cliffs, NJ: Prentice Hall.

Kantowitz, B. H. (1974). Double stimulation. In B. H. Kantowitz (Ed.), *Human information processing: Tutorials in performance and cognition* (pp. 83–131). Hillsdale, NJ: Erlbaum.

Kim, H., & Baron, R. S. (1988). Exercise and illusory correlation: Does arousal heighten stereotypic processes? *Journal of Experimental Social Psychology, 24,* 366–380.

Kruglanski, A. W., & Freund, T. (1983). The freezing and unfreezing of lay inferences: Effects on impression primacy, ethnic stereotyping, and numerical anchoring. *Journal of Experimental Social Psychology, 19,* 448–468.

Lippman, W. (1922). *Public opinion.* New York: Harcourt & Brace.

Logan, G. D. (1979). On the use of concurrent memory load to measure attention and automaticity. *Journal of Experimental Psychology: Human Perception and Performance, 5,* 189–207.

Macrae, C. N., Hewstone, M., & Griffiths, R. J. (1993). Processing load and memory for stereotype-based information. *European Journal of Social Psychology, 23,* 77–87.

Marcel, A. J. (1983). Conscious and unconscious perception: Experiments on visual masking and word recognition. *Cognitive Psychology, 15,* 197–237.

Navon, D., & Gopher, D. (1979). On the economy of the human processing system. *Psychological Review, 86,* 214–255.

Neisser, U. (1976). *Cognition and reality.* San Francisco: Freeman.

Neuberg, S. L., & Fiske, S. T. (1987). Motivational influences on impression formation: Outcome dependency, accuracy-driven attention, and individuating processes. *Journal of Personality and Social Psychology, 53,* 431–444.

Ogden, G. D., Levine, J. M., & Eisner, E. J. (1979). Measurement of workload by secondary tasks. *Human Factors, 21,* 529–548.

Perdue, C. W., Dovidio, J. F., Gurtman, M. B., & Tyler, R. B. (1990). Us and them: Categorization and the process of intergroup bias. *Journal of Personality and Social Psychology, 59,* 475–486.

Perdue, C. W., & Gurtman, M. B. (1990). Evidence for the automaticity of ageism. *Journal of Experimental Social Psychology, 26,* 199–216.

Posner, M. I., & Boies, S. J. (1971). Components of attention. *Psychological Review, 78,* 391–408.

Pratto, F., & Bargh, J. A. (1991). Stereotyping based upon apparently individuating information: Trait and global components of sex stereotypes under attention overload. *Journal of Experimental Social Psychology, 27,* 26–47.

Rolfe, J. M. (1973). The secondary task as a measure of mental load. In W. T. Singleton, J. G. Fox, & D. Whitfield (Eds.), *Measurement of man at work* (pp. 135–148). London: Taylor & Francis.

Rosenthal, R. (1978). Combining results of independent studies. *Psychological Bulletin, 85,* 185–193.

Rosenthal, R., & Rubin, D. B. (1979). Comparing significance levels of independent studies. *Psychological Bulletin, 86,* 1165–1168.

Rothbart, M., Fulero, S., Jensen, C., Howard, J., & Birrell, P. (1978). From individual to group impressions: Availability heuristics in stereotype formation. *Journal of Experimental Social Psychology, 14,* 237–255.

Sherman, S. J., & Corty, E. (1984). Cognitive heuristics. In R. S. Wyer, Jr., & T. K. Srull (Eds.), *Handbook of social cognition* (Vol. 1, pp. 189–286). Hillsdale, NJ: Erlbaum.

Sherman, S. J., Judd, C. M., & Park, B. (1989). Social cognition. *Annual Review of Psychology, 40,* 281–326.

Showers, C., & Cantor, N. (1985). Social cognition: A look at motivated strategies. *Annual Review of Psychology, 40,* 281–326.

Smith, G. J., Spence, D. P., & Klein, G. S. (1958). Subliminal effects of verbal stimuli. *Journal of Abnormal and Social Psychology, 59,* 167–176.

Srull, T. K., & Wyer, R. S., Jr. (1989). Person memory and judgment. *Psychological Review, 96,* 58–83.

Stangor, C., & Duan, C. (1991). Effects of multiple task demands upon memory for information about social groups. *Journal of Experimental Social Psychology, 27,* 357–378.

Stangor, C., & McMillan, D. (1992). Memory for expectancy-congruent and expectancy-incongruent social information: A meta-analytic review of the social psychological and social developmental literatures. *Psychological Bulletin, 111,* 42–61.

Tajfel, H. (1969). Cognitive aspects of prejudice. *Journal of Social Issues, 25,* 79–97.

Taylor, S. E., & Crocker, J. (1981). Schematic bases of social information processing. In E. T. Higgins, C. P. Herman, & M. P. Zanna (Eds.), *Social cognition: The Ontario symposium* (Vol. 1, pp. 89–134). Hillsdale, NJ: Erlbaum.

Tetlock, P. E. (1983). Accountability and complexity of thought. *Journal of Personality and Social Psychology, 45,* 74–83.

Tetlock, P. E., & Kim, J. I. (1987). Accountability and judgment processes in a personality prediction task. *Journal of Personality and Social Psychology, 52,* 700–709.

Tooby, J., & Cosmides, L. (1990). The past explains the present. *Ethology and Sociobiology, 11,* 375–424.

Trope, Y. (1986). Identification and inferential processes in dispositional attribution. *Psychological Review, 93,* 239–257.

Turvey, M. T. (1973). On peripheral and central processes in vision: Inferences from an information-processing analysis of masking with patterned stimuli. *Psychological Review, 80,* 1–52.

Wickens, C. D. (1976). The effects of divided attention in information processing in tracking. *Journal of Experimental Psychology: Human Perception and Performance, 2,* 1–13.

Wickens, C. D. (1980). The structure of processing resources. In R. Nickerson (Ed.), *Attention and performance VIII* (pp. 239–257). Hillsdale, NJ: Erlbaum.

Wickens, C. D. (1984). *Engineering psychology and human performance.* Columbus, OH: Charles E. Merrill.

Received August 21, 1992
Revision received August 6, 1993
Accepted August 11, 1993 ■

PART 8

Motivational Effects on Information Processing

Introduction and Preview

It is quite possible to surface after brief immersion in the literature on "social perception" with the impression that people, when they are with other people, are preoccupied with the cognitive task of assessing each other's fundamental nature.

(Jones & Thibaut, 1958, p. 151)

Although Jones and Thibaut (1958) made this observation over 40 years ago, you may be having similar thoughts after progressing to this stage of the book. Up to this point we have explored a number of different facets of how people process, represent, and use information that they encounter in the social world. We have learned that people, as information processors, have limits on how much they can attend to at any given moment, and therefore they selectively process some portion, but not all, of the information available to them; they interpret that information and give it meaning; they evaluate what they are learning and elaborate on it by drawing inferences; and they represent that expanded new knowledge in a mental representation that is stored in memory. That cognitive representation then becomes the "fount of knowledge" on which the individual can draw in the future for making judgments, guiding decisions, and orienting behavior. And as we have seen, limitations in the cognitive system can result in a variety of biases and shortcuts as people process and use that information.

All of this is very impressive, and social cognition research has made great progress in understanding "how the mind works." However, there are additional parts to the story. In much of what we have seen thus far, people are often portrayed as rather impartial processors of social information. However, one important element in social perception is the fact that perceivers typically are *not* neutral observers of the people and interactions they encounter. That is, people are motivated to see and to interpret events in ways that are favorable to themselves, and these *self-serving motives* can influence their processing and use of social information. We are motivated to believe that we are attractive, intelligent, and witty, that others evaluate us favorably, that we have performed admirably on tasks, that we are well liked. More generally speaking, people care about the people they interact with, about the events in which they become involved, even about the ongoing flow of life that they observe. They care — often deeply — about their own successes and failures, they have goals that they want to attain, and they care about being well liked by others. And they are not impartial in the ways they think about people that they like and dislike. The research evidence documenting these biases in perception is substantial and compelling (Kruglanski, 1996; Kunda, 1990).

A similar bias occurs in perceptions of groups. As emphasized in Social Identity Theory (Tajfel & Turner, 1979), people derive important aspects of their self-esteem from the groups with which they identify. Because they are motivated to have a positive self concept, they are therefore motivated to view their ingroups more favorably than other groups. The resulting tendency to evaluate "us" as being better than "them" — even in the absence of objective criteria or evidence for such a comparison — is known as the *ingroup bias* (Brewer, 1979), and permeates our perceptions of our own and other groups. As with an individual's self-serving motives, the ingroup bias not only can influence evaluative judgments of both ingroups and

outgroups, but also can guide interpretation of behavior and events. Moreover, and importantly for our concerns in this book, these motives influence the ways in which people process and use the information relevant to those concerns. How this happens is the focus of this part.

Consider some examples of the effects of these motives in everyday life.

● We want to feel good about our abilities, yet we get good grades in some, but not all courses. Our desire for positive self-evaluation can lead us to be convinced that those courses in which we did well are really "the important" courses, whereas those in which we did poorly are less important.

● Unlike courses where we receive grades as explicit evaluations of our performance, in many domains of life it can be unclear how well we're doing, how "good" we are. We often gauge our performance by comparing ourselves with others. But who is the appropriate person for such comparison? When self-serving motives are at stake, it can be beneficial to compare our own performance with that of someone who is less talented and has done poorly, rather than someone who typically excels.

● We want to believe that our opinions and the decisions we make are "correct" and well justified. Consequently, when we hear someone offering views compatible with our own, we accept them without much thought and we feel good about this confirmation of what we think. In contrast, we will critically evaluate and challenge the arguments offered by someone holding views contrary to our own.

● We derive some sense of "who we are" from the groups we belong to, so we are motivated to view our ingroups as good and important. To facilitate that evaluation, we derogate the value and worth of outgroups.

In all of these instances, it is clear that our motives and goals are guiding what, how much, and how we process information.

The readings in Part 8 provide useful illustrations of the variety of ways and contexts in which these effects can occur. Moreover, they demonstrate the kinds of evidence that social scientists have generated to document these effects. Reading 30, by Hastorf and Cantril (1954), demonstrated motivational effects on perceptions of a real-life event. An important football game between two rival universities, Dartmouth and Princeton, turned out to be not only hard fought but also very rough, with many penalties being called for foul play and some players on each side suffering major injuries. In the days and weeks following the game, there was much discussion and debate about the way the game was played and who was at fault. Students at each school, identifying with and showing allegiance to their own university, blamed the players on the other school's team for inordinately foul play. To study how motives influence perception and interpretation, Hastorf and Cantril showed the same film of the game to students at both universities and asked the students to indicate any infraction of the rules that they saw and also whether these infractions were "mild" or "flagrant." Students at both universities leveled primary responsibility for the rough play on the opposing team. Moreover, whereas Princeton students "saw" Dartmouth players commit many more flagrant fouls than Princeton players, Dartmouth students "saw" both teams make comparable numbers of infractions.

In discussing their findings Hastorf and Cantril highlight several themes that we have mentioned in previous chapters. For example, they emphasize that events that we witness take on specific meaning only after we have imposed some interpretation on them. And their results show that people do not observe and interpret the events they witness in a neutral, impartial manner. Rather, they are motivated to "see" events through rose-colored lenses that are consistent with favored outcomes. In effect, the fans of each team "saw" two entirely different games, their perceptions being driven by their own motives and allegiances. These results document the more general point that our identification with certain groups can lead to an ingroup bias which, in turn, can color and guide the way we interpret and use information about our own and other groups.

The other two readings in this part reveal in more detail some of the cognitive mechanisms by which motives have these effects. As we have seen in previous chapters, people often generate explanations or causal theories to account for events that they witness, including their own outcomes. Kunda's (1987) research shows that self-serving motives can influence the nature of the causal theories we intuitively generate. For example, in one study participants read a description of a person who had gone to professional school (law, medicine) and who had done well or poorly. Participants were asked to estimate how important each of several background characteristics of the person (e.g., youngest or oldest child, close or distant relationship with father) was for their eventual success (or not) in professional school. Participants rated those characteristics on which they themselves matched the target person (e.g., oldest child) as being more important for a successful outcome than those attributes on which they and the target person differed. If this result truly reflects a self-serving motive, then it should be seen most prominently in judgments made by students who themselves are planning to go to professional school after graduating from college. In fact, the importance estimates for matching and not-matching characteristics were significantly different for those intending to pursue professional degrees, but not for those who did not have such plans. Thus, our motives can guide our views of what characteristics are important for success, and — guess what — those tend to be the very characteristics that we ourselves possess!

In another study, Kunda (1987) demonstrated another effect of self-serving motives on the way information is processed, specifically, how those motives can bias the way we evaluate evidence relating to our preferred causal theories. Participants read a newspaper article reporting new scientific evidence about the adverse effects of caffeine on health. Kunda found that people who are not heavy coffee drinkers were more persuaded by the arguments made in the article than were people who do drink a lot of coffee. Again, this effect occurred only for those participants for whom the issue was relevant. Thus the extent to which evidentiary information is viewed as valid, is accepted, and has impact on people depends in part on whether it is consistent or inconsistent with personal preferences.

Do these findings imply that we are totally focused on "seeing" only what we want to see? Do we simply ignore or routinely dismiss information that contradicts our self interests? Reading 32 by Ditto and Lopez (1992) carries us a step further, and their research demonstrates another mechanism by which desired outcomes and viewpoints can be preserved. They point out a difference in how thoroughly people process and analyze information that is compatible or incompatible with their own self-interests. Specifically, they argue that there is an asymmetry in the *extent* of processing, such that information consistent with self-interest or a favored viewpoint is less likely to trigger analytic thinking, whereas information that challenges such views will be critically evaluated. That is, people may actively try to refute opposing views, whereas they make

little or no effort to evaluate the veracity of messages that are consistent with their opinions or desired outcomes. For example, in one of Ditto and Lopez's (1992) studies, participants could select any number of pieces of information before making a judgment of another person's intelligence. When that person was personally relevant and appeared to be of lower intelligence, then participants read and studied more information prior to making that judgment. In another study, participants learned about an enzyme ("TAA"), a deficiency of which supposedly could cause disorders of the pancreas. Participants then took a saliva test that presumably would measure their TAA level. Through an experimental manipulation, some participants learned that they had TAA deficiency, whereas others learned that they did not (participants were actually randomly assigned to these conditions). Participants who believed they were TAA deficient took longer to evaluate the results of the saliva test, and often would take the test again, before seemingly accepting the conclusion. On the other hand, participants whose test showed they were not TAA deficient accepted the result without question or effort to verify the result. TAA deficiency participants were also more skeptical about the seriousness of this health condition than were people who believed they had no such deficiency. Thus, self-serving motives can have several effects. First, they can bias the way we generate explanations for and evaluate information relevant to our own personal interests (Kunda, 1987). Second, they can influence the extent to which we critically evaluate the evidence on which feedback with self-relevant implications is or is not accepted (Ditto & Lopez, 1992).

Ditto and Lopez's (1992) findings are important for another reason as well. Their results demonstrate that, rather than merely ignoring or easily dismissing information that contradicts self interests, people devote considerable attention to it. Moreover, Ditto and Lopez (1992) argue that, if the contradicting information is clear and compelling, people will, under some conditions, accept a conclusion that is inconsistent with the favored position. People's processing may be driven by self-serving motives, but they do not adopt defensive "blinders" when confronted with information that challenges their favored view. They critically assess the information, they may develop their own arguments against it, and they may resist its implications. However, when these strategies do not work, people can then be open to accepting that information and its message.

Discussion Questions

1. How do the individual's current motives and goals influence the way he or she processes information?
2. How might the motives discussed in this part influence processes discussed in earlier parts, for example, inferences and attributions (Part 5), representation and memory (Part 2), impression formation (Part 6)?

Suggested Readings

Kruglanski, A. W. (1996). Motivated social cognition: Principles of the interface. In E. T. Higgins & A. W. Kruglanski (Eds.), *Social psychology: Handbook of basic principles* (pp. 493–520). New York: Guilford.

Kunda, Z. (1990). The case for motivated reasoning. *Psychological Bulletin, 108,* 480–498.

McDonald, H. E., & Hirt, E. R. (1997). When expectancy meets desire: Motivational effects in reconstructive memory. *Journal of Personality and Social Psychology, 72,* 5–23.

Devine, P. G., Sedikides, C., & Fuhrman, R. W. (1989). Goals in social information processing: The case of anticipated interaction. *Journal of Personality and Social Psychology, 56,* 680–690.

They Saw a Game: A Case Study

Albert H. Hastorf and Hadley Cantril

On a brisk Saturday afternoon, November 23, 1951, the Dartmouth football team played Princeton in Princeton's Palmer Stadium. It was the last game of the season for both teams and of rather special significance because the Princeton team had won all its games so far and one of its players, Kazmaier, was receiving All-American mention and had just appeared as the cover man on *Time* magazine, and was playing his last game.

A few minutes after the opening kick-off, it became apparent that the game was going to be a rough one. The referees were kept busy blowing their whistles and penalizing both sides. In the second quarter, Princeton's star left the game with a broken nose. In the third quarter, a Dartmouth player was taken off the field with a broken leg. Tempers flared both during and after the game. The official statistics of the game, which Princeton won, showed that Dartmouth was penalized 70 yards, Princeton 25, not counting more than a few plays in which both sides were penalized.

Needless to say, accusations soon began to fly. The game immediately became a matter of concern to players, students, coaches, and the administrative officials of the two institutions, as well as to alumni and the general public who had not seen the game but had become sensitive to the problem of big-time football through the recent exposures of subsidized players, commercialism, etc. Discussion of the game continued for several weeks.

One of the contributing factors to the extended discussion of the game was the extensive space given to it by both campus and metropolitan newspapers. An indication of the fervor with which the discussions were carried on is shown by a few excerpts from the campus dailies.

For example, on November 27 (four days after the game), the *Daily Princetonian* (Princeton's student newspaper) said:

> This observer has never seen quite such a disgusting exhibition of so-called "sport." Both teams were guilty but the blame must be laid primarily on Dartmouth's doorstep. Princeton, obviously the better team, had no reason to rough up Dartmouth. Looking at the situation rationally, we don't see why the Indians should make a deliberate attempt to cripple Dick Kazmaier or any other Princeton player. The Dartmouth psychology, however, is not rational itself.

The November 30th edition of the *Princeton Alumni Weekly* said:

> But certain memories of what occurred will not be easily erased. Into the record books will go in indelible fashion the fact that the last game of Dick Kazmaier's career was cut short by more than half when he was forced out with a broken nose and a mild concussion, sustained from a tackle that came well after he had thrown a pass.
>
> This second-period development was followed by a third quarter outbreak of roughness that was climaxed when a Dartmouth player deliberately kicked Brad Glass in the ribs while the latter was on his back. Throughout the often unpleasant afternoon, there was undeniable evidence that the losers' tactics were the result of an actual style of play, and reports on other games they have played this season substantiate this.

490

Dartmouth students were "seeing" an entirely different version of the game through the editorial eyes of the *Dartmouth* (Dartmouth's undergraduate newspaper). For example, on November 27 the *Dartmouth* said:

However, the Dartmouth-Princeton game set the stage for the other type of dirty football. A type which may be termed as an unjustifiable accusation.

Dick Kazmaier was injured early in the game. Kazmaier was the star, an All-American. Other stars have been injured before, but Kazmaier had been built to represent a Princeton idol. When an idol is hurt there is only one recourse—the tag of dirty football. So what did the Tiger Coach Charley Caldwell do? He announced to the world that the Big Green had been out to extinguish the Princeton star. His purpose was achieved.

After this incident, Caldwell instilled the old see-what-they-did-go-get-them attitude into his players. His talk got results. Gene Howard and Jim Miller were both injured. Both had dropped back to pass, had passed, and were standing unprotected in the backfield. Result: one bad leg and one leg broken.

The game was rough and did get a bit out of hand in the third quarter. Yet most of the roughing penalties were called against Princeton while Dartmouth received more of the illegal-use-of-the-hands variety.

On November 28 the *Dartmouth* said:

Dick Kazmaier of Princeton admittedly is an unusually able football player. Many Dartmouth men traveled to Princeton, not expecting to win—only hoping to see an All-American in action. Dick Kazmaier was hurt in the second period, and played only a token part in the remainder of the game. For this, spectators were sorry.

But there were no such feelings for Dick Kazmaier's health. Medical authorities have confirmed that as a relatively unprotected passing and running star in a contact sport, he is quite liable to injury. Also, his particular injuries—a broken nose and slight concussion—were no more serious than is experienced almost any day in any football practice, where there is no more serious stake than playing the following Saturday. Up to the Princeton game, Dartmouth players suffered about 10 known nose fractures and face injuries, not to mention several slight concussions.

Did Princeton players feel so badly about losing their star? They shouldn't have. During the past undefeated campaign they stopped several individual stars by a concentrated effort, including such main-stays as Frank Hauff of Navy, Glenn Adams of Pennsylvania and Rocco Calvo of Cornell.

In other words, the same brand of football condemned by the *Prince*—that of stopping the big man—is practiced quite successfully by the Tigers.

Basically, then, there was disagreement as to what had happened during the "game." Hence we took the opportunity presented by the occasion to make a "real life" study of a perceptual problem.[1]

Procedure

Two steps were involved in gathering data. The first consisted of answers to a questionnaire designed to get reactions to the game and to learn something of the climate of opinion in each institution. This questionnaire was administered a week after the game to both Dartmouth and Princeton undergraduates who were taking introductory and intermediate psychology courses.

The second step consisted of showing the same motion picture of the game to a sample of undergraduates in each school and having them check on another questionnaire, as they watched the film, any infraction of the rules they saw and whether these infractions were "mild" or "flagrant."[2] At Dartmouth, members of two fraternities were asked to view the film on December 7; at Princeton, members of two undergraduate clubs saw the film early in January.

The answers to both questionnaires were carefully coded and transferred to punch cards.[3]

Results

Table 30.1 shows the questions which received different replies from the two student populations on the first questionnaire.

Questions asking if the students had friends on the team, if they had ever played football themselves, if they felt they knew the rules of the game well, etc. showed no differences in either school and no relation to answers given to other questions. This is not surprising since the students in both schools come from essentially

---

[1] We are not concerned here with the problem of guilt or responsibility for infractions, and nothing here implies any judgment as to who was to blame.
[2] The film shown was kindly loaned for the purpose of the experiment by the Dartmouth College Athletic Council. It should be pointed out that a movie of a football game follows the ball, is thus selective, and omits a good deal of the total action on the field. Also, of course, in viewing only a film of a game, the possibilities of participation as spectator are greatly limited.
[3] We gratefully acknowledge the assistance of Virginia Zerega, Office of Public Opinion Research, and J. L. McCandless, Princeton University, and E. S. Horton, Dartmouth College, in the gathering and collation of the data.

TABLE 30.1. Data from First Questionnaire

Question	Dartmouth Students (*N* = 163) %	Princeton Students (*N* = 161) %
1. Did you happen to see the actual game between Dart-mouth and Princeton in Palmer Stadium this year?		
Yes	33	71
No	67	29
2. Have you seen a movie of the game or seen it on television?		
Yes, movie	33	2
Yes, television	0	1
No, neither	67	97
3. (Asked of those who answered "yes" to either or both of above questions.) From your observations of what went on at the game, do you believe the game was clean and fairly played, or that it was unnecessarily rough and dirty?		
Clean and fair	6	0
Rough and dirty	24	69
Rough and fair*	25	2
No answer	45	29
4. (Asked of those who answered "no" on both of the first questions.) From what you have heard and read about the game, do you feel it was clean and fairly played, or that it was unnecessarily rough and dirty?		
Clean and fair	7	0
Rough and dirty	18	24
Rough and fair*	14	1
Don't know	6	4
No answer	55	71
(Combined answers to questions 3 and 4 above)		
Clean and fair	13	0
Rough and dirty	42	93
Rough and fair*	39	3
Don't know	6	4
5. From what you saw in the game or the movies, or from what you have read, which team do you feel started the rough play?		
Dartmouth started it	36	86
Princeton started it	2	0
Both started it	53	11
Neither	6	1
No answer	3	2

TABLE 30.1. (*Continued*)

Question	Dartmouth Students (*N* = 163) %	Princeton Students (*N* = 161) %
6. What is your understanding of the charges being made?**		
Dartmouth tried to get Kazmaier	71	47
Dartmouth intentionally dirty	52	44
Dartmouth unnecessarily rough	8	35
7. Do you feel there is any truth to these charges?		
Yes	10	55
No	57	4
Partly	29	35
Don't know	4	6
8. Why do you think the charges were made?		
Injury to Princeton star	70	23
To prevent repetition	2	46
No answer	28	31

* This answer was not included on the checklist but was written in by the percentage of students indicated.
** Replies do not add to 100% since more than one charge could be given.

TABLE 30.2. Data from Second Questionnaire Checked while Seeing Film

Group	N	Total Number of Infractions Checked Against			
		Dartmouth Team		Princeton Team	
		Mean	SD	Mean	SD
Dartmouth students	48	4.3*	2.7	4.4	2.8
Princeton students	49	9.8*	5.7	4.2	3.5

* Significant at the .01 level.

the same type of educational, economic, and ethnic background.

Summarizing the data of Tables 30.1 and 30.2 we find a marked contrast between the two student groups.

Nearly all *Princeton* students judged the game as "rough and dirty" — not one of them thought it "clean and fair." And almost nine-tenths of them thought the other side started the rough play. By and large they felt that the charges they understood were being made were true; most of them felt the charges were made in order to avoid similar situations in the future.

When Princeton students looked at the movie of the game, they saw the Dartmouth team make over twice as many infractions as their own team made. And they saw the Dartmouth team make over twice as many infractions as were seen by Dartmouth students. When Princeton students judged these infractions as "flagrant" or "mild," the ratio was about two "flagrant" to one "mild" on the Dartmouth team, and about one "flagrant" to three "mild" on the Princeton team.

As for the *Dartmouth* students, while the plurality of answers fell in the "rough and dirty" category, over one-tenth thought the game was "clean and fair" and over a third introduced their own category of "rough and fair" to describe the action. Although a third of the Dartmouth students felt that Dartmouth was to blame for starting the rough play, the majority of Dartmouth students thought both sides were to blame. By and large, Dartmouth men felt that the charges they understood were being made were not true, and most of them thought the reason for the charges was Princeton's concern for its football star.

When Dartmouth students looked at the movie of the game they saw both teams make about the same number of infractions. And they saw their own team make only half the number of infractions the Princeton students saw them make. The ratio of "flagrant" to "mild" infractions was about one to one when Dartmouth students judged the Dartmouth team, and about one "flagrant" to two "mild" when Dartmouth students judged infractions made by the Princeton team.

It should be noted that Dartmouth and Princeton students were thinking of different charges in judging their validity and in assigning reasons as to why the charges were made. It should also be noted that whether or not students were spectators of the game in the stadium made little difference in their responses.

Interpretation: The Nature of A Social Event[4]

It seems clear that the "game" actually was many different games and that each version of the events that transpired was just as "real" to a particular person as other versions were to other people. A consideration of the experiential phenomena that constitute a "football game" for the spectator may help us both to account for

the results obtained and illustrate something of the nature of any social event.

Like any other complex social occurrence, a "football game" consists of a whole host of happenings. Many different events are occurring simultaneously. Furthermore, each happening is a link in a chain of happenings, so that one follows another in sequence. The "football game," as well as other complex social situations, consists of a whole matrix of events. In the game situation, this matrix of events consists of the actions of all the players, together with the behavior of the referees and linesmen, the action on the sidelines, in the grandstands, over the loud-speaker, etc.

Of crucial importance is the fact that an "occurrence" on the football field or in any other social situation does not become an experiential "event" unless and until some significance is given to it: an "occurrence" becomes an *event* only when the happening has significance. And a happening generally has significance only if it reactivates learned significances already registered in what we have called a person's assumptive form-world [1].

Hence the particular occurrences that different people experienced in the football game were a limited series of events from the total matrix of events *potentially* available to them. People experienced those occurrences that reactivated significances they brought to the occasion; they failed to experience those occurrences which did not reactivate past significances. We do not need to introduce "attention" as an "intervening third" (to paraphrase James on memory) to account for the selectivity of the experiential process.

In this particular study, one of the most interesting examples of this phenomenon was a telegram sent to an officer of Dartmouth College by a member of a Dartmouth alumni group in the Midwest. He had viewed the film which had been shipped to his alumni group from Princeton after its use with Princeton students, who saw, as we noted, an average of over nine infractions by Dartmouth players during the game. The alumnus, who couldn't see the infractions he had heard publicized, wired:

> Preview of Princeton movies indicates considerable cutting of important part please wire explanation and possibly air mail missing part before showing scheduled for January 25 we have splicing equipment.

The "same" sensory impingements emanating from the football field, transmitted through the visual mechanism to the brain also obviously gave rise to different

---

[4] The interpretation of the nature of a social event sketched here is in part based on discussions with Adelbert Ames, Jr., and is being elaborated in more detail elsewhere.

experiences in different people. The significances assumed by different happenings for different people depend in large part on the purposes people bring to the occasion and the assumptions they have of the purposes and probable behavior of other people involved. This was amusingly pointed out by the New York *Herald Tribune's* sports columnist, Red Smith in describing a prize fight between Chico Vejar and Carmine Fiore in his column of December 21, 1951. Among other things, he wrote:

> You see, Steve Ellis is the proprietor of Chico Vejar, who is a highly desirable tract of Stamford, Conn., welterweight. Steve is also a radio announcer. Ordinarily there is no conflict between Ellis the Brain and Ellis the Voice because Steve is an uncommonly substantial lump of meat who can support both halves of a split personality and give away weight on each end without missing it.
>
> This time, though, the two Ellises met head-on, with a sickening, rending crash. Steve the Manager sat at ringside in the guise of Steve the Announcer broadcasting a dispassionate, unbiased, objective report of Chico's adventures in the ring … .
>
> Clear as mountain water, his words came through, winning big for Chico. Winning? Hell, Steve was slaughtering poor Fiore.
>
> Watching and listening, you could see what a valiant effort the reporter was making to remain cool and detached. At the same time you had an illustration of the old, established truth that when anybody with a preference watches a fight, he sees only what he prefers to see.
>
> That is always so. That is why, after any fight that doesn't end in a clean knockout, there always are at least a few hoots when the decision is announced. A guy from, say, Billy Graham's neighborhood goes to see Billy fight and he watches Graham all the time. He sees all the punches Billy throws, and hardly any of the punches Billy catches. So it was with Steve.
>
> "Fiore feints with a left," he would say, honestly believing that Fiore hadn't caught Chico full on the chops. "Fiore's knees buckle," he said, "and Chico backs away." Steve didn't see the hook that had driven Chico back … .

In brief, the data here indicate that there is no such "thing" as a "game" existing "out there" in its own right which people merely "observe." The "game" "exists" for a person and is experienced by him only in so far as certain happenings have significances in terms of his purpose. Out of all the occurrences going on in the environment, a person selects those that have some significance for him from his own egocentric position in the total matrix.

Obviously in the case of a football game, the value of the experience of watching the game is enhanced if the purpose of "your" team is accomplished, that is, if the happening of the desired consequence is experienced — i.e., if your team wins. But the value attribute of the experience can, of course, be spoiled if the desire to win crowds out behavior we value and have come to call sportsmanlike.

The sharing of significances provides the links except for which a "social" event would not be experienced and would not exist for anyone.

A "football game" would be impossible except for the rules of the game which we bring to the situation and which enable us to share with others the significances of various happenings. These rules make possible a certain repeatability of events such as first downs, touchdowns, etc. If a person is unfamiliar with the rules of the game, the behavior he sees lacks repeatability and consistent significance and hence "doesn't make sense."

And only because there is the possibility of repetition is there the possibility that a happening has a significance. For example, the balls used in games are designed to give a high degree of repeatability. While a football is about the only ball used in games which is not a sphere, the shape of the modern football has apparently evolved in order to achieve a higher degree of accuracy and speed in forward passing than would be obtained with a spherical ball, thus increasing the repeatability of an important phase of the game.

The rules of a football game, like laws, rituals, customs, and mores, are registered and preserved forms of sequential significances enabling people to share the significances of occurrences. The sharing of sequential significances which have value for us provides the links that operationally make social events possible. They are analogous to the forces of attraction that hold parts of an atom together, keeping each part from following its individual, independent course.

From this point of view it is inaccurate and misleading to say that different people have different "attitudes" concerning the same "thing." For the "thing" simply is *not* the same for different people whether the "thing" is a football game, a presidential candidate, Communism, or spinach. We do not simply "react to" a happening or to some impingement from the environment in a determined way (except in behavior that has become reflexive or habitual). We behave according to what we bring to the occasion, and what each of us brings to the occasion is more or less unique. And except for these significances which we bring to the occasion, the happenings around us would be meaningless occurrences, would be "inconsequential."

From the transactional view, an attitude is not a predisposition to react in a certain way to an occurrence or stimulus "out there" that exists in its own right with certain fixed characteristics which we "color" according to our predisposition [2]. That is, a subject does not simply "react to" an "object." An attitude would rather seem to be a complex of registered significances reactivated by some stimulus which assumes its own particular significance for us in terms of our purposes. That is, the object as experienced would not exist for us except for the reactivated aspects of the form-world which provide particular significance to the hieroglyphics of sensory impingements.

REFERENCES

1. Cantril, H. *The "why" of man's experience*. New York: Macmillan, 1950.
2. Kilpatrick, F. P. (Ed.) *Human behavior from the transactional point of view*. Hanover, N. H.: Institute for Associated Research, 1952.

Received October 9, 1952. ■

Motivated Inference: Self-Serving Generation and Evaluation of Causal Theories

Ziva Kunda

The results of four studies suggest that people tend to generate and evaluate causal theories in a self-serving manner: They generate theories that view their own attributes as more predictive of desirable outcomes, and they are reluctant to believe in theories relating their own attributes to undesirable events. As a consequence, people tend to hold theories that are consistent with the optimistic belief that good things will happen to them and bad things will not. I argue that these self-serving biases are best explained as resulting from cognitive processes guided by motivation because they do not occur in the absence of motivational pressures.

Most people tend to approach life with an optimistic stance. In general, we expect more desirable outcomes to be more likely (Irwin, 1953; Marks, 1951; Parducci, 1968; Pruitt & Hoge, 1965). We also think that we are more likely than our peers to experience positive outcomes and less likely than they to experience negative outcomes. Such optimism has been shown for a wide range of life domains, including beliefs about financial, professional, interpersonal, health-related, and crime-related outcomes (Weinstein, 1980, 1983, 1984; for a review see Perloff, 1983). Because logically we cannot all be better off than our peers, our belief that we are is bound to be unrealistic.

This article is based on a doctoral dissertation submitted to the Department of Psychology of the University of Michigan. I am especially grateful to the chairs of my doctoral committee, Hazel Markus and Richard Nisbett, for their advice, and to John Jemmott and Edward Jones for comments on an earlier version of the article.

Correspondence concerning this article should be addressed to Ziva Kunda, Psychology Department, Green Hall, Princeton University, Princeton, New Jersey 08544.

Where, then, does this unrealistic optimism come from? The present approach assumes that people do not merely proclaim that good things will happen and bad things will not. Rather, they support and maintain their optimistic beliefs through a network of interrelated theories about the causal determinants of positive and negative outcomes. They construct elaborate theories to explain how different attributes are related to various outcomes, but these theories are biased in a self-serving manner: People believe that their own attributes are more likely than other attributes to facilitate desired outcomes and to hinder feared outcomes. Such biased theories allow people to believe that they are more likely than others to experience the desired outcomes and to avoid the feared ones. In this article, I explore two potential sources for such biased theories: Self-serving generation and self-serving evaluation of causal theories.

The first process assumes that people use their stored world knowledge to generate theories about the causes of positive and negative outcomes in a self-serving manner, favoring those theories that could help maintain optimism about their own likelihood of incurring such outcomes. For example, upon hearing that the divorce rate in this country is 50%, people might attempt to convince themselves that they will not fall victim to this misfortune. They could do this by searching through their knowledge about themselves and the world for factors that predispose them toward a happy marriage. Some people may remember, for example, that they have had several serious romantic relationships. They may then theorize that the understanding of others and of themselves gained through these relationships will make it easier for them to establish a stable relationship with their spouse.

The problem with such theorizing is that people possessing the opposite traits can just as easily generate theories about how their own traits predict happy marriage. Someone with no early romantic relationships might take comfort in the belief that entering marriage without any baggage of prior assumptions or hostility left over from earlier relationships is conducive to happy marriage. Thus no matter what people's attributes are, they may come to believe that their attributes will help them achieve desired outcomes and avoid feared outcomes.

Such self-serving theory generation is possible because people have great facility in generating causal theories linking any attribute to just about any outcome (Anderson & Sechler, 1986; Fischhoff, 1975; Kunda, 1985), and they have no way of determining the correctness of their theories. Indeed, they come to believe in the validity of any theory that they have been induced to generate (Anderson, Lepper, & Ross, 1980; Anderson & Sechler, 1986). Consequently, if people set out to generate a theory linking their own attributes to a desired or a feared outcome, they should be able to do so easily, no matter what their attributes are or what the outcome is. Once they generate such theories, these theories are likely to persist because people have enhanced memory for theories that they generate themselves (for review see Greenwald, 1981), because the arguments generated to support the theories remain available (Anderson, New, & Speer, 1985), and because people are not likely to generate alternative, contradictory theories spontaneously (Koriat, Lichtenstein, & Fischhoff, 1980).

The second form of self-serving processing examined here assumes that when confronted with evidence that has implications for optimistic beliefs, people evaluate it in a self-serving manner, applying more stringent criteria to evidence with less favorable implications to the self. For example, evidence implying that one is likely to incur health problems might be subjected to extensive scrutiny and criticism, whereas evidence implying good health might be accepted at face value.

Such self-serving evidence evaluation is possible because people are capable of applying different inferential rules on different occasions (Kunda & Nisbett, 1986; Nisbett, Krantz, Jepson, & Kunda, 1983). Also, people are sadly lacking in the clear criteria needed to determine the appropriateness of a given rule to a given problem (Nisbett & Ross, 1980). When evaluating evidence, they may therefore apply to it only those inferential rules likely to produce a self-serving evaluation.

Through the repeated exercise of self-serving generation and self-serving evaluation of causal theories, people may come to possess a biased set of theories according to which their own attributes can cause desirable outcomes and deter undesirable ones. Such theories may help sustain unrealistic optimism.

There is now considerable evidence indicating that people use self-serving beliefs and processes in a variety of domains, including perception (Erdelyi, 1974), memory (Greenwald, 1980; Greenwald & Pratkanis, 1984), attribution of responsibility for one's own behaviors (Miller & Ross, 1975; Tetlock & Levi, 1982; Zuckerman, 1979) and for other people's behaviors (Lerner, 1980), value assessment (Tesser & Campbell, 1983), and social comparison (Pyszczynski, Greenberg, & LaPrelle, 1985; Taylor, 1983). But there is little evidence concerning self-serving biases in inferential processes involving generation and evaluation of causal theories, although it is here that self-serving biases could have some of their most pervasive and consequential implications because of the dramatic and accumulating effects of such biases on beliefs. As a result of such biases, initially mildly optimistic beliefs could become increasingly polarized as one selectively generates and evaluates evidence (cf. Lord, Ross, & Lepper, 1979).

If self-serving biases in the generation and evaluation of evidence are found, it would also be interesting to determine whether these biases result from cold cognition processes or from hot cognition processes. Many of the biases initially introduced as resulting from hot, motivational processes have been reinterpreted in terms of entirely cold, cognitive processes. It has been argued that people may display such biases through no particular intention or effort of their own. Rather, the environment provides them with predominantly positive information, and their general inferential shortcomings lead them to act on this information so as to reason in an apparently self-serving manner (Miller & Ross, 1975; Nisbett & Ross, 1980).

Because most relevant self-serving biases can be interpreted in both cognitive and motivational terms, some theorists have argued that the hot-versus-cold cognition controversy cannot be resolved empirically (Ross & Fletcher, 1985; Tetlock & Levi, 1982). But others have argued that it is essential to assume motivational processing because many self-serving biases have been shown to occur only in the presence of arousal (e.g., Zanna & Cooper, 1976).

The present approach takes into account both motivational and inferential factors. In this view, the cognitive apparatus is harnessed in the service of motivational ends. People use cognitive inferential mechanisms and processes to arrive at their desired conclusions, but motivational forces determine which processes will be used in a given instance and which evidence will be considered. The conclusions therefore appear to be rationally supported by evidence, but in fact the evidence itself is tainted by motivation; its production and evaluation are guided by motivation (cf. Darley & Gross, 1983).

This position assumes that in order to generate causal theories about the relations between attributes and outcomes, one needs to search one's memory for beliefs about the attributes, the outcomes, and the world in general that could be woven together into a coherent theory. Also, in order to evaluate the validity and generalizability of evidence, one needs to search through memory for appropriate inferential rules. It has been shown that on different occasions people may access different facts and rules: They may make different social judgments (Higgins & King, 1981; Higgins, King, & Mavin, 1982), endorse different attitudes (Salancik & Conway, 1975; Snyder, 1982), assume different self-conceptions (Fazio, Effrein, & Falender, 1981; Markus & Kunda, 1986), and apply different inferential rules (Kunda & Nisbett, 1986; Nisbett et al., 1983). It seems possible that motivation may help determine which rules and facts people access when generating and evaluating causal theories and thus influence the content of these theories.

Several theorists have proposed similar processes to account for self-serving biases in other domains, but the implications of these ideas to the domain of theory generation and evaluation have not been elaborated, and there is little direct evidence for motivationally guided accessing of long-term memory in any domain (although considerable evidence suggests that motives may affect encoding, organization, and use of information coming from external sources; for a review see Srull & Wyer, 1986). The notion that motivational forces may drive inferential processes follows from dissonance theory (Festinger, 1957), but very little of the dissonance research was concerned directly with theory generation and evaluation. Most dissonance research examined the effects of motivational pressures resulting from choosing between equally attractive alternatives and from performing behaviors that would normally be avoided (for a review see Wicklund & Brehm, 1976). With few exceptions (e.g., Kassarjian & Cohen, 1965), the dissonance paradigm provided little direct support for the hypothesis that people rely on motivationally directed inferential processes to sustain optimistic beliefs.

More recently, similar formulations, in which motivation is assumed to guide cognitive processes, have been proposed to account for self-serving attributions for one's own behavior (Anderson & Slusher, 1986; Pyszczynski & Greenberg, in press) and for phenomena such as stereotyping, anchoring, and primacy effects (Kruglanski & Freund, 1983). The aim of the present research is to extend the notion of motivated inference to a broader range of phenomena and to make a start at spelling out the cognitive mechanisms underlying such processes.

In this article, I examine whether people generate and evaluate causal theories in a self-serving manner and whether such biases are due to motivational factors. I argue that the motivational interpretation of such biases would be strengthened if they occurred only in the presence of motivational forces resulting from personal involvement with the outcomes in question.

Self-Serving Theory Generation

Study 1: Generating Self-Serving Theories About the Causes of Divorce

Study 1 examines whether people tend to generate theories in a self-serving manner so as to support the optimistic view that their own attributes predict good life outcomes but not bad ones. Do people believe that their own attributes are more predictive of desired outcomes than are other attributes? Do people possessing a given attribute view it as a better predictor of desired outcomes than do people who do not possess it?

It is important to study these processes in the context of highly desirable and undesirable outcomes about which people have little concrete information that would allow objective assessment of their odds. Young people's beliefs about the future outcomes of their marriages seem to fit these criteria. Almost everybody wants to be happily married and never to have to face the prospect of divorce. Yet few people, if any, have any way of assessing the actual likelihood that they will get divorced.

Nevertheless, most young people are quite convinced that they will remain married to their first spouse until death does them part (Lehman & Nisbett, 1985). This is so despite their awareness of the well-publicized base rate: About half the marriages in the United States end in divorce. Such unrealistic optimism could be sustained by self-serving theorizing about the causal relation between one's attributes and the outcome of marriage.

To examine whether people engage in such self-serving theorizing, subjects read a description of a target person, consisting of one of two opposite sets of attributes, and were asked to assess the extent to which each of these attributes might have contributed to the outcome of the target's marriage. At the end, subjects were asked for their own standing on each of these attributes.

People were expected to judge their own attributes as better for marriage than the opposite attributes. Thus people who shared a given attribute with the target person were expected to judge that attribute as better for marriage than were people who possessed the opposite attribute. Within subjects, each person was expected to judge the subset of attributes that he or she shared with the target as better for marriage than the remaining attributes.

Subjects were also asked about the likelihood that they would get divorced, so as to verify that they were unrealistically optimistic in this regard.

Method
Subjects were 103 University of Michigan undergraduates of both sexes enrolled in introductory psychology. They participated in groups of 4 to 6 subjects.

The study was presented as concerned with people's memory, opinions, and beliefs. Subjects read a cover sheet that began with a reminder that the divorce rate in the United States was 50% and continued with a description of a research project designed to detect personality and background factors related to marriage outcomes. The researchers were said to have gathered information about the background factors of individuals who had attended the University of Michigan in the 1960s (almost half of whom were already divorced) and to have found some of the factors to be related to marriage outcomes. Because the researchers were also interested in people's beliefs about these issues, the study was to examine whether people knew which factors were likely to facilitate divorce and which were likely to hinder divorce.

Subjects then read a description of a person said to be one of the actual participants in the original study. The description consisted of one of two opposite sets of six attributes. Half the subjects read that (a) the person's mother was never employed outside the home; (b) as a college student the person was introverted and (c) independent; (d) the person was nonreligious; (e) the person identified with liberal political views; and (f) the person had at least one serious relationship with a member of the opposite sex before entering college. The other half of the subjects read that the person had the opposite set of attributes (employed mother, extravert, dependent, religious, conservative, no early romantic involvement). Half the subjects read that the person was male and half that the person was female. This variable had no effect on the dependent measures and will not be discussed further. A third of the subjects read that the target person was divorced, a third that the person was happily married, and a third were given no information about the outcome of the target person's marriage.

Subjects were next asked to indicate how each of the target person's attributes might have contributed to the eventual outcome of the target person's marriage on a 9-point scale ranging from 1 (*made divorce much more likely*) through 5 (*had no influence*) to 9 (*made stable marriage much more likely*).

After responding to a series of unrelated questionnaires, subjects were asked about the probability that they would incur a number of positive and negative events, including divorce. At the end, subjects were asked to indicate their own standing on each of the background attributes (i.e., whether their own mother had been employed outside the home, etc.).[1]

Results and Discussion
For each attribute, people who matched the target person on that attribute (i.e., possessed that attribute themselves) were expected to view it as better for the target person's marriage than were people who did not match the target person (i.e., possessed the opposite attribute). Table 31.1 shows that this pattern was found for 9 of the 12 possible comparisons. For example, subjects whose own mothers had been employed outside the home viewed having had an employed mother as better for

---

[1] Subjects' self-reported attitudes were not affected by the target's outcome. For each outcome condition, the percentage of subjects who indicated that they matched the target on each attribute was calculated, and these percentages were averaged across attributes. On average, the percentage of subjects indicating that they matched the target in the happily married, divorced, and no-information conditions was 53, 55, and 53, respectively.

TABLE 31.1. Mean Rating of the Effect of Each Attribute on the Target Person's Marriage Given by Subjects Who Did and Who Did Not Match the Target Person on These Attributes

Target's Attribute	Match	N	No Match	N	Coef[a]	t
Employed mother	5.53	17	4.40	35	.40	2.75**
Nonemployed mother	4.96	28	4.48	23		
Introvert	3.65	17	4.37	30	−.09	.40
Extravert	5.70	37	5.30	10		
Independent	4.50	46	2.25	4	.36	1.14
Dependent	4.92	12	5.03	36		
Nonreligious	4.80	20	4.12	32	.29	1.98**
Religious	6.81	27	6.33	24		
Liberal	4.81	32	4.74	19	−.22	1.53
Conservative	4.89	18	5.73	30		
Early relationship	6.47	40	5.75	12	.40	2.29*
No early relationship	4.43	23	3.57	28		

Note: Ratings were made on a scale ranging from 1 (*made divorce much more likely*) to 9 (*made stable marriage much more likely*).
[a] These are multiple regression coefficients obtained in the prediction of subjects' responses from whether or not they matched the target person.
* $p < .05$. ** $p < .01$.

marriage and having had a nonemployed mother as worse for marriage than did subjects whose mothers had not worked outside the home.

A multiple regression was performed for each of the six items. In each case, subjects' responses were predicted from the target person's attribute (e.g., employed or nonemployed mother), the subject's attribute, and whether the subject matched the target person on this attribute. The key question was how the match/no-match variable (which was a dummy variable coded as 1 for *match* and as −1 for *no match*) contributed to the prediction of subjects' responses. As seen in Table 31.1, four of the six regression coefficients were positive, indicating that subjects who matched the target person on a given attribute viewed that attribute as better for marriage than did subjects who did not match the target person. Three of these positive coefficients were significant at the .05 level or lower. Neither of the two negative coefficients was significant. This analysis is a between-subjects analysis comparing the responses of subjects possessing opposite positions on each dimension.

Subjects were also expected to view attributes that they possessed as better for marriage than attributes that

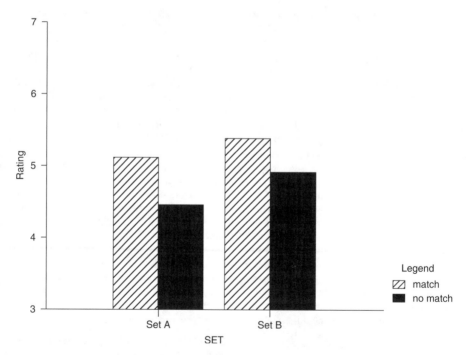

FIGURE 31.1 ■ For Each Attribute Set, Mean Ratings Given by Subjects for the Effects On the Target Person's Marriage of Attributes On Which They Did and Did Not Match the Target person.

they did not possess. Thus each subject was expected to rate the subset of attributes on which he or she matched the target person as better for the target person's marriage than the remaining attributes on which he or she did not match the target person. To examine this, the mean rating of the items on which he or she matched the target person and the mean of the items on which he or she did not match the target person were calculated for each subject.[2] As seen in Figure 31.1, subjects judged items on which they matched the target person as better for marriage than items on which they did not match the target person. This was significant for each of the opposite attribute sets, pair-wise $t(50) = 2.73, p < .01$, and $t(48) = 2.04, p < .05$, as well as for both sets combined, $t(99) = 3.40, p < .01$.

Because of the combination of unequal cell sizes and unequal means for individual items, the effect may be somewhat exaggerated. To control for this, all items were standardized and the same analyses were carried out on the standardized scores. This procedure actually underestimates the magnitude of the effect. Nevertheless, these comparisons were all significant at $p < .05$.

Information about the outcome of the target's marriage did not interact with whether subjects matched the target ($p > .20$), but it did have a significant main effect on responses: Attributes were judged as best for marriage when the target was said to be happily married (5.82), as worst when the target was said to be divorced (4.38), and as intermediate when no information was given (4.62), $F(2, 97) = 27.78, p < .001$. This suggests that subjects' theories about the causal determinants of divorce were not merely retrieved from memory. Rather, subjects appear to have generated the theories on the spot to meet the demands of the particular situation.

This main effect could be due to demand characteristics because subjects may have concluded that at least some of the attributes had to be related to the target's outcome. Also, their theories about these relations may have remained specific to the target person rather than becoming more general theories about the causes of divorce. However, in a follow-up study (Kunda, 1986), there was a similar main effect in the absence of such constraints. After explaining why a specific target was happily married or divorced, subjects indicated, in a setting made to appear unrelated so as to counteract demand, that they had generated general theories about the relations between target attributes and divorce.

These findings corroborate other research indicating that people are capable of generating theories linking any attribute to just about any outcome (Anderson & Sechler, 1986; Fischhoff, 1975). They are willing to do this even on the basis of a single instance (cf. Anderson, 1983), suggesting that people are constantly revising and updating their causal theories as they encounter individuals who have experienced various outcomes. The causal theories that are generated following exposure to such individuals appear to be shaped not only by these individuals' attributes and outcomes and by general world knowledge but also by personal motivations and goals.

It seems that when generating theories about the influence of different attributes on marriage, people enhance the positive influence of their own attributes at the expense of other people's attributes. This process could enable people to maintain unrealistic optimism about the eventual outcomes of their own marriages. Indeed, even though subjects were reminded at the beginning of the study that the probability of divorce was 50%, subjects believed, on average, that the probability that they would get divorced was only 20%. These data suggest that this unrealistic optimism may be sustained at least in part through the selective generation of theories concerning the precursors of divorce when optimistic beliefs are questioned. If one believes that one's attributes are positively related to stable marriage, it follows that one is unlikely to get divorced. Motives, therefore, may exert their influence on reasoning by directing the memory search through relevant world knowledge and leading to greater activation and use of those knowledge structures that can support self-serving theories and beliefs.

Study 2: Generating Self-Serving Theories About Success in Professional School

Study 1 suggests that the mere possession of a given attribute leads one to view this attribute as more positively related to desired outcomes and less predictive of feared events. Thus people appear to generate causal theories in a self-serving manner. However, it is not clear that these findings necessarily imply motivationally directed theory generation. It is also possible, for example, that people with different attributes have different histories of unintentional exposure to information about these attributes and that this selective exposure highlights the positive aspects of these attributes in general and in relation to particular outcomes. If this were true, the effect could be due to purely cognitive factors (cf. Nisbett & Ross, 1980).

---

[2] Only subjects with at least one match response and at least one no-match response were included in the within-subjects analyses in this and the following study.

This alternative explanation implies that people's tendency to enhance the positivity of the relation between their own attributes and particular outcomes should be independent of the extent to which they are personally concerned about these outcomes. If it could be shown that people with different attributes have different beliefs about the relations between these attributes and outcomes only if they care about these outcomes, this alternative interpretation would be rendered less plausible, and the view that such differential beliefs result from motivationally directed theory generation would be strengthened.

Study 2 replicated Study 1, but this time the outcome concerned success or failure in a professional school such as for law or medicine. In this domain, it was possible to identify people who had no motivational involvement with the outcomes, namely those students who did not plan to go on to professional school. Unlike motivationally driven subjects, these disinterested subjects were not expected to consider their own attributes to be more predictive of success than other attributes.

Method

Subjects were 138 University of Michigan undergraduates of both sexes enrolled in introductory psychology. They participated in groups of 4 to 6 subjects.

Subjects read a cover sheet explaining that the study was part of a research project concerning the actual and believed causes of success and failure in professional schools such as for law, medicine, and business. They next read that the researchers had collected information about the background factors of many University of Michigan graduates who had gone on to professional schools and that some of these were found to be related to how well the students had done in professional school, even when grade point averages and Scholastic Aptitude Test (SAT) scores were held constant. The study was supposed to examine whether people knew which factors were likely to facilitate success in professional school and which were likely to hinder it.

Subjects then read a description of a person said to be one of the actual participants in the original study. The description consisted of one of two opposite sets of attributes. Half the subjects read that the person (a) was Catholic, (b) was the youngest child in his or her family, (c) had a mother who was never employed outside the home, (d) had a distant relationship with his or her father, (e) had at least one serious relationship with a member of the opposite sex before entering college, and (f) was insecure. The other half of the subjects read that the person had an opposite set of attributes (Protestant,

oldest child, employed mother, close relationship with father, no early romantic relationship, secure). The person was said to be either male or female. This variable had no effect on the dependent measures and will not be discussed further. A third of the subjects read that the person had done very well in professional school, a third read that the person had done very poorly, and a third were given no information about how well the person did.

Subjects were next asked to indicate how each of the target person's attributes might have contributed to the person's performance in professional school, on a 9-point scale ranging from 1 (*made poor performance much more likely*) through 5 (*had no effect*) to 9 (*made excellent performance much more likely*). After responding to a series of unrelated questionnaires, subjects were asked to indicate their own standing on each of the background attributes.[3] Finally, subjects were asked to indicate, by checking *yes, no,* or *maybe,* whether they planned to attend a professional school after they graduated.

Results and Discussion

Table 31.2 shows that the pattern of responses given to individual items replicates Study 1: In 10 of the 12 possible comparisons, subjects who matched the target person on a given attribute rated that attribute as better for the target person's success in professional school than did subjects who did not match the target person on that attribute.[4]

The results of the multiple regression analyses performed on each item also replicated Study 1. Subjects' responses to each item were predicted from the target's attribute, the subject's attribute, and whether the subject matched the target on this attribute. As seen in Table 31.2, five of the six regression coefficients obtained for the match variable were positive, indicating that subjects who matched the target person on a given attribute viewed that attribute as better for success than did subjects who did not match the target person. Two of these positive coefficients were significant at the .05 level or lower. The only negative coefficient was not significant.

---

[3] Subjects' self-reported attitudes were not affected by the target's outcome. On average, the percentage of subjects indicating that they matched the target in the good-performance, poor-performance, and no-information conditions was 48, 46, and 47, respectively.

[4] Self-ratings for the last two items were obtained on 9-point scales. Subjects who placed themselves at the scale midpoints were excluded from the analyses for these items.

TABLE 31.2 Mean Rating of the Effect of Each Attribute on the Target Person's Success in Professional School Given by Subjects Who Did and Who Did Not Match the Target Person On These Attributes

Target's Attribute	Match	N	No Match	N	Coef[a]	t
Catholic	5.67	21	5.21	48		
Protestant	5.20	15	5.52	54	−.01	.02
Youngest child	5.58	31	4.84	38		
Oldest child	6.51	33	6.36	36	.36	2.09*
Nonemployed mother	5.74	34	4.76	33		
Employed mother	5.58	31	5.84	38	.17	1.13
Early relationship	5.51	47	5.50	22		
No early relationship	5.19	31	4.92	38	.07	.60
Insecure	4.38	13	3.89	44		
Secure	7.47	57	6.75	8	.29	1.10
Distant father	5.50	16	3.78	45		
Close father	6.62	42	6.00	14	.59	3.75**

Note: Ratings were made on a scale ranging from 1 (*made poor performance much more likely*) to 9 (*made excellent performance much more likely*).

[a] These are multiple regression coefficients obtained in the prediction of subjects' responses from whether or not they matched the target person.

* $p < .05$. ** $p < .001$.

As expected, the within-subjects analysis replicated Study 1 only for subjects who planned to attend professional school or who were considering the possibility, as seen in Figure 31.2. These subjects rated items on which they matched the target person as better for success in professional school than items on which they did not match the target person. Planned comparisons yielded $t(126) = 2.77$, $p < .01$, and $t(126) = 2.93$, $p < .01$, respectively, for subjects who answered the question about whether they planned to attend professional school with *yes* and *maybe*. No such difference was found for subjects who did not plan to attend professional school, $t(126) = .27$. A 2 (match) × 2 (plans) repeated measures analysis of variance (ANOVA) in which responses of subjects replying *yes* and *maybe* were combined yielded a significant interaction, $F(1, 127) = 3.89, p < .05$, in addition to a significant main effect for the match variable, $F(1, 127) = 5.12, p < .05$. Analysis of standardized scores yielded similar results.

As in Study 1, information about the target's performance in professional school did not interact with whether subjects matched the target ($p > .20$) but did

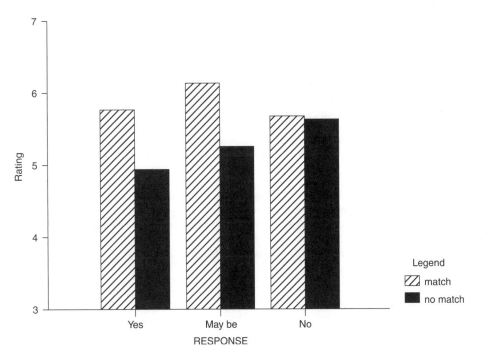

FIGURE 31.2 ■ Mean Ratings Given by Subjects Who Thought that They Would Definitely, Would Probably, and Would Not Attend Professional School of Attributes on which They Did and Did Not Match the Target person.

have a significant main effect on responses ($p < .001$). Attributes were judged as most conducive to success when the target was said to have done well (6.38), as least conducive to success when the target was said to have done poorly (4.71), and as intermediate when no information was given (5.51). This suggests once again that subjects were generating the theories on the spot.

These data suggest that people's tendency to view their own attributes as better than other attributes is probably due to motivational processes. It appears that people generate theories favoring their own attributes to reassure themselves that they will obtain desired goals or avoid feared outcomes by virtue of the goodness of their attributes. Thus the motivation to obtain success may lead people to search memory for world knowledge that could support theories in which their own attributes are viewed as conducive to success. People with different attributes will access different world knowledge and generate different theories about the causes and determinants of success. This differential generation of theories seems closely tied in with concern about one's own likelihood of obtaining motivationally loaded outcomes because when people do not care about the outcome in question, they do not bother to generate theories favoring their own attributes.

The data do not, however, completely rule out the possibility that these biases are due to entirely cognitive processes. It is possible, for example, that in comparison with people who are not concerned with a given outcome, people who are concerned with this outcome possess far more elaborate cognitive structures relevant to this outcome and that information contained in these structures is biased toward a favorable view of the causal consequences of their own attributes. Of course, one wonders whether the differential formation of such structures would not itself require motivationally guided inferential processes. Nevertheless, more conclusive arguments for the role of motivation in theory generation await research in which different theories are generated under different motivational conditions by the same subjects or by subjects randomly assigned to conditions and therefore assumed to possess similar knowledge structures.

Self-Serving Evidence Evaluation

So far, it has been suggested that optimistic beliefs may be maintained through self-serving theory generation. The following section focuses on whether optimistic beliefs may also be maintained through self-serving

biases in the evaluation of evidence coming from an external source. Do people judge, evaluate, and believe scientific theories differentially, depending on the theories' implications for the self? And if they do, are these processes driven by motivational forces?

Study 3: Caffeine Consumption and the Evaluation of Evidence About Negative Effects of Caffeine

Study 3 examines whether people evaluate scientific evidence in a self-serving manner. Are people less likely to believe evidence linking an attribute to a negative outcome if they possess this dangerous attribute? Although other researchers have addressed similar questions (e.g., Kassarjian & Cohen, 1965; Pyszczynski & Greenberg, in press), there has been little attempt to examine biased evidence evaluation while attempting to rule out the possibility that the biases are produced entirely by prior beliefs (cf. Nisbett & Ross, 1980).

Subjects read an article about the negative effects of caffeine consumption on health. Heavy caffeine drinkers were expected to be less willing to believe the article than were people who did not consume much caffeine, because only the former would be personally threatened if the article were true. However, such results could be due to different prior beliefs about caffeine and its effects held by people who did and did not consume caffeine rather than to motivationally directed differential processing of evidence. In order to rule out this possibility, the negative effects were said to be specific to women. This allowed male subjects to serve as controls. Presumably, male and female heavy caffeine drinkers hold the same prior beliefs about caffeine, but only women should be motivated to disbelieve the evidence presented in this study because only they are personally threatened by it. Consequently, if the reduced willingness of caffeine drinkers to believe the article's contents is specific to women, it is probably due to motivational processes and not to prior beliefs.

Method
Subjects were 112 female and 104 male University of Michigan undergraduates enrolled in introductory psychology. Subjects who indicated that they had heard about the disease discussed in the study were eliminated from the analyses, leaving a total of 75 women and 86 men (the pattern of results remained identical when the other subjects were included in the analyses).

The study was presented as concerned with people's memory, opinions, and beliefs. Subjects read an article said to be adapted from the science section of *The New York Times* (in fact, the bulk of the article was adapted from a medical journal article, though the results were later disputed by other researchers). The article said that a recent review of research about the negative effects of caffeine consumption suggested that women were endangered by caffeine and were strongly advised to avoid caffeine in any form. The major risk for women was said to be fibrocystic disease, reportedly associated with often painful lumps in the breast that could go unnoticed in the early stages but that grew progressively worse with age. The disease was said to be serious because it was associated in its advanced stages with breast cancer. Women who regularly drank three or more cups of caffeine a day for a period of one year or longer were said to be at serious risk of contracting the disease. The article stated that caffeine induced the disease by increasing the concentration of a substance called cAMP in the breast, and this concentration was higher than normal in women with fibrocystic disease and still higher in women with breast cancer.

The article then said that the damage caused by caffeine was either reversible (by eliminating caffeine from the diet) or irreversible. This variable had no significant effects on the dependent measures and will not be discussed further.

When subjects finished reading the article, they handed it back to the experimenter and were given a questionnaire concerning their recall of different portions of the article. These questions served to ascertain that subjects understood the connection between caffeine consumption and fibrocystic disease. The key dependent measures were embedded among these questions. Subjects were asked to assess the probability that within the next 15 years they would develop fibrocystic disease. After they were asked about the nature of these connections, they were asked to indicate how convinced they were of the connection between caffeine and fibrocystic disease and of the connection between caffeine and the dangerous substance cAMP on a 6-point scale ranging from 1 (*not at all convinced*) to 6 (*extremely convinced*).

Finally, subjects were asked whether they had heard before about fibrocystic disease. Subjects who indicated that they had were eliminated from the analyses. At the very end, subjects were asked to indicate their own level of caffeine consumption by checking *heavy, moderate, low*, or *no consumption*.

Following the study, subjects were fully debriefed, and the controversial nature of the study was explained to them.

TABLE 31.3 Mean Estimates Given by Male and Female Heavy and Low Caffeine Consumers for the Likelihood That They Would Develop Fibrocystic Disease

Sex	Caffeine consumption	
	Heavy	Low
Female		
M	39%	11%
n	43	32
Male		
M	7%	2%
n	32	54

Results and Discussion

Responses of subjects indicating that they consumed heavy or moderate amounts of caffeine were grouped together, as were responses of subjects who indicated that they consumed low or no amounts of caffeine. These two groups will be referred to as heavy and low caffeine consumers, respectively.

As seen in Table 31.3, female heavy caffeine consumers thought that they were more likely to develop the caffeine-related disease than did female low consumers, suggesting that they were responsive to the threatening evidence. The comparable effect for men, who were not threatened by the evidence, was considerably smaller. The Sex × Caffeine Consumption interaction was highly significant, $F(1, 157) = 18.21$, $p < .0001$.

Despite this responsiveness of female heavy consumers to the evidence, Figure 31.3 shows that these women were not as convinced by the evidence as were female low consumers. Planned comparisons yielded $t(155) = 2.31$, $p < .05$, and $t(153) = 1.92$, $p < .05$, respectively, for the connection between caffeine and fibrocystic disease and the connection between caffeine and the dangerous substance cAMP. As expected, no such effects were found for men, most of whom realized that they were not personally threatened by the research even if they were heavy caffeine consumers (both $ps > .50$). The Sex × Caffeine Consumption interactions were marginal for both variables, $F(1, 155) = 3.62$, $p < .10$, and $F(1, 153) = 2.40$, $p = .12$.

Thus it appears that those subjects who stood to suffer personal implications if the evidence were true were more likely to doubt its truth. Perhaps the motivation to maintain an optimistic view of their future health led these subjects to access those inferential rules and background beliefs that would allow them to reduce the

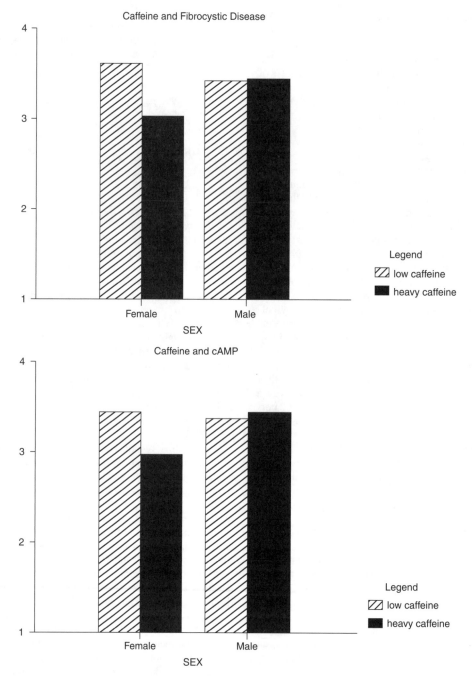

FIGURE 31.3 ■ Study 3: Mean Responses Given by Female and Male Heavy and Low Caffeine Consumers to Questions About the Extent to which They were Convinced by Information About the Negative Effects of Caffeine.

credibility of the threatening research. However, the data do not allow for direct examination of these mediating processes.

Study 4: Reducing Motivational Pressures to Doubt Undesired Evidence

Study 3 showed that people who are personally threatened by negative evidence do not totally ignore this evidence, but they are not as convinced by it as are disinterested people. The reluctance of female heavy caffeine consumers to be convinced by the threatening evidence is probably due to motivational processes designed to preserve optimism about their future health rather than to different prior beliefs about the effects of caffeine. This is because male heavy caffeine consumers, who presumably hold the same prior beliefs about caffeine held by female heavy caffeine consumers but for whom no motivational pressure to disbelieve the evidence existed, did not show the same reluctance to be convinced by the evidence.

Still, a staunch critic of motivational processes might argue, female heavy caffeine consumers might hold different prior beliefs about caffeine than do male heavy caffeine consumers, and the results may be due to these differences in prior beliefs. If this were true, there should be similar differences in subjects' readiness to be convinced by the evidence even when the motivational pressures were greatly reduced. On the other hand, if the differences found are due to motivation, reducing the motivational pressures should reduce or eliminate the effect (cf. Miller, 1976). Study 4 addresses this issue.

Motivational pressures to disbelieve the article were reduced by making the negative implications of caffeine consumption seem much milder. The article stated that the disease said to be facilitated by caffeine was extremely common, so much so that doctors felt that it shouldn't even be considered a disease; more than 65% of women were said to suffer from it. The design was identical in all other respects to that used in Study 3.

Results and Discussion

As seen in Table 31.4, subjects' beliefs about their likelihood of developing the caffeine-related disease replicated Study 3. Female heavy caffeine consumers thought that they were considerably more likely to develop the disease than did female low caffeine consumers, whereas the comparable effect for men was considerably smaller. The Sex × Caffeine Consumption interaction was highly significant, $F(1, 59) = 7.42, p < .01$.

TABLE 31.4 Mean Estimates Given by Male and Female Heavy and Low Caffeine Consumers for the Likelihood That They Would Develop Fibrocystic Disease

	Caffeine Consumption	
Sex	Heavy	Low
Female		
M	46%	15%
n	16	16
Male		
M	6%	1%
n	18	13

Unlike in Study 3, female heavy consumers were no less convinced by the evidence than were female low consumers. As seen in Figure 31.4, the slight differences between the groups were actually in the opposite direction, but these differences did not approach significance on either measure (both ps > .50). Sex × Caffeine Consumption ANOVAS yielded no significant effects for either variable.

Thus when motivational pressures to disbelieve evidence are reduced, subjects who are personally threatened are less likely to disbelieve it. These data suggest that the reluctance of threatened subjects to believe the evidence presented in Study 3, where the motivational pressures were greater, was due to these motivational pressures. If it were due to different prior beliefs, it should have been found in Study 4 also because the relevant prior beliefs here should not differ in any significant way from those in Study 3.

Taken together, these studies suggest that people do engage in motivationally directed inferential processes, but only when the levels of motivation are high. Even when motivation is high, they do not completely ignore negative evidence; they are responsive to it, but not as responsive as they might have been in the absence of motivational involvement.

General Discussion

These studies suggest that people tend to generate and evaluate causal theories in a self-serving manner; they spontaneously generate theories that view their own attributes as more predictive of desirable outcomes and are reluctant to believe in theories that imply that their own attributes might be related to undesirable events. As a consequence, people tend to hold theories that are consistent with the optimistic belief that good things will

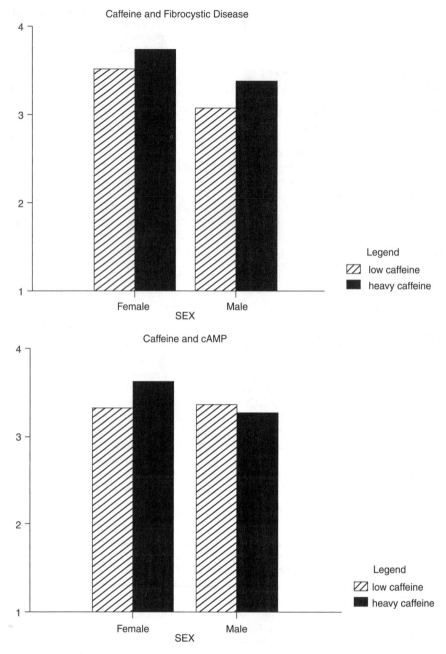

FIGURE 31.4 ■ Study 4: Mean Responses Given by Female and Male Heavy and Low Caffeine Consumers to Questions About the Extent to which They Were Convinced by Information About the Negative Effects of Caffeine.

happen to them and bad things will not. These self-serving tendencies seem to be explained best as resulting from cognitive processes guided by motivational ends.

It is clear that motivational forces do not completely blind people to undesirable evidence or information. When generating causal theories to explain other people's life outcomes, people often do acknowledge that their own attributes might be related to undesirable outcomes. For example, subjects who had no early romantic relationships seemed to believe that this attribute was likely to be causally related to divorce (but they didn't believe the link to be as strong as did subjects who had early romantic relationships). Similarly, heavy caffeine consumers who read that caffeine consumption could lead to a disease thought they were more likely to suffer this disease than did low caffeine consumers. Thus, motivational forces could lead people to play down negative information but not to ignore it.

It is also clear, however, that it is difficult to account for people's optimistic beliefs without assuming some motivational biases. People's tendency to generate self-serving theories linking their attributes to desirable outcomes does not seem to be due to purely cognitive mechanisms, because this tendency was found only for people who cared about the outcomes. Only those subjects who considered attending professional school believed that their attributes were more likely than other attributes to be related to success in professional school. These findings do not, however, completely rule out an entirely cognitive interpretation, because they could also be explained in terms of preconceptions if one assumes that people who are concerned with an outcome also possess elaborate and biased cognitive structures related to this outcome.

The data supporting self-serving biases in the evaluation of evidence provide stronger support for the notion of motivationally driven processes and do not appear to lend themselves easily to alternative cognitive explanations based on prior beliefs. The results showed that people threatened by undesirable evidence were reluctant to believe this evidence, but only when its implications were perceived as serious. Thus female heavy caffeine consumers were less likely than female low consumers to be convinced by evidence indicating that caffeine consumption leads to disease in women, but only when the disease appeared serious. This effect was not due to differential prior beliefs held by heavy and low caffeine consumers because the effect was not found for male heavy caffeine consumers, who presumably possess the same prior beliefs about caffeine as do female heavy caffeine consumers but who were not

personally threatened by the evidence in question. Furthermore, the effect was not found for female caffeine consumers when the implications of caffeine consumption were made to appear less serious, even though these women clearly held the same prior conceptions about caffeine as did their counterparts who believed the implications to be more serious.

Taken together, these two sets of studies suggest that people generate and evaluate causal theories in a self-serving manner only when they are motivated to do so. Such self-serving biases in inference may result from the influence of motivational forces on the choice of inferential procedures used in the generation and evaluation of evidence. People do rely on evidence when formulating their beliefs and do so in a seemingly rational way, but the evidence itself and the inferential rules used to evaluate it are tainted by self-protective motivational forces. Thus, the motivation to view oneself as likely to obtain desirable outcomes and avoid feared outcomes can trigger a memory search that is likely to activate information capable of supporting theories that view one's own attributes as conducive to obtaining the desirable outcome as well as inferential rules that could refute threatening evidence and validate reassuring evidence.

This view of motivation as guiding inference by influencing the search through memory for knowledge structures suggests a new way of investigating motivational biases. Rather than concentrating on the outcomes of such biases, that is, the biased conclusions people arrive at, it might be more fruitful to concentrate on investigating the underlying mechanisms responsible for these biases, that is, the biased activation and use of memories and rules (cf. Tetlock & Levi, 1982). Once these mechanisms are better understood, it should be possible to accumulate a body of literature capable of withstanding the cognitive critique that has shed doubt on the role of motivation in producing the self-serving biases documented to date.

References

Anderson, C. A. (1983). Abstract and concrete data in the perseverance of social theories: When weak data lead to unshakable beliefs. *Journal of Experimental Social Psychology, 19*, 93–108.

Anderson, C. A., Lepper, M. R., & Ross, L. (1980). Perseverance of social theories: The role of explanation in the persistence of discredited information. *Journal of Personality and Social Psychology, 39*, 1037–1049.

Anderson, C. A., New, B. L., & Speer, J. R. (1985). Argument availability as a mediator of social theory perseverance. *Social Cognition, 3*, 235–249.

Anderson, C. A., & Sechler, E. S. (1986). Effects of explanation and counterexplanation on the development and use of statistical theories. *Journal of Personality and Social Psychology, 50*, 24–34.

Anderson, C. A., & Slusher, M. P. (1986). Relocating motivational effects: A synthesis of cognitive and motivational effects. *Social Cognition, 4*, 270–292.

Darley, J. M., & Gross, P. H. (1983). A hypothesis-confirming bias in labeling effects. *Journal of Personality and Social Psychology, 44*, 20–33.

Erdelyi, M. H. (1974). A new look at the new look: Perceptual defense and vigilance. *Psychological Review, 81*, 1–25.

Fazio, R. H., Effrein, E. A., & Falender, V. F. (1981). Self-perceptions following social interaction. *Journal of Personality and Social Psychology, 41*, 232–242.

Festinger, L. (1957). *A theory of cognitive dissonance.* Stanford, CA: Stanford University Press.

Fischhoff, B. (1975). Hindsight does not equal foresight: The effects of outcome knowledge on judgment under uncertainty. *Journal of Experimental Psychology: Human Perception and Performance, 1*, 288–299.

Greenwald, A. G. (1980). The totalitarian ego: Fabrication and revision of personal history. *American Psychologist, 35*, 603–618.

Greenwald, A. G. (1981). Self and memory. In G. H. Bower (Ed.), *The psychology of learning and motivation* (pp. 201–236). New York: Academic Press.

Greenwald, A. G., & Pratkanis, A. R. (1984). The self. In R. S. Wyer & T. K. Srull (Eds.), *Handbook of social cognition* (pp. 129–178). Hillsdale, NJ: Erlbaum.

Higgins, E. T., & King, G. A. (1981). Accessibility of social constructs: Information-processing consequences of individual and contextual variability. In N. Cantor & J. F. Kihlstrom (Eds.), *Personality, cognition, and social interaction* (pp. 69–121). Hillsdale, NJ: Erlbaum.

Higgins, E. T., King, G. A., & Mavin, G. H. (1982). Individual construct accessibility and subjective impressions in recall. *Journal of Personality and Social Psychology, 73*, 35–47.

Irwin, F. W. (1953). Stated expectations as functions of probability and desirability of outcomes. *Journal of Personality, 21*, 329–335.

Kassarjian, H. H., & Cohen, J. B. (1965). Cognitive dissonance and consumer behavior. *California Management Review, 8*, 55–64.

Koriat, A., Lichtenstein, S., & Fischhoff, B. (1980). Reasons for confidence. *Journal of Experimental Psychology: Human Learning and Memory, 6*, 107–118.

Kruglanski, A. W., & Freund, T. (1983). The freezing and unfreezing of lay inference: Effects on impressional primacy, ethnic stereotyping, and numerical anchoring. *Journal of Experimental Social Psychology, 19*, 448–468.

Kunda, Z. (1985). *Motivation and inference: Self-serving generation and evaluation of causal theories.* Unpublished doctoral dissertation, University of Michigan, Ann Arbor.

Kunda, Z. (1986). *Generating theories from single instances.* Unpublished manuscript, Princeton University, Princeton, NJ.

Kunda, Z., & Nisbett, R. E. (1986). The psychometrics of everyday life. *Cognitive Psychology, 18*, 195–224.

Lehman, D., & Nisbett, R. E. (1985). *Effects of higher education on inductive reasoning.* Unpublished manuscript, University of Michigan, Ann Arbor.

Lerner, M. J. (1980). *The belief in a just world: A fundamental delusion.* New York: Plenum Press.

Lord, C. G., Ross, L., & Lepper, M. R. (1979). Biased assimilation and attitude polarization: The effects of prior theories on subsequently considered evidence. *Journal of Personality and Social Psychology, 37*, 2098–2109.

Marks, R. W. (1951). The effects of probability, desirability, and "privilege" on the stated expectations of children. *Journal of Personality, 19*, 332–351.

Markus, H., & Kunda, Z. (1986). Stability and malleability of the selfconcept. *Journal of Personality and Social Psychology, 51*, 858–866.

Miller, D. T. (1976). Ego involvement and attributions for success and failure. *Journal of Personality and Social Psychology, 34*, 901–906.

Miller, D. T., & Ross, M. (1975). Self-serving biases in attribution of causality: Fact or fiction? *Psychological Bulletin, 82*, 213–225.

Nisbett, R. E., Krantz, D. H., Jepson, C., & Kunda, Z. (1983). The use of statistical heuristics in everyday inductive reasoning. *Psychological Review, 90*, 339–363.

Nisbett, R. E., & Ross, L. (1980). *Human inference: Strategies and shortcomings of social judgement.* Englewood Cliffs, NJ: Prentice-Hall.

Parducci, A. (1968). The relativism of absolute judgments. *Scientific American, 219*, 890.

Perloff, L. S. (1983). Perceptions of vulnerability to victimization. *Journal of Social Issues, 39*, 41–61.

Pruitt, D. G., & Hoge, R. D. (1965). Strength of the relationship between the value of an event and its subjective probability as a function of method of measurement. *Journal of Experimental Psychology, 69*, 483–489.

Pyszczynski, T., & Greenberg, J. (in press). A biased hypothesis testing approach to motivated attribution distortion. In L. Berkowitz (Ed.), *Advances in experimental social psychology.* New York: Academic Press.

Pyszczynski, T., Greenberg, J., & LaPrelle, J. (1985). Social comparison after success & failure: Biased search for information consistent with a self-serving conclusion. *Journal of Experimental Social Psychology, 21*, 195–211.

Ross, M., & Fletcher, G. J. O. (1985). Attribution and social perception. In G. Lindzey & E. Aronson (Eds.), *Handbook of social psychology* (pp. 73–122). New York: Random House.

Salancik, G. R., & Conway, M. (1975). Attitude inference from salient and relevant cognitive content about behavior. *Journal of Personality and Social Psychology, 32*, 829–840.

Snyder, M. (1982). When believing means doing: Creating links between attitudes and behavior. In M. P. Zanna, E. T. Higgins, & C. P. Herman (Eds.), *Consistency in social behavior: The Ontario Symposium* (Vol. 2, pp. 105–130). Hillsdale, NJ: Erlbaum.

Srull, T. K., & Wyer, R. S. (1986). The role of chronic and temporary goals in social information processing. In R. M. Sorrentino & E. T. Higgins (Eds.), *Handbook of motivation and cognition* (pp. 503–549). New York: Guilford Press.

Taylor, S. E. (1983). Adjustment to threatening events: A theory of cognitive adaptation. *American Psychologist, 38*, 1161–1173.

Tesser, A., & Campbell, J. (1983). Self-definition and self-evaluation maintenance. In J. Suls & A. Greenwald (Eds.), *Social psychological perspectives on the self* (Vol. 2, pp. 1–31). Hillsdale, NJ: Erlbaum.

Tetlock, P. E., & Levi, A. (1982). Attribution bias: On the inconclusiveness of the cognition-motivation debate. *Journal of Experimental Social Psychology, 18*, 68–88.

Weinstein, N. D. (1980). Unrealistic optimism about future life events. *Journal of Personality and Social Psychology, 39*, 806–820.

Weinstein, N. D. (1983). Reducing unrealistic optimism about illness susceptibility. *Health Psychology, 2*, 11–20.

Weinstein, N. D. (1984). Why it won't happen to me: Perceptions of risk factors and susceptibility. *Health Psychology, 3*, 431–457.

Wicklund, R. A., & Brehm, J. W. (1976). *Perspectives on cognitive dissonance*. Hillsdale, NJ: Erlbaum.

Zanna, M. P., & Cooper, J. (1976). Dissonance and the attribution process. In J. H. Harvey, W. J. Ickes, & R. F. Kidd (Eds.), *New directions in attribution research* (Vol. 1, pp. 199–217). Hillsdale, NJ: Erlbaum.

Zuckerman, M. (1979). Attribution of success and failure revisited, or: The motivational bias is alive and well in attribution theory. *Journal of Personality, 47*, 245–287.

Received July 17, 1986
Revision received March 12, 1987
Accepted March 27, 1987 ■

Motivated Skepticism: Use of Differential Decision Criteria for Preferred and Nonpreferred Conclusions

Peter H. Ditto and David F. Lopez

Three experiments show that information consistent with a preferred conclusion is examined less critically than information inconsistent with a preferred conclusion, and consequently, less information is required to reach the former than the latter. In Study 1, Ss judged which of 2 students was most intelligent, believing they would work closely with the 1 they chose. Ss required less information to decide that a dislikable student was less intelligent than that he was more intelligent. In Studies 2 and 3, Ss given an unfavorable medical test result took longer to decide their test result was complete, were more likely to retest the validity of their result, cited more life irregularities that might have affected test accuracy, and rated test accuracy as lower than did Ss receiving more favorable diagnoses. Results suggest that a core component of self-serving bias is the differential quantity of cognitive processing given to preference-consistent and preference-inconsistent information.

In her book *On Death and Dying*, Elisabeth Kubler-Ross (1969) described the initial reaction of a patient on being informed of her terminal illness (p. 38). The patient reacts first by considering the possibility that her

The results of Study 1 were presented at the 1991 Annual Convention of the American Psychological Society, Washington, DC. The results of Studies 2 and 3 were presented at the 1991 Annual Convention of the Midwestern Psychological Association, Chicago. This research was supported by funds supplied by the Applied Psychology Center at Kent State University.

We thank the many undergraduate research assistants who served as experimenters and coders for the studies reported here: Angela Battaglia, Bob Boughman, Mike Hovancek, Sunny Metzger, Scott Nevel, Scott Norris, Debbie Owens, Tony Ryland, Lisa Siciliano, Tim Strach, and Patrick Wise. We also thank James Hilton, Charlie Perdue, Bill von Hippel, Allen Townsend, and three anonymous reviewers for their helpful comments on earlier versions of this article.

Correspondence concerning this article should be addressed to Peter H. Ditto, Department of Psychology, Kent State University, Kent, Ohio 44242–0001.

X-rays were "mixed-up" with those of another patient. When that explanation cannot be confirmed, the patient leaves the hospital and seeks out a succession of new physicians in hopes of receiving a "better explanation" for her medical condition.

The image of denial portrayed in this anecdote is quite consistent with the more general view of motivated reasoning presented in this article. When confronted with threatening or otherwise objectionable information, a search for more palatable alternative explanations often ensues. It seems only natural, for example, that an individual faced with an unfavorable medical diagnosis would actively search for more benign interpretations of this unwelcome news. Because this search is likely to be at least partially "successful" — plausible alternative interpretations can be generated for virtually any piece of data — additional medical opinions are likely to be required before the individual is willing to accept the validity of the unfavorable diagnosis.

Contrast this image with that of an individual receiving a favorable medical diagnosis. Misassigned X-rays and misdiagnoses are equally plausible alternative explanations for both favorable and unfavorable medical forecasts. Yet, an individual given a favorable report seems unlikely to even consider the possibility that such factors might account for their diagnosis. Rather, favorable information seems much more likely to be accepted at face value without need for further corroboration. Several doctors may be required to provide convincing proof of illness, but one is generally enough to provide convincing proof of health.

This article examines the notion that people are less skeptical consumers of desirable than undesirable information. Three experiments are reported that examine the hypothesis that information consistent with a preferred judgment conclusion is examined less critically than information inconsistent with a preferred conclusion, and consequently, less information is required to reach a preference-consistent conclusion than a preference-inconsistent one. More generally, our goal in this article is to integrate research on the selective nature of cognitive resource allocation with that on the historically problematic issue of motivational biases in judgment by suggesting that one central way that motivational factors affect judgments is through their tendency to affect how critically people examine information that they do and do not wish to receive.

The Problem of Motivated Reasoning

The intuition that hopes, wishes, apprehensions, and fears affect judgments is compelling and persistent. Turning this intuition into a viable empirical and theoretical fact, however, has proved to be one of the most recalcitrant problems in the history of experimental psychology (Erdelyi, 1974; Miller & Ross, 1975).

Yet, after reaching its nadir with the publication of Tetlock and Levi's (1982) essay on the intractability of distinguishing "cognitive" and motivational explanations for self-serving attribution biases, progress in conceptualizing the role of motivational factors in judgment processes has resurged (Higgins & Sorrentino, 1990; Sorrentino & Higgins, 1986). At the empirical level, a variety of methodological strategies have been used to support the motivated nature of self-serving judgments either by documenting the mediational role of arousal (Brown & Rogers, 1991; Gollwitzer, Earle, & Stephan, 1982; Stephan & Gollwitzer, 1981) or by using one of a number of techniques of manipulating the motivational significance of information while holding potentially confounding informational differences constant (Ditto, Jemmott, & Darley, 1988; Holton & Pyszczynski, 1989; Kunda, 1987; Liberman & Chaiken, in press).

At the theoretical level, several researchers have responded to Tetlock and Levi's (1982) call for greater specificity in the conceptualization of the mechanisms underlying motivational bias (Kruglanski, 1980, 1990; Kunda, 1987, 1990; Pyszczynski & Greenberg, 1987). The goal of these researchers is to move beyond the simple assertion that motivations affect judgments and to attempt to identify the specific point or points at which motivational processes enter into, and how exactly they perturb, the generic information-processing sequence. A recent review of the motivated-bias literature (Kunda, 1990), however, reveals considerably more empirical support for the proposition *that* motivational factors affect judgments than direct evidence for exactly *how* this process occurs (Liberman & Chaiken, in press).

Within the motivated-judgment literature, the empirical finding that has received the greatest amount of attention and controversy in recent years is the robust tendency of individuals to perceive information that is consistent with a preferred judgment conclusion (preference-consistent information) as more valid than information that is inconsistent with that conclusion (preference-inconsistent information). Thus, whether the information concerns one's intelligence (Wyer & Frey, 1983), social sensitivity (Pyszczynski, Greenberg, & Holt, 1985), professional competence (Beckman, 1973), or vulnerability to future illness (Ditto et al., 1988; Kunda, 1987), preference-consistent feedback (e.g., information suggesting high intelligence or low vulnerability to illness) is perceived as valid, accurate, and internally caused, whereas preference-inconsistent feedback (e.g., information suggesting low intelligence or high vulnerability to illness) is perceived as less valid, less accurate, and more likely to be externally explainable.

This is not to say, however, that individuals never acknowledge the validity of preference-inconsistent information. Albert perhaps reluctantly, most people accept a variety of negative beliefs about themselves (Markus & Wurf, 1987) and even among individuals confronted with diagnoses of cancer, profound denial reactions are clearly the exception rather than the rule (Aitken-Swan & Easson, 1959; Gilbertson & Wangensteen, 1962). As originally noted by both Heider (1958) and Festinger (1957), the "rational" aspects of "rationalization" cannot be ignored. Judgments seem best characterized as a compromise between the wish to reach a particular conclusion and the plausibility of that conclusion given the available data (Heider, 1958; Kunda, 1990; Pyszczynski & Greenberg, 1987). Any analysis of motivated information processing, therefore, must account for both differential perceptions of the validity of preference-consistent and preference-inconsistent information and the ultimate responsiveness of individuals to preference-inconsistent conclusions.

A Quantity of Processing View of Motivated Reasoning

One deceptively simple explanation that can account for both aspects of this delicate balance is that information consistent with a preferred conclusion is subjected to a less extensive and less critical cognitive analysis than is information inconsistent with that conclusion.

A central theme underlying the past 2 decades of social cognition research is that individuals think more deeply about information in some situations than in others. Emerging out of mid-1970s research documenting the of time "mindless" nature of human action (e.g., Langer, 1978; Tversky & Kahneman, 1974), the notion that individuals selectively allocate their cognitive resources has become a central tenet of major theoretical treatments of persuasion (Chaiken, 1987; Petty & Cacioppo, 1986) and social judgment (Bargh, 1984; Chaiken, Liberman, & Eagly, 1989; Fiske & Neuberg, 1990). Research both within and outside these theoretical frameworks has documented a host of situational factors that seem to affect the degree to which incoming information is subjected to effortful cognitive analysis, including the personal relevance of the information (e.g., Borgida & Howard-Pitney, 1983; Petty, Cacioppo, & Goldman, 1981), the extent to which individuals must justify their conclusions to others (e.g., Tetlock, 1983, 1985), and the consistency of the incoming information with prior expectations (e.g., Hilton, Klein, & von Hippel, 1991; Pyszczynski & Greenberg, 1981).

More specific to the current point, the evaluative implications of incoming information have also been shown to affect how extensively that information is processed. A diverse body of research suggests that negative social information is more likely than positive social information to trigger cognitive analysis. Within the attributional framework, for example, research on "spontaneous" causal reasoning has shown that individuals report more attributional thought in response to failure feedback than success feedback (e.g., Wong &

Weiner, 1981). This tendency has been shown to be independent of subjects' expectations for receiving the different types of feedback (Bohner, Bless, Schwarz, & Strack, 1988).

Using a very different methodological approach, Pratto and John (1991) found longer color-naming latencies in a Stroop (1935) color-interference paradigm when subjects named the color of desirable trait words. Pratto and John argued that attentional resources are automatically directed toward negative social information, probably the result of the adaptive significance of monitoring undesirable outcomes.

Assuming that preference-consistent information induces a more positive affective response than preference-inconsistent information, research on the effects of mood on information processing provides additional support. Schwarz (1991) reviewed a variety of studies in the areas of decision making, problem solving, and persuasion showing that experimentally induced negative affect initiates effortful, detailed-oriented cognitive analysis, whereas positive affect is associated with less effortful, heuristic-based analysis (e.g., Bless, Bohner, Schwarz, & Strack, 1990; Isen, 1984; Mackie & Worth, 1989; Worth & Mackie, 1987). Naturally occurring negative affect (i.e., depression) has similarly been shown to result in relatively vigorous analytical and information-seeking strategies (Marsh & Weary, 1989).

The notion that preference-consistent and preference-inconsistent information may receive differential amounts of processing is also consistent with recent theoretical models of motivated judgment. Kruglanski (1980, 1990) argued that because the information-processing sequence has no natural termination point, motivations (or what he refers to as *epistemic goals*) can affect judgment outcomes by delaying or hastening the "freezing" of the epistemic search. More specific to the current point, he suggested that the desire to reach a particular judgment conclusion (i.e., the need for specific closure) results in individuals engaging in a more extensive search for alternative explanations (i.e., delayed freezing) when incoming information is inconsistent with the desired conclusion than when it is consistent with the conclusion.

The same assymetry is implicit in Psyzczynski and Greenberg's (1987) biased hypothesis-testing model of motivated inference. Psyzczynski and Greenberg (1987) argued that when individuals encounter information with unfavorable implications for the self, they are more likely to generate multiple hypotheses for testing, engage in a more extensive search for mitigating information, and devote greater processing capacity to evaluating relevant evidence than when confronted with information that is more palatable to the self.

An eclectic body of theory and research, therefore, supports the conclusion that information consistent with a preferred judgment conclusion is less likely to initiate intensive cognitive analysis than is information inconsistent with that conclusion. This assymetrical quantity of processing should, in turn, lead individuals to be less critical consumers of the former than of the latter. Because preference-consistent information is relatively unlikely to initiate causal thinking, alternative explanations for the information are unlikely to be considered. Consequently, the validity of preference-consistent information should tend to be rather uncritically accepted. The negative affect generated by information perceived to be preference inconsistent, on the other hand, should be more likely to initiate an effortful correction process (Gilbert, Pelham, & Krull, 1988; Quatrone, 1982) in which the initial characterization is adjusted to take into account additional factors that may plausibly be considered to explain the outcome. Assuming that more extensive analysis is likely to reveal multiple plausible explanations for virtually any piece of data (Kruglanski, 1990), preference-inconsistent information is more likely than preference-consistent information to be perceived of as "confounded" (i.e., explainable in more than one way) and its validity perceived to be less certain.

This analysis does not suggest, however, that individuals will never acknowledge the validity of preference-inconsistent information. In sharp contrast to a defensive inattention conceptualization of motivated information processing, the current perspective suggests that individuals are quite attentive to preference-inconsistent information, and if confronted with information of sufficient quantity or clarity, should eventually acquiesce to a preference-inconsistent conclusion. Rather than leading individuals to believe whatever they prefer to believe, the differential quantity of processing initiated by preference-consistent and preference-inconsistent information should bias judgments more subtly by affecting the amount of information required to reach valenced conclusions.

Stated another way, people may be said to use differential decision criteria for preference-consistent and preference-inconsistent conclusions. Because individuals are relatively unlikely to consider alternative explanations for preference-consistent information, relatively little information (or information of relatively poor quality) should be required for people to arrive at a preference-consistent conclusion. In contrast, individuals

should approach preference-inconsistent information more skeptically. Because any given piece of preference-inconsistent information is more likely to be perceived of as confounded, it should require somewhat more information (or information of relatively high quality) to reach a preference-inconsistent conclusion.

From this perspective, the differential perceptions of the validity of preference-consistent and preference-inconsistent information occurs because of the stricter criteria applied to the latter. Within the self-serving attributional bias paradigm, for example, there seems little doubt that if experimenters persisted in presenting failure feedback, subjects would eventually relent to an internal attribution for their poor performance. The differential attributions of success- and failure-feedback subjects for a single test result, in the current view, simply reflect the more skeptical stance taken (i.e., the stricter decision criterion used) by subjects presented with information inconsistent with their preferred conclusion. Once again, one test result may be enough information for an individual to accept a preferred conclusion but may not be enough to convince an individual of the validity of a nonpreferred one.

No research has examined the prediction that less information is required to reach a preference-consistent conclusion than a preference-inconsistent one. Because virtually all research on motivational bias is interested in differential judgment as its primary dependent measure, experimental designs are used in which the amount of information presented to subjects is held constant and differences in judgments are measured. To obtain a direct measure of the amount of information required to reach preferred and nonpreferred conclusions, however, the opposite approach needs to be taken. In Study 1 therefore, an attempt is made to "hold the judgment constant" and measure the amount of information required to make that judgment. Consistent with the proposed analysis, it is predicted that subjects will use differential decision criteria for preferred and nonpreferred judgment conclusions. That is, subjects presented with preference-consistent information should require less information to reach a preferred conclusion than subjects presented with preference-inconsistent information should to reach a nonpreferred one.

Study 1

The goal of Study 1 was to confront some subjects with a judgment situation in which they had a clear preference for one conclusion over another, present them with information that was either consistent or inconsistent with their preferred conclusion, and then obtain some measure of the amount of information needed to arrive at the preference-consistent or preference-inconsistent conclusion, respectively. To do this in a way that effectively ruled out alternative explanations based on differential information available to different groups of subjects, we chose to examine our hypotheses within the context of an interpersonal judgment (e.g., Holton & Pyszczynski, 1989). Interpersonal judgments are particularly useful in ruling out information-based counter explanations for motivational effects for the simple reason that it is much easier to control what subjects know about a fictitious stimulus person than it is to control what they know about themselves.

Method

Subjects
Subjects were 67 female undergraduates from general psychology courses at Kent State University who participated for course credit. One subject was excluded for failure to understand the experimental instructions. Another 6 subjects were excluded for failing to meet an additional inclusion criterion (discussed later), leaving a total of 60 subjects, 15 in each of four experimental conditions.

College Admissions Cover Story
On arriving at the laboratory room, subjects had their photograph taken and were then given 10 min to complete an 18-question analogy test. An experimenter explained that the picture and test were for another part of the study that subjects would be told more about in a few minutes.

When subjects had completed the analogy test, it was explained that the present study would consist of two tasks designed to mirror a college admissions decision. First, subjects would be presented with information about two fellow general psychology students and asked to make a decision regarding which one was the more intelligent. Second, subjects would engage in a short problem-solving task with the individual they chose as most intelligent (both of the "contestants" were ostensibly in a nearby room). The problem-solving task was described as "not difficult — but it does require that you and your partner work closely together — and that you learn to trust your partner with your feelings and intuitions." The whole session, it was said, was an attempt to mimic a scenario in which a college admissions official must use limited information to evaluate individuals' intelligence, and then those evaluated as most intelligent would "come to your university and work with you on a more personal level."

Finally, it was explained that this was only Part 1 of the study. Subjects were told that they had the option of coming back for Part 2 of the study in which they would serve as one of the contestants. Thus, it was explained that both of the contestants to be evaluated had previously participated in Part 1 of the study.

Intelligence Evaluation Task
Subjects were told that they would see information packets about the two contestants consisting of (a) a photograph of each contestant (just like the photograph that had previously been taken of the subject), (b) each contestant's high school GPA, and (c) an evaluation form completed about each contestant by that contestant's partner in the problem-solving task that each had participated in when they were in Part 1 of the study.

Finally, subjects were told that they would also be shown each contestants' performance on an 18-question analogy test (just like the test subjects had completed). Their inspection of these exam performances, however, would be complicated by one final fact. Admissions officials, it was said, are under tremendous time pressures and must make their decisions quickly while not forsaking accuracy. To simulate this speed-accuracy compromise, subjects were told that they would be shown the contestants' responses one question at a time. Each contestant's test questions had been separated and each question taped to an index card. On each card, the contestant's response was circled (ostensibly by the contestant), along with an indication (in red) of whether the question was answered correctly or incorrectly (if the response was incorrect, the correct response was circled in red). Subjects were told to examine both contestants' responses to the first question, then to turn to the second question, and so on. Both contestants responded to the same set of analogy questions but a different set than those answered by the subject herself. The key section of the instructions then went on as follows:

> What we want you to do is to look at these items *one question at a time* — without looking back through them — and *as soon as you feel that you have seen enough items to make a decision* — STOP — and make your decision regarding which contestant is most intelligent. In other words, we want you to try and make your decision looking at as *few of the questions as possible ... but at the same time still try to make that decision with a reasonable degree of accuracy*. [emphasis in original]

When the experimenter was assured that the subject understood the task, the subject was given a few minutes to review the pictures, GPA information, and evaluation forms. The subject was then given the stacks of analogy questions and told to let the experimenter know when she had made her decision.

Dependent Measures
After the decision, the experimenter made note of which contestant the subject chose as most intelligent and the *number of cards the subject required to make their intelligence decision.* Subjects then rated their *surprise regarding the outcome of their intelligence decision* on a 9-point scale (1 = *not at all surprised* and 9 = *very surprised*). More specifically, subjects were asked "Did the individual that you expected to be the most intelligent actually turn out to be the most intelligent? In other words, how surprised were you by which contestant turned out to be the most intelligent?" Subjects next rated both *contestants' performances* on the analogy questions on a 9-point scale (1 = *very poor/below average* and 9 = *very good/above average*), estimated the *percentage of analogy questions that each contestant had answered correctly*, and evaluated each contestant on four dimensions (intelligent–unintelligent, logical–illogical, likable–dislikable, and attractive–unattractive) on 9-point scales.

Preference Manipulation
The goal of Study 1 was to confront some subjects with a judgment situation in which they had little or no preference for one conclusion over another and others with a situation in which they had a clear a priori preference for one conclusion. This was accomplished by creating a contingency between the intelligence decision and future interaction and having some subjects decide which of two equally likable contestants was most intelligent and facing other subjects with a choice between a likable contestant and a thoroughly dislikable one.

The likability of the contestants was manipulated using the evaluation forms that had supposedly been completed about them by their previous partner. The evaluation forms consisted of three sections of 9-point rating scales in which the contestant's partner ostensibly rated *the problem-solving task* on three dimensions (e.g., enjoyable–unenjoyable), their *feelings during the problem-solving task* on three dimensions (e.g., anxious–calm), and their *partner in the problem-solving task* (i.e., the contestant) on eight dimensions (e.g., intelligent–unintelligent and likable–dislikable). In addition, there was a space at the end of the form for additional comments.

For subjects assigned to the *no-preference conditions*, the likability of both contestants reflected by the partners' evaluation forms was equal and quite high (overall $M = 7$, where 9 represents the positive pole of each scale). Nothing was written on either contestants' form in the space left for additional comments.

In contrast, subjects assigned to the *preference conditions* read evaluation forms suggesting two contestants who differed dramatically in likability. For one contestant (the comparison contestant), the evaluation form was identical in both the no-preference and preference conditions (i.e., suggesting high likability). For the other contestant (the target contestant), however, the evaluation form in the preference conditions suggested that he was quite dislikable. For example, the target contestant's partner rated the problem-solving task as unenjoyable (2 on a scale where 9 was most enjoyable) and the target contestant himself as dislikable (1 on a scale where 9 was most likable). In addition, in the space for additional comments, the following comment appeared (in handwriting intended to suggest a female partner): "i think the task would probably have been fun if it weren't for my partner. He thought he was never wrong and he made me feel stupid (like I didn't know what I was talking about). *Rude!!!"* (emphasis in original).

The dislikability of the target contestant conveyed by the preference-condition evaluation form, in conjunction with the contingency of future interaction with whomever was chosen as most intelligent (i.e., the problem-solving task), was intended to create a preference in these conditions for the target contestant to be seen as less intelligent. That is, all else being equal, subjects in the preference conditions would rather the analogy questions reveal that the target contestant was the less intelligent contestant (and therefore that they need not interact with him in the future) than that the target was the more intelligent contestant. In contrast, subjects in the no-preference conditions, faced with a choice between two equally likable contestants, should have little or no preference for one contestant or the other to be more intelligent.

Performance Manipulation
The second variable manipulated was the performance quality of the two contestants on the analogy test questions. The 18 analogy questions were conceived of as three sets of 6 questions and within each of the three 6-question sets, two different performance patterns were constructed. In the positive performance pattern, the responses circled on the cards indicated that the contestant answered *5 out of every 6 questions correctly.*

In the negative performance pattern, the contestant answered only *3 out of every 6 questions correctly*. In the *target-positive* conditions, the target contestant was seen to give the positive test performance and the comparison contestant the negative performance. In the *target-negative* conditions, on the other hand, the target contestant was seen to give the negative performance and the comparison contestant the positive performance.

Recall that one goal of this study was to "hold the judgment constant," that is, lead all subjects to make the same judgment while measuring how much information was required to make it. Thus, it was intended that the performance patterns in the current study be distinct enough such that subjects examining the cards would all be led to conclude that the contestant associated with the positive performance pattern was the most intelligent. This judgment pattern is critical if the amount of information required to make the judgments is to be compared across conditions and to rule out the possibility that subjects were simply choosing the individual they most wanted to work with as most intelligent. Thus, it was established at the outset that only those subjects choosing the contestant associated with the positive test performance as most intelligent would be considered in the primary analyses.

Design
Overall then, this study used a 2 (preference vs. no preference) × 2 (target-positive performance vs. target-negative performance) between-subjects design. Stated another way, combining the preference and performance manipulations created two preference conditions: (a) a *preference-consistent condition* in which the subject prefers that the dislikable target contestant perform poorly and he, in fact, performs poorly; (b) a *preference-inconsistent condition* in which the subject prefers that the dislikable target contestant perform poorly and he, in fact, performs well; and (c) two corresponding control/no-preference conditions: *one corresponding to the preference-consistent condition* (i.e., the likable target contestant performs poorly) and *one corresponding to the preference-inconsistent condition* (i.e., the likable target contestant performs well). The key dependent measure was the number of analogy question cards subjects required to make their decision regarding which contestant was most intelligent.

Controlling Intelligence Information
In this study, as in many other real-world and research situations, the judgmental consequences of differential expectations exactly mimic those of differential preferences (cf. Miller & Ross, 1975; Tetlock & Levi, 1982). Just as we predict that individuals will require more information to reach a preference-inconsistent conclusion than a preference-consistent conclusion, research has shown that individuals require more information to reach an expectancy-inconsistent conclusion than an expectancy-consistent one (e.g., Darley, Fleming, Hilton, & Swann, 1988).

We took several steps to control subjects' expectancies regarding the intelligence of the contestants and, in fact, to set them slightly against ourselves by conveying the image that the target contestant was slightly more intelligent than the comparison contestant. First, 21 female undergraduates rated 10 pictures of male students as to their perceived intelligence and likability. The picture rated highest in intelligence ($M = 8.05$ on a 9-point scale) was used as the target contestant. A second picture somewhat lower in perceived intelligence ($M = 7.19$) but comparable in perceived likability was chosen for use as the comparison contestant. Second, the target contestant was given a slightly higher high school GPA (3.0) than the comparison contestant (2.9). Third, the preference manipulation itself was designed to convey dislikability in a way that did not also convey a lack of intelligence. All partner evaluation forms indicated the same rating of the contestants' intelligence (7 on a 9-point scale). Also, the comments on the target contestant's evaluation form in the preference conditions conveyed the image of the target as a "know-it-all," thus suggesting high intelligence as much or more so than low intelligence.

Finally, a post hoc measure of subjects' expectations was included in the dependent measures in the form of subjects' self-reported surprise regarding which contestant turned out to be more intelligent. Thus, if we were successful at conveying the image that the target contestant was more intelligent than the comparison contestant, this should be revealed in relatively elevated surprise ratings in the target-negative conditions (i.e., when the target contestant performs more poorly than the comparison contestant).

Results

Preliminary Analyses and Manipulation Checks
Six subjects chose the contestant associated with the poor performance as most intelligent. All 6 of these subjects were in the preference, target-positive (i.e., preference-inconsistent) condition. Afterward, *t* tests comparing these 6 subjects with the 15 preference-inconsistent subjects choosing the target contestant as

most intelligent were conducted on all dependent measures, and no significant differences were found. In addition, Preference (preference vs. no preference) × Performance (target positive vs. target negative) analyses of variance (ANOVAs) were conducted on all dependent measures both including and excluding these 6 subjects, and all results were identical. This suggests that the differential attrition rate across conditions does not pose interpretive problems for the current study and is perhaps best viewed as support for the effectiveness of the preference manipulation. Some subjects chose to ignore the intelligence evaluation task rather than to work with the dislikable target contestant.[1]

Additional support for the effectiveness of the preference manipulation comes from subjects' ratings of the likability and attractiveness of the target contestant. Preference × Performance ANOVAs revealed that the target contestant was rated as significantly less likable in the preference conditions ($M = 4.6$) than in the no-preference conditions ($M = 6.6$), $F(1, 56) = 29.80$, $p < .001$, and significantly less attractive in the preference conditions ($M = 3.8$) than in the no-preference conditions ($M = 5.0$), $F(1, 56) = 8.93$, $p < .01$. The only other significant effect in these two ANOVAs was that the target contestant was seen as significantly more likable when he performed well ($M = 6.0$) than when he performed poorly ($M = 5.2$), $F(1, 56) = 4.24$, $p < .05$. Ratings of the likability and attractiveness of the comparison contestant revealed no significant effects.

The performance manipulation was also successful. Subjects' ratings of the quality of the contestants' analogy test performances, the percentage of analogy questions answered correctly by both contestants, as well as their ratings of the intelligence and logical ability of both contestants all revealed only main effects for performance (all $ps < .001$), suggesting that whomever was associated with the positive performance was seen as performing better, more intelligent, and so forth.

Amount of Information Required to Make the Intelligence Decision

All subjects in the main analyses chose the contestant performing best on the analogy questions as most intelligent. The key dependent measure in this study, however,

was the number of analogy questions required by subjects to make this decision. Overall, subjects in the no-preference conditions required significantly more cards to make their decision ($M = 9.3$) than did subjects in the preference conditions ($M = 7.8$), $F(1, 56) = 4.43$, $p < .05$. This main effect, however, was qualified by a significant Preference × Performance interaction, $F(1, 56) = 6.14$, $p < .02$, showing that, as predicted, the perceived likability of the target contestant affected the amount of information required by subjects to make their intelligence decisions. Figure 32.1 presents the mean number of analogy questions required to make the intelligence decisions across the four conditions. Simple effects analyses showed that in the no-preference conditions (i.e., when both contestants were equally likable), there was no difference in the number of cards required to decide that the target contestant was less intelligent (when he performed relatively poorly; $M = 9.9$) than that he was more intelligent (when he performed relatively well; $M = 8.8$), $F(1, 56) = 1.12$, $p = .29$. However, in the preference conditions (i.e., when the target was dislikable), subjects required significantly fewer cards to make the preference-consistent decision (i.e., decide that the dislikable target was less intelligent; $M = 6.6$) than to make the preference-inconsistent decision (i.e., decide that the dislikable target was more intelligent; $M = 9.1$), $F(1, 56) = 5.99$, $p < .02$.

Interestingly, simple effects analyses comparing the two target-positive and two target-negative conditions

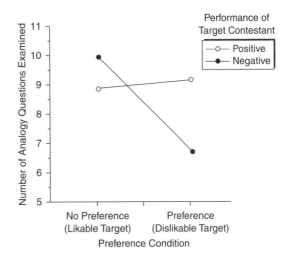

FIGURE 32.1 ■ Number of Analogy Questions Required for Intelligence Decision by Experimental Condition (Study 1).

---

[1] That these subjects ignored the intelligence information is suggested by the fact that all 6 excluded subjects rated the target contestant as more intelligent than the comparison contestant. Thus, it was not that these subjects disregarded the incoming data and chose to believe what they wanted to believe but rather that they simply disregarded the assigned task and chose to interact with the contestant with whom they wanted to interact.

revealed that preference and no-preference subjects differed significantly from each other only in the target-negative cells, $F(1, 56) = 10.50$, $p < .01$. No other effects in the ANOVA were significant.

Self-Reported Surprise
Consistent with our intention of leading subjects to expect the target contestant to be somewhat more intelligent than the comparison contestant, subjects' self-reported surprise regarding which contestant turned out to be more intelligent revealed only a significant performance main effect, $F(1, 56) = 8.80$, $p < .01$. Subjects reported being more surprised when the target contestant performed relatively poorly (preference $M = 4.4$ and no-preference $M = 5.6$) than when the target contestant performed relatively well (preference $M = 3.9$ and no-preference $M = 3.4$).

Discussion

The results of Study 1 provide strong support for the hypothesis that individuals use differential decision criteria for preferred and nonpreferred judgment conclusions. Subjects presented with performance information suggesting that the dislikable contestant was less intelligent than his competitor required fewer analogy questions to make their decision than subjects presented with information suggesting that the dislikable contestant was the more intelligent of the two. A similar pattern did not emerge when the contestants were portrayed as equally likable. Thus, subjects' preference for the dislikable contestant to be less intelligent (and consequently to avoid additional contact with him) resulted in their requiring less information to arrive at this conclusion than to arrive at the less preferred conclusion.

Importantly, the results of Study 1 cannot be explained as a function of differential performance expectations regarding the two contestants. Subjects in both the preference and no-preference conditions reported being more surprised when the target contestant performed relatively poorly than when he performed relatively well. Although self-reported surprise after receiving information is by no means a perfect indicator of preinformational expectations, the most obvious interpretation of the surprise data is that subjects expected the target contestant to be more intelligent and thus reported a relatively high degree of surprise when the test performances suggested that he was not.

Finally, although the results of Study 1 provide clear support for the differential criteria prediction, stronger support was found for subjects' "freezing" their decision process relatively quickly when faced with preference-consistent information than for their persisting in their analysis when faced with preference-inconsistent information. In other words, the clearest effect in Study 1 is that subjects needed relatively few cards to decide that the dislikable contestant was the less intelligent contestant. No evidence was obtained that subjects faced with preference-inconsistent information required more information to make their judgment than no-preference subjects faced with the identical information.

The analysis of motivated reasoning presented here should not be misinterpreted as predicting that the source of "bias" in the processing of preference-relevant information resides exclusively in the hypercritical processing of preference-inconsistent information. The core of our analysis concerns the relative difference in the quantity of processing given to preference-consistent and preference-inconsistent information. In fact, the pattern of results found in Study 1 might be interpreted as consistent with past research showing better evidence for self-enhancement biases than self-protective biases (Miller & Ross, 1975). Self-enhancement biases involve the ready acceptance of preference-consistent information, whereas self-protective biases involve a reluctance to accept preference-inconsistent information. It is also consistent with a large body of research showing that subjects in positive moods tend to use less complete and effortful cognitive strategies than do subjects in more neutral moods (Bless et al., 1990; Isen, 1984; Mackie & Worth, 1989; Worth & Mackie, 1987). In this view, much of the bias in the perception of preference-relevant information may result not from a tendency to be hypercritical of preference-inconsistent information, but rather from a tendency to quickly and uncritically accept information with desirable implications.

Study 1 examined the differential decision criteria hypothesis within the context of an interpersonal judgment. Although there is little reason to make distinctions between intrapersonal and interpersonal judgments in terms of how preferences are likely to operate, most research on motivational biases examines judgments where the motivational power is generated by presenting individuals with information that is somehow threatening to their self-image. Study 2 examines the differential decision criteria prediction in this more traditional judgmental domain.

Study 2

There are perhaps few things more disturbing than discovering that one might be ill. Most people in most situations clearly prefer health to sickness (Ware & Young, 1979). This general preference is supported by a variety of experimental studies demonstrating "defensive" reactions of individuals confronted with unfavorable medical diagnoses (e.g., Croyle & Sande, 1988; Ditto et al., 1988; Jemmott, Ditto, & Croyle, 1986). These studies show that compared with individuals receiving a "healthy" diagnosis, individuals receiving an unhealthy diagnosis downplay the seriousness of the diagnosed disorder and its consequences, augment the perceived commonness of the diagnosed disorder and its consequences, and derogate the accuracy of the diagnostic test.

Study 2 takes advantage of this powerful preference by comparing subjects' reactions to information suggesting either health or illness. The general prediction is that given that people generally prefer health to illness, more information should be required for people to accept a seemingly unhealthy diagnosis than a seemingly healthy one.

Method

Subjects
Subjects were 51 undergraduates from general psychology courses at Kent State University who participated for course credit. The results from 3 subjects were discarded after participation because they voiced suspicions about the experimental manipulations. The final sample consisted of 48 subjects, 29 women and 19 men.

Procedure
The experimental procedure used in this study has been described in detail elsewhere (see Croyle & Ditto, 1990, for a lengthy discussion of its development and validation). It is described here with an emphasis on those aspects of the procedure that are unique to this study.

On arrival at the laboratory suite, subjects were told that the study was concerned with "the relationship between psychological characteristics and physical health" and would consist of them completing some health and personality questionnaires and taking some simple medical tests. An experimenter then measured subjects' blood pressures and gave them a packet of "personality questionnaires" to complete. This packet contained a 14-item hypochondriasis scale (Pilowsky, 1967). Three subjects answered 8 or more questions in the hypochondriacal direction. These subjects were told that they were in a control condition, given their full experimental participation credit, and excused.

After completing the questionnaires, the experimenter read a description of a fictitious medical condition called "TAA deficiency" in which an enzyme called thioamine acetylase (TAA) is absent from the body. TAA deficiency was said to cause individuals who have it to be "relatively susceptible to a variety of pancreatic disorders" later in life.

The experimenter went on to state that about 6 months ago a chemically coated test paper was developed that reacts to the presence of TAA in saliva. Subjects assigned to the *deficiency condition*, were told that if TAA reactive paper comes in contact with saliva in which TAA is absent (indicating TAA deficiency) it will show *no color reaction*, but if it comes in contact with saliva containing TAA, it would change from its *normal yellow color to a dark green*. Subjects assigned to the *no-deficiency condition*, on the other hand, were told just the opposite. These subjects were told that the TAA paper would change from yellow to green if TAA was absent in saliva but show no color reaction if TAA was present.

Subjects were then told how to self-administer the test. Subjects were told to place a small amount of saliva in a cup and to rub a strip of the test paper in their saliva. Color development in the moistened test strip was said to "take anywhere from 10 seconds to one minute but is generally complete within 20 seconds." As soon as their test result was clear, subjects were told that it was important for them to "as quickly as possible" place their test strip in a small envelope to "provide us with a permanent record of your test result."

After the experimenter checked to make sure all subjects understood the testing procedures, subjects were left alone to conduct the test and told to complete the next packet of questionnaires (containing the dependent measures described later) as soon as the test was completed.

When subjects administered their TAA saliva reaction test, the test strip (made of yellow construction paper) always remained yellow. Because of what they had previously been told about the nature of the test, however, deficiency subjects interpreted this lack of reaction as an indication that they *had TAA deficiency*, whereas no-deficiency subjects interpreted it as indicating that they *did not have TAA deficiency*.

Dependent Measures
Measures of "defensiveness." Subjects completed a packet of questionnaires asking them to indicate their beliefs about a series of different health disorders. There were five key dependent measures embedded in the questionnaire packet: subjects' ratings of the *seriousness of TAA deficiency and pancreatic disease* on a scale from 0 (*not serious/can be ignored*) to 100 (*very serious/life threatening*), subjects' percentage estimates of the *prevalence of TAA deficiency and pancreatic disease*

in the college-age population, and subjects' ratings of the *accuracy of the TAA saliva reaction test* on a 9-point scale (1 = *extremely inaccurate* and 9 = *extremely accurate*).

Coded videotape measures. Subjects' behavior was surreptitiously videotaped during the experimental session. The raw videotapes were edited to remove all indications of assigned condition, and these segments were viewed by two judges. The judges' key task was to record the amount of time each subject required to decide that his or her TAA test was complete, that is, that no color reaction was going to take place. Behavioral markers were built into the TAA test to facilitate this judgment. Judges were told that the subjects' decision process would be framed on one side by the dipping of the test strip in the saliva and on the other by the sealing of the test strip in the provided envelope. The judges were able to reliably make this judgment (Spearman-Brown coefficient = .85), and so the two judges' times were averaged to form a decision latency index. The judges were also asked to make a note of all subjects engaging in multiple testing of their saliva sample (e.g., redipping the test strip in the saliva after observing the initial result). Judges showed very high agreement on these judgments, dis-agreeing in only two instances (96% agreement rate). Only those behaviors on which both judges agreed were considered.

Debriefing

On completion of the dependent measures, subjects were put through a careful process debriefing (Ross, Lepper, & Hubbard, 1975). Subjects indicated little if any distress regarding the procedure during the debriefing.

Results

Test Result (deficiency vs. no deficiency) × Gender (male vs. female) ANOVAs on all dependent measures revealed no main effects or interactions involving gender. Thus, unless otherwise noted, all analyses reported are independent t tests comparing the deficiency and no-deficiency groups.

Defensiveness Measures

Consistent with past research using this paradigm, subjects confronted with the unfavorable diagnostic information showed relatively optimistic assessments of the meaning of their test result. As can be seen in Table 32.1, deficiency subjects perceived TAA deficiency as less serious, $t(45) = -3.80$, $p < .01$, and more common, $t(44) = 4.53$, $p < .01$, than did no-deficiency subjects;

pancreatic disease as less serious, $t(43) = -1.98$, $p < .05$, and more common, $t(43) = 2.86, p < .01$, than did no-deficiency subjects; and the TAA saliva reaction test as a less accurate indicator of TAA status, $t(45) = -2.43$, $p < .05$, than did no-deficiency subjects.[2]

Coded Videotape Measures

The key dependent measure in the current study was the amount of time subjects required to decide that their TAA saliva reaction test was complete. Quite consistent with the deficiency subjects' posttest indications of defensiveness, inspection of the videotape records revealed evidence of deficiency subjects' reluctance to accept their unfavorable diagnosis. Deficiency subjects took almost 30 s longer on average to decide that their TAA test was complete ($M = 104.8$ s) than did no-deficiency subjects ($M = 76.5$ s), $t(45) = 2.60, p < .02$.

One possible explanation of this decision latency difference is that deficiency subjects were simply stunned by the unfavorable diagnosis and thus that this extra decision time was characterized by a relatively passive disbelief rather than by a vigorous analysis of preference-inconsistent information. This explanation is undermined, however, by evidence suggesting that subjects faced with the unfavorable diagnosis actively engaged in a variety of behaviors designed to test and retest the validity of their test result. The bottom row of Table 32.1 shows the number of subjects in each condition who, after initial examination of their test result (i.e., no color change), retested themselves. Thirteen of 25 deficiency subjects (52%) engaged in some sort of retesting behavior as opposed to only 4 of 22 no-deficiency subjects (18%), $X^2(1, N = 47) = 5.79, p < .05$.[3]

The most common form of retesting observed was a simple redipping of the original test strip in the original saliva sample after observing the initial lack of color reaction. All 4 of the no-deficiency subjects displayed this simple redipping behavior. Deficiency subjects, however, often went to much greater lengths to examine the validity of their test result. Three subjects conducted a second test with a new test strip (1 of whom placed the second strip in her shirt pocket — perhaps for later examination). Four tested a second saliva sample. Others engaged in a variety of different testing behaviors, such as placing the test strip directly on their

---

[2] The differential degrees of freedom reported are due to missing values for some measures.
[3] Because of equipment failure, 1 no-deficiency subject was not videotaped.

TABLE 32.1. Condition Means for All Dependent Measures (Study 2)

Measures	Diagnosis Condition	
	Deficiency	No Deficiency
Posttest		
Seriousness of TAA deficiency	31.7	49.8
Seriousness of pancreatic disease	54.8	67.3
Prevalence of TAA deficiency	38.8	16.6
Prevalence of pancreatic disease	23.0	13.1
Accuracy of TAA saliva test	4.9	6.2
Videotape		
Decision latency (in seconds)	104.8	75.5
No. of subjects' multiple testing	13 (52%)	4 (18%)

Note: Seriousness judgments were made on a scale from 0 (*not at all serious/can be ignored*) to 100 (*very serious/life threatening*). Prevalence judgments represent the percentage of the college-age population estimated to have had each disorder. Accuracy judgments were made on a scale from 1 (*extremely inaccurate*) to 9 (*extremely accurate*). TAA = thiamine acetylase (fictitious medical condition).

tongue, multiple redipping of the original test strip (up to 12 times), as well as shaking, wiping, blowing on, and in general quite carefully scrutinizing the recalcitrant nature of their yellow test strip.

Discussion

Study 2 provides support for the differential decision criteria hypothesis in a second domain and with a second operationalization of information quantity. Presented with an unchanging yellow test strip, subjects believing this lack of color change to be an indication of an enzyme deficiency required more time to decide that no color reaction was going to take place than did subjects believing this lack of color change to be an indication of normal enzyme presence. This extra time was not spent idly. Deficiency subjects were also more likely than no-deficiency subjects to conduct replications of the original test to check on its validity. This can be seen as an experimental analog of the anecdote in the introduction to this article. When unsatisfied with an initial diagnosis, individuals tend to "seek a second opinion." Interestingly, both common sense and the results of Study 2 suggest that people are more likely to consult a second opinion when faced with an unfavorable diagnosis than with a favorable one.

The results of Study 2 are consistent with both those of Study 1 and with our major prediction. Whether the unwanted outcome is illness or the prospect of an unpleasant social interaction, whether amount of information is defined as a decision latency or as the

number of analogy questions examined, less information seems required to reach a preferred conclusion than a nonpreferred one. In addition, Study 2 provides some direct evidence that preference-inconsistent information is more likely to be carefully scrutinized than preference-consistent information.

Study 2, unfortunately, is ultimately vulnerable to amotivational counterexplanations. At the most general level, it might be argued that subjects in Study 2 required more time to accept the unhealthy diagnosis than the healthy one not because the unhealthy diagnosis was unwanted but simply because it was unexpected. Enthusiasm for this and related counterexplanations should be tempered by the fact that previous research using the same experimental paradigm has provided data difficult to explain from a purely informational standpoint (see Croyle & Ditto, 1990, and Ditto et al., 1988, for more detailed discussions). Nevertheless, one of the goals of Study 3 was to provide additional evidence against expectancy-based counter-explanations.

The second and more central goal of Study 3, however, was to provide more direct evidence for the notion that individuals are more likely to generate alternative explanations for preference-inconsistent than preference-consistent information. Although data exist to suggest that preference-inconsistent information receives more processing than preference-consistent information, no direct evidence supports Kruglanski's (1990) idea that this additional processing includes a greater consideration of alternative explanations. The link between any such differential processing and judgment outcomes has also yet to be empirically demonstrated.

Study 3

As in Study 2, subjects in Study 3 were presented with diagnostic information regarding the TAA enzyme condition. The primary dependent measure in Study 3 was subjects' generation of possible alternative explanations for their diagnostic test result. Elaborating on a measure used by Ditto et al. (1988), subjects were asked to list any recent irregularities in their lives that they believed might have affected the accuracy of their test result. Subjects' beliefs about the overall accuracy of the diagnostic test were also measured.

Study 3 attempted to disentangle expectancy-based and motivational explanations for the results of Study 2. The design flaw in Study 2 is that sickness is statistically less common than health, leading to a confound between preference consistency and expectancy consistency (deficiency feedback being both preference inconsistent and expectancy inconsistent). Study 3 avoided this problem by leading all subjects to believe they had a relatively rare enzyme condition but manipulating the perceived healthfulness of the condition (e.g., Ditto & Jemmott, 1989). That is, subjects were presented with diagnostic outcomes that were equally unexpected and differed only in terms of their consistency with subjects' preferences.

Study 3 also included two control groups designed to be similar to the no-preference groups in Study 1. As in Study 2, the key groups in Study 3 evaluated the diagnostic information after receiving their diagnosis. Study 3 included another set of subjects who evaluated the diagnostic information after the diagnostic test was described but *before* receiving their diagnostic results. These subjects should lack the motivation hypothesized to drive any differential consideration of the validity of the diagnostic test. The inclusion of a prediagnosis judgment group also provided a convenient way of checking on subjects' expectations regarding the likelihood of receiving the different kinds of diagnoses.

Method

Subjects

Subjects were 93 undergraduates from general psychology courses at Kent State University who participated for course credit. The results from 3 subjects were discarded after participation because they voiced suspicions about the experimental manipulations. The results from 3 others were discarded because of procedural errors made during the course of the experiment. The participation of 8 additional subjects was terminated after each exceeded our hypochondriasis screening cutoff. The final sample consisted of 79 subjects, 49 women and 30 men.

Procedure and Manipulations

Two small procedural changes were made to facilitate the current cover story and manipulations. First, the TAA enzyme condition in Study 3 was described as the presence of the TAA enzyme ("TAA positivity") rather than its absence ("TAA deficiency"; Ditto & Jemmott, 1989). Second, all subjects were led to believe that they had this condition by telling them that if the TAA

enzyme was present in their saliva their test strip would turn from yellow to green and rigging their test paper to show this color reaction.[4] These changes were incorporated to present subjects with the simplest possible cover story — presence of the enzyme being indicated a presence of the color reaction.

The valence manipulation. The desirability of TAA positivity was manipulated by leading some subjects to believe that TAA positivity had *unhealthy consequences* (e.g., "people who are TAA positive are 10 times more likely to experience pancreatic disease than are people whose secretory fluids do not contain TAA.") and others to believe that it had *healthy consequences* (e.g., "people who are TAA positive are 10 times less likely to experience pancreatic disease than are people whose secretory fluids do not contain TAA.") To control subjects' expectations about the likelihood of being TAA positive, all subjects were given identical base-rate information stating that preliminary research indicated that TAA positivity was found in "about *1 out of every 20 people (5%)*" (emphasis in original).

Timing of dependent measures. Half of the subjects completed the dependent measure packet immediately after the TAA saliva test was described but before taking the test and receiving their test result (*prediagnosis conditions*). The other half of the subjects completed the dependent measures immediately after self-administering the TAA saliva reaction test and receiving their test result (*postdiagnosis conditions*).

Dependent Measures

Subjects in the prediagnosis and postdiagnosis conditions completed slightly different versions of the dependent measures. The items completed by all subjects are described first, followed by those completed by the prediagnosis and postdiagnosis subjects only.

All subjects. The first question included the statement "the accuracy of diagnostic tests can be affected by person-specific factors such as irregularities in diet, stress, sleep pattern, or activity level." Subjects were then asked to write down in a provided space "any such irregularities that have been true for you during the last 48 hours that might affect the accuracy of your TAA test result." The number of test-affecting life irregularities listed by each subject was summed. All subjects also rated (a) the *clarity of the experimenter's explanation* of the testing procedures on a 9-point scale (1 = *very unclear/difficult to understand* and 9 = *very clear/easy to understand*) and (b) their opinion regarding the *overall accuracy of the TAA saliva reaction test* on a 9-point scale (1 = *very inaccurate* and 9 = *very accurate*).

---

[4] The color reaction is created by using glucose-sensitive paper as the TAA test paper and spiking subjects' mouthwash with a small amount of sugar (e.g., Jemmott, Ditto, & Croyle, 1986).

Prediagnosis subjects only. Two additional items were included in prediagnosis subjects' dependent measure packets. First, subjects were asked to indicate whether there was anything in their personal or family medical history that "makes you think that you may have TAA positivity?" If so, subjects were asked to explain. Second, subjects were asked to estimate their *overall likelihood of being TAA positive* on a 9-point scale (1 = *very unlikely* and 9 = *very likely*).

Posttest subjects only. In addition to being asked to note any life irregularities that might have affected their test, postdiagnosis subjects were asked to write down any problems they had administering the TAA saliva reaction test that they thought might have affected the accuracy of their test result. The number of problems listed by each subject was summed.

On completion of the dependent measures, subjects were put through a careful process debriefing, thanked, and dismissed. Subjects indicated little if any distress regarding the procedure during the debriefing.

Results

Condition Valence (healthy vs. unhealthy) × Timing of Dependent Measures (prediagnosis vs. post-diagnosis) × Gender (male vs. female) between-subjects ANOVAs revealed no main effects or interactions involving gender on any dependent measure. Thus, unless otherwise noted all analyses reported are Condition Valence × Timing of Dependent Measures ANOVAs.

Perceived Likelihood of TAA Positivity
No prediagnosis subject indicated anything in their personal or family history that made them think they might be TAA positive. Subjects told that TAA positivity had desirable health consequences did not differ in their perceived likelihood of being TAA positive ($M = 3.3$) from subjects told that TAA positivity had undesirable health consequences ($M = 3.1$), $F < 1$.

Generation of Alternative Explanations
No differences were found in subjects' ratings of the clarity of the experimenter's explanation of the testing procedures. Subjects uniformly rated the experimenter's explanation as very clear (overall $M = 8.3$ on a 9-point scale). Similarly, only 4 out of 40 postdiagnosis subjects listed problems with administering the test as possibly affecting their test result, and only 1 cited more than one. All 4 of these subjects were in the unhealthy diagnosis condition.

Subjects who believed TAA positivity to be unhealthy cited more test-affecting life irregularities ($M = 1.4$) than did subjects who believed TAA positivity to be healthy ($M = .9$), $F(1, 75) = 5.56$, $p < .05$. This main effect, however, was qualified by a significant Valence × Timing interaction, $F(1, 75) = 7.50$, $p < .01$, showing that, as predicted, this healthy–unhealthy difference was limited to the postdiagnosis conditions. Figure 32.2 presents the mean number of test-affecting life irregularities cited across the four experimental conditions. Simple effects analyses showed that in the prediagnosis conditions there was no difference in the number of life irregularities cited by subjects in the healthy ($M = 1.3$) and unhealthy conditions ($M = 1.2$), $F < 1$. In the postdiagnosis conditions, however, subjects given the unhealthy diagnosis cited significantly more life irregularities that could have affected the results of their test ($M = 1.7$) than did subjects given the healthy diagnosis ($M = .5$), $F(1, 75) = 13.16$, $p < .01$.

Simple effects analyses comparing the two healthy and two unhealthy conditions revealed that the difference between the two healthy conditions was somewhat more reliable, $F(1, 75) = 5.14$, $p < .05$, than that between the two unhealthy conditions, $F(1, 75) = 2.59$, $p < .12$. No other effects in the ANOVA were significant.

Perceived Accuracy of the TAA Saliva Reaction Test
Subjects' ratings of the accuracy of the TAA saliva reaction test were very consistent with the life-irregularity

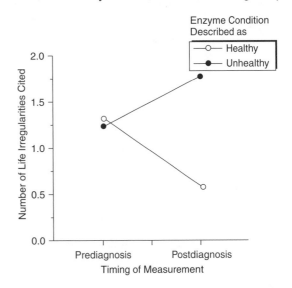

FIGURE 32.2 ■ Number of Test-affecting Life Irregularities Cited by Experimental Condition (Study 3).

citings. Overall, subjects who believed TAA positivity to be unhealthy rated the TAA test as less accurate ($M = 6.1$) than did subjects who believed TAA positivity to be healthy ($M = 7.1$), $F(1, 73) = 7.74$, $p < .01$. This main effect, however, was qualified by a significant Valence × Timing interaction, $F(1, 73) = 4.01$, $p < .05$, showing that this healthy-unhealthy difference was again limited to the postdiagnosis conditions. Figure 32.3 presents the mean accuracy ratings across the four experimental conditions. Simple effects analyses showed that in the prediagnosis conditions there was no difference in the perceived accuracy of the TAA test in the healthy ($M = 6.9$) and unhealthy conditions ($M = 6.6$), $F < 1$. In the postdiagnosis conditions, on the other hand, subjects given the unhealthy diagnosis rated the diagnostic test as significantly less accurate ($M = 5.6$) than did subjects given the healthy diagnosis ($M = 7.3$), $F(1, 73) = 11.31$, $p < .01$.

In contrast with the same analyses on life-irregularity citings, simple effects analyses comparing the accuracy ratings of the two healthy and two unhealthy conditions revealed that the difference between the two healthy conditions was less reliable ($F < 1$) than that between the two unhealthy conditions, $F(1, 73) = 4.25$, $p < .05$. No other effects in the ANOVA were significant.

Finally, the correlation between the number of life irregularities cited and perceived accuracy of the TAA saliva reaction test was negative and significant ($r = -.42$, $p < .0001$). The more life irregularities subjects generated, the less accurate they perceived the

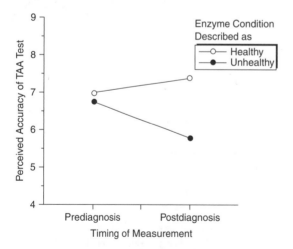

FIGURE 32.3 ■ Perceived Accuracy of Thioamine Acetylase (TAA, a fictitious medical condition) Saliva Reaction Test by Experimental Condition (Study 3).

TAA diagnostic test to be. The within-cell correlations were as follows: prediagnosis, healthy ($r = -.37$); prediagnosis, unhealthy ($r = -.37$); postdiagnosis, healthy ($r = -.06$); and postdiagnosis, unhealthy ($r = -.38$).

Discussion

The results of Study 3 provide additional evidence that people are less critical consumers of preference-consistent than preference-inconsistent information. Consistent with the predictions of Kruglanski (1990), subjects generated fewer alternative explanations for a diagnostic test result indicating a healthy medical condition than for one indicating an unhealthy medical condition. This occurred even though subjects asked before receiving their diagnosis rated the healthy and unhealthy diagnoses as equally unexpected. The fact that prediagnosis subjects did not show an assymetry in the number of life irregularities cited also attests to the motivated nature of the obtained results.

Consistent with past research (e.g., Ditto et al., 1988), postdiagnosis subjects rated the unhealthy diagnosis as less accurate than the healthy diagnosis. That these differential accuracy ratings are a product of a difference in how vigorously alternative explanations for the diagnosis were considered is suggested by the negative correlation between the number of life irregularities cited and overall accuracy ratings. The causal direction of this relation is, of course, ambiguous. It is possible that subjects simply decided how accurate they wanted the test to be and then provided the number of life irregularities that would justify that position. It is important to note, however, that the correlation is just as evident in the prediagnosis conditions, where subjects have no decision to justify, as it is in the postdiagnosis conditions, where they do. The only cell where the negative correlation does not emerge is in the postdiagnosis, healthy condition probably because both the life irregularities and test accuracy measures have relatively small variances in that cell. Thus, the results of Study 3 are consistent with the mediational role of processing intensity in differential validity perceptions; however, future research needs to provide more conclusive evidence.

The fact that no effects were found on measures related to the quality of the experimenter's test instructions and only a very few subjects cited problems with the test's administration is consistent with the general notion that the effect of preferences on information processing and judgments is constrained, ultimately, by the clarity of the information itself. As concerned researchers, we took great pains to train our experimenters to give clear instructions and to devise compelling manipulations and cover stories. That subjects overwhelmingly rated the experimenter's instructions as clear and had few problems following those clear instructions to complete a simple test suggests that we may have left even motivated subjects with little room to find fault with these aspects of the diagnosis. The informational panorama presented by 48 hr of a college student's life, on the other hand, is likely to have provided much more grist for a motivated cognitive mill. Motivational factors do not operate in a cognitive vacuum. The predicted effects likely reveal themselves most strongly on the life-irregularity measure because this measure provided subjects with a more fertile ground of plausible alternative explanations for the test result than the other measures (see Dunning, Meyerowitz, & Holtzberg, 1989, for a similar result).

Like the analogous results of Study 1, the simple effects comparing the life-irregularity citings of the two healthy conditions are more reliable than those comparing the two unhealthy conditions. The opposite pattern of simple effects, however, is found in subjects' perceived accuracy ratings. For both the life-irregularity and perceived accuracy findings, it seems plausible that the specific pattern of simple effects observed is a function of differential ceiling effects in particular conditions. The number of life irregularities cited by postdiagnosis, unhealthy subjects may have been mitigated by subjects' inability to plausibly generate more than a few such irregularities (or perhaps their reluctance to report more than a few because of self-presentational concerns). Similarly, the accuracy ratings of postdiagnosis, healthy subjects were likely constrained by the fact that accuracy ratings were quite high overall (see Figure 32.3), and thus, these subjects had relatively little room to adjust their accuracy ratings upward.

Perhaps the best interpretation of the results from Study 3 is that the effects appear relatively symmetrical for preference-consistent and preference-inconsistent information. This type of symmetrical pattern would again be quite consistent with the larger body of research on the role of affect in information processing. This literature suggests both that positive affect results in relatively truncated processing compared with more neutral moods (Mackie & Worth, 1989) and that negative affect results in more intensive processing compared with neutral moods (Schwarz, 1991).

From this perspective, the different pattern of results found in Study 1 and Study 3 may be attributable to differences in the affective responses subjects had to the information provided in the two studies. The informa-

tion provided subjects in Study 3 would be expected to produce relatively symmetrical affective responses. Subjects told they had a rare and beneficial enzyme condition should have experienced positive affect; those told they had a rare and unhealthy enzyme condition should have experienced negative affect. Relatively symmetrical processing effects would, in turn, be expected. The preference-inconsistent condition in Study 1, however, may have produced relatively little negative affect. Although subjects clearly preferred not to work with the dislikable contestant, they did not report an intense dread of this possibility. If they also went into the intelligence evaluation task expecting to work with the dislikable contestant (given the information about his higher intelligence), then the discovery that the expected was in fact true may have produced relatively little negative affect (Feather, 1969). In contrast, subjects discovering that the dislikable contestant was less intelligent may have found this information an unexpected, and therefore relatively pleasant, surprise. The asymmetrical decision criteria effects would follow directly from these asymmetrical affective consequences.

General Discussion

The question facing new look researchers in the early 1950s and self-serving bias researchers in the early 1980s was *whether* motivational factors could be shown to affect judgments. Now that the case for motivated biases in judgment seems rather well made (Kunda, 1990), the pressing issue of the early 1990s concerns the careful specification of exactly *how* motivational factors enter into and affect judgment processes. From early research within the cognitive dissonance (Festinger, 1957) and fear and persuasion (Janis & Feshbach, 1953) frameworks to several recent theoretical treatments of motivated judgment (Kruglanski, 1990; Kunda, 1990; Pyszczynski & Greenberg, 1987), many conceptualizations of the mechanisms underlying motivated reasoning have been suggested. Although these conceptualizations are clearly more complementary than antagonistic, important differences in emphasis exist that make some comparison between the views valuable in highlighting issues to be addressed in future research.

Motivated Skepticism and Selective Exposure

Our contention that more attention and thought is allocated to preference-inconsistent than preference-consistent information may initially seem incompatible with research within the selective exposure tradition (Festinger, 1957) showing that individuals will sometimes preferentially expose themselves to preference-consistent (i.e., "consonant") information over preference-inconsistent (i.e., "dissonant") information. Pyszczynski, Greenberg, and LaPrelle (1985), for example, found that subjects receiving negative feedback on a social sensitivity test indicated greater interest in social comparison information when they expected that information to show others to perform poorly compared with themselves than when they expected that information to show others performing relatively well (see also Frey & Stahlberg, 1986).

Quite the contrary, however, the idea that attention is initially directed toward preference-inconsistent information is perfectly compatible with recent research regarding the circumscribed nature of selective exposure effects. In his review of over 3 decades of research, Frey (1986) presented an image of selective exposure moderated by adaptive concerns. Initially, according to Frey, individuals direct attention toward unwanted information in an attempt to refute it (Wyer & Frey, 1983). As several researchers have argued, it makes adaptive sense that negative social information should be particularly likely to draw attention and careful, detail-oriented cognitive analysis (Pratto & John, 1991; Schwarz, 1991). This tendency to be at least equally interested in preference-inconsistent information as in preference-consistent information persists as long as the preference-inconsistent information is perceived to be refutable (Frey, 1981a) or the decision itself is perceived to be reversible (Frey, 1981b). In the Frey and Stahlberg (1986) study cited earlier, for example, subjects led to believe that an unflattering intelligence test result might be invalid were quite evenhanded in their interest in information they expected to disparage the test's validity and information they expected to support it.

Frey's (1986) analysis suggests that the tendency to preferentially expose oneself to information consonant with a desired judgment outcome is most likely to emerge relatively late in the decision process, when initial processing suggests that alternative explanations for preference-inconsistent information can no longer be plausibly entertained (see Jones & Gerard's, 1967, discussion of the "basic antinomy"). Thus, although selective inattention to threatening information was one of the first mechanisms posited to underlie defensive judgments (Janis & Feshbach, 1953; Janis & Terwilliger, 1962), there is neither empirical nor theoretical support for the notion that the tendency to

perceive preference-inconsistent information as less valid than preference-consistent information is mediated by selective inattention to the former. Reluctance to acknowledge the validity of preference-inconsistent information seems to stem from its tendency to receive more rather than less attention than preference-consistent information.

The current research is fundamentally concerned with this initial process of validity assessment. Motivational forces, however, do not cease to operate once the validity of preference-relevant information has been tentatively accepted (Frey, 1986). It is at this point, for example, that selective exposure effects should become evident. Once the validity of preference-inconsistent information has been accepted, further exposure to validity-supporting information should no longer be perceived to be useful, although the individual should still be interested in seeing information undermining that validity. Individuals who have accepted the validity of preference-consistent information may also become relatively uninterested in information that would lead them to reassess that conclusion, particularly if they have behaviorally committed to this interpretation (Frey, 1986).

It is also the case that even though an individual may accept the validity of preference-inconsistent information, he or she may still engage in processes that soften its implications, such as downplaying the relevance of the aspect of self to which the information pertains (Tesser & Paulhus, 1983) or engaging in compensatory enhancement of some other aspect of self (e.g., Steele, 1988). Seeking self-enhancing social comparison information (Pyszczynski, Greenberg, & LaPrelle, 1985; Wills, 1981) is also best construed as softening the implications of threatening information rather than challenging its validity. Many writers have made a distinction between *denial of fact* (i.e., denying the validity of a threatening piece of information) and *denial of implication* (i.e., accepting the validity of the information but denying its threatening implications; Janis, 1958; Lazarus, 1983; Weisman, 1972), most suggesting that individuals attempt the first before resorting to the second. This is quite consistent with the available data. Confronted with unwanted information, the first "line of defense" seems to be a relatively thorough analysis of its validity. It is only if this initial analysis suggests that the validity of the information must be accepted, that the individual begins to direct attention away from additional information that might confirm that validity and toward a careful consideration of the implications of this information within the context of the broader social and self-systems.

The Quality Versus Quantity of Processing Distinction

Another point on which various conceptualizations of motivated reasoning differ concerns whether the processing of preference-consistent and preference-inconsistent information is thought to differ in quality or merely in quantity (e.g., Kunda, 1990). The current analysis and Kruglanski's (1980, 1990) theory of lay epistemology emphasize the quantitative nature of this difference, suggesting that the central way that motivational factors affect judgments is through their effects on how extensively preferred and nonpreferred information is analyzed. Kunda (1990), on the other hand, argued explicitly that the processing of preference-consistent and preference-inconsistent information differs not simply in degree but also in kind. Like Pyszczynski and Greenberg (1987), Kunda's work relies heavily on a hypothesis-testing model of inference processes and argues that different hypotheses are generated for testing in response to preference-consistent and preference-inconsistent information, and different inference rules are used to evaluate these hypotheses.

A quantitative perspective is consistent with a hypothesis-testing conceptualization of inference processes. The theory of lay epistemology, in particular, is quite explicitly couched in hypothesis-testing language. In addition, a quantitative perspective would not dispute the fact that motivational factors may result in different hypotheses or inference rules being considered in response to preference-consistent and preference-inconsistent information. Where the quantitative and qualitative perspectives do differ, however, is in whether these differences are thought to occur directly as a function of motivational factors or indirectly as a function of the quantitative processing differences caused by motivational factors.

According to Kunda (1990), individuals "directly" access those beliefs and strategies that they consider "most likely to yield the desired conclusion" (p. 480). The quantitative view, on the other hand, would conceive of any such differences as arising only indirectly as a product of the relatively greater processing given to preference-inconsistent information. That is, an individual may very well be more likely to test the hypothesis that a diagnostic test is inaccurate when it yields a seemingly unfavorable result than when it yields a seemingly favorable one. However, this difference may not occur directly but rather because the initial characterization of the favorable diagnosis as accurate is readily accepted, whereas the negative affect generated by

the initial characterization of the unfavorable diagnosis as accurate is likely to motivate the more effortful cognitive process of considering other possible attributional influences.

This description is quite consistent with the view of mental systems posited by Gilbert (1991), in which the provisional acceptance of information is thought to occur relatively effortlessly as part and parcel of the comprehension process, whereas the process of "unaccepting" information is thought to be more effortful. It is also consistent with Pyszczynski and Greenberg's (1987) statement that before any motive can create the affect necessary to influence the choice of hypotheses for testing (or indeed any other aspect of information processing), the individual must consider the possibility, however fleetingly, that the undesirable hypothesis is true (see also Spence, 1983). In the quantitative view then, the same initial hypotheses are considered in response to both preference-consistent and preference-inconsistent information; that is, there is no direct or qualitative difference in the initial hypothesis chosen for testing. The difference in the hypotheses ultimately "tested" in response to preference-consistent and preference-inconsistent information arises only as an indirect product of a quantitative difference in processing; that is, because more hypotheses are considered in the latter case than in the former. A similar reasoning follows for any differences in the inference rules used for testing those hypotheses.

One implication of conceiving of motivational bias from a quantitative rather than qualitative perspective is the relative lack of self-deception implied by the former. Although the general concept of self-deception is no longer the theoretical and empirical "bugaboo" it once was (Erdelyi, 1974; Sackheim & Gur, 1978), in one form or another the issue of self-deception has dogged research on motivated judgment since the 1950s (Fingarette, 1969; Howie, 1952; Luchins, 1950). The very concept of motivated inference necessitates that the undesirable nature of incoming information be represented at some level by the cognitive system. If the negative nature of the information is subsequently diminished somehow by that cognitive system, to what degree is the individual aware of how (or even that) this process has taken place?

The direct effects implied by qualitative models of motivated inference suggest that the individual must at some level "know" what an inference strategy will yield before choosing to use it. Without knowledge regarding which strategies are likely to yield the desired conclusion and which are likely to yield a less desirable one, it is impossible for an individual to opt for one and forgo the other. In the qualitative view then, people are conceived of as having different goals when considering preference-consistent and preference-inconsistent information, consequently choosing different inference strategies in the two cases based on their expectation regarding the answer that inference strategy is likely to produce vis-á-vis that goal.

The quantitative view, on the other hand, conceives of the difference between the processing of preference-consistent and preference-inconsistent information more as a difference in *drive* than a difference in goals. Individuals faced with preference-consistent information are conceived of as simply less motivated to critically analyze the available data than are individuals faced with preference-inconsistent information and, consequently, are less likely to consider multiple possible explanation for it. No need for individuals to knowingly opt for one hypothesis or inference rule over another is implied. In a sense, the quantitative view sees the goal of the cognitive process as the same in both instances — people are attempting to construct an accurate view of themselves and their world — it is the vigor with which that goal is pursued in the two situations that differs.

This is not to say, of course, that motivated inference strategies are never informed and shaped by expectations. Research on the self-enhancing nature of social comparison seeking strategies (e.g., Pyszczynski, Greenberg, & LaPrelle, 1985), for example, clearly shows that they are. What we are suggesting, rather, is that much of the biasing effect that preferences have may occur without the deliberate construction process inherent in the qualitative perspective. In a sense, the current analysis simply relocates some portion of motivational bias effects by suggesting that rather than exclusively affecting how preference-relevant information is processed, preferences may have much of their effect before this point by affecting whether (or perhaps more accurately, how deeply) such information is processed. Thus, rather than always having to assume a deliberate and necessarily self-deceptive construction process, wants and fears may often bias judgments more passively because of the simple fact that preference-consistent information is accepted "at face value," whereas preference-inconsistent information tends to trigger more extensive cognitive analysis.

Conclusions

Perhaps the most resonant finding in the last 2 decades of social cognition research is that people think more deeply about information in some situations than in others (Bargh, 1984; Chaiken et al., 1989; Isen, 1984; Petty & Cacioppo, 1986; Tetlock, 1983, 1985). The research presented here is an attempt to integrate theory and research on self-serving biases in judgment with this large body of research emphasizing the selective allocation of cognitive resources.

The view of self-serving bias presented here also serves to integrate this research with that on other types of motivated inference processes. Accuracy motivation is generally thought to affect information processing by altering the quantity of cognitive effort an individual allocates to a judgment task (Chaiken et al., 1989; Kruglanski & Freund, 1983; Simon, 1957). Intensity of processing has also been posited as the mechanism underlying the effects of control motivation on attributional judgments (Pittman & D'Agostino, 1985). Thus, another advantage of a quantitative view of self-serving bias is its position that a single mechanism may underlie many different motivational influences on judgment (see Kruglanski, 1990, for a similar view).

Implied in all of this integration, of course, is the fact that numerous factors can affect how deeply a given piece of information is processed, and consequently, any or all of these factors can potentially moderate the effects that an individual's preferences will have on a given judgment. It seems that judgment is more often than not "multiply motivated" and consists of desires for an accurate view of the world and for a particular view of the world that combine to determine the course and outcome of the information-processing sequence (Heider, 1958; Kruglanski, 1990). This view of the human thinker as fundamentally constrained by adaptive concerns and human judgment as ultimately a compromise between preferences and plausibility is central to the current analysis of motivated inference.

It is neither the case that people believe whatever they wish to believe nor that beliefs are untouched by the hand of wishes and fears. Both passion and reason are characteristic of human thought. The research presented here continues the process of recognizing this duality and conceptualizing the passionate side of human judgment within the more general information-processing framework from which it was once banished.

REFERENCES

Aitken-Swan, J., & Easson, E. C. (1959). Reactions of cancer patients on being told their diagnosis. *British Medical Journal, 1*, 779–783.

Bargh, J. A. (1984). Automatic and conscious processing of social information. In R. S. Wyer, Jr., & T. K. Srull (Eds.), *Handbook of social cognition* (Vol. 3, pp. 1–44). Hillsdale, NJ: Erlbaum.

Beckman, L. (1973). Teachers' and observers' perceptions of causality for a child's performance. *Journal of Educational Psychology, 65,* 198–204.

Bless, H., Bohner, G., Schwarz, N., & Strack, F. (1990). Mood and persuasion: A cognitive response analysis. *Personality and Social Psychology Bulletin, 16,* 331–345.

Bohner, G., Bless, H., Schwarz, N., & Strack, F. (1988). What triggers causal attributions? The impact of valence and subjective probability. *European Journal of Social Psychology, 18,* 335–345.

Borgida, E., & Howard-Pitney, B. (1983). Personal involvement and the robustness of perceptual salience effects. *Journal of Personality and Social Psychology, 45,* 560–570.

Brown, J. D., & Rogers, R. J. (1991). Self-serving attributions: The role of physiological arousal. *Personality and Social Psychology Bulletin, 17,* 501–506.

Chaiken, S. (1987). The heuristic model of persuasion. In M. P. Zanna, J. M. Olson, & C. P. Herman (Eds.), *Social influence: The Ontario symposium* (Vol. 5, pp. 3–39). Hillsdale, NJ: Erlbaum.

Chaiken, S., Liberman, A., & Eagly, A. H. (1989). Heuristic and systematic information processing within and beyond the persuasion context. In J. S. Uleman & J. A. Bargh (Eds.), *Unintended thought* (pp. 212–252). New York: Guilford Press.

Croyle, R. T., & Ditto, P. H. (1990). Illness cognition and behavior: An experimental approach. *Journal of Behavioral Medicine, 13,* 31–52.

Croyle, R. T., & Sande, G. N. (1988). Denial and confirmatory search: Paradoxical consequences of medical diagnoses. *Journal of Applied Social Psychology, 18,* 473–490.

Darley, J. M., Fleming, J. H., Hilton, J. L., & Swann, W. B., Jr. (1988). Dispelling negative expectancies: The impact of interaction goals and target characteristics on the expectancy confirmation process. *Journal of Experimental Social Psychology, 24,* 19–36.

Ditto, P. H., & Jemmott, J. B. III. (1989). From rarity to evaluative extremity: Effects of prevalence information on evaluations of positive and negative characteristics. *Journal of Personality and Social Psychology, 57,* 16–26.

Ditto, P. H., Jemmott, J. B., III, & Darley, J. M. (1988). Appraising the threat of illness: A mental representational approach. *Health Psychology, 7,* 183–200.

Dunning, D., Meyerowitz, J. A., & Holtzberg, A. D. (1989). Ambiguity and self-evaluation: The role of idiosyncratic trait definitions in self-serving assessments of ability. *Journal of Personality and Social Psychology, 57,* 1082–1090.

Erdelyi, M. H. (1974). A new look at the new look: Perceptual defense and vigilance. *Psychological Review, 81,* 1–25.

Feather, N. T. (1969). Attribution of responsibility and valence of success and failure in relation to initial confidence and task performance. *Journal of Personality and Social Psychology, 2,* 129–144.

Festinger, L. (1957). *A theory of cognitive dissonance.* Stanford, CA: Stanford University Press.

Fingarette, H. (1969). *Self-deception.* New York: Routledge, Chapman & Haul.

Fiske, S. T., & Neuberg, S. L. (1990). A continuum model of impression formation from category-based to individuating processes: Influences of information and motivation on attention and interpretation. In M. P. Zanna (Ed.), *Advances in experimental social psychology* (Vol. 23, pp. 1–74). San Diego, CA: Academic Press.

Frey, D. (1981a). Postdecisional preferences for decision-relevant information as a function of the competence of its source and the degree of familiarity with this information. *Journal of Experimental Social Psychology, 17,* 621–626.

Frey, D. (1981b). Reversible and irreversible decisions: Preference for consonant information as a function of attractiveness of decision

alternatives. *Personality and Social Psychology Bulletin, 7,* 621–626.

Frey, D. (1986). Recent research on selective exposure to information. In L. Berkowitz (Ed.), *Advances in experimental social psychology* (Vol. 19, pp. 41–80). San Diego, CA: Academic Press.

Frey, D., & Stahlberg, D. (1986). Selection of information after receiving more or less reliable self-threatening information. *Personality and Social Psychology Bulletin, 12,* 434–441.

Gilbert, D. T. (1991). How mental systems believe. *American Psychologist, 46,* 107–119.

Gilbert, D. T., Pelham, B. W., & Krull, D. S. (1988). On cognitive busyness: When person perceivers meet persons perceived. *Journal of Personality and Social Psychology, 54,* 733–740.

Gilbertson, V. A., & Wangensteen, O. H. (1962). Should the doctor tell the patient that the disease is cancer? In *The physician and the total care of the cancer patient* (pp. 80–85). New York: American Cancer Society.

Gollwitzer, P. M., Earle, W. B., & Stephan, W. G. (1982). Affect as a determinant of egotism: Residual excitation and performance attributions. *Journal of Personality and Social Psychology, 43,* 702–709.

Heider, F. (1958). *The psychology of interpersonal relations.* New York: Wiley.

Higgins, E. T., & Sorrentino, R. M. (1990). *Motivation and cognition: Foundations of social behavior* (Vol. 2). New York: Guilford Press.

Hilton, J. L., Klein, J. G., & von Hippel, W. (1991). Attention allocation and impression formation. *Personality and Social Psychology Bulletin, 17,* 548–559.

Holton, B., & Pyszczynski, T. (1989). Biased information search in the interpersonal domain. *Personality and Social Psychology Bulletin, 15,* 42–51.

Howie, D. (1952). Perceptual defense. *Psychological Review, 59,* 308–315.

Isen, A. M. (1984). Toward understanding the role of affect in cognition. In R. Wyer & T. Srull (Eds.), *Handbook of social cognition* (pp. 179–236). Hillsdale, NJ: Erlbaum.

Janis, I. L. (1958). *Psychological stress.* New York: Wiley.

Janis, I. L., & Feshbach, S. (1953). Effects of fear-arousing communications. *Journal of Abnormal and Social Psychology, 48,* 78–92.

Janis, I. L., & Terwilliger, R. F. (1962). An experimental study of psychological resistances to fear arousing communications. *Journal of Abnormal and Social Psychology, 65,* 403–410.

Jemmott, J. B., III, Ditto, P. H., & Croyle, R. T. (1986). Judging health status: Effects of perceived prevalence and personal relevance. *Journal of Personality and Social Psychology, 50,* 899–905.

Jones, E. E., & Gerard, H. B. (1967). *Foundations of social psychology.* New York: Wiley.

Kruglanski, A. W. (1980). Lay epistemology process and contents. *Psychological Review, 87,* 70–87.

Kruglanski, A. W. (1990). Motivations for judging and knowing: Implications for causal attribution. In E. T. Higgins & R. M. Sorrentino (Eds.), *The handbook of motivation and cognition: Foundations of social behavior* (Vol. 2, pp. 333–368). New York: Guilford Press.

Kruglanski, A. W., & Freund, T. (1983). The freezing and unfreezing of lay-inferences: Effects on impressional primacy, ethnic stereotyping, and numerical anchoring. *Journal of Experimental Social Psychology, 19,* 448–468.

Kubler-Ross, E. (1969). *On death and dying.* New York: Macmillan.

Kunda, Z. (1987). Motivation and inference: Self-serving generation and evaluation of evidence. *Journal of Personality and Social Psychology, 53,* 636–647.

Kunda, Z. (1990). The case for motivated reasoning. *Psychological Bulletin, 108*, 480–498.

Langer, E. J. (1978). Rethinking the role of thought in social interaction. In J. H. Harvey, W. Ickes, & R. F. Kidd (Eds.), *New directions in attribution research* (Vol. 2, pp. 35–58). Hillsdale, NJ: Erlbaum.

Lazarus, R. S. (1983). The costs and benefits of denial. In S. Breznitz (Ed.), *The denial of stress* (pp. 1–30). Madison, CT: International Universities Press.

Liberman, A., & Chaiken, S. (in press). Defensive processing of personally relevant health messages. *Personality and Social Psychology Bulletin.*

Luchins, A. S. (1950). On an approach to social perception. *Journal of Personality, 19*, 64–84.

Mackie, D. M., & Worth, L. T. (1989). Processing deficits and the mediation of positive affect in persuasion. *Journal of Personality and Social Psychology, 57*, 27–40.

Markus, H., & Wurf, E. (1987). The dynamic self-concept: A social psychological perspective. In M. R. Rosenzweig & L. W. Porter (Eds.) *Annual Review of Psychology* (Vol. 38, pp. 299–337). Palo Alto, CA: Annual Reviews.

Marsh, K. L., & Weary, G. (1989). Depression and attributional complexity. *Personality and Social Psychology Bulletin, 15*, 325–336.

Miller, D. T., & Ross, M. (1975). Self-serving biases in attribution of causality: Fact or fiction? *Psychological Bulletin, 82*, 213–225.

Petty, R. E., & Cacioppo, J. T. (1986). The elaboration likelihood model of persuasion. In L. Berkowitz (Ed.), *Advances in experimental social psychology* (Vol. 19, pp. 123–205.) San Diego, CA: Academic Press.

Petty, R. E., Cacioppo, J. T., & Goldman, R. (1981). Personal involvement as determinant of argument-based persuasion. *Journal of Personality and Social Psychology, 41*, 847–855.

Pilowsky, I. (1967). Dimensions of hypochondriasis. *British Journal of Psychiatry, 113*, 89–93.

Pittman, T. S., & D'Agostino, P. R. (1985). Motivation and attribution: The effects of control deprivation on subsequent information processing. In J. H. Harvey & G. R. Weary (Eds.), *Attribution: Basic issues and applications* (pp. 117–143). San Diego, CA: Academic Press.

Pratto, F., & John, O. P. (1991). Automatic vigilance: The attention-grabbing power of negative social information. *Journal of Personality and Social Psychology, 61*, 380–391.

Pyszczynski, T., & Greenberg, J. (1981). Role of disconfirmed expectancies in the instigation of attributional processing. *Journal of Personality and Social Psychology, 40*, 31–38.

Pyszczynski, T., & Greenberg, J. (1987). Toward an integration of cognitive and motivational perspectives on social inference: A biased hypothesis-testing model. In L. Berkowitz (Ed.), *Advances in experimental social psychology* (Vol. 20, pp. 297–340). San Diego, CA: Academic Press.

Pyszczynski, T., Greenberg, J., & Holt, K. (1985). Maintaining consistency between self-serving beliefs and available data: A bias in information evaluation following success and failure. *Personality and Social Psychology Bulletin, 11*, 179–190.

Pyszczynski, T., Greenberg, J., & LaPrelle, J. (1985). Social comparison after success and failure: Biased search for information consistent with a self-serving conclusion. *Journal of Experimental Social Psychology, 21*, 195–211.

Quatrone, G. A. (1982). Overattribution and unit formation: When behavior engulfs the person. *Journal of Personality and Social Psychology, 42*, 593–607.

Ross, L., Lepper, M. R., & Hubbard, M. (1975). Perseverance in self perception and social perception processes. *Journal of Personality and Social Psychology, 32*, 880–892.

Sackheim, H. A., & Gur, R. C. (1978). Self-deception, self-confrontation, and consciousness. In G. E. Schwartz & D. Shapiro (Eds.) *Consciousness and self-regulation: Advances in research* (Vol. 2, pp. 139–197). New York: Plenum Press.

Schwarz, N. (1991). Feelings as information: Informational and motivational functions of affective states. In E. T. Higgins & R. M. Sorrentino (Eds.), *The handbook of motivation and cognition: Foundations of social behavior* (Vol. 2, pp. 527–561). New York: Guilford Press.

Simon, H. (1957). *Models of man: Social and rational.* New York: Wiley.

Sorrentino, R. M., & Higgins, E. T. (1986). *Handbook of motivation and cognition: Foundations of social behavior* (Vol. 1). New York: Guilford Press.

Spence, D. P. (1983). The paradox of denial. In S. Breznitz (Ed.), *The denial of stress* (pp. 103–123). Madison, CT: International Universities Press.

Steele, C. M. (1988). The psychology of self-affirmation: Sustaining the integrity of the self. In L. Berkowitz (Ed.), *Advances in experimental social psychology* (Vol. 21, pp. 261–302). San Diego, CA: Academic Press.

Stephan, W. G., & Gollwitzer, P. M. (1981). Affect as a mediator of attributional egotism. *Journal of Experimental Social Psychology, 17*, 443–458.

Stroop, J. R. (1935). Studies of interference in serial verbal reactions. *Journal of Experimental Psychology, 18*, 643–662.

Tesser, A., & Paulhus, D. (1983). The definition of self: Private and public self-evaluation maintenance strategies. *Journal of Personality and Social Psychology, 44*, 672–682.

Tetlock, P. E. (1983). Accountability and the perseverance of first impressions. *Social Psychology Quarterly, 46*, 285–292.

Tetlock, P. E. (1985). Accountability: A social check on the fundamental attribution error. *Social Psychology Quarterly, 48*, 227–236.

Tetlock, P. E., & Levi, A. (1982). Attribution bias: On the inconclusiveness of the cognition-motivation debate. *Journal of Experimental Social Psychology, 18*, 68–88.

Tversky, A., & Kahneman, D. (1974). Judgment under uncertainty: Heuristics and biases. *Science, 185*, 1124–1131.

Ware, J. E., & Young, J. (1979). Issues in the conceptualization and measurement of value placed on health. In S. J. Mushkin & D. W. Dunlop (Eds.) *Health: What is it worth?* (pp. 141–166). New York: Pergamon Press.

Weisman, A. D. (1972). *On dying and denying.* New York: Human Sciences Press.

Wills, T. A. (1981). Downward comparison principles in social psychology. *Psychological Bulletin, 90*, 245–271.

Wong, P. T. P., & Weiner, B. (1981). When people ask "why" questions, and the heuristics of attributional search. *Journal of Personality and Social Psychology, 40*, 650–663.

Worth, L. T., & Mackie, D. M. (1987). The cognitive mediation of positive affect in persuasion. *Social Cognition, 5*, 76–94.

Wyer, R. S., & Frey, D. (1983). The effects of feedback about self and others on the recall and judgments of feedback-relevant information. *Journal of Experimental Social Psychology, 19*, 540–559.

Received July 10, 1991
Revision received March 20, 1992
Accepted March 27, 1992 ■

PART 9

Reconstructing the Past, Anticipating the Future

Introduction and Preview

We live in the ongoing flow of time. Although we are often preoccupied with the present, we also have histories and futures. Moreover, our knowledge of our pasts and our hopes and plans for our futures are important elements in our current functioning. We use that knowledge of the past to understand how we got where we are; and we use that knowledge to guide our thoughts and actions in trying to get where we want to be. Social cognition research has investigated several important aspects of how people understand the past and look to the future. The readings in Part 9 are concerned with those questions and issues.

Reconstructing the Past

Reconstructive Memory

Events that have already happened are, by definition, in the past. They had a brief existence, a reality at the time they occurred, and now the mental representations of those events are stored in memory. Intuitively it might seem that those memories, when accessed and retrieved, can provide us with accurate recollections of the people and events we have experienced in the past. However, just as the processing of current information can be selected, interpreted, and elaborated in various ways that can alter its meaning, likewise our retrieval of the past can be guided, reinterpreted, and biased in various ways. When looking to the past, the present can often provide a filter, a lens through which our own history is seen. In particular, our current beliefs, desires, and goals can lead us to *reconstruct* our understanding of who we were and what we did in the past.

In many situations, we believe in the consistency and stability of our personality attributes, our attitudes, and our abilities. In other cases, we believe that we have undergone change as a result of recent experiences. These effects have been demonstrated in research investigating people's intuitive theories of change (Ross, 1989). As illustrated in Reading 33 by McFarland, Ross, and Giltrow (1992), when we believe that our attributes will change over time, we recollect that we were quite different at an earlier age than we are now. In contrast, for those characteristics we believe are quite stable, we do not revise our sense of how we were in an earlier era. In effect, people reconstruct their past to fit with their current theories about how they may or may not have changed over time (Conway & Ross, 1984; Ross, McFarland, & Fletcher, 1981). Our memories, then, can be quite malleable.

These studies show that people's recollections of the past may be biased, differing in systematic ways from the actual events that took place or misremembering the way we were. But is "memory" flexible enough to recall events that in fact never occurred? Can we generate "memories" of the past that are not merely slanted in one way or another but in fact are *creations* of our minds? Questions of this nature became quite important, as well as quite controversial, in the 1990s when a number of cases of "repressed memories" were widely reported. These cases often involved a person having vivid memories, arising for the first time in adulthood, that she had been sexually abused when she was very young. In some instances these reports entailed memories of events that, based on what we know about

memory, were very unlikely to be true (e.g., detailed memories of events that occurred during the first two years of life — a time period that people typically cannot recall at all). The question then became "How would such memories come about?" One disturbing possibility is that these memories were the product of suggestion, based on questions posed to patients by their well-intentioned therapists, in the course of the therapeutic hour. Think about a possibility long enough, imagine it as clearly as possible, and it becomes real — and consequently is later "recalled" as something that actually happened (Loftus, 1993).

The possibility that memories could be totally fabricated, without a basis in reality, then led researchers to conduct experiments in which they tried to study whether such false memories could be created in an experimental context. Reading 34 by Loftus (1997) summarizes some of this research. In these studies, participants are asked to recall events from their childhood, some of which were known to have been actual childhood experiences and some of which (based on consulting with parents, close friends, etc.) were known not to have occurred. When encouraged to recall these past events, participants had no difficulty generating descriptions of the "real" events, but a sizeable portion of them were also able to produce descriptions (sometimes quite vivid and detailed) of the events that had never taken place. Thus people reported "false memories."

This research demonstrates that memory is more than a passive and verbatim cognitive record of the past. Memory is an active process that does more than simply reproduce the past; it *reconstructs* the past. Moreover, that reconstruction process means that this cognitive system — memory — can be influenced by numerous social psychological factors, such as one's current beliefs, goals, and motives as well as by social influence (e.g., through suggestion and social pressure).

Counterfactual Thinking

Sometimes we know what has happened and, rather than reconstructing it to make it fit our wishes, we instead consider alternatives to what has happened. That is, we ponder an alternative reality, we engage in a "what if" style of thinking. Specifically, we consider what might have happened differently so that the outcome we have experienced would have been different. This kind of thought is called *counterfactual thinking* (Kahneman & Miller, 1986).

Imagine that a popular musical group is coming to town and you're eager to hear them. There are, of course, a limited number of tickets, and you know they'll go quickly. The tickets went on sale yesterday, and they may sell out today. The ticket window opens at 10:00, and you leave home in what you think is plenty of time. But just as luck would have it, the route to downtown is torn apart for road repairs, requiring a detour through little side streets, all of which have become thoroughly clogged with an enormous traffic jam. As you sit in bumper-to-bumper traffic, you're getting increasingly nervous about getting downtown in time to get tickets. When you finally arrive at 11:30, you learn, to your distress, that the last tickets were sold at about 11:00. In your disappointment, you "relive" the events that "caused" this disaster. "If only I had skipped a class and gone downtown yesterday, I would have gotten tickets for sure." "If I had gotten an earlier start this morning . . ." "If only I had taken a different route . . ." "If only I hadn't forgotten about those road repairs . . . I should have known . . ." When you "look back" in this way, you are mentally creating alternatives to what actually

happened — "counter to fact" — and hence are engaged in counterfactual thinking.

Missing out on those concert tickets quite reasonably leads to such thoughts. But obviously, we don't do this all the time; we don't spend our days reliving events that have already transpired and are over. This realization leads to some interesting questions: When do we engage in counterfactual thinking? What triggers such thoughts? Why do we do it at all? What consequences follow from such counterfactual thinking? These questions have been the focus of a lot of research in the last decade.

What circumstances initiate such thought? Events that deviate from our goals and expectations are likely to trigger counterfactual thinking (Roese, 1997). When things don't turn out as expected, we often try to understand what went wrong and how things could have been different. Miller, Turnbull, and McFarland (1990) suggested that people have "mental models" of events and situations, and these mental models include causal relations that provide us a basis for understanding and anticipating what is likely to happen. When something unexpected happens, we can compare the immediate situation with elements of the mental model as a basis for imagining how things might have been different.

Counterfactual reasoning, then, involves creating a different reality from the one that is represented in our mental model of an event. How do we construct such alternate realities? What principles guide the way we generate them? Research has identified several factors that play a role in this process. For example, some elements of a mental model seem to be more easily changeable than others. In my example it seems easier to imagine leaving 30 min earlier than to imagine that there was no road construction. Also, the counterfactuals we generate focus on elements that are controllable by the person involved, rather than uncontrollable factors. You could control which day you went to buy the tickets, and you could control what time you left in the morning, but you couldn't control the fact of road repairs and the resulting traffic jam. In fact, in one study (Davis, Lehman, Wortman, Silver, & Thompson, 1995), researchers interviewed people whose spouse or child had been killed in a car accident. They found that, although a high percentage of them still (4–7 years after the incident) had counterfactual "If only . . ." thoughts, those counterfactuals always focused on what the interviewee or the victim could have done differently. There wasn't one case in which the interviewee mentioned thinking of what the other driver (who in most cases had been negligent) might have done differently.

Counterfactual thinking involves a comparison process — a comparison of the known reality (the event that actually occurred) with some alternate reality (mentally generated by the individual). As Markman, Gavanski, Sherman, and McMillan (1993) discuss in Reading 35, these comparisons can be either upward counterfactuals or downward counterfactuals. In *upward counterfactuals* one compares the current outcome to an alternative that improves on the result; by leaving earlier, you would have gotten downtown in time to buy the tickets. This typically is "If only I'd . . ." thinking. In *downward counterfactuals*, the comparison is with some worse alternative; being too late for the tickets would have been far worse if you had been in a car accident in all that traffic. This typically is "At least I didn't . . ." thinking. Markman et al. point out that these two kinds of counterfactual thinking can lead to different emotional reactions. Upward counterfactuals focus on a better outcome that didn't happen, and therefore can lead to feelings of regret, sadness, and disappointment. Downward counterfactuals, in contrast, focus on a worse possibility that could have happened (but didn't). This process can generate feelings of relief and can lead to feelings of relative

well-being. Reading 36 by Medvec, Madey, and Gilovich (1995) provides an interesting demonstration of the emotional reactions that follow from both upward and downward focus among Olympic athletes.

Markman et al. (1993) also highlight another important difference between upward and downward counterfactuals. In addition to inducing different affective reactions, these two kinds of counterfactuals can serve different functions for the individual. Upward counterfactuals, by imaging the elements that might have led to a better alternative, can provide a basis for learning and for increasing one's preparation for the future, when similar circumstances may occur again. On the other hand, downward counterfactuals, by focusing on worse alternatives that didn't occur, can aid in coping with and adjusting to serious losses (see also Spellman & Mandel, 1999). Thus, counterfactual thinking, by looking back at what has happened and considering what might have been, can be beneficial in preparing oneself for the future (Roese, 1997).

Anticipating the Future

Much of the material we have discussed in this book might create the impression that social cognition is concerned only with information we have acquired about things that have already happened or are presently occurring. For example, in the Introductory Overview chapter I described a variety of ways people process and use information — encoding, elaboration, representation, retrieval — and most of these processes are focused on information with which the person is currently engaged. At other times, the emphasis seems to have been on people's use of information about past events. For example, we have learned how people represent and store information in cognitive structures (Part 2) that record the products of their past experiences. We've examined how people form first impressions (Part 6) and stereotypes (Part 7), which summarize and represent the main themes of what we have learned about persons and groups. We've learned how people are sometimes led to question why something has happened, why someone did what he did, and they then attribute the event or behavior to a specified cause (Part 5). And in the first half of this section I have discussed ways in which people look back at what has happened in the past, how they can reconstruct their memory of those events and can ponder alternatives to what actually happened. All of these topics might lead one to think that the cognitive system is geared primarily toward understanding the past. However, drawing such a conclusion would be a serious error.

In fact, a more accurate conclusion would be just the opposite, namely, that all of the processes and phenomena that we have covered in this book are oriented toward the future. That is, the cognitive system processes information that is available in the present, works on it in various ways to more fully comprehend its meaning, stores it in memory, and sometimes reconsiders those past events for one primary purpose: to be better prepared to anticipate the future. True, cognitive structures represent our accumulated knowledge from past experience, but we use that stored knowledge to comprehend the present and to anticipate future events. Similarly, we sometimes engage in attributional analysis aimed at understanding why something happened, but we do so in the belief that such events may happen again in the future, and to the extent that we understand the causal relations underlying them now, we can better anticipate their reoccurrrences. We form impressions of individuals and stereotypes of groups not merely as convenient summaries of the diverse information we've learned, but rather because they provide a basis for anticipating how a person or group member might behave. In all of these cases, the information processed and stored from past experiences provide us with expectancies for the future, and those *expectancies* guide us in numerous ways. The final two readings in Part 9 illustrate important ways that expectancies can shape our thoughts, feelings, and behaviors as we move toward the future.

Self-Fulfilling Prophecies

We have already seen considerable evidence of the influence of expectancies on information processing in previous articles. For example, expectancies can guide the inferences we make (Dunning & Sherman, 1997, Reading 3), they can guide the way we interpret new information (Darley & Gross, 1983, Reading 27) and construe our past (McFarland, Ross, & Giltrow, 1992, Reading 33), and they can influence how we make decisions to act (Correll, Park, Judd, & Wittenbrink, 2002, Reading 28). Moreover, information that violates our expectancies captures our attention (White & Carlston, 1983, Reading 2) and is often better remembered (Srull, 1981, Reading 23). Thus, by this point in reading this book, you already know that expectancies have broad and diverse effects on us.

All of these examples reveal important ways that expectancies can influence our perceptions and judgments. In addition, expectancies can manifest themselves in social behavior. A *self-fulfilling prophecy* occurs when (a) an expectancy held by one person (Alex) about another person (Bill) (b) influences Alex's behavior toward Bill, (c) which in turn influences Bill's behavior in response, and (d) Bill's behavior confirms the original expectancy held by Alex. Suppose, for example, that Alex thinks that Bill is aloof and unfriendly. Given that expectancy, Alex is likely to be a bit reserved and "standoffish" when he interacts with

Bill. Bill in turn might interpret Alex's behavior as being cold and distant, and hence is likely to reciprocate with similar reserve. Alex, in turn, would see Bill's response as consistent with his initial expectancies — "I've always thought of Bill as being rather aloof, not very outgoing." Thus Alex's initial expectancy has been confirmed by Bill's behavior.

In contrast to the effects of expectancies cited earlier, in which those expectancies actually bias our perceptions of other people and their behavior, in this case Alex's perceptions are accurate: Bill in fact behaved in a reserved and distant manner. What Alex is likely *not* aware of, however, is the fact that his own behavior, guided by his initial belief, actually induced that expectancy-confirming behavior from Bill. For this reason I have always thought of the self-fulfilling prophecy as a particularly insidious effect of expectancies, in that the perceiver (Alex) actually has his belief confirmed, but is *not* cognizant of the fact that he himself played a central role in producing that outcome. Reading 37 by Snyder, Tanke, and Berscheid (1977) provides a compelling demonstration of the self-fulfilling prophecy in social interaction.

Affective Forecasting

One of the difficulties in knowing what the future will be like is that it is, in fact, in the future — it hasn't happened yet. Therefore, in anticipating the future, we're engaged in "guesstimating" what is likely to happen. Our expectancies, derived from our past experiences, provide a potentially very useful basis for looking ahead. If the future "behaves" much like the past has been, then what we've learned from experience should be a useful guide for what is likely to be. And in many cases it is. However, like so many other topics we've considered in previous chapters, things are not so simple. There are systematic biases in the way we use our

knowledge of the past to anticipate the future, those expectancies themselves may be somewhat distorted, and we may be using the "wrong" expectancy to anticipate the future. These aspects of our cognitive functioning can lead us astray, and the consequence can be some misperceptions (in this case, "misanticipations") of what the future will be like.

Imagine that you bought what turned out to be a winning raffle ticket, and therefore you have won a brand new sports car — a gorgeous convertible with all the latest gizmos and gadgets that car makers have dreamed up. Obviously you're feeling great! You can now get rid of your present car, which clearly has seen better days. Now you'll easily be able to travel to new and interesting places you've never been to, you'll be more popular than ever as your friends will want to ride (and hang out) with you, you'll have more (and better) dates. Yes, winning this new car will make quite a difference — life is going to be great! All of these reactions are quite normal and appropriate. Now think about how your life is going to be 3 years from now. If you're like other people, you probably feel that it will continue to be great — better than it has been, for sure. Yes, this new car will be the start of a lot of good changes in your life.

Now imagine instead a different scenario. You get a call from home — your dad has had an accident, is disabled, and no longer can work. Your family now faces serious financial hardships, and your mom can't do everything herself. You're needed at home, and this means that you'll have to drop out of college. You need to get a job to help out — without your college degree, it won't be a high-paying job, but you really have no choice. It is, after all, your family. So you're feeling very badly, not only about your dad but also about the implications of this turn of events for your life — no college degree, your hopes for going to law school are now out the window, etc. Quite understandably, you're feeling extremely low. Now once again, look ahead 3 years and imagine how you'll be feeling about your life. Again, if you're like other people, you probably feel that the present changes will have an enduring effect on you, that life will not be all that you'd hoped for.

It's clear that major life events such as these have strong and powerful impacts on our feelings — at least in the short term. And as these scenarios illustrate, in many cases we believe that these effects will be long lasting. However, a considerable amount of research has shown that people who experience new highs do not remain euphoric forever, and more importantly, their lives are not forever changed. Before too long, their emotional lives have returned to normal. Similarly, people who have experienced a tragedy, a physical injury, or the loss of a loved one are not permanently damaged. With the passage of time they manage to rebound, to cope and adjust, and to move on with their lives. In fact, the affect associated with negative life events fades more quickly than does the affect associated with positive experiences (Skowronski, Gibbons, Vogl, & Walker, 2004). In both cases, then, people often overestimate the long-term effects of emotion-laden events — positive or negative — on their future affective states.

Affective forecasting refers to people's ability to predict their overall emotional level of happiness in the future. Research by Gilbert, Wilson, and their colleagues (Gilbert & Wilson, 2000) has demonstrated a *durability bias*, that is, people's tendency to believe that their current affective state will continue to influence their lives (including their emotions) well into the future. Their studies have documented several factors that underlie this bias. For example, as shown in Reading 38 by Wilson,

Wheatley, Meyers, Gilbert, and Axom (2000), people are often focused on the emotions that they are feeling at the moment. When asked how the present event will influence their long-term emotional experience, this "focalism" results in their not considering a variety of other factors that can influence their overall affective states in the future. With the passage of time many, many other events will occur and will affect one's emotional state and level of adjustment. Those events — many of them trivial, some of them momentous — will generate their own affective reactions, and those experiences will reshape not only the direction of one's life but also how the person is feeling about life at the moment. These intervening events diminish the continuing impact of today's affect-defining outcomes, but because they are in the future, we are not cognizant of them or of their role in (re)shaping our affective experience. Moreover, we generally are not aware of the many ways that our minds can protect us from the threatening implications of unpleasant experiences (Gilbert, Pinel, Wilson, Blumberg, & Wheatley, 1998). We are quite adept at rationalizing and redressing the negative events we have experienced. These cognitive mechanisms can also alleviate the long-term consequences of present experiences, and hence we overestimate their long-term implications for our emotional life.

Predicting the future is always tricky business (just ask the weatherman or a stockbroker!). The past is often a good source of clues to how things may play out in the future, and therefore our expectancies based on past experience can provide a useful framework for anticipating future events. However, those expectancies can be biased by a variety of factors, and hence can generate views of the future that aren't always accurate.

Discussion Questions

1. What is reconstructive memory? What principles guide our reconstruction of our past?
2. How is counterfactual thinking similar to and different from attributional thinking (Part 5)?
3. What is a self-fulfilling prophecy? Can you think of an example of a self-fulfilling prophecy in your own experiences?
4. What is the durability bias in affective forecasting? Why does it occur?

Suggested Readings

Johnson, M. K., & Sherman, S. J. (1990). Constructing and reconstructing the past and the future in the present. In E.T. Higgins & R. M. Sorrentino (Eds.), *Handbook of motivation and cognition* (Vol. 2, pp. 482–526). New York: Guilford.

Olson, J. M., Roese, N. J., & Zanna, M. P. (1996). Expectancies. In E. T. Higgins & A. W. Kruglanski (Eds.), *Social psychology: Handbook of basic principles* (pp. 211–238). New York: Guilford.

Kahneman, D., & Miller, D. T. (1986). Norm theory: Comparing reality to its alternatives. *Psychological Review*, 93, 136–153.

Roese, N. J., & Olson, J. M. (Eds.) (1995). *What might have been: The psychology of counterfactual thinking*. Mahwah, NJ: Erlbaum.

Allison, S. T., Mackie, D. M, & Messick, D. M. (1996). Outcome biases in social perception: Implications for dispositional inference, attitude change, stereotyping, and social behavior. In M. P. Zanna (Ed.), *Advances in experimental social psychology* (Vol. 28, pp. 53–93). New York: Academic Press.

Biased Recollections in Older Adults: The Role of Implicit Theories of Aging

Cathy McFarland, Michael Ross, and Mark Giltrow

This research explored how older adults recall the traits they possessed at an earlier age. It was hypothesized that older adults' recollections would be related to their theories about aging. In Study 1, a group of older Ss provided their theories concerning how various traits change with age. Another group of older Ss rated their current status on these traits and recalled the status they possessed at a younger age. In addition, a group of younger adults rated their current status on the same traits. On traits theorized to increase with age, older Ss recalled themselves as possessing lower levels at an earlier age than the younger group reported possessing. On traits theorized to decrease with age, older Ss recalled themselves as possessing higher levels at an earlier age than the younger group reported possessing. Study 2 indicated that this effect is obtained regardless of trait positivity.

How good was my memory 20 years ago? Was I happier when I was younger? Although people may query themselves about the past at any point in the life cycle, the answers they provide may become particularly important when they enter into late adulthood and evaluate the meaning of their lives (Buhler & Massarik, 1968;

This research was supported in part by a grant from the Gerontology Research Center at Simon Fraser University, by a Social Sciences and Humanities Research Council of Canada (SSHRCC) research grant, and by an SSHRCC Research Fellowship. We wish to express our appreciation to the staff and patrons of the Dogwood Pavilion Senior Citizens Center in Coquitlam, British Columbia, Canada, for their cooperation. In addition, we are grateful to Elinor Ames, Meredith Kimball, Darrin Lehman, Marlene Moretti, and three anonymous reviewers for their helpful comments on an earlier draft. Finally, we thank Anita Bloy and Shelley Loptson for their help with the second study.

Correspondence concerning this article should be addressed to Cathy McFarland, Department of Psychology, Simon Fraser University, Burnaby, British Columbia, Canada V5A IS6.

Butler, 1963; Cohler, 1982; Haight, 1988; Hausman, 1981; Molinari & Reichlin, 1985). In the present investigation, we explored the process by which older individuals recall what they were like at an earlier stage of life.

An investigation of older persons' recollections is important at this time in light of the growing interest in the phenomenological approach to the study of aging (Neugarten, 1977; Reker & Wong, 1988; Ryff, 1986; Whitbourne, 1985). Various theorists have proposed that as individuals age, they continually formulate general conceptions or summary representations of the course that their lives are taking. These "life stories" (Whitbourne, 1985), "life narratives" (McAdams, 1988), "personal narratives" (Cohler, 1982), "self-narratives" (Gergen & Gergen, 1983), or "autobiographies" (Birren & Hedlund, 1987) represent people's attempts to organize the experiences of their lives into a coherent, internally consistent sequence.

Although people may formulate these story-like representations of the past at any point in the life cycle, they may do so more frequently during later life (Butler, 1963; Butler & Lewis, 1982; Cohler, 1982; Hyland & Ackerman, 1988; Lieberman & Falk, 1971; Taft & Nehrke, 1990). To cope with the prospect of death, people may need to evaluate the meaning and value of their existence (Boylin, Gordon, & Nehrke, 1976; Erikson, 1950; Reker & Wong, 1988). In the course of this analysis, individuals may review their lives to establish their strengths and weaknesses, areas of decline and improvement, and so forth.

The constructions of the past that are arrived at through the life review process may have important consequences for the psychological adjustment of older individuals (Lewis & Butler, 1974; Merriam, 1980). For example, an older person who perceives his or her physical and mental abilities to be declining through the years may experience depression and a sense of hopelessness regarding the future. People's recollections of the qualities they possessed in the past may influence not only their current emotional reactions, but their behaviors and expectations for the future as well (Gergen & Gergen, 1983; Pipp, Shaver, Jennings, Lamborn, & Fischer, 1985; Ryff, 1984, 1986, 1989a; Thomae, 1970; Whitbourne, 1985). Recent research investigating memory self-efficacy (i.e., individuals' beliefs concerning their own memory abilities and changes in those abilities [Hertzog, Hultsch, & Dixon, 1989]) illustrates this latter point. Studies indicate that (a) older adults are more likely than younger adults to report declines in their memory ability (Hultsch, Hertzog, & Dixon, 1987), and (b) the perception of decline in memory ability relates to predictions and actual performance levels on memory tasks (Cavanaugh & Poon, 1989; Dixon & Hultsch, 1983; Hertzog, Dixon, & Hultsch, 1990). An exploration of older adults' recollections of the abilities and other personal characteristics they possessed earlier in life should help illuminate the nature of the life review process and its potential consequences for adjustment.

The voluminous literature pertaining to aging and memory appears to contain no previous research focusing specifically on older individuals' recollections of the personal qualities they possessed in various phases of their lives. In the typical study on aging and memory, two or more age groups are compared in terms of their ability to encode and retrieve information that has little personal relevance to their own lives — for example, nonsense syllables, words, or stories (for reviews, see Hertzog, Dixon, & Hultsch, 1990; Hultsch & Dixon,

1984; Poon, 1985). This type of research has documented some deficits in the memory performance of older adults, but the findings may not be that applicable to understanding the type of long-term recall that concerns us here.

There are some studies that have explored age differences in memory of material that has greater personal relevance. In a line of research exploring remote memories, older and younger individuals have been compared in terms of their ability to remember public, objectively verifiable, information such as news events from various time periods or the names of high school classmates (e.g., Bahrick, Bahrick, & Wittlinger, 1975; Botwinick & Storandt, 1974, 1980; Perlmutter, Metzger, Miller, & Nezworski, 1980; Poon, Fozard, Paulshock, & Thomas, 1979). In addition, researchers have explored age differences in (a) memory skills applicable to everyday life (e.g., the ability to remember to carry out certain actions, the ability to find lost objects, etc.; Herrmann & Neisser, 1979; Rabbitt & Abson, 1990; Sinnot, 1986; Tenney, 1984) and (b) people's memories of events in their own lives (Fitzgerald, 1988; Fitzgerald & Lawrence, 1984; Hyland & Ackerman, 1988; Rubin, Wetzler, & Nebes, 1986). In none of these studies, however, have older subjects been asked to recall their own attributes. The psychological processes that guide the recall of personal attributes may differ from those that guide the recall of specific objects or events.

In studies most pertinent to present concerns, researchers have explored people's conceptions of how various psychological characteristics change over the life course (Ryff, 1982, 1984, 1986; Ryff & Heincke, 1983). Older adults were asked to evaluate their current status on some personal characteristic (e.g., attitudes, values, or personality traits) and to recall their status at some earlier age. The difference between these two evaluations was used as a measure of self-perceived change. This type of design has helped researchers to (a) identify those qualities that are perceived by older individuals to change with age and (b) assess whether laypersons' conceptions of aging correspond to those of psychological theorists.

Unfortunately, this type of research design does not provide information concerning the accuracy with which older adults recall their past states or help identify the factors that may lead to inaccuracies. To assess the degree of bias inherent in older persons' recollections, one must compare their memories of their status at an earlier age with either their own self-conceptions measured at that age or the current self-conceptions of a comparable group of individuals who are presently that earlier age. Furthermore, to assess the potential causes of inaccuracies in memory, one must assess the relation between biases in recall and factors presumed to mediate such biases.

Although the accuracy with which older individuals recall their past characteristics and the recall strategies they use are topics that have not been investigated, a well-known study by Woodruff and Birren (1972) exploring middle-aged individuals' recollections of their youth provides considerable insight into these issues. Individuals completed the California Personality Inventory, a test of personal and social adjustment, at two time points. They were first tested when they were about 20 years of age, and they were tested a second time when they were about 45 years of age. At the end of the second testing session, they completed a retrospective version of the personality inventory in which they were required to respond to the questions as they thought they had 25 years earlier. The results indicated that the average level of social–personal adjustment in these individuals had not changed significantly over the years; nonetheless, middle-aged individuals recalled themselves as being less well-adjusted at age 20 than they had reported originally. Apparently, subjects perceived a change in personality that had not actually occurred.

Woodruff and Birren (1972) considered two potential explanations of this phenomenon. First, people may want to believe that they become better adjusted with age and thus construct a past that allows them to see improvement in themselves. Alternatively, people may hold stereotypes regarding the qualities possessed by various age groups and the ways in which these qualities change with age. Middle-aged individuals may use their stereotypes of adolescence to help them construct an image of what they must have been like at that stage of life.

Although Woodruff and Birren did not obtain data that would allow them to evaluate the validity of these two interpretations, recent work by Ross and his colleagues (Ross, 1989) offers considerable support for this second interpretation. According to these authors, the long-term recall of personal characteristics is a reconstructive process involving two steps. To characterize their prior status on some dimension, individuals first assess their present standing on that dimension and then attempt to judge whether their prior status differed in any way from their current status. To make this judgment, individuals make use of implicit theories regarding the inherent stability of personal attributes and the factors that may produce changes in those characteristics.

For example, a person may believe that aggressiveness is a quality that remains relatively stable over time, but that various factors (e.g., therapy, competitive events, age) have the potential to alter an individual's level of aggressiveness. In constructing how aggressive he or she was 5 years ago, the person is hypothesized to assess whether any events that could plausibly produce change have occurred during that time interval. If no such events can be identified, individuals use a *theory of stability* in constructing the past, assuming that their prior status is similar to their present status. On the other hand, if an event can be identified, individuals use a *theory of change* to recall the past, assuming that their prior status differs from their present status.

According to this analysis, people's memories will be accurate to the extent that the theory they use to recall the past is accurate. Systematic biases in memory should occur when the theory used fails to reflect the actual degree of change that has taken place over time. Previous research supportive of this model indicates that people overestimate the similarity between their present and past states when they invoke theories that assume stability in the face of actual change (McFarland & Ross, 1987); in contrast, people overestimate the difference between their present and past states when they invoke theories that assume change in a context in which they have actually remained stable (Conway & Ross, 1984; McFarland, Ross, & DeCourville, 1989).

This model of autobiographical memory can help explain the distorted recollections of Woodruff and Birren's (1972) middle-aged subjects and provides a basis for making predictions concerning the biases in recall that older adults might produce. Presumably, subjects in the Woodruff and Birren study possessed the erroneous theory that personal–social adjustment increases as people progress from adolescence to middle age. Along these lines, Ross (1989) found that university students hold the theory that adjustment improves from adolescence to middle age. Use of this inaccurate theory to construct the past may have led Woodruff and Birren's subjects to underestimate the degree of social–personal adjustment that they reported at age 20.

There is considerable evidence that older adults possess beliefs about how various personal qualities change as people grow older (Heckhausen, Dixon, & Baltes, 1989; Kite & Johnson, 1988; Rothbaum, 1983; Ryff, 1984, 1986, 1989a). It seems reasonable to propose that older individuals may use these theories to construct what they were like at a younger age. Under some conditions, the application of these theories will lead to biases in memory. Suppose a personal quality actually remains stable with age. When older individuals possess the theory that this quality increases with age they should underestimate the amount of the quality that they possessed at an earlier stage of life. Alternatively, when they possess the theory that this quality decreases with age they should overestimate the amount of the quality that they possessed at an earlier stage of life. Finally, when they believe that this quality is not affected by age their memories concerning the amount of the quality that they possessed in the past should be relatively unbiased.

Study 1 was designed to test these hypotheses concerning the factors that may influence older individuals' recollections. Our research was focused on biases in recall not because we believe that biased recollections are more common than accurate recollections or that people's theories of aging are generally inaccurate, but because (a) they provide an indication of the processes that guide recall, and (b) they may have important consequences for the well-being of older adults.

Study 1

Overview

In this study, we assessed (a) a group of older individuals' theories regarding the degree to which a variety of personality and physical characteristics change with age, (b) a different group of older individuals' self-perceptions of their current standing on these dimensions and their recollections of their standing at a younger age, and (c) a group of younger individuals' self-perceptions of their current standing on these dimensions. Our strongest predictions pertain to people's recollections of qualities that do not appear to change in any systematic way with age. Thus, we assessed age differences on each dimension (by comparing the older individuals' ratings of their current standing with the younger individuals' ratings to their current standing) and preselected those items for which no age differences were revealed. These characteristics were then subdivided into three categories on the basis of older individuals' theories of aging: qualities believed to increase with age, qualities believed to remain stable with age, and qualities believed to decrease with age.

A measure of memory bias for each personal characteristic was created by comparing the older individuals' recalled standing with the average current standing of individuals in the younger group. We hypothesized that older subjects' recollections would be biased on those traits for which theories of aging exaggerated the amount of change. Specifically, we expected that for qualities that are believed to increase with age yet remain stable, older individuals would recall themselves as exhibiting lower levels at an earlier age than the younger group reported possessing at that age. For qualities that are believed to decrease with age yet remain stable, they would recall themselves as exhibiting higher levels at an earlier age than the younger group reported possessing at that age. For those qualities that are believed to remain stable with age, older individuals' recollections should not vary systematically from the levels reported by the younger group.

Because a longitudinal design was impractical we chose to test our hypotheses using the cross-sectional method. The key feature of this approach is that we used the younger group's current standing as a representation of what the older group was like at a younger age. For example, memory bias is calculated by comparing across groups (i.e., by comparing the older group's recollections with the younger group's current ratings) rather than within individuals (i.e., by comparing older individuals' recollections of the past with their own past ratings). Although we acknowledge that terms such as *bias* and *accuracy* are more appropriate when used in reference to within-subject comparisons, we use them here because (a) our hypotheses focus on bias and (b) between-groups comparisons are the only method (albeit indirect) for assessing bias in the cross-sectional method. We should note that there are other limitations to this method; we discuss these at various points in this article.

Method

Subjects
There were two separate groups of older adults in the study: one group provided an assessment of older persons' theories regarding the impact of aging on a variety of dimensions (the theory assessment group); the other provided an assessment of older persons' current and recalled standing on these dimensions (the recall assessment group). We used two separate groups for these assessments to ensure that individuals would not feel compelled to report memories consistent with their own theories of aging. The subjects in both of these groups were approached individually at a local recreation center for senior citizens and asked to complete a questionnaire. On the recommendation of the staff, we thanked the subjects for their participation by providing them with coupons that could be used at the snack bar located

in the center. The recall assessment questionnaires were collected 2 weeks before the theory assessment questionnaires. Individuals who had completed a recall questionnaire were not allowed to complete a theory questionnaire. There were 21 women and 24 men in the theory assessment group and 29 women and 14 men in the recall assessment group. The average age of subjects in the theory assessment group was 68.6 years (ranging between 59 and 81 years), and the average age of subjects in the recall assessment group was 67.7 years (ranging between 55 and 78 years). Both groups of subjects were asked to rate their economic level (1 = upper class, 2 = middle class, and 3 = lower class) and educational level (1 = elementary, 2 = junior high, 3 = high school, and 4 = university or college). The average economic levels of these two groups were comparable (theory assessment group $M = 1.57$; recall assessment group $M = 1.67$, $t < 1$). The average educational level of the recall assessment group was somewhat higher ($M = 3.07$) than that of the theory assessment group ($M = 2.63$), $t(86) = 2.40$, $p < .05$.

The individuals in the younger group provided ratings of their current standing on the same dimensions rated by the older groups. In an attempt to achieve comparability between the younger and older samples, we approached younger individuals who resided in the neighborhood surrounding the community center. The majority of the seniors attending the recreation center lived within a radius of a few miles. The younger individuals were approached at their homes and were asked to complete the questionnaire. They were paid $5 for their participation. There were 22 women and 24 men in the younger group. The average age of individuals in this group was 38.20 years (ranging between 31 and 45 years), their average economic level was 1.94, and their average educational level was 3.52. The mean educational and economic levels of the younger group were significantly higher than those of both older groups ($ps < .05$). The implications of these age differences in education and economic status for the interpretation of our results is addressed later in this article.

Selection of Groups

The mean age of the younger group was approximately 38 years, and the mean age of the two older groups was approximately 67 years. We did not select for these particular age levels on an a priori basis. We were offered access to a large sample of older adults through a local community center. The mean age of the patrons happened to be 67 years. To recruit the younger sample, we went to homes in the neighborhood surrounding the center

and asked if there was anyone in the household between 30 and 54 years of age who would be willing to complete a questionnaire. The mean age of the volunteers happened to be 38 years. By selecting subjects in this age range, we hoped to obtain a sample that would be clearly differentiated from the older group in terms of age, but similar to the older group on other dimensions (e.g., settled into careers, marriages, and lifestyle). Note that for the purpose of testing our hypotheses concerning long-term recall over several decades, it was not critical for the older and younger samples to be prototypical of middle age and old age.

The three groups were contacted in the following order: (a) younger group, (b) recall assessment group, (c) theory assessment group. The younger group was tested first so that we could establish the age level that the recall assessment group would be asked to recall. The recall assessment group was tested next so that we could establish the time span (i.e., 38 years vs. 67 years) to be used in the questions provided to the theory assessment group.

Procedure

Assessment of older adults' theories of aging. On the first page of the questionnaire, subjects in the theory assessment group were informed that the purpose of the study was to assess their beliefs concerning the degree to which people undergo changes on a variety of personal characteristics between the ages of 38 and 67. In one section of the questionnaire, subjects were asked to rate the degree to which each of 42 personal characteristics changes between the ages of 38 and 67. The 42 characteristics are presented in Table 33.1. These characteristics were selected on the basis of an examination of previous research investigating changes associated with aging. We chose items that would reflect each of the following personal attribute domains: abilities, personality traits, and physical characteristics. Half of the subjects (men and women) were asked to rate the changes they believed would occur in the average man; the other half (men and women) rated the changes they believed would occur in the average woman. Below each trait item listed, there was a scale ranging from 1 (*extreme decrease in the level of the trait between the age of 38 and 67*) to 7 (*extreme increase in the level of the trait between the age of 38 and 67*). The value 4 on the rating scale indicated *no change between the age of 38 and 67*.

In addition to assessing subjects' theories regarding changes occurring in the average person, we assessed their theories concerning changes occurring in themselves. We measured both types of theories because either type could be used by subjects as an aid in recollecting

TABLE 33.1. Mean Perceived Age Changes in Self and Average Other and Actual Age Differences

Item	Actual Age Difference			Theories of Age Change in Average Other			Theories of Age Change in Self		
	Overall	Men	Women	Overall	Men	Women	Overall	Men	Women
1. Leadership ability	−.33*	.05*	−.32*	4.51_n	4.30_n	4.70_n	4.54_i	4.91_i	4.15_n
2. Independent	.60	.14*	.97	5.26_i	4.90_i	5.57_i	5.57_i	5.78_i	5.30_i
3. Forceful	−.57	−1.17	−.09*	4.23_n	4.20_n	4.26_n	4.46_i	4.30_n	4.65_i
4. Masculine	−.65*	−.31*	.07*	3.70_n	3.85_n	3.55_n	3.48_d	3.78_n	3.06_d
5. Understanding	.32*	.68*	.02*	5.80_i	5.67_i	5.91_i	5.64_i	5.87_i	5.45_i
6. Involved in politics	.56*	.86*	.47*	4.16_n	4.00_n	4.30_n	4.03_n	4.52_n	3.40_d
7. Willing to stand up for beliefs	.37*	.19*	.52	5.46_i	5.14_i	5.74_i	5.55_i	5.48_i	5.55_i
8. Affectionate	−.36*	.87	−1.28	4.98_i	5.05_i	4.91_i	5.10_i	4.87_i	5.40_i
9. Shy	−.60*	−.70*	−.61*	3.64_n	3.24_d	4.00_n	2.77_d	2.74_d	2.85_d
10. Successful	.03*	.31*	−.10*	4.35_n	4.65_n	4.09_n	4.71_i	5.09_i	4.30_n
11. Quick-thinking	−.69	−.59*	−.62*	3.41_d	3.33_d	3.48_n	3.73_n	3.74_n	3.70_n
12. Kind	.05*	.40*	−.24*	5.59_i	5.52_i	5.65_i	5.47_i	5.61_i	5.35_i
13. Relaxed	.53*	.24*	.84	4.80_i	5.19_i	4.44_n	5.14_i	5.48_i	4.95_i
14. Rugged	.09*	−.01*	.50*	3.18_d	3.29_d	3.09_d	3.02_d	3.04_d	2.95_d
15. Satisfied with life	.47*	.47*	.47*	5.07_i	5.05_i	5.09_i	5.20_i	5.26_i	5.10_i
16. Happy	−.16*	−.07*	−.30*	4.51_n	5.25_i	3.87_n	4.64_i	4.87_i	4.55_n
17. Active	−.09*	.04*	−.20*	3.28_d	3.00_d	3.52_n	3.05_d	2.64_d	3.50_n
18. Outgoing	.30*	.56*	.13*	4.17_n	3.85_n	4.45_n	4.25_n	4.13_n	4.40_n
19. Concerned about others	.56	.39*	.57	5.42_i	5.30_i	5.52_i	5.30_i	5.00_i	5.70_n
20. Pride in oneself	.15*	.17*	.12*	4.84_i	4.65_n	5.00_i	4.61_i	4.78_i	4.45_i
21. Capable	−.34*	−.59*	−.20*	4.24_n	3.80_n	4.67_n	3.95_n	3.83_n	4.10_n
22. Well-adjusted	.15*	.33*	.02*	5.12_i	4.90_i	5.33_i	4.81_i	4.96_i	4.70_i
23. Intelligent	−.19*	.03*	−.12*	4.64_i	4.50_n	4.77_i	4.48_i	4.39_n	4.60_i
24. Ability to remember news events of 10 years previous	−.24*	−.03*	−.10*	3.57_n	3.50_n	3.64_n	3.43_d	3.30_d	3.50_n
25. Ability to remember faces and names of acquaintances of 20 years ago	.12*	.21*	.22*	3.50_n	3.65_n	3.36_d	3.33_d	3.32_n	3.35_n
26. Ability to remember to do everyday activities	.04*	−.61*	.40*	3.50_d	3.55_n	3.46_n	4.12_n	4.00_n	4.25_n
27. Ability to remember a name or phone number (right after hearing it)	−.09*	−.04*	.14*	2.79_d	2.65_d	2.91_d	2.88_d	2.82_d	2.90_d
28. Ability to detect pain	.19*	.21*	.12*	4.62_i	4.25_n	4.96_i	4.21_n	4.32_n	4.10_n
29. Sensitivity to hot temperatures	1.21	.32*	1.82	4.70_i	4.35_n	5.00_i	4.67_i	4.68_n	4.70_n
30. Sensitivity to cold temperatures	1.14	1.71	.64*	5.02_i	4.85_i	5.17_i	4.88_i	5.64_i	4.05_n
31. Ability to taste sweet and salty foods	.38*	.74*	−.04*	4.02_n	3.95_n	4.09_n	4.23_n	4.17_n	4.25_n
32. Degree of physical discomforts	.28*	−.06*	.52*	4.93_i	4.95_i	4.91_i	4.84_i	5.00_i	4.60_i
33. Worried about physical problems	.51*	.21*	.68*	4.81_i	4.40_n	5.17_i	4.57_i	4.83_i	4.20_n
34. Worried about stomach problems	.51*	.32*	.77*	4.56_i	4.15_n	4.91_i	4.20_n	4.30_n	4.00_n
35. Worried about chest pain	.31*	.11*	.75*	4.88_i	5.05_i	4.74_i	4.63_i	4.91_i	4.16_n
36. Depressed	.68	−.04*	1.16	4.43_n	4.45_n	4.41_n	4.29_n	4.35_n	4.10_n
37. Importance of being attractive	.14*	−.15*	.04*	3.91_n	4.00_n	3.83_n	4.05_n	4.04_n	4.05_n
38. Positive about body	.42*	.29*	.47*	3.93_n	3.85_n	4.00_n	4.19_n	4.05_n	4.32_n
39. Intensity of emotions (how strongly one experiences feelings)	.27*	.35*	−.02*	4.79_i	4.20_n	5.30_i	4.50_i	4.70_n	4.30_n
40. Duration of emotions (how long it takes to return to normal)	.37*	.24*	.30*	4.61_i	4.80_i	4.44_n	4.36_n	4.48_n	4.15_n
41. Emotional excitability	−.16*	.26*	−.65	3.88_n	4.10_n	3.70_n	4.05_n	4.22_n	3.80_d
42. Mood swings (in a given day)	.11*	−.18*	.25*	3.95_n	4.25_n	3.70_n	3.52_n	3.35_n	3.70_d

Note. Positive values on the age difference measure indicate that the older group had a higher average current rating than the younger group. Negative values on the age difference measure indicate that the older group had a lower average current rating than the younger group. Numbers higher than 4 on the theories measure indicate that subjects believed the quality to increase with age. Numbers lower than 4 on this measure indicate that subjects believed the quality to decrease with age. The value 4 indicates that subjects believed the quality to remain stable over time. Subscript i = theory of increase item; subscript n = theory of no change; subscript d = theory of decrease.
* $p > .05$.

their pasts. Subjects indicated the degree to which they personally had changed since they were 38 years old on the 42 personal dimensions. The order of the self and average other ratings was counterbalanced.

Assessment of older adults' current and recalled standing. The second group of older subjects was informed on the first page of the questionnaire that we were interested in how they see themselves at this point in their life on a variety of personal characteristics and in how they remembered being at the age of 38 on these same characteristics. Subjects were presented with the list of 42 personal characteristics and asked to rate both their present standing on each trait and the standing that they recalled themselves having at age 38. Below each trait label were two scales, each ranging from 1 (*no amount of the quality*) to 7 (*extreme amount of the quality*). Subjects rated their present standing on the first scale and their recalled standing on the second scale.

Assessment of younger adults' current standing. Subjects were informed on the first page of their questionnaire that we were interested in how they see themselves at this point in their life on a variety of personal characteristics. They were asked to rate their current standing on the 42 dimensions listed in Table 33.1 on the same 7-point rating scales that were used to evaluate the older individuals' current standing.

Subjects in each of the three groups were assured of the anonymity of their responses and were encouraged to ask questions if they encountered any problems. The instructions appear to have been quite clear; no subjects reported any difficulties in understanding the task.

Results

Age Differences on Personal Characteristics
Initially, we needed to assess which of the 42 characteristics remain stable during adulthood. For each trait, we performed *t* tests to examine whether there was a significant difference between the mean of the younger individuals' current ratings of self and the mean of the older individuals' current ratings of self. The age differences obtained on the 42 trait dimensions are presented in the first data column of Table 33.1. Age differences on each trait were calculated by subtracting the mean of the younger group from the mean of the older group. Positive values indicate that the older group reported a higher level on the trait than the younger group; negative values indicate that the older group reported a lower level on the trait than the younger group. Analyses revealed significant age differences (at the .05 level of significance) on only 7 of the 42 characteristics.

The 35 characteristics that did not show a significant age difference are noted in Table 33.1 with an asterisk.

The above analyses were collapsed across subject sex. We performed additional analyses to assess age differences within each sex. Analyses comparing the men in the younger group with those in the older group on each trait dimension revealed 39 characteristics for which no significant age difference was obtained. Similar analyses comparing the women in each group yielded 34 characteristics for which no significant age difference was obtained. The age differences observed on each trait in men and women are presented in the second and third data columns of Table 33.1. Again, those characteristics revealing no statistically significant age differences are indicated by an asterisk.

Theories of Aging
Subjects' theories regarding age changes on each of the 42 dimensions are presented in Table 33.1. The theory assessment group rated both the degree to which the average other man (or woman) changes with age, and the degree to which they themselves changed with age. The mean ratings of the average man (collapsed across subject sex), the average woman (collapsed across subject sex), and the average other person (collapsed across target sex and subject sex) are presented in data columns 4, 5, and 6. The mean self ratings provided by men, women, and the overall sample are presented in data columns 7, 8, and 9.

For each target type, we subdivided the items into 3 categories: *theory of increase* items were those for which the mean rating was significantly greater (at the $p < .05$ level) than 4 (the point on the scale representing no perceived age change), *theory of decrease* items were those for which the mean rating was significantly lower (at the $p < .05$ level) than 4, and *theory of no change* items were those for which the mean rating did not differ significantly from the value of 4. Theory of increase, decrease, and no change items are noted in Table 33.1 with subscripts i, d, and n, respectively.

Items were classified as theory of no change items when the mean did not differ significantly from 4 (the value on the rating scale labeled *no change*). We examined the frequency distribution of scores on each of these items to assess whether scores were normally distributed about the mean. It would be inappropriate to classify an item as one for which subjects expect no change if scores on the item were bimodally distributed (i.e., if there was a high percentage of scores at the two extremes of the distribution). For each item, we calculated the percentage of responses falling at each of the seven scale values. Across all theory of no change items (theories of the average other), the average percentage of responses at each value was the following: 1–12%, 2–5%, 3–13%, 4–40%, 5–12%, 6–8%, 7–10%. The corresponding figures for the theory of no change items pertaining to self were: 1–12%, 2–5%, 3–7%, 4–45%, 5–11%, 6–10%, 7–10%. Examination of these percentages indicates that the distributions of scores on the theory of no change items tended to be normally distributed about the mean. Furthermore, the percentage of responses at the value 4 was substantially higher than the percentage of responses at any other single scale value. Thus, it seems justifiable to portray these items as ones for which older adults expect little change over time.

Relation Between Theories of Aging and Recall Bias
Primary analysis. We predicted that the direction and degree of bias in older persons' recollections would depend on theories of aging. In the main analysis relevant to this prediction we explored recall bias in the overall sample (collapsed across subject sex) as a function of older individuals' theories of the average person. The 35 items that did *not* show age differences (see data column 1 of Table 33.1) were divided into the three theory of aging categories, yielding the following breakdown: theory of increase items (items 5, 7, 8, 12, 13, 15, 20, 22, 23, 28, 32, 33, 34, 35, 39, and 40), theory of no change items (items 1, 4, 6, 9, 10, 16, 18, 21, 24, 25, 31, 37, 38, 41, and 42), and theory of decrease items (14, 17, 26, and 27). We then created a measure of memory bias on each item for each subject by subtracting the average of the younger individuals' current ratings on that item from each older subject's rating of his or her recalled standing on that trait. A measure reflecting recall bias for each of the three item types was created by averaging across individual items in each category. Positive values on this measure indicated that subjects recalled themselves as having more of a trait at age 38 than the younger group reported having. Negative values indicated that subjects recalled themselves as having less of a trait at age 38 than the younger group reported having.

A one-way repeated measures analysis of variance (ANOVA; theory of aging in the average person: increase vs. no change vs. decrease) performed on this measure of recall bias revealed a significant effect for theories of aging, $F(2, 84) = 14.09$, $p < .0001$ (see Table 33.2 for relevant means). Consistent with our predictions, subjects' recollections appear to reflect theories of aging. Specifically, subjects' recollections of qualities believed to increase with age were more biased ($M = -.21$, in the direction of recalling themselves as

TABLE 33.2. Mean Biases in Recall as a Function of Theories of Aging in Men, Women, and the Overall Sample

Theory Target and Subsample	Theory of Aging		
	Theory of Increase	Theory of No Change	Theory of Decrease
Theories of average other			
Overall	$-.21_a$	$.04_b$	$.51_c$
Men	$-.30_a$	$.27_b$	$.33_b$
Women	$-.17_a$	$-.09_a$	$.74_b$
Theories of aging in the self			
Overall	$-.27_a$	$.17_b$	$.22_b$
Men	$-.27_a$	$.27_b$	$.54_b$
Women	$-.29_a$	$-.09_a$	$.38_b$

Note. Within rows, means *not* sharing a common subscript differ significantly ($p < .05$). Positive values on the recall bias measure indicate that subjects recalled possessing a higher amount of the quality at an earlier age than the younger group reported having at that age. Negative values on the recall bias measure indicate that subjects recalled possessing a lower amount of the quality at an earlier age than the younger group reported having at that age.

possessing less of the characteristic at age 38 than the younger group reported possessing) than their recollections of qualities believed to remain stable ($M = .04$), $t(84) = 2.10$, $p < .05$. Similarly, subjects' recollections of qualities believed to decrease with age were more biased ($M = .51$, in the direction of recalling themselves as possessing more of a characteristic at age 38 than the younger group reported possessing) than their recollections of qualities believed to remain stable with age ($M = .04$), $t(84) = 3.92$, $p < .001$.[1]

---

[1] Earlier, we reported that the education and economic levels of the recall assessment group were significantly lower than those of the younger group. We conducted an additional analysis to assess whether the relation between theories of aging and recall is obtained when educational and economic levels are held constant. An analysis of variance using theories of aging (increase vs. no change vs. decrease) and age group–measure (older subjects' recalled standing vs. younger subjects' current standing) as predictors and using education and economic levels as covariates was performed on subjects' ratings of their attributes. This analysis revealed a significant interaction between theories of aging and age group–measure, $F(2, 168) = 10.20$, $p < .0001$. The pattern of adjusted means associated with this interaction supports the conclusion that theories are related to recall, independent of the influence of economic and educational levels. On the theory of decrease items, the older group's recalled standing ($M = 5.02$) was significantly higher than the younger group's current standing ($M = 4.32$), $t(82) = 3.03$, $p < .01$. On the theory of increase items, the older group's recalled standing ($M = 4.30$) was somewhat lower than the younger group's current standing ($M = 4.53$), $t(82) = 1.90$, $p < .07$. On the theory of no change items, the older group's recalled standing ($M = 4.58$) was comparable to the younger group's current standing ($M = 4.46$), $t < 1$.

Subsidiary analyses. The above analysis revealed a highly significant relation between theories of aging and recall bias. Additional analyses were conducted to explore whether this relation would be obtained if we used alternative methods for classifying items into the theory of aging categories.

In the primary analysis there was an unequal number of items in each theory category, and there were relatively few items in the theory of decrease category. We created three equal-sized categories by (a) rank ordering the 35 items used in the primary analysis in terms of the mean theory rating, and (b) performing a tertile split. This procedure yielded the following classification: theory of increase items (5, 7, 8, 12, 13, 15, 20, 22, 32, 33, 35, and 39), theory of no change items (1, 6, 10, 16, 18, 21, 23, 28, 31, 34, 40, and 42), and theory of decrease items (4, 9, 14, 17, 24, 25, 26, 27, 37, 38, and 41). The ANOVA based on this new classification revealed a significant effect for the theories of aging variable on the recall bias measure, $F(2, 84) = 10.75$, $p < .0001$.

In both of the above analyses, there were some items in the theory of no change category that had relatively higher variabilities (i.e., a relatively lower percentage of subjects falling at exactly the value 4) on the theory measure. Thus, we conducted an analysis using a more stringent criterion for assigning items to the theory of no change category. For this analysis, an item was classified as a theory of no change item if 40% or more of the theory responses fell at the value of 4. This procedure yielded the following classification scheme: theory of increase items (1, 5, 6, 7, 8, 12, 13, 15, 16, 20, 21, 22, 32, 33, 34, 35, 39, and 40), theory of no change items (4, 10, 18, 23, 28, 31, and 38), and theory of decrease items (9, 14, 17, 24, 25, 26, 27, 37, 41, and 42). Again, the ANOVA revealed a significant effect for the theory of aging variable, $F(2, 84) = 8.65$, $p < .001$.

The primary analysis, as well as the ones just reported, focused on theories of aging in the average person (collapsed across target sex). Additional analyses were conducted for theories of aging in the average man and woman, as well as for older individuals' theories of how they themselves changed with age (relevant means are presented in Table 33.2). Each analysis yielded a highly significant effect for the theories of aging variable and results comparable to those obtained in the primary analysis.[2] Taken together, the subsidiary analyses suggest that the primary finding is robust: a relation between theories of aging and recall bias is obtained across various methods of theory categorization, as well as across various target groups.

---

[2] A separate report of these analyses is available from the first author.

Study 2

Study 1 offered support for the prediction that older persons' recollections of the characteristics they possessed at an earlier age would be influenced by their theories of aging. Specifically, the biases in recall shown by these individuals appear to be consistent with their theories of how people change with age.

The purpose of Study 2 was to clarify two issues. First, we collected data that would allow us to assess the role that motives for self-enhancement play in biases in older individuals' recollections. Various authors have proposed that people may at times construct their pasts in ways that serve to bolster self-esteem (Clark & Isen, 1982; Greenwald, 1980; Ross, 1989; Sanitioso, Kunda, & Fong, 1990; Swann, 1987; Taylor & Brown, 1988). If self-esteem concerns influence the recollections of older people, we would expect the relation between theories of aging and recall bias to reflect the favorability of the characteristic being recalled. Specifically, biases in recall should be greater for positive qualities theorized to increase with age than for positive qualities theorized to decrease with age, and greater for negative qualities theorized to decrease with age than for negative qualities theorized to increase with age. This pattern of bias would support the theory that people improve with age, and therefore, might enhance self-esteem (Woodruff & Birren, 1972). In Study 2, we obtained older individuals' evaluations of the favorability of the 42 characteristics used in Study 1. We then reanalyzed the recall data of Study 1, exploring the impact of trait favorability on the relation between theories of aging and recall bias.

The second purpose of this study was to assess the validity of a potential alternative account of the findings of Study 1. Our position is that in recalling their pasts, older subjects invoked theories that specified greater age changes in their personal qualities than had actually occurred. An alternative possibility, however, is that respondents' theories and recollections were accurate, whereas the assessment of age changes in personal characteristics was not. Individuals' assessments of current status might reflect a normalization of the response scale that renders the ratings of the older and younger individuals non-comparable. When evaluating their current standing, older individuals may have compared themselves with other older persons, whereas younger individuals may have compared themselves with other younger persons. To the extent that subjects rated their current status "relative" to same-aged peers, genuine age differences in personal qualities may have been obscured. For example, an older man may evaluate his degree of physical discomfort relative to that of other older men, whereas a younger man may evaluate his physical discomfort relative to other younger men. Thus, a rating of 4 on a 7-point scale by each individual could mean different things because they are using different standards (Biernat, Manis, & Nelson, 1991; Higgins & Lurie, 1983). The general absence of age differences in the present data is consistent with this alternative interpretation of the findings. Accordingly, in Study 2, we attempted to examine more closely the process by which people evaluate their current standing on personal dimensions.

Method

Subjects
Seventy-one older individuals (20 men and 51 women) were approached at the same local community centre used in Study 1 and asked if they would volunteer to complete a questionnaire. The mean age of these individuals was 65.9 years (ranging between 55 and 79 years), their mean educational level was 3.03, and their mean economic level was 2.37. Again, the subjects were offered snack bar coupons in thanks for their participation.

Procedure
In the first section of the questionnaire, subjects were asked to respond to questions designed to help clarify the process by which subjects in Study 1 may have evaluated their current status on the personal attribute dimensions. On the first page, they were informed (as were the younger and older subjects [recall assessment group] in Study 1) that one purpose of our research was to explore how they see themselves at this point in their life. They were to rate the degree to which they possessed a variety of personal qualities at their current age. In addition, they were told (as were the older subjects in Study 1) that we were interested in how they recalled being at age 38. Subjects then provided ratings (on the same scales used in Study 1) of their current and recalled standing on 6 characteristics selected at random from the list of 42 characteristics investigated in Study 1 (satisfied with life, physical discomforts, involved in politics, mood swings, ability to remember to do things, and active). They were then asked to respond to either an open-ended or forced-choice question assessing *how* they evaluated their current status. The open-ended assessment required subjects to briefly describe how they went about rating their current standing on one characteristic (satisfied with life). Subjects

receiving the forced-choice assessment were informed that people might use two strategies in order to evaluate their present standing on the 6 personal qualities: (a) compare themselves with what they were like in the past or (b) compare themselves with other people of their own age group. We provided these two response options because our intuition was that they would be the most common types of comparisons used by subjects. Respondents were asked to indicate which of these two strategies they mainly used when evaluating their current standing on the 6 qualities. The ordering of the two response options was counterbalanced.

In the second half of the questionnaire, subjects were asked to evaluate how positive it is for the average woman (or average man) of their age to possess each of 42 qualities. Below each of the characteristics was a scale ranging from 1 (*extremely negative quality to have*) to 7 (*extremely positive quality to have*). Half of the subjects (both men and women) evaluated the average woman; the other half (both men and women) evaluated the average man.

Results

Process of Evaluating Current Status
We obtained subjects' descriptions of how they evaluated their current status to establish the degree to which these evaluations were influenced by comparisons with same-age peers. Responses to the open-ended question were placed into one of three categories. The first category was labeled *past focus*. A response was placed in this category if the subject made reference to the past or to changes occurring over time in evaluating his or her current status (e.g., "Being medically unable to work has changed my life a lot," or "Since retirement, life has changed dramatically and a certain amount of dissatisfaction is occasioned by close proximity to my spouse 24 hrs a day"). The second category was labeled *present focus*. A response was placed in this category if a subject considered his or her present life conditions in evaluating his or her current status (e.g., "Having good friends helps me," "Our whole family has good health," or "Just to live in a country like Canada is a privilege"). The third category was labeled *peer focus*. A response was placed in this category if the subject reported comparing himself or herself with same-age peers. Interrater reliability was high: 85% of the responses were categorized identically by two raters. All responses were codable into one of these three categories. The percentage of responses in each category was the following: 48% for past focus, 52% for present

focus, and 0% for peer focus. These results indicate that at least for the characteristic "satisfied with life," subjects do not appear to evaluate their current status by comparing themselves with same-age peers.

Analyses of the forced-choice question indicated that 72% of the subjects reported that they evaluated their current status on the six dimensions mainly by referring to the past; only 28% reported making comparisons with same-age peers, $\chi^2(1, N = 36) = 7.10, p < .01$. Overall, the findings on these two measures indicate that, at least in the present context, people do not appear to evaluate their current standing by comparing themselves with same-age peers. Thus, these results offer evidence against the "change in standards" interpretation of the age difference findings of Study 1.

We found little evidence of social comparison in our open-ended data. This result may seem surprising in light of research on social comparison processes. This work indicates that people do compare their attributes with those of others and that self-evaluations and affective reactions are influenced by such comparisons (see Suls & Wills, 1991, and Wood, 1989, for reviews). For the most part, however, social comparison research has assessed subjects' reactions to structured opportunities for comparison rather than spontaneous social comparisons (as we did here). There are some notable recent exceptions to this general rule. Researchers exploring the coping process in various victim groups (e.g., cancer patients, arthritis patients) have used open-ended methodologies to assess comparison strategies. They have obtained evidence for spontaneous social comparison (Affleck & Tennen, 1991; Wood, 1989). There are two important differences between our study and those that have obtained evidence of spontaneous social comparison. First, our subjects were not victims and were therefore not experiencing personal threat. Threat has been shown to be a major factor influencing the social comparison process (Suls & Wills, 1991). Second, our subjects were older adults. It has been proposed that older individuals may be less likely to engage in social comparison than younger individuals (Suls & Mullen, 1982). Further research is needed to assess (a) the frequency of spontaneous social comparison in nonthreatened samples, (b) age differences in spontaneous social comparison, and (c) the relative frequency of social versus other types of comparison in self-evaluation.

Although our data suggest that older adults may not use same-age peers as a basis of comparison in evaluating their personal attributes, we do not wish to imply that their judgments are made without reference to standards. Individuals' expectations concerning old age, for exam-

ple, may serve as comparative baselines against which current status is evaluated. A particular experience may be judged as more or less extreme, depending on (a) the level of one's prior expectations and (b) whether one's experiences are assimilated to, or contrasted with, the prior expectation (Manis, Nelson, & Shedler, 1988). We focused our attention on the "same-age peer" standard because of its relevance for explaining the large number of nonsignificant age differences in our data. Note that the use of prior expectations as evaluative standards could just as easily produce exaggerated age differences as it could diminished ones.

Trait Favorability and the Relation Between Theories of Aging and Recall Bias

To explore the potential role that self-esteem concerns play in recall, we reanalyzed the recall bias data from Study 1. Specifically, we assessed whether the relation between older individuals' theories of aging and recall bias changed as a function of the favorability of the trait being recalled.

Our initial analysis collapsed across subject sex. The items in each of the three theory of aging categories (i.e., theories of the average other person) were subdivided further into two additional categories based on Study 2 subjects' ratings of the favorability of the traits in that category: positive traits and negative traits. Within each theory category, the traits were rank-ordered from the most positive to the least positive. Half of the traits (those with the highest rankings) were classified as positive; the remainder were classified as negative. This procedure yielded six item categories: positive theory of increase items, negative theory of increase items, positive theory of no change items, negative theory of no change items, positive theory of decrease items, and negative theory of decrease items. The items in each category are presented in Table 33.3. A measure of recall bias for each individual (on each item type) was calculated by subtracting the average of the younger group's current rating on an item from each subject's recalled rating and then averaging across the items in each category. A 3×2 repeated measures ANOVA (Theory of Aging: increase vs. no change vs. decrease $\times$ Trait Favorability: positive vs. negative) performed on this measure yielded a main effect for theories of aging, $F(2, 84) = 14.04, p < .0001$, that was not qualified by an interaction effect between theories and trait favorability ($F < 1$). The main effect of trait favorability was also nonsignificant ($F < 1$).

An examination of the pattern of means presented in the first two data rows of Table 33.4 reveals little support

TABLE 33.3. Personal Attributes Classification as a Function of Theory Type and Positivity

Theory of Increase	Theory of No Change	Theory of Decrease
	Positive attributes	
5. Understanding	1. Leadership ability	17. Active
7. Willing to stand up for beliefs	10. Successful	26. Ability to remember to do everyday activities
	16. Happy	
8. Affectionate	18. Outgoing	
12. Kind	21. Capable	
13. Relaxed	31. Ability to taste sweet and salty foods	
15. Satisfied with life		
22. Well-adjusted	37. Importance of being attractive	
23. Intelligent	38. Positive about body	
	Negative attributes	
20. Pride in oneself	4. Masculine	14. Rugged
28. Ability to detect pain	6. Involved in politics	27. Ability to remember a name or phone number (right after hearing it)
32. Degree of physical discomforts	9. Shy	
33. Worried about physical problems	24. Ability to remember news events of 10 years previous	
34. Worried about stomach problems	25. Ability to remember faces and names of acquaintances of 20 years ago	
35. Worried about chest pain	41. Emotional excitability	
39. Intensity of emotions (how strongly one experiences feelings)	41. Emotional excitability	
40. Duration of emotions (how long it takes to return to normal)	42. Mood swings (in a given day)	

for the proposition that older peoples' recollections are more biased when they support theories of improvement than when they support theories of decline. For example, the bias in recall of characteristics believed to decrease with age was similar for positive ($M = .45$) and negative ($M = .57$) characteristics ($t < 1$).

Similar analyses were conducted on the male and female subsamples. The results of these analyses were comparable to those obtained on the overall sample. The main effects for theories of aging — male subsample, $F(2, 26) = 8.27$, $p < .005$; female subsample, $F(2, 56) = 8.72$, $p < .001$ — were not qualified by interactions between theories of aging and trait favorability ($Fs < 1$). In addition, the main effects for trait favorability were nonsignificant ($Fs < 1$).

In the analyses reported above, half of the personal attributes within each of the theory type categories were classified as positive, and the remainder were classified as negative. A potential problem with this method of categorization is that some of the items classified as

TABLE 33.4. Mean Biases in Recall as a Function of Theories of Aging and Positivity of Characteristics

Sample and Positivity of Trait	Theory of Aging		
	Theory of Increase	Theory of No Change	Theory of Decrease
Overall			
Positive	−.29	.01	.45
Negative	−.14	.07	.57
Men			
Positive	−.23	.35	.50
Negative	−.38	.18	.17
Women			
Positive	−.36	−.18	.79
Negative	.05	.01	.66

Note. Positive values on the recall bias measure indicate that subjects recalled possessing a higher amount of the quality at an earlier age than the younger group reported having at that age. Negative values on the recall bias measure indicate that subjects recalled possessing a lower amount of the quality at an earlier age than the younger group reported having at that age.

negative were ones that did not receive particularly low favorability ratings. Thus, we conducted an additional analysis using a categorization in which only those items that received low favorability ratings (below 4 on the favorability rating scale) were classified as negatively valued attributes (items 4, 9, 14, 32, 33, 34, 40, 41, and 42). The results of this analysis were comparable to those based on the original categorization. The pattern of means was similar to that reported in Table 33.4 (theory of increase positive items, $M = -.23$; theory of no change positive items, $M = .12$; theory of decrease positive items, $M = +.49$; theory of increase negative items, $M = -.17$; theory of no change negative items, $M = -.17$; theory of decrease negative items, $M = .57$. Furthermore, the main effect of theories of aging was significant, $F(2, 84) = 8.5$, $p < .01$, and the interaction and the main effect of trait favorability were both nonsignificant ($Fs < 1$).

General Discussion

The present investigations were designed to explore the process by which older individuals recollect the personal attributes they possessed in the past. The results of Study 1 supported the hypothesis that older adults' recollections would be influenced by culturally shared theories about the changes that people experience as they grow older. For those qualities theorized to increase with age (but that appear to remain stable), older individuals recalled themselves as possessing a lower amount of the attributes at an earlier age than the younger group reported possessing at that age. For qualities theorized to decrease with age (but that appear to remain stable), older people recalled themselves as possessing a greater amount of the attributes at an earlier age than the younger group reported possessing at that age. The results of Study 2 indicated that theories of aging predicted recall of both positively and negatively valued personal attributes. Biases in recall that would support theories of improvement with age were no larger than those that would support theories of decline.

Limitations

Before the implications of these findings are addressed, it is important to discuss two aspects of our research that may limit the generalizability of the results. The first set of problems derives from the fact that we used a cross-sectional design to test our hypotheses. The nature of this design leads to concerns about the validity of two of our measures: the age difference measure (which was calculated by comparing the older group's current ratings with the younger group's current ratings) and the recall bias measure (which was calculated by comparing older individuals' recalled ratings with the average of the younger group's current ratings). The validity of both of these assessments rests on the assumption that the younger group's current ratings were an adequate representation of what the older group was like at an earlier age. Unfortunately, this may not be the case. The older group and the younger group represent different cohorts and thus were exposed to different historical-cultural forces — forces that could potentially influence the types of characteristics explored in our research.

Although we recognize the potential validity of these concerns, there are reasons to believe that the younger group's current ratings may not be an inaccurate reflection of what the older group was like at a younger age. In our study, we obtained no significant age differences on the vast majority of traits investigated. In general, this finding is consistent with the findings of previous researchers. For approximately 75% of the attributes we studied that revealed no age differences, there are previous studies that obtained similar results.[3] The consistency of our findings with those of other researchers offers some support for the validity of our measures.

Additional interpretational problems arise because of the correlational nature of the design. We explored the relation between naturally occurring theories of aging and recall bias. Because we did not experimentally manipulate older persons' theories of aging, it is possible that a third variable is operating in conjunction with our theories of aging variable. That is, the set of traits theorized by older people to increase with age may differ

---

[3] The relevant studies (for each personal quality) are: Feldman, Biringham, & Nash (1981; personal characteristics 1, 4, 5, 7, 8, and 9); Monge (1975; 10 and 14); Nehrke, Hulicka, & Morganti (1980; 15, 20, 21, and 18); Douglas & Arenberg (1978; 16 and 42); Costa & McCrae (1988; 5, 8, 13, 16, 17, 18, and 36); Poon, Fozard, Paulshock, & Thomas (1979; 24); Schaie (1979; 23); Bahrick, Bahrick, & Wittlinger (1975; 25); Poon (1985; 26 and 27); Plutchik, Weiner, & Conte (1971; 32, 33, 34, and 35); Berscheid, Walster, & Bohrnstedt (1973; 37 and 38); Schultz (1982; 39); Cameron (1975; 16); Bengtson, Reedy, & Gordon (1985; 20 and 21); Sinnot (1986; 26); Havighurst, Neugarten, & Tobin (1968; 15). It is noteworthy that some of these studies (Costa & McCrae, 1988; Douglas & Arenberg, 1978; Schaie, 1979) used longitudinal designs (cross-sequential/time-sequential) to assess maturational effects.

from those theorized to decrease with age on a variety of dimensions (e.g., controllability, importance). Thus, it is possible that these extraneous factors are responsible for the observed pattern of recall distortion. Furthermore, we have no evidence pertaining to the direction of the relation between theories of aging and recall bias. Our position is that the use of theories of aging led to the observed biases in recall. However, it is possible that systematic biases in recall produced by alternative factors may lead older people to formulate particular theories of aging.

Implications

Although we acknowledge the above limitations of our design, we believe that the findings of the present research offer some additional support for the model of personal attribute recall proposed by Ross and his colleagues (Ross, 1989). Presumably, the older participants found it difficult to recall the qualities they possessed some 30 years earlier. Consequently, they may have made use of currently available information (specifically, their current status on personal attributes and their implicit theories of aging regarding those attributes) in an attempt to reconstruct their prior status. Because many of their theories specified greater change over time than actually occurred, the use of these theories to help them estimate their past status may have produced the observed systematic biases in memory.

The current studies extend previous work relevant to Ross's model in several ways. First, they offer additional evidence of a direct relation between theories of personal change and recall. Although the results of many previous studies are consistent with the model (see Ross, 1989, for a review), before the present investigation there were only two studies offering direct evidence of a relation between theories of personal change and recall of personal attributes (Hirt, 1990; McFarland, Ross, & DeCourville, 1989).

Second, the present research explored the processes that influence the recall of personal attributes over several decades. In previous work relevant to the model, the recall period was a matter of minutes or weeks. Our results indicate that the factors that guide the recall of attributes over lengthy periods of time are similar to those that guide recall over shorter periods.

Finally, the present study is the first to explore explicitly the role that motives for self-esteem protection may play in influencing people's recollections of their standing on personal attributes. The results offered

no support for the assumption that biases in recall that could serve to enhance a positive self-image are stronger than those that might serve to lower self-esteem. Older adults construct support for cultural theories of aging from their own developmental histories even when the theories (a) appear to be erroneous and (b) may have negative implications for current self-views. The lack of self-servingness in the recollections of these older adults is consistent with the findings of other studies that we have conducted using younger adults (McFarland & Ross, 1987; McFarland, Ross, & DeCourville, 1989). Thus, it seems inappropriate to consider this effect to be age related. Although some studies have demonstrated what appear to be motivated biases in recall (Parrott & Sabini, 1990; Sanitioso, Kunda, & Fong, 1990), the conditions under which the recall process is influenced by self-serving motives have not been clearly identified. An exploration of these conditions represents an interesting avenue for future research.

The present findings have implications for our understanding of how people's recollections of the past influence their adjustment during later life. Recent reviews of research exploring the influence of life review and reminiscence on adjustment and life satisfaction indicate that these processes do not inevitably have positive consequences (Merriam, 1989; Molinari & Reichlin, 1985; Moody, 1988; Thornton & Brotchie, 1987). Our findings suggest that life review may increase or decrease one's sense of well-being, depending on the particular trait domain being recalled. For some attributes, specifically those for which older adults possess theories of improvement, the recall process may serve to enhance current feelings of competence and well-being (Gergen & Gergen, 1983). For other traits, however, specifically those for which older adults possess theories of decline, the recall process may serve to undermine positive self-feelings. It is noteworthy that the attributes for which older people appear to exaggerate decline are ones that are extremely important for everyday functioning: physical health, memory, and emotional stability.

The reasoning presented above rests on the assumption that the construction of an idealized past has detrimental consequences. Presumably, the contrast between their current selves and a glorified image of their past selves may lead individuals to experience negative affective reactions (Brickman, Coates, & Janoff-Bulman, 1978). There are no doubt occasions, however, when idealization has the opposite effect. For instance, people can contemplate the "good old days" without explicitly comparing their past and present lives. This form of reminiscence might be expected to enhance their current moods. Indeed, there is some evidence indicating that reminiscing about positive past events may increase positive affect in older individuals (David, 1990; Fallot, 1979; Haight, 1988; Havighurst & Glasser, 1972; Hyland & Ackerman, 1988).

Even the direct comparison between an idealized past and the present may not inevitably produce negative responses. There are several reasons why this may be the case. First, even when individuals perceive that they have declined on some dimension, they may still believe (a) that their current capacities are adequate for dealing with day-to-day life (Sunderland, Watts, Baddeley, & Harris, 1986), (b) that the adversity has benefited their lives in some way (e.g., they have learned from the negative experience or improved their coping skills; Taylor, 1983; Taylor & Brown, 1988), or (c) that declines in functioning are normal and to be expected (Ryff, 1989a). Second, some personal qualities may be valued to a greater degree in the earlier stages of life (e.g., being rebellious, having athletic ability). By exaggerating their prior status on these dimensions, older people can take pride in having met the requirements of that phase of life. Finally, there may be times when older individuals' reconstructions are influenced by their desire to cope with a current stressor. After a failure experience, for example, they might idealize their prior qualities to reassure themselves that they possess the abilities or personality traits that are important for coping in the future. Similarly, when faced with the possibility of death, idealizations of the past may allow them to preserve the belief that their lives have been meaningful (Butler, 1963; Molinari & Reichlin, 1985).

We have argued that idealizations of the past may produce either positive or negative emotional reactions. The same may be true for negative constructions of the past. To the extent that recalling a negative past allows people to see improvement in themselves (Conway & Ross, 1984; Ryff, 1989b; Strack, Schwarz, & Gscheidinger, 1985) or allows them to gain a better understanding of themselves (Butler, 1963; Romaniuk, 1981), it should have positive consequences for their emotional states. However, dwelling on the negative features of one's past (e.g., failure experiences, regrets, unresolvable conflicts) might be expected to produce negative reactions (Blaney, 1986; Butler, 1963; Shute, 1986). In summary, there may be no simple relation between the positivity of recollections and current affective reactions. Future research may delineate the factors that mediate this relation. Such research should help to clarify the conditions under which life review and reminiscence will have positive consequences for older adults.

In addition to contributing to our understanding of recall processes, the present findings have implications for the study of individuals' conceptions of developmental changes occurring during adulthood. Consistent with previous research, we observed that their theories of aging are not entirely negative: individuals expect both declines and improvements with age (Heckhausen et al., 1989; Ryff, 1984; Schonfield, 1982). In addition, our findings imply that these theories are not completely accurate. Our subjects expected some degree of change in over 50% of the attributes that appear to remain stable with age. Finally, older adults expect similar age changes in themselves and others. Statistical tests comparing subjects' ratings of how they themselves changed with age with their ratings of how the average person changes revealed only one significant difference (shyness). Thus, older adults' perceptions of aging appear to be neither self-enhancing nor self-depreciating.

In conclusion, we believe that our findings offer preliminary support for the proposition that older individuals' recollections may be guided by their implicit theories of aging. Further studies using longitudinal designs seem warranted; such research should clarify the nature of the relation between people's stereotypes about the aging process and their recollections of their own lives.

REFERENCES

Affleck, G., & Tennen, H. (1991). Social comparison and coping with major medical problems. In J. Suls & T. A. Wills (Eds.), *Social comparison: Contemporary theory and research* (pp. 369–391). Hillsdale, NJ: Erlbaum.

Bahrick, H. P., Bahrick, P. P., & Wittlinger, R. P. (1975). Fifty years of memory for names and faces: A cross-sectional approach. *Journal of Experimental Psychology, 104*, 54–75.

Bengtson, V. L., Reedy, M. N., & Gordon, C. (1985). Aging and self-conceptions: Personality processes and social contexts. In J. E. Birren & K. W. Schaie (Eds.) *Handbook of the psychology of aging* (2nd ed., pp. 544–593). New York: Van Nostrand Reinhold.

Berscheid, E., Walster, E., & Bohrnstedt, G. (1973, November). The happy American body: A survey report. *Psychology Today*, pp. 119–131.

Biernat, M., Manis, M., & Nelson, T. E. (1991). Stereotypes and standards of judgment. *Journal of Personality and Social Psychology, 60*, 485–499.

Birren, J. E., & Hedlund, B. (1987). Contributions of autobiography to developmental psychology. In N. Eisenberg (Ed.), *Current perspectives in developmental psychology* (pp. 394–415). New York: Wiley.

Blaney, P. H. (1986). Affect and memory: A review. *Psychological Bulletin, 99*, 229–246.

Botwinick, J., & Storandt, M. (1974). *Memory, related functions, and age.* Springfield, IL: Charles C Thomas.

Botwinick, J., & Storandt, M. (1980). Recall and recognition of old information in relation to age and sex. *Journal of Gerontology, 35*, 70–76.

Boylin, W., Gordon, S. K., & Nehrke, M. F. (1976). Reminiscing and ego integrity in institutionalized elderly males. *Gerontologist, 16*, 118–124.

Brickman, P., Coates, D., & Janoff-Bulman, R. (1978). Lottery winners and accident victims: Is happiness relative? *Journal of Personality and Social Psychology, 36*, 917–927.

Buhler, C., & Massarik, F. (1968). *The course of human life.* New York: Springer.

Butler, R. N. (1963). The life review: An interpretation of reminiscing in the aged. *Psychiatry, 26*, 65–76.

Butler, R. N., & Lewis, M. I. (1982). *Aging and mental health: Positive psychosocial and biomedical approaches.* St. Louis: Mosby.

Cameron, P. (1975). Mood as an indicant of happiness: Age, sex, social class, and situational differences. *Journal of Gerontology, 30*, 216–224.

Cavanaugh, J. C., & Poon, L. W. (1989). Metamemorial predictors of memory performance in young and older adults. *Psychology and Aging, 4*, 365–368.

Clark, M. S., & Isen, A. M. (1982). Toward understanding the relationship between feeling states and social behaviour. In A. H. Hastorf & A. M. Isen (Eds.), *Cognitive social psychology* (pp. 73–108). New York: Elsevier/North Holland.

Cohler, B. J. (1982). Personal narrative and life course. In P. B. Baltes & O. G. Brim (Eds.), *Life-span development and behaviour* (Vol. 4, pp. 205–241). San Diego, CA: Academic Press.

Conway, M., & Ross, M. (1984). Getting what you want by revising what you had. *Journal of Personality and Social Psychology, 47*, 738–748.

Costa, P. T., & McCrae, R. R. (1988). Personality in adulthood: A six-year longitudinal study of self-reports and spouse ratings on the NEO personality inventory. *Journal of Personality and Social Psychology, 54*, 853–863.

David, D. (1990). Reminiscence, adaptation, and social context in old age. *International Journal of Aging and Human Development, 30*, 175–188.

Dixon, R. A., & Hultsch, D. F. (1983). Metamemory and memory for text relationships in adulthood: A cross-validation study. *Journal of Gerontology, 38*, 689–694.

Douglas, K., & Arenberg, D. (1978). Age changes, cohort differences, and cultural change on the Guildford Temperment Survey. *Journal of Gerontology, 33*, 737–747.

Erikson, E. (1950). *Childhood and society.* New York: Norton.

Fallot, R. D. (1979). The impact on mood of verbal reminiscing in later adulthood. *International Journal of Aging and Human Development, 10*, 385–400.

Feldman, S. S., Biringham, Z. C., & Nash, S. C. (1981). Fluctuations of sex-related self-attributions as a function of stage of family cycle. *Developmental Psychology, 17*, 24–35.

Fitzgerald, J. M. (1988). Vivid memories and the reminiscence phenomenon: The role of a self narrative. *Human Development, 31*, 261–273.

Fitzgerald, J. M., & Lawrence, R. (1984). Autobiographical memory across the life-span. *Journal of Gerontology, 39*, 692–698.

Gergen, K. J., & Gergen, M. M. (1983). Narratives of the self. In T. R. Sarbin & K. E. Scheibe (Eds.), *Studies in social identity*, New York: Praeger.

Greenwald, A. G. (1980). The totalitarian ego: Fabrication and revision of personal history. *American Psychologist, 35*, 603–618.

Haight, B. K. (1988). The therapeutic role of a structured life review process in homebound elderly subjects. *Journal of Gerontology, 27*, 245–253.

Hausman, C. P. (1981). Life review therapy. *Journal of Gerontological Social Work, 3*, 31–37.

Havighurst, R. J., & Glasser, R. (1972). An exploratory study of reminiscence. *Journal of Gerontology, 27*, 245–253.

Havighurst, R. J., Neugarten, B. L., & Tobin, S. S. (1968). Disengagement and patterns of aging. In B. L. Neugarten (Ed.), *Middle age and aging* (pp. 161–172). Chicago: University of Chicago Press.

Heckhausen, J., Dixon, R. A., & Baltes, T. B. (1989). Gains and losses in development throughout adulthood as perceived by different adult age groups. *Developmental Psychology, 25*, 109–121.

Herrmann, D. J., & Neisser, U. (1979). An inventory of everyday memory experiences. In M. M. Gruneberg, P. Morris, & R. N. Sykes (Eds.), *Practical aspects of memory* (pp. 35–51). San Diego, CA: Academic Press.

Hertzog, C., Dixon, R. A., & Hultsch, D. F. (1990). Relationships between metamemory, memory predictions and memory task performance in adults. *Psychology and Aging, 5*, 215–227.

Hertzog, C., Hultsch, D. F., & Dixon, R. A. (1989). Evidence for the convergent validity of two self-report metamemory questionnaires. *Developmental Psychology, 25*, 687–700.

Higgins, E. T., & Lurie, L. (1983). Context, categorization, and memory: The "change of standard" effect. *Cognitive Psychology, 15*, 525–547.

Hirt, E. R. (1990). Do I see only what I expect? Evidence for an expectancy-guided retrieval model. *Journal of Personality and Social Psychology, 58*, 937–951.

Hultsch, D. F., & Dixon, R. A. (1984). Memory for text materials in adulthood. In P. B. Baltes & O. G. Brim (Eds.), *Life-span development and behaviour* (Vol. 6, pp. 77–108). San Diego, CA: Academic Press.

Hultsch, D. F., Hertzog, C., & Dixon, R. A. (1987). Age differences in metamemory: Resolving the inconsistencies. *Canadian Journal of Psychology, 41*, 193–208.

Hyland, D. T., & Ackerman, A. M. (1988). Reminiscence and autobiographical memory in the study of the personal past. *Journal of Gerontology, 43*, 35–39.

Kite, M. E., & Johnson, B. T. (1988). Attitudes toward older and younger adults: A meta-analysis. *Psychology and Aging, 3*, 233–244.

Lewis, M. I., & Butler, R. N. (1974). Life review therapy: Putting memories to work in individual and group psychotherapy. *Geriatrics, 29*, 165–169.

Lieberman, M. A., & Falk, J. M. (1971). The remembered past as a source of data for research on the life cycle. *Human Development, 14*, 132–141.

Manis, M., Nelson, T. E., & Shedler, J. (1988). Stereotypes and social judgment: Extremity, assimilation and contrast. *Journal of Personality and Social Psychology, 55*, 28–36.

McAdams, D. P. (1988). Biography, narratives, and lives: An introduction. *Journal of Personality, 56*, 1–18.

McFarland, C., & Ross, M. (1987). The relation between current impressions and memories of self and dating partners. *Personality and Social Psychology Bulletin, 13*, 228–238.

McFarland, C., Ross, M., & DeCourville, N. (1989). Women's theories of menstruation and biases in recall of menstrual symptoms. *Journal of Personality and Social Psychology, 57*, 522–531.

Merriam, S. (1980). The concept and function of the reminiscence: A review of the research. *The Gerontologist, 20*, 604–609.

Merriam, S. (1989). The structure of simple reminiscence. *The Gerontologist, 29*, 761–767.

Molinari, V., & Reichlin, R. E. (1985). Life review reminiscence in the elderly: A review of the literature. *International Journal of Aging and Human Development, 20*, 81–92.

Monge, R. H. (1975). Structures of the self-concept from adolescence through old age. *Experimental Aging Research, 1*, 281–291.

Moody, H. (1988). Twenty-five years of the life-review: Where did we come from? Where are we going? *Journal of Gerontological Social Work, 12*, 7–21.

Nehrke, M. F., Hulicka, I. M., & Morganti, J. B. (1980). Age differences in life satisfaction, locus of control, and self-concept. *International Journal of Aging and Human Development, 11*, 25–33.

Neugarten, B. L. (1977). Personality and aging. In J. E. Birren & K. W. Schaie (Eds.), *Handbook of the psychology of aging* (pp. 626–649). New York: Van Nostrand Reinhold.

Parrot, W. G., & Sabini, J. (1990). Mood and memory under natural conditions: Evidence for mood incongruent recall. *Journal of Personality and Social Psychology, 59*, 321–336.

Perlmutter, M., Metzger, R., Miller, K., & Nezworski, T. (1980). Memory of historical events. *Experimental Aging Research, 6*, 47–60.

Pipp, S., Shaver, P., Jennings, S., Lamborn, S., & Fischer, K. W. (1985). Adolescents' theories about the development of their relationships with parents. *Journal of Personality and Social Psychology, 48*, 991–1001.

Plutchik, R., Weiner, M. B., & Conte, H. (1971). Studies of body image 1: Body worries and body discomforts. *Journal of Gerontology, 26*, 344–350.

Poon, L. W. (1985). Differences in human memory with aging: Nature, causes, and clinical implications. In J. E. Birren & K. W. Schaie (Eds.), *Handbook of the psychology of aging* (pp. 427–462). New York: Van Nostrand Reinhold.

Poon, L. W., Fozard, J. L., Paulshock, D. R., & Thomas, J. C. (1979). A questionnaire assessment of age differences in retention of recent and remote events. *Experimental Aging Research, 5*, 401–411.

Rabbitt, P., & Abson, V. (1990). "Lost and found": Some logical and methodological limitations of self-report questionnaires as tools to study cognitive aging. *British Journal of Psychology, 81*, 1–16.

Reker, G. T., & Wong, P. T. P. (1988). Aging as an individual process: Toward a theory of personal meaning. In J. E. Birren & V. L. Bengston (Eds.), *Emergent theories of aging* (pp. 214–246). New York: Springer.

Romaniuk, M. (1981). Reminiscence and the second half of life. *Experimental Aging Research, 7*, 315–336.

Ross, M. (1989). Relation of implicit theories to the construction of personal histories. *Psychological Review, 96*, 341–357.

Rothbaum, F. (1983). Aging and age stereotypes. *Social Cognition, 2*, 171–184.

Rubin, D. C., Wetzler, S. E., & Nebes, R. D. (1986). Autobiographical memory across the life-span. In D. C. Rubin (Ed.), *Autobiographical memory* (pp. 202–221). Cambridge, England: Cambridge University Press.

Ryff, C. D. (1982). Self-perceived personality change in adulthood and aging. *Journal of Personality and Social Psychology, 42*, 108–115.

Ryff, C. D. (1984). Personality development from the inside: The subjective experience of change in adulthood and aging. In P. B. Baltes & O. G. Brim (Eds.), *Life-span development and behaviour* (Vol. 6, pp. 243–279). San Diego, CA: Academic Press.

Ryff, C. D. (1986). The subjective construction of self and society: An agenda for life-span research. In V. W. Marshall (Ed.), *Later life: The social psychology of aging* (pp. 33–74). London: Sage.

Ryff, C. D. (1989a). In the eye of the beholder: Views of psychological well-being among middle-aged and older adults. *Psychology and Aging, 4*, 195–210.

Ryff, C. D. (1989b). Happiness is everything, or is it? Explorations on the meaning of psychological well-being. *Journal of Personality and Social Psychology, 57*, 1069–1081.

Ryff, C. D., & Heincke, S. G. (1983). Subjective organization of personality in adulthood and aging. *Journal of Personality and Social Psychology, 44*, 807–816.

Sanitioso, R., Kunda, Z., & Fong, G. T. (1990). Motivated recruitment of autobiographical memories. *Journal of Personality and Social Psychology, 59*, 229–241.

Schaie, K. W. (1979). The primary mental abilities in adulthood: An exploration in the development of psychometric intelligence. In P. B. Baltes & O. J. Brim (Eds.), *Life-span development and behaviour* (Vol. 2, pp. 67–115). San Diego, CA: Academic Press.

Schonfield, D. (1982). Who is stereotyping whom and why? *The Gerontologist, 22*, 267–272.

Schultz, R. (1982). Emotionality and aging: A theoretical and empirical analysis. *Journal of Gerontology, 37*, 42–51.

Shute, G. E. (1986). Life review: A cautionary note. *Clinical Gerontologist, 6*, 57–58.

Sinnot, J. D. (1986). Prospective, intentional and incidental everyday memory. *Psychology and Aging, 1*, 110–116.

Strack, F., Schwarz, N., & Gscheidinger, E. (1985). Happiness and reminiscing: The role of time perspective, affect, and mode of thinking. *Journal of Personality and Social Psychology, 49*, 1–10.

Suls, J., & Mullen, B. (1982). From the cradle to the grave: Comparison and self-evaluation across the life-span. In J. Suls (Ed.), *Psychological perspectives on the self* (Vol. 1, pp. 97–125). Hillsdale, NJ: Erlbaum.

Suls, J., & Wills, T. A. (1991). *Social comparison: Contemporary theory and research.* Hillsdale, NJ: Erlbaum.

Sunderland, A., Watts, K., Baddeley, A. D., & Harris, J. E. (1986). Subjective memory assessment and test performance in elderly adults. *Journal of Gerontology, 41*, 376–384.

Swann, W. B. (1987). Identity negotiation: Where two roads meet. *Journal of Personality and Social Psychology, 53*, 1038–1051.

Taft, L. B., & Nehrke, M. F. (1990). Reminiscence, life review and ego integrity in nursing home residents. *International Journal of Aging and Human Development, 30*, 189–196.

Taylor, S. E. (1983). Adjustment to threatening events: A theory of cognitive adaptation. *American Psychologist, 38*, 1161–1173.

Taylor, S. E., & Brown, J. D. (1988). Illusion and well-being: A social psychological perspective on mental health. *Psychological Bulletin, 103*, 193–210.

Tenney, Y. (1984). Aging and the misplacing of objects. *British Journal of Developmental Psychology, 2*, 43–50.

Thomae, H. (1970). Theory of aging and cognitive theory of personality. *Human Development, 13*, 1–16.

Thornton, S., & Brotchie, J. (1987). Reminiscence: A critical review of the literature. *British Journal of Clinical Psychology, 26*, 93–111.

Whitbourne, S. K. (1985). The psychological construction of the life-span. In J. E. Birren & K. W. Schaie (Eds.), *Handbook of the psychology of aging* (pp. 594–618). New York: Van Nostrand Reinhold.

Wood, J. V. (1989). Theory and research concerning social comparisons of personal attributes. *Psychological Bulletin, 106*, 231–248.

Woodruff, D. S., & Birren, J. E. (1972). Age changes and cohort differences in personality. *Developmental Psychology, 6*, 252–259.

Received May 20, 1991
Revision received August 15, 1991
Accepted August 30, 1991 ■

Memory for a Past That Never Was

Elizabeth F. Loftus[1]

For most of this century psychologists have been examining the imperfections of memory. The science of memory has educated us about the kinds of human experiences that Akira Kurosawa expressed in his film *Rashomon*, in which four individuals tried to recall a violent episode that they had previously experienced. Although the recollections differed greatly, each of the various rememberers maintained a strong conviction in his or her own particular version of the past. The history of psychologists' study of memory was well reviewed by Daniel Schacter in the opening chapter of his edited volume on memory distortion, and he used *Rashomon* nicely to ponder the extent to which memory can ever really tell us the truth about what has happened in the past (Schacter, 1995).

The early demonstrations of distorted memory often involved the observation that a true event was remembered, but in a somewhat mistaken way. Visual forms were remembered as being more regular and symmetrical than they really were. Memory of a story was distorted after multiple retellings. Remembered word lists sometimes included words that had not been studied but were strongly associated with words that had been studied (Deese, 1959; see Roediger & McDermott, 1995, for recent demonstrations of this phenomenon).

Later empirical demonstrations showed that people sometimes had an accurate memory but were wrong about the source of that memory. Other work with more

complex events showed that people remembered an event itself, but were wrong about some of the details — even details that might be considered critical (see Loftus & Ketcham, 1994).

It is only in the last decade of the 20th century that researchers have seriously turned their attention to the question of how far they can go. Rather than tinkering with a detail here and there, can they actually create entirely false memories for the past? Could they make people believe and remember that they were hospitalized when they were not, or that they were lost and frightened when they had not been? This line of research into false memory shows that it is indeed possible to create complex and elaborate false memories in the minds of research subjects, and that subjects are confident that these false memories are real. Here is how it has been done.

Planting Childhood Memories

Once upon a time, there was a case history involving a 14-year-old boy named Chris. He had been misled to believe and remember that he had been lost in a shopping mall at about the age of 5, that he had been frightened and was crying, and that he had ultimately been rescued by an elderly person and reunited with his family (Loftus, 1993). Chris was partly responsible for inspiring a variety of empirical efforts to create entirely false memories of childhood.

At the University of Washington, my collaborators and I conducted a study using a simple method that was

[1] Address correspondence to Elizabeth Loftus, Department of Psychology, Box 351525, Seattle, WA 98195-1525; e-mail: eloftus@u.washington.edu.

similar to the one Chris had experienced (Loftus, Coan, & Pickrell, 1996; Loftus & Pickrell, 1995). The subjects were 24 individuals who were asked to recall events that were supposedly supplied by a close relative. Three of the events were true, and one was a false event about getting lost in a shopping mall, department store, or other public place. The subjects, who ranged in age from 18 to 53, thought they were taking part in a study of childhood memories. At the outset, each subject completed a booklet said to contain four short stories about events from his or her childhood provided by a parent, sibling, or other older relative. Three events had actually happened, and the fourth, always in the third position, was false. Each event was described in a single paragraph.

The false event was constructed from information provided by the relative, who was asked where the family would have shopped when the subject was about 5 years old, which members of the family usually went along on shopping trips, and what kinds of stores might have attracted the subject's interest. The relative was also asked to verify that the subject had not been lost in a mall around the age of 5. The false events always included the following elements: That the subject (a) was lost in a mall, large department store, or other public place for an extended period of time at about the age of 5, (b) cried, (c) was found and aided by an elderly woman, and (d) was reunited with the family.

Subjects completed the booklets by reading about each event and then writing what they remembered about each event. If they did not remember an event, they were told to write, "I do not remember this."

When the booklets were returned, subjects were called and scheduled for two interviews that occurred approximately 1 to 2 weeks apart. Subjects thought the study was about how their memories compared with those of their relative. Across the interviews, subjects remembered something about 68% of the true events about which they were questioned. The rate of "remembering" the false event was lower: 25% remembered the event, fully or partially.

Could researchers create false memories about events that were more unusual than getting lost? Using a similar procedure, Ira Hyman and his colleagues at Western Washington University successfully implanted in the minds of adult subjects some rather unusual childhood memories (Hyman, Husband, & Billings, 1995). In one study, college students were asked to recall actual events that had been reported by their parents and one experimenter-crafted false event. The false event was an overnight hospitalization for a high fever and a possible

ear infection or else a birthday party with pizza and a clown. Parents confirmed that neither of these events had happened, yet subjects were told that they had experienced one of the false events at about the age of 5.

Subjects tried to recall childhood experiences that they thought had been supplied by their parents, under the belief that the experimenters were interested in how people remember shared experiences differently. All events, both the true ones and the false one, were first cued with an event title (e.g., "family vacation," "overnight hospitalization") and an age. In all, subjects remembered something about over 80% of the true events. As for the creation of false memories, 20% of the subjects adopted the false memory by the time of the second interview. One subject "remembered" that the doctor was a male, but the nurse was female — and also a friend from church.

In a second study, Hyman's group tried to implant memories for three new false events that were unusual, such as attending a wedding reception and accidentally spilling a punch bowl on the parents of the bride. In this study, more intense pressure was exerted on subjects to provide more complete recall. Overall, subjects remembered something about approximately 90% of the true events. Subjects did not remember the false events during the first interview, but approximately 25% did so by the time the third interview was completed. For example, one subject initially had no recall of the wedding accident, stating, "I have no clue. I have never heard that one before." By the second interview, the subject said: "It was an outdoor wedding, and I think we were running around and knocked something over like the punch bowl or something and, um, made a big mess and of course got yelled at for it."

Who is especially susceptible to these sorts of suggestions? One answer came in a study that used the false event involving the punch bowl. False memories — either full or partial — were expressed by 27% of the subjects during the second interview. One subject, for example, remembered extensive detail about the unfortunate man who got punch spilled on him:

> … a heavyset man, not like fat but like tall and … big beer belly, and I picture him having a dark suit on, like grayish dark, and like having grayish dark hair and balding on top, and, uh, I picture him with a wide square face, and I just picture him getting up and being kind of irritated or mad … .

Two variables related to personal characteristics correlated strongly with the creation of false memories. The first was score on the Dissociative Experiences Scale, which taps into the extent to which a person has lapses in memory and attention or fails to integrate awareness, thought, and memory (Bernstein & Putnam, 1986). Also correlated was score on the Creative Imagination Scale, which is a measure of hypnotizability, and also can be construed as a self-report measure of the vividness of mental imagery (Wilson & Barber, 1978).

Although it happened in the particular studies just cited that 25% of adult subjects accepted the false memory of being lost, 20% accepted the false memory of being hospitalized, and approximately 25% accepted the false memory of knocking over a punch bowl, these studies cannot support any firm claims about the percentage of people in the population who might be able to be misled in this way. It might be higher or lower depending on the particular method used and the characteristics of the sample. For example, Mary Devitt (1995), from the University of North Dakota, found lower percentages of 14- to 24-year-old subjects creating false memories of being lost at age 6 or hospitalized at age 5, with more subjects accepting the hospitalization suggestion than the getting-lost suggestion. Kathy Pezdek (1995), from Claremont University, tried to instill a false memory about getting lost and also a false memory about receiving a rectal enema. She succeeded in the former case (with 15% of subjects accepting the false suggestion about getting lost) but not in the latter (with no subject accepting the false suggestion). What is clear in each of these studies, however, is that false memories took root after strong suggestions, at least in a minority of subjects, showing that researchers are capable of creating quite complex childhood memories in research subjects.

Impossible Memories

One could argue that the suggestions used to plant memories of being lost or hospitalized cause subjects to take some genuine experiences and combine them with other factual details to create distorted memories of true experiences. Perhaps this is so in some instances. A stronger case for implantation of false memories could be made if subjects were induced to remember the impossible. Although there are numerous cases of people remembering false experiences in the real world, such as being abducted by aliens and transported away on spaceships, memories that many people consider impossible, it would be desirable to demonstrate that impossible memories could be planted experimentally.

Recently, researchers have devised some clever ways of getting people to remember experiences that are highly unlikely to be genuine. These studies use various methods to get people to believe that they are remembering episodes from the 1st year of life. Given that adults are exceedingly unlikely to have genuine episodic memories from this period, researchers have confidence that such methods have produced truly false memories.

Remembering Mobiles

A clever procedure for planting false memories was developed by Nick Spanos and his collaborators at Carleton University (Spanos, 1996; Spanos, Burgess, Burgess, Samuels, & Blois, 1997). Subjects were first administered several questionnaires, which were then apparently analyzed by a computer that gave all subjects the same false feedback that they had been classified as "High Positive Cognitive Monitors." This profile suggested that they had specially coordinated eye movements and visual exploration skills that probably were established in the first few days after birth. They were further falsely informed that they had probably been born in hospitals that had special programs in place to hang swinging colored mobiles over the heads of infants to facilitate this eye coordination.

Experimental techniques were then used to "confirm" whether the subjects had been born into such programs. Half were hypnotized and mentally guided back to the day after birth (i.e., age regressed), and asked to describe their experiences. After they were probed for memories of their birth experiences, they were "returned" to their adult age and asked more questions, including questions designed to determine whether they thought the memories they had produced were real or were fantasy. One week later, they came back to the lab for further questioning, having been warned that during the interim they might find that they had been primed by the regression experience to feel itching near the umbilicus or have thoughts and dreams about infancy. During the second lab session, they again discussed and rated the reality of their "memories" and also reported on any interim experiences.

Half the subjects were not hypnotized at all, but engaged in a "guided mnemonic restructuring" procedure, which they were assured would aid them in recalling their infant memories. They were mentally guided back to shortly after birth, and were also actively encouraged to use imagery to recreate experiences from infancy. Otherwise these subjects were treated the same as the hypnotized group, and both were compared with control subjects who did not undergo any memory procedures but simply completed the various other questionnaires.

Spanos and his collaborators found that the vast majority of their subjects were susceptible to these memory-planting procedures. Both the hypnotized subjects and the subjects who engaged in guided mnemonic restructuring reported infant memories, with the latter group doing so somewhat more often than the former (70% vs. 95%). The researchers attempted to hypnotize all the subjects in the group selected for this treatment, regardless of their previously measured levels of hypnotizability.

Both groups remembered the suggested mobile at a relatively high rate (46% of the hypnotized subjects, 56% of the nonhypnotized group). People who had received low scores on the measure of hypnotizability were less likely to include the mobile (31%) in their memory reports than were people with medium and high scores on the measure of hypnotizability (62%).

Did subjects believe they were having real memories, or were they aware that their experiences were fantasies? First, it is worth noting that all control subjects indicated that the experiences were fantasy or else said they were unsure. Second, the hypnotized and guided subjects were far more likely to say that the experiences were truly memories rather than fantasies. Of those who reported memories from infancy, nearly half (49%) classified them as real memories, as opposed to 16% who claimed that they were merely fantasies.

Susan DuBreuil, Maryanne Garry, and I adapted and extended the false-feedback paradigm developed by Spanos (DuBreuil, Garry, & Loftus, in press). Approximately half of our subjects were induced to develop memories of the 1st day of life, as Spanos's group had done, but the rest were induced in a similar fashion to remember specific experiences from the 1st day of kindergarten. We accomplished these inductions with false feedback suggesting that the subjects fit a particular profile; those in the kindergarten group were told that this was probably due to being exposed, on the 1st day of kindergarten, to spiral disks that were hung in the classroom to stimulate coordinated eye movements and visual exploration, and subjects in the infancy group were told what Spanos's group had told their subjects. The infancy subjects were age regressed to ascertain whether they experienced the day after birth and the dangling mobile, and the kindergarten subjects were age regressed to ascertain whether they experienced the spiral disks. The hypothesis was that subjects might be even more readily induced to falsely remember spiral disks from kindergarten than mobiles from infancy

because people believe they can remember their early childhood but not their infancy.

The hypothesis was not supported: The results did show that more than 80% of subjects reported remembering some experience at the target age. Approximately 60% of the infancy group claimed some memory of the mobile, and only 25% of the kindergarten group claimed some memory of the spiral disk. Thus, the latter subjects were less likely to create a false memory for the suggested stimulus. One possible reason is that they had some actual memories from the target period that they could describe, so they had something to say, and thus felt less compelled to produce a report about the suggested stimulus.

Many of the false memory reports were quite detailed. An example from a subject in the infancy group gives the flavor of these responses:

> There are little paper baby bottles hanging from the ceiling, and there's a yellow bow tied to somebody's, um, crib, but I don't know why, and the crib I'm in is like, um, a clear plastic thing and there's like, uh, red … along the side. And actually I remember there's a mobile. If I'm laying on my back, it's hanging from the left corner. But it seems to be pastel colors. It's nothing bright.

These findings are consistent with the idea that people can be led to experience complex, vivid, detailed false memories via a simple procedure that leads them to expect that they harbor unconscious hidden memories and that special procedures will help unlock these memories. Hypnosis clearly is not a requirement. Even when subjects did not recall the specific mobile that was suggested, many recalled other items — doctors, nurses, bright lights, cribs, bars, masks — just the kinds of things you would expect to encounter in a hospital setting of this kind.

Remembering Early Infancy

Using a very different method, a research group at Ohio University also succeeded in getting reports of "impossible" memories, ones that supposedly occurred in the 1st year of life (Malinoski & Lynn, 1996). In this research, subjects were asked to report their earliest memory, and the instructions emphasized the importance of reported memories being real memories, not memories based on family stories, photos, or other people's accounts. An interviewer allowed each subject 1 min to recall his or her earliest memory; subsequently, the subject reported the memory and rated its clarity and his or her confidence in its accuracy. Next, the experimenter probed for even earlier memories and again obtained subjective ratings of clarity and confidence. The process continued until the subject twice denied having any earlier memories. Next, the subject received misinformation: That most young adults can remember very early events, including their second birthday, if they close their eyes and try hard to visualize, focus, concentrate, and "let themselves go." After a 1-min pause for the subject to visualize, focus, and concentrate, the interviewer asked for the subject's memories of his or her second birthday, with clarity and confidence ratings. If the subject reported having no such memories, the interviewer encouraged him or her to try again.

At the outset, the mean age of earliest memory report was 3.7 years. When instructed to visualize and concentrate, close to 60% of subjects reported a memory of the second birthday. After repeated probes and verbal reinforcement, more than three quarters of the subjects reported memories at or prior to age 24 months, a third reported memories within their first 12 months, and the mean age of earliest memory report was 1.6 years. Early memory reports correlated with hypnotizability; the more hypnotizable a person was, the earlier the memory he or she reported.

Although the researchers could not prove that the memory reports were false, the age of many of the reports makes it doubtful that they were actual memories of events at the claimed age of occurrence. Were subjects simply making things up to please the experimenter? Most subjects explicitly denied doing so. Moreover, confidence ratings indicated that many subjects truly believed in the memories that they reported.

Memories or Memory Reports?

The four individuals who tried to recall the violent episode in *Rashomon* gave four different versions. Were these different memories of the same event or simply different reports? Was each narrative consciously constructed to describe an event in a particular way, even if the truth of the event was crystal clear to the teller? Or had each of the four narrators developed a genuine belief in the story he or she was telling?

These questions can be asked not only of *Rashomon*, but also of the subjects who partake in the studies of "false memories." When 25% of subjects say they remember events either fully or partially, how does one know they actually remember the events? Perhaps they learned about the events from family members and later came to remember not the events themselves but the fact that the events happened. Perhaps subjects only claim to remember because they want to be helpful. These are thorny questions for which there are no fully satisfying answers. But researchers in this area have taken steps to determine whether the subjects who say they remember actually do. Are they confident about the memories? In many cases, yes. Do they elaborate upon the memories, providing details that go far beyond what was suggested to them? In many cases, yes. Are they willing to talk about the memories with other individuals they believe are unconnected to the experiment? In certain cases, yes. These are some of the reasons why researchers believe that subjects in the studies of false memories have subjective experiences that feel just like real memories.

Final Remarks

Planting memories is not a particularly difficult thing to do. It can be done not only with strong external suggestion, as in the cases in which relatives helped to convince subjects that they were lost or hospitalized. It can be done with pressure to remember more and more, as in the case in which subjects were convinced they had memories from the 1st year of life. It can also be done in more subtle ways, as when people are induced to simply imagine that they had experiences in the past that they never actually had (Garry, Manning, Loftus, & Sherman, 1996; Goff, 1996; Goff & Roediger, 1996). Researchers still have much to learn about the generalizability of the false memory findings obtained thus far, as well as about the degree of confidence subjects have in these memories and the characteristics of false memories created in these ways. As research continues, it is probably important to heed the cautionary tale in the data already obtained: Mental health professionals, interviewers, and other investigators need to know how much they can potentially influence participants in research, clinical, and forensic contexts, and take care to avoid that influence when it might be harmful.

REFERENCES

Bernstein, E. M., & Putnam, F. W. (1986). Development, reliability, and validity of a dissociation scale. *The Journal of Nervous and Mental Disease, 174*, 727–735.

Deese, J. (1959). On the prediction of occurrence of particular verbal intrusions in immediate recall. *Journal of Experimental Psychology, 58*, 17–22.

Devitt, M. K. (1995). *The effects of time and misinformation on memory for complete events*. Unpublished doctoral dissertation, University of North Dakota, Grand Forks.

DuBreuil, S. C., Garry, M., & Loftus, E. F. (in press). Tales from the crib. In S. J. Lynn & K. M. McConkey (Eds.), *Truth in memory*. New York: Guilford Press.

Garry, M., Manning, C., Loftus, E. F., & Sherman, S. J. (1996). Imagination inflation. *Psychonomic Bulletin & Review, 3*, 208–214.

Goff, L. M. (1996). *Imagination inflation: The effects of number of imaginings on recognition and source monitoring*. Unpublished master's thesis, Rice University, Houston, TX.

Goff, L. M., & Roediger, H. L., III. (1996, November). *Imagination inflation: Multiple imaginings can lead to false recollection of one's actions*. Paper presented at the annual meeting of the Psychonomic Society, Chicago.

Hyman, I. E., Husband, T. H., & Billings, F. J. (1995). False memories of childhood experiences. *Applied Cognitive Psychology, 9*, 181–197.

Loftus, E. F. (1993). The reality of repressed memories. *American Psychologist, 48*, 518–537.

Loftus, E. F., Coan, J. A., & Pickrell, J. E. (1996). Manufacturing false memories using bits of reality. In L. Reder (Ed.), *Implicit memory and metacognition* (pp. 195–220). Mahwah, NJ: Erlbaum.

Loftus, E. F., & Ketcham, K. (1994). *The myth of repressed memory*. New York: St. Martin's Press.

Loftus, E. F., & Pickrell, J. E. (1995). The formation of false memories. *Psychiatric Annals, 25*, 720–725.

Malinoski, P. T., & Lynn, S. J. (1996). *The plasticity of very early memory reports*. Unpublished manuscript, Binghamton University, Binghamton, NY.

Pezdek, K. (1995, July). *Childhood memories: What types of false memories can be suggestively planted?* Paper presented at the biennial meeting of the Society for Applied Research in Memory and Cognition, Vancouver, Canada.

Roediger, H. L., III, & McDermott, K. B. (1995). Creating false memories: Remembering words not presented in lists. *Journal of Experimental Psychology: Learning, Memory, and Cognition, 21*, 803–814.

Schacter, D. L. (1995). Memory distortion: History and current status. In D. L. Schacter (Ed.), *Memory distortion: How minds, brains, and societies reconstruct the past* (pp. 1–43). Cambridge, MA: Harvard University Press.

Spanos, N. P. (1996). *Multiple identities and false memories*. Washington, DC: American Psychological Association.

Spanos, N. P., Burgess, C. A., Burgess, M. F., Samuels, C., & Blois, W. O. (1997). *Creating false memories of infancy with hypnotic and nonhypnotic procedures*. Unpublished manuscript, Carleton University, Ottawa, Canada.

Wilson, S. C., & Barber, T. X. (1978). The Creative Imagination Scale as a measure of hypnotic responsiveness: Applications to experimental and clinical hypnosis. *American Journal of Clinical Hypnosis, 20*, 235–249.

The Mental Simulation of Better and Worse Possible Worlds

Keith D. Markman, Igor Gavanski, Steven J. Sherman, and Matthew N. McMullen

Counterfactual thinking involves the imagination of non-factual alternatives to reality. We investigated the spontaneous generation of both *upward counterfactuals*, which improve on reality, and *downward counterfactuals*, which worsen reality. All subjects gained $5 playing a computer-simulated blackjack game. However, this outcome was framed to be perceived as either a win, a neutral event, or a loss. "Loss" frames produced more upward and fewer downward counterfactuals than did either "win" or "neutral" frames, but the overall prevalence of counterfactual thinking did not vary with outcome valence. In addition, subjects who expected to play the game again made more upward counterfactuals and were less satisfied with the outcome than were subjects who did not expect to play again. However, once subjects saw the cards from which they could have selected had they "hit" again (two winning cards and two losing cards), all subjects generated primarily upward counterfactuals and showed a corresponding decrease in satisfaction. These results implicate both cognitive and motivational factors in the generation of counterfactuals and tell us something about the functional value of counterfactual thinking: downward counterfactuals provide comfort; upward counterfactuals prepare one for the future. © 1993 Academic Press, Inc.

We live in neither the best nor the worst of possible worlds. Few people would maintain that their governments, jobs, marriages, health, or wealth are as good as they possibly could be. But for the most part, they would also deny that these life conditions are as bad as they could be. Thus, most people can imagine both better and worse alternatives to their present reality.

The imagination of alternatives to reality is called *counterfactual thinking* (Kahneman & Miller, 1986; Kahneman & Tversky, 1982). In the current research we investigated the generation of counterfactuals that either improve on or worsen reality. Our goals were to determine the conditions under which people compare their reality to better or worse possible alternatives and to examine some cognitive and emotional consequences of these different counterfactual comparisons.

Research conducted over the past few years has examined the cognitive rules that govern counterfactual thinking. This research has shown, for example, that

This research was supported in part by Biomedical Research Support Grant BRSG S07 RR07301 from the National Institutes of Health to Igor Gavanski and by National Institute of Mental Health Grant MH17146 to Steven J. Sherman. Portions of this research were presented at the 31st annual meeting of the Psychonomic Society, New Orleans, November, 1990. We thank Kendy Braynard, Karen Galambos, Karen Klineman, and Debra McClintock for their help with this research. We are grateful to Russell Fazio for his comments on a previous version of this manuscript. Correspondence and reprint requests to any of the authors can be addressed to Department of Psychology, Indiana University, Bloomington, IN 47405.

people are generally more likely to imagine what might have been different about exceptional (i.e., surprising or unexpected) events than about normal events (Kahneman & Miller, 1986; Kahneman & Tversky, 1982). In addition, counterfactual thinking has been found to influence both social judgments and feelings, including regret, perceived happiness, victim compensation, suspicion, and event causality (e.g., Johnson, 1986; Kahneman & Miller, 1986; Kahneman & Tversky, 1982; Landman, 1987; Miller & Gunasegaram, 1990; Wells & Gavanski, 1989).

Although understanding the cognitive rules that govern the availability of various counterfactuals is important, we believe that a full understanding of counterfactual thinking processes also requires consideration of how they might serve people's motives and goal states. What are the costs and benefits of imagining what could have been (but can no longer be)? Here we consider several possible benefits.

Standards of Comparison

For learning about ourselves, for judging our opinions and abilities, and for understanding, predicting, and coming to grips with the outcomes of the situations in which we find ourselves, we often compare ourselves and our situations to certain standards of comparison. Often these standards are other individuals who can serve as reference points or as sources of information. Thus, for students assessing their test scores, for athletes evaluating their performance levels, or for people suffering from a disease who are trying to judge their coping effectiveness or their prognosis, social comparison is an important process. In most situations multiple people are available as potential standards and targets for social comparison. Some of these others are better off than we are, and some are worse off. Of these many potential standards of comparison, who is most likely to be chosen for social comparison? Social comparison theory has examined factors that govern people's selection of different standards of comparison (see, e.g., Festinger, 1954; Wills, 1981; Wood, 1989). Festinger (1954) believed that the primary purpose of social comparison is accurate self-evaluation — people compare themselves to others in order to evaluate their opinions and abilities. Accordingly, people generally prefer to compare themselves to similar others. In addition, people strive to improve themselves, so they may compare themselves to slightly better-off others (Wheeler, 1966; but see Hakmiller, 1966). Interestingly, Festinger also

pointed out that such "upward" social comparisons may lead to feelings of failure and inadequacy.

Wills (1981), on the other hand, has argued for the predominance of "downward" social comparison, which involves comparison with a worse-off other (e.g., "I may have gotten a C– on the exam, but I did better than Bob"). Wills maintains that downward social comparison is initially evoked by negative affect, and that people engage in this process in order to protect and enhance their subjective well-being.

Despite the importance of specific other individuals who serve as standards of comparison, specific others are not the only possible reference standards. We propose that counterfactual comparisons involving the self may serve the same functions as social comparisons. Thus, for social comparison one might compare a grade of C– on an exam to the F that one's roommate received. Alternatively, one might compare the grade to an imagined alternative to reality (e.g., "I may have gotten a C– on the exam, but if I hadn't done that one hour of studying, I might have gotten an F"). In both cases the standard is an exam with an even worse performance. We argue that the generation of counterfactuals may be determined by the same motives as determine the selection of standards for social comparison.

Just as we can generally find comparison people who are better or worse off than us, most outcomes also allow the imagination of both better and worse possible alternatives. We use the term *upward counterfactual* to describe alternatives that improve on reality and the term *downward counterfactual* to describe alternatives that worsen reality. Upward counterfactuals often take the form of "if only ..." statements. Consider, for example, the disgruntled owner of a "lemon" who thinks, "If only I had bought a Honda, I wouldn't be at the service station every other week."[1] Such counterfactuals may devalue the actual outcome and make us feel worse. However, by simulating routes to imagined better realities, we may learn to improve on our outcomes in the future (Taylor & Schneider, 1989; Wells, Taylor, & Turtle, 1987). Just as upward social comparison can help us improve our tennis game or our coping with a disease by focusing on someone who is doing better, so can the generation of upward counterfactuals help us learn and prepare for the future by pointing out how a given outcome might have been better. The car owner who thinks, "If only I had bought a Honda ..."

---

[1] Of course, it is not only bad outcomes that allow upward counterfactuals. Even when something good happens, we might wonder "how might this have been even better?"

may benefit from this counterfactual in that he or she learns to buy a Honda (or car of similar quality) the next time. Unfortunately, both upward social comparison and upward counterfactual generation are likely to make us unhappy with the current state of affairs, which could have been better.

The generation of worse alternatives to reality, or downward counterfactuals, has received less attention. Downward counterfactuals often take the form of "at least ..." statements as in the example of a student who receives a C– on an exam and thinks "at least I didn't fail." Such a downward counterfactual may make one feel better — in comparison to the F one could have gotten, a C– seems pretty good. Taylor, Wood, and Lichtman (1983) speculated that many accident victims enhance their present reality by comparing it to a hypothetical worse reality. Johnson and Sherman (1990) suggest that downward counterfactual generation can help in coping with stressful events. However, although downward counterfactuals may provide comfort, they leave one ill-prepared for the future.[2] The student who simulates how a C– might have been even worse may be comforted but will not identify alternative strategies to improve the grade on future occasions. Thus, both downward social comparison and downward counterfactual generation can serve the function of enhancing coping and feelings of relative well-being by highlighting how the situation or outcome could easily have been worse.

In sum, both upward and downward counterfactuals hold trade-offs for the individual: the upward counterfactual prepares one for the future at the expense of immediate feelings of dissatisfaction, whereas the downward counterfactual enhances satisfaction, often at the expense of leaving one unprepared for the future.

Repeatability and Counterfactuals

If people generate upward counterfactuals primarily to prepare for the future and downward counterfactuals primarily to comfort themselves, this suggests some conditions under which each kind of counterfactual might be preferred. In particular, people who experience a particular outcome (e.g., a C– on an exam; the purchase

of a "lemon" car) and who foresee the possibility of being in a similar situation in the near future (e.g., taking another exam in the course, buying another car) might be expected to generate primarily upward counterfactuals, with the goal of improving on that outcome.[3] On the other hand, for a one-time event (e.g., one's only visit to Las Vegas; one's only time in graduate school) preparation for a better "next time" is largely irrelevant. The best one can do is to feel better about one's current outcomes and situation — by downward comparison ("It could have been worse; I could have lost more money.") Accordingly, we would expect the potential repeatability of an outcome to influence people's tendency to imagine better or worse possible counterfactual outcomes (or to use upward vs downward social comparisons).

In addition, people's desire either to improve upon an outcome or to obtain comfort and maximize the value of the obtained outcome may depend on their initial impressions of how good or bad the outcome is. In the following section, we consider possible influences of outcome valence on counterfactual thinking.

Outcome Valence and Counterfactuals

Several theorists have suggested that people are generally more likely to engage in counterfactual thinking and to imagine what might have been different about bad than about good outcomes (e.g., Gavanski & Wells, 1989; Gleicher, Kost, Baker, Strathman, Richman, & Sherman, 1990; Kahneman & Miller, 1986; Landman, 1987). Kahneman and Miller (1986) posit that it is harder to imagine how a favorable reality might have been worse (downward counterfactual) than to imagine how an unfavorable reality might have been better (upward counterfactual).

However, previous research has not provided strong tests of the effects of outcome valence on counterfactual thinking. In much of this work, subjects have been instructed or otherwise directed to produce a specific change to a factual outcome (i.e., to make a bad outcome better or to make a good outcome worse). Such procedures have several deficiencies from our standpoint: (a) they do not tell us how outcome valence influences the *spontaneous* generation of counterfactuals;

---

[2] One could argue that imagination of how things could have been worse helps to avoid future negative outcomes, but we would argue that avoidance of such worse outcomes is more economically attained by pursuing the same actions that resulted in the better factual outcome on this occasion.

[3] We restrict this generalization to the *near* future because of the large body of research showing that people sharply discount delayed rewards and punishments (see, e.g., Rachlin, Logue, Gibbon, & Frankel, 1986).

(b) they overlook the possibility that outcome valence may have different effects on the generation of upward and downward counterfactuals.

In addition, in most previous research, outcome valence has been at least partially confounded with the ease of generating different kinds of counterfactuals. For example, several studies have examined counterfactual thinking about scenarios that culminate in the death of the protagonist (e.g., Kahneman & Tversky, 1982; Wells & Gavanski, 1989). It is easy to imagine how such outcomes could have been better (upward counterfactual) but rather difficult to imagine how they could have been worse (downward counterfactual). In other research, only two possible outcomes have been explicitly described — either a favorable factual outcome paired with an unfavorable counterfactual outcome or an unfavorable factual outcome paired with a favorable counterfactual outcome (e.g., Gavanski & Wells, 1989; Gleicher et al., 1990). In each of these cases, bad outcomes are paired with a better counterfactual *default event* (cf., Wells & Gavanski, 1989), whereas good outcomes are paired with a worse counterfactual default. But most outcomes that we experience in our daily lives allow imagination of both better *and* worse possible alternatives (although the availability of these two kinds of counterfactuals is probably somewhat correlated with the valence of the factual outcome). Under such conditions we predict that outcomes that are experienced as dissatisfying will activate a desire for something better and thus will stimulate upward counterfactuals; outcomes experienced as satisfying will lead to the desire to enjoy the outcome and will stimulate downward counterfactuals.

Overview of the Research

Our goals were to determine, first, whether the motives to improve upon one's outcome in the future or to gain maximum satisfaction from the obtained outcome influence the nature of the counterfactuals that people generate and, second, whether the relative strengths of these motives depends on the repeatability of the event and on people's initial perceptions of how good or bad the outcome was.

The scenario paradigms that have been used in previous work, in which uninvolved observer subjects read hypothetical stories and make inferences about the protagonists, are not well suited to studying the questions we address. Such paradigms are unlikely to activate either self-improvement or self-protection motives and,

at best, they evoke only weak affect in subjects. Accordingly, we developed a paradigm that allowed us to examine the *spontaneous* generation of counterfactuals by people in an actual situation involving the self. Subjects played a computer-simulated blackjack game. The objective outcome was the same in all conditions: subjects tied the dealer and ended up with $5. This allowed all subjects the opportunity to make either upward (I could have won more money) or downward (I could have lost) counterfactuals.

To examine the effects of the motives to improve future outcomes or to enhance obtained outcomes on counterfactual thinking, we manipulated subjects' perceptions of the *repeatability* of the outcome. Some subjects (*repeaters*) were led to believe that they would be playing three more hands of blackjack after the first hand. Other subjects (*no-repeaters*) believed that they would be going on to an unrelated task after playing one hand of blackjack. Repeaters should be motivated primarily by a desire to improve their outcomes in the future, whereas no-repeaters should be motivated by a desire to make the best of their obtained outcome. Hence, the former group should tend to simulate how the outcome could have been better (upward counterfactual), whereas the latter group should simulate how the outcome could have been worse (downward counterfactual). Moreover, these differences in counterfactual generation should have a predictable effect on satisfaction: repeaters should be *less satisfied* than no-repeaters with the outcome they obtained. This is because repeaters will be focused on how their outcome could have been better, whereas no-repeaters will focus on how things might have been worse.

In addition, we varied subjects' perceptions of outcome valence through a framing manipulation (see Kahneman & Tversky, 1979). This manipulation enabled us to study spontaneous counterfactual generation in reaction to three differently perceived valences of an identical outcome: positive, neutral, and negative. If negative outcomes are more likely to evoke counterfactual thinking, then subjects in "lose" frames should be most likely to imagine how the outcome might have been different whereas subjects in "win" frames should be least likely to do so. If, on the other hand, outcome valence influences only the generation of particular kinds of counterfactuals, then subjects in all conditions should be equally likely to simulate alternative outcomes, with the differences arising in the relative proportions of upward and downward counterfactuals. Subjects in "win" frames should generate relatively more downward counterfactuals, whereas subjects in "lose" frames should generate relatively more upward counterfactuals. If repeatable outcomes activate motives for improvement only to the extent that subjects are initially dissatisfied with the outcome, then this will show up as an interaction between outcome repeatability and outcome framing, with repeatable outcomes leading to relatively more upward counterfactuals than non-repeatable outcomes only in the case of negative framing.

Finally, we were interested in whether there was a difference between the counterfactuals that people generate when they simply speculate on what outcomes might have resulted had particular actions occurred (e.g., "What would have happened if I had selected the first card?") versus when they actually know what outcomes would have resulted from the actions (e.g., "If I had selected the first card, I would have won [lost]"). Accordingly, near the end of the procedure, we allowed subjects to see the values of the cards from which they could have selected had they chosen to hit again. Some of these cards would have resulted in subjects winning the game (i.e., beating the dealer) and others would have resulted in subjects going over 21 and losing the game. Thus, we obtained data concerning subjects' counterfactuals and levels of satisfaction during two discrete time intervals of the experiment: after subjects discovered their outcomes, but *before* they saw the values of the cards from which they could have selected, and *after* subjects saw the values of these cards.

Method

Subjects and Design

Eighty-eight introductory psychology students participated in partial fulfillment of a course requirement. Subjects were randomly assigned to conditions of a 3 (Frame: win, neutral, lose) × 2 (Repeat vs No-repeat) factorial design. Seeing the cards from which they could have selected (before–after) was a within-subjects factor. Data from two additional subjects, assigned to the win, no-repeat cell, were discarded due to a procedural error. As well, data from three subjects who "busted" during the experiment were discarded.

Procedure

Subjects were told that the study concerned "what people think about as they gamble." Subjects were informed that they would be asked to "think aloud" as they played blackjack. They were given a practice

TABLE 35.1. Starting Points and Potential Payoffs ($) for Subjects in the Three Framing Conditions

	Frame		
	Win	Neutral	Lose
Subjects start with	0	5	20
"Possible" Outcomes			
Beat dealer	+ 20	+ 15	0
Tie dealer	+ 5	0	−15
Lose to dealer	0	−5	−20
Net gain with tie	+ 5	+ 5	+ 5

Note. All subjects tied the dealer and ended up with $5.

thinking-aloud task to allow them to become comfortable speaking into a tape recorder and were given detailed instructions on how to play the game, regardless of whether or not they were familiar with blackjack.[4] Subjects then saw a visual demonstration on a Macintosh SE computer of how the game was going to operate. When the demonstration was completed, subjects were informed of their potential payoffs. These payoffs are shown in Table 35.1.[5]

The game was programmed so that all subjects would tie the dealer and end up with $5. However, we used a framing manipulation to create in subjects a perception of *gaining* $5 in the win condition, *neither gaining nor losing* in the neutral condition, and *losing* $15 in the lose condition. In *win* conditions, subjects started off with no money. They were told that if they won (beat the dealer's hand) they would receive $20. If they tied (matched the dealer's hand), they would receive $5. If they lost (went over 21 or failed to beat or tie the dealer), they would receive nothing. In *neutral* conditions, subjects were given $5 to start with. They were told that if they won, they would receive an additional $15. If they tied, they would keep their $5. If they lost, they would lose the $5 that they were initially given. In

[4] One small change was made to the usual rules of blackjack: the dealer had to *stay* on 16 or more (the usual rule is that the dealer must *hit* on 16 or less). This rule change was made so that it would be possible for the dealer and subject to achieve a tie at 16.

[5] As shown in Table 35.1, the difference in the payoffs between winning and tying ($15) is greater than the difference between tying and losing ($5). This asymmetry was decided upon because Kahneman and Tversky (1979) have shown that the slope of the value function (i.e., the increment or decrement in the perceived value of an outcome) is steeper for perceived losses than for perceived gains. In other words, a gain of $5 has less impact on value and satisfaction than an equal loss of $5. The specific magnitudes of the payoffs for win, neutral, and lose conditions were decided upon based on pilot testing with a separate group of subjects.

lose conditions, subjects were given $20 to start with. They were told that if they won, they would keep the $20. If they tied, they would lose $15 of the $20. If they lost, they would lose all $20. As can be seen, the potential and actual outcomes (i.e., the net gains) were objectively the same across the win, neutral, and lose conditions.

After being informed of the potential payoffs, subjects in *repeat* conditions were told that this would be the first in a series of four similar blackjack games that they would play. Subjects in *no-repeat* conditions were told that after playing this one hand of blackjack they would go on to an unrelated task that did not involve gambling. Subjects talked into the tape recorder as they played the game.

Subjects first saw the cards being "shuffled" on the computer screen. The subjects' and the dealer's cards were then dealt from the shuffled deck. In addition, four face down cards were dealt on the right side of the screen. The game was "fixed" in the following way: subjects were always dealt 16 to start off. (The number 16 was chosen because of the uncertainty it provides the players as to whether to stay or take another card.) The dealer was dealt a queen face up and one down card. Figure 35.1 shows the screen display that was visible to subjects at this point.

If subjects decided to hit (take another card), they were instructed to choose one of the four face-down cards. This card would become an ace (for a total of 17), regardless of which was chosen. The deck of cards was again shuffled on the computer screen and four new face-down cards were dealt to the side of the screen. If subjects hit again, the same sequence of events transpired, that is, subjects received another ace (18). If subjects hit yet again, they "busted" and the data were discarded (this occurred only three times). At whatever point subjects stayed, the dealer's face down card was revealed to show that the dealer had matched the subjects' hand (16, 17, or 18).

After subjects finished recording their thoughts to this point, the nature of the possible counterfactual alternatives was revealed. The four face-down cards on the side of the screen (from which subjects might have selected had they decided to hit again) were turned over to reveal a *two, ten, three,* and *king.* Note that the two and three would have won the game whereas the ten or king would have lost. The positions of the winning and the losing cards on the screen was counterbalanced. Subjects were instructed to continue recording their thoughts.

Subjects' spontaneous verbalizations during the thought-listing procedure served as our primary dependent measures. However, we also collected questionnaire data at the end of the experiment. Subjects indicated, on scales of −2 (extremely dissatisfied) to +2 (extremely

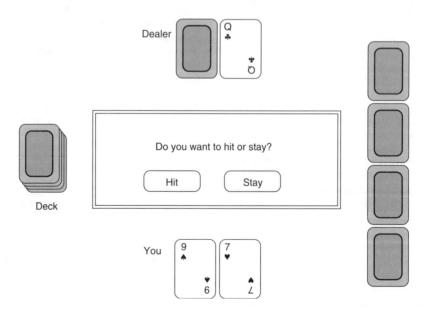

FIGURE 35.1 ■ Computer Screen Display at Outset of Game.

satisfied), how satisfied they were with the outcome. In addition, they wrote down what might have occurred differently so that the outcome of the game would have been different. Finally, subjects completed a questionnaire that assessed suspiciousness and familiarity with the game of blackjack. Subjects were then debriefed and asked to keep the nature of the study confidential until all the data had been collected.

Coding

From the transcribed protocols, two judges who were blind to the experimental hypotheses and conditions independently coded the number and direction of the spontaneous *counterfactuals* generated by subjects ($+1$ = upward counterfactual; 0 = no counterfactual; $+1$ = downward counterfactual). Examples of responses coded as upward counterfactuals are: "maybe I should have taken another card," "I was hoping the dealer had a 6 or a 7 'cause he has to stay with 16 or 17"; "if I had gotten the 2, I would have beaten the dealer"; "Ooh ... 3 would have been nice!"; "Wow, if I had picked the last one or second one I could've won." Examples of responses coded as downward counterfactuals are: "i get to keep the $5 instead of losing"; "it's better than losing it all, I guess"; "at least I didn't lose"; " ... five dollars is better than nothing"; "Oh, a ten and a king ... I'm happy I stayed."; "If I had gotten the king, I would have lost to the dealer."

The judges agreed 93% of the time as to whether or not subjects had generated at least one counterfactual during each interval of the game (i.e., both before and after subjects had seen the cards from which they could have selected had they hit again). Agreement concerning the presence of additional counterfactuals was somewhat lower, but acceptable (78% overall). Interjudge agreement on the *direction* of these counterfactuals was only moderate ($r = .69$ for the first counterfactual coded after subjects discovered the outcome of the game; $r = .67$ for the first counterfactual after subjects saw the cards from which they could have selected). The disagreements in direction appear to have arisen, at least in part, from cases where the judges had coded different statements as the first counterfactual. Accordingly, in cases where one judge had coded an upward counterfactual whereas the other had coded a downward counterfactual, the disagreement was resolved by a third judge. When both judges had agreed, either a $+1$ (upward) or -1 (downward) was assigned; when one judge had coded a counterfactual whereas the other had not, either a $+.5$ or $-.5$ was assigned. When neither judge had coded a counterfactual, a 0 was assigned. Because reliability was generally highest for the first counterfactuals that the judges coded both before and after subjects saw the cards from which they could have selected, our primary analyses concentrated on these counterfactuals.

The judges also coded any explicit expressions of *outcome satisfaction* on a scale ranging from -2 (extremely dissatisfied) to $+2$ (extremely satisfied). Subjects who gave no indication of satisfaction or dissatisfaction received a score of 0. Interjudge reliability was high for the satisfaction ratings ($r = .84$ for the interval after subjects discovered their outcomes; $r = .94$ for the interval after subjects saw the cards from which they could have selected). Analyses were performed on the mean satisfaction ratings.

Results

In a preliminary analysis, we examined the number of "hits" that subjects took while playing the game. Of the 88 subjects, 24 stayed at 16, 48 took one additional card, and 16 took two cards (mean number of hits = .86). An analysis of variance (ANOVA) showed that the number of "hits" was not influenced by either Outcome Repeatability, $F(1, 82) = 1.66$, $p = .20$, or Outcome Frame, $F(2, 82) = 1.91$, $p = .15$; interaction, $F < 1$.

We initially analyzed the counterfactuals that subjects had generated immediately after discovering the outcome of the game (*before* they had seen the values of the cards that they could have selected from had they hit again). After discovering the outcome of the game, 82 of the 88 subjects spontaneously generated at least one codable counterfactual. Of these subjects, 28 generated two counterfactuals and 22 generated three counterfactuals. The average number of counterfactuals was 1.5. The overall number of counterfactuals was not significantly influenced by either Outcome Repeatability, $F(1, 82) = 1.55$, $p = .22$, or Outcome Frame, $F(2, 82) < 1$; the interaction between these factors also did not attain significance, $F(2, 82) < 1$.

Direction of Counterfactuals

We then examined the *direction* of the counterfactuals that subjects generated immediately upon discovering the outcome of the game, with upward counterfactuals coded as $+1$ and downward counterfactuals coded as -1. In accordance with previous research (e.g., Kahneman & Tversky, 1982; Wells & Gavanski, 1989), we analyzed the first counterfactual that each subject generated. Six subjects, relatively evenly distributed among conditions, generated no codable counterfactuals and were omitted from the analysis. Figure 35.2 shows the mean direction-of-counterfactual score for subjects in all conditions. As shown in this figure, subjects tended to make downward counterfactuals, in that the mean direction-of-counterfactual score was negative in all but the lose-repeat condition. However, the relative incidence of upward and downward counterfactuals varied substantially by condition. An ANOVA showed significant effects of both Outcome Repeatability, $F(1, 76) = 5.32$, $p < .05$, and Outcome Frame, $F(2, 76) = 7.27, p < .01$. The Repeatability X Frame interaction was not significant, $F < 1.$[6]

As seen in Fig. 35.2, the proportion of upward to downward counterfactuals was greater for subjects who anticipated playing the game again (repeaters) than for subjects who did not anticipate playing the game again (no-repeaters). In addition, subjects in lose frames generated a higher proportion of upward to downward counterfactuals than did subjects in either neutral or win frames. Individual comparisons showed that the mean direction-of-counterfactuals for lose conditions significantly differed from that in both neutral and win conditions, $ps < .05$, and that the latter two conditions did not significantly differ.

Satisfaction with Outcome

We next examined subjects' spontaneous expressions of satisfaction with the outcome of the game (coded on a scale ranging from $+2$ = very satisfied to -2 = very dissatisfied). Satisfaction varied predictably with the pattern of counterfactuals. A 2 (Repeatability) $\times$ 3 (Frame) ANOVA on the satisfaction measure showed significant effects of both Outcome Repeatability, $F(1, 82) = 7.88$, $p < .01$, and of Outcome Frame, $F(2, 82) = 17.51$, $p < .001$. Figure 35.3 shows the mean satisfaction scores for subjects in all conditions. As shown in this figure, repeaters expressed less satisfaction with the outcome than did no-repeaters. In addition, subjects in lose frames were significantly less satisfied than were subjects in either neutral or win frames, $ps < .05$; the latter two groups did not differ in satisfaction. The Repeat X Frame interaction approached significance on this measure,

---

[6] The same pattern of effects is obtained when this analysis is done including subjects who did not generate counterfactuals (these subjects received a score of 0: Frame, $F(2, 82) = 7.51$, $p < .01$; Repeatability, $F(1, 82) = 5.34, p < .05$; interaction, $F(1, 82) < 1$.

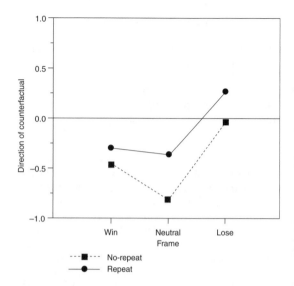

FIGURE 35.2 ■ Mean Direction-of-counterfactuals (pre-card). Positive Numbers Indicate Relatively more Upward than Downward Counterfactuals; Negative Numbers Indicate Relatively more Downward than Upward Counterfactuals.

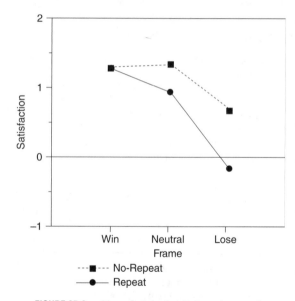

FIGURE 35.3 ■ Mean Satisfaction Ratings (pre-card).

$F(2, 82) = 2.77$, $p = .07$. As seen in Fig. 35.3 repeatability had relatively strong effects on subjects' satisfaction in the lose and neutral conditions but not in the win condition. Note that this pattern is paralleled by a nonsignificant tendency for the effects of repeatability on the direction of counterfactuals to be weaker in win conditions than in either neutral or lose conditions.

These results suggest a close relation between direction of counterfactual comparison and outcome satisfaction — subjects in conditions that evoked the highest proportion of upward to downward counterfactuals were least satisfied with the obtained outcome. To further examine this relation, we calculated the correlation between direction-of-counterfactuals and outcome satisfaction, partialling out the contributions of the independent variables (i.e., Repeatability and Frame) to this relation. This analysis allows us to determine whether direction of counterfactuals and satisfaction are related independently of the effects of framing and repeatability on both of them. The correlation was significant, $r(72) = -.62$, $p < .01$, indicating that satisfaction decreased as the proportion of upward to downward counterfactuals increased.

After the Cards were Revealed

We next examined what happened to subjects' counterfactuals and expressions of satisfaction after they had seen the cards from which they could have selected had they "hit" again. Again, the majority of subjects (82 of 88) generated at least one counterfactual after seeing the cards. Of these, 16 generated two counterfactuals and 56 generated three.

To examine the effects of seeing the cards on the direction of subjects' counterfactuals, we performed a mixed ANOVA, with Before/After as a within-subjects factor. Recall that two of the four cards would have resulted in the subject beating the dealer and two would have resulted in the subject "busting" and losing the game. Hence, subjects again had the opportunity to make either upward or downward counterfactuals. However, subjects overwhelmingly generated upward counterfactuals after seeing the cards. As shown in Fig. 35.4, the direction-of-counterfactuals score was positive in all conditions. The change in the direction of counterfactuals from before to after seeing the cards was significant, $F(1, 76) = 30.90$, $p < .001$.

With the "after-card" data included, neither Framing nor Repeatability produced significant main effects on the direction-of-counterfactuals measure, Framing $F(2, 76) = 2.65, p = .08$; Repeatability $F(1, 76) = 1.15$, $p = .29$. However, the effect of seeing the cards showed marginally significant interactions with both Framing, $F(2, 76) = 2.92, p = .06$, and Repeatability, $F(1, 76) = 2.99, p = .09$. These interactions reflect that seeing the

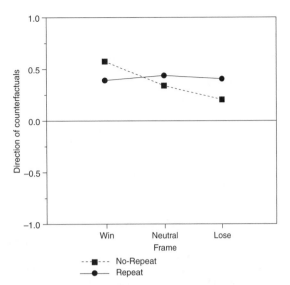

FIGURE 35.4 ■ Mean Post-card Direction-of-counterfactuals. Positive Numbers Indicate Relatively More Upward than Downward Counterfactuals; Negative Numbers Indicate Relatively More Downward Than Upward Counterfactuals.

cards eradicated the effects of Framing and Repeatability on the direction of the counterfactuals that subjects generated. ANOVA revealed no significant effects of these manipulations on subjects' "post-card" counterfactuals, $Fs < 1$.

One possible interpretation for the prevalence of upward counterfactuals after the cards were revealed is that subjects were surprised to discover that they would have had a 50% chance of winning with an additional card. Hence, they generated counterfactuals about this unexpected (exceptional) possible outcome. If so, then one might expect that subjects who had taken more hits, for whom the outcome should have been more surprising, would have generated relatively more upward counterfactuals. (The actual probabilities of not busting with another hit from a fair deck were .41 when the subject had 16 showing, .31 when the subject had 17 showing, and .21 when the subject had 18 showing.) In order to test this possibility, we included number-of-hits as a pseudo-factor in the design. This analysis showed no significant main or interaction effects of number of hits, all $ps > .20$. The degree to which the winning cards were improbable does not seem to have mediated the tendency toward upward counterfactuals.

Subjects also expressed significantly lower satisfaction after seeing the cards than before seeing the cards,

$F(1, 82) = 12.18$, $p < .01$. However, on this measure, the main effects of Outcome Frame and Outcome Repeatability were still significant, Frame $F(2, 82) = 11.77$, $p < .001$; Repeat $F(1, 82) = 5.47$, $p < .05$. No interaction effects attained significance. When we performed an ANOVA on the post-card satisfaction alone, the effect of Frame remained significant, albeit substantially weaker, $F(2, 82) = 4.50$, $p < .05$. The effect of Repeatability was no longer significant, $F(1, 82) = 2.38$, $p = .13$. The interaction was not significant, $F(2, 82) = 1.18$, $p = .31$. Figure 35.5 shows subjects' mean post-card satisfaction scores.

At this point, there is a difficulty in interpreting the reduction in satisfaction brought about by seeing the cards. The way that satisfaction was coded, 0s might reflect either ambivalence (i.e., some statements of satisfaction and some of dissatisfaction) *or* a lack of explicit statements about satisfaction. Hence, the drop in satisfaction after seeing the cards might simply reflect that subjects, having already expressed their levels of satisfaction earlier, made few statements concerning satisfaction after seeing the cards. Arguing against this possibility, only a small minority of subjects had actually received scores of 0 on either the pre- or post-card satisfaction measures. Of the 88 subjects, 5 received satisfaction scores of 0 before seeing the cards whereas 8 received satisfaction scores of 0 after seeing the cards (2 subjects received 0s on both the pre- and

post-card measures). When we repeated the analysis omitting the 11 subjects who had received 0s on *either* the pre- or post-card satisfaction measure, the reduction in satisfaction brought about by seeing the cards remained significant, $F(1, 74) = 5.89$, $p = .02$.

Questionnaire Data

Subjects' questionnaire data, obtained at the end of the study, followed a similar pattern to the verbal protocol data from the time interval *after* subjects had seen the cards from which they could have selected. That is, there was a significant effect of Outcome Frame on satisfaction, $F(2, 82) = 31.35$, $p < .001$, such that subjects reported greater satisfaction in the win and neutral frames than in the lose frame. In addition, there was a marginally significant effect of Outcome Repeatability, $F(1, 82) = 3.06$, $p = .08$, such that subjects were more satisfied in no-repeat conditions than in repeat conditions. As with the post-card verbal protocols, the counterfactuals that subjects wrote on the questionnaires failed to show consistent effects of the manipulations. There were no significant effects involving Outcome Frame, $ps > .50$. The first counterfactual listed did show a marginally significant effect of Repeatability, such that subjects generated relatively more *upward* than downward counterfactuals in the no-repeat conditions, $F(1, 82) = 3.65$, $p = .06$. However, this pattern was reversed with the second counterfactual, with subjects generating relatively more downward counterfactuals in the no-repeat conditions, $F(1, 82) = 7.10$, $p < .01$.

Discussion

Previous work in the area of counterfactual generation has focused primarily on the cognitive rules that govern the availability of different counterfactuals. This work has informed us of important factors that determine which counterfactual is most likely to be generated under various situations. For example, we know that the timing of events is very much related to counterfactual generation. People are likely to mentally undo the initial event in a causal chain (Wells et al., 1987) and to undo the final event in a temporal chain (Miller & Gunasegaram, 1990). In addition, counterfactuals are more likely to develop around exceptional or surprising events as opposed to normal events (Kahneman & Miller, 1986) and around actions rather than inactions (Landman, 1987).

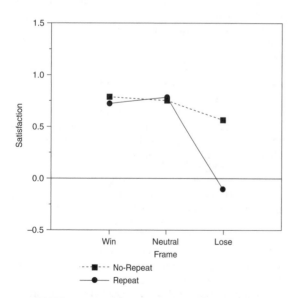

FIGURE 35.5 ■ Mean Post-card Satisfaction Ratings.

Although findings such as these have helped us to understand important antecedents and consequences of counterfactual thinking, the current study suggests that a fuller understanding of counterfactual generation will require more than the cognitive rules that govern the availability of various counterfactual scenarios. We must, in addition, consider how counterfactual thinking serves people's motives and goal states. Counterfactual generation has functional value, and people tend to generate those counterfactuals that hold the greatest psychological value for them in a given situation.

We have identified two important values of counterfactual thinking: improvement of one's outcomes in the future and the provision of comfort and the ability to deal with stressful or negative situations. The motivations for these two goals will be differentially activated in different kinds of situations and will determine the direction of counterfactual generation. We have investigated two factors that affect one or the other of these motivations. The repeatability of an event induces the goal of improving upon one's outcomes in the future. This leads one to think about how things might have been better "if only — ." Such thinking will ensure that one tries to bring about the "if only" situation in the future so that better outcomes might be achieved. For one-time events, preparation for a better future is irrelevant. The predominant goal is thus to make the best of whatever outcome occurred. This goal is best met by generating counterfactuals that allow one to see that things could have been worse and that at least those very negative outcomes did not occur. Interestingly, the attainment of each goal comes with its cost. Preparing for the future leaves one focused on the inadequacy of current outcomes and leads to feelings of dissatisfaction. The comfort obtained by thinking about how things could have been worse comes at the expense of being unprepared in the future should the same or a similar situation happen to arise.

In addition to repeatability, outcome valence also affects the goal or motive that is activated. Outcomes experienced as negative focus one on the inadequacy of the current situation and thus on the possibility of better outcomes that might have been or could be. Positively experienced outcomes focus one on the goodness of these outcomes compared to other things that could have been. These findings suggest that optimists and pessimists, who may view the very same outcome in positive or negative terms respectively, may well generate different counterfactuals as a consequence of their psychological framing. The optimist may be satisfied and happy, and yet may be ill-prepared to improve upon circumstances in the future. The pessimist, on the other hand, may be well set up for improvement in the future, but may never enjoy the fruits of improvement due to the predominance of upward counterfactual generation.

In identifying two of the important functions of counterfactual generation, the current findings have illuminated the importance of the direction of counterfactual thought. Upward counterfactuals are activated by the goal of future improvement. This focus on better possible worlds allows one to avoid mistakes in the future. Downward counterfactuals are activated by the goal of coping with the present. Worse alternative worlds allow one to feel relatively satisfied and fortunate, despite the absolute level of the negativity of an outcome.

Given the close link between counterfactual thinking and causal attribution (Gavanski & Wells, 1989; Kahneman & Tversky, 1982; Lipe, 1991), it is interesting to consider how the different counterfactuals evoked by repeatable versus non-repeatable outcomes may influence the nature of people's causal attributions. Repeatable outcomes evoke upward counterfactuals. Upward counterfactuals about one's own behavior and performance at a task (i.e., what could I have done differently to improve the outcome?) may lead to lower estimates of one's ability; upward counterfactuals about the task (i.e., what could have been different about the task that would have improved the outcome?) may lead one to view the task as more difficult than would otherwise be the case. Hence, one might expect that repeatable outcomes would lead to lower ability attributions *and* higher task-difficulty attributions than non-repeatable outcomes. Interestingly, one causal attribution study (Wortman, Costanzo, & Witt, 1973) did manipulate the potential repeatability of an outcome and found exactly this pattern. Although Wortman et al. did not interpret their results in terms of counterfactual thinking processes, our research suggests that different directions of counterfactuals may well have mediated the effects of outcome repeatability on the subjects' causal attributions.

In focusing on upward and downward counterfactuals, the present work has helped us to see some important links between principles of counterfactual generation and social comparison principles. The literature on social comparison has pointed out that people can choose for social comparison purposes either those who are better off than themselves (upward social comparison) or those who are worse off (downward social comparison). Upward social comparison is typically associated with the motive of self-improvement (Festinger, 1954; Wheeler, 1966), although focusing on those who are better off might well make one feel inadequate. Downward social comparison is typically associated with self-protection, although a focus on people who are worse off may prevent one from improving or learning to be better. Thus, whether the comparisons are with other specific individuals (in the case of social comparison) or with alternative possible worlds (in the case of counterfactual generation), the goals that drive the motivational processes and the outcomes of these processes seem very similar indeed.

These parallels between social comparison principles and counterfactual generation imply that work in each area, although separately developed historically, may well have benefits for the other. For example, one principle of social comparison is that people generally tend to compare themselves to similar others. This implies that counterfactuals that involve subjectively small changes (similar realities) will be more likely than counterfactuals that require large changes. In fact, counterfactuals involving relatively small changes do appear to be more likely (Kahneman & Tversky, 1982). Many other findings in the social comparison literature identify when different types of others will and will not be chosen for comparison purposes (for overviews, see Wills, 1981; Wood, 1989). The factors identified in these studies may suggest when certain counterfactual worlds as opposed to other possible worlds will be generated, for both cognitive and motivational reasons.

Similarly, consideration of the literature on counterfactual generation may lead to important suggestions about when and why certain social comparisons as opposed to others are likely to occur. Literature on counterfactual generation and the exceptionality of events suggests that the unexpectedness or surprisingness of people's outcomes may make them especially likely targets for social comparison. Or perhaps people who do things rather than those who maintain the status quo are likely to be chosen for social comparison. In any case, it seems likely that these two areas of work have much to offer each other both in the way of specific predictions and in the way of conceptual clarification.

Aside from the general principles of counterfactual generation that the present study has suggested, several of the more specific findings are worthy of comment. With regard to the effects of positive vs. negative framing of outcomes, we found that the former led to relatively more downward counterfactuals. However, we did not find a greater number of counterfactuals in response to negative outcomes as previous literature might have suggested (Gavanski & Wells, 1989; Gleicher et al., 1990; Landman, 1987). There are several possibilities for this seeming discrepancy. In the first place, past research has employed scenarios where the possible alternatives were limited in terms of number and direction, and perhaps these limitations were more severe for the positive outcome scenarios. Our situation clearly allowed for counterfactuals in both directions, and the objective outcome was identical. Other studies had employed quite different positive and negative scenarios rather than simply manipulating the framing of a constant outcome. A second possibility is that positive outcomes do generally lead to fewer counterfactuals because they are more expected and less surprising. People don't usually expect to fail or to have negative events occur. In the current study, however, whether the outcome was framed as positive, negative, or neutral, it was a quite unusual and surprising event — an exact tie with the dealer (cf. Kahneman & Varey, 1990). It may have been the novelty of this outcome that allowed for the large and equal number of counterfactuals in all the framing conditions.

Another finding of note concerns the effects of subjects seeing the cards that they would have received had they taken another hit. Recall that after subjects had chosen not to take a further hit, they were shown the cards from which they could have chosen. Two of these cards would have led to a win, and two would have led to a loss. Upon seeing these cards, subjects in *all* conditions focused on the potentially winning cards and they overwhelmingly generated upward counterfactuals (and showed a corresponding decrease in satisfaction with the outcome).[7] Seeing the actual values of the cards also erased the effects of framing and repeatability on the counterfactuals that subjects generated (note, however, that the initial effects of these manipulations on subjects' satisfaction with the outcome persisted to some extent). There are two possible interpretations of these effects. First, subjects may have been surprised that as many as two of the four cards would have led to a win and hence generated counterfactuals about this surprising outcome. The fact that the tendency toward upward counterfactuals was not influenced by the objective probabilities of a winning card (i.e., whether the subject had 16, 17, or 18 showing) argues against this possibility. However, because we did not assess

---

[7] Interestingly, some subjects actually expressed reluctance to see the cards from which they could have selected. Presumably they did so in anticipation of the possibility that seeing the cards might reduce their satisfaction with the outcome. Research currently underway is exploring conditions under which people are likely to either seek out or avoid information about counterfactual alternatives.

subjective probabilities of winning with another card, it cannot be ruled out.

An alternative and interesting possibility is that counterfactual thinking processes differ when people simply speculate on what outcomes might have resulted had particular actions occurred (e.g., "What would have happened if I had selected the first card?") and when they actually know what outcomes would have resulted from the actions (e.g., "If I had selected the top card, I *would* have won"). In the former case, subjects' counterfactuals seem to be determined by the motives that are activated by situational circumstances — better possible worlds with repeatability and negative outcomes, worse possible worlds with no repeatability and with positive outcomes. In the latter case, once subjects know for sure that a better world *was* possible if a particular choice had been made, these positive possibilities dominate attention and lead to upward counterfactual generation and the consequences of such generation. This distinction between situations where the consequences of counterfactuals are imagined (e.g., what would have happened had Lincoln not been shot?) and situations where the consequences are known (e.g., if I had bought stock X as opposed to stock Y, I would now be $50,000 better off) is one that is certainly worth pursuing.

In addition to specifying the conditions under which upward or downward counterfactuals are likely, the present study also demonstrated the close correspondence between the type of counterfactual generated and the type of affect experienced. Upward counterfactuals were associated with dissatisfaction, whereas downward counterfactuals were associated with feelings of satisfaction. Although we suspect that the relation between counterfactuals and affect is reciprocal (i.e., initial satisfaction influences type of counterfactuals *and* type of counterfactuals influences subsequent satisfaction), our results provide evidence for the causal influence of counterfactuals on affect. It is difficult to imagine (simulate) how the potential repeatability of an outcome would directly produce the patterns of satisfaction that were obtained, independently of counterfactual thinking processes. In fact, repeatability in our experiment meant a chance to win *more* money in the future, so if anything one would expect subjects in repeat conditions to be happier. In addition, the finding that seeing the "counterfactual inducing" cards produced sharp reductions in satisfaction is hard to explain without positing that the counterfactuals that subjects generated actually caused them to become less satisfied.

Finally, we wish to point out other ways in which the current study has gone beyond previous work on counterfactual thinking. Much of the previous research (e.g., Johnson, 1986; Kahneman & Tversky, 1982; Landman, 1987; Wells & Gavanski, 1989) has examined situations involving extreme and dramatic outcomes (e.g., death, serious injury, winning a lottery). One unfortunate consequence of this focus on dramatic-outcome situations might be to encourage the impression that counterfactual thinking guides cognitive and emotional responses only in a highly circumscribed set of circumstances. We have here demonstrated the importance of counterfactual thinking in response to relatively mundane outcomes of the kind that are common in people's day-to-day living.

In addition, most previous work on counterfactual generation has involved hypothetical scenarios in which the self was not directly included. The amount of personal involvement in such scenarios is likely to be minimal. By including the self directly in outcomes that have self-relevance and meaning, we were able to examine counterfactual generation as it occurs more naturally. Moreover, past work has generally directed subjects to generate counterfactuals that might undo a given outcome. Such direction leaves open the possibility that spontaneous counterfactual generation may not be very likely and may operate by a quite different set of principles. We were able to observe spontaneous counterfactual generation and thus to identify factors that lead people not simply to respond to imperatives to undo an outcome but that lead them to generate such alternative worlds on their own.

In short, we believe that this research brings us closer to understanding the interplay of cognition and affect in the kinds of counterfactual thinking processes that are an integral part of our day-to-day existence; they provide insight into both *when* people will imagine certain alternatives to reality, as opposed to others, and *why* people bother to imagine these counterfactual alternatives in the first place.

REFERENCES

Festinger, L. (1954). A theory of social comparison processes. *Human Relations*, **7**, 117–140.

Gavanski, I., & Wells, G. L. (1989). Counterfactual processing of normal and exceptional events. *Journal of Experimental Social Psychology*, **25**, 314–325.

Gleicher, F. H., Kost, K. A., Baker, S. M., Strathman, A., Richman, S. A., & Sherman, S. J. (1990). The role of counterfactual thinking in judgments of affect. *Personality and Social Psychology Bulletin*, **16**, 284–295.

Hakmiller, K. L. (1966). Need for self-evaluation, perceived similarity and comparison choice. *Journal of Experimental Social Psychology,* **1** (Suppl.), 45–49.

Johnson, J. T. (1986). The knowledge of what might have been: Affective and attributional consequences of near outcomes. *Personality and Social Psychology Bulletin,* **12**, 51–62.

Johnson, M. K., & Sherman, S. J. (1990). Constructing and reconstructing the past and future in the present. In E. T. Higgins & R. M. Sorrentino (Eds.), *Handbook of motivation and cognition: Foundations of social behavior* (Vol. 2, pp. 482–526). New York: Guilford Press.

Kahneman, D., & Miller, D. T. (1986). Norm theory: Comparing reality to its alternatives. *Psychological Review,* **93**, 136–153.

Kahneman, D., & Tversky, A. (1979). Prospect theory: An analysis of decisions under risk. *Econometrica,* **47**, 263–291.

Kahneman, D., & Tversky, A. (1982). The simulation heuristic. In D. Kahneman, P. Slovic, & A. Tversky (Eds.), *Judgment under uncertainty: Heuristics and biases* (pp. 201–208). New York: Cambridge University Press.

Kahneman, D., & Varey, C. A. (1990). Propensities and counterfactuals: The loser that almost won. *Journal of Personality and Social Psychology,* **59**, 1101–1110.

Landman, J. (1987). Regret and elation following action and inaction. *Personality and Social Psychology Bulletin,* **13**, 524–536.

Lipe, M. G. (1991). Counterfactual reasoning as a framework for attribution theories. *Psychological Bulletin,* **109**, 456–471.

Miller, D. T., & Gunasegaram, S. (1990). Temporal order and the perceived mutability of events: Implications for blame assignment. *Journal of Personality and Social Psychology,* **59**, 1111–1118.

Rachlin, H., Logue, A. W., Gibbon, J., & Frankel, M. (1986). Cognition and behavior in studies of choice. *Psychological Review,* **93**, 33–45.

Taylor, S. E., & Schneider, S. K. (1989). Coping and the simulation of events. *Social Cognition,* **7**, 174–194.

Taylor, S. E., Wood, J. V., & Lichtman, R. R. (1983). It could be worse: Selective evaluation as a response to victimization. *Journal of Social Issues,* **39**, 19–40.

Wells, G. L., & Gavanski, I. (1989). Mental simulation of causality. *Journal of Personality and Social Psychology,* **56**, 161–169.

Wells, G. L., Taylor, B. R., & Turtle, J. W. (1987). The undoing of scenarios. *Journal of Personality and Social Psychology,* **53**, 421–430.

Wheeler, L. (1966). Motivation as a determinant of upward comparison. *Journal of Experimental Social Psychology,* **1** (Suppl.), 27–31.

Wills, T. A. (1981). Downward comparison principles in social psychology. *Psychological Bulletin,* **90**, 245–271.

Wood, J. V. (1989). Theory and research concerning social comparisons of personal attributes. *Psychological Bulletin,* **106**, 231–248.

Wortman, C. B., Costanzo, P. R., & Witt, T. R. (1973). Effect of anticipated performance on the attributions of causality to self and others. *Journal of Personality and Social Psychology,* **27**, 372–381.

Received March 23, 1992 ■

When Less Is More: Counterfactual Thinking and Satisfaction Among Olympic Medalists

Victoria Husted Medvec, Scott F. Madey, and Thomas Gilovich

Research on counterfactual thinking has shown that people's emotional responses to events are influenced by their thoughts about "what might have been." The authors extend these findings by documenting a familiar occasion in which those who are objectively better off nonetheless feel worse. In particular, an analysis of the emotional reactions of bronze and silver medalists at the 1992 Summer Olympics — both at the conclusion of their events and on the medal stand — indicates that bronze medalists tend to be happier than silver medalists. The authors attribute these results to the fact that the most compelling counterfactual alternative for the silver medalist is winning the gold, whereas for the bronze medalist it is finishing without a medal. Support for this interpretation was obtained from the 1992 Olympics and the 1994 Empire State Games. The discussion focuses on the implications of endowment and contrast for well being.

So we have the paradox of a man shamed to death because he is only the second pugilist or the second oarsman in the world. That he is able to beat the whole population of the globe minus one is nothing; he has "pitted" himself to beat that one; and as long as he doesn't do that nothing else counts. (James, 1892, p. 186)

Victoria Husted Medvec and Thomas Gilovich, Department of Psychology, Cornell University; Scott F. Madey, Department of Psychology, University of Toledo.

This research was supported in part by grants from the National Institute of Mental Health (MH45531) and the National Science Foundation (SBR9319558).

We would like to thank Todd Bickford, Theresa Buckley, Nancy De Hart, Deborah Fidler, Nina Hattiangadi, Allison Himmelfarb, Elena Jeffries, Danielle Kaplan, Talia Korenbrot, Renae Murphy, Sara Sirlin, and Shane Steele for their help in editing the videotapes and collecting data.

Correspondence concerning this article should be addressed to Thomas Gilovich, Department of Psychology, Uris Hall, Cornell University, Ithaca, New York 14853-7601.

James's (1892) observation represents an early statement of a fundamental principle of psychology: A person's objective achievements often matter less than how those accomplishments are subjectively construed. Being one of the best in the world can mean little if it is coded not as a triumph over many, but as a loss to one. Being second best may not be as gratifying as perhaps it should.

Since James's time, of course, this idea has been both theoretically enriched and extensively documented. Social psychologists have shown that people's satisfaction with their objective circumstances is greatly affected by how their own circumstances compare with those of relevant others (Festinger, 1954; Suls & Miller, 1977; Taylor & Lobel, 1989). A 5% merit raise can be quite exhilarating until one learns that the person down the hall received an 8% increase. Psychologists have also demonstrated that satisfaction with an outcome likewise depends on how it compares with a person's

579

original expectations (Atkinson, 1964; Feather, 1967, 1969). Someone who receives a 5% raise might be happier than someone who receives an 8% increase if the former expected less than the latter. Often it is the *difference* between the actual outcome and the expected outcome, or the actual outcome and the outcomes of others, that is decisive (Crosby, 1976; Olson, Herman, & Zanna, 1986).

More recently, psychologists have discovered a third way in which the determinants of satisfaction are relative. In particular, people seem to be greatly affected by how their objective outcomes compare to imagined outcomes that "might have been" (Kahneman & Miller, 1986; Kahneman & Tversky, 1982b; Markman, Gavanski, Sherman, & McMullen, 1993; Miller, Turnbull, & McFarland, 1990; Roese, 1994; Roese & Olson, in press). The intensity of people's reactions to events appears to be proportional to how easy it is to conjure up greater or lesser outcomes that "almost happened." An 8% return on one's investment might exceed expectations and yet be disappointing if one is reminded of an alternative investment one "almost" made that yielded a substantially higher return. The critical comparison in this case is a postcomputed response to what has occurred, rather than a precomputed representation of what seems likely, *ex ante*, to occur (Kahneman & Miller, 1986).

Most of the research on counterfactual thinking has held outcome constant and examined the reactions of people contemplating different counterfactual alternatives. For example, Kahneman and Tversky (1982b) asked their participants to imagine the reactions of two travellers who both missed their scheduled flights, one by 5 minutes and the other by 30 minutes. The outcome is the same — both must wait for the next flight — but it is easier to imagine a counterfactual world in which the first traveller arrives on time. Studies such as this have repeatedly shown that the same outcome can produce strikingly different reactions as a function of the ease of generating various counterfactual alternatives (Johnson, 1986; Kahneman & Miller, 1986; Kahneman & Tversky, 1982a, 1982b; Miller & McFarland, 1986; Miller et al., 1990; Turnbull, 1981; Wells & Gavanski, 1989).

We wished to take this a step further. We were interested in whether the effects of different counterfactual comparisons are sufficiently strong to cause people who are objectively *worse* off to sometimes feel better than those in a superior state. Moreover, we were interested not just in documenting isolated episodes in which this might happen, but in identifying a specific situation in

which it occurs with regularity and predictability. The domain we chose to investigate was athletic competition.

We chose this domain of investigation because in athletic competition outcomes are typically defined with unusual precision. Someone finishes first, second, or third, for example, thereby earning a gold, silver, or bronze medal. With all else equal, one would expect the athletes' levels of satisfaction to mirror this objective order. We suspected, however, that all else is not equal — that the nature of athletes' counterfactual thoughts might cause their levels of satisfaction to depart from this simple, linear order.

Consider the counterfactual thoughts of bronze and silver medalists. What might their most compelling counterfactual thoughts be? One would certainly expect the silver medalist to focus on almost winning the gold because there is a qualitative difference between coming in first and any other outcome. Each event has only one winner, and to that victor belongs the considerable spoils that the modern commercial-athletic world bestows (R. H. Frank & Cook, 1995). Moreover, for the silver medalist, this exalted status was only one step away. To be sure, the silver medalist also finished only one step from winning a bronze, but such a downward social comparison does not involve much of a change in status (i.e., neither the bronze nor silver medalist won the event, but both won medals), and thus does not constitute as much of a counterfactual temptation.

In contrast, bronze medalists are likely to focus their counterfactual thoughts downward. Like the qualitative jump between silver and gold, there is a categorical difference between finishing third and finishing fourth. Third place merits a medal whereas the fourth-place finisher is just one of the field. This type of categorical difference does not exist in the upward comparison between second and third place.

Because of this asymmetry in the direction of counterfactual comparison, the person who is objectively worse off (the bronze medalist) might nonetheless feel more gratified than the person who is objectively better off (the silver medalist). Like William James's (1892) pugilist, silver medalists may torment themselves with counterfactual thoughts of "if only …" or "why didn't I just. …" Bronze medalists, in contrast, may be soothed by the thought that "at least I won a medal." The net result is that with respect to athletic competition, there may be times when less is more.

We conducted three studies to examine this question. First, we analyzed the affective reactions of bronze and silver medalists as they won their medals in the 1992 Olympic games in Barcelona, Spain. Second, we had participants evaluate the Olympians' postcompetition interviews to see whether silver medalists seemed to be focused on the medal they almost won whereas third-place finishers appeared to relish the pleasure simply of being medalists. In the third study, we asked athletes themselves about the nature of their counterfactual thoughts.

Study 1

We videotaped all of the National Broadcasting Company (NBC) coverage of the 1992 Summer Olympic games in Barcelona, Spain. From this footage, two master tapes were constructed. The first showed the immediate reactions of all bronze and silver medalists that NBC chose to televise at the time the athletes learned how they had finished. Thus, the tape shows Janet Evans as she touched the wall of the pool and discovered she had come in second, and Jackie Joyner-Kersey after she completed her last long jump and earned a bronze medal. The second tape consisted of all bronze and silver medalists whom NBC showed on the medal stand during the award ceremony. For example, this tape shows Matt Biondi receiving a silver medal for his performance in the 50-m freestyle, and the Lithuanian men's basketball team (in uniforms designed by *The Grateful Dead*) after they received their bronze medals.

Each tape was shown to a separate group of participants who were asked to rate the expressed emotion of each athlete. Because of the asymmetry in the likely counterfactual comparisons of the bronze and silver medalists, we expected those who finished third to be demonstrably happier than those who finished second.

Method

Participants
Twenty Cornell University undergraduates served as participants. Only people who indicated they were uninterested in and uninformed about sports were recruited. This ensured that their ratings would not be affected by any preexisting knowledge about the athletes or their performance in the Olympic games.

Stimulus Materials
The tape of the athletes' immediate reactions included shots of 23 silver and 18 bronze medalists. Not surprisingly, given NBC's main audience, most of these shots (25) were of Americans. To create the master tape, we simply copied all footage of the finish and immediate

aftermath of all silver and bronze medal winners. These shots tended to be rather brief ($M = 14.4$ s; $SD = 8.3$ s), and we stayed with the scene for as long as NBC did. Because the issue of what footage to include involved minimal judgment, we did the editing ourselves.

This was not the case for the medal stand videotape. Here there were too many editing decisions to be made. Should a shot of the athlete *leaving* the medal stand be included? Should a certain "head and shoulders" shot on the medal stand be included or not? To eliminate the possibility of our expectations guiding these editorial decisions, we turned the job over to someone unaware of our hypothesis. We identified all medal stand shots of second- and third-place finishers in NBC's coverage, and asked our editor to copy those moments that best captured the emotion that the athletes appeared to be feeling. This resulted in a master tape of 20 silver and 15 bronze medal winners. The average length of each shot was 14.7 s, with an SD of 13.8 s. In this case fewer than half of the shots (15) were of American athletes.[1]

Two versions of each tape were created, with the order of presentation of the athletes varied across versions. Blank spaces were inserted between shots of the different athletes to provide participants with time to complete their ratings.

Procedure. Participants arrived at the laboratory in groups and were told that they would be watching a videotape of athletes from the 1992 Olympic games. They were informed that they were to rate the expressed emotions of each athlete on a 10-point "agony to ecstasy" scale. The participants were first asked to watch a few shots of athletes without making any ratings in order to give them an idea of the range of emotions shown on the tapes. After participants were familiar with the format of the videotape, the rating session commenced.

Five participants rated each version of each of the two videotapes. The tapes were shown without sound to eliminate the chance that commentators' remarks might affect their evaluations of the athletes' expressed emotions. A 1.5-inch (3.8 cm) strip of paper was affixed to the bottom of the video screen to occlude various graphics used by NBC to indicate the athlete's order of finish.

---

[1] The reason that Americans were not as overrepresented in this tape as they were in the other is that for many of our medal stand segments, it is the gold medal winner who is being featured by NBC and the silver and bronze medalists who are pictured incidentally. Thus, there were many instances in which NBC was focused on an American gold medalist, and we were able to capitalize on their ancillary coverage of a silver or bronze medalist from another country.

Results

Participants' ratings were highly reliable, for both the immediate-reactions videotape (Spearman-Brown index = .97) and the medal stand tape (Spearman-Brown index = .96). Thus, the ratings of all participants viewing the same tape were averaged to create an index of the happiness of each of the athletes. Preliminary analyses revealed no effect of order of presentation, so the data were collapsed across the two versions of each tape.

The mean happiness ratings are presented in Figure 36.1. As predicted, bronze medalists appeared happier on average than their counterparts who won silver medals. When assessing the athletes' immediate reactions, participants assigned the bronze medalists a mean happiness rating of 7.1 (SD = 2.0) but the silver medalists a mean rating of only 4.8 (SD = 1.9). When examining the athletes on the medal stand, participants assigned the bronze medalists a mean rating of 5.7 (SD = 1.7) and silver medalists a mean rating of only 4.3 (SD = 1.8). These data were analyzed with a 2 (type of medal: bronze vs. silver) × 2 (tape: immediate vs. medal stand) analysis of variance (ANOVA). This analysis revealed two significant main effects, but no interaction. The main effect of tape, $F(1, 72) = 4.78$, $p < .05$, indicates that the athletes on the whole looked happier immediately after their performances than when they were on the medal stand. More important, the main effect of type of medal, $F(1, 72) = 18.98$, $p < .001$, indicates that the athletes who finished third looked significantly happier than those who finished second.

There is a potential artifactual explanation of these results, however. In certain Olympic events, the competition is structured such that bronze medalists have just won a match or a game whereas silver medalists have just lost. A bronze medalist in wrestling, for example, would have just defeated the fourth place finisher, and the silver medalist would have just lost to the gold medal winner. We were concerned that being in the immediate aftermath of victory or defeat might have contaminated our comparison of bronze and silver medalists. Fortunately, most Olympic events (such as those in track, swimming, and gymnastics) are not structured in this way. In these events the athletes simply finish first, second, and third depending on how well they do.

To eliminate this "just won"–"just lost" artifact, we reanalyzed the data excluding all athletes involved in sports with this structure. This reduced our pool of 23 silver and 18 bronze medalists in the immediate-reactions videotape to 20 and 15, respectively. Similarly, it reduced our pool of 20 silver and 15 bronze medalists in the medal-stand tape to 14 and 13, respectively. A 2 × 2 ANOVA of these data yielded the same significant main effect of type of medal as before, $F(1, 58) = 6.70$, $p < .02$. Bronze medalists appeared happier both immediately after their events ($M = 6.7$) and on the medal stand ($M = 5.6$) than their counterparts who had won silver medals ($Ms = 5.0$ and 4.7). Consistent with our thesis, impartial judges viewed bronze medalists as being happier than silver medalists, and this effect was not limited to those few events in which bronze and silver medalists were in the immediate aftermath of a victory or a defeat, respectively.[2]

Is there any other alternative interpretation of these data? Might these results be due to differences in the *ex ante* expectations of bronze and silver medalists rather than — as we propose — their *ex post* thoughts about what might have been? We think not. First of all, there is no reason to believe that bronze medalists as a whole tended to exceed their expectations or that silver medalists

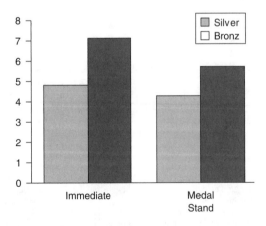

FIGURE 36.1 ■ Mean Happiness Ratings.

[2] One other aspect of the data should be noted. Because seven of the athletes pictured in the immediate-reactions videotape are also shown on the medal stand tape, the data are not all strictly independent and the ANOVA reported is not completely accurate. However, the results are not changed when this overlap is deleted from the analysis. We did this two ways: first, by keeping these athletes' immediate-reactions data and deleting their medal stand data; second, by deleting their immediate reactions and keeping their data from the medal stand. Regardless of which analysis we used to eliminate the redundancy, the bronze medalists were still rated significantly happier than the silver medalists.

on average tended to fall short of theirs. To be sure, our sample of silver medalists probably entered the Olympics with higher expectations on average than our sample of bronze medalists, but they also *performed* better as well. There is certainly no compelling reason to believe that one group over-or under-performed relative to their initial expectations.

This alternative interpretation can also be dismissed on empirical grounds. We obtained an unbiased measure of the athletes' likely expectations prior to the Olympics and then used a regression analysis to examine the effect of medal won (bronze or silver) after initial expectations were controlled statistically. The athletes' likely expectations were derived from *Sports Illustrated's* Olympic preview (Verschoth, 1992). *Sports Illustrated* predicted the likely bronze, silver, and gold medal winners of every Olympic event the week before the games began. Athletes who were expected to win gold, silver, or bronze medals were assigned expectation scores of 1, 2, and 3, respectively. Those not predicted to win a medal were assigned an expectation score of 4. As anticipated, the athletes in our samples who won silver medals were originally expected to do better ($M = 2.8$) than those who won bronze medals ($M = 3.0$), although not significantly so, $t < 1.0$. More important, however, is that a comparison of actual and anticipated performance argues against the claim that our results are due to differences in initial expectations of bronze and silver medalists. Silver medalists as a whole did better than anticipated (actual = 2.0; anticipated = 2.8), and therefore should have been relatively happy. Bronze medalists, on the other hand, performed on average exactly as expected (actual and anticipated = 3.0).

More formally, we entered the expected finish of each athlete into a regression equation that predicted the agony–ecstasy ratings from the medal won (silver or bronze), the medal predicted (gold, silver, bronze, or none), and the type of videotape segment (immediate reactions or medal stand). This analysis revealed that the effect of medal won remained significant when expectations were statistically controlled, $t(72) = 4.3$, $p < .0001$.[3] Silver medalists looked less satisfied with their performances than did bronze medalists, and they did so for reasons unrelated to how well they were expected to perform.

---

[3] This effect remains significant when the athletes from the just won–just lost events are excluded and when the redundancy created by the 7 athletes who appear on both tapes is removed.

Discussion

Our first study highlights a reliable context — Olympic competition involving bronze and silver medal winners — in which those who perform better nonetheless feel worse. On the surface this result is surprising because an underlying premise of all serious athletic competition is that athletes should strive as hard as they can, and that the higher they finish the better they feel. When examined with an eye toward the athletes' counterfactual thoughts, however, our findings seem less surprising. To the silver medalist, the most vivid counterfactual thoughts are often focused on nearly winning the gold. Second place is only one step away from the cherished gold medal and all of its attendant social and financial rewards. Thus, whatever joy the silver medalist may feel is often tempered by tortuous thoughts of what might have been had she only lengthened her stride, adjusted her breathing, pointed her toes, and so on. For the bronze medalist, in contrast, the most compelling counterfactual alternative is often coming in fourth place and being in the showers instead of on the medal stand.

But can we confidently attribute these results to the athletes' counterfactual thoughts? Although the data from Study 1 are consistent with this claim, it is important to examine directly the proposed asymmetry in the athletes' counterfactual comparisons. The following two studies were designed to do exactly that. Do silver medalists tend to think about how they almost won the gold? Do bronze medalists focus on how close they came to missing out on a medal altogether? What exactly do athletes think about after they learn their medal standing?

Study 2

To examine the nature of Olympic medalists' counterfactual thoughts, we turned once again to NBC's coverage of the 1992 Summer Olympic games. NBC's sportscasters interviewed numerous medal winners immediately following their events, and from this footage we developed a master tape of all of NBC's interviews of bronze and silver medalists. Participants were shown the tape and asked to assess the extent to which the athletes seemed preoccupied with thoughts of how they *did* perform versus how they *almost* performed.

Method

Participants

Ten Cornell University students served as participants. As in the first study, we recruited students who considered themselves to be nonsports fans because we did not want any prior knowledge about the athletes to affect their ratings.

Stimulus Materials

NBC interviewed 13 silver medalists and 9 bronze medalists immediately after their events, and these 22 interviews comprised the stimulus tape for this study. Two versions of the tape were created, with the order of presentation of the athletes varied across the versions. The average length of each interview clip was 27 s (SD = 14 s). Blank spaces were inserted between the interviews to allow participants time to complete their ratings.

Procedure

Participants arrived at the laboratory in groups and were told that they would be watching a videotape of athletes from the 1992 Olympic games. They were asked to watch and listen to each interview carefully and to rate each athlete's comments in two ways. First, they rated the apparent content of each athlete's thoughts on a 10-point scale ranging from "at least I ..." (1) to "I almost ..." (10). To clarify the meaning of this scale, participants were given an example of how a student who receives a B in a course could have various thoughts ranging from "at least I didn't get a C" to "I almost got an A."

Second, participants were asked to assess the extent to which the apparent content of the athlete's thoughts fell into three categories: (a) "Athlete seems focused on how he/she could have done worse; makes a comparison with one or more competitors who finished behind;" (b) "Athlete seems focused on how he/she could have done better; makes a comparison with one or more competitors who finished ahead;" (c) "Athlete seems focused on what he/she accomplished; no comparison to competitors." Participants were asked to indicate the percentage of the athlete's thoughts that seemed focused on each of the three categories. They could assign any number from 0 to 100% to each of the three categories, but the percentages they assigned had to add up to 100% for each athlete. The participants were asked to watch a number of clips without making any ratings so that they were aware of the types of comments they would be evaluating. Once participants were familiar with the format of the videotape and the rating scales, the rating session began.

Five participants rated each of the two versions of the videotape. As in the first study, a 1.5-inch (3.8 cm) strip of paper was affixed to the bottom of the video screen to occlude various graphics depicting the athlete's order of finish.

Results

The interrater reliability of participants' ratings was acceptably high (Spearman-Brown index = .74 and .93 for the first and second measures, respectively[4]), and so the ratings were averaged for each scale to create indices of the apparent thoughts of each athlete. Preliminary analyses of these data revealed no effect of order of presentation, so the data were collapsed across the two versions of the tape.

As predicted, silver medalists' thoughts were rated as being more focused on "I almost" than were those of bronze medalists. On the 10-point "*At least I*" to "*I almost*" scale, participants assigned silver medalists' thoughts an average rating of 5.7 (SD = 1.5) and bronze medalists' thoughts an average rating of only 4.4 (SD = 0.7), $t(20) = 2.37, p < .03$.

The data from the second measure were less clear cut. First, participants thought that only a small percentage of the athletes' thoughts were focused downward on those they beat. The average assigned to this category was only 7.5% and did not differ between bronze and silver medalists. The percentages assigned to the other two categories conformed more closely to our predictions. Participants rated silver medalists as being more focused on upward comparisons (M = 38%) than bronze medalists (M = 20%), whereas bronze medalists were judged to be more focused on their own performance (M = 73%) than silver medalists (M = 54%). Because these data are not independent (the percentage assigned to all categories must equal 100%), our test of significance was based on an index that combined the last two categories. Specifically, the percentage assigned to the category "looking upward" was subtracted from the percentage assigned to the category "focusing on one's own performance." As predicted, this index was higher for bronze medalists (M = 53%) than for silver medalists (M = 16%), although the difference was only marginally significant, $t(20) = 1.57, p < .15$.

Discussion

The results of the second study provide support for the hypothesized difference in the counterfactual thoughts of the bronze and silver medalists. Silver medalists seem to be focused on the gold medal they "almost"

---

[4] The .93 is the average Spearman–Brown index for the last two components of the second dependent measure, which, as we discuss in the main text, are the focus of our analysis.

won, while bronze medalists seem content with the thought that "at least I did this well." This asymmetry can thus explain the observed differences in the athletes' expressed emotions in Study 1. This can be seen most clearly through an analysis that combines the data from Studies 1 and 2. Fifteen of the 22 athletes whose counterfactual thoughts were assessed in Study 2 were on the immediate-reactions videotape in Study 1 and thus were also rated on the agony–ecstasy scale. As we predicted, the two ratings correlated significantly: The more focused the athletes were on almost finishing higher, the less happy they seemed ($r = -.56$, $p < .05$).[5] This relationship was also observed when the data for silver ($r = -.51$; $n = 10$) and bronze ($r = -.34$; $n = 5$) medalists were considered separately, although the sample sizes were then too small to yield statistical significance. Thus, by focusing on what they achieved, bronze medalists are rather happy; in contrast, a concern with what they failed to achieve makes the silver medalists seem less so.

In this study we did not have direct access to the athletes' thoughts; we had participants infer them on the basis of the athletes' comments. It is certainly possible, of course, that the athletes had various thoughts they did not verbalize. To overcome this limitation, we conducted a third study that examined bronze and silver medalists' own reports of their thoughts following an athletic competition.

Study 3

In designing Study 3, we sought an athletic forum with significant stakes where we could gain access to bronze and silver medalists immediately after their events. The 1994 Empire State Games provided such a forum. The Empire State Games have been a prominent amateur athletic event in New York State for the last 17 years. Athletes from across the state compete on a regional basis to qualify for the Empire State Games. Notable participants have included such athletes as Olympic gold medalists Dianne Roffe-Steinrotter and Jeff Blatnick and NBA basketball stars (and "Dream Team" members) Christian Laettner and Chris Mullin. In 1994,

more than 5,000 athletes from across New York State competed in the 4-day event.

Method

Participants

One hundred fifteen Empire State Game medalists participated in this study. All of the participants won bronze ($n = 55$) or silver ($n = 60$) medals in swimming or track events. The athletes competed in either the Scholastic Division (composed exclusively of students up to 12th grade; $n = 31$ males and 34 females) or the Open Division (consisting mainly of college students; $n = 25$ males and 25 females).

Procedure

The athletes were approached individually following their events and asked to rate their thoughts about their performance on the same 10-point scale used in Study 2. Specifically, they were asked to rate the extent to which they were concerned with thoughts of "*At least I …*" (1) versus "*I almost*" (10). Special effort was made to ensure that the athletes understood the scale before making their ratings. This was accomplished by mentioning how athletes might have different thoughts following an athletic competition, ranging from "I almost did better" to "at least I did this well."[6]

Results

As predicted, silver medalists' thoughts following the competition were more focused on "I almost" than were bronze medalists'. Silver medalists described their

---

[5] We used the data from the immediate-reactions videotape in Study 1 rather than those from the medal stand tape simply because there was more overlap with the athletes interviewed in Study 2 for the former (15) than for the latter (7). Furthermore, 5 of the overlapping 7 from the medal stand tape also appeared on the immediate-reactions tape.

[6] We had hoped to include a question similar to the second measure used in Study 2 in which participants divided the athletes' thoughts into three categories by assigning the appropriate percentage to each. We thought this might be difficult for the athletes to do the moment they emerged from the heat of competition, however. We therefore tried to simplify matters by presenting the task spatially: The athletes were shown a plexiglass board in which we had carved a triple-pronged "pitchfork." The athletes were to distribute 10 metal tokens contained in the handle of the pitchfork into the categories represented by each prong. The three prongs were labeled "Who I Beat," "No Comparisons," and "Who Beat Me," and the athletes were told to apportion the tokens so as to represent the extent to which their thoughts were focused on each. Unfortunately, the measure proved to be exquisitely ineffective. Some athletes, particularly a number of shivering swimmers who had just emerged from the pool, seemed unable to comprehend it; others managed to dislodge the tokens; and the responses of still other athletes were contaminated by the comments of onlookers who found the device fascinating and offered unsolicited advice.

thoughts with a mean rating of 6.8 ($SD = 2.2$), whereas bronze medalists assigned their thoughts an average rating of 5.7 ($SD = 2.7$), $t(113) = 2.4$, $p < .02$.

Discussion

The data from this study are consistent with the findings from Study 2: Following a competition, silver medalists tend to focus more on what they failed to achieve than do bronze medalists. This asymmetry in counterfactual comparisons explains why bronze medalists tend to be happier than silver medalists. While bronze medalists can find contentment in thinking "at least I won a medal," silver medalists are often confronted with an imagined outcome that *almost* occurred — a preferred outcome in which they are the winner and have the gold medal hanging around their neck. Imagining what might have been can lead those who do better to feel worse than those they outperform.

General Discussion

The purpose of this research was to examine whether there are reliable situations in which those who are objectively better off nonetheless feel worse than those in an inferior position. Athletics offered an ideal context in which to test this question for the same reason that it offers a useful context for investigating many psychological hypotheses — the availability of data of unusual objectivity and precision (Baumeister & Steinhilber, 1984; M. G. Frank & Gilovich, 1988; Gilovich, Vallone, & Tversky, 1985; Lau & Russell, 1980). In addition, athletics was chosen as the domain of investigation in this case because performance in athletics often yields a clearly defined rank order: Someone enters the record books as the first-, second-, or third-place finisher.

It should be clear, however, that the significance of the present results extends far beyond the playing field or the medal stand. There are many other situations in which the same processes documented here can likewise cause those who are better off to feel worse. A student who misses out on an A—by one point and earns a B+ could easily feel less satisfied with the grade than someone who is in the middle of the pack of Bs. Or consider a person who correctly guesses all but one number in a lottery. Such an individual misses out on the jackpot, but usually wins a modest sum for coming close. The prize no doubt provides some enjoyment, but the knowledge of having just missed the jackpot is bound to

come up from time to time and ruin otherwise blissful moments. More generally, as our opening quote from William James suggests, being one of the best may not be as satisfying as it might seem. The existence of a rival "best" can turn a gratifying appreciation of what one *is* into a disquieting focus on what one is *not*.

The hedonic impact of such a rival "best" raises the question of the extent to which social comparison processes rather than (or in addition to) counterfactual thoughts may have been responsible for our findings. We believe that our results are best situated in the research on counterfactual thinking for two reasons. First, we obtained evidence for the hypothesized asymmetry in the direction of counterfactual comparisons in Studies 2 and 3, but as yet no such evidence exists to support an asymmetry in the direction of social comparisons. Second, there is nothing in social comparison theory per se that would predict upward comparisons on the part of silver medalists and downward comparisons on the part of bronze medalists. Although such a pattern could certainly be made to fit with social comparison theory, it requires extratheoretical elements to do so. In contrast, the present pattern of results was originally derived from the work on counterfactual thinking and the psychology of "coming close" (Kahneman & Varey, 1990; Miller et al., 1990).

This does not mean, of course, that social comparison processes are never activated in the immediate aftermath of Olympic competition, or that such processes contributed nothing to the present findings. Social comparison processes and counterfactual thoughts are doubtless frequently intertwined. Social comparisons can be a source of counterfactual thoughts about "possible worlds" that one would not have otherwise, and counterfactual thoughts can make salient particular social comparisons that would otherwise remain hidden. Unfortunately, it is presently unclear how much of the asymmetry in counterfactual thinking we documented in this context was intertwined in this way with significant social comparisons.

Although the predicted findings were originally derived from previous research on counterfactual thinking, they also extend the work in this area in two important respects. First, as we stated at the outset, past research has held outcome constant and shown that the same outcome can give rise to very different reactions as a function of the counterfactual thoughts that are generated. Our results take this a step further: There are contexts in which people's counterfactual thoughts are sufficiently powerful to lead those who are objectively worse off to be reliably happier than those in a better position.

Our results also extend previous findings in this area by emphasizing the "automatic" or "imposed" nature of many counterfactual thoughts. Much of the recent work on counterfactual thinking has emphasized a person's ability to choose the most strategic counterfactual comparisons (Markman et al., 1993; Roese, 1994). "Counterfactual generation has functional value, and people tend to generate those counterfactuals that hold the greatest psychological value for them in a given situation" (Markman et al., 1993, p. 103). Downward comparisons (i.e., thinking about a worse outcome) are thought to provide comfort, whereas upward comparisons (i.e., thinking about a better outcome) are thought to improve future performance. Indeed, it has been shown that people who expect to perform again in the future are more likely to generate upward counterfactuals than those who expect to move on (Markman et al., 1993).

Although many counterfactual thoughts are doubtless strategically chosen in this way, such motivational considerations cannot account for the present findings. On the whole, the silver and bronze medalists at the Barcelona Olympics were at the peak of their athletic careers and therefore likely to continue to engage in similar high-level competitions in the future. From a motivational perspective, then, both groups should have made upward counterfactual comparisons in order to prepare for future contests. The asymmetry in counterfactual comparisons that we observed implies that many counterfactuals are imposed by the nature of the events experienced.

Indeed, Kahneman (in press) outlined a continuum of counterfactual thinking that ranges from "automatic" to "elaborative." Elaborative counterfactual processing is partly brought on through the exercise of choice, and its direction and intensity is influenced by the individual's motives and intentions. Automatic counterfactual thinking, in contrast, is "initiated by the occurrence of an event and … [is] … explainable largely in cognitive terms" (Kahneman, in press). The counterfactual thoughts that distinguish silver and bronze medalists shade toward the latter end of this continuum. Coming close to winning the gold, for example, appears to automatically activate frustrating images of having almost won it all.

We are not suggesting, of course, that finishing second or coming close to a cherished outcome always leads to less satisfaction than a slightly more modest performance. Finishing second is truly a *mixed* blessing. Performing that well provides a number of direct benefits that increase our well being — recognition from others, boosts to self-esteem, and so on. At the same time, it can indirectly lower satisfaction by the unfortunate contrast with what might have been. Thus, the inconsistent effect of finishing second is analogous to the "endowment" and "contrast" polarity that Tversky and Griffin (1991) claimed affects the hedonic significance of *all* experienced events. According to their analysis, any experience has a direct effect on well-being by what it brings to one's endowment — that is, the pleasure or pain derived from the event itself. But a person's experiences also have an indirect effect on well being by altering the adaptation level against which future experiences are contrasted. Their contrast (in which the event itself establishes a new standard against which future events are compared) is different than the one at work here (in which the events' proximity to a better outcome causes one to lose sight of what is and focus on what might have been). The core idea is the same, however. In both cases, the direct effect of the event itself is offset by a comparison process with the opposite effect, be it a comparison of future outcomes to the present, or the present outcome to a counterfactual alternative that was almost attained.

Tversky and Griffin (1991) have delineated some of the general rules that govern the relative weighting of endowment and contrast, and thus whether the net effect of a given event enhances or diminishes well being. They acknowledged, however, that the degree to which a given event evokes endowment and contrast can be highly idiosyncratic. As a consequence, when applied to a problem such as ours it can be difficult to predict exactly when those who are better off will nonetheless feel worse than those who are less fortunate.

Another unresolved issue, this one more tractable, concerns the duration of the effects we have documented here. We have established that bronze medalists are happier than silver medalists in the short run, but does this effect hold up over time? As yet there are no data to answer this question. Nevertheless, one of the most noteworthy features of life's near misses seems to be their durability. Consider the account of finishing second that Nicholson Baker (1991) provides his wife:

> [I] told her my terrible story of coming in second in the spelling bee in second grade by spelling *keep* 'c-e-e-p' after successfully tossing off *microphone*, and how for two or three years afterward I was pained every time a yellow garbage truck drove by on Highland Avenue and I saw the capitals printed on it, 'Help Keep Our City Clean,' with that impossible irrational K that had made me lose so humiliatingly …

Or consider the case of Abel Kiviat, the 1,500 m silver medalist in the 1912 Olympics in Stockholm. Kiviat had the race won until Britain's Arnold Jackson "came from nowhere" to beat him by one-tenth of a second. "I wake up sometimes and say, 'What the heck happened to me?' It's like a nightmare." Kiviat was 91 years old when he said this in an interview with the *Los Angeles Times* (cited in Tait & Silver, 1989, p. 351). It appears that thoughts about what might have been may plague us for a very long time.

REFERENCES

Atkinson, J. W. (1964). *An introduction to motivation*. Princeton, NJ: Van Nostrand.

Baker, N. (1991). *Room temperature*. New York: Vintage.

Baumeister, R. F., & Steinhilber, A. (1984). Paradoxical effects of supportive audiences on performance under pressure: The home field disadvantage in sports championships. *Journal of Personality and Social Psychology, 47*, 85–93.

Crosby, F. (1976). A model of egoistical relative deprivation. *Psychological Review, 83*, 85–113.

Feather, N. T. (1967). Valence of outcome and expectation of success in relation to task difficulty and perceived locus of control. *Journal of Personality and Social Psychology, 7*, 372–386.

Feather, N. T. (1969). Attribution of responsibility and valence of success and failure in relation to initial confidence and task performance. *Journal of Personality and Social Psychology, 13*, 129–144.

Festinger, L. (1954). A theory of social comparison processes. *Human Relations, 7*, 117–140.

Frank, M. G., & Gilovich, T. (1988). The dark side of self- and social perception: Black uniforms and aggression in professional sports. *Journal of Personality and Social Psychology, 54*, 74–85.

Frank, R. H., & Cook, P. (1995). *The winner-take-all society*. New York: Free Press.

Gilovich, T., Vallone, R. P., & Tversky, A. (1985). The hot hand in basketball: On the misperception of random sequences. *Cognitive Psychology, 17*, 295–314.

James, W. (1892). *Psychology*. New York: Holt.

Johnson, J. T. (1986). The knowledge of what might have been: Affective and attributional consequences of near outcomes. *Personality and Social Psychology Bulletin, 12*, 51–62.

Kahneman, D. (in press). Varieties of counterfactual thinking. In N. Roese & J. Olson (Eds.), *What might have been: The social psychology of counterfactual thinking*. Hillsdale, NJ: Erlbaum.

Kahneman, D., & Miller, D. T. (1986). Norm theory: Comparing reality to its alternatives. *Psychological Review, 93*, 136–153.

Kahneman, D., & Tversky, A. (1982a). The psychology of preferences. *Scientific American, 2*, 160–173.

Kahneman, D., & Tversky, A. (1982b). The simulation heuristic. In D. Kahneman, P. Slovic, & A. Tversky (Eds.), *Judgment under uncertainty: Heuristics and biases* (pp. 201–208). New York: Cambridge University Press.

Kahneman, D., & Varey, C. A. (1990). Propensities and counterfactuals: The loser that almost won. *Journal of Personality and Social Psychology, 59*, 1101–1110.

Lau, R. R., & Russell, D. (1980). Attributions in the sports pages: A field test of some current hypotheses about attribution research. *Journal of Personality and Social Psychology, 39*, 29–38.

Markman, K. D., Gavanski, I., Sherman, S. J., & McMullen, M. N. (1993). The mental simulation of better and worse possible worlds. *Journal of Experimental Social Psychology, 29*, 87–109.

Miller, D. T., & McFarland, C. (1986). Counterfactual thinking and victim compensation: A test of norm theory. *Personality and Social Psychology Bulletin, 12*, 513–519.

Miller, D., Turnbull, W., & McFarland, C. (1990). Counterfactual thinking and social perception: Thinking about what might have been. In L. Berkowitz (Ed.), *Advances in experimental social psychology* (Vol. 22, pp. 305–331). San Diego, CA: Academic Press.

Olson, J. M., Herman, P., & Zanna, M. P. (1986). *Relative deprivation and social comparison: The Ontario symposium* (Vol. 4). Hillsdale, NJ: Erlbaum.

Roese, N. J. (1994). The functional basis of counterfactual thinking. *Journal of Personality and Social Psychology, 66*, 805–818.

Roese, N. J., & Olson, J. M. (in press). *What might have been: The social psychology of counterfactual thinking*. Hillsdale, NJ: Erlbaum.

Suls, J. M., & Miller, R. L. (1977). *Social comparison processes: Theoretical and empirical perspectives*. New York: Wiley.

Tait, R., & Silver, R. C. (1989). Coming to terms with major negative life events. In J. S. Uleman & J. A. Bargh (Eds.), *Unintended thought* (pp. 351–382). New York: Guilford Press.

Taylor, S. E., & Lobel, M. (1989). Social comparison activity under threat: Downward evaluation and upward contacts. *Psychological Review, 96*, 569–575.

Turnbull, W. (1981). Naive conceptions of free will and the deterministic paradox. *Canadian Journal of Behavioural Science, 13*, 1–13.

Tversky, A., & Griffin, D. (1991). Endowment and contrast in judgments of well-being. In R. J. Zeckhauser (Ed.), *Strategy and choice* (pp. 297–318). Cambridge, MA: MIT Press.

Verschoth, A. (1992, July 22). Who will win what. *Sports Illustrated*.

Wells, G. L., & Gavanski, I. (1989). Mental simulation of causality. *Journal of Personality and Social Psychology, 56*, 161–169.

Received January 10, 1994
Revision received May 8, 1995
Accepted May 10, 1995 ■

READING 37

Social Perception and Interpersonal Behavior: On the Self-Fulfilling Nature of Social Stereotypes

Mark Snyder, Elizabeth Decker Tanke, and Ellen Berscheid

This research concerns the self-fulfilling influences of social stereotypes on dyadic social interaction. Conceptual analysis of the cognitive and behavioral consequences of stereotyping suggests that a perceiver's actions based upon stereotype-generated attributions about a specific target individual may cause the behavior of that individual to confirm the perceiver's initially erroneous attributions. A paradigmatic investigation of the behavioral confirmation of stereotypes involving physical attractiveness (e.g., "beautiful people are good people") is presented. Male "perceivers" interacted with female "targets" whom they believed (as a result of an experimental manipulation) to be physically attractive or physically unattractive. Tape recordings of each participant's conversational behavior were analyzed by naive observer judges for evidence of behavioral confirmation. These analyses revealed that targets who were perceived (unknown to them) to be physically attractive came to behave in a friendly, likable, and sociable manner in comparison with targets whose perceivers regarded them as unattractive. It is suggested that theories in cognitive social psychology attend to the ways in which perceivers create the information that they process in addition to the ways that they process that information.

Thoughts are but dreams
Till their effects be tried

— William Shakespeare[1]

Research and preparation of this manuscript were supported in part by National Science Foundation Grants SOC 75-13872, "Cognition and Behavior: When Belief Creates Reality," to Mark Snyder and GS 35157X, "Dependency and Interpersonal Attraction," to Ellen Berscheid. We thank Marilyn Steere, Craig Daniels, and Dwain Boelter, who assisted in the empirical phases of this investigation; and J. Merrill Carlsmith, Thomas Hummel, E. E. Jones, Mark Lepper, and Walter Mischel, who provided helpful advice and constructive commentary.

Requests for reprints should be sent to Mark Snyder, Laboratory for Research in Social Relations, Department of Psychology, University of Minnesota, 75 East River Road, Minneapolis, Minnesota 55455.

[1] From *The Rape of Lucrece*, lines 346–353.

Cognitive social psychology is concerned with the processes by which individuals gain knowledge about behavior and events that they encounter in social interaction, and how they use this knowledge to guide their actions. From this perspective, people are "constructive thinkers" searching for the causes of behavior, drawing inferences about people and their circumstances, and acting upon this knowledge.

Most empirical work in this domain — largely stimulated and guided by the attribution theories (e.g., Heider, 1958; Jones & Davis, 1965; Kelley, 1973) — has focused on the processing of information, the "machinery" of social cognition. Some outcomes of this research have been the specification of how individuals identify the causes of an actor's behavior, how individuals make inferences about the traits and dispositions of the actor, and how individuals make predictions about the actor's future behavior (for reviews, see Harvey, Ickes, & Kidd, 1976; Jones et al., 1972; Ross, 1977).

It is noteworthy that comparatively little theoretical and empirical attention has been directed to the other fundamental question within the cognitive social psychologist's mandate: What are the cognitive and behavioral consequences of our impressions of other people? From our vantage point, current-day attribution theorists leave the individual "lost in thought," with no machinery that links thought to action. It is to this concern that we address ourselves, both theoretically and empirically, in the context of social stereotypes.

Social stereotypes are a special case of interpersonal perception. Stereotypes are usually simple, overgeneralized, and widely accepted (e.g., Karlins, Coffman, & Walters, 1969). But stereotypes are often inaccurate. It is simply not true that all Germans are industrious or that all women are dependent and conforming. Nonetheless, many social stereotypes concern highly visible and distinctive personal characteristics; for example, sex and race. These pieces of information are usually the first to be noticed in social interaction and can gain high priority for channeling subsequent information processing and even social interaction. Social stereotypes are thus an ideal testing ground for considering the cognitive and behavioral consequences of person perception.

Numerous factors may help sustain our stereotypes and prevent disconfirmation of "erroneous" stereotype-based initial impressions of specific others. First, social stereotypes may influence information processing in ways that serve to bolster and strengthen these stereotypes.

Cognitive Bolstering of Social Stereotypes

As information processors, humans readily fall victim to the cognitive process described centuries ago by Francis Bacon (1620/1902):

> The human understanding, when any proposition has been once laid down ... forces everything else to add fresh support and confirmation ... it is the peculiar and perpetual error of the human understanding to be more moved and excited by affirmatives than negatives. (pp. 23–24)

Empirical research has demonstrated several such biases in information processing. We may overestimate the frequency of occurrence of confirming or paradigmatic examples of our stereotypes simply because such instances are more easily noticed, more easily brought to mind, and more easily retrieved from memory (cf. Hamilton & Gifford, 1976; Rothbart, Fulero, Jensen, Howard, & Birrell, Note 1). Evidence that confirms our stereotyped intuitions about human nature may be, in a word, more cognitively "available" (Tversky & Kahneman, 1973) than nonconforming evidence.

Moreover, we may fill in the gaps in our evidence base with information consistent with our preconceived notions of what evidence should support our beliefs. For example, Chapman and Chapman (1967, 1969) have demonstrated that both college students and professional clinicians perceive positive associations between particular Rorschach responses and homosexuality in males, even though these associations are demonstrably absent in real life. These "signs" are simply those that comprise common cultural stereotypes of gay males.

Furthermore, once a stereotype has been adopted, a wide variety of evidence can be interpreted readily as supportive of that stereotype, including events that could support equally well an opposite interpretation. As Merton (1948) has suggested, in-group virtues ("We are thrifty") may become outgroup vices ("They are cheap") in our attempts to maintain negative stereotypes about disliked out groups. (For empirical demonstrations of this bias, see Regan, Straus, & Fazio, 1974; Rosenhan, 1973; Zadny & Gerard, 1974).

Finally, selective recall and reinterpretation of information from an individual's past history may be exploited to support a current stereotype-based inference (cf. Loftus & Palmer, 1974). Thus, having decided that Jim is stingy (as are all members of his group), it may be all too easy to remember a variety of behaviors and incidents that are insufficient one at a time to support an attribution of stinginess, but that taken together do warrant and support such an inference.

Behavioral Confirmation of Social Stereotypes

The cognitive bolstering processes discussed above may provide the perceiver with an "evidence base" that gives compelling cognitive reality to any traits that he or she may have erroneously attributed to a target individual initially. This reality is, of course, entirely cognitive: It is in the eye and mind of the beholder. But stereotype-based attributions may serve as grounds for predictions about the target's future behavior and may guide and influence the perceiver's interactions with the target.

This process itself may generate behaviors on the part of the target that erroneously confirm the predictions and validate the attributions of the perceiver. How others treat us is, in large measure, a reflection of our treatment of them (cf. Bandura, 1977; Mischel, 1968; Raush, 1965). Thus, when we use our social perceptions as guides for regulating our interactions with others, we may constrain their behavioral options (cf. Kelley & Stahelski, 1970).

Consider this hypothetical, but illustrative, scenario: Michael tells Jim that Chris is a cool and aloof person. Jim meets Chris and notices expressions of coolness and aloofness. Jim proceeds to overestimate the extent to which Chris' self-presentation reflects a cool and aloof disposition and underestimates the extent to which this posture was engendered by his own cool and aloof behavior toward Chris, that had in turn been generated by his own prior beliefs about Chris. Little does Jim know that Tom, who had heard that Chris was warm and friendly, found that his impressions of Chris were confirmed during their interaction. In each case, the end result of the process of "interaction guided by perceptions" has been the target person's *behavioral confirmation* of the perceiver's initial impressions of him.

This scenario makes salient key aspects of the process of behavioral confirmation in social interaction. The perceiver (either Jim or Tom) is not aware that his original perception of the target individual (Chris) is inaccurate. Nor is the perceiver aware of the causal role that his own behavior (here, the enactment of a cool or warm expressive style) plays in generating the behavioral evidence that erroneously confirms his expectations. Unbeknownst to the perceiver, the reality that he confidently perceives to exist in the social world has, in fact, been actively constructed by his own transactions with and operations upon the social world.

In our empirical research, we proposed to demonstrate that stereotypes may create their own social reality by channeling social interaction in ways that cause the stereotyped individual to behaviorally confirm the perceiver's stereotype. Moreover, we sought to demonstrate behavioral confirmation in a social interaction context designed to mirror as faithfully as possible the spontaneous generation of impressions in everyday social interaction and the subsequent channeling influences of these perceptions on dyadic interaction.

One widely held stereotype in this culture involves physical attractiveness. Considerable evidence suggests that attractive persons are assumed to possess more socially desirable personality traits and are expected to lead better lives than their unattractive counterparts (Berscheid & Walster, 1974). Attractive persons are perceived to have virtually every character trait that is socially desirable to the perceiver: "Physically attractive people, for example, were perceived to be more sexually warm and responsive, sensitive, kind, interesting, strong, poised, modest, sociable, and outgoing than persons of lesser physical attractiveness" (Berscheid & Walster, 1974, p. 169). This powerful stereotype holds for male and female perceivers and for male and female stimulus persons.

What of the validity of the physical attractiveness stereotype? Are the physically attractive actually more likable, friendly, and confident than the unattractive? Physically attractive young adults are more often and more eagerly sought out for social dates (Dermer, 1973; Krebs & Adinolphi, 1975; Walster, Aronson, Abrahams, & Rottman, 1966). Even as early as nursery school age, physical attractiveness appears to channel social interaction: The physically attractive are chosen and the unattractive are rejected in sociometric choices (Dion & Berscheid, 1974; Kleck, Richardson, & Ronald, 1974).

Differential amount of interaction with the attractive and unattractive clearly helps the stereotype persevere, for it limits the chances for learning whether the two types of individuals differ in the traits associated with the stereotype. But the point we wish to focus upon here is that the stereotype may also channel interaction so that it behaviorally confirms itself. Individuals may have different styles of interaction for those whom they perceive to be physically attractive and for those whom they consider unattractive. These differences in interaction style may in turn elicit and nurture behaviors from the target person that are in accord with the stereotype. That is, the physically attractive may actually come to behave in a friendly, likable, sociable manner — not because they necessarily possess these dispositions, but because the behavior of others elicits and maintains behaviors taken to be manifestations of such traits.

Accordingly, we sought to demonstrate the behavioral confirmation of the physical attractiveness stereotype in dyadic social interaction. In order to do so, pairs of previously unacquainted individuals (designated, for our purposes, as a perceiver and a target) interacted in a getting-acquainted situation that had been constructed to allow us to control the information that one member of the dyad (the male perceiver) received about the physical attractiveness of the other individual (the female target). To measure the extent to which the actual behavior of the target matched the perceiver's stereotype, naive observer judges, who were unaware of the actual or perceived physical attractiveness of either participant, listened to and evaluated tape recordings of the interaction.

Method

Participants

Fifty-one male and 51 female undergraduates at the University of Minnesota participated, for extra course credit, in a study of "the processes by which people become acquainted with each other." Participants were scheduled in pairs of previously unacquainted males and females.

The Interaction Between Perceiver and Target

To insure that participants would not see each other before their interactions, they arrived at separate experimental rooms on separate corridors. The experimenter informed each participant that she was studying acquaintance processes in social relationships. Specifically, she was investigating the differences between those initial interactions that involve nonverbal communication and those, such as telephone conversations, that do not. Thus, she explained, the participant would engage in a telephone conversation with another student in introductory psychology.

Before the conversation began, each participant provided written permission for it to be tape recorded. In addition, both dyad members completed brief questionnaires concerning such information as academic major in college and high school of graduation. These questionnaires, it was explained, would provide the partners with some information about each other with which to start the conversation.

Activating the Perceiver's Stereotype
The getting-acquainted interaction permitted control of the information that each male perceiver received about the physical attractiveness of his female target. When male perceivers learned about the biographical information questionnaires, they also learned that each person would receive a snapshot of the other member of the dyad, because "other people in the experiment have told us they feel more comfortable when they have a mental picture of the person they're talking to." The experimenter then used a Polaroid camera to photograph the male. No mention of any snapshots was made to female participants.

When each male perceiver received his partner's biographical information form, it arrived in a folder containing a Polaroid snapshot, ostensibly of his partner. Although the biographical information had indeed been provided by his partner, the photograph was not. It was one of eight photographs that had been prepared in advance.

Twenty females students from several local colleges assisted (in return for $5) in the preparation of stimulus materials by allowing us to take Polaroid snapshots of them. Each photographic subject wore casual dress, each was smiling, and each agreed (in writing) to allow us to use her photograph. Twenty college-age men then rated the attractiveness of each picture on a 10-point scale.[2] We then chose the four pictures that had received the highest attractiveness ratings ($M = 8.10$) and the four photos that had received the lowest ratings ($M = 2.56$). There was virtually no overlap in ratings of the two sets of pictures.

Male perceivers were assigned randomly to one of two conditions of perceived physical attractiveness of their targets. Males in the attractive target condition received folders containing their partners' biographical information form and one of the four attractive photographs. Males in the unattractive target condition received folders containing their partners' biographical information form and one of the four unattractive photographs. Female targets knew nothing of the photographs possessed by their male interaction partners, nor did they receive snapshots of their partners.

The Perceiver's Stereotype-based Attributions
Before initiating his getting-acquainted conversation, each male perceiver rated his initial impressions of his partner on an Impression Formation Questionnaire. The questionnaire was constructed by supplementing the 27 trait adjectives used by Dion, Berscheid, and Walster (1972) in their original investigation of the physical attractiveness stereotype with the following items: Intelligence, physical attractiveness, social adeptness, friendliness, enthusiasm, trust-worthiness, and successfulness. We were thus able to assess the extent to which perceivers' initial impressions of their partners reflected general stereotypes linking physical attractiveness and personality characteristics.

The Getting-acquainted Conversation
Each dyad then engaged in a 10-minute unstructured conversation by means of microphones and headphones

---

[2] The interrater correlations of these ratings of attractiveness ranged from .45 to .92, with an average interrater correlation of .74.

connected through a Sony TC-570 stereophonic tape recorder that recorded each participant's voice on a separate channel of the tape.

After the conversation, male perceivers completed the Impression Formation Questionnaires to record final impressions of their partners. Female targets expressed self-perceptions in terms of the items of the Impression Formation Questionnaire. Each female target also indicated, on 10-point scales, how much she had enjoyed the conversation, how comfortable she had felt while talking to her partner, how accurate a picture of herself she felt that her partner had formed as a result of the conversation, how typical her partner's behavior had been of the way she usually was treated by men, her perception of her own physical attractiveness, and her estimate of her partner's perception of her physical attractiveness. All participants were then thoroughly and carefully debriefed and thanked for their contribution to the study.

Assessing Behavioral Confirmation

To assess the extent to which the actions of the target women provided behavioral confirmation for the stereotypes of the men perceivers, 8 male and 4 female introductory psychology students rated the tape recordings of the getting-acquainted conversations. These observer judges were unaware of the experimental hypotheses and knew nothing of the actual or perceived physical attractiveness of the individuals on the tapes. They listened, in random order, to two 4-minute segments (one each from the beginning and end) of each conversation. They heard *only* the track of the tapes containing the target women's voices and rated each woman on the 34 bipolar scales of the Impression Formation Questionnaire as well as on 14 additional 10-point scales; for example, "How animated and enthusiastic is this person?", "How intimate or personal is this person's conversation?", and "How much is she enjoying herself?". Another group of observer judges (3 males and 6 females) performed a similar assessment of the male perceivers' behavior based upon only the track of the tapes that contained the males' voices.[3]

[3] We assessed the reliability of our raters by means of intraclass correlations (Ebel, 1951), a technique that employees analysis-of-variance procedures to determine the proportion of the total variance in ratings due to variance in the persons being rated. The intraclass correlation is the measure of reliability most commonly used with interval data and ordinal scales that assume interval properties. Because the measure of interest was the mean rating of judges on each variable, the between-rater variance was not included in the error term in

Results

To chart the process of behavioral confirmation of social stereotypes in dyadic social interaction, we examined the effects of our manipulation of the target women's apparent physical attractiveness on (a) the male perceivers' initial impressions of them and (b) the women's behavioral self-presentation during the interaction, as measured by the observer judges' ratings of the tape recordings.

The Perceivers' Stereotype

Did our male perceivers form initial impressions of their specific target women on the basis of general stereotypes that associate physical attractiveness and desirable personalities? To answer this question, we examined the male perceivers' initial ratings on the Impression Formation Questionnaire. Recall that these impressions were recorded *after* the perceivers had seen their partners' photographs, but *before* the getting-acquainted conversation.[4] Indeed, it appears that our male perceivers did fashion their initial impressions of their female partners on the basis of stereo-typed beliefs

calculating the intraclass correlation. (For a discussion, see Tinsley & Weiss, 1975, p. 363). Reliability coefficients for the coders' ratings of the females for all dependent measures ranged from .35 to .91 with a median of .755. For each dependent variable, a single score was constructed for each participant by calculating the mean of the raters' scores on that measure. Analyses of variance, including the time of the tape segment (early vs. late in the conversation) as a factor, revealed no more main effects of time or interactions between time and perceived attractiveness than would have been expected by chance. Thus, scores for the two tape segments were summed to yield a single score for each dependent variable. The same procedure was followed for ratings of male perceivers' behavior. In this case, the reliability coefficients ranged from .18 to .83 with a median of .61.

[4] These and all subsequent analyses are based upon a total of 38 observations, 19 in each of the attractive target and unattractive target conditions. Of the original 51 dyads, a total of 48 male-female pairs completed the experiment. In each of the remaining three dyads, the male participant had made reference during the conversation to the photograph. When this happened, the experimenter interrupted the conversation and immediately debriefed the participants. Of the remaining 48 dyads who completed the experimental procedures, 10 were eliminated from the analyses for the following reasons: In 4 cases the male participant expressed strong suspicion about the photograph; in 1 case, the conversation was not tape recorded because of a mechanical problem; and in 5 cases, there was a sufficiently large age difference (ranging from 6 years to 18 years) between the participants that the males in these dyads reported that they had reacted very differently to their partners than they would have reacted to an age peer. This pattern of attrition was independent of assignment to the attractive target and unattractive target experimental conditions ($\chi^2 = 1.27$, *ns*).

about physical attractiveness, multivariate $F(34, 3) = 10.19$, $p < .04$. As dictated by the physical attractiveness stereotype, men who anticipated physically attractive partners expected to interact with comparatively sociable, poised, humorous, and socially adept women; by contrast, men faced with the prospect of getting acquainted with relatively unattractive partners fashioned images of rather unsociable, awkward, serious, and socially inept women, all $Fs(1, 36) > 5.85$, $p < .025$.

Behavioral Confirmation

Not only did our perceivers fashion their images of their discussion partners on the basis of their stereotyped intuitions about beauty and goodness of character, but these impressions initiated a chain of events that resulted in the behavioral confirmation of these initially erroneous inferences. Our analyses of the observer judges' ratings of the women's behavior were guided by our knowledge of the structure of the men's initial impressions of their target women's personality. Specifically, we expected to find evidence of behavioral confirmation only for those traits that had defined the perceivers' stereotypes. For example, male perceivers did not attribute differential amounts of sensitivity or intelligence to partners of differing apparent physical attractiveness. Accordingly, we would not expect that our observer judges would "hear" different amounts of intelligence or sensitivity in the tapes. By contrast, male perceivers did expect attractive and unattractive targets to differ in sociability. Here we would expect that observer judges would detect differences in sociability between conditions when listening to the women's contributions to the conversations, and thus we would have evidence of behavioral confirmation.

To assess the extent to which the women's behavior, as rated by the observer judges, provided behavioral confirmation for the male perceivers' stereotypes, we identified, by means of a discriminant analysis (Tatsuoka, 1971), those 21 trait items of the Impression Formation Questionnaire for which the mean initial ratings of the men in the attractive target and unattractive target conditions differed by more than 1.4 standard deviations.[5] This set of "stereotype traits" (e.g., sociable, poised, sexually warm, outgoing) defines the differing perceptions of the personality characteristics of target women in the two experimental conditions.

We then entered these 21 stereotype traits and the 14 additional dependent measures into a multivariate analysis of variance. This analysis revealed that our observer judges did indeed view women who had been assigned to the attractive target condition quite differently than women in the unattractive target condition, $Fm(35, 2) = 40.003$, $p < .025$. What had initially been reality in the minds of the men had now become reality in the behavior of the women with whom they had interacted — a behavioral reality discernible even by naive observer judges, who had access *only* to tape recordings of the women's contributions to the conversations.

When a multivariate analysis of variance is performed on multiple correlated dependent measures, the null hypothesis states that the vector of means is equal across conditions. When the null hypothesis is rejected, the nature of the difference between groups must then be inferred from inspection of group differences on the individual dependent measures. In this case, the differences between the behavior of the women in the attractive target and the unattractive target conditions were in the same direction as the male perceivers' initial stereotyped impressions for fully 17 of the 21 measures of behavioral confirmation. The binomial probability that at least 17 of these adjectives would be in the predicted direction by chance alone is a scant .003. By contrast, when we examined the 13 trait pairs that our discriminant analysis had indicated did *not* define the male perceivers' stereotype, a sharply different pattern emerged. Here, we would not expect any systematic relationship between the male perceivers' stereotyped initial impressions and the female targets' actual behavior in the getting-acquainted conversations. In fact, for only 8 of these 13 measures is the difference between the behavior of the women in the attractive target condition in the same direction as the men's stereotyped initial impressions. This configuration is, of course, hardly different from the pattern expected by chance alone if there were no differences between the groups (exact binomial $p = .29$). Clearly, then, behavioral confirmation manifested itself only for those attributes that had defined the male perceivers' stereotype; that is, only in those domains where the men believed that there did exist links between physical attractiveness and personal attributes did the women come to behave differently as a consequence of the level of physical attractiveness that we had experimentally assigned to them.

Moreover, our understanding of the nature of the difference between the attractive target and the unattractive target conditions identified by our multivariate analysis of variance and our confidence in this demonstration of

---

[5] After the 21st trait dimension, the differences between the experimental conditions drop off sharply. For example, the next adjective pair down the line has a difference of 1.19 standard deviations, and the one after that has a difference of 1.02 standard deviations.

behavioral confirmation are bolstered by the consistent pattern of behavioral differences on the 14 additional related dependent measures. Our raters assigned to the female targets in the attractive target condition higher ratings on *every* question related to favorableness of self-presentation. Thus, for example, those who were thought by their perceivers to be physically attractive appeared to the observer judges to manifest greater confidence, greater animation, greater enjoyment of the conversation, and greater liking for their partners than those women who interacted with men who perceived them as physically unattractive.[6]

In Search of Mediators of Behavioral Confirmation

We next attempted to chart the process of behavioral confirmation. Specifically, we searched for evidence of the behavioral implications of the perceivers' stereotypes. Did the male perceivers present themselves differently to target women whom they assumed to be physically attractive or unattractive? Because we had 50 dependent measures[7] of the observer judges' ratings of the males — 12 more than the number of observations (male perceivers) — a multivariate analysis of variance is inappropriate. However, in 21 cases, univariate analyses of variance did indicate differences between conditions

(all $ps < .05$). Men who interacted with women whom they believed to be physically attractive appeared (to the observer judges) more sociable, sexually warm, interesting, independent, sexually permissive, bold, outgoing, humorous, obvious, and socially adept than their counterparts in the unattractive target condition. Moreover, these men were seen as more attractive, more confident, and more animated in their conversation than their counterparts. Further, they were considered by the observer judges to be more comfortable, to enjoy themselves more, to like their partners more, to take the initiative more often, to use their voices more effectively, to see their women partners as more attractive and, finally, to be seen as more attractive by their partners than men in the unattractive target condition.

It appears, then, that differences in the level of sociability manifested and expressed by the male perceivers may have been a key factor in bringing out reciprocating patterns of expression in the target women. One reason that target women who had been labeled as attractive may have reciprocated these sociable overtures is that they regarded their partners' images of them as more accurate, $F(1, 28) = 6.75, p < .02$, and their interaction style to be more typical of the way men generally treated them, $F(1, 28) = 4.79, p < .04$, than did women in the unattractive target condition.[8] These individuals, perhaps, rejected their partners' treatment of them as unrepresentative and defensively adopted more cool and aloof postures to cope with their situations.

Discussion

Of what consequence are our social stereotypes? Our research suggests that stereotypes can and do channel dyadic interaction so as to create their own social reality. In our demonstration, pairs of individuals got acquainted with each other in a situation that allowed us to control the information that one member of the dyad (the perceiver) received about the physical attractiveness of the other person (the target). Our perceivers, in anticipation of interaction, fashioned erroneous images of their specific partners that reflected their general stereotypes about physical attractiveness. Moreover, our perceivers had very different patterns and styles of interaction for those whom they perceived to be physically attractive and unattractive. These differences in

---

[6] We may eliminate several alternative interpretations of the behavioral confirmation effect. Women who had been assigned randomly to the attractive target condition were not in fact more physically attractive than those who were assigned randomly to the unattractive target condition. Ratings of the actual attractiveness of the female targets by the experimenter revealed no differences whatsoever between conditions, $t(36) = .00$. Nor, for that matter, did male perceivers differ in their own physical attractiveness as a function of experimental condition, $t(36) = .44$. In addition, actual attractiveness of male perceivers and actual attractiveness female targets within dyads were independent of each other, $r(36) = .06$.

Of greater importance, there was no detectable difference in personality characteristics of females who had been assigned randomly to the attractive target and unattractive target conditions of the experiment. They did not differ in self-esteem as assessed by the Janis-Field-Eagly (Janis & Field, 1973) measure, $F(1, 36) < 1$. Moreover, there were no differences between experimental conditions in the female targets' self-perceptions as reported after the conversations on the Impression Formation Questionnaire ($Fm < 1$). We have thus no reason to suspect that any systematic, pre-existing differences between conditions in morphology or personality can pose plausible alternative explanations of our demonstration of behavioral confirmation.

[7] Two dependent measures were added between the time that the ratings were made of the female participants and the time that the ratings were made of the male participants. These measures were responses to the questions, "How interested is he in his partner?" and "How attractive does he think his partner is?".

---

[8] The degrees of freedom for these analyses are fewer than those for other analyses because they were added to the experimental procedure after four dyads had participated in each condition.

self-presentation and interaction style, in turn, elicited and nurtured behaviors of the target that were consistent with the perceivers' initial stereotypes. Targets who were perceived (unbeknownst to them) to be physically attractive actually came to behave in a friendly, likable, and sociable manner. The perceivers' attributions about their targets based upon their stereotyped intuitions about the world had initiated a process that produced behavioral confirmation of those attributions. The initially erroneous attributions of the perceivers had become real: The stereotype had truly functioned as a self-fulfilling prophecy (Merton, 1948).[9]

We regard our investigation as a particularly compelling demonstration of behavioral confirmation in social interaction. For if there is any social–psychological process that ought to exist in "stronger" form in everyday interaction than in the psychological laboratory, it is behavioral confirmation. In the context of years of social interaction in which perceivers have reacted to their actual physical attractiveness, our 10-minute getting-acquainted conversations over a telephone must seem minimal indeed. Nonetheless, the impact was sufficient to permit outside observers who had access only to one person's side of a conversation to detect manifestations of behavioral confirmation.

Might not other important and widespread social stereotypes — particularly those concerning sex, race, social class, and ethnicity — also channel social interaction so as to create their own social reality? For example, will the common stereotype that women are more conforming and less independent than men (cf. Broverman, Vogel, Broverman, Clarkson, & Rosenkrantz, 1972) influence interaction so that (within a procedural paradigm similar to ours) targets believed to be female will actually conform more, be more dependent, and be more successfully manipulated than interaction partners believed to be male? At least one empirical investigation has pointed to the possible self-fulfilling nature of apparent sex differences in self-presentation (Zanna & Pack, 1975).

---

[9] Our research on behavioral confirmation in social interaction is a clear "cousin" of other demonstrations that perceivers' expectations may influence other individuals' behavior. Thus, Rosenthal (1974) and his colleagues have conducted an extensive program of laboratory and field investigations of the effects of experimenters' and teachers' expectations on the behavior of subjects in psychological laboratories and students in classrooms. Experimenters and teachers led to expect particular patterns of performance from their subjects and pupils act in ways that selectively influence or shape those performances to confirm initial expectations (e.g., Rosenthal, 1974).

Any self-fulfilling influences of social stereotypes may have compelling and pervasive societal consequences. Social observers have for decades commented on the ways in which stigmatized social groups and outsiders may fall "victim" to self-fulfilling cultural stereotypes (e.g., Becker, 1963; Goffman, 1963; Merton, 1948; Myrdal, 1944; Tannenbaum, 1938). Consider Scott's (1969) observations about the blind:

> When, for example, sighted people continually insist that a blind man is helpless because he is blind, their subsequent treatment of him may preclude his even exercising the kinds of skills that would enable him to be independent. It is in this sense that stereotypic beliefs are self-actualized. (p. 9)

And all too often it is the "victims" who are blamed for their own plight (cf. Ryan, 1971) rather than the social expectations that have constrained their behavioral options.

Of what import is the behavioral confirmation process for our theoretical understanding of the nature of social perception? Although our empirical research has focused on social stereotypes that are widely accepted and broadly generalized, our notions of behavioral confirmation may apply equally well to idiosyncratic social perceptions spontaneously formed about specific individuals in the course of every day social interaction. In this sense, social psychologists have been wise to devote intense effort to understanding the processes by which impressions of others are formed. Social perceptions are important precisely because of their impact on social interaction. Yet, at the same time, research and theory in social perception (mostly displayed under the banner of attribution theory) that have focused on the manner in which individuals process information provided them to form impressions of others may underestimate the extent to which information received in actual social interaction is a product of the perceiver's own actions toward the target individual. More careful attention must clearly be paid to the ways in which perceivers *create* or *construct* the information that they process in addition to the ways in which they *process* that information. Events in the social world may be as much the *effects* of our perceptions of those events as they are the *causes* of those perceptions.

From this perspective, it becomes easier to appreciate the perceiver's stubborn tendency to fashion images of others largely in trait terms (e.g., Jones & Nisbett, 1972), despite the poverty of evidence for the pervasive cross-situational consistencies in social behavior that the existence of "true" traits would demand (e.g., Mischel, 1968). This tendency, dubbed by Ross (1977) as the "fundamental attribution error," may be a self-erasing error. For even though any target individual's behavior may lack, overall, the trait-defining properties of cross-situational consistency, the actions of the perceiver himself may produce consistency in the samples of behavior available to that perceiver. Our impressions of others may cause those others to behave in consistent trait-like fashion for us. In that sense, our trait-based impressions of others are veridical, even though the same individual may behave or be led to behave in a fashion perfectly consistent with opposite attributions by other perceivers with quite different impressions of that individual. Such may be the power of the behavioral confirmation process.

REFERENCE NOTE

1. Rothbart, M., Fulero, S., Jensen, C., Howard, J., & Birrell, P. *From individual to group impressions: Availability heuristics in stereotype formation.* Unpublished manuscript, University of Oregon, 1976.

REFERENCES

Bacon, F. [*Novum organum*] (J. Devey, Ed.). New York: P. F. Collier & Son, 1902. (Originally published, 1620.)

Bandura, A. *Social learning theory.* Englewood Cliffs, N. J.: Prentice Hall, 1977.

Becker, H. W. *Outsiders: Studies in the sociology of deviance.* N. Y.: Free Press, 1963.

Berscheid, E., & Walster, E. Physical attractiveness. In L. Berkowitz (Ed.), *Advances in experimental social psychology* (Vol. 7). New York: Academic Press, 1974.

Broverman, I. K., Vogel, S. R., Broverman, D. M., Clarkson, F. E., & Rosenkrantz, P. S. Sex-role stereotypes: A current appraisal. *Journal of Social Issues*, 1972, *28*, 59–78.

Chapman, L., & Chapman, J. The genesis of popular but erroneous psychodiagnostic observations. *Journal of Abnormal Psychology*, 1967, *72*, 193–204.

Chapman, L., & Chapman, J. Illusory correlations as an obstacle to the use of valid psychodiagnostic signs. *Journal of Abnormal Psychology*, 1969, *74*, 271–280.

Dermer, *M. When beauty fails.* Unpublished doctoral dissertation, University of Minnesota, 1973.

Dion, K. K., & Berscheid, E. Physical attractiveness and peer perception among children. *Sociometry*, 1974, *37*(1), 1–12.

Dion, K. K., Berscheid, E., & Walster, E. What is beautiful is good. *Journal of Personality and Social Psychology*, 1972, *24*, 285–290.

Ebel, R. L. Estimation of the reliability of ratings. *Psychometrika*, 1951, *16*, 407–424.

Goffman, E. *Stigma: Notes on the management of spoiled identity.* Englewood Cliffs, N.J.: Prentice Hall, 1963.

Hamilton, D. L., & Gifford, R. K. Illusory correlation in interpersonal perception: A cognitive basis of stereotypic judgments. *Journal of Experimental Social Psychology*, 1976, *12*, 392–407.

Harvey, J. H., Ickes, W. J., & Kidd, R. F. *New directions in attribution research.* Hillsdale, N.J.: Erlbaum, 1976.

Heider, F. *The psychology of interpersonal relations.* New York: Wiley, 1958.

Janis, I., & Field, P. Sex differences and personality factors related to persuasibility. In C. Hovland & I. Janis (Eds.), *Personality and persuasibility.* New Haven, Conn.: Yale University Press, 1973.

Jones, E. E., & Davis, K. E. From acts to dispositions: The attribution process in person perception. In L. Berkowitz (Ed.), *Advances in experimental social psychology* (Vol. 2). New York: Academic Press, 1965.

Jones et al. *Attribution: Perceiving the causes of behavior.* Morristown, N.J.: General Learning Press, 1972.

Jones, E. E., & Nisbett, R. E. The actor and the observer: Divergent perceptions of the causes of behavior. In E. Jones, D. Kanouse, H. Kelley, S. Valins, & B. Weiner (Eds.), *Attribution: Perceiving the causes of behavior.* New York: General Learning Press, 1972.

Karlins, M., Coffman, T. L., & Walters, G. On the fading of social stereotypes: Studies in three generations of college students. *Journal of Personality and Social Psychology*, 1969, *13*, 1–16.

Kelley, H. H. The process of causal attribution. *American Psychologist*, 1973, *28*, 107–128.

Kelley, H. H., & Stahelski, A. J. The social interaction basis of cooperators' and competitors' beliefs about others. *Journal of Personality and Social Psychology*, 1970, *16*, 66–91.

Kleck, R. E., Richardson, S. A., & Ronald, L. Physical appearance cues and interpersonal attraction in children. *Child Development*, 1974, *45*, 305–310.

Krebs, D., & Adinolphi, A. A. Physical attractiveness, social relations, and personality style. *Journal of Personality and Social Psychology*, 1975, *31*, 245–253.

Loftus, E., & Palmer, J. Reconstruction of automobile destruction. *Journal of Verbal Learning and Verbal Behavior*, 1974, *13*, 585–589.

Merton, R. K. The self-fulfilling prophecy. *Antioch Review*, 1948, *8*, 193–210.

Mischel, W. *Personality and assessment.* New York: Wiley, 1968.

Myrdal, G. *An American dilemma.* New York: Harper & Row, 1944.

Raush, H. L. Interaction sequences. *Journal of Personality and Social Psychology*, 1965, *2*, 487–499.

Regan, D. T., Straus, E., & Fazio, R. Liking and the attribution process. *Journal of Experimental Social Psychology*, 1974, *10*, 385–397.

Rosenhan, D. L. On being sane in insane places. *Science*, 1973, *179*, 250–258.

Rosenthal, R. *On the social psychology of the self-fulfilling prophecy: Further evidence for pygmalion effects and their mediating mechanisms.* New York: M.S.S. Information Corp. Modular Publications, 1974.

Ross, L. The intuitive psychologist and his short-comings: Distortions in the attribution process. In L. Berkowitz (Ed.), *Advances in experimental social psychology* (Vol. 10). New York: Academic Press, 1977.

Ryan, W. *Blaming the victim.* New York: Vintage Books, 1971.

Scott, R. A. *The making of blind men.* New York: Russell Sage, 1969.

Tannenbaum, F. *Crime and the community.* Boston: Ginn, 1938.

Tatsuoka, M. M. *Multivariate analysis.* New York: Wiley, 1971.

Tinsley, H. E. A., & Weiss, D. J. Interrater reliability and agreement of subjective judgments. *Journal of Counseling Psychology*, 1975, *22*, 358–376.

Tversky, A., & Kahneman, D. Availability: A heuristic for judging frequency and probability. *Cognitive Psychology*, 1973, *5*, 207–232.

Walster, E., Aronson, V., Abrahams, D., & Rottman, L. Importance of physical attractiveness in dating behavior. *Journal of Personality and Social Psychology*, 1966, *4*, 508–516.

Zadny, J., & Gerard, H. B. Attributed intentions and informational selectivity. *Journal of Experimental Social Psychology*, 1974, *10*, 34–52.

Zanna, M. P., & Pack, S. J. On the self-fulfilling nature of apparent sex differences in behavior. *Journal of Experimental Social Psychology*, 1975, *11*, 583–591.

Received December 6, 1976 ■

Focalism: A Source of Durability Bias in Affective Forecasting

Timothy D. Wilson, Thalia Wheatley, Jonathan M. Meyers, Daniel T. Gilbert, and Danny Axsom

The durability bias, the tendency to overpredict the duration of affective reactions to future events, may be due in part to focalism, whereby people focus too much on the event in question and not enough on the consequences of other future events. If so, asking people to think about other future activities should reduce the durability bias. In Studies 1–3, college football fans were less likely to overpredict how long the outcome of a football game would influence their happiness if they first thought about how much time they would spend on other future activities. Studies 4 and 5 ruled out alternative explanations and found evidence for a distraction interpretation, that people who think about future events moderate their forecasts because they believe that these events will reduce thinking about the focal event. The authors discuss the implications of focalism for other literatures, such as the planning fallacy.

The pleasures and pains, joys and sufferings, which people actually experience, often fall short of what they had anticipated ... In anticipating a coming event we have it alone in mind, and make no provision for other occurrences. (Tatarkiewicz, 1962/1976)

Editor's Note: This article reported five experiments. Experiments 1, 3, and 4 are reported here.

Timothy D. Wilson, Thalia Wheatley, and Jonathan M. Meyers, Department of Psychology, University of Virginia; Daniel T. Gilbert,Department of Psychology, Harvard University; Danny Axsom, Department of Psychology, Virginia Polytechnic Institute and State University.

We gratefully acknowledge the support of research Grant RO1-MH56075 from the National Institute of Mental Health. We thank Alesha Pelter, Jeff Smith, and Reggie Tyree for their help in conducting the research.

Correspondence concerning this article should be addressed to Timothy D. Wilson, Department of Psychology, Gilmer Hall, University of Virginia, Charlottesville, Virginia 22903. Electronic mail may be sent to tdw@virginia.edu.

If a genie popped out of a lamp and offered you three wishes, would you attain lasting happiness? Most of us think that, like Aladdin, we would become happier people. Perfect health, true love, and untold riches would be ours for the asking, and who would not enjoy blessings such as these? To obtain lasting happiness, however, people have to know what to wish for. In the present studies, we tested the hypothesis that people often think about the future in ways that reduce the accuracy of their affective forecasts.

Undoubtedly, people know a great deal about what will make them happy. Most of us recognize that it would be better to ask the genie for good health, true love, and lots of money than for severe arthritis, a dysfunctional marriage, and the minimum wage. However, predictions about the affective consequences of future events may not always be correct. *Miswanting* is the case in which people do not like or dislike an event as much as they thought they would (Gilbert & Wilson, 2000; Mitchell, Thompson, Peterson, & Cronk, 1997).

Gilbert and Wilson (2000) identified a number of sources of miswanting. Sometimes, for example, an affective forecast is based on a faulty understanding of exactly what the event will entail. When people think about winning a million dollars, they probably imagine spacious mansions, round-the-world trips, and a cavalier attitude toward their children's college tuition. They might not anticipate the difficulty of maintaining relationships with envious friends, the hundreds of annoying phone calls from needy people seeking handouts, and the late-night worries about taxes and investments. The events that we imagine occurring are often quite different from the events that actually occur (Griffin & Ross, 1991).

Even if people know exactly what will happen, however, they can still make inaccurate forecasts about the affective consequences of that event. This is particularly true when people think about the duration of their affective reactions. They may know exactly what winning a million dollars entails and may accurately predict that they will be ecstatic when Ed McMahon arrives at their doorstep and hands them a check with lots of zeros. They might overestimate, however, the duration of this ecstasy. Gilbert and Wilson (2000) argued that people often overestimate the duration of their emotional reactions to future events. This *durability bias* is important, because people typically wish for and work toward events that they believe will cause lasting happiness, not just a moment's pleasure. If they overestimate how long their pleasure will last, they might be working toward the wrong things.

Gilbert, Pinel, Wilson, Blumberg, and Wheatley (1998) found evidence for the durability bias in six studies that examined the accuracy of people's affective forecasts. In one study, assistant professors predicted that their tenure decision would have an impact on their happiness for several years, whereas former assistant professors who had achieved tenure were no happier than former assistant professors who had not. In another study, voters in a gubernatorial election predicted that they would be significantly happier a month after the election if their candidate won than if their candidate lost. In fact, the supporters of the winning and losing candidates were just as happy a month after the election as they were before the election. Wilson, Meyers, and Gilbert (1999) replicated this result in a study of the 1996 presidential election. Democrats predicted that they would be substantially happier the week after the election if President Clinton were victorious; in fact, they were no happier following the election than they had been before. Republicans predicted that they would be substantially less happy if President Clinton were victorious; in fact, they were only slightly less happy

than they were before. The durability bias has proved to be a robust phenomena, obtained in diverse samples of people who made predictions about both short-term and long-term events (Gilbert et al., 1998; Wilson et al., 1999).

One cause of the durability bias is *immune neglect*, which is the failure to take into account how much one's psychological immune system will ameliorate reactions to negative events. When something bad happens, people work hard to reconstrue the event in ways that make it less painful. Because the psychological immune system operates largely outside of awareness, people do not take it into account when forecasting their future emotional reactions. They overpredict the duration of their reactions to future negative events because they do not appreciate the extent to which they will transform the events psychologically in a way that blunts their impact.

Gilbert et al. (1998) noted that immune neglect is not the only cause of the durability bias. Indeed, because the psychological immune system works to ameliorate negative affect but not positive affect (Taylor, 1991), immune neglect explains only mispredictions about the duration of reactions to negative events. Consistent with this prediction, Gilbert et al. (1998) found a stronger durability bias in reaction to negative than to positive events. There was, however, a positive durability bias in some of their studies. In subsequent research, we have found significant positive durability biases, such as the Wilson et al. (1999) study in which Democrats overpredicted how happy they would be after President Clinton's 1996 reelection. Clearly, an additional mechanism is needed to explain these findings.

We suggest that there is also a problem of *focalism*, whereby people focus too much on the occurrence in question (termed the focal event) and fail to consider the consequences of other events that are likely to occur.[1] People think about the focal event in a vacuum without reminding themselves that their lives will not occur in a vacuum but will be filled with many other events. As noted by Tatarkiewicz (1962/1976, p. 111) in the opening quote, people "make no provision for other occurrences" when predicting their happiness following a positive or negative event.

Other occurrences can mitigate the effects of a focal event in a number of ways, such as by reducing how much people think about the event, causing people to reframe the event, and by triggering affective reactions

---

[1] Schkade and Kahneman (1998) have independently called this a focusing illusion.

that compete with or nullify the consequences of the event. We will focus on the first of these possibilities, namely that by failing to consider the occurrence of other future events, people overestimate how much the focal event will occupy their thoughts and influence their happiness. When imagining a positive tenure decision, for example, assistant professors might not think about other events that will compete for their attention, such as the upcoming deadline for the chapter they have yet to write, the dinner party they are hosting in a week, and the fact that their car needs a new battery. By failing to consider other occurrences such as these, they will overestimate how much they will think about their tenure decision.

Given that some aspects of people's lives are predictable — for example, professors know what their teaching schedule will be the following semester and that they will have to endure several boring committee meetings — people are capable of taking some nonfocal events into account when predicting their future happiness. Because many aspects of the future are unpredictable, it would be unfair to chastise people for not taking into account events that they cannot know will occur. How could people anticipate that their car battery will die the week after their tenure decision? Our point is that whatever happens after the event will compete for people's attention, regardless of whether these events are unpredictable (the demise of a car battery) or predictable (boring committee meetings, playing with our children, reading a good book, or puttering around the vegetable garden). Research on subjective well-being suggests that people's attention turns quickly to their current concerns, reducing the impact of past events on their happiness (Frederick & Loewenstein, 1999; Suh, Diener, & Fujita, 1996). People do not have to be clairvoyant to appreciate this fact when making affective forecasts.

The focalism hypothesis is related to other well-known instances in which people give disproportionate weight to accessible information (Higgins, 1996; Schwarz, 1990). For example, when people explain why a given hypothesis might be true, they focus too much on reasons supporting the hypothesis and too little on reasons for alternative hypotheses. Similarly, when asked to imagine a specific behavior, such as giving blood, people focus too much on ways in which the behavior could occur and too little on ways in which the behavior might not occur (for reviews see Anderson, Krull, & Weiner, 1996; Koehler, 1991). Even when asked to think about ways in which an event might not have occurred, people tend to focus on a limited range of alternatives that are easy to bring to mind, at the expense of alternatives that are more difficult to imagine

(Kahneman & Miller, 1986; Kahneman & Tversky, 1982; Roese & Olson, 1997). People are often content to focus on what comes to mind easily, without making the effort to think about alternative explanations, scenarios, outcomes, or beliefs (Gilbert, 1991).

Similarly, when people forecast their future happiness after an emotional event, they focus too much on that event. People could, in principle, go beyond what is accessible and think about the many other things that will occupy their future lives. Consistent with the research just mentioned, however, we hypothesize that when making affective forecasts, people focus too much on the focal event and too little on other events that will also transpire and require their attention.

If so, then it should be possible to reduce the durability bias by inducing people to think about the many other events that will transpire in the future. That is, if focalism is a cause of the durability bias, then reducing focalism (by inducing people to think about nonfocal events) should reduce this bias. If people are thinking not only about their tenure decision but also about what their future teaching schedule will be like and how often they will have to attend committee meetings, they should make more accurate estimates of the extent to which their tenure decision will influence their happiness. This hypothesis follows directly from studies in other areas that have asked people to go beyond the most accessible explanation or hypothesis that comes to mind, by thinking about alternative explanations and hypotheses (e.g., Hirt & Markman, 1995). Our studies followed the same logic, by asking people to think about other events that would transpire in the future, in addition to the focal event.

Specifically, we asked people to predict their overall level of happiness after an emotional event, with the expectation that they would overestimate how long that event would have an impact on their happiness (the durability bias). Before making their predictions, some participants completed a prospective "diary" (ostensibly as part of another study), in which they rated how much time they would spend on a variety of everyday activities on a specific future date. We hypothesized that people who completed the diary would predict that they would think less about the focal event in the future and that it would have less impact on their future happiness than would people who did not complete the diary. In studies 1–3 we tested these hypotheses with college football fans who predicted how happy they would be after a win and a loss by their college football team, whereas in Studies 4–5 we examined people's predicted happiness after hypothetical national events such as a space tragedy in which several astronauts were killed.

Study 1: They Foresaw a Game

Method

Overview

College football fans at the University of Virginia (UVA) and Virginia Polytechnic Institute and State University (Virginia Tech) predicted what their level of overall happiness would be immediately after the UVA–Virginia Tech football game and on each of the succeeding few days if their school lost and if their school won the game. They also predicted how much they would think about the game. Prior to making these predictions, some participants completed a prospective diary questionnaire, on which they rated how much time they would spend on a variety of everyday activities in the days after the football game. We hypothesized that people in the diary condition, relative to people in a no diary control condition, would predict that their happiness would not be as influenced by the outcome of the game and that they would think less about the game.

Participants

Participants were 36 students (19 women, 17 men) from UVA and 52 students from Virginia Tech (27 women, 25 men) who indicated that they were football fans and cared about the outcome of their school's football games (that is, they were above the median on the average of these two measures, which were highly correlated, $r = .71$). The students participated for partial fulfillment of a requirement in an undergraduate psychology course.

Procedure

Participants completed a prediction questionnaire 1–2 months prior to the 1995 football game between UVA and Virginia Tech in small groups or during class meetings. They were told that the packet contained questionnaires from different research projects and that they should go through the packet one page at a time without looking ahead.

Diary manipulation. Approximately half the participants (randomly assigned) first received a questionnaire labeled "diary study," on which they were asked to think about a specific day later in the semester and to estimate what they would be doing that day. They estimated the number of hours they would spend on 10 activities (e.g., going to class, socializing with friends, studying, eating meals) on a 7-point scale that ranged from *no time* to *four or more hours*. They then filled in 24 blanks, 1 for each hour of the day, according to what they thought they would be doing at that time. Participants completed the measures for either Monday,

November 20 (2 days after the UVA–Virginia Tech football game) or Tuesday, November 21 (3 days after the football game). Participants in the control condition did not receive these measures. To equalize the length of the study and to be consistent with the cover story that they would be completing different questionnaires, control participants received a personality scale after completing the dependent measures.

Dependent measures. As a baseline measure of happiness, people were first asked, "How happy would you say you are these days?" They responded on a 9-point scale that ranged from 1 (*not happy*) to 9 (*very happy*). This question has been used in past studies and has been found to correlate highly with other scales of happiness and life satisfaction. For example, Gilbert et al. (1998) found that this item was correlated with items from Diener, Emmons, Larsen, and Griffin's (1985) Satisfaction With Life Scale ($r = .86$) and with Kamman and Flett's (1983) Affectometer 2 scale ($r = .83$). Participants were then reminded that UVA and Virginia Tech would play each other in football on Saturday, November 18, and were asked to predict what their "general level of happiness" would be right after the game and on each of the following 7 days, if their team lost and if their team won. Participants made their predictions on the same scale on which they had rated their current happiness. People also predicted how much they would think about the game right after it ended and on each of the following 7 days, if their team won and if their team lost. These predictions were made on 9-point scales that ranged from 1 (*not at all*) to 9 (*very often*). The order of the happiness and thought predictions was counterbalanced.

Results and Discussion

We asked people to predict their happiness and thoughts on the day of the football game and on each of the subsequent 7 days. This length of time was arbitrary because we did not know how long people believed a football game would impact their happiness. As it happened, people's predictions started to level off on the fourth day after the game, and there were few differences between conditions from this day onward. To simplify the presentation of the data, and to be consistent with subsequent studies, we report only people's predicted happiness right after the game and on the next 3 days. (The significant effects involving the diary manipulation remain significant when all days are entered into the analyses.) Initial analyses also revealed that there were no significant interactions between the diary manipulation and gender, whether participants were students at UVA or Virginia Tech, or whether happiness or thought predictions were made first. We thus collapsed across these variables in subsequent analyses.

Happiness Predictions
There were no significant differences in baseline happiness between the control and diary conditions ($M = 6.47$, $SD = 1.51$ vs. $M = 6.67$, $SD = 1.41$, respectively), $t(86) < 1$, *ns*. To control for individual variation in initial happiness, we subtracted participants' baseline scores from their predictions to create an index of predicted change in happiness.

The scores were analyzed with a 2 (diary: diary vs. control) $\times$ 2 (outcome: predictions following a win vs. loss) $\times$ 4 (time: predictions for after the game and for the next 3 days) between-within analysis of variance (ANOVA).[2] Not surprisingly, there was a strong main effect of outcome, reflecting the fact that people predicted they would be happier if their team won than if their team lost, $F(1, 85) = 103.64$, $p < .001$ (see Figure 38.1). There was also a main effect of time, reflecting the fact that people predicted that their happiness would improve as time passed, $F(3, 255) = 11.62$, $p < .001$, and a significant Outcome $\times$ Time interaction, reflecting the fact that the difference in predicted happiness after a win versus a loss became smaller over time, $F(3, 255) = 102.29$, $p < .001$.

Of greater theoretical interest was the significant Diary $\times$ Outcome $\times$ Time interaction, $F(3, 255) = 4.23$, $p < .03$. As seen in Figure 38.1, this interaction reflects the fact that people in the diary conditions made more moderate (i.e., closer to baseline) affective predictions, at least on some days. A closer look at this interaction revealed that the diary had its strongest effects on people's predicted happiness on the 3 days after the football game. On predictions for the day of the game (Saturday), neither the main effect of diary nor the Diary $\times$ Outcome interaction was significant, $Fs(1, 86) < 1.33$, *ns*. On predictions for the 3 days after the game, the Diary $\times$ Outcome interaction was significant, $F(1, 85) = 4.05$, $p < .05$.

Thought Predictions
People's predictions about how much they would think about the game were analyzed with the same 2 (diary) $\times$ 2 (outcome) $\times$ 4 (time) between-within ANOVA. Not

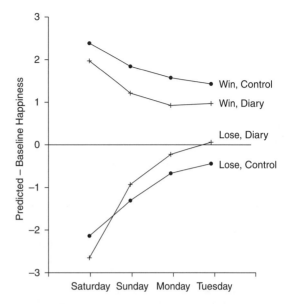

FIGURE 38.1 ■ Study 1: Effects of Diary on Affective Predictions. The Higher the Number, the Happier People Predicted They Would be, Relative to their Baseline Level of Happiness.

surprisingly, the main effect of time was significant, $F(3, 258) = 212.17$, $p < .001$, reflecting the fact that people said they would think less about the game as time passed (see Figure 38.2). The main effect of outcome was also significant, $F(1, 86) = 99.82$, $p < .001$, reflecting the fact that people said they would think about the game more after a win than a loss. These main effects were qualified by an Outcome $\times$ Time interaction, $F(3, 258) = 8.51$, $p < .001$, reflecting the fact that the difference in predicted thought following a win versus a loss got larger over time.

Of greater theoretical interest was the main effect of the diary manipulation, $F(1, 86) = 9.65$, $p < .005$ and a significant Diary $\times$ Time interaction, $F(3, 258) = 7.20$, $p < .001$. As seen in Figure 38.2, there was no effect of the diary on the amount of predicted thought right after the game (on Saturday). As expected, however, people in the diary condition predicted that they would think about the game less on succeeding days.[3]

---

[2] In a repeated measures design with several measurements, it is possible to have an inflated Type 1 error due to a violation of symmetry assumptions. To avoid this problem, the *p* levels for all effects involving a repeated measures factor with more than 2 degrees of freedom, in all analyses in this article, were corrected using the Greenhouse–Geisser adjustment.

[3] The diary manipulation appears to have had a somewhat larger effect when people were predicting a win than when they were predicting a loss, though neither the Diary $\times$ Outcome nor the Diary $\times$ Outcome $\times$ Time interactions reached conventional levels of significance, $F(1, 86) = 1.13$, *ns*, and $F(3, 258) = 2.56$, $p = .08$, respectively. The latter trend may be due to a floor effect, given that there was less room to move down on the scale when people made predictions about a loss than when people made predictions about a win.

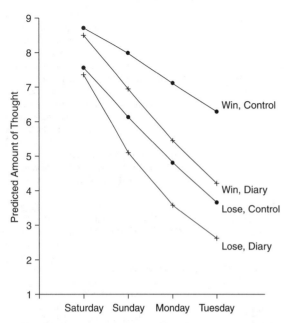

FIGURE 38.2 ■ Study 1: Effects of Diary on Thought Predictions. The Higher the Number, the Greater the Amount of Predicted Thought about the Football Game.

TABLE 38.1. Tests of the Mediating Role of Predicted Thought

Path	Study 1	Study 3	Study 4	Study 5
Diary condition → predicted thought	−0.530* (.171)	−0.574* (.214)	−1.043* (.467)	−1.473* (.564)
Predicted thought → predicted happiness	0.461* (.151)	0.942* (.490)	−0.412* (.104)	0.256 (.295)
Diary condition → predicted happiness (unmediated)	−0.369 (.250)	−1.613* (.551)	1.057* (.449)	−1.475 (.894)
Diary condition → predicted happiness (mediated)	−0.124 (.252)	−1.073 (.594)	0.627 (.423)	−1.086 (1.003)
z^a	2.12*	1.50	1.90	0.77

Note. The values shown are the unstandardized beta weights and their standard errors (in parentheses). The beta between predicted thought and predicted happiness controls for diary condition. The first beta weight between diary condition and predicted happiness does not control for predicted thought, whereas the second beta weight does. A meta-analysis of the mediation effect across the four studies was significant, $z = 3.15$, $p = .002$.
[a] The test of the reduction of the unmediated path from diary condition to predicted happiness, when predicted thought is added as a mediator (Kenny, Kashy, & Bolger, 1998).
* $p < .05$.

Mediation Analyses

We tested the hypothesis that the effect of the diary manipulation on predicted happiness was mediated by its effects on how much people said they would think about the game, using multiple regression (as described by Kenny, Kashy, & Bolger, 1998). As an overall index of predicted thought, we averaged people's thought forecasts over time and outcome. As an index of predicted happiness, we averaged people's happiness forecasts over time and then subtracted their predictions after a loss from their predictions after a win. (Thus, the larger the score on the happiness index, the more people thought that their happiness would be influenced by the outcome of the football game.) As seen in the first column of Table 38.1, there was a significant negative relationship between the dummy-coded diary condition (*control* = 0, *diary* = 1) and predicted thought (this is similar to the main effect of diary on predicted thought already reported, whereby people in the diary condition predicted that they would think less about the football game). The relationship between predicted thought and predicted happiness was also significant, adjusting for the effects of the diary condition. Table 38.1 also shows the relationship between the diary condition and predicted happiness, before and

after adjusting for the amount of predicted thought. The reduction in beta weight after controlling for predicted thought was significant ($z = 2.12$, $p = .03$), supporting the hypothesis that predicted thought mediated the effects of the diary manipulation on predicted happiness (Kenny et al., 1998).

Summary of Results

As hypothesized, people in the diary condition predicted that, as time passed, they would think less about the football game than did people in the control condition. They also predicted that their happiness would return more quickly to baseline levels. These results, and the mediation analyses just reported, are consistent with the focalism hypothesis. One reason that people make enduring predictions about the impact of future events on their happiness may be that they overestimate how much they will think about those events.

Because Study 1 did not include a measure of people's actual happiness after the football game, we cannot conclude that people in the diary condition made more accurate affective forecasts. On the basis of our previous research, we assumed that people in the control condition overestimated how long the football game would have an impact on their happiness and that this durability bias was corrected, at least in part, by completing the prospective diary.

In Study 3, we used a within-subjects design in which the same participants predicted how happy they would be after a football game and reported their actual happiness after that game. We hypothesized that people in the diary condition would make more moderate affective forecasts and would predict that they would think less about the football game than would people in the control condition. Further, we hypothesized that the forecasts of people in the diary condition would be more accurate.

Study 3: They Foresaw and Experienced a Game

Method

Overview
College football fans at UVA predicted how happy they would be and what they would be thinking about on the days following a football game between UVA and the University of North Carolina at Chapel Hill (UNC). As in Study 1, some participants completed a prospective diary questionnaire prior to making these predictions. On the day after the football game, participants rated their actual happiness.

Participants
Participants were 27 students (19 women, 8 men) from UVA who indicated that they were football fans, on the same measures used in Studies 1 and 2. The students participated in an initial session for partial fulfillment of a requirement in an undergraduate psychology course.

Procedure
Predicted happiness and thought. The procedure was identical to that of Study 1 with the following exceptions: Students participated approximately 2 months before the football game between UVA and UNC that was played on November 16, 1996. Those randomly assigned to the diary condition first completed the same diary questionnaire as in Study 1. The day they were asked to think about was Monday, November 18. All participants then predicted what their overall level of happiness would be following the football game (November 16) and on each

of the succeeding 3 days (November 17, 18, and 19) if UVA lost and if UVA won the game.

We changed the way in which people predicted their thoughts in two ways. First, people were asked to predict not only how much they would think about the football game but also how much they would think about other matters. Half the participants were randomly assigned to make these predictions on the same 9-point scales used in Study 1. After rating how much they would think about the game, people rated how much they would think about their school work, social life, leisure time activities, paying job, family, and any other things not listed. The remaining participants received an open-ended question that asked them to complete the sentence, "I will be thinking mostly about these things." All participants predicted what they would think about after a UVA loss and a UVA win for each of three time periods (after the football game on Saturday, November 16, and each of the next two days).

Actual happiness. We assessed people's actual happiness on the day after the football game. Beginning a week before the game, participants were contacted and asked to pick up an envelope containing a questionnaire they could complete for credit or payment. We made no mention of the prediction part of the study that students had already completed. Participants were instructed to open the envelope on Sunday, November 17 (the day after the football game), after 5 p.m. Participants rated their overall level of happiness on the same scale on which they made their predictions at Time 1.

On subsequent pages of the questionnaire we included exploratory measures of how much people had been thinking about the game and their recall of their happiness immediately after the game. By necessity, these questions followed a mention of the football game (e.g., the thought question asked people how much they had been thinking about the UVA–UNC game). Because the reference to the football game might have triggered people's memory of the earlier, prediction part of the study, thereby contaminating their answers to the questions, these measures were exploratory.

Results and Discussion

Happiness Predictions
People in the diary and control conditions reported similar levels of baseline happiness ($M = 7.46$, $SD = 1.27$ and $M = 6.71$, $SD = 1.54$, respectively), $t(25) = 1.37$, $p > .18$. To control for individual variation in initial happiness, we subtracted baseline ratings from predictions to create an index of predicted change in happiness.

As in Study 1, we performed a 2 (diary: diary vs. control) $\times$ 2 (outcome: predictions following a win vs. loss) $\times$ 4 (time: predictions for after the game and for the next 3 days) between-within ANOVA on these scores. Not surprisingly, there was a strong main effect of outcome, reflecting the fact that people predicted they would be happier if their team won than if their team lost, $F(1, 25) = 53.94$, $p < .001$ (see means in Figure 38.3). There was also a main effect of time, reflecting the fact that people predicted that their happiness would improve as time passed, $F(3, 75) = 8.75$, $p < .001$, and a significant Outcome $\times$ Time interaction, reflecting the fact that the difference in predicted happiness after a win versus a loss got smaller over time, $F(3, 75) = 60.68$, $p < .001$.

Of greater theoretical interest were the significant Diary $\times$ Outcome and Diary $\times$ Outcome $\times$ Time interactions, $F(1, 25) = 8.30$, $p < .01$, and $F(3, 75) = 4.00$, $p < .03$, respectively. As in Study 1, these interactions reflect the fact that people in the diary conditions made more moderate (i.e., closer to baseline) affective predictions. In the control condition, both the effect of Outcome and the Outcome $\times$ Time interactions were

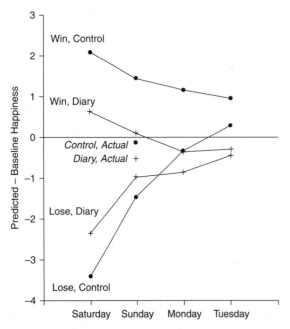

highly significant, $F(1, 25) = 54.29$, $p < .001$, $\eta = .83$ and $F(3, 75) = 49.04$, $p < .001$, $\eta = .81$. Although still significant, these effects were, as predicted, smaller in the diary condition, $F(1, 25) = 9.61$, $p = .005$, $\eta = .53$ and $F(3, 75) = 16.82$, $p < .001$, $\eta = .63$.

Accuracy of Happiness Predictions

People's actual happiness ratings, made the day after the football game, are also shown in Figure 38.3. Because UVA won the football game, these happiness ratings were compared with people's predicted happiness following a win, with a 2 (diary: control vs. diary) $\times$ 2 (discrepancy: predicted vs. actual ratings) between-within ANOVA. As predicted, the simple effect of discrepancy was significant in the control condition, $F(1, 25) = 16.46$, $p < .001$, reflecting the fact that people in this condition predicted that they would be happier than they in fact were ($M = 1.43$, $SD = 1.34$ vs. $M = -0.14$, $SD = 1.46$). Also as predicted, the simple effect of discrepancy was not significant in the diary condition, $F(1, 25) = 2.34$, $p = .14$, reflecting the fact that there was little difference between predicted and actual happiness in this condition ($M = 0.08$, $SD = 1.38$ vs. $M = -0.54$, $SD = 1.27$). The Diary $\times$ Discrepancy interaction was marginally significant, $F(1, 25) = 2.93$, $p = .10$. A focused contrast that tested the precise pattern of predicted means was significant, $F(1, 25) = 10.03$, $p < .005$. This contrast assigned a weight of 3 to the mean in the control–predicted happiness cell and a weight of -1 to the means in the other three cells.[4]

Thought Predictions

We assessed people's predicted thoughts in two ways: With an open-ended measure in which people described what they would be thinking about after the game and on each of the two succeeding days, and on a rating scale on which people rated how often they would be thinking about the game and several other topics during the same time periods. The responses to the open-ended measure were coded by a research assistant, who counted the number of thoughts about the game and not about the game. To check the reliability of these codings a second assistant independently coded the thoughts of 10 participants. The correlation between the codings of the first and second

FIGURE 38.3 ■ Study 3: Effects of Diary on Affective Predictions. The Higher the Number, the Happier People Predicted They Would be, Relative to Their Baseline Level of Happiness.

---

[4] Because this contrast involved both between-subjects and within-subjects effects, and the corresponding error terms differed by more than a factor of 2, we adopted the conservative approach of using the larger (between-subjects) error term when computing this contrast (Rosenthal & Rosnow, 1985).

assistant was .97 for both game-related and other thoughts. To compare responses on the open-ended and rating scale measures, all scores were converted to standard scores. Because initial analyses revealed no significant effects of the type of thought measure people completed, we collapsed across this variable.

People's predicted thoughts about the game were analyzed with a 2 (diary) × 2 (outcome) × 3 (time) between-within ANOVA. Not surprisingly there was a strong main effect of Time, $F(2, 50) = 56.03, p < .001$, reflecting the fact that people said they would think less about the game as the days passed (see means in Figure 38.4). There was also a main effect of the diary manipulation, $F(1, 25) = 7.20, p < .01$. As hypothesized, people in the control condition predicted that they would think more about the game than did people in the diary condition. The Diary × Time interaction was nearly significant, $F(2, 50) = 3.00, p = .06$, reflecting the fact that the differences between the diary conditions became smaller over time. The Diary × Outcome interaction was also marginally significant, $F(1, 25) = 3.08, p = .09$, reflecting the fact that the

effects of the diary manipulation were slightly stronger for predictions following a loss than a win.

People's predicted thoughts about other matters were analyzed with the same ANOVA. Although people in the diary condition tended to say they would think about other matters more than did people in the control condition ($M = 0.27, SD = 0.95$ vs. $M = -0.25, SD = 0.75$) the main effect of diary was not significant, $F(1, 25) = 2.42, p = .13$. The only significant effect in this ANOVA was a main effect of time, $F(2, 50) = 6.51, p < .003$, reflecting the fact that people said they would think less about other matters right after the game ($M = -0.26, SD = 0.86$), than on the succeeding two days ($M = 0.14, SD = 1.01$ and $M = 0.12, SD = 0.99$).[5]

Mediation Analyses
In the same manner as in Study 1, we tested whether the effects of the diary condition on predicted happiness were mediated by predicted thought. The results of this mediation analysis are shown in Table 38.1. As expected, the relationship between diary condition and predicted thought was significant, and the relationship between predicted thought and predicted happiness was significant, after controlling for diary condition. Further, the relationship between diary condition and predicted happiness was significant when we did not control for predicted thought and nonsignificant when we did. However, unlike in Study 1, the drop in this beta weight was not significant ($z = 1.50, p = .13$), possibly due to the substantially smaller sample size in Study 3.

Summary of First Three Studies
College football fans overestimated the extent to which the outcome of a football game would influence their overall happiness, replicating the durability bias found by Gilbert et al. (1998). As expected, completing a prospective diary about one's future daily activities significantly

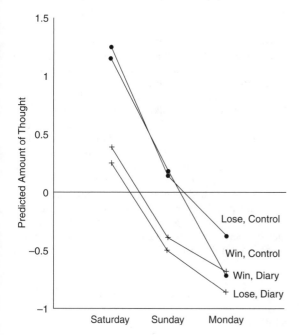

FIGURE 38.4 ■ Study 3: Effects of Diary on Thought Predictions. Predictions are Standard Scores, such that the Higher the Number, the Greater Amount of Predicted Thought about the Football Game.

---

[5] As mentioned earlier, we included exploratory questions on the follow-up questionnaire, handed out the day after the football game, that asked people how much they had been thinking about the game and how happy they had been the day before. Because these questions came after a mention of the football game, we were concerned that they might trigger people's memory of the earlier, prediction part of the study, causing them to respond similarly to their predictions. This is what appears to have happened. For example, people in the control condition reported that they had been thinking more about the game than people in the diary condition did, which, as just seen, matched their earlier predictions. Although it is possible that the diary questionnaire people filled out 2 months earlier influenced how much they actually thought about the game, it seems more likely that the mention of the game on the questionnaire reminded people of their predictions, contaminating their responses.

moderated the durability bias. The simple reminder that one's day would be full of normal activities, such as going to class and socializing with friends, was enough to correct the durability bias, at least to some extent. The mediation analyses were in the predicted direction, providing evidence that it was a change in how much people anticipated that the game would dominate their thoughts that mediated the change in their affective forecasts. Combined across Studies 1 and 3, this mediation analysis was significant ($z = 2.56$, $p = .01$).

These results provide evidence for the focalism hypothesis, which argues that people focus too much on the focal event and fail to consider the consequences of other events that are likely to occur. Study 3 suggested that the diary manipulation reduced focalism by lowering people's anticipated thought about the focal event, and not by increasing people's anticipated thought about other events (as evidenced by the fact that the diary manipulation had no significant effects on people's predicted thoughts about other matters). Questions remain, however, about precisely how the diary manipulation led people to believe that they would think less about the focal event. We tested two possible mechanisms in Study 4.

First, it is possible that people who completed the diary realized that other events would dominate their thoughts and distract them from thinking about the game, which caused them to moderate their affective forecasts. According to this *distraction hypothesis*, people who think about future events moderate their forecasts because they believe that these events will occupy their thoughts and reduce thinking about the focal event.

Alternatively, it is possible that people focus more on the affective consequences of other events than on their distracting qualities. Not only do daily events take our mind off a focal event such as a football game, they also produce affective reactions that might "cancel out" or dilute the effects of the game. For example, when people think about the fact that they will have a lot of studying to do on Sunday and Monday, they might believe that the tediousness of studying will eliminate any lingering positive affect caused by Saturday's football victory. According to this *affective competition hypothesis*, it is not a reduction in predicted thought about the game that mediates the change in affective forecasts, but people's belief that the affect triggered by other events will nullify the affect caused by a football victory or loss. Although it might seem that the mediation analyses performed in Studies 1 and 3 (see Table 38.1) rule out this possibility, such analyses cannot definitely rule out the reverse causal order (Kenny et al., 1998). It is possible that the diary manipulation caused people first to lower their estimates of how much the game would influence their happiness, and then to lower their estimates of how much they would think about the game.

Another reason that Studies 1 and 3 cannot distinguish between these different mechanisms is that the diary manipulation asked people to rate positive (e.g., socializing with friends), negative (e.g., studying), and neutral (e.g., eating) events. According to the distraction hypothesis, the valence of these events was inconsequential because many future events, regardless of their valence, will be seen as distracting. According to the affective competition hypothesis, people focused on the fact that some of the activities would cause affect opposite to that triggered by the football game and would thus neutralize their mood.

The purpose of Study 4 was to test these mechanisms by manipulating the valence of the events that people rated on their diary questionnaires. As in the previous studies, participants were asked to predict how happy they would be after an event in the future. Prior to making these forecasts, people received one of two different versions of a diary manipulation. One was similar to the manipulation used in Studies 1 and 3, which asked people to rate how much time they would spend on positive, negative, and neutral activities. The other asked people to think exclusively about neutrally valenced activities such as cooking.

We asked people to predict their happiness following a negative event (a hypothetical accident in space in which several astronauts were killed). The affective competition hypothesis predicts that only the mixed diary manipulation will moderate people's forecasts, because it involves thinking about activities of the opposite valence to the focal event. According to this hypothesis the neutral diary manipulation should be less effective, because people will not think about events that will produce affective reactions opposite to those caused by the focal event. In contrast, we predicted that both the mixed and neutral diary manipulations would moderate people's forecasts. Consistent with the distraction hypothesis, people were expected to believe that the activities would take their mind off the focal event, even if they were all relatively neutral in valence.

Study 4: They Foresaw a Space Tragedy

Method

Overview

People were asked to imagine that a tragic accident, in which several astronauts were killed, occurred 12 weeks in the future. They estimated their level of overall happiness right after hearing about the event and on each of the next 3 days. They also rated how much they would think about the accident after it occurred. Before reading about the accident, people completed one of two diary questionnaires or no questionnaire. The events people were asked to think about on the diary questionnaires were either of mixed or neutral valence.

Participants

Participants were 73 students (33 women, 40 men) at UVA who participated in partial fulfillment of a requirement in an undergraduate psychology course. The sample size for some of the data presented below is slightly lower because of missing data.

Procedure

The procedure was identical to Studies 1 and 3 except for the following changes. People rated their current level of happiness "compared to how happy you are ON AVERAGE" by circling a number from 1 to 9, where 1 = *below average happiness*, 5 = *average happiness*, and 9 = *above average happiness*. Several studies have found that when people are asked to rate their overall level of happiness, most people rate themselves as happy (Myers & Diener, 1995). We asked people how happy they are compared with their average level of happiness in an attempt to reduce the skewness of people's responses.

People were asked to imagine that the following event occurred on a Sunday 12 weeks in the future:

The space shuttle *Columbia*, which was launched from the Kennedy Space Center in Florida the previous week, attempts to dock with *Mir*, the Russian space station. The goal of the mission is to transfer an American astronaut from *Mir* to the space shuttle, to bring him home. Due to pilot error on the part of one of the American astronauts on board the *Columbia*, a tragedy occurs. The space shuttle slams into *Mir* with such force that the Russian space station is destroyed, killing everyone aboard. The impact also tears a large hole in the space shuttle. The crew frantically tries to repair the damage but it is too late. All seven astronauts on board perish from a lack of oxygen.

Participants rated what their "general level of happiness" was likely to be right after hearing about the accident and on each of the succeeding three days, on the same scale on which they rated their current happiness. Finally, participants completed the same predicted thought scales as used in Study 3, on which they estimated how much they would think about the *Mir* accident and several unrelated things (e.g., their school work), immediately after the accident and on each of the 2 succeeding days.

Diary manipulations. Participants were randomly assigned to one of three conditions. The control condition was the same as in the first two studies. The procedure in the diary conditions was similar to the previous studies, except that we varied the valence of the activities people were asked to rate. In the mixed diary condition, 6 of the activities were positive (e.g., socializing with one or more friends, attending the lecture of a favorite class, and talking to a friend long distance), 6 were negative (e.g., attending their least favorite class, feeling stressed about their social life, and getting into a fight with a same-sex friend), and 4 were neutral (e.g., cooking or preparing food and watching TV). In the neutral diary condition, all of the activities were relatively neutral in valence. The specific activities were chosen on the basis of responses by pretest participants, who rated the positivity or negativity of 54 everyday activities. We chose events that occur frequently in students' lives and were rated by pretest participants as very positive or very negative (in the mixed diary condition) or near the midpoint of the scale (in the neutral diary condition).

Results and Discussion

Happiness Predictions

As in the previous studies there were no significant differences between conditions in people's baseline level of happiness, $F(2, 70) < 1$, *ns*. The means in the control, mixed diary, and neutral diary conditions were 5.58 ($SD = 1.55$), 5.18 ($SD = 1.50$), and 5.48 ($SD = 1.29$), respectively. We subtracted participants' baseline scores from their happiness predictions to obtain an index of predicted change.[6] As hypothesized, people in the mixed and neutral diary conditions made less extreme affective forecasts than people in the no diary condition did (see Figure 38.5). A planned comparison revealed that predictions made by people in the two diary

---

[6] Given that we asked people to predict how happy they would be compared with their average level of happiness, it might seem redundant to subtract their baseline level of happiness from their predictions. We believe that it is still best to subtract baseline levels because doing so corrects for individual differences in initial happiness. As it happened, it made little difference either way; the results were very similar (and equally significant) when the analyses were performed on people's raw predictions.

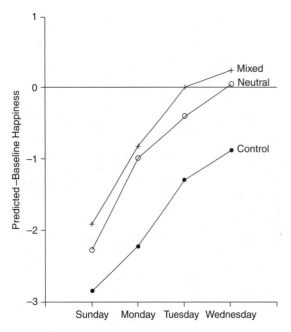

FIGURE 38.5 ■ Study 4: Effects of Mixed Versus Neutral Diary Events on Affective Predictions. The Higher the Number, the Happier People Predicted They Would Be, Relative to their Baseline Level of Happiness.

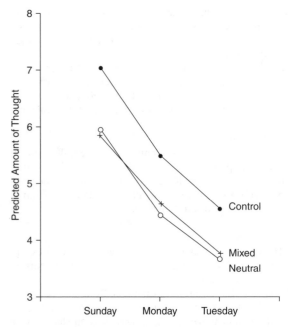

FIGURE 38.6 ■ Study 4: Effects of Mixed Versus Neutral Diary Events on Predicted Thought about the Space Tragedy. The Higher the Number, the Greater the Amount of Predicted Thought.

conditions were significantly less extreme than predictions made by people in the no diary condition, $F(1, 70) = 5.38, p = .02$. The predictions in the two diary conditions did not differ significantly from each other, $F(1, 70) < 1, ns$. Neither of these contrasts interacted significantly with time, $Fs(3, 210) < 1.46, ps > .23$.

Thought Predictions
People in the two diary conditions predicted that they would think less about the *Mir* accident than people in the no diary condition did (see Figure 38.6). A planned comparison revealed that people in the two diary conditions predicted that they would think about the accident significantly less than did people in the no diary condition, $F(1, 70) = 4.94, p = .03$. The predictions in the two diary conditions did not differ significantly from each other, $F(1, 70) < 1, ns$. Neither of these contrasts interacted significantly with time, $Fs(2, 140) < 1, ns$.

As in Study 3, there were no significant effects of the diary manipulation on people's predicted amount of thought about things other than the focal event, $F(2, 70) < 1, ns$. There was a significant main effect of

time, $F(2, 140) = 8.93, p < .001$, reflecting the fact that participants in all conditions predicted that they would think more about other matters as time passed. The Diary Condition × Time interaction was not significant, $F(4, 140) < 1, ns$.

Mediation Analyses
As in Studies 1 and 3, we tested whether the effect of the diary condition on predicted happiness was mediated by predicted thought. People in the control condition received a 0 on the dummy coded variable whereas people in the mixed and neutral diary conditions received a 1. As seen in Table 38.1, the relationship between diary condition and predicted thought was significant and the relationship between predicted thought and predicted happiness was also significant, after controlling for diary condition. Further, the relationship between diary condition and predicted happiness was no longer significant after controlling for predicted thought. The difference between these beta weights was nearly significant ($z = 1.90, p = .057$), which is consistent with the hypothesis that predicted thought mediated

the effects of the diary manipulation on predicted happiness (Kenny et al., 1998).[7]

The fact that the mixed and neutral diary manipulations were equally effective supports the distraction hypothesis, that people who think about future events moderate their forecasts because they believe that these events will occupy their thoughts and reduce thinking about the focal event. The affective competition hypothesis, that people believe that the affect triggered by future events will nullify the affect caused by the focal event, was not supported. It is possible, of course, that affective competition exists in other contexts. Surely people believe that the affect caused by one event (e.g., a job promotion) can nullify the affect caused by an event of the opposite valence (e.g., a loss by one's favorite sports team). It appears, however, that the affective competition process is not a necessary condition for focalism to reduce the durability bias. It is sufficient for people to believe that future events, even ones neutral in valence, will reduce the extent to which they will think about the focal event.

General Discussion

The results of five studies provide evidence for the durability bias (the tendency to overpredict the duration of affective reactions to future events), a mechanism responsible for this bias (focalism, whereby people think too much about the focal event and fail to consider the consequences of other events that are likely to occur), and a way of reducing the durability bias (asking people to think about other future events that are likely to occupy their thoughts). Specifically, when people were first asked to think about the amount of time they would spend on several everyday activities, they made less extreme (and more accurate) affective forecasts. The mediation analyses suggested that the effects of the diary manipulation on affective forecasts were mediated by its effects on how much people believed they would think about the focal event, as predicted by the focalism hypothesis.

Before discussing the implications of our findings, it is important to address a possible alternative explanation. This alternative concerns our interpretation of the results in the control conditions in which people overestimated the duration of their happiness following affective events. We have argued that this result is evidence for the durability bias. Alternatively, it is possible that the inaccurate forecasts were an artifact of the way in which we asked people to predict their future happiness and report their actual happiness. When asked to predict their future happiness, people's attention was drawn to the focal event (e.g., the football game), which might have led them to interpret the overall happiness question to mean "How happy will I be when I am thinking about the game?" Because we did not draw people's attention to the focal event when we asked how happy they were after the game, they might have reported something different (their general level of happiness) than they predicted (their happiness when thinking about the game). Perhaps the durability bias was due to this "apples and oranges" problem, namely that the predicted and actual happiness measures tapped different states.

There is a sense in which this interpretation of our results is not an artifact but the point of the focalism hypothesis: When people make affective forecasts they exaggerate how much the event will be focal in their thoughts and thus overestimate how much it will influence their happiness. There is another sense, however, in which the "apples and oranges" problem could be an artifact. According to this interpretation, people know that they will not think about the event very often and know that their overall level of happiness will not be affected for very long. Further, they know that when they do think about the event, their temporary moods will be affected. Because people in our studies did not have the opportunity to express the belief that the events would have momentary effects on their moods, they expressed this belief on the general happiness questions. That is, because they were constrained by the kind of question we asked, they interpreted it differently than we intended (to mean that the events would influence their temporary mood while thinking about the event, but not their general level of happiness).

We have evidence from other studies that rules out this artifactual explanation of our results. In one study,

---

[7] The signs of some of the beta weights in this study were the opposite of the signs in the other studies because people made predictions about a negative event only. For example, the more participants said they would think about the space accident, the less happy they predicted they would be, resulting in a negative beta. In Studies 1 and 3, people made predictions about both positive and negative events (wins and losses of a football game), and the data were coded such that the more people said they would think about the event, the happier they said they would be after a win relative to how happy they said they would be after a loss (resulting in a positive beta). Similarly, in Study 4, people in the control condition (dummy coded as 0) predicted they would be less happy after the accident than did people in the diary conditions (dummy coded as 1), resulting in a positive beta. In Studies 1 and 3, people in the control conditions predicted that they would be happier after a win relative to how happy they would be after a loss than people in the diary conditions did, resulting in a negative beta.

people predicted how happy they would be if Bill Clinton or Bob Dole won the 1996 presidential election. When we measured people's actual happiness after the election, we reminded them of the focal event (the election) and still found evidence for the durability bias (Wilson et al., 1999). Thus, if people had interpreted the prediction question to mean, "how happy I will be when thinking about the election," they were wrong. When reminded of the election, they were still not as happy or unhappy as they had predicted they would be.

In another study, there was very little delay between the time people made their predictions and the occurrence of the focal event. In Study 6 by Gilbert et al. (1998), people were asked to predict how happy they would be immediately after learning that they did not get a desirable job and 10 min after learning that they did not get the job. Participants then found out that they did not receive the job and reported how happy they were at that moment and 10 min later. Consistent with the durability bias, people predicted that they would be more unhappy at both time points than they in fact were. Given that participants made their actual ratings only a few minutes after predicting their happiness, it is reasonable to assume that the focal event (not getting the job) was still very much in their thoughts. Thus, even if people interpreted the prediction question to mean, "How happy will I be when thinking about not getting the job?", they were incorrect.

Finally, we conducted a study that attempted to clear up the "apples and oranges" problem in a different way. If people know that focal events will have temporary effects on their moods (as opposed to their general happiness), then they should be more accurate if we asked them to predict how often they would be in good and bad moods after the event. To find out, we asked a sample of UVA students to predict the frequency of their good and bad moods on the days following the 1998 football game between UVA and Virginia Tech. The day after the game, we asked participants to report the actual frequency of their good and bad moods. Because UVA won the football game, we could test the accuracy of people's predictions following a win. As hypothesized, we still found a durability bias. People predicted that they would be in good moods more often than they in fact were ($M = 7.80$, $SD = 0.86$ vs. $M = 6.47$, $SD = 1.85$), $t(14) = 2.55$, $p = .02$. They predicted that they would be in bad moods less often than they in fact were ($M = 1.80$, $SD = 0.56$ vs. $M = 3.53$, $SD = 2.23$), $t(14) = -2.76$, $p = .02$. A 2 (good vs. bad mood) × 2 (predicted vs. actual) within-ANOVA revealed a significant interaction, $F(1, 14) = 7.57$, $p = .02$.

Thus, the "apples and oranges" problem does not appear to be a viable explanation of the durability bias. When we were more explicit about what we were asking people to predict, they still overestimated the duration of their emotional reactions to the focal event. When we measured happiness only minutes after the event such that it was still focal in people's thoughts, they still overestimated their emotional response to the event.

Returning to our finding that completing prospective diaries reduces the durability bias, the careful reader will have noted that the form of this effect differed somewhat across studies. Specifically, the diary manipulation influenced predictions about positive outcomes somewhat differently than it influenced predictions about negative outcomes. For positive events, there was a main effect of the diary manipulation ($z = 3.42$, $p < .001$) and no interaction with time ($z = -.01$, ns; averaged across studies). For negative events, there was a nearly significant main effect of the diary manipulation ($z = 1.78$, $p = .08$), which was qualified by a significant Diary × Time interaction ($z = 2.81$, $p < .005$). The results of Study 1 exemplify this pattern of results (see Figure 38.1). For positive events, people in the diary condition made consistently more moderate predictions, both for the day of the event and subsequent days. For negative events, the diary manipulation changed people's forecasts only for the days after the event. For the day of the event, there was little difference between the diary and no diary conditions.

We offer the following speculation about the reason for this asymmetry in the results. There is evidence that positive emotional states are relatively fragile (e.g., more disrupted by distracting events) than negative emotional states are (e.g., Kanouse & Hanson, 1972). For example, thinking about how busy and distracted one will be the next day is probably more likely to ruin a good mood than it is to improve a bad mood. When predicting how happy they would be right after a focal event, the diary participants seem to have appreciated this fact. It is as if they were saying, "Right after the game I'll have a lot of things on my mind besides football, and that will bring me down from the high of a football victory. It will not, however, make me feel better about a football loss." Because we did not measure people's actual happiness immediately following the focal events (e.g., the football games), we cannot test the accuracy of these differential predictions for positive versus negative events on the day the events occurred. We can say that diary participants made more moderate forecasts for the days following positive and negative events, and, on the basis of the results of Studies 2 and 3, that these forecasts were more accurate than the forecasts made by control participants.

It is good news that we have found a way to make affective forecasts more accurate. When imagining how long they will feel sad after a negative event, it might be to people's advantage to remind themselves that life does, indeed, go on. They might think about the many daily activities that will compete for their attention in the days after experiencing the negative event. This mental exercise might well lead people to conclude that the negative event will fade from their thoughts relatively quickly and thus will not influence their happiness for as long as they might otherwise think.

We hasten to add, however, that the mental diary manipulation we have explored is not likely to be a magical cure for all durability biases. In Study 1, for example, the diary manipulation moderated people's forecasts but did not correct them completely (judging by people's actual happiness ratings in Studies 2 and 3). Furthermore, the kinds of focal events people imagined in our studies were relatively mild, compared with the major disappointments and extraordinary successes they sometimes experience. Imagining one's daily life might be well-suited to correct predictions about minor emotional events such as the outcomes of football games, but ill-suited to change predictions about major emotional events such as winning the lottery or becoming paralyzed in an accident. Focalism might be more difficult to correct in such instances, even though there is evidence that these life-changing events do not influence people's happiness for as long as they think (Brickman, Coates, & Janoff-Bulman, 1978; Wortman & Silver, 1989).

A Broader Look at Focalism

The tendency to think about a focal event, at the expense of other, unrelated events, is likely to influence judgments other than affective forecasts. In fact, there is evidence showing that focalism applies to thoughts about past emotional events and to predictions about nonemotional events.

Focalism and Postdictions About Past Affect
An interesting question is whether people display the durability bias when thinking about their past emotional lives and if so, whether focalism is one of the culprits. Gilovich and Medvec (1995) and Ross (1989) have noted that as time passes, people remember less about their actual experiences and rely more on their theories

about what they must have been feeling and thinking. Consequently, when thinking about the duration of an emotional experience in the past, people might focus too much on a focal event and not enough on other events that influenced their thoughts and feelings, thus producing a retrospective durability bias. However, focalism might be weaker in retrospect than prospect. People might remember other events that were occurring at the time of the focal event and competing for their attention (e.g., "I remember that when the Broncos won the Super Bowl I had just changed jobs and was working 16-hour days.") Even if people cannot recall exactly what else was going on in their lives when thinking about a focal event, the past may be perceived as less of a vacuum than the future. People know that it was filled with many events and activities, even if they cannot remember precisely which ones.

Consistent with these hypotheses, Wilson et al. (1999) found that (a) people focused too much on a focal event even when thinking about the past, producing a retrospective durability bias (e.g., overestimating how happy they were after the 1996 presidential election); and (b) this retrospective durability bias was less extreme than it was when people predicted in advance how happy they would be after the event, possibly because the past seemed like less of a vacuum than the future did.

Focalism and Regrets About Past Inactions
Focalism is similar to a mechanism offered by Gilovich and Medvec (1995) to explain temporal patterns of regret. In their studies, people were most likely to regret errors of commission in the recent past (actions they wished they had not performed) but errors of omission in the more distant past (actions they wished they had performed but did not). "Forces that restrain human action may be inherently less salient than forces that compel action" (p. 390), they argued, especially over time as people forget the reasons they did not do something. This process bears some similarity to focalism, in that it involves too much focus on what is easy to bring to mind (the failure to act in a certain way and the reasons that action would have turned out well) and too little focus on what is more difficult to bring to mind (reasons the course of action would not have turned out well). If so, the present research suggests a way of reducing regret for foregone opportunities: Ask people to think about all of the other things happening in their lives at that time. Doing so might trigger the realization that there were myriad forces making it difficult to act in the desired way.

Focalism and the Planning Fallacy

Buehler, Griffin, and Ross (1994) found that people underestimate how long it will take them to complete future tasks, such as homework assignments. They identified two mechanisms underlying this bias: A cognitive one, whereby people focus too much on the future task and not enough on past experiences with similar tasks, and a motivational one, whereby people engage in "wishful thinking," minimizing possible roadblocks that will get in their way (Buehler, Griffin, & McDonald, 1997). The first mechanism is similar to focalism, to the extent that people focus too much on a focal event when making a prediction about the future. However, this mechanism differs from focalism in what it is that people are said to neglect to think about. Buehler et al. (1994) suggest that people would make more realistic predictions if they thought more about past experiences similar to the focal event; that is, if they made more of a connection between their past and future experiences. Although this is surely true, the focalism hypothesis suggests that people would also make more realistic estimates if they thought more about nonfocal events in the future that would impede their progress, such as other assignments they have that week, how busy their social life will be, and whether their parents will be visiting that weekend. Note that such mental correction does not necessarily involve thinking about past experiences. People could correct their predictions in this manner even if they did not have any previous experiences with the task.

Focalism and the Near Versus Distant Future

An issue we have not addressed is whether focalism is more likely to influence forecasts in the distant versus the near future. Although we are unaware of research that directly addresses this question, it seems likely that the focalism bias is worse when predicting the distant future. When people imagine how they will feel next week, they are likely to recognize that their lives will be full of other activities, such as their upcoming dentist appointment and soccer game. When imagining how they will feel next year, they probably think about the focal event in more of a vacuum, without considering the fact that their lives will be just as full then as they are now.

There are two sources of evidence consistent with this hypothesis. First, Liberman and Trope's (1998) temporal construal theory states that people use low-level construals when thinking about the near future and high-level construals when thinking about the distant

future. In one study, for example, people were asked how many hours they would spend on academic and nonacademic activities during the next week or a week 1 year in the future. When thinking about the following week, people took into account how busy their lives would be and estimated that they would spend relatively little time on each activity. When thinking about a week in the distant future, people focused more on the desirability of the activities and less on how busy they would be with other activities. That is, consistent with our results, people making distant predictions focused more on the focal event they were considering and less on the other activities that would fill up their lives.

Similarly, Gilovich, Kerr, and Medvec (1993) found that people are more confident that they will do well on a task the further in time they are from the event, either in prospect or retrospect. They point to a number of reasons for this finding, such as the fact that people feel more accountable for their performance when the task is close in time, which makes them focus more on reasons why they might do poorly on the task. Consistent with temporal construal theory, it might also be that the further people are from the task the more they think about it in a vacuum, without considering the many other factors that will compete for their attention. When predicting how they will do on an exam they will take in 3 months, for example, people might think exclusively about the test and how likely they are to know the material. They might not think about other factors that will be going on in their lives that could influence their performance, such as how much sleep they will get the night before, how healthy they will feel, and other demands on their time. If so, then a manipulation similar to our prospective diary questionnaire might make people think more about other events that will impede their performance, thereby moderating their predictions.

In sum, focalism appears to be a quite general process that helps explain several phenomena, such as the durability bias and the planning fallacy. Any time people think about how an event in the future or the past will or did affect them, they are likely to focus too much on that event and not enough on other occurrences that will or did occupy their thoughts and influence their behavior. Whereas we agree with Buehler et al.'s (1994) statement that "The act of prediction, by its very nature, elicits a focus on the future rather than the past" (p. 367), we would add an addendum. By its very nature, prediction and postdiction focus attention on the focal event, at the expense of other occurrences that influence people's emotions, judgments, and behavior.

REFERENCES

Anderson, C. A., Krull, D. S., & Weiner, B. (1996). Explanations: Processes and consequences. In E. T. Higgins & A. W. Kruglanski (Eds.), *Social psychology: Handbook of basic principles* (pp. 271–296). New York: Guilford Press.

Brickman, P., Coates, D., & Janoff-Bulman, R. J. (1978). Lottery winners and accident victims: Is happiness relative? *Journal of Personality and Social Psychology, 36,* 917–927.

Buehler, R., Griffin, D., & MacDonald, H. (1997). The role of motivated reasoning in optimistic time predictions. *Personality & Social Psychology Bulletin, 23,* 238–247.

Buehler, R., Griffin, D., & Ross, M. (1994). Exploring the "planning fallacy": Why people underestimate their task completion times. *Journal of Personality and Social Psychology, 67,* 366–381.

Diener, E., Emmons, R. A., Larsen, R. J., & Griffin, S. (1985). The Satisfaction With Life Scale. *Journal of Personality Assessment, 49,* 71–75.

Frederick, S., & Loewenstein, G. (1999). Hedonic adaptation. In E. Diener, N. Schwartz, & D. Kahneman (Eds.), *Well-being: The foundations of hedonic psychology* (pp. 302–329). New York: Russell Sage Foundation.

Gilbert, D. T. (1991). How mental systems believe. *American Psychologist, 46,* 107–119.

Gilbert, D. T., Pinel, E. C., Wilson, T. D., Blumberg, S. J., & Wheatley, T. P. (1998). Immune neglect: A source of durability bias in affective forecasting. *Journal of Personality and Social Psychology, 75,* 617–638.

Gilbert, D. T., & Wilson, T. D. (2000). Miswanting. In J. Forgas (Ed.), *Thinking and feeling: The role of affect in social cognition* (pp. 178–197). Cambridge, England: Cambridge University Press.

Gilovich, T., Kerr, M., & Medvec, V. H. (1993). Effect of temporal perspective on subjective confidence. *Journal of Personality and Social Psychology, 64,* 552–560.

Gilovich, T., & Medvec, V. H. (1995). The experience of regret: What, when, and why. *Psychological Review, 102,* 379–395.

Griffin, D. W., & Ross, L. (1991). Subjective construal, social inference, and human misunderstanding. In L. Berkowitz (Ed.), *Advances in experimental social psychology* (Vol. 24, pp. 319–359). San Diego, CA: Academic Press.

Higgins, E. T. (1996). Knowledge activation: Accessibility, applicability, and salience. In E. T. Higgins & A. Kruglanski (Eds.), *Social psychology: Handbook of basic principles* (pp. 133–168). New York: Guilford Press.

Hirt, E. R., & Markman, K. D. (1995). Multiple explanation: A consider-an-alternative strategy for debiasing judgments. *Journal of Personality and Social Psychology, 69,* 1069–1086.

Kahneman, D., & Miller, D. T. (1986). Norm theory: Comparing reality to its alternatives. *Psychological Review, 93,* 136–153.

Kahneman, D., & Tversky, A. (1982). The simulation heuristic. In D. Kahneman, P. Slovic, & A. Tversky (Eds.), *Judgment under uncertainty: Heuristics and biases* (pp. 201–208). New York: Cambridge University Press.

Kamman, R., & Flett, R. (1983). Affectometer 2: A scale to measure current level of general happiness. *Australian Journal of Psychology, 35,* 257–265.

Kanouse, D. E., & Hanson, L. R., Jr. (1972). Negativity in evaluations. In E. E. Jones, D. E. Kanouse, H. H. Kelley, R. E. Nisbett, S. Valins, & B. Weiner (Eds.), *Attribution: Perceiving the causes of behavior* (pp. 47–62). Morristown, NJ: General Learning Press.

Kenny, D. A., Kashy, D. A., & Bolger, N. (1998). Data analysis in social psychology. In D. T. Gilbert, S. T. Fiske, & G. Lindzey (Eds.), *The handbook of social psychology* (4th ed., Vol. 1, pp. 233–265). New York: McGraw-Hill.

Koehler, D. J. (1991). Explanation, imagination, and confidence in judgment. *Psychological Bulletin, 110,* 499–519.

Liberman, N., & Trope, Y. (1998). The role of feasibility and desirability considerations in near and distant future decisions: A test of temporal construal theory. *Journal of Personality and Social Psychology, 75,* 5–18.

Mitchell, T. R., Thompson, L., Peterson, E., & Cronk, R. (1997). Temporal adjustments in the evaluation of events: The "rosy view." *Journal of Experimental Social Psychology, 33,* 421–448.

Myers, D. G., & Diener, E. (1995). Who is happy? *Psychological Science, 6,* 10–19.

Roese, N. J., & Olson, J. M. (1997). Counterfactual thinking: The intersection of affect and function. In M. Zanna (Ed.), *Advances in experimental social psychology* (Vol. 29, pp. 1–59). San Diego, CA: Academic Press.

Rosenthal, R., & Rosnow, R. L. (1985). *Contrast analysis: Focused comparisons in the analysis of variance.* New York: Cambridge University Press.

Ross, M. (1989). Relation of implicit theories to the construction of personal histories. *Psychological Review, 96,* 341–357.

Schkade, D. A., & Kahneman, D. (1998). Would you be happy if you lived in California? A focusing illusion in judgments of well-being. *Psychological Science, 9,* 340–346.

Schwarz, N. (1990). Feelings as information: Informational and motivational functions of affective states. In R. Sorrentino & E. T. Higgins (Eds.), *Handbook of motivation and cognition* (Vol. 2, pp. 527–561). New York: Guilford Press.

Suh, E., Diener, E., & Fujita, F. (1996). Events and subjective well-being: Only recent events matter. *Journal of Personality and Social Psychology, 70,* 1091–1102.

Tatarkiewicz, W. (1976). *Analysis of happiness* (E. Rothert & D. Zielińska, Trans.). Warszawa, Poland: PWN/Polish Scientific Publishers. (Original work published 1962).

Taylor, S. E. (1991). Asymmetrical effects of positive and negative events: The mobilization–minimization hypothesis. *Psychological Bulletin, 110,* 67–85.

Wilson, T. D., Meyers, J. M., & Gilbert, D. T. (1999). [The durability bias in prediction and postdiction]. Unpublished raw data.

Wortman, C. B., & Silver, R. C. (1989). The myths of coping with loss. *Journal of Consulting and Clinical Psychology, 57,* 349–357.

Received May 26, 1998
Revision received October 28, 1999
Accepted October 28, 1999 ■

Appendix: How to Read a Journal Article in Social Psychology

Christian H. Jordan and Mark P. Zanna

When approaching a journal article for the first time, and often on subsequent occasions, most people try to digest it as they would any piece of prose. They start at the beginning and read word for word, until eventually they arrive at the end, perhaps a little bewildered, but with a vague sense of relief. This is not an altogether terrible strategy; journal articles do have a logical structure that lends itself to this sort of reading. There are, however, more efficient approaches — approaches that enable you, a student of social psychology, to cut through peripheral details, avoid sophisticated statistics with which you may not be familiar, and focus on the central ideas in an article. Arming yourself with a little foreknowledge of what is contained in journal articles, as well as some practical advice on how to read them, should help you read journal articles more effectively. If this sounds tempting, read on.

Journal articles offer a window into the inner workings of social psychology. They document how social psychologists formulate hypotheses, design empirical studies, analyze the observations they collect, and interpret their results. Journal articles also serve an invaluable archival function: They contain the full store of common and cumulative knowledge of social psychology. Having documentation of past research allows researchers to build on past findings and advance our understanding of social behavior, without pursuing avenues of investigation that have already been explored. Perhaps most importantly, a research study is never complete until its results have been shared with others, colleagues and students alike. Journal articles are a primary means of communicating research findings. As such, they can be genuinely exciting and interesting to read. That last claim may have caught you

Preparation of this paper was facilitated by a Natural Sciences and Engineering Research Council of Canada doctoral fellowship to Christian H. Jordan. Thanks to Roy Baumeister. Arie Kruglanski, Ziva Kunda, John Levine, Geoff MacDonald, Richard Moreland, Ian Newby-Clark, Steve Spencer, and Adam Zanna for their insightful comments on, and appraisals of, various drafts of this paper. Thanks also to Arie Kruglanski and four anonymous editors of volumes in the series, Key Readings in Social Psychology for their helpful critiques of an inital outline of this paper. Correspondence concerning this article should be addressed to Christian H. Jordan, Department of Psychology, University of Waterloo, Waterloo, Ontario, Canada N2L 3Gl. Electronic mail can be sent to chjordan@watarts.uwaterloo.ca.

off guard. For beginning readers, journal articles may seem anything but interesting and exciting. They may, on the contrary, appear daunting and esoteric, laden with jargon and obscured by menacing statistics. Recognizing this fact, we hope to arm you, through this paper, with the basic information you will need to read journal articles with a greater sense of comfort and perspective.

Social psychologists study many fascinating topics, ranging from prejudice and discrimination, to culture, persuasion, liking and love, conformity and obedience, aggression, and the self. In our daily lives, these are issues we often struggle to understand. Social psychologists present systematic observations of, as well as a wealth of ideas about, such issues in journal articles. It would be a shame if the fascination and intrigue these topics have were lost in their translation into journal publications. We don't think they are, and by the end of this paper, hopefully you won't either.

Journal articles come in a variety of forms, including research reports, review articles, and theoretical articles. Put briefly, a *research report* is a formal presentation of an original research study, or a series of studies. A *review article* is an evaluative survey of previously published work, usually organized by a guiding theory or point of view. The author of a review article summarizes previous investigations of a circumscribed problem, comments on what progress has been made toward its resolution, and suggests areas of the problem that require further study. A *theoretical article* also evaluates past research, but focuses on the development of theories used to explain empirical findings. Here, the author may present a new theory to explain a set of findings, or may compare and contrast a set of competing theories, suggesting why one theory might be the superior one.

This paper focuses primarily on how to read research reports, for several reasons. First, the bulk of published literature in social psychology consists of research reports. Second, the summaries presented in review articles, and the ideas set forth in theoretical articles, are built on findings presented in research reports. To get a deep understanding of how research is done in social psychology, fluency in reading original research reports is essential. Moreover, theoretical articles frequently report new studies that pit one theory against another, or test a novel prediction derived from a new theory. In order to appraise the validity of such theoretical contentions, a grounded understanding of basic findings is invaluable. Finally, most research reports are written in a standard format that is likely unfamiliar to new readers. The format of review and theoretical articles is less standardized, and more like that of textbooks and other scholarly writings, with which most readers are familiar. This is not to suggest that such articles are easier to read and comprehend than research reports; they can be quite challenging indeed. It is simply the case that, because more rules apply to the writing of research reports, more guidelines can be offered on how to read them.

The Anatomy of Research Reports

Most research reports in social psychology, and psychology in general, are written in a standard format prescribed by the American Psychological Association (1994). This is a great boon to both readers and writers. It allows writers to present their ideas and findings in a clear, systematic manner. Consequently, as a reader, once you understand this format, you will not be on completely foreign ground when you approach a new research report — regardless of its specific content. You will know where in the paper particular information is found, making it easier to locate. No matter what your reasons for reading a research report, a firm understanding of the format in which they are written will ease your task. We discuss the format of research reports next, with some practical suggestions on how to read them. Later, we discuss how this format reflects the process of scientific investigation, illustrating how research reports have a coherent narrative structure.

Title and Abstract

Though you can't judge a book by its cover, you can learn a lot about a research report simply by reading its title. The title presents a concise statement of the theoretical issues investigated, and/or the variables that were studied. For example, the following title was taken almost at random from a prestigious journal in social psychology: "Sad and guilty? Affective influences on the explanation of conflict in close relationships" (Forgas, 1994, p. 56). Just by reading the title, it can be inferred that the study investigated how emotional states change the way people explain conflict in close relationships. It also suggests that when feeling sad, people accept more personal blame for such conflicts (i.e., feel more guilty).

The abstract is also an invaluable source of information. It is a brief synopsis of the study, and packs a lot of information into 150 words or less. The abstract contains information about the problem that was investigated, how it was investigated, the major findings of the study, and hints at the theoretical and practical implications of the findings. Thus, the abstract is a useful summary of the research that provides the gist of the investigation. Reading this outline first can be very helpful, because it tells you where the report is going, and gives you a useful framework for organizing information contained in the article.

The title and abstract of a research report are like a movie preview. A movie preview highlights the important aspects of a movie's plot, and provides just enough information for one to decide whether to watch the whole movie. Just so with titles and abstracts; they highlight the key features of a research report to allow you to decide if you want to read the whole paper. And just as with movie previews, they do not give the whole story. Reading just the title and abstract is never enough to fully understand a research report.

Introduction

A research report has four main sections: introduction, method, results, and discussion. Though it is not explicitly labeled, the introduction begins the main body of a research report. Here, the researchers set the stage for the study. They present the problem under investigation, and state why it was important to study. By providing a brief review of past research and theory relevant to the central issue of investigation, the researchers place the study in a historical context and suggest how the study advances knowledge of the problem. Beginning with broad theoretical and practical considerations, the researchers delineate the rationale that led them to the specific set of hypotheses tested in the study. They also describe how they decided on their research strategy (e.g., why they chose an experiment or a correlational study).

The introduction generally begins with a broad consideration of the problem investigated. Here, the researchers want to illustrate that the problem they studied is a real problem about which people should care. If the researchers are studying prejudice, they may cite statistics that suggest discrimination is prevalent, or describe specific cases of discrimination. Such information helps illustrate why the research is both practically and theoretically meaningful, and why you should bother reading about it. Such discussions are often quite interesting and useful. They can help you decide for yourself if the research has merit. But they may not be essential for understanding the study at hand. Read the introduction carefully, but choose judiciously what to focus on and remember. To understand a study, what you really need to understand is what the researchers' hypotheses were, and how they were derived from theory, informal observation, or intuition. Other background information may be intriguing, but may not be critical to understand what the researchers did and why they did it.

While reading the introduction, try answering these questions: what problem was studied, and why? How does this study relate to, and go beyond, past investigations of the problem? How did the researchers derive their hypotheses? What questions do the researchers hope to answer with this study?

Method

In the method section, the researchers translate their hypotheses into a set of specific, testable questions. Here, the researchers introduce the main characters of the study — the subjects or participants — describing their characteristics (gender, age, etc.) and how many of them were involved. Then, they describe the materials (or apparatus), such as any questionnaires or special equipment, used in the study. Finally, they describe chronologically the procedures of the study; that is, how the study was conducted. Often, an overview of the research design will begin the method section. This overview provides a broad outline of the design, alerting you to what you should attend.

The method is presented in great detail so that other researchers can re-create the study to confirm (or question) its results. This degree of detail is normally not necessary to understand a study, so don't get bogged down trying to memorize the particulars of the procedures. Focus on how the independent variables were manipulated (or measured) and how the dependent variables were measured.

Measuring variables adequately is not always an easy matter. Many of the variables psychologists are interested in cannot be directly observed, so they must be inferred from participants' behavior. Happiness, for example, cannot be directly observed. Thus, researchers interested in how being happy influences people's judgments must infer happiness (or its absence) from their behavior — perhaps by asking people how happy they are, and judging their degree of happiness from their responses: Perhaps by studying people's facial expressions for signs of happiness, such as smiling. Think about the measures researchers use while reading the method section. Do they adequately reflect or capture the concepts they are meant to measure? If a measure seems odd, consider carefully how the researchers justify its use.

Oftentimes in social psychology, getting there is half the fun. In other words, how a result is obtained can be just as interesting as the result itself. Social psychologists often strive to have participants behave in a natural, spontaneous manner, while controlling enough of their environment to pinpoint the causes of their behavior. Sometimes, the major contribution of a research report is its presentation of a novel method of investigation. When this is the case, the method will be discussed in some detail in the introduction.

Participants in social psychology studies are intelligent and inquisitive people who are responsive to what happens around them. Because of this, they are not always initially told the true purpose of a study. If they were told, they might not act naturally. Thus, researchers frequently need to be creative, presenting a credible rationale for complying with procedures, without revealing the study's purpose. This rationale is known as a *cover story*, and is often an elaborate scenario. While reading the method section, try putting yourself in the shoes of a participant in the study, and ask yourself if the instructions given to participants seem sensible, realistic, and engaging. Imagining what it was like to be in the study will also help you remember the study's procedure, and aid you in interpreting the study's results.

While reading the method section, try answering these questions: How were the hypotheses translated into testable questions? How were the variables of interest manipulated and/or measured? Did the measures used adequately reflect the variables of interest? For example, is self-reported income an adequate measure of social class? Why or why not?

Results

The results section describes how the observations collected were analyzed to determine whether the original hypotheses were supported. Here, the data (observations of behavior) are described, and statistical tests are presented. Because of this, the results section is often intimidating to readers who have little or no training in statistics. Wading through complex and unfamiliar statistical analyses is understandably confusing and frustrating. As a result, many students are tempted to skip over reading this section. We advise you not to do so. Empirical findings are the foundation of any science and results sections are where such findings are presented.

Take heart. Even the most prestigious researchers were once in your shoes and sympathize with you. Though space in psychology journals is limited, researchers try to strike a balance between the need to be clear and the need to be brief in describing their results. In an influential paper on how to write good research reports, Bem (1987) offered this advice to researchers:

> No matter how technical or abstruse your article is in its particulars, intelligent nonpsychologists with no expertise in statistics or experimental design should be able to comprehend the broad outlines of what you did and why. They should understand in general terms what was learned. (p. 74)

Generally speaking, social psychologists try to practice this advice.

Most statistical analyses presented in research reports test specific hypotheses. Often, each analysis presented is preceded by a reminder of the hypothesis it is meant to test. After an analysis is presented, researchers usually provide a narrative description of the result in plain English. When the hypothesis tested by a statistical analysis is not explicitly stated, you can usually determine the hypothesis that was tested by reading this narrative description of the result, and referring back to the introduction to locate a hypothesis that corresponds to that result. After even the most complex statistical analysis, there will be a written description of what the result means conceptually. Turn your attention to these descriptions. Focus on the conceptual meaning of research findings, not on the mechanics of how they were obtained (unless you're comfortable with statistics).

Aside from statistical tests and narrative descriptions of results, results sections also frequently contain tables and graphs. These are efficient summaries of data. Even if you are not familiar with statistics, look closely at tables and graphs, and pay attention to the means or correlations presented in them. Researchers always include written descriptions of the pertinent aspects of tables and graphs. While reading these descriptions, check the tables and graphs to make sure what the researchers say accurately reflects their data. If they say there was a difference between two groups on a particular dependent measure, look at the means in the table that correspond to those two groups, and see if the means do differ as described. Occasionally, results seem to become stronger in their narrative description than an examination of the data would warrant.

Statistics *can* be misused. When they are, results are difficult to interpret. Having said this, a lack of statistical knowledge should not make you overly cautious while reading results sections. Though not a perfect antidote, journal articles undergo extensive review by professional researchers before publication. Thus, most misapplications of statistics are caught and corrected before an article is published. So, if you are unfamiliar with statistics, you can be reasonably confident that findings are accurately reported.

While reading the results section, try answering these questions: Did the researchers provide evidence that any independent variable manipulations were effective? For example, if testing for behavioral differences between happy and sad participants, did the researchers demonstrate that one group was in fact happier than the other? What were the major findings of the study? Were the researchers' original hypotheses supported by their observations? If not, look in the discussion section for how the researchers explain the findings that were obtained.

Discussion

The discussion section frequently opens with a summary of what the study found, and an evaluation of whether the findings supported the original hypotheses. Here, the researchers evaluate the theoretical and practical implications of their results. This can be particularly interesting when the results did not work out exactly as the researchers anticipated. When such is the case, consider the researchers' explanations carefully, and see if they seem plausible to you. Often, researchers will also report any aspects of their study that limit their interpretation of its results, and suggest further research that could overcome these limitations to provide a better understanding of the problem under investigation.

Some readers find it useful to read the first few paragraphs of the discussion section before reading any other part of a research report. Like the abstract, these few paragraphs usually contain all of the main ideas of a research report: What the hypotheses were, the major findings and whether they supported the original hypotheses, and how the findings relate to past research and theory. Having this information before reading a research report can guide your reading, allowing you to focus on the specific details you need to complete your understanding of a study. The description of the results, for example, will alert you to the major variables that were studied. If they are unfamiliar to you, you can pay special attention to how they are defined in the introduction, and how they are operationalized in the method section.

After you have finished reading an article, it can also be helpful to reread the first few paragraphs of the discussion and the abstract. As noted, these two passages present highly distilled summaries of the major ideas in a research report. Just as they can help guide your reading of a report, they can also help you consolidate your understanding of a report once you have finished reading it. They provide a check on whether you have understood the main points of a report, and offer a succinct digest of the research in the authors' own words.

While reading the discussion section, try answering these questions: What conclusions can be drawn from the study? What new information does the study provide about the problem under investigation? Does the study help resolve the problem? What are the practical and theoretical implications of the study's findings? Did the results contradict past research findings? If so, how do the researchers explain this discrepancy?

Some Notes on Reports of Multiple Studies

Up to this point, we have implicitly assumed that a research report describes just one study. It is also quite common, however, for a research report to describe a series of studies of the same problem in a single article. When such is the case, each study reported will have the same basic structure (introduction, method, results, and discussion sections) that we have outlined, with the notable exception that sometimes the results and discussion section for each study are combined. Combined "results and discussion" sections contain the same information that separate results and discussion sections normally contain. Sometimes, the authors present all their results first, and only then discuss the implications of these results, just as they would in separate results and discussion sections. Other times, however, the authors alternate between describing results and discussing their implications, as each result is presented. In either case, you should be on the lookout for the same information, as outlined above in our consideration of separate results and discussion sections.

Reports including multiple studies also differ from single study reports in that they include more general introduction and discussion sections. The general introduction, which begins the main body of a research report, is similar in essence to the introduction of a single study report. In both cases, the researchers describe the problem investigated and its practical and theoretical significance. They also demonstrate how they derived their hypotheses, and explain how their research relates to past investigations of the problem. In contrast, the separate introductions to each individual study in reports of multiple studies are usually quite brief, and focus more specifically on the logic and rationale of each particular study presented. Such introductions generally describe the methods used in the particular study, outlining how they answer questions that have not been adequately addressed by past research, including studies reported earlier in the same article.

General discussion sections parallel discussions of single studies, except on a somewhat grander scale. They present all of the information contained in discussions of single studies, but consider the implications of all the studies presented together. A general discussion section brings the main ideas of a research program into bold relief. It typically begins with a concise summary of a research program's main findings, their relation to the original hypotheses, and their practical and theoretical implications. Thus, the summaries that begin general discussion sections are counterparts of the summaries that begin discussion sections of single study reports. Each presents a digest of the research presented in an article that can serve as both an organizing framework (when read first), and as a check on how well you have understood the main points of an article (when read last).

Research Reporting as Story Telling

A research report tells the story of how a researcher or group of researchers investigated a specific problem. Thus, a research report has a linear, narrative structure with a beginning, middle, and end. In his paper on writing research reports, Bem noted that a research report:

> . . . is shaped like an hourglass. It begins with broad general statements, progressively narrows down to the specifics of [the] study, and then broadens out again to more general considerations. (1987, p. 175)

This format roughly mirrors the process of scientific investigation, wherein researchers do the following: (1) start with a broad idea from which they formulate a narrower set of hypotheses, informed by past empirical findings (introduction); (2) design a specific set of concrete operations to test these hypotheses (method); (3) analyze the observations collected in this way, and decide if they support the original hypotheses (results); and (4) explore the broader theoretical and practical implications of the findings, and consider how they contribute to an understanding of the problem under investigation (discussion). Though these stages are somewhat arbitrary distinctions — research actually proceeds in a number of different ways — they help elucidate the inner logic of research reports.

While reading a research report, keep this linear structure in mind. Though it is difficult to remember a series of seemingly disjointed facts, when these facts are joined together in a logical, narrative structure, they become easier to comprehend and recall. Thus, always remember that a research report tells a story. It will help you to organize the information you read, and remember it later.

Describing research reports as stories is not just a convenient metaphor. Research reports *are* stories. Stories can be said to consist of two components: A telling of what happened, and an explanation of why it happened. It is tempting to view science as an endeavor that simply catalogues facts, but nothing is further from the truth. The goal of science, social psychology included, is to *explain* facts, to explain *why* what happened happened. Social psychology is built on the dynamic interplay of discovery and justification, the dialogue between systematic observation of relations and their theoretical explanation. Though research reports do present novel facts based on systematic observation, these facts are presented in the service of ideas. Facts in isolation are trivia. Facts tied together by an explanatory theory are science. Therein lies the story. To really understand what researchers have to say, you need to consider how their explanations relate to their findings.

The Rest of the Story

There is really no such thing as research. There is only search, more search, keep on searching. (Bowering, 1988, p. 95)

Once you have read through a research report, and understand the researchers' findings and their explanations of them, the story does not end there. There is more than one interpretation for any set of findings. Different researchers often explain the same set of facts in different ways.

Let's take a moment to dispel a nasty rumor. The rumor is this: Researchers present their studies in a dispassionate manner, intending only to inform readers of their findings and their interpretation of those findings. In truth, researchers aim not only to inform readers, but also to *persuade* them (Sternberg, 1995). Researchers want to convince you their ideas are right. There is never only one explanation for a set of findings. Certainly, some explanations are better than others; some fit the available data better, are more parsimonious, or require fewer questionable assumptions. The point here is that researchers are very passionate about their ideas, and want you to believe them. It's up to you to decide if you want to buy their ideas or not.

Let's compare social psychologists to salesclerks. Both social psychologists and salesclerks want to sell you something; either their ideas, or their wares. You need to decide if you want to buy what they're selling or not — and there are potentially negative consequences for either decision. If you let a salesclerk dazzle you with a sales pitch, without thinking about it carefully, you might end up buying a substandard product that you don't really need. After having done this a few times, people tend to become cynical, steeling themselves against any and all sales pitches. This too is dangerous. If you are overly critical of sales pitches, you could end up foregoing genuinely useful products. Thus, by analogy, when you are too critical in your reading of research reports, you might dismiss, out of hand, some genuinely useful ideas — ideas that can help shed light on why people behave the way they do.

This discussion raises the important question of how critical one should be while reading a research report. In part, this will depend on why one is reading the report. If you are reading it simply to learn what the researchers have to say about a particular issue, for example, then there is usually no need to be overly critical. If you want to use the research as a basis for planning a new study, then you should be more critical. As you develop an understanding of psychological theory and research methods, you will also develop an ability to criticize research on many different levels. And *any* piece of research can be criticized at some level. As Jacob Cohen put it, "A successful piece of research doesn't conclusively settle an issue, it just makes some theoretical proposition to some degree more likely" (1990, p. 1311). Thus, as a consumer of research reports, you have to strike a delicate balance between being overly critical and overly accepting.

While reading a research report, at least initially, try to suspend your disbelief. Try to understand the researchers' story; that is, try to understand the facts — the findings and how they were obtained — and the suggested explanation of those facts — the researchers' interpretation of the findings and what they mean. Take the research to task only after you feel you understand what the authors are trying to say.

Research reports serve not only an important archival function, documenting research and its findings, but also an invaluable stimulus function. They can excite other researchers to join the investigation of a particular issue, or to apply new methods or theory to a different, perhaps novel, issue. It is this stimulus function that Elliot Aronson, an eminent social psychologist, referred to when he admitted that, in publishing a study, he hopes his colleagues will "look at it, be stimulated by it, be provoked by it, annoyed by it, and then go ahead and do it better ... That's the exciting thing about science; it progresses by people taking off on one another's work" (1995, p. 5). Science is indeed a cumulative enterprise, and each new study builds on what has (or, sometimes, has not) gone before it. In this way, research articles keep social psychology vibrant.

A study can inspire new research in a number of different ways, such as: (1) it can lead one to conduct a better test of the hypotheses, trying to rule out alternative explanations of the findings; (2) it can lead one to explore the limits of the findings, to see how widely applicable they are, perhaps exploring situations to which they do not apply; (3) it can lead one to test the implications of the findings, furthering scientific investigation of the phenomenon; (4) it can inspire one to apply the findings, or a novel methodology, to a different area of investigation; and (5) it can provoke one to test the findings in the context of a specific real world problem, to see if they can shed light on it. All of these are excellent extensions of the original research, and there are, undoubtedly, other ways that research findings can spur new investigations.

The problem with being too critical, too soon, while reading research reports is that the only further research one may be willing to attempt is research of the first type: redoing a study better. Sometimes this is desirable, particularly in the early stages of investigating a particular issue, when the findings are novel and perhaps unexpected. But redoing a reasonably compelling study, without extending it in any way, does little to advance our understanding of human behavior. Although the new study might be "better," it will not be "perfect," so *it* would have to be run again, and again, likely never reaching a stage where it is beyond criticism. At some point, researchers have to decide that the evidence is compelling enough to warrant investigation of the last four types. It is these types of studies that most advance our knowledge of social behavior. As you read more research reports, you will become more comfortable deciding when a study is "good enough" to move beyond it. This is a somewhat subjective judgment, and should be made carefully.

When social psychologists write up a research report for publication, it is because they believe they have something new and exciting to communicate about social behavior. Most research reports that are submitted for publication are rejected. Thus, the reports that are eventually published are deemed pertinent not only by the researchers who wrote them, but also by the reviewers and editors of the journals in which they are published. These people, at least, believe the research reports they write and publish have something important and interesting to say. Sometimes, you'll disagree; not all journal articles are created equal, after all. But we recommend that you, at least initially, give these well-meaning social psychologists the benefit of the doubt. Look for what they're excited about. Try to understand the authors' story, and see where it leads you.

Acknowledgments

Preparation of this paper was facilitated by a Natural Sciences and Engineering Research Council of Canada doctoral fellowship to Christian H. Jordan. Thanks to Roy Baumeister, Arie Kruglanski, Ziva Kunda, John Levine, Geoff MacDonald, Richard Moreland,

Ian Newby-Clark, Steve Spencer, and Adam Zanna for their insightful comments on, and appraisals of, various drafts of this paper. Thanks also to Arie Kruglanski and four anonymous editors of volumes in the series, Key Readings in Social Psychology for their helpful critiques of an initial outline of this paper. Correspondence concerning this article should be addressed to Christian H. Jordan, Department of Psychology, University of Waterloo, Waterloo, Ontario, Canada N2L 3G1. Electronic mail can be sent to chjordan @watarts.uwaterloo.ca.

REFERENCES

American Psychological Association (1994). *Publication manual* (4th ed.). Washington, D.C.

Aronson, E. (1995). Research in social psychology as a leap of faith. In E. Aronson (Ed.), *Readings about the social animal* (7th ed., pp. 3–9). New York: W. H. Freeman & Company.

Bem, D.J. (1987). Writing the empirical journal article. In M.P. Zanna & J.M. Darley (Eds.), *The compleat academic: A practical guide for the beginning social scientist* (pp. 171–201). New York: Random House.

Bowering, G. (1988). *Errata*. Red Deer, Alta.: Red Deer College Press.

Cohen, J. (1990). Things I have learned (so far). *American Psychologist, 45*, 1304–1312.

Forgas, J.P. (1994). Sad and guilty? Affective influences on the explanation of conflict in close relationships. *Journal of Personality and Social Psychology, 66*, 56–68.

Sternberg, R.J. (1995). *The psychologist's companion: A guide to scientific writing for students and researchers* (3rd ed.). Cambridge: Cambridge University Press.

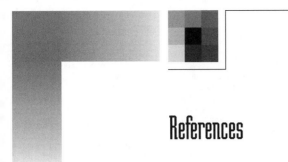

References

Abelson, R. P. (1981). The psychological status of the script concept. *American Psychologist, 36,* 715–729.

Allison, S. T., Mackie, D. M., & Messick, D. M. (1996). Outcome biases in social perception: Implications for dispositional inference, attitude change, stereotyping, and social behavior. In M. P. Zanna (Ed.), *Advances in experimental social psychology* (Vol. 28, pp. 53–93). San Diego, CA: Academic Press.

Allport, G. W. (1954). *The nature of prejudice.* Reading, MA: Addison-Wesley.

American Psychological Association (1994). *Publication manual* (4th Ed.) Washington, D.C.

Aronson. E. (1995). Research in social psychology as a leap of faith. In E. Aronson (Ed.), *Readings about the social animal* (7th ed., pp. 3–9). New York: W.H. Freeman and Company.

Asch, S.E. (1946). Forming impressions of personality. *Journal of Abnormal and Social Psychology, 41,* 258–290.

Bargh, J. A. (1994). The four horsemen of automaticity: Awareness, intention, efficiency, and control in social cognition. In R. S. Wyer & T. K. Srull (Eds), *Handbook of social cognition: Basic processes* (Vol. 1, pp. 1–40). Hillsdale, NJ: Erlbaum.

Bargh, J. A. (1999). The cognitive monster: The case against the controllability of automatic stereotype effects. In S. Chaiken & Y. Trope (Eds), *Dual-process theories in social psychology* (pp. 361–382). New York, NY: Guilford Press.

Bargh, J. A., Bond, R. N., Lombardi, W. L., & Tota, M. E. (1986). The additive nature of chronic and temporary sources of construct accessibility. *Journal of Personality and Social Psychology, 50,* 869–879.

Bargh, J. A., & Chartrand, T. L. (1999). The unbearable automaticity of being. *American Psychologist, 54,* 462–479.

Bargh, J. A., Chen, M., & Burrows, L. (1996). Automaticity of social behavior: Direct effects of trait construct and stereotype activation on action. *Journal of Personality and Social Psychology, 71,* 230–244.

Bargh, J. A., & Pietromonaco, P. R. (1982). Automatic information processing and social perception: The influence of trait information presented outside of conscious awareness on impression formation. *Journal of Personality and Social Psychology, 43,* 437–449.

Bassili, J. N., & Smith, M. C. (1986). On the spontaneity of trait attribution: Converging evidence for the role of cognitive strategy. *Journal of Personality and Social Psychology, 50,* 239–245.

Bem, D. J. (1987). Writing the empirical journal article. In M. P. Zanna & J. M. Darley (Eds.), *The compleat academic: A practical guide for the beginning social scientist* (pp. 171–201). New York: Random House.

Biernat, M. (1995). The shifting standards model: Implications of stereotype accuracy for judgment. In Y. Lee, L. J. Jussim, & C. R. McCauley (Eds), *Stereotype accuracy: Toward appreciating group differences* (pp. 87–114). Washington, DC: American Psychological Association.

Blair, I. V. (2002). The malleability of automatic stereotypes and prejudice. *Personality and Social Psychology Review, 6,* 242–261.

Blascovich, J. (2000). Using physiological indexes of psychological processes in social psychological research. In H. T. Reis & C. M. Judd (Eds), *Handbook of research methods in social and personality psychology* (pp. 117–137). Cambridge, UK: Cambridge University Press.

Bowering, G. (1988). *Errata.* Red Deer, Alta.: Red Deer College Press.

Brewer, M. B. (1979). In-group bias in the minimal intergroup situation: A cognitive-motivational analysis. *Psychological Bulletin, 86,* 307–324.

Brewer, M. B., Dull, V., & Lui, L. (1981). Perceptions of the elderly: Stereotypes as prototypes. *Journal of Personality and Social Psychology, 41,* 656–670.

Bruner, J. S. (1957). On perceptual readiness. *Psychological Review, 64,* 123–152.

Cacioppo, J. T., Berntson, G. G., & Crites, S. L., Jr. (1996). Social neuroscience: Principles of psychophysiological arousal and response. In E. T. Higgins & A. W. Kruglanski (Eds), *Social psychology: Handbook of basic principles* (pp. 72–101). New York: Guilford.

Cacioppo, J. T., Berntson, G. G., Lorig, T. S., Norris, C. J., Rickett, E., & Nusbaum, H. (2003). Just because you're imaging the brain doesn't mean you can stop using your head: A primer and set of first principles. *Journal of Personality and Social Psychology, 85,* 650–661.

Carlston, D. E., & Skowronski, J. J. (1994). Savings in the relearning of trait information as evidence for spontaneous inference generation. *Journal of Personality and Social Psychology, 66,* 840–856.

Carlston, D. E., Skowronski, J. J., & Sparks, C. (1995). Savings in relearning: II. On the formation of behavior-based trait associations and inferences. *Journal of Personality and Social Psychology, 69,* 429–436.

Carlston, D. E., & Smith, E. R. (1996). Principles of mental representation. In E. T. Higgins & A. W. Kruglanski (Eds), *Social psychology: Handbook of basic principles* (pp. 184–210). New York, NY: Guilford.

Chen, M., & Bargh, J. A. (1997). Nonconscious behavioral confirmation processes: The self-fulfilling consequences of automatic stereotype activation. *Journal of Experimental Social Psychology*, *33*, 541–560.

Cohen, J. (1990). Things I have learned (so far). *American Psychologist*, *45*, 1304–1312.

Conway, M., & Ross, M. (1984). Getting what you want by revising what you had. *Journal of Personality and Social Psychology*, *47*, 738–748.

Correll, J., Park, B., Judd, C. M., & Wittenbrink, B. (2002). The police officer's dilemma: Using ethnicity to disambiguate potentially threatening individuals. *Journal of Personality and Social Psychology*, *83*, 1314–1329.

Darley, J. M., & Gross, P. H. (1983). A hypothesis-confirming bias in labeling effects. *Journal of Personality and Social Psychology*, *44*, 20–33.

Darwin, C. (1998). *Expression of the emotions in man and animals* (3rd ed.). New York: Oxford University Press. (Original work published in 1872.)

Davis, C. G., Lehman, D. R., Wortman, C. B., & Silver, R. C. (1995). The undoing of traumatic life events. *Personality and Social Psychology Bulletin*, *21*, 109–124.

Devine, P. G. (1989). Stereotypes and prejudice: Their automatic and controlled components. *Journal of Personality and Social Psychology*, *56*, 5–18.

Devine, P. G., & Baker, S. M. (1991). Measurement of racial stereotype subtyping. *Personality and Social Psychology Bulletin*, *17*, 44–50.

Devine, P. G., Sedikides, C., & Fuhrman, R. W. (1989). Goals in social information processing: The case of anticipated interaction. *Journal of Personality and Social Psychology*, *56*, 680–690.

Dijksterhuis, A., & van Knippenberg, A. (1998). The relation between perception and behavior, or how to win a game of Trivial Pursuit. *Journal of Personality and Social Psychology*, *74*, 865–877.

Ditto, P. H., & Lopez, D. F. (1992). Motivated skepticism: Use of differential decision criteria for preferred and nonpreferred conclusions. *Journal of Personality and Social Psychology*, *63*, 568–584.

Dovidio, J. F., Kawakami, K., Johnson, C., Johnson, B., & Howard, A. (1997). On the nature of prejudice: Automatic and controlled processes. *Journal of Experimental Social Psychology*, *33*, 510–540.

Duncan, B. L. (1976). Differential social perception and attribution of intergroup violence: Testing the lower limits of stereotyping blacks. *Journal of Personality and Social Psychology*, *34*, 590–598.

Dunning, D., Leuenberger, A., & Sherman, D. A. (1995). A new look at motivated inference: Are self-serving theories of success a product of motivational forces? *Journal of Personality and Social Psychology*, *69*, 58–68.

Dunning, D., & Sherman, D. A. (1997). Stereotypes and tacit inference. *Journal of Personality and Social Psychology*, *73*, 459–471.

Fazio, R. H., Jackson, J. R., Dunton, B. C., & Williams, C. J. (1995). Variability in automatic activation as an unobstrusive measure of racial attitudes: A bona fide pipeline? *Journal of Personality and Social Psychology*, *69*, 1013–1027.

Fazio, R. H., Powell, M. C., & Herr, P. M. (1983). Toward a process model of the attitude-behavior relation: Accessing one's attitude upon mere observation of the attitude object. *Journal of Personality and Social Psychology*, *44*, 723–735.

Fazio, R. H., Sanbonmatsu, D. M., Powell, M. C., & Kardes, F. R. (1986). On the automatic activation of attitudes. *Journal of Personality and Social Psychology*, *50*, 229–238.

Festinger, L. (1957). *A theory of cognitive dissonance*. Palo Alto, CA: Stanford University Press.

Fischhoff, B. (1975). Hindsight = foresight: The effects of outcome knowledge on judgment under uncertainty. *Journal of Experimental Psychology: Human Perception and Performance*, *1*, 288–299.

Fiske, S. T. (1980). Attention and weight in person perception: The impact of negative and extreme behavior. *Journal of Personality and Social Psychology*, *38*, 889–906.

Fiske, S. T. (1989). Examining the role of intent: Toward understanding its role in stereotyping and prejudice. In J. S. Uleman & J. A. Bargh (Eds), *Unintended thought* (pp. 253–283). New York, NY: Guilford.

Fiske, S. T. (1998). Stereotyping, prejudice, and discrimination. In S.T. Fiske, D. T. Gilbert, & G. Lindsey (Eds.), *The handbook of social psychology* (Vol 2, pp. 357–411). New York, NY: McGraw-Hill.

Fiske, S. T., & Neuberg, S. L. (1990). A continuum of impression formation, from category-based to individuating processes: Influences of information and motivation on attention and interpretation. In M. P. Zanna (Ed.), *Advances in experimental social psychology* (Vol. 23, pp. 1–74). New York: Academic Press.

Fiske, S. T., & Taylor, S. E. (1991). *Social cognition* (2nd ed.) New York: McGraw-Hill.

Forgas, J. P. (1994). Sad and guilty? Affective influences on the explanation of conflict in close relationships. *Journal of Personality and Social Psychology*, *66*, 56–68.

Garcia-Marques, L., Hamilton, D. L., & Maddox, K. B. (2002). Exhaustive and heuristic retrieval processes in person cognition: Further tests of the TRAP model. *Journal of Personality and Social Psychology*, *82*, 193–207.

Gilbert, D. T., & Malone, P. S. (1995). The correspondence bias. *Psychological Bulletin*, *117*, 21–38.

Gilbert, D. T., Pelham, B. W., & Krull, D. S. (1988). On cognitive business: When person perceivers meet persons perceived. *Journal of Personality and Social Psychology*, *54*, 733–740.

Gilbert, D. T., Pinel, E. C., Wilson, T.D., Blumberg, S. J., & Wheatley, T. P. (1998). Immune neglect: A source of durability bias in affective forecasting. *Journal of Personality and Social Psychology*, *75*, 617–638.

Gilbert, D. T., & Wilson, T. D. (2000). Miswanting: Some problems in the forecasting of future affective states. In J.P. Forgas (Ed.), *Feeling and thinking: The role of affect in social cognition* (pp. 178–197). New York, NY: Cambridge University Press.

Gilovich, T., Vallone, R., & Tversky, A. (1985). The hot hand in basketball: On the misperception of random sequences. *Cognitive Psychology*, *17*, 295–314.

Hamilton, D. L. (1998). Dispositional and attributional inferences in person perception. In J. M. Darley & J. Cooper (Eds), *Attribution and social interaction: The legacy of Edward E. Jones* (pp. 99–114). Washington, DC: American Psychological Association.

Hamilton, D. L., & Garcia-Marques, L. (2003). Effects of expectancies on the representation, retrieval, and use of social information. In G. V. Bodenhausen & A. J. Lambert (Eds), *Foundations of social cognition: A Festschrift in honor of Robert S. Wyer, Jr.* (pp. 25–50). Mahwah, NJ: Lawrence Erlbaum Associates.

Hamilton, D. L., & Gifford, R. K. (1976). Illusory correlation in interpersonal perception: A cognitive basis of stereotypic judgments. *Journal of Experimental Social Psychology*, *12*, 392–407.

Hamilton, D. L., Katz, L. B., & Leirer, V. O. (1980). Organizational processes in impression formation. In R. Hastie, T. M. Ostrom, E. B. Ebbesen, R. S. Wyer, Jr., D. L. Hamilton, & D. E. Carlston (Eds), *Person memory: The cognitive basis of social perception*. Hillsdale, NJ: Lawrence Erlbaum Associates.

Hamilton, D. L., & Sherman, J. W. (1994). Stereotypes. In R. S. Wyer, Jr., & T. K. Srull (Eds), *Handbook of social cognition* (2nd ed., Vol. 2, pp. 1–68). Hillsdale, NJ: Lawrence Erlbaum Associates.

Hamilton, D. L., & Sherman, S. J. (1996). Perceiving persons and groups. *Psychological Review, 103*, 336–355.

Hamilton, D. L., Sherman, S. J., & Castelli, L. (2002). A group by any other name — The role of entitativity in group perception. In W. Stroebe & M. Hewstone (Eds), *European review of social psychology* (Vol. 12, pp. 139–166). Chichester, England: Wiley.

Hamilton, D. L., Sherman, S. J., & Lickel, B. (1998). Perceiving social groups: The importance of the entitativity continuum. In C. Sedikides & J. Schopler (Eds), *Intergroup cognition and intergroup behavior* (pp. 47–74). Mahwah, NJ: Lawrence Erlbaum Associates.

Harmon-Jones, E., & Devine, P. G. (Eds.) (2003). Special section: Social neuroscience: Promise and caveats. *Journal of Personality and Social Psychology, 85*, 589–671.

Hastie, R. (1980). Memory for behavioral information that confirms or contradicts a personality impression. In R. Hastie, T. M. Ostrom, E. B. Ebbesen, R. S. Wyer, Jr., D. L. Hamilton, & D. E. Carlston (Eds), *Person memory: The cognitive basis of social perception* (pp. 155–177). Hillsdale, NJ: Erlbaum.

Hastie, R. (1984). Causes and effects of causal attribution. *Journal of Personality and Social Psychology, 46*, 44–56.

Hastie, R., & Kumar P. A. (1979). Person memory: Personality traits as organizing principles in memory for behaviors. *Journal of Personality and Social Psychology, 37*, 25–38.

Hastie R., & Park, B. (1986). The relationship between memory and judgment depends on whether the judgment task is memory-based or on-line. *Psychological Review, 93*, 258–268.

Hastie, R., Ostrom, T. M., Ebbesen, E. B., Wyer, R. S., Jr., Hamilton, D. L., & Carlston, D. E. (Eds.) (1980). *Person memory: The cognitive basis of social perception*. Hillsdale, NJ: Erlbaum.

Hastorf, A. H., & Cantril, H. (1954). They saw a game: A case study. *Journal of Abnormal and Social Psychology, 49*, 129–134.

Hawkins, S. A., & Hastie, R. (1990). Hindsight: Biased judgments of past events after the outcomes are known. *Psychological Bulletin, 107*, 311–327.

Heider, F. (1944). Social perception and phenomenal causality. *Psychological Review, 51*, 358–374.

Heider, F. (1958). *The psychology of interpersonal relations*. New York: Wiley.

Heine, S. J., & Lehman D. R. (1997a). Culture, dissonance, and self-affirmation. *Personality and Social Psychology Bulletin, 23*, 389–400.

Heine, S. J., & Lehman, D. R. (1997b). The cultural construction of self-enhancement: An examination of group-serving biases. *Journal of Personality and Social Psychology, 72*, 1268–1283.

Higgins, E. T., King, G. A., & Mavin, G. H. (1982). Individual construct accessibility and subjective impressions and recall. *Journal of Personality and Social Psychology, 43*, 35–47.

Higgins, E. T., Rholes, W. S., & Jones, C. R. (1977). Category accessibility and impression formation. *Journal of Experimental Social Psychology, 13*, 141–154.

Hilton, J. L., Fein, S., & Miller, D. T. (1993). Suspicion and dispositional inference. *Personality and Social Psychology Bulletin, 19*, 501–512.

Jones, E. E. (1979). The rocky road from acts to dispositions. *American Psychologist, 34*,107–117.

Jones, E. E. (1990). *Interpersonal perception*. New York: Freeman.

Jones, E. E., & Davis, K. E. (1965). From acts to dispositions: The attribution process in person perception. In L. Berkowitz (Ed.), *Advances in experimental social psychology* (Vol. 2, pp. 220–266). New York: Academic Press.

Jones, E. E., & Harris, V. A. (1967). The attribution of attitudes. *Journal of Experimental Social Psychology, 3*, 1–24.

Jones, E. E., & Nisbett, R. E. (1972). The actor and the observer: Divergent perceptions of the causes of behavior. In E. E. Jones, H. H. Kanouse, R. E. Kelley, S. Nisbett, S. Valins, & B. Weiner (Eds), *Attribution: Perceiving the causes of behavior* (pp. 79–94). Morristown, NJ: General Learning Press.

Jones, E. E., & Thibaut, J. W. (1958). Interaction goals as bases of inference in interpersonal perception. In R. Tagiuri & L. Petrullo (Eds), *Person perception and interpersonal behavior* (pp. 151–178). Palo Alto, CA: Stanford University Press.

Kahneman, D., & Miller, D. T. (1986). Norm theory: Comparing reality to its alternatives. *Psychological Review, 93*, 136–153.

Kelley, H. H. (1967). Attribution theory in social psychology. In D. Levine (Ed.), *Nebraska symposium on motivation* (Vol. 15, pp. 192–240). Lincoln: University of Nebraska Press.

Kim, H. S. (2002). We talk, therefore we think? A cultural analysis of the effect of talking on thinking. *Journal of Personality and Social Psychology, 83*, 828–842.

Klein, S. B., & Kihlstrom, J. F. (1998). On bridging the gap between social-personality psychology and neuropsychology. *Personality and Social Psychology Review, 2*, 228–242.

Klein, S. B., & Loftus, J. (1990). The role of abstract and exemplar-based knowledge in self-judgments: Implications for a cognitive model of the self. In T. K. Srull & R. S. Wyer Jr. (Eds), *Advances in social cognition* (Vol. 3, pp. 131–139). Hillsdale, NJ: Lawrence Erlbaum Associates.

Kruglanski, A. E. (1996). Motivated social cognition: Principles of the interface. In E. T. Higgins & A. W. Kruglanski (Eds), *Social psychology: Handbook of basic principles* (pp. 493–520). New York: Guilford.

Kruglanski, A. W., & Webster, D. M. (1991). Group members' reactions to opinion deviates and conformists at varying degrees of proximity to decision deadline and of environmental noise. *Journal of Personality and Social Psychology, 61*, 212–225.

Kruglanski, A. W., Webster, D. M., & Klem, A. (1993). Motivated resistance and openness to persuasion in the presence or absence of prior information. *Journal of Personality and Social Psychology, 65*, 861–876.

Kunda, Z. (1987). Motivated inference: Self-serving generation and evaluation of causal theories. *Journal of Personality and Social Psychology, 53*, 636–647.

Kunda, Z. (1990). The case for motivated reasoning. *Psychological Bulletin, 108*, 480–498.

Loftus, E. F. (1993). The reality of repressed memories. *American Psychologist, 48*, 518–537.

Loftus, E. F. (1997). Memories for a past that never was. *Current Directions in Psychological Science, 6*, 60–65.

Loftus, E. F., & Palmer, J. C. (1974). Reconstruction of automobile destruction: An example of the interaction between language and memory. *Journal of Verbal Learning and Verbal Behavior, 13*, 585–589.

Lord, C. G., Ross, L., & Lepper, M. R. (1979). Biased assimilation and attitude polarization: The effects of prior theories on subsequently considered evidence. *Journal of Personality and Social Psychology, 37*, 2098–2109.

Mackie, D. M., Hamilton, D. L., Susskind, J., & Rosselli, F. (1996). Social psychological foundations of stereotype formation. In C. N. Macrae, C. Stangor, & M. Hewstone (Eds), *Stereotypes and stereotyping* (pp. 41–78). New York: Guilford Press.

Macrae, C. N., Milne, A. B., & Bodenhausen, G.V. (1994). Stereotypes as energy-saving devices: A peek inside the cognitive toolbox. *Journal of Personality and Social Psychology, 66*, 37–47.

Mandel, D. R., & Lehman, D. R. (1996). Counterfactual thinking and ascriptions of cause and preventability. *Journal of Personality and Social Psychology, 71*, 450–463.

Markman, K. D., Gavanski, I., Sherman, S. J., & McMullen, M. N. (1993). The mental simulation of better and worse possible worlds. *Journal of Experimental Social Psychology, 29*, 87–109.

Markus, H. (1977). Self-schemata and processing information about the self. *Journal of Personality and Social Psychology, 35*, 63–78.

Markus, H. R., & Kitayama, S. (1991). Culture and the self: Implications for cognition, emotion, and motivation. *Psychological Review, 98*, 224–253.

Mayseless, O., & Kruglanski, A. W. (1987). Accuracy of estimates in the social comparison of abilities. *Journal of Experimental Social Psychology, 23*, 217–229.

McArthur, L. Z., & Post, D. L. (1977). Figural emphasis and person perception. *Journal of Experimental Social Psychology, 13*, 520–535.

McFarland, C., Ross, M., & Giltrow, M. (1992). Biased recollections in older adults: The role of implicit theories of aging. *Journal of Personality and Social Psychology, 62*, 837–850.

Medin, D. (1989). Concepts and conceptual structure. *American Psychologist, 12*, 1469–1481.

Medin, D. L., & Shoben, E. J. (1988). Context and structure in conceptual combination. *Cognitive Psychology, 20*, 158–190.

Medvec, V. H., Madey, S. F., & Gilovich, T. (1995). When less is more: Counterfactual thinking and satisfaction among Olympic medalists. *Journal of Personality and Social Psychology, 69*, 603–610.

Menon, T., Morris, M. W., Chiu, C., and Hong, Y. (1999). Culture and the construal of agency: Attribution to individual versus group dispositions. *Journal of Personality and Social Psychology, 76*, 701–717.

Miller, D. T., Turnbull, W., & McFarland, C. (1990). Counterfactual thinking about what might have been. In M. P. Zanna (Ed.), *Advances in experimental social psychology* (Vol. 23, pp. 305–331). New York: Academic Press.

Nisbett, R. E., Peng, K., Choi, I., & Norenzayan, A. (2001). Culture and systems of thought: Holistic versus analytic cognition. *Psychological Review, 108*, 291–310.

Nisbett, R. E., & Ross, L. (1980). *Human inference: Strategies and shortcomings of social judgment.* Englewood Cliffs, NJ: Prentice-Hall.

Nisbett, R. E., & Wilson, T. D. (1977). Telling more than we can know: Verbal reports on mental processes. *Psychological Review, 84*, 231–259.

Northcraft, G. B., and Neale, M. A. (1987). Experts, amateurs, and real estate: An anchoring-and-adjustment perspective on property pricing decisions. *Organizational Behavior and Human Decision Processes, 39*, 84–97.

Olson, J. M., Roese, N. J., & Zanna, M. P. (1996). Expectancies. In E. T. Higgins & A. W. Kruglanski (Eds), *Social psychology: Handbook of basic principles* (pp. 211–238). New York, NY: Guilford Press.

Payne, B. K. (2001). Prejudice and perception: The role of automatic and controlled processes in misperceiving a weapon. *Journal of Personality and Social Psychology, 81*, 181–192.

Pendry, L. F., & Macrae, C. N. (1996). What the disinterested perceiver overlooks: Goal-directed social categorization. *Personality and Social Psychology Bulletin, 22*, 249–256.

Peng, K., & Nisbett, R. E. (1999). Culture, dialectics, and reasoning about contradiction. *American Psychologist, 54*, 741–754.

Plous, S. (1989). Thinking the unthinkable: The effects of anchoring on likelihood estimates of nuclear war. *Journal of Applied Social Psychology, 19*, 67–91.

Pratto, F., & John, O. P. (1991). Automatic vigilance: The attention-grabbing power of negative social information. *Journal of Personality and Social Psychology, 61*, 380–391.

Roese, N. J. (1994). The functional basis of counterfactual thinking. *Journal of Personality and Social Psychology, 66*, 805–818.

Roese, N. J. (1997). Counterfactual thinking. *Psychological Bulletin, 121*, 133–148.

Roese, N. J., & Olson, J. M. (1997). Counterfactual thinking: The intersection of affect and function. In M.P. Zanna (Ed.), *Advances in experimental social psychology* (Vol. 29, pp. 1–59). San Diego: Academic Press.

Ross, L. (1977). The intuitive psychologist and his shortcomings: Distortions in the attribution process. In L. Berkowitz (Ed.), *Advances in experimental social psychology* (Vol. 10, pp. 174–221). New York: Academic Press.

Ross, L., Amabile, T. M., & Steinmetz, J. L. (1977). Social roles, social control, and biases in social-perception processes. *Journal of Personality and Social Psychology, 35*, 485–494.

Ross, M. (1989). The relation of implicit theories to the construction of personal histories. *Psychological Review, 96*, 341–357.

Ross, M., McFarland, C., & Fletcher, G. J. O. (1981). The effect of attitude on the recall of personal histories. *Journal of Personality and Social Psychology, 10*, 627–634.

Ross, M., & Sicoly, F. (1979). Egocentric biases in availability and attribution. *Journal of Personality and Social Psychology, 37*, 322–336.

Rothbart, M., & John, O. P. (1985). Social categorization and behavioral episodes: A cognitive analysis of the effects of intergroup contact. *Journal of Social Issues, 41*(3), 81–104.

Sagar, H. A., & Schofield, J. W. (1980). Racial and behavioral cues in Black and White children's perceptions of ambiguously aggressive acts. *Journal of Personality and Social Psychology, 39*, 590–598.

Schneider, D. J. (1973). Implicit personality theory: A review. *Psychological Bulletin, 79*, 294–309.

Schwarz, N., Bless, H., Strack, F., Klumpp, G., Rittenauer-Schatka, H., & Simons, A. (1991). Ease of retrieval as information: Another look at the availability heuristic. *Journal of Personality and Social Psychology, 61*, 195–202.

Skowronski, J. J., Gibbons, J. A., Vogl, R. J., & Walker W. R. (2004). The effect of social disclosure on the intensity of affect provoked by autobiographical memories. *Self and Identity, 3*, 285–309.

Slovic, P., & Lichtenstein, S. (1971). Comparison of Bayesian and regression approaches to the study of information processing in judgment. *Organizational Behavior and Human Performance, 6*, 649–744.

Smith, E. R. (1994). Social cognition contributions to attribution theory and research. In P.G. Devine, D.L. Hamilton, & T.M. Ostrom (Eds), *Social cognition: Impact on social psychology* (pp. 77–108). San Diego: Academic Press.

Snyder, M. (1981). On the self-perpetuating nature of social stereotypes. In D.L. Hamilton (Ed.), *Cognitive processes in stereotyping and intergroup behavior* (pp. 183–212). Hillsdale, NJ: Erlbaum.

Snyder, M., Tanke, E. D., & Berscheid, E. (1977). Social perception and interpersonal behavior: On the self-fulfilling nature of social stereotypes. *Journal of Personality and Social Psychology, 35*, 656–666.

Spellman, B. A., & Mandel, D. R. (1999). When possibility informs reality: Counterfactual thinking as a cue to causality. *Current Directions in Psychological Science, 8*, 120–123.

Srull, T. K. (1981). Person memory: Some tests of associative storage and retrieval models. *Journal of Experimental Psychology: Human Learning and Memory, 7*, 440–463.

Srull, T. K., & Wyer, R. S., Jr. (1979). The role of category accessibility in the interpretation of information about persons: Some determinants and implications. *Journal of Personality and Social Psychology, 37*, 1660–1672.

Srull, T. K., & Wyer, R. S., Jr. (1989). Person memory and judgment. *Psychological Review, 96*, 38–83.

Stangor, C., & McMillan, D. (1992). Memory for expectancy-congruent and expectancy-incongruent information: A review of the social and social developmental literatures. *Psychological Bulletin*, *111*, 42–61.

Sternberg, R. J. (1995). *The psychologist's companion: A guide to scientific writing for student and researchers* (3rd Ed.). Cambridge: Cambridge University Press.

Strack, F., & Mussweiler, T. (1997). Explaining the enigmatic anchoring effect: Mechanisms of selective accessibility. *Journal of Personality and Social Psychology*, *73*, 437–446.

Stroessner, S. J., & Plaks, J. E. (2001). Illusory correlation and stereotype formation: Tracing the arc of research over a quarter century. In G. B. Moskowitz (Ed.), *Cognitive social psychology* (pp. 247–259). Mahwah, NJ: Erlbaum.

Tajfel, H. (1969). Cognitive aspects of prejudice. *Journal of Social Issues*, *25*(4), 79–97.

Taijfel, H., & Turner, J. C. (1979). An integrative theory of intergroup conflict. In W. G. Austin & S. Worchel (Eds), *The social psychology of intergroup relations*. Monterey, CA: Brooks/Cole.

Tajfel, H., & Turner, J. C. (1986). The social identity theory of intergroup behavior. In S. Worchel & G. Austin (Eds), *Psychology of intergroup relations*. Chicago: Nelson-Hall.

Taylor, S. E. (1981). A categorization approach to stereotyping. In D. L. Hamilton (Ed.), *Cognitive processes in stereotyping and intergroup behavior* (pp. 88–114). Hillsdale, NJ: Erlbaum.

Triandis, H. C. (1995). *Individualism and collectivism*. Boulder, CO: Westview.

Trope, Y. (1986). Identification and inferential processes in dispositional attribution. *Psychological Review*, *93*, 239–257.

Tversky, A., & Kahneman, D. (1974). Judgment under uncertainty: Heuristics and biases. *Science*, *185*, 1124–1131.

Tversky, A., & Kahneman, D. (1983). Extensional versus intuitive reasoning: The conjunction fallacy in probability judgment. *Psychological Review*, *90*, 293–315.

Uleman, J. S., Newman, L. S., & Moskowitz, G. B. (1996). People as flexible interpreters: Evidence and issues from spontaneous trait inference. In M. P. Zanna (Ed.), *Advances in experimental social psychology* (Vol. 28, pp. 211–279). San Diego, CA: Academic Press.

Webster, D. M., & Kruglanski, A. W. (1994). Individual differences in need for cognitive closure. *Journal of Personality and Social Psychology*, *67*, 1049–1062.

White, J. D., & Carlston, D. E. (1983). Consequences of schemata for attention, impression, and recall in complex social interactions. *Journal of Personality and Social Psychology*, *45*, 538–549.

Wilder, D. A. (1981). Perceiving persons as a group: Categorization and intergroup relations. In D. L. Hamilton (Ed.), *Cognitive processes in stereotyping and intergroup behavior* (pp. 213–257). Hillsdale, NJ: Erlbaum.

Willingham, D. T., & Dunn, E. W. (2003). What neuroimaging and brain localization can do, cannot do, and should not do for social psychology. *Journal of Personality and Social Psychology*, *85*, 662–671.

Wilson, T. D., Wheatley, T., Meyers, J. M., Gilbert., D.T., & Axsom, D. (2000). Focalism: A source of durability bias in affective fore-casting. *Journal of Personality and Social Psychology*, *78*, 821–836.

Winter, L., & Uleman, J. S. (1984). When are social judgments made? Evidence for the spontaneousness of trait inferences. *Journal of Personality and Social Psychology*, *47*, 237–252.

Wittenbrink, B., Gist, P. L., & Hilton, J. L. (1997). Structural properties of stereotypic knowledge and their influences on the construal of social situations. *Journal of Personality and Social Psychology*, *72*, 526–543.

Yzerbyt, V., Rocher, S., & Schadron, G. (1997). Stereotypes as explanations: A subjective essentialistic view of group perception. In R. Spears & P. J. Oakes (Eds), *The social psychology of stereotyping and group life* (pp. 20–50). Oxford, UK: Blackwell.

Author Index

Subject Index